HARMSWORTH
HISTORY
OF THE WORLD

THE STATUE OF LIBERTY

Erected on Bedloe's Island in New York Harbour, this colossal statue was presented to the United States by the people of France.

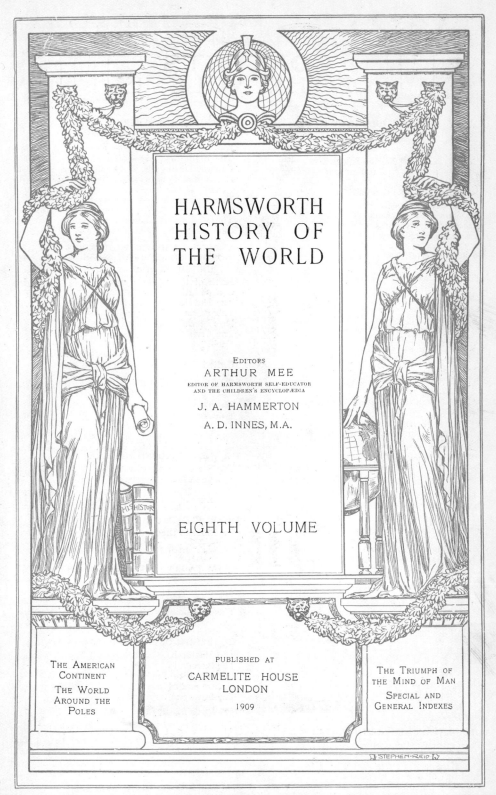

HARMSWORTH HISTORY OF THE WORLD

Editors
ARTHUR MEE
EDITOR OF HARMSWORTH SELF-EDUCATOR
AND THE CHILDREN'S ENCYCLOPÆDIA

J. A. HAMMERTON

A. D. INNES, M.A.

EIGHTH VOLUME

The American
Continent
The World
Around the
Poles

PUBLISHED AT
CARMELITE HOUSE
LONDON
1909

The Triumph of
the Mind of Man
Special and
General Indexes

CONTENTS
OF THIS VOLUME

HARMSWORTH HISTORY
OF THE WORLD
SEVENTH GRAND DIVISION
AMERICA

STEPHEN REID

SEVENTH GRAND DIVISION
AMERICA

We have now arrived at the last grand geographical division in the world's history ; a division which, as far as land is concerned, includes a hemisphere. But its written history covers little more than a period of four centuries, and the monumental records are meagre and vague.

In some regions a civilisation far from despicable existed perhaps for some centuries before Columbus ; but when we compare this with the three thousand years of written records in the Eastern Hemisphere, and the monumental records which may have survived for ten thousand years, it becomes obvious that American history forms but a small part in the history of the world.

In it, however, we include what anthropological inquiry can tell us of the primitive races which peopled two continents, and what is known of the civilisations which came into being during our European "Middle Ages."

But the main part of our story deals with the expansion of the dominion of one European people in the southern and central portion of the two continents, the expansion and rivalry of two other European peoples in the northern portion, the supremacy achieved by the British race, and the development of the twin Powers of that race partly under the Union Jack and partly under the Stars and Stripes.

To this is added the study of the world around the Poles, which completes our survey of the Oceans as well as of the Continents of the globe ; and thence we pass finally to touch in closing on some of those inquiries which are suggested by the story we have told.

PLAN

AMERICA BEFORE COLUMBUS
By Professor Konrad Haebler

THE COLONISATION OF THE CONTINENT AND THE AMERICAN NATION
By A. G. Bradley, Dr. H. F. Helmolt, W. H. Woodward, and Prof. Haebler

SOCIAL CONDITIONS AND THE SOCIAL FUTURE IN THE UNITED STATES
By H. G. Wells

THE WORLD AROUND THE POLES
By George Sandeman, M.A.

For full contents and page numbers see index

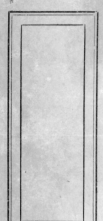
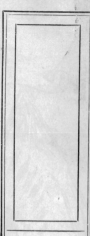

AN OJIBWA BRAVE   AN OJIBWA CHIEF   IROQUOIS ADOPTED AS OJIBWA CHIEF
A SUB-CHIEF OF THE UTES   A CHIEF OF THE APACHES

INDIAN TYPES OF NORTH AMERICA

Reproduced from direct colour photographs by Detroit Photographic Co

TO FACE PAGE 5675

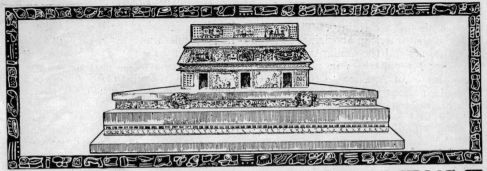

AMERICA BEFORE COLUMBUS
PRIMITIVE RACES OF THE CONTINENT
By Professor Konrad Haebler

WHERE DID AMERICAN MAN COME FROM?

THE problem how the first men may have come to America has always given much food for reflection to both learned and unlearned. Many could not imagine that a continent should exist with countless different races for whom no place could be found in the genealogy of Genesis, and for want of a better way out of the difficulty they assumed that the inhabitants of America were the descendants of the ten lost tribes of Israel. This naïve assumption did direct service to science itself by offering occasion to some intelligent observers to go thoroughly into the manners and customs of the American Indians, in the hope of discovering analogies which might serve them as proofs.

A second hypothesis regarding the origin of the Americans has received a far more scientific colouring. The fabulous island-world of the Western ocean, the oldest evidence of which is the mythical Atlantis of Plato's Timæus, exercised an indirect influence on the discovery of the New World, in so far as even Columbus was under the spell of belief in it. Whether it was based on any historic or prehis-

Was there a Land-bridge over the Atlantic?

toric fact has not hitherto been proved. But men of science are not wanting who answer this question in the affirmative, and who see in a land-bridge over the Atlantic Ocean the way by which the first men came to the American continent.

Modern research no longer takes up so naïve a position on this question as the old Spaniard who therewith attributed to the Indians a Keltiberian origin. The sinking of a continent between Europe and America in an age when our part of the earth was inhabited by peoples whose traces are still to be found must in any case have left some signs which could not have escaped the advanced investigation of the earth's surface. The attempt to trace the outlines of this continent from the cliffs and

The First Route to America

shoals of the Atlantic Ocean is also worthless trifling. On the other hand, geologists of note believe that they can prove that the northern part of the Atlantic Ocean was not always covered by water, and they think it was by this way that man came from the Old World to the New, in times when the climatic conditions of our part of the globe were still considerably different from those of history.

Finally, still a third hypothesis exists for the population of America. It would be the simplest of all did not the same science which admits the possibility of a North Atlantic land-bridge having existed dispute the same possibility for this. Nowhere do the continents of the Old and New World approach nearer to one another than in North-west America, where Bering Strait separates them by only a narrow arm of water, and the Aleutian Islands also make it possible for a navigator provided with but the most primitive appliances to cross from one to the other.

At all times vessels of the inhabitants of the Asiatic coasts have occasionally been tossed by wind and weather as far as the shores of Alaska, and that an immigration took place in this direction even in historic times is almost a certainty. The resemblance of the American aborigines to Mongolian peoples and the similarity of certain ethnological peculiarities in races of the Pacific states of America to those of the civilised nations of Asia have long brought this hypothesis many adherents. Some, indeed, would find direct proof of

America's Earliest Inhabitants intercourse between the Chinese and America in the accounts of the land of Fu-schan, and on the strength of this would boldly claim the Aztec civilisation to have been an offshoot of the Chinese. Such inferences, however, have not been able to stand the test of strict examination.

In the ages which we can connect with even the earliest Chinese epochs America was certainly not populated by this means; and if the geologists are right who assert that the far north-west did not rise from the waves of the Pacific Ocean—which once flowed with a boundless expanse to the North Pole—until after the Glacial Period, then the first inhabitants of America certainly did not get there in this way, for by this time the bones of many generations were already bleaching on the soil of the New World.

Since it has been proved that the human race on American soil can be traced back to the same periods of the earth's history as in the Old World, the question whence the first men came there has lost much of its importance. It is true that the cradle of the human race can hardly have been in America; to cite one objection, the anthropoid apes, which are indispensable to the theory of evolution as the connecting link between the animal world and man, have at no time been native there, any more than they are now, as the fossil finds in all American excavations have proved.

But, however, if the first men came over during periods in which the distribution of land and water on the earth's surface was still quite different from that

Problem of America's First Man shown by history, then geology will one day, at least, be able to give an answer to our question. Yet even this negative result is of unqualified scientific importance, for it puts all those in the wrong who pretend to see in the customs of the savage and civilised races of America the influences of certain ethnographic units familiar to our ideas. If the first man made his home in America at the time when his fellow in the Old World still vied with the

beasts in gnawing the bones of the game he had killed, and if a hollow in the hills was the only shelter he knew, the dispute as to whether the civilisations of America are to be traced to Aryan or Semitic influences may be given up as idle. For this much at least is irrefutably proved by the palæontology and history of the New World—that its development from the times of the mammoth to its discovery by Christopher Columbus was continuous and was not influenced from without.

America is also highly interesting to the student of the early history of the human race as well as to the geologist, in that it preserved the witnesses of a past of which we find in the Old World only scanty and often obliterated traces until a later time. This later time did not, it is true, possess such a developed method of research as the present day, but in its accounts, and in the memorials that it handed down to posterity, it has consigned to us far richer material for research than has the Old World, and has given us information of events and conditions in the early history of man which we should otherwise seek in

The Stone Age in America vain. Even the most highly civilised races of America were only at the beginning of the Copper Age when they were discovered, while most of the inhabitants of the New World still lived entirely in the Age of Stone.

Americans once asserted that they had dug human bones out of strata of the Tertiary Period; but, like those who had made similar assertions regarding finds in the Old World, they failed to give scientific proof. On the other hand, human relics have come to light there, as they have here, that belong to the Interglacial Period; nor are such relics, although naturally not very numerous, limited to a small area, but are found both in the mountainous regions of California and in the vast plains of the Argentine pampas. In America, too, man was the contemporary of the mammoth and other ancient gigantic species of animals, and at a later but still prehistoric period the New World even had a population which in places was fairly considerable.

That this was the case is evident from the considerable number and unusual size of the refuse accumulations of prehistoric man that are known by the name of "kitchen-middens." These refuse mounds exist in North and South America, on the shores of the ocean, on the inland seas, and on the banks of the great rivers, and, besides their scientific name, are called "shell-mounds" in the North and "sambaquis" in the South. They consist of accumulations of the inedible parts of fish and other aquatic animals, especially shellfish, and naturally contain among this refuse fragments of objects that were used by the men who inhabited their sites. That these objects belong chiefly to the earliest human culture, the Palæolithic, was to be anticipated, but it must not be forgotten that refuse mounds are also met with, especially in South America, which belong not only to the Neolithic Period, beyond which the wild Indian of Eastern South America has never advanced, but even with certainty to historic times.

What number of people and what time it may have taken to throw up these mounds, which are often hundreds of feet long, and of considerable height, we have as yet no reliable means of determining. But it can scarcely be assumed that they were formed very slowly, for otherwise the action of the elements, especially on the sea-coasts, would scarcely ever have allowed accumulations to be made **History from** which have stood the test of **the Ancient** thousands of years. We are, **Shell-mounds** therefore, undoubtedly justified in concluding, from the large extent and wide distribution of these mounds, that large areas of the continent were thickly populated even in prehistoric times.

This fact must especially be kept in view, in order to estimate at their proper value the hypotheses regarding the civilising influences of the peoples of the Old World on those of the New; for if in times when even Asia and Europe still possessed an exclusively uncivilised population America was already inhabited by man in exactly the same manner, then, considering the geographical conditions of the continent, foreign influences can only be called in to account for culture phenomena when the supposition of independent development is insufficiently strong.

If we now view the American continent in its entirety on its appearance in historic times, it affords us surprising confirmation of the extraordinary influence of geographical position on the development of human culture. The comparatively narrow strip of coast which accompanies the mountain-chain of the Cordilleras—the backbone of America, as it has been significantly called—at its western foot, with the terraces in which these mountains rapidly rise to considerable height, was almost in its whole extent, from Alaska down to Chili, the seat of civilised and half-civilised races; at any rate, their degree of civilisation was far above the level of that of the population of the vast plains and extensive lowland **Primitive** through which, east of the Cor- **North** dilleras, the mightiest rivers of **Americans** the earth roll their waters to the sea. Here lay the two great centres of civilisation of Peru and Mexico, the latter of which, it is true, spanned the American continent from ocean to ocean near its narrowest part.

In the regions east of the Cordilleras, which probably form three-fourths of the whole area of the continent, man was still, at the beginning of the sixteenth century, in a primitive stage of civilisation. North America showed him then at best as beginning to rise from his state of "natural man"; whereas in the southern continent no traces of this are to be discovered. The clever paradox that hunger is the father of all progress, because it forces man to fight with his surroundings, has probably nowhere been more strikingly confirmed than in South America. The Peruvian of the mountains, for example, on a soil from which he wrung his living by energetic toil, created one of the most ingeniously organised of bodies politic in the world's history, while his eastern neighbour, revelling in the luxuriant wealth of tropical Nature, roved about in a condition which did not even bring before his mind the principal difference between man and beast.

It is true that Nature held the Indian back, keeping him at the lowest possible stage of civilisation, not only through its bounteous gifts, but also by reason of other and less beneficent influences. On the vast plains which accompany the great rivers far along their upper courses Nature denied to man even a permanent **Nature's** abode, one of the most neces- **Influence** sary conditions for the develop- **on Man** ment of progress in culture. The floods which recurred periodically, placing areas of many square miles under water for weeks and months, compelled the Indian—who had to build his hut close to the banks of the rivers on account of the fish that gave him food—regularly to abandon his dwelling and leave it to destruction. It is no wonder that he became an indefatigable swimmer, an excellent boatman, and an expert fisherman ; but his mind became as little associated as his body with the soil he lived on, and the water that washed away his light hut effaced also from his mind any remembrance of his past history. Historical research was for a long time helpless as regards these primitive races.

Features of the Aborigines Attempts were first made to pick out from the endless mass of races and tribes the groups that were more or less closely related to one another ; but even these attempts encountered the greatest obstacles. The outward appearance of the aborigines, their complexion, and the form of their skulls and bodies, were first tried as distinctive marks. It proved that races of different complexions exhibited signs of relationship, whereas the same complexion and figure were repeated in races that were not related at all ; and the skull measurements often gave every gradation from the dolichocephalic to the brachycephalic among the individuals of a single small tribe.

The only guide that has hitherto proved at all trustworthy is the linguistic one. On the bases that we obtain with its aid is founded, almost exclusively as regards South America, the little we know of the history of these races, or rather the little we know in the way of facts. The uncivilised Indian knows nothing of the history of his tribe. He rarely knows more than the names—and perhaps, in the country not subject to floods, the dwellings—of his father and grandfather. After a few generations the knowledge of long migrations fades away into a dim tradition, and in his legends the overgrowth of mythological fantasies completely stifles clear historical recollection.

This also explains how the Indians so easily changed under the influence of new surroundings. Language alone followed this process of transformation comparatively slowly, and contained elements of persistency which asserted themselves more lastingly amid all change. But far more importance must be attached to the influence exercised by mixture on the languages of the Indians. It will seldom have resulted from peaceable intercourse. The Indian in his natural state, while looking on the beasts of the forest almost as his equals, considered every strange man, on the other hand,

The Mixed Languages of the Indians

much as game, and every man was strange to him who was not of his clan. This explains the war of " all against all " that existed among most of the Indian tribes.

Whether we have to regard this same conception as accounting for the anthropophagy which seems at times to have existed throughout the whole American continent, from one end to the other, may perhaps be disputed. In any case the Indian pursued his human enemy with the same unmercifulness as he pursued his worst enemies in the animal world, and his war was, as far as the male portion of the hostile tribe was concerned, a war of annihilation. But he behaved otherwise towards the women. In the restless life of the nomadic Indian a great share of the daily toil and care fell to the female sex, and the Indian knew well how to appreciate the faithful services of his women.

Thus, when he succeeded in capturing the women of a hostile tribe in battle, it was only rarely that he wreaked his wrath on them ; far oftener he saw in them a welcome addition to the hands that provided for his bodily well-being. It is clear that these strange women who were adopted into the tribe must also have exercised an influence for change upon it under certain circumstances, especially if such adoptions happened repeatedly. It must often have come to pass that a tribe, whose outward circumstances were favourable rapidly increased, so that at last all its members could no longer find room within its circle. It was then naturally the youngest members—those in the first stage of manhood—whom the uneasy pressure first affected, and whom must have first migrated. Only a few women, or none at all, would have followed them on their journey into the unknown, for their diligent hands could far less be spared at home than the surplus warriors.

How New Tribes were Formed

So that, in order to establish a home, these warriors would have to resort to the abduction of women. The nearest village would then be attacked ; the men that could not escape would be slaughtered ; but with the women the band of warriors would combine to form a new tribe, which must naturally show in every respect the mixture of different elements. This formation of new tribes is not only logically quite admissible, but it is also verified by historical instances among the many races of South America.

PREHISTORIC SOUTH AMERICA
THE EARLY PEOPLES & THEIR CIVILISATIONS

FROM the few historical facts that we are able to glean with the help of the sciences of language, ethnology, and anthropology, we are still only able to ascertain in rough outline the past of the chief races of South America. Of those that we can still recognise the Tapuyas are considered to be the oldest. "Tapuya" is really not a name at all, but the term in the Tupi language for all "strangers," or "enemies." Karl von den Steinen, an authority to be frequently cited, calls this group that of the Ges tribes; others follow the example of some of their Indian neighbours and call them the Crens, meaning the "old" or "ancient ones."

They have become most popular under the name of Botocudos, from the lip-peg (botoque), which, however, is worn as an ornament of distinction not only by them but also by most of the other primitive races of South America; even **Prehistoric Tapuyas of Brazil** the warriors of the Chibchas, who must be unconditionally reckoned among the civilised races, stuck as many pegs through their lower lips as they had killed enemies in battle. The name "Tapuya" recommends itself most, because in history it has been specially applied to the Ges tribes, and did not, like all the other names, actually belong only to a small number of the tribes that are called by it. The age of these tribes is shown by the fact that their neighbours, who have driven them farther and farther from their former abodes, call them "the ancients."

The most decisive proof that they have lived in the regions of Brazil from the earliest times, long previous to history, is the circumstance that the palæozoic skulls from Lagoa Santa, which Lund brought to light in the caves there, exhibit all the characteristics peculiar to the Tapuya skull. On the other hand, it is doubtful whether the "sambaquis," or refuse-mounds, of Brazil are also attributable to them, because the Tapuyas seem at all times to have been, as they are to-day, a nomadic race of hunters, and never a race of navigators and fishermen. Only such a race, and a comparatively sedentary race, too, could have consumed such quantities of shell-fish as form the mounds of the sambaquis. The **Territory Ruled by the Tapuyas** Tapuyas have played an historical part only passively. They were probably once the sole masters of the whole of Brazil, from the watershed of the Amazon down to the Parana; but probably even in prehistoric times they were hemmed in on all sides so that at the time of the Spanish conquest they ruled practically only the hill-country of the interior of Brazil.

Tribes of them were also drawn into the great racial migration which, several centuries before their discovery by the Spaniards, set out from the east to make an onset upon the more highly civilised races of the Andean highlands; but the Semigaes, who on this occasion penetrated into the region of the upper tributaries of the Amazon, became differentiated in character from their race, and so assimilated themselves with the surrounding Tupi and Carib tribes that only their name and their language still show their old connection.

There have probably never been any races of the Tapuya stock on the north side of the Amazon. Here, until a few centuries before Columbus, one of the most extensive races of the New World, the Aruacs, held unlimited sway. They, too, belong indisputably to the oldest nations of America. Where **Where the Aruacs Held Sway** their real original abodes may have been can be only approximately determined. The Aruacs also represent the type of an inland race. Although in later times many of their tribes were quite at home on the water as navigators and fishermen, their primitive culture points unconditionally to an inland home. And although they were subsequently the undisputed masters of the vast regions north of the Amazon from the Andes to the shores of the ocean, their original abodes cannot have been in the luxuriant, tropical lowlands of the great river territories of South America ; on the contrary, the characteristics we find common to all their widespread branches, as the original elements of their culture, lead us to the conclusion that their home was situated above the region of periodical floods, and yet was still in tropical climes. Now, as we find them on the eastern slopes of the Cordilleras, from the peninsula of Goajira in the north down to the borders of Chili, and in specially large numbers in Eastern Bolivia, the original home of all these tribes is probably to be sought in this direction.

The tribes of the Aruac group, among which must also be counted those called the Nu tribes by Karl von den Steinen, ranked far higher in civilisation than the Tapuyas ; and although Tupis and Caribs subsequently became fully their equals, the civilisation of the Aruacs was founded much earlier than theirs. There is abundant proof that the Aruacs were the teachers of their younger conquerors.

When the Aruac group may have begun to spread from the hill country of Eastern Bolivia to the north-east, east and south-east, and whether in its advance it found the basins of the Orinoco and Amazon and their tributaries still unpeopled or inhabited by other races, cannot be ascertained even approximately. It is probable that it found these new regions uninhabited, because Aruac races have formed a uniform substratum over large areas of Northern South America, which substratum of race reappears wherever the later conquerors did not completely fill the area. But to judge from its extent, and from the great deviations in the language of its various branches, this group of races took not only hundreds but thousands of years for its migrations. In spite of this the Aruacs were not a rude, savage race when this process began, for even the original race knew an

Migrations of the Aruac Races

A GROUP OF INDIAN ARUACS, ONE OF AMERICA'S EARLIEST RACES

Until a few centuries before the coming of Columbus, the Aruacs, one of the most extensive races of the New World, held unlimited sway on the north side of the Amazon. Higher in civilisation than the Tapuyas, this group was by no means a rude, savage people, for even the original race knew an agriculture that cannot be called quite primitive.

THE ELABORATE HEAD DECORATIONS AND UTENSILS OF THE INDIAN ARUACS

agriculture that cannot be called quite primitive. In large parts of South America the agricultural Indians live not only on maize, which is grown all over America, but even to a greater extent on the tuberous root of a species of *euphorbiaceæ*, the manioc (*Manihot plum.*) or cassava.

In the raw state these roots are highly poisonous, owing to their containing prussic acid ; otherwise they are rich in nutritious properties. Now, in early times some unknown Indian tribe made the discovery that the manioc is deprived of its poisonous properties by squeezing the sap out of the root and preparing the latter in a suitable manner : a discovery of far-reaching importance, considering that the manioc afterwards formed almost the sole means of subsistence of hundreds of thousands of Indians. As the manioc shrub does not flourish in the tropical and flood-exposed lowlands, neither the Tupis nor the Caribs, both of whom probably were originally pure fish-eaters, can have been the inventors of this process ; still less the Tapuyas, who did not practise agriculture at all. It does not naturally follow that the honour of this discovery is due to the Aruacs, whose probable original abodes

Far-Reaching Discovery of an Indian Tribe

certainly correspond to the special climatic conditions necessary for the manioc : it is conceivable that they, too, were first instructed in the art of preparing the manioc by a still more highly civilised race. But this certainly took place in the original home of the race, which, with its gradual expansion, spread the cultivation of the manioc, so that finally the Indians of other stocks also learned the art from them.

The Aruac races are further distinguished by their skill in making earthen vessels. This is still so characteristic of them at the present day that, of the races of Central Brazil, Karl von den Steinen classes those of the Aruac stock under the name of "potter tribes." It is certainly not a coincidence that, the farther one goes from the east coast of the continent towards the mountains, the better and finer the pottery becomes. All the races that inhabit the eastern slopes of the Cordilleras were comparatively far advanced in the working of clay, and the products of their industry are distinguished by variety of form and purpose and by elegance of decoration—which ranges from simple lineal ornament to the plastic imitation of living things—from the products of the primitive races of the lowlands. This distinction is certainly not limited to the Aruac races. South of them, among the races of the Gran Chaco, which are still regarded as belonging to other stocks, the same thing is observed, and the pottery which has been dug up from the ruins of the old Indian settlements in Catamarca vies with that produced by many civilised nations. There can be scarcely any doubt that with the Aruacs it is not a case of independent development but of an influence exercised by the ancient civilised races of the Peruvian highlands or their eastern neighbours. But this influence must also belong to an extraordinarily early period, for even the Aruac races, who have never risen to a higher mode of life, and still live at the present day, hundreds of miles away from their ancestral home, in the state of almost pure savages, are the providers and teachers of their neighbours in the matter of pottery.

The Aruac races have acquired quite a special claim to a comparatively higher culture from the fact that anthropophagy had long been absent from their ranks, whereas round about them it still existed, at least as a religious rite, even among races of an unquestionably higher civilisation. It is remarkable that the great mass of the Aruac races, in spite of the fact that some of their tribes lived for generations in the closest contact among whom the enemies killed or captured in war were regularly eaten, never relapsed into this barbarous custom.

This progress in culture also must have belonged to the period that preceded the migrations of the Aruac races, because it was common to every tribe. When we consider that this ancient race was already familiar with agriculture, skilled in the preparation of earthen vessels, and disinclined to anthropophagy, we are almost tempted to look for the ancestors of the Aruacs among the civilised nations that

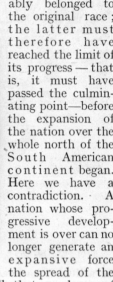

peopled the high valleys of the Cordilleras long centuries before the founding of the Inca dynasty. But an important circumstance stands in the way of this hypothesis. The Aruacs, as we meet them in history, never developed a really higher civilisation than, as we have shown, probably belonged to the original race ; the latter must therefore have reached the limit of its progress — that is, it must have passed the culminating point—before the expansion of the nation over the whole north of the South American continent began. Here we have a contradiction. A nation whose progressive development is over can no longer generate an expansive force

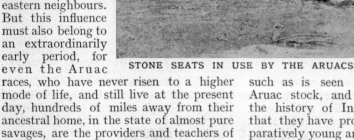

STONE SEATS IN USE BY THE ARUACS

such as is seen in the spread of the Aruac stock, and all that we know of the history of Indian migrations shows that they have proceeded only from comparatively young and rising races.

We shall therefore have to explain the historical process thus. At a period when their original stock on the plateaus of Bolivia began to develop vigorously, the Aruacs were raised from the pure natural state by the cultural influences of the more highly civilised races in the west, and were advanced in a manner that indirectly served to strengthen the aspiring power of the race. In the old home there was no scope for this abundant energy, and so the emigration began. Whether this moved simultaneously in a southern and northern direction cannot be ascertained. We meet with detached tribes of this family south of their original abodes and likewise in the far east. But they throw no light on the date and direction of their migrations. On the other hand, we can trace the northern current for a long time, and fairly clearly. As the Aruacs had already begun to till the ground in their home, their migrations will, on the one side, have progressed much more slowly than those of races that

The Tribes in Search of New Lands

did not know any artificial means of procuring food; on the other side, they must certainly have moved first in a direction that did not compel them to accommodate themselves to other habits. This was only possible if they followed the spurs of the Cordilleras northward. We find them in the sixteenth century in the mountains between Santa Marta and Venezuela, and at the present day in the peninsula of Goajira, their most northern continuation. The Carios in the neighbourhood of Coro also practised agriculture on **Aruac Tribes on the Sea** Venezuelan soil, and lived in permanent abodes at the time of the discovery. At the Cabo de la Vela, Nature checked their northern advance; but their migration was continued in an easterly direction, and reached, still centuries before the discovery of America, the mouth of the Orinoco.

Meanwhile, a change had taken place in respect to part of the race—Aruac tribes had become used to the water, and had become navigators and fishermen. Whether this change began among the coast tribes or among those which had penetrated from the old home into the flood districts of the upper tributaries of the Orinoco is doubtful; the latter appears the more probable, as the sea offers too many difficulties for elementary navigation. Moreover, Aruac tribes are repeatedly found scattered in the basin of the Orinoco. At any rate, the race must still have possessed a considerable power of expansion, for even the ocean on the east coast set no limit to its migrations. The Aruac navigators ventured out from the mouth of the Orinoco upon the open sea, and gradually gave the whole island-world of the Caribbean Sea what is supposed to have been its first population. A little farther, and they would have reached the North American continent from the islands and made the connection

between it and the southern continent, which does not seem ever to have been effected. Meanwhile, their brother tribes on the mainland still followed the sea coast in their new change of direction. Through Guiana they turned again to the south, and even the Amazon did not prove an insuperable obstacle to them. Aruacs are found, with the sure signs of an immigration from the north, as far as the watershed between the tributaries of the Amazon and of the Paraguay.

The migrations of the Aruacs came to a standstill only when they were met by other races with the same desire for expansion. This probably took place comparatively early, the tribes that were advancing south-eastward coming upon the Tupi races. At a later period they encountered the Caribs, to whom finally, in a struggle which lasted for centuries, the majority of the northern Aruacs fell victims.

Although the Tupis have had uninterrupted intercourse with the white man from the first discovery of Brazil down to the present day, the methodical investigation of this race is considerably behind that of others. The reason for this lies in the fate that awaited the race upon the occupation of the land by Europeans. At an early date the missionaries formed, from a dialect of the Tupi language, the so-called *lingua geral*, in which a series of grammars, translations, etc., have been written. It is due to this that the study of the wild Tupi languages, if they may be so termed as opposed to the *lingua geral* cultivated under European influence, has been improperly neglected, and thus one of the best means of ascertaining the ancient history of the Tupi stock has been withheld from us. The same circumstance—long familiarity with the race—has also kept ethnologists from giving their closer attention to the Tupis, whose characteristics have, meanwhile,

TOMBS OF THE ARUAC PEOPLES

been gradually succumbing to the influence of civilisation, so that for the ethnographical and historical study of the best-known stock of the South American Indians we are restricted to inadequate material.

The original home of the Tupis has also been said to have been in the highlands of the interior, but this is based on quite unreliable data and is in contradiction to what is shown by the characteristics of the race in historic times. The mother country of the Tupi races is presumably to be sought not very far from where Europeans first met them, although their expansion and migrations had then been going on in different directions for centuries. Their original home was, in any case, in the region of the northern affluents of La Plata, but scarcely on the other side of the watershed from which the rivers run northward to the Amazon. In contrast to the Aruacs, the Tupis are a decided water-race. Although most of their tribes, but not all, also tilled the ground to a limited extent, in the sixteenth century they still lived almost exclusively by fishing and hunting. On the Paraguay and its tributaries, and on the rivers of the regions of which their wandering hordes further took possession, they boldly launched their canoes in peace and war. In early times they peopled the few islands that lie at inconsiderable distances from the coast, and they were evidently at home on the sea itself so far as their small craft permitted. Even the Tupi tribes who went far into the interior in their migrations still remained navigators and fishermen. A map of the races of South America shows at once the direction in which the Tupi race expanded. It first followed the affluents of La Plata in a southerly direction to the ocean, but only slowly so long as

A CARIB IDOL
The idol represented in the above illustration, which throws an instructive sidelight on the worship of the Caribs, was discovered in 1792 in a cave in Carphenter's Mountain, Jamaica.

it had no special need of expansion. On the other hand, the migration of the Tupis along the coast of the Atlantic Ocean in a northerly direction seems to have proceeded, comparatively speaking, much more rapidly. Up to the mouth of the Amazon they never occupied a broad area, but satisfied themselves with driving the old Tapuya races from a narrow strip of the coast-land, on which, always with an eye to the water, they settled.

That their territory at the time of the conquest still formed an exceedingly narrow strip as compared with its length, but one which was nowhere broken by the return of the hostile nations they had displaced, goes to prove that its occupation took place quickly and at no very remote period. The migrations of the Tupis must have been of a considerably different character from those of the Aruacs. Whereas the latter evidently proceeded slowly and without serious fighting (in the territory of the Aruacs we scarcely ever find clear traces of a strange population not merged in them by assimilation), the migrations of the Tupis bear throughout the stamp of having been warlike in their nature. Even the name Tapuya (strangers or enemies), which they gave to all races with which they came in contact, is historical evidence of this. In their intercourse with Europeans the Tupis by no means proved to be a particularly savage and cruel race; they were the good friends of the first settlers, and subsequently became tractable material in the hands of the Jesuit missionaries. But in their relations with their Indian neighbours they seem to have been preeminently the aggressors, and with proud self-consciousness the southern Tupis called themselves Guaranis (warriors). Nor must we forget that with few exceptions,

REMNANTS OF AN ANCIENT RACE: PRESENT-DAY CARIBS AT HOME

The youngest of South American races, the Caribs were at one time a powerful people, with a degree of civilisation exceedingly low. Eating their enemies was so characteristic of the Caribs that their name of "cannibal" has become identical with the term for man-eaters. The Caribs of the present day bear little resemblance to their remote ancestors.

to be explained by special circumstances, the Tupi tribes were given to cannibalism. It was certainly no longer a scarcity of food that made them cannibals, nor was it a sacred ceremony springing from religious conceptions, such as we find among several civilised races of ancient America. The Guarani ate the prisoners he made in battle to celebrate his victory over his enemies. The custom observed in this connection is almost a characteristic of the Tupi tribes.

The prisoners were not put to death immediately upon their captors' return from the warpath, but were first kept for some time in by no means severe imprisonment, which became lighter and lighter the nearer the time of their end approached, and terminated with most luxurious living, during which the prisoner was not only abundantly provided with the best of food and drink, but was even married to the daughters of the tribe. Meanwhile, without his being aware of it, preparations were made for the feast which was to be crowned by his death. In the middle of the ceremonial dances of his enemies

he received the fatal blow; immediately thereupon followed the definitely prescribed dissection of the corpse, and the distribution of the portions among the members of the tribe. The women and even the sick who were prevented from attending the feast also received their share. In this form of cannibalism it is obvious that the characteristic features of different stages of culture come into contact. It still contains reminiscences of the time when the flesh of an enemy, like that of a wild beast, served to appease hunger. But it is already pre-eminently the expression of proud triumph over the conquered enemy, for we have special testimony that the feast bore the character of the celebration of a victory. But finally, ceremonial influences also begin to show themselves to such an extent that the transition from the cannibalism of the Tupis to the human sacrifices of the Aztecs appears near at hand.

As anthropophagy, in this or in a similar form, is a common trait of almost all Tupi tribes, it must have begun in the original home of the race. This is a further argument against the Tupis having come from the highlands of Bolivia. The Tupi tribes which live nearest to this region, and should accordingly present the most archaic forms, are the only ones which have entirely done away with cannibalism, and have generally reached the highest degree of civilisation of any members of the race : these are the **The Early Tribes in Conflict** Omaguas between the Putumayo and Caquetá, and the Cocamas at the confluence of the Marañon and Ucayali. How these tribes of the Tupi stock could be cut off so far from the others is not difficult to explain. The Aruacs coming from the north halted at the great waterway of the Amazon at about the same time as the Tupis from the south reached its other bank.

So that, to the difficulties that Nature set in the way of a farther advance, was here added the hostility of new and powerful tribes. It was probably this, even more than the river with its innumerable sluggish arms—which is no grave obstacle to a race familiar with boats—that was the chief reason why the main body of the Aruacs could not advance any more to the south bank than the main body of the Tupis could advance to the north bank. That attempts could not have been wanting on both sides is shown by the small detached tribes of each nationality that are met with in turn on the hostile bank. But, on the whole, the division is sudden and sharp. To the Aruacs it meant the end of their onward movement. They seem still to have possessed the power to offer the Tupis an invincible resistance, but not to continue their advance in a new direction.

But the Tupis continued to advance. Their traditions show that they followed the Amazon and its tributaries upward ; and that the passage up the Amazon did not appear an impossibility to these Indians was proved in the year 1641, when some of them served the Portuguese as **Peoples who Sailed the Amazon** guides during the first expedition of the kind undertaken by the latter. Owing to the enormous extent of the Amazon, it no longer appears possible to follow the Tupi migration upward in its basin, but probably even the tribes of the Xingu and Tapajoz did not come down from the watershed to the Paraguay, but from the Amazon up its tributaries. For, in contrast to the Aruacs and Tapuyas, traces of Tupi tribes only occur where there was

sufficient water to allow them to remain true to the characteristic of their race. Numerous hordes of Tupis may have been scattered and destroyed in the network of the Amazon, and we cannot now ascertain to what circumstance it was due that the ancestors of the Omaguas and Cocamas managed to break through the central mass of the Nu-Aruac tribes and penetrate almost to the foot of the Cordilleras. Probably the report of a rich cultivated land led them up the Amazon and its tributaries, as in later times the legend of the Omaguas and of the ever-vanishing Eldorado led the Spaniards down the same way.

According to the traditions of the Spanish chroniclers the remembrance of an invasion by the hostile population of the lowlands had not quite died out even among the Indians of the civilised states. Between the immigration of the Omaguas to their later abodes and the discovery of America there must in any case have been a considerable space of time, for the Omaguas not only rose far above the average degree of civilisation of the Tupi races under the influence of more highly **Caribs and Their Civilisation** civilised peoples, so that they renounced cannibalism, tilled the ground, and occupied permanent dwelling-places—indeed, even founded large towns—but the knowledge of all these achievements had even had time to spread abroad among their less civilised neighbours, who reported the name of the Omaguas to the Spaniards as being a race of fabulous wealth and extraordinary power.

The youngest of the races of South America is that of the Caribs. It is partly due to this circumstance, and to good fortune in the field of ethnographic research, that we know its history somewhat better than that of the other groups. The original abodes of the Carib race probably lay near the original home of the Tupi race. As the latter peopled the upper affluents of the Paraguay, the Caribs peopled the upper basin of the Tapajoz and of the rivers flowing in the same direction to the lower Amazon. The degree of civilisation attained here by the Caribs must be described as extraordinarily low ; their language could not count farther than three, really only to two, and we must imagine that their other conditions of life corresponded to this poverty of ideas. Even here mutual intercourse will have taken place between them and the Tupis, which may have had lasting influence on both races. Their development was so similar that one of the first investigators in this field, Karl von Martius, even regarded the Tupis and Caribs as brother tribes and descendants of a common race. At present, however, one is more inclined to the view that the Tupis and Caribs came from different stocks, but were early and closely co-related.

The Caribs were likewise chiefly a race of fishermen, and their relations to the world of water were those which earliest reached a higher development. They, too, like the Tupis, the more the old home became too small for them, followed the rivers of their native land downward, so that they gradually got to the Amazon itself and so to the open sea. The traces of their migration in this direction are obliterated, and it is not impossible that their arrival at the mouth of the Amazon preceded the appearance of the Tupis.

But in that case it was probably also the Caribs, and not the Tupis, who first checked the advance of the Aruac races ; indeed, the enmity between the Caribs and the Aruacs has left **A Check to the Aruacs** widespread traces, whereas between the latter and the Tupis contact took place at comparatively few points only. What may have given the impulse to the migrations of the Caribs is no clearer than the causes of all the other great movements of the races of the American continent. On the other hand, we are better informed as to the manner of their progress, owing to the fact that it was still fresh in the memory of the generation of aborigines found by the Spaniards when they discovered America. Of all Indian races the Caribs were by far the most feared. Even to the Europeans these dauntless sons of the wilderness offered a stubborn resistance, and indeed frequently came off victorious in their bloody battles with the first bands of discoverers, but only to fall, later on, before better equipped expeditions. The Caribs were ruthless in their warfare, not only with Europeans, but also with the Indian population, before the white men appeared.

At what period they were transformed from a comparatively harmless race of fishermen, as Karl von den Steinen found them in the original home of the race on the Upper Xingu, into the nation of bold and savage water-pirates, spreading terror far around, as we find them in the fifteenth century, is, of course, a mystery. But the fact that the Caribs made their language prevail over almost the whole region north of the Amazon, including a large part of the Antilles, and this, so far as tradition leads us to infer, by violent methods alone, shows that the race must **The Caribs Known as Man-Eaters** have possessed quite extraordinary power. When the Caribs began their migrations they were still at the stage when the flesh of their enemies was welcome food ; and they apparently never rose above this rather rude standpoint of anthropophagy.

Eating their enemies was so characteristic of the Caribs that among the Spaniards their name was identical with the term for man-eaters, and in its corruption to " cannibals " this term has become the common property of all civilised nations. This circumstance has fatally affected historical research, as, of course, races of other origin also adhered to the custom of anthropophagy, and it was generally sufficient for the dicoverers of the sixteenth century to ascertain that a race was given to cannibalism to count it at once among the Caribs. It was only later and often most recent research that succeeded in bringing order into this confusion. In the cannibalism of the Caribs, as in that of the Tupis, there are no signs of the beginning of a refined conception. It is true that actual hunger will have but rarely driven them to it, for as fishermen and hunters they knew how to gain their livelihood from a bountiful Nature ; moreover, as soon as their expansion over Aruac territory began, their women probably continued the agriculture practised by these tribes, although on a more limited scale.

But it is chiefly the expression of warlike triumph that serves to explain their cannibalism, and their wars with all hostile tribes were wars of extermination, in **The Shy and Peaceable Aruacs** which no male captives were made, but all the adult men were put to death. The shy and peaceable Aruacs could not have been dangerous opponents ; they even met the Europeans upon their first appearance with respectful timidity, which was only changed to fearful flight after they had learned by years of suffering what bitter experiences were in store for them in intercourse with the white man. So that even weak parties of Carib warriors must often have succeeded in overcoming far superior bands of their opponents. But if the Carib on the warpath behaved with ruthless ferocity towards the male portion of hostile tribes, he, too, spared the women. On the restless expeditions that he undertook, often for considerable distances, in his narrow canoe, women could not accompany the warrior ; they would have been a far greater hindrance to him than on expeditions by land. But as at least the longer expeditions were not undertaken exclusively for the purpose of spoil and plunder—although the warlike expeditions of the Caribs are often decidedly distinguishable from migrations—but had for their object the founding of new settlements, the Caribs probably mixed extensively with the women of another race. And it is only owing to the circumstance that the Carib expeditions were made exclusively on territory inhabited by Aruac races that the intermixture did not become more multiform.

Settlements Founded by the Caribs

The time of the Carib migrations can be somewhat more precisely judged than that of any other similar event. We have already indicated that the advance of the Caribs to the mouth of the Amazon seems to have preceded the arrival of the Tupis at that river. But the Tupi races must also have been pretty near the same goal at that time. Otherwise it can scarcely be explained why the Caribs should have extended their conquests exclusively in a direction in which they got farther and farther from the tribes they had left behind, so that finally they lost all touch with them. The discovery of these almost venerable remains of a people at the most primitive stage of development on the Xingu is really due to mere chance. From there to the Amazon the Tupi population forms a perfectly continuous mass in which sprinklings of the Carib stock are nowhere to be found. So that it must have been the advance of the Tupis that gave the Carib movement its northerly direction, and the weak resistance of the Aruacs must then have enticed the Caribs farther and farther, and have allowed them to spread over the north of South America very much more quickly than we can assume to have been the case with the migrations of the Aruacs, or even with those of the Tupis. In spite of this, it was, of course, centuries before the Caribs could

Spread of the Aruac Tribes

make their race the prevailing one from the mouth of the Amazon to the lagoon of Maracaibo. Their extreme outposts broke through the belt of the Cordilleras, presumably at no great distance from the northern sea-coast—even in the basin of the river Magdalena there is still a tribe of Carib origin, although rather as a detached horde amid nations of other races.

But, generally speaking, the higher civilisation of the races in the mountain regions of the Andes placed an insuperable obstacle in the way of their progress. In the basin of the Orinoco, whose tributaries they navigated in their canoes far into their upper courses, right to the foot of the mountains, spreading fear and terror among the dwellers on their banks, Carib tribes seem to have settled only to a limited extent ; but at its mouth we find them numerously and almost exclusively represented.

That here they established their dominion on a stratum of Aruac races is unquestionable, although direct proof of it is not so clear as in other parts. The last conquest of the Caribs, which had not come to an end at the time of the discovery of America, was that of the Antilles. When the Cordilleras checked his advance westward, the Carib, whose continual roving into new lands for centuries had become to him a necessary of life, looked around for new objects. While some made their raids up the Orinoco, others made their aim the small islands lying off the Venezuelan coast, often within sight, of whose Aruac population they presumably had heard from the coast-tribes of the mainland. It was probably here that they made a further and—for American conditions—important advance in the art of navigation : they learned to use the sail, an art probably known by none of all the other aborigines of the New World except the Maya races, but by these more perfectly.

The Last Conquest of the Caribs

The circumstance that the conquest of the islands took place in such recent times is of special importance in judging the nature of Indian migrations. On the large islands of the Antilles the first Spanish settlers found an almost unmixed population of the Aruac race—a peaceable, friendly, good-natured people, living on the abundant produce of their agriculture, with a little hunting and fishing added. But even these Aruacs already lived in constant fear of the Caribs, who sprang up on the coasts in their fast-sailing canoes, sometimes here, sometimes there, and plundered and burned one settlement of the Aruacs after another, murdering the men and carrying off the women.

The Aruacs were well aware, from the fate that had befallen the smaller islands in the course of the last generation, what the ultimate issue of this unequal struggle would be. When the continual raids had sufficiently weakened the male population of an island, the Caribs no longer appeared merely as flying robbers, but came in larger bands to crush the last resistance of the islanders. A war of extermination would then be waged upon the occupants of a permanent settlement on the island, and after the massacre or probably the flight of the last of these the settlement furnished a new centre of expansion to the unscrupulous Caribs. On the Lesser Antilles the Spaniards found almost everywhere the remarkable phenomenon that the language of the women was different from that of the men. In early times this gave rise to every possible kind of incorrect conjecture, until a closer study of the linguistic elements revealed the fact that the language of the women was a dialect of Aruac, while that of the men was Carib.

Linguistic Phenomenon Explained

This discovery, in connection with the stories told by the islanders of the invasion of the Caribs, showed that the Antilles had been conquered during the existing generation, and that the women of the Caribs, with their different language, were none other than the female portion of the Aruacs, who had become the wives of the conquerors. To the historical student of Indian migrations this fact was of no ordinary significance, for it shows us, in the first place, how slowly the expansion of one race over the territory of another proceeded, it having taken generations to fill districts so small in extent as the islands of the Antilles. On the other hand, it gives us the key to the explanation of the extraordinary multiplicity of the American languages, and to the bounds, effaced almost beyond recognition, between the races of one independent linguistic stock and those of another. For, though not in the conquering generation, in the offspring proceeding from the intermixture with strange women both the anthropological-physical and the ethnic and linguistic elements must naturally have blended in such a manner as, attaining a new fixity, to form a new race. The question has been much discussed whether the excursions of the Caribs may not have extended to the mainland of North America, which is at no great distance from the Antilles, and thereby have brought the native populations of the northern and southern continents in contact with one another, of which there is no trace on the isthmus connecting the two parts. But what one was inclined to regard as Carib influence in the art productions of northern Indians has not stood the test of scientific investigation.

Limits of Carib Excursions

It is certainly singular that the two parts of the American continent—on which for thousands of years man had been making slow progress in the development of his faculties—not only remained uninfluenced and unknown by mankind of the other continents, but should also have remained equally strange and unknown to each other, in spite of isthmus and island-bridge. And yet it seems to have been so. The line dividing the northern and southern races on the land bridge of Central America certainly does not come at the narrowest part; on the contrary, the territory occupied by the nations of southern origin extends to the primitive sphere of culture of Central America. But the line is a sharp one: different races do not overlap one another here, as we so frequently find to be the case in the interior of nearly every continent. Neither can we trace the slightest influence of any consequence having been exercised by the inhabitants of the one half on those of the other.

The Line Between North and South

The Avondale Mounds in Washington County, Mississippi

The De Soto Mound in Jefferson County, Arkansas

NORTH AMERICAN MOUNDS AND THEIR PURPOSES

The American mounds were sometimes used for burial purposes by the primitive peoples. But the mound also entered into their worship, and the third illustration shows a religious ceremony centring round a small mound with symbolic shell and reversed arrows, while the chief huts of the village are burning. How large some of the mounds were is well illustrated in the second picture, some of them having from three to seven million cubic feet of material.

AMERICA
BEFORE
COLUMBUS

PRIMITIVE
RACES
OF AMERICA
III

RACES OF THE NORTH AND EAST

THE STORY OF THE PAST AS REVEALED BY THE ARTIFICIAL EARTHWORKS

LIKE the southern half, North America also witnessed extensive migrations in prehistoric and even in historic times, but the investigator who seeks to trace them is in a much more unfavourable position on the soil of the northern than of the southern continent. The civilisation brought to the New World from Europe has already extended its victorious march over almost the whole of the United States, a triumph which has filled the mother civilisation with undivided admiration and the daughter with pride.

This victorious march has swept away with unusual inconsiderateness the traces left of the ancient civilisation of the aboriginal population. Whereas in South America we still find the Indian master of vast regions, under conditions of life that evidently form to a large extent analogies to the peculiar aboriginal civilisation found by the first Europeans, in **Driving the Indian from North America** North America the Indian has for centuries been continuously driven by the white man from the neighbourhood of his settlements ; only in isolated cases have there been men in North America in earlier times who took a benevolent interest in the Indian, and attempted to reconcile him to the new civilisation and win him over to the new conditions.

It is only in the last few decades that the American people have also recognised that they were on the point of destroying their solitary and last opportunity of ascertaining the earlier history of their home, and, with that liberality which we so often find there, works have now been undertaken on a large scale, some of which have already been brought to a successful conclusion, with the object of ascertaining the historical meaning of the ethnographical relics in the territory of the United States. It is, moreover, true that

the Indians themselves no longer play any part in large portions of this territory. Where they have not already been quite exterminated or absorbed by civilisation, their traditions, although not generally quite so scanty as those of the Indians of South America, are still of very limited value ; for, apart from the remembrance of their struggles for generations **History From Excavations** with the white man, their shadowy reminiscences of the time when the Indian was still sole lord of wood and prairie have been almost entirely effaced. Here, too, the most valuable part of our material is, on the one hand language, and on the other hand what the oldest writers were able to ascertain from the Indians when they first met them.

To this are added the results of excavations, which have been undertaken on a larger scale than in South America. But down to the present day the American has had erroneous ideas concerning the most important marks of the earlier history of his land, the famous artificial mounds of the pre-Columbian period. A far wider gap separates the history of recent from that of olden times in the northern than in the southern continent.

Both for geographical and for historical research North America falls into three groups, not always sharply defined, but clearly perceptible. The first is formed by the lands in the extreme north of the continent, extending from Alaska to **Ice-bound Lands of the North** Greenland, which are broken up by numerous flowing and standing waters, though these are rigidly ice-bound for a considerable part of the year. It has been supposed that these lands did not always bear the inhospitable character with which the long-continued cold and gloom of the Polar winter has stamped them in the present period of the earth's history. But if this supposition is at all correct, it refers at best to times that are not separated from us by historical, but by geological periods; and if, perchance, the first man came to America by way of these most northern lands, this event was certainly followed by thousands of years in which his passage

Where did the Innuits Come from? was sunk in absolute oblivion. Not until times rather later than the decline of the Roman Empire did a new migration take place here, which is of very little importance in the general history of mankind, but has left some slight traces behind.

The Esquimaux—or, as they call themselves, the Innuits—have been taken by many for an American race, or for descendants of those Indians who had had a special development under the influence of Polar nature. If certain resemblances in build and in mode of life between them and the most northern Indian tribes of the Pacific coast, the Haidahs and Thlinkits, are not to be traced to mutual influence, we are certainly driven to such a conclusion. But, considering the strikingly Mongolian character of the Innuits and the still closer relationship that connects them with the races of Northern Asia, it is far more probable that their home is to be sought in Asia; as immigrants they have always been treated with hostility by the Indians. The custom of the Indians, by no means confined to South America, of annihilating the men in their tribal wars, but of incorporating the women in their own tribe, involved the formation of mixed peoples where the different races were in close contact for a great length of time.

In this case it was the north-west coast of Alaska, opposite the Asiatic continent, and in a more favoured climatic situation, which, at all events, afforded the first home to a large number of Innuit tribes which gradually came over, or else mutual influences have been at work

America Peopled by Indians which explain the analogous manners and customs of the Innuits and the Indians of North-west America. In any case, the Innuits found the American continent already peopled by Indians up to the latitude of Bering Strait; otherwise in their further migrations they would scarcely have turned to the inhospitable north, over whose vast area their traces extend in scanty relics of houses and implements. Whether they

made other attempts at a southward advance elsewhere cannot be ascertained from these finds; but in any case they must have met with the same hostile reception from the races of Indian blood as met them in the north-west.

Such a contact between the races cannot have been of long duration, as otherwise ethnographic proofs would have been found, as in the extreme west. Those who regard the Innuits as an Indian tribe, gradually driven toward the Pole, would find proof of their view in the fact that the northern sagas which relate the voyages of Eric Rauda to Vinland ascribe the destruction of the settlements there to the Skraelings, a name given by the northern settlers in Greenland to the Esquimaux.

Now, it is an undoubted historical fact that the Vikings undertook voyages to the north-east coast of America as far back as the year 1000, but owing to the saga's poetic dress, in which alone the little information relating thereto is preserved, we do not know with certainty where these settlements were, nor the character of the population found there.

Expansion of the Innuits The difference between the Skraeling, the Viking's enemy in Greenland, and the skin-clad North Indian, with whom he fought under similar conditions in Vinland, might easily make so little impression on the Viking's mind, used to the dress and manners of North European civilisation, that both would appear as one to the bard who recited Viking deeds in saga song.

In spite of this the sagas give us a clue to the date of the migrations of the Innuits. They doubtless made their way to Greenland from the American coast or from the islands lying north of it. As the Innuits were at war with the northerners of Greenland about 1200, and succeeded in driving them away during the course of the two following centuries, we may conclude with a fair amount of certainty that the expansion of the Innuits over the North American Continent must have come to an end about the same time.

The migrations of the Esquimaux have no connection with the history of the rest of America, whereas, on the other hand, there was frequent contact between the Indian races of North America, as there was between the races of South America. For the northern as well as for the southern half of the continent the eastern chains of the Cordilleras formed an unmistakable boundary of culture. In the north as well as in the south the region of higher civilisation lies on the Pacific side of the mountains, not on the Atlantic side. But the further step in assuming a connection between northern and southern civilisation and between the northern and southern primitive races is not justified.

If the Indian in the basin of the Mississippi is more closely related, ethnographically, to the Indians in the basin of the Amazon or Orinoco than to his western neighbours on the other side of the Cordilleras, this fact is sufficiently explained by the similarity of their conditions of life. Man at a low stage of civilisation is everywhere, both in the Old and New Worlds, dependent in the highest degree on his natural surroundings, and where these produce similar conditions the development of man will also tread similar paths.

On the whole, the Indian population of North America east of the Cordilleras exhibits a far greater uniformity of race than is the case in South America, and, although with the aid of language a number of largely different stocks may be **New World's** distinguished (which presuppose a separate development **Thousand** for hundreds if not thousands **Languages** of years), the division of the North American races is more recent than that of the South American. This is shown by the mere fact that, of the thousand or so different languages and dialects of the New World named by Brinton in his " History of the American Race," about 750 belong to the part south of the Isthmus of Panama and only 250 to Central and North America. But at the same time the multiplicity of the latter races is also so great as to have required an extraordinary length of time.

The most important problem of the pre-Columbian history of North America is formed by the question: Who were the builders of the so-called mounds ? These mounds of earth, or, more rarely, stones, erected by the hand of man, often with a considerable expenditure of labour, are scattered more or less numerously over the greater part of the United States. We find them in the north near the Great Lakes and far into the territory of Canada. And although towards the south, from the confluence of the Mississippi and Arkansas, they become rarer, their traces may be found not only as far as the mouth of the Father of Waters, but even in the most southern regions of the peninsula of Florida. On the west side the southern limit of the mound region has not yet been ascertained with certainty, but even there it extends to Texas and Mexico, touching the region of civilisation of the Pueblo Indians and the races of Central America. Its bounds are scarcely narrower

Home of the Mound-Builders in an east-and-west direction, for while the artificial mounds almost reach the 70th degree of longitude in the State of Maine in the east, their most western outposts in the north are beyond the 101st parallel. Now, the mounds in this vast area are certainly not numerous everywhere or equally distributed. On the other hand, it seems as if the real home of the mound-builders lay in the basin of the central and upper Mississippi and its eastern affluents, especially the Ohio, while the groups of such erections lying outside this region are characterised more or less as radiations from this centre.

When more careful attention was first given to the earthworks in the states of Ohio, Illinois, and Wisconsin in the early part of this century, people were quite astonished at their large number, the considerable size attained by some of them, and the original forms, sometimes bordering on the regularity of mathematical figures, which they exhibited in many instances. Astonishment grew when the interest that was thus awakened led to earthworks of like or allied character being constantly discovered in new parts, and when the excavations, which were at first made at only a few places, yielded inexplicable results. Thus the conviction gradually dawned upon scientific and lay investigators that the mounds must be the relics of a long-vanished nation.

Those whose conjectures were aided by a vivid imagination did not hesitate to connect the race of the mound-builders directly with the Toltecs, the race that for a long **Earthworks** time was held to be the stan- **a Proof of** dard-bearer of every civilisation **Civilisation** discovered on the soil of North and Central America. But even the more cautious were convinced that these erections proved the existence of a highly developed civilisation in an epoch thousands of years back. Unquestionably the artificial mounds were the work of a sedentary race, for the Indian who roved about in the state of a nomad could not possibly have had time, power, or inclination to erect even the most insignificant of these earthworks, not to speak of the structures—not very numerous, but of imposing dimensions—of Etowah, Cahokia, etc., the largest of which had a content of 3,000,000 to 4,000,000 cubic feet. To erect such structures required a population not only of far greater density than had ever **Fortifications** been found anywhere on the **on the** North American Continent, **Mississippi** but one that must also have been excellently organised to be able to subject such labour as these gigantic works entailed to a common will. But what a race, what a state must that have been which not only produced these structures but protected the banks of the chief river-courses for many miles with extensive fortifications, such as would seem in early times to have accompanied the Mississippi in an almost uninterrupted chain from the mouth of the Arkansas up to the Illinois. And an almost incredible range of territory is given to this state if, instead of merely taking into account the region most thickly covered with such earthworks, we extend its boundaries as far as the earthworks can be found.

A sedentary population of such density must naturally have been mainly dependent on a cultivated food supply, and that the mound-builders had been agriculturists was evident from all that was brought to light in the excavations made in the mound region. Not only were ears and grains of maize found, with the vessels and implements necessary for its preparation, but the excavations, or inferences from them, proved that other seeds and fruits were also possessed by the mound-builders.

Indeed, their agriculture must have been already highly developed, for careful investigation revealed not only irrigation works and aqueducts of considerable extent in places, but, in the valleys of the great rivers, even cultivated patches, on which the excess of moisture had been counter- **Mound-Builders** acted by a raising of the **and Their** ground in beds. The mound- **Advanced Arts** builders must also have possessed rich experience in handicraft. Their pottery exhibited not only a great variety of forms, adapted to the most different purposes, but in the better articles attained great technical perfection. Here, too, no trace could be found of the use of the potter's wheel, but some vessels seemed to have been given a glaze of very fair quality. The excavations could

naturally not give a very definite idea of the people's accomplishments in weaving, on account of the greater perishability of all fabrics, but even of this art both coarse and fine specimens were by no means wanting. It was thought that special proof of a higher civilisation was given by the specimens of copper orna-ments brought to light in the earthworks. The whole of America was in the Stone Age when Columbus discovered it, so that if worked copper was found here, although in no considerable quantity, it must neces-sarily have belonged to a race of higher civilisation, and long periods must have elapsed since the decay of this race for its progress in culture to have been entirely lost again to after-ages.

The race had certainly had a special knowledge of architecture. This was proved not only by the almost incredible number of earthworks erected by them, and the astounding massiveness of the large mounds, but, above all, by the variety of form that they had been able to give to their works. It is true that the structures were often merely accumulations of earth **Earthworks** of truncated conical form, or **Tell the Story** oblong-oval or rectangular **of the Past** mounds or terraces, but in other places they exhibited the most surprising forms. The outlines of some of them were unmistakable repre-sentations of living creatures—snakes, birds, and mammals, and even the human form. If this proved that this ancient race possessed an artistic eye, another kind of earthwork was still more calculated to inspire respect for its achieve-ments in culture. Earthworks were dis-covered which reproduced the mathematical figures of the circle, rectangle, square, and polygon with an accuracy which investi-gators pronounced to be quite inconceivable without the use of instruments.

In its religious ideas such a people must certainly also have risen far above the naturalism and animism of uncivilised races, and of this, too, the remains seemed to offer proof. If a considerable part of the earthworks had served as fortifications, dwellings, and cultivated land, there were innumerable others which, from their position and form, would not have been suited for these purposes. Many of them proved to be graves, either of single persons or of whole families, and there were even graves for large numbers and burial-grounds like cemeteries. The manner in which the dead had almost always been interred with articles used in their earthly occupations left no room for doubt that the race of the mound-builders believed in a second existence. It even seemed as if religion played an extraordinarily important part among them in all the concerns of life. Almost everywhere that earthworks occurred with any frequency there were mounds of a certain kind which could not be explained at the first glance. These mounds, generally of conical form, had at their base, or even in their higher strata, a horizontal layer of firmly beaten clay or clayey earth, which, upon the removal of the overlying masses, in general proved to be a carefully levelled surface like a floor, rather inclined towards the middle, in the centre of which the traces of fire were often found.

The discoverers of this form of mound thought themselves justified in regarding these floors as sacred places, and the remains of fire as affording traces of sacrifices; and as human bones were repeatedly found in ashes, human sacrifices were supposed to have played an important part in the mound-builders' religious **Religious Rites of the Mound-Builders** rites, as in many other parts of the New World. The discoverers therefore gave these earthworks the name of altar-mounds, and from their frequency they drew the conclusion that the old civilised state must have possessed a numerous and influential sacerdotal caste, to which presumably the most imposing of the great earthworks, the terraced pyramids for sanctuaries honoured by special worship, owed their origin.

Thus the picture of the race that erected the earthworks was no longer shadowy and indistinct; on the basis of these discoveries, and with the aid of the analogies of the civilisations found on American soil by the first Europeans, fairly definite ideas had been arrived at. But it was thought that quite an extraordinary age must be ascribed to this race, because at the time of the discovery of America all memory of these peoples had already vanished, and, from the high stage of civilisation they had occupied, it was thought that their gradual decline and the extinction of all their traditions must have taken a considerable space of time.

On the other hand, a particularly remarkable discovery had been made. One of the mounds representing living things was discovered in the neighbourhood of Bloomington, Wisconsin; and several of the older archæologists thought they recognised in it the form of an elephant or some other animal with a trunk. Now, among the pipe-bowls in the form of animals that have been found in large numbers in excavations in the mound region, the representation of an **America's Prehistoric Animals** animal provided with a real trunk—as distinguished from the trunk-like snout of the tapir, which in Chiapas is a sacred animal —also occasionally occurs; they were therefore convinced that the builders of that mound must at least have had a traditional recollection of the form of an elephant or mastodon. But as the proboscidians were extinct on American soil long before historic times, the tradition of the mound-builders must have gone back to the ages to which the mastodon skeletons of the Missouri valley belonged. From the arrow-heads that were found with those skeletons it was assumed that the animals had been killed by man.

Although the above view of the mound-builders was formerly the predominant one, for a long time scholars have not been wanting who, doubting the existence of a prehistoric civilised race on the soil of North America, are of opinion that the ancestors of the same Indians who inhabit the United States to-day erected these mounds in comparatively recent times. The more the ancient history of the New World was subjected to methodical investigation, the greater became the number of the mounds. In the course of the last few years the sytematic examination of the earthworks in the different parts of the Union, which has been undertaken on a very extensive scale by the North American Bureau of Ethnology at Washington, has proved irrefutably that the mounds really possess neither the age commonly attributed to them nor all the peculiarities demanded. On **The Mounds Under Examination** the contrary, they are not the work of one race, but are probably the relics of the different Indian races which inhabited the territory of the United States before and after the discovery of America by Columbus.

The inferences as to the age of the mounds drawn from the "elephant mound" had not met the approval even of many who still did not doubt that the builders of this mound intended to represent an animal with a trunk. But after recent investigations this too seems by no means certain. The soil of the mound has undoubtedly been under cultivation for years, but its form, although not so clear, has remained quite recognisable. It now appears that the ground is very light sand, and that the trunk has probably been

Mounds as Monuments of the Past formed at the head-end merely by the long-continued influence of the elements, especially of the wind. The mound was presumably meant to represent the bear, an animal often used as a totem. In a like manner the most recent surveys have done away with other old erroneous ideas.

There is, at all events, no denying that a number of earthworks in the valley of the Ohio, especially those of the so-called Newark group, exhibit forms of almost mathematical regularity; but the circumstance that of all the circular circumvallations only one or two are almost perfectly round, while the great majority only imperfectly attain this evidently desired end, goes to prove that they were built experimentally rather than with the help of instruments of precision. It likewise proves quite erroneous to regard the artificial mounds over the whole extent of their range as uniform, and therefore as the relics of a single race. Closer investigation shows rather that a number of different groups of mounds can be so clearly distinguished by their form and contents that in certain districts we are even able to trace the settlements of two different mound-building populations at one and the same place.

The hypothesis of a particular ancient civilised race being the mound-builders collapses. The mounds remain to us as a class of highly important monuments, from which we can derive information of the earlier history of the North American Indians that no other source can give. Starting from the assumption that the

The State of Indian Civilisation state of Indian civilisation had remained practically the same since the discovery of America, if it had not advanced through intercourse with the white man, the Indians were considered to have been almost without exception nomadic races of hunters, whose unconquerable love of unrestrained freedom would never and nowhere have permitted them to form large communities and erect permanent dwellings. This conception is perfectly unhistorical. In large tracts of North America there were, even in the sixteenth century, restless hordes of Indians, who lived almost exclusively by hunting, of which they were passionately fond.

But near to them, or separating them, and probably throughout the greater part of the present United States, there were also Indian races which had made, compared with them, quite considerable progress in the path of their culture development. So far as there are still any descendants of these races in existence, the policy of the Anglo-American colonists towards the Indians, which has been guided merely by self-interested motives, has certainly reduced them again to a stage of civilisation little different from that of their nomadic and savage fellows.

The Indian mounds and graves have left us evidences of a civilisation that tell an undeniable tale; and an impartial examination of the oldest accounts of the first meeting of the white man and the red man on North American soil confirms in numerous particulars what the mound-finds lead us to suppose. Individual re-

The Light of Research on the Dark Ages searches are certainly not yet far enough advanced for the valuable material of the discoveries to be used wholly and fully. We know too little of the ancient migrations of the pre-Columbian Indians to be able with certainty to connect the boundaries that archæology traces in certain districts with definite racial boundaries. But where this has become possible the antiquities serve materially to clear up historical hypotheses, and a combination of the different methods of research will further reduce the uninvestigated area year by year.

The whole basin of the Mississippi—a broad strip of land beginning at the Great Lakes in the north and extending to the lowlands of the lower Mississippi—was in earliest times peopled by tribes comprised under the common name of Algonquins. Of the better known Indian tribes belonging to them are the Chippewas in the north, the Delawares, Mohicans, and Ottawas in the north-east, and the Shawnees in the south-east. From their traditions it is supposed that their original home is to be sought in the north-east, beyond the Great Lakes, although they had been driven thence before the time of Columbus by the nations of the Iroquois race. Their migrations from the north seem to have proceeded by two separate branches. The one went in a south-easterly direction, mainly along the sea-coast; not, like the Tupis in South America, peopling only a narrow strip, but spreading out widely, and following the rivers that flow into the sea far into the Alleghany Mountains. In spite of their being near the water, the Algonquins were scarcely ever exclusively a race of fishermen. Whether they were already agriculturists when they moved down the east coast is doubtful.

Even the eastern Algonquins practised agriculture in later times, but their fellows who moved along the Great Lakes on their way westward, and in earlier times inhabited their banks, certainly did so even at the time of the migration. As was always the case, the farther the tribes were led apart by their migrations, which continued slowly for centuries, the more differentiated they became in customs and mode of life. If it were not for the unmistakable sign of a kindred language, one would scarcely suppose that the Chippewas of the north-west and the Shawnees in the south were brothers of one and the same race. A number of nations

The Algonquin Civilisation and Religion of the Algonquin race are distinguished from all other Indians of North America by their comparatively advanced civilisation. There is no doubt that even in early times they had taken to a settled mode of life and devoted themselves to agriculture.

Nor is it mere chance that in several points their religious ideas border on those of their neighbours in the extreme north-west. From certain peculiarities in this respect one might be inclined to seek their home in the north-west rather than in the east, for many of them remind us of the Tinnés on the one hand, and the Pueblo tribes on the other. The Chippewas and Lenapés already possessed, in their painted wooden tablets or sticks, a system of interchange of ideas that had advanced beyond the purely pictorial character to a kind of hieroglyphic symbolism, which was specially employed for preserving the remembrance of sacred rites. Their religious system, with the worship of the sun and the four cardinal points as the homes of the wind-gods, we shall find further developed among the Pueblo Indians.

A further resemblance to the latter obtains in the cult of the totems, or clan tokens, which we meet with not only in the Pueblos but also among many other Indian tribes of the Pacific coast as far as the Thlinkits and Haidahs on the borders of Alaska. For this reason we may, at all events, regard races of this stock as the builders of the peculiar earthworks known as effigy mounds. It is an interesting fact that all the animals—bear, snake, various birds, fishes, etc.—from which most of the

Builders of Effigy Mounds designations and sacred objects of the clans (the totems) were derived are represented in these mounds. As these earthworks did not serve as burial-places, and were little adapted for fortifications, we may perhaps regard them, like the meeting-hall of the Iroquois or the "kiva" of the Pueblo Indians, as the centre of the cult of the clan. Whether Indians of the Algonquin race were also the builders of the mounds on the central Mississippi and on the Illinois we would rather doubt, especially as this district exhibits mounds of various types that are all different from those of Wisconsin. If a not very reliable tradition of the Lenapés or Delawares can be credited, the answer would have to be decidedly in the negative.

In spite of their great progress in the paths of civilised life, the Algonquins did not manage to build durable dwellings. This is the more peculiar, as they might have seen those of the neighbouring Pueblo Indians, with whom commercial relations seem to have existed. But we may not place them lower in the scale of civilisation solely on this account. The erection of stone buildings—which are better able to defy the destructive influence of time than wooden huts at best only coated with lime, and even than mounds of loose earth—creates only too easily an erroneous idea of the degree of civilisation of a race.

At the lower stages of civilisation man is, however, primarily dependent on his natural surroundings, and if the limestone and sandstone plateaus of the west offered the Pueblo Indians the opportunity

Primitive Copper Workers of easily becoming no mean builders, the wooded hill regions of the lake district denied to the Algonquins the opportunity of handing down to posterity similar impressive proofs of their civilisation. But the Algonquins achieved something that scarcely any other race of North Atlantic Indians did: they knew and worked copper. It certainly occurred in such purity in the hills between Lake Superior and Lake Michigan that in the best specimens it could even be shaped by hammering in the cold state. Probably, however, they also knew a primitive and not very efficient method of smelting and welding, with the help of which they formed beads and small plates of the metal, while they were able to emboss the latter with figures. The bands of the Algonquins

Race Named After the Savannah who were advancing south-eastward, having crossed the Savannah River, came upon solid masses of strange Indians, who rendered the continuation of their migration in the same direction impossible. This probably led first to a temporary halt, but, space eventually proving too limited for the gradually increasing numbers of the Algonquins, their migrations were resumed in a westerly direction. The Indians who marched up the Savannah, crossed the Alleghanies, and began to spread over the valleys of the Green River and Tennessee, were called after the Savannah by their neighbours, from their long sojourn on this river, and as " Savannees "—which with time has become " Shawnees "—have preserved the remembrance of this stage of their migrations down to historic times.

The Shawnees and related Delaware tribes are proved to have taken an important part in the erection of the earthworks that occur throughout Tennessee and the neighbouring states on the lower tributaries of the Ohio. A large number of such mounds in this district have been erected for burial purposes, sometimes singly, but generally in groups, and very often in connection with larger earthworks and circumvallations, and the manner of interment has so characteristic a stamp that in it we find undoubtedly a racial peculiarity.

Whereas in other parts of the mound area the dead were frequently buried in a crouching position, like the mummies of South America, or in bone-heaps after removal of the flesh, the mode of interment

Burial Customs of the Tribes practised here reminds one greatly of that usual in Europe. The bottom and four side-walls of a hole in the earth were lined with flat stone slabs, and the corpse was laid in it, lying full length on its back. Flat stones served to close the sarcophagus, and, if there was any fear of the earth falling through the spaces between them, these spaces were often covered by a second layer of smaller slabs. Such graves are repeatedly found, even without mounds

over them, but they are especially numerous in the small conical mounds on the southern tributaries of the lower Ohio, where the Shawnees and kindred Indian races lived down to historic times. We should expect these Shawnees to have been the builders of the graves and the earthworks connected with them, and we are able to prove it. We thus obtain an important argument in judging of the age of many groups of earthworks, in opposition to the fanciful theory of a past of thousands of years.

The custom of interring the dead in stone receptacles, as above described, has been practised by Shawnee Indians not only in historic times, but, where there was suitable stone, down to the last century, and has been observed by numerous writers in different places independent of one another. In accounts of earlier times the erection of a mound a few feet in height and of conical form is repeatedly mentioned. Moreover, if excavations have revealed that burial-places of this particular kind have repeatedly contained articles of undoubted European

Check to the Algonquin Advance origin among the things placed with the dead, the mounds of this type are certain proof that the particular localities were at some time occupied by members of the Shawnee group of the Algonquin race, whose migrations have been going on in this region down to historic and even post-Columbian times.

The Indians who checked the advance of the Algonquins in a southerly direction belonged, presumably, to the group of the Muskokis, whose best-known representatives were the Creeks and Chickasaws. Although these Indian tribes were the first to come in contact with Europeans at the time of the discoveries— the best part of De Soto's adventurous expedition from Florida to the Mississippi having been made through the territory of Indians of the Muskoki race—they have hitherto been more neglected by research than the more northern tribes.

As descendants of this race have been found only on the banks of the rivers flowing into the Gulf of Mexico parallel to the Mississippi, and as in this district they formed a compact body unmingled with foreign tribes down to the discovery of America, we must assume that they were less given to migration than most of the other Indians. The land occupied by them in the sixteenth century was presumably the ancient home of the race; we may, perhaps, behold in them descendants of the earliest inhabitants of Eastern North America. In early times their abodes near the Mississippi undoubtedly extended much further northward, and possibly even further east; so that there may be some truth in the tradition of the Lenapés that they drove the Muskokis from their more northern settlements on the Mississippi.

The Muskokis were also by no means at the low level of civilisation that, judging by modern views, is usually attributed to the earlier Indian population of the continent. They tilled the ground on the most extensive scale, and their agricultural produce excited the admiration of De Soto's Spaniards. Their settlements were called " towns " by the Spaniards, and some of them contained a large number of inhabitants. They, too, took a large part in the erection of the artificial mounds, and the characteristics of their work are speaking witnesses to the progress they had made. In the district **Practical** of the Muskokis are some of the **Uses of the** largest mounds that the whole **Earthworks** region of the mound-builders can boast. These earthworks —which probably bore at the same time the dwellings of the foremost members of the tribe, and formed a place of refuge for the whole tribe when attacked by enemies—are not, like the smaller mounds, round or conical in form, but remind one rather of the terraced erections on which rose the temples and palaces of the civilised races of Central America. The De Soto mound, although it is not absolutely proved that it was erected by the Muskokis, gives a fair idea of this type.

The most imposing erection of this kind is the Etowah mound in the south of Georgia, and it can be proved that it was still inhabited by Muskoki tribes at the beginning of the sixteenth century, being used as a palace and fortress by their chiefs. As it is surrounded by a large number of smaller mounds, which are enclosed by a kind of fortification, partly rampart and partly moat, we can form from this an idea of old Indian towns which agrees in so many respects with Le Moyne's description that a great degree of reliability may be accredited to the latter. The Muskokis had acquired a degree of civilisation that

leads us to infer that they had been a sedentary race for a very long time. Although the ground of the district they occupied did not afford them suitable material for massive buildings, yet they, almost alone among the Indians of the East, built stronger dwellings than could be erected of purely vegetable materials.

How the Indians Built Their Houses The most recent investigations and excavations have proved that some of the mounds that, by reason of their floor-like layers of clay and the remains of bones and ashes found in and beneath these, were pronounced by their first discoverers to be altar-mounds, in reality bore the houses of the Muskoki Indians.

The ruins of these houses, which appear here and there to have been round, but generally square, show that these Indians constructed their dwellings of a framework of wooden posts, between which the ground-work for a stucco-like wall-plaster was formed with cross-beams and interwoven twigs and branches. The plaster was left rough outside, but inside it was smoothed and whitewashed, as in the archaic buildings of the Pueblo Indians. It was applied only to the side-walls, on which it seems to have reached rather above the height of a man; above rose an arched roof borne by the thin ends of the posts and by pliant staves, and covered with vegetable matter—a reminiscence of the leaf-hut that had been usual among most Indian races, and also in earlier times among the Muskokis. The bones and heaps of ashes in the mounds are explained by the custom of consigning a man's house to the flames when he died.

In Le Moyne's description the deceased seems unquestionably to have been buried outside the village circle, under a mound which, on account of its smallness, we may perhaps regard as only the nucleus and beginning of the one to be erected. But among the Muskokis the deceased **Peculiar Burial Customs** was generally buried in the house itself, and, as soon as the fire had so far consumed the walls that the building collapsed, the place was covered up with earth. This peculiar mode of burial, of which traces may likewise be found in historic times, characterises in its turn, like the stone graves of the Shawnees, an ethnographic district, and enables us to throw a ray of light into the darkness that almost completely veils the earlier history

expansion of the Iroquois. The races that erected the effigy-mounds were, therefore, probably past their prime, and had perhaps even settled in other parts, when the races of the Iroquois family received the impulse that helped them to expand over the greater part of northernmost America. On the other hand, the separation of the Cherokees from the main race belongs to a much earlier period. The direction of their migrations agrees admirably with the theory that the original home of the race was in the extreme north-east. The Cherokees would then have moved off as a first wave in a southerly direction, so that in course of time they came to the basin of the Ohio, where they are proved to have long had their abodes. They do not seem to

of the Indian races. As in the south, so also in the north the territory of the Algonquins was bordered by foreign races of Indians. The land around the great North American lakes and their outlet to the sea, the River St. Lawrence, was the abode of the races of the Iroquois stock. Of all the Indians, these were most distinguished by their fine physical development and—probably as its consequence—by bravery, love of fighting, and warlike virtues, which long made them the most dreaded enemies. The real Iroquois, however, only became an important factor in the history of these districts in the last few centuries before the colonisation of North America. In earlier times the race of the Cherokees had seceded from them, and played no less important a part in the earlier history of America than they did subsequently in the time of colonial rule. The original home of the common race of the Iroquois and Cherokees is supposed to have been in the farthest north-east of the territory they afterwards occupied. It is true that in historic times the whole Lake region, including the districts bordering it on the south and west, was occupied by the Iroquois and the kindred race of the Hurons.

But this removal cannot have occurred in very early times, for these races seem to have taken but little part in the erection of artificial mounds. We are, therefore, forced to ascribe the earthworks of Michigan and Wisconsin to an earlier occupation of this district by Algonquins. And as these northern works are but rarely of a defensive character, it seems as if they were erected earlier than the period of struggle which must have attended the

A "PREHISTORIC" SCENE OF TO-DAY

The above illustration of a Pueblo woman engaged in making pottery is from a drawing made by an artist in Mexico recently, and illustrates a scene which is no doubt the same to-day as before the dawn of American history, for the Pueblo Indians are a primitive people existing in a land where modern invention has attained its highest.

have found these districts uninhabited; on the contrary, it is certain that Algonquin tribes not only sojourned there temporarily before them, but, as they did farther south and west, built permanent settlements and tilled the ground. At least some of the mounds in the farther course of the Ohio may owe their origin to the latter; and under Algonquin influence, but also in consequence of continual fighting, the Cherokees in turn proceeded to build artificial mounds, which once more form a special province,

of the Cherokee district, and we must assume that the cultivation of tobacco played an important part in the

PRIMITIVE PUEBLO WATER-CARRIERS

This scene, like that on the opposite page, is drawn from life of the present day, and is yet in every sense worthy to be regarded as a scene from prehistoric America.

agriculture of the whole region. But the upper valley of the Ohio furnishes not only the most numerous, but also, to judge from their forms, the oldest types of the Indian pipe, and shows the uninterrupted course of its further development so clearly that we must suppose it to have been the abode of a race closely connected with the history of the tobacco-pipe, as the Cherokees were. The mounds furnish the most remarkable instances of circumvallations of almost mathematical regularity. But as these are not exclusively limited to the upper course of the Ohio, it remains doubtful whether the greater number of them may not have been erected by the earlier inhabitants of the valley for protection against the advance of the Cherokees, but have been restored by the latter, after the conquest, to serve the same purpose. Cherokee graves certainly occur in connection with many of these groups of mounds, and at least bear witness to the fact that the invaders adopted the manners and customs of the conquered as far as the earthworks were concerned; what part they may have taken themselves in developing this

within the vast mound region, by their ethnographic peculiarities. Two things are characteristic of the Cherokee mounds : in the first place, the dead are buried in a lying position, but only in a more or less perishable covering (bark or stuffs), and generally in mounds that served as burial-places for large numbers ; in the second place, pipes, ranging from the most archaic to almost modern forms, such as are peculiar to the Indians, occur in these graves. Pipe-smoking is found in the mound region far beyond the borders

primitive architecture is of course difficult to ascertain. The migration of the Cherokees through the valley of the Ohio took place practically in pre-Columbian times, but it had not yet come to an end when the white man entered this district.

Only a little farther south, in the valley of the small river Tennessee, the agreement between the still existing groups of mounds and the position of the so-called "overhill towns" of the Cherokees, as recorded by the earliest visitors, testifies that these

5701

Indians, having once adopted the custom of mound-building, remained true to it even on their further migrations.

Yet another large branch seems to have been detached from the Iroquois race in the Hurons, who expanded in a westerly direction along the south bank of the River St. Lawrence as far as the lakes.

Five Nations of the Iroquois and Tuscaroras Whether this took place at a time prior to the migrations of Iroquois tribes to the south cannot be proved, but is very probable; for whereas the "Five Nations" of the Iroquois and the Tuscaroras in the far south had so strong a consciousness of belonging to the same stock that at the beginning of the eighteenth century the latter returned to the north and were received into the league as a sixth nation, even in the time of the first settlers there existed between Iroquois and Hurons a bitter enmity which had lasted from time immemorial, and which had a decided influence on the settlement of the land by Europeans in colonial times.

As regards civilisation, these Iroquois races were doubtless behind the Cherokees in most respects. They also were agricultural and sedentary to a small extent. When the first colonists ascended the River St. Lawrence, Hochelaga was decidedly a town-like settlement of permanent character. Nor are earthworks entirely wanting in this district that mark the sites of old Indian settlements. But they do not bespeak the higher civilisation of the more southern districts.

They are clearly defensive works, and therefore were probably not built until the real Iroquois undertook the forcible extension of their dominion over the territory of their neighbours. But this cannot have been long before the discovery of America, as these wars were still going on when the first white men began to penetrate from the coast into the interior. By "Iroquois," in the narrower sense, are

Tribes that Inhabited Canada meant only the tribes that inhabited the most northern states of the Union and the neighbouring districts of Canada down to the time of early colonisation. These, too, seem to have occasionally erected earthworks—a proof that even they did not lead an entirely unsettled life, although permanent dwellings and agriculture—these bases of progress in civilisation—play a smaller part with them than with most of the other nations. Of all

the races that the first European settlers found on American soil the Iroquois best represent the type that has erroneously been regarded as characteristic of the whole Indian population of North America.

In the main the Iroquois were still a race of hunters, and one that pursued its human game with the same cruelty and ruthlessness as its animal game. As they were an inland race, navigation and fishing did not play the same part in their economy as it did with the Tupis and Caribs, although they constructed excellent canoes of the bark of trees, and possessed a skill in damming up streams, for the purpose of catching the fish, that told of long experience. But their element was hunting and war. In build the Iroquois were superior to most of their neighbours, and to their comparatively wild life they owe a development of their physical powers such as was no longer possible even at the beginning of a civilised life.

By their strength, and still more by their bloodthirstiness and savage cruelty, they had made themselves a terror to all their neighbours far and wide. That racial relationship did not prevent them

Savage and Dreaded Iroquois from displaying their warlike propensities is proved by the struggles between them and the Hurons, in which the latter, despite their equality in numbers, on account of their more peaceable disposition were forced to retreat farther and farther before their enemies. But the warlike expeditions of the Iroquois extended by no means exclusively, perhaps not even mainly, westward. Their southern neighbours had also to suffer severely from their hostility, and in all probability their invasions were the cause of the latest American migration, which we have still to mention, namely, that of the Sioux-Dakotas, which must probably have taken place only in the last few centuries before Columbus. It is a characteristic sign of the superiority of the Iroquois in war that the only bands that pushed southward seem to have been small in numbers; at any rate they were able only to establish tribes of moderate size in the conquered districts, such as the Conestogas, and the Susquehannas on the banks of the river of the latter name.

What has made the Iroquois specially famous is the league in which the five tribes that remained in the old home combined with one another for attack and

HIAWATHA, THE GREAT ONONDAGA CHIEF

Hiawatha, who among the American Indians was regarded as a person of miraculous birth, was supposed to have been sent on earth to teach man the arts of civilisation. It was he who first discovered the value of maize as food, and taught his people the sciences of navigation and medicine. When the white man landed in America to preach Christianity, Hiawatha exhorted the Indians to receive the words of wisdom, and then departed to Ponemah, the land of the "Hereafter." Longfellow's great poem has given to Hiawatha an abiding place in literature.

From the drawing by J. Walter Wilson, R.I.

defence. This has been regarded as proof of a special talent for statesmanship, and as showing consequently a higher degree of intellectual development than the other Indians possessed.

But weighty reasons are opposed to such an interpretation. In the first place, it is by no means certain that this league was **Famous** the product of the uninfluenced **Iroquois** mental development of the **League** Indians. Hitherto it has been pretty generally assumed that the league of the Iroquois was concluded in the fifteenth century—about 1430. But the further the examination of Indian tradition with regard to underlying facts has been proceeded with, the more we have been convinced that all that seemed to appertain to the savage of an infinitely remote past, without history or record, in reality only applies to a few generations back. According to the latest calculation, the league was probably not made until about 1560; this assumption is strengthened by the stories of dissensions between the various Iroquois nations, which can scarcely belong to so remote a past as would result if the league was created about 1430.

If the alliance came about at so late a date, the earliest contact with the white man must have preceded it ; whether this was of a hostile or amicable kind, it must have exercised a different influence on the origin of the idea of an alliance if the latter had grown out of purely Indian conditions. Too much honour has been done to the chiefs who formed the league by the conception that has been spread of its purposes. The idea that the league was intended to do away generally with the state of war, and bring about perpetual peace among all Indians, is in such striking contradiction to the whole history of the Iroquois race before and after it was made, that this interpretation may unhesitatingly be pronounced an erroneous one. The exaggerated manner the Indians **Hiawatha** have of expressing themselves **in History and** may certainly be credited **Literature** with having formulated it in such grandiloquent terms, although no more was intended by them than to put an end to the dissensions between the small Iroquois tribes, which had previously been only too frequent.

Even so, there still remains sufficient in the League of the Five Nations to assure to the Onondaga chief Hiawatha,

who is considered to have been the father of the idea, quite as prominent a place in history as has been prepared for him in literature by Longfellow's immortal poem. In the whole history of the American nations, and the civilised races by no means excepted, there is not on record a second instance of the natives having had the insight to subordinate their sense of independence, which was carried almost to the point of unruliness, for any length of time to higher considerations.

Among the Mexicans we also find alliances of kindred races ; but these neither rested on so intelligent a basis as the league of the Iroquois, nor were they destined to last so long or to exercise a similar influence on the fortunes of the nation. In the case of the Iroquois, the self-denying act of their chiefs had as its consequence the maintenance of their supremacy among their neighbours until the time when the latter, even earlier than they themselves, sank into insignificance before the invasion of the white man.

If the nations of the Iroquois league exhibit at the present day the highest percentage of natives who have not suc- **The Iroquois** cumbed to European civili- **Races at the** sation, but have been able to **Present Day** reconcile themselves to it and become good citizens of a modern state, they owe this mainly to the wise foresight of their forefathers, who, by forming the league, created the first basis of a political order, from which accrued to them power over their kind, and respect and consideration on the part of the new immigrants.

When the races of Iroquois stock began to expand southward—a process which, as we have mentioned, belongs to the last few centuries before the discovery of America—they not only became involved in hostilities with the Algonquins, but another race was also driven by them from its abodes and forced to seek new districts. This was the Sioux or Dakota race, which certainly does not seem to have possessed in those times the importance that it afterwards acquired under the government of the United States. That the original home of these Indians, noted for the resistance they offered to settlers in the Far West in the course of the last century, was also east of the Alleghanies— in Virginia and North Carolina—is a discovery for which historical research has to thank linguistics. For, in the language

A SCENE FROM THE PRESENT THAT ILLUSTRATES THE PAST
A Pueblo hunter of Katzimo on the look-out.

of the long-neglected Indians of the central states, older forms of the same linguistic stock have been found whose later dialects are spoken in the vast region of the Sioux and Dakotas west of the Mississippi. Even in the east **The Sioux a Race of Hunters** the nations of this group were almost exclusively restricted to hunting; it seems that they never seriously took to agriculture or possessed permanent dwelling-places. A race that grew so little attached to the soil as these restless hunters must naturally have retired more quickly before the energetic advance of an enemy than the agricultural Algonquins and Cherokees.

Whether they fought with the latter in the valley of the Ohio we cannot tell from the obscure tradition of the Sioux tribes regarding this migration from the east. The migration certainly belongs to a later period than the secession of the Cherokees from the main race of the Iroquois. But probably the courses of the two races came but little in contact, as the Sioux, coming down the Big Sandy, reached the Ohio at a point lying on the south-west border of the territory over which the Cherokees expanded. As soon, however, as they were beyond reach of the hostility of the Iroquois the migration of the Sioux would also have assumed a slower pace, names of places and rivers confirming the tradition that they settled for some time in different parts of the Ohio valley. But they never seem to have settled permanently; for Europeans who followed the Ohio downward came across no nations of this race on its banks. The names given by the Sioux themselves to the different groups reflect a long separation between the upper and lower part of the river. But when De Soto crossed the American continent he came upon nations of the Sioux race only on the other side of the Mississippi—a proof that the whole migration of the races from the eastern states to the borders of the region they still occupied in this century took place in pre-Columbian times. Probably many other races peopled these vast regions when the first white men set foot on American soil; but what we know of them is infinitely little.

Even what has been brought to light, by laboriously following up scarcely perceptible traces, regarding the great races of the Algonquins, Muskokis, Iroquois, and Sioux, is so scanty that it can scarcely be called their history. The extensive and **Scanty Results of Research** zealous researches that have only recently been begun on American soil will surely bring to light many other memorials to which even historical attributes may be given; but unfortunately more than a few main features in the pre-history of the American Indians science will scarcely ever be able to trace.

CHIEFS OF THE SIOUX RACE OF AMERICAN INDIANS

AMERICA
BEFORE
COLUMBUS

PRIMITIVE
RACES
OF AMERICA
IV

AMERICAN PEOPLES OF THE WEST
THE LIFE, CUSTOMS AND CIVILISATION
OF THE PREHISTORIC CLIFF-DWELLERS

IF we cross the Rocky Mountains from the east, we enter the region of a development in culture of an evidently different kind. This difference is most striking if we cross by the Upper Rio Grande and the affluents of the Colorado from the hunting-grounds of the buffalo-hunters into the territory of the Pueblo Indians. On closer examination, however, it appears that all the races of the Pacific coast, up to the borders of the Esquimaux region in Alaska, exhibit close agreement in the evolution of their customs, so that, in spite of linguistic differences, they are more closely related to one another than to their eastern neighbours.

The inhabitants of the far North-west—the Thlinkits, Haidahs, and Nootkas—are almost exclusively races of fishermen, a not very frequent occurrence on North American soil. It is evident, moreover, **Inhabitants of the Far North-West** that they were not driven to this mode of life by their natural surroundings, but developed thus from the very beginning. This we may infer from the fact that, in spite of their racial individuality being comparatively highly developed, they have no traditions indicating an earlier and different state of development. When they first came in contact with Europeans they had developed, independently of foreign influences, a number of institutions that told of a very long period of gradual progress in culture. That they were expert navigators and fishermen and skilled boat-builders was too natural under the prevailing conditions to justify us in basing general conclusions upon it.

Like some of the Indians of the East, the natives of the North-west also attached chief importance, not to the family, but to the gens, or clan; accordingly they, too, did not occupy single houses, but built one house for all the families of a clan, in which each had only a compart-ment. The same community also ruled their life outside the house : common the work, common the benefit. A special feature with them was the system of totems, or clan symbols derived from living things, for which a reverence similar to **Slavery Among the Indians** fetishism was shown by all the members of the clan, but only by them. These totems certainly also had their share in developing the artistic efforts of the race, for the representations of the clan fetishes —sometimes of huge dimensions, as on the wooden totem-posts of the Haidahs and Bellacoolas—are among the most frequent proofs of their artistic sense, which exercised itself on the most diverse raw materials, such as wood, stone, and bone, but not clay. Now, with time a more highly developed social system had grown out of the gentile system.

Almost all the Indians of the North-west were familiar with slavery, and that in its most pronounced form, according to which the slave is the chattel and therefore the saleable property of his master. This presupposes a higher development of the ideas of clan, family, and property than we find among many other Indian races, whose slaves were almost exclusively captives taken in war, who either met a painful death or were amalgamated with the tribe. The same development is shown by the fact that almost all these races carried on a more or less extensive trade—the Sahaptins journeyed from the **Shell-Money as a Medium of Exchange** upper Columbia to the Missouri—and even used shell-money as a standard medium of exchange, which seems to have been recognised throughout the greater part of the Pacific coast to the borders of the Mexican states. Finally, all the Pacific tribes, although agriculture was either entirely unknown to them in consequence of the climatic conditions, or only played a subordinate part, were sedentary, but with this peculiarity: they possessed permanent winter dwellings built of stone and earth, but in the fishing-seasons they erected also temporary summer dwellings at different places. In all these peculiarities there prevails among the Indians of Western North America, always excepting the sprinkling of tribes of much lower development in Central California, a very general agreement, which is by no means limited to the coast tribes who live by fishing, but extends to the agricultural tribes living farther south and east.

South and south-east of the territory of the north-west Indians, and separated from them by a number of small tribes, some of them still at a very low stage of development, is another large region of a similarly developed culture, which from the earliest times has interested scholars in no common degree—the region of the Pueblo Indians. Remains of these races have been preserved through all the vicissitudes of colonial wars down to the

present day, and under circumstances which make it still possible to study among them the traces of their early civilisation.

The boldest historical conjectures have been made about these races. Like the mound-builders, they, too, were supposed to have formed in prehistoric times a mighty and extensive empire with a highly developed civilisation. Such theories con-

History of the Aztec Peoples

nected them, far more directly than was possible in the valleys of the Ohio and Mississippi, with the Central American civilised states of the Toltecs and Aztecs. A peculiar tradition of the latter supported this in a very remarkable manner. When the Spaniards, after the conquest of Mexico, inquired of the Aztec priests and scribes the early history of their race, they gave the following account. At a remote period they had set out from a place called Aztlan, which lay on a great lake in the far north; had wandered for countless years, during which they had been split up into several tribes, and

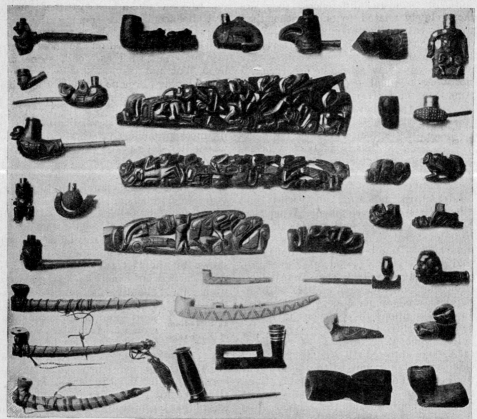

COLLECTION OF INDIAN CARVED PIPES OF NORTH-WEST AMERICA   Mansell

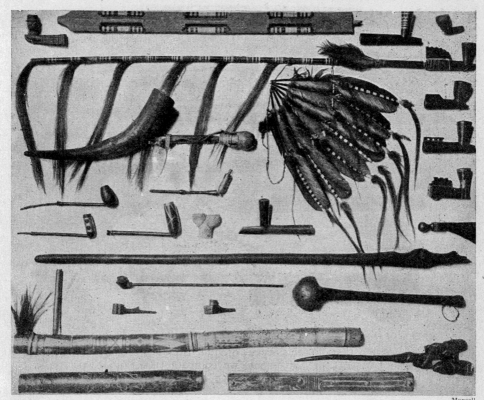

INDIAN IMPLEMENTS, ORNAMENTS AND PIPES, SHOWING THE VARIETY IN USE

founded temporary settlements at the various places, and had finally settled on the Lake of Mexico, to found the town of Tenochtitlan. This tradition has supplied food for the imagination for centuries.

In the great water on which Aztlan lay was seen a resemblance of the region of the great North American lakes, and an enterprising American even gave a group of earthworks in Wisconsin the name of Fort Aztlan. All erections of an unexplained type that occurred north of

The Aztecs and Their Neighbours the borders of the Mexican empire as far as the Lake district were considered to have been stations of the Aztecs. But whether any actual facts can be proved to underlie this tradition is doubtful. As regards the direction in which a higher civilisation spread, we find in the history of the Central American races facts that are difficult to reconcile with the Aztec tradition. But the idea that an indistinct knowledge of a prehistoric relationship between the civilised race of the Aztecs and their less civilised northern neighbours may be reflected in the legend must not be rejected offhand.

It is thought that linguistic affinity with the races of the Nahua stock, among whom the Aztecs of Mexico became most famous, can be traced into the heart of the Pueblo region, as far as the group of towns called by the Spaniards "Tusayan," but better known at the present day by the name of the chief place, Moqui. Resemblances in customs, religious ideas, and old traditions are unmistakable in all these races. But quite as unquestionable, if not more important, are similarities of this character between the Pueblo Indians and their northern neighbours, so that we should finally arrive at the result that in the whole mass of races, from Alaska nearly to the Isthmus, we have the members of one great family, which, however, seeing that its linguistic disunion is so great as almost to deny all connection, must have been broken up into different branches in very early times.

Considering how firmly half-civilised races in particular cling to everything connected with their religious ideas, often even when the original conditions on which the traditional institutions were founded have long disappeared, it is

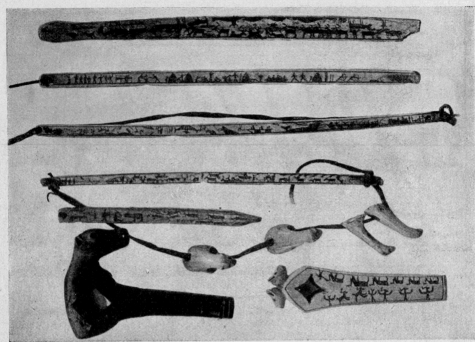

EXAMPLES OF DRILL BOWS USED BY THE EARLY INHABITANTS OF AMERICA   Mansell

certainly noteworthy that in this very respect remarkable points of agreement have been discovered between the Indians of the North-west and the Pueblo races. In the whole region of the latter the sacred hall in which a great part of the religious ceremonies are held, and the others at least prepared for, is the "estufa," erroneously so called by the Spaniards from its peculiar structure. The Pueblo Indians call it kiva. In structure the kiva differs very considerably from all the other buildings of the Pueblo Indians in the most important points. It always lies more or less away from the rooms of which a pueblo (village) is composed, and which are built close to and over one another. It has the peculiarity that it is at least partly, and often entirely, sunk below the ground, and is only accessible by a ladder from an entrance built in the middle of the roof.

The kiva is to the Indians of the pueblos what their meeting-house is to the eastern Indians; here the men assemble to discuss common affairs, but especially to prepare for and to perform their religious rites. Even to-day there exist in the pueblos still inhabited by Indians a large number of such underground meeting-houses, which, so far as missionary activity has not yet done away with the remains of the

original rites, serve their old purposes. If we compare these kivas with those that occur in the remains of old Indian towns that have long been in ruins, it appears that centuries of intercourse with the white man have made scarcely any change in the kiva.

In the inhabited pueblos, and even in many that in all probability have sunk into ruins without being trodden by European foot, the kiva is a rectangular hall; on the other hand, the older the ruins are the more exclusively do we find kivas of circular form, although we all the dwelling-rooms of the same ruins are rectangular, and circular build-

How the Kivas were Built ings occur only rarely throughout the Pueblo region in the form of towers. The circular kivas undoubtedly represent an older type; for whereas the four-sided kivas are lined with stone, carefully coated with plaster, and neatly whitewashed up to the posts forming the roof, the stone wall of the round kivas reaches to only three-fourths of the whole height. This is then completed by horizontal beams fitting into one another, which approach roundness owing to the number of angles they form, and are constructed exactly like those of the log-house type of building which the pioneers of the West learned from the Indians. This form of the kiva is certainly a reminiscence of the time when the Pueblo Indians were not the skilled builders they afterwards became. Its being sunk below the ground, a custom by which the Indians of various parts sought to give their dwellings greater height and better protection from the elements, and its beam-work point unmistakably to other conditions of life; but we can well understand how it is that only in these halls that served for religious purposes, long unintelligible to the Indians themselves, the memory of conditions has been preserved of which almost all trace has been lost in their general life. Now, it is undoubtedly very remarkable that round and square houses, partly dug in the ground, lined with stone slabs, and, at least in some cases, only accessible by an opening in the roof, occur as dwellings among various Indian races of California who are not particularly closely related to the Pueblo Indians either linguistically or ethnographically. Moreover, these same Californian races, like the Pueblo Indians,

Religious Dances of the Tribes

make a great feature in their religious ceremonies of certain dances reminding one almost of theatrical performances, which in both cases, if not exclusively performed in the common dwelling-hall, were prepared in a part of it curtained off temporarily for the purpose. As in these dances almost similar masks, fashioned as snakes, skeletons, etc., occur in both cases, we are justified in assuming that these races have a common stock of traditional customs that is not due to late adoption or transmission, but to an original relationship.

That the stone structures of the cliff-dwellers, in the almost inaccessible cañons of the rivers that cut their way through the central plateau, are to be regarded as dwellings of the same races whose last remnants now inhabit the pueblos of the regions of Cibola and Tusayan under the name of Zuñis and Moquis, is beyond all doubt. The transition between the architectural forms is unmistakable, and the connection between cliff-dwellings and houses, both on the

STONE ARROWHEADS, KNIVES AXES AND HAMMERS FROM DIFFERENT PARTS OF AMERICA

plateau and in the river valleys, has also been clearly proved by excavations, as has also the chronological sequence. We must certainly not overlook the fact that the migrations of the Pueblo Indians also proceeded slowly, in consequence of their living almost exclusively by agriculture. Indeed, at times events occurred which **Pueblos as Expert Potters** positively caused a retrograde movement, and to such an extent that the wanderers returned to parts they had left long ago and occupied anew their partly ruined dwellings. Such occurrences are even related in the traditions of the present Pueblo Indians of times certainly later than their first meeting with the Spaniards about the middle of the sixteenth century.

But although the most northern evidences of the Pueblo civilisation, the cave-ruins, reveal an architectural development that is in no respect inferior to that displayed by the carefully built pueblos of the valleys of the Chaco and Chelley, yet the other antiquities show an earlier type in the north, and furnish evidence of a later development that continued down to the time of those degenerate Pueblo Indians whom we know to-day.

Pottery especially affords us a further glimpse of the early history of these races. It is not chance that the North Californian tribes, who could work wood and stone skilfully, and otherwise occupied by no means the lowest rung of social culture, had no pottery. The potter's art develops only where Nature is not bountiful with that necessary, water, and man has to procure and preserve a supply. For races that live by fishing, wickerwork, more easily produced, suffices, and for this Nature had given them a suitable material in the reed and other aquatic creeping plants.

Of these they made baskets, which were often utilised as vessels in which fish could be cooked in water heated by the primitive method of throwing red-hot stones **Process of Pottery Evolution** into it. But water could not be kept in these receptacles for any length of time, and when these races migrated into drier districts their need of pottery led to its manufacture. The evolution of their pottery from spinning and basket-making is unmistakable from the manner, peculiar to the Indians of both north and south, of building their pots from an endless thread of clay. If the far North-west is the common home of the Californian and Pueblo

Indians, the latter evidently did not develop into potters until after the separation of the groups. This stage has not yet been discovered from the antiquities. We find the Pueblo races, even in their earliest northern abodes, at a respectable stage of development, not only as architects, but also as potters. In the central Pueblo regions, on the Chaco and Chelley, we then perceive a further advance, while the culmination of their artistic activity was reached at Sikyatki, not far from Moqui, which was destroyed only shortly before the arrival of the Spaniards.

We are not without an explanation of this. As is commonly known, the races of the west in the latitude of the Californian peninsula are divided up by the nations in the lowest stage of civilisation. Not only do the traces of a struggle with these occur in the south, in the cave-dwelling and the pueblos built on easily blockaded spurs of the plateaus, but dwelling-places agreeing remarkably with the pueblos also occur in the north as far as the Haidahs, a proof that the Pueblo races sought to protect themselves from the aggression of **Opposing Races in Contact** hostile tribes. This first attack by Athabascan or Tinné tribes —for as such we must regard them, in spite of the scanty proofs of linguistic affinity—although not the immediate cause, probably decided the direction and subsequent development of the tribes that were driven south, which are first met with in history at the Mesa Verde and the river San Juan.

The theory that the whole region of the Pueblos, from the river Mancos in the north to the mouth of the Gila in the south, and from the Rio Pecos in the east to the Colorado in the west, ever constituted a united body politic is quite as untenable as the similar hypothesis regarding the region of the mound-builders. The statesmanship of the American natives has scarcely anywhere been great enough to form, much less maintain, an extensive state.

In the territory of the Pueblos there prevailed, probably during the whole period of their social prosperity, the same system of small communities based on the gens that the Spaniards found existing there at the discovery; its remains may still be recognised without difficulty from the traditions of the Pueblo Indians, in spite of the mixtures caused by the fusion of the population. It has its root in the soil. Their primitive agriculture, which is

TIGHTLY PLAITED WILLOW BASKETS

BASKET OF WOVEN YUCCA   COILED JAR FOUND IN CLIFFS

LARGE VASES OF THE COILED AND INDENTED VARIETY

WORK OF THE CLIFF-DWELLERS: EXAMPLES OF BASKET-MAKING AND POTTERY

Investigations among the cliff dwellings of the Mesa Verde have brought to light from graves and refuse-heaps many articles which help us to understand the people and their customs. The above examples of basket-making and pottery show in a most interesting manner how the latter was modelled on the former. The baskets were coated on the outside with a substance composed of clay mixed with rather coarse sand, stopping all the interstices and rendering them watertight, and the pottery, as shown in the illustrations, was made to resemble in its outward appearance the baskets.

certainly said to have supplied in a good year crops sufficient to last for two or three years, did not suffer any great number of people in one place, owing to the unfavourable climatic conditions. The Pueblo region was certainly more thickly populated in earlier times than it is now, but when the Spaniards first entered it its period of prosperity seems to have been over. For although the earliest accounts give the number of large and small towns of the Pueblo Indians at seventy or seventy-one, these lie exclusively in the southern and eastern parts of the Pueblo

must also be assumed in quantity. For the height of development in culture often comes after the first traces of decline in a nation, but it scarcely ever precedes the culmination of the material development.

The petty jealousies and feuds of the small communities with one another had a fateful influence on the history of the Pueblo Indians. Occasion for these was incessantly given by outward circumstances—in the limited areas fit for cultivation, and the insufficient quantity of moisture, the most careful use of which could alone make the soil productive and

RUINS OF A CLIFF-DWELLING: "SPRUCE-TREE HOUSE" IN THE MESA VERDE, COLORADO

In a great plateau, thirty miles long and twelve or fifteen wide, situated largely in the Indian Reservation, and called the Mesa Verde, have been unearthed many examples of the communal cliff dwellings of the early inhabitants of America. The cliff-dweller has been described as "a dark-skinned fellow." His hair was usually black, and moderately coarse and long. He was of medium stature, and the back of his skull was flattened by being tied firmly against a board in infancy. He had fair teeth, much worn as the years grew upon him from munching ill-ground corn. This and illustrations on pages 5713, 5715, and 5717 are from Nordenskiöld's "Cliff-Dwellers of the Mesa Verde."

region, the same as are still partly peopled by the descendants of the old natives, while the central and northern parts, in which the most architecturally perfect buildings have been found, seem to have been then, as they are to-day, forsaken and in ruins.

Although it is quite probable that many of the southern pueblos may not have existed when the more northern ones were built and inhabited, the circumstance that the latter are also technically the most perfect is a certain sign that the southern races already show the beginning of a decline which, as it is displayed in quality,

the land inhabitable. These outward conditions had an influence on the development of the Pueblo civilisation similar to the influence they had on the inhabitants of Peru, who had to fight with the same climatic difficulties. We therefore not only find here, as we do there, surprisingly ingenious and extensive irrigation works, but, from the analogy to Peruvian conditions and from the existing customs of the present Pueblo races, we may also infer that a water law was carefully made and enforced among the old Pueblo peoples. A continual struggle with drought is not

THE MESA SUMMIT AT THE TOP OF THE OLD TRAIL

THE ENCHANTED MESA AS VIEWED FROM THE NORTH

IN THE LAND OF MESAS: THE STRANGE TABLE-LANDS OF MEXICO

The natural formation of these mesas, or table-lands, of Mexico appealed to prehistoric man as suitable sites for his dwelling-places, and in the stone age of America many communities made their dwellings on the tops and in the clefts of these table-lands, where, owing to the difficulty of access, they could enjoy comparative safety from attacks.

indicated solely by the recollections of the present Indians, or by the ruins of the old works, but dependence on the fertilising moisture plays so prominent a part in the whole pronounced religious system of these races that we must suppose that the climatic conditions were little different then from what they are now.

Excavations in the ruins have often proved the existence of old sources of water in or near them, and it has often required only moderate labour in removing sand and rubbish to increase considerably the yield of these springs. That a race whose whole existence depended on obtaining water would have spared no pains to increase it is testified beyond doubt by the discovery of artificial reservoirs and similar works. In spite of this it would be wrong to see in variations of the sources of a water supply the only reason for the migrations of the Pueblo races, because these migrations were not from the dry districts to the more favoured ones, but exactly the reverse—from the woodland farther and farther into the arid sand-steppe.

If it were a mere hypothesis that the southward movement of the Pueblo Indians was brought about from an invasion of the Central Californian savages, there can scarcely be any doubt that the aggression of similar hostile races decided the further course of these migrations. And if some of the magnificent ruins of the valleys of the Chaco and Chelley are not well adapted for a prolonged defence, it only proves that at the time of their erection the pressure of hostile races had not yet begun. But this is easily accounted for by assuming that the buildings in these valleys, among which even cave-buildings are fairly numerous, were erected at a time when the more

northern settlements—which almost entirely lay protected, especially the numerous and extensive cave-dwellings on the Rio Mancos and other northern affluents of the San Juan—were still inhabited, and were adapted to form a barrier against marauding savages.

According to European ideas we are much inclined to think cave-dwellers men at the lowest stage of culture. But the cliff-dwellers of Western North America were not this at all. Sedentary, living almost solely by agriculture, they had already reached the stage of rearing **Culture of the Cliff-Dwellers** domestic animals, and as basket-makers, weavers, and potters they were superior to almost all their neighbours. It was they who, like the Mexicans, produced those original feather-covered webs that excited the great astonishment of the Europeans. Their pottery is quite equal, in purity and simplicity of form and decoration, to that of their neighbours.

But there was one art in which the Pueblo Indians were superior to all the other races of the northern continent, including the Aztecs—the Mayas, in part, excepted—namely, the art of building. A race that was able to erect buildings in caves like the Cliff Palace discovered by Gustaf Nordenskiöld [see page 172] in a side valley of the Mancos was no longer rude and primitive; it was 'a race which, if not to be numbered among civilised peoples, was at least well on the way to become one. Nature herself had certainly gone a long way toward making the inhabitants of this district builders. In the sandstone that encloses the narrow valleys of most of the waters of the north-western plateau-land in layers of varying resistance, the natives were offered a material

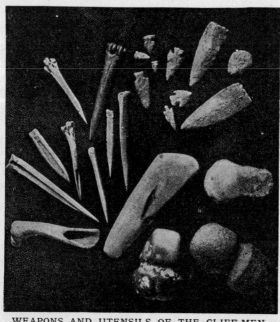

WEAPONS AND UTENSILS OF THE CLIFF-MEN

REMAINS OF THE GREATEST BUILDING OF THE CLIFF-DWELLERS

On page 172 of the History appears a remarkable illustration of a palace under a cliff in Cliff Palace Cañon, Colorado, indicating how considerable was the culture of those early people of America, and another view of that striking monument of the Stone Age is given in the above picture. "Literally hanging from a tremendous cliff," the buildings were inhabited by the first settlers of Colorado, who had every reason to feel themselves secure in their inaccessible homes.

that can almost be shaped of itself. This stone broke down to a considerable extent, under the influence of atmospheric forces, in pieces that required but little working to make them fit for house-building. The rudest buildings—sub-structures—such as are also to be seen at the Cliff Palace, were therefore probably constructed merely by piling up stones selected for the purpose; but of these simplest beginnings only a few traces have been preserved. The material is for the most part brought into the proper shape with great care, the layers secured by an almost invisible but sufficiently strong cement, and every joint so carefully faced with small stones that the outer surfaces of the buildings have not merely withstood the action of the weather for centuries, but even at the present day seem to be firm and smooth.

Buildings of the Pueblo Indians

Moreover, the Pueblo Indians had two other architectural accomplishments in which few races of the New World equalled them: layering the material in strips of equal size—an advance which they probably learned from the long layers in the stone of their native valleys—and mortising the joints, an art not even known by the Maya architects of Chichen-Itza. Such skill naturally presupposes long practice in the art, but we cannot trace its development. Besides the great assistance rendered by Nature, the migrations of the Pueblo Indians undoubtedly furthered the development of their architectural knowledge to an extraordinary degree, by giving them occasion to use the experience gained in the course of a building period whenever they erected a new settlement.

The migrations which we have had to assume as having been from north to south, in historic times, have not to be included in this respect. On the contrary, the buildings of the northern and central Pueblo regions—for instance, the Cliff Palace, and the ruins of Kintiel, Pueblo Bonito, and Nutria in the Chaco valley—while bearing traces of greater age, exhibit the highest development of Pueblo architecture, whereas the later settlements of the same regions and farther south are not so carefully built, although this

HOPI INDIAN GIRLS GRINDING CORN

INDIAN GIRLS WEAVING BASKETS

Underwood

CAVE-DWELLER IN DANCING ATTIRE

AN INDIAN POTTER AT WORK

SCENES IN THE PRIMITIVE INDIAN HOMES OF AMERICA

Some of the customs of America's early Indian inhabitants are here illustrated. In the first of these pictures there is represented a home scene at Shonghopavi, Arizona, where Hopi girls are shown in the act of grinding the shelled corn by rubbing it under flat stones of granite. The extraordinary fashion of hair-dressing depicted in the second illustration belongs exclusively to the maidens of the tribe, as after marriage the hair is arranged differently.

AN INDIAN RESERVATION   INDIAN VILLAGE SCENE

A MORNING PROMENADE   PLAZA "PUEBLO" OF MISHONGINOVI

AMONG THE CLIFF-DWELLERS OF TO-DAY: SCENES IN AN INDIAN RESERVATION

Six hundred feet above the desert, in the Hopi Indian Reservation, Arizona, stands the picturesque village of Wolpi, shown in the two upper views on this page. The people inhabiting these rocky eminences are also depicted, the third illustration showing women and children of Oraibi, situated in the same reservation as Wolpi. Mishonginovi, a view of which is given in the last picture, is the second largest village of the ancient cliff-dwellers in Arizona.

is by no means explained by a want of material. Thus there is no alternative but to assume that the latter buildings were erected at a time when the conditions under which the Pueblo Indians lived had already changed for the worse. But as even these buildings belong to a period prior to the dicovery by the Spaniards,

The Native Methods of Defence we come once more to the conclusion that the golden age of the Pueblo races was already past in the sixteenth century. Here we are led to the further inference that the migrations of the Pueblo Indians cannot have been spontaneous.

Ideas drawn from modern warfare have been applied too much to ancient times, and consequently the defensive strength of the Pueblo towns has been declared so inadequate that the purpose of defence has been positively denied them. But we have only to consider the offensive and defensive weapons of the Pueblo Indians, who were in any case considerably superior to their opponents in social culture, to see at once that very primitive means of defence must have sufficed. The war waged by the Indians upon one another has always consisted in surprises ; the idea of a siege, if only of days, or of the artificial cutting off of indispensable resources, especially of water, which became a dangerous weapon as the art of war advanced, need scarcely be seriously considered in the wars to which the Pueblo Indians were exposed. The attacks of the enemy had for their object plunder that was of immediate use and easy to carry away, and, if possible, prisoners, especially women and young persons.

The enemy, moreover, would certainly have tried to damage the crops of the Pueblo Indians in these wars ; but to gather in the ripe fruit was a comparatively long business with the means at the disposal of these primitive races, and so the plundering Apache or Navajo

Combination for Defensive Purposes would let the Pueblo Indian himself do this first ; he preferred to fetch the stored-up crop from the house rather than the ripe crop from the field. But even the pueblos that did not lie in the inaccessible caves of the cañons or on the easily blockaded spurs or ledges at the edges of the plateau, but on the level ground of the river valleys or in the plains at the foot of the tableland, afforded sufficient protection from a sudden attack. Owing

to the massive style in which they were built, a larger number of inhabitants would be always threatened at the same time, and therefore could easily combine for common defence.

Furthermore, the older pueblos are far more closely built even than those now inhabited, so that outside they show an unbroken wall several stories high, while inside the stories rise in terraces from a central court. The entrance to this court was in most cases easily defended ; further, the ground floor had no entrances opening on to the court, access being obtained to the rooms of the occupants solely from the first platform, which could be reached only by ladders.

The enemy were also educated by the continual struggle, and if the danger of their attacks and their numbers increased in the same measure as the strength of the defenders diminished through unfavourable outward circumstances, the more civilised and physically weaker Pueblo Indians would have eventually to yield to the more robust and hardy sons of the desert. But this would take place

Savage and Brutal Peoples through circumstances mainly independent of the strength of the settlements. So at least we must imagine the war that gradually crushed out the civilisation of the Pueblo races over a considerable part of their ancient territory. They were surrounded north and east by Indian races that belonged to the most savage and brutal of the whole continent. The Apaches and Navajoes made themselves a terror even to the Anglo-Saxon pioneers of the West in the present century, and they were nations of the same stocks that surrounded the Pueblo region on various sides. Even when the Spaniards first entered this region they heard of the deadly enmity between the Pueblo Indians and their neighbours, and were themselves sympathetically drawn into the struggle.

Just as the peaceable inhabitants of the pueblos were at continual war with the flying robbers of the prairie in historic times, so, too, did their forefathers fight with their enemies' forefathers for their existence. From the circumstance that a marked relationship exists in build and in various customs between the Navajoes and the Northern Pueblo Indians at the present day some would draw the conclusion that the former are to be regarded, not so much as a tribe hostile to the Pueblo

Indians, but rather as a kindred tribe that once itself occupied settlements in the Pueblo region, and became a roving race of robbers only through hostile oppression. Although the fact remains that the Pueblo civilisation succumbed to the invasion of hostile neighbours, these must certainly have been other than the Navajoes. It is true that since the last century these Navajoes have been known as a tribe that practises agriculture, though to a limited extent ; that possesses the largest numbers of horses and sheep of any Indians of the west ; and whose squaws weave the finest coloured cloths of sheep's wool. But all these are acquirements that belong to times subsequent to contact with the white man. Moreover, the social progress

to south, we have left a whole group of Pueblo ruins—and that the most southern of all—unnoticed. The attention of the first Spaniards who entered the Pueblo region from Mexico was attracted by a number of ruins that met their eye in the basis of the Gila River, the most southern affluent of the Colorado. These were remains of settlements which unmistakably bear the character of the Pueblos, although they constitute a group of themselves.

The Gila valley, however, did not offer its inhabitants the suitable building material that had made the Pueblo Indians in the upper parts of the table-land such excellent builders. The ruins of this and the adjacent valleys are therefore distinguished by the material used,

WOODEN MASKS AND RATTLES OF THE NORTH-WEST COAST OF AMERICA

of the Navajoes rests chiefly in the hands of their women, whereas among the Pueblo Indians the main burden of tilling the ground falls to the men. This civilising influence of the female sex may be traced, however, in its ultimate origin, to the Pueblo Indians, whose women, captured in their raids, have been their teachers. This intermixture explains also the physical affinities of the races and resemblances in their languages.

One more point in the early history of the Pueblo races needs mention : their relations to their southern neighbours, the civilised races of Mexico. If in the foregoing we have assumed that the Pueblo civilisation progressed from north

which is a kind of brick made of mud mixed with vegetable substances and air-dried ; a material known in many parts by the Spanish name of " adobe," and frequently used in historic times and even to the present day. But otherwise these buildings are also distinctly the work of Pueblo tribes. Here, too, we have towns consisting mainly of a single solid mass of houses, or really only rooms ; these rooms, built over one another in storeys, enclose an inner court, from which they rise in terraces, while the outer walls are mostly perpendicular. This is therefore exactly the character of the more northern settlements of stone, such as we found from the cave-buildings on the San Juan to the open

D

towns of the Moquis and Zuñis. These buildings must have been erected by the same races that built the more northern ones, or by races nearly related to them.

Now, as these towns were found forsaken and in ruins by the Spaniards at a time when the central pueblos were still largely inhabited, they must certainly belong to an earlier period than many of the stone pueblos. But no conclusions may be drawn from this antagonistic to the view that the Pueblo civilisation developed generally from north to south. The race that built the ruins of the Gila valley, generally known as Casas Grandes, certainly did not learn its architecture here.

Generally speaking, the material, owing to its comparatively poor resistance to atmospheric influences, is by no means calculated to induce man to erect hollow buildings above ground. In the ruins on the Rio Gila we can perceive only the endeavour to retain architectural forms that had gradually become a need of the race, even in districts in which the natural conditions were considerably less favourable. The race that erected them separated from the body of the Pueblo Indians only when the latter had fully developed its characteristic civilisation farther north, on the plateaus of the sandstone mountains, and as no traces of the same civilisation occur farther south, it appears that this race, whether it was harassed by hostile peoples, or induced by natural causes again to change its abodes, rejoined the more northern members of the race before historic times. In the legends of the Indians who have

settled in the vicinity of these ruins since the last century they are almost exclusively called houses, palaces, or fortresses of Montezuma, and we shall scarcely be far wrong if we regard this as the survival of an indistinct recollection of the deeds of Mocteuzoma I. Ilhuicamina.

But such a tradition was certainly not developed until after the conquest of Mexico by the Spaniards. This is obvious, not only from the fact that the empire of

Development of Native Architecture Mexico-Tenochtitlan never extended to anywhere near these parts, but above all from the circumstance that there is absolutely no style of architecture like that of the ruins of the Gila within the sphere of civilisation of the Central American states, and that the resemblances to the architecture of the Central American are much less within the Pueblo region than, for instance, in the region of the mound-builders. It may be considered historically proved that the spheres of civilisation of the Pueblo Indians and of the Maya and Nahua races, at least during the time that their respective characteristic architectures were developing, were entirely exclusive of one another and had no connection whatever. But in all probability this was not always so. Although the legends of an original home in the far Aztlan of the north, in the form in which they became known to the Spaniards, referred only to comparatively unimportant changes of abode made by the various nations of the Nahua race at no very remote period, this does not preclude the

Underwood

THE HANDICRAFT OF INDIAN WORKERS
In this illustration are shown the artistic creations of Indian weavers and potters in a Hopi house, Grand Cañon, Arizona.

TREES CUT DOWN BY PREHISTORIC MAN: REMARKABLE FIND IN ARIZONA

This unique picture illustrates an extraordinary discovery near Phœnix, Arizona, where, in recent times, a petrified forest was unearthed. It is supposed that the tree blocks, some of which are here shown, were chopped thousands of years ago by the prehistoric inhabitants of the country, becoming petrified in the course of the long ages.

possibility that in the very earliest times races lived even as far down as the region of Mexico who exhibited a racial relationship to all the other nations inhabiting the Pacific coast of North America.

Besides wide-spread linguistic resemblances there is the recurrence of religious ideas and customs, which are too peculiar to have been the result of simultaneous independent development in different places. The simultaneous worship of the sun and fire is certainly in itself an idea so familiar to the primitive races of all ages and all lands that from its occurrence in different tribes we could not infer that they were related, even if it were not practised in like manner in other neighbouring tribes. On the other hand, it is very remarkable that both among the Pueblo Indians and among the civilised races of Central America all the fires throughout the tribe had to be extinguished at regular intervals ; and that at one place only, amid elaborate religious ceremonies, priests appointed for the purpose, by rubbing two sticks, obtained the new fire, which was then spread from this one centre by speedy messengers. Another highly characteristic religious idea common to these same races is that of the feathered snake. Apart from the fact that Nature

Primitive Religious Ceremonies

itself furnishes no creatures as patterns for such a form, the snake is often one of the most dangerous enemies of man in the legends of American races. Among the Pueblo Indians it is also most closely connected with the deities of fertilising moisture, which to them is the essence of all good. Besides these there are a whole number of other resemblances.

We may mention a parallel of a non-religious character. Feathers, especially those of the gorgeously coloured tropical birds, or of the eagle as the symbol of power, have played an important part in the ornament of all primitive races. But only in very few parts of the earth has the attempt been made by primitive races to imitate, by weaving, the feather coat that adorns and protects the birds.

The races of the Mexican Empire brought this art to a perfection that has never since been attained, so that it is most singular that of all the American races only the Pueblo Indians practised a similar art, although considerably more primitive, and that not as a comparatively late acquirement, but where we first found them, on the northern borders of their territory, farthest from the Mexican borders, dwelling in the caves of the Mancos valley, and producing their characteristic archaic pottery.

5723

GRANARIES OF THE INDIANS OF THE COLORADO DESERT

MOQUI INDIAN WOMEN BUILDING HOUSES

Among the Moqui Indians of America the customs of the sexes with regard to the division of labour are different from those generally prevailing among other tribes, the women performing heavy tasks, such as house-building, while the men undertake the lighter household duties and engage in such occupations as blanket-weaving.

SCENES IN THE LIFE AND CUSTOMS OF AMERICAN INDIANS

ANCIENT CIVILISATIONS of CENTRAL AMERICA
THE LAND AND THE PEOPLES
AND THE CULTURE OF THE MAYA RACES

AT the Isthmus of Panama, the Cordilleras, the backbone of the American continent, sink so far below the level of the sea that only their highest points rise above the waters to form a narrow range of inconsiderable height; but a few degrees farther north they begin again to tower mightily aloft. The district known to-day as Northern Panama and Costa Rica is a mountainous country; its highest points even there rise nearly 7,000 feet above the sea-level. However, the range is again interrupted in its northward advance.

The marshes of Nicaragua and the Isthmus of Tehuantepec form two more depressions of great depth, and here, rather than at the narrowest point, we should place the true line of demarcation **The Division** between the peoples of North **Between North** and of South America. **and South** Between these two points is the only place where Central America seems to have made the attempt at continental expansion so characteristic of the eastern portions of the two great half-continents. But the Isthmus of Yucatan, a thickly wooded, hilly country lying before the mountain plateau of Guatemala, has no developed river system on any large scale; and to its position between the Bay of Campeche and that of Honduras it owes the favourable character of its climate, lying low as it does in the tropic latitudes.

Above the Isthmus of Tehuantepec the northern continent begins to expand, but for nearly ten degrees of latitude farther north it is formed by the Cordilleras, which spread wider and wider, leaving only a narrow strip of shore at their feet on the east and west, and filling up the main portion of the continent with their peaks. Hence the peculiar character of the Mexican climate. Although the district of ancient Mexico lies entirely within the tropics, yet only on the seaboard is the real tropic temperature encountered, which, if it brings the advantage of **Mexico's** Nature's fullest glory, in- **Peculiar** volves also the disadvantage **Climate** of a dangerous climate. This disadvantage is nullified by the nature of the country, which consists of a high plateau rising sufficiently high above the sea to be free from the dangers of malaria, and yet only so high as to enjoy an almost uninterrupted springtime and to provide for man's necessities with generous hand, and reward his toil with richest bounty. The main mountain-range, however, rises boldly and majestically to the regions of the everlasting snow which shines down from the peaks of Popocatepetl and the summit of Orizaba upon the eternal springtide at their feet.

In the immediate neighbourhood of this highest point the Cordilleras divide into an eastern and a western range. Between these there stretches a highland studded with numerous lakes, of moderate size, but extraordinarily fruitful— **Home of the** the Mexican highland. Here **Oldest** was played out to its close **Civilisations** the little-known drama of the ancient civilisation of America. The country from the Lake of Nicaragua to the northern parts of the valley of Mexico has been the home of one of the oldest civilisations of the New World. It is as yet wholly impossible to give any exact dates for its beginnings in the past, and impossible it will probably remain, even if success should crown the attempt to interpret those undeciphered memorials which now look down upon our efforts to solve their riddle. But if anyone, starting with the conception of the " New " World, considers this civilisation as moderately young, he does it great injustice—nearly

Unreliable Histories of America
as great as do those who place its most flourishing period more than 11,000 years in the past. The native authors who have written the history of the peoples of Central America, working in the first century after the conquest, and aided by the old traditions and the pictorial sculptures, occasionally place these beginnings as far back as the last century before the Christian era.

There is little congruity in their productions, which do not inspire us with confidence. The dynasties which have been deciphered from the pictorial decorations previous to the time of Columbus agree with the Spanish and Nahuatlac sources of information, and go back in a great number of individual states from 700 to 800 years before the discovery of America. Only these testify to an almost invariable character of the civilisation, even in the earliest times, and certainly do not go back as far as that primal starting-point at which we are entitled to place the beginnings of the history of these peoples.

We can probably get nearer to the truth with the help of the chronological indications which can now be gathered from the memorials of the Maya civilisation. The Maya were accustomed to reckon from an established point in the past, exactly as we reckon from the birth of Christ ; and not only the year, but the actual day, which forms the starting-point of their chronology has been satisfactorily made out. This was June 28th, according to our reckoning, of a certain year dating back more than 3,750 years before the erec-

Memorials of Maya Civilisation
tion of the monument which forms the basis of these cal- culations. Even here, however, we unfortunately have no sure foundation for chronological limitations— for we do not know by our reckoning the time at which the inscription in question was set up, nor can we be certain whether that day marked a real event in the remote history of the people, or whether it represents a point on which to base calculation and inference, resembling in this respect

the Jewish chronology, which goes back to the creation of the world. We must therefore attempt to gain a conception of the earliest history of these civilisations by other means ; and their memorials, which have come safely down to us through the storms of centuries, afford richer and more copious information, although it be not entirely complete.

The highly painted pictorial work which the Spanish conquerors of Montezuma's kingdom have handed on to us has induced men for centuries to consider the civilisation of the peoples of Central America as Mexican. This is a great historical error. The Mexicans—or the Aztecs of Mexico-Tenochtitlan, to give them their proper ethnographic name—are neither the founders nor yet the most important representatives of this civilisation to which their name has been unfortunately attached by the sport of circumstance.

Shortly before the Spanish invasion of the district they had obtained a leading position among the peoples of the country. A consciousness of the fact that their civilisation was not the result of their

Obstacles to the Progress of Discovery
own efforts, but was inherited by them from others, was inhe- rent in the Aztecs themselves, and appears in the chronicles of their native historians ; yet so cloudy is it, so interwoven with error, that we could scarce have arrived at the truth with nothing but these indications to help us. That truth became plain only when the ruined monuments were dis- covered of another civilisation, older and more highly developed than the Aztec, and when something of its language had been learned. But progress in this direc- tion did not begin before the close of the eighteenth century ; and even to-day we have advanced only half-way towards the full understanding and appreciation of these highly important historical materials.

The chief obstacle to the progress of discovery has been the fact that historical investigation had taken a wrong direction until recent times. The errors thereby produced were further disseminated by two great visionaries, the Indo-Spanish historian, D. Fernando de Alba Ixtlilxochitl (pronounced Ishtlilshotshitl) and the French missionary and author, the Abbé Brasseur, of Bourbourg. The first-named, during the last ten years of the sixteenth century, was the author of a large number of historical treatises concerning the

SCENE ON THE MEXICAN SOUTHERN RAILWAY

A VALLEY IN CENTRAL MEXICO, NEAR THE TOWN OF TAMPICO

TYPICAL SCENERY ON THE ANAHUAC TABLELAND

CHARACTERISTIC LANDSCAPES IN CENTRAL AMERICA

countries of ancient Mexico, based upon extensive investigations into the several modes of writing current among the ancient Indians of the country, and also into the physical characteristics of the western peoples of his own time. In these works he gives an exhaustive account of the civilisation presumed to be the most ancient in Central America, that of the Toltecs; and he traces back to their civilising influence almost all the intellectual development of the ancient nations of Central America. This theory obtained credence far and wide, and to an extraordinary extent.

The Toltecs Pioneers of Culture

The rediscovery of the old ruined cities brought about the search for fresh material. It aroused intense enthusiasm in the youthful missionary Brasseur, whom chance had brought to the seat of these old civilisations. Eagerly, but without thorough historical and philological training, he collected Central American antiquities and quickly published a series of works upon the subject. He was not content to pile all the culture of ancient America upon the Toltecs; he hinted also at vague connections with the civilisations of Egypt and India, and attributed to this race an extent of knowledge that the peoples of to-day could scarcely attain again.

American ethnology is a science still in its youth. But the methods of historical criticism have been brought to bear upon the ancient history of Central America; and one of the first results has been to clear away the wild speculations of the Abbé Brasseur and to shatter the tradition of the all-prevailing influence of Toltec civilisation. Two facts are now incontestably established. Among the numerous peoples and constitutions which rapidly followed one another, and which played an important part upon the tableland of Anahuac, there existed, probably towards the end of the first thousand years of the Christian era, a kingdom and a dynasty of rulers who were known as Toltecs, from the name of their capital, Tollan or Tula. They are mentioned in almost all the native historical documents. The particular historical facts handed down by these documents are extraordinarily scanty; we shall come back to them in treating of the history of Anahuac.

The Riddle of Ancient America

Neither the date at which they existed, nor their relations to the surrounding peoples, afford us the smallest justification for considering these transitory nationalities as the creators, or even as the chief exponents, of that great civilisation whose highly developed monumental art is rightly the astonishment of the latter-day world. The little principality of the Toltecs was situated at a considerable distance from the seat of that civilisation; moreover, the nationality to which it has given its name belonged to the great mass of Nahuatl-speaking races, to which also the Aztecs of Mexico-Tenochtitlan belonged. The oldest and most highly developed memorials of this civilisation bear unmistakable tokens of its being derived from another race.

This brings us to the second historical fact that has been indisputably established. The whole of Central America has undoubtedly passed through a uniform process of civilisation. Its foundations, and most of the development that has been built upon those foundations, belong to an era in the remote past; and that particular civilisation with which we meet in all Central America was already in existence, complete in all its details, before the peoples of Nahua origin came down from the north and invaded the district of Central American civilisation; or, at any rate, it was thus complete before the peoples of this civilisation and those of the Nahua race had so closely cohered as to make it possible to speak of them as exercising each an influence upon the other. But if this old civilisation did not originate in the Nahua race, then the Toltecs could not have originated there either. A Nahua race has been their origin; grant this, and the whole Toltec legend, which has so long played a great part in the more ancient history of America, collapses utterly.

Yucatan the Cradle of Civilisation

The peoples to whom Central America owes the peculiarly high development of its civilisation belong to the Maya race. The name Maya-Indian is now the usual designation of the natives of the Yucatan peninsula, and this limited application of the term has been in force since the time of the discovery of America. Consequently the Yucatan peninsula has been regarded as the cradle of this civilisation for a considerable period. This is, however, a mistake; in the scientific sense the name Maya race included all the peoples speaking a language distinguished by marked differences from the Nahua tongue. The purest dialect of this is the true Maya, but

THE MOUNTAINS ABOVE COJUTEPEQUE IN SALVADOR

THE POPOCATEPETL VOLCANO

VOLCANOES OF FUEGO AND ACETENANGO   VOLCANO OF COLIMA IN MEXICO

THE SNOW-COVERED MOUNTAINS ABOVE ESTELI IN NICARAGUA

THE MOUNTAINOUS SCENERY OF CENTRAL AMERICA

its kindred dialects were spoken in the whole district between the Cordilleras and the Atlantic Ocean from the Isthmus of Tehuantepec to Nicaragua. In the luxuriant tropical districts which spread from the foot of the Cordilleras to the Bay of Tabasco, and are watered by the river Usumacinta and Rio de la Pasion, in the modern province of Chiapas in the Mexican republic, and in the neighbouring portions of the small republics of Central America—in these it is that we must locate, if not the birthplace, at any rate the habitation of the Maya peoples, who there brought the civilisation peculiar to their race to a high pitch of development.

Maya History and Tradition

Even to-day it is wholly impossible to write the history of the Maya peoples. Such of their old traditions as have come down to us through the medium of the Spaniards are quite insufficient and far scantier than what we learn of the history of their more northern neighbours, the Nahua peoples ; even there, and in the few historical texts written in the Maya language, the traditions of the people are still distorted and warped. As, in political life, the Nahua not only pressed upon and crowded the Maya, but to some extent scattered and absorbed them, so, in their historical picture-designs, much is due to the influence of the traditions of these more powerful neighbours. Moreover, these designs, as far as history is concerned, go back only one or two hundred years ; the more extensive chronological register of " ahaus " (periods) unfortunately refers only to Yucatan ; this province must, upon internal evidence, be considered as conquered comparatively late.

Thus for the earlier history we are almost entirely thrown back on such information as we can gain from the monuments which have come down to us. These are of great richness and extraordinary importance. On the conquest of the Mexican kingdom the Spaniards were so dazzled by this nationality which confronted them, to all seeming, in full vigour, that they concentrated their attention exclusively upon it, and hardly deigned to bestow a glance upon the states of Tlazcala and Tezcuco in the immediate neighbourhood. Hence we cannot be surprised that they give us no information of these monuments of the ancient Maya kingdom, hidden in the boundless forests, although they far sur-

The Spanish Conquest of Mexico

passed in splendour all that Montezuma's kingdom could display. In the real Aztec district but one single building of monumental character has been preserved (the ruins of Xochicalco, pronounced Shotshicalco), whereas the ancient Maya cities of Chiapas and the neighbouring district afford hundreds of temples and palaces for inspection.

Later again, when the Spaniards entered into closer relations with the Maya peoples on the peninsula of Yucatan, they became acquainted with some, at least, of the interesting buildings which served the early needs of these peoples, yet they did not fully grasp their importance. While the land of Mexico offered them its boundless treasures, the temples of the Maya and the land which loving Maya toil had changed into a garden contained nothing which the greed of the conquerors could have reft away.

Only when the destructive floods of the conquest and its confusion had passed by, and when the first friars came over, did it begin to dawn upon the Spaniards what testimonies of the past lay hidden among this people, insignificant though they had become. Here it was that they found, what they never met with again on the whole of this recently discovered continent, a people that had learned to preserve its thoughts in written text. The Maya characters still remain one of the most interesting problems in American antiquarian science. Although some of the early Spanish friars in Yucatan had been able to acquire a knowledge of them sufficiently extensive to enable them to read and, within limits, to write them, yet in the course of time this knowledge has been so entirely lost that the most skilled American antiquarians of to-day cannot agree upon the system to which the Maya writing should be ascribed. To some extent controversy upon the point is futile ; the Spanish clergy who were able to learn the writing from the inhabitants have confirmed its phonetic character.

The Lost Maya Writing

As a comparison of the two shows at a glance, the writing of the Nahua peoples, who probably derived the use of written characters from the Maya, is far in the rear of the Maya system. As they also had already formed a system more or less phonetic for the writing of proper names, all attempts to reduce the Maya writings to the level of ideographic or purely hieroglyphic characters are pronounced erroneous once and for all. On the other hand, it would apparently be just as erroneous for us to attempt to reduce this writing to an alphabet in the way that the Spanish clergy of the sixteenth century reduced it, selecting individual elements from the old Maya writing for use in instructing their catechumens. Success has now rewarded the efforts to establish the Maya arithmetical system. Their system of figures employed only four signs altogether; the point for unity, a horizontal stroke for the number 5, and two conventional signs for 20 and 0. This arithmetical equipment is not particularly impressive, and the Maya might be thought far behind many older and newer nations whose systems can employ figures of greater value and in larger number. But the ingenious method has been discovered by which the Maya, with these simple aids— and no use is made of the 20 in this method —can write figures up to the equivalent of many millions, and we rightly feel a high respect for their intellectual penetration. In the Maya arithmetical notation, exactly as in ours, it is the position of the sign that gives it its value; but they placed their signs in a vertical line—whereas we write them horizontally—and employed one of them as a decimal multiplier. In fact the lowest figure of a column had the arithmetical value which it represented; the figures in

A PAGE FROM THE DRESDEN MAYA MS.
The memorials of the Maya civilisation which have been handed down to us show that these people had an extraordinary fancy for adorning their buildings, their sculptures, and even their earthenware with pictorial decorations and inscriptions of considerable length.

the second, fourth, and each following place had twenty times the value of the preceding figure; while figures in the third place had, for reasons based upon the Maya calendar system, only eighteen times the value of those in the second place. With this notation, which is absolutely unlimited, the Maya were ahead of not only all the peoples of America, but even of the Greeks and Romans. It is certainly to be expected that this people would have employed some ingenious method for writing words; and the delicate signs of their script, the firm execution of their inscriptions in lapidary style, confirm this conjecture, though the inscriptions are unintelligible to us. In spite of this their script is a valuable help in investigation, for it affords the only criterion by which we can precisely separate the districts of Maya and Nahua civilisation, which are often with difficulty distinguished, owing to constant communication and their interacting influence one on another. For even though the Mexicans had also formed a hieroglyphic system capable at least of describing concrete objects intelligibly, yet it was so clumsy in comparison that a glance at a manuscript, together with a complete examination of inscriptions carved in stone, inform us at once to which of those two civilisations the creators of any given monument belonged. As we cannot understand the historical writings, and cannot rely upon the oral tradition handed down by the Spaniards, the Maya script is the only means of defining the extent of the district which was subject to the civilising influences of their culture in ancient times. In this connection the greatest importance attaches to the fact that the Maya peoples

The Maya Pictorial Decorations had an extraordinary fancy for adorning their buildings, their sculptures, and even their earthenware, not only with pictorial decorations of more or less richness, but also with inscriptions of considerable length. We owe it to this fact that we can ascribe buildings which show unmistakable affinities with Maya architecture to their real founders, and, on the other hand, can attribute many a monument to the Maya which lay entirely outside of the dominions which they are known to have inhabited.

The number of the ascertained sites of the Maya civilisation, the ruins of which lie hidden in the impenetrable forests of Chiapas, Honduras, Yucatan, etc., continues to increase year by year ; more abundant opportunities are thereby afforded us for investigating the life of this forgotten people. Now and again an unexpected discovery extends the known area of the Maya civilisation beyond its previous limits in one or another direction ; but, upon the whole, the boundaries of this area are tolerably well settled. In the first place, the whole of the Yucatan peninsula belongs to it, with the numerous islands which lie along the coast and were taken over by the Maya, obviously with a view to civilisation.

On the north-west of Yucatan their district has not spread so far, and at most reached to the Isthmus of Tehuantepec. However, in this district, in Chiapas, on the banks of the Usumacinta, and in the low-lying valleys of its numerous tributaries, we must place not only the highest

The Home of Maya Civilisation development of the Maya civilisation, but also its original home. Here lay and here still lie the famous ruined cities of Palenque, of Ococingo, of Menché, and the recently discovered Piedras Negras group, all remarkable for the splendid richness of their artistic decorations and the extent of their inscriptions. Here, too, on internal evidence, must be placed the home of that most important and most beautiful among the few Maya manuscripts that

have been preserved for later generations, the Codex Dresdensis ; the remaining two—the Codex Perezianus in Paris, and the Tro-Cortesianus in Madrid— are of later date and very probably of Yucatan origin.

The illustration on the preceding page throws an interesting light on the Maya inscriptions and pictorial decorations, which, as we have seen, were frequently of very considerable length. This reproduction of a page from the famous Maya MS. in the Royal Free Library at Dresden, shows a section of the so-called " tonalamatl," a sacred season of 260 days, constantly met with in manuscripts and employed for prophetic purposes. But while the drawings partly tell their own story, the writing cannot be deciphered, even the most skilled American antiquarians of the present day, as already stated, being unable to agree to any definite extent upon the system to which it should be ascribed.

On the south-west of Yucatan the Maya district spreads up into the Cordilleras ; and though we cannot follow the traces of this nationality on to the Pacific seaboard in any direction, yet it

Famous Maya Ruins board in any direction, yet it was only a narrow strip of coast which they failed to bring under their influence, for the mountain range shows traces of their settlements up to and beyond its watershed. The southern boundary of the Maya district is perhaps as yet the most uncertain. On the Atlantic coast two of the most famous Maya ruins, Quirigua and Copan, are hidden by the valley walls of the Motagua in Guatemala and Honduras ; and the whole of Guatemala up to the boundaries of the republic of San Salvador seems at one time to have been inhabited by people of the Maya race.

On the north the characteristic memorials of the Nahua element make a sharp division of areas possible ; but on the south the style of the neighbouring peoples was of no definite character, and so it has not yet been settled whether coincidences and similarities in this district are due to the neighbouring influence of the Maya or to a real ethnological connection with them. Within these boundaries the area of Maya civilisation embraces an extent of about 7,000 square miles—that is, rather more than the kingdom of Prussia ; in more than half of this, traces of an unusually large population are apparent.

AMERICA
BEFORE
COLUMBUS

ANCIENT
CIVILISATIONS
OF CENTRAL
AMERICA
II

REMARKABLE CIVILISATION OF A VANISHED RACE

THE LIFE AND CUSTOMS OF THE MAYA

WAS this district ever a united Maya kingdom ? There is no difficulty in arriving at the assumption that it was. The half-mythological, half-historical traditions which have been transmitted to us in the dialects of Kakchiquel and the Maya of Yucatan mention a great kingdom on many occasions. Now it is the Nachan kingdom, the kingdom of the great snake, a mythological symbol which meets us over and over again in the whole district of Maya civilisation. In another legend it is the kingdom of Xibalbay, the kingdom of a mighty and powerful ruler from whom the heroes of the legend won their independence after much toil and struggle.

Historical coincidences have been observed in both these stories, and the capital of the Nachan kingdom has been identified with Palenque, that of the Xibalbay kingdom with the Zapotec Mitla. Even if these conjectures were justified, and they are still in dispute, it need not necessarily follow that these kingdoms had ever embraced the whole or even the greater part of the Maya district. In the disruption which is so prominent a feature in the ancient constitutional history of Central America, a power of very moderate dimensions according to modern ideas, proved a sufficient foundation for the legend of a mighty kingdom. The historical circumstances of later times, at any rate, afford no evidence in favour of a previous political confederacy of the little Maya principalities.

The District of Maya Civilisation

The Maya language, moreover, not only in recent times, but at the period of the Spanish conquest, was divided into a set of dialects sharply differentiated each from the rest. When the monks began to study individual dialects for purposes of communication, they recognised in them that relationship to a common source which the natives themselves had totally forgotten. This fact obliges us to place the disruption of the Maya in a remote antiquity, and to suppose a long period of separate existence to the several communities wherein the different dialects were formed. More careful examination of the Maya memorials has led to a similar result. The monuments of Copan in Honduras, of Palenque in Chiapas, of Chichen-Itza in North Yucatan, of Peten and Tical on the boundary of the Guatemala tableland —in short, all the monuments that are scattered over the district of Maya civilisation—bear the marks of a uniform development of that civilisation.

What the Maya Monuments Reveal

Only a more particular study of their individualities has made it equally unmistakable that all these buildings do not belong to one and the same period, and that the coincidences they display are not such as to enable us to ascribe their foundation to any one people or to any one constitutional unity. Under these circumstances the fact becomes all the more important that it was not merely one member or a few individual members of this nation that rose to the perfection manifested in their ingenious system of writing, of arithmetical notation, and of chronology.

On the contrary, on the highlands of Guatemala, in Copan and Chama, in the lowlands of the Usumacinta, in the valley of the Motagua, in the Far East, in the island of Cozumel, all the peoples of Maya origin could record their traditions in the same script, and controlled the complicated calculation of their festivals by the same astronomical rules—rules that presuppose observation over a great lapse of time. In a word, the astonishing achievements of the Maya peoples in civilisation—

Similarity of the Maya Script

achievements absolutely unparalleled in the New World—must belong to an epoch previous to the period of disruption. Only one branch of the Maya people had no share in these achievements—the Huasteca, on the north coast of Mexico, who had been driven to the estuary of the Panuco River. This fact is important for the criticism of the legends of the Nahua migration. In historical times the Huasteca were divided from their southern kinsfolk by a wide district peopled generally by the Nahua, though these were divided into numerous small states.

Whether the Huasteca had migrated into the Nahua district, or whether immigrations of the Nahua had cut them off from their parent stem, the fact remains that

and from the pictorial decorations of their architecture. In no single district, with the exception of the Yucatan peninsula, has the attempt as yet been successful to trace a connection between the Maya states of the sixteenth century (the history of which can be retraced some ten generations, that is, two or three hundred years) and the states which centre round the great ruined sites. It is only during the last twenty years that these have been carefully investigated.

To-day nearly all these places lie far from the roads which the traffic of later times has opened up; they are hidden in the wild depths of the tropical forest, where vegetation springs up with such overpowering vigour that often a few years after an

ZAPOTEC REMAINS AT MITLA: IDOLS TWO THOUSAND YEARS OLD

at one period the Maya and the Nahua must have found themselves in opposition, and this at a time when the Maya had not completed the most important part of their progress. Otherwise, either the Huasteca would have shared in the Maya civilisation, or else, isolated in the midst of Nahua peoples, they would not have retained their national peculiarities undisturbed. Such a case of arrest upon the lower planes of civilisation is only possible when the neighbouring elements are in a state of mutual repulsion.

Until the key to the inscriptions has been found, we can draw conclusions as to the circumstances and conditions of life among the peoples of antiquity only from the general character of the Maya cities

expedition has cut paths and made the ruins accessible the next expedition finds that the jungle has again reconquered the whole. Under these circumstances it is hopeless to try and infer the age of the ruins from that of the trees under which they are hidden; all the more so, as historical tradition tells of more than one ruined city that the Spaniards found hidden in tropical vegetation when they made their first discoveries in the sixteenth century. Even then the imposing erections with which the soil of Chiapas is thickly sown were, for the natives as well as for the Spaniards, merely the long-silent witnesses of a remote past to which there was attached neither the traditions of history nor the legends of romance. The very names of these

RUINS SHOWING THE FIRST DEPARTURE FROM THE VERTICAL ARCHITECTURE

REMAINS OF A ZAPOTEC FORTIFICATION ON A HIGH HILL NEAR MITLA

Recent excavations at Mitla have brought to light many extensive ruins of ancient palaces, tombs, and other edifices—relics of its pre-Columbian period—many of them displaying considerable architectural beauty.

SCENES AT MITLA, THE ANCIENT CAPITAL OF THE XIBALBAY KINGDOM

places had long been completely forgotten; the appellations that later times have accepted have no original authority,

THE HALL OF MONOLITH COLUMNS

instance, the Mexican read as "Cinacatan," in his language, "the Town of the Bat" (probably a totemistic denomination of a little Maya state that was still in existence in the time of Cortes); but the Maya vocalised the same concept as "Tzutuhil." Each of these names was equally employed and equally well understood in the one district as in the other—a proof of the intimate association of the Maya and Nahua peoples. Now, at the time of the discovery of America, the area of the oldest Maya civilisation had been already abandoned by the Maya; the Spaniards undertook the colonisation of the land under the guidance and with the help of the Nahua. Consequently, in the case of a district that for hundreds of years was the home of the highest Maya civilisation, and had never entirely fallen into the

but rest upon Spanish tradition or have been transmitted to us by the wild Indian tribes of the neighbourhood. A peculiar characteristic of the old Indian peoples has contributed not a little to this result. The names of their towns, of their persons, and even of their gods, were taken without exception from material objects; hence they could easily be represented by hieroglyphs of a conventional and universally intelligible nature. Of this we have countless instances in the manuscripts of Nahuatlac origin. This mode of writing was intelligible over the limited region where it persisted, but its phonetic interpretation was by no means everywhere the same. For

Underwood

PREHISTORIC RUINS AT MITLA: HALL OF MOSAICS

hands of the Nahua, we find in our authorities only place-names of Nahua origin. Hence, the ruined places of Chiapas are designated without exception by Spanish and Nahuatlac names; yet these places show indisputable signs of their Maya occupation in the style of their pictorial decorations, and, above all, in the numerous inscriptions in the Maya character.

To judge from extent, from beauty, and from technical perfection, an important, if not the central, point of the civilisation of this people must have been situated on the eastern slope of the Cordilleras, in Chiapas. Separated by no great distance,

religious element must have been of transcendent importance ; so much so that to some, at least, of the old Maya cities a government by the priestly caste has been attributed. The analogy of neighbouring conditions and the scanty counter statements of historical tradition do not confute the theory. The migration legends of the Central American peoples are of great importance ; for the settlements, even of those peoples that had made a considerable advance in civilisation, were only of relative duration. In the legends we constantly meet with the story that the peoples, under the

MAYA COPY OF THE GREAT TEMPLE OF CHICHEN-ITZA IN NORTHERN YUCATAN

reaching from the foot of the mountain to the sea, the ruined sites remain of Ococingo, Palenque, Menché, and Piedras Negras. Each of these must once have formed a large town, a centre of religious and political life, round which a thick population clustered. To us there remains little save the sites of the temples and perhaps of one or two palaces. It is a characteristic peculiarity of all Central American civilisation to have practically no profane buildings to show, but a large number of religious erections of great extent and particular beauty. At once the conclusion offers itself that in the political life of the old Maya towns the

guidance of their national god, wandered about until the god, speaking himself or through one of his servants, ordered the people to settle definitely on a certain spot and to build him a dwelling-place.

This merely means that the priests were the ruling class, as being the servants and representatives of the godhead ; the fact is confirmed by our own historical knowledge of peoples who were ruled by religious and not by warrior leaders. We consider the almost exclusive preponderance of religious buildings in Palenque, in Menché, and other ruined places ; we observe the pictorial decorations remaining in these temples, which

E   28   D

we find to be almost entirely composed of divinities and priests in nearly every case with the insignia of temporal dominion—the sceptre and a peculiar head-dress of richest featherwork ; and hence we conclude that the same conditions must have prevailed to an unlimited extent in these old Maya towns. Certainly, centres of political power might have existed elsewhere and have left behind them fewer and less-enduring memorials. We might be led to this conclusion by the analogy of the neighbouring Nahua district, where Teotihuacan and Cholula were recognised centres of religious life and were adorned with greater buildings than many a royal capital, without being in any unusually close connection with the political life of those districts. But the old Maya towns, with the extensive precincts of their temples, are very numerous, and are not very widely separated ; hence it is impossible to find room either near or between them for the existence of such independent political centres as would form the natural counterpoise to this high development of the priestly forces. One, at least, of the ruined cities, Palenque, bears traces within and around itself which admit the possibility of other than sacred conceptions attaching to the ground.

Within the limits of the ruins are to be found constructions for bringing water and serving it throughout the district which are too extensive to have been connected with the temple buildings alone. The remains of an ancient Indian town are not great, even though the town was of considerable extent and population. The common folk were occupied by their agricultural labours at a distance from

THE TEMPLE OF THE SUN AT PALENQUE
The worship of the sun occupied a foremost place in the Maya religious observances, this illustration showing a temple erected to that deity.

the town for most of the year. The monuments themselves show us how thorough and extensive ancient Maya agriculture was ; many of the elements current in their hieroglyphic script were borrowed from agricultural implements ; in their religion the divinities of fruitfulness played a most important part and are adorned with symbols relating to agriculture.

The reports of the Spaniards further confirm the fact : in the districts inhabited at their time they found everywhere a dense population supporting itself by careful tilling of the soil. As winter caused but a short interruption of agricultural operations, the population had no permanent habitations in the immediate neighbourhood of the temples, their houses for their daily needs being placed in the middle of their fields. Their frail dwellings, built of wood and wattle-work, straw and matting, offered no resistance to the march of time, and left no traces of their ruin which could have survived the lapse of centuries. On the environs of Palenque, in the depths of that forest which has covered the town more or less since historical times, there are, it is true, concealed memorials of antiquity, isolated and at a distance from the town ; probably, therefore, when Palenque was a flourishing town, its neighbourhood was also inhabited by an industrious agricultural population. We know, from the figures which have been transmitted to us of the state of things in Mexico-Tenochtitlan, what large crowds of people were occupied in the temple services of the Central American peoples. So, as the temples in each of the old Maya cities are always numerous and often of considerable extent, we have in this fact an exact correspondence with the traditions.

A VIEW OF THE OUTER WESTERN FACADE OF THE PALACE

EASTERN FACADE OF THE INNER WING OF THE PALACE

REMAINS OF THE ANCIENT MAYA PALACE AT PALENQUE IN MEXICO

At the same time the extent and importance of the temples are evidence for the strong powers of the ruling priestly castes.

The Maya buildings, which we must consider, without exception, as monumental buildings in our sense of the word, were almost always erected upon a foundation in the form of a hill, displaying

The Maya Style of Architecture many resemblances to the mounds of the North American Indians. Here and there, where the ground was favourable, natural hills were employed for this object, and cut down to the size of the designed erection. But generally the whole mound or terrace was artificially constructed of boulders, rubble, gravel, or earth, according to the nature of the material at hand.

In countless cases these mounds, known as " ku " in the Maya tongue, are all that remain to tell of an ancient building. In such cases we must suppose that the mound was crowned by an open altar, or a construction of some perishable material, of which all traces have disappeared. Kus without buildings upon them are found in Chiapas only in connection with more permanent erections ; but in Yucatan, where the Maya architecture can be traced in many other directions, there stand, or stood, unnumbered kus in complete isolation, and these in the later Spanish period often formed the only memorials of the ancient Indian settlements. All the larger temple sites of the Maya show a number of earth terraces ; these were arranged in an exactly parallel order, and formed the four sides of a lower court in the midst.

But in the case of such groups of mounds the sides are usually covered with flagstones or with smooth plaster spread over them ; and the terraces almost invariably support buildings which may be of considerable size. At the eastern foot of the Cordilleras, both in Chiapas and on the boundaries of Honduras, Nature provided the

Maya Peoples Ignorant of the Arch Maya with a hard sandstone of an argillaceous kind. This was an ideal material for their purposes. It could be quarried in large blocks without trouble ; being only moderately heavy, its transport offered no insurmountable difficulties, and it was capable of being worked even with their inadequate instruments. For the Maya, in spite of their artistic cleverness, apparently made no use of metal tools in their work, although they seem to have had some knowledge of copper work for decorative productions. Their ignorance of the arch is a fact of importance for the Maya architecture. They overcame the difficulty by making each new course overhang the one beneath it until the opening became small enough to be closed by a single slab. However, this kind of arch could cover only a moderate breadth, could hardly be built firmly enough to support a second building, and obliged the construction of the roof to be extremely massive. The consequence was that the fore-wall of the building that composed the roof provided a surface often more than half the size of the storey beneath it.

The Maya architects were in the habit of using this surface for ornamental decoration, and it became so important an architectural feature that the monuments of the highest development often retain it without the massive roofing behind, merely as an isolated ornament to finish off the building. A façade of this kind, which really contained but one floor of rooms, often produced the appearance of a three-storied building. The Maya could only place

Buildings Like Terraced Pyramids one storey upon another in tower-shaped buildings of considerable extent ; on the other hand, they have built many temples in another style of two or more storeys. This was done in pyramidal form. The foundation upon which they were raised gave all the Maya buildings the appearance of a terraced pyramid. The building did not stand exactly upon the edges of the artificial mound ; an open space ran around every side of it. If a second storey was to be raised, it was only necessary to increase the height of the mound at the back of the building until it was upon a level with the roof. This roof then formed an open space before the door, and in the centre of the mound thus raised a second storey could be erected.

Entrance to this could be gained either from the sides of the mound which were not built upon, or by a stairway against one of the sides of the building. The Maya architects were invariably obliged to construct buildings of considerable breadth, because bold and lofty erections were unattainable with the means at their disposal. The heaviness of the broad and massive roof is dispelled only by the rich ornamental design of the sides and the façade. The boldness of design and the scrupulous finish of detail are extraordinary.

The Maya buildings entirely exclude the supposition that they were formed by merely putting together any material at hand. They are, without exception, the result of uniform design, and their arrangement most certainly implies previous survey and full calculation. The sculptures are even stronger evidence for this fact; they often rise a considerable height from the ground, and their design occupies many yards of wall space. This is especially the case with the stone carvings. It is wholly inconceivable that these masses of stonework should have been

and in Yucatan (especially Uxmal and Chichen-Itza). But the sculptured figures in each of these several districts have such strongly marked characteristics that they require separate description. In the ruined cities of Chiapas, the oldest district of Maya civilisation, the bas-relief is the prevailing feature of their sculpture. At one place it is a form of relief in clay or stucco, a development of the potter's art; instances are the altar slabs of Palenque and a long row of interesting examples. Elsewhere it is relief in stone, requiring far greater artistic skill. For instance, the

THE IMPOSING REMAINS OF AN AZTEC TEMPLE IN YUCATAN

begun only when the blocks had been placed in position; on the contrary, it is plain from the manner of their insertion that they were previously worked apart. This implies a previous capability for planning and disposing ornamental designs which is possible only to the highest powers of the surveyor and calculator.

All these architectural peculiarities are to be found, though with certain local differences, among all those Maya races which have left buildings of any importance behind them. They are to be found not only in the ruins of Chiapas, but also in Guatemala (Tikal), in Honduras (Copan),

famous altar-pieces of Palenque, and the splendid slab from Menché-Tenamit. If we leave out of sight the fundamental peculiarities of style, the skill of the Maya in each of these materials must excite our highest admiration, both for the designs conceived and for the technical perfection of execution. With them are to be ranked by right of birth the artists in the neighbouring district, forming the modern republic of Guatemala.

The true Guatemala highland need not be considered with reference to the most ancient Maya civilisation. At the beginning of the sixteenth century in that district

5741

the Spaniards certainly met with the independent Maya states, Quiché, Kakchiquel, and Tzutuhil. But there is hardly a doubt that these states first came into existence in later centuries. On the other hand, the lowland on the east of Guatemala, on the borders of Yucatan, was in the occupation of the Maya at the height of their

The Height of Maya Civilisation civilisation. The states of Tikal and Peten certainly belong to a far earlier period of development than do Utatlan, Iximché, and Cinacatan, the capitals of the three principalities previously named. The highly carved wood panels which have travelled from the ruins of Tikal to the museum of Basel, if allowance be made for difference of material, must certainly, by their design and execution, be placed in the same category as the Chiapas memorials.

Unless we are to conceive entire independence for each separate Maya state, the towns of Chiapas and those of Lower Guatemala must have been more closely connected with each other than they were with the rest of the Maya district. At any rate, in this district remains of old Maya roads can be traced here and there, whereas such roads are rarer towards the south and reappear in any number only around a central point in Yucatan.

The most southerly ruined sites, Quirigua and Copan on the Honduras boundary with their numerous characteristics, form another district of civilisation still wider in extent. Quirigua, on account of the stiffness and clumsiness of its artistic figures, is considered one of the oldest states of the Maya civilisation. It may perhaps be older than Copan, which was more advanced and which probably contained the germs of an early destruction; but it is certainly of later date than the northern Maya settlements, for its art is more advanced than the art of the north was, and has closer affinities with the art of Copan. With the exception of two

Statues and their Inscriptions efforts in Yucatan, Quirigua and Copan are the only states which rose to the full portrayal of the human form; real statues there are certainly none, but we find caryatids and memorial pillars of human shape. These unmistakably represented particular individual personalities, though trammelled by symbolical and stereotyped accessories. Each of these stelæ is covered with extensive inscriptions; but though these cannot be deciphered as a whole,

their value is manifest from the fact that they have already made us acquainted with seven dates which are calculated from the fixed point of time before referred to, 3,750 years before the erection of the oldest of these pillars. The dates upon these seven monuments are important, inasmuch as the respective ages of the pillars give us a minimum length of time for the Copan civilisation which erected them.

The difference between the earliest and the latest date amounts to 108 years; we may therefore conclude that the destruction and fall of Copan formed the conclusion of this period; for it is improbable, given the continuance of certain conditions and the absence of any counteracting cause, that the established custom of erecting portrait memorials should have been dropped. This train of argument certainly does not lead to much; the time and circumstances which brought about the fall of Copan are as little known to us as are the same circumstances in the case of the other Maya states. When the Spaniards entered the continent, Copan was already in ruins, a mystery overgrown

Variety of Maya Divinities by the primeval forest. So entirely had it fallen into oblivion that Cortes with his band was able to march past it at the distance of but a few miles, while his Indian guides, who must have informed him of all the wonders of the country, never mentioned it even once.

As almost all the monumental buildings in the Maya district with which we are acquainted consist of temples, we see that religion must have played a most important part in the public life of the ancient Maya. The Maya possessed a large number of different divinities, without reckoning the little fetishes, or household gods which every house possessed, and which were known here, as in the Antilles, by the name of "zemes." Their polytheism was, however, of a limited character compared with that of other peoples; this is the more likely, owing to the probability that many of the different names of the gods which have come down to us were current among different Maya races to denote similar conceptions.

Moreover, the varied representations of the gods in the monuments and in manuscripts were certainly to some extent only different forms of one and the same divine power. The missionaries were able to describe this consciousness of an

MAYA HIGH-PRIEST SACRIFICING TO THE GOD KUKULKAN

This illustration from the bas-relief in stone from Menché-Tenanit, now in the British Museum, shows the god habited in the royal insignia, the sceptre and the rich feather dress, while before him kneels the high-priest in the act of sacrifice, the rich clothing and the feather head-dress denoting his office. The sacrifice consists in tearing the tongue with the thorns of the rope the priest holds in his hands, and allowing the blood to drop into the sacrificial vessel.

underlying unity in the case of the god Hunabku, who was invisible and supreme ; naturally their zealous orthodoxy saw here some fragmentary knowledge of the one God.

Hunabku does not appear very prominently in the Maya worship or mythology ; of this the sun is undoubtedly the central point. Kukulkan and Gukumatz—probably in his essence Itzamna also

The Place of the Sun in Worship —are only variant names, originating in difference of race, for the power of the sun that warms, lights, and pours blessings upon the earth. As the sun rises in the east out of the sea, so the corresponding divinity of the traditions comes over the water from the east to the Maya, and is the bringer of all good things, of all blessings to body and soul, of fruitfulness and learning. In the last character the divinity is fully incarnated. He appears as an aged greybeard in white flowing robes ; as Votan he divides the land among the peoples and gives the settlements their names ; as Kabil, the " Red Hand," he discovers writing, teaches the art of building, and arranges the marvellous perfection of the calendar. This part of the myth has undoubtedly a historical connection with the sun-myth, the real centre of all these religious conceptions, and is further evidence of the powers of the priesthood and of the fact that their influence was exercised to advance the progress of civilisation. Fully realistic is a conception of that particular deity which is represented in the Maya art by the widely prevailing symbol of the feathered snake. This is also a branch of the sun-worship. In the tropical districts, for a great part of the year the sun each day, at noon, draws up the clouds around himself ; hence, with lightning and thunder, the symbols of power, comes down the fruitful rain in thunderstorms upon the thirsty land.

Thus the feathered snake, perhaps even a symbol of the thunder, appears among the Maya, on the highland of Central America, among the Pueblo Indians, and also among some Indian races of the North American lowland. It represents the warm, fruitful power of the heavens, which is invariably personified in the chief luminary, the sun. The symbols of the snake and of Quetzal, the sacred bird with highly coloured plumage are attributes of more than one Maya divinity.

Under different shapes in the Tzendal district, in Yucatan to a large extent, and particularly in Chichen-Itza, they have so coloured the religious and the artistic conceptions of the Maya that we meet with traces of this symbolism in almost

Good and Bad Gods every monument and every decoration. The dualism of the Maya Olympus also originates in a mythological interpretation of natural phenomena. The representatives of the sun—light and life—are opposed to those of the night —darkness and death ; both have nearly equal powers and are in continual conflict for the lordship of the earth and of mankind. Moreover, the good gods have been obliged to abandon man after expending all their benefits upon him, and have made him promise of a future return, to support him in the struggle, and to assure him of victory at the last. Around these central mythological conceptions, which in different forms are practically common property among most early peoples, are grouped, in the case of the Maya, a large number of individual characteristics, each diversely developed. Not only was human life subject to the power of the gods in a large and general way, since the gods had created and formed it, but also religion—or, to be more exact, the Maya priesthood—had contrived a special system whereby man's life was

MAYA TEMPLE OF THE CROSS
Originally an oratory, this building, the work of early Americans, is of very remote antiquity. The cross had a symbolical meaning among the ancient Maya other than as an emblem of Christianity.

RELIGIOUS CUSTOMS OF THE MAYA: THE GROUP OF THE CROSS

This picture represents a religious custom obtaining among the Maya peoples, who inhabited districts of Central America in the pre-Columbian days. To avert supposed calamities and on religious festivals it was usual to sacrifice newly-born children and offer their bodies to the gods. Such an offering the priest on the right is holding in his hands. A remarkable fact concerning this tablet is that it was executed with the aid of blunt instruments of flint.

ostensibly under the permanent influence of the gods, even in the most unimportant trifles. Upon this subject the quarters of the heavens and the constellations were of decisive importance; careful and keen observation, lasting apparently over a great period of time, had put the Maya priesthood in possession of an astronomical knowledge to which no other people upon a corresponding plane of civilisation has ever attained.

Their calendar still bears traces of its development; in earlier times it consisted of eighteen months of twenty days each, as with many other American peoples. At the time of the discovery of America the Maya knew how to correct the solar year by means of five intercalary days, a piece of knowledge which the Nahua peoples also possessed; but they were also aware that this did not correspond with the real length of the solar year, and corrected the error with greater accuracy than the Old World **Astronomical Laws known to the Maya** had done previous to Gregory's alteration of the Western calendar. Herein they were superior to the Spaniards, who destroyed their civilisation without suspecting this fact. This carefully corrected solar year was then considered in relation to all other possible annual calculations, and upon it the priestly caste established a number of astronomical laws more carefully worked out than in any other nation. Of nearly equal, if not of even greater, importance to the solar year was the ritual year of twenty weeks with thirteen days each; each division of it belonged to a particular divinity. Here the four quarters of the heavens played an important part, since to each of them a quarter of the ritual year belonged. But in all this diversity the consciousness of a higher unity clearly existed; evidence for this is the special symbol of the four quarters of the heaven—the cross—which the Spaniards were highly astonished to find everywhere in the Maya temples, as an object of particular veneration. Moreover, an influence upon the motions of the earth was certainly attributed to the morning and evening stars and to the Pleiades. Perhaps also the periods of revolution for Venus, Mercury, and Mars were approximately known and employed in calculation.

The knowledge of these minute astronomical calculations was the exclusive possession of the highest priesthood, though at the same time they exercised a certain influence upon the whole national life. Upon these calculations the priests arranged the worship of the gods. The Maya worship is sharply divided from that of the Nahua, and in particular from the bloody idol-worship of the Aztecs, which

5745

has been erroneously considered as almost the typical form of Central American worship. However, human sacrifice does not seem to have been entirely excluded from the Maya religion. But in earlier times, before communication with the Nahua peoples and their lower forms of civilisation had exercised a deteriorating influence upon the Maya culture, human sacrifice was practised most rarely, and the Maya knew nothing of the cannibalism which, even among the Aztecs, accompanied these sacrifices. It was only on the high festival, when, at the outset of a new year, the Maya kindled the fire anew to symbolise the commencement of a period, that a human victim was offered to the gods. The Maya were certainly fully aware of the high value of blood as a sacrifice; only the power of atonement was not inherent in the blood of a slaughtered victim, but in that of a living man.

Cannibalism Unknown to the Maya

The blood was shed in honour of the god, with fasting and discipline, by tearing the tongue or some other sensitive portion of the body with thorns or other instruments of torture. Yet this happened only upon high occasions. The usual offerings were of a wholly inoffensive kind, and consisted of the first-fruits of the huntsman's spoil or of the produce of the ground. The most widely spread of all forms of offering was the censing with burning copal resin, a religious use which continued to the time of Christianity, and, in individual cases, until recently; upon the discovery of outlying Maya ruins, traces of such incense offerings of quite recent time have been found. Peacefully, with no shedding of blood, the life of this people passed by; under the unlimited but mildly exercised administration of a priestly aristocracy they passed a life that was laborious but free from care. Upon their memorials, weapons of war appear only as attributes of the gods.

Amid the blessings of prosperity and advancing civilisation they came to know the dark side of life. Long and careful cultivation of the fruitful tropic soil had given them a kingdom which they increased by an extensive trade. It may have been a merchant ship from a harbour in the Maya district that met with Columbus and his comrades upon their fourth voyage over the Atlantic between Jamaica and the mainland; its sails, its well-clothed crew, and its cargo may have pointed to the existence of a higher civilisation behind the district of the Antilles and the naked savages who inhabited it. But prosperity was fatal to the nation. Phallic worship, reverence to a divinity of unnatural lust, are signs of moral decay among the ruling classes of this people; and so it is intelligible that they went down before an external shock, though it was the shock of an enemy which was by no means of overpowering strength.

Prosperity Fatal to the Nation

STATUE OF TLALOC, THE GOD OF RAIN, FOUND AT CHICHEN-ITZA

END OF THE MAYA CIVILISATION
AND THE COMING OF THE SPANIARDS

IT was about the ninth century of our era—perhaps a century or two earlier—that the peace of the Maya states of Chiapas and Tabasco was broken by the invasion of the Nahua peoples. A manuscript of Kuikatec origin informs us of a wave of conquest which passed from the south-west of Central America to the Isthmus of Tehuantepec, then turned towards the east, troubled some part of Guatemala, and finally penetrated to the Acalan district, directly bordering on the Yucatan peninsula. The enemy was then situated in the rear of that group of states to which Palenque, Menché, and other centres of Maya civilisation belonged.

The reason that we cannot recognise these ancient names in the lists of the Kuikatec conquest is, perhaps, simply because the documents have not been deciphered. At any rate, invading hordes of the kind did not spare the Maya district, which was easy of access and possessed all the allurements of a high civilisation. It is doubtful whether hard fighting took place or not between the unwarlike Maya and the fierce, invading Nahua. The ruins of Chiapas and Tabasco show scarce a trace of wilful destruction such as is unmistakable in the case of Mayapan (Yucatan). It was far less difficult for this people to give up their wonted habitations than it would have been for a more civilised race. It was only for their gods that they built permanent edifices; they were themselves satisfied with frail thatched huts in which they slung their hammocks, almost their only furniture, for the night.

Invasion of the Nahua Peoples

It is just possible that Copan, with its one century of flourishing civilisation, was only a temporary halting-place of the Maya peoples, who had abandoned their more northerly settlements in the Usumacinta lowland before the invasion of the advance guard of the Nahuatlac migration. If this be the case, then there also they were left only a few generations

in peace. The later devastation of this district by numerous and compact bodies of Nahua races would show that the conquerors followed later the tracks of their flying adversaries, and there also put an end to their peaceful existence. The final result, however, of the struggle between these two different races, a struggle which apparently lasted a considerable time, was to shatter the old Maya civilisation and to divide the races belonging to it into two essentially distinct groups, the Maya people of Yucatan and those of the Guatemala branch.

Shattering the Old Maya Civilisation

Upon their invasion the Maya found Yucatan still uninhabited, whether this invasion followed upon their flight before the Nahua peoples or was an event of earlier times. Probably Yucatan offered no great or immediate attractions to them. Thanks to its position between two seas, the climate of the peninsula was healthy; the sea-breezes also brought moisture sufficient for the needs of a luxuriant vegetation. But running water —that indispensable condition of a permanent settlement—is scarce to be found on the whole peninsula.

A search for the precious liquid in subterranean caverns, the collecting of it in reservoirs, and the transport of it often to the height of three or four hundred feet up steps and ladders, is an undertaking not lightly entered upon by any people that can find more suitable ground at its disposal. Undoubtedly, Yucatan was first settled by the Maya far later than Chiapas or Tabasco. All the remains that have been brought to light by the manifold excavations, even those from the lowest strata, point to the highly advanced civilisation of the inhabitants; traces of a gradual development of this civilisation there are none. The immigrating people must therefore have gained their culture elsewhere, as is demonstrable in the case

What the Excavations Reveal

of the Maya in the neighbouring districts farther west. In Yucatan, also, a considerable portion of the civilised districts was in ruins at the time of the Spanish invasion;

Features of the Ancient Maya Art but other towns and temples, which fully correspond in character with those destroyed, were then in full perfection. And tradition was certainly able to give a more or less connected account of the cities that had been abandoned and destroyed. The Yucatan buildings display an art of an undoubtedly late period compared with the art of the more westerly states; the execution is not so careful, and there is a certain admixture of foreign elements. In place of the simple design of the old monumental buildings, where the sole decorations were the carved slabs and their accompanying inscriptions, we have here, partly resulting from the nature of the material employed, an excess of ornamental detail, a wilfully exaggerated symbolism, the existence of which is far more intelligible in the case of an older people than it is in a nation advancing by the

GIGANTIC MAYA SCULPTURE AT ITZAMAL IN MEXICO

strength of youth. The lavish employment of stereotyped forms leaves but meagre space for inscriptions, so that this valuable adjunct of the ancient Maya art is here almost entirely wanting.

In the sculpture and wall paintings the influence of elements of Nahuatlac origin is unmistakable; this brings the foundation of the Yucatan ruins nearer to the time when the two races came in contact. The calendar of the Yucatan Maya also shows traces of a later origin, and diverges

in many points from that of the Maya race of Chiapas. These differences have a particular importance, as they show the Yucatan people in concord with the Nahua, who certainly developed their civilisation later, and in divergence from their own original race. Tradition also—though often, after the manner of tradition, returning upon the creation of all things—does give grounds for that supposition that the occupation of Yucatan was the result, in the first instance, of the collapse of the old Maya civilisation.

Yucatan appears to have been originally divided into a number of small individual states, each with its own separate traditions; consequently the history of the peninsula contains a large number of different traditions which cannot be traced to a common source, and do not show sufficient points of contact among themselves to enable us to construct a general history of the Maya race. We may, however, conclude that the emigrations and the settlements in Yucatan were not the result of one uniform leadership, but that separate little bands, independent of one another, had fled beyond the thick woods that bound Yucatan. Individuals among these groups retained the old institutions under which they had seen happier times in their more western home. The god Itzamna was named as the founder and the first ruler of the sacred town Itzamal. Similarly Kukulkan, who was certainly only the incarnation of a similar group of ideas, is said to have been the first king of Mayapan to have carried on for many

RESTORATION OF THE MAYA TEMPLE OF KAB-UL AT THE SACRED TOWN OF ITZAMAL IN MEXICO

On a pyramid to the east of Itzamal rose a temple dedicated to Izamat-ul, Izamna, or Zamna, the great founder of the ancient Maya empire. "To him were brought," says one historian, "the sick, the halt, and the dead, and he healed and restored them all to life by the touch of his hand," hence the appellation Kab-ul, the Miraculous Hand, applied to him.

years a rule of peace and prosperity, and to have been the origin of the princely house of the Cocomes. This means that the bands of Maya who chose Itzamal and Mayapan for their new abode were still under the government of their old priestly caste. On the analogy of Mexico we may conclude that these priests had marched at

The Sacred Town of Itzamal the head of the emigrants with the holy images of the gods, and had finally given them commands, presumed to be from heaven, for the colonisation and the building of the new towns. In Itzamal the priestly caste seems to have been pre-eminent until the town was absorbed in the neighbouring states, which were rapidly extending under a secular rule. Mayapan in the course of time took a predominating position among these. The fact, however, that the race of kings in that town traced their origin from Kukulkan himself is a proof that this royal house either owed its origin to a secularisation of its priestly rulers, or, at any rate, was founded with the help and approval of the priesthood of their national god.

Circumstances seem to have been somewhat different, even from the beginning, with those bands of the Maya who were known as Itzaes, and who founded and gave its title to the town of Chichen-Itza. In this case, even at the outset of their emigrations, a secular government appeared in place of their priestly leadership; for although the Tutul Xius are occasionally mentioned as holy men, they appear everywhere as a family of warriors and princes. Their traditions most distinctly point to their origin from the Maya states of the west; the land of Nonoual is particularly mentioned as a starting-point of their migrations; that is, the Nonohualco of the Nahua, the coast-line of Tabasco. Starting at that point, they arrived, after long wanderings, at Chacnouitan, the most southerly part of

Settlements of the Maya Peoples Yucatan, and they founded their first important town in Ziyan Caan on the lake which was afterwards called Bacalar. In later times, as also appears in the annals of the Tutul Xius, the historical interests of Yucatan gravitated to the north of the peninsula; only on the lake Bacalar the Spaniards, under Montejo, met with a numerous Maya population in several extensive towns. For something like sixty years the rulership of the Tutul Xius lasted

in Ziyan Caan; then they also marched northward and eventually chose Chichen-Itza for their residence. Chichen-Itza is a town which has played a considerable part among the sacred places of Yucatan, a part resembling that of Teotihuacan in Anahuac; its fortunes had no lasting connection with the race of the Tutul Xius which had founded it.

In the meantime, the territorial principalities in the whole neighbourhood had been greatly strengthened, and their conflicting interests brought war and destruction upon the rising towns. It seems to have been the Cocomes, the rulers of Mayapan, who overthrew the throne of the Tutul Xius in Chichen-Itza after a government of 120 years; the town itself they made loosely dependent upon their own state, but the governors and their followers were obliged to start upon a fresh emigration. According to these traditions, Yucatan owes to this same race of princes another of its noblest towns and the rich artistic decorations with which it is adorned. At any rate, the Tutul Xius fled in a slanting direction across the whole peninsula as far as the northern coast, and

Nahuatlac Soldiers in Yucatan Wars settled in Champoton, where they are said to have ruled for more than 250 years. This fact is confirmed by the extensive burial-grounds of a Maya people which have been discovered on the little islands which lie opposite to the town of Champoton, or Potonchan, known later as a site of Nahuatlac population.

Apparently it was here that the Maya people who were subjects of the Tutul Xius entered into relations with the Nahua people, who had gained accessions of strength in the meantime. In the fourteenth century troops of Nahuatlac soldiers played an important part in the internal wars of Yucatan; and that it was not, as tradition relates, only the Cocomes of Mayapan who availed themselves of the services of these strangers is proved by the artistic style of the productions with which we meet even in the territory of the enemies of the Cocomes, especially in Chichen-Itza; here chiefs and warriors are repeatedly immortalised in an art the style of which betrays its affinity to the pictorial art of the Aztec manuscripts at the very first glance.

Such confederations as these enabled the Tutul Xius to extend their rulership from Champoton towards the north and east. They entered into treaties of peace with the princes of Mayapan ; and families of ruling princes again held the sceptre in Itzamal and Chichen-Itza. At this time the Tutul Xius changed their residence from Champoton to Uxmal (pronounced Ushmal). Their splendid state buildings in that district are sure evidence of a long period of peace, which they utilised to advance further their civilisation.

The different little states were under a rulership that was at least mild, but forced them to keep peace with one another ; the artistic energy resulting from this peace expended itself in the countless monumental ruins with which we meet upon the soil of Yucatan. It was in this period, too, that the country was opened up, as was formerly the district between Palenque and its neighbouring towns, by the extensive and carefully made system of highroads, remains of which have been found in the most widely separated places.

Religious purposes were the chief object of this work. According to the traditions, the roads led from the chief temple of Chichen-Itza and Itzamal out into the country in all directions, as far and wide as people prayed and made pilgrimages to **Chief of the Maya Deities** Kukulkan, the feathered snake, unmistakably the chief among the Maya deities of later times. Chichen-Itza was specially connected with Cozumel, an island town not far from the eastern coast, which seems to have formed a wide circle of temples in the whole of its extent ; it was here that the Spaniards first found the cross, the symbol of the god who ruled the four quarters of the heaven.

The Indian summer of the Maya civilisation was not fated to last long in Yucatan. The yoke of the Cocomes was heavy upon land and people. At the beginning of their rule, in order the better to secure their position, they had created an aristocracy which was obliged to give personal service to the government ; for this, however, they were recompensed by rich grants of land and people, which they ruled—or, more exactly, plundered—through their representatives.' The result was that the Cocomes introduced, probably in imitation of Nahuatlac predecessors, the institution of slavery, which had hitherto been unknown to the Maya. They based their rights on the principle of conquest. The state of Mayapan owed a considerable portion of its extent to the sternness of this rule ; in this way Chichen-Itza became tributary to the government of Mayapan. The iron hand of government growing heavier and heavier may very well, in the course of time, have brought it about that the position of the common people, who were subject to the tributary caciques, degenerated into a kind of subjection not very different from slavery. Moreover, the **Revolts Against the Cocomes** ruling classes abandoned themselves to the unlimited enjoyment of life ; even the legends of the founding of their state speak of acts of dreadful immorality. The result was that the rulers did not feel their position secure, though they were situated in the midst of a nobility bound to themselves by common interests.

After the manner of tyrants, they thought they would find their surest protection in a foreign bodyguard, and they took warriors of the Nahua race from the district of Tabasco into their service. Even with this help they were not entirely successful in suppressing manifestations of dissatisfaction. One of the first to revolt against the tyranny of the Cocomes was the prince of Uxmal, but the fortune of war decided against him, and factions which broke out in Uxmal itself resulted in the abandonment of the royal town by its inhabitants, though not in its destruction. The remainder of the Tutul Xius were again obliged to retreat, and founded a new principality in Mani, which, however, never attained the splendour and importance of the imperial towns of Chichen-Itza and Uxmal.

The rising of the Tutul Xius had, however, set the example of revolt, and soon found imitators among the petty kings who were hard pressed by the Cocomes, though not so hard as had been the aristocracy of Mayapan. The next to refuse the respect he owed to the tyrant of Mayapan was the prince of Chichen-Itza. But he also was brought to punishment. A man of extraordinary energy sat upon the **Hunac Eel the Tyrant of Mayapan** throne of the Cocomes. Hunac Eel was certainly an even harsher tyrant than his predecessors had been, but he was also a far-seeing politician. He knew very well that he could not rely upon the fidelity and dependence of his subjects; therefore he sought protection for his rule outside of his kingdom. The chronicles speak of a treaty which Hunac Eel had made with the governors of the kings of Mexico in Tabasco and Xicalango ; this is certainly an anachronism, for at the time when Hunac Eel was king of Mayapan the Aztec rulers of Mexico-Tenochtitlan were fighting to win their own independence from the Tecpanec kings of Azcaputzalco.

But the fact is certainly well attested that Hunac Eel entered into alliance with the warlike Nahua of the neighbouring principality. In spite of his great display of power—Hunac Eel entered upon his campaign against Chichen-Itza with thirteen tributary princes—the result of his expedition was far less decisive than had been his war against Uxmal, but Chichen-Itza succumbed to overpowering forces. The town, however, retained its own princes, who were to some extent dependent upon the Mayapan government. For some time past the kingdom of Cocomes had been in a state of internal war. The uncertainty of the chronological calculations of Yucatan history does not make it plain how long these internal struggles in the kingdom of Mayapan had continued ; apparently about a century passed by before the crash came. This was, however, brought about by continual revolts in Chichen-Itza. Religious motives may have been at the bottom of this invincible animosity, or may at least have stimulated it. Mayapan and the priestly town of Itzamal, which were in close alliance, reverenced Itzamna as their divine founder, while Chichen-Itza by degrees had become the central point of the whole district of Maya civilisation for the worship of Kukulkan, the feathered snake, representations of which are a predominating characteristic in Chichen art. The rivalry between Itzamal and Chichen-

REMAINS OF THE ROYAL PALACE AT UXMAL
During the era of Mexican civilisation many stately buildings were erected at Uxmal, but when a revolt broke out against the tyranny of the Cocomes the royal town was abandoned by its inhabitants.

Itza gave occasion for complications resulting in hostilities between the states ; it certainly gave considerable impulse to the animosity with which the people of Mayapan were accustomed to regard the rival they had never entirely subdued. But the Cocomes were also blind to their own real interests ; they allowed the spirit of division to make further and further inroads into their kingdom, until at last even their foreign mercenaries could no longer cope with the power of the enemy. An alliance was concluded between the Tutul Xius, who had retreated to their highlands of Central Yucatan, the rulers of Chichen-Itza, and the enemies in the immediate neighbourhood of the Cocomes, and neither the bands of Nahua warriors nor the fortifications with which Mayapan had long since been surrounded could make head against the united forces of so many opponents. The Cocomes kingdom collapsed, and with it disappeared the last trace of a Maya confederation. The proud capital which for nearly 500 years had been the central point of the kingdom —a kingdom whose boundaries had embraced the greater part of the Yucatan peninsula—was utterly destroyed by its revengeful enemies. Though this is a most important occurrence in Yucatan history during the century which preceded the Spanish conquest, yet its date remains quite uncertain.

Apparently the decisive battles took place about the year 1436, after a previous period of nearly twenty years had passed almost without any cessation of hostilities. That this conflict must have consisted

THE GOVERNOR'S PALACE, THE MOST MAGNIFICENT MONUMENT OF CENTRAL AMERICA

COURTYARD OF THE NUNS' HOUSE AND ELLIPTICAL PYRAMID

Built by the Maya peoples in the great days of their prosperity, Uxmal, which some writers are prepared to regard as the home of the earliest civilisation, is to-day so many heaps of ruins from which we may learn much of the past

PREHISTORIC RUINS AT THE IMPERIAL TOWN OF UXMAL IN YUCATAN

rather of a series of revolutionary combats than of a continuous war is certainly to be inferred from the change in circumstances which had taken place. Even the hated Nahua body-guards were not involved in the tyrant's fall, but were spared by the conquerors. They were even allowed to settle in the province of Aculan,

Fall of the Cocomes Power

in the neighbourhood of Campeche, and there to form a little Nahua state. But this was apparently soon absorbed by the Maya, who surrounded it on all sides, for, a century later, at the time of the conquest, not a single Nahua-speaking inhabitant was to be found on the peninsula.

The conquerors, too, left equally unmolested a last branch of the Cocomes race, which was in Ulua at the time of the revolution, apparently attempting to enlist fresh Aztec reinforcements for the help of its mother state. It may have collected around itself the last surviving dependents of the old dynasty, and have founded another small state with their help ; by this means the name of Cocomes survived to future generations. The province of Zotuta, with its capital Tibulon, situated deep in the forests of the central regions, was the scene of its rule until the Spaniards made their way there also.

It is not easy to explain the nature of the influence which the fall of the Cocomes power exerted upon the two rival priestly towns of Itzamal and Chichen-Itza. Under its king Ulmil, Chichen-Itza had been for a long time the central point of the resistance offered to the kings of Mayapan; consequently the vials of the royal wrath had repeatedly been poured out upon town and land. In spite of this, up to the time of the destruction of Mayapan, the king of Chichen-Itza invariably appears as a powerful ally of the revolted party. One would have expected that the holy town of the feathered snake would now increase in strength and vigour. On the

Yucatan Split into Kingdoms

contrary, its name entirely disappears from the traditions ; upon the division of Yucatan into seven little kingdoms, a condition of things which the Spaniards found upon their conquest, Chichen-Itza appears no longer as an independent kingdom. The abandoned ruins of the town, which were speedily covered by a luxuriant vegetation, were offered by the kings of Itzamal as a resting-place for the first small Spanish troop which made its way into Yucatan. A possible explanation of this remarkable fact may be found in the legend that a prince of Chichen-Itza had abandoned the land, with the greatest part of his people, in one of the many revolutions which disturbed the last days of the Mayapan dynasty.

He is said to have turned again to the original dwelling-places of the Maya in the far west, hoping thus to avoid these scenes of war and oppression. The Maya state of Peten-Itza, on the lake of Peten, in Guatemala, is reputed to owe its origin to him. On his expedition to Honduras, Ferdinand Cortes visited its capital, which was situated on the island of the Peten lake called by the Spaniards the Isla de Flores. In this district, also, ruins of Maya towns have been recently discovered which would not disgrace the architects of Chichen-Itza, supposing them really to have been the founders of a second younger civilisation in this district, which was, for the Maya, classic ground.

Another curious tradition is connected with the little kingdom of Peten-Itza. The favourite horse of Cortes is said to have been so ill in that place that it could

The Coming of the Spaniards

go no farther. It was, therefore, handed over to the Maya, with orders to look after it carefully, that it might be given over to the next Spaniards who should come that way. But the Indians, whose reverential awe of the horse—an animal with which they were entirely unacquainted—is known to us from many episodes of the conquest, thought that the best way to look after the horse was to pay him the honours due to a god, to quarter him in a temple, and to feed him with sacrifices. This worship continued until the noble charger was killed by this unusual food, and must then have been replaced by a facsimile in clay.

The Maya state of Pente was the longest to maintain its independence against the Spaniards. The remoteness and isolation of the district in which the last Itzaes had set up their habitation were their best protection. Here, for more than a century after the visit of Cortes, the worship of the old gods, the practice of the ancient art, and the study of the old sacred books were maintained ; more than one attempt on the part of missionaries and governors to destroy this last retreat of heathendom came to an inglorious end in the extensive jungles which spread their sure defences around the little kingdom of Peten on all sides. It was only in 1671 that a simultaneous attack upon different sides succeeded in uniting a sufficient force at the lake of Peten ; even then the Maya, who had learned the arts of war in their century of battles, resisted with the courage of despair ; but the Indians and their rude and almost primitive implements of destruction could not make head against protective armour and better weapons. And so destruction came upon the last town in which the most ancient civilisation of the New World had gained a respite for its independence.

many generations, also provided secular rulers for the newly rising principality. The Cheles did not probably attempt to revive the aggressive policy of the Cocomes.

Nevertheless, their state, next to the state of Zachi, was by far the most extensive which the Spaniards found in the peninsula, and embraced, with the exception of the little Nahua territory of Campeche, the whole of the north and east. The district of this principality, in which the Spaniards found a friendly reception from the outset, became later the germ of the Spanish province of Yucatan ; Merida, the capital of this province, was built upon the site

RUINS OF A BEAUTIFUL TEMPLE AT UXMAL, SHOWING THE ELABORATE CARVINGS

Long before this time a similar fate had befallen all the other Maya kingdoms. Strangely enough, that town had gained the most profit from the revolution against Mayapan, which should have been most deeply involved in the fall of the Cocomes, as being their closest ally. The greatest part of the district which formed the old kingdom of Mayapan did not fall into the power of the Itzaes of Chichen, or the Tutul Xius of Mani, but to the old priestly town Itzamal ; and the race of the Cheles, from which the high-priesthood of the kingdom of Mayapan had been drawn for

of the ancient Tiho, only a few miles from Itzamal. Chiefly in consequence of their foolish conduct, the Spaniards had many a hard battle to fight before they subjugated the whole Maya district of Yucatan ; but when once peace and order had been firmly re-established in the country, the native population, which was even then numerous, displayed all the virtues peculiar to the ancient race. The docile, pliable, and frugal Maya-Indians tilled the soil for their Christian lords and priests with the same industry which they had displayed under their ancient masters, and the clever architects and sculptors now erected temples and palaces upon modern designs with all their ancient skill.

It is doubtful whether the Maya kingdom of Guatemala, and the later kingdoms of Quiché, of Kakchiquel, and of Tzutuhil, were first populated when the inroads of the Nahua race menaced the old civilisation of the Tzendal district. It is far more probable that the acquisition of these territories by Maya peoples belongs to an earlier period. The connection of kindred nations in their immediate neighbourhood in so momentous a fashion naturally could not fail to have an influence upon these kingdoms; at any rate, the people of the western highland gained then a strong additional element, which was more advanced than they in civilisation and consequently must have had a considerable influence upon these races.

Ancient Maya Kingdoms

The Maya people of Guatemala also had a full share in the important acquisition which the civilisation of their race had gained. They were well acquainted with the art of writing in the hieroglyphic signs peculiar to the Maya civilisation. Their legendary traditions, which have come down to us in even greater number than have those of their most advanced kinsfolk on the east, show the same number of religious conceptions; the same gods, with now and then even the same names, are prominent here as there. The complicated astronomical calendar, which must count among the most important scientific achievements of the Maya peoples, was for them also the governing principle in religious and civic life.

But the habits of their daily life, and the buildings thereby developed, were different, and resulted in a sensible difference in the artistic character of the district. This is especially the case with their architecture, which cannot but surprise us, supposing it to have been exclusively derived from the architects of Palenque, Menché, etc. The highlands of Guatemala, in which the capital town of Quiché and its related governments were situated, offered, for the expression of their artistic tendencies, a material of the same value and nature as the Maya had at their disposition in the lower districts. Nevertheless, the architecture of the western races never even approximated to the rich

Architecture of the Western Races

decorations of the east, and the number of memorials in the plastic art, the highland origin of which is indisputable, is very small. However, from the numerous examples of pottery found in the highlands and in the western district of Guatemala, we observe that these Maya peoples did not break away, as did the Huastecs, from the specific Maya civilisation of the original race, but that they had shared in every form of its development. On pottery ware from Quiché and related towns inscriptions and calendars have been transmitted to us which we are accustomed to find carved in stone or moulded in stucco as architectural decorations among the other Maya races.

The number of sites in the western Maya district, the ruins of which have been discovered, is by no means small, and remains of massive stone buildings, though without the usual artistic decoration, are by no means lacking. But the preponderance of fortifications in the sites of the west distinguishes them in a marked way from those of the lowlands and the Yucatan peninsula. Among the buildings of the lowlands are to be found many the position of which was certainly chosen with a view to resisting hostile attacks. But consideration of strategical necessities is nowhere very conspicuous, and in many places entirely wanting. In Guatemala quite the contrary is the case. The choice of site here shows that strategical considerations were generally of the first importance. Walls, fortresses, and citadels, often of considerable extent, which could have been reduced only by the combined attacks of large forces of men, are the most remarkable remains in the district of Quiché.

Maya Wars With the Nahua Peoples

The Maya in the lowlands were of a distinctly peaceful disposition; possibly in the course of time an entire change in their national character was brought about by their continual wars with the warlike Nahua races, some of which can be demonstrated to have made their way even as far as Nicaragua. It is, however, more probable that from the outset differences existed between the peaceful races of the flourishing coast-land and the more primitive peoples of the mountains, differences derived from the internal divisions of the district, which did not manifest themselves within the historical epoch. The old town Tulan continually appears

EXAMPLES OF THE EARLY RELIGIOUS SCULPTURES OF CENTRAL AMERICA

Religious worship played an important part in the lives of the Santa Lucians, one of the early races who inhabited America. Among their many deities the most prominent were the sun and moon, both of which in works of sculpture were represented with human forms. The bent staff emanating from the mouth of the worshipper in the first picture represents a petition or prayer which he is making to an aged divinity. The second picture shows a worshipper, the image of death reminding him of the end of his days, adoring a flaming deity, probably the sun.

as a source of all emigrations, and must be sought for in the district of Tabasco, if by Tulan we may understand an individual town. From this town Nima-Quiché—the great Quiché—emigrated with three brothers, and turned his steps westward to the mountains, as we learn from the traditions of the western peoples. The

Tradition of the Western Peoples brothers are said to have then divided the land so that one obtained the district of Chiapas (Quelenes), the other obtained Verapaz (Tezulutlan), and the third the district of Mames and Pocomams (on the north-west of Guatemala), while he himself gained the land of Quiché, Kakchiquel, and Tzutuhil ; the royal house of this kingdom traced its origin from him.

In spite of its Nahua influences this tradition clearly shows the consciousness of a national unity, even among such Maya peoples as have played no further part in history ; and it also refers their origin to a time when this national consciousness had not been so wholly deadened as it afterwards was. Chiapas now appears as one of the four Maya kingdoms, and there is nothing to show that this district had already fallen into the hands of foreign conquerors ; therefore this division of peoples must be regarded as belonging to a time long before the flight of the Maya from Chiapas.

The later history of the race is hopelessly confused. Continual internal wars, constant emigrations and change of place, revolts against tyrannical power, and confederations of peace are its chief constituents. The very dynasty of the Quiché race is by one historian given as consisting of eleven generations, by another as consisting of seventeen, and even sometimes as of twenty-three. However, the kings of Quiché certainly held an important position among the ruling races of Guatemala, and a chronicler declares that the Quiché kings date back to the era of

Founder of the Quiché Kingdom the Aztec rulers of Mexico-Tenochtitlan, adding at the same time that the Quiché kingdom was not merely equal to the Aztec kingdom in extent, but that it was even far superior to it. For the disruption of the small kingdoms of Kakchiquel and Tzutuhil, different reasons are suggested. The succession to King Acxopil, the successor of the Nima-Quiché, the real founder of the Quiché kingdom, may possibly have led to the

disruption. The rulers of the smaller kingdoms remained, however, in honourable relations with the chief kingdom of Quiché, and were even interested in the maintenance of the supreme power in consequence of the mode of succession peculiar to these American kingdoms.

Acxopil during his lifetime handed over to his eldest son the government of the kingdom of Kakchiquel, and to the younger the government of Tzutuhil, with the stipulation that after his death the elder son should govern the whole kingdom, including Quiché, the second son should govern Kakchiquel, and a third should rule over Tzutuhil. The object of this arrangement was that each ruler, before obtaining the highest position in the state, should undergo a training for supremacy in positions of gradually increasing importance. It does not appear, however, that this regulation was strictly observed after his death.

Icutemal, the elder of the sons of Acxopil, got possession of the throne of Quiché ; but he handed over the rulership of Kakchiquel to his own elder son, and not to his brother.

An Era of Internal Struggles This was a signal for the outbreak of protracted internal struggles, which lasted uninterruptedly almost up to the Spanish conquest. In this case also the neighbouring Nahua races were enlisted as allies in the wars of these related Maya kingdoms. Their influence was here so strongly pronounced that the bloody human sacrifices and the cannibalism practised by the Nahua were also adopted by the Maya. At any rate, all our information testifies that the Maya people in Guatemala were far more extensively commingled with Nahua elements than in Yucatan.

The three kingdoms continued mutually independent and in a state of constant internal struggle until the arrival of the Spaniards. In 1492 a number of the chiefs of Kakchiquel revolted against Cay Hunahpu, who had again attempted to extend his empire at the expense of his neighbours. He was defeated, and atoned for his aggression by his death. In this there is nothing extraordinary ; but the Kakchiquel attached such importance to this victory that they made it the starting-point of a new chronology. In true revolutionary style they abolished the whole of the old priestly calendar and created a year of 400 days, divided into twenty months of twenty days each. They are

THE SYMBOLICAL SCULPTURES OF THE SANTA LUCIANS

That the Santa Lucians had attained a highly developed state of culture is evidenced from their works of art. Although most of their sculptures represent some form of worship, there are many depicting scenes of ordinary day life. To the latter belongs the centre picture, where two men of the nobler classes are seen conversing. The other two show sick men, one of whom is visited by a medicine man in the guise of a deer, which is a reminder of the moderate number of years he has lived, thus bidding him be of good hope; the other an elderly man finding himself in the presence of death.

the only race of Central America which abandoned the scientific astronomical calendar of the Maya. It requires no great penetration to see that their new year was no advance upon the old one, but was an act as futile as it was arbitrary.

The Years of Aztec Dominion In spite of numerous relations with the Nahua races, there seems to have been no real connection between the Maya kingdom and the Aztec kingdom of Montezuma. The existence of each was known to the other, and embassies may have been exchanged between them even before the arrival of the Spaniards. The Aztec conquests certainly came extremely close to the boundaries of the Maya kingdom in the last ten years of Aztec dominion ; this did not conduce to any close connection between the two groups of states.

The Quiché were so much occupied with warding off the attacks of hostile kinsfolk within the boundaries of their own kingdom that they could not turn their attention to foreign conquest, which might have brought them into conflict with the Aztecs. When the Spaniards began to encroach upon the Aztec kingdom, Montezuma II. is said to have sent a great embassy to the king of Kakchiquel ; they do not, however, seem to have been able to come to an understanding. Before the Spaniards had undertaken the subjugation of the Maya kingdom of Guatemala, emissaries of the king of Kakchiquel appeared in Mexico, which was the first kingdom to fall before Cortes, and asked for his help against the Quiché.

Naturally this help was gladly lent in view of future possibilities. In the year 1524 the Adelantado Pedro de Alvarado appeared in Iximcat, and, in alliance with the Kakchiquel, began a war against the Quiché, and conquered them in several bloody conflicts. The Tzutuhil had remained neutral, trusting to the inaccessibility of their kingdom, and had refused their help, not only to the Quiché, but also to the Spaniards. This fact provided a pretext for Alvarado to turn his forces against them ; and neither the resources of Nature nor those of art could avail to protect the Tzutuhil against the power of Spain. The Kakchiquel learned too late that they had gained a Spanish alliance, for which they had so much sought, at the price of their own freedom.

Alliance at the Price of Freedom When they tried to shake off the yoke which was imperceptibly laid upon them, the moment had long since passed when their resistance could have been attended with any hopes of success. The blood that they shed in vain could only expiate their criminal action in being the first to throw open their country to the foreign invader.

FRONT AND BACK VIEWS OF BURIAL MASKS OF THE ANCIENT MEXICANS
These masks, generally made of copper or wood, were used among the Maya peoples for the purpose of covering the face of the dead, thus keeping away the demons while their wearers made their journey to the "abode of the clouds."

ADVANCE OF THE NAHUA PEOPLES
THE LEGEND OF TOLTEC CIVILISATION

IN the sixteenth century the Spaniards found a numerous population of Nahua, people who had been settled for many hundreds of years, in a territory which lies upon the north of the districts of Maya civilisation, and stretches to the borders of the Pueblo Indians—that is, from the Isthmus of Tehuantepec up to the boundaries of Texas and New Mexico.

These peoples did not, however, consider their country as their original home ; in fact, there was there a remnant of a foreign population which had, in general, followed the steps of Nahua civilisation. The migration legends which were widely extant among the Nahua give very consistent narratives, and point to the home of the race having been situated in the far north upon a great water. In this legend the place-names Aztlan (the Town on the Water) and Chicomoztoc (the Seven Caves) play a great part. This legend has evoked a whole literature. **Emigration of the Nahua Peoples** From the coast of the Pacific Ocean to the North American lakes, from Bering Strait to the Plain of Mexico, scarcely a spot can be found which one or another inquirer has not connected with the emigrations of the Aztecs from Aztlan-Chicomoztoc to Mexico-Tenochtitlan.

The traces of emigration of the Nahua peoples in a northerly direction, other than those of a legendary nature, are extremely inadequate. The district which lay a little to the north of the later centre of Nahua civilisation—that is, the plateau of Anahuac—was populated in comparatively early times by the race of the Pueblo Indians. Their civilisation shows some points of resemblance to the Nahua culture ; but the fundamental differences are so striking or extreme that it is impossible to suppose a Nahua migration through this region even in remote times. Traces of the Nahua language have certainly been found in proper names, or, as it were, fossilised in the dialects of the Pueblo peoples in Sinaloa, and as much farther north as the Hopi or Moqui or Tusayan. Even in the district of Maya civilisation we are surprised to find in the chronicles of the sixteenth century many names of places derived from the Nahua speech. But we are well assured that the reason for this is not that the Nahua district extended into this territory, but that the Spaniards were guided into this district by Indians who were only acquainted with Nahua power and with Nahua names for the places. These names have thus been stereotyped by tradition, and confirmed by the preponderance of the Nahua element in the midst of the Spanish colonisations. A similar state of things must undoubtedly have come to pass on the north also. **Indians as Guides to the Spaniards**

The historical traditions of the Nahua race invite the conclusion that their original home was certainly situated in the northern portion of the district in which the Spaniards found their race predominant. Not only the hieroglyphic designs, which were partially complete before the period of conquest, but also the Spanish chroniclers, who collected their information from the natives, point to the fact that the Nahua races had long lived as a wholly uncivilised fishing and hunting people within those boundaries where they were discovered in the sixteenth century. Even then there were individual related peoples who had not yet obtained a share in the civilisation of their more favoured brethren, and only a short time had elapsed, if we may believe tradition, since certain races who at the time of the Spanish conquest stood high in the scale of general civilisation had given up their wandering lives and turned to agriculture and the blessings of progress. **Wandering Races Turn to Agriculture**

The desire for a settled life was certainly not prominent among the Nahua, and least of all among the Aztecs, and it is a tendency which we cannot consider to have been gained by imitating civilised predecessors, even in the case of the most civilised peoples of America

Like the Maya, the Indians of Central America made no difficulty about abandoning their habitations, where for generations they had been settled and had worked, supposing their political circumstances to have altered for the worse. The wanderings of the Aztecs are of themselves evidence that they were the last to leave their common home, Aztlan-Chicomoztoc. For at least ten years in historical times they wandered among the different nations of the Nahua race, which ages ago had obtained a secure settlement and made great advances in civilisation. That tradition should have remained pure in the case of such inequality of development, under the unfavourable circumstances which the nomad life of an uncivilised people involves, is wholly incredible; mythological and religious conceptions have much more probably formed the basis of the legends of the migration of the Nahua from Aztlan-Chicomoztoc. Constantly and for all time the Nahua have been an inland race. Both on the Atlantic and also on the Pacific coasts at a late period they drove out an older population which does not seem to have been akin to themselves. But even after some of their peoples had settled in the tropical climate of their coast-land they still retained the objection of an inland race to the "great salt water." The Maya engaged in an extensive maritime commerce from their own harbours; the Nahua peoples engaged in commerce, too, but their extensive traffic was carried on exclusively on the high-roads, although many of the Nahua people were acquainted with the construction of fishing-boats. Yet in their history we find the Nahua, with all their objection to the sea,

unmistakably associated with the water. A legend which places their birthplace on a great water is evidence of this, and in their history the lakes on the highlands of Anahuac play a most important part. Even without this lake district a number of centres of Nahua development were also situated on the shores of lakes—as,

A PYRAMIDAL BUILDING OF THE AZTECS IN OAXACA
The western slopes of the Cordilleras are particularly rich in architectural antiquities, relics of the early Aztecs, who at one time inhabited these regions. Our knowledge of the significance of these relics is necessarily limited, as for centuries they remained buried, and have only been excavated within recent times.

for instance, Tezcuco, Chalco, and Tenochtitlan. Over and over again, in history and in legend, we meet with the water and that which it brings forth.

The nature of their environment had made the Nahua a people of hunters and fishers; it had also created in them a further characteristic, a fierce warlike spirit. It is true that under the snowy peaks of the Cordilleras an everlasting spring reigned in the deep valleys of Mexico; the climate was far more suitable for a people of careless enjoyment than for a race of ferocious warriors. Hunting, moreover, could not have exercised a very hardening influence; in the whole kingdom there was no wild animal which could have been particularly dangerous to huntsmen, when armed even with the simplest of weapons. It was the ancient inhabitants of the land that made the Nahua a nation of warriors.

Upon their immigration they did not find their future country uninhabited, as the Maya had done in Yucatan. That they found there a trace of inhabitants foreign to themselves may be concluded from the traditions, although the inadequacy of our information makes it impossible to establish the ethnological character of this race. In the myths of the Nahua giants of superhuman size and unbounded strength appear, and though we cannot put a literal interpretation on this, as did the old Spanish chroniclers, who identified the bones of antediluvian animals with the skeletons of this giant race, we may none the less conclude that the Nahua had a long and bitter struggle with a powerful enemy, and that they must have exerted their utmost resources and carried on a war of unceasing destruction before they succeeded in winning a territory where their race might develop to its full strength. It was in this warfare that that fierce warrior spirit was implanted in this untutored people.

The Nahua a Race of Warriors

We find the Nahua everywhere a race of warriors, alike fearful and feared, and we come across some of them outside their later district, as, for instance, in Yucatan and Guatemala; but the traditions within their own territories are of an equally warlike character. Battle and victory, conquest and destruction are the dominant features of their art; and in their case war was closely connected with religion—religion in its most horrible and frightful form, as it appeared in the bloody worship of the Aztecs for their national god Huitzilopochtli. In the strange horrors of this worship inquirers have attempted to trace the influence of peoples earlier than the Nahua; they have ascribed the cult to the temporary stay of the Aztecs in the district of Tarasca. But even leaving out of sight the fact that a remote branch of the Nahua race was possibly settled even in Tarasca, this cruel worship, with its numerous human sacrifices, is by no means peculiar to the Aztecs.

It appears in a more or less horrible form among almost all the Nahua people, and it is no external accessory of divine worship; it is rather the typical form of that worship. Let us suppose that the majority of this race were not under the influence of similar conceptions; we have then to ask by what possibility that compact could have been brought about between Mexico, Tlazcala, and Huexotzinco, the provisions of which regulated wars for these three states, with a view to providing a sufficient number of captured enemies for sacrifice to their gods

REMAINS OF AN ANCIENT AZTEC BUILDING NEAR TEHUANTEPEC IN OAXACA

That the ancient Aztecs possessed many claims to civilisation is demonstrated by the majesty and dignity of their architectural designs, which often attain enormous dimensions. The specimen on this page was concealed for ages within a luxuriant growth of vegetation, so dense that people living in the near vicinity were unaware of its existence.

upon given occasions. War, human sacrifice, and ceremonial cannibalism are characteristic of the Nahua. The special influences that led the national character of the race in this direction must certainly be placed in a period long anterior to the disruption of the Nahua people into its separate branches, and still further anterior to the supposed stay of the Aztecs among the people of Tarasca.

At the time of the Spanish invasion the Nahua certainly were no longer that nation of fishermen, hunters and fierce warriors which had begun to develop at the outset in the highlands of Anahuac. On the contrary, a development, lasting for centuries, had resulted in a civilisation which in many districts could compete with the civilisation of the Maya, and the external splendours of which completely dazzled the Spaniards. This civilisation, however, as almost all our sources of information consistently assert, was not the result of slow development on the part of the people themselves, but was acquired and imported from without. The Nahua races of the valleys of Mexico, the traditions of which are known to us, were proud to consider themselves Chichimecs, and almost all the Chichimec races appear originally as half-wild, wandering, ill-clothed tribes of huntsmen, who received their first introduction into the ways of civilisation by communication with older nations who were already firmly settled in confederate towns and states, and were occupied in agriculture. The different histories of the race, which were not confused by any attempt to harmonise the Christian and old American chronologies, go back some six or seven centuries into the past. Many a race which has later

THE AZTEC GOD OF DEATH AND WAR

played an important part in the history of Central America must have given up its wild and wandering life, and have gained its first impulse to civilisation within that short period ; these traditions, which almost without exception avail themselves of long dynasties to serve their chronological necessities, imply the previous existence of several civilised states.

The Toltecs, as the chief exponents of Nahua civilisation, appear to some extent in the more ancient sculptures, and still more often in the later histories which were modelled upon European examples. According to the later legends which have come down to us, the Toltecs were a branch of the Nahua race, and also came from the north, from Chicomoztoc to the town Huehuetlapallan, about the fourth century of our era. At the beginning of the sixth century they are said to have been settled on a tableland of Mexico, Tula being the capital of their kingdom, and soon to have risen to a fabulous development of civilisation. Here all their esoteric knowledge is said to have been acquired, and it was also here that the scentific regulation of the calendar, which became an example for all other peoples, was carried out by the Toltec priests and kings. Moreover, the Toltecs are also said to have compiled the history of the past and to have established an authentic text of it. But, above all, they are reputed to have been the teachers of all later nations in the sphere of art, especially in architecture and sculpture.

The buildings which adorned their settlements displayed a splendour and a magnificence almost unrivalled by the famous palace towns of later times, such as Tezcuco and Tenochtitlan. After an existence of several centuries the Toltec

A TOLTEC KING SEATED ON HIS THRONE

To recent research we owe much of our knowledge with regard to the Toltecs, a prehistoric people of
Mexico and Central America who had attained a high level of civilisation, and were advanced in arts.
The above picture, by a French artist, is based upon the suggestions as to costume and decorations, as
well as the actual physical characteristics of the people, obtained from their sculptured remains.

"THE STONE OF THE SUN": A RELIC OF AMERICA'S ANCIENT CIVILISATION

This interesting relic of the past, known as Tizoc's Stone, or the Stone of the Sun, consists of a block of trachyte measuring over eight feet in diameter, thirty-one feet in circumference, and two feet six inches in depth, the surface being ornamented with two figures ingeniously portrayed in fifteen different attitudes, recalling the victories of the Emperor Tizoc, who in every one of the groups is represented holding the vanquished by the hair.

kingdom is supposed to have collapsed, about the year 1055, as a result of internal struggle and external attacks. Its territory fell into the hands of the other neighbouring states. The Toltec nobles, however, who fled into every district of Anahuac upon the fall of the kingdom, were everywhere the missionaries of that advanced civilisation which was acquired by the other peoples of the Nahua as a direct result of the fall of this kingdom. These are the general features of the legend; the details, however, are terribly confused. Even in the case of the Indian historian Ixtlilxochitl, the author of the Toltec legend, who has depicted it in two different places, the chronology of the names and the details are anything but consistent in his two accounts. A great part of the Toltec stories is mere legend, in which we can unmistakably recognise a

AZTEC CALENDAR STONE

Discovered near Zecateces in Mexico, this primitive calendar of early American civilisation is now in the National Museum at Mexico City.

strong mythological element. For instance, there is said to have been a decree that the rule of each individual monarch should last neither more nor less than fifty-two years; if he lived longer, he was obliged, after a reign of fifty-two years, to abdicate in favour of his eldest son; supposing he died before that period, a council of the elders continued the government in his name until the legal term was fulfilled. Fifty-two years, however, was the period of the great Mexican cycle of years which was used to make the ritual calendar coincide with the solar year; at the beginning of this period, the holy fire was again kindled with ceremonial festival, under the belief that by that means the existence of the world was again insured for a like period. The further we retrace the story, however, the more doubtful do the facts become, and the

THE TOLTEC GORGE: IN PREHISTORIC TIMES A POPULOUS CENTRE

At the Toltec Gorge, so called because of its association with the Toltec civilisation of Central America, large quantities of instruments and weapons have been discovered, these throwing considerable light on the customs of the past.

stronger is the mythological element. Excavations have certainly laid bare ancient ruins upon the site of the presumed settlement of that famous Toltec kingdom in the town of Tula, some miles north of Mexico, but these ruins are neither extensive nor imposing. The artistic value of the ruined buildings upon the soil of

Quetzalcoatl King of the Toltecs the old Nahua states sensibly diminishes as we advance from north to south—a fact in opposition to the Toltec legend. Moreover, with the exception of the foundation and destruction of cities, almost everything that we know of the Toltecs centres round the personality of a king, Quetzalcoatl.

But this name, denoting the feathered snake, like the Maya Kukulkan, is also the name of a divinity which in later times was worshipped far and wide throughout the Nahua kingdom; his appearance makes us the more suspicious, as other names in the dynasty also coincide with the names of gods, and several kings have been deified by tradition. For these reasons the historical substratum of the Toltec legend becomes more and more hypothetical. Once, perhaps, there may have existed a Toltec principality, with Tula for its capital, which may have played a certain part in the racial feuds of the little Nahua kingdom; but the Toltecs have no right to the importance which has been ascribed to them as being the chief civilising influence of Anahuac.

The name " Tulan " also appears in the original legends of the Maya; it does not, however, denote any one particular place, but it is a general designation for a large royal settlement richly adorned; the legend also alludes to no less than four Tulans existing at the same time. If we could venture to identify the Tula of Nahua tradition with the similarly named Maya towns, and could then consider the Maya people themselves as the Nahua

The Toltecs Related to the Nahua Toltecs, this would be the easiest solution of the problem. Unfortunately there are great difficulties in the way of such an explanation. The Toltecs are invariably a people related to the Nahua, and therefore speaking their language; and their habitations upon the north of the later Nahua district—the plateau of Mexico—are in accordance with this fact; neither of these can be brought into connection with the Maya by any means. If,

however, we cannot venture to identify the Maya with the Toltecs, we may consider the connection between Maya and Nahua civilisation as indisputable. We have now to ask in what manner the advance in civilisation which the Maya had gained also fell to the share of the Nahua peoples, and how these peoples advanced from the coast of Tabasco up into the northern heights of the Mexican tableland.

The political circumstances which the Spaniards found on the Mexican tableland at the conquest have brought it about that we possess reliable information concerning the history only of those people who lived in Anahuac ; that is, in the neighbourhood of the Mexican lakes. The numerous related nations that had settled on the north, and even more extensively on the south, of the tableland were almost as much strangers to the Aztecs and their related nations of Anahuac as the Maya peoples were. In historical times the immediate neighbours of the Maya of Guatemala were the Zapotecs, the Mixtecs, and the Kuikatecs. Even if their habitations remained unchanged, as they appa-

Facts from a Recent Discovery rently did, throughout the period that the Nahua settlements of Anahuac lasted, we can, nevertheless, suppose a long-existing connection between the Maya and this branch of the Nahua nation, and this all the more because the necessary indications which we have at our disposal for the reconstruction of the earlier history of this race point to a close connection.

An illuminated manuscript of Kuikatec origin that has only recently been discovered informs us that the Kuikatecs, under the guidance of their racial god, apparently entitled " Maollin," wandered and fought for six centuries in the district which formed the boundary between the Maya and Nahua peoples in ancient times. The localities mentioned in the manuscript cannot all be certainly identified, but they point to the districts of Guatemala and Chiapas. The migrations then continued in a southerly direction not far from the Pacific coast.

There the Kuikatecs finally met with an insurmountable obstacle, and therefore turned aside in an easterly direction, crossed the north of Guatemala, and finally arrived safely in Chiapas, in a territory of Acalan, a district immediately bordering upon Yucatan. Probably these and similar migrations of the Nahua races brought about the fall of the flourishing Maya towns of Chiapas and Tabasco. The majority of the Maya peoples may have abandoned their old home to this enemy; but some of their members there certainly were who either became the subjects of the new arrivals, as their tributary vassals, or were prevented by force from escaping the new dominion. It is in these causes that we must seek the interchange of civilisation between the Maya and the Nahua teristic. Their invasion into the district of Maya civilisation cannot be affirmed with the same certainty; but in later times we meet with them in the immediate neighbourhood of the Maya, and settled upon a portion of that district the antiquities of which indisputably point to a previous settlement of the Maya peoples. On the Zapotecs the influence of Maya civilisation was extremely powerful. Even their language has undergone a strong admixture of Maya words and forms. It

AN UNDECIPHERED PAGE FROM THE VIENNA NAHUA MANUSCRIPT OF ZAPOTEC ORIGIN
The page here reproduced belongs to the series of Codex Viennensis, in which regular pictorial designs appear in connection with dates. It is, therefore, presumed that these hitherto inexplicable designs are of a historical character.

races. The well-known precedents of the Germanic migrations upon our own continent make us familiar with the fact that a people in a high state of civilisation may collapse helplessly before the vigorous attacks of a less cultured race, but that in a short time their own higher culture leavens the mass of the conquerors and again brings the old civilisation to the front. How far the Kuikatecs were influenced by Maya civilisation we cannot exactly define; but in the case of the Zapotecs this influence is very charac- would, however, be a mistake to dispute their connection with the Nahua race; for the Spanish chronicles regard the Zapotecs as a nation foreign to the Maya and connected with the peoples of Mexico.

Moreover, even the scanty accounts which we learn from this people themselves show that they must be placed among the nations of the Nahua race. Among these nations, however, they were at any rate one of those peoples who very early gave up the savage life of the old hunting races for a more civilised mode of existence.

for centuries they have unmistakably taken a leading position in all the acquisitions of civilised progress among the Nahua peoples. A considerable portion of the literary treasures which have come down to us from the time when the Nahua civilisation was developing independently belongs to the Zapotecs. Their manuscripts are not written in Maya script, but, with the exception of some small characteristic divergences, coincide with the mode of writing found in Aztec and other undoubtedly Nahuatlac documents. Probably the Zapotecs, or their kinsfolk, formed their mode of writing, which later became the property of all the Nahua peoples, under the influence and in imitation of that with which the Maya had made them acquainted.

The Maya Religious Calendar

A further relationship is visible between the Maya manuscripts and those of Zapotec origin in the extensive representations which are concerned with the religious calendar, in which, as we know, the Maya have given proof of astonishing astronomical knowledge. The peculiar sacred calendar system of the Maya shows the combination of the numbers 20 and 13—a combination which appears nowhere else in the world. This system was adopted in its main elements by the Zapotecs and four other Nahua peoples.

Moreover, careful examination has established the fact that the titles for each particular day, which are invariably taken from the objects of daily life, are essentially the same in the case of every language the calendar names of which are known to us. So close is this coincidence that even the names of the days with which the sacred or ritual year might begin (a year composed of 13 by 20 equals 260 days, in combination with the solar year) hang together, in the case of Maya and Nahua peoples respectively, in such a way that a more ancient group of names in combination among the Maya of Chiapas and Tabasco, and the Zapotecs and related nations, can be distinguished from a more recent combination in use among the Maya of Yucatan and the Aztec-Nahua. It is plain that these are no chance coincidences, and when we consider the remarkable development which astronomical science had reached among the Maya, it is equally plain in this case who it was that gave and

Science Among the Maya

who it was that received. Finally, the Zapotecs were instructed by the Maya in another department—that of architecture. The old Zapotec district, which is to-day the Mexican province Oaxaca, contains ruins of ancient Indian buildings in different places ; but most of these are so dilapidated that we can draw only the vaguest conclusions as to their original condition.

The ruins of Mitla are an exception to this rule, chiefly because their stronger buildings made them more capable of resisting the attacks of time. Mitla is only the Mexican name for the town which the Zapotecs themselves called Yopaa ; both names mean " the Place of the Dead." Possibly the Xibalbay of the Maya, which also means "Town of the Dead," is the most ancient name of this town, and goes back to an epoch when this district was also in possession of the Maya peoples. At any rate, there is no particular proof of this in the paintings which exist in the rooms of the temple-building of Mitla and are still in good condition ; they are undoubtedly of later origin and belong to the Nahua civilisation. On the contrary, the architectural style of the building —partly below and partly above ground, with its decorated rooms and its roof of over-hanging courses—resembles far more nearly the Maya architecture than that of the younger Nahua peoples. For instance, the temple buildings of the Aztecs consist almost entirely of high pyramids artistically faced, on which there are no buildings at all, or erections of only a temporary nature.

Mitla in Ruins

Our historical information about the Zapotec kingdom goes back only a few decades—certainly not a century—before the Spanish conquest. When the Aztec kingdom began to extend in a southwesterly direction, the Zapotecs appear in the circle of the Aztec princes. About the year 1484, Ahuitzotl, the seventh king of Mexico-Tenochtitlan, made an invasion far into the Zapotec district in the direction of Tehuantepec, and in the fortress Huaxyacac he laid the basis of further conquest. At that time different Zapotec towns or principalities became either subject or tributary to the Aztecs ; and on this occasion Mitla also, the sacred town of the Zapotecs, was conquered and destroyed by the Mexicans.

AMERICA
BEFORE
COLUMBUS

ANCIENT
CIVILISATIONS
OF CENTRAL
AMERICA
V

NAHUA RELIGION AND MYTHOLOGY
THE GODS AND HUMAN SACRIFICES

THE Central American civilisation, with the changes which the Zapotecs had imposed upon it, made its way northward, and finally became the common property of almost all the Nahua peoples. The individual steps of this progress cannot be recognised in the scanty remains which have come down to us from the Nahua races which were settled between the Zapotecs and the highland of Anahuac.

As to the Mixtecs, we know that they also built terraced pyramids, on which were raised the altars of their gods; they too had learned to hand down to posterity the histories of their gods and princes in those written characters with which we first meet among the Zapotecs. They measured the lapse of their days and the recurrence of their festivals by a calendar founded upon the same principles as that of Central America. It is impossible, however, to give any more accurate de-**Culture of the Mixtecs** scription of the position which this race held among the advancing civilisations. As we go farther north, this civilisation assumes a more general character, and can be designated as the Aztec offshoot of Central American culture. It is a civilisation which certainly has affinities with the ancient Maya, though it struck out a line of its own in those centuries when its progress was free from external influence.

Once more in the northern districts we meet with traces which recall to our minds the southern origin of the Mexican civilisation; these are in the town of Cholula. The famous pyramid which has been named after this town, and which excited the astonishment and amazement of the Spanish conquerors, has been for a long time in such a ruined condition that it is impossible to assign its position in American art from its artistic style. The old chroniclers, however, inform us that, unlike the Aztec temple pyramids, which were usually crowned by an open altar of the god, this pyramid bore a roofed-in building on its summit. This reminds us of the architectural style of the more southern races, and the name of the god to whom the temple was dedicated points in the same direction; his name was Quetzalcoatl—that is, the feathered snake.

God of the Feathered Snake The religious conception on which the symbol of the feathered snake is based is so widely spread over American soil that we cannot at once assume it to have been borrowed from any similar neighbouring worship; the analogous development of the mythological conceptions of the American peoples would lead us to a complete explanation of this occurrence of identical symbols. However, in Cholula, and in the cult of the god Quetzalcoatl, we have to deal, not only with an observed similiarity to the Kukulkan or Gukumatz of the Maya, but we have also to consider the complete identity of the god, his mythology and his worship, which could not be established without some internal communication.

According to Mexican tradition, Quetzalcoatl came to the country in a boat, passing over the western ocean with a few companions; he is said to have landed upon Mexican soil in the far north of the country, on the River Panuco. To the naked savages who then inhabited the land he was a marvellous apparition, a figure clothed in shining raiment, and wearing a beard, an appendage unusual among the natives. Quetzalcoatl soon taught them the arts of peace, in particular agriculture and weaving; he gave them **The Legend of Quetzalcoatl** writing to preserve his teaching, and the calendar to regulate his worship. After he had established a well-ordered state in the land where formerly only wandering huntsmen dwelt, he disappeared, with the promise that he would again revisit his people. This legend in every particular coincides so exactly with the Maya legend of Kukulkan that we cannot doubt the

PYRAMIDS OF THE SUN AND THE MOON AT TEOTIHUACAN, IN MEXICO

The pyramids of the sun and the moon, at Teotihuacan, belong to that early period when, like Mitla, Teotihuacan was not only a place of pilgrimage for the living, but also a sacred place, in which to be buried was to be sure of salvation.

one being borrowed from the other. There is a further point to be considered. The custom of human sacrifice is a characteristic feature in Nahua worship ; at the bottom of it was the religious belief that the offering to the god was sanctified by its sacrifice, and that to some extent transubstantiation into the divine essence took place. Consequently the sacrifice—often before its death—became an object of veneration. Thus, too, it was that the corpse was eaten, in order that everybody who tasted of it should assimilate a portion of the divine substance ; and for this reason again the skin of the victim served as a sacred covering for the image of the god himself, or for his earthly representatives, the priests.

Human Sacrifices in Worship

These ideas are entirely Nahuatlac, and are altogether wanting among the Maya of ancient times who had not been influenced by the Nahua ; also among younger nations of the same origin, among whom the custom of human sacrifice was in restricted use, the particular Nahua adoptions of it are nowhere to be found. Quetzalcoatl, in Maya consciousness, has always been a divinity who not only objected to human sacrifice in his own worship, but entirely abhorred the characteristic Nahua use of the offering, and this at the time when it gained its highest importance and extent under the Aztec

dominion. The worship of Quetzalcoatl was carried on in a closed temple-chamber with penance and discipline, but only with inoffensive victims. It formed a kind of secret worship in opposition to the bloody sacrifice openly made to Huitzilopochtli and Tezcatlipoca ; and to it the last king of the Aztecs, Montezuma, resorted as soon as his own gods and their priests had proved helpless before the stranger who had come forth from the waters of the west, with his beard and his armour of gleaming brass.

In one other place we find a wide district of Mexico thickly covered with the ruins of old buildings—that is, on the eastern coast-line, north of Vera Cruz, in the district of the Totonacs. It is possible that these Nahua architects also had Maya neighbours upon their borders ; these must have been the Huastecs, who had been driven northward far from the mass of the Maya people. But the ruins that have been found in their own district are very inadequate, and our knowledge of their history is extremely scanty ; it would therefore be a bold conclusion to assign the existence of the numerous architectural remains in the district of the Totonacs to the influence of their civilisation. Moreover, the position of the buildings is here of a different character from those in the Maya district. The terraced

The Work of Nahua Architects

A NEARER VIEW OF THE PYRAMID OF THE SUN
This closer view of the pyramid of the sun illustrates the striking manner in which Nature has regained mastery over the works of man, the huge mound being now entirely covered with shrubs and other natural growth.

pyramid here, too, forms the foundation of that space which was consecrated to the worship of the gods, following the universal character of the pyramids in the Maya and Nahua territories. But the heavy flights of steps, and a wall running round the upper terrace, are a distinct divergence from the normal type ; they excite particular attention, as they remind us of the strategical purposes so strongly marked in all the Totonac cities.

Generally the Totonac pryamids do not seem to have been crowned with a massive temple of stone, and in this respect they have approached the Hahua type ; but in the few cases where the upper platform is decorated with a stone temple, a coincidence with the style of the Central American architecture is apparent in the unusually heavy roof rising above a building which is low and narrow in comparison with the main mass of the erection ; the impression of **Towns that Surprised the Spaniards** heaviness thus given is only dispelled by the prominent facade which crowns the whole. We should be the better able to decide how far the Nahua peoples succeeded in independently developing their highest civilisation and their artistic style after the Spanish arrival if more extensive ruins had been left of those great towns which the astonishment of the conquerors has painted for us in such brilliant colours, at the time when a systematic examination of them was at length undertaken. The few antiquities that have been found upon these ancient centres of progress are so little consonant with the glowing descriptions of the conquistadores that we must either suppose their surprise **Sacred Town of the Nahua Races** led them into considerable exaggeration, or we must assume that a large portion of the ornamental buildings was constructed of far more perishable material than was the case elsewhere. Of the ruined sites of pure Nahuatlac origin only two are worth particular consideration, namely, Teotihuacan and Xochicalco.

Teotihuacan is a striking example, clearly demonstrating how short was the historical recollection of the different Nahua royal families in spite of all the long genealogies that have been put forward. This town has already become mythical to the generation with which the conquerors came into contact, and yet for centuries it had been the religious centre and the sacred town for the Nahua races of the tableland of Anahuac, even as Mecca is for the Mohammedans, or Jerusalem for the Christians. Our historical sources give us no information as to whether it played any part in politics under the most ancient Chichimec dominion ; but they ascribe its foundation to the remotest antiquity ; they put it

5773

forward consistently and invariably as the holiest and most venerated of temples, with the most influential priesthood. The question may be left undecided as to whether the modern designations of the most important pyramids of Teotihuacan —as " the hill of the sun," " the hill of the moon," etc.—have been justified

The Striking Pyramids at Teotihuacan by archæological inquiry ; at any rate, the name " path of the dead " is correct for the long range of little hills which stretches out behind the larger pyramids. Teotihuacan was, like Mitla, not only a place of pilgrimage for the living, but also a sacred place, in which to be buried was to be sure of salvation. Even in the most recent times the neighbourhood of the ruins has been an inexhaustible hunting-ground for the little pots and clay figures which formed the offerings with which the dead were usually committed to the earth. Moreover, the other names mentioned are in entire accord with the ancient Nahua civilisation.

The Nahua religion was founded upon those startling manifestations of Nature which have struck the imagination of men in every part of the world. Nature-worship, under later influences, was wholly changed to an anthropomorphic realisation of religious conceptions, and by degrees many accessory notions fastened themselves around individual divinities. Yet, almost without exception, the gods of the different Nahuatlac nations can be traced back to particular phenomena of Nature. Even Huitzilopochtli, the fearful war-god of the Aztecs, whose worship was accompanied by a shedding of human blood that has never been equalled elsewhere, originally sprang from an entirely inoffensive conception of Nature.

He is the incarnation of the sun's beneficent power, which in the early spring begins a fruitful reign, and in the autumn fades away and dies before the burning heat

War God of the Aztecs and the drying winds. Legend tells of his miraculous procreation, of his battle with the hostile twins, and of his death, proceeding in exactly the same manner as among the most different peoples in the Old and New Worlds. The sacred symbol of Huitzilopochtli is the colibri, the feathers of which decorated the god's left leg, according to the legend, to remind him of the fact that his mother Coatlicuë received him in the form of a bunch of feathers which she carried unwittingly in her bosom. To the Mexican highlands, however, the colibri is what the swallow is to the temperate zones—the messenger who announces that Nature again awakes from her winter sleep. In autumn the image of the god was every year destroyed by a priest of another godhead by shooting at it with an arrow to the accompaniment of particular religious ceremonies ; this was the end of the good part of the year, the return of which was celebrated in the spring as the return of Huitzilopochtli.

Under the form of the colibri he had also been the guide of the Aztecs on their migrations ; he had continually called them on with his cry : " Tiui, tiui ! " until they had come to the seat of their power. Here was the first impulse to anthropomorphism ; for along with the bird, the image of the god and his representatives, the priests, had accompanied the people. These conceptions then became so confused that the belief finally arose that Huitzilopochtli was only a casual historical personality who had been exalted to the height of a racial god. Human sacrifices

The Nahua People's Chief God played an essential part in all Nahuatlac worship ; but the great extent to which they were carried in the Aztec worship of Huitzilopochtli arose from the unusually ferocious disposition of the Nahua national character.

The real chief god of the Nahua people is Tezcatlipocá. He is much more easily recognisable as an incarnation of the sun, and this not in its beneficial character as the bringer of all good, of light and warmth and fruitfulness, but also in its dangerous and destructive power, as hot drought and devouring fire. In its first character Tezcatlipocá was no doubt originally to the Nahua that which Kukulkan-Quetzalcoatl had been to the Maya people—the father of civilisation and culture. But when in the course of time the worship of the feathered snake as Quetzalcoatl made its way among the Nahua, then the legend began to be formed of the enmity between these two divinities ; with a recollection of the previous power of Tezcatlipocá, the legend ends with a victory of this god over the foreign intruder, but shows him more and more in the light of a hostile, cruel god, while all the ideas concerning beneficent kindly powers group themselves around Quetzalcoatl, notwithstanding his defeat.

RUINS OF THE PYRAMID STEPS OF XOCHICALCO IN THE DISTRICT OF CHOLULA IN CENTRAL AMERICA

The ruins of Xochicalco, shown in the above illustration, are the remains of an extensive fortified position. Investigations have shown that the pyramid consisted only of a foundation, and of a temple which rose thereon and was perhaps unroofed, its sloping outer walls giving the appearance of a second pyramid. The whole building was overlaid with large, highly sculptured plates of trachyte, while the space within was filled with rubble. On the western side a flight of steps, now largely ruined, led up to the temple entrance, while the entire exterior of the building was adorned with rich decorative work which covered the sloping walls of the two pyramidal erections, and also the horizontal frieze which lay between them.

The numerous gods of the beneficent powers of Nature and of the fruitful soil are a peculiarity of the Nahua religion. On the one hand they show the important influence of animism on the conceptions of Nahua mythology ; upon the other hand they make it evident how important was the part that agriculture played in the

Influence of Agriculture on the Peoples life of these peoples at the time when their conceptions of the gods were coming into existence. In this there is matter for surprise, inasmuch as in later historical times we meet with individual Nahua races upon a lower plane of civilisation.

A confusion of the divinities of different races had unmistakably taken place in a considerable portion of their mythology as it existed at the time of the Spanish conquest and has come down to us. Every people that rose to an important position in this civilisation contributed its own national divinities to the common stock of conceptions ; in worship and legend it created for them an important position, but side by side with their worship it worshipped and preserved all the more ancient deities. This is the simplest mode of explaining the extraordinary number of the gods in the Aztec Olympus, which the ancient historians have also described with expressions of astonishment.

After the power of the sun, which warms the earth and makes it fruitful and flourishing, the most important element of the Mexican highland climate was the rain. The success of every crop depended entirely upon the opportuneness and the sufficiency of this heavenly gift. The old historical sculptures of the different Nahua races of the east often describe the pregnant effects upon the general life of the people consequent on years of drought. Hence we need not be surprised if the gods of water, of moisture, and of the clouds that pour forth rain, take a significant place in the national worship.

Tlaloc the God of Rain There are but few divinities of which we have so many and such extensive sculptures as of Tlaloc, the god of rain. He was depicted in a peculiar position, semi-recumbent, with the upper part of the body raised upon the elbows, and the knees half-drawn up, perhaps with the intention of symbolising the fructifying influence of moisture upon the earth. By his side there was also a goddess with similar essential characteristics ; as a symbol of fruitfulness she had presented him with numerous children. In addition to this, the fruitfulness of the soil was represented by a large number of independent divinities, for the most part of the female sex. Coatlicuë, who had brought up Huitzilopochtli, as being the mother of the colibri, was the goddess of flowers and fruit. The legend of the Aztec goddess of the fruitful corn-land, Centeotl, was especially detailed. In the narrower sense she represents—and to a larger extent than Xilonen, who appears as her daughter—the maize, the staple food of the Americans, the yellow colour of which was sacred to her. The fact that the maize plays a large part in the hieroglyphic writing of both the Maya and the Nahua testifies to the importance of this grain in the domestic economy of ancient America.

As the goddess of fruitfulness, Centeotl is also the protector of women in childbirth ; in spite of this her worship was accompanied with far more human sacrifices than were customary for all the remaining Nahua divinities. The idea which runs throughout the Aztec sacrifice

The Sacred Town of the God of Death —namely, that the victim, even before his death, by being dedicated to the god, becomes a part of the god and is one with him, is especially to be recognised in her worship ; in this the numerous female victims received a share of the reverence paid to the goddess in a complicated ceremonial which took place before their death.

The god of death has already appeared among the Zapotecs ; his sacred town, Yopaa (or Yapooh), became famous under its Mexican title, Mitla. Mitla is a popular reduction of the form Mictlan, and is at once the name both of the god of death and of his kingdom. He also is accompanied by a female goddess, easily to be recognised in the pictorial representations of Mitla by the invariable death-mask with its prominent row of teeth. As in the case of most peoples, the conception of death is connected with the ideas of the north and of darkness. His kingdom is situated in everlasting darkness within the earth ; his worship was carried on by the priests at night, clothed in black or in dark-coloured raiment.

According to Aztec ideas the kingdom of death was not the inevitable end of all life. The common herd—that is, everybody who had not been able during his life upon earth to make good his claim to a better lot—found his way to Mictlan sooner or later. It was not, however, as in the Christian hell, a life of endless torture which was there prepared for the departed. The journey was certainly long and surrounded with every kind of danger. For this reason they never forgot to bury food, drink, and all kinds of amulets—especially strips of aloe paper—together with the corpse; but of the final fate of the dead man, who passed after all his journeyings into the ninth division of the lower world, the Mexicans themselves could give no adequate account.

Far different was the fate of those who, according to the conceptions of these peoples, had shown particular merits in upon the most important festival of their gods in order to be witnesses of his honour. There came into the kingdom of Tlaloc not only those who were sacrificed to him, but also all those who were drowned or struck by lightning. The manner of their death was a sign that the god loved them and took them to himself. The highest heaven—for the heaven also rose in nine divisions above the earth—was that of the sun and his incarnations Huitzilopochtli, Tezcatlipocá, and Quetzalcoatl.

Hither came the souls of the kings and the mighty, of the priests and the nobles, who had been able during their earthly life to approach more nearly to the gods than common men; but, above all, the souls of those went to the sun who

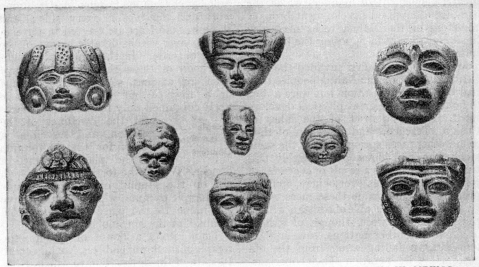

COLLECTION OF MASKS AND HEADS FOUND AT TEOTIHUACAN, IN MEXICO

life or death. All the offerings brought to the gods entered, as we know, into immediate and close connection with the godhead; this connection was naturally continued in the future life, where such victims shared in the joys of heaven, in the service and the company of their gods.

The nature of these pleasures had been fully detailed for us in the case of those who entered into connection with Tlaloc. They went up to the summits of the highest mountains, the abode of the clouds, where a splendid garden awaited them, in which all the waters of the world had their source and cooled and refreshed the whole neighbourhood. There they lived among everlasting feasts and games, and could even descend again to the earth had fallen in battle; and by these means many were able to lay claim to the heaven from which they would have been naturally excluded. Hither, too, came all those who had been sacrificed to the sungods as prisoners of war or had fallen in religious struggles; and this conviction of the meritorious nature of death in battle contributed not a little, as among the Mohammedans, to nourish the warlike spirit of these peoples. Finally, there came to the sun the souls of all women who had died in childbirth. There they all carried on a life of unending pleasure; with song and dance they accompanied the sun on his course; and when he sank in the west, in holy sleep, they renewed their strength to begin their work anew upon the morrow.

As we see, the religion of the Nahua peoples was by no means without its mild and kindly side. Their peculiar conception of the consubstantiation of the victim with the divinity deprived human sacrifice of much of its native horror, and the desire to win a life of everlasting joy induced many to offer themselves as willing victims

Willing Victims to the Gods to the god. The continued practice of cannibalism rested upon a similar conception. By tasting the victim, which had become to some extent divine, the eater of it also shared in the godhead ; similarly, with certain ceremonies, an image of the god which was not offered in sacrifice, but formed of eatable material, was broken and consumed by the worshippers. The greater refinement of manners which the advance of civilised development brought to many of the Nahua races may also have had a share in opposing the horrible human sacrifices.

When the Aztecs first invaded the particular district of the Nahua peoples they had but little civilisation but were a race of bold warriors of great physical development. In the district of the lakes of Chalco, Tezcuco, and Zumpango they found other races springing from the same stock who had developed a highly cultured civilisation as a result of centuries of residence. Here, as everywhere, civilised progress had not made these races either stronger or more capable of resistance ; and the attacking Aztecs, though of similar origin to the other nations, saw in their refinement a falling away from the old customs—a degeneration. Their consciousness of their superiority, the success that invariably attended their efforts, were to them proofs of the good-will of the gods, who preferred to be worshipped in the old fierce manner rather than with the modern milder cult ; and by degrees this idea tended more and more to bring back the dreadful form of worship. The

Wide Range of the Aztec Power Aztec Power extended over countries containing the most different peoples, who had been more or less subjugated ; from these their religious ideas led them to exact that awful tribute which made them hated by every nation that was dependent on them.

These peculiar circumstances were neither of long historical duration nor very widely spread, but have none the less greatly contributed to throw back our

knowledge of the preceding history of the Central American district, and to spread abroad false ideas concerning it. The chief task, at the moment, for Mexican archæology is to distinguish what is transitory and isolated from what is characteristic and universal.

The name Teotihuacan, representing the company of the Nahua gods, leads us naturally to the consideration of their religious conceptions ; similarly, the name Xochicalco, the last of the ruined towns that we need mention, affords an excellent opportunity for some remarks upon Nahua art. In their general character the ruins of Xochicalco are very similar to those in the district of the Totonacs. Spurs running out into the plain from the main mountain range have been made defensible by stonework and trenches on every side ; and these works of art are erected in terracefashion over a considerable extent of the mountain side. In the immediate neighbourhood of these there seems to have been an ancient settlement, a village or a town ; but the fortified space itself contained only temples and palaces

Temple of the Flower Goddess and the dwellings of the garrison, and served as a refuge for the inhabitants of the place in time of danger. Within the fortifications, though not on the summit of the hill, stands the temple pyramid which certainly gave the name to the place—for Xochicalco means " in the house of flowers."

There stood a house of flowers, the temple of the flower goddess, Xochiquetzal. In spite of the destruction to which it has been subjected in the course of centuries, this building is still one of the finest that has been discovered upon American soil. Ancient chronicles would have us believe that at the time of its completion the temple pyramid of Xochicalco had five storeys ; examinations of the position have proved that it never had more than one, and that the storey which can now be seen. Upon this, following the sloping rise of the pyramid, a building without a roof, running round three sides of the pyramid, but open in front, contained a sacred temple space, but was not itself a properly enclosed temple. This particular form of building is certainly connected with the worship of the Nahua peoples, whose religious ceremonies were almost entirely carried on under the open heaven and in the full light of day.

THE CHICHIMEC SUPREMACY
NAHUA DOMINION IN LEGEND AND HISTORY

IT was within the boundaries of the civilisation described that the history of the Nahua peoples was developed. If we would pass a right judgment upon this history, we must, above all things, keep one point in view—the extreme narrowness of the conditions within which the early ancient history of Mexico was brought to a close.

The limits of the older historical traditions nowhere overpass the mountain range which on almost every side surrounds the valley of Mexico proper ; places like Tula and Tulancingo, only a few miles distant from the central point of Nahua history, the Lake of Tezcuco, are lost in avenues of distance. The main portions of those peoples who spoke the Nahua language were entirely unknown to this tradition ; in the last century, at the time when the Aztec warlike expeditions penetrated into more remote districts, one or two names of individual kings are men-

The Seat of Empires and Dominions tioned. The district in which the ancient Mexican history ran its course according to tradition is little more than 6,500 square miles in area. Separated by a distance of but a few miles were here situated the capitals of all the states which succeeded to the empire of the district of Mexican civilisation during the last century of the ancient régime, and it is these towns which the Spanish historians describe as the seat of so many empires and dominions.

According to tradition the oldest inhabitants of Anahuac are the Olmecs—or Ulmecs—and the Xicalancs. These apparently were regarded as the giant people the conquest of whom cleared the way for the settlements of the Nahua race ; more often, however, the Olmecs and Xicalancs are considered as the conquerors of the giants, and as the founders of the oldest sacred towns Teotihuacan and Cholula. That these names were invariably used to designate the Nahua peoples at large is proved by the fact that their names are always to be found in that district whither the seven races were led who left their common home, the seven caves of Chicomoztoc, in order to seek the promised land. The Olmecs are said to have been accompanied on their migrations by the Zapotecs

The Olmecs Settle in Anahuac and Mixtecs ; to these are occasionally added the Totonacs, and even the Huastecs, who spoke a Maya dialect. By this we may understand that the settlement of the Olmecs in Anahuac was supposed to be contemporaneous with the settlement of the other people of the same race who did not form the focus of the Nahua interests ; that is, the people with whom we meet as intruding upon and shattering the Maya civilisation. Beyond this, tradition has nothing to say of the Olmecs and Xicalancs ; no royal name, no event, was preserved in their history. But the fact that they were closely connected with the seat of the highest and most ancient priestly knowledge shows that we must not think of them as a rude hunting tribe, but that their arrival marked an epoch of civilisation for the highland of Anahuac.

The next group of Nahua races that found their way into Anahuac and became of historical importance were the Chichimecs. The ancient historians employed this name in a double sense. In its general meaning it denotes the whole group of the later Nahua people ; in this sense our historical sources speak of the Teo Chichimecs—the inhabitants of the

Races of Nahuac Origin district of Tlazcala—the Toltec Chichimecs, the Colhua Chichimecs, and the Aztec Chichimecs. In this case the name means neither more nor less than those peoples who were of true Nahuac origin and belonged to a great group of Nahua-speaking races ; these races were called savages—this is the sense of the word—when other related races had already undergone the influence of civilisation, and so had grown out of their ancient national characteristics. These changes took place under the influence of a foreign nationality —that of the Maya, as we already know ; hence the name Chichimec gained the meaning of " unadulterated," " pure," and in this sense it was a term applied to all the Nahua peoples who could claim purity of origin. We learn that no individual Nahua race was originally called by this name from the fact that the Teo Chichimecs, the Toltecs, the Colhua, the Aztecs, but never the Chichimecs, are mentioned as having come among the seven races from the caves of Chicomoztoc.

Emperor of the Chichimecs

In spite of this, in the course of time, and as a result of long traditional transmission, the name Chichimec came to be the designation of a race, or, more properly, of a certain body politic. For a time this body must have played an important part among the peoples of Anahuac. We have mention of kings of the Toltecs, of the Colhuas, and of the Aztecs ; but in the case of the Chichimecs an emperor is mentioned, and the title Chichimecatl Tecuhtli —" the lord of the Chichimecs "—was the highest to which a governor of the different Nahua states could lay claim.

Eleven kings, including Chichimecatl, had apparently already reigned over this people when the Toltecs of Tula sent an embassy to the Chichimec court and offered the government of their country to the king's second son ; there is here a vague recollection of some family connection between the Chichimecs and Toltecs. The first Chichimec prince who is said to have ruled after the fall of the Toltec kingdom—the king Xolotl—is said to have had a reign of nearly 300 years. The artistically conceived system of ancient Mexican chronology has been traced far into the past by native writers who were influenced by Christianity, and for this reason they went back only far enough to make the chronologies of the Old and New Worlds coincide, and to connect their people with the confusion of tongues at the Tower of Babel. The chronologies proposed for the history of the old kingdoms have no scientific value whatever.

Legendary Kings in Anahuac

The tradition of numerous peoples of Anahuac preserved the legend of a long row of kings or princes who are said to have ruled the land ; and in many cases these genealogies are connected with the gods,

or include such gods in the genealogical tree. Certain authors like Ixtlilxochitl, and probably many before him of whose writings he availed himself, arranged a number of such dynasties in a vertical line instead of in parallel columns ; however, by their means we have been able to trace back Mexican history right to the beginning of the Christian era, or even further.

The kingdom of Toltec civilisation is one of the unhistoric legends which originated in the manner we have described ; its legendary source is betrayed by the fact that its kings constantly bear the names of gods, and that the town Tollan (Tula), from which the name Toltec is supposed to have been derived, can scarcely have been the capital of a Toltec kingdom. In the Toltec legend is reflected a recollection of the historical importance of a state the central point of which was Culhuacan.

This cannot be traced back into those remote times in which the Toltec kingdom has been placed, but belongs to an historical period ; at that time a large number of other Chichimec states, together with Tezcuco, had a flourishing existence, and then it was that the youngest branch of the Nahua race, the Aztec, began to attract attention to itself. Such knowledge as has come down to us of the ancient kingdom—extending over a period from the sixth century, in which tradition places its beginnings, up to the thirteenth century, in which its historical period begins—is of importance in only this respect : it shows us in abstract form, little influenced by the realities of the time, those conceptions and ideas which the Nahua people themselves held concerning their common civic life. Thus far the legends throw light on the internal history of the race, both in ancient and in more modern times.

Flourishing Chichimec Communities

The tradition of the oldest times, speaking as it does of numerous reigning deities, would of itself show us the important influence of the priestly caste among the older Nahua races, even if we had no examples from historical times of the energy and tenacity with which the priests struggled against the inevitable inroads of a secular power. The gods, partly under their own sacred names, and sometimes appearing as princes who ruled for centuries and were canonised after their death, are the constant guides of the Nahua races on their migrations, or laid the foundation of particular prosperity and unusual growth during their periods of settled existence; this fact proves that theocracy and a rule of priests under the special protection of heaven was a typical characteristic among the Nahua, and also among the Maya peoples, for a long period of their development.

It was at this time that most of the great temple pyramids were founded; and their foundation under such a government explains to us why tradition has considered them, for the most part, anterior to the founding of a secular state, or has ascribed them to some earlier people. As long as nations of a common origin and similar religious conceptions were in exclusive contact with one another, so long were the priests able to keep the peace without great difficulty. There was certainly rivalry among the priests of divinities belonging to different races, and this now and then led to those animosities which the legend represents as the battles of the gods among themselves;

Gods Fighting Among Themselves at the same time peace and prosperity were well-nigh universal and gave every necessary encouragement to a rapidly spreading civilisation. But the spread of this civilisation, however, threatened the priestly states with a twofold danger. Among their subjects there were to be found now and then certain people outside of the sacerdotal caste who realised the true state of affairs and objected to a monopoly of profit on the part of the priests. Moreover, increasing prosperity invited attacks from less civilised neighbours, with which the priestly power alone could not cope.

Thus there grew up, side by side with the priests, the class of "caciques," the military power. The importance of this class increased in proportion to the growth of danger from without, and to the value of their services in repelling it, until at length the military leaders recognised that they were indispensable and declined to surrender to the priests that power which they had with difficulty acquired. Civilisation thus enters upon a fresh struggle— that of the secular and religious powers. At the outset the priestly caste often succeeded in frightening their superstitious people with threats of divine wrath; every defeat in battle, every failure of the crops, every devastating plague, enabled them for a time to keep the balance of power between the secular and the religious forces. Here we have the cause of those repeated long interregnums with which we meet at the beginnings of almost every dynasty. In many cases the secular power attempted

Secular and Religious Powers in Conflict to win over the religious power and to reconcile it to the new state of things by means of liberal concessions; but the natural result everywhere came to pass. The military class, when once they had gained the upper hand, concentrated the power more and more in themselves, declined to resign it in times of peace, and by degrees created a military nobility which acted as a counterpoise to the priestly power and invariably led to the establishment of a dynasty in which succession was regulated either by election or by inheritance.

Among the related peoples these changes were accomplished in a gradual and uniform manner. The mere fact that one little race had shaken off the priestly yoke and chosen a king for itself demanded a similar development on the part of its neighbours, and at an early period the Caciques became connected by a comunity of interest with the dynasty, both in their political and family relations. Only when their common enemy, the priestly caste, had finally been forced into a secondary position did the desire for empire on the part of the secular rulers become obvious. This ambition led to the wars of conquest among the petty princes who from time to time rose from one or other of the nations of Anahuac to be a dominant power.

The nations of Mexico were incompetent to organise a large empire, and, like almost all the peoples of the New World, remained thus divided up until the Spanish arrival. Even the greatest monarchs exer-

Mexico's Divided Nations cised lordship over only the immediate neighbourhood of their residences. The outlying districts, even when closely connected with the central state, were invariably ruled by feudal princes, whose fidelity was not proof against many external temptations. If the ruling monarch were strong enough to subdue his disobedient vassals, then his kingdom not only extended over his own territories, but included those lying without it; but, the larger the number of these subject kings, the greater became the danger that this loosely constructed political organisation might entirely collapse. As a matter of fact, it is in this fashion that one empire after another, Chichimec, Colhua, and Tezcucan, came into existence and fell to pieces again; and if the Spaniards at the beginning of the sixteenth

The Supreme Power of the Kings century had not brought the whole system to an end, the Aztec empire would undoubtedly have suffered a like fate. Naturally, under these circumstances, the yoke of the central government was generally light. When a disobedient vassal was subdued, or when the king with his army passed through the subject province to make fresh conquests, then his hand was heavy upon the land, and the life and property of his people were at his disposal.

But the contributions which in time of peace were sent up to the seat of power in acknowledgment of subjection were in few cases more than nominal gifts, and were generally only a half-voluntary tribute, rather symbolic than real. So easy was this rule that the lords of neighbouring, and also of more distant, districts occasionally preferred to recognise the dominion of some other prince, and to pay him a voluntary tribute, in order to assure themselves against the possibility of his forces being turned against themselves. This is the explanation of those kingdoms, nominally of large extent, being so often overthrown by a mere handful of people in a very short space of time.

For as soon as the prestige of the king, which was founded upon the imagination of his people, had been shattered, then all who had paid him tribute shook off his feeble yoke and declared themselves independent until a new potentate from another race succeeded in making himself a terror in the land. Although numbers of princely houses imagined, as we have

Kingdoms and Their Capitals said, that they could trace their genealogy uninterruptedly through six or seven centuries, yet it is only at the beginning of the twelfth century that history begins. At that time a number of so-called kingdoms were already in existence in Anahuac; among these the Chichimec kingdom, with its capital Tenayocan, on the west side of the lake of Tezcuco, held the leading position. The next in importance was the kingdom of Acolhua, with its capital Culhuacan, lying to the north of the lake of Chalco; it had apparently inherited the Toltec civilisation and was the chief centre of the culture of the time. Its ruling dynasty traced its origin to Topiltzin, the last Toltec king. In the middle of the century this line of kings had to struggle against an unexpected attack from the Chichimec power, and to make way for a dynasty from that race, which paid a nominal allegiance to the lords of Tenayocan.

Atzcaputzalco, Coatlichan, and Xaltocan are named as being other kingdoms under the protection of the one we have mentioned; all these places are to be found in the immediate neighbourhood of the central lakes. Moreover, the states of Tlazatlan, Zacatlan, and Tenamitec are also named as being countries which were subject to the authority of the Chichimec dynasty, so that this Chichimec power seems to have extended nearly over the whole valley of Mexico. All these principalities had made long strides in civilisation, an advance generally attributed by the chroniclers to Toltec influences. The

Nahua Races Living in Savagery invasion of fresh Nahua races still living in unreclaimed savagery threatened this civilisation with unmistakable dangers towards the end of the century. The Tecpanecs and Chalca obviously were sprung from Chicomoztoc—" the seven caves "; the consciousness of their relationship with the Nahua races already settled in the valley of Mexico had never been lost, and consequently Tollan also appears as one of the resting-places of their migration.

Then they appear in Anahuac proper, at Chapultepec, but in spite of their numbers they do not seem to have pressed the Chichimecs either very long or very hardly. A short time later they formed a political community completely organised in the most southerly portion of the lake district, and here the Chalca states attained an importance in the next century before which the fame of the Chichimecs and of Acolhua began to pale.

At that time also the youngest of the Nahua races—the Aztecs—had appeared in the lake district; their own traditions relate that they had been the last to leave the " seven caves," and that their migrations had lasted longer and their wanderings been more extensive than those of the other races related to them. At that time they were entirely under the government of their priests, who carried the image of their national god, Huitzilopochtli, upon a litter before them, and issued their orders as commands from heaven. The race cannot have been numerous when it first obtained permission from the Chichimec lords to make a settlement in Chapultepec, but the addition of numerous related tribes and the acquisition of friendly contingents from neighbouring towns increased their importance every year, and their warlike prowess began to make them famous— even notorious—in the unending wars of the different dynasties, in which they played a considerable part as allies of one or the other party.

Up to this point they had remained true to their institutions; in spite of all the chances of war, and the changes which it brought, the priests of Huitzilopochtli continued to hold the power. It was then that this god began to undergo a metamorphosis from the character of sun-god to that of war-god. But even the Aztecs could not resist the influence exercised upon them by the exigencies of their **Aztecs'** position and the example of **First Secular** neighbouring races; and in **Monarch** spite of the vigorous objections of the priesthood they chose their first secular monarch, Huitzilihuitl, about the year 1250. Like the princes of the neighbouring states he had a king's title and exercised a king's power within his own race, but he was not successful in founding an Aztec dynasty.

He had entered into an alliance with the Cacique of Zumpancoa against the Tecpanecs of Xaltocan, had started upon a campaign, but had only succeeded in exciting the opposition of the other Tecpanec princes to his Aztecs. As he declined to pay tribute to the Tecpanecatl Tecuhtli, the ruling monarch of the race who resided in Atzcaputzalco, he was attacked on every side by the subjects and the allies of the Tecpanecs, and after numerous losses and a vain attempt to summon to his aid the Chichimec king of Tezcuco, he was obliged to abdicate. The priestly caste again obtained the power and succeeded in making peace with their neighbours, though at the sacrifice of that independence which Huitzilihuitl had defended.

The ruling powers of Anahuac had meanwhile become more or less weakened; the Chichimec ruler, Tlotzin Pochotl, and his successor, Quinantzin, did not succeed in keeping their territory intact. Their inclinations were rather towards arts of peace than feats of war. They had turned their attention chiefly toward the decoration of their capitals, and had neglected to protect their boundaries, so that the reins of power fell from their hands. The ties which bound the subject kings of Atzcaputzalco, Xaltocan, and **Royal** other states, to the central **Court in** government grew looser and **Tezcuco** looser. Owing to the circumstances under which the Aztecs appear among these states, scarcely any traces are left of a defensive alliance between the Tecpanec states and the kingdom of the Chichimecs. The direction which their development took was largely influenced by the change of settlement from Tenayocan to Tezcuco under Quinantzin.

Tezcuco, under the preceding government, had become a dangerous rival of the old capital, while the Chichimec princes were devoting their attention to the decoration and adornment of their palaces and gardens. The government of the important province of Tezcuco fell into the hands of the presumptive successor of the emperor, Chichimecatl Tecuhtli. As governor, Quinantzin had already held a royal court in Tezcuco; while still in Tenayocan he had established his position as emperor, and had then entrusted the government of his present capital to another's hands and gone back to his chosen Tezcuco. In consequence of this change of capital from the western to the eastern side of the lake the whole Chichimec kingdom naturally enough gravitated in that direction.

At that time the boundaries of the Chichimec kingdom stretched far away over the valley to the east. Tlazcala, Huexotzinco, and other states upon the eastern tableland, were then governed by princes of Chichimec race. But as the kingdom gained ground in the east it became enfeebled on the west and **Lost Ground** abandoned the field to the **of the Chichimec** Tecpanec states. The **Kingdom** change of residence to Tezcuco did not entirely commend itself to all the Chichimecs, and as Quinantzin could not rely on the fidelity of his satraps a great confederacy was soon formed against him, which was secretly fostered by the Tecpanecs and tended to the separation of the whole of the western portion of the kingdom of Tezcuco. Once again a Chichimec state was formed about the ancient capital Tenayocan, in which a relation of Quinantzin usurped the title of Chichimecatl Tecuhtli. The emperor himself seemed little disturbed at this occurrence. He made sure of his power in the east; on the west he allowed things to take their course, as he was not strong enough to control them. The rival state was,

Chichimec Power Established however, of no long duration; within a short time the opposition king was attacked by the Tecpanecs, who had succeeded in bringing the Aztecs to their help. After the fall of Tenayocan the Chichimec power was firmly established in the western districts.

This state of affairs very soon after received the sanction of an international confederacy which was formed between the Tecpanec king of Atzcaputzalco, as emperor of all the Tecpanec states, and Quinantzin. To Quinantzin the Tecpanec king yielded the predominant position of Chichimecatl Tecuhtli, but by thus cleverly renouncing the appearance of power he gained a signal advantage in reality, for Quinantzin in return admitted all his claims to the ancient territory of the Chichimecs and confirmed him in their undisputed possession.

These battles had so entirely broken up and confounded every element in the Nahuatlac nationality that the new kingdoms were founded on a territorial far more than on a national basis. Thus we find Tezcuco the capital of districts that had been named by the different Nahua races. Tecpanecs, Aztecs, Colhua contributed at least as much to their population as did the Chichimecs and the eastern races.

The Aztecs were in the worst position; their habit of offering their services in war to the highest bidder, the wild ferocity with which they carried on their warfare, which had been the chief factor in forming their religion with its infamous sacrifices of human blood, made them the objects of universal hostility. The

The Aztec Race Broken up wars which ravaged the country on the north of the lake district at the end of the thirteenth or the beginning of the fourteenth century brought destruction upon their capital Chapultepec; and the Aztec race, like many another, was broken up and dispersed. Scattered companies of them entered again into the services of the neighbouring states as mercenaries, with the intention of gaining permission to form fresh settlements as a reward for their prowess in war. But only two races—the Mexica and the Tlatelulca—kept their lineage sufficiently pure in the following ages to have a clear remembrance of their origin, until their turn for rule also came in the course of time. They had, however, much ground for thankfulness to the prince of Colhuacan, who had offered a refuge for their wanderings in Tizaapan or in Iztacalco.

The Tecpanecs had gained the chief advantage from the troubles of these times. The western portion of the lake of Zumpango from the north, as far as Chalco on the south, had become their almost undisputed territory. The eastern portion belonged similarly to the kings of Tezcuco. But the weak point of all these American states—their inability to organise a government over a large extent of country—became apparent here also. Atzcaputzalco, as the early centre of the whole Tecpanec kingdom, for some time retained considerable importance, and for a number of years its kings bore the title of Tecpanecatl Tecuhtli. But imperceptibly the centre of gravity of the polit-

Centres of Tecpanec Government ical world shifted more and more toward the south. While the ancient Culhuacan again flourished next to Atzcaputzalco and Tenayocan, and quickly surpassed them both in importance, Chalco, Tenanco, and Amequemecan rose in the south as fresh centres of Tecpanec government.

Circumstances threw the leadership into their hands when, about a century later, a common enemy of all the states of the lake district appeared in the Mexica people. At the time of their greatest development the Tecpanec states are said to have been no fewer than twenty-five in number; many of these were closely bound together by ties of relationship. A feeling of close connection was certainly alive among them all, and this sentiment became the more vigorous when the very existence of the race was threatened. But, in the meantime, individual Tecpanec kings had been fighting as furiously among themselves as the princes of the Chichimec race under similar circumstances had fought and were continuing to fight with all other kings.

In the first half of his reign, Quinantzin, the Chichimec emperor, was apparently indifferent to the loss of the western province of his kingdom; but he had not finally renounced his claims upon it. For the time being he had concentrated all his powers on strengthening the newly formed kingdom on the eastern tableland. When signs of insurrection became visible even there, he met them with an unusual display of energy, and was generally able to restore order. When this was done he again turned his attention to the province he had lost. His first attack was upon the prince of Xaltocan, whose kingdom, owing to its inaccessible situation, had never been made tributary to the Tecpanecs. The well-organised forces of the united kingdom of Tezcuco easily overcame all attempts at resistance on the part of the Xaltocans.

After this victory the Tecpanec emperor did not think it expedient to allow the possession of this loosely connected province to be contingent upon the uncertain results of a war. With a view to strengthening this connection he offered peace and alliance to the Chichimecs, and declared himself ready to recognise their claims to the dominion of the whole lake district, and to acknowledge their overlordship, which was in his case to be merely formal. Quinantzin was satisfied with this result. He allowed the Tecpanecs the possibility of pursuing their peaceful and statesmanlike projects while he exercised at least a nominal suzerainty over a district which was far wider than any that his forefathers had possessed. When he died, in the year 1305, no less than seventy subject kings were present at the magnificent ceremonies which attended his burial in Tezcuco ; no less than seventy kings paid homage to Techotl, the youngest son of the deceased monarch, whom he had nominated as his successor, for the elder brothers had lost all claims to the throne by participation in an attempt at revolt.

Death of the Great King Quinantzin

The most remarkable feature of the government of Techotl is that he first in Central America attempted to introduce a general change in the organisation of the states, which had hitherto been of a loose and wholly unstable character. Hitherto every subject king had reigned in his own province as free and unfettered as the Chichimecatl Tecuhtli himself had in his government of the central portion of the kingdom; so long as he paid the moderate tribute and in time of war offered no opposition to the passage of an army through his dominions, he might be sure that no heavier burdens would be laid upon him by his feudal lord. Quinantzin's reign had repeatedly displayed the serious dangers to the continuance of a united kingdom which were involved in such a state of affairs. The old king himself had, by sternly suppressing any attempt at insubordination, done much to increase the security of the political unity. Techotl energetically followed out these views. He contrived to gather most of the vassal kings together in Tezcuco, and to keep them in his immediate neighbourhood, under the honourable pretext of forming a council of state ; their representatives, who ruled in their places, owed even greater allegiance to their feudal master.

Techotl's System of Government

Moreover, a new division of the country was arranged, the old racial boundaries were definitely abolished, the number of districts for the purposes of government was increased almost threefold, and thereby the danger that local insurrections might spread far and wide was largely diminished. Finally, Techotl, by means of a number of ordinances that were binding throughout his realm, kindled a spirit of unity among his people.

All these arrangements could only have been valid for his dominions on the east of the lakes ; the west, which was almost as closely united, though perhaps not so strictly organised, under the Tecpanec king Tezozomoc, was almost beyond the reach of any kind of aggression. The state of nominal vassalage which Quinantzin had established remained undisturbed under the rule of Techotl ; but after an energetic and ambitious monarch, in the person of Tezozomoc, had ascended the Tecpanec throne the danger of rivalry between the Chichimec kingdom, now known as Acolhuacan, and the Tecpanec kingdom became gradually more threatening. It was under the son and successor of Techotl, the king Ixtlilxochitl, that the storm broke. The satraps whose powers had been limited by Techotl's reforms, and who entertained for him an animosity not difficult to comprehend, made all kinds of excuses to avoid taking part in his funeral ceremonies.

New King on Tecpanec Throne

Their passive resistance was of little danger ; more important was the attitude of the Tecpanecatl Tecuhtli. Tezozomoc openly declined to recognise the suzerainty of the young Chichimec prince, and was unmistakably striving to throw off a yoke that had been sensibly relaxed. With the careless patience, which for generations was a striking characteristic of the Chichimec rulers, Ixtlilxochitl bore with the equivocal behaviour of his most powerful vassal. On the other hand, however, he appeared to be firmly deter-

Intrigues Against the King mined to settle his dubious relations with the Tecpanec king in the spirit of his father's reforms. Tezozomoc met this straightforward policy with craft and dissimulation of every kind. As soon as Ixtlilxochitl threatened to enforce his demands, Tezozomoc declared himself ready to fulfil all claims.

But as soon as he had appeased him by a show of submission he declined to fulfil the responsibilities he had accepted, under pretexts of the most trivial kind. It was a mistake fraught with important consequences that Ixtlilxochitl permitted these intrigues to continue year by year. He shook the confidence of his own friends and allies, and gave his opponent time, not only to make proper preparations in every direction for a decisive conflict, but also to make allies of some of those vassals whose fidelity was weakening.

According to tradition, Tezozomoc, in three successive years, had sent a heavy tribute of raw cotton to Tezcuco, and had first requested, then required, and finally commanded that this tribute should be redelivered at Atzcaputzalco ready woven into stuff. Twice were his commands fulfilled ; but the third time an embassy was returned to the effect that the Chichimec ruler had received the tribute with thanks, and would use it to arm his warriors, who were determined to punish their disobedient vassals.

Even then Ixtlilxochitl proceeded to wait for the attack of the Tecpanecs. Tezozomoc sent his army twice across the lake into

Tecpanecs Defeated in Battle the district of Tezcuco, but twice suffered a heavy defeat at the hands of adversaries whose numbers continually increased. In spite of all this he unconditionally rejected all the offers of the Tezcucan emperor to make peace on condition of recognising his superiority, and now openly advanced the claim that the title of Chichimecatl Tecuhtli belonged to him, in the first place, as being the direct successor of the founder of the Chichimec empire, the king

Xolotl. In spite of this he would undoubtedly have been defeated if Ixtlilxochitl could have made up his mind to follow up with vigour the advantages he had won. Repeated victories brought to his side many of the little kings who had hitherto remained neutral ; and many of the allies of Tezozomoc were beginning to weaken in their fidelity.

Thus when Ixtlilxochitl made his attack, he could easily collect a considerable army ; and in the province of Tepotzotlan he won a brilliant victory against a hostile army of 200,000 men. It is difficult to understand how Ixtlilxochitl allowed himself to be again befooled by the cunning Tezozomoc. After a four months' siege the capital of Atzcaputzalco was incapable of offering further resistance. Tezozomoc agreed to an unconditional surrender and begged for pardon, appealing to the sentiment of kinship. Although he had been so many times deceived, Ixtlilxochitl was once again satisfied with mere promises. Without completing the work of conquest he withdrew his victorious army from the walls of his enemy's capital. This was a

Conquering Chichimec Emperor signal for a general collapse. Expectation of booty or reward in some form or other had brought certain waverers to his side to fight against the dreaded Tecpanecs ; but they had no idea of exposing themselves to the revenge of Tezozomoc, who had been left in possession of his princely power, without themselves gaining any corresponding advantage.

An ominous stillness greeted the Chichimec emperor when he returned to his capital. Reports soon began to come in that Tezozomoc was making fresh preparations ; and when he at last invited the king and his son, Nezahualcoyotl, to come to Chiuhnauhtlan to receive his oath of allegiance, the king no longer dared to trust himself in the traitor's hands. But his prudence came too late. When Tezozomoc perceived that his cunning plan had been laid bare, he hastened to Tezcuco by forced marches. While defending his capital, Ixtlilxochitl was captured and expiated the many mistakes of his life with his death. His son and heir, Nezahualcoyotl, only with the greatest difficulty escaped the sentence of death which Tezozomoc, the newly crowned Chichimecatl Tecuhtli, passed upon him.

AMERICA
BEFORE
COLUMBUS

ANCIENT
CIVILISATIONS
OF CENTRAL
AMERICA
VII

THE RISE OF THE AZTECS
AND THE FORTUNES OF THE MEXICAN KINGDOMS

THE fall of the Chichimec kingdom of Acolhuacan took place in the year 1419. We must, however, go back for a century to pick up the threads required for the understanding of its further development. We have seen that the Mexica had been deprived of their refuge, Chapultepec, which they gained upon the change of the Chichimec capital to Tezcuco, and that it was with difficulty that they obtained from the Tecpanec ruler permission to settle elsewhere.

The priests may have explained their misfortunes as due to the wrath of the gods at the deposition of the theocracy and the choice of a king ; at any rate, they did not succeed in regaining the favour of heaven for their people, though for a considerable time they had been in undisputed possession of power. While the Mexica were feared among all their neighbours for their plundering raids, they were constantly **The Mexica in Peace and War** sought for as allies in time of war. But in times of peace the chief anxiety of their neighbours was to keep these restless strangers as far off as possible. They probably then paid the Tecpanec princes an unusually heavy tribute, and submitted to a certain measure of degradation, for their presence was barely tolerated, and they were sent about from one settlement to another.

Thereupon Tenoch, a priestly guide of the Mexica, once again exhorted them to migrate in the name of the god Huitzilopochtli, and led the scanty remnants of his people forth from their flourishing towns into the marshy coast-land on the west of the lake of Tezcuco. There, being warned by an omen from heaven, he probably founded that town which in the course of time became the capital of the Aztec kingdom, Mexico-Tenochtitlan. Almost at the same time the related Tlatelulca withdrew from the tyrannical oppression of the Tecpanecs, and founded a second settlement in their immediate

neighbourhood, Tlatelulco, which later on became a keen rival of Tenochtitlan, but was at last outstripped by and incorporated into the rival town. This migration to Tenochtitlan, which is placed in the year 1325, had not gained independence for the Mexicans. There, too, they found themselves within the dominion of a **The Aztecs Strengthened by Fugitives** Tecpanec king, were obliged to obtain his permission to settle, and continued to owe him tribute. As they had fixed their capital at a distance and settled in an uncultivated district considered almost uninhabitable, they did, however, by degrees, free themselves from his crushing tyranny.

In spite of its unfavourable situation the sister town developed with unexpected rapidity. The Mexicans were not the only people who were trying to escape from the dominion which had so long oppressed them. The reforms of the Tezcucan kings were felt to be as unsatisfactory as the tyranny of the Tecpanecs, and from both kingdoms numerous fugitives streamed into the barren wilderness and were readily received by the Aztecs of Tenochtitlan and Tlatelulco, eager to increase their strength. Thus these towns entirely lost their national character, and their population was composed of elements more and more diverse. The new arrivals, while they gladly fell in with the civilisation and the customs of the ancient inhabitants, exerted a refining influence upon the harshness of the Aztec customs, began **Refining Influences on the Aztecs** to amalgamate the latter with their own institutions, and contributed in no small degree to soften the deep hatred with which the worshippers of Huitzilopochtli were regarded by all their neighbours. From the outset Tlatelulco far outstripped the neighbouring Tenochtitlan

It was to Tlatelulco that the emigrants from the country of the Tecpanecs turned by preference, and we can easily understand that the relations of the ruling prince gained concessions more easily than outsiders. Thus it was a special mark of favour that the king of Atzcaputzalco agreed to set up a member of his family as a feudal prince in Tlatelulco when the town was strong enough to demand a king of its own. On the other hand, numerous emigrants from Culhua turned their steps toward Tenochtitlan. The ancient Culhuacan capital had long ago obtained an almost independent position under the suzerainty of the Tecpanecs, and had repeatedly played an important part in the political history of the whole kingdom.

Internal dissensions had broken out at last somewhere about the time when the Mexicans had founded their new capital. Numerous peoples of the Culhua, who had been driven from their homes by that revolution, made their way to Tenochtitlan, where within a short time their nationality was more strongly represented than was that of the Aztecs. The newly founded state owed to these circumstances its first important revolution. Mexico had been founded under the guidance of the priests; the name of Tenochtitlan (the town of Tenoch) was derived from the priestly guide who had led the people thither. But the traditions of centuries had made the Culhua accustomed to a monarchy; and though in religious matters they yielded to the custom of the country, in temporal affairs they declined to submit permanently to priestly government. Several members of the old royal family had come to Mexico among the fugitives.

A compromise between the old inhabitants and the new colonists finally led to the choice of a king in the town of Tenoch, and the colonist element was sufficiently strong to bring about the election of Acamapichtli, the son of the king who bore the name of Culhuacan. After the fall of his father's dynasty he had fled to Tezcuco, and had there married a princess of Chichimec race, Ilancueitl. The connection of these dynasties has an extraordinarily strong influence upon all the later history of the Aztec kingdom of Tenochtitlan, and we have here the primary explanation of many facts that would be wholly unintelligible if we were to consider the town and the kingdom only from the Aztec point of view.

Mexico a Vassal Kingdom

Mexico now remained, in spite of its friendly relations with Tezcuco, a Tecpanec vassal kingdom. Acamapichtli was obliged to obtain the confirmation of his election in Atzcaputzalco; it was in the service of Tezozomoc that the young king of Mexico made his early expeditions, which were so successful that he soon became highly respected among the vassal kings. The first campaign that he undertook in the Tecpanec service was in a southerly direction against the Chalca.

AZTEC BRIDGE OF PETRIFIED WOOD ACROSS THE TEMASOPE RIVER IN MEXICO

A PRESENT-DAY RAILWAY THROUGH A PREHISTORIC CUTTING

This illustration depicts a striking section of the Mexican Nochistlan railway, which, according to a recent report, rejoices in ebony sleepers, and ballast of silver ore drawn from prehistoric and disused mines beside the track; these ancient mines being of Aztec origin, as is also the remarkable hand-hewn cutting shown in the picture.

These people, although related to the Tecpanecs, had founded a kingdom on the southern shore of the Lake Tezcuco, and on the lake which they called the Lake of Chalco. This state had grown so large that it had split up into numerous vassal states. The Mexican chronicles of these wars describe them as the exploits of the Mexican kings only, but, until the fall of the Tecpanec kingdom, the kings of Mexico acted only as allies in these wars.

Acamapichtli died in the year 1403, without having left any commands as to the succession; this fact probably marks the ascendancy of the priestly caste, which was once again making despairing efforts to restore the theocracy. But **The Early Races at War** foreign elements, accustomed to a dynasty of monarchs, had already become too strong; though the priestly caste succeeded in making a succession dependent upon a new election, they could not prevent the choice from falling upon the son of Acamapichtli, Huitzilihuitl. We are particularly told of him, too, that he was obliged to obtain a confirmation of his election from the Tecpanec ruler. As subject to Tezozomoc he took part, in the following year, in the war which led to the

overthrow of Ixtlilxochitl and of the Chichimec kingdom, although this king was closely connected with him by his marriage with his sister. Even allowing for the exaggerations of the chroniclers, we see very plainly that the kings of Mexico had become at that date most important vassals, from the fact that the king of Tlatelulco was commander-in-chief of Tezozomoc, and therefore also of the troops of Huitzilihuitl. These two kings did not live to the end of the wars. The ruler of Tlatelulco fell in one of the battles in which the Tezcucans were victorious; Huitzilihuitl died in 1417 in Tenochtitlan, the town which he had striven to extend without and to organise within. The result of his efforts was that his half-brother Chimalpopoca succeeded to the throne unopposed, representing his country upon the fall of Ixtlilxochitl.

We must suppose that it was only by force of circumstances that Huitzilihuitl and Chimalpopoca continued to fight on the side of Tezozomoc, for they had far greater advantages to expect from the success of Ixtlilxochitl, who was their friend and connection by marriage, than from the victory of their tyrannical emperor. They could not, however, have given the

5789

Tecpanec king the smallest grounds for suspicion. When this monarch proposed to increase and organise his kingdom by uniting it with the Tezcucan territories, the Mexican Chimalpopoca was regarded as one of the six subject kings, together with the rulers of Chalco, Tlatelulco, Acolman, Coatlichan, and Huexotla.

Tezozomoc's intention to make his kingdom more secure both within and without was only incompletely realised. The conditions imposed upon the vassal kings were most oppressive; two-thirds of the income from their provinces they were obliged to send to the king, retaining only a third for themselves. Consequently they felt the unjust burden of this tribute far more than the honour of their promotion, and they expressed their dissatisfaction with no attempt at concealment. The newly crowned Chichimecatl Tecuhtli was not successful in obtaining recognition of his power throughout the kingdom of Ixtlilxochitl.

The distant provinces on the north and east, however, gladly seized the opportunity of refusing all payment of tribute and declaring their independence; and so strong was the hostility of the Tlazcalans against Tezozomoc that they received the exiled heir of Tezcuco, the prince Nezahualcoyotl, and offered him a refuge in their mountains until the intervention of the Mexican king Chimalpopoca was successful in obtaining the repeal of the sentence of death that had been passed upon him. Tezozomoc was already advanced in years when he united the whole of Anahuac under his rule; he enjoyed the fruits of victory for eight more years before his death, and named his son Tejauh as his successor. But by this act he sowed the seeds of dissension in both his family and his kingdom. Among all the sons of Tezozomoc, Maxtla, who had been appointed regent of Coyohuacan, was unquestionably the one who was most like his father, though he had not inherited his tenacity and his calmness in addition to his energy, bravery, and

cunning. He took it as an insult that he should have to content himself with a second place in his father's kingdom, and the indifference of Tejauh enabled him, after a few months, to drive his brother from the throne, and to set himself up as Chichimecatl Tecuhtli, the king of the whole of Anahuac. This revolution was bloodless, but not so its results.

A Bloodless Revolution in Anahuac The vassal kings had already borne the yoke of the aged Tezozomoc, the hero of a hundred fights, with the greatest impatience, and they considered it wholly intolerable to become the vassals of Maxtla, a young prince who, in his own government in Coyohuacan, had only succeeded in making himself thoroughly hated by his subjects and the neighbouring princes.

It was by an act of violence against the legitimate ruler that he had thrust himself into his place. The kings of Mexico and Tlatelulco placed themselves at the head of the dissatisfied subjects; Tejauh had fled to Tenochtitlan, and so it was there arranged to surprise Maxtla at a festival, to overthrow him, and to reinstate Tejauh. But the conspiracy was betrayed, and the victim of it was not Maxtla, but Tejauh. Maxtla did not know with which of the

A CHARACTERISTIC EXAMPLE OF AZTEC CARVING
This colossal head carved in stone is part of an Aztec ruin discovered at Itzamal, in Yucatan, and illustrates the high quality of the artistic work of this very early and, in many respects, primitive race of people which inhabited Central America in the pre-Columbian days. The design was probably executed with blunt flint.

Aztec kings he would have to deal first; without waiting, therefore, for further developments, he attacked with swift decision first the Mexicans and then

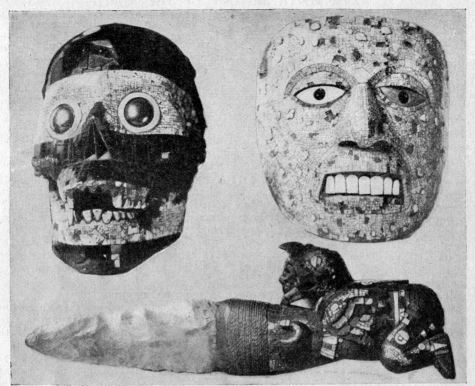

RELICS OF PRIMITIVE TIMES: AZTEC MASKS AND KNIFE   Mansell

These further examples of the artistic workmanship of the primitive Aztec peoples represent mosaic death masks and a flint knife with ornamental handle, set with stones. The mask on the right is encrusted with turquoise mosaic.

Tlatelulco. So successful was he in each of these campaigns that both kings were overthrown and their cities and countries laid waste. They would, perhaps, have been destroyed for all time if revolt had not broken out in every part of Maxtla's kingdom against his rule of lawlessness and oppression. The sympathies which a large portion of the eastern provinces felt for the ancient royal house were greatly strengthened by Maxtla's aggrandisement. As his hands were entirely tied by the wars, the Chichimec Nezahualcoyotl considered that the time had come to make some attempt to regain his father's kingdom. Tlazcala and Huexotzinco willingly placed their bands of warriors at his disposal.

Maxtla's Rule of Lawlessness and Oppression

The feeble opposition with which he met in most of the provinces of his father's kingdom enabled him to reconquer a large part of it, but the capital, Tezcuco, offered an unconquerable resistance. Tezozomoc had here set up the prince of the old royal house as his representative. This prince knew very well that he had nothing to hope from the mercy of the lawful heir of the Chichimec kingdom if he were once defeated; he therefore made the most vigorous and ultimately successful efforts to maintain himself in the capital. But as long as he remained unsubdued the position of Nezahualcoyotl was untenable, chiefly on account of the moral impression conveyed. The campaigns that had been begun with such brilliant success ended in a manner not very far removed from defeat.

The first result of this half success was that a number of allies began to weaken in their fidelity, so that Nezahualcoyotl must have begun to fear that attack of Maxtla which he would certainly have to withstand. In this dangerous position the allies whose aid he most desired—the Aztecs—offered their help. After Maxtla had retired from Mexico they had at once re-established the empire. For a moment their choice had wavered between Itzcopuatl, the brother of Chimalpopoca, and his nephew Montezuma, who, though young, had already been crowned with the laurels of many victories. Fortunately, their constitution was wide enough for more than one vigorous man to make himself useful in it. The kingdom still bore unmistakable traces of its development from an aristocracy. Apart from the priesthood, still most influential, the king had by him two high temporal dignitaries, the tlacatecatl (lord of the armies) and the tlacochcalcatl (lord of the arrow). Montezuma was called to

Confederacy Against the Tecpanecs
the first of these two positions; he was able thereby to satisfy his ambition and also to expend his energy in acting with his royal uncle for the good of the realm. Recent events pointed with sufficient clearness to the direction his energies should take, for Maxtla unconditionally refused to recognise the choice that had been made, and was threatening a new attack. Thus a common enemy again brought the Mexicans and the Chichimecs together.

Montezuma went to Nezahualcoyotl and formed a confederacy with him against the Tecpanecs, which confederacy was at once joined by the newly chosen king of Tlatelulco. It was immediately agreed that they should carry the war as soon as possible into the enemy's country. Nezahualcoyotl openly announced his intention of re-establishing the old royal house in Tezcuco, thereby certainly estranging many friends who had hoped to gain their own independence if they stood by him in the hour of misfortune. But by entering into alliance with all the enemies of the Tecpanec tyrant he was fully compensated for the dangerous elements in his own situation. The campaign which he led in person along with the Mexicans was finally decisive after many victories on either side. With the support of the king of Tlacopan the allied Aztecs and Tezcucans gained a complete victory over the Tecpanecs.

Atzcaputzalco was captured and destroyed, and Maxtla fell, either in battle or afterwards, beneath the blows of his

The Fate of Anahuac
opponents. Those who had thought that with the fall of the Tecpanec tyranny freedom had come for Anahuac were cruelly undeceived. The more prudent of the dependents of Nezahualcoyotl had remained neutral in the decisive battles, and now they openly revolted. But the power of the allies increased no further; and the division of political power which had been arranged after the capture of Atzcaputzalco, at the festivities which

took place in Tenochtitlan to celebrate the victory, was now immediately carried out. Anahuac was divided between the kings of Mexico and Tezcuco. Nezahualcoyotl, who had not even yet been able to effect an entrance into his ancient capital, obtained the whole of his father's kingdom, which had embraced the eastern half of Anahuac, and also the title of Chichimecatl Tecuhtli. The historical importance of this title still gave its recipient the right to claim the first place and the highest rank among the allies. The part played by the Mexicans had hitherto been of too little importance to enable them to dispute about this position; they had to thank their long friendship and relationship with the monarchs of Tezcuco for the fact that an important portion of the booty fell to their share.

With the exception of the district of Tlacopan, which had been exempted from destruction to provide lands for those who had given their help against Maxtla, the whole kingdom of the Tecpanecs, in which the Mexicans themselves, like the

Conquered Kingdom of the Tecpanecs
other kings, had hitherto been only vassals, now fell into their power, which at first they were obliged, no doubt, to enforce with arms. Their position in the councils of the allies became still more prominent; here they were considered as having equal rights with the Tezcucans, while the king of Tlacopan, the third member in this new triple alliance, remained independent, but was obliged to recognise the unconditional superiority of the two other members. In the future these conditions were to remain unchanged; it was arranged also that all future conquests should be divided between the allies, so that the king of Tlacopan should obtain a fifth part of the spoil and the rest should be divided in equal portions between the rulers of Tezcuco and Tenochtitlan. Such were the contents of the treaty between the leading nations of Anahuac.

These political relations continued to the time of the Spanish invasion; the confederation that would eventually have broken up remained undisturbed until the time of the conquest. The three allied kings carried on a number of wars, especially against their immediate neighbours on the south; no doubt the booty was then divided in accordance with the provisions of their compact. The Mexicans seem, however, to have gained greater accessions of territory even in these cases of common conquest. But each of the allied kings undertook isolated wars of conquest against adjoining territories. Consequently, the division of the kingdom into eastern and western territories is not strictly adhered to ; we meet with the Tezcucans on the west and on the coast of the Pacific Ocean, and similarly we find the Aztecs on the east as far as the shores of the Gulf of Mexico.

The most important change which the lapse of time brought about within the confederacy consisted in the fact that the kings of Tenochtitlan began more and more to take a leading part. Though keeping strictly to the legal conditions of the confederation, the kings of Tezcuco allowed themselves to be pushed into the background by the kings of Tenochtitlan ; the reason lay solely in a national peculiarity of both peoples and their leaders.

The kings of Tezcuco had always been more renowned for the care they expended upon the internal well-being of their kingdom than for their warlike **A Famous King of Tezcuco** expeditions. This reputation was supported by both of the kings who held the throne at the time of the confederation, Nezahualcoyotl and his son Nezahualpilli. It was not that they were lacking in warlike vigour ; when it was a question of maintaining their authority or preserving the integrity of their kingdom, they were fully equal to the task ; but they never undertook wars of conquest. Under no circumstances was war an end in itself to the kings of Colhuacan ; it was invariably the means to higher ends.

During the first ten years Nezahualcoyotl concentrated his attention upon the reorganisation of his kingdom, which had been greatly shattered by revolutions following upon the death of Ixtlilxochitl. He kept in view that feudal system which his father, and his grandfather, Techotl, had introduced ; and this in spite of the sad experience which both he and his predecessors had had of it. Similarly he followed the steps of his ancestors with regard to the organisation of a judicial system ; his decrees were long respected by the Spaniards as being particularly valuable. Above all, he resembled the earlier kings in his love for the fine arts ; temples and palaces, gardens and baths,

streets and bridges, arose under his care, both in the capital and in the provinces. Wherever in the whole valley of Mexico more important artistic buildings were taken in hand, the finished art of Nezahualcoyotl and his architects became the guiding principle of their construction. He showed his thankfulness to the Mexicans **Songs of the Poet King** for the support which they had given him in the hour of necessity by his erection of the aqueduct which brought spring water in pipes of clay enclosed in stone from Chapultepec to the capital of the Aztecs situated among the marshes ; and when, in the year 1445, continuous rains had made the lake rise to a threatening height, and had almost flooded the whole of Tenochtitlan, he it was who built a wide mole of a semicircular form, and kept the low-lying water round the town from uniting with the lake which was threatening danger.

Nezahualcoyotl also devoted uninterrupted attention to intellectual progress. He was himself one of the foremost poets that the ancient American civilisation produced ; his melancholy songs passed from mouth to mouth long after his race and his kingdom had disappeared from the face of the earth. The maturity of his intellect is to be seen in the traditions that we have of his religious ideas. His predecessors had been accustomed to exercise a wide tolerance toward the religious conceptions of their various subjects, which often differed materially from one another. But in this matter Nezahualcoyotl far surpassed the fame of his ancestors.

In the very capital of his kingdom, in the city of Tezcuco, he allowed temples to be erected to the most different divinities, even a temple to Huitzilopochtli, although he was as averse to the blood-stained worship of this divinity as were his forefathers. Being **The Centre of Intellectual Life and Progress** thus convinced of the inadequacy and incompleteness of the worships of his people, he arrived at the conception of the one God who created and sustains the world. Perhaps it would be a bold comparison to call the Tezcuco of Nezahualcoyotl the Athens of Central America ; but in his time Tezcuco certainly was the one great centre of all the intellectual life, progress, and learning to be found in these kingdoms.

A MEXICAN DIVINITY

A VASE FROM HONDURAS

FEMALE FIGURE IN VOLCANIC STONE   MEXICAN STATUE IN VOLCANIC STONE

EXAMPLES OF ANCIENT CENTRAL AMERICAN CARVING IN STONE

AMERICA
BEFORE
COLUMBUS

ANCIENT
CIVILISATIONS
OF CENTRAL
AMERICA
VIII

THE MEXICAN SUPREMACY
AND THE POWERFUL EMPIRE OF MONTEZUMA

ALTHOUGH Nezahualcoyotl had a large number of sons by different women, it was only in the year 1463 that he entered upon lawful wedlock with the princess Azcaxochitl of Tlacopan. There was one son of their union, Nezahualpilli, who was eight years old at the death of his father, which took place in 1472.

Brought up under the care of the king Axayacatl, in Mexico, he remained the true son of his great father in his intellectual capacities. He was not allowed to take the same important position in the triple alliance as his father had held, who was older than his Aztec confederates, and whose age and intellectual endowments had been a check on the encroachment of the neighbouring kingdom. His son was obliged to take the second place within the confederacy; for now not only might and splendour, but also the preponderance of age and experience were on the side of the Mexicans.

Mexicans Held in Fear The development of the kingdom of Tenochtitlan was different in many essential details. Its equality with Tezcuco in the confederation of 1431 had not been entirely deserved; immediately before the gates of the capital lay the sister state Tlatelulco, governed by its own independent monarch. And although the Mexicans were more feared for their prowess in arms than respected over a wide district, they yet had first to subdue that kingdom before they could lay claim to suzerainty over the Western Anahuac.

A famous line of royal heroes, the sons and nephews of Huitzilihuitl, had devoted themselves successfully to this task. At first their expeditions were directed chiefly toward the south; after Xochimilco and Cuitlahua had been incorporated, the endless wars against the states of Chalca began. The Mexicans had already overcome the people of Chalca many times when they were in the service of the Tecpanecs; but these had not yet been entirely subdued,

and at the time of the revolution they had again recovered their independence, as had many other portions of the Tecpanec kingdom. Even now the people of Chalca offered an invincible resistance to the Mexicans alone. But their provocations had also driven Nezahualcoyotl into the ranks of their enemies; and the numerous Chalca states were unable to offer any prolonged resistance to the united armies of the three allied kingdoms. For nearly twenty years—1446-1465—three successive kings of Mexico took the field yearly against the Chalca with varied success, until they succeeded in reducing their last fortress, the town of Chalco. From 1465 the Chalca were reckoned among the states tributary to Tenochtitlan.

Mexican Kings on the Battlefield

In the year 1440, Itzcohuatl, who had helped to found the confederacy of 1431, died, and his nephew Montezuma (more correctly "Mocteuzoma") Ilhuicamina, succeeded him on the throne; this was the king who did most to extend the Aztec dominions. The war against Chalco, which was brought to a successful end in the last years of his reign, claimed most of his attention, but at the same time he extended the boundaries of his kingdom in other directions also. Moreover, he made most important improvements in the internal organisation of the state.

Even under the government of Itzcohuatl his high position enabled him to exercise great influence, for he had been at the same time commander-in-chief of the army and high-priest of Huitzilopochtli. Nor was it for nothing that he had been the intimate friend of Nezahualcoyotl. The capital owed to him the most important of those buildings which excited the astonishment of the conquerors; the dykes which connected the town with the mainland; the canals which served as its high-roads; the temples, and in particular the temple of Huitzilopochtli, to which

Montezuma's Great Work for his Kingdom

generations had made additions, and which was not even ended on Montezuma's death, although he brought out the final plans. In religious matters Montezuma showed some sympathy with that toleration practised by the kings of Tezcuco. In Tenochtitlan there were already numerous temples to foreign divinities, and it

The Mexicans' Blood-stained Hecatombs speedily became the custom to celebrate every victory over another race by transplanting its gods and its worship to the capital. As a matter of fact, these importations exercised no material influence upon the peculiar character of the Aztec worship; on the contrary, the higher the power and the fame of the Mexicans rose, the more eagerly did they continue their horrible sacrifices of human blood.

They were possessed with the idea that their successes, which became more brilliant year by year, were owing to the favour of heaven, which they had gained by their numerous sacrifices; and in order to retain this favour they increased their blood-stained hecatombs in proportion to the growth of their power. Every national festival, every victory, every recommencement of the cycle of years, every coronation, and every dedication of a temple was celebrated with bloody sacrifices; the greater the occasion, the more numerous the victims. Nor was it only a question of thankfulness to the gods whose favour they had won; by these means they attempted to make atonement to those whose anger they had incurred.

When, in the year 1445, a famine which lasted several years came upon the whole of Anahuac, the Aztec desire for sacrifice rose almost to the pitch of frenzy. At first they were themselves sufficiently strong to make captives of their foes in border warfare; the brave hearts of these prisoners, which were torn still palpitating from the breast which the obsidian knife had cleft, were considered as the most welcome offering to the gods.

Anahuac Under a Great Famine But at length their necessities became greater, and their warriors thinned in number, and, exhausted by famine, were neither available for sacrifice nor equal to the fatigues of a campaign. The rulers of the state, trembling before the wrath of heaven, then conceived an idea unparalleled in the history of the world. They concluded a formal contract with the warlike states of the east, the Tlascalans

and the Huexotzincos, upon whom the famine had pressed less severely, to hold an annual sham fight in a particular place, between an equal number of warriors, apparently with the idea of providing the necessary victims for the services of the gods from the prisoners who should then be taken. As a matter of fact, during the years of famine such battles took place several times; but after that time had passed by the warlike disposition of the Aztecs provided a number of sufficient victims from real warfare, and mimic warfare became superfluous.

The greater the power and prestige of the Mexicans grew, the more oppressive they found it to have exactly in front of the gates of their capital an almost independent community ruled by its own kings, the sister town of Tlatelulco. The time when this state could have rivalled Mexico in glory and splendour had long passed away, but there remained a hostile disposition which was apparent in all kinds of little animosities. The Mexicans, naturally, only waited for a favourable opportunity to take their revenge for these; but, con-

The King of Tlatelulco Overthrown sidering the number of enemies that they had both within and without their realm, it was a hazardous act to endanger peace at the gates of the capital by any show of aggression. It fell out exactly in accordance with their wishes that the king of Tlatelulco entered into a most traitorous compact with their enemies at a time when the wars against the Chalca claimed the undivided attention of the Mexicans.

When Montezuma again returned to Tenochtitlan from the successful campaign in the south, he turned his overpowering forces on Tlatelulco; and, in the battles which followed, the allies, as usual, failed to come to the help of its short-sighted king, who lost his throne and his life. In spite of this the Mexicans were satisfied with setting up a vassal king of Tlatelulco in the person of a governor who was unconditionally subject to themselves. But although Moquihuix owed his elevation entirely to his uncle, Montezuma, the deeply rooted aversion of the people of Tlatelulco from their more fortunate rivals won him over in the course of time.

When Axayacatl, in the year 1468, ascended the throne of Tenochtitlan after the death of Montezuma, Moquihuix made the attempt to win back the independence of his little state by force of arms. The struggle is said to have lasted full five years before the powerful Mexicans succeeded in definitely crushing the resistance of their neighbour. We see by this fact how the singularly loose organisation of the states allowed a little band of brave and determined warriors to threaten the existence even of a powerful kingdom, so long as they could rely upon the sympathies of its remaining subjects. After the subjection of Moquihuix, the Mexicans did not again commit the folly of planting the seeds of disunion so close to the centre of their kingdom. Tlatelulco ceased to exist as an individual town ; it was incorporated with Tenochtitlan, from which it had long been divided only by a canal, and those of its inhabitants who did not submit to the new order of things were banished.

Tenochtitlan, by its union with Tlatelulco, now acquired a considerable extension of territory, security against continually threatening danger, and an extraordinary increase of power. In the whole of Central America down to the Isthmus of Tehuantepec, and northward from that **Extent of Mexican Power** point, the Tlatelulca had been energetic traders, and nearly all the commerce between the north and the south had passed through their hands. Of all the states in and around Anahuac the Tlazcaltecs were almost their only rivals in this department, although their traffic was carried on rather among the states upon the gulf than upon the Pacific coast.

Hitherto the feeble character of their home policy had at times unfavourably influenced the commercial undertakings of the Tlatelulca, but after the Mexicans had gained possession of the town the business interests of its inhabitants were also under Mexican protection. From this time onward the Mexican merchants play an important part as forming the reconnoitring and intelligence department of the Mexican armies, and as opening the way for acts of aggression in all their wars.

Under Axayacatl the kingdom of Tenochtitlan reached its widest extent. The Mexican power went at least so far northward as to overpass the mountain range which surrounds the high valleys of Anahuac. Here Tula and Tulancingo represent the extreme outposts, the connection of which with the Aztec kingdom was neither firm nor lasting. Moreover, upon the west the Mexicans made

conquests at a late period and of no great extent. Only the portions of Michuacan on their immediate boundaries were subject to their rule ; with the Tarascos, who dwelt farther west and extended to the seaboard, they never really measured their strength. On the Pacific coast the influence of the central states spread first **Widespread Aztec Influence** toward the south. But it was not exclusively the kings of Tenochtitlan who made towns and princes tributary to themselves in this district ; the Tezcucans also had vassals here. It has been already observed that the Mexican power was confined to a few fortified towns in the Zapotec country ; but on the north-west and south, beyond the Isthmus of Tehuantepec, numerous vassal princes seem to have recognised their suzerainty.

On the east wide districts were subject to the central power. If originally the kings of Tezcuco had here overshadowed the Aztecs, yet the latter, in course of time, had gained the upper hand, owing to the peaceful inclinations of the princes of Tezcuco, and by availing themselves of every opportunity which the Mexicans afforded them. The king of Tenochtitlan undoubtedly may be reproached for having traitorously employed his regency during the minority of Nezahualpilli to aggrandise himself at the expense of the allied kingdom ; but, in fact, even upon the east, the influence of the Aztecs was preponderant and overspread the states on the coast of the Mexican Gulf from Panuco in the north, through the district of the Huastecs and Totonacs, as far south as Xicalanco and Nonohualco to the borders of Yucatan.

However, in the immediate neighbourhood of these allied central powers there existed a point of continual disturbance which was a refuge for all those who wished to escape the ever-increasing tyranny of the Aztecs ; this was the kingdom of Huexotzinco and the republic of Tlazcala. In earlier times **Tyranny of the Aztecs** both had belonged to the Chichimec kingdom of Tezcuco, and in the period of persecution had lent their support to the legal heir of that country, Nezahualcoyotl. But when he entered into alliance with the Aztecs, with a view to recovering his kingdom, his earlier allies broke away from him, and from that time forward created uninterrupted disturbances upon the boundaries of the kingdom. As a result of a whole series of campaigns, Huexotzinco seems to have been made tributary—at any rate, for some time. But whenever the allied kings forced their way into the mountainous country of the Tlazcaltecs, and obtained some apparent result by devastating it with fire and sword, the lawless spirit of this brave little people invariably survived all the attacks of the

How the Aztec Kingdom was Organised motley vassal armies of the kings of Anahuac. Though shut in on every side, the Tlazcalans maintained their independence until the arrival of the Spaniards; and the ferocious hatred with which they regarded their neighbouring persecutors made them the firmest allies of Cortes against Tenochtitlan.

The organisation of the Aztec kingdom was essentially the same as that of the other Central American states. When they had firmly subjugated territories, they made tributary vassal kingdoms of them, and attempted to secure the fidelity of their subject kings by setting up therein members of the royal family, or its connections by marriage. But the Mexicans attempted to secure their hold, not only upon the thrones of their conquered kingdoms, but also upon the land itself. Each successful campaign was followed by free gifts of land and people to all those whose warlike prowess had contributed to the success; at times we should be correct in speaking of an actual colonisation of the conquered district.

Bravery in war was thus stimulated by the prospect of a brilliant reward which was within the reach of even the humblest warrior; and this newly founded feudal aristocracy provided a protection and a counterpoise to any yearnings for independence that the vassal kings might have had. The colonisation and organisation of conquests in this manner did not, however, extend beyond the country of Anahuac and the districts in the immediate vicinity of its southern border. Want of

Provinces Conquered by the Mexicans men chiefly prevented the extension of a similar form of government over the more distant provinces. But even there a victorious campaign was immediately followed by the deposition of the reigning monarch and his dynasty, and the installation of a subject king. Provided a specified tribute were paid, the conquered province remained in other respects almost as independent as before. Every year the

messengers came from Tenochtitlan to collect a tribute, in cases where they were not permanently settled at the court of the vassal king; and, in order to ensure obedience and respect to the king and to his land, particular points on the most important lines of communication were strongly fortified and powerfully garrisoned.

These posts formed a meeting-place for the collectors and for merchants in times of peace and a basis for resistance in case of revolt. We have particular notice of such garrisons in the outlying provinces of the Mixtec and Zapotec territory on the south, and in the district of the Huaztecs and Tontonacs on the east. With all these provisions the Mexicans did not succeed in preventing frequent insurrections, sometimes of a dangerous nature; but in spite of the burning hatred with which they were regarded by a great part of their subjects, on account of their bloody and tyrannical rule, during a whole century these subjects never succeeded in seriously endangering the existence of the empire by a general insurrection.

Montezuma II. on the Throne of Tenochtitlan Axayacatl, who died in the year 1477, after a short but glorious reign, was followed by two monarchs who did not attain the fame of their forefathers. Tizocic and Ahuitzotl did indeed lead the armies of the Aztecs to victory in different directions beyond their borders; but they had neither the personal qualities nor the good fortune to confer any particular benefits upon the state, the extent of which made it more and more difficult to rule. But in the person of Montezuma II. a monarch again ascended the throne of Tenochtitlan who seemed capable of reviving the great traditions of the past.

Before he ascended the throne he had already covered himself with military glory, and he made it his particular object to justify the hopes which were set upon his rule; but fortune was not particularly favourable to him. In the last years of Ahuitzotl's reign belief in the invincible powers of the Mexican arms had begun to grow visibly weak; the Zapotecs had recovered their complete independence, and in Tlazcala the Mexicans had again received a defeat. A few isolated successes did not enable Montezuma, by means of a sensational victory, to remove the impression of the discomfitures they had suffered.

PAINTED BOWLS AND CUP FROM THE ISLAND OF SACRIFICIOS

SPECIMENS OF POTTERY, WITH PAINTED DESIGNS

VASES OF TERRA-COTTA FROM TOMBS IN NICARAGUA

CHARACTERISTIC EXAMPLES OF ANCIENT MEXICAN POTTERY

Mansell

Prospects for the future within the realm were also threatening; the alliance between Mexico and Tezcuco, upon which the power of the central states had hitherto chiefly rested, began to grow weaker and weaker. Nezahualpilli, although his bravery had been proved upon many a field, had, like his predecessors,

Montezuma Guilty of Treachery been no lover of war; and it was owing, for the most part, to the influence of the confederation that he had supported the Mexicans in their restless desire for extension of territory, while at times he had stood aside and remained neutral. So it was no wonder if the kings of Tenochtitlan became more and more convinced that they were the sole repositories of strength and power, and that the other confederates had no right to equal prestige or to an equal share in the spoil. Their exaggerated opinion of themselves led to arrogance; and this produced distrust upon both sides, resulting in secret enmity.

The Mexicans began to conceive the plan of attacking their previous confederates upon the first opportunity, and reducing them to the position of vassal states. During an unsuccessful war against Tlazcala in the year 1512, which the Aztecs and Tezcucans undertook in common, Montezuma is said to have carried his faithlessness so far as to have left the confederates in the lurch during a battle, and to have even entered into treasonable correspondence with the Tlazcalans. Nezahualpilli did not find courage to avenge this insult by an open declaration of war, but from this time the confederates regarded one another as enemies, and when Nezahualpilli died, four years later, hostilities broke out openly.

The king of Tezcuco had neglected to choose his successor during his lifetime, so Montezuma was able to obtain the election of a prince whom he hoped to use according to his desires. Cacama was

The New King of Tezcuco Montezuma's own nephew, and if he were a man of strong character the fact had never yet been made manifest. Character, indeed, was far more apparent in his brother Ixtlilxochitl, who, though younger, had made a name for himself as a warrior during his father's lifetime. But all his attempts to prevent the election of Cacama were unsuccessful; and as he regarded his nephew merely as Montezuma's tool, Ixtlilxochitl might suppose

himself fighting for the independence of his father's kingdom when he openly raised the standard of revolt. He did not succeed in maintaining himself any length of time in Tezcuco; but in the northern provinces he found numerous supporters.

There he might reckon upon the help of all those who feared that the victory of Cacama would mean the establishment of an exclusively Mexican dominion; and so he succeeded not only in utterly defeating an army that Montezuma sent against him but also in making progress, slowly but steadily, forward, until he so threatened Tezcuco that Cacama preferred to conclude peace with him on condition of dividing their father's kingdom.

The kings of Anahuac must undoubtedly have heard long ago of the appearance of wonderful foreigners who had come oversea from the east into the neighbouring district. The extensive trade and the admirable organisation of traffic in the kingdom of Anahuac and the neighbouring provinces would certainly have brought them rumours, and perhaps particular information, concerning the first appearance and the further progress

Spaniards Assisted by Natives of these foreigners who for the last twenty-five years had been spreading over the islands and on the south. What superstitious ideas were excited by this occurrence can be understood from the important place given to discussions in the later historians as to whether the appearance of the Spaniards had any connection with the old prophecies, which spoke of an entire revolution of their conditions of life, which should come forth from the east. At any rate, as regards the Spaniards, the belief of the natives that their appearance was connected in some way with the promised return of Quetzalcoatl was to them a help no less important than was the universal enmity with which the nations of Central America regarded the Mexican dominion.

This hatred brought to their side the large bands of native allies who helped them to overcome all the difficulties which confronted the passage of a few hundred men into the centre of these extensive states, while the religious awe in which they were held afforded them a friendly reception and a firm footing on the coast-land, and cleared the way for their entrance into Mexico—an entrance which implied the fall of the ancient kingdoms of Central America.

NATIVE CIVILISATIONS of SOUTH AMERICA

MANNERS AND CUSTOMS OF THE VANISHED RACES

THE CHIBCHAS IN HISTORY AND LEGEND

THE southern extremity of the Cordilleras or the Andes is formed of one mountain chain ; but twenty-six degrees south of the equator they divide into two ranges which diverge more widely as they proceed northward. At first these enclose only a narrow tableland, on which one or two lake systems are to be found ; afterwards the mountain ranges become more complex. Between the main ridges and parallel with them long valleys form a river-bed to which the streams on the heights at either hand contribute until the river is strong enough to force a passage through some outlet in these mountain walls. On the west the rivers, after a precipitous descent, rush wildly down across the narrow strip of barren coast-land to the ocean. On the east, after a fall quite as abrupt, they reach the wooded lowlands and feed the great river system of La Plata, the Amazon, and the Orinoco.

Many of the valleys lie at very considerable heights—the level of Lake Titicaca is more than 12,600 feet above the sea ; Quito has an elevation of 9,380 feet ; and Bogota 8,750 feet. Yet it is not difficult to understand why it was only here that the native South American civilisation could take root and develop. With the exception of occasional tracts, the narrow

Cradle of South American Civilisation strip of coast-land lying between the mountains and the sea upon the west is not actually sterile, or at least is not wholly incapable of cultivation. But the almost entire absence of rainfall throughout the year, and the heat of a tropical sun, whose rays are here

nearly vertical, destroy all beginnings of vegetation before they have sufficiently established themselves to afford shade and protection to their own roots or to undergrowth. At intervals, in the

The Natural Features of the Country long stretch of coast-line, streams and rivers descend from the mountains, but the scanty limits of the level country afford them no space for development. So at the melting of the snows they rush down as devastating torrents to the sea, while in the dry seasons they are either dried up entirely or contain so little water that a narrow belt of vegetation in the immediate neighbourhood of their banks is all that can find a bare subsistence.

If on the western side it is the almost entire absence of rainfall which precludes human habitation and progress, upon the east the excessive rainfall is equally unfavourable to human industry. Here, too, for the most part, the mountain face descends abruptly. But beneath it spreads a boundless expanse of lowland over which the rivers flow but gently. When the mountain streams are swollen by the melting snow, these rivers rise high above their banks ; districts of such extent are then so inundated that the boundaries even between the most important river systems disappear, and a canoe can be borne from one river to the next. Here also primitive man, with his rude implements, could gain no sufficient footing to enable him to wrest from Nature the means of life. Nor was any such struggle necessary ; from the wealth of her tropical abundance Nature afforded him only too easily the

A FAMILIAR SIGHT ON THE SLOPES OF THE ROCK-STREWN ANDES

A GIGANTIC GROUP OF PEAKS RANGING FROM 15,000 TO 23,000 FEET IN HEIGHT

THE MOUNTAIN CHAIN OF THE ANDES IN SOUTH AMERICA

A MOUNTAIN PASS, SHOWING THE HEAD WATERS OF THE RIVER AMAZON

REST HUT BUILT FOR THE USE OF TRAVELLERS CROSSING THE MOUNTAINS

CHARACTERISTIC SCENES AMONG THE ANDES

means of satisfying his modest requirements, and he became a wanderer with no definite or settled dwelling-place.

Thus there remained for man's habitation only that huge mountain mass which bears in its long folds the peaks and ranges of the Cordilleras, and forms low valleys between its mountain arms. It rises above **Primitive** the sea-level to a height of **Man's** several thousand feet, almost to **Habitation** the snow-line of the Alps; but the temperature that prevails even at this height in tropical latitudes is by no means unfavourable to man and to his requirements. Primitive man here found that most indispensable of all requisites, water — water in sufficient abundance to fertilise the soil, and yet not so abundant as to be an invincible enemy; water, too, that presented him with provision in the fish which were found in the greater and smaller lakes, into which brook or river swelled when its course was dammed; and these fish could be caught even with the primitive implements of early times.

Here the forest offered him a refuge, and, in the next stage of his progress, material for his inventions. The rocks which the mountain torrents brought down to him were ready for him to build with. In the Cordilleras of South America he found two more precious gifts, which had the greatest influence upon the development of his civilisation—the potato, which grew even upon the heights where the maize could not flourish; and the llama, the household animal of the American continent, which bore man's burdens, clothed him with its wool, and fed him with its meat.

All these conditions were perhaps not equally favourable over the whole of that great stretch of country which forms the region of the South American civilisation; yet it is plain from what has been already said that the natural conditions contributing to the development of a civilisa- **How Nature** tion were at hand. At any rate, **Assisted** even in the remotest anti- **Development** quity, these conditions raised culture to a higher plane than it attained at that time among the inhabitants of the rest of South America. The knowledge of the proper mode of preparing the manioc and skill in pottery ware seem to spring from those ancient civilised influences which proceeded from the peoples of the Cordilleras, apparently from the range of Bolivia, where they were

more widely extended than elsewhere. It is in this region that we must seek for the early home, not only of many uncivilised peoples of South America, but also of all the civilised peoples; as is apparent from the fact that in South America all tradition points to the progress of civilisation from south to north, whereas in the districts of Central America the contrary was the case. The civilisation actually attained, though its development was by no means uniform, is, on the whole, of a higher standard as we penetrate southward. For this reason, and also because in the extreme north this civilisation existed undisturbed at the time of the Spanish invasion, while at the same time in the south numbers of older states had been absorbed by the Incas, we shall begin our narration of the ancient history of these civilisations from the north.

The most northerly of the civilised districts of South America is that of the Chibchas. For philological reasons attempts have been made to show the relation of the Chibchas to other races, and in particular to those that inhabit the most southerly regions of Central America **Home of** immediately on the north of **the** the Isthmus of Panama; it **Chibchas** has thus been inferred that the Chibchas emigrated to their later settlements from the north. Others, also, have attempted to identify scattered Chibcha bands in Costa Rica, which are said to have arrived there from the south. But if even their connection with races living outside their boundaries should be established, yet the peculiar nature of the Chibcha civilisation in Colombia justifies us in disregarding the historical importance of these, and confining our attention to the Chibchas themselves.

Their district lay upon the eastern bank of the central river of Magdalena, from which it was divided by a high range of mountains stretching from Rio Funza on the south as far as Carare and Sogamoso on the north and penetrated by no river of any importance. On the east it borders on the Cordilleras themselves. In a few places there were passes across those mountains, known to the Chibchas even then, and on the north-easterly corner, in the later San Juan de los Llanos, there seems to have been from early times communication between the inhabitants of the highland and those of the lowland upon the east. A high tableland, intersected

ANTIQUITIES OF THE VANISHED PEOPLE OF PERU

This collection of antiquities represents artistic handicrafts of the ancient peoples of Peru. The mummy of a Peruvian woman is shown in the foreground, while the poncho represented at the top of the page was an article of apparel much worn in bygone days and is still in vogue among certain American races. Other articles shown are vases and idols.

by numerous rivers, for the most part of small importance, covered with a great number of large or small lakes, and bounded by the two river systems above mentioned—such is the district of the Chibchas. It has an area of about 500 square miles, and was tolerably thickly populated at the time of the conquest. In the Chibcha

Chibcha Legend of Man's Creation traditions there is nothing to lead us to conclude that their immigration into this district was of a late date. Their religious ideas invariably preserve the tradition of an early period of development ; and so closely were their conceptions bound up with the localities in which the Spaniards met with them that they seem to have considered themselves as autochthonous. This is their legend concerning the creation of man.

After Chiminigagua had created heaven and earth, and had sent out the birds that brought light into all countries, a lovely woman named Bachue, or Furachogue, is said to have risen from the lake of Iguaque, on the north-east of Tunja, with a child three years old upon her arm, and to have built for herself a hut not far from there in a flowery valley, to have cultivated the ground, and to have carefully brought up the child. When the boy had become a man she is supposed to have married him, and to have presented him with a progeny so numerous that the surrounding country was occupied and peopled by it. When they grew old, the couple wandered back to the lake of Iguaque, and there took leave of their posterity, and disappeared again, in the form of two giant snakes, into the lake from which they had first come forth.

In spite of this and similar legends it is doubtful whether the first home of the Chibchas is rightly to be placed in the river district of the Magdalena. ' It must be noticed that they were there surrounded by people with whom they were in a state of continual war, and whose language

The Chibchas Surrounded by Enemies was in no way related to their own. Moreover, the character of their civilisation was so entirely different that we can hardly believe the Chibchas to be a branch of the race surrounding them which had attained a higher cultivation under the influence of more favourable conditions. It is impossible, also, to establish any connection between the Chibchas and the other civilisations of the south. They were divided from their nearest civilised

neighbours, the Quitus, by the deep depression which the valley of the Ica River and the lake of Cocna makes in the Cordilleras at the sources of the Magdalena, and there are no coincidences in religion or civilisation to point to an earlier close connection between these peoples. Similarly upon the north there is absolutely no race or district which the Chibchas can be shown to have reached, carrying with them germs of the civilisation which brought forth a rich harvest in the river system of the Magdalena.

From the earliest times the Chibcha district must have been divided into a number of little communities about as numerous as the towns were later on ; for over each of these settlements, with the districts surrounding them, a cacique continued to rule in later times. At first, all of these towns were of an equal importance, were independent of each other, and perhaps were connected in groups merely by their common veneration of certain sacred shrines ; but in the course of time some of these petty monarchs began to enrich themselves at the expense of their

A Period of Racial Struggle neighbours. Around each nucleus thus formed, other families had gathered by degrees, under compulsion or persuasion, until at last five caciques divided the government of the district, almost all the other local caciques being dependent upon them. This distribution was not definitely settled once for all, but each of the five head caciques (the " kings " of the Spaniards) was continually attempting to aggrandise himself at the expense of the others. The period immediately preceding the Spanish arrival was one of furious struggle ; its result would undoubtedly have been the closer incorporation of the political groups upon the highland of Bogota if the Spaniards had not indiscriminately subjugated all the kings and extended their power over a district which reached far beyond the boundaries of the old Chibcha kingdom.

Of the five states which divided the district of Chibcha in the century immediately preceding the arrival of the Spaniards, the first was known as Zippa, or Bogota, after the name of its governor, which is said to mean the sun ; the Spaniards gave this name to the capital of the country. The four others were as follows : the state of Zaque or Hunsa, with its capital Tunja ; the state of

VIEW IN THE CORDILLERAS BETWEEN MENDOZA AND CHILI

SCENE ON THE RIVER CHILLAN IN THE SOUTH OF CHILI

MOUNTAIN AND RIVER SCENES IN THE SOUTH AMERICAN CONTINENT

Sogamoso, the priestly kings of which bore the title of Iraca ; Guatabita, which lay on the lake of the same name ; and lastly Tundama, to which belonged the extreme north-east of the district, from the line of the Cordilleras to the later San Juan de los Llanos. Although in later times the central point of political power was to be found in the states of Tunja and Bogota, yet the tradition of the Chibchas recorded that this condition of affairs was of recent establishment. Between the states of Tundama, Sogamoso and Guatabita the traditions made no difference as regards the period of their foundation.

Mythological Hero of the Chibchas

But if their religious and mythological circumstances be considered, we may assert that Tundama was rather on the circumference of the Chibcha civilisation, of which Sogamoso formed the political centre, during that period which immediately preceded the rise of Zaque and Zippa ; whereas Guatabita formed the oldest religious centre of the whole area of Chibcha population. Here, on the lake of Guatabita, tradition placed all those events of the past which served to explain the conditions of the present. Here in particular was placed the battle between the mythological hero of the Chibchas, Bochica, who was certainly an incarnation of the sun, and his wife Chia, an incarnation of the moon, who was as wicked as she was beautiful. According to tradition, the Chibchas, at their first appearance, were mere savages living in the valley of the Funza River, which was then entirely surrounded by mountains upon the south.

Bochica came to bring them the blessings of civilisation ; he taught them how to cultivate the maize and potato, to make them garments by spinning yarn, and to live as an organised community. But Chia everywhere opposed his efforts towards civilisation, and when she saw that in spite of her energy the work of Bochica became more and more successful, she dammed up the outflow of the Funza until its waters filled up the whole valley, and only a few of the inhabitants succeeded in escaping to the highest peaks. Thereupon anger overcame Bochica. He banished Chia from the earth, and put her into the heaven as the moon ; then with his lightning he split the enclosing valley wall, so that the waters rushed out in the mighty waterfall of Tequendama, and

The Flood in Chibcha Legend

only the lake of Guatabita remained as a memorial of the universal flood. The details of this legend reflect a high veneration for the powers of Nature which is a characteristic feature in the religion of the Chibchas. Mountain and rock, tree and shrub, but especially water, brooks and lakes, were considered by them as inhabited by divine beings, and were objects of particular veneration.

This veneration showed itself especially in pilgrimages, dances, and the burning of incense, and in the bringing of costly presents. The Chibchas offered these divinities objects peculiarly suitable for decoration and sacrifice, since their district provided them with many precious stones, especially emeralds, and also with gold. They had the greatest skill in beating out gold and then tastefully inlaying it with jewels. Hence their offerings were especially suitable for the service of the gods, and the habit of making these offerings turned their artistic tendencies into particular channels. This custom no doubt contributed not a little to the unusually high development of the goldsmith's art among the Chibchas. The sites of their worship—both of the gods and of the dead who were connected with them—caves, lakes, and similar places, consequently provide a rich hunting-ground, and one only too easily attainable, for the costly antiquities of the Chibcha civilisation. From the Spanish conquest to the most recent times treasures to a large amount have been gathered from such places, for the most part to be melted down and coined into money. It is only in more recent times that greater respect has begun to be shown to these remains of a remarkable civilisation. Fortunately, a sufficient number of the inexhaustible and valuable antiquarian relics of the country has come down to us to enable us to form a judgment about them.

Relics of a Remarkable Civilisation

The lakes—and especially the lake of Guatabita—were localities much frequented for the purpose of making religious offerings. The festival sacrifices which the newly elected monarch offered in the lake of Guatabita even in later times gave rise to the fairy legend of El Dorado, the golden man, who is said to have been thrown into the lake of Guatabita. The proceedings were as follows : In all the Chibcha states the accession of a new monarch was celebrated with prolonged religious ceremonies. His coronation was preceded by long and strict fasting ; and at the end of this time of penance, sacrifices and festivals of unusual extravagance took place. But in Guatabita the following ceremony closed the festival.

The inhabitants of the whole land came together in procession to the shores of the lake, and on the day of coronation the priests brought the young ruler from his place of penance to the lake, where a vessel awaited his arrival, richly loaded with the most expensive offerings of gold and emeralds. The four most important caciques, clothed in their richest and most brilliant robes, entered the vessel ; on the shore of the lake, to the accompaniment of offerings of incense, which were continued throughout the whole crowd of people there gathered together, the new monarch was clothed in festival robes by the priests, smeared with a sticky kind of earth, and then powdered from head to foot with gold dust. Gleaming like the sun—and in most of the Chibcha states the kings were considered as descended from the sun— he, too, entered the vessel, took his place **Chibchas'** among his caciques, and was **Sacrifices to** then rowed out upon the lake. **their Gods** In the middle of the lake the boat was stopped, and now the monarch offered to the gods, who were supposed to inhabit the lake, the rich store of offerings, while the people on shore celebrated the sacrifice by dancing to the accompaniment of musical instruments until the monarch reached the land again, and then for the first time began to take part in a festival continued for many days.

Though this mode of sacrifice was peculiar to Guatabita, yet the holy sacrificial spots were constantly visited by both the rulers and the subjects of the other Chibcha states. There were a large number of sacred lakes which were regarded as proper places for sacrifice, and were connected by high roads carefully kept in repair for the convenience of the pilgrims. Upon all extraordinary occasions—famines and epidemics, victorious battles, and at other times also—the kings of the different states ordained festival pilgrimages in which almost the whole people took part ; for such pilgrimages were not only a duty that they owed to the gods, but were at the same time a festival for the people, who were then allowed free indulgence in all sensual pleasures. The main objective of all pilgrimages was Guatabita, the spot

most highly and widely revered in the whole Chibcha district. Probably even now the lake contains immense riches, which were poured into it in the shape of offerings. Repeated attempts to drain it have twice been partially successful. Search upon the districts around the banks has brought to light gold to the **A Lake of** value of thousands of pounds, **Boundless** although it was only the ordi- **Treasures** nary inhabitants who offered their gifts upon the shore. What boundless treasures must be hidden in that lake ! For not only the rulers of Guatabita, but each " usaque," " guecha," and, in fact, everybody of any social position whatever, was rowed out a short distance upon the lake and made his offering as nearly as possible at the central point of the sacred locality.

When the Spaniards came into the Chibcha district, Guatabita had lost its independence, and formed a part of the kingdom of Zippa, or Bogota. But that the religious centre was situated originally in Guatabita, and not in the new seat of power, is proved by the fact that Bogota is never mentioned in the mythological and legendary traditions, while the most extensive and most elaborate cycle of legends centres round Guatabita.

Side by side with Guatabita, Sogamoso (Sugamuxi) undoubtedly possessed some religious importance. The little state which bears this name lay on the eastern boundary of the Chibcha district, where two difficult passes over the eastern Cordilleras make communication possible with the lowland of Llanos. The development of many religious customs shows that the two states here came into contact, and that their communication was not without influence upon the Chibchas.

The bloodless worship which the Chibchas offered to Nature, natural objects, and especially water, held the first place in Guatabita. But their religion was by no **Sun-worship** means entirely composed of **Among the** such harmless conceptions ; **Chibchas** human sacrifice formed an integral portion of their sun-worship. They certainly believed that the sun had been created by Chiminigagua. But this inexplicable creator seems never to have enjoyed divine honours, while the worship of the sun is everywhere to be found, as in the case of the Dorado ceremonies at Guatabita. The especial servants of the sun were the priesthood,

MOUNT ILLIMANI RISING TO A HEIGHT OF 21 190 FEET, IN BOLIVIA

ON THE FRONTIER BETWEEN BOLIVIA AND PERU

SOUTH AMERICAN VIEWS: SCENES IN BOLIVIA AND PERU

Photos: Edwards and E. N. A.

A TYPICAL PRAIRIE SCENE IN THE ARGENTINE

THE FAMOUS IQUAZU FALLS IN THE ARGENTINE

"SUGAR LOAF" ROCK AT RIO JANEIRO, WITH THE CORCOVADO MOUNTAIN IN DISTANCE

THE DIVERSIFIED SCENERY OF THE SOUTHERN CONTINENT

Photos: Edwards and Rider Noble

the " jeques," who were well organised and united by strict rules ; as in the case of all early peoples, they exercised a wide influence upon the country and its inhabitants. The training to which the jeques were obliged to submit reminds one of the manner in which the medicine-man of the North American savages was forced

Fetishes in Chibcha Households to gain a reputation for holiness ; but in this case the process was more systematic. Not every man was at liberty to proclaim himself as an intermediary between God and man. The priestly caste was already one of the estates of the realm : the position passed from uncle to nephew, the usual line of succession among the Chibchas. A period of penance and preparation extending over many years had to be passed through, and the permission of the monarch obtained.

Among the Chibchas every house had its own fetishes : these were little shapeless human figures, in the case of the rich families made of gold, while those of the poor were of clay; they almost always contained an interior receptacle for offerings. Besides these there was a large number of inferior divinities, to which no especial priests were attached, but which special classes of the people worshipped—a worship which might become universal on particular occasions. The temples with their priests were employed for a very anthropomorphic form of sun-worship, and all the celestial bodies were considered as the satellites of the sun.

Sacrifices of blood, and particularly human offerings, appear almost exclusively in the sun-worship. The mode of sacrifice was peculiar. The chosen victim was conveyed to a mountain-top upon which the rays of the rising sun smote. Here he was killed at the moment when the sun rose above the horizon, and the rock was smeared with his warm blood so that the sun could immediately derive nourish-

Cruel Forms of Human Sacrifices ment therefrom. A similar conception lay at the bottom of another peculiarly horrible form of sacrifice. In this case the victim was brought to the appointed place, bound to the top of mastlike poles, and slowly done to death with arrows and spears, while the priests caught the blood that streamed down and offered it to the images in the temple. Greater refinement is apparent in another mode of human sacrifice, where the idea that the

victim is identified with a divinity is prominent. This idea is borrowed from Aztec customs. It is remarkable that for this purpose there were chosen only boys who belonged to the races living in Llanos, on the east.

This circumstance is also connected with the fact that the sun rises in the east and points to the eastern origin of the primitive Chibchas. From the later San Juan de los Llanos there was carried on a regular trade in small boys, whose navels were cut immediately after their birth as a mark that they were destined for sacrifice to the sun. When six or eight years old, they were brought into the towns by merchants, and the caciques purchased one or more of these sacred boys in proportion to their wealth. Until fifteen years of age they were honoured almost like divinities. They lived in the temples, where the priests were their servants ; they acted as intermediaries between God and man in the case of suppliants ; and if they ever left the temple buildings, which did not often happen, they were carried in litters, like kings and nobles,

Youths Kept for Sacrifice in order that their holy feet might not touch profane ground. Thus they lived until they became of age. If such a sacrificial youth found an opportunity to commit an act of unchastity, he became unfit for sacrifice : he was driven out, and sank to the level of an ordinary mortal; but otherwise his earthly career ended with a great feast in which the Chibchas gave full rein to their passion for display in processions and musical performances.

The sacrificial youth was the central point of the festival, and when it was at its height the heart and entrails were suddenly torn from the victim's body amid a deafening uproar from the mob, his head was struck off, and his blood and heart were carried to the feet of the gods as rapidly as possible. It was supposed, therefore, that the gods were supported by the flesh and blood of the victim. Both the Chibchas and their priests seem never to have practised cannibalism ; the corpse was secretly buried by the latter, who gave out that the sun had eaten it.

One of the duties of the priests naturally consisted in the regulation of the calendar. All that has been said of the complicated chronology of the Chibchas, of their three different and concurrent methods of reckoning the year, is a figment of the

A PULQUERO EXTRACTING PULQUE FROM THE MAGUEY PLANT IN MEXICO

A PACK-TRAIN OF LLAMAS, WITH INDIAN DRIVER, IN PERU

THE LIFE AND CUSTOMS OF SOUTH AMERICAN PEOPLES

Underwood & Underwood

imagination, and the pretended calendar signs of the Chibchas are a feeble attempt at deception. Writing was absolutely unknown to the Chibchas; even the mnemonic system of the Peruvians—the "quipus"—was never used by them. Their year consisted of twelve lunar months, which were divided into smaller divisions according to the phases of the moon. It is also entirely false that they devoted ten days to religious contemplation and retirement, ten to work, and ten to pleasure. A year of 360 days would naturally have brought them into obvious contradiction with the seasons; and as, for religious reasons, the priests carefully watched the sun, they were probably able to make the year coincide with the

Misconceptions With Regard to the Chibchas

a little plateau on the right bank of the upper Magdalena River, are to be found remains of an ancient American civilisation presenting peculiar characteristics. The ruins are now named San Agustin, after a miserable village which was founded in the previous century by the natives who felled the quina-wood; but what its ancient name was, and who the people were who left such remarkable memorials behind them, are still wholly uncertain.

The Chibcha civilisation never extended so far, but with no other of the races with which the Spaniards came in contact can these antiquities be connected. At the time of the Spanish conquest, and also according to Chibcha traditions, though these do not go back very far, this district was inhabited by the wild hordes of the

THE STRAIT OF MAGELLAN, AT THE SOUTHERN EXTREMITY OF CHILI

sun, though perhaps by arbitrary methods. The pillars found among people whose architecture has advanced very little have frequently been considered as dials or gnomons. It is certainly remarkable that in the Chibcha district, where stone architecture was entirely unknown up to the time of the conquest, numbers of stone pillars have been found, well set up and rounded, which apparently fulfilled no particular purpose; they lie there as if they had been casually left on the road.

These may be considered as sun-dials; but the entire lack of information as to their use, and also the fact that there are no traces of them in places which are well known to have been thickly populated, make the theory very doubtful, On the south of the Chibcha district. and only a few miles distant from it, on

Paeces, a race of cannibals and restless hunters, upon the lowest planes of civilisation, and accounted the most dangerous neighbours of the Chibchas. The memorials of the San Agustin civilisation must even then have been in ruins and have remained abandoned in the depths of the primeval forest, as they continued for another three centuries, until certain wood-cutters penetrated into this jungle in their search for quina-trees, and, in order to prove the truth of their marvellous accounts of numerous temples of human figures, brought forth from the darkness of the forest the monuments which to-day adorn the market-place of San Agustin.

Memorials of San Agustin Civilisation

Upon the wooded hills at the upper course of the stream which flows through San Agustin and takes its name from the

THE ROCKING STONE AT TANDIL, PROBABLY USED IN HUMAN SACRIFICE

THE ANCIENT CARVED DEVIL GATES AT TANDIL

TRACES OF THE ANCIENT INHABITANTS OF ARGENTINA

town, the wood-cutters found a number of little temples, the construction of which is without parallel upon American soil. The people who erected them were making their first attempts at architecture. They were unable to work or to build into walls the stones which the mountain streams brought down to the tableland which they inhabited; they therefore sunk their temples half in the ground. Great blocks of stone were set up side by side in the manner of dolmens, forming a four-cornered room small enough to be roofed in by a huge slab. One might be tempted to consider these cell-like constructions as burial-places. But nothing has been found to justify this theory; on the contrary, the general character of their position shows undoubtedly that they were intended for temples. It also appears that they were never closed in upon every side; but the monuments clearly show sculptured pillars which formed the entrance, upon the back of which a large picture of a god was occasionally drawn.

Primitive Temples of San Agustin

At the present time scarcely a temple remains in a sufficient state of preservation to enable us to get an accurate plan of it; but from the descriptions and drawings of the first discoverers we are forced to conclude that the numerous carved stones which are now lying about in the woods, and some of which have been brought down to San Agustin, were at one time united into a single area of temples consisting of little consecrated chambers; and the considerable number of these monuments points to a rich population.

The memorials of San Agustin fall into three classes—supports or pillars, which formed the temple entrance; altar-stones sculptured with pictures of the gods in human form; and monuments of various kinds to which no particular place in the temples can be assigned. The temple pillars display the art of this unknown people at its highest development. Though their architectural capabilities were extremely limited, yet their plastic art had attained such a pitch of perfection as to imply a long previous period of development. In their representations of the gods, symbolical tendencies confined the makers to archaic types; on the other hand, the pillars show a realism and a characterisation which tempt us to suppose that they were

The Art of an Unknown People

portraits of realities. But in this case the artists laid stress only upon the face and its expression; the rest of the body is never drawn with freedom, but for the most part is carved in relief upon the supports, the pillars, or the stones, and the figures are usually disproportioned.

The clothed legs and the bare feet are often much reduced in size and occasionally disappear in the foundations. Their pictures of the human frame display a peculiar kind of clothing, now reminding us of flowing robes and now merely showing a waist-cloth. But the torso is nearly always portrayed as clothed with a sleeved garment terminating in a band at the wrist. As in the case of nearly all South American civilisations, the sculptures of San Agustin never display the head bare—from the square helmet to the carefully wound turban we have before us almost all the head-coverings which appear in the gold-work of the Chibchas and the clay figures of the Peruvians.

The realistic character of these heads enables us to form some general conclusions upon the features of this unknown nation. The noses are strongly proportioned with broad cartilages, the cheek-bones are prominent, the lips remarkably protruding and giving an impression of sensuality where this is not the result of the artistic mode of representing the mouth. The eyes, for the most part, are large, with strongly accentuated pupils, of almond shape, covered by eyebrows often well marked. The most carefully carved pillars which formed corresponding pairs display above the head-dress the symbolic picture of an animal, the head of which is broad and rather flat, the body thick, and the tail long and annulated.

Sculptures of San Agustin

The representation has resemblances to the chameleon or to a stumpy lizard; but as it displays many correspondences with memorials of a third race, which have occasionally been considered as apes, but are more properly identified with the puma or American lion, this is probably the correct interpretation here. Lastly, these " protectors of divinity " grasped weighty clubs in their hands; and when the figures of the gods are armed, they, too, carry only clubs and staves. The figures of the gods are far less realistic; the living element in them is constantly overpowered by ornamental tendencies proceeding from symbolism. Only occasionally are nose and eyes depicted with any reality, and the contour of the face is constantly indicated merely by three small right angles; of this there are many examples in Chibcha gold-work.

The most important feature of the gods is the mouth; this, too, is often drawn at right angles, but almost invariably displays a double row of powerful teeth from which the four eye-teeth in the upper and lower jaws protrude. This peculiar arrangement of teeth depicted in almost all their representations is an important indication for the solution of the riddle as to the origin of the monuments: it appears again in a large number of clay vessels with faces on them, of Peruvian origin, which have been found in the valleys on the coast-line from Chimu to Santa. If we retrace the conceptions upon which this facial representation was founded, a clay figure from Tiahuanaco leads us to the conclusion that the jaws of the puma were thus depicted. Thus, we are here concerned with a divinity to whom the qualities of this bloodthirsty beast of prey were attributed. An excellent support for this theory is seen in the fact that occasionally even the images of San Agustin hold tiny figures of human victims in their hands, which for that reason must be children who had not yet been destined to sacrifice. These results are also important for the identification of the monuments of the third race. Here the animal in one instance appears with its long annulated tail above a human victim of such small proportions that it holds it in its forearms. In this figure investigators have seen an

THE SUN-GOD OF THE CHIMU PEOPLES
The piece of terracotta here illustrated, showing the sun-god of the ancient peoples of Chimu, was discovered near Trujillo by Mr. T. Hewitt Myring. Its antiquity is undoubted, dating possibly to 5000 B.C.

ape in the act of copulation; and, as at least two undoubtedly phallic representations have been found in a district of this unknown people, an attempt has been made to connect them with the powers of procreation. But in this case, too, we have to deal with the god incarnate in a sacred animal, the puma, which is devouring the victim that is brought to him. Among similar representations there exists a fish in the hand of a divine figure, and similarly a snake; and in another instance the snake is being devoured by a very realistic owl. The number of sculptured stones around the ruins of San Agustin is considerable; but in other directions similar stones are found in isolation between the Magdalena River and Popayan, and also in the neighbourhood of this town. In Quito we have no instances of stone sculptures of this character, but all the traditions concerning the worship of the bloodthirsty god Supay and his temples correspond so well with the ruins of San Agustin that earlier relations between these peoples can very well be presumed. In the middle of Peru the Marañon and the Santa flow for a time northward in two parallel valleys, until they pass through the Cordilleras; here we shall also meet with a civilisation the monuments of which so constantly remind us of San Agustin as to lead us to the conclusion that in ancient times there was one single people of a uniform civilisation which inhabited the high valleys from ten degrees south latitude as far as several degrees north of the equator, and that it is the remains of these that can be observed in the inhabitants of the Santa Valley of Quito and of the upper Magdalena.

AMERICA
BEFORE
COLUMBUS

NATIVE
CIVILISATIONS
OF SOUTH
AMERICA
II

THE STATES OF THE MAGDALENA
AND THE END OF THE CHIBCHA KINGDOM

THE oldest historical traditions of the Chibchas are connected with Sogamoso. A king, Nompanem, is said here to have immediately succeeded Bochica, and to have reduced the teaching of that hero to legal form. But the purity of the old teaching was lost among his successors. Idacansas, **In the Days of the Legendary Kings & Heroes** related by the legends to have been the most famous ruler of Sogamoso, is said to have kept his subjects in check far more by treachery and deceit than by virtue and valour. In later times we only hear of quarrels for the dominion of Iraca among the different caciques who were subject to the kingdom, and at the time of the conquest the political importance of Sogamoso was entirely overshadowed by Zaque and Zippa.

Side by side with Guatabita and Sogamoso, which may be considered as an older group of states, owing to the connection of their historical traditions with their religious ideas, the kingdoms of Zaque of Tunja, and the kingdom of Zippa, or Bogota, form a more recent group of states, founded on a purely political basis. Tradition intimates that they originated in a revolt against the ancient kingdoms. The first ruler of Tunja, or Hunsa, is said to have been set up there by a king of Sogamoso; according to some authorities the capital, Hunsa, was so called from his name Hunsahua, while others assign Ramiriqui as the ancient residence of the rulers of Tunja. At any rate, these rulers, by means of their prowess in war, obtained in a short period not only considerable prestige, but also **A King of Monster Shape** entire independence. When the kingdom began to extend its boundaries in all directions, its ruler was no longer satisfied with the title " Usaque," which he had hitherto borne, a title which belonged to most of the independent and tributary caciques; he therefore assumed the title of "Zaque," by which the rulers of Hunsa are better

known than by their proper names. Of the successors of Hunsahua but little is told us, and that little is chiefly legendary. For instance, Tomagata is said to have been a kind of human monster with four ears and a long rat's tail, who by means of his piety acquired all kinds of magical powers, which he did not employ, for the benefit of his subjects.

Another ruler, whose government lasted until the arrival of the Spaniards in South America, though not in the Chibcha district, has been shrouded in legend. He is said to have sprung directly from the sun, the rays of which made a daughter of the cacique of Guacheta pregnant. As a child of the sun he enjoyed reputation for many years before he gained any temporal power. But when the ruling zaque made himself hated by his people for his tyranny, Garanchacha placed himself at the head of the revolt and easily gained a victory which at once gave him **A Son of the Sun** the position of a zaque. A change of residence from Ramiriqui to Tunja (Hunsa) has been ascribed to him, and the isolated stone pillars, to which reference has been made, have been connected with his rule. He is said to have proposed to build a magnificent temple to his father, the sun-god, in the neighbourhood of Hunsa, and for this reason he had those pillars brought from a distance; they were transported only by night, that the people might believe that the gods themselves created the material for their temples. But before the work was ended news came to the king of the arrival of the Spaniards on the lower Magdalena River, and for this reason temple building was suspended.

Fully to estimate the value of this tradition it is highly important to observe that a zaque named Garanchacha can find no place in the dynasty of the kings of Tunja, at any rate in so far as their names have been transmitted to us in the histories of the battles with the Zippas.

The only kingdom in the Chibcha districts upon the history and civilisation of which we have any detailed information is that of Bogota. Its kings played a part similar to that of the Aztecs in Mexico and the Incas in Peru, and, like them, so attracted the attention of the conquerors that other races and states were wholly disregarded. It is true that even in this case the traditions do not go back very far; and if we consider the entire lack of any aids to the memory we cannot be surprised at the fact. Originally the ruler of Bogota (Bacata) was merely a vassal (usaque) of the king of Guatabita. He was, however, obliged to protect the south-west boundaries of his kingdom from the constant incursions of the savage cannibal Muzos and Panches. The military power developed in these efforts very soon gave him a considerable preponderance over the other usaques, and he became, as it were, the generalissimo of the combined forces of Guatabita.

To protect their boundaries the Chibcha rulers in early times formed a special regiment of warriors, the guechas. This force **The Warrior Caste** was recruited from the whole dominion, underwent special training under the king's personal observation, and was then stationed on the borders. As the usaques, or caciques, were taken exclusively from the warrior caste, the road to high position lay open to every man who could distinguish himself by especial bravery, although, as a rule, the usaque nobility stood aloof from the lower orders. A kind of military organisation existed in times of peace; the usaques upon the borders were the commanders of the portions of the warrior class there stationed, and brought up their contingents if war broke out in another part of the district, however distant from the boundary entrusted to themselves. For this object the separate usaques carried different standards by which they could be recognised both in battle and in camp.

The guechas also had a particular dress assigned to them. Like all members of the Chibcha races, they never wore their head bare. They wore a head-dress not unlike a cap, the hair being closely cropped; and it was a special privilege of their rank to pierce their ears, their nostrils, and their lips. For each enemy that a guecha killed in battle he was allowed to fasten a golden ornament in his under lip, a decoration which considerably increased his ferocious appearance. The guechas were armed with long spears, axes, slings, and throwing-sticks, from which they could sling short, sharply pointed arrows. A declaration of war, which was generally accompanied with particular formalities, was preceded by weeks of religious ceremonies; then the usaques and the **Mummies Carried into Battle** guechas put on their most brilliant apparel, which consisted of waving feather garments, gold and precious stones; and they marched out followed by an endless company of women, who conveyed provisions and large quantities of the intoxicating chicha for their use.

It was a peculiar custom to carry with them into battle the mummies of famous warriors; these were borne into the thickest part of the fight upon a richly covered litter surrounded by a chosen band of picked warriors. As in the case of their sacrifices, processions, singing and shouting, the unpleasant din of their instruments played an important part in war. The victory was celebrated with weeks of festivals and dances and rich thank-offerings to the gods; but a defeat, too, was the occasion for expiatory offerings to appease the divinities whose anger had presumably been aroused.

From the band of usaques to whom the protection of the southern boundary was entrusted arose, some two centuries before the Spanish arrival, the ruler of Muqueta, who is distinguished with the title of Zippa and Bogota after his kingdom had become the most important in the Chibcha district. He is said to have won his independence from Guatabita by availing himself of a festival at the sacred lake to make an attack. He may have been invited to the festival from motives not wholly disinterested; at any rate, it enabled him to win an easy victory over his master. He next proceeded to extend the boundaries of his king **An Upstart Kingdom of Antiquity** dom at the expense of the hostile races on the south and west, and his rapid successes soon gave him the preponderance over the other members of the race. Partly by force of arms, and partly by the voluntary help of such provinces as were not satisfied with their own rulers, the Zippa kingdom increased so rapidly that it was soon able to consider itself as uniting the whole Chibcha race under its sway. The usual line of succession among the

Chibchas, as among many American peoples, was from uncle to nephew on the sister's side. It was not, however, the royal race of Bogota but the race of usaques of Chia who appointed the Zippa, as appears from the following legend.

The brother of a cacique of Chia had entered upon a liaison with one of the cacique's wives, and when this was discovered and he was threatened with death on the sacrificial mast, he fled to the court of the Zippa. Here he made himself so invaluable by his military capacity that he was appointed to the succession in default of any legal heir. When his brother attained this high position, the ruler of Chia began to fear for his personal safety. Thanks to the intervention of the mother and the sister of the two princes, a compact was made according to which the son of this sister should succeed the cacique of Chia, and should also succeed the Zippa in the event of his death; and this mode of inheritance is said to have endured for all future time. At the bottom of this peculiar custom, which is certainly also found among the Kakchikel, but with a different origin, lies the desire to give greater security to a kingdom composed of many little districts of doubtful fidelity. This could be done by appointing a mighty vassal, and especially a near relation, as the future successor, and by providing him with the means of seizing the power at the critical moment. Everyone who was destined to govern a district, small or large, had to pass through a long period of probation. The test of continence thereby involved had much in common with the probation of the priests; and the priests, too, superintended the ordeal. At the close of it the ornaments for the ears and nose were put upon the young warrior in token of his high position, and his accession then took place accompanied by the most licentious festivities. The power which a cacique exercised when once he was recognised was practically unlimited. Each usaque possessed in his own province powers **Ordeal of the Warrior** similar to those of his master in his central dominion. To him the usaques owed unconditional obedience, but they had a power of appeal from their master, whereas the ordinary subject had none. The position passed from uncle to nephew, and though each succeeding ruler had to be confirmed in his position by the monarch, yet the latter could only nominate a prince of his own to the throne in the event of a family of caciques becoming extinct, or in case of treachery and rebellion. The gifts and the tribute paid to the governor did not press heavily upon the people, and consisted chiefly of gold and woven cloth. Arrears, however, were rigorously exacted. In the kingdom of Zaque emeralds formed a costly portion of the tribute. The rich mines of Muzo, which were then in the power of hostile savages, were but little worked. These precious stones formed an important medium of exchange, commerce being carried on side by side with conflict, not only among the several Chibcha states, but also far beyond their boundaries. Almost every third day was a market day, and in particular places in the Chibcha district fairs were held at special times, to which merchants came in with their special wares from the most remote districts. Long measure and dry measure are said to have been in use; the medium

Mansel
SPECIMEN OF ANCIENT AYMARA POTTERY

Mansell

AYMARA ART: TERRA-COTTA FIGURES FROM BOGOTA, COLOMBIA

In art the Aymara were in advance of most semi-barbarous peoples. Examples of their pottery, given on this and the preceding page, show, both in ornamentation and modelling, that their art had passed the rudimentary stage.

of exchange consisted of a coinage made of fine beaten gold ; and interest was paid upon trade debts from the day on which they were contracted. Although in this manner the most beautiful and costly precious stones came into the hands of the Chibchas, yet they themselves undertook mining operations in search of them. In Somondoco traces have been found showing that they knew how to lay bare those veins in the rock which contained the emeralds, and to pick out the veins with sharp instruments until they yielded the precious stones.

During the last half-century before the conquest all the splendours of Chibcha art were concentrated at the courts of the Zaque in Tunja, and Zippa in Bogota. It is true that the palaces of these rulers were constructed of only wood and straw, but the splendid proportions of their design impressed even the Spaniards. A double wall of palisades surrounded the palace quarters, which were **Splendid** of considerable extent, and, **Palaces of Wood** being covered with a roof **and Straw** of waterproof tapestry, formed a dry promenade. The outer stockade was interrupted at intervals with masts. It was further decorated with little pieces of gold plate ; these moved with every breath of wind, glistened in the sunlight, and made a metallic noise as they clashed together. The interior of the court was kept scrupulously clean, and contained a

large number of rooms wherein the ruler and his court resided and where his treasures were kept. The buildings in which the ruler received his subjects were naturally fitted up at the greatest expense.

As in the case of the temples, so also in the palaces of the Zippa, the foundations of the main pillars were laid upon the corpses of victims who were apparently buried alive and crushed to death when the pillar was raised ; the offering of their blood to the gods was supposed to preserve the house from ill fortune. The walls were constructed of wood and the roofs of straw, but of these materials nothing was visible from within. The floor was thickly covered with clean mats ; the walls and roof were hung with different coloured tapestry, decorated with golden ornaments and richly adorned with precious stones. The ruler sat upon a throne of wood which was richly overlaid with gold, surrounded by the highest priests and dignitaries.

No subject dared approach him without bringing some gift, and then he was allowed to enter only with head bowed and eyes fixed on the floor. He was obliged either to maintain this posture or to turn away from the king as long as he remained in his presence ; no one was sufficiently honourable to look him in the face, as to be placed face to face with the monarch was equivalent to a sentence of death. The ruler's feet were never allowed to touch the floor ; if the necessities of religion or war obliged him to leave his palace, he changed his throne for an open litter, decorated no less richly with gold and precious stones, which was carried on the shoulders of four men. A numerous escort invariably accompanied the monarch. At the head of the procession were

A King with Two Hundred Wives servants who swept the streets before him and laid down carpets ; then followed a band of musicians and a numerous bodyguard composed of priests and dignitaries. The common people, for whom each exit of the ruler was a festival, brought up the rear.

In the immediate neighbourhood of the palace, though not within its limits, were the dwellings of the king's wives; of these the last Zippa is said to have had as many as two hundred. Only one among these ranked as a legal wife, and her privileges were by no means insignificant ; among others she is said to have had the right of enforcing a prescribed period of continence upon her husband at her death. It is related of the wives of the usaques, each of whom is said to have had a considerable number, that they were allowed to punish misconduct in their husbands with stripes, as they were not subject to the laws which governed the common people. Adultery among women was visited with stern punishment upon both them and their paramours ; upon mere suspicion, upon an incautious word, the outraged husband might kill his wife.

The position of the ruler, as well as of individual caciques, was inherited by nephews and not by sons, only the personal property of the dead man coming to the wife and children. Among the Chibchas, on the death of the king and the more important dignitaries, certain women and servants also followed them into the other world. The corpse was quickly embalmed and forced into a sitting posture, while

Strange Burial Customs of the Chibchas the funeral ceremonies went on for days with singing and drinking; then the priests took the corpse by stealth to a secret place and buried it in a deep grave —first the mummy, with its costly raiment and valuable offerings of gold and precious stones, and then, upon a thin covering of earth, were laid the women who were to accompany the dead man. These women were made almost unconscious by means of stupefying drugs, and upon them

more earth was laid and then a number of slaves. The earth was often piled into a mound above the whole. After the burial the funeral lamentations lasted some days longer, being also renewed upon the anniversary ; but the general interest was quickly concentrated on the new ruler, who had meanwhile been undergoing the ordeal previously mentioned.

In the year 1470 Saguanmachica sat upon the throne of Bogota. As the rules of the succession ordained, he had governed the district of Chia until his predecessor's death. Even at that time the kingdom of Zippa had attained important dimensions. Saguanmachica, however, contributed not a little by his conquests to gain for it that leading position among the Chibchas which it retained until the arrival of the Spaniards. His predecessors had already turned their arms against the foreign states around them, and had also subdued many of the kindred Chibcha peoples. Saguanmachica attacked the caciques of Fusagasuga on the farther side of the Pasca River and easily won a brilliant victory. But it led to important

Nemequene the Great Zippa King consequences ; the king of Guatabita felt himself insecure and opened hostilities himself to anticipate a Zippa attack. Saguanmachica energetically repulsed him and penetrated into the land of Guatabita ; but his victorious career was checked by the most powerful Chibcha king, the Zaque Michua, of Hunsa, who came to the help of Guatabita and threatened the boundaries of Bogota.

Neither of these warriors seems to have been prepared for a decisive battle. Affairs relapsed to their former position, and the robber inroads of the neighbouring savage tribes gave the Zippa king so much to do that he was obliged to put off his campaign of revenge against the zaque from year to year. As soon as Saguanmachica had re-established peace upon his borders, he again overran the land of Guatabita and menaced the Hunsa boundaries from that point. But before he reached their country Michua marched against him with a powerful army, and both leaders perished in the furious battle which ensued.

Success finally rested with the Bogota, but, panic-stricken at the death of their king, they eventually relinquished the fruits of victory and returned home. The successor to the Zippa throne was Nemequene, the most important ruler that the land ever possessed. He, too, had previously been cacique of Chia, and his nephew, Tisquesusa, succeeded him in that position. The Fusagasugas, who had recently been subdued, considered this a favourable opportunity to regain their independence ; at the same time the Zipaquira, the Nemza, and those hereditary enemies, the savage Panches, made an inroad into the country.

Nemequene showed himself equal to every danger ; with one army he repulsed the external enemy while Tisquesusa subdued the rebels with another. After that he took up Saguanmachica's plans for conquest. Guatabita fell into his hands rather by treachery than by force. The people of Guatabita were the cleverest goldsmiths in the Chibcha district ; they displayed the highest skill in covering stone figures with finely beaten gold, on which those artistic little engravings peculiar to the Chibcha art were produced, representing men and beasts individually and in groups. Consequently, every king, every usaque, every cacique, was anxious to have one or more of the Guatabita goldsmiths.

Two Warriors for One Goldsmith But the monarch desired to turn the artistic skill of his subjects to his own advantage, and demanded that two warriors should enter his service in return for every goldsmith that he sent abroad. This fact gave the Zippa his opening.

He and his caciques suddenly expressed a desire for numerous goldsmiths ; and the best warriors of Bogota went to the court of Guatabita in their place. There they not only formed a combination among themselves, but by means of persuasion and presents succeded in winning over numerous allies among the other foreigners. By these means the Zippa got the border fortress of Guasca into his power, and when one day he suddenly appeared before the capital of Guatabita there was no one to oppose him. The king and his escort were killed in the palace, and his territory was incorporated with the kingdom of Bogota, and placed under the government of a brother of Nemequene.

The next object of Nemequene's attacks was the ruler of Ubaque. It was only after several months of fierce warfare that he made his submission to the Zippa and gave him his two daughters to wife ; but the conclusion of peace brought a considerable accession of territory to the Zippa kingdom, although he left the ruler of Ubaque in possession of his dominions as a vassal prince. While Nemequene was thus rounding off the boundaries of his kingdom by these little conquests, a grave danger was threatening its internal peace. The brother of the monarch, who had been made governor of Guatabita, succeeded, partly by treachery and partly by force, **Fate of a Robber Governor** in getting possession of the fortress where the prince of Ubaque kept his rich treasures. But before the robber could carry off his booty he was surrounded by the troops of the Ubaque, reduced to starvation, and finally killed in an attempt to break through the lines of the besiegers, after throwing the treasures into a neighbouring lake. Though his attack was entirely justified, the Ubaque was afraid of the anger of the Zippa, whose brother, the governor, had been killed. The rich presents which he sent to Nemequene were not received until he had appeared at court to plead his cause in person. But when he related to the monarch a full and truthful account of the circumstances, Nemequene recognised the injustice that his brother had committed, and took no action against the Ubaque.

Nemequene's love of justice was equal to his reputation as a warrior ; all the laws that were in force in the Chibcha district at the time of the Spanish conquest were ascribed to him. The number of these regulations was certainly limited, and the punishments assigned were severe. Death in different forms was the punishment for murder, desertion, rape, incest, and sodomy ; a coward was clothed in woman's garments and given woman's work to do. The apparel and the ornaments of high rank were forbidden to the common people ; only the usaques were allowed to bore their ears and noses for the wearing of ornaments. To be carried in a litter was the exclusive privilege of the king and of those to whom he might grant permission. Among the **A Rude Law- Giver** regulations of the civil law which testify to greater progress in the idea of justice we have the following : The property of a man who died without heirs invariably came to the monarch ; if a wife died in childbed, and the child also, the husband was obliged by law to recompense his wife's family, though, however, no such recompense was necessary if the child lived, he being then responsible only for its maintenance.

Throughout his rule Nemequene had never forgotten to prepare for a decisive battle with the Zaque. Quemuenchatocha, a boy aged eighteen years, had succeeded Michua in Tunja, and no doubt it was owing to his youth that war was not begun on his side first. But Nemequene could not resign the traditional claims of his predecessors to supremacy. He therefore, with a powerful army, began the subjugation of the vassals of the Zaque. After his first successes, he sent a message to the Zaque, advising him to recognise his supremacy if he did not wish to risk being driven from his kingdom. But the Zaque was not a man to be easily frightened.

Zippa versus Zaque

He knew that he might reckon upon the support of all those who, like himself, were threatened with the encroachments of the Zippa; a powerful army soon came to him from the Iraca of Sogamoso. The battle was hotly disputed and for a long time remained indecisive; both monarchs were visible far and wide as they were borne in their gleaming litters above the heads of the multitude, hurrying among the bands of warriors, and exciting them to the highest displays of courage. Then the Zippa advanced too far to the front, and received an enemy's arrow in the breast. In vain did he exhort his men to stand fast. The news spread rapidly through their ranks, and the troops of the Zaque attacked with redoubled vigour, and won a complete victory. The defeated army was finally obliged to return to Bogota after abandoning all its previous conquests, the Zaque making only a show of pursuit.

Nemequene returned to his capital still alive, but five days afterwards he succumbed to his wound. His successor, Tisquesusa, who had already won a high reputation as governor of Chia, immediately upon his accession resumed the war with the Zaque. His first campaign brought about the subjection of a number of usaques who had hitherto been the vassals of the king of Tunja. He was already preparing for a decisive conflict with his adversary when news came to him that an invasion had been made into the Chibcha district by a powerful foreign enemy—the expedition of Queseda and his comrades. Here, as everywhere, the Spaniards won a brilliant victory at the first onset, and this they chiefly owed to the fear which their horses inspired in the natives. Tisquesusa fled into the woods; but his retreat was betrayed and he was crushed. His successor submitted to the foreign enemy. The Zaque awaited the Spaniards in haughty neutrality without offering resistance; for that reason he was not deprived of the throne, but died a natural death soon afterwards.

Many of the rulers continued an obstinate resistance; but after the main kingdom had been subjugated to the foreign dominion, their efforts were useless, and only provoked that ferocity which so often stained the Spanish conquests in cases where the natives did not offer a ready submission. Upon the death of Tisquesusa, the loosely organised kingdom of the Chibchas collapsed. The people never again were strong enough to attempt the recovery of their independence. In a very few years the Spaniards obliterated the last traces of the native civilisation, with its peculiar characteristics, as much by their oppression of the natives as by the material improvements which they brought into the empire; their introduction of fresh blood rapidly modified the Chibcha race.

Coming of the Spanish Conquistadors

ANCIENT INCA BRIDGE NEAR GUARANDA   Rau

MIXED RACES OF THE WEST COAST
THEIR LIFE, CUSTOMS AND RELIGIONS

AN intersecting system of mountains, where the Magdalena and the Cauca take their rise, is all that separates San Agustin from the most northerly province which belonged to the Inca kingdom at the time of the Spanish conquest. This range stretches uninterruptedly over thirty degrees of latitude, reaching almost everywhere from the coast of the Pacific Ocean to the eastern slope of the Cordilleras, whence numerous streams rush down into the great plains of South America. Here the Spaniards found for the second time a rich and well-organised civilisation in their newly discovered world.

The most mistaken ideas have prevailed until recently concerning the Inca kingdom of Tahuantinsuyu, and, as in Central America, mainly through the fault of the native chroniclers. In Mexico we saw that Don Fernando de Alba Ixtlilxochitl introduced an unhistoric factor into the ancient **Ancient Peru in History** history of the country in his account of the Toltecs; Garcilaso de la Vega has done the same for the South American provinces, by which we mean the different groups of states which are incorporated in the great Inca kingdom at the end of the fifteenth century; this historian is generally known as "el Inca," in order to distinguish him from other authors of the same name, and in reference to his descent from the royal house of Cuzco.

During the sixteenth century he wrote a history of Peru in which such unbounded and unreasonable confidence has been placed, owing to the author's connection with the natives, that the accounts of other chroniclers of greater impartiality have, until recently, been entirely neglected. The work of Garcilaso is nothing more than an enthusiastic panegyric of the dominion of the ancient native rulers; it displays all their exploits in the clearest light, but sometimes fails to see, or entirely neglects, the shady side of their history. In particular the struggles which must have endured during thousands of years of previous development are dismissed as being the work of the Incas, although their dominion was only a few centuries old, and although their state was certainly the youngest among the **Civilisation Under the Incas** different civilisations of South America. The extensive district which was afterwards subject to the Inca rule contained numerous centres of civilisation from the earliest times. It is as difficult here as in the case of the northern civilisation to decide whether the amount of culture which they all possessed, and which shows their connection with a particular civilisation, enables us to conclude the exact amount of culture that had been attained by the inhabitants before this disruption into separate races and peoples.

In the history of human development the same phenomena continually occur under different circumstances; and care must be exercised in deciding whether coincidences and connections belong to a previous relationship or are rather results of earlier collateral influences. If such an early relationship existed at all, it must at any rate be referred to times earlier than the foundation of the kingdom of Peru, which is said to have taken place at the beginning of the Christian era.

This tradition is due to the influence of that desire so remarkable among the Mexican chroniclers to make the history of their own country synchronise with the history of the Old World. The different civilisations within the Inca kingdom were **Light on Ancient Races** situated in districts inhabited by at least three races which can be clearly distinguished on linguistic grounds. Geographical causes gave such a peculiar character to the development of each of these that the possibility of their common origin is counterbalanced by the difference in their monuments. Perhaps closer relations existed between special groups of these nations. The kingdoms of Quito, of Chanchan, and the more southern provinces on the coast, seem to have been in closer connection with one another than with the Peruvians of the highlands, the Quechua and Aymara. It can hardly be doubted that these latter were the originators of that civilisation which the Incas later made the common pro-

Traces of the Aymara Civilisation perty of all their subjects. In recent times the Aymara ran the risk of having a part ascribed to them in South America similar to that which was attributed to the Toltecs in Central America.

Early settlements on the most northern boundary of this civilised district have been ascribed to them, and to the influence of their migrations has been attributed all traces of unusual culture which have been discovered from Colombia as far south as Chili and beyond the eastern Cordilleras into the Argentine district of Catamarca. On the other hand, we may consider it as proved that the Aymara were the authors of the remains of a particular civilisation, and one by no means despicable, existing upon the south-east of Tahuantinsuyu around the lake of Titicaca. We may also ascribe to the influence of this ancient civilisation the existence of the fine, artistically wrought pottery that has been brought to light upon the borders of Gran Chaco, now almost inaccessible to the white man, in a district that has been inhabited only by nomad Indians within human memory. This pottery displays ornamentation, not only in colours but also in modelling, of a kind that has been met with but rarely without the boundaries of the ancient civilised peoples.

But the peculiarities of the Aymara civilisation are so distinct and so entirely consequent upon the geographical conditions of their early home that they do not justify us in attributing the origin of all civilisation exclusively to this people.

Evolution of the Quito State That of the Aymara must rather be considered with the civilisation of the Quitu and of the Yunga as merely one of the factors which go to make up the general picture of South American civilisation. Among those states which were incorporated with the Inca kingdom at the time of the Spanish conquest, but which could point to a long period of independent development, the most northerly was Quito. Its inhabitants were called Cara.

They did not, however, consider their origin to have been in this district, but supposed themselves to have invaded, between the ninth and tenth centuries of our era, the territory which they possessed about the sixteenth century. Here they founded a new state. They were by no means certain of their original home.

Migrating from a southerly district, they are said to have followed the coast to the Pacific Ocean ; they then entered the province of Manta, somewhat inland, but continued their migrations along the coast-land, which offered but few attractions for settlement. Finally, the Esmeralda River enabled them to gain the richer and healthier valleys of the mountains. The population in these was dense, but uncivilised, and could offer no lasting resistance to the more highly developed military skill of the Cara, and about the year 1000 a king named Quitu firmly established their rule. He created the organisation of the country, one of those close oligarchical monarchies which are found almost everywhere among the early races of America. He introduced the worship of the sun and moon among all

Dynasty Founded by Quitu the peoples he subjugated, and was the founder of a dynasty which ruled for several centuries over the Quito kingdom. His successors at first proceeded to extend the boundaries of the kingdom upon the north ; the peoples in that direction were as primitive as those which had been subjugated in the centre of the kingdom, and conquest in this direction was limited only by the difficulty of establishing lines of communication with their base of operations.

Matters were different toward the south. The later Scyris, the kings of Quito, soon began to turn their arms in that direction, but in the well-organised state of Puruha they soon met with a resistance which entirely barred their progress. After the two rulers had measured their strength, with indecisive results to either side, they concluded a treaty which was to do away with all possibility of hostilities for the future. Up till now the throne of Quito had descended eleven times from father to son, or, failing an immediate heir, from uncle to nephew, according to the custom of the land. Chance then brought it about that the Scyri possessed neither son nor nephew to take up the reins of government, but only a daughter. At such a conjuncture the princes and caciques of the realm had the right to elect a new Scyri ; but the king was able to persuade them to alter these rules for the succession, and made a compact with the king of Puruha according to which his son was to marry the princess and ascend the throne of Quito, thereby fusing the two kingdoms into one. In this newly formed kingdom the town of Quito remained the capital, and all the more so as upon the southward the clouds of Peruvian conquest began to lower threateningly.

Quito was a kingdom not only extensive and rich, but also well organised and civilised—a prize to excite the desires of any monarch anxious for conquest. Though the Cara did not understand, as the Peruvians did, the art of laying down high-roads and building bridges in their country, they were by no means despicable architects. The king had laid out gardens and built palaces in Liribamba among a number of little lakes connected by canals ; and these formed not only a royal palace worthy of a mighty prince, but also a strong fortress in which an army of thousands of warriors might offer **The Cara and Puruha in Warfare** a vigorous resistance to their opponents. The soldiers of the Cara and Puruha were armed only with spear and sling, but they used these weapons with most astonishing accuracy, as the Inca warriors were to learn when their turn came.

Prowess in war had become somewhat impaired under the later Scyris; a generation of peace had produced much advance in wealth and material comforts, but had not called forth the fierce virtues of war. Consequently, when the Inca Tupak Yupanki first turned his arms against the Quitu he met with but little resistance. The outlying provinces, which were only loosely connected with the kingdom, were for the most part won over by the promises of peace which the Inca held out to them as he advanced threateningly at the head of his veteran army.

When Tupak Yupanki invaded the kingdom of Puruha every step of progress was bought at the price of blood ; but when the Scyri general, trusting to superior numbers, gave battle in the open, he suffered such a decisive defeat that the Inca gained possession of all Puruha almost without striking another blow. However, he did not at once invade the district of Quito ; after establishing garrisons in the territory he had conquered he returned to Cuzco in 1460, as his attention was claimed elsewhere. The Scyri died a few years after these events. His life had been peaceful, and he had grown old, before the attack of Tupak Yupanki had invested him with heavier responsibilities at a time when he was not strong enough to resist. But a year of **Inca Victory Through Treachery** battles had aroused those qualities in his son for which his ancestors had been distinguished. As soon as he had obtained possession of his father's kingdom he began a campaign against the invaders ; and although he did not succeed in regaining the whole extent of his kingdom, yet he rapidly drove the Inca-Peruvians out of that district which had formed the nucleus of his father's realm. Many years passed before the Incas again turned their eyes northward.

At last, in the year 1475, Huaina Capak appeared on the boundaries of Quito, but found them better guarded than they had been in the time of Tupak Yupanki. The Puruha had strongly fortified the bank of the Achupalla ; and the unfailing accuracy of their slingers wrought terrible havoc in the ranks of the enemy and entirely neutralised their superiority in tactics and armament. But the Inca obtained by treachery what he could not win by force of arms ; on this occasion, also, promises of peace made a great impression upon the subjects of the proud Scyri, and before the powerful Inca army many caciques began to waver. Treachery of this kind revealed an unfortified ford over the Achupalla ; and when once the river had been crossed the Puruhas were obliged to evacuate their fortress and retreat.

They again attempted to oppose the Peruvians, but so decisive was their defeat, and so general the desertion of their vassals, that the Scyri was obliged to abandon almost the whole territory, with his capital, Quito, and his summer residence, Liribamba. He fled to Hatun **The Scyri Dies Fighting** Taqui, in the country of Otabalo, and, after unconditionally rejecting the propositions of peace which the Inca held out, he perished fighting for the last remains of his kingdom. Huaina Capak then considered that his conquests were complete. But immediately after the death of the Scyri resistance was renewed around the person of Paccha, the daughter and heiress of the king. She did not openly oppose the Inca's power, but she made it clearly understood that new dangers would be continually threatening him from her. In order to win her over without bloodshed, he added her to the number of his legal wives. As Quito and Puruha had formerly been united by this means, he incorporated the country with his own kingdom, and the histories of the two states are henceforward indissolubly united.

If the Cara of Quito had really migrated northward from another people on the coast of the Pacific Ocean, as their legend relates, this people must have been the Muchik, who are called Yunga by the Inca-Peruvians, the Chimu by the Spaniards. From the Gulf of Guayaquil southward to the neighbourhood of the modern Callao the whole seaboard had long been in their power. Farther southward people speaking another language and with another political centre were situated on the borders of the provinces of the Chimu kingdom. Their civilisation, however, showed so many points of resemblance to that of their more northern neighbours that the Incas denoted all the

peoples on the coast by the collective name of Yunga ; moreover, between the peoples of the northern and the southern coast political relations were so close that it is impossible accurately to divide the little that is known of their histories.

The very fact that an important group of states could be developed on the coast of Peru is evidence that this people had made considerable strides in their **States on the Coast of Peru** struggle for existence ; or the country over which the Chimu kingdom extended was certainly unfavourable to a dense population. The ground of the narrow coast-line between the spurs of the Cordilleras and the sea is not wholly barren ; but there is an almost entire lack of rainfall, and the burning rays of the tropical sun have made the country nearly a desert. Oases exist here and there, where the rapid torrents that flow down from the neighbouring range bring sufficient moisture with them to support some vegetable life. These rivers, in their unchecked fury, are even dangerous to mankind.

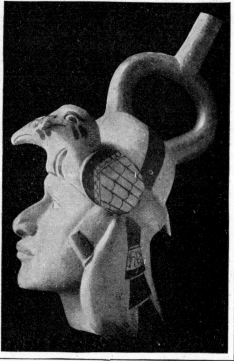

REMARKABLE POTTERY FOUND IN A CHIMU TOMB

Of all the ancient pottery discovered in America this wonderfully preserved Greek-like head, found in a Chimu tomb in Peru, is without doubt the most beautiful. It is the gem of Mr. T. Hewitt Myring's recently made collection. The head-dress probably indicates that it represents an influential priest or a wealthy law-giver. The strong suggestion of Græco-Egyptian art certainly gives considerable support to the theory of an early intercourse with the East.

THE BURIAL CUSTOMS OF ANCIENT AMERICA

The custom of preserving the bodies of the dead prevailed largely among the early peoples of America. The first illustration shows a mummified body prepared for burial, the ball at the top representing the face, which is covered with a red material, over which is thrown a primitive wig. In the second picture is seen the body as it actually reposes inside the case.

During the dry season the thirsty ground so entirely absorbs the moisture that often no single drop reaches the sea; but when a thunderstorm bursts with tropical fury above the spurs of the Cordilleras the rivers rise high above their banks in a few hours, and in their resistless course sweep away every barrier to their power. The period must have been long before man sought a refuge in this dangerous strip of country; but he succeeded in overcoming all difficulties and in wresting from Nature the means to support a population far more numerous than that of to-day. For this the extensive remains of the ancient towns which are to be found at the mouth of almost every valley leading from the mountains to the sea are evidence.

Man's Fight with Nature

The first requirement for a lasting settlement of the country was the power of controlling the water. The people that settled there may have had experience in their earlier home in the art of draining, an art widely diffused of old in the mountainous districts of Peru, and practised here, at any rate, with brilliant success. Where the river passed from the mountains to the plain it was divided or drawn off in great canals which followed the course of the river and led into a complication of smaller tributaries. By this means of irrigation a much larger extent of country could be cultivated for maize, sweet potatoes, yuccas, and cotton, and also the great danger of inundation was overcome. The labyrinth of water-courses broke the power of the flood and turned the extraordinary fury of the rivers into an extraordinary blessing for the land.

A further evidence for the agricultural activities of the coast peoples is their knowledge of the excellent effects of guano. As guano was used for manure by the Inca-Peruvians, they must have learned its value from the coast races, who possessed inexhaustible supplies of this article, for they alone were sufficiently skilled in navigation to import it from the islands. It is certain that at the earliest times only individual valleys

5829

A TOMB OF THE ANCIENT AMERICANS IN THE SANTA VALLEY

on the coast were populated, and as the long, wild stretches of sand which separate the belts of vegetation around the river courses from one another made communication by land almost impossible, these individual settlements lived for a long time in complete isolation. But the more the population increased in such an oasis the more urgent became the necessity of bringing new portions of land under cultivation. As differences of climate, and the hostility between the mountain and the coast peoples, confined these river settlements within exceedingly narrow limits, the Yunga sought along the sea-coast for fresh districts which were capable of cultivation, and gradually obtained possession of almost all the valleys which run down from the Cordilleras.

According to tradition their extensions of territory were made from the north southward. Against this there are archæo-logical reasons. We have already noticed a tradition of migration from the south among the Cara of Quito; it would be difficult to explain the relationship between their civilisation and that of San Agustin with the civilisation of Central Peru if the centre from which these movements proceeded was situated in the neighbourhood of Guayaquil. And as the Chimu peoples extended their dominion no farther south than Lima, how is it possible that a civilisation similar down to the smallest details could have occurred in districts even farther south? It is much more probable that the settlements on the coast proceeded from the south and drove the northern people more and more into their civilised districts, or pushed them northward away from the coast-line into the mountains. At any rate, there was a uniform zone of civilisation in existence at an early period, which embraced the

STRIKING EXAMPLES OF ANCIENT CHIMU POTTERY

The artistic powers of the ancient Peruvians were almost exclusively devoted to their pottery. The examples given above, discovered by Mr. T. Hewitt Myring in the Chimu valleys, display a remarkable taste in decoration and modelling.

coast-land from Rio Maule as far as the Gulf of Guayaquil and contained certain highland races upon the north-east. This civilisation was ancient, and had begun to fade before the Incas became important in the highland.

Individual kingdoms and races broke away from the community ; no political unity ever existed. The unities of religion and language disappeared under local influences, until a new centre of power was formed near the northern boundaries in the valley of Chimu. Here a number of powerful kings undertook to proceed in a contrary direction and extend their power

and Huacho became incorporated in the Chimu kingdom partly individually and partly in groups which had enjoyed a uniform civilisation for a long time. On the south the priestly state of Pachacamak, which was tributary to the Cuismancu, and the group of valleys which was ruled by the Chupimancu, formed smaller states ; either they were obliged to offer an armed resistance to the Chimu conquest, or, like Pachacamak, they owed their further independence probably to the reverence paid to their temple towns. At any rate, they display rich and carefully decorated ruins of that old civilisation which had

AN INCA-PERUVIAN STONE BRIDGE IN THE SANTA VALLEY
In architecture the Inca-Peruvians were considerably in advance of their American forerunners. In the absence of fords, most of their more important rivers were crossed at various points by bridges of stone, which were built with a singular degree of mathematical precision and accuracy. Where stone bridges were impracticable, as in mountain ranges, suspension bridges of hempen rope and woven lianas took their places.

southward, and again to unite in a political unity peoples already closely related. This course of events was in progress along the coast when the Incas began a similar career of conquest in the highland. Recollections of this, which were still fresh at the time of the Spanish conquest, are the cause of the mistaken idea that the civilisation of the coast-land proceeded in the same direction. In the sixteenth century it was perfectly well known that the kings of Chimu had extended their power southward and subdued a number of smaller states. Thus, the valleys of Viru, Santa, Nepeña, Huarmey, Supe,

attained such a high and uniform pitch of civilisation and culture upon the north and south of the Chimu kingdom.

Both before and at the time of the Incas the coast district must have been extremely thickly populated. Chanchan, the capital of the Chimu kingdom, in the neighbourhood of the modern Trujillo, is by no means the only site which has an area of about 250 acres. Ruined sites of equal size are situated in Pachacamak and in Huadca; and the cemetery of Ancon, near Lima, an inexhaustible hunting-ground for Peruvian antiquities, also points to a long-continued and dense population of the country.

FUNERAL POTTERY OF THE ANCIENT CHIMU

PORTRAIT HEADS IN TERRACOTTA FROM EARLY PERUVIAN GRAVES

PERUVIAN POTTERY OLDER THAN THE INCA CIVILISATION

At different times examples of an early Peruvian pottery, much ante-dating the Inca civilisation, have come to light, but the finest and most complete collection is that which Mr. T. Hewitt Myring brought to England in April, 1909, numbering over 1,000 specimens, all in a fine and undamaged condition. They were found in Huacho tombs, dating from the extraordinary Chimu civilisation, one authority placing them at the latest 5000 B.C. The examples given above show a wonderful power of realistic expression, the quality of the work varying with the wealth of the deceased.

PAINTED TERRACOTTAS FROM THE TOMBS OF EARLY PERU

MISCELLANEOUS CHIMU FUNERAL POTTERY, PERHAPS 7,000 YEARS OLD

OTHER ADMIRABLE EXAMPLES OF THE EARLY PERUVIAN POTTERY

More of the fine Huacho terracottas discovered by Mr. Myring. Their splendid condition is due to the rainless climate of the Chimu valleys, the absolute dryness preventing injurious chemical action. The painted terracottas probably come from tombs of persons unable to afford the sculptor's or modeller's fee. Below are various pieces of funeral pottery, including clever bird representations, especially the sacred owl, and three of the open vases with false bottoms which are very frequently found. In all cases the false bottom contains a piece of gold or silver.

Almost all these sites are of similar appearance, since most of the buildings in the extensive ruins are right-angled in construction and disposed at right angles to one another. As the coast does not provide sufficient stone or wood to be used as building material, the coast peoples erected their buildings for the most part of little bricks made chiefly of pounded clay. The walls in consequence had to be made of considerable thickness ; but the breadth decreased towards the top, so that the roofs and ceilings were wider than the floors. This was the case, at any rate, with the temples and palaces, the only buildings of which the walls display traces of decoration in the form of ornamental stucco-work. Concerning the mode of roofing, we can only draw doubtful conclusions. The few roofs that remain are

ANCIENT PILLARS NEAR TIAHUANACO
The origin and use of these relics are unknown, but they were probably connected with Titicaca civilisation.

also composed of worked clay ; but the great halls which exist among the ruins can hardly have been covered by such perishable means. Windows were entirely unknown ; the rooms were generally built around a court, and air and light were admitted by the door, which often took up the whole of the front side. The most important ruins, however, are not dwelling-

houses. These would be made of clay for the chief classes ; the houses of the common people must have been made of reeds and canes, as wood was entirely lacking. The extensive ruins of walls, which can still be seen to have embraced the ancient cities, are partly the great walls of defence of which most towns possessed a double row with entrances at the angles, and are partly the weaker walls which divided the town into a number of districts like courts ; these are supposed to have been inhabited in common by particular clans and also by officials. The palaces and temples seem for the most part to have been erected around the circumference of the town ; in the case of temples we constantly meet with terraces rising in steps, the walls of which were interrupted now and then by rooms and were built of brick, the interior being filled with rubble. Many of the temple pyramids also served as tombs, but only for the kings and the highest priests. Extensive cemeteries like that of Ancon are to be found in many places, particularly on the south of the Chimu kingdom. Here the mummies were placed, fastened in a sitting position, sometimes alone, sometimes in

A STONE GIANT DISCOVERED ON THE SHORES OF LAKE TITICACA

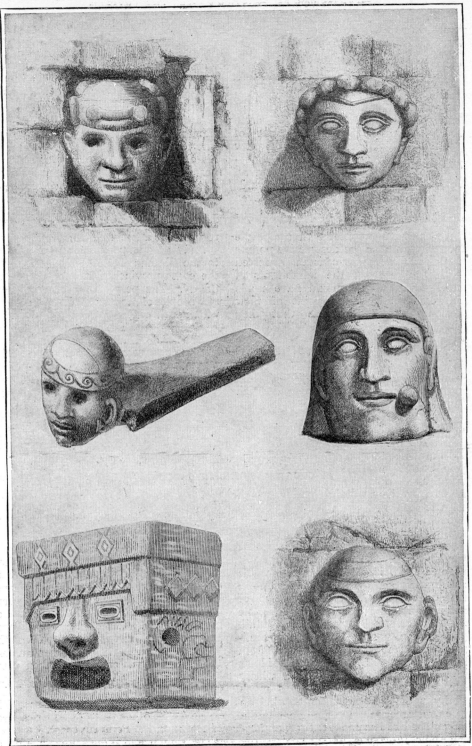

EXAMPLES OF THE ADVANCED SCULPTURE OF PRIMITIVE SOUTH AMERICA
Although much of the sculpture which has been discovered in the Inca kingdom is often attributed to the Incas, it is probably the remains of a much earlier and less known race of people who inhabited these regions. Among the Incas, sculpture was almost entirely forbidden, and in their buildings it was rarely that any decorative carvings found a place.

groups, in vaulted graves, or in enormous jars, occasionally with no protection at all, and often in tiers one upon the other, but always decorated as well as possible and provided with the implements of their earthly profession. Often, however, a common man could not afford the expense of such a resting-place ; he buried

The Moon as the Chimu's Chief Deity his dead in the floor of his dwelling, and the city grounds are often honeycombed with such graves. A people who showed such piety towards their dead must naturally have believed in a future life corresponding in some degree to their earthly existence.

We can hardly conceive that a people upon whose notice the destructive powers of the sun were so constantly forced as they were upon the inhabitants of the Peruvian coast should have made sun-worship the central point of their religion ; it is intelligible that they should have regarded water as the chief object of their veneration, for their livelihood depended entirely upon its beneficent influences. The Chimu are certainly said to have reverenced the moon as their chief deity, and also the Pleiades and the three stars which form Orion's belt. But they also considered the sea to be a divine power, which helps to feed men with its fish, makes communication possible between nations, and moderates the sun's destructive glow with its refreshing breeze. A similar worship, either of the sea or of water of some kind, is spread over the whole coast-line. Fishes also obtained reverence, as being created by the water ; the god of Pachacamak, the chief divinity of the whole coast district, was depicted with a fish's tail.

In Pachacamak we find a body of religious conceptions which proceed from different sources. In the highlands of Peru we shall presently meet with a widely extended worship which displays much affinity with the Quetzalcoatl-Kukulkan of Central America. Originally perhaps a sun-god, he had become so entirely anthropomorphic in course of time, that the people thought of him only in his human form as a law-giver and a civiliser, and as in opposition to the sun-worship of the

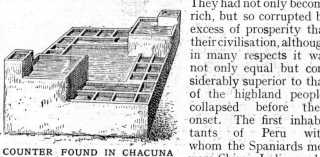

COUNTER FOUND IN CHACUNA

Incas. The Pachacamak of the coast peoples was originally a similar divinity ; as the son of Con he is mythologically connected with the highland god and represents the same idea, the origin of all created things, including probably the idea of divinity, since all other deities are only emanations from him. On the coast the elements of the water-worship were brought into connection with him ; thus he spreads his cloak upon the waves as a boat and passes out of sight over the sea, or in the roaring of the stream he delivers oracles as Rimak (the rushing one). Consequently, he could be represented with a fish's tail, and the fish, as being his symbol, was regarded as a fetish.

Phallic worship has also been ascribed to the Chimu ; figures of clay found in the coast provinces seem to confirm the theory. The peoples on the coast were also peoples of decaying civilisation, among whom such conceptions invariably recur. They had not only become rich, but so corrupted by excess of prosperity that their civilisation, although in many respects it was not only equal but considerably superior to that of the highland people, collapsed before their onset. The first inhabitants of Peru with whom the Spaniards met were Chimu Indians who had ventured a considerable distance from the coast in their rude vessels. As the stretches of land which divided the separate coast valleys from one another were incapable of cultivation, that communication between the towns, which their size and prosperity would have led us to expect, could not be carried on by land. The migration legends speak of the first inhabitants of almost all the coast-land as having come from the sea ; and the con-

Conquests of the Chimu quests of the Chimu, to whom the llama of the mountains was unknown, can have taken place only by sea. Wood, however, was lacking just as much for shipbuilding as for architecture, and the canoe, so widely employed in other parts of America, was unknown on the Peruvian coast.

The Chimu and Yunga used a kind of raft which rested on strong bundles of canes, the air contained in the canes giving it sufficient buoyancy. On the coast of

A TEMPLE OF THE SUN ON THE ISLAND OF TITICACA

STANDING STONES AT TARATO NEAR TO LAKE TITICACA

RUINS OF INCA MONUMENTS IN THE NEIGHBOURHOOD OF TIAHUANACO

REMAINS OF THE INCA CIVILISATION IN BOLIVIA

Peru the Pacific Ocean fully justifies its name, and thus by these primitive means a constant communication, attended with little danger, could be carried on. Those vessels, similar in construction, which the inhabitants on the lake of Titicaca used, were no doubt built for the first time by colonists from the coast district who had

Races Under the Inca Dominion been transported thither after the Inca conquest ; for Nature there offered material far more suitable for shipbuilding in the mighty trees which were apparently employed by the exponents of the oldest civilisation, the builders of Tiahuanaco.

The races of the coast-line came under the Inca dominion at different times. Pachacutek had already subdued the valleys on the south without encountering any obstinate resistance. Similarly, in later times, Cuismancu and Chupimancu gave in their submission to the Inca-Peruvians at the first demand, hoping with their help to escape the oppressive dominion with which the Chimu kings threatened them. The sacred town of Pachacamak also submitted to the Inca without bloodshed ; for the Inca had already learned to attract the adherence of other peoples by religious toleration.

Near the temple of Pachacamak they erected a new and more splendid building for the sun, but they also made offerings to the god of the conquered people, and for this the priests expressed their thanks in favourable prophecies. From this point the Incas and the Chimu came into collision, but after long and bloody battles the fortune of war enabled the Inca Tupak Yupanki to advance, after his first campaign against the Quitu, towards the centre of the Chimu kingdom, the town of Chanchan in the valley of Otuzco. The ruler of the kingdom continued to offer a despairing resistance, but his satraps abandoned him one after the other, and bought the favour of the Inca by their submission,

The Chimu's Submission to the Incas and when he threatened to interrupt the flow of water to the coast, the Chimu saw the uselessness of further resistance, and unconditionally surrendered himself and his kingdom on the field of Cajamarca. In at least two places on the highlands of Peru, before the times of the Incas, a civilisation existed which had attained a considerable pitch of development. In the centre of Peru, where the Santa River runs for a long distance parallel with the Marañon River between the dark slopes and the snow-white peaks of the Cordilleras, until the former stream turns aside to the Pacific Ocean, a powerful, warlike people, who were also acquainted with the arts of peace, founded a great kingdom.

Historical traditions give us practically no information about this ; it must remain doubtful for the present whether the Cuismancu of Conchucos, already mentioned, is not the result of some apparent misunderstanding. Conchucos, which is situated on a little tributary of the Marañon, does at any rate belong to this civilisation ; and the ruins of Sipa, which are not far distant, with its great tombs formed out of cubical stone blocks, is one of the most interesting points whence a conception can be gained of the manner in which this race developed.

The kingdom of the Cuismancu, which was subdued without opposition by the Inca Tupak Yupanki on his campaign against the Chimu, is placed by most chroniclers upon the coast ; and the central point of the kingdom of which Conchucos formed a part did not lie on the Marañon, but in

Architecture in the Santa Valley the Santa valley, the upper portion of which, notwithstanding the bleak aspect and the unfruitful nature of its highlands, contained the capital of the country, known by the Peruvians as Puna. Proceeding up stream the traveller arrives at Huaraz, Chavin de Huantar, and finally at the watershed at the sources of the Pasco ; in Huanaco there are traces of ancient towns, fortresses and temples which certainly have strong affinities with one another and with the ruins existing in the valley of the Marañon, but show strong points of difference from those in the neighbouring district.

The people of the Santa Valley had attained considerable skill in architecture, no doubt partly through the influence of their geographical situation. The mountains afforded them admirable material of granite and sandstone, which the torrents brought down in blocks and slabs to the very gates of their town when the melting of the snows sent the streams roaring down to the lowland. Their art, however, had long passed the stage of merely employing material ready to hand. They understood how to work their stones carefully ; they laid them upon beds of mortar which have endured for hundreds of years ; and the enormous cubes of

AN ARCHITECTURAL RELIC OF THE ANCIENT PERUVIANS: THE MONOLITHIC GATE OF AK-KAPANA IN PERU

Of all the remarkable architectural relics of the ancient Peruvians the most extraordinary is the Monolith Gate shown above, forming, as it originally did, the boundary stone, or entrance, to a sacred enclosure. The rich sculptured decorations which adorn it represent the god Huiracocha, in his capacity as the bringer of light and the awakener of life, receiving adoration from the high priests. The heaviest and largest of all gates in existence, close examination shows that the design is conceived from the "weaving" pattern of the early Peruvian pottery.

which their temple walls are partly built can have been laid in position only through long experience in the art of transporting heavy masses. The most important of their sites is Huanuco. But as the place was already populated with Inca-Peruvians we cannot decide so easily in this case as we can in others which elements

The Famous Temple of Chavin are of Peruvian origin and which belong to the ancient civilisation. On the other hand, Chavin de Huantar, with its famous temple, was destroyed and abandoned by the Incas. The temple is said to have been built with no less than five storeys of rooms and corridors ; it stands so close to the mountain wall that it has been thought to be partly underground, although its foundations undoubtedly rested upon the surface of the valley.

A characteristic feature is that its sanctuaries are all plunged in darkness, no sunbeam ever entering the sacred chamber ; in these chambers we again find pictures of the gods with a double row of grinning teeth, which terminate at either extremity with the two overlapping fangs. We have already seen in the case of San Agustin that this arrangement of the teeth originated from the puma. The theory is again confirmed by the fact that the puma continually recurs to an extraordinary extent among the sculptures of Chavin, Huaraz, and Huanuco, and is occasionally apparent in place-names, such as Pumacayan, Pumacancha. The sculptures of the Santa Valley also remind us of those of San Agustin in so far as the proportions of the human frame are reduced and the head is sculptured in ornamental style. This can be no chance coincidence.

The kings of this territory pushed forward their boundaries to the coast at the point where the Santa River emerges from the Cordilleras, and, a little before its entry into the coast plains, remains are to be found of temples and fortifications

Temples Destroyed by the Incas built of granite blocks like those in the upper valley. The same remark applies to the valleys of Casma and Nepeña. The large number of fortifications invites the theory that there was a continual state of war between the rulers of the highlands and the kings of Chimu, who were in possession of the coast. But the utter destruction which is unmistakably visible in the temple ruins of Mojeque in the Casma Valley, and of Chavin in the

Santa Valley, must be ascribed, not to the Chimu, but to the Incas. After their conquests they took all possible pains to destroy the seats of the gloomy worship which the peoples of the Santa Valley carried on, and to introduce in its place the worship of their sun-god.

The second district of highland civilisation before the time of the Incas has been more closely examined, and here tradition is not entirely silent. Its site is upon the southern and western shores of the lake of Titicaca, and its most splendid ruins are those of Tiahuanaco. The many questions which research in this district has raised will probably never be answered. It is pretty certain that it was an ancient nation of the Aymara race which erected these buildings. One portion of the ruins which bears the name Ak-Kapana was certainly a temple enclosure, consisting of a terrace in the form of a pyramid of moderate height, at the foot of which was a sacred enclosure of stone pillars. In the case of Ak-Kapana these pillars enclose a square room, while similar constructions in the neighbourhood of the lake of Umayo

The Splendid Ruins at Tiahuanaco are circular ; but we may consider them both identical. Whether these erections have anything to do with stone-worship, which was widely spread in this district of the Peruvian highlands, is very doubtful ; the ruins of Tiahuanaco are evidence against rather than for the theory.

At any rate, the gods that were worshipped here were certainly conceived as being of human form. Evidence of this fact exists in the remains of statues which are still to be found among the ruins ; of these, according to the ancient chroniclers, there must have been a much greater number in earlier times. The statues of this ancient epoch, with their artistic stiffness, remind us of those of Chavin and San Agustin. Here also, as in the case of all peoples not fully developed, we find an excessive preponderance of the symbolic and a devotion to a particular style which entirely preclude any attempt at realism. But the gods of Tiahuanaco were other and milder than those of the afore-mentioned civilisation ; their human forms are not the same, and, moreover, their worship was hidden from the light of day.

Tiahuanaco holds also an important position in the domain of architecture. Extensive as the ruins are, not a single closed building is to be seen. That the

A CHIMU MUMMY IN A SITTING ATTITUDE

A COLLECTION OF MUMMIES IN A CHIMU CEMETERY

The Chimu peoples had a great reverence for their dead. Dotted over their kingdom were extensive cemeteries where the mummies were placed in a sitting position, as shown in the above illustrations. Sometimes they were deposited in their vaulted graves in groups, sometimes alone, and often with no protection at all. Decorated as well as the means of their surviving relatives would allow, they were often provided with the earthly implements of their profession.

THE CHIMU PEOPLES' METHODS OF BURYING THE DEAD

architects were able to erect such buildings of several storeys is proved by a block upon which the facade of a two-storied building has been carved as a model. But the great blocks of stone lie about like those in Pumapungu, the other ruined town of Tiahuanaco, and certainly never formed a building. Many stones have

Ancient Monolith Gates undoubtedly been worked according to plan, and prepared for fitting in with other stones, but nothing can be constructed out of the whole. Certainly the monolith gates which have earlier attracted particular attention must not be considered as part of the building, but, like the Egyptian pylons, as boundary stones and entrances to the sacred enclosure, as can be seen from their situation in Ak-Kapana.

The most remarkable of these gateways also belongs to this enclosure. If it is not the most massive of the blocks scattered about Tiahuanaco, it is the largest and the heaviest of all the gates in existence, and at the same time is the only one which has been adorned with rich sculptured decorations. Its sculptures are conceived in a style known to us from other Peruvian patterns—those, for instance, used in weaving—and it shows a large picture of a god in its centre, apparently receiving adoration from side figures.

From certain appendages upon and near the figures it has been concluded that the picture has reference to the worship of Huiracocha; and as this or a similar worship was universal among the other peoples of Peru, on the highland as well as on the coast, we need not be surprised at finding traces of it in a memorial which must have belonged to the most ancient Peruvian civilisation. Huiracocha—or in the fuller form, which occurs at times, Con-Ticsi-Huiracocha—was also originally a sun-god, but in his capacity as the bringer of light and awakener of life he became in course of time the creator of mankind and

Widespread Worship of Huiracocha the father of all civilisation. In this character he himself or his messengers passed through all the districts of Peru from Tiahuanaco onward, bringing the arts of peace and civilising the people, until at last he disappeared in the far north on the shores of the sea that surrounds the world.

No divinity, even under different names, enjoyed so wide a worship as his. The Incas, who had at first been exclusively sun-worshippers, became wholly devoted to the worship of Huiracocha, and he was the only god among the divinities of the peoples they subdued that they worshipped. They admitted him to honour, not only in their sun-worship but made him an integral part of their mythological system. But his true origin is in the southern district in which Tiahuanaco held the most important position.

In the immediate neighbourhood of the lake of Titicaca a number of other sacred towns are situated. It is necessary to explain the closeness of their connection with the civilisation of Tiahuanaco, because in later times they were converted to the Inca sun-worship. This is especially true of the islands of the lake of Titicaca. Legends of the Inca period pretend that the sun-worship had its origin in these islands, but that the sacred towns were none the less neglected until the Inca Tupak Yupanki began to make pilgrimages to them and restored them to their proper position. The fact from which this theory proceeds is that Tupak Yupanki was one of the first Incas to visit the shrine of Huiracocha on the lake of Titicaca and

Legends of the God Huiracocha recognise his divinity. The southern shore of the lake, with its islands, was up to that time obstinately defended against the Inca-Peruvians by the Collas, one of the races peculiarly hostile to them ; so there can be no question here of an earlier possession and a later neglect of the shrine by the Incas. In later times they erected numerous monumental buildings there ; but on the most sacred site, near the rock behind which the sun stood still until the creator, Huiracocha, set it in motion again, appear remains of a character antecedent to Incan architecture. The sanctuary, moreover, is not a temple, but, like Ak-Kapana, an open enclosure surrounded only by a palisade.

Another site in connection with the worship of Huiracocha was Cacha, situated in the valley of Huilcanota half-way between Cuzco and the lake of Titicaca. From their architectural peculiarities the ruins in the temples in that place do not go back beyond the Inca period. Here there was a temple of Huiracocha, erected, according to the legend, in memory of the fact that the god had sent flame down from heaven and set the mountains on fire, to punish the resistance which the Canao-Indians offered to his teaching until they recognised his divinity.

RISE OF THE GREAT INCA KINGDOM
THE BEGINNINGS OF AN ERA OF CONQUEST

UPON the ruins of these civilisations, and subject to the influences of each of them in a greater or lesser degree, rose the kingdom of the Incas. The history of this empire at its greatest extends over an extremely small period, scarcely two centuries of the time during which the various peoples that composed that empire were working out the particular civilisations they reached.

But as, at the moment of the conquest, the Incas happened to be the leading power in South America, later generations have concentrated their attention entirely upon their history and upon that of peoples related to them. The Incas were not the exponents of a particular nationality or of a specially high civilisation, but they imposed their laws and customs upon a large area of country, and upon the basis of the ancient civilisations they made individual and extraordinary advances. In their kingdom, **Insignificant Origin of the Incas** which was finally composed of a large number of peoples speaking different languages, they introduced the Quechua (pronounced Kétschua) language as the official dialect. However, this was not their mother tongue. The Incas were, on the contrary, a clan of the Aymara race, the ancient civilisation of which we have observed in Tiahuanaco.

Upon the collapse of this kingdom they may have turned northward and settled in the valley of Huilcamayo, whence they entered upon their career of conquest "towards the four quarters of the heavens." As they could not reveal to the eyes of men the insignificance of their origin, they created a legend upon the subject in which a common origin was pretended both for their temporal power and their religious convictions, raising them far above ordinary mortals to the level of the gods. Long before the arrival of the Incas—thus the legend runs—the peoples of the Peruvian highlands were living in complete savagery. They did not understand agriculture ; they had no settled dwelling-places ; and their only clothes were the skins of the beasts upon the raw flesh of which they fed. At last the sun-god, Inti, had pity on them ; and so he put two of his children upon the islands of Lake Titicaca, which his sister and wife, **Legend of Sun-God's Children** Quilla, the moon-goddess, had borne to him, namely, the Manco Capak, with the latter's sister and wife, Mama Ocllo. He gave them a golden staff and ordered them to follow the valley northward until the golden staff disappeared in the earth at the point where it should touch it. There they were to settle, to convert the inhabitants to sun-worship, and to acquaint them with the blessings of civilisation ; and he promised them his protection and support until their bountiful influence should be extended over all the peoples of the earth. Brother and sister, with this commission, started upon their wanderings down the valley of Huilcamayo.

A few miles from Cuzco, near the mountain of Guanacaure, the golden staff suddenly disappeared. Here Manco Capak proceeded to build a house for himself and his sister wife. He then began to till the ground, which he planted with potatoes, quinoa, and other plants ; and Mama Ocllo worked within the house, cooking, spinning, weaving, and practising all the **Manco's Mission to the Natives** arts which her divine parents had taught her. When they had thus looked after their own comfort Manco began to fulfil his divine mission to the natives. The inhabitants of Cuzco were astounded at the sight of himself and his sister, who were clothed in bright garments and decorated with shining ornaments ; they listened suspiciously to the message of the sun-god. When, under his guidance, they began to share in the blessings of civilisation, when the men had learned to till the ground and to build houses, and the women to spin and to weave—then they recognised what benefits they owed to the mission of Manco Capak. They readily chose him to be their ruler, and the sun-god to be their god, and the little town which formed around the hut of this first child of the sun grew and increased visibly under the protection of his heavenly father. This legend may be called the later official form of the legend of Indian origin. As to its connection with the lake of Titicaca we may conclude that this did not take place until the sun-worship of the Incas had become reconciled to the Huiracocha worship of the highlanders, who had their sacred temple upon the lake of Titicaca. As this religious compromise took place only under the Inca Huiracocha, the eighth in the Inca dynasty, this version of the legend was not more than a hundred years old when the Spaniards reached Peru.

The Legend in an Older Form

The older form of the legend gives a different account of the circumstances preceding Manco's settlement. One day, from the heights of Paccaritambo, nine Spanish miles south of Cuzco, there appeared four sets of twins who were also called children of the sun; among these were Ayar Manco and Mama Ocllo. Now, the biggest and strongest of these was Ayar Cachi, the husband of Mama Huaco; and his sister, being afraid of him, determined to get rid of him. They were certainly clothed in festal robes and richly adorned when they made their appearance; but they had left treasures far greater and more splendid behind them in the mountain cave.

She now asked Ayar Cachi to fetch these out; but as soon as he had disappeared in the cave she rolled great blocks of stone to the mouth and shut him in. His rage was terrible when he discovered the traitorous deception : he shattered in pieces the mountain which rose above the cave, and the earth trembled far and wide with the shock ; but he could find no way out, and finally became changed to a mountain stone. The other twins now moved farther north and ultimately settled at the mountain Guanacaure, until they finally determined to move nearer to Cuzco. When they left Guanacaure, another brother, Ayar Utschu, voluntarily

Children of the Sun

changed himself into stone, and the others promised to pray to him in the future. However, he put on mighty stone wings and flew up to their common father, the sun ; whence he returned with the message that Ayar Manco was to take over the leadership of the twins, as Manco Capak, after which they moved down to Cuzco and there began their civilising mission ; but Ayar Utschu remained on Guanacaure as a block of stone, in order to act as future intermediary between them and their father, the sun.

In this version of the legend two points are of importance. Upon the mountain Guanacaure there was, even at the time of the Spanish arrival, one of the most sacred temples of the whole kingdom of Tahuantinsuyu, the foundation of which was naturally connected with the legends of the race. In later times this temple, like all the official sanctuaries of the Incas, was dedicated to the sun ; but the legends of its foundation undoubtedly point to the fact that in this case, as in the case of the cave of Paccaritambo, we have to do with a sanctuary belonging to the epoch of stone-worship. This worship was preponderant not only among the Collas on the south and west of the lake of Titicaca, but also in the district of Cuzco and still farther north, until the Incas spread the sun-worship. On this theory are to be explained the peculiar steps and platforms hewn out of the rock of Monte Rodadero, in the immediate neighbourhood of Cuzco, and other memorials of a like nature undoubtedly connected with stone-worship ; such, for instance, as those at Concacha in the upper valley of the Apurimac ; the stone chair of Huillcas Huaman in the Pampas valley ; and a supposed throne of the Inca in Cajamarca in the far north.

Striking Monuments of Stone-Worship

All these sites, which were continual objects of veneration at the Inca period, make it probable that the Incas did not persecute stone-worship as assiduously as they did that of some other divinities; and when we remember the tradition of the transformation of the two children of the sun into stone, and the manner in which their worship was brought into connection with the sun-worship, the inference becomes irresistible that the earliest Incas made a religious and political compromise with the stone-worship which was flourishing around them. For political reasons a compromise was made, a century later, with regard to the cult of Huiracocha. While the opposition between stone-worship and sun-worship died away, it is possible that the former has always been deeply ingrained in the Peruvian natives from Inca times to the present day. And now every native porter who travels over one of the numerous passes from valley to valley in the country adds a new stone to the heap of those which his predecessors have piled up as an offering to the Apacheta, "who gives him strength to bear his burden."

The information that the legend gives us concerning the settling of the Incas in Cuzco is equally important. Before their arrival the locality must have been thickly populated, and the people must have long passed out of the state of barbarism which the official traditions ascribe to all the Peruvians before the Inca period, and have attained a settled mode of life; for the town of Cuzco was the residence of the ruler, by name Alcaviza, who also ruled over the district in the immediate neighbourhood of the town. It was from him that **The Incas Settle in Cuzco** Manco Capak and his little company asked permission to settle in the vicinity. When this had been accorded to them, they soon made their proximity unpleasant. Directly they had obtained a firm footing in one of the quarters of Cuzco they set up an opposition to the ruler and to the priests of the worship that had hitherto been carried on in the ancient Cuzco, and began to make proselytes to their own worship, which was exclusively that of the sun. This separation of parties soon degenerated into open war, the result of which was that Alcaviza and his dependents were driven out. Thus, the Inca-Peruvians got possession of the town which was to become the centre of their extensive kingdom in the course of centuries.

Peruvian tradition does not enable us to determine even approximately the date at which the first rulers of the Inca race got possession of the power. The "quipus," those bundles of different-coloured threads which the learned Peruvians used as a *memoria technica*, seem to have been of no help for chronological purposes; and all their permutations could in no way compensate for an ignorance of the art of writing. Oral tradition upon historical events certainly formed an important part of the education imparted to the young Inca nobles and the chosen nobility of the allied and subject races in the schools of the Amauta, the learned class. But all that remained of such knowledge in the Spanish period does not help us to a chronological record of the origin of the **Lost Link in Inca History** Inca kingdom. The number of rulers who held the throne of Cuzco from Manco Capak until Atahualpa is not even agreed upon. The estimates of the chroniclers variously give ten or thirteen rulers as predecessors of the brothers Huascar and Atahualpa; there were at least eleven of them.

It is a remarkable fact that this uncertainty does not attach to the earliest period; the succession of the first five Inca kings has been made out with tolerable certainty. Discord then appears to have sprung up in the royal family and to have disturbed the legal order of succession. Efforts to hide this fact have produced two different accounts concerning the Inca rulers in the intermediate period, which contradict each other in many details and make it extremely difficult to discover the real state of affairs. Moreover, the later Incas were much better known by their first names than by their proper names, which changed very little; but these lists of names are differently connected in the case of the three or four predecessors of Huaina Capak, so that the reign of this latter king is the first of the events which can be regarded as possessing chronological and historical certainty.

If an average reign of thirty years be ascribed to the eleven Inca kings —the legal succession was from father to son—their establishment in Cuzco would have taken place about the year 1200 of the Christian era. Upon its collapse the Inca kingdom would then have existed about 330 years—an estimate of time which is perhaps too long rather than too **Duration of the Inca Kingdom** short, if we consider the instability of the institutions of ancient America. Although Manco Capak is not really a proper name, yet the bearer of it must be considered as an historical personality. Perhaps the Amauta purposely allowed his proper name to be forgotten, in order to conceal the historical connection of the Inca rulers with the other states of ancient America, and to strengthen the popular idea of their direct origin from the sun-god.

"Capak," in the Quechua language, the official dialect of the Inca state, means "kingdom" and "mighty," and is a royal title which other chiefs assumed before and at the time of the Incas. The same is true of the word "Manco." Its origin and proper meaning are not altogether so clear, but tradition speaks of a number of Mancos who were kings, in particular of those districts which were situated in the westerly and northerly parts of the Inca kingdom. "Manco Capak" must consequently be translated "mighty king"—a name wholly suited to impress the people and to deceive them concerning the lowly origin of the Inca rulers in Peru. Of Manco Capak's rule after his establishment in Cuzco we have only the general tradition that he instructed his people in civilisation, introduced sun-worship, and increased his boundaries rather by the arts of peace than by force of arms. The legend attributes to him the foundation of all those institutions which left their impressions upon the later Inca kingdom, although a large number of the laws ascribed to him would have been useless and incapable of execution in the limited extent of the original realm. The Inca

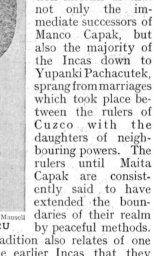

Mansell

A STONE SEAT OF ANCIENT PERU

kingdom, which roused the astonishment of the sixteenth-century conquerors, and to-day justly claims the greatest interest, was essentially the work of the four great rulers, Huiracocha, Yupanki (also called Pachacutek), Tupak Yupanki, and Huaina Capak. These certainly built upon the foundations which their predecessors had laid, but they also entirely altered the general character of the kingdom. Consequently, it is extremely difficult to gain a trustworthy idea of the condition of the Inca kingdom before the time of these monarchs.

The traditions give us as little definite information concerning the first three successors of Manco Capak as they do about himself. All our sources agree in naming them Sinchi Roca, Lloque Yupanki, and

Maita Capak, and they are said to stand to one another in the relationship of father and son. But traditions are wholly at variance concerning the names and relationships of their wives and mothers.

We have the official tradition that the marriage of Manco Capak with his sister, Mama Ocllo, was in fulfilment of a command of the sun-god, following the precedent of the marriage of the sun with his sister-planet, the moon; but this is most obviously derived from the ancient decree of the Inca kingdom, also well known in the later period, according to which that Inca son alone could legitimately ascend the throne whom the father has begotten of his own sister, or, failing a sister, of the next nearest relation of pure Inca blood. On the contrary, another and apparently reliable tradition informs us that not only the immediate successors of Manco Capak, but also the majority of the Incas down to Yupanki Pachacutek, sprang from marriages which took place between the rulers of Cuzco with the daughters of neighbouring powers. The rulers until Maita Capak are consistently said to have extended the boundaries of their realm by peaceful methods. The official tradition also relates of one or two of the earlier Incas that they did not choose their "coya" from the Inca family, but raised daughters of the neighbouring kings to the throne of the Inca kingdom. We cannot understand how Huaina Capak would have dared, after his conquest of Quito, to have included the princess who was heiress to the throne among the number of his own wives, if a religious decree had been in force from the foundation of the dynasty that marriage should be with the sister or with a mate of the closest relationship.

Moreover, such a policy on the part of the Incas is easily intelligible. They had entered the valley of Huillcanota as a little band of foreign invaders, and their forcible expulsion of the Cuzco ruler was

THE INCAS IN PERU: REMAINS OF A BYGONE CIVILISATION

In Peru, the ancient home of the Incas, are to be found many remains of that race, these testifying to the advanced standard of civilisation in America before the conquering Spaniards landed on its shores. The above pictures illustrate, 1, ruins near Lima; 2, a burial tomb; 3, ruins of the temple of Virococha; and 4, an ancient seat of justice.

Photos: N. P. Edwards, E. N. A., and others

hardly likely to win over the sympathies of the neighbouring races, many of whom had apparently entered upon connections of friendship and marriage with Alcaviza. Furthermore, they remained foreigners by their continual opposition to the universal religion of the highlands, stone-worship, and the worship of Huiracocha ; and in

The First Century of Inca Rule
the place of this they had introduced a worship which attracted less sympathy among the people as being less intelligible to them. For the first century of their rule the Incas were nothing else than little territorial princes among a crowd of others. They were totally incapable of imposing their political and religious customs upon their neighbours, and were probably thankful themselves to be left unmolested.

In such circumstances that policy recommended itself which was likely to ensure their position by means of alliance ; by setting up family relationships they attempted to destroy the recollection of their foreign and late invasion of the territory of the highland kings. We may believe the ancient traditions from the fact that they succeeded by these means in imposing their higher civilisation upon peoples who were less cultivated though not entirely savage, while the obvious advantages they attained by their careful tilling of the soil and their division of labour won over adherents to them who abandoned the neighbouring provinces and settled under the Inca protection.

In thankfulness for the material improvement in their position, these last accepted a religion which they scarcely understood, and perhaps regarded the progress and prosperity of the Inca district as evidence of the higher powers of their god. But the extensions of the Cuzco kingdom under the first four Inca kings were very limited. At that time the Chancas were independent of the Inca kingdom ; they possessed a district upon

The Incas Without Real Power
the immediate west of the valley of Cuzco between Andahuailas and Ayacucho, which at that period was far more powerful than the Inca state. Independent also were the Quechua, whose language in later times became the official Inca idiom ; they lived on the north of the Incas in the times of Maita Capak. The Cana and Canche also, who dwelt between Cuzco and the lake of Titicaca, were then wholly independent. Even in the immediate neighbourhood of their capital the Incas at that time possessed no real power. They were connected with all the little dynasties lying over a radius of from twelve to twenty miles around Cuzco, who considered themselves of royal power, only by means of a compact concluded on a basis of equality of justice, which compact Huiracocha, the eighth ruler on the Inca throne, changed into a real dominion.

Finally, Maita Capak was at one time by no means securely settled in his capital ; for the Alcaviza, the successors of the race who had exercised the chief power in Cuzco before the arrival of Manco Capak, looked enviously upon their more fortunate rival. Under the fourth Inca king a bloody battle took place in order finally to banish from the town the restless dependents of the ancient dynasty.

The battle in which Maita Capak overcame the rebel Alcaviza is expressly noted as the first occasion upon which an Inca extended his power by the sword. Things were very different under the successors to the throne. The three following Incas, Capak Yupanki, Inca Roca, and

Founders of the Kingdom's Greatness
Yahuar Huacac, whose collective reigns probably embraced about a century, were the founders of the greatness of the kingdom. With them begins the policy of conquest by which the Incas extended the boundaries of their power in every direction. In their immediate neighbourhood they seem to have preserved the confederation that had been set on foot, but they enlisted the youthful warriors of the allied kingdoms in their service and accustomed them to regard themselves as their leaders. By this means, and through the rich booty they took in war, they imperceptibly gained a preponderance over the other confederates which, in course of time, inevitably became a dominion.

Capak Yupanki began his rule by assuring his position at home. Maita Capak had left many sons whom he had set up in almost independent positions in the neighbouring districts. When Capak Yupanki gave them clearly to understand that he wanted their obedience, not their friendship, they made a conspiracy to depose him, and to set up a ruler in his place more in accordance with their own views. But their compact was betrayed : instead of the Inca, most of the conspirators fell by the sword ; and in order to erase the impression of this tragedy, and to turn the energy of the youthful Incas into some useful direction, Capak Yupanki began that series of campaigns which led him speedily to the north (Condesuyu) and north-east (Andesuyu) along the course of the streams.

From that time the Incas became particularly aggressive and expansive. Hardly in the entire world has a power been seen which remained so moderate and humane in its warfare as the Incas, although generation upon generation grew up in the service of arms. Always ready to appeal to the sword, and gifted with heroic bravery, the Incas none the less invariably attempted peaceful methods before proceeding to attack. Their campaigns were not rapid surprises, like those of the wild and half-civilised peoples in the west of America, when the greatest possible number of the opponents were killed in order that they, laden with the enemy's spoil, might get home again as quickly as possible. Their warfare was systematic. The Incas never took an enemy by surprise; their armies invariably sent out ambassadors inviting a willing submission to their mild rule.

The Incas in Peace and War They said that the Inca, the child of the sun-god, had come to them, not to do them harm, but to free them from all that was ancient and bad, and thereby to make them acquainted with the blessings of a more civilised mode of life and a higher religion.

The more the Inca kingdom increased in power and extent, the wider spread the certainty, even among remote nations, that this message was no empty pretence, but that in reality the position of subjects in the Inca realm was far superior to the lot of those who opposed their rule in any district. Hardly ever did the Incas depose a ruler who voluntarily subjected himself to their government. Incorporation in the Inca kingdom certainly altered the position of the monarch, who became a vassal of the sun's child in Cuzco instead of an independent ruler. The relations of the king to his previous subjects were also largely remodelled upon the organisation of the leading power, but the Incas never appeared as fanatical doctrinaires.

They invariably respected national peculiarities as far as these were consistent with their political necessities; but in course of time the influence of the ruling power threw such peculiarities into the background, and tended to obliterate them entirely.

Upon religious questions the earliest Incas did not practise this conciliatory policy. The first races which they subdued were obliged to receive a common form of worship without exception. Maita Capak is said to have once ordered the subjects of the neighbouring regions to bring all their stone images to Cuzco, **Bloodless Campaigns of the Incas** alleging as his motive the preparation of brilliant festivities to their common gods; but when all these stone gods had been collected he had them broken in pieces and built into the walls of the temple of the sun, in order to show the people the powerlessness of the gods which they worshipped. But even on this side their policy became far more diplomatic in the course of time, chiefly under the influence of political necessities.

The Inca campaigns often ended without the shedding of a drop of blood, in spite of the great display of power they involved. They were, however, always ready to break down the most obstinate resistance. The difficulties of communication in that wide realm imposed a slow retreat upon the numerous Inca armies. Especially in later times, when the kingdom had become of considerable extent, it was not unusual for a campaign to last two or three years or even more. The army was furnished not only for the necessities of war, but also for its own maintenance.

As in the case of those armed garrisons which were established by the Incas in districts where obedience could only be enforced by arms, so the army, when marching out to attack, could till the soil with weapons at their sides if the campaign threatened to last long. But it was only in exceptional cases that an army was obliged to have recourse to these means. Not only the organisation of the troops for attack, but also the commissariat, the transport of reinforcements, and the withdrawal of troops, were marvellously well arranged. The **Sagacious Inca Government** trades which were everywhere carried on in the Inca kingdom enabled the rulers in times of peace to make important provision of food, clothing, and other necessary articles. These were collected in great magazines in every province, and in times of war, famine, or pestilence, these stores were opened. Such an organisation, together with that prestige which the Incas so rapidly acquired, enables us to understand that it was often unnecessary to appeal to arms in struggles with the less civilised races in the mountain valleys and on the inhospitable coast. The feeling of absolute helplessness among their powerless enemies was the best ally to the Incas.

Even in cases where their invitation to voluntary subjection was rejected, the Incas did not give up their policy of conciliation. An attack immediately followed from their side, and the superiority of their organisation and equipment almost invariably gave them the victory. But then the Inca ambassadors immediately renewed their peace proposals, and even then the native rulers were generally left in their positions, provided they had not

conquest the soil of Peru showed unmistakable traces of the fact that the Incas were ready to wage unsparing war when necessary. In those cases they had no hesitation, with an army of extraordinary strength, in destroying fortresses like that of Mojeque, the gigantic blocks of which form a mighty field of ruins even to-day, or temples such as that of Chavin de Huantar, in spite of, or even on account of, the extensive reverence paid them; and here their object was not only to leave the enemy no opportunity for future rebellion, but also to make an impression upon him by their ruthless destruction of that which had cost so much trouble to build. And where a people persisted in

RUINS AT OLLANTAYTAMBO, SHOWING PRESENT-DAY QUECHUA, OR INCA INDIANS

continued their resistance to the last. Hardly any kingdom with which the Incas came in contact during their career of conquest was sufficiently closely organised to make the war one of extermination. Individual rulers who considered themselves equal to the Incas certainly thought it shameful to buy a continuation of their power by recognising the Inca superiority, and they at least felt the full weight of their anger. Yet even in those cases the Incas generally found certain vassals, loosely dependent upon their opponents, who were ready to listen to their enticing propositions and to give them their aid in bringing the war to a successful conclusion. But at the time of the Spanish

revolting against the mild Inca rule they had a still more efficacious method at hand. They not only built numerous fortresses and kept them ready prepared in such conquered districts, but they also broke down the resistance of the peoples they had subdued by taking the most youthful warriors who would have been the most likely to revolt, and settling them in distant provinces among races of tried fidelity.

This picture of the warlike policy of the Incas was not realised to the fullest extent during the rule of Capak Yupanki. His armies were not so large, and his campaigns were not so distant, as to demand a highly organised military system. His successor, the Inca Roca, contributed

INCA SEATS CUT OUT OF THE SOLID ROCK AT OLLANTAYTAMBO

AN OLD BURIAL PLACE OF THE INCAS NEAR CUZCO

SCENES IN CUZCO, THE MOST ANCIENT OF THE PERUVIAN CITIES

perhaps, no less to the later greatness of the kingdom of Cuzco than Capak Yupanki ; but his efforts took another direction. We are certainly told of him and of Yahuar Huacac that they undertook occasional campaigns beyond the boundaries of their dominion, but they both seem to have been men of peace at heart. On the other hand, the beginnings of the extensions and improvements in the capital of Cuzco are ascribed to the Inca Roca. The work carried on under his government makes it quite certain that even in his time the Incas were in a position to employ their subjects in the execution of immense designs. To him and to his coya, or queen, is ascribed the installation of the most ancient water-service, which brought to the town of Cuzco fresh spring water at a time when it was growing more civilised in its necessities and of greater importance.

An Age of Advanced Civilisation

This water-service, however, is not to be confounded with the sluice-gates and irrigation works which were necessary for the soil of the Inca kingdom in most districts to make that high cultivation of the land possible under its climatic conditions which the dense population of the empire demanded. With regard to this irrigation, the Incas continued their long-sighted, careful policy by the erection of works which aroused the greatest astonishment. They are, however, by no means the first to have discovered the art of irrigation ; this was practised to a considerable extent by almost all their subject peoples before they became members of the Inca kingdom. We see, then, that the legend is in no way worthy of credence which depicts Manco Capak as the discoverer and expounder of that mode of cultivation which became peculiar to the Inca realm.

The work which forms the chief memorial, and is in fact an imperishable monument of Inca Roca, is the palace which he began to erect in his capital. Architecture, before the Inca period, had attained considerable perfection uninfluenced by Inca models ; and the Incas certainly do not merit any praise for having further developed an art which they found already at the highest stage of its earlier progress. In comparison with the technical perfection which the immense ruins of Tiahuanaco display, the art of the Inca architects of Cuzco was certainly something of a retrogression. Tia-

The Great Palace of Inca Roca

huanaco is the work of architects who employed enormous blocks of stone, similar to those of the cyclopean buildings which are found in all parts of the world, and who were even at that remote period able to prepare every single detail with accurate measurements and plans.

On the other hand, the walls of the palace of the Inca Roca are cyclopean buildings in the ordinary sense of the term ; the blocks are of the largest size which could be handled with the limited appliances of the time, and are often most wonderfully shaped to suit the necessities of the site on which they were erected ; a particularly remarkable stone displays, for instance, no less than twelve corners.

Moreover, the fitting of these blocks thus carefully shaped, the outer surface of which was generally smoothed, is so exact, in spite of their irregular forms, that even to-day the blade of a knife can scarcely be driven into their joints, although no mortar or other cohesive material was employed. A later Inca once pulled down a portion of the town of Cuzco in order to rebuild it upon a uniform plan. But large numbers of buildings were exempted from this destruction, as is shown by the number of constructions built with irregular polygon blocks, which can be clearly distinguished from the architecture of the later Inca, standing at the present day. The most important monument in this style is the palace of Inca Roca, which was situated in a street of Cuzco now known as the Calle del Triunfo ; its walls, artistically composed of many cornered blocks, were used by the modern builders of later times as a welcome foundation.

Inca Triumphs in Architecture

The architectural perfection of the Inca-Peruvians advanced considerably in later times. Their preference for large blocks of stone invariably persisted, and this to such an extent that even where Nature did not provide the ordinary material of hard rock and obliged them to build with smaller stones, as their subject nations had done, their buildings can still be distinguished from those of earlier times by the fact of their displaying individual stones of unusually large dimensions. But at the chief period of the Inca power, temples and palaces were built with cubes of stone worked with extraordinary care, and laid with such exactitude that the courses upon the front of the building present, upon a close examination, the appearance of level bands. From a point of view at a moderate distance, the whole wall of the building appears as though it were made of one stone. In spite of this marvellous technical perfection, the Inca buildings were never very beautiful ; in their long, massive, heavy walls, proportion is almost entirely wanting ; and as the Incas were never capable of constructing a vaulted roof in the primitive mode of the Central Americans, the length of their buildings in comparison with their moderate height produces a disagreeable impression.

Furthermore, in the kingdom of Tahuantinsuyu, sculpture was almost entirely forbidden. Very rarely in Inca buildings are to be seen any decorative carvings whatever ; the few gates above which a decoration of pumas' heads appears are probably only remains of buildings antecedent to the Incas, which they had pulled down, and the material of which their architects had used for their own purposes. The Inca worship forbade any kind of sculptural decoration, and in ancient times waged a bitter war of extermination against the idols of the subject races; it thus

Decorations Forbidden by Inca Worship became a rule that living beings should, under no circumstances, be depicted in stone. Their buildings display extraordinary skill in working even the hardest rock, and their pottery-ware shows equally clearly that they found no difficulty in depicting real life with proportion and vigour ; but every sculpture that has been found on Peruvian soil is antecedent to the time of the Inca kingdom. The artistic tendencies of the Incas have made it easy to distinguish their work from that of their predecessors and successors. Generally an examination of the stone-work is sufficient to settle any question as to the origin of an Inca building ; for neither before nor after them were blocks fitted together with that exactness which proclaims most careful polishing.

Another characteristic feature in the Inca architecture is that all openings were in trapezoidal form. Windows in their buildings are rather the exception than the rule, a circumstance which increases the gloomy appearance of their houses. However, upon the inside walls of their buildings are constantly to be found niches which served them as cupboards, and these, as well as the doors, which looked into an open court in a long row, and admitted light and air to the rooms

grouped around it, display the peculiarity that the posts lean in towards one another, so that the lintel is rather narrower than the threshold. The Inca architects clung to this peculiarity, whatever the diversity of material and situation ; from the lake of Titicaca up to Quito, and from Cuzco to the shore of the Pacific Ocean, this

The First Inca Schools distinctive feature can be recognised without difficulty. Their mode of roofing must have made the Inca buildings appear doubly strange and ugly. For that purpose they could not use stone, and trees were too scarce to provide sufficient material for solid constructions of wood.

Consequently, the roofs of even their most ornamental buildings were composed of canes and straw, which were supported by wooden posts of moderate strength. The exterior of the buildings was decorated by plates and artistically worked pieces of precious metal, but this would be true only of the temples, and to a limited degree of the palaces; for gold and silver were worthless to the common people, and served mainly as gifts to the gods, and to the kings, who were considered almost equal to them.

The foundation of the first schools in the kingdom was also ascribed to the Inca Roca. The Peruvians had their own learned class, the Amauta ; but these formed only a subordinate division of the Inca caste. Far from desiring to spread education throughout the ranks of the people, the Incas were of the opinion that too much knowledge and power could produce only dissatisfaction, and were consequently unsuitable for the common people.

Hence it was that only scholars of the Inca blood could be received into the classes of the Amauta ; and besides the youths of the Inca race, their schools in Cuzco were attended only by such children of the vassal princes as the special favour of the Incas allowed to come—a favour which also served political purposes, as

How the Young were Trained it made the young princes acquainted with those particular conceptions upon which the Inca power was founded. In these schools the young people obtained solid and valuable instruction ; bodily exercises and intellectual training went on side by side ; and the difficult problem of developing body and mind to an equal degree was thus solved sufficiently to meet the requirements of the time. Languages formed an important department in their instruction. The Incas of the royal families are said to have spoken a language of their own ; this was known to the Amauta, but upon the destruction of the Inca race, before and during the Spanish conquest, the knowledge of it was so entirely lost that at the time of the Inca Garcilaso there was no one living who knew it. This lan-

Forgotten Language of Inca Rulers guage cannot have been a wholly isolated dialect, as Garcilaso would have us believe, but was probably a dialect of the Aymara, which was spoken by Manco Capak and the race which was destroyed upon the migration of the Incas to Cuzco.

It was an act of far-seeing policy that the Incas did not make these rude, uncultivated dialects the official language of their realm, but used the Quechua, which was widely spread upon the north and west of Cuzco, and the sounds and forms of which were less harsh and more easily acquired. Under their rule this speech became native to all the subjects of their empire, so that it is even now spoken throughout the area of the former kingdom of Tahuantinsuyu, while only a few remains have survived of the national languages of the subject races, and some dialects have become altogether extinct.

The higher learning was naturally exclusively reserved to the Amauta ; it was pursued only in particular schools. Thus, none but the Amauta understood the system of quipus, the different-coloured

Ideal of the Inca Government strings arranged in a row upon a cross-string, which served as the only existing help to the memory. This system may have been very well suited for that fixed condition of things which was the ideal of the Inca government, but it could not compensate for the lack of a proper handwriting as a real means of exchanging thoughts or of stereotyping expression. In the high schools of the Amauta the preservation of historical traditions was earnestly

pursued. Epic and lyric poems are said to have been preserved by the Amauta during the Inca period ; but these were undoubtedly transmitted entirely by word of mouth—no use being made of the quipus, many examples of which are in existence, but none of which have been explained or translated. It has been established that the Ollanta drama, which was supposed to be a product of ancient Indian intellect, came into existence in the seventeenth century, and is therefore owing to Spanish influence.

Finally, the Amauta became the repositories of priestly knowledge, with which, as is usual to, and characteristic of, a kingdom of sun-worshippers, astronomical knowledge was closely connected. The Inca calendar seems to have been in a much earlier stage of development than that of many other American peoples ; the Incas were probably too proud to borrow the discoveries

Peruvians' Chief Festival of other nations, while their own civilisation was of too short a growth to have arrived at the discovery of an accurate calendar. Their chief festival, upon which their chronology was founded, the "Inti Raimi," was celebrated upon a date settled by observation of the sun ; this was the day on which the shadow of the gnomon, known as "Inti huatana," showed that the northerly procession of the sun had ceased—that is, that the winter solstice had begun, the day being about June 21st ; consequently a difference between the actual year and the state year was impossible.

The Peruvians do not seem to have gained these results by calculation; almost all their festivals were regulated by the position of the sun and the phases of the moon ; they also knew and reverenced the Pleiades and the morning and evening star, under the name of "Chasca." Pachacutek, the Inca, was the first to divide the year into twelve months.

THE PATHWAY OF THE DEAD AND THE PYRAMID OF THE MOON IN MEXICO

GROWING POWER OF THE INCAS
AND THE REVIVAL OF NATIONAL RELIGIONS

THE institutions ascribed to the Inca Roca show that the Inca kingdom under his government had arrived at a high pitch of intellectual and material prosperity ; but, as will be seen from the following occurrences, its organisation was still extremely loose and in no way corresponded with the political ideals which our sources show us to have prevailed at the time of the conquest. It was the immediate successors of Inca Roca who really founded and centralised the Inca kingdom.

The government of the Inca Yahuar Huacac Yupanki was considered as a period of misfortune by the Peruvian Amauta ; his name denotes " the man who weeps tears of blood." The history of the first six Inca rulers is related by all our sources with great consistency and but few discrepancies ; but with regard to the kings between Inca Roca and Inca Yupanki Pachacutek there is such confusion in the ancient traditions **Strife in the Inca Kingdom** that the number, names, and exploits ascribed to individual kings cannot be brought into any sort of harmony. It can only be asserted that during this period both the Inca dynasty and the Inca kingdom underwent heavy shocks and were frequently subject to internal strife.

The dangers with which the Inca kingdom was threatened resulted from efforts to strengthen their rule over the races in their immediate neighbourhood, who had hitherto been rather their allies than their subjects. Yahuar Huacac had made a step in this direction by demanding tribute from the races of the high valleys, who had been in the habit of making voluntary presents to the Incas ; this was the signal for a revolt which brought the Inca kingdom to the verge of destruction for a second time. The Chanca, a warlike race spread upon the north-west of Cuzco between Andahuailas and Arequipa, marched against Cuzco, under the leadership of their king, Uscovillca, with such overpowering force that Yahuar Huacac did not venture to await the enemy in his unfortified town, but fled southward.

The dangers which threatened the Inca state from without come at this point into connection with those which were originated by the internal conditions of the dynasty. The narratives make **Inca State in the Midst of Dangers** it tolerably plain that the legal line of succession was again interrupted. The official accounts, which always attempt to conceal any disturbance of the political law and order, represent matters as if the legal heir to the throne had, by his youthful haughtiness, excited the anger of his father to such an extent that he threatened to disinherit his son, and reduced him to the humble position of shepherd to the sacred flocks in the mountains. There one of his ancestors, a prince of the royal house, by name Huiracocha, is said to have appeared to him one day in a dream, and told him of the great dangers which threatened the kingdom, owing to the revolt of the Chanca.

Thereupon the prince hastened to the capital, in spite of his father's prohibition. His father did not receive his explanation, but when he had fled before the approaching enemy, the king's son is said to have inspired the timid citizens of the capital with fresh enthusiasm, and finally to have repulsed the attacks upon Cuzco. Moreover, with the help of the divine warriors whom Huiracocha sent to his assistance he defeated the enemy in open battle, and subjected them for ever to the Inca **Legend of a Brave Prince** rule. The legend then continues to relate how the victorious prince declined the proposals of his thankful comrades to accept the crown, and proceeded to conciliate his royal father by submission until the latter voluntarily abdicated and duly announced himself as the first of his son's vassals. However, the real course of events was probably as follows. The courage of the reigning king, and of the Incas around him, failed before the threatening advance of the Chanca. The state was so dislocated that he could not rely upon the greater portion of his subjects ; and as the town of Cuzco and its environs offered no secure refuge, the Inca and his closest dependents determined to conceal themselves and their treasures in the mountains.

The supporters of the pre-Incan dynasty among the citizens who were now thus abandoned—that is, the worshippers of the old god Huiracocha—rose to power upon the cowardly flight of their ruler ; even without the Chanca they would certainly have put an end to the rule of the foreigners if the long and prosperous government of the later dynasty had not formed among the people a strong party which was favourable to the Incas. Under these circumstances a youth of the Inca race appeared among the waverers ; he had no legal right of succession to the throne, but was a man of Inca blood and Inca courage. The immediate necessity was to do away with the opposition between the remnant of the ancient inhabitants and the Inca dependents, which had broken out with greater vigour upon the flight of the ruler. For this purpose he invented the legend of the appearance of the god Huiracocha.

He said that the god of the ancient people had chosen him, the Inca, as the saviour of his people. By this means he obtained allies among the neighbouring highland races, who helped him to victory. This favourite of Huiracocha was naturally disinclined to lay the palm of victory at the feet of those Incas in whose absence he had won his success ; but he was equally unable openly to usurp the power of the Inca king in the face of a strong party of allies who had materially contributed to his success. The consequence was that for many years the lawful ruler, who was greatly despised by his people for his cowardice, set up his court far from Cuzco, while his more fortunate rival held the reins of power in the capital without venturing to assume the royal title.

A new King on the Inca Throne Finally, a compromise was brought about which enabled the aged king to spend his remaining years in peace and gave the real ruler the legal title he had won. The Inca who took the name of the god Huiracocha had to thank his southern neighbours, the Canes and Cancha, for the salvation of Cuzco and for his victory over the Chanca.

But there was collected beneath his standard, not a body of vassals, but a confederation which expected a rich recompense from the spoils of war. Here we have another proof of the fact that the Inca kingdom, both in extent and in internal compactness, was still far removed from its later perfection. But important strides were made under the rule of the far-seeing Huiracocha. In the first place, the subjugation of the

RUINED TEMPLE OF HUIRACOCHA, BETWEEN CUZCO AND THE LAKE OF TITICACA
The Temple of Huiracocha marks the beginning of that scepticism among the Incas and Amautas concerning their gods, to counteract which the more faithful of Huiracocha's worshippers caused a number of temples to be erected, this being the most important of them. Most of these temples also served as tombs, but only for the kings and high priests.

A WAYSIDE SHRINE BELOW THE WALLS OF AN ANCIENT INCA FORTRESS

In the above picture the distant past is united with modern times, as it illustrates a wayside Calvary erected by some devout Roman Catholics near the ancient walls of an Inca fortress. The few descendants of the Incas to-day preserve, to some extent, their old religious forms, but many have been won over to Catholicism by the missions of the Church.

Chanca provided him with a numerous body of warriors immediately dependent upon him, whom he raised to honour and position. On the other hand, there were many little dynasties in the neighbourhood of Cuzco loosely dependent upon the Inca state who were disinclined to give in their allegiance to the new ruler, and had regarded his predecessors upon the throne with displeasure. Huiracocha, with extraordinary cleverness, now changed the feeble suzerainty of the ruler of Cuzco into a virtual dominion. The dependents of the previous Inca did not find courage for an open display of hostility, and as the individual dynasties were unable to unite for common purposes they were reduced to the position of vassal states. The Canes and Cancha, when they refused to recognise the sovereignty of the Inca by sending him tribute, were attacked and subdued after a vigorous resistance.

Canes and Cancha Subdued

They later became the most faithful, loyal and reliable subjects of the Inca; to them was reserved the honourable duty of providing bearers for the king's litter; for the Inca, like the princes of the Chibchas and Quitus, was invariably carried on a litter when he went on a journey. During a long rule the Inca Huiracocha carried his arms successfully against enemies in the most various directions; but his success was due as much to his political skill as to the bravery of his armies.

We have a particular proof of this in his interference in the quarrels of the Colla. On the western and southern shores of the lake of Titicaca, two rulers, Cari of Chucuito, and Zapana of Hatun-Colla, were struggling for pre-eminence, and each was short-sighted enough to invite Huiracocha's help. That gave him the opportunity of being the first of the Inca race to press forward to the sacred islands of Titicaca and the ruined cities of Tiahuanaco. He took the side of the weaker and more remote Cari, who readily became a kind of vassal to the Inca, in order to repel his more powerful opponent; and thereby he prepared the incorporation of both districts in the Inca state, an incorporation which a rising in that district enabled his grandson, Tupak Yupanki, to complete.

A fundamental reason for the rapid and brilliant success of the new Inca lay in the alteration of his religious policy. The sun-worship which the Incas had set up

5857

as the religion for the state and the people could hardly appeal to the inhabitants of the highlands. It was a mixture of reverence for the powers of Nature and of ancestor-worship, which latter feature made it an important element in the Inca family life, strong emphasis being thereby laid upon the difference between the Inca race and

Inti the Sun-god of the Incas the peoples subject to them, and so this cult became rather an opportunity for expressing dis-gust than an occasion for wor-ship. The sun, with his beneficent influences of warmth and fruitfulness, was certainly an eminently suitable deity for the inhabitants of the bare, rough highlands, and Huira-cocha, as he was originally worshipped by the Quechua and other neighbouring peoples, was no doubt an offshoot from a sun divinity. Although the Incas must have conceived of the sun-god, Inti, as their forefather in a human form, they none the less banished from their worship every kind of anthropomorphism. When worship was not directly offered to the luminary, as it invariably was on great feast-days, the god was represented only by a bright golden shield.

Pictorial representation was systematic-ally objected to by the Incas, not only in their own worship, but also in that of all other gods. In their campaigns against hostile peoples the destruction of temples and images was considered an important duty. The peoples who reluctantly bowed to the yoke of the Inca dominion were not brought into any closer sympathy with their religion when they saw the hall of the sun-god in the temple at Cuzco changed into a hall of ancestors; along the walls stood the embalmed mummies of dead rulers, a band of solar children grouped around their father, the sun-god.

There can be no question that this worship contributed to raise a barrier between the Incas and their subjects. The worship of Huiracocha now resolved upon by the new

Worshippers of the God Huiracocha Inca, who borrowed his name from that of the god, implied a complete breach with the re-ligious policy that had hitherto obtained. But this Inca, who was too cultivated to find any satisfaction for his own religious needs in sun-worship, could not afford to set up such a primitive idolatry as the ancient worship of the highland god must have been. The god whom the Amautas and Incas worshipped under the name of Huiracocha, as the

almighty creator of all things, whom they honoured more than Inti, the sun-god, as being the source of all life, was no stone image; he defied all representation, pic-torial and otherwise, as he worked and lived under no concrete form, existing as the mighty power which penetrates the whole world. Upon the occurrence of one of those religious ceremonies with which the rising orb of day was greeted, and which were crowned by the presence of the king, the Inca Huiracocha is said to have asked the priests and Amautas collected around him whether it was conceivable that Inti was the highest god and the ruler of all things, as he invariably accomplished his course around the earth in a manner both regular and fatiguing. Supposing he were free and powerful, would he not at some time feel a desire to take a rest or to strike out another path than the one of which his daily routine must have made him thoroughly weary?

Similar beginnings of scepticism and eclecticism not difficult to understand, are related of his successors, and afforded an opportunity for the introduction of the

Revival of National Religions ideas which the Incas attached to their worship of Huira-cocha. In Cacha they erected a famous temple of Huiracocha for the benefit of the people; its ruins show strong divergences from the archi-tectural style of the Incas, and also from that of all the other Peruvian peoples, and remain standing to-day as an unsolved problem. In Cuzco and other places altars were erected to the god, and his image was placed before them, generally in the form of an old man in flowing robes.

Other national religions, which had been repressed hitherto, now celebrated their revival. In the version of the legend about the conquest of the Chanca, who are said to have been overcome with the help of the Pururauca, those stone statues of warriors which started into life and rushed into the ranks of the enemy at the Inca's call, we see at least a reminiscence of the revival of stone-worship. In the case of the succeeding Inca there is even better evidence of this, in the fact that after a visit to Tiahuanaco he ordered similar memorials to be set up in the neighbourhood of Cuzco; the results of this order were the peculiar steps, plat-forms, and sites hewn in the rock of Monte Rodadero near Cuzco. The worships of other subject peoples were also recognised later by the Incas, and transported to Cuzco ; as, for instance, the worship of Pachacamak, the chief god of the peoples on the coast of the Pacific Ocean. At the time of the Spanish conquest Cuzco was a meeting-place, not only for princes and governors, but also for the gods and priests of every race which belonged to the Inca kingdom—a regular arsenal of idols, differing widely in shape and meaning.

It was important for the Inca Huiracocha to find a successor to the throne who could continue and bring to perfection the work which he had begun. The rule of the Inca Yupanki, who was also called Pachacutek, was an open progress of almost uninterrupted triumph. On the east he extended the boundaries of his kingdom to the point where the mountain streams moderate their impetuous course in the boundless llanos. On the south he won several victories over the king of Hatun-Colla, and added the king of Chucuito to the number of his vassals. Upon the north he extended his dominion as far as Cajamarca and Conchucos ; and as his father had left him no more room for conquest upon the **Inca Rule Extended to the Sea** west of the mountain valleys, he advanced to the shores of the Pacific Ocean and subdued the whole seaboard as far as the Rimak valley. His campaigns, which he sometimes led in person and sometimes entrusted to his brothers, and later to his successor, often lasted for years ; under him was completed the military organisation to which we have already referred.

The war upon the coast called for special precautions. Previous attempts to press forward in that direction had caused the Inca unusually heavy losses. His highland warriors could not endure the hot coast climate, and fevers were enemies against which they were almost powerless. But by relieving the armies fighting on the coast with fresh divisions at short intervals, and by removing the warriors to the highlands to recruit, he succeeded in extending his rule to the sea. When once this was accomplished, he found reliable soldiers in the races on the coast, and soldiers, too, who were inured to the climate.

The principle of leaving an easy retreat open to the enemy against whom he marched was also followed by him. Numerous races and princes in the mountains and on the coast submitted to his display of power without obliging him to make them feel the sharpness of his sword. Among those which submitted voluntarily was the priestly state of Pachacamak in the valley of Lurin. The times when the Incas overthrew the temples had long since passed away. Pachacutek worshipped in person the gods who were honoured as far and wide upon the coast-land as Huiracocha **Honouring the Inca God** was in the mountains, and left the temples and their treasures undisturbed ; to these latter he even sent costly presents. The only condition he laid upon the conquered people was that upon the heights which overlooked the town and temple of Pachacamak a new and more splendid temple should be erected to his own god Inti, the sun, and he ordered a similar temple to be built in Cuzco for Pachacamak.

The Inca power had not been so firmly established in these extensive and recently subdued districts that Pachacutek did not have to deal now and again with revolts. The Chanca reluctantly bore the Inca yoke. Neither permanent fortifications in their land, nor the fact that their ranks had been repeatedly weakened by the transportation of their warriors into more peaceful parts of the kingdom, served to break or to appease their haughty spirit. On the contrary, they determined, when they were convinced of their weakness, to abandon their ancient home rather than give up their independence. The whole tribe started on a migration in a north-easterly direction, and founded a settlement in Chachapoyas, which was only again united with the kingdom under the last Inca ruler.

Pachacutek had also other battles to fight within his realm, but these did not seriously endanger it. Among the men of Inca blood there were still many remaining who knew to what change of succession the dynasty from which Pachacutek was sprung owed the throne of Cuzco. Thus an extensive conspiracy had **Plot and Counterplot in the Inca Palace** been formed with the secret object of deposing the Inca Pachacutek and setting up in his place a descendant of the ancient royal family, the Inca Urco. But Pachacutek was informed in time of these treasonable designs, and before the conspirators had the least suspicion that their plans were known the Inca Urco suddenly and mysteriously disappeared in the royal palace, from which he was never again to issue.

ORNAMENTAL VASES EXECUTED IN BLACK TERRACOTTA

TERRACOTTA VASES IN THE FORM OF ANIMALS

OTHER SPECIMENS OF WORKMANSHIP IN BLACK TERRACOTTA

DECORATIVE POTTERY OF THE INCAS: ANTIQUE SPECIMENS FROM PERU

Photos Mansell

AMERICA
BEFORE
COLUMBUS

NATIVE
CIVILISATIONS
OF SOUTH
AMERICA
VI

THE FLOURISHING OF THE INCAS
THEIR SOCIAL AND RELIGIOUS LIFE

PACHACUTEK won great fame for himself by his victorious campaigns towards the four quarters of the heavens; and with just pride he named his territory Tahuantinsuyu—the four cardinal points. But he left a still greater memorial of himself in the internal organisation of the Inca kingdom, an organisation that far surpassed anything else of the kind in existence upon American soil. To consider Peru under the Incas as a kingdom founded upon a basis of socialism is to misunderstand entirely the facts of the case.

The Inca rule was an absolute theocracy, at the head of which was the Inca, who concentrated temporal and religious functions in his own person as being the child of the sun-god and the chief priest of that divinity. His power was absolute over body and soul, property and person, of his subjects; the only laws that were binding upon him were his own will and pleasure, and **The Inca Lord of Life and Death** these he might change to any extent he pleased. A consequence of this powerful position was that the Inca alone possessed real property; the whole extent of the kingdom belonged to him, with every living creature in it; other men had only the usufruct of his property. It appears a hard ordinance that, as our historical sources inform us, a third of the produce of the country was appropriated for the support of the ruler, another third for the service of the sun, while only a third remained for the people. But the oppression of this law is only apparent; the Inca and the sun represented the financial department of modern times, and a large proportion of the people lived at their expense.

Moreover, those portions of the land assigned to the people lay in the neighbourhood of the villages and places of population; as such settlements had been made purposely on land that was capable of cultivation, the best third of the land was in the hands of the people.

The extensive tablelands of the Puna, the high mountain ranges, were included in the land belonging to the sun and to the Inca, where the low temperature precluded agriculture. Here was the home of the great herds of llamas, which belonged to the Inca or **Home of the Llama** to the sun. The possession of these animals was forbidden to the common people. The llama is the only large domestic animal which the American natives possessed. Different kinds of fowl, and in many districts little dogs, were tamed and bred; but they were of use to mankind only as food; their possession was a compensation for the increasing difficulty of gaining a living by hunting. The llama alone has the character of a domestic animal, in the full sense of the word, among the ancient Americans, for it alone was of use to man during its lifetime.

In early times it was never used for riding or drawing vehicles. However, the Peruvians of the highlands—for the climate of the coast is fatal to the llama, and for that reason the animal was never used there in Inca times—made constant use of it as a beast of burden. The llama was equally valuable for its wool. Like the sheep, it can be shorn from time to time without occasioning the least injury to its health; and in the Inca kingdom its wool was always woven into stuffs.

The llamas, in common with all living animals, were the exclusive property of the Inca—that is, of the state. State servants performed the shearing, and **Work of the Sun Maidens** officials divided the raw wool among the people according to their powers of working it and their necessities. The wool was not only woven for the clothing of the people, but a portion of it served in lieu of taxes. A kind of factory for wool-weaving went on in the abodes of the ladies of the sun, the Acllas; these were monastical retreats where hundreds of girls were constantly employed in spinning and weaving. Here was also worked the finer wool of the vicuna, a variety of the llama which ran wild and was driven into herds only at shearing-time. These fine stuffs were not intended for the common people, but were invariably worn by the Incas. For the royal families,

Llamas on the Royal Table and especially for the ruling Inca, the sun-maidens were obliged to provide large supplies of the finest stuffs; for state ceremonial exacted from the king that he should always be clothed in spotlessly new garments. In the provinces, also, the Acllas worked the coarser wool of the llama, and thereby contributed to supply the royal storehouses, in which large quantities of woollen garments were collected for the use of the army in time of war.

The llama was also important as a food supply; game was neither plentiful nor varied, and the people could not have supported themselves thereby. Most of the inhabitants certainly kept and bred fowls in and near their houses. But beyond this there existed only the flesh of the llama, and a number of these animals were daily slaughtered for the Inca's table. But the herds were so numerous and increased so rapidly, that now and again a large number of them were slaughtered and divided among the people, who were thus feasted by the monarch. The llama had descended from its wild forefathers, the guanaco and the vicuna, and had become a permanent species. Such a development must have required an extremely long period of time for its accomplishment, and consequently the llama must have been tamed long previous to the Inca rule.

But although this acquisition of civilisation was not due to the Incas, yet they were the first peoples to systematise the breeding and the use of the animal. On one of his first campaigns of conquest the Inca Pachacutek subdued the district

Gold in the Inca Kingdom of Huilcabamba, and found that the veins of gold there situated were already being extensively worked by the natives. Although they could work only the upper strata, and with their primitive implements could naturally extract the gold from only the richest lodes, yet the astonishing amount of gold and silver which the Spaniards found in the Inca kingdom shows that the work was profitable. The people were obliged to pay their

tribute to the Inca from these mining operations. The work demanded of them was not hard; they were always allowed sufficient time to satisfy their own personal requirements. But the mountain peoples had as little claim to the precious metal which they brought forth to the light of day as had the owners of the corn in the lowland, or the shepherds of the llamas, to the possession of these goods; for real property belonged to the Inca alone.

Gold and silver, the medium of exchange in the whole civilised world, brought neither power nor influence into the Inca kingdom, but were employed for the decoration of the gods and kings and were worthless in the hands of individuals. A state which had no money and practically no property had also nothing wherewith to pay taxes. But the citizen himself was the property, the slave, of the state, and consequently he owed a certain portion of his labour to the state. In the larger settlements a considerable number of the inhabitants paid their tribute in different kinds of manufacture, in which, in some cases, they had attained

Agriculture a Divine Service considerable skill. The ancient Peruvian weaving, both of woollen and cotton stuffs, though carried on with very simple implements, is of high quality in respect of both fineness and durability; and the weavers understood the employment of large and artistic patterns by the use of different coloured threads. Still more remarkable is the Peruvian pottery-ware, with its great variety of decoration, which is invariably tasteful, and with its rich and artistic colouring. Their artistic powers were almost exclusively exercised upon this pottery; and ware that has been shaped into realistic but very fantastic forms has come down to us from almost all the provinces of the Inca kingdom.

The country people were employed in herding the flocks of llama, or in cultivating the lands belonging to the Inca and the sun. The plough was unknown to the Peruvians; they turned up the soil with an implement like a spade, and, as they invariably worked in large numbers, digging in rows, their fields must have had a furrowed appearance. Agriculture was the foundation of the Inca kingdom; it was regarded as divine service, and every subject of the kingdom was entrusted with its accomplishment. When the season for tilling the soil had come round, the Inca himself, followed by all his court, proceeded in great pomp to a field which was dedicated to the sun in the neighbourhood of Cuzco, and began the agriculture in person with religious ceremonies. Each of his courtiers had to follow his example.

The order was then transmitted by officials through the country that the subjects should begin the year's work upon the land. The head of every family was in annual possession of a particular plot of land proportioned to the needs of his household; if his family increased, so did his plot, a piece half the size of the original allotment being given him for each son, and a quarter of the original size for each daughter. But the land remained state property, and upon the death or migration of the occupant it reverted to the Crown. Cultivation was carried on in common and under the superintendence of overseers. First were tilled the lands of the sun; then those of individual citizens, including the allotments of the poor, the sick, and the officials; and finally the lands of the Inca were cultivated. In the milder districts of the kingdom a number of

Methods of Inca Agriculture varieties of maize were raised. The mandioc, several kinds of pumpkins, beans, and some other vegetables, were grown more in the gardens around the houses than in the fields. But in many districts of the Inca kingdom the cold climate was unfavourable to these vegetables. In such cases potatoes formed the staple of agriculture.

The Inca-Peruvians carried on agriculture not only extensively, but also with great energy. The use of manure, for which purpose, after they had conquered the sea-coast, they used guano, was as little a discovery of theirs as was the science of irrigation. In the narrow valleys of the highlands they increased the ground available for agriculture by making terraces for miles, at a great expense of labour, in the precipitous mountain heights, which were then carefully irrigated by canals from the river running down the valley.

Land that was in this way brought under cultivation naturally belonged only to the Incas; the amount of work necessary for its success was far more than individual sources could provide, and presupposed a strong and close organisation. A family of at least ten inhabitants formed the smallest administrative unity in the kingdom; an inferior official superintended

this, whose business it was to care for and watch over it. Ten of such unities formed a "hundred"; here the superintendent was obliged to keep an eye upon the districts of his ten inferior officials, besides the care of his own office. The next political unity was formed of ten "hundreds," and a "ten thousand" was

How the Kingdom was Governed generally equivalent to a province of the kingdom. The highest power naturally lay in the hands of the Inca, who had a consultative council in Cuzco. But besides this council the governors of the provinces —who were generally chosen from the Inca class when political necessities had not left the rule in the hands of one of the old conquered princes—and also the officials of smaller districts, were obliged from time to time to appear personally before the central power, or to send in their reports with the help of the quipus.

By this means the government was fully informed concerning the inhabitants of each province and their capabilities, and also concerning the supplies and provisions which every district was obliged to make, to meet its own necessities, and even to have a surplus in hand. Moreover, the overseers were constantly inspected by officials of a higher class. In cases where faults were discovered, the guilty person was punished, and so also were his superiors, who ought to have informed the subjects of their obligations and to have assured themselves that these were fulfilled.

As the common man, the "hatunruna," possessed no real property, he might also pay his taxes in military service. The Incas did not maintain a standing army, and any careful or extensive training in the use of arms seems to have been the privilege of the Incas alone, and of the sons of the nobles from the subject provinces. It is by no means clear in what manner the hatunruna obtained the training necessary to enable him to fulfil

Taxes paid in Military Service his part in the constant and distant campaigns of the Incas. There was, however, a system for regularly relieving the garrisons that were maintained in unsettled quarters, as well as for conveying reinforcements to the battlefields; an arrangement must consequently have been on foot somewhat similar to the old Prussian system of relief, according to which the hatunruna returned to his agricultural pursuits after a short period of active service, until he was again called out in due course, though generally only for a very limited space of time.

An important duty of the overseers of the " hundreds " was to see that the people performed their allotted portion of work ; the women were included under this decree. Their essential duties in their households consisted in the care of the garden and of the poultry ; but most important were the spinning and weaving, which they were obliged to practise beyond the mere satisfaction of their household necessities, as we have already stated. Idleness was a punishable offence in the Inca kingdom. Even when women made visits to their neighbours they took their work with them, unless the person visited was of higher rank than her visitor ; in this case it was the duty of the visitor to ask for permission to take her work. It was the business of the local overseers to apportion as much land to each inhabitant as would suffice for the maintenance of himself and his wife. If, as happened in exceptional cases, the land belonging to the community did not suffice, the inhabitants had a claim upon the lands of the Inca ; but when the population of a province rose to such an extent that the land was no longer capable of supporting them, colonists, known as " mitimaes," were sent out into less thickly populated or new provinces. The state undertook the duty of providing for the support of each individual, but avoided poverty, with its evil results of beggary and vagabondism, which was, in fact, entirely obviated by the necessity of labour and the prohibition

which was laid upon an unauthorised change of residence. The state also recognised its duty of providing for its subjects in extraordinary cases ; and, thanks to the general industry, the storehouses situated in every province were sufficiently full of supplies to meet all necessities.

The conception of private property was not wholly unfamiliar to the inhabitants of the Inca state. Houses and land were, it is true, the property of the community, to which they reverted at the death of the holder. But so ample was the provision made for the support of the individual that he was able to put aside some savings, and to lay out these economies as he wished, even in the purchase of luxuries, as the state, or community, provided his necessities. The objects found in the Peruvian cemeteries show us that luxuries were not altogether unknown even among the common people, and this personal property was almost invariably interred with its dead owner. As new members were born into the family, the land allotted to it was increased. The young Inca citizens passed a long and tranquil childhood. It was incumbent on their parents to give them a practical education and to train them in domestic duties, but it was not till the completion of their twenty-fourth year that the state made any claim upon the young people. At twenty-five they were married. Marriage was also strictly controlled by the law, which denied the Inca Peruvian any opportunity of personal initiative from the cradle to the grave. The public officials were required to keep a register of persons

ANCIENT AMERICA'S DOMESTIC ANIMAL

The only large domestic animal possessed by the American natives, the llama was much prized by them, the Peruvians of the highlands making constant use of it as a beast of burden, while it was also valuable on account of its wool, which was woven for the clothing of the people.

PRESENT-DAY DESCENDANTS OF THE ANCIENT INCA PEOPLES OF PERU

of both sexes who every year attained a marriageable age in their districts. Each year a day was appointed for the celebration of marriages throughout the kingdom.

The young men and maidens, clad in their best attire, appeared before the officers of their district, who publicly, but with little in the way of ceremony, assigned to each youth a young maiden. On the same day, at Cuzco, the Inca himself officiated for those of noble blood. The consent of the young people was superfluous in the eyes of the law, but, when possible, their inclinations were considered. No one, however, might marry outside of his own district. The usual allotment of land was now made to the young couple, and the community saw to the building of their simple and primitive dwelling. In this way they entered the ranks of the hatun-runas, accepting all the responsibilities involved, except that for the first year—the honeymoon of their married life—they remained exempt from public service. The duties of labour were obligatory up to the age of fifty; after that time the community, as also in cases of temporary or permanent disablement, became responsible

for their support to the end of their lives. While military service was demanded of the men, another tax was levied by the Inca upon the women. Every year the officials were required to select from the number of young maidens the best and most beautiful for the service of the ruler and of the sun. In each province the Inca had his palace and a house attached to it, in which these maidens led a privileged if a laborious existence. Whenever the Inca came into residence it was from their number that he chose the partner of his couch. If the connection resulted in pregnancy, the young mother returned to her native home, where great respect was paid both to her and to the child.

Very different was the lot of those selected for the service of the sun. Like the royal wives, they led a favoured but industrious life in religious seclusion. But in their case the law against incontinence was inviolable, and a cruel death awaited the sun-maiden and her seducer if this statute was transgressed. That the Incas should occasionally have taken children from their parents in their tenderest years for sacrifice to the sun-god is hardly probable.

Such sacrifices may in earlier times have been offered to the sun-god and to the deities of many of the peoples afterwards subdued. But such a usage is wholly inconsistent with the spirit of the national religion as it was practised under the later Incas. In the Inca state religion was much more a matter of politics than of dogma. The late Incas therefore imposed no restrictions upon the various races of their subjects as to the number of gods they might desire to worship. It was also from political motives that they established at Cuzco the temples and priests of the various religions; for thus they were in continual touch with the forces which they knew to exercise a great influence upon the masses.

Politics in the Inca Religion

The introduction into every newly acquired province of sun-worship as a supreme and universal form of religion was also meant to serve their political ends. Although there was at Cuzco a high priest of the sun-god, who exercised a kind of control over priests of all denominations throughout the country, yet the real head of the church was the Inca. As descendant of the sun-god he stood nearer to the deity than his highest priest, while as child of the sun he was himself entitled to divine honours after his death, upon which he returned to his ancestor. Dissensions between king and priesthood, which recur so frequently in the communities of Central America, were rendered impossible by the semi-divine character of the Inca. For this reason the decided revolution which the Inca Huiracocha brought about in the domain of religious politics never at any place or time caused the slightest difficulty, although it raised at once a host of formidable rivals to the priesthood of the sun.

The privileged position, and the endowment of a third of the land, remained their exclusive right; but even the Inca kings made numerous and costly offerings to the temples of Huiracocha and Pachacamak.

Feasts in Honour of the Sun-God

The laborious life of the masses was relieved only by the festivals which were celebrated in honour of the sun-god; once at least in each month the inhabitants of each locality were summoned by the officials to a feast. Upon these occasions the flesh of the llama, set apart by the Inca for the people, was certainly consumed; at the same time large quantities of the maize beer called " aka," were drunk, and dance and song contributed to the enjoyment. Similar holidays followed the completion of all the more important tasks; the cultivation of the fields, the gathering in of the harvest, or any exceptional undertaking—house-building, roadmaking, and the like. Besides these, however, there were four high festivals common to all the land: the Hatun Raimi, the Cusqui Raimi, the Situa Raimi, and the Huaracuy.

The Hatun (or Inti) Raimi was celebrated at the time of the winter solstice (the 21st of June), and was the first and principal festival by which the year was reckoned. Lasting for nine days, it celebrated the return of the source of life and heat, the sun having reached and passed its extreme northern declination. The first three festival days were devoted to preparation; every inhabitant of the Inca kingdom was obliged to abstain from all food, with the exception of a little uncooked maize and water, and, if married, from conjugal intercourse; all fires were extinguished. During these days it was the duty of the young unmarried women in each household, and of the sun-maidens for the use of the Inca and his court, to prepare the sacred bread, the first food that might be taken after the fast. The principal ceremony took place on the morning of the fourth day. At the approach of dawn the whole population poured out of their houses into the open space where the priests were awaiting the sunrise. Here the thronging multitude crouched barefooted in a wide circle around the priests, and, no one daring to rise, awaited the moment when the sun's orb should appear above the horizon, to greet it with solemn sacrifice.

Religious Ceremonies at Cuzco

Naturally it was at Cuzco that the feast was celebrated in its most magnificent form. Here, upon that day, the square of Haucaipata, around which stood the royal palaces, was thronged with the highest and noblest from every province of the kingdom. Clothed in festal attire, but barefooted and in the same attitude of humility, they, too, awaited the moment of sunrise. Thereupon the Inca king was the first to rise; upon this day, as being the child of the sun, he himself performed the office of high-priest. In either hand he held a cup inlaid with gold, filled to the brim with aka. While he addressed a solemn greeting to the rising luminary, he emptied the cup in his right hand into a golden basin that stood before him, whence golden pipes conveyed the libation to the Temple of the Sun.

The cup in his left hand he put to his own lips, and then invited his nearest relatives, and any on whom he wished to confer distinction, to take from this cup, with small golden chalices, a portion for themselves. Then, together with the higher priests and dignitaries, the Inca entered the temple in order to pay his adoration to the image of the god. The Temple of the Sun had undergone, at the hands of the Inca Pachacutek, a thorough restoration and extension ; since which time, owing to its rich adornment with precious metals, it had been known by the name of Coricancha, " the Golden Precinct."

It was an extensive group of buildings, encircled by walls of squared masonry, lying somewhat nearer the mountains than the market-place. In and around the great court were a number of edifices, the most sacred of which was the Hall of the Sun. Here, on the wall at the back **The Sacred Hall of the Sun** of the temple, so placed as each morning to catch the rays of the rising sun, was the great golden disc, encircled with rays, which constituted the Holy of Holies. Walls and roof, as well as the altars before this and the other shrines of the temple, were richly overlaid with gold, while along the walls, seated in their litters and wrapped in the most costly fabrics, stood the perfectly preserved mummies of the dead Incas. Behind the Hall of the Sun a similar room contained the image of the moon and the mummies of the coyas, the imperial wives who had given to the kingdom an heir to the throne. Here all ornamentation was in silver. Then followed smaller sanctuaries for the other heavenly bodies, the divine retinue of Inti, and for his earthly followers, the priests.

After libations and incense had been offered at these shrines also, the Inca returned to the square, where the rest awaited him ; for on this day the great sacrifices were performed not in the enclosed court of the temple, but in the open market-place. The priests now led forth a young black llama. Black animals, as being more uniform in colour, were more highly prized than white ones, which as a rule showed darker patches ; moreover black was the sacred colour and was specially favoured by the Inca. While the unbound victim was held by priests of lower grade, the high-priest cut open the body with an obsidian knife and tore out the heart and entrails. From these he foretold the events of the year that was just beginning. The body was now divided, and, in order to burn it as **How the Festivals were Observed** a sacrifice, the high-priest lighted with a burning-glass, which he wore on his right wrist, the new fire from which all the hearths in the city were kindled afresh. This concluded the more important ceremonies, which now gave place to general rejoicings. Numbers of the common llamas were slaughtered, but only the blood and entrails were offered to the god ; the flesh was assigned to the people for food. The remaining days of the festival were spent in eating and drinking, dancing and singing, and revels of every description, the freedom of which often degenerated into licence. For the people the feast closed on the ninth day, after six days of rejoicing.

The Inca and his attendants seem to have continued the celebrations for a month, and even then to have lamented their brief duration. The second of the common festivals, the Cusqui Raimi, was connected with agriculture. It was celebrated before the beginning of harvest, and was a sort of procession in honour of the sun-god, who, after everything in mortal power had been done to secure the success of the crops, was implored with his divine favour to bless and increase the harvest. This feast also was followed by days of continuous and unrestrained revelry, meant, no doubt, to provide the people with recreation after the labours of the field.

Of a different character was the third feast, or Situa Raimi, which fell at the time of the spring equinox, in September. The assumption that every calamity or unexpected event which befell the individual or **The Place and Power of Evil Spirits** the community was due to some transgression was current in the Inca kingdom as elsewhere, and was reflected in the laws. But if the guilt of the individual might be expiated by atonement or punishment, it still adhered to the community, which had likewise to bear the weight of all the terrors which threatened it from the evil spirits with which earth and air were peopled. To appease or drive away these was the object of the feast. It was preceded, like the others, by a three-days' fast and the preparation of sacred bread. In addition, however, to those intended for food, other loaves were baked, mixed with the blood of sacrifice. With this bread each man, on the fourth day at sunrise, rubbed his body, after bathing in running water, in order to purify himself. On the

The Great Day of the Festival morning of the great day of the festival the crowning ceremony took place at the fortress of Sacsahuaman. This was a huge fortification built of enormous blocks of stone, which rose in five tiers on one of the heights commanding the city from the north-east. Its erection had been commenced by the Inca Huiracocha at the time when the Chanca invasion had threatened the as yet utterly defenceless city with extinction. The Inca Pachacutek had successfully completed the mighty structure. From the gate of the fortress, at the Situa Raimi, issued four youths of the Inca race, clad in complete armour. Brandishing their spears, they ran at full speed through town and country in the direction of the four cardinal points. Everywhere the gaily clad multitudes flocked from their dwellings to meet them and greeted them with loud shouts and waving of garments. At fixed distances others of the Inca race, similarly attired, waited to receive the lance in turn, and carried it farther and farther until the boundary of the district was passed. There the lance was driven deep into the earth, and it was supposed that the evil spirits had thus been expelled from the soil. During the night the Incas waved burning torches, which they extinguished on the farther side of the boundary in the streams that flowed out of the country. In this way the powers of darkness were also put to flight, and the following days were devoted to festivity.

While at the Situa Raimi the chief actors were the Inca youths, who symbolically **Attaining Manhood's Privileges** delivered the people from the dangers that threatened them. The fourth great feast, the Huaracuy, was almost exclusively confined to the Inca class, and the people could participate only in the general rejoicings. This feast marked the conclusion of the probations which the children of Inca descent, as well as the sons of the noblest families in the provinces, had to undergo before they might be admitted to the privileges of manhood.

THE LAST INCA RULER: ATAHUALPA FALLS BEFORE THE SPANIARDS   *Rau*

The story of Atahualpa is told at length in the chapter which begins on the next page. A son of Huaina Capak, he became ruler of the kingdom of Quito on his father's death, and found occasion to go to war with his brother Huascar, who had succeeded to the Inca throne. Victory resting with Atahualpa, he was acknowledged as the ruler of the dual kingdom; but the Inca power was nearing its end, and Atahualpa fell before the conquering march of the Spanish forces.

LAST DAYS OF THE INCA KINGDOM
THE LANDING OF THE SPANIARDS IN AMERICA

IN spite of the efforts of the Incas to maintain the belief that the whole of the Inca class was descended from Manco Capak, and through him from the sun-god himself, they had not been able to banish from the memory of men the fact that a part of the caste could establish no blood-kinship with the founder of the dynasty. In the earliest times, in addition to the ruler of Cuzco, many other small dynasties of the Peruvian highlands had assumed the designation of Inca, which, like " Manco " and " Capak," was originally a mere title and not the name of a race. Whether these, on their incorporation into the empire of the son of the sun, maintained the name and privileges of the Inca is doubtful.

Thus arose a new class in the community, which, though unable to establish any blood-relationship with the Incas, shared all their privileges. When Manco Capak came to Cuzco, he was attended by a small **Alcavizas Driven From Cuzco** band of dependents, with whose help he drove the Alcavizas from the city. In the infancy of the state these naturally formed a privileged class, and when, later, the constant extension of the empire brought to the capital a mixed population of every conceivable element, they and their posterity, the aristocracy of Cuzco, were admitted to all the essential privileges enjoyed by those of pure Inca blood.

On the other hand, the Inca stock increased with great rapidity by the natural process of reproduction. Among the masses no man was permitted to marry more than one wife, but from this law the whole of the Inca caste was exempt, and the ruler might also grant dispensation to others. For himself, especially, it was not only a privilege to possess a number of wives, but also a duty to leave behind him as numerous a progeny as possible. Only one, however, of the ruler's wives shared his royal rank; she bore the name of coya, and took an important part in the public ceremonial that was incumbent upon the Inca. The

Inca Pachacutek was the first to enact that the natural sister or the nearest female relation of the ruling Inca should always be chosen as the coya, in order as far as possible to preserve the blood of the children of the sun from contamination. In addition to the coya, the Inca might take **Marriage Laws of the Incas** as many wives as he wished; if they belonged to the Inca class, they and their children were considered legitimate. The Inca also sought daughters in marriage from his vassal princes; this was considered a high honour, and no less so if the Inca married one of his illegitimate daughters to a dignitary or a vassal prince. Marriage between men and women of the Inca class was celebrated in the same way as that of the people, with the exception that the Inca ruler in person performed the ceremony in Cuzco. Youths of Inca blood might take only one wife of their own accord, though they might also have numerous concubines; but after the completion of an important task, or upon the occasion of a feast, the ruler often rewarded his kinsmen with one or more wives.

Individual rulers are said to have left as many as a hundred children, or even more. Each of these became the founder of a family, the connection of which with the common stock was preserved in their name and insignia; such families united to worship the mummy of their ancestor in the Temple of the Sun. By law the Inca king was as completely master of the bodies and souls of the Incas as of **The Incas Specially Favoured** his other subjects; but, as a matter of fact, the Inca class obtained special privileges in the kingdom of Tahuantin-suyu. The duty of labour, which was incumbent upon everybody in the Inca state, was not binding upon them. A memorial of the time when the Incas formed a small band in the middle of a foreign race was preserved in the right which they had of eating at the ruler's table ; later this right became so extended that the Inca was obliged to support the whole of the Inca caste, and also all the officials of the kingdom who were not Incas, with the produce of that third of the land which belonged to him. The highest temporal and religious offices were filled with sons of the Inca race ; and the

Education Among the Incas

man who could show his value in such a position was certain of the monarch's favour. To this many of the Inca sons owed their large palaces and bands of attendants both in the capitals and in the provinces. The education imparted to the Inca caste justified their special privileges. In the case of the young girls known as " ñusta," their education was a more refined type of that received by the daughters of the people and the sun-maidens.

On the other hand, the young men, the "auqui," not only received a careful intellectual training, as previously mentioned, but were also obliged to undergo a thorough course of physical exercise. This was concluded, when the auqui had reached his sixteenth year, with the ordeal which preceded the feast of Huaracuy, and gave him the right of assuming the name and the insignia of an Inca. These competitions consisted of a foot-race, individual contests with weapons, similar contests between two bands, and finally a battle between two army corps, one of which had to defend a fortress while another attacked it. They also had to prove that they were able to bear pain and toil without complaining, and had to show their capability of making their own clothes and equipment.

When these tests had been gone through successfully, the youthful band would be led before the king by their masters, who were highly experienced Incas and Amautas. He invested them with the insignia of their new position, and henceforward they were no longer called auqui, but took the title of Inca. The

Spaniards' Name for the Incas

king bored the lobe of each one's ear with a golden needle, and from that time he might wear gold and silver ear ornaments. This habit was carried to such an extent that the Spaniards gave the Incas the name of Orejones, " large-eared," because the weight of their ornaments had drawn out the lobes to a remarkable extent. Up to this point the youths had been clothed simply and almost inadequately ; but on their festival day their nearest relations put upon them fine sandals, as they were worn by grown-up Incas, fastened the " huara " of fine vicuna wool around their loins, and placed the head-covering, " llautu," upon their hair, which was now closely cropped. The marks of rank worn by the ruler coincided very nearly with these ; only his llautu was bordered with a fine fringe of red wool—in the case of heirs to the throne of full age, the colour was yellow— which descended to the eyebrows, and a thick tassel of similar colour, the " paicha," adorned his right temple.

A juristic system can scarcely exist in a kingdom where the ruler is the source of all law and of every decree ; the officials to whom the Inca deputed the rule of certain portions of the people decided what matters were punishable and what could be allowed. As there was no real property, there could be no pecuniary troubles and no fines. Anyone who was guilty of an offence had outraged the laws of the Inca, the representative of the highest god, and was therefore almost invariably punished with death ; that is to say, he was either strangled, knocked on the head,

The Severe Punishment of Law-Breakers

shot with arrows, or thrown from the rocks. The sun-maidens guilty of incontinence were walled up alive ; but their seducers, and also the entire family which had brought up such an adept in wickedness, were put to death, and the place where their house had stood was sown with salt and left deserted for ever.

The greater became the extent of the Inca kingdom, the more important became the means of quick communication. In early times the Incas had confronted the question of crossing the high mountain ranges which divided one highland valley from another, and the watercourses which rushed furiously down the deeper valleys. When the Inca Pachacutek marched against Huilcabamba, his enemy broke down the bridges over the Urubamba, and thought thereby to oppose an impassable obstacle to the advance of the Inca army ; but the Inca called up engineers and workmen from the capitals and from the whole country to his aid, and a new bridge was completed after a few weeks.

The Inca Pachacutek, who here showed his great faculty for organisation, had a high-road built from Cuzco as far as Cajamarca, a distance of nearly a hundred miles ; it ran over passes and through valleys, over marshes and through rocks, and its remains are in existence to-day. In the time of the Spanish rule this high-road formed the main entry of the country, as did a similar high-road built by the Inca Yupanki, running on the west of Pachacutek's road down to the coast, which it followed as far as Tumbez, the most northern settlement of the Inca kingdom on the sea, lying not far from the Gulf of Guayaquil.

As the Peruvians were totally unacquainted with vehicles, the roads were intended only for the traffic of men, and at most for the llamas that were used as beasts of burden; consequently they were only eighteen to twenty-two feet broad, and were enclosed on either side by a parapet of some height. Upon deep precipices they became narrower, and flights of steps occasionally crossed the ranges which divided the several valleys. Where there were no fords, the rivers were crossed by bridges of stone, which in the mountain ranges gave place to suspension bridges constructed of hempen rope and of woven lianas. Long boarded paths gave a footing across the marshes of the Paramos and the watersheds. At

Resting-places in the Mountains regular intervals resting-places were built near the road, called "tambos"; they consisted of a walled-in courtyard intended for beasts of burden, to which adjoined two open rooms for the travellers themselves. Smaller refuges at shorter intervals on all the most important lines of communication were established for the public service. In them were stationed the foot-messengers, known as "chasquis," by whose help news of important events, from the remotest provinces, could be brought to the capital in a short space of time.

How highly swiftness of foot was valued can be seen from the fact that it was included in the tests which the sons of the Incas had to undergo. Thus even among the common people the foot-messenger was a privileged person. Several runners were invariably stationed in the little post-houses; as often as a messenger came in, wearied by the rapidity with which he had passed over his section, one of those waiting took over his message, which was delivered either by word of mouth or by means of the quipus, to take it on to the next station at an equal speed. The service is said to have been so admirably organised that fresh sea-fish were by no means a rarity at the ruler's table.

It may be an injustice to the merits of the other Inca kings to ascribe nearly all valuable institutions to the Inca Pachacutek; but his name shows that he must have established the lion's share of these. "Pachacutek" means "world-organiser." He was succeeded upon the throne of Tahuantinsuyu by his eldest son, Tupak

Extension of Inca Territory Yupanki, who, like his father, united military reputation to a capacity for keen and vigorous government at home. Under his rule the Inca kingdom was extended in nearly every direction until it recovered that territory which it possessed at the time of the conquest. He completed the subjugation of the kingdom of Chimu, and pressed his conquest forward to Quito.

On the other side he changed the confederation with the princes round the lake of Titicaca into a firm dominion over them, while he also extended his power into Chili as far as the Rio Maule. It was never the Inca policy to introduce the organisation of the ancient provinces, in all its carefully thought out details, into new districts immediately upon their subjugation. Where similar institutions already existed, as they did in the kingdom of Chimu, the process of assimilation was probably distinctly rapid. But other provinces, whose institutions showed marked differences, could only by slow degrees be incorporated in the social organism of the Inca state, as is proved by the frequent recurrence of revolts under the Inca régime. The Inca rulers found colonisation the best means of repressing these; Tupak Yupanki is said constantly to have practised it.

At the time of the Spanish conquest the language of the Yunca had not entirely died out upon the lake of Titicaca, among the mitimaes whom Tupak Yupanki had settled there after the conquest of the Chimu kingdom. This Inca was a zealous worshipper of Huiracocha; after the con-

The Spaniards on American Soil quest of Hatun-Colla he made a pilgrimage to his shrine on the lake of Titicaca, and adorned it with new buildings in his honour, though these included a sun-temple and a house for the sun-maidens. At the same time he prosecuted those unifying religious tendencies which the Incas had made their guiding principle since the time of the Inca Huiracocha. When his son, Huaina Capak, ascended the throne, the Spaniards had already got a footing upon American soil; reports of their arrival can hardly have failed to reach Cuzco. The subjects of the Inca upon the coast land carried on an extensive traffic upon the Pacific seaboard, exchanging their products for those of their northern neighbours, and such traffic must have been under the control and protection of the government.

Conquest of the Quito Kingdom But the Incas were too entirely convinced of their own superiority to have had any suspicion that their period of prosperity was coming to a rapid end. The reign of Huaina Capak is full of those relations with the kingdom of Quito which were to exercise such influence upon the fate of his dynasty.

The first act of his government was to take revenge upon the inhabitants of Quito for the blood of the Inca-Peruvians who had been slain upon the revolt of the provinces conquered by Tupak Yupanki. This business kept him far from the capital for many years. At that time the Inca developed a strong preference for the milder climate on the north of his kingdom; in Tumebamba, which he had fitted up as his headquarters during the campaign, he built palaces, temples, and gardens of a splendour almost equal to those of Cuzco. And when he eventually succeeded in completing the conquest of the kingdom of Quito he married the Princess Paccha, the only daughter of the last ruler, in order to unite the province more closely to his person and to his kingdom.

Huaina Capak was not very fortunate in his domestic life. While his father was alive he held the position of heir to the throne, according to the new laws of succession, and had therefore chosen his eldest sister to be his legal wife; but she bore him no children. Thereupon he took two other wives of the Inca race, a younger sister and a cousin, on the condition that the one who first bore him a son should receive the privileges of the coya. Shortly afterwards his sister presented

Heir to the Inca Throne him with a successor, Huascar. But while he was absent in Quito he began to forget the mother and child; and Paccha, whom he had made a legal wife in defiance of the law which governed his domestic affairs— for this princess was not of the Inca race— became doubly dear to him when she presented him with a boy whose lively spirit won his father's heart even in his childhood. Huaina Capak was naturally

obliged to return at intervals to Cuzco, that being still the central point of the kingdom; but as soon as he had performed his state duties he again returned to his beloved Quito, and there he spent the greater portion of his life.

The Inca kingdom was at this time capable of extension only upon its northern boundary. On the west the ocean formed the boundary of the country for hundreds of miles. In the south the kingdom extended into Chili, where the highlands, which became wilder and wilder at every step, seemed scarcely worth the trouble of conquest. On the east every single inhabitant of the fruitful valleys of the Cordilleras was subject to his rule.

The boundless primeval forest which bordered the lowland was inhabited only by wandering tribes of savages who avoided every attempt to subdue them by vanishing without a trace as soon as the Inca armies approached; and the unhealthy climate, and the impossibility of following their usual mode of life, induced the Incas to renounce all plans of conquest in this direction. Upon the north, however, they were enticed by a valuable territory

Domestic Troubles of Inca King where the conditions of life were very similar to those of their home. Huaina Capak turned his arms more than once in this direction; and Quito was an admirable base of operations for expeditions northward. It does not appear that Paccha ever accompanied her husband to Cuzco; the feeling among the Incas, who were so zealous to preserve the purity of their race, was anything but favourable towards her. It is equally unlikely that the mother of Huascar accompanied her husband to Quito; but the young prince was summoned there at least once, with many of his elder relations, to learn from his father's mouth the manner in which he desired the government to be conducted in the event of his death.

He could not persuade himself entirely to exclude his favourite son from the succession. Atahualpa, who had grown up to the entire satisfaction of his father, accompanied him everywhere on his journeys and campaigns, and his lively manners had made him the favourite of the army. On the other hand, Huascar developed but slowly: his character was serious and quiet; the court which the ruler had abandoned, the coya who was scorned and rejected, and the danger that he himself might be disinherited —all these facts tended to darken his early years. Huaina Capak did not venture upon the extreme step of changing the succession; but he stipulated that the kingdom of Quito should be held in independence by his favourite Atahualpa, and that Huascar should inherit the Inca kingdom, even as Huaina Capak had himself received it upon his accession.

Huascar gladly agreed not to disturb his brother in his possessions, and to remain on terms of friendship with him; the arrangement was for him a relief from long anxiety. But Atahualpa had also reason for satisfaction: he was better provided for than an Inca's inferior son had ever been, and in his person was revived the royal house of Quito. It was only the legitimist party at the court of Cuzco who were dissatisfied; they thought it was a disgrace that the unity of the kingdom should be endangered by the caprice of Huaina Capak, that a province should be lost again to the Sun state which had been bought with the blood of its subjects under two kings, and all for the sake of a child who had neither position nor right. However, such objections were naturally not ventured in face of the unlimited powers of Huaina Capak, and when he died a few years later, in the prime of life, in an epidemic of smallpox in Quito, he was able to close his eyes in the belief that he had secured the welfare of his kingdom and of his favourite.

Atahualpa had developed early, and, after sharing for years in all his father's business of war and peace, had become fully acquainted with the duties of a ruler. He immediately undertook the government of the state to which his father had destined him, and there remained at his side all those who had served Huaina Capak in his lifetime. In Cuzco, on the other hand, people clung obstinately to the old regulations. Huascar was not

Huascar   Atahualpa

THE LAST OF THE INCAS

The sons of Huaina Capak by different mothers, Huascar received the kingdom of Peru at his father's death, while Atahualpa obtained the kingdom of Quito. In a war between the brothers, Atahualpa was victorious, but was subsequently strangled by the Spaniards.

yet of age, and a council of the oldest relations of the dead monarch held the reins of power. In their eyes the capricious dispositions of Huaina Capak did not hold good, because they violated the succession of the house; they were willing to recognise Atahualpa only as the representative of the Inca for the province of Quito. The obligation of presenting himself in Cuzco to pay allegiance to the new king was as binding upon him as upon all the members of the royal family. The regents did not, however, venture to answer Atahualpa's contemptuous silence by an open attack. It was only when Huascar had been proclaimed monarch in Cuzco, after undergoing the customary period of preparation, and with all the usual brilliant festivities, that a different policy was begun. In order to make trial of the feeling entertained in Quito towards the claims of the legitimists, Huascar demanded of Atahualpa that he should send to Cuzco the wife and the treasures of the late monarch which were still in Quito. Atahualpa rejected this demand, appealing to the last wishes of Huaina Capak; yet he allowed it to be clearly understood that he was ready to continue negotiations. The embassy that Huascar had sent to Quito proposed to Atahualpa that he should put in an appearance as quickly as possible in Cuzco; he only asked to be allowed to make his entry with the ceremonial that befitted his rank, to be given a space of time for preparation, and to be permitted to bring a large company of retainers.

These demands the Inca was foolish enough to concede. A period of feverish energy now began in Quito. All the old generals of Huaina Capak who had remained in Quito from inclination to the prince and respect to his father's will were now called up to Atahualpa and ordered to reorganise their contingents. It was not difficult, with the treasures of the old king, to provide the equipment of a powerful army ; and small divisions of this force started toward Cuzco under pretext of forming the retinue of Atahualpa, who was coming to offer his allegiance. When the Inca's eyes were at last opened, it was not difficult for him to call his subjects together in arms in great

The Last of the Incas at War numbers ; but these contingents did not form an army. A few miles from Cuzco, not far from the place where once the Inca Huiracocha had beaten the Chanca in a bloody conflict, the armies of the brothers met. The young troops of Huascar could not withstand the superior tactics of the enemy ; Huascar himself fell into the hands of the conquerors as he was trying to cut his way through their ranks to Cuzco. Thereupon all resistance ceased throughout the kingdom, and the capital surrendered unconditionally to the victorious army. Atahualpa made a cowardly use of his victory. Under the pretence of settling the limits which should divide his power from that of Huascar, he summoned every member of the Inca blood to Cuzco ; but every person who entered the town was immediately arrested, and slain by his generals, who held the town under martial law.

Atahualpa had not been able to forget that the Incas were not willing to recognise his equality, as he was the son of a foreigner ; those alone were spared who had favoured him from the outset. But Cuzco was no longer the heart of the kingdom. Atahualpa disliked visiting the scene of his dreadful vengeance ; such departments of the government as had to be carried on in Cuzco were undertaken by his officials. He himself made a journey of inspection through the central provinces of the kingdom. But before he had returned from this expedition, news reached him that strangers had landed in the extreme north

Landing of Pizarro in America of his kingdom. These were Pizarro and his following. The Spaniards have often been reproached with their ruthless destruction in the New World of a civilisation which was but little inferior to their own, and afforded the best hopes for future prosperity. The romantic enthusiasm for the manners and customs of the past which possessed men in the first half of our century extended also to the New World. The organisation of the Aztec states, and

still more that of the Inca kingdom, appeared to be the ideal of a polity in which king and people, in their mutual relations, had solved with complete success the great difficulty of all political science— namely, to make the freedom and prosperity of individuals exactly correspond with the general good.

It is already sufficiently plain, from what we have said, that such a theory is refuted by an examination of the actual conditions of the Inca kingdom. Undoubtedly the Inca state succeeded to a remarkable extent in solving the problem of an extensive state control for the good of each individual subject ; but this success was attained only by means of an unparalleled system of surveillance which reduced individuals to the position of helpless instruments in the community, and entirely destroyed all personal freedom.

Equally erroneous is the idea that anything remarkable was to be expected from a further development of the ancient American civilisation. Neither the Aztec nor the Inca kingdom represented the highest point of an uninterrupted develop-

The Decadence of Aztec and Inca Civilisations ment. The sites of civilisation in the new continent were the scene of the rise and fall of peoples, of their exodus, and of their immigration even as was the case in wide districts inhabited by uncivilised races, and the rise of a people implied a retrogression in civilisation no less in the New World than in the Old. Both the Aztec and the Inca kingdoms were in their decadence at the time of the Spanish invasion. The Inca kingdom had certainly passed through more than one internal dynastic revolution without receiving any important check to its development. But it would not so easily have survived the revolution which must have followed upon the fall of the Inca race—a fall brought about by the passionate hatred of Atahualpa.

Moreover, even here the size of the kingdom, in spite of the wonderful centralisation of the government, had almost reached the limits of what was possible at that period. The extraordinarily rapid successes of Cortes and Pizarro, who were able to shatter mighty kingdoms with a handful of hungry adventurers, can be explained only by the fact that both civilisations were in their decadence and bore the germs of destruction within themselves.

DISCOVERY of AMERICA & THE SPANISH CONQUEST

THE LURE OF THE GOLDEN EAST
AND HOW IT LED TO WESTERN DISCOVERY

THE ideas prevailing in the fifteenth century as to the formation of the earth's surface left no room for the existence of a new continent; although the learned had withdrawn their opposition to the theory of the earth being round, yet this doctrine had hardly penetrated the minds of the public, and a number of other erroneous ideas still prevailed both in learned and in illiterate circles. Petrus de Alliaco's "Imago Mundi" was still the text book for the science of geography, and no more modern work on this subject could seriously claim precedence over it.

The interest taken in the subject, moreover, remained for a long time very limited. The constructive method of the scholars of the day satisfied people so entirely that they did not consider it worth their while to acquaint themselves practically with that which lay outside their range of experience. Nor, indeed, was it eventually the science of the time from which proceeded that impulse which in its final consequences led to the knowledge by mankind of the habitable globe.

Even the Crusades, which were undoubtedly an important factor in the extension of man's knowledge of the earth and of its inhabitants, affected that knowledge only within the limits **The Crusades** of the world as it was already **as an Aid** known through the traditions **to Knowledge** of antiquity. The Crusades might, indeed, serve to render such knowledge more real, and to reconnect those threads which had been severed by the events of the intermediate centuries; but they neither chiefly nor directly enlarged the stock of geographical knowledge.

Such a knowledge was, however, evolved by the more intimate contact between the Christian and Mohammedan civilisations which the Crusades had brought about. The teaching of Mohammed had then already extended beyond the limits of the **The First** world which had been disclosed **Voyages to** to previous ages. The brisk in- **the East** tercourse between the holy city of Mecca and all the districts inhabited by the followers of Mohammed, which was the natural consequence of the prophet's precepts in the first instance, not only enriched the knowledge of the Arabs, but also, through them, became the means of its extension in the Old World, and thus gave rise to the first voyages undertaken by two enterprising Italian merchants, Niccolo de Conti and Marco Polo, into the remotest regions of the East.

The news of the immense wealth of the kingdom of the Great Khan, of the town of Cathay, and of the island of Zipangu—that is to say, in China and Japan—which these travellers had either seen personally or heard from eye-witnesses, gave a powerful stimulus in mercantile circles to the extension of the knowledge, enterprise, and business of the time. This impulse was, moreover, not confined to those circles. The development of closer relations with the East led to the knowledge that Christianity had advanced further than had hitherto been imagined.

In place of the legendary tales of the journeys of the Apostle St. Thomas, who was said to have preached the gospel to the heathen in the Farthest East, came the story of the Christian realm of Prester John, which was reputed to have a remote but happy and brilliant existence on the other side of that great desert which formed the boundary of the Old World of civilisation. The desire to join hands with these distant fellow believers, and with their help to open up new regions for the spreading of the gospel, which mission in the Old World was continually suffering reverses from

Fabulous Treasures of the East

Mohammedan rule, was combined with the thirst felt by adventurers and merchants for the fabulous treasures of the East. The first attempts to discover a route to the Indies sprang from these motives. The Italians were the chief originators of such ideas, but the political disruptions of their country proved a hindrance to the carrying out of any extensive enterprises on the part of Italy.

It was rather the small kingdom of Portugal which, through accidental circumstances, became the focus of these ideas. This kingdom, which on the land side was cut off by the Spanish states, was, both by Nature and by political necessity, dependent on the sea, and a large colony of foreigners, among whom the Italians were numerously represented, quickened the spirit of enterprise of its own people and brought them into contact with all that went on in the wider circles of the civilised world. It was a peculiarly fortunate circumstance that in the person of the infante Henry—to whom posterity has given the name of " the Navigator," although he had scarcely ever been on board a ship—a man arose who brought energy and organising capacity to bear on the efforts to procure for Christianity a wider extension, and for the Old World a more direct connection with the legendary East.

When, at length, such voyages of discovery, originally undertaken entirely on Prince Henry's account, no longer merely involved sacrifices without returning anything save purely theoretical gains, Portuguese vessels pushed farther and farther

Prince Henry the Patron of Discovery

along the coasts of Africa, at first, entirely at Henry's instigation, taking the course indicated by him, with the definite object of discovering a way to the riches of India and to the land of Prester John. They did not, it is true, attain their goal until after the New World had arisen from the waters of the Atlantic Ocean before the astonished eyes of Columbus and his companions ; nevertheless, it was their action as pioneers which alone

rendered possible the feat of Columbus. Cristoforo Colombo or Colon—or, as we will here call him by his more familiar name, Christopher Columbus—the son of a weaver and innkeeper, Domenico Colombo, by his wife, Susanna Fontanarossa, was born about the year 1447. As his father travelled backward and forward several times between Genoa and Savona, Christopher's birthplace cannot be fixed, for he appears to have looked on both towns as his home. All the pretensions of the numerous other towns are without justification. He was the eldest of Domenico's five children, three brothers and one sister being born after him. The weavers of Genoa had their own guild school, which, no doubt, Christopher attended.

Naturally, the education which he received there was not very advanced, and the knowledge which he acquired in this period—and for those times it was not inconsiderable—was due to his bright intelligence and unusual energy. The boy had early to assist his father in his trade, although he seems to have had but slight inclination for the work, and even after

Character of Christopher Columbus

he had succeeded in obtaining a berth on a merchant ship and had made some voyages, on his return home he was again obliged to resume his former occupation. It is certain that up to his twenty-fifth year he had not been able to free himself permanently. In 1474 he disappeared from Genoa, and some years later he reappeared at Lisbon as a sailor, making every endeavour to conceal the fact that he had ever been anything else.

Columbus was not one of those great geniuses who, in the certain consciousness of their own worth, look back upon their path with peace and satisfaction. Like many of his contemporary countrymen, he was an aspirer in whom a fair amount of self-complacency and boastfulness was joined to cleverness and energy—a combination which in hundreds of cases produces a charlatan, and in rare instances a true man. He was ashamed of his low origin and of his humble trade ; but if we were to rely only on his own words we should assume that he had been of gentle birth and a sailor from his youth. As we can prove to have been untrue, we may also doubt his alleged naval achievements. It is quite possible that he sailed across the Mediterranean Sea as far as the Levant, and had seen the harbours on the coasts of the Atlantic, from England on the north to the coasts of Guinea on the south—the southern limit of the Portuguese voyages. Evidently he did not always sail as a peaceful merchant, for he claims to have gone as a privateer in the service of King René, which must have been about the year 1472, when René supported the rebellious people of Barcelona ; and in 1476 he is said to have been shipwrecked o the Portuguese coast at the time when the Venetian gondoliers were engaged in severe battles with the dreaded French pirate Coullon. His naval activity can, however, have been neither of long duration nor very conspicuous, for the accounts of his career give no time for the former, and the practical proofs of his nautical skill were inade-

CHRISTOPHER COLUMBUS
Born about 1447, Columbus earned undying fame by his discovery of America. From a picture painted in the fifteenth century.

quate to support the idea of long and profound training. Columbus passed a number of uneventful years in Portugal, during which time he married Felipa Moniz, in whose veins the Italian blood of the renowned Perestrello flowed. This connection may possibly have had its influence on the formation of his life. In Portugal he evolved the plan fcr the western passage to India, and for this purpose the influence which he may have acquired through his wife's relations possibly proved of some use to him. The story that he had received from a dying sailor the secret of the discovery of a whole western continent, as a Christmas legacy at the house of his mother-in-law in the Azores, is so clumsy a fabrication that it is surprising that it has been so long credited. Truly such a gift was not needed to assist Columbus in his plan. The idea that the Indies might be reached by a horter route by sailing around the globe in a straight westerly direction seemed more feasible to the

PAOLO TOSCANELLI
A celebrated Portuguese physician and cosmographer, he prepared a document on the practicability of a western passage to Asia, and by following his directions Columbus discovered America.

Portuguese the more their discoveries led them to realise that the African continent stretched itself out in a southerly direction, necessitating a deviation from the eastern course. No doubt, in the first instance, the practicability of a western passage to the Indies was primarily taken into serious consideration by Portuguese circles ; and as the opinions of Portuguese sailors were not considered sufficient evidence, the advice of foreign authorities on the cosmography of that region was also obtained. Fernam Martin, the king's confessor, consulted the celebrated physician and cosmographer, Paolo dal Pozzo Toscanelli, concerning this question. Following up this inquiry, the great Florentine drew up a somewhat lengthy document on the practicability of a western passage to Asia. It was this pamphlet that, probably for the first time, gave a chart illustrative of that part of the unexplored world which was to be opened up by the western passage. By means of this letter and the accompanying chart, which later on—probably by illegal means —came into the hands of Columbus, Toscanelli became the actual originator of the discovery of America. He realised as little, of course, as did Columbus to what results his instructions were destined to lead, but, taking into consideration the almost slavish dependence with which Columbus allowed himself to be guided in his voyage of discovery by the map and directions of Toscanelli, one cannot help crediting the latter with a very considerable share in the solution of the problem of the western passage. Stress must more especially be laid upon this point because Toscanelli's share did not consist of a combination of crude ideas and fatalism which, as in the case of Columbus, might lead an adventurer to sacrifice his life in the pursuit of a foolhardy idea; it was the result of well-founded and careful scientific research, which, though not proving to be absolutely correct, was nevertheless, in its principles, completely justified. Columbus's whole plan probably first originated through his having received **Columbus's Indebtedness to Toscanelli** information of Toscanelli's statements, and then in his adopting and giving out these views as his own. Such an origin of the plan nullifies the statement that the account of the voyages of the Icelanders and Esquimaux to the North American continent had influenced the development of Columbus's ideas.

Columbus certainly maintained that he had penetrated in a northerly direction a hundred miles beyond Thule; but, considering that Thule was by no means an established geographical fact during the fifteenth century, the whole bears the stamp of a swaggering invention. The Arctic archipelago no doubt forms a bridge between the old and the new continents in the extreme north, and we know for certain that a connection, apart from Columbus's achievement, has been established in both directions, from west to east and from east to west, between the inhabitants of both continents, the Esquimaux having penetrated as far as Greenland; the Icelanders, on the other hand, having been driven by east winds to the coasts of northern America.

About 1000 A.D. Leif Eriksen—and some years after, his widow with Thorfinn Karlsevni—founded colonies of Norse Vikings on American soil, which are mentioned in the Northern Sagas. Through unfavourable circumstances, however, these colonies after a few years died out. It is impossible that the northern Scandinavian bards had the slightest idea that Finland and Huitramannaland—for so they called the newly discovered regions **What Columbus Sought** —were anything but a continuation of the chain of islands extending from Iceland and Faröe and beyond Greenland, and it is equally improbable that, even if it had reached the ears of Columbus, it would have proved of any significance to the furtherance of his plan for a western passage to the treasures of India.

The sailors' tales were of far greater value, not only to Columbus, but also to the council commissioned by the king to consider the possibility of a western passage. The Atlantic Ocean had cast up on many different parts of the Old World coasts specimens which showed that it also washed a completely different world; and the fact that these objects thrown up were often in good preservation strengthened the idea that the trans-Atlantic distance of the east coast of Asia, which was regarded as the only possible home of these objects, could not be insurmountably great.

The same inference was drawn from the reports of the few travellers who had penetrated as far as the Great Khan. These had purposely somewhat exaggerated the distances, and had unintentionally overrated the deviations from the direct course, so that people had been led to the conviction that the distance from Europe by land to Quinsay and Zaitun must greatly exceed the half circumference of the globe, and accordingly the distance by sea, calculated in the western passage, would prove decidedly less. The great difficulty presenting itself, however, was that the greater part of the passage would have to **The Dangers of the Unknown Seas** be traversed without coming in sight of land, and, as a matter of fact, this really meant more than was then assumed. At that time people had indeed dared to attempt to cross the Mediterranean irrespective of the land, all its basins being well known in every direction, and the ships trading between the Mediterranean and Flanders, England and the Baltic countries, sometimes lost sight of land for days; but in general, in crossing the ocean from Guinea to England, the vessels always coasted, for the sailor kept within reach of land in case of threatening danger.

There were supposed to be numerous more or less extensive islands in the Atlantic Ocean, and these were duly entered on the ancient maps. Among these were Antilia, the remnant of the continent whose destruction Plato describes in "Timæus," St. Brandan's Isle, and the Island of the Seven Cities, besides many others. Yet, although they appeared plainly on the maps, the sailors who had for days been driven out of their course on the ocean had never seen more than mere tracts of land on the farthest horizon, which invariably vanished from view on nearer approach. Columbus did not allow himself to be scared by such considerations; though conscious that he might go for

COLUMBUS EXPLAINING HIS PROJECT TO THE MONKS OF LA RABIDA
From the paining by Izquierdo, photo Lacoste

BEFORE THE COUNCIL OF SALAMANCA: COLUMBUS PLEADING HIS CAUSE

Columbus pleaded long and earnestly before he persuaded people to assist him in his maritime expeditions by providing the necessary means. His first assured partisans were the guardians of the Franciscan monastery, La Rabida,
at Huelva, and the doctor of the neighbouring little town of Palos, Garcia Fernandez. He pleaded in vain before
a learned assembly at Salamanca, and was about to journey abroad, in order to offer his plans to foreign monarchs,
when in Queen Isabella he found a staunch friend, whose influence procured him the use of ships for his voyage.
From the painting by Julius Röting

weeks and months without discovering land, he was resolved to navigate the boundless ocean: this was the one peculiarity of his plan, and, above all, it merits recognition and regard.

There are no means of ascertaining the truth of Columbus's claim that he urged his project for the western passage upon the King of Portugal during fourteen years. It is, on the contrary, quite certain that he stayed in Portugal for only eight and not for fourteen years, and that during his stay there he was often absent from court for long periods, occupied with other concerns. As a matter of fact, we begin to know more about him and his projects only from the time when he left Portugal.

Columbus's Flight from Portugal

Neither did Columbus leave voluntarily, but because he had committed an offence for which he could expect only severe punishment. On account of this he deserted his wife and children, and, accompanied solely by his four-year-old son, Diego, fled the country. The nature of his offence is not recorded. Doubtful financial affairs and disputes with the royal officials have been surmised; but probably his crime was more closely connected with his project, for which he had appropriated Toscanelli's letter and chart, the materials most essential to his plan. The commentators of the Toscanelli correspondence have always had to face great difficulties, because the only correct and comprehensible portion is that addressed to Fernam Martin, while the alleged postscript to Columbus, which, as well as the former portion, is known only through a copy by Columbus, is filled with impossibilities.

Why, then, should not the man who disowned his ancestors and his antecedents, and invented a coat of arms and a noble pedigree for himself, also have invented the postscript to a letter of which Toscanelli is said for years—if Columbus's representations be correct—to have preserved the rough draft, and even to have stupidly kept the address and signature—a thing which Columbus did not even do in his forgery? This is also the explanation why King John was so willing to exempt Columbus from punishment and then assure his return when it became apparent that an attempt was to be made from Spain to carry out the project which John, with his seamen, had privately attempted. The plans of Columbus did not meet with

The Case Against Columbus

an immediate friendly reception in Spain. He had in this country also to strive with precarious circumstances for some years before he succeeded in gaining a small number of trustworthy followers who, allowing themselves to be convinced by him, assisted in his endeavour to gain a hearing from the king. During this time he made his living by the sale of books and maps, and no doubt, while carrying on this trade, he acquired that singular knowledge of books which, later on, is so prominent in all his writings. An attachment to a young lady of Cordova, Beatrice Enriquez, for a time bound him to the old city of the caliph, but he proved as faithless to his mistress as he had been to his wife.

During the whole of his life he retained an interest in the son whom he had had by her, Fernando Colon, who in course of time became celebrated for his writings and for his library, which are still preserved in Seville. Of his mistress he thought again, and then with remorse, only when, face to face with death, he was making his will. The children did not accompany him on his wanderings. Little Diego was in charge of a brother-in-law in Huelva, and Fernando remained for a time with his mother. It was not until after Columbus had attained his desire of gaining over the Spanish rulers in favour of his voyage of discovery that his sons entered the royal service as pages, and from that time they shared their father's successes and failures.

The First Supporters of the Explorer

The first assured partisans whom Columbus gained for his plans were the guardian of the Franciscan monastery, La Rabida, at Huelva, Fray Juan Perez de Marchena, and the doctor of the neighbouring little town of Palos, Garcia Fernandez. Both voluntarily occupied their leisure hours with cosmographical studies, and when Columbus, during his flight from Portugal, sought shelter in the monastery, a friendship founded on mutual interests soon sprang up between these men, which was to prove of extraordinary value to Columbus in later years.

At that time he travelled on, after a brief sojourn, in order to make his own way independently, but it was many years before he again found anyone else to take so intelligent an interest in his plans, which were then shrouded with fantastic superfluities. Not until the year 1486 did Celi, Duke of Medina, espouse his cause. The duke probably would have entrusted him with a ship for a trial voyage from his seaport town of Santa Maria, near Cadiz, had not Queen Isabella, in consequence of the duke's reports, manifested her interest and summoned Columbus to the court. The position of Columbus at that time, with his imperfectly constructed and unscientifically formed ideas, was naturally a difficult one in the presence of the ecclesiastical and secular authorities whom Ferdinand and Isabella had assembled at their court. He was universally pronounced to be an Italian boaster, and the proofs which he gave were not considered convincing either in Cordova or in Salamanca, where he was also permitted to explain his plans before a learned assembly.

It so happened that the final removal of the last remnants of Moorish power on the Iberian Peninsula formed the immediate aim of the Spanish ruler, and demanded the consolidation of all the forces of the country hitherto so imperfectly developed.
Columbus Waiting for Assistance Columbus therefore had to remain satisfied, for although the further consideration of his plans was postponed to a more favourable time, the queen's interest, once aroused in his behalf, was the means of procuring him a yearly allowance. It is true that in his impatience the time of waiting seemed long; and he had already formed the resolution to continue his journey and to offer his plans to other monarchs, when at last a combination of various circumstances brought about the fulfilment of his desire, which meanwhile had grown into a fixed idea. He returned to the monastery, La Rabida, with the intention of fetching his son Diego from Huelva, and then travelling to France.

His friends there were so impressed by his projects, which in the course of the negotiations had gained much in clearness and distinctness, that the warden invited him to remain while he made another and final attempt on his behalf. Fray Juan Perez de Marchena had in former years been father-confessor to the queen, and on the strength of this he undertook to press

Columbus's enterprise most warmly upon her attention. The words of the priest fell upon fruitful soil. His message reached the queen while in the camp of Santa Fé before the Moorish capital of Granada, just at the time when the fall of the last hostile bastion and the final consummation of the great life-work of the Spanish nation was looked forward to with feelings of exultation. Columbus was once more summoned to the court, and received the assurance that after the fall of Granada he should be provided with means for his attempt. He arrived in time to witness the removal of the crescent from the towers of the Alhambra, and the substitution of the cross, which, shining from afar, was raised on the Moorish citadel. In spite of all, the negotiations were, at the last moment, almost frustrated.

The Mighty Ambitions of the Explorer

Columbus's plans had seemed so sure to his own mind that he, penurious adventurer as he was, conducted himself as though he had kingdoms to give away, and made demands on his own behalf which, if he were to attain his object, would make him richer than the rulers from whom he was now obliged to beg a few hundred pounds. He not only desired a certain share for all time in all the material gain which might accrue through his discoveries, but he also claimed for himself and his descendants the hereditary dignity of a royal admiral over the entire ocean, besides the position of a vice-king in all lands which might be added to the kingdom through his discoveries.

King Ferdinand was particularly enraged by this presumption. All transactions were broken off, and Columbus left the camp; but in spite of this, Queen Isabella prevailed upon her husband to agree to the conditions imposed by this extraordinary man. The treaty was drawn up to meet Columbus's demands, and the town of Palos, which was by chance under the obligation of providing certain ships for the royal service, received the order to place them at Columbus's disposal.

The Help of Queen Isabella

THE PINTA, WHICH WAS COMMANDED BY MARTIN ALONZO PINZON

THE NIÑA, WHICH WAS UNDER THE COMMAND OF VINCENT YANEZ PINZON

The ships shown on this page are exact models of the two little caravels which accompanied the Santa Maria on her famous voyage of discovery, and give an excellent idea of the style and size of the tiny vessels which braved the waters of the Atlantic. In 1892 these models set out from Palos to America, following the same route as that taken by the great admiral himself four hundred years before, and were exhibited at the World's Fair at Chicago.

COLUMBUS'S FAMOUS VOYAGE OF DISCOVERY

THE DISCOVERY OF AMERICA
THE THREE FAMOUS VOYAGES OF COLUMBUS

NEVERTHELESS, all difficulties were not yet overcome. Columbus had to bind himself, on his part, to share the cost, for which he, at that time, actually did not possess the means; and the manning of the three vessels caused considerable difficulties as soon as their destination became known. By interesting the influential naval family of Pinzon, at Palos, in his plans, and gaining their material support for the undertaking by promising them a share of his chartered rights, he succeeded in fitting out and manning the ships for the daring voyage. The little fleet—consisting of the Santa Maria, piloted by Columbus himself; the Pinta, under Martin Alonzo Pinzon; and the Niña, with Vincent Yanez Pinzon—was able to put to sea on August 3rd, 1492. These caravels of Columbus were not large vessels—the Santa Maria had a tonnage of only 120; the Pinta, 100; and the Niña, 80—but they proved so exceptionally fitted for the special purpose of these voyages that they were soon after regarded as models when the much larger vessels which had been employed during the first delirium of success proved to give inferior results.

Start of the Famous Voyage

Columbus had taken Toscanelli's chart on board as part of his equipment, and treated it with the absolute and blind faith of a fanatic. After having lost almost three weeks on the Canary Islands while making necessary repairs, he sailed out into the unknown ocean on September 6th. Thence he took a decidedly westerly course, and he was so firmly convinced of its correctness that he would not permit himself to be diverted from this route even by apparent signs of the nearness of land, although he believed they coincided absolutely with Toscanelli's calculations on the chart. He kept a double record of the distance traversed, in order that the sailors should not become fully conscious of the adventurous nature of the voyage. In the public one he purposely minimised the distances; while in the private one, for his own use, his course followed the chart in order that he might ascertain the position of the land. In spite of all, he was not able to keep the courage of his ignorant sailors unshaken. He had reached the region of the monsoons, and the fact that a strong wind from the east swelled the sails day by day without bringing a sight of the daily promised land made the inexperienced men anxious about the possibility of their return. More than once their fear took the form of animosity against the unknown stranger, who proudly boasted of his authority and was by no means remarkably fitted for seafaring life.

The Trials of the Fateful Voyage

His heart gradually grew heavy, as, morning after morning, the waste of water sparkled with unceasing monotony in the rays of the rising sun. But he did not lose courage or hope, and although the pilots of the other vessels began to lose faith in his ultimate success, they stood firmly by their admiral and assisted him in suppressing the attempts at insubordination which were not infrequent among the crew of the Santa Maria. At last, at the beginning of October, the signs which announced to the sailors the approach of land began to increase, and Columbus impressed on the look-out man the necessity for special care, promising a reward to the one who should first sight the land. During the twilight of October 11th Columbus and several others believed they saw lights across the water in the distance; but night approached before a shot from the Pinta in the lead gave the sign that land had actually been sighted. The sails were hurriedly furled and the course altered, but a whole long night withheld from the expectant sailors the final certainty that the land which had so often been announced, only to vanish once more, was this time no phantom.

Land in Sight at Last

In the dawn of October 12th, 1492, Columbus and his companions saw a fairly large and well-wooded island rising from the sea ; and before they had manned the boats and gained the island, they had been noticed from its shore. Brown, scantily clad men and women watched the approach of the strangers with un-

Where Columbus First Landed mistakable astonishment, and when the land was reached they proved to be good-natured and harmless people, though practically uncivilised, leading a miserable existence as fishermen and hunters. The land was the island of Guanahani (the modern Watling Island), and its inhabitants, whom the Spaniards, in their conviction that the eastern end of Asia had been reached, had called "Indios," were the Aruac Indians, who had not yet been supplanted by the Caribs.

Although the reality compared unfavourably with the expectations which had been cherished, yet Columbus by the discovery of land had succeeded in his undertaking. Information which he obtained from the natives, in spite of imperfect means of intercourse, showed that this was not an isolated island in the ocean. With solemn public worship he took possession of the land, on behalf of the Catholic rulers of Castile and Aragon, and received the oath of allegiance as viceroy and governor from the crew, who from cowardice and hostility had veered round to the opposite extreme.

During the next few days almost every hour brought fresh surprises. After the ships had run up to a series of small islands, a larger expanse of land, the eastern end of Cuba, was sighted on October 28th, and was called by Columbus Isla Fernandina. After following up the coast in a westerly direction for some days without reaching its termination, he returned to the first anchorage, sailed round the eastern point, and, taking a south-easterly course, came upon a second ex-

Discovery of Hispaniola panse of land, to which he gave the name of Hispaniola. The novelty of the impressions received, and the tropical luxuriance of Nature, easily tempted the discoverers to disregard the fact that they had not discovered the slightest trace of the great commercial towns of Eastern Asia, Zaitun, and Quinsay, which they had set out to find. When, in addition to this, the discovery of gold was made by the aid of the inhabitants of Hispaniola, Columbus

was far more anxious to return to Spain, in order that he might bask in the sunshine of the triumph consequent upon success, than to prosecute his discoveries.

He was not to return, however, without tasting the first drop of bitterness in his cup of happiness. On the morning of November 22nd the Pinta made no reply to the signal from the admiral's ship. Martin Alonzo Pinzon had deserted his superior officer, and had set out in search of adventures on his own responsibility, surmising, from the gestures of the natives, the proximity of a region rich in gold. It was the first instance of self-seeking treachery, which, in the course of colonial explorations, was to be followed by many similar ones. This proved the more unfortunate, as the Santa Maria ran aground and had to be abandoned, and thus the Niña, the smallest of the vessels, alone remained to Columbus for the return voyage.

Strange to say, while preparations were being made for the homeward voyage, the Pinta returned, and the admiral, probably more from prudence than from conviction, accepted Pinzon's excuses ;

Columbus Returns in Triumph and on January 14th, 1493, he set sail for home, leaving a small company of voluntary settlers behind. Until they reached the Azores the weather proved extraordinarily favourable for the return, but on nearing their native shore the waves again threatened to engulf the secret of the newly discovered continent. The Pinta was driven far towards the north, and finally entered Vigo harbour. Columbus, having escaped the dangers of the storm, arrived at Lisbon, and had the proud satisfaction of flying the colours of Castile on entering the royal harbour of that king whose belief in his now brilliantly vindicated plans he had failed to gain. His journey to the Spanish court, which was then at Barcelona, resembled a triumphal procession across the kingdom, and he stood in triumph before the rulers from whom he had previously departed as a beggar.

Preparations for a second voyage across the ocean, planned on a much larger scale, were begun almost at once after Columbus's landing. Whereas for the first voyage the great difficulty had been to raise a sufficient number of sailors, in this case it was to know how to select the right men from among the thousands who were anxious to go. The first regulations for

COLUMBUS TAKING LEAVE OF THE PRIOR OF LA RABIDA ON HIS VOYAGE OF DISCOVERY TO THE UNKNOWN WEST

From the painting by R. Balaca, photo by Lacoste

the ordering of the colonisation date from the rules then drawn up. On September 25th a fleet consisting of seventeen large vessels, with more than 1,500 men on board, sailed from Seville for the newly discovered land, and was, as in the first instance, favoured by splendid weather. They first reached the island of Dominica by a slightly different course, and then, passing many new islands, they arrived at Hispaniola. Here, however, disenchantments began. The colonists who had remained behind had failed to maintain friendly relations with the natives, whose animosity they had aroused by their brutality, and through their recklessness they had succumbed to a man. Columbus, in order to lessen the impression that this news might make on the new arrivals, chose a different position for the founding of a permanent colony.

Fate of the First Spanish Colony

The first town on the soil of the New World received the name of Isabella, and through the united exertions of the colonists it rapidly rose above the ground. Not until after Bartholomew Colon had removed the colony and deserted the old town was the name of San Domingo given to the now existing capital. In spite of everything done, most of the settlers were filled with disappointment ; they found neither treasures nor riches, and the reward of each man's work and duty seemed likely to be reaped only by future generations. The reports of those who returned home, therefore, sounded anything but encouraging. The value of the new discovery was doubted more and more, and the general feeling of enthusiasm which among all classes of society had preceded Columbus's second voyage was probably never again manifest during the entire history of Spanish colonial enterprise.

Having established a firm footing on Hispaniola, the admiral himself started out for fresh discoveries. As the coast of Cuba had been followed for weeks without its farthest point being reached, Columbus felt convinced that he had arrived at the Asiatic continent, and he thereupon drew up an authentic report which later on was frequently turned into ridicule. On his return to San Domingo he found that public opinion had quite changed. His authority among the disillusioned colonists was greatly shaken, and was still more weakened by the influence of the news of

Columbus Mistaken in his Discovery

the failure of his latest expedition to discover any rich, populous and civilised regions, such as were believed to exist in Eastern Asia. Further reinforcements led by his brother Bartholomew also brought him the news from home that his reputation at court had suffered. When, in addition to all this, discord and rebellion broke out among the colonists, he deemed it advisable to retreat, and to return to Spain, in order to vindicate himself.

This time Columbus was able to leave his brother as his substitute at the head of the youthful colony ; and as the latter, of all the brothers, possessed the greatest administrative talent, the admiral could cherish the hope that no such dire consequences would threaten the second colony as those that befell the first on his previous departure. When, without serious difficulty, he had succeeded, before the court of the Spanish rulers, in disproving the charges against him and had justified his actions, the government again placed three ships at his disposal, and he could not resist the desire to start once more with them on a voyage of discovery. On this third occasion he kept farther to the south than during his previous attempts, and, coming in touch with only a few islands, he reached the coast of the continent of South America just where it takes a decidedly western course. He followed it up for some distance, but at the highest point of the island Margarita he turned towards the north, more especially because he was himself ailing and in need of rest.

The Third Voyage to America

After a more or less uneventful voyage around the islands of the Antilles he arrived safely at Hispaniola. As proof of how vague and unscientific Columbus's cosmological observations were, is his report of his discoveries. In this, led astray by the huge quantity of pure water which the torrent of the Orinoco carries far into the Caribbean Sea, he gave himself up to the most fantastic speculations, believing that he had arrived at the environs of Paradise, and that his mission as the bringer of salvation appointed by God had been visibly established.

Bartholomew Colon had, during his brother's absence, held the reins of government with a firm hand, though he succeeded only in a measure in maintaining peace and order by banishing the most insubordinate members from the colony. Soon all those who for any reason whatever were dissatisfied with Colon's government had joined them, and Columbus actually found two hostile camps in place of his peaceful settlement. But the means which he employed to put an end to this state of affairs were the most unfortunate that he could have chosen. He drew up a covenant with the dissatisfied, and he certainly achieved the return of these doubtful factors to his dominion not merely by pardoning the leaders, but by re-establishing them in the positions which they had forfeited through their own fault. By doing this he irretrievably lost the confidence of those who desired the re-establish-

one who had frequently distinguished himself in the Moorish wars; but he proved by no means the right person to deal with the abnormal circumstances in the colonies.

Hatred of the specially favoured strangers, who possessed almost unlimited power in the colony, but did not always make a just use of it, inspired the malcontents, and no doubt Bobadilla participated in this feeling even before he reached Hispaniola. The full judiciary powers, also, over the vice-regent himself with which he had been accredited by the Spanish ruler without doubt gave him a formal right to deprive Columbus

THE CLOSE OF A GREAT CAREER: DEATH OF CHRISTOPHER COLUMBUS
Dying at Valladolid on May 21st, 1506, the body of Christopher Columbus was first buried within the precincts of the Franciscan monastery at Valladolid, but, at the instigation of his son, it was eventually removed to a small church in Seville, and thence, in 1537, to San Domingo. In 1798 the discoverer's bones were taken to Havana, and laid to rest in the cathedral there. When, however, Spain lost the remainder of her American colonies in the war of 1898, the remains of the great navigator were brought back to Granada and buried close to those of the Roman Catholic sovereigns.
From the painting by F. Ortego

ment of law and order. While, therefore, one party forced him to make concession after concession, and so led him further from the paths of justice, the other party refused him their support, and turned with complaints toward their native land.

Columbus, in the midst of this confusion, was at his wits' end, and finally joined his entreaties to the complaints of the colonists, requesting the Crown to send an official across the ocean with full powers to examine into the administration of the vice-regent and to re-establish law and order in the unsettled colony. Ferdinand entrusted Francesco de Bobadilla with this difficult mission, as he was a man experienced in native administrative affairs, and

and his brothers of their office. The vice-regent not only submitted unconditionally to the royal decree, but also prevailed upon the less submissive Bartholomew to consent to a similar mode of action. Bobadilla, not content with putting the brothers in chains and transporting them to Spain, confiscated their joint property in the colony in the name of the Crown, and incurred at least the suspicion of party animus, from which he was wholly unable to free himself in spite of the fact of his having inflicted heavy punishments on numerous friends as well as on opponents of the admiral, among whom were many Spaniards. It was a truly humiliating spectacle to behold the man who a few years previously had returned in triumph to lay a newly discovered world at the feet of his sovereigns now land in chains to sue for the intervention of those rulers against the official whom they had endowed with their authority to act as vice-regent. The order which was sent immediately to Seville, that Columbus should instantly be set at

Columbus Fallen on Evil Days liberty and despatched to the court with all the honours due to his rank, was as much instigated by gratitude as by justice; and of Bobadilla's recall there could be no doubt. But he had to rest content with the recognition of the validity of all his rights, and to see a new man—the choice of the rulers fell upon Nicolas de Ovando—appointed to conduct the inquiry into the grievances of the colonists, while he himself was strictly forbidden, until further notice, to set foot in the colony.

Columbus was not the man to remain passive while a point of law was being decided which might be most unfavourably misconstrued by his inaction. The sovereigns had already given to others leave to undertake voyages of discovery, in spite of the wording of his contracts and without the knowledge and co-operation of Columbus. The best way in which most securely to preserve his rights of viceregal power over the whole region opened up by his discovery seemed to him to be to take as keen an interest as possible in the exploration of the land, which still presented many enigmas to him. The rulers placed no difficulties in his way, and for the fourth time he was entrusted with vessels fitted out for voyages of discovery—four in number—and in the event of necessity he received permission to run up to Hispaniola, but only on his return. How little attention Columbus paid to his duty is shown by the fact that he sailed almost straight to San Domingo and

Columbus Again in America demanded permission to enter the harbour, a demand which Ovando justly enough refused, as it would most certainly only have tended to endanger the peace which had in a measure been restored.

After he had weathered a severe storm in the shelter of the island—a storm that to his satisfaction had engulfed a number of ships just fitted out for a voyage home, and with them his enemy Bobadilla, because Ovando had not seen fit to pay any attention to his warnings regarding it—he turned to the south-west, reached the Gulf

of Honduras, and coasted for months toward the east, the south, and again to the east as far as the Gulf of Darien, where the Central American isthmus joins the southern continent. On this voyage he first heard rumours of another ocean in the west, but as far as Columbus personally was concerned, he only reaped bitter want and privation. These reached their culminating point when the last of the four vessels ran aground on the then uncolonised Jamaica, and he had to wait for months without resources until he succeeded in sending news by a fishing-boat to San Domingo summoning help. When Columbus now actually again set foot in his viceregal residence, he was both mentally and physically too crushed to become a source of danger to the country. He returned to Spain after a short stay and found a fresh blow awaiting him there.

Queen Isabella, to whom he owed the achievement of his first voyage, and who had always proved his kind and sympathetic patroness, was dead, and a dispute for the regency of Castile now arose between King Ferdinand, as husband of the late queen,

Death of the Great Discoverer and his son-in-law, Philip the Handsome, of Burgundy, as the husband of her daughter and heiress, the crazy Joanna. While on the point of paying court to the youthful Philip, to whom Castile deserted when he, contrary to Ferdinand's wish, took over the regency on behalf of his mentally afflicted wife, the heiress to the Castilian throne, Columbus became ill at Valladolid and died there, May 21st, 1506, little noticed and mourned by few. His body in death was destined to be as unresting as he himself had been in life. His corpse, first buried in the Franciscan monastery at Valladolid, was, at the instigation of his natural son Fernando, conveyed to the small church of Santa Maria de las Cuevas in Seville, and thence, in 1537, when his heirs had again been restored to the viceregal administration, to San Domingo.

In 1798, when the Spaniards had to abandon the island of Hispaniola, the discoverer's bones were taken to Havana, and until lately reposed in the cathedral there. When, however, in the war of 1898, Spain lost the remainder of her American colonies, the remains of the great navigator were brought back across the ocean and buried close to the Roman Catholic sovereigns at Granada, the city in which the explorer's hopes were first realised.

THE COMING OF THE CONQUISTADORS
BEGINNING OF THE SPANISH COLONISATION

COLUMBUS had died with the firm conviction that the country which he had discovered formed part of the continent of Asia. Even during his fourth voyage he intimated that there was another ocean on the western coast of the Isthmus of Panama, and this prediction would only have been correct had he found himself on a peninsula of Farther India, whose other coast was washed by the waves of the Indian Ocean. The discoveries of other navigators had already begun, even during his lifetime, to shake this conviction.

While Columbus in 1492 was carrying on the negotiations with the Spanish sovereigns, and was almost despairing of a favourable termination, his brother, Bartholomew, was endeavouring to interest the King of England in the project, and had almost achieved a favourable settlement when he received the news of the success of the Spanish deliberations. He thereupon broke off the negotiations ; but Henry VII., whose interest had been fully aroused, soon after empowered another Italian, Giovanni Gabotto —more familiarly known to us as John Cabot—to set out in a westerly direction on a voyage of discovery under the protection of the English flag. In two voyages, which succeeded each other very rapidly, Cabot discovered the part of Northern America reaching from Newfoundland almost down to Florida.

John Cabot Discovers North America

After Columbus's third voyage, several Spanish sailors who had taken part in the admiral's voyages obtained leave to take an independent share in the extension of further discoveries. Among these were Hojeda, with the celebrated and oldest geographer of the New World, Juan de la Cosa, and the Florentine, Amerigo Vespucci, whose clear but unreliable descriptions of his experiences first popularised a knowledge of the New World and gave rise to the idea of calling the new continent by his name. Peralonso Niño and Cristobal Guerra had in the same year (1499) sailed as far as the northern coast of South America, beyond the borders which Columbus had himself reached. Vincente Yañez Pinzon, and after him Diego de Lepe, penetrated to the south as far as Cape St. Augustine, and were the first to discover the delta of the river Amazon. Another accidental discovery, however, proved of greater importance to posterity. On March 19th, 1500, the Portuguese Pedralvarez Cabral had sailed from Lisbon with thirteen ships with the intention of going to the East Indies by way of the Cape of Good Hope, where the Portuguese two years previously had arrived during their voyages of discovery. In order to avoid the dangerous passage along the west coast of Africa he had turned aside in the open ocean far towards the west, and, being driven farther in that direction by easterly winds, he came in sight of the coast of Brazil on April 22nd. After following the coast-line for a time, he took possession of it in the name of his king.

Brazil Claimed by Portugal

This mode of procedure was based on the agreement regarding the settlement of a line of demarcation which had been signed between Spain and Portugal almost immediately after Columbus's discovery. That is to say, the rulers of Portugal had, in order to prevent any legal disputes, made Pope Nicholas V. invest them, at the beginning of their era of active discovery, with all lands which they might discover during their voyages to the south and east. It so happened that Columbus's enterprise was directed towards the same India which, at the time of his first voyage, had not yet been reached by the Portuguese ; the Spanish sovereigns therefore hastened, after the return of Columbus, to have their claims also sanctioned by the Pope. This was done in the following manner : Pope Alexander VI. awarded to the Spaniards all the land to the west

Claims Sanctioned by the Pope

of the degree of longitude which extended from pole to pole one hundred miles on the other side of the islands of the Azores, and to the Portuguese all that which was situated to the east. Subsequent negotiations between the interested Powers led to an alteration, the line of division being removed 370 Spanish miles

New Territories of Spain and Portugal to the west, on the farther side of the Cape Verd Islands. The Spaniards imagined, according to the position of the discoveries at that time, that they were surrendering to the Portuguese at the most some islands in the ocean, whereas they hoped to secure for themselves, by the displacement of the line, vast districts in the unknown eastern part of Asia.

Not until the discovery of Cabral was it proved to what extent the South American continent jutted out towards the east as compared with the latitudes reached by Columbus, so that a considerable portion of the newly discovered land belonged thereby to the Portuguese. Moreover, the latter were at first so much occupied with the extension and security of their East Indian territory that they gave but little heed to their western colonial possessions. King Manuel, for state reasons, authorised two voyages in order to gain information about the domains which had devolved on him ; but as they did not lead to the discovery of any treasures, either in precious stones or rare spices, he left all subsequent exploration of these countries to the spirit of enterprise in general. During several decades certain Portuguese merchants alone undertook occasional western voyages in order to bring Europe colonial products, especially the highly valuable logwood, " brasil," from which the country in later times received its name.

One of these voyages led to the discovery of the river La Plata in the year 1514 ; but so trifling was the attention paid by

The One Town Founded by Columbus Portugal to events there that the claims of the discoverers were never seriously formulated or protected. The last years of Columbus's life, as well as those following his death, were not taken up so much in new discoveries as with organising colonies in the land which had been acquired. Columbus had personally founded only the one town of San Domingo, on Hispaniola. He was averse to the division of the settlements over the entire island, because he feared that the colonists would thereby be removed from his control, and he deprecated any encroachment on his rights.

During his last voyage Columbus had determined on a second settlement on the coast of Veragua ; but it had to be relinquished almost before it had been decided upon, owing to the hostility of the natives. Nicolas de Ovando, who, not without design, in all questions of organisation advised exactly the opposite to that which Columbus ordered, as being the most serviceable to his own interests, first gave an impetus to the extension of the Spanish colonies in the New World. Not only do a number of new towns on Hispaniola owe their existence to him, but Puerto Rico was at least colonised by his order by Juan Ponce de Leon in 1510. No doubt he would have achieved much more in this direction had not the uncertainty of the colonial conditions of government exercised a deadening influence on him.

During his lifetime Columbus had proposed to King Ferdinand to renounce the enjoyment of his rights on condition that

The Claims of Columbus's Descendants his son Diego should be permitted forthwith to possess them in their entirety. Diego urgently reiterated this demand on the death of his father, and as at first only a few financial concessions were granted to him, and the principal point at issue remained unsettled, he lodged a complaint against the government. Even so the settlement might have been long protracted had not Diego Colon—Columbus— by forming ties of relationship with the ducal house of Alva, gained influential intercessors with King Ferdinand. At any rate, Diego accomplished so much that in 1509 he was again permitted to take over the government of the newly discovered islands, with the title of Royal Governor and Admiral of the Indies. When, in 1511, judgment was passed on his appeal by the Court of First Instance, he was awarded all the official positions, titles, honours and privileges promised to his father in all the countries discovered by him.

Diego Colon was, however, in no wise satisfied with this ; he and his descendants had, moreover, for many years been at law with the Crown in order to secure the extension of their claims, not only over all the land which had been discovered by Columbus himself, but also over that which had, in addition to his father's discoveries, been won for the Spaniards by others. This lawsuit, however, was mixed up with every imaginable sort of unnecessary litigation, which rendered it practically interminable and anything but honourable for either side, so that it lost its actual significance soon after Diego Colon's death in 1526. His legal successor, who was an utter scamp, surrendered the greater part of the prerogatives so that he might extricate himself from all manner of immoral transactions.

After Diego Colon had again attained his viceregal rights, he endeavoured to extend the province which had been secured by actual colonisation; and his first step in this direction was the founding of a Spanish settlement on the island of Cuba by Velasquez, Diego's friend of long standing, who was commissioned to carry it out. Diego, however, experienced the same fate with him as did his father with Martin Alonzo Pinzon. Velasquez undertook the management of the expedition, for which the vice-regent paid the expenses; but no sooner had he established himself in Cuba than he sent reports of his successes direct to the court, representing his achievements in such glowing colours that his authorisation as governor of the island as well as vice-regent, for which he had sued, was not denied to him. The first settlement on the continent also followed close upon the discoveries of Columbus.

Gold on the Coast of Veragua

The eyes of the government, as well as of the lovers of adventure, had been turned to these regions by the gold which he had found in larger quantities on the coast of Veragua. Already in 1508 Alonzo de Hojeda, a veteran explorer, and Diego de Nicuesa had received permission to found two new colonial provinces which were to extend from the Gulf of Uraba to the east, and from ocean to ocean in the west; but their undertakings had been followed by severe misfortune for many years. Not until both leaders had lost their lives through the vicissitudes incidental to their attempts at colonisation was the foundation of a modest settlement achieved on the coast of Darien, receiving the name of Santa Maria la Antigua.

This settlement also might have been ruined, owing to the lack of necessaries and the passive resistance of the natives, if Vasco Nuñez de Balboa had not made a specially suitable leader, who understood how to turn the undertaking into a success. Balboa wanted an accredited legal title for his influential position. While, on the one hand, he turned to Spain in order to have his leaderless companions' selection of himself confirmed, on the other hand he strove to commend himself to the government by some prominent deed. To him, as to Columbus, the Indians had given information about another ocean. The solution of this problem seemed particularly appropriate at a time when the necessity for a farther advance towards the west began to be felt. Partly through his personal ability in managing the Indians, and partly also by the extreme severity with which he met every attempt at insubordination, Nuñez de Balboa succeeded in confining the difficulties incidental to the crossing of the isthmus almost exclusively to bodily hardships and privations, which are unavoidable on a march through sparsely populated and tropically unhealthy forest-land.

De Balboa Discovers the Pacific

Even so he lost many of his followers before he, as the first European, caught sight of the Pacific Ocean from the last mountain range in the west, and was able some days later, on arriving at the coast, to take possession of it and all the islands situated within it. On account of the treasures of gold and pearls which resulted from this expedition, his discovery proved to be highly important. He was not permitted to reap the fruits of his labours, for, before the news of his discovery reached Spain, Pedrarias Davila had sailed as governor of the province of Darien, and by his jealous distrust had prepared a somewhat inglorious end for Balboa.

The country, however—the Isthmus of Panama and the adjoining northern territories—became the oldest most important continental province of the Spanish colonial kingdom, and on account of its treasures it received the name of Castilla del Oro, "Golden Castile." The question whether it was actually the eastern border of the Asiatic continent which Columbus had discovered received the first convincing answer through Balboa's discovery. Although people were soon certain that South America was separated from and different from the well-known regions of Asia, a considerable time elapsed before they were willing to concede the same with regard to the northern half of the American continent. On the whole, the knowledge

Spain's Rich Colonial Kingdom

of South America made far more rapid progress than that of North America. The mediæval superstition that the produce of the soil increased in value the nearer one got to the equator had in this case a distinct influence; and the rivalry between Spain and Portugal, though it was shortly given up, had its share in directing the expeditions of discovery in the direction of the equator. To it we are indebted for the voyages of Amerigo Vespucci (1502) and of Gonzalo Coelho (1503) on the part of Portugal, and for those of Juan Diaz de Solis (1515) on behalf of Spain, which opened up the coasts of South America far beyond the mouth of La Plata. They paved the way for the epoch-making achievement of Fernando de Magalhães, who, during his search for a south-western passage to the east Asiatic Moluccas, or Spice Islands, which had in the meantime become better known to the Portuguese, sailed through the archipelago at the southern extremity of America.

The Great Discovery of Magalhães

By actually reaching the Asiatic islands Magalhães irrefutably exposed Columbus's error and first brought his project to complete realisation. When, after his death, his crew returned home by way of the Cape of Good Hope, the problem of the spherical form of the earth first received a practical solution. This voyage was infinitely more productive of scientific results than the achievement of Columbus.

Up to that time the colonies of the western Indies had hardly fulfilled the hopes which had been centred on their discovery. Many profitable tropical products had been found, and their importation into Spain, as well as the maintenance of the colonists already scattered over extensive tracts of land, who yet depended almost exclusively on their native country for support, had led to tolerably brisk trade intercourse, in which, as the mother country was hardly equal to the whole task of colonisation, the traders of foreign nations took an active part. The colonies had, however, proved by no means profitable to the state. The equipment of so many expeditions, and the establishment of the necessary administrative apparatus at home and abroad, entailed considerable expense. In spite of the attempt which had been made to raise an adequate revenue by means of duties and taxes, among which the royalty of a

Spain's Unprofitable Colonies

twentieth part on all ore discovered ranked first, yet these had so far yielded but moderate profits. Auriferous sand had, indeed, been discovered on Hispaniola and Cuba and in several places on the continent, and washing for gold had begun; but, owing to the poor quality of the sand, the labour was by no means combined with large profit.

Moreover, the colonies suffered through this discovery; for the natives, overburdened with hard work, diminished with astonishing rapidity, and already in the first third of the sixteenth century threatened, on the islands first inhabited, to become altogether extinct. The colonists, who sought only to enrich themselves by the gold washings as quickly as possible and at any cost, in order that they might lead an idle life of debauchery, extravagance at home or in the settlements, were another dangerous element in the community.

The government must by no means be held entirely responsible for the fact that this state of affairs afterwards assumed such proportions that the Spanish colonies could even with exaggeration have been described as "mining colonies." Ever since the second voyage of Columbus it had been made a universally binding rule that all vessels conveying emigrants to the new continent should carry with them an equal cargo not only of indigenous cereals and seeds, but also of shrubs, trees and useful plants for the colonies' experimentation in the various territories.

European Animals in the New World

The European domestic animals, the greater number of which throve in the New World, were first imported by the Spaniards. America possessed but few, and of these not many were productive. The horse not only became, in many districts of America, an almost indispensable possession, but it even propagated through wild breeding. Cattle also throve exceedingly well on American soil; not only did they, as livestock, form one of the most marketable articles for trade in the colonies, but their hides constituted one of the staple commodities for export to Europe.

Nothing, however, increased as rapidly among the Indians as did poultry; after the middle of the century the pioneers of western civilisation were greeted by the crowing of a cock, even in districts where the foot of a European had never been before. Experiments with less simple cultivation had also early been made in the colonies

THE
DISCOVERY
OF
AMERICA

AND
THE SPANISH
CONQUEST
IV

THE SPANIARDS IN MEXICO

THE VICTORIOUS CAMPAIGNS OF CORTES

THE fact that the interest of the government became more and more centred upon the quest for precious ores was chiefly due to the development of the discoveries during the thirteenth and fourteenth centuries. Columbus had ascribed but trifling importance to the encounter with the Yucatan trading bark.

He assumed that because the traders had no ore on board none was to be found in their native country or in the land of their destination. The comparative development of civilisation with which the explorers had here first come in touch thus remained unnoticed. Not until the superficially explored coasts of the Gulf of Mexico had been submitted to a closer examination was this half-forgotten trading nation again discovered, and while the newcomers were following in their track the first of the American fairy-lands was disclosed to the view of Europeans. After Diego Velasquez had, during his personal attempts to colonise **Spanish Expeditions in Mexico** Cuba, achieved such important results, it is not surprising that he showed inclination and courage for further enterprise. Not many years after, in 1517, he sent a small fleet, in command of Francisco Fernandez de Cordoba, with orders to coast along the continent and barter with the natives.

The ships reached the peninsula of Yucatan, not far from its south-eastern extremity ; then followed it in a northerly and westerly direction, and only turned back on meeting with hostility from the natives. They gave astonishing accounts of massive temples in which the cross was adored side by side with stone idols ; of towns in which thousands of people lived, following their respective trades. They also reported that the latter did not go about half-naked, like most of the natives whom they had hitherto come across, but were completely clothed, many wearing rich and costly garments almost like Europeans. These accounts sounded so extremely tempting that Valesquez in the following year decided on sending a second and larger expedition to the same regions, placing his nephew, Juan de Grijalva, at the head. The new fleet sighted land off the island of **Spaniards Trading on the Coast** Cozumel. When the Spaniards found that the coast there extended towards the south, as it did in the west, they were confirmed in their idea that Yucatan must be an island, and they sailed round in the wake of the previous expedition.

Not until they had seen the rising land appear behind the coast, while following the yet undiscovered shores of Mexico farther to the north, did they believe that they had reached the mainland. A vessel returned to Cuba with this intelligence. Grijalva himself, with the remainder of the crews, sailed along the entire coast of the Mexican realm, beyond Panuco in the north, trading and gathering information, without, however, venturing to attempt a settlement. For this, on his return, he had to bear serious reproaches from Diego Velasquez, although his mode of action had been in strict accordance with the terms of the instructions he had received.

The remote possibility that someone else might precede and anticipate him in the discovery awakened in Diego Velasquez the most painful anxiety when the rumours of the discoveries by Cordoba and Grijalva had begun to circulate in the colonies. The preparations for the fitting out of a fresh expedition commenced upon the arrival of **Cortes in Command of New Enterprise** the first ship, and when Grijalva returned they were carried on with increased energy. Velasquez had already found a leader for this new expedition. His choice had fallen on Fernando Cortes, who, after spending fifteen years in the colonies, where he had gained abundant experience and manifested singular fitness, was alcalde of the capital

5893

Santiago, and one of the most distinguished men of the island. Fernando Cortes is one of the most congenial of all the personalities who have taken part in the extension of the Spanish dominion on American soil. He was descended from a distinguished family of Medellin, had the advantage of a superior education, and had even studied law for two years. Impelled by enthusiasm, he had, in 1504, gone to the newly discovered country, and had accompanied Velasquez during the first colonisation of Cuba, acting for a long time as his private secretary. The prospect of taking part, from that time under better circumstances, in the discovery of a new and promising tract of land was suited both to his temperament and to his desires; and he willingly agreed to share the cost of the expedition out of his own fortune. Velasquez, filled with jealousy, became suspicious of the enthusiasm which Cortes manifested in the affair. Even before the preparations were concluded he repented of his choice of Cortes, and, foolishly enough, allowed this to become apparent; but Cortes was resolved not to be displaced. For this reason he sailed to Trinidad, a western harbour on the island, without awaiting the equipment of his eleven ships. The order which he there received from Velasquez, not to leave until he had joined him for a further conference, served only to hasten him in continuing his journey. He suggested that Cape San Antonio, the western point of Cuba, should be the meeting-place of the fleet.

As the time needed for equipping the vessels threatened to result in dangers for him, he took the risky step of forcibly detaining two ships intended for the conveyance of provisions to Santiago and completed his equipment with their cargo, referring them for payment to Velasquez, whose servant he still nominally was. Cortes was able to put to sea in the middle of February, 1519, with rather more than 400 Europeans on board his eleven ships, with about 200 Indians, sixteen horses, and fourteen guns in addition. It was but a small troop considering all he accomplished

Velasquez Jealous of Cortes

FERNANDO CORTES
After conquering Mexico, this Spanish soldier developed the mining and agricultural interests of the country, and inaugurated a beneficent system of colonisation.

with it, although, indeed, it was looked upon at that time as one of the most imposing and powerful forces that had ever been sent forth to found a new colony.

The voyage was at first along a well-known route to Cozumel, and around Yucatan to Tabasco. During the preceding expeditions the explorers had met chiefly with animosity from the natives at the latter place, so Cortes resolved to punish them. A footing had, however, first to be gained by fighting; but with the help of the muskets, and more especially of the guns and horses, the resistance of the people of Tabasco was overcome. Having felt the edge of the Spanish sword, these natives altered their previous demeanour, and, bringing presents, submitted themselves to him. Two further strokes of fortune succeeded this good beginning. A Spaniard was rescued from Indian captivity on the coast of Yucatan, where he had been shipwrecked years before with several companions, of whom he remained the only survivor. His knowledge of the dialects and customs of the country proved most useful to Cortes, more especially during the first part of his enterprise. He received similar assistance at Tabasco. There happened to be an Aztec woman among the twenty slaves whom, besides other things, the natives had presented to Cortes as a peace-offering; and this woman, who received the name of Donna Marina in baptism, rendered most valuable service to Cortes as an interpreter. From her, with whom he had become closely connected as his mistress, he first heard of the kingdom of the Aztecs and of the political conditions which then prevailed there. This information enabled him to form the daring plans for their subjection which he carried into effect with almost inconceivable success. Cortes sailed from Tabasco along the coast as far as the small island of San Juan de Ulloa, and founded not far distant from it the first Spanish colony on American soil, naming it Villarica de la Vera Cruz. He was accorded a friendly reception by the Aztec chiefs on landing. The news of the events in

Cortes Among the Aztecs

CORTES IN MEXICO: A STIRRING EPISODE IN THE SPANISH CAMPAIGN

Receiving costly presents from the Emperor Montezuma II., Cortes sent these to Spain, with reports of his doings, requesting at the same time for himself and his followers the governorship of the country, which he intended to subjugate to the Spanish crown. Then, desiring to be independent of Velasquez, who was associated in the expedition, Cortes, after despatching the best ship to Spain, ordered the destruction of the other vessels, and here he is seen giving orders for the burning of the boats. That accomplished, the followers of Cortes elected him as their commander-in-chief.

From the painting by F. Sans

Tabasco had spread to Montezuma's capital, and opinions as to the reception to be accorded to the strangers had, at the king's council, been very much divided. But the dismay which the defeat of the people of Tabasco had created strengthened their superstitious ideas, according to which Quetzalcoatl was said to have prophesied his return to his people across the eastern ocean. The Spaniards, who had as their attendants the lightning which flashed from the cloud, and the horse which sped along with lightning-like rapidity, seemed to give proof that they were the children of the God of Thunder-clouds and of the Wind. The governor of the coast was therefore ordered to give the strangers a peaceful reception and to meet their demands as far as possible.

The ships, guns, and horses of the Spaniards astonished the natives; but the amazement of the court of Montezuma was still greater, owing to the skill of the Aztec scribe who made faithful sketches of the Spaniards for the illustration of the report sent to the capital. Cortes added a statement to the governor's message, saying that he was the envoy of a great king in the far east, and the bearer of presents to the ruler of Mexico, as well as of a commission which could be delivered only by word of mouth. Montezuma's reply was not long delayed. It was accompanied by costly presents of gold and beautiful feathers; but it was to the effect that Cortes should be satisfied with these gifts and abstain from a personal visit to the capital.

That, however, was not the intention of the Spaniards, nor did the gifts suffice to induce them to decide on a fruitless return. Cortes repeated his request to be permitted to appear before Montezuma, at the same time making preparations for accomplishing his visit to Mexico in spite of the ruler's desire. He looked around for confederates for such a contingency, more especially as the attitude of the Aztec governor at the coast began to assume unmistakable signs of unfriendliness. The Totonacs, who inhabited the neighbouring country along the shore more to the north, and who had but recently submitted reluctantly to the yoke of the Aztecs, had from the beginning been in touch with the Spaniards, and had repeatedly invited them to visit their capital, Cempoalla. Cortes went there with part of his crew, and, returning to Vera Cruz, was

The Totonacs Friendly to the Spaniards

more than satisfied that he could now, with this cover for his line of retreat, safely venture upon a march into the interior. Before all things it was necessary to establish a feeling of unity in his small force. Cortes had no intention of allowing Diego Velasquez to reap the fruits of his labours after the evident signs of animosity which the latter had, at the last, shown towards him ; and the majority of his followers were of the same opinion.

Velasquez now himself experienced what he had brought on Diego Colon during the colonisation of Cuba. Cortes sent Montezuma's costly presents straight to Spain with detailed reports, and at the same time demanded for himself and for his followers the governorship of the country, which he intended to subjugate to the Spanish Crown. The pilot, Alaminos, who had directed all the voyages of discovery along this coast, was sent with the best ship, as the bearer of this message, and, in order to prevent any attempt at desertion, the remainder of the fleet was declared to be no longer seaworthy, and was therefore stranded and destroyed. As soon as this had been accomplished, the followers of Cortes declared themselves independent of Velasquez, and again chose Cortes as their commander-in-chief. The followers of Velasquez at least made some show of opposition, but they were defeated by the majority. After the leaders had been severely punished by way of example, the remainder submitted to the inevitable. Cortes, having made sure of his men, started for the interior with a numerous retinue of native Indians. The farther, however, that he advanced, the more urgently Montezuma warned him against this visit to the capital; and as the Spaniards were repeatedly told by the Indians who accompanied them of the treacherous plans which had been laid by order of the Aztec ruler, the explorers advanced in continual anticipation of war. They first met with open hostility on entering Tlazcala's territory. These brave

mountaineers, who had for centuries successfully repelled all the attacks of their neighbours, would not now submit to the newcomers. This meant a long and bitter struggle, entailing heavy losses for the Spaniards also, to convince the people of Tlazcala that even their fearless bravery could avail nothing in the face of firearms. They therefore sued for peace and became true and trusty friends of the Spaniards on hearing from the Totonacs that these strangers also entertained anything but friendly feelings for the Aztec ruler, and that they were resolved to put an end to his tyranny in one way or another. After the Spaniards had rested in Tlazcala's territory from the fatigues of the march and battles, and had reinforced their army with additional men from among the Tlazcalas, they resumed their march and first reached Cholula. Here they were again met by Montezuma's messengers, who forbade them to remain and advised their return. Cortes at the same time learned from his Indian confederates that the intention was to attack him and his followers on their departure. In order to anticipate this he seized the hostile ringleaders and gave up the town to his Indian allies to pillage. This they accomplished so thoroughly that even the great pyramid of the Temple of Quetzalcoatl was thrown into a heap of ruins. Montezuma, intimidated, denied all knowledge of the outrage, and did not again venture to oppose the Spaniards.

MONTEZUMA II
Aztec emperor of Mexico, he became a prisoner in the hands of the Spaniards, and was killed by his own subjects for demanding that their enemies should depart unmolested.

Unmolested, they climbed over the mountain ridge of Popocatepetl down into the valley of Mexico, and through the highway leading from Iztapalapan they entered Tenochtitlan, which is washed by the sea. Thousands of the natives stared at them with scarcely less astonishment than they themselves felt at the advanced state of civilisation which they encountered at every step. Montezuma, attended by a numerous retinue, met them almost humbly, and assigned to them as their quarters the palace of his father, which, owing to the thick walls surrounding the

THE SPANISH CONQUEST OF MEXICO: THE VICTORY OF CORTES OVER THE AZTECS AT OTUMBA

From the painting by Manuel Ramirez

whole building, was adapted for defence as well as for a dwelling-place. At first the intercourse between the king and the Spaniard was to all appearances quite friendly. Montezuma, nevertheless, with quiet dignity, rejected all attempts at his conversion ; on the other hand, he declared his willingness to acknowledge the

Montezuma and the Spaniards Emperor Charles V. as his sovereign and to pay him a high tribute in ores and costly materials. Notwithstanding, his mode of dealing was not straightforward. An attack which had in the meantime been made by the Mexicans on the Spaniards remaining at Vera Cruz was proved to have been instigated by Montezuma, and this treachery served the Spaniards as a pretext for compelling the king to move out of his palace into the Spanish quarter, where he was treated more or less as a prisoner. He was forced to do homage to the emperor with solemn ceremony, and had actually to transfer the government to the Spaniards, who, after the suppression of one attempt to raise another descendant of the royal family to the throne as ruler, began to assume the government and administration of the country in an entirely peaceable manner. The transition would have been accomplished without bloodshed if disturbances from without had not intervened.

Although Alaminos had received orders to sail straight to Spain without touching at the colonial harbours, he could not refrain from stopping at Cuba, though but hurriedly and in secret, to circulate the news of Cortes' extraordinary success. The greater the prize the keener became Velasquez' desire not to allow it to be wrested from him. For this reason he did not content himself with reporting the disloyal conduct of Cortes to Seville, but used every endeavour to fit out a second fleet for an expedition to deprive Cortes of the prize before he could gain a

Rival Fleets of the Spaniards footing in the new country. Panfilo de Narvaez, to whom Velasquez entrusted the duty of humbling Cortes and bringing him back to a sense of obedience, headed a force which, though considerably superior to that of Cortes, yet lacked cohesion. The vice-regent, Diego Colon, had, without infringing the law, absolutely forbidden Velasquez to endanger Cortes' brilliant achievement by a forcible invasion, and the repeated protests of his envoy, who

accompanied Narvaez' fleet to Vera Cruz, were not without influence on the crew, whose confidence Narvaez, who was less popular as a man than Cortes, failed to gain by his personal qualities.

To the challenge that the town Villarica should be surrendered to him Cortes' representative replied by sending on the messengers to his commander in Mexico. Cortes, from his personal interviews, soon realised that there would not be much difficulty in drawing the men away from their allegiance to Narvaez. He therefore openly entered into negotiations with him for combined action, based upon a division of the administrative powers ; but at the same time he collected all his available military forces and moved hurriedly forward to meet Narvaez, leaving a strong garrison, under Pedro de Alvarado, in the capital. As he had been exceedingly well informed by deserters, he was able to surprise Narvaez during a dark night, meeting with hardly any resistance. When the latter leader, who had lost an eye in the battle, had been taken prisoner, almost the whole force which he had

Cortes and his Army in Danger brought with him joined Cortes, only a few, like Narvaez, taking advantage of a permission to return to Cuba. This victory more than doubled Cortes' forces, for Narvaez had brought far more horsemen and riflemen than had Cortes himself.

Meanwhile, a threatening ferment had begun to show itself in Tenochtitlan immediately after the departure of Cortes, and when, during the celebration of a great festival, Alvarado was informed that the crowds were to be incited to attack the Spaniards and liberate Montezuma, he concluded that it would be highly advisable to anticipate such a stroke, and therefore he attacked the rejoicing multitude and dispersed it after a terrible massacre. The Mexicans now on their part changed to open hostility, and surrounded the Spaniards so closely that Alvarado had to summon Cortes to his aid as quickly as possible.

Cortes hastened to Mexico as soon as he had again reorganised his forces. The Spaniards, of course, perceived everywhere a changed and unfriendly disposition towards them, but as they did not find their movements barred, they were able to join the besieged after a sharp fight. Cortes recognised, when too late, that he had gained nothing thereby, but that instead he had made the Spaniards' supremacy, which had been won under such difficulty, dependent upon the issue of a single battle. As soon as he entered the town all paths were closed to him, and the reinforced host of Spaniards found themselves now as hopelessly menaced as Alvarado's division had been.

At first the Spaniards attempted to gain the mastery over their adversaries by open fight, and in spite of the fact that they overthrew thousands of the badly armed natives, the latter seemed continually to increase. Cortes thereupon endeavoured to shelter himself under the authority of the imprisoned king, and the appearance of the latter on the battlements of the palace actually led to a short armistice. When Montezuma asserted that he was not a prisoner and commanded that the Spaniards were to be allowed to depart unmolested, then the rage of his subjects turned on him, and he was struck and wounded by so many stones that he died within a few days.

With him vanished the Mexicans' last remnant of consideration for their opponents. It now became evident to Cortes **The Tragic Fate of Montezuma** that he would have to get out of the town, cost what it might. The investment by the enemy was so close that it was not even possible to make secret preparations. Each step of the retreat along the causeway over the lake, which was one and a quarter miles long, had to be gained by fighting. Cortes started, hoping thus to lessen the danger. The enemy, having long foreseen such a contingency, were at once prepared, and pressed forward vigorously, fighting from boats on both sides of the causeway, which was broken through in various places, sending a shower of missiles after the retreating men. Cortes had thrown a portable bridge over the first of the three canals that intersected the causeway, which his men actually succeeded in crossing ; but by the time the second canal was reached discipline had already been so weakened by the severity of the attack on all sides that the bridge was no longer available ; in fact, it had not even been carried forward. The crowd of fugitives now rushed on, over the bodies of those in advance, and when the mainland was at length reached, order was re-established to some extent.

A cypress-tree marks the spot where the rout ended, and is still preserved as a monument of the " noche triste " (sad night).

Two-thirds of the Spaniards and an even greater proportion of their native allies had either been killed or taken prisoners there, and the latter were bled to death on the altars of the idols. All the artillery, most of the muskets, and forty-six out of the sixty-seven horses were destroyed. Cortes subsequently despatched only a fifth of **Spanish Prisoners on Aztec Altars** the golden treasures as a royalty for the Spanish king, the remainder was handed over to the soldiers ; but almost everything had been lost in the terrible fight. Those who had escaped were almost without exception wounded and were in a critical position, for they were still many hundreds of miles from the nearest friendly district.

Cortes, thinking that the enemy would have rendered the old road impracticable for him in various ways, marched round the lakes on the northern shore, and actually reached Otumba via Teotihuacan before fresh numbers were added to the pursuing enemy, who intended attacking him in front. There the Spaniards had once more to fight for their lives against an overwhelmingly superior force (Cortes estimated the number of his enemies at 200,000), and the hardly won victory was no doubt due to the circumstance that they were able to kill the enemy's leader in the midst of his warriors. After the battle the Spaniards were, at any rate, able to continue the retreat under less pressure, but not until they entered the territory of Tlazcalan could they consider themselves safe, the Tlazcalans having remained faithful to the covenant which they had made with the Spaniards.

Months passed before the Spaniards had recovered from the terrible fatigues of the retreat, and been so far reinforced by contingents from the islands that Cortes could once more think of taking the offensive. He left the hospitable Tlazcalans during the last weeks of the year 1520, and endeavoured, by the subjection of the neighbouring tribes, to restore the **Cortes as an Organiser** prestige of the Spanish arms. He then attacked Tezcuco, intending to make it the strategic basis from which to prepare for the conquest of the island town of Tenochtitlan. In consequence of the political situation which had been computed by Anahuak, Cortes found confederates at Tezcuco after the banishment of the Aztec governor. Cortes now proved himself to be as good an organiser as he had hitherto been a leader. While carrying on the war against the coast towns, chiefly with the aid of his allies, who were in command of small Spanish divisions, he made a canal from Tezcuco to the Gulf of Mexico, and in a practically unassailable position he built a fleet of thirteen ships, which, on the opening of the canal, put to sea, so that he was able to ward off the troublesome invasion of hostile vessels. Attacks on one coast town after another were now undertaken from both land and sea, those towns which commanded the entrance to the canal being the last to fall. As the fleet at the same time gained a decisive victory over the Mexican fleet of boats, which accordingly now no longer existed as a fighting sea force, the Spaniards were in a position to turn to the invasion of the capital itself. Cuitlahuac, the king who had led the battles of the "noche triste," had died in the city after a reign of only four months. He was succeeded by Quauhtemoctzin —Guatemocin— who, as a brave ruler, proved in no wise inferior to him. After a few unsuccessful attacks, the Spaniards had to acknowledge the impossibility of taking the town by storm, but the systematic siege to which they had reluctantly resorted proved both tedious and difficult. Every inch of the ground, as

well as every house, was defended with the greatest courage by the natives, who were crowded together in overwhelming numbers in Tenochtitlan; and so long as the entrances to the town on the water side were not completely in the hands of the Spaniards, Cortes' ships were not in a position entirely to prevent provisions from reaching the besieged. In spite of this, the Spaniards advanced slowly but surely, and, after a siege lasting almost ten weeks, succeeded in confining the enemy to a small portion of the town by pulling down the surrounding houses, so as to ensure the deployment, during the battle, of the artillery and cavalry which largely formed the Spanish strength. Quauhtemoctzin then, realising the impossibility of holding the starved-out town, attempted to escape by sea, but fell into the hands of the Spaniards. The besieged then also gave up all resistance, and on August 13th, 1521, the heroic defenders quitted the ruins of Tenochtitlan. Immediately after this success, Cortes resumed the activity which had been interrupted by the appearance of Narvaez on the coast. Montezuma's record of taxes enabling him to form as correct an idea as possible of the extent and constitution of the kingdom, he organised the territory and

THE CHRISTIAN CROSS ON AN AZTEC ALTAR
In this reproduction of a beautiful piece of statuary, Cortes, the conqueror of Mexico, is represented placing the Christian Cross on an Aztec altar, supplanting in so doing the native image, greatly to the dismay and indignation of the Mexican chief, who has in vain endeavoured to prevent what to him is an act of sacrilege.
From the statue by Molto y Such

THE SPANIARDS IN MEXICO: BATTLE SCENE FROM AN OLD DRAWING

Of the many battles fought by the Spaniards in Mexico, perhaps the most desperate was that with the inhabitants of Michuacan, towards the middle of the sixteenth century, when the Spanish forces under Cortes were joined by the Tlazcalans, who brought their famous war-dogs to bear upon the struggle. This engagement was the outcome of Indian treachery, which is typified by the figure of a man hanging in the background of the picture. That the battle ended in a victory for the Spaniards and their allies is signified by the mutilated body of an Indian champion in the right-hand corner.

regulated the taxes on this basis. The news of a rich and highly civilised country which had at last been discovered on American soil, and was secured to the Spanish Crown by his energy, proved exceedingly useful to Cortes, for an impetus was thereby given to the desire for emigration such as had not existed since the second voyage of Columbus. The capital of Mexico, which, with his wonted energy, Cortes at once rebuilt, numbered, after a few years, several thousands of inhabitants, and from thence a network of smaller European settlements spread over the whole of Montezuma's territory.

During this period the return of the Victoria, the only ship out of Magalhaēs' fleet to complete the voyage around the world by the southern points of America and Africa, had directed attention to the Spice Islands. These were pre-sumably situated within the Spanish sphere of authority ; and the question of finding a shorter route than the one discovered by Magalhaēs arising, two ships were immediately built at Zacatula, and shortly after began a systematic and careful exploration of the Pacific coast of Mexico.

Cortes for a time indulged in the hope of discovering a passage through Central America. This desire, and the wish to ascertain the southern boundaries of the country conquered by him as quickly as possible—for an invasion from the colonies of Darien might with certainty be expected, in consequence of the impression which his conquests had created—led him to equip two fresh expeditions as soon as circumstances in the interior of the province allowed of such a step. One, under the command of Pedro de Alvarado, advanced from the southern

Pacific territories of Mexico into the province of the Maya tribes, who occupied the mountain districts to the north of the Isthmus, which is the Guatemala of to-day. Alvarado was able to take advantage of the same conditions which had proved of such assistance to Cortes in gaining the victory, and through the jealousies of the various chiefs he was able to incite one tribe against the other.

Though occasionally encountering an obstinate resistance, he was obliged to concede that the bravery of the natives equalled the courage shown at the defence of Tenochtitlan; but they were not able, either here or elsewhere, to hold their own permanently against the Spaniards, and the campaign proved rich not merely in glory but also in material results. The other expedition, which Cortes sent at the same time along the coasts of the Atlantic to the south, was less successful. The leader, Cristobal de Olid, from the beginning gave rise to the suspicion that he intended to serve Cortes in the same manner as the latter had served Velasquez. He had indeed, at Puerto de Caballos, after circumnavigating the peninsula of Yucatan, taken possession of the country in the name of Cortes, and founded a colony which he called Triunfo de la Cruz.

Then he evinced the desire of securing for himself a small territory between Castilla del Oro, now an organised province of Central America, and the Mexican territory belonging to Cortes. He began by attaching to himself all the restless and adventurous elements in both provinces, and with their help he either got rid of or intimidated the conscientious ones. It so happened that several contingents which Cortes had sent after Cristobal de Olid disappeared and never reached their destination, so that the commander-in-chief only heard rumours of his proposed defection. Cortes, however, foresaw no serious danger. His efforts to gain from the king his recognition as governor had not been crowned with entire success; therefore, had Olid, in league with Velasquez, succeeded in establishing himself independently in the south, it would certainly have cost Cortes the greater part, if not the whole, of his governorship.

Cortes, therefore, with the quick determination peculiar to him, quitted Mexico in October, 1524, and sailed along the Atlantic coast as far as Usumacinta. From thence traversing Yucatan where the peninsula joins the mainland, he crossed Lake Isabel and reached Olid's colony on the coast. The object of his journey had been attained before his arrival: Olid had been removed, and the colony had returned to obedience. During his march, **Cortes in Unexplored Regions** passing through considerable regions of unexplored country, Cortes had become acquainted with the towns and countries of the Maya tribes of the east, establishing his claims on this country in such a way that all danger of foreign intervention was removed. The subjection of the peninsula of Yucatan, the seat of the last tribes who still adhered to the ancient, genuine Maya traditions, was not, it is true, seriously attempted until some years later by

Edwards

A PRESENT-DAY VIEW OF THE AQUEDUCT BUILT BY CORTES IN THE CITY OF MEXICO

Francisco de Montejo, and it was carried through comparatively slowly and with varying success. After the peninsula had been explored on all sides, both by land and sea, its acquisition was but a question of time, as its principal secrets had been disclosed by Cortes. For a number of years, until new discoveries drew attention in other directions, the "flotas de Yucatan" sailed there from time to time from Seville, bringing back rich treasures. But while Cortes advanced into the jungle to punish the insubordination of his subjects, they boldly held up their heads in the capital. Cortes was looked upon as dead, and his enemies—the energetic, unscrupulous conquistador possessed an abundance of them in men who found that he had not been able to fulfil their exaggerated hopes— were so superior in force that they were soon able to annul the regency which he had instituted, and to seize the reins of government for themselves. This rival government, however, collapsed upon the approach to the town of the returning commander, who in the meantime had been constituted governor and commander-in-chief of the province of New Spain by Charles V. But the germs of discontent which compelled him in 1527 to go over to Spain in order to lay his case personally before the court date from these circumstances. In spite of endless lawsuits he succeeded in acquitting himself well before the Council of the Indies, but, like Columbus, he, too, was not reinstated in his former position. When he returned to Mexico in 1530 he was

The Proud Conqueror Superseded forced to tolerate a new governor placed immediately over himself, and this weighed heavily on the proud conqueror. During this period he gave a fresh impetus to discoveries in a north-westerly direction. He sent ships along the Pacific coast and also discovered the Bay of California. In the year 1535 he himself once more penetrated far up the coast of the Californian peninsula. Although he was not the discoverer of the desired north-west passage any more than he had previously been the discoverer of Central America, he furthered

FERNANDO DE SOTO

A Spanish discoverer, he greatly distinguished himself in the Nicaragua expedition and in the conquest of Peru, being subsequently appointed governor of Cuba.

a knowledge of the truth that North America was not connected with the continent of Asia, even in higher latitudes. Long before the middle of the century the Spaniards had also pushed on far into the interior of the regions to the

Where Life was Gay and Luxurious north-west of Mexico. Nuño de Guzman had, in addition to the subjection of the northern districts of the Aztec kingdom, advanced, in 1530, into the subsequent New Galicia—the provinces Durango and Sinaloa of to-day—with an army composed of Spanish and Indian warriors. Rumours of towns rich in gold had enticed him to these districts. They received apparent confirmation when a few of the followers of Fernando de Soto, who had gone from Florida straight through the southern provinces of the United States as far as Texas and Mexico, told of colonies where the houses were many storeys high and where life was even as gay and as luxurious as in Mexico itself. They called the largest of these towns Eibola. It became the goal of an expedition which Juan Vasquez de Coronado undertook in 1535 from Culiacan in a north-westerly direction. After he and his companions had, with many struggles and privations, wandered through the arid regions between the Great Colorado and the Rio Grande, they did, in fact, arrive at the towns of the Pueblo Indians, which had umistakably given rise to the rumours, but they failed to discover the reported treasures in possession of the homely husbandmen of Zuñi, Walpi, and Moqui, even as they had failed to find Nuño de Guzman. The reputed City of Gold now received a new name.

Even after many centuries the phantom of the treasures of Quivira still lured the Spaniards into the desert prairie land of the Llano Estacado. The Spanish power, in reaching the Pueblo towns, had practically attained its northern boundary, beyond which it advanced only indirectly during the nineteenth century, when the opening of the Far West set in motion on all sides a great stream of immigrants for California.

PIZARRO DESCRIBING TO CHARLES V. OF SPAIN THE TEMPTING RICHES OF PERU

Immediately after the discovery of America by Columbus, the golden land of the Indian tribes who inhabited Peru held a strange fascination for Spanish adventurers, of whom at once the most unscrupulous and the most brilliant was Francisco Pizarro, an erstwhile pig-tender of Estremadura. Returning to Spain after one voyage with a glowing account of the Inca kingdom, with its reputed wealth of gold and other precious minerals, he found no difficulty in persuading Charles V. to grant him the exploring rights for the conquest of the new province.

From the painting by Lizcano

THE
DISCOVERY
OF
AMERICA

AND
THE SPANISH
CONQUEST
V

THE SPANISH CONQUEST OF PERU
PIZARRO'S BRUTAL METHODS WITH THE INCAS

NOT only had new life been infused into emigration by the achievements of Cortes, but they had also inspired the desire for fresh discoveries. The Council of the Indies had never previously been so occupied with requests for permission to make fresh attempts at colonisation as during the years subsequent to the conquest of Mexico. There was now no longer any need for the government officially to continue exploration in the new regions of the world ; the enterprising spirit of its subjects competed for pre-eminence in the matter of discoveries.

Of course, all the adventures for which the Council of the Indies had granted concessions were not actually undertaken, while some, again, proved such absolute failures that the holders renounced their claims within a short time, and even colonies which, like Santa Marta, had subsisted for a number of years, had occasionally declined so rapidly that they required to be completely reconstituted. Even though vast tracts of land on the confines of the Spanish colonies remained for more than a century still unreclaimed—tracts over which the Spaniards were never in a position to exercise more than a formal claim—yet scarcely an unexplored region of larger dimensions was left in the southern half of the New World, with the exception of those lowlands to the south of the river Amazon, which to this day are still almost unknown. In isolated instances the explorers pushed far forward into regions which up to now had not been identified with certainty, because no white man who could give an account of his experiences has ever again advanced so far.

The Spanish Explorations in South America

The Spaniards had presumably heard vague rumours from the Indians in Central America of the existence of rich and powerful states both in the north and also in the south, and when the expansion of the Central American province to the north was closed by the conquest of Mexico, their attention was naturally directed towards the south. The voyages along the Pacific coast had so far resulted only in the knowledge of various races who were in an unusually low state of civilisation, and no doubt it was on that account that so long a time elapsed before the Spaniards guessed at the existence of the country of the Incas. Through a misunderstanding, the name of Peru was again assigned to it. Biru was the name of a small kingdom on the bay of San Miguel, at the south-western end of the isthmus. Balboa had already touched there, and it had been the goal of an expedition which Pascual de Andagoya undertook in 1522. The direct result did not surpass what the expeditions into the regions of Darien had led men to expect. The natives, however, who had by that time become more intelligible, made it clearer than ever to the gold-seeking Spaniards that there existed great kingdoms in the south on the Pacific coast, where they would find the yellow ore in plenty. This news could apply only to the kingdom of the Incas.

Spaniards' Lust for Gold

The assertions of the Indians had made an indelible impression, especially on one of the followers of Andagoya. Francisco Pizarro was an adventurer of the ordinary type. He had tended the pigs at his home in Estremadura, but when still a youth he had, with Hojeda, crossed the ocean in 1508, and had also shared in all the dangers which preceded the founding of the Darien colony. After its annexation he was numbered among the constant participators in all voyages of discovery. In this way he had gained vast experience in all kinds of difficult positions, and manifested throughout quiet but almost inflexible perseverance, which was highly appreciated by his superiors and comrades. While evolving the plan for the discovery of the golden land of the Indians, these same qualifications also proved of immense

Pizarro's Voyages of Discovery

service to him. As his means were insufficient for the equipment of an expedition, in spite of fifteen years' service in the colonies, he turned to the colonists for assistance. Diego del Almagro, a man of the same type as Pizarro, brought him a host of resolute comrades, but, like Pizarro, he did not possess the necessary financial means. These, nevertheless, were also found. The vicar of the church of Panama, Fray Hernando de Luque, not only possessed a small fortune himself, which he was prepared to stake on the undertaking, but his relations with the governor, Pedrarias Davila, and with other notabilities of the colony, made it possible for him to smooth the way for the enterprise in every direction, so that Pizarro was able to make the first advance into the south in 1524.

Pizarro's Gold-seeking Expedition

The result of the expedition was by no means remunerative. Both Pizarro, who had sailed in advance, and Almagro, who followed him some months later, reconnoitred the coast from Panama about halfway up to the northern boundary of the kingdom of the Incas, and gained but little treasure as a reward for great hardships. Pizarro, however, again gave brilliant proofs of his imperturbable powers of endurance. Twice he sent his ship back to Panama, remaining behind on the totally strange coast with a little band of followers ; and when he finally decided on a return, it was only with the object of attaining, through personal influence, the equipment for his expedition which seemed indispensable to him for such distances.

The conquest of Peru now became the object of a financial speculation for which a thoroughly business-like agreement was drawn up. Luque and his sureties found the money, while Pizarro and Almagro staked their lives, and the division of the proceeds was regulated accordingly. Not many months after his return Pizarro was able once more to put to sea, this time accompanied by Almagro, in order again to resume the exploration of the coast on the southern spot which had been previously reached. This time, as a result of the better equipment and the more favourable time of year, more rapid progress was made ; but, in spite of all, their provisions ran short before they reached the more densely populated regions. Once again reinforcements and

Spanish Adventurers in a Plight

provisions had to be procured from Panama, and even thus the expedition threatened to become completely frustrated. Upon hearing the accounts of the disappointed men who returned, the governor decided that a continuation of the undertaking was only a useless waste of money and lives ; he therefore sent to Pizarro and his followers on the Isla del Gallo and ordered their return. Pizarro remained immovable, and for seven months held out on the island with only twelve companions, until his partners were in a position to send him a ship and provisions.

With these he energetically resumed his voyage to the south and finally reached the Inca kingdom. He got on friendly terms with the natives of Tumbez on the Gulf of Guayaquil, and was at length able, with his own eyes and ears, to investigate the truth of the rumours circulated by the Indians. The greatness of his discovery actually far exceeded all his hopes and necessitated another return home. This was no task which could be accomplished with the funds provided by his partners, and on this account a basis with extensive capital had to be established. On his return with the news of his discoveries in Panama he had no difficulty in convincing his partners of the necessity for first acquiring in Spain the exploring rights for the conquest of the province, and it became evident to them that he would be the most suitable person to lay this proposition before the Council of the Indies. In the spring of 1528 he travelled over to Seville and presented himself at court. When he returned to Panama, two years later, he carried with him the nominations for himself as " adelantado," for Almagro as commandant, and for Luque the reversion of the first bishopric.

Pizarro at the Court of Spain

Almagro, to be sure, felt that he had been slighted by the unequal division of the honours between him and his partners, but for the moment he was appeased. Apparently on the best of terms, they led a band of about 200 Spaniards towards the south. Even before they reached Tumbez the expedition was strengthened by more than one reinforcement. Their reception by the natives there was again peaceful, the more so as Pizarro delivered them from their hostile neighbours, the inhabitants of the island of Puno, whom, incited thereto by the people of Tumbez, he defeated completely. He there also heard of the war between the brothers Huascar and Atahualpa, which had just terminated, and of the seeds of discontent which the latter had sown. This information made Pizarro hasten to the scene before the favourable opportunity for intervention had passed. When he had founded a colony—San Miguel—for the adjustment of the trade, he started for the interior, and made straight for the spot where, according to the accounts of the natives, he might expect to find the Inca Atahualpa.

To advance to meet a host of ostensibly 40,000 men, in quite an unknown country, with 168 Spaniards without any confederates, was most foolhardy. The smallness of the number may have been the means of his success, as the Inca-Peruvians did not consider it necessary to place hindrances in his way or to arm themselves for resistance. Atahualpa, on the contrary, seemed almost anxious to make the acquaintance of the Spaniards, to whom he repeatedly sent messengers with presents and an invitation to appear before the Inca. Unmolested, Pizarro climbed up into the mountains from the plains of the coast, and at last reached the town of Cajamarca, near which the army of the Inca was encamped. The town was deserted—a circumstance which was not unwelcome to the Spaniards, enabling

FRANCISCO PIZARRO
An adventurer of the ordinary type, he conquered Peru on behalf of Spain, employing the most brutal and cruel methods in his campaigns against the Incas.

them, at any rate, to prepare unnoticed for defence, and also to make arrangements for their attacks. On the day after their arrival Pizarro sent to the camp a small division, composed entirely of horsemen under Hernando de Soto, and through them invited the Inca to honour the Spaniards with a visit. He had arrived at the conviction that it would be foolish to measure the strength of his own forces with those of the Inca in open battle. All his hopes were set on getting possession of the Inca's person, and then, as Cortes had done with great success in Mexico, under cover of his authority, to get the country into his power. Atahualpa evinced unmistakable interest in the appearance

The Wily Tactics of Pizarro

of the horsemen, a novel sight for him, though he took scant notice of the message which Soto brought him ostensibly in the name of the Emperor Charles. He promised, however, to appear in Cajamarca on the following day, in order to make the acquaintance of the other Spaniards and of their commander-in-chief. It became evident to Pizarro that the following day would decide the issue of his undertaking, and his suggestion that they should at once fall upon the Peruvians and take Atahualpa a prisoner at the earliest opportunity was received with universal satisfaction. All the preparations for the success of the daring plan were carefully made. With growing impatience the Spaniards watched the greater part of the next day pass without a single person coming within reasonable distance from the camp of the Incas, and they began to fear that, in spite of all the precautions which had been taken, their plan had been discovered. Late in the afternoon, however, a procession began to move towards Cajamarca, and in a moment every Spaniard was at his post. The town seemed deserted when the Inca entered; he was able to proceed as far as the market-place without seeing a soul, and the market, too, was at first empty. When the Inca, carried in an uncovered litter, halted, he was met by a monk, Fray Pedro de Valverde, accompanied by two natives whom Pizarro had enrolled among his followers on his first voyages and had taken to Spain, where they were trained to be interpreters. The monk made the customary speech to the Inca which by command of Charles V. had to be interpreted to the natives each time before force might be used towards them.

Atahualpa Among the Spaniards

Beginning with the creation of the world, he told of the vicariate of the Pope over the globe, and deduced from the papal deed the claim of the Spanish rulers to the obedience of his Indian subjects. Atahualpa listened to the address without change of countenance, and, as Valverde repeatedly referred to the Bible, which he carried open in his hand, the Inca desired to see the book. Not perceiving anything extraordinary in it, he threw it contemptuously on the ground, after turning over its leaves. It needed only the exclamation of indignation which this conduct evoked from the cleric to give the signal for the attack to

The Inca Taken Prisoner
the Spaniards, who had been following the proceedings with the keenest interest. The two small field culverins, which had been placed in such a position that they swept the market-place, were discharged; the horsemen, standing near their saddled steeds at the back of the adjacent houses, mounted and dashed forward toward the market-place and the litter of the Inca, knocking down everything which happened to come in their way.

The musketeers and unmounted warriors at the same time endeavoured to prevent the followers of the Inca, numbering several thousand men, from going to the assistance of the combatants in the market-place. The daring plan was carried out most satisfactorily during the confusion which followed upon the sudden and unexpected attack. As the bearers were thrown down, the Inca fell from the litter and was secured by the Spaniards without injury. His followers undoubtedly fought with great bravery in order to liberate him, but the large expanse of ground which had been most cunningly chosen gave them no opportunity. After a short but cruel and ferocious battle the Peruvians, of whom about 2,000 are said to have been killed, were forced to retire and leave the Inca to his fate.

By the success of this daring feat the conquest of the kingdom of the Inca had practically been accomplished. The tribe dispersed and left the country open to the Spaniards, who, secure under the authority of the Inca, obtained the realisation of all their desires. Atahualpa at

Treasures for the Spaniards
once recognised that force could avail nothing. He was treated with every consideration, being waited on by his wives and household, but he was not permitted to leave Cajamarca, where he was lodged in one of the strongest buildings and carefully watched. He hoped to gain his liberation by means of negotiation. When he perceived with what greed the Spaniards fawned for gold and treasures, he offered to fill the room which he inhabited, as

high as a man could reach, with gold and silver, on condition that he might be permitted to return to the throne of his ancestors. The Spaniards took care not to reject so good an offer, and watched with delight and astonishment while, at the order of the Inca, the treasures actually poured into Cajamarca from all directions. The doubts which they had at first felt as to the possibility of such a promise ever being fulfilled vanished.

But this did not prevent them from continuing the attempt to conquer the country, which was their goal, by other means. Pizarro had, in the meantime, collected further information about the dispute concerning the succession, and found that Huascar, the rightful Inca, still lived. He was too valuable a tool not to be secured, but Atahualpa did not remain in ignorance of the design. In order to remove his dangerous rival he gave the secret order that Huascar should be immediately executed. He little guessed that in so doing he had sealed his own fate. As the collection of the ransom did not proceed fast enough to please either the

Unopposed March of the Spaniards
Inca or the Spaniards, it was decided to send a contingent to the sanctuary at Pachacamac. Pizarro placed his brother Fernando at the head of this troop, which was the first to penetrate farther into the Inca kingdom. The real object of the expedition was not attained.

Fernando Pizarro found the temple practically robbed of its treasures, and could do nothing but destroy the mud idol and replace it by the cross. On his return he again gave glowing accounts of the high state of civilisation and of the excellent administration of the kingdom. His reports were surpassed by those of two other Spaniards who had also pushed on as far as Cuzco with a safe-conduct from the Inca on account of the ransom. Nowhere was the slightest sign of resistance shown, and now, as before, gold flowed into the Inca's room. The sight of such treasures, however, proved too much for the avaricious eyes of the adventurous troop, and even before the ransom was completed a division was decided on.

The amount of gold and silver which had accumulated may be computed from the fact that the royalty for the Spanish king was worth a sum approaching £400. From that time Atahualpa, who now claimed his liberty, was regarded only

CONQUEST AND EXTERMINATION: PIZARRO SEIZING THE INCA OF PERU

The barbarous method of colonisation, by which the inhabitants of a country were driven out or murdered by new conquerors, was employed in the great days of Spain's colonising. The settling of a new land began with wholesale slaughter. The picture, by Millais, shows Pizarro seizing the Inca of Peru and putting the natives to the sword.

as an encumbrance. The strength of the Spaniards had been almost doubled by the addition of considerable reinforcements brought by Almagro. Upon the advice of several of his followers Pizarro put Atahualpa on his trial as a usurper and fratricide, and ordered his execution; **Atahualpa Executed by the Spaniards** he then nominated another member of the royal family as Inca, in order to secure the continued obedience of the natives. This object was, however, only partially attained. After the death of both Inca kings the bond of obedience was severed in this realm also. The natives withdrew more and more from the Spaniards, and at times even showed open hostility.

Pizarro then decided upon leaving Cajamarca. He led the main force towards the south in order to occupy the capital, Cuzco, and at the same time sent a smaller troop, under the command of Benalcazar, in a northerly direction to take possession of Atahualpa's capital and with it the kingdom of Quito. This was a very important step, as the report of the treasures of Peru had already aroused the envy of other Spaniards. Pedro de Alvarado, Cortes's confederate in the conquest of Mexico, and now governor of Guatemala, arrived in Peru some weeks later, accompanied by a host of adventurers, with the avowed intention of securing for himself in Quito a wealthier dominion than the one he had found in the north. The spectacle presented by Cortes and Narvaez in Mexico was almost

repeated here, though Alvarado showed less consideration. He entered into negotiations with Pizarro and Almagro, and finally transferred the whole equipment to them in consideration of an indemnity; which agreement was accepted by his confederates, for the kingdom of the Inca was large and rich enough to hold out the prospect of further spoils for them also.

Up till then the Spaniards only once had to draw sword. Pizarro found, when pushing on to Cuzco, that the way was barred by a hostile force which only retreated after heavy fighting wherein the Spaniards suffered great losses. They were, however, again able to establish themselves without resistance and founded a Spanish colony in Cuzco, but Pizarro did not again constitute it the capital. Its position in the south-east of the realm and its distance from the coast precluded it from becoming a suitable spot for Spanish purposes. The arrival of Alvarado necessitated Pizarro's hasty return to the coast, and there the future seat of the provincial government was established—the modern **Pizarro's Further Discoveries** Lima, on the river Rimac, the Ciudad de los Reyes. The continual reinforcements which Pizarro's forces were continually receiving placed him in the enviable position to continue his discoveries in every possible direction, and soon to push beyond the borders of the old Inca kingdom. Almagro began a series of expeditions, soon after the colonisation of Cuzco, by advancing towards the south between the

THE RUINS OF THE FIRST SPANISH SETTLEMENT IN PERU   Edward

THE FATE OF PIZARRO: ASSASSINATION OF THE CONQUEROR OF PERU

A succession of civil wars broke out in the Peruvian province between the Pizarrists and Almagrists, and during these Almagro was defeated and executed in 1538. Three years later the Almagrists, led by Almagro's son, had their revenge, a party of them falling upon Francisco Pizarro at Lima and assassinating him when he offered resistance.
From the painting by J. Laguna, photo Lacoste

two Cordilleras, through the present Bolivia. In doing so, he subjugated without difficulty the provinces round the lake of Titicaca, and then marched on over the mountains towards the south, enduring untold hardships, cold and hunger finally necessitating the risk of crossing the icy crest of the western Cordilleras in order to regain the less impracticable coast. He followed it beyond Coquimbo, in the region of Copiapo. On his return along the seashore, he had once more to undergo the severest privations in the desert of Atacama. In spite of all this the only gain from his expedition was the exploration of a great part of modern Chili, and the conviction that there were no treasures there which could be carried away with ease. Almagro returned just in time to rescue the Spaniards in Cuzco from a great danger. The Inca whom Pizarro had nominated in Cajamarca had soon after died, and Manco Inca had been made king in his place. The Spaniards, however, not meeting with resistance anywhere from the submissive natives, regarded him as superfluous. They paid so little attention

Escape of the Inca King

to him that he was easily able to escape from Cuzco into the north-eastern highlands, whence he planned a far-reaching conspiracy against the Spaniards. The weak garrison of Cuzco was surprised and fell into great straits, Fernando Pizarro's impetuous bravery alone saving them from complete destruction. While Almagro had been suffering useless privations in Chili, Spain had at least done him justice, for Charles V. made him governor of a province to the south of the Peruvian kingdom, which extended from a westerly and easterly direction about 750 miles to the south from the river Santiago (in modern Ecuador), to undefined southern latitudes, and Almagro was of the opinion that Cuzco belonged to this province. Fernando Pizarro refused to acknowledge this, and as deliberations led to no decision, Almagro in the end forcibly entered Cuzco and took Fernando Pizarro and his brother Gonzalo prisoners, while Francisco Pizarro made the attempt to liberate the brothers by force. When, however, the contingent which had been sent was also beaten by Almagro, he agreed to negotiations, which he immediately afterwards annulled,

5911

as his attempts to liberate the brothers had been crowned with success. A succession of civil wars now began in the Peruvian province, which terminated only when all the leading members of the "conquista" had met a cruel end. First Fernando Pizarro engaged in battle with Almagro, and, beating him at Las Salinas,

Civil Wars in the Peruvian Province had him executed in a most summary manner. When he returned to Spain, in order to lay his brother's case before the court, he was himself placed on his trial, and it was only because of his imprisonment for life that he survived his brothers. For the purpose of re-establishing justice and order, the Council of the Indies sent the licentiate Vaca de Castro, with supreme authority, to undertake the government of the province. His arrival closed another scene in the cruel drama. Almagro's faction, led by his son, had fallen upon Francisco Pizarro, and slain him when he offered resistance. The younger Almagro had no wish to be nominated to the governorship of the whole of Peru, but he laid claim to at least the southern province which had been assigned to his father.

Upon Vaca de Castro's refusal to grant this, he rose against him, and a large number of the conquistadors were only too ready to follow his leading. Fate, however, did not treat him kindly, for his party suffered a severe defeat in the battle of the Chupas, not far from Huamango, in 1542, and he was himself treacherously delivered over to his opponents and paid the penalty of his mutiny by death. Of the representatives of both conquerors only Pizarro's youngest brother, Gonzalo, still remained at liberty. Since

1540 he had been governor of Quito, and in the battles of Vaco de Castro against Almagro he had remained in faithful allegiance to the former. When, however, in 1544, Blasco Nuñez Vela was entrusted with the regency—chiefly in order to procure a happier lot for the natives, who, during the period of the fierce party wars, suffered must unjust oppression—he also could not resist temptation. To the rough Peruvian settlers, the protection of the natives seemed synonymous with the loss of their own rights.

Therefore, as Blasco Nuñez showed a great want of tact in the discharge of his commission, even the judges of the Audiencia, the Supreme Court of Lima, joined against the government in the insurrectionary movement of which, at his own instigation, Gonzalo Pizarro was elected leader. The more prudent among the colonists immediately returned to obedience when Blasco Nuñez was followed by Pedro de la Gasca, a priest who proved himself a discreet and energetic successor.

Gonzalo Pizarro became intoxicated by the consciousness of his power, and prolonged his resistance until, thanks to Gasca, his position became untenable and his case hopeless. During the battle which

Gasca Goes Back to His Monk's Cell ensued most of his false friends deserted him, and he was taken prisoner, together with the ringleaders of his faction, and was put to death. Gasca, who had reached Panama in 1544 without troops (it was then still subject to Pizarro) in six years established quiet and orderly conditions in Peru for the first time, then asked for a successor, and retired to a monk's cell, from which he had been summoned by the command of Charles V.

INCA WARRIORS: A REPRODUCTION FROM AN ANCIENT PERUVIAN PEDESTAL

LAST OF THE SPANISH CONQUESTS
THE VAIN SEARCH FOR EL DORADO

FRANCISCO PIZARRO had also turned his attention to the southern province which had been discovered by Almagro. After the execution of his rival he considered it a constituent part of his own governorship, from which he sought to exclude all foreign intervention. For this purpose he despatched an officer, Pedro de Valdivia, his faithful ally, with a commission to usurp governmental power by the establishment of a Spanish colony.

Valdivia chose the same road as Almagro, but during a more favourable time of year, so that though he had to contend less with natural difficulties he came more into contact with the enmity of the natives, who were anything but friendly after their experiences with the Spaniards. The inhabitants of the newly founded town of Santiago led a wretched existence on that account during the first years, although reinforcements were frequently sent there **The Aruacs' Fight for Independence** from Peru, especially after rich mines had been discovered and started in the valley of Quillota. Valdivia made use of the reinforcements more especially in order to continue the exploration of the country to the south. Commissioned by him, the Genoese, Pastene, sailed along the coast in the year 1544 until he reached the western outlets of the Straits of Magellan, which had been set as the southern boundary of the province.

When Pedro de la Gasca eventually took over the governorship of Peru he gave Valdivia his continued support, because, during the periods of unrest, the latter had rendered him valuable service. He was then able to continue his advance by land into the more southern regions of the province. The foundation of the town of Concepcion, on the borders of the district inhabited by the warlike Arauca Indians, followed in 1550. The battles with this tribe, which for quite ten years fought with wonderful bravery for its independence, have been celebrated in

song by more than one poet. But the heroic deeds which were performed on both sides during this period were quite out of proportion to the reward gained by the Spaniards' victory. This country, which Spain had won with such **Spanish Advance in America** bloodshed, was certainly fruitful and possessed a good climate, yet the advantages which it offered did not by any means equal those of many other parts of the Spanish colonial kingdom, so that its colonisation and usefulness at first promised to make but very slow progress.

The Spaniards had, in addition to the conquest of Peru, advanced beyond the borders of the Inca kingdom in two other directions. There is no easier approach from the west coast of America to the vast lowlands of the east than the one to the south of Lake Titicaca, where the eastern Cordilleras extend into a series of moderately high mountain ranges which together surround and break into the highlands of modern Bolivia. Reference has been made in a previous chapter to the great part which this country played as the cradle of the races of primitive times.

By this road also the Incas seem to have carried their conquests beyond the sources of those rivers which flow, some through the Madeira to the Amazon, and some through the Pilcomayo to the La Plata. Almagro came into touch with those regions in 1535, during his expedition to Chili; but their exploration was systematically undertaken a few years afterwards, when Blasco Nuñez **Undiscovered Treasures of Potosi** Vela, during his short period of office, entrusted the governorship of the provinces of Charcas and Tucuman to Captain Francisco de Rojas. The first explorers passed the immense treasures of Potosi, not suspecting their existence, and pushed on far into the lowlands in a south-easterly direction, through the provinces of Jujuy, Calchaqui, and Catamarca, fighting not only with the natives, but frequently quarrelling also among themselves, until at the river Tercero they came upon traces of the Spaniards who had advanced thus far from the east. This completed the transit of the continent.

After the Portuguese had, in 1514, discovered the mouth of La Plata, and

The First Explorer of the Paraguay

extended their exploration to the south far beyond it, without, however, attempting to found a settlement there, the Spaniards hastened to secure, by actual usurpation, their claims to these districts in the face of the adjoining kingdom. Diego de Solis was the first to explore a tract of the Paraguay in 1515, but after he had been killed in battle with the natives his followers returned to Spain. Then Sebastian Cabot and Diego Garcia, one after the other, quickly appeared on the river and carried on a lucrative trade with the natives, in consequence of which it received the name of Rio de la Plata —Silver River—but they also were not able to found a settlement. Owing to the reports which they brought back, Pedro de Mendoza undertook the colonisation of these regions in 1534. His fleet of fourteen ships is said to have had no less than 2,000 men on board, who became the progenitors of the Spanish population of the Argentine provinces.

After Mendoza had founded the first colony in Buenos Ayres, and had for months unsuccessfully endeavoured to secure the conditions essential to its continuance, he was discouraged and gave up the attempt. The men, however, whom he had left to carry on the undertaking, understood what was needed in order to vitalise the colony. Ayolas, the first of his deputies, resolutely forsook the low ground down stream, and founded the town of Asuncion, more than 100 miles higher up, at the confluence of the Pilcomayo and the Paraguay, and it became the centre of the gradually developed

Asuncion the Centre of Development

province. He himself lost his life in the endeavour to extend his explorations farther to the west; but his worthy successor, Domingo de Irala, again took up his plans, and Francisco de Rojas' comrades found traces of his journeys near the Tercero. On a subsequent expedition he advanced from the Upper Paraguay, through the territory of the Chiquitos, as far as the regions which had been colonised from Peru; and though he had again

to return thence in obedience to an order from Gasca, the establishment of Santa Cruz de la Sierra as an intermediate station for trade communication between the Atlantic Ocean and Peru is the direct result of his achievements.

Only one other incident in the earlier history of the colony of La Plata is of importance in connection with the exploration of the South American continent, and this was the arrival there of Alvar Nuñez Cabeza de Vaca, in 1540, to take up the governorship of the province in succession to Pedro de Mendoza. It seemed to him to be an unnecessarily circuitous route to sail first to the south as far as the mouth of the river La Plata, and then again up the river; so he landed with most of his 400 followers opposite the island Santa Caterina, and pushed on from there in a westerly direction through the wooded lowlands as far as Asuncion. It was only due to specially favourable circumstances that the march was accomplished at all, for both he and his followers had to pass through untold struggles and privations, and had, except for the opening

Relations of Spaniards with the Natives

up of the country, achieved no results. Some years later, however, when the colonists compelled him to resign his office in favour of Irala and return to Spain, he involuntarily discovered the easier approach by way of Buenos Ayres.

The colony of Asuncion—or Paraguay, as it is more familiarly called—occupied a special position among all the Spanish provinces, because there the Spaniards' relation to the natives developed most unusually. The Spaniards, from the beginning, had been accorded a friendly reception by the Guaranis about Asuncion, and as these terms continued in the future the consequence was that there, more than elsewhere, they married the daughters of the natives. The colonists everywhere made the Indian girls their concubines, especially before the influx of European women had increased. Actual marriages, also, often took place between the various races, more especially with the wives and daughters of the caciques, and resulted in an increase in the number of half-castes. In Paraguay the difficulty the Spaniards had in communicating with their native country, together with exceptionally friendly relations with the natives, combined to produce conditions especially favourable to the crossing of races. An

SOUTH AMERICA IN THE 16TH CENTURY: MAP OF THE SPANISH CONQUESTS AND COLONIES

The conquest of Peru by the Spaniards about the year 1528 marks a new era in the history of South America. Previous to that time the country had been practically immune from invasion by Europeans, and, although large tracts still remained unexplored, it possessed a not inconsiderable population of Indians. The above map shows the Spanish conquests and colonies, and the direction of the routes of exploration in the first half of the sixteenth century.

endeavour has been made, even to quite recent times, to trace the results of these conditions in the peculiar characteristics of the inhabitants of the province and subsequent republic of Paraguay.

Just as the La Plata and the Paraguay had in the south suggested to the Spaniards the way from the coast to Peru, so, in like **Expeditions into the Interior** manner, another of the great rivers led them, almost against their will, farther to the north from Peru to the sea. During the few years of peace which succeeded the downfall of Francisco Pizarro, his younger brother, Gonzalo, to whom had fallen the governorship of Quito in the place of Benalcazar, undertook an expedition.

The rumours of a wealthy kingdom in the depths of the continent decided its destination, and gave rise to a whole series of adventurous expeditions far into the interior, part of which has not even to this day again been thoroughly explored. If the crest of the Cordilleras through one of the passes from Quito is crossed in an easterly direction, it is quite evident that one must come upon one or other of the rivers which flow to the Rio Napo, and then with it to the Amazon. Later on, in the time when the missions instituted by various clerical orders in the regions of the Upper Amazon called forth a noble spirit of emulation for the conversion and domiciliation of the natives, the road to Quito over the Embarcadero de Napo became a much-frequented highway.

Almost a hundred years previously, when Gonzalo Pizarro led the first Spaniards by this road, they naturally, also, met with only the ordinary fate of all explorers— weariness, hunger, and sickness ; so that Gonzalo, in order to facilitate the departure of his band, decided on placing the sick and weak, with the baggage, on rafts, and, with the stronger, to follow along the banks of the river. Often, when the provisioning became more and more **Famous Voyage on Rafts** difficult, he sent the vessels far in advance, so that they might send or bring back food for those following by land. In doing this, however, the track was once lost just where the raft had been carried on especially far ahead, before known regions had been reached, and Gonzalo and his followers were obliged to turn back without being able to communicate with the others. Gonzalo had appointed Francisco de Orellana pilot of the raft. When the latter realised that he had been abandoned, and saw the impossibility of taking his raft back against the current, he formed the daring resolve to drift along with it, knowing that it would finally bring him to the sea somewhere or other.

With only fifty companions on rafts which they had had to construct themselves, he drifted down the Napo into the Amazon, and then not only on to the ocean, but also some distance along the coast to the north, until, after a water journey of seven months, he reached the first European settlement on the island of Cubagua. In spite of many battles he lost only a few of his followers, and not many other conquistadors have had to endure greater sufferings than they endured, or had to contend with such dangers as they overcame.

This same expedition from Peru was again undertaken in the sixteenth century. In the year 1559 the Marquess of Cañete, then vice-regent of Peru, after hearing the accounts of an Indian who had come from Brazil to Peru, out of the Marañon and Huallaga, and was supposed to have discovered inhabited and wealthy towns **A Tragic Voyage of Discovery** on the way, organised a voyage of exploration under the leadership of Pedro de Orsua. This expedition gave him an opportunity of getting rid of numerous unruly spirits who, since the various risings, had threatened the security of the province. These malcontents, however, gave quite an unexpected turn to the undertaking.

As soon as they had advanced far enough into the unknown district to be secure from pursuit, they murdered Orsua and completed the voyage up the river under the leadership of Lope de Aguirre, whom they had themselves chosen. After this they turned to Venezuela, and, having tyrannised over the province for months, they were at length overpowered in a battle near Barquisimeto, and the greater part of them were slain. The Amazon first became a permanent public road after the Portuguese had, in 1641, advanced with a great expedition from Para as far as Quito. This was the beginning of the methodical exploration of the mighty river system in detail, which came to an end when the Indians became extinct and the missionary activity on their behalf had consequently terminated.

The north-eastern portion of South America had at length become not quite an unknown region. Although Columbus had there first come in touch with the American continent, and almost the oldest attempts at colonisation on the continent itself had also been made on the northern coast, it had for a considerable time remained comparatively neglected, because it held out no prospect of unusual wealth and the natives were more warlike there than elsewhere. It was the tribes of the Caribs belonging to this coast who had greeted the first Spaniards with poisoned arrows, and then vanished into the dense forests of the interior, in order to conquer by passive resistance the opponent whom they were not prepared to meet in open battle. Their name was so terrible to the Spaniards that it became the typical designation of all warlike and hostile races, and in its altered form, " cannibals," has become synonymous all the world over with " man-eater."

A considerable number of attempts at colonisation in the territory between the mouths of the Orinoco and of the River Magdalena were entirely frustrated before the Spaniards succeeded in gaining a footing in the region of the coast. However, this **The Hunting-Ground for Slaves** territory only played an important part in Spanish colonial affairs when, owing to the rapid decline of the population on the islands of the Antilles, it became, on a large scale, the hunting-ground for slaves, while the island of Cubagua, on the coast, served as the principal market-place for the spoil. Not until the first twenty years of the sixteenth century did Rodrigo de Bastidas succeed in founding a settlement in Santa Marta which promised to result in a permanent usurpation of the country. But it is possible that upon his violent death it, too, might again have been lost had it not received support from the neighbouring province, which the first Spaniards had already named Venezuela—Little Venice—after its native lake-dwellings on Lake Maracaibo.

The great German merchants had taken part in almost the first voyages of exploration to the West Indies as well as to the East Indies, and the accession of Charles V. in Spain enabled them to secure for themselves an important and permanent share in colonial trade. Besides these mercantile agents, numbers of adventurous young Germans had also gone there, many of them passing through almost all the phases of discovery of the Conquista. It is small wonder, therefore, that two Germans once

sued for and gained a concession for colonial discoveries. The Ehingers were closely connected with the house of Wels, whom many members of the family had served. When, therefore, they received from Charles V. the right to colonise the interior from Cape Maracapana as far as the extreme end of the Guajiro Peninsula, **Pioneer Germans in Venezuela** from one ocean to the other, they counted with certainty on the help of the Welses, and some years later they transferred their prerogative to them. The Germans did only the pioneer work in colonising Venezuela, and helped forward the development of this province by the Spaniards.

This establishment of a colony was of peculiar importance in connection with the opening up of the unknown interior of South America, as it, in the first place, prevented the complete destruction of the colony founded by Bastidas in Santa Marta, and thereby formed the basis of the successful expedition of Gonzalo Jimenez de Quesada up the River Magdalena, besides becoming itself the starting-point of a succession of voyages of discovery. Almost simultaneously with Quesada and Benalcazar, Federmann led an expedition on to the plateau of Bogota, while George Hohermuth and Philip von Hutten started along the eastern foot of the Andes ; and, although they did not, as has often been asserted, advance as far as the River Amazon, they were the first Europeans who came upon its mighty northern tributaries, the Caqueta, and probably also the Putumayo.

The rumour of the existence of another country rich in gold was still maintained after the conquest of Peru, and the accounts of the natives pointed to the northern regions beyond the Inca kingdom. Ambrosius Ehinger—whom the Spaniards called Dalfinger—had already explored the valley of Upare and along the Magdalena on the strength of these rumours, and **Vain Searches for the Land of Gold** had almost reached the boundary of the Chibcha kingdom when he decided to return. His successors, starting from the eastern Llanos, sought in vain for the entrance to the land of gold. George Hohermuth reached the entrance to the territory of the Chibchas while he was resting in San Juan de los Llanos, which region carried on a continuous trade with the Chibchas. Nicolas Federmann was the first to discover the pass from Llanos across the Cordilleras, but on setting foot in the country of the Bacata he found the kingdom had been overthrown and was in the possession of the Spanish victors.

The fortunate conqueror of this province, which, under the name of Nuevo Reino de Granada, became the pearl in the crown of Spanish colonial possessions,

The Pearl of Spain's Possessions was Gonzalo Jiminez de Quesada. He had come to Santa Marta in the year 1536 with the governor, Pedro Fernandez de Lugo, and was by him immediately afterwards deputed, with several hundred followers and three small vessels, to explore the River Magdalena up stream, and to advance upon the powerful ruler who, according to the stories of the natives, dwelt there. Near the river itself Quesada only met with the same fortunes as his predecessors, who, after many hardships, had discovered single Indian villages which were, no doubt, occasionally rich in spoils. The winter floods at length compelled him to leave the valley and ascend to the mountains. After he had with much toil advanced through the Sierra de Oppon, he came almost by chance upon the country of the Chibchas, in the neighbourhood of the subsequent Velez, for since he had quitted the river he could find no intelligible guide.

The resistance which the Spaniards met with from the rulers of the states and provinces of the Chibchas, who were divided among themselves by all kinds of rivalries, did not prove serious, and during three years Quesada gained almost fabulous treasures with comparatively small loss. He had just organised the newly acquired province and was on the eve of departure, when, within a few weeks of each other, Nicolas Federmann from the east, and Sebastian de Benalcazar from the south, appeared upon the scene. How the former arrived there has already been referred to. Benalcazar had, as is well

A Trio of Unsuccessful Spaniards known, at first taken possession of the kingdom of Quito on behalf of Pizarro, and later on he, too, was induced, by precisely the same rumours which had guided the other two conquistadors, to undertake a voyage on his own account.

None of the three attained the object which they had desired—the regency of the rich province of Chibcha. Federmann ended in prison, a fate he well merited owing to the perfidy which he had shown on all sides. Benalcazar had to be satisfied with the governorship of Popayan, to which was added the territory to the west of the Magdalena. Quesada did not reap the fruit of his conquests either, for he had to relinquish the governorship of Santa Marta and New Granada in favour of the unworthy son of Lugo, who in the meanwhile had died. After many years spent in legal proceedings he returned to the scene of his early conquests with the title of marshal, and died there, at a great age, after many adventures. Although with the conquest of the Chibcha kingdom the land had come into the possession of the Spaniards, in whose Institutions the legend of "El Dorado," the Golden Man, originated, yet the voyages in search of El Dorado were never pursued with greater zeal than during the next following decades.

Philip von Hutten, Hernan Perez de Quesada, brother of the conqueror of Chibcha, and finally the latter himself, sought for the Golden Man in Llanos des Caqueta and Putumayo; but after an enormous loss of life they came in contact with only a few half-civilised Indian races. In consequence of this the kingdom of El Dorado was trans-

The New Era of Colonial Administration ferred to a lake of Manoa, which was sought for between the lower reaches of the Orinoco and the Marañon. On this occasion Quesada's son-in-law undoubtedly for the first time threw light on the river system of the Orinoco from New Granada as far as its estuary—during the sixteenth and seventeenth centuries the Guaviare was universally regarded as the river source of the Orinoco. In Trinidad he fell into the hands of Raleigh, who had recommenced his journey to the land of gold from the mouth of the Orinoco towards the Andes, and who, by his account of the expedition, has assisted more than his predecessors to spread abroad in Europe an idea of the geographical configuration of these regions. As a matter of fact, however, his whole expedition was only through a region which had long since been explored by the Spaniards.

The hope of finding El Dorado was gradually abandoned, for in the vast colonial territory owned by the Spaniards there was no space left for it. Love of exploration could no longer find an outlet for its activity, and it was succeeded by the serious and difficult task of organising the extremely vast regions which had at least become known, if only superficially.

SPAIN'S EMPIRE IN AMERICA
ORGANISATION OF THE COLONIES
AND THE PROBLEM OF THE SLAVE TRADE

ACCORDING to the interpretation which Columbus believed he might put upon his prerogatives the whole of the vast colonial empire of Spain in America should have constituted a great empire over which he and his descendants should exercise almost unlimited authority as hereditary viceroy, governor, and admiral, united in one person ; while the Crown in the meanwhile should possess in the right of suzerainty only a limited influence in the appointment of officials and a certain share of the revenue. Not only was this view held by the explorer, but his descendants also, in a lawsuit against the Crown, upheld the claim that the documentary concessions extended not only to islands and lands which had become known through the personal activity of Columbus, but also to all land which, during subsequent trans-Atlantic voyages of discovery undertaken by the First Admiral, should become the possession of the Spanish Crown.

The lawsuit terminated in a very simple manner—for the descendants of Columbus proved so utterly unfit for the duties imposed upon them by their claims that they finally themselves renounced their acknowledged documentary rights, because they had by vulgar debauchery incurred **Failures of the Great Columbus** punishment at the hand of justice, and had consequently fled. Apart from this, the point of law which was at issue proved by no means a simple one, for Columbus, on his part, had failed in more than one direction to fulfil the conditions of the Treaty of Santa Fé. He had neither gained the object which had formed the aim of the entire undertaking, nor had he been able, or even

shown a serious desire, to discharge the financial obligations which had been imposed upon him by the negotiations of 1492. Though he left the equipment of the expeditions to the government, he would nevertheless not give up all claim to the **Columbus's Colonial Ambitions** share in the profits which had been assigned to him only as compensation for his proportionate share in the expenditure. Within a very short time the question was transferred from the footing of a theoretical and legal debate to purely practical jurisdiction.

The prospect which lay in store for the colonies under the government of Columbus, between the second and third voyages of the explorer, had already become evident. The colonial method which had been adopted by the Portuguese on the coast of Guinea appeared to the First Admiral as the only feasible model—with this one exception, however, that he wished to be lessee of the general monopoly in the West Indies— that is to say, he desired to occupy the position which the Infante Henry had filled before his rights had reverted to the Crown. But he was entirely wanting in that keen spirit of enthusiasm which induced the infante, for many years, to make one sacrifice after another for the discovery of new countries and for the extension of Christendom ; moreover, his one object was, in a mean-spirited way, not to miss any possible gain for himself.

For this reason he would not permit the settlers of San Domingo to spread themselves over the continent, and then, at their own risk, to undertake the search for precious ores and other trade commodities.

He feared that by such means a portion of the spoil would escape his control and diminish his share in the profits. For the same reason, also, when sufficiently large quantities of other staple trade commodities were not procurable, he did not hesitate to freight his ships with stolen natives, in order to sell them to the mother country, after the example of the Portuguese. Not even the humane laws of the Spanish Government had power to prevent the rapid extinction of the native population in the Antilles, and it is obvious that a similar result would have been the immediate and inevitable consequence of Columbus's ideas on colonisation.

Columbus's Weakness as a Ruler

The first attempt at a slave trade with Spain had been checked by the categorical inhibition of Ferdinand and Isabella, and as Columbus was incapable of maintaining order in his only settlement, this afforded the government an opportunity for a breach with his entire colonial system. He requested the assistance of an officer of the Crown to re-establish order, and the subsequent investigation showed how impossible it would have been to entrust the government of the entire territory to the explorer, although he claimed it as his prerogative.

It is evident the government of Ferdinand and Isabella had originally planned a colonial undertaking according to the Portuguese model, and Columbus's expedition had given rise to the expectation that the discovery of flourishing and well-organised states would result in Spain's carrying on an extensive and successful trade with them. The real object of Columbus's expedition was not so much to acquire territory as to divert the costly and much sought after products of the Far East from the existing trade routes, and to establish the monopoly of the Spanish harbours. The extension of Christianity in these far-off realms was doubtless a second object. The Spaniard, who had for centuries carried on a dreadful war upon the soil of his native land for the extension of Christianity among unbelievers, without doubt did not shrink from pursuing the same object by identical means in far-distant lands. If Columbus had really reached the harbours of Zaitun and Quinsay, with their treasures, their trade, and their organisation, most probably Spanish rule would have been established there in the same manner in which the

Spanish Wars to Extend Christianity

Portuguese ruled in the East Indies. In this way the first " Institution " established by the Spanish rulers for the benefit of colonial affairs—the " Casa de Contratacion," or the " House for Commerce," intended primarily for all commercial undertakings—was, in essentials, a copy of the " Casa da India " at Lisbon.

The Casa de Contratacion was, on its foundation in 1503, intended to watch over the interests of the Crown in colonial matters, more especially over commercial intercourse with the colonies. At that time the administrative powers were, according to the contracts of 1492, almost exclusively in the hands of Columbus, and the establishment of the Casa de Contratacion is sufficient evidence that the government in no way aimed at disputing these prerogatives, although Columbus had then already been suspended from the absolute power of exercising them and a governor had been nominated by the administration. But the foundation of settlements over the whole of Hispaniola and on the neighbouring islands, and the subdivision of the land among the colonists, as well as the advance into the interior of the island, portended a breach with Columbus's colonial system, for his plan had been to draw the mercantile profits of the land only from permanent ports on the coasts. The Crown's second decree for the Casa de Contratacion already showed an altered face, though mercantile interests still occupied the foreground.

The Founding of New Settlements

The realisation of the profits which the government confidently anticipated from direct participation in the colonial trade is therein less prominently dealt with, and it now becomes more a question of the ordering and control of navigation and mercantile intercourse between the mother country and the colonies generally, whether carried on at the expense of the Crown or by the private individual. As the Casa de Contratacion developed into a court of administration, direct and judicial powers accrued to it. At least one lawyer is referred to in the regulations of 1511, besides the manager, treasurer, and book-keeper, as being in its employ.

The control of the correspondence, which was transferred to the Casa, formed the most important extension of power which was accorded during that year, and laid the foundation for its future significance. Not only all the letters which arrived for the government from the colonies had to be opened and read, but all the government deeds intended for the colonies had also to be registered in the books of the institution, the officials even receiving orders to enter protests against such governmental instructions as seemed to them injudicious or risky and to suspend their execution. By reason of these powers the Casa de Contratacion became more and more a board of administration. The qualifications necessary for such a board were in later years also specially assigned to it ; in less important matters the decision of the Casa was regarded as final, whereas upon greater and more important questions the Consejo de Indias could be referred to as a superior court.

In spite of the far-reaching prerogatives which had, according to agreement, been assigned to Columbus as viceroy, governor, and admiral of the Indies, colonial affairs, from the beginning, required extensive supervision and guidance on the part of the government. These increased considerably in importance from the moment when Columbus was suspended from the full enjoyment of his authoritative powers, and when a Crown official was appointed in the interim to act for him provisionally. Ferdinand the Catholic, in order to secure the necessary uniformity and continuity of the colonial policy, had then already transferred the business connected with these powers to one distinct person. The Archbishop Fonseca was the authority on colonial affairs in the Privy Council ; Secretary Gricio first acted as Under-Secretary, but after a short time he was succeeded by Lope de Conchillos, then already known for his unfortunate share in the quarrel about the succession between Ferdinand the Catholic and Philip the Handsome.

Administering the Spanish Colonies

During the years 1509 to 1512 Don Diego Colon was reinstalled in the prerogatives of his father, but only to a limited extent. The division of the continually expanding colonial kingdom was then already in prospect, by which division only those countries which had been won for Spain by the direct invasion of the First Admiral were ceded to his descendants under the conditions of the treaty of Santa Fé. Even so these prerogatives were not granted without limitations, though the heirs were permitted to retain, as had been stipulated, the power to exercise jurisdiction, in the first instance, throughout the entire range of the country assigned to them. On the other hand, in 1511, by the establishment of the " Audiencia " of San Domingo, a court of appeal was instituted more especially for the entire colonial department, where appeals could be made against the decisions of the vice-regal courts of justice. The court was authorised to give judgment directly in the king's name, and it could eventually even summon the vice-regent himself before its bar. Owing to the fact that in all departments of national life government and the administration of justice had not as yet become detached from each other, each magistrate not only pronouncing judgment, but also executing it throughout the circuit of his authority, the Audiencia, in its capacity of a court of appeal for the legal settlement of all kinds of colonial affairs, became an important factor in colonial administration.

A Court of Appeal Established

This importance grew in proportion as the government recognised the necessity of creating a counterpoise to the vast prerogatives of the vice-regent and governor, and of constituting an authority in touch with the governor, by which to control him, and act under the immediate direction of the government in the colonial territories which were not administered according to the treaty of Santa Fé. The government provided itself with another influence in the clergy. At first priests belonging to a religious order were almost exclusively sent to the islands to watch over religious interests and promote missionary work among the natives.

Almost immediately upon their advent conflicts arose between them and the temporal authorities. Fray Bernal Boil, who had accompanied Columbus on his second voyage as vicar-general, had, like the latter, soon to be recalled, because he became too argumentative in defending his own version of the official duties against the officials. As soon as the government had convinced itself of the vast extent of the newly acquired possessions, it also became seriously concerned about the organisation of religious matters. At Ferdinand's suggestion Pope Alexander VI., in the year 1502, founded the first two bishoprics in San Domingo and La Vega on the island of Hispaniola. Almost immediately upon the definite settlement

Missionary Work Among the Natives

the erection of new dioceses ensued, and soon an extensive network of archbishoprics, bishoprics, and parochial dioceses was spread over the whole colonial territory. The possibility arising, however, that the Church, not being a state within a state, might become dangerous to the power of the government, care was taken that the

Colonies the Property of the Spanish Crown Crown should receive, from the Pope himself, the right of presentation to all benefices in the New World, in order to make the clergy of the colonies entirely dependent on the government, so that they even became a strong and influential support in all the vicissitudes of colonial events.

When, therefore, in the year 1516, Charles V. inherited from his grandfather the extensive colonial possessions with the Spanish Crown lands, he found the colonial government under safe guidance ; indeed, one might almost say that the government had already begun to shape for itself a system for its colonial policy. As the discovery of America had been due exclusively to the initiative of Queen Isabella, the colonies, by political law, formed an integral and constituent part of the Crown of Castile. In the idea of a colony the sixteenth century conceived a country that was almost exclusively the private property of the Crown, at least so far as the possession of all privileges was concerned. The Spanish Government, therefore, after the abolition of the prerogatives belonging to the Colons, regarded the colonies as a domain whose revenue should accrue exclusively to it and be employed at its discretion. One consequence of this idea was that the government issued strict regulations for admission to the colonies.

In order seriously to control the execution of this decision, the entire intercourse between the mother country and the colonies was confined to the town of Seville, with the outer harbour of San Lucar de Barrameda. The disadvantages for trade,

The Mother Country and Her Colonies which were the natural consequence of this monopoly by Seville, soon became evident. During the first years of Charles V.'s reign, an especially vigorous agitation arose, no doubt as a consequence of the union of the Spanish kingdom with the German and Dutch territories under one and the same sceptre ; and this was the means of procuring a considerable mitigation of the system, if not an advance in the participation also of these nations in

the trans-Atlantic trade. For a time this counter-current was successful, and it probably gave rise to a hope for still greater success hereafter ; but the fiscal interests finally conquered, and Seville's monopoly of the colonial trade was rigorously maintained for a considerable time.

The fiscal and monopolist system, though characteristic, does not exclusively distinguish Spanish colonial policy, but it has, as in the case of the other states which have recognised it, left its special marks. But the most remarkable feature of the Spanish policy is its attitude towards the aborigines of the colonies. Columbus also considered the natives from the Portuguese point of view—that is to say, he regarded them either as a power with whom war could be waged and a treaty concluded ; or as a commodity, like other colonial products, to be bought or sold, according to the requirements of commercial interests.

In any case, the natives were, from this point of view, either foreign persons or foreign things. As a result, Columbus, on his third voyage, endeavoured to cover his unsuccessful search for gold, spices and other

Spain's Humane Treatment of the Natives costly wares by freighting the home-sailing vessel with a cargo of slaves, to be sold in Seville. But in this he met with opposition from the Spanish Government, and more especially from Queen Isabella of Castile, as sovereign of the colonial kingdom. Immediately upon the news of the arrival of the living cargo, the officials in Seville received an order to stop the sale and to wait for a decision as to whether the slavery of the Indians was permissible according to the laws, human and divine.

It was followed by an order that the Indians should be taken back to their native country and set at liberty. This was a decision on the highest principles and of the widest scope, and it inaugurated a colonial policy such as had up to that time nowhere been attempted. It is probable that King Ferdinand, a politician of temperate views, who by no means regarded the whole colonial enterprise of his consort and co-regent with favour, would have decided differently had his own view of the matter served as a standard.

One is strengthened in this belief by the insistence with which Queen Isabella, in her will and its codicil, urges upon her husband the protection of the natives. This codicil is the next significant step in the legislation of the native question.

Although short and concise, its statements regarding the natives are so far of great importance, that the latter are therein recognised as subjects of equal birth, and their lives and property as under the protection of the Crown ; and it is especially urged upon King Ferdinand, as executor, to repress and make compensation for any possible injustice which the natives might have to suffer.

The practical treatment of this question did not quite attain the high level of the theoretical decision. The declaration that the Indians were to enjoy the privileges of free subjects provoked opposition not only from the colonists, but also from the colonial officials and even from the clergy. It was impossible to form any conception of the revenues and produce of the colonies without having sufficient working material in the shape of native labour. Without a certain amount of compulsion, however, the native could not be induced, either to perform a sufficient amount of work to meet the requirements of the colonies, or to remain on a permanently friendly footing with the settler ; yet this was indispensable if the civilising influence,

The Natives Under a Form of Bondage and more especially the conversion of the natives to Christianity, which had from the beginning of the history of discoveries been so strongly emphasised, were to be carried on with any degree of success.

For this reason, both the temporal and spiritual authorities were unanimous in declaring that the granting of unlimited freedom to the natives would mean the ruin of the colonies, from both a spiritual and an economic point of view. The " Repartimientos " and " Encomiendas " were finally the result of the negotiations which were carried on with regard to these matters. The personal liberty of the natives was therein specially recognised, but in order to promote their education by European methods of civilisation and to secure their conversion to the Christian doctrine, they were assigned (repartir) to the charge of individual colonists and placed under their protection (encomendar). The latter thereby acquired a certain measure of patriarchal authority over their protégés which, according to the letter of the law, was most humanely designed, though in reality it created for the native almost everywhere a sure state of bondage ; and this bondage, along with the simultaneous existence of Indian slavery, often made the well-meaning designs of the law-makers entirely illusory for certain classes of the natives.

The law required certain moral guarantees from the holder of a repartimiento, and, on the other hand, quite definitely fixed the maximum of work to be done by the natives. The governors of the various colonial districts, and, above all, of those territories which had been newly discovered, and had yet to be colonised, could not, however, under the pressure of the actual circumstances, evade the claims made upon them to reward, by the bestowal of the repartimiento, the services of the colonists who had first taken possession of the country. During the voyages of discovery and conquest it was not generally men of specially high morality who gained the highest honours for their comrades and country.

Difficulties in the Way of Government

As, however, these expeditions made such great demands upon the participators, as to both daring and powers of endurance, naturally these characteristics preponderated among the recruits, who had nothing to lose and everything to gain. It is only natural that anyone who had so schooled himself as to face famine and death at the hand of the enemy for months should not be particularly disposed to treat with lenience and consideration the lives of beings whom he was easily induced to regard as creatures of an inferior order, creatures who could be brought to a peaceful state of subjection to the European yoke only after cruel and devastating wars.

Even with the best intentions of the favourably disposed governors, it was almost impossible to carry through a conscientious administration of the laws of the encomiendas. In the districts which were but sparsely populated by Europeans these rough settlers, who could hardly be dispensed with for the extension of the Spanish power, in numerous instances mutinied against the officials when the latter, in pursuance of the law, endeavoured to seize what the former looked on as the well-earned wage of their own superhuman exertions and privations. More than one governor was killed by his unruly followers, owing to his efforts to enforce respect for the law.

Fate of Law-respecting Governors

That great evils existed in the treatment of the natives in the extensive regions of the " Conquista " is certainly undeniable, although it is also incontestable that the horrors of the Indian oppression have been extremely exaggerated by the agitators for the rights of humanity, among whom Bishop Bartolomé de las Casas occupies a prominent place. The Indians were undoubtedly often overburdened by toil, and thousands of them succumbed; yet, from the point of view of self-interest, it **Antilles Inhabited by Aruacs** was of great importance to the colonists that those peoples under their protection should be preserved; unscrupulous exploitation cannot therefore be taken as the universal rule. The native population on the first discovered and colonised Antilles diminished with extraordinary rapidity; but, no doubt, this was brought about by many different causes.

In the first instance their number had been considerably overrated. Columbus made a point of doing this in order to enhance the value of his discovery, and the vehement agitation for the freedom of the Indians, which had already begun twenty years after the discovery, did still more to falsify ideas as to the number of the natives. If one remembers that the Antilles were only gradually populated by the Aruac race from the continent, and that this race of fishermen and hunters has nowhere else founded larger or more densely populated settlements; and if one also bears in mind that this race had for generations to suffer from a war of extermination with the dreaded native pirates, the Caribs, a dense population on the Antilles at the time of their discovery would be an impossible assumption.

The natives, however, soon realised that the newly arrived Spaniards would prove far more dangerous enemies than the Caribs had been. For this reason many of them fled from their villages into the jungle, where they suffered great loss among themselves and in war with the Christians. To these factors were further added those of unaccustomed kinds of labour, a change **Factors in the Depopulation of the Antilles** of food and manner of life, and finally maladies which had been imported by the Europeans and became epidemic among the natives, causing fearful devastation. The combination of all these influences must be held responsible for the depopulation of the Antilles.

This depopulation in one sense became of importance to the entire native question, as it led to a rupture with the general principle of the universal liberty of the Indians. In 1505 Ferdinand the Catholic had already allowed the natives who by arms might oppose civilisation and Christianity to be attacked and enslaved. Possibly this permission may in the first instance have been aimed at the Caribbean races, but the more apparent the retrogression of the native population became, when the larger islands grew to be more densely populated by Europeans, the more was this licence employed as a cloak for the concealment of an extensive Indian slave trade.

Nothing was easier than by a defiant bearing to provoke the natives to take up arms so that without a violation of the law they could be dragged away as slaves. By these means the smaller Antilles, on which no Spanish settlements had been established, became within a short time entirely depopulated. But natives who had been exported to the larger islands as slaves, and there branded on the thighs with hot irons—a curious consequence of a law designed to be humanitarian—in order to prevent their exchange with peaceable Indians, were soon, also, no longer able to supply the ever-increasing demand for **Slave-hunts on the Continent** labourers and to replenish their own reduced numbers. The slave-hunts were then extended to the continent and more especially to the northern coast of South America, whose inhabitants, of kindred origin with the island population, showed an unusually violent and lasting opposition to the first attempts at colonisation.

At this stage the doings of the slave-hunters assumed such proportions that they gave rise to the first movements of opposition, and these soon became of great power, as points of view were brought to bear upon the question which had nothing actually to do with the matter itself. The clergy of the colonies, as has already been mentioned, had at first not considered themselves in the least obliged to interfere on behalf of unlimited liberty for the Indians. Not only the secular priests, but also the Franciscans, who since the days of Columbus—when he also had belonged to the order as a lay brother— had played a prominent part in colonial administration, did not regard it as scandalous that the Indians were compelled by moderate pressure to join the Christians, or, in cases of resistance, were enslaved and treated as enemies. The Dominicans maintained a different attitude. The antithesis between the two points of view also aroused the opposition of the one order against the other, and thus, no doubt, contributed not a little to the aggravation of the question. The first who ventured to stigmatise from the pulpit, as a disgrace and outrage, the hitherto existing treatment of the natives was the Dominican brother Pedro de Cordoba, who thereby became distinguished far beyond his own diocese of San Domingo, where he preached.

Bartolomé de las Casas, who at that time was himself a keeper of slaves in Cuba, was won over to his views. His impetuous spirit took up the cause of the natives with such zeal that he became one of the best known among the champions of native liberty. Las Casas presented himself at the Spanish court, for the first time, shortly before the death of Ferdinand the Catholic. Though his vivid descriptions of the horrors practised in the treatment of the natives were met by the public with mixed feelings, he was the means of bringing about the decision that a special commission should be sent out to hold an inquiry into the actual circumstances. The native question had by that time become such an object of contention between the Franciscans and Dominicans that both orders were, on principle, excluded from election to the commission ; but as the question was intended to be treated purely as a matter of conscience, and had for this reason been placed in the hands of the clergy, it was finally agreed that three Hieronymite monks should be chosen and sent to the islands with discretionary powers.

Outcry Against Slavery

Las Casas vehemently impugned the impartiality of the three fathers because they refused to take his point of view, but he certainly wronged them. As a universal remedy he proposed the formation of self-governed and self-administered communities of Indians, to which only the clergy from among the Spaniards should be admitted as leaders in religious matters, and this was also attempted by the Hieronymites. Las Casas, a few years later, failed to colonise, on the same plan, a tract of the Paria coast, far removed from intercourse with the white man ; and the Hieronymites, contending against still more unfavourable conditions, were equally unsuccessful in their attempt to colonise San Domingo. No doubt, however, the fact of their being sent greatly increased the opposition of the religious orders among themselves, so that the government was forced at last to take the matter entirely out of the hands of the clergy and entrust it to a secular official.

The licentiate Rodrigo de Figueroa kept quite aloof from all theoretical points of view and regulated the native question solely from the standpoint of the hitherto formulated laws on that point. These guaranteed a certain amount of liberty to the peaceable Indians, but permitted the enslavement of the hostile ones. In order to do this he first of all had to settle which Indians were to be regarded as hostile. As he was guided by entirely disinterested and well-intentioned ideas, he considerably circumscribed the territory remaining to the slave-hunters. The improvement in the treatment of the Indians as a whole, in the repartimientos and encomiendas, was the necessary consequence of the increased attention which was paid to the regulations bearing upon it.

Circumscribed Area of the Slave-hunters

An economic revolution was, in addition to this, carried out about the same time, at any rate in the island colonies. In spite of all efforts to the contrary on the part of the government, the Spanish settlements had for a long time been little more than permanent trade factories ; all valuable objects which could be got from the natives by barter were collected, and with native help precious ores were dug and washed. But whenever the government sent seeds and plants across the ocean, their cultivation was not a success, because the natives did not understand their treatment, and the colonists considered it beneath them to have anything to do with the matter.

As therefore only a limited amount of the valuable products of the soil could be found, the exchange trade soon also collapsed, and though the new discoveries revived the carrying trade of San Domingo, it at the same time continuously withdrew the labourers from the island, thus diminishing its individual importance. The settlements suffered much in consequence until, by the cultivation of the sugar-cane, new and profitable livelihood was found for the colonists. Labourers were also required for this, and though the necessary work was not as irksome as gold-washing, it entailed a settled mode of life and continuous work for the colonists, whereas the other implied only an uncertain search for fortune.

Profits of the Sugar-cane

The cultivation of sugar-cane had an important share in maintaining the vitality of the Spanish colonies up to the time when, through the great extension of these colonies, further opportunities for gaining a livelihood arose. Besides this, it was also of immense importance in their development, because it gave the impulse **Negro Slaves** to the importation of negro **Imported to** slaves. These had, in isolated **the Colonies** instances, been imported in the service of their Spanish masters from the time of the discovery of America. It was not long before it became evident in the colonies that the negroes became acclimatised exceedingly well there, and far surpassed the Indian natives in their capacity for work.

The government did not regard the importation of negroes with favour. It was feared that they, being but recently baptised, would be only half-hearted adherents of Christianity, and might have a bad influence upon the conversion of the Indians; so on that account the African negroes were entirely excluded from the colonies, and the immigration of black house slaves was also restricted as much as possible. The repeated petitions of the colonists for a plentiful supply of black labourers disclosed to the government the importance of this matter, so that it gradually came to be regarded in quite another light when Las Casas, from motives of philanthropy, urgently recommended the introduction of negro slaves in order to rescue the Indians from slavery. Although on this point the government still maintained the principle of inhibition for negro importation, it was now only on account of fiscal interests.

It is a fact that since 1516 about 4,000 negroes alone were almost annually transported by the agents of the slave monopoly from the coast of Guinea to the New World—exclusive of the considerable number who reached the colonies by **The New** special license, and in later **World's Trade** times through smuggling. No **in Slaves** doubt the negroes, and the half-castes who had already sprung from the union of whites with blacks and Indians, constituted in the middle of the sixteenth century a very important element in the agricultural population, and, as such, demanded special attention. These negroes had received, even less than the Indians, the merest semblance of a civilising education from the colonists,

and, as they were by nature far less submissive, they were more inclined to forsake their masters and revert to the manners and customs of their native life in the jungle. In 1550 the Spaniards had already to suppress dangerous insurrections of the negro population. These again recurred from time to time, until, after a successful insurrection in the year 1808, the negroes even succeeded in founding an independent state on the western half of the island of San Domingo in the Republic of Haiti.

The mixing of races was comparatively of less importance in Spanish America. In most of the colonies during the first years savage marriages with the native women were no doubt the rule, so long as European women did not go there or could not, under the circumstances, be imported; and wherever this continued, as was the case in Paraguay, it naturally resulted in a greater mixing of the races. In Mexico and Peru, as well as also in Bogota, the marriages of Spanish conquistadors with women of the native nobility were more often made from political considerations, and the Spanish **Blending** kings acknowledged this aristo- **of** cracy by giving it an equal **the Races** standing with the Spanish nobility. On the whole, however, the Spaniards in the colonies guarded the purity of their blood with no less care than in the mother country, and the creoles to this day regard it as the highest distinction to be the descendants of grandfathers and great-grandfathers of pure Spanish blood. Although the colonists of European descent, on the one hand, felt themselves the living antithesis of the native races, yet, owing to changed conditions of life, an altered climate, and different social circumstances, in course of time an indistinctly recognised but later on fully appreciated variation on the Spanish type was developed, the pure-bred Spaniards remaining in the colonies only temporarily as merchants, soldiers and officials, and never losing the feeling of being aliens.

On his accession Charles V. found the native question at its height, and for a time he let it run its course. The bitter paper war between Las Casas and Sepulveda about the admissibility of native slavery belongs to the first years of his reign, as well as the unsuccessful attempt at colonisation by the Dominican who had been elected patron of the Indians. The institution of a special advocate for the natives also became general, and in every colony a spiritual chief pastor was then charged with the protection of the natives. The laws, also, for the treatment of the Indians were permanently altered and developed in a more decided recognition of their interests, until the Edict of Granada, of November 17th, 1526, included in six paragraphs all the regulations bearing upon their treatment.

The edict still distinguished between two classes of Indians, friendly and savage, and permitted the enslavement of the latter, while special officials were charged with the decision of each individual case. From that time this law became the

government, therefore, confined itself to freeing the system of the encomiendas more and more from all the imperfections which adhered to it, and to watching more and more carefully over its conscientious execution. The principle of promoting the social advancement of the Indians by a closer union with the Spaniards, and of granting to the conquistadors and their descendants, as a reward and recognition, the supervision of Indian wards, was adhered to. All the Indians were, however, by no means divided into encomiendas.

From the beginning the Crown had retained certain portions both of the land and of the population of every province

VICTORS AND VANQUISHED: A GROUP OF SPANIARDS AND PERUVIANS
From the painting by H. P. Briggs in the National Gallery

standard for the treatment of the natives, not only in all the colonies, but also in all the agreements concerning discoveries. It was nevertheless followed, in rather rapid succession, by further regulations in favour of the Indians. In 1530 Indian slavery was definitely abolished, after many disputes both for and against it.

In the same way the government made several attempts to abolish the encomiendas, but this regulation was never carried through, for two reasons: first, because it threatened to be prejudicial to the material advantage of the colonist; and, second, because it hindered the advancement of the civilisation of the Indian. The

and district, which were destined for the service of the Crown and not for the use of the individual colonist. Beyond this, the more the misuse of the encomiendas was attacked, the greater grew the difficulty of extending the system, so that finally only those Indians who were in the immediate neighbourhood of the places founded at the time of the conquest remained under the protection of the colonists. The vast territories which had not been so densely populated by Europeans remained, as before, the free land of the Indians, whose conversion and civilisation were almost exclusively transferred to the religious societies and to the missionaries sent out by them.

MISSIONARY ENTERPRISE IN BOLIVIA: A JESUIT SETTLEMENT AT SAN JOSE

The warlike Guaranis for long resisted the religion and customs of their Spanish invaders, and towards the middle of the sixteenth century Jesuit missionaries were sent to Paraguay in aid of the first Christian preachers. So successful were their efforts that in a few years the entire control of the province, civil and religious, was handed over to them. They founded a number of villages, at each of which a settlement in charge of two priests was erected. The above picture shows such an edifice, with a portion of an Indian village.

THE JESUITS IN SOUTH AMERICA
AND THE CIVILISING OF THE NATIVE RACES

THE merits of the Spanish clergy on Spanish territory can hardly be rated too highly. The mysticism of the Renaissance united with the enthusiasm for the natural conditions of human society which had arisen from Romanticism in casting upon the Spanish missionaries the reproach that they, with blind fanaticism, had annihilated the last remnants of sacred antiquity in the New World and had brought to the people of America only spiritual servitude instead of spiritual salvation.

It had been purely an act of necessity for the missionaries and clergy in the provinces, where they were confronted by a well-developed system of religion and an influential hierarchy, to interfere radically and energetically with the inhuman customs which they frequently found to exist among the natives ; as, for example, in Mexico. It can certainly not be disputed that in so doing they had occasionally destroyed ob-**The Vandalism** jects of heathen adoration, **of the Spanish** which destruction has been **Missionaries** deplored by modern ethnographical science. On the other hand, it was just these clergy, and in many provinces only they, who considered it worth their while to investigate, collect, and record the language, customs, and traditions of the natives, so that modern science is indebted to them for the most copious and valuable material for philological and ethnological research. No doubt, few of them were fully conscious of the services they were rendering to latter-day research, as they were more engrossed by their immediate aim, the civilisation and conversion of the Indians.

Wherever the temporal and spiritual governments were in line in their treatment of the natives, one naturally hears less of the successful activity of the monks ; although the fact of the appearance of the Dominicans and of Las Casas, besides the existence of numerous isolated notes in the official records and in the secular and clerical chronicles, prove that their activity extended in the same measure into territories other than those in which they were more especially active. They have raised for themselves an immortal monument, more especially in the history **Missionaries** of these latter parts. After **the Pioneers of** the whole of the new conti-**Civilisation** nent had been superficially explored during the period of the conquest, Spanish colonial activity was, towards the close of the sixteenth century, concentrated on those regions whose agricultural development promised immediate advantages from a European point of view.

But wide tracts of land, where it was assumed that, owing either to climatic, political, or trade reasons, no remunerative cultivation was possible, remained almost entirely untouched. The greater part of the South American continent to the east of the Cordilleras and to the north of the mouth of the river La Plata belonged to this rejected territory. In this vast district, through which the mighty Amazon, with its tributaries, the Paraguay and other tributaries of the river La Plata, flowed, the work of cultivation and of introducing and maintaining European standards of civilisation were almost exclusively the work of missionaries.

At first it was chiefly the Franciscans and Augustinians who, from the monasteries and colleges of the Peruvian highlands, undertook the conversion of the Indians living farther down stream and along the rivers flowing from the Cordilleras towards the east. These spiritual fathers, with incomparable self-sacrifice and **Converting** self - forgetfulness, wandered **the American** among the savage natives, **Indians** often only gaining, after months and years of activity, the means for the closer understanding which laid the foundation for their material and religious labour of civilisation. Recognising that the wandering life of the Indians was extremely fatal to all enduring spiritual influence, and that to gather them together in fixed settlements was an essential condition of their progress in civilisation, the missionaries invariably aimed, first of all, at finding and pointing out to the Indian tribes whose conversion was in contemplation likely dwelling-places which would suit not only their propensities,

Villages Closed against Europeans

but also the requirements of civilisation. In doing this they intentionally avoided the proximity of European settlements, in spite of the laws which prohibited to Europeans in general a prolonged sojourn in the Indian villages.

Moreover, in quite early times they covered the upper and middle valleys of the tributaries of the Marañon, and during the seventeenth century the valleys of this river also, as well as of other great rivers of South America, with a network of Indian villages and hamlets. The greater number of these fell into ruin in course of time, owing either to the retrogression of the native population, which became evident there also, or to the persecution which was afterwards stirred up against the activity of the spiritual fathers. But they had laid the actual foundation for the advance of European civilisation throughout the entire territory.

The sphere and the character of the missions to the Indians of South America became most familiar through the Jesuits, who, in the second half of the sixteenth and the beginning of the seventeenth centuries, extended their missionary activity, which had been inaugurated by the devout Francis Xavier in the east, to the New World in the west. One must not, however, overlook the fact that the peculiar constitution of the so-called " reductions " and " missions " was neither invented by the Jesuits nor ever exclusively maintained by them. Its conception has been more especially attributed to their order because the Jesuit missions of Brazil and Paraguay have influenced

The Jesuits Active in Paraguay

the political history of the South American continent as no other order has done. The Jesuits, in concurrence with other religious associations, early began their activity as missionaries, if anything, in a greater degree perhaps in the Portuguese than in the Spanish territory. But they only assumed an exceptional position when, in the year 1608, a special district in Paraguay was assigned to them, free from all civil authority, where they were able to carry out the attempts at the civilisation and conversion of the Indians on a larger scale. There was no special motive attached to the fact that the government, in so doing, endowed them with an unusual amount of independence.

The Bull of Alexander VI. with reference to the line of demarcation had in principle established the boundaries of the Spanish and Portuguese colonial sphere, but its general and indefinite wording was quite inadequate for a really political demarcation. Both governments soon recognised this when the mouth of the river La Plata was discovered simultaneously by rival explorers. Several attempts at a diplomatic understanding were made in consequence of this, but, in point of fact, both Powers still attached far too little importance to the unexplored and unpromising territory whose possibilities seemed doubtful.

With time these circumstances assumed real importance, chiefly through the dissimilar colonial policy pursued by the two Powers in these border districts. Asuncion, on the Paraguay, was the chief

Portuguese in South America

of all the Spanish colonies, where from the beginning the relations between the natives and the colonists had been especially friendly, and where the best spirit of Spanish legislation for the Indians found expression regardless of outward circumstances. Bonds of friendship were formed between the brave and honest Guarani and the confederates of Irala which, during the course of centuries, were scarcely ever seriously doubted. The covenant with this mighty and widely dispersed Tupi tribe soon brought out the underlying contrast between the Spanish colonists and their eastern neighbours, the Portuguese.

The powers of little Portugal were so entirely engrossed by East Indian politics that the Brazilian colonial territory was, scarcely ten years after its discovery by Cabral, given over entirely to private enterprise. In this way a number of small settlements were founded in the Bahia de Todos os Santos, at Cape St. Vincent, and on the island of St. Caterina in the bay of Rio de Janeiro. These were at first regarded as Portuguese colonies, but, besides the few actual Portuguese and Portuguese Jews in the colony, there were a number of questionable characters, the subjects of every realm, who carried on trade of a very doubtful merit, and whose products were sent, not only to Lisbon, but also, if they succeeded in evading the customs, to French, English, and even Hanseatic harbours.

While the foreign merchants dealt principally in brazil-wood, sugar, and similar colonial products, the Portuguese chiefly carried on a brisk trade in Indian slaves, whom they did not take so much to Lisbon as to the colonial harbours, irrespective of whether these natives belonged to Portuguese or to Spanish territory. As was the case everywhere else, the consequence of the slave-hunts was that the natives retired farther and farther from the coast. The slave-hunters, however, followed their prey into the interior by the most accessible paths—that is, by the waterways; and thus they soon also came in conflict with the Guarani, and through them, indirectly, with the Spanish colonists.

In order to put an end to these lawless conditions, and to draw greater advantages from this colonial possession, the Portuguese Government decided on a change in its colonial system. **Portugal's New System of Administration** In the year 1531 a great part of Brazil was divided into so-called " capitanries "— vast tracts of land for which the rights of feudal lords, as in the Old World, were granted to the owners in return for an insignificant royalty payable to the Crown. This colonial system was also tried by the English in a part of Northern America.

The thirty-five capitanries which arose under this system had this advantage— that they brought about actual attempts at settlements in many places, and in this way the first sugar plantations, with their refineries, and the first farms were established. On the whole, however, the system did not work satisfactorily. Many of the capitanries were relinquished by the owners; others dragged on a weary existence. Above all, the illegalities in the trade with foreign countries and the sorties of the slave-hunters still continued, even when a central authority had been established for the separate districts, and a vice-regent had been sent over to occupy the residence at Bahia.

The attempt at colonisation by the French Protestants, under Villegaignon, proves how little real authority the Portuguese had over their Brazilian possession. The French expedition was the result of the trade which had for a considerable time been carried on illegally, yet unhindered, between Dieppe and the coast of Brazil. Those lovers of adventure who were anxious to emigrate imagined they could easily found a new home there, and annex a valuable portion of colonial territory for their mother country without difficulty. As a matter **Underhand Methods of the French** of fact, they were in possession of the bay of Rio de Janeiro for almost five years. If internal disputes and altered political conditions at home had not come fortuitously to the aid of the Portuguese, a long time might have elapsed before the future capital of Brazil had once more become Portuguese property.

The French, retiring more and more towards the north, repeatedly attempted to gain a footing on Brazilian soil, and for this purpose made most clever use of the policy which they had so successfully carried through on a larger scale in their settlements on the St. Lawrence. They allied themselves with the natives, not only to gain peace with them, but also that they might incite them against their colonial rivals. This policy was easy in Brazil, because, in the eyes of the Portuguese, the native continued to be a commodity to be employed to the best advantage.

The union of Portugal with Spain in the year 1580 was not to be without influence on colonial legislation, although the government of Portugal and its colonies remained entirely separate, in spite of the conquest by Philip II. Many laws were formulated which in principle tended towards the personal liberty of the Indians. They were, nevertheless, almost entirely without influence on the actual circumstances, for the colonists always managed so that their property in Indian slaves should remain judicially unassailed. The conditions for the native were improved only farther towards the interior, **Brazil a Mission Field of Jesuits** where even to this day the views held are very divergent. The Jesuits, of whom the first came to Brazil in 1549, found an extended field of labour there. That they were at first less harassed by the slave-hunters in the northern provinces may be due to the fact that the latter were principally kept in the south owing to long-standing custom, as well as from the insecurity of the political boundaries and other circumstances. There they soon developed into a perfect scourge, not only to the Indians, but also to the Spanish colonists. The remarkable state creation of the missions of Paraguay originated when the Jesuits inaugurated their efforts in favour of the natives in the south also; about which, then and to this day, opinions have been so divided.

The Jesuits with a Free Hand The Jesuits' object was to save the Guarani from the persecution of the Europeans. As they had, however, made the discovery that the colonists and colonial officials of Asuncion and Buenos Ayres frequently made common cause secretly with the Portuguese slave-traders for their own advantage, they did not remain satisfied, as they had done elsewhere, with going into the jungle and gathering the natives around them there, but they induced Philip III., who was ruler of Spain and Portugal simultaneously, to transfer to them a tract of land to the east of Paraguay as far as to the Uruguay.

Here they were permitted to do as they liked, almost without interference from either temporal or spiritual authority. Their efforts to bring the Indians of the surrounding regions under their benevolent control were immediately crowned with extraordinary success, for the inhabitants of their reductions soon numbered more than 100,000 souls. It was not exclusively Guaranis who gained admission there, but, as the tribes belonged almost without exception to the Tupi race, the Jesuits had no difficulty in making Guarani the general language. They attempted and achieved this also in the north Brazilian missions. The Guarani which they developed is actually the *lingua geral* which still is the universal language of the civilised natives of Brazil.

The social order which the Jesuits instituted in the mission districts made a more marked impression both on contemporaries and on posterity. That they,

Developing the New Communities in so doing, acted from philosophical standpoints, and that they attempted to realise Campanella's "City of the Sun," are probably only surmises which were introduced subsequently. The models by which the Jesuits were inspired were of considerably greater consequence to them. The extensive landed property of the religious communities was, on the one hand, managed, if not generally, at any rate in isolated instances, directly by the

brotherhood. But the model of the Inca-Peruvian social organisation, with its renunciation of private property and its universal labour obligation, had an even greater influence in the development of the most important characteristics of the Jesuit community.

The conception of personal property was then but very little developed among most of the uncivilised Indian tribes, and labour in common was the rule. It is not surprising that the missionaries experienced no difficulty in instituting the same arrangements, for they offered the Indian a number of things besides, which he coveted and prized, but which, under previous forms of association, he had but seldom enjoyed; these were regular and plentiful food and continued protection from his fellow-savage as well as from his white enemies. The clergy followed the sensible plan for the mission to the heathen by making civilisation the first step to conversion.

The mental capacity of the savage is unable to grasp the higher matters of Christian dogmas, and the civilised Indian must often enough have formed very extraordinary conceptions of them; and in order to be able to make him a Christian, even if only in seeming, a start had first to be made by civilising him. In consequence of the cruel slave-hunts of the Portuguese, and the often scarcely better treatment which the natives received from the Spanish colonists, the Jesuits succeeded, in a surprisingly short time, in collecting a considerable number of natives on the territory which had been assigned to them. They thus founded a number of districts, each of which contained at least 2,000 inhabitants, but they all manifested a very typical conformity among themselves.

The church formed the centre of each reduction. As the colony quickly acquired considerable agricultural wealth, which was allowed to be employed only for the benefit of the missions themselves, a number of almost monumental church buildings were raised in these Indian villages in the remote jungle. In other respects these districts must have given a very monotonous impression. Next to the church there was a large open square surrounded by the most important buildings—the dwelling of the padre and the store and meeting-houses. From it straight streets started rectangularly, and

THE FAMOUS CHURCH OF SAN IGNACIO, BUILT BY THE INDIANS 150 YEARS AGO

SIDE ENTRANCE OF THE SAME CHURCH AND ANOTHER MISSION BUILDING

HISTORIC REMAINS OF JESUIT MISSION BUILDINGS IN ARGENTINA

the prospect was in every instance formed by a chapel standing on the border of the common. The simple huts of the Indians were situated along these streets, and all the buildings were erected by the community and remained its property. The inhabitants had only the use of the dwellings, and of the small gardens situated

Socialism in Jesuit Settlements near them they partly had personal possession. The garden was the only thing which the family supervised themselves, and, it is said, generally very badly. The extensive maize and cotton fields adjoining the common, and the considerable herds of oxen and sheep, which constituted the chief wealth of the reduction, were cultivated and managed according to the directions of the missionaries for the benefit of the community.

The entire produce found its way into the granaries, whence it was then distributed by the padres to each individual household. In the same way the regulation of the work depended upon them, each inhabitant being pledged to do some, according to his trade and capacity. With such labourers it was but a trifling matter for the missionaries to provide for the necessary requirements of shelter, clothing and sustenance ; they also introduced many cultured arts, such as carving, watchmaking and even printing. It is no doubt due to the steady method of their instruction, as well as to an actual mental deficiency, that the Indian, in all his training, never succeeded in getting beyond imitation, and never made any inventions or progress, in spite of the discipline of civilisation which had influenced him for more than a hundred years.

The Jesuits defended themselves against the attacks of those who reproached them for having intentionally crushed the human liberty of their charges with the assertion that it had been impossible to force the Indian from his condition of perpetual child-

The Natives Happy with the Missionaries ishness, and that a greater degree of personal liberty would only have injured the individual and the general good. There may be much truth in this ; at any rate, it is certain that the natives were actually contented under the guidance of the missionaries, and that they not only rendered them almost unconditional obedience, but also took serious pains to retain their spiritual rulers when the government thought it advisable to recall them.

The authority of the missionaries was, it is true, directly as well as indirectly almost unlimited. There were in each reduction only two Europeans, both regular priests, of whom one, the actual leader, supervised the spiritual, while the other managed the material concerns of the settlement. They were assisted by a kind of municipality founded upon the model of the Spanish colonial towns, which, though it depended upon the election of the community, was always absolutely subservient to the missionaries.

The fact that there was hardly a temporal judicial authority proves how entirely the Jesuits had their charges under control. The inhabitants were governed almost exclusively by the power of the confessional, and the Jesuits have themselves shown that actual sins came to their knowledge but very rarely through the confessional. The Jesuits also naturally represented their communities abroad, for they had made them, as far as possible, independent of the outer world, both politically and economically. An outsider rarely found his way to the missions ; and the twofold

Prosperity a Source of Danger reason why the stranger became exclusively the guest of the padres was first in order to prevent his closer acquaintance with the natives, and secondly to preserve the latter from unfavourable outside influences. One of the missionaries left the settlement at long intervals, accompanied by one of the most reliable of the natives, for the purpose of exchanging, in the Spanish settlements, the surplus of their productions, consisting principally of cotton and hides, for anything which the reductions did not themselves produce ; but even then contact with the European was avoided as much as possible.

The reductions increased rapidly in Paraguay and soon possessed a large population, and this circumstance in itself threatened to become fatal. All the settlements were unprotected, and the missionaries themselves considered it a decided advantage to calm the warlike tendencies of the Guaranis, who had once been celebrated for their daring bravery ; besides this, a law which was generally valid forbade the arming of the Indians. Thus the Portuguese slave-robbers, who in the seventeenth century already had at their disposal a well-organised and well-armed force, experienced no difficulty when the idea occurred to them, in the year 1637, of taking their Indian slaves from the missions instead of having to track them laboriously in the jungle. This development was indeed an eventful one for the Jesuits. Forthwith, in consideration of the prevailing circumstances, they secured for their native charges the suspension of the law against the carrying of firearms, and thereafter the friars brought up the natives to be good and thorough soldiers.

They not only easily repelled the attacks of other savage natives, but also beat the Paulists—so the Portuguese slave-hunters were called, after their native place, the Province San Paulo—so completely that they were forced to transfer the field of their activity farther into the northern continent. They also proved themselves extremely trustworthy and well-drilled fighting material whenever, through risings in the interior or hostilities on the borders, the Spanish settlements were threatened by other Europeans.

The Jesuits thus carried on the work of the conversion of the natives for more than a century without interruption, with the exception of the dissensions with the spiritual and temporal authorities of the neighbouring districts. In the meantime the tendency of the spirit of the age in the Old World had become more and more opposed to their order, and this attitude of things finally affected their settlements in the remote jungle also. The first impulse, it is true, arose from purely political motives. With the continuous opening up and development of the South American continent, Spain and Portugal at length in the same way felt the necessity for a more distinct demarcation of their colonial possessions. The personal union of the two kingdoms which had been established by Philip II. was again annulled by the Portuguese protest of 1640, and in 1668, after long-standing animosities, Spain was forced to acknowledge the supremacy of the house of Braganza in Portugal and her colonies. Soon afterwards the Spanish Crown passed to the Bourbon dynasty. When Ferdinand VI. began from within to reorganise the state, which had been ruined by long mismanagement and by the prolonged war of succession, a newer, freer, and clearer impulse was also given to colonial progress.

The desire for the regulation of the Brazilian boundary was one of the issues. The Portuguese had repeatedly laid claim

Separation of Spain and Portugal

to the left shore of the mouth of the La Plata. They had founded a town, Colonia, opposite to Buenos Ayres, and had often attempted to extend their settlements in this region ; and this became an especial thorn in the flesh to the government at Madrid, because these settlements were exclusively for the purpose of illegally breaking through the bounds by which Spain sought to secure her trade with the colonists. As Portugal, however, possessed only a slight interest in these advanced coast towns, she readily agreed that Spain should exchange considerable plains of land in the interior, part of which formed the left bank of the Uruguay—on which were seven of the missions carried on by the Jesuits—for the left bank of the mouth of the La Plata.

Breaking up the Mission Settlements

The agreement provided that the natives should quit the territory under the guidance of their spiritual leaders, and should travel farther into the Spanish territory. When, however, the boundary commissioners at length began to carry out the agreement on this spot, they were not only met by the Jesuits with urgent remonstrances, but the natives by force of arms offered a resistance which was at first successful. The Jesuits soon again submitted to the order for obedience which had proceeded from Spain, and with the same spirit brought their influence to bear upon the natives. These could not, however, readily make up their minds to give up the loved home for whose defence they had taken up arms, and though it did not actually result in a serious battle, yet it required the approach of a considerable force, which had been collected by Spain and Portugal together, to convince them of the fruitlessness of their attempt.

The incident was in itself so simple and harmless that it scarcely offered a ground for complaint against the Jesuits ; but in the hands of the all-powerful Portuguese minister, the Marquess de Pombal, who then already sought an occasion to attack the influential Jesuit order, it assumed the guise of a heavy accusation. It was not difficult, by means of torture, to force from two captive Indians belonging to the mission the confession that the Jesuits had urged and goaded them on to armed resistance against the order of the allied monarchs. Then a baptised Guarani, whose name was Nicholas, gathered

Pombal the Fierce Enemy of the Jesuits

together the remaining Indians, who permanently disobeyed the order to leave, and formed them into a band of homeless outlaws. With these he continued the war of robbery and plunder against the European settlements on both sides of the frontier. This gave rise to the fable of that independent kingdom which yielded obedience to no temporal power, which the Jesuits, with the help of the natives, were supposed to have striven to establish in the interior of South America. This accusation was of great importance in connection with the expulsion of the Jesuits from Portugal, so much desired and finally accomplished by Pombal.

The Jesuits Fallen on Evil Days

It is also possible that it may have had some influence upon the deliberations of Charles III. and his Ministers when it became a question of taking a stand against the Society of Jesus in the conflict which was waged throughout the whole world. Unquestionably, neither Pombal nor any other far-seeing and intelligent statesman seriously believed in such an accusation ; it was, at the most, brought up as an expedient in the agitation in order to conceal the purely worldly and political motives which determined the expulsion of the Jesuits from Portugal and Spain.

Moreover, the Jesuits have not left the slightest proof that the accusations brought against their missionary activity, where only their own personal interests were in question, were well merited. Both in Brazil and Paraguay they submitted with dumb resignation to the order which recalled them suddenly and without any preparation from the field of action where they had successfully laboured for a hundred years. Even the unworthy and revengeful manner in which the order was carried out by the officials appointed for this purpose did not in a single instance force them from their purely passive role of endurance. In obedience to the order they vanished from all places where either the welfare of their charges was threatened or where they foresaw that want and death would be inevitable for themselves. History has justified them in one respect. No matter how one may judge of their system with regard to the treatment of the natives, they at any rate perfectly understood how to take care of their individual well-being, and to teach them to become absolutely submissive and useful subjects.

How History has Justified the Missionaries

Those who succeeded to their inheritance in a few years again alienated the Indians from all the progress in civilisation which they had made under the Jesuits, and by a wrong treatment turned them once more into wandering savage tribes. And thus they have remained wherever the bare jealousy of the more highly civilised European presumes to see in the Indian, who, mentally, has not yet grown out of the fetters of centuries of ancient prejudices, a creature of an inferior order.

The expulsion of the Jesuits is the last important phase in the native policy of latinised South America. From that time the care of the Indians in the sphere of missions was transferred to temporal authorities. While in the other provinces they had been gradually learning actually to carry into effect the well-intentioned aims of the native legislation, these first-mentioned provinces had once more to go through the entire range of experience with regard to the treatment of the natives, and their natural development, which had taught the others tolerance. With regard to the position of the Indians, scarcely any confirmed grounds of complaint existed in general during the last twenty years of Spanish colonial rule. Where there remained dependence and a certain lack of enterprise, this was rather the result of a natural propensity inculcated by the generations that had previously followed old customs than the effect of a perverted application of the law.

The Indians Backward in Development

The greater proportion of the Indians do not, even in the present day, completely understand the European's hypothesis of a progressive civilisation, or his attitude and mental outlook, even though for two generations past this development in progress has been maintained by free citizens of free republics with every imaginable guarantee of personal liberty. These are, however, conditions which have unavoidably manifested themselves, and will continue to do so as a necessity of nature, wherever two nations, holding entirely different theories concerning civilisation, and having such marked differences in the degree of culture, come into conflict. It is possible that certain specially gifted individuals might be able to raise themselves at length to a complete equality of culture, but the large proportion of less highly civilised people will always remain, both mentally and physically, dependent upon the more advanced race.

SPAIN'S GOLDEN ERA IN AMERICA
AND THE DAYS OF THE BUCCANEERS

WHILE it must be acknowledged that the policy of the Spanish Government regarding the native question was the most enlightened and well-intentioned of any which had been put into practice anywhere, this cannot be affirmed with reference to their trade policy. The fact that the entire trade communication with the colonies was monopolised by the one harbour of Seville was as much the result of the arrangements made with Columbus as an imitation of the Portuguese model.

The explorer had, according to agreement, stipulated that he should receive, besides the right of participation in all subsequent colonial voyages, a share in the clear profit from the combined colonial undertakings. In order to fulfil this stipulation, it became an unavoidable necessity that all colonial enterprises should be strictly controlled with reference to their cost and profit. This would naturally have been impossible if the ships destined for the colonies had been allowed to sail from every harbour of the Spanish peninsula, which was surrounded by the sea on three sides. As is well known, it was not until far into the sixteenth century that a definite understanding was arrived at, after long law-suits and repeated agreements between the government and the heirs of Columbus.

Seville's Exclusive Trade Monopoly

The fact, however, that the exclusive monopoly of the trade by Seville, and the strict regulations of the customs, were adhered to, was undoubtedly the consequence of the political views which on this subject prevailed with the government. The land which came to the Crown of Castile as an integral and permanent part through the discovery of Columbus was not regarded so much as a territorial accession of land as an increase of the Crown domains belonging to the kings of Castile. This acceptation was shared in the sixteenth and seventeenth centuries by all the Powers who carried on any colonial policy whatever, the remains of which can be traced almost everywhere. In Spain they have been maintained so strongly that modern Spain cannot quite free herself from them, in spite of three generations of progressive revolutions.

According to such an acceptation of the law it naturally depended upon the pleasure of the government, or of those to whom the government had transferred their rights, as to who should be admitted to the colonies, either with the object of settling there or for the purposes of trade. The restrictions were then also, from the beginning, very numerous, and they were, with the exception of several fundamental amplifications instituted during the first decades, maintained with, if anything, almost too great severity. As the colonies belonged to the Crown of Castile, the Castilians possessed, in the first instance, the natural right to trade therein, but this prerogative had also been conceded to the Aragonese since 1495.

Restricted Entry to the Colonies

The privilege received yet further expansion after the accession of Charles V. Considerations of an agricultural nature were principally responsible for the resolution to permit all subjects of the many kingdoms ruled by the Spanish king to have access to the colonies. Spain was endowed with extensive colonial possessions at a moment when such a national property could, and did, become extremely dangerous. Hardly had the political unity of the actual Spanish soil been established by the removal of the last Moorish kingdom, and scarcely had Ferdinand and Isabella taken the first steps to lead the country—whose agricultural development had been much impaired by the continued war against the Moors—to a greater expansion of its natural resources, when a new and dangerous enemy to its national industry arose. Thus the discovery of America removed thousands upon thousands of strong labourers from

The Spanish Rush to America

the national work of the by no means large population, and created serious competition between the life of hazardous colonial profits and the slow but certain and advancing field of labour in both agriculture and handicraft at home. Although the agricultural development was successfully carried on upon the foundations laid by the Catholic rulers, yet the mother country could not, under such difficult conditions, carry on the exclusive maintenance of the colonial territory, which rapidly increased from century to century. From the time of the proclamation of the law in question, the exclusion of strangers had already been disregarded in favour of those who knew how to take care of the interests of the state and of the colonies while seeking their own gain.

An Open Door in the New World

That Charles V., in opening up the New World to all his subjects, acted from the standpoint that the solution of the agricultural problems which had been imposed upon the colonies by the government lay in gaining new forces is more especially evidenced by the fact that he called upon all the most powerful agricultural factors of his most distant Spanish dominions to co-operate in the colonial enterprises. From Germany he summoned the Hanses and the Augsburgers, and from Italy, more especially, the great merchants.

The laws of the country concerning the trade with the colonies were, of course, also binding upon these. They, too, were obliged first to enter Seville with their ships and wares, pay the entrance duty, and also submit to the compulsory registration which was supervised by the Casa de Contratacion, according to which no person or trade commodity was permitted to enter the colony without satisfying the legal demands. Like the Spaniards, they were also bound to return to Seville and again go through the same formalities. All costly articles from the colonies, more especially ores, also came under this prohibition, which forbade such articles being taken out of Spain. As Spain, with its colonies as well as through them, consumed considerably more trade commodities than it was able to supply to foreign countries, this regulation could not be enforced permanently, as in time became evident to the government, engrossed as it was in mercantile questions. However,

Spain's Trade Relations with Her Colonies

it neither knew how to remedy the evil nor recognised the fact that, owing to the entirely altered conditions created by the production of ores in the New World, gold and silver had dropped in their exchange value to the trade level for wares, the price of which no human laws can fix. Trade with the colonies during the earlier years was burdened by no customs duties, but as commercial intercourse increased, export and import duties were introduced, such as had been imposed between the several Spanish territories. As precious ores were not wares, they were not affected; but the state, by levying a royalty on the profits from their sale, secured a share for itself.

It was of the utmost importance, more especially at first, that the government should revive the trade with the colonies. For this purpose it readily granted, through the Casa de Contratacion, the necessary passes to every ship which proposed sailing across the ocean, and sold such charts as could be supplied. It also established its own court of pilots as a school for helmsmen and as a centre for examination. The rigour of the law was at first often suspended, and incidentally the number of ports of departure was considerably increased, the Canary Islands securing exemption from the enforced call at Seville. Forced registration, also, was not strictly maintained. It was a well-known fact that the returning vessels often secretly deposited a considerable portion of their costly freight on the shores of the Portuguese Azores, in order to escape the customs, and Philip II., during the first years of his reign, instructed his councillors not to interpose the full severity of the law against this practice, in so far, at all events, as his own subjects were concerned.

Traders who Escaped the Customs

Naturally these restrictive regulations were particularly burdensome to the colonies. By preventing free competition, they, in combination with the superabundance of gold and silver, caused the prices between the colonies and the mother country, at the end of the sixteenth century, to be in the ratio of three to one, and even as five to one. The agitation for the removal of the trade restrictions was at that time enormously powerful there. But it was the absolute impossibility of preventing in any way the misuse of measures intended to procure alleviation in a distant land, and over an endless extent of thinly populated coast, that caused the government to adhere with even greater severity to the system of enforced registration.

Before any harbour for imports in the New World, besides San Domingo, could become of importance for trade purposes, political circumstances in the mother country led to a fresh organisation of her commercial intercourse with the colonies. These proved of extraordinary service to the system of control pursued by the government, without tending to make the disadvantages connected with it perceptible to the colonists. The results which the Spaniards and Portuguese achieved with the aid of their trans-Atlantic maritime power were not without reaction on the remaining European Powers. French and English sailors, often guided during their first voyages by Italian pilots, soon also ventured to cross the ocean ; their discoveries in North America are dealt with elsewhere.

So long as Spain remained at peace with the rest of the world, and its colonies yielded only moderate compensation in return for the disbursement made, this intermeddling of foreign Powers in the colonial sphere remained comparatively unimportant. When, however, under Charles V., the plans for the government of the world by Spain became more and more sharply defined, violent antagonism arose, at first against France under Philip II., and also against England. This gave rise to open enmity, which led to repeated wars in Europe, daring privateering voyages on the ocean, and finally, also, to those buccaneering expeditions and attacks on the other side of the ocean from which the colonial ports had long to suffer, until at length the foreign Powers succeeded in securing portions of the ancient Spanish colonial possessions.

The Days of Buccaneering Expeditions

When this enmity first became apparent through the capture of single and unarmed ships sailing between Spain and the colonies, Charles V. issued the decree, in the year 1526, that in times of war the ships should no longer set sail and return singly, but should, under the leadership of competent captains, be combined into fleets capable of resistance. This was the origin of the celebrated " plate-fleets " and galleons, which for two centuries carried on the trade exclusively between Spanish America and the remainder of the civilised world. This measure was at first introduced only with reference to the security of trans-oceanic commerce ; that it rendered the most important services to the Crown's fiscal control was certainly soon proved and acknowledged by all interested parties. The diffusion of the Spanish race in the New World had not reached its termination when the fleets were introduced. Several phases in the development of this institution had to be passed through before it received its permanent establishment, after which it remained approximately as follows.

The Celebrated Plate-fleets and Galleons

The ships which intended sailing to the West Indies assembled annually in the months of March and September at Seville, or, when their draught did not allow of it, at San Lucar de Barrameda, or, later on, at Cadiz. They had to be at least ten in number, otherwise the fleet was not permitted to set sail. As a rule, there were between thirty and forty, and in some cases a great many more ships. In the year 1589, no less than ninety-four vessels going from Panama to the South were required to transport all that the fleet had brought to Portobello. Ships of less than a hundred tons were, as a rule, excluded from participation in the voyage to the Indies, and all, even the heavily freighted merchantmen, were obliged to carry at least four heavy and sixteen light guns, and every man on board carried weapons.

Two of the largest vessels were selected as " capitana " and " almiranta " ; the first, carrying all the highest in command of the whole fleet, sailed in advance, while the admiral's ship formed the rear-guard with the special duty of keeping the fleet together. The capitana and almiranta were more strongly built than the other ships, and, in order to increase their powers of action in battle, they were not allowed to be freighted to the same extent as the merchantmen. Besides these, the fleet was at first accompanied by at least one, and later on by several larger ships—the galleons—whose chief duty it was to watch over the safety of the fleet. They had a tonnage of at least two hundred to three hundred, were powerfully equipped, and were allowed only light freight.

Guardians of Spain's Treasures

They were at the same time intended to bring back in safety to Spain the gold and silver which were due to the Crown as taxes and duty. In times of war the Indian fleets, upon which the entire wealth of Spain depended, were not even thus considered sufficiently well guarded. A protecting fleet, consisting of galleys and galleons, was therefore also equipped out of the revenue from the additional tax which had been levied upon the Indian trade for this purpose, and these had to accompany the

Spain's Great Merchant Fleets trading fleets on the high seas and escort the returning ones in the same way. Finally, several lighter and smaller ships — despatch-vessels, called " avisos "—were attached to each fleet, their duty being to go in advance, so as to discover threatening dangers and to prepare the officials on either side for the arrival of the fleet.

The combined fleet sailed from Seville to San Domingo, where the official control to which they had been submitted at the port of sailing was renewed. The ships which were to sail via Porto Rico and Havana to Vera Cruz formed the so-called " Fleet of New Spain " ; they then separated from those which first sailed through the Gulf of Mexico to Cartagena and thence to Portobello. The latter, called the " Continental Fleet," was by far the more important of the two, as it carried all the merchandise from the whole southern continent of America. All direct commercial intercourse with the mother country, except through these fleets, was not only forbidden to all the provinces, but was also so fettered by customs restrictions and trade rules that the colonies were at the most only permitted to exchange certain products of their own soil, but never European trade commodities.

The Continental Fleet, in the first instance, supplied Peru and Chili, starting from Portobello, but soon after also Tucuman and Paraguay, the countries of the modern Argentina. The anomaly that the merchandise for the south-east of America had to traverse the watershed between the Atlantic and Pacific oceans

The Humble Beginnings of Buenos Ayres twice before arriving at its place of destination arose from there being no noteworthy colony at the mouth of the La Plata. Buenos Ayres had, it is true, been founded in the year 1535, but it was almost immediately dissolved, its final colonisation taking place in 1562. It was, however, for the time being of no importance, owing to its great distance from the centres of Spanish colonial government, and its

exposed position on a coast which was difficult to defend, and also because of its immediate proximity to the Portuguese, who claimed the opposite shore of the bay as their territory. The Spanish Government did not consider it advisable to recognise the town as a harbour in the trans-oceanic trade intercourse. This region was first organised in 1617 as a special colonial district, and remained for a considerable time the seat of an extensive but illegal trade with foreign nations before the government decided, in conjunction with the alteration in the trade with Chili and Peru by way of Cape Horn, to include Buenos Ayres also among the places to be affected by the trade of the fleets.

Up to that time the principal traffic was confined to the route via Portobello. As a settlement this town was of no importance, and it remained uninhabited during the greater part of the year, owing to its unhealthy climate. At all events, the greatest business transactions and the wildest speculations of the whole of South America were made there during the forty days' market, or fair, that followed the arrival

The Perils of the Trading Vessels of the fleet. A luxurious life of pleasure, incidental to easily won gains, reigned for a short time in the town, which consisted of hastily erected tents and huts. When, however, at the conclusion of the fair, preparations were made for the return, the population of Portobello vanished, not to come back again within another half or whole year, or even longer period, when the same scene was reenacted. The regularity of the fleets left much to be desired ; there never was a lack of adventurous vessels, but conditions of the weather and political complications often prevented the regular carrying out of the despatch of the fleets in sailing. More than once the fair of Portobello had to be postponed or stopped altogether, because the expected ships had been wrecked or had fallen into the hands of hostile privateers.

Thus it happened that though the optional sailings of the fleets had at first been joyfully welcomed as a sign of progress, the inconvenience caused by the ships arriving far too seldom to meet the colonists' requirements became a heavy burden, which was felt all the more when an extraordinary rise in the price of all trade commodities resulted. Nevertheless, owing to the ever-increasing insecurity on the ocean, the government strictly

BUCCANEERS ATTACKING A SPANISH TREASURE SHIP

To the European settlers in the West Indies the seventeenth century was a period of outlawry. Bands of buccaneers, originally smugglers and pirates, mostly recruited from convicts transported to the islands from England and France, were the terror of the Caribbean Sea. Composed of almost all nationalities, with the exception of Spain, they pursued everything Spanish with a deadly hatred. In 1630 their headquarters in San Domingo were destroyed, but in a few years the adventurers returned in force and for the next seventy years fattened on European trade and property.

enforced the regulations which had been drawn up. It might have given way by allowing the departure of the fleets from Europe to take place at any time, and it did, as a matter of fact, make several concessions in this respect, but it had such a prominent interest in the safe return of the entire fleet that it never thought of the possibility of forgoing it.

Pirates on the Watch for Spoil These fleets were actually the only means of communication between the two worlds, for the entire official and private correspondence was carried by them ; but a still more important point was that only with their assistance could all the colonial revenues, which were indispensable for the state budget, reach the government exchequer.

All the colonial offices sent their reports to the respective ports for the custody of the fleets, where the letters and valuables were entrusted to the soundest and safest vessels. Three months after their arrival at San Domingo, the ships of the New Spain and Continental Fleets were instructed to reassemble once more at Havana. The galleons and the equipped convoys filled up the interval with occasional pirate expeditions, until they had once more to undertake the safe-conduct of the united fleets on their return, sailing under similar precautionary measures through the Bahama Sea into the open ocean. This part of the voyage was by far the most dangerous. Spain's political enemies, as well as the pirates, always turned their attention to catching the returning fleet, which, on account of its transport of precious metals, was called the " plate," *ie.*, silver fleet. Occasionally the enemy succeeded completely in this design, but generally only in part.

The colonies, from the beginning, yielded the mother country all kinds of products. Besides the logwood which was much exported from all parts of America, various drugs, and, later on, large quantities of sugar and hides, formed the freight of the returning vessels. The most valuable portion of the cargo always consisted of gold, silver, pearls and precious stones. Columbus had already found gold in moderate quantities with the natives. As soon as they had become convinced that it was of indigenous origin, the settlers began gold mining and washing. The gold mines, in which, owing to the primitive manner of work-

America's Unprofitable Gold Mines

ing, but comparatively little was achieved in spite of a great expenditure of labour, were the real places of torture for the Indians. At all times and in all places the flotsam and jetsam of human society have assembled among gold-diggers. In the presence of such elements all laws for the protection of the natives were powerless, because each official risked his own life in endeavouring to enforce respect for the law from such an assembly.

But during the whole time of the conquista the actual wealth was not derived from gold and silver mines, but through barter with the natives. Appreciating this fact, the government always willingly encouraged mining industry by granting an abatement of taxes and sending over experienced miners, mostly Germans ; but, as always, it demanded and collected the fifth part of all gold gained by barter or on marauding expeditions.

The mining industry did not become remunerative until after the conquest of Mexico. The silver-mines of Sultepeque, and more especially of Guanajuato, yielded such rich ores that they were permanently worked. The Spaniards also found treasures of fabulous value in possession of the natives of Peru ; but there, as in all other provinces, the store of precious metals attainable by barter was exhausted comparatively early, and the prospects of the gold and silver mines were, for the moment, decidedly less favourable than in the north, until the silver-mines of Potosi were discovered, quite by chance, in the year 1545. This mining district proved of untold wealth for a long period, and it is chiefly due to it, in combination with the Mexican silver-mines, that the production of precious metals in the New World has been maintained permanently on a comparatively high level.

Discovery of Potosi's Silver Mines

The first primitive method of procedure made the working of only the richest ores remunerative. The discovery of a process of amalgamation, however, made it possible to gain more extensive profits from the rocks of Mexico and Peru. A German miner, who, owing to a fire which burned out the quicksilver mines of Almaden, had become penniless, was, according to the most recent research, the inventor of amalgam. He went into partnership with a Spaniard, Bartolomé de Medina, for the realisation of his discovery.

However, as the Inquisition permitted only the latter, and not his German master, to go over to Mexico, the Spaniard so entirely assumed the credit of the discovery that not even the name of the German has become known.

The process of extracting silver by means of quicksilver brought about a complete revolution in the mining industry of Mexico. The mine proprietors promised to freight the ships of the New Spain fleet as high as the masts if they could only obtain sufficient quicksilver, and the price of it increased enormously. The monopoly of the profits from the pits of Almaden, which were the largest in the world, and, next to those of Idria, the only ones then worked, had already been acquired previously, and the Spanish government now also claimed the monopoly of the trade. It leased the pits to the Fuggers, who, by an intelligent process of working, under German direction, produced approximately one hundred per cent. of profit during half a century. They were obliged to relinquish all the gains to the government, who sold the

Huge Profits from the Silver Mines quicksilver in America to the mine-owners for three and four times as much as the purchase-money. Thenceforward the galleys, which on the return voyage brought the treasures of gold and silver from America, on the outward voyage carried from 150 to 250 tons of quicksilver. From 1563 to 1641—that is to say, as long as the Fuggers were the leaseholders of the pits of Almaden—silver worth £50,000,000 is said to have been gained from 12,658 tons of quicksilver which they had extracted. The royalty on this alone amounted to over £10,000,000.

In the whole export trade that Spain carried on with its colonies there was only one other article which equalled quicksilver in importance, and that was the negro slave. Reference has already been made to the fact that access to the colonies had, in accordance with the oldest legislation, been closed to these slaves, but that the government was not strict in granting exceptions. The negroes did not begin to play an important part in the organisation of the colonies and in colonial trade until Las Casas, with his narrow philanthropic ideas, recommended the importation of negro slaves as a means of liberating the Indians from their state of servitude. If, as was evidently the clear

intention of the Spanish Government, the colonies were to be organised for other purposes than to serve as fulcrums for barter and trade, as had been established by the Portuguese in the Indies, then undoubtedly provision for labourers had to be made. It was quite evident that there were not enough Europeans for this

Strict Laws with Regard to Emigration purpose. On the one hand, the climate enfeebled their working powers, and, on the other hand, the disproportion between the number of the European colonists and the expansion of the colonial possessions was such that to surmount the difficulties of colonisation by European forces alone was quite out of the question.

Added to this, the conception which the Spanish Government had of their duty to the colonies forbade Spain's deportation of criminals or doubtful subjects. Columbus wished to attempt the discovery of America with discharged convicts. Portugal, in the irregular method of her colonial policy, had made some experiments with convict settlements in Brazil, but the Spanish laws permitted only the nation's free men to emigrate, and the government, in single instances only, transported misdemeanants at the request of special colonial groups. Even with their help it would have been impossible to carry on mining, cattle-raising and plantations in the colonies simply for this reason, that many kinds—and more especially the higher kinds—of labour always remained to be done by the Europeans. If, therefore, the Indian—who, owing to his indolence and his spirit of independence, could scarcely be induced to do the work voluntarily, according to European standards—was to be exempt from all compulsion, then another supply of labour had to be imported into the colonies.

Las Casas' proposal, that negroes should be used for this purpose in the same manner in which they were employed on

The Colonies' Demand for Cheap Labour the islands on the coasts of Africa, was favourably received by the government. For fiscal reasons the Crown nominally maintained the prohibition of negro importation, but, in consideration of the payment of certain fees, single individuals or companies were allowed to supply to the harbours of the colonies a fixed number of negroes annually. The colonial authorities had been called upon to give a report in respect to their annual requirements. In the beginning 4,000 were named, but in the course of the long period during which the " Asiento "—the contract for the monoply of the importation of slaves—lasted, the number was at various times increased or diminished. The colonists, however, always complained that the supply of negro slaves for the

Privileges Enjoyed by the Slave-ships

New World fell far short of the actual demand, and the trade in this valuable commodity was at all times the favourite business of the illegal smuggling trade which was carried on by foreign shipowners. There is no doubt that this matter permanently engrossed the attention of the government.

The slave-ships enjoyed certain privileges, inasmuch as they were allowed, by the deposit of a security, to sail from the coast of Guinea, where they purchased their black merchandise from Portuguese dealers, straight to America, where a few ports were open to them for the landing of the negroes. The oldest Asientists already enjoyed certain privileges for the requirements of their trade, and in the return from Spain of their profits in the shape of colonial goods ; but they remained bound by the obligation to return to Seville, as well as to be registered in the same manner as all other merchants. As control of them was far more difficult than of the voyages of the fleets and galleys, the Crown's toleration of the Asientists was very soon taken advantage of for the general evasion of the oppressive colonial trade laws and for extensive and growing smuggling.

Though the slave monopoly was at first in the hands of the Genoese and the Germans, it was comparatively little abused, and it was only slightly prejudicial to the legitimate trade in general ; yet in time these conditions changed when other nations, with less friendly intentions, took the monopoly into their hands.

Widespread Traffic in Slaves

The idea of leasing the sole rights in the traffic of slave importation to the Portuguese was not bad in itself, as the Portuguese were in undisputed possession of the *materia prima* of the negroes themselves. The Portuguese merchants received the Asiento at the time when Portugal was bound to Spain by a personal union, and they retained it after the revolt of the Braganzas until the acknowledgment of Portuguese independence by the treaty of

peace in 1667. Then the merchants of Seville temporarily obtained the Asiento for themselves. The Guinea Company, in which Louis XIV. himself had a share, possessed the monopoly of the slave-trade after Spanish America, until political circumstances necessitated the retirement of France.

This was not advantageous to Spain, however, one of the conditions of the Treaty of Utrecht expressly stipulating the cession of the Asiento to the English, who undoubtedly profited most thoroughly by it. The English at the same time received a guarantee for the right to send annually to the colonies, which were closed to the trade of all the other colonies under privileged conditions, two vessels of modest dimensions freighted with European trade commodities, in addition to the slave-ships. It has, however, been reported that these vessels, while they discharged their cargo openly and in sight of the harbour officials during the day, were again freighted by night from larger ships which did not disembark, but rode at anchor outside for no apparent reason. In this way three and four times the bulk

Profits of the Slave Trade

of their actual merchandise was landed. These were serious evils, which finally induced Ferdinand VI. to repurchase the Asiento contract from the English, even before its legal termination. The reason that the government was so long in deciding upon this step was not alone due to the fact that it was immediately interested in the profits of the English association, nor because the English alone had succeeded in transporting the prescribed number of slaves to the colonies ; but it was chiefly owing to the large sums which accrued to the state exchequer by means of these transactions and played an important part in the revenue of the Indies.

The original tax of eight shillings per head, by means of which the first holders of the trade monopoly bought the licence, was in time raised to from three to four pounds. The importation of 3,000 to 4,000 slaves annually thus became also perceptible in the colonial budget of the eighteenth century, when the royalties from the gains of precious metals had diminished considerably. The question has often been discussed as to what amount of gold, silver, and other valuables the Spanish state and country had derived from its trans-Atlantic colonial possessions, but it has never been satisfactorily settled, owing to the utterly incomplete reports of the trade of Spain and its colonies which have hitherto been obtainable. While it has been asserted that the development of Spanish America was retarded for a hundred years by the colonial policy of Spain, an attempt has been made to attach the responsibility for Spain's economic downfall to the very abundance of precious metals, by the assertion that the gold from the

into the eighteenth century to make use of them in any other way, is a point of view which all the colonial Powers of that age had in common. Probably Spain's attitude would not have changed to this day if the powerful revolutionary agitations which in the New World led to the complete severance of the United States from England and of very nearly the whole of Latin America from Spain, had not forced her to a very different polity

THE LOSS OF THE REVENGE: SIR RICHARD GRENVILLE'S LAST FIGHT

Forming one of the squadron of queen's ships despatched to the Azores in 1591 to look out for the homeward-bound treasure fleet of Spain, the Revenge, under the command of Sir Richard Grenville, was cut off from the admiral and the rest of the squadron by a powerful Spanish fleet. With "her hundred fighters on deck and her ninety sick below," the little Revenge made a brave fight against the fifty-three ships of Spain, but was ultimately captured and her gallant commander mortally wounded. So impressed was the Spanish admiral by the heroic stand of the English that he sent his barge to take Sir Richard Grenville to his own ship, the San Pablo, where he died a few days later.
From the painting by Sir Oswald Brierley, by permission of the Art Union of London, 112, Strand

New World corrupted and eventually ruined Spain. That, however, like the previous statements, is an exaggeration.

If Spain had been a sound economic state, there would have been as little likelihood of her corruption by the superfluity of gold and silver as there was of England's being injured by the treasures of India. That Spain did not allow her colonies a freer and more individual life, but regarded them as essentially an asylum for the mother country, and refused until far

The Spanish colonies fulfilled their object until the eighteenth century. They provided the mother country with such abundant means of gold, which was indispensable to her political position in the concert of Europe, that it aroused the envy of all other countries, and tempted them, on the one hand, to embark in colonial enterprises themselves, while, on the other hand, it made them take from the Spaniards as much of their colonial treasures as possible.

VALPARAISO THE CHIEF PORT OF THE CHILIAN REPUBLIC

THE NEW PLAZA IN THE CAPITAL CITY OF SANTIAGO

A CHARACTERISTIC STREET SCENE IN VALPARAISO

SCENES IN THE CAPITAL AND PRINCIPAL PORT OF CHILI

SPAIN'S FIGHT FOR HER EMPIRE
AGAINST THE RIVAL EUROPEAN POWERS

FROM the position which the Spanish colonies held in relation to the mother country it naturally follows that they possessed no independent history. Their history comprised the change of officials, the incidental alterations in their administrative organisation, and the regulations for the furtherance of the economic interests instituted far more for the benefit of Spain than for that of the colonies. It was owing to Spain's dependence on them that they became involved in all the political complications of the mother country. The history of all that the colonies had to suffer, as part of the Spanish kingdom, at the hands of Spain's opponents is the nearest approach to a general history of the colonial empire.

When Spain came into warlike conflict with neighbouring European states, the latter did not fail to damage the trade and **Spain and her Enemies** the naval power of their opponent, on her far-reaching seacoasts, by means of privateers. In the year 1512 ships were captured by the French, in the course of such attacks, while struggling towards the harbour of Seville on their return from the colonies. A state of war, at times open and at other times latent, prevailed continuously against France during the reigns of Charles V. and Philip II., and it spread the more on the sea because, by the opening up of Mexico and Peru, the colonial trading vessels had become more desirable prey than they had been at the beginning of the century.

The Spanish regents were, however, not blind to this fact. The enemies' attacks upon the South American fleets helped in no small degree the development of that maritime supremacy which Spain maintained during the greater part of the sixteenth century. This ascendancy might perhaps have been more firmly established if Charles V. had not possessed such convenient sources of help

in his great European dominions. The same thing happened here as with the colonial trade, for Spain was unable, during the first years of traffic, to satisfy her colonies' demands, so that she granted participation in maritime trade **The Spanish Fleet Supreme on the Sea** to all the allied nations— the Italians, Dutch and Germans. Owing to the abundance of treasure which the country drew from her colonies, this arrangement became permanent, and the fatal consequences which in such a state of affairs must arise from a defection of her allies were not taken into account.

For the time being, at any rate, the Spaniards succeeded by these means in making themselves the ruling maritime Power. No nation could have dared, before 1580, to meet the Spanish fleet openly on the ocean. Even during the small naval war which the privateers, more especially the French privateers, carried on with the Spaniards the latter were undoubtedly at first superior. It was only due to the exceptionally unfavourable position in which the country, with her colonies, found herself when face to face with the enemy that the latter, in spite of many losses, reaped rich benefit and many advantages from the privateering wars.

The arrangements to safeguard the voyages of the trading fleets, and for their convoy along the coast provinces by the naval ships, soon drove the corsairs away from the Andalusian coast and from Cape St. Vincent, where they might often **Spain's Fights with the Corsairs** have become dangerous to the ships returning to Seville. They were obliged to transfer their scene of action farther off, to regions where the home squadrons could not so readily come to the aid of the trading fleets. But they were not able to remain on the Canary Islands, or on the Azores or the Cape Verde Islands, which they had chosen as their centre.

The Spanish measures of defence finally even forced the enemy to seek for spoil in the very quarters where the Spaniard obtained his—that is to say, in the colonies. The pirates did not long remain in ignorance of the sailing routes appointed for the Spanish fleets, because they, too, depended on the ocean currents. In

Privateers' Harbours of Refuge the same way they soon learned that many of the smaller Antilles, and even great tracts on the shores of the larger islands, had been entirely abandoned by the colonists and were therefore " no man's land." Thus the privateers had no great difficulty in finding harbours of refuge, where they could equip themselves for their unexpected attacks, repair the damages incurred, and place the spoils gained in security.

Only a step remained between the capture of the Spanish ships in the trans-Atlantic waters and the attack and plunder of the colonial settlements. The first stages of open hostility followed during the third Franco-Spanish War in the 'forties of the sixteenth century. The daring of the privateers—who, with the secret assistance of the French Government, had been extremely well equipped—was so great that they not only plundered and laid under contribution the small and isolated colonial coast places, but also attacked Santa Maria and Cartagena in 1542. In 1555 they seized the capital of Cuba, Havana, and occupied it for twenty-six days. In the face of such conditions all that the government could do was to order the coast towns to be fortified as far as possible, and whenever this could not be done the settlements near the sea-coast were to be abandoned and transferred farther into the interior.

New enemies then arose for the colonies. Up to that time it had been chiefly the French who had done their utmost to injure the colonial trade and the

England's Rupture with Spain settlements of their traditional enemies. When Queen Elizabeth of England ascended the throne which Philip II. had shared with her sister, the rupture between England and Spain increased year by year, and developed into open hostility, which became all the greater when Elizabeth firmly showed her Protestant tendencies. The English Navy was then far inferior to the Spanish, and was not in a position to contend with it on the

ocean ; and, moreover, the English seamen did not then appear to be conducting active naval warfare against the Spaniards. They endeavoured, however, to break through the strict embargo laid on the Spanish colonies' direct trade with the Old World, and in so doing they did not scruple to attack the Spanish ships openly. Soon afterwards they turned their attention to those settlements where their opponents were weak, and where the colonial authorities had opposed their illegitimate trade.

The tactics they generally employed were first to plunder a shipload of negro slaves of the Portuguese on the coast of Guinea, for which they were certain of securing a market in the colonies, often with the connivance of the Spanish authorities. At the same time, they knew thoroughly how to seize any opportunity of striking a blow, and if it proved favourable they were at no loss to know how to provoke the Spaniards so that they themselves could always plead that they had taken up arms only in self-defence. Richard Hawkins had, in 1530, already laid the foundation for the wealth which in later years enabled his cele-

Plundering Voyages of Drake and Hawkins brated son, John Hawkins, to carry on privateering as a slave merchant, with his own flotilla. This mode of trading was, during the 'sixties, carried on by numerous English ships. If they reached unknown coasts, they exchanged wares with the natives. They forcibly extorted permission to trade in the Spanish settlements if it was not willingly granted. But such measures had seldom to be resorted to, except for the sake of appearance.

When, however, the Spaniards once gained the upper hand, they naturally did not deal very leniently with them, as Hawkins and Drake experienced at Vera Cruz in 1568. The English did not scruple, when opportunity favoured them, to make an actual attack, such as Drake attempted without complete success on Nombre de Dios and Panama in 1572. A few years later, Drake was the first enemy to advance through the Straits of Magellan into the Pacific Ocean, and to plunder the entirely defenceless coast districts of Chili and Peru, thus gaining an enormous amount of spoil. In order that these spoils might not be exposed to the risk of being seized by the Spaniards, who were on the look-out for him on the return voyage, he brought them safely to London by way of the southern point of Africa. There Queen

Elizabeth, on account of his exploits, knighted him, in spite of the Spanish protests. Though the peace between England and Spain, which until then had not been officially declared, had imposed a certain amount of caution upon the English "pirate," this was done away with when, in 1585, both countries were at open war.

In this same year Drake went to sea with twenty-three ships and 2,500 men, and, apart from numerous privateering feats, plundered the towns of San Domingo and Cartagena, destroyed San Agustin in Florida, and brought back 240 guns from the conquered ships and from the subjugated coast districts, besides rich treasures. From that time until the death of Queen Elizabeth scarcely a year passed in which more or less richly equipped fleets did not set sail, either to plunder the coasts of Spain or to ravage the colonies. It was because the English sailors had been thoroughly tried on their daring privateer voyages that they distinguished themselves in the battle against the "invincible" Armada. After the halo which until then had surrounded the Spanish Navy had been **Founders of England's Naval Supremacy** dispelled by this battle, the English came forward as serious rivals for the supremacy of the sea. This struggle, which began with the victory over the Armada at Gravelines, terminated at Trafalgar with their complete triumph. The foundation of England's supremacy at sea was laid by the English seamen, who, like Hawkins and Drake, began as smugglers and pirates.

They first convinced the government of the importance of the supremacy of the sea for the prosperity of England, who from her geographical position is dependent upon the sea. Then Walter Raleigh, while the acknowledged favourite of Queen Elizabeth, made the English aspirations for maritime supremacy acceptable at court. Raleigh himself made the first attempts at colonisation on American soil, though they had no immediate or permanent results. The expeditions to Guiana which he undertook in 1595, 1597 and 1616 were the first really serious attempts by foreigners on the southern continent, not only to become possessed of the coast, but also to advance into the interior.

As in the north, they gave the impulse to foreign Powers to establish themselves within the Spanish-Portuguese colonial sphere. Fresh competitors with Spain had appeared in the meanwhile, and these proved the more dangerous because their position as subjects of the Spanish Crown gave them opportunity of becoming acquainted with the conditions of colonial trade. When the first ships belonging to the Netherlands, which at that time had not yet revolted, brought their trade commodities **The Dutch Trade with America** to America, the colonists recognised the advantage gained, and made every kind of representation to the Spanish Government, requesting it to concede to the Dutch, in the same way as to the inhabitants of the Canary Islands, the privilege of sailing straight to the colonies from Dutch ports, so making the call at Seville obligatory for only the return voyage.

The Council of the Indies would never agree to this, but it often permitted the Dutch as well as the German and Italian ship-owners and merchants to participate in the colonial trade, even after the general permit of Charles V. had ceased to exist, and the strong seaworthy Dutch hulks were often hired in the service of the king for the official voyages across the ocean. This commercial privilege was seriously endangered when the Protestant provinces rebelled against the Spanish yoke; but the attitude which Philip II. assumed in connection with this insurrection was of advantage to the Dutch. He still desired that only his own, though rebellious, subjects should trade with the South American provinces, and so he continued to grant a share in the Spanish and colonial trade to those shipowners and merchants of the northern provinces who had not been directly implicated in the rebellion.

Thus the Dutch were able, as before, to carry on their business openly and under the Spanish flag, both at Seville and in the colonies, although it was notorious that in this way the money gained flowed into the money chests of the rebels. Not until 1603 was this anomaly abolished—at any rate, in **How the Dutch Enriched Themselves** part—when the Dutch trade was burdened with a special tax of 30 per cent. ad valorem, until it, too, was again withdrawn during the twelve years' armistice (1609–1621). In spite of this, the Dutch, besides carrying on a legal trade, soon attempted to enrich themselves from the colonies by illegal means. Sometimes they captured Spanish ships, while at other times, by evading the forced registration, they traded directly with America—partly with the Spanish-Portuguese settlements, but more frequently with the Indians in the then still uncolonised regions.

The reason why they, like the English, turned chiefly towards the coast districts, between the Orinoco and the Amazon, was probably because they still believed the famous legend of El Dorado, who

The Elusive Treasures of El Dorado was looked for between these rivers; though, with the practical disposition which is characteristic of their race, they did not forget to profit by an inferior but more certain gain while seeking for treasures. The actual activity of the Dutch as colonists in America began only with the renewal of the war with Spain. Then, in the year 1621, a West India Company was formed upon the model of the East India Company. However, in the first instance, it made it its business to plunder and damage the Spanish-Portuguese colonies, establishing at the same time a number of small settlements on the Oyapok, the Berbice and the Essequibo, which afterwards developed into the colony of Dutch Guiana.

The West India Company came more into prominence through the attacks upon Brazil, which was then still subject to the king of Spain. It succeeded, in a surprisingly short time—during the first thirty years of the seventeenth century—in gaining a firm footing in Olinda and Recife, and gradually the Portuguese were almost completely driven from the northern provinces of Brazil. By means of a clever policy of religious and international tolerance, the company succeeded in making the greater part of the old settlers accept the new order of things unconditionally, while it retained their services for the new community, which soon flourished and experienced no difficulty in resisting the Spanish-Portuguese attacks.

The colony was in its prime during the regency of Count Johann Moritz of Nassau (1637–1644), who not only made

Brazil in its Prime his residence, Moritzstadt, the centre for commerce, but also a home for serious scientific studies, such as had never previously been carried on elsewhere on American soil. The altered political conditions first had a disturbing influence when Portugal, separating from Spain in 1640, made a treaty with the Netherlands. The West India Company at first maintained its claim to its Brazilian conquests, and received the support of the States-general.

The eagerness for the retention of the disputed possession subsequently subsided, so that the Spanish colonial party, which had been considerably strengthened since 1640, succeeded in confining the Dutch more and more to the coast, finally even conquering the coast also, with the assistance of the Portuguese. The Dutch, in the treaty of peace in 1661, also officially renounced all their Brazilian pretensions for an indemnity. From that time attention was once more directed to the so-called savage coast of Guiana. The more ancient settlements of Berbice and Essequibo were ceded to England in 1814, but, on the other hand, the Netherlands possess up to the present day, in Surinam, a remnant of the land which had been colonised under the auspices of the West India Company.

The example which the Netherlands had set by the foundation of state-aided trading companies excited the attention of the rest of Europe, more especially on account of the great results of their East India Company. The French also founded a privileged trading company with the title of " The American Islands Company,"

France's West India Colonies almost simultaneously with the establishment of the West India Company. To this France owes her present West India colonies—Martinique, Guadeloupe, and her smaller dependencies—although her first possession was St. Christopher, which now belongs to England. Its fortunes were very variable before they finally came under the direct control of the state. The first company collapsed as early as 1650, and saved itself from complete bankruptcy only by disposing of its territorial rights to individual proprietors, who for a long time exercised an almost unlimited sovereignty, as had been the case in the Portuguese and North American capitanries.

Colbert then supported the system of privileged companies with great zeal, repurchased the West India Islands, and handed them over, with other territories, to the French West India Company, which also became ruined during the first decades of the eighteenth century, in consequence of political complications. Denmark and Sweden also, for a short time, acquired their colonial possessions in the Caribbean Sea by means of privileged trading companies, and in part endeavoured to retain them. Although, with the English, the impulse for colonial activity had been the result of personal and individual initiative,

"FROM SOUTHERN SEAS AND THE SPANISH YOKE"

The seventeenth century was a period rich in adventure. English seamen betook themselves to Southern seas on voyages of piracy, sometimes returning after amassing huge fortunes, when they escaped death at the hands of the Spaniards. In the above we see a returned sailor telling a group of merchant-adventurers the story of his capture and escape.

From the painting by Edgar Bundy, by the artist's permission

it was by the union of their forces into privileged trading companies that they also first achieved greater results.

The inevitable consequence of the mighty expansion of the Spanish colonial kingdom was that the Lesser Antilles, which were but sparsely endowed with natural treasures, soon became entirely neglected, though they comprised the **Expansion of Spanish Colonies** land which Columbus first discovered in the New World. In the beginning of the sixteenth century they had been occasionally visited by Spanish slave-hunters. When the latter, however, no longer reaped any benefit through these expeditions, most of the smaller islands remained entirely uninhabited, and at the most served as hiding-places for the freebooters of all nations who lay in wait for the Spanish ships. It was no wonder that at a time when, through the example of the Dutch, the desire for colonial conquests had been aroused, these uninhabited islands should have been regarded as suitable for the purpose. Some Englishmen had, in 1605, already taken possession of the completely deserted island of Barbados, without colonising it at the time.

When St. Christopher had developed into a settlement in 1623, a speculator was also found for Barbados, and he induced the king to grant him the right of a " capitan " over the island and its trade. During the following years the English, French and Dutch took possession of almost all the Lesser Antilles. England's colonial possessions attained a further expansion in the time of Cromwell. The Lord Protector, in the year 1655, attacked San Domingo with an important array of military forces, and though he was defeated there, he was more successful in Jamaica, which became the permanent possession of the English. Until then Spain had regarded all other foreign settlements as a usurpation of her sphere of power, and it **England's Colonial Acquisitions** was not till 1670, when peace had been concluded with England, that she recognised the validity of England's colonial acquisitions. The same occurred in her relations with France during the subsequent conclusions of peace.

In spite of all, this was a period of outlawry for the Antilles. The English and French had adhered to the unusual custom of procuring labourers for the settlers by transporting convicts, on con- dition that they should do compulsory labour for the colonists for a specified number of years. Even though there were many among the number who had been convicted for political or religious offences, there was no lack of men of an infamous kind who made the worst possible use of their regained liberty. The renowned buccaneers and filibusters were recruited from their ranks, and, at the time when the European trading companies were almost completely ruined, and when the English also were entirely occupied by wars at home, they became pirates and were the terror of the Caribbean Sea.

Thus they once more revived the days of Hawkins and Drake by their daring attacks upon the Spanish colonial coasts as far as the Pacific Ocean. These homeless and lawless bands of robbers were composed of the subjects of all countries, Spain alone finding no place in their company ; and while they were not in conflict with other nations, they pursued everything that was Spanish with the most deadly hatred. For this reason the enemies of Spain often made use of and protected them, but, for the same reason also, the change **A New Dynasty in Spain** in European politics consequent upon the accession of the Bourbons to the throne soon put an end to their doings. The filibusters then attached themselves to either the English or the French, according to the preponderance in force of either nation. Thus, the best elements among them were assimilated by the colonial settlements, while the incorrigible ones gradually fell victims to their trade or at last received well-merited punishment.

Spain's change of dynasty, from the Hapsburgs to the Bourbons, which kindled in Europe a universal conflagration of more than ten years' duration, did not bring to the colonies any more serious shocks. The latter were content to take upon themselves unconditionally the consequences of the events in the mother country, as they had done previously at the union with Portugal, as well as at its revolt, which was a proof that they had not even then awakened to a life of their own. During the first decades the policy of the new dynasty was entirely occupied with European concerns.

Not until various occurrences had led to the conviction that Spain was in need of reorganisation from within, if she was to occupy a place in the council of the Powers compatible with her great past, did the colonies also assume a higher value in the eyes of the government. Although, owing to the pressure of circumstances, she became nationalised in a surprisingly short time, yet much of the French spirit was infused into the country which till then had been kept in an extraordinary state of isolation. Without the least doubt the revolution which the system of colonial administration underwent under Ferdinand VI. and Charles III. is essentially the direct product of French ideas. The

But the times when the caravels were considered the most suitable vessels for colonial trade were irrevocably past, and the enforced registration at Seville meant only delay and disadvantages for the larger ocean ships which had long since come into favour.

The transference in 1715 of the staple Indian trade to Cadiz, whose bay and harbour were able to shelter the larger vessels and fleets, was at any rate an adaptation to the actual requirements, though it actually meant no

A TYPICAL SCENE IN MODERN CHILI: THE FAIR AT A COUNTRY TOWN

altered conditions of trade and intercourse had in the meanwhile caused the mother country to suffer in as great a degree as the colonies from the restrictions which fettered the colonial trade. The first breach in the old system was still immaterial. Seville was not a suitable point of departure for an extensive transAtlantic trade such as had been developed in the eighteenth century. In this matter it is of no consequence whether or not the navigable water of the Lower Guadalquivir had really deteriorated from neglect.

real advance one way or the other. The monopoly of the trade with the Indies was soon seriously and generally taken in hand. The government felt keenly that it was an anachronism that the trade between the mother country and the colonies was still essentially confined to the fleets which traded, at the most, twice in the year. A sense of the value of time also began to manifest itself in the political sphere, quite apart from the fact that the increase of the colonial commerce had proved the impossibility

5953

of meeting its requirements by the rare and uncertain arrival of the fleets and by having to encourage an illegal trade intercourse on an extensive scale, to meet the difficulty. For this reason it was regarded as a beneficial sign of progress on both sides, when monthly traffic from Corunna, by means of single fast-sailing vessels,

Spain's Expanding Commerce was instituted between Spain and America under Ferdinand VI. Although these ships, in the first instance, were intended to meet the requirements of the government, they were also available for private trade as far as their cargo space permitted. This measure had scarcely any appreciable influence on the fleets, which had lost considerably in importance, but it had the beneficial effect of making it possible to satisfy the needs of the colonies upon a more peaceful basis, and one which would frustrate the smuggling trade of foreigners.

The excellent results which were thereby gained finally inspired the enlightened government of Charles III. courageously to break completely with all former systems. In 1774, the trade of the colonial provinces among themselves became enfranchised under certain limitations which aimed at the protection of Spanish produce, and thus a larger sphere of activity was opened up for the beginnings of a colonial industry. Four years later, 1778, the trans-Atlantic trade was also entirely reorganised. The trading of the fleets was suspended, and the Cadiz-Seville monopoly was annulled. In place of it, it was decided that the nine important harbours of the mother country should have the right to be starting-ports of the ships for the colonies, while on the other side of the ocean no less than twenty-two harbours were opened for direct traffic with Spain.

A new table of rates, wisely adapted to the circumstances, was at the same time drawn up, so that, even though the smuggling of the English and the Portuguese could not

The Rise of Buenos Ayres be entirely suppressed, the essential part of the trading intercourse was once more placed on a legal footing. The markets which had long since ceased to meet the requirements of Portobello therewith also came to an end, and the traffic which had once followed the road from Panama, via Peru and Chili to Tucuman and Buenos Ayres, was now completely revolutionised. Buenos Ayres, owing to its natural situation, became,

with the new order of things, the specially favoured harbour for the trade of the southern colonies with Spain, as the ships intended for Chili and Peru, after running up to Buenos Ayres, now followed the route round Cape Horn, in order to reach the harbours of the Pacific Ocean. The province of Buenos Ayres until then had been the step-child of the government; under the new laws it was placed on an equal footing with the richest colonial province of Spain, because of the wealth of its plantations and sheep-farms.

The facilities offered to trade brought about an important revolution in commerce. The farmer and planter found it easier to procure a remunerative market for the product which could be drawn in unlimited abundance from the soil, owing to its luxuriant fruitfulness. The facilitated trade therefore reacted in a forcible manner upon agriculture and manufacture. The government under Charles III. was, moreover, eager to make up in every way for the persistent neglect of the past. Scientific expeditions were sent out to make exact surveys, not only of the coasts, but also of the entire surface of the coun-

Humboldt's Scientific Journeys tries, and they were at the same time commissioned to examine carefully the mineralogical, botanical and zoological peculiarities of the New World. This was the origin of the great collections of colonial products in Madrid, the precursors of the botanical gardens and natural history museums, which to-day find a place in all our large cities and towns.

These researches have enriched science with many indispensable features, and we have to thank them for quinine, whose extraction has carried an industry far into those regions from which the European settler had not until then understood how to gain any advantage. How these events have influenced mankind, and what never-to-be-forgotten achievements of science they have matured, may be characterised under one name. By order of the Spanish Government, Alexander von Humboldt undertook his journeys of many years' duration through Central and South America. The scientific results of these travels inaugurated a new era in the history of geography and natural science, which he directed into those new channels where they have to this day remained, thus making the Spanish colonial policy one of the most enlightened of its time. KONRAD HAEBLER

INDEPENDENCE of SOUTH & CENTRAL AMERICA

SPAIN'S COLONIES IN REVOLT

BOLIVAR, "THE LIBERATOR OF THE COUNTRY"

ONE of the weightiest reasons why Spain could not adequately support the action of France in favour of the British colonies struggling for independence was her consideration for her own colonies. The government of Charles III. could not maintain the plan of completely preventing intercourse between the colonies and the outside world, and for this reason it was doubly afraid of the influence which might be exerted in these colonies by the spectacle of Spain's aiding the subjects of another state to oppose by force the introduction of institutions which one had always maintained in her own colonies, and was extremely reluctant to abolish. Thus, though in alliance with France, Spain began war against England only in Europe and in the West Indies, main-

Spain's Lost Colonies taining a most reserved attitude towards the United States. Spain had for long been convinced of the impossibility of excluding foreign influence from the Antilles, and had to a certain extent abandoned them to it.

In comparison with Spain's colonial empire on the mainland, they were of small importance, and their value decreased from year to year. The greater number of these islands had already freed themselves from the Spanish dominion, and those remaining became of importance only when Spain had lost all her possessions on the mainland. To these earlier losses was added, in 1795, that of San Domingo. When the repeated changes introduced by French revolutionary governments had led to a general war in the west half of the island which belonged to France, Spain did not disdain

to pave the way to the recovery of a part of the island by an alliance with the insurgent blacks. On making peace with the re-established republican government in 1795, Spain was punished for this by having to cede the eastern half of the

Antilles Surrendered by Spain island to France. The Spanish Government, which did not place a very great value on the Antilles, did not find the sacrifice very difficult, and gave up the island. But the bones of the discoverer of the New World, which had till then lain in the cathedral of the capital, San Domingo, were not left in possession of the foreigner. They were ceremoniously exhumed, placed on board the frigate Descubridor, and taken to Havana. In the cathedral of that city they found a resting-place under the Spanish flag until 1898.

But the peace with France, bought by the sacrifice of San Domingo, was destined to have more momentous consequences for the Spanish colonial possessions. Spain renewed the policy of friendship with France which the Bourbon Family Compact had rendered traditional, and even went so far as to enter into an alliance with Napoleon when all Europe combined to resist his growing power. The immediate

The Spanish Fleet Destroyed at Trafalgar consequence of this was the destruction of the Spanish fleet at the Battle of Trafalgar, October 21st, 1805. An English attack on the Spanish colonies in America immediately followed. Through information supplied by General Miranda, of New Granada, who had served in the French revolutionary army but had afterwards been exiled, the

English were led to believe that the Spanish colonies desired nothing more earnestly than an opportunity to throw off the yoke of the mother country and to establish themselves as independent states. It cannot be denied that, under the influence of the North American War of Independence and the French Revolution,

Unsuccessful Preachers of Revolt a few hot-headed individuals were carried away by an enthusiasm for political liberty for which they were as yet quite unprepared. And these, of course, held the same opinion as Miranda; but the mass of the Spanish-American population had no sympathy whatever for such ideas, as the English learned to their cost when they acted on Miranda's suggestion and endeavoured to kindle the flame of insurrection in Spanish America.

Of all the Spanish coast-towns none was more suitable for such an undertaking than Buenos Ayres. The mouth of the La Plata had always been the seat of an extensive illicit trade. The authorities had been able to limit this only by relaxing the old strict trade regulations in favour of this harbour. Thus, Buenos Ayres, as the headquarters of the party of commercial revolution, made rapid progress, and there were, perhaps, within its walls more enlightened minds than in the other settlements. No harbour had profited more by the permission to trade unrestrictedly with all nations, which Spain temporarily granted to its colonies in 1797, in view of the permanent insecurity of the seas.

But, in spite of this promising situation, the British found no confirmation of Miranda's reports. After the conquest of the Cape of Good Hope, in 1805, a part of the British fleet, with 1,600 men, was sent, under General Beresford, to make an attack on Buenos Ayres. The Spanish governor had been fearing a British attack since the spring; but he thought its

The Changing Fortunes of Buenos Ayres object would be, not Buenos Ayres, but Montevideo. He had accordingly collected the scanty means of defence available at the latter place. Thus it came about that not only the governor, but the whole population, lost their heads when Beresford landed two miles south of Buenos Ayres, moved next day into the suburbs, and the third day into the capital itself. But there was not the least sign of enthusiasm for the British rule

which Beresford forthwith proclaimed; on the contrary, a decidedly hostile spirit pervaded the community from the beginning.

While the town apparently submitted to its new rulers without much show of resistance, crowds of determined patriots were assembling in secret in the suburbs and on the neighbouring haciendas; and when Captain Jacques de Liniers succeeded, under cover of a thick morning mist, in leading a small body of troops across the river, these formed the nucleus of an attacking force which in its swift onset drove the British from the streets of the town into the market-place and forced them first to take refuge in the fortress and then to capitulate. Thus, Buenos Ayres was recovered by a blow as rapid as that by which it had been lost.

It is true that only a small portion of the British force had been destroyed; and the news of Beresford's initial successes had led to the despatch of considerable reinforcements, which arrived in rapid succession. In order to secure a safe base for their operations the British now directed their attack against Monte-

Montevideo in the Hands of the British video. Though heroically defended, the town could not hold out against the enemy's superiority in numbers and weapons. After the whole east coast had fallen into their power, the British considered themselves strong enough to recover Buenos Ayres from the patriots.

The latter, who had made Liniers, the saviour of the town, captain-general, were quite unable to face the British in the open; but when General Whitelock, forming his force into three divisions, attempted a concentrated attack through the streets on the market and the fortress, he was, after two days' fighting, so thoroughly defeated that in the capitulation which followed he had to agree to evacuate Montevideo and the east coast. The captured British officers made fruitless attempts to awaken the spirit of independence among the colonists; even so enthusiastic a patriot as Belgrano had but one answer for such suggestions: " Either our old king or none."

The history of the South American revolution is usually considered from a false standpoint. The simultaneous occurrence of revolutionary movements in almost all the Spanish colonies in the years 1809 and 1810 is generally supposed to indicate that the whole of South

America was ripe for freedom; that a longing for independence had everywhere taken possession of the minds of the people, and now, all at once, found expression throughout the continent. But at the beginning of the nineteenth century, despite the influence of the colonial war in North America and of the French Revolution, the idea of an independent South America really existed only in the heads of a few men who had grown up in the centres where foreign influence was most felt, and who, during their travels abroad, had become enthusiastic for modern ideas without comprehending the presuppositions involved in them.

At any rate, up to the year 1808 all their attempts to loosen the bond between Spain and her colonies met with the same fate as the attack of the British on Buenos Ayres. Such was Miranda's experience on two occasions, when, supported by the British, he landed on the coast of Venezuela, his native province. The first time he failed to gain a footing; the second time he succeeded in taking forcible possession of the town of Coro; but, in **Schemes of the Great Napoleon** the face of the indifference of the mass of the people and the hostility of the better classes, there was no prospect of success, and he was soon forced to give up the attempt at a rising. The revolution that occurred in 1809 was not due to a change in the opinions of the Spanish Americans, but to the state of affairs in Spain. When Napoleon, by the crafty comedy at Bayonne, had persuaded both Ferdinand VII. and Charles IV. to renounce their claims to the Spanish throne in order to create a kingdom for his brother Joseph, there arose in all the colonies, as well as in Spain itself, a hatred of their hereditary foe that neither the Bourbon succession nor the Family Compact could eradicate.

But the colonies maintained a quiet and expectant attitude. Even Liniers—who, though a Frenchman by birth, had been made Spanish viceroy of the province in return for having twice saved Buenos Ayres—dared not listen to the enticing proposals which Napoleon made him in order to secure the recognition of Joseph, because he well perceived the impracticability of any such plan at that moment. But had Napoleon succeeded in getting Joseph unanimously accepted as king in Spain, and in securing his recognition by

the other European Powers, it is probable that the change of dynasty would have proceeded as smoothly in America at the beginning of the nineteenth century as it had at the beginning of the eighteenth. It was only the political events conjured up by the " Dos de Mayo " (May 2nd, 1808) that aroused the spirit which led in **Spain Angry at Napoleon's Treachery** Spain to the Utopian constitution of 1812, and in the colonies to the separation from the mother country— a step politically quite premature. When Junot, in November, 1807, occupied Lisbon in order to force Napoleon's policy on Portugal, the Portuguese Court and Government crossed the ocean, protected by the all-powerful British fleet, chose Rio de Janeiro as capital, and gave Brazil a constitution on similar lines to that of the mother country, in order to bind it more closely to its head.

These events were much talked of in the neighbouring Spanish colonies, but exerted no immediate influence on their politics Still, the colonies joined enthusiastically in the protest made by Spain against Napoleon's treachery and the attempt to force King Joseph on her. A spark of the national enthusiasm which accompanied the accession of Ferdinand VII. at Madrid, March 19th, 1808, extended to the colonies. The latter resolved, despite the French occupation of the mother country, to continue the government as then constituted on behalf of Ferdinand VII.

But the reports of the national rising, of the victory of Baylen, and of the capture of Madrid, were soon followed by the crushing news of the flight of the regency to Seville, of the formation of the general junta, and the subjugation of all Spain with the exception of Isla de Leon. A question here arose which was all-important for the future history of the colonies. The regency and the junta had proved themselves utterly incapable **Succession of Spanish Misfortunes** of defending the country against the national enemy, and their authority was unconditionally rejected by the few provinces that still were able to keep off the French yoke. Under these conditions, were the regency and the junta to be looked upon as representatives of Ferdinand VII., to whom the colonies owed loyalty and obedience? The obligation itself was disputed neither by the Creoles nor by the Peninsulars—Spaniards who had immigrated. However, the latter, to a still greater extent than the former, took as a precedent the example set them in the mother country. There every successful partisan who succeeded in snatching a small district from the French,

Unrest in the Spanish Colonies

or in defending it against their attacks notwithstanding the breaking up of all established authority, formed a junta of his townsmen and adherents, declared the old officials incapable, and replaced them by his friends. Similarly, in the colonies a feeling of discontent with the representatives of the old form of government spread among both Spaniards and Creoles. Led on by a desire for power, politicians who knew they had a large following rose against the viceroys and governors, and compelled them to renounce the authority which had expired on account of the captivity of their prince. They then formed regencies and juntas of their own, everywhere considering themselves the representatives of Ferdinand VII., and in all respects the legal successors of the Spanish officials they had displaced. Such was the course of events in Quito, in Caracas, in Buenos Ayres and in Mexico. Now, as was inevitable, the governors and their following soon came to the conclusion that it was by no means the will of the whole people by which they had allowed themselves to be intimidated.

They accordingly began a struggle against the newly established rulers, and succeeded either in gaining a complete victory, as in Quito, or in regaining at least a part of their official authority, as in the case of the governor of Buenos Ayres, who established himself in Montevideo. The abolition of the traditional legal authority brought with it the danger that all law would be disputed. The revolutionary movement had by no means always placed the best men of the people at the head of the various governments, and after an authority had once been set up by a tumultuous assembly, it was

BOLIVAR, THE GREAT LIBERATOR
Born in 1783 and dying in 1830, Simon Bolivar, by a series of remarkable and often brilliant campaigns, was largely instrumental in securing for the South American republics their much desired independence from Spain.

natural that every party which had any power whatever over the populace also had hopes of seeing its own ambitions fulfilled, not immediately, but at any rate during the course of further developments.

The revolution had led more and more to the predominance of such elements as had been working for the independence of the colonies, at first unconsciously, but ever with more definite aim. The risings of 1809 bore the stamp of loyalty; the colonists revolted on behalf of Ferdinand VII. without understanding clearly who really represented his authority, and many a governor fell, as did Liniers, solely because he was suspected of being ready to recognise any established government, even were it that of Joseph Bonaparte. As time went on, American national influences made themselves unmistakably felt. The differences between the Creoles, or colonists born in America, and the " chapetones," or Spanish immigrants, had become more and more accentuated ever since the governments of Charles III. and Charles IV.—on account of some unimportant revolutionary attempts among the colonial-born population —had begun to maintain more strictly than before the principle of keeping in the hands of men born in Spain all offices to which power and influence were attached. This exclusion from all important public positions was felt more keenly by the Creoles than were many other oppressive measures enforced by the mother country. Accordingly, when the regular course of government had once been interrupted, the Creoles saw no reason why they should not

The Initial Stage of the Revolution

aspire to more profitable and important positions. Thus, for example, in Buenos Ayres, the first overthrow of established authority was soon followed by a second, which aimed at giving the government a more national—that is, a more Creole— character. But still more happened in this stage of the revolution. The boundaries between the different Spanish colonies

VIEW OF CARACAS, THE CAPITAL OF VENEZUELA

LA GUAYRA, ONE OF THE TWO PRINCIPAL PORTS

GENERAL VIEW OF CARACAS, SHOWING THE PRESIDENT'S PALACE

SCENES IN THE SOUTH AMERICAN REPUBLIC OF VENEZUELA

were not always justified by ethnographic and economic considerations. This was especially so in the great provinces of Bogota and Buenos Ayres. There were great radical differences between the various districts. Though the governments that had sprung up so suddenly claimed the right of managing their own affairs, they

Civil War in Buenos Ayres were by no means disposed to allow the scope of their authority to be limited by the principles on which they based their rights to power. Where conflicting elements had been held together by the power of the law only, it was but natural that upon the dissolution of the legally established governments they should demand consideration for their own interests. Thus civil war broke out in Buenos Ayres and in New Granada a few years later.

The chaos produced in the Spanish Cortes owing to the supremacy of doctrinaires could but create greater confusion in colonial relations. By the Spanish Constitution of 1812 the legal position of the colonies was completely altered. Though there was scarcely ever any close connection with the colonial delegates, crowded together in Cadiz and selected by party influence, and the districts they represented, nevertheless the doctrines concerning the rights of man proclaimed by the popular orators in Cadiz made dangerous progress among the colonial population, which was both politically and economically far less advanced than the people of Spain.

The revolutionary movement assumed the most serious character in Mexico. Here, too, the political changes in Spain had led to the overthrow of the government. But the movement among the Creoles was at its very beginning completely lost in a rising of the lower classes of the population, led by a fanatical priest. The latter threatened not only the Spanish authorities, but all who refused to

The Mexican Revolt submit unconditionally to the rule of the populace, composed principally of native Indians. This in itself rendered a permanent success impossible. With a rapidly assembled army of nearly 100,000 men, the priest, Dionysio Hidalgo, leader of the fanatical masses, was able to attack and plunder the towns of Guanajuato, Valladolid, and Guadalajara ; but, notwithstanding his great superiority in numbers, he was unsuccessful in his

assault on the capital, which Spaniards and Creoles united in defending. For his undisciplined army retreat was synonymous with dissolution. Though he received several severe checks while falling back, he was still able to rally a large force under his banner and again to take the offensive ; but, as he was quite unable, with his horde of robbers and cut-throats, to establish any permanent government in place of the one he was opposing, his prestige rapidly decreased. During a second retreat he was betrayed to the Spaniards by his own officers, and shot.

The movement was not yet completely suppressed ; but none of the leaders who placed themselves at the head of the Indian population in the different provinces after Hidalgo's death succeeded in making the revolt as dangerous as it had been at its beginning. The movement had only served to unite all conservative forces for the common purpose of defence, and had placed the struggle for liberty in so unfavourable a light that for years afterwards the province of New Spain was a stronghold of the royalists.

Victory of the Royalists It was only lost to them later on, when, in blind self-confidence, they allowed a conspiracy to be formed which merely borrowed the name of the liberty gained by the other provinces after a hard struggle, and in reality only replaced the country's lawful self-government by an illegal administration.

During the Napoleonic wars the revolutionary movement persisted in only two places in the South American continent. After temporary successes on the part of the republicans, Quito and Chili fell back completely into the power of the royalists ; in New Granada and the neighbouring colony, Venezuela, the efforts to win freedom attained a certain importance, while in the La Plata states they led to permanent independence. But the forces producing the various movements differed widely from each other.

The members of the junta of Creoles which forced the captain-general to resign at Caracas, April 19th, 1810, considered themselves the loyal subjects of Ferdinand VII. They accordingly sent envoys, including Bolivar, the future hero of the South American War of Independence, to England, the nation which was at that time giving the most valuable support to the adherents of the king in the

PANORAMIC VIEW OF LA PAZ THE CAPITAL CITY OF BOLIVIA

THE CUSTOMS HOUSE 16,000 FT. ABOVE SEA-LEVEL, BETWEEN CHILI AND BOLIVIA

THE CATHEDRAL OF CAPACABANAS

SCENES IN THE SOUTH AMERICAN REPUBLIC OF BOLIVIA

peninsula. The object of this embassy was to agree with England upon a common course of action against the enemy of their country. The delegates returned with only conditional promises from the British Government; but at La Guayra they were met by General Miranda. Under the influence of this veteran in the struggle for colonial freedom there was established at Caracas a republican government which preserved the rights of Ferdinand VII. in theory only. This government, it is true, was supreme for a time in the capital and in the central provinces; but even there it did not find the least support in the people, while the east, the west, and still more the great plains of the south—the llanos—were decidedly hostile to it. Thus it was that the royalists were soon able to proceed to the offensive. Their attack was so overpowering that Miranda was obliged to limit himself entirely to the defence. Misfortune produced dissension among the champions of liberty. Miranda was appointed dictator, but had no success; he was finally betrayed and handed over to the royalists by the very men who called themselves champions of freedom. Bolivar, also being entangled in the affair, years afterwards died in prison at Cadiz.

Republican Government at Caracas

The instigators of this heroic deed fled abroad, but did not abandon their plans. As the junta of New Granada still remained independent, many Venezuelans—among them Bolivar—entered its service. Bolivar proposed anticipating the attack on New Granada, which the Spaniards threatened to take from Venezuela, by carrying war into the latter province. In accordance with his wish, the junta authorised him to wrest the border provinces Merida and Trujillo from the hands of the royalists. After succeeding in this in a surprisingly short time, he carried the war into the heart of the country, without authorisation, thinking that the possession of the capital, Caracas, would decide the issue of the contest. With this step the war in the north assumed its special character. Simon Bolivar is the type of those pronunciamento generals who until quite recently have played so great a part in the history of Spain, and a still greater in that of the Spanish-American republics. It may be granted that Bolivar was not quite

Bolivar's Struggles for Liberty

so devoid of conscience as many of his imitators; but no one can fail to see that the idea for which he fought had no existence apart from his own personality. By his fiery, florid eloquence he may often have succeeded in deceiving himself as well as those he tried to convince. In any case, he considered liberty and freedom, whose blessings he eulogised in the most extravagant terms, merely as foundations on which to build up his own fame; and he held himself more than justified in ruthlessly persecuting and crushing all men who would not accept freedom as inaugurated by Bolivar.

With the exception of a small part of the town population, almost all Venezuela was royalist, or at least heartily sick of civil war. Thus, as he advanced, Bolivar met sometimes with secret opposition, sometimes with stolid apathy; and only where his arms were victorious was he able to excite a fictitious enthusiasm for the ideal blessings he professed to be fighting for. He entered Caracas with theatrical pomp as liberator; but the kind of freedom he brought to the Venezuelans betrayed its true character in his completely overlooking the civil authorities and assuming the powers of a dictator with the pompous title of "Libertador de la Patria" (Liberator of the Fatherland). But he failed to deceive even his immediate followers, chiefly persons whose interests were bound up in his own.

"Liberator of the Fatherland"

He was not the only one, even in Venezuela itself, who was working on this plan. In the extreme east, on the boundary of Guiana, another liberator, Mariño, had arisen; but instead of combining against their common enemies, the Spaniards, each of these saviours of the people desired nothing more ardently than the defeat of his rival, that he might then appear as sole emancipator and obtain undisputed supremacy.

Yielding to the pressure of the half-breeds, Bolivar had made the fatal mistake of declaring a war of extermination against the Spaniards; and all men were reckoned as Spaniards who did not willingly agree to all the demands of the so-called patriots. This savage warfare naturally led to reprisals on the part of the European population; but while they had on their side an excuse for retaliation, Bolivar, by his action, disgraced the principles he professed to be fighting for and did himself great injury, inasmuch as he had far less power at his disposal than that possessed by his enemies. Thus the war assumed an especially bloody character. Murder and robbery, the weapons employed by both parties, set free the lowest passions and brought to the fore the worst elements of the population. Bolivar meanwhile did not distinguish himself as a general; he had no plan of campaign, and he had drawn up no constitution. The Spanish flag still waved over Puerto Cabello, the strongest point on the coast; battles were fought at Barquisimeto and on the Araure with varying results. Finally, Bolivar himself had to fall back upon Caracas.

Here the hostility of the Llaneros completed his ruin. It was in vain that he sought to give his dictatorship a legal basis by calling together a congress at Caracas; it was in vain that he now concluded an alliance with the dictator of the eastern provinces, fully recognising his authority. Even their combined forces could not temporarily withstand the ever-increasing troops of horsemen which the fierce Boves brought from the southern plains in support of the Spaniards.

Bolivar Branded as a Traitor Matters had gone so far that far-sighted persons assisted the latter, in anticipation of their speedy victory. First Mariño, then Bolivar himself, was repeatedly and so severely beaten that his retreat degenerated into flight. When he reached the coast of Cumana, the Liberator had so little means of resistance that he fled with the ships that contained his war material.

When his compatriots had again assembled, and he endeavoured to rejoin them, he was branded as a traitor and with difficulty escaped the fate which he himself, under similar circumstances, had prepared for General Miranda. The result of the campaign of 1813 was that the whole of Venezuela fell once more into the hands of the royalists. The latter were now free to bring about a similar state of affairs in the republic of New Granada, which was divided against itself, and from which Bolivar had withdrawn the greater part of its military resources for the purposes of his Venezuelan enterprise.

In the south, too, the revolutionary movement had by this time exhausted itself. The rising in the La Plata states was at its beginning conducted in a spirit which contrasted very favourably with that characteristic of the Venezuelan movement. The bulk of the people were, it is true, as indifferent to the revolution as in Venezuela; but there was a decidedly more progressive spirit among the middle and upper classes in Buenos Ayres than in Caracas. On the news of the dissolution of the government in Spain, the viceroy at Buenos Ayres was deposed. On May 25th, 1810, a junta declared the province independent of the junta of Seville. But it continued to rule, as did the governments that developed from it in the course of years, in the name of Ferdinand VII. There was even a party ready to invite to Buenos Ayres as regent Ferdinand's sister, the Infanta Carlota, who had married a Portuguese prince. The plan, however, which led to long and complicated intrigues in Rio de Janeiro and Montevideo, came to nothing.

Viceroy of Buenos Ayres Deposed

The newly formed government considered that its first task was to obtain the recognition of its authority throughout the La Plata province; but in this it met with serious resistance. The royalists had chosen Montevideo as their headquarters; and the arrival of support from the mother country not only rendered the city impregnable against the limited means of attack at the disposal of the junta, but gave the royalists command of the bay and the mouth of the river flowing into it.

But little by little the supremacy of the Spaniards was limited to the town itself; their naval schemes were brought to naught by the aid of the Brazilians and British, who were friendly to the junta; and finally, when the Spanish ships had been defeated by the newly created rebel fleet, the fortress of Montevideo capitulated. But meanwhile there had arisen in the province of Buenos Ayres the general confusion that in all the colonies followed the abolition of legally constituted authority; and the east bank of the river La Plata also was only nominally under the rule of the various governments that rapidly succeeded one another in Buenos Ayres. In reality the division was springing up which finally led to the establishment of the "Republica Oriental del Uruguay." A similar course of events had also occurred in another part of the old province.

Chaos in the Spanish Colonies

In December, 1810, the junta of Buenos Ayres sent General Belgrano to secure the recognition of the new government in the district of Paraguay; but the attempt ended in complete failure. Belgrano was enticed far into the deserted land before any enemy faced him ; then at Paraguay he received a check that necessitated a dangerous retreat. It was only then that the liberal idea occurred to him of letting the province itself decide whom it would obey. Accordingly he concluded with the defenders of Paraguay a capitulation at Tacuary which allowed him to retire without further injury being done. The consequence was that progressive ideas were disseminated so rapidly in the province that it took its fate into its own hands, and in 1814 chose as executive Dr. José Gaspar Tomas Rodriguez da Francia. His was a rule of force, more ruthless and bloody than had ever been seen on American soil; but it was an enlightened despotism. By destroying the power and wealth of the priests, and promoting agriculture and industry in every possible way, he rendered the state independent of the outside world. Thus the independence of Paraguay was rendered secure even after his death in 1840.

Paraguay Under a Ruthless Despotism

The government of Buenos Ayres had now to contend with movements not unlike that to which it owed its existence. It was repeatedly occupied in combating efforts at decentralisation in various parts of its territory even after the Argentine Republic had actually secured its independence. But Buenos Ayres also played an important part in the struggle against the common enemies of all the provinces, the Spanish royalists. The authority of the junta met with the most serious opposition in the district of Upper Peru, the modern Bolivia, which was then governed from Buenos Ayres. The first rising against Spanish dominion had taken place there in 1809, but had been easily put down by an expedition from Peru proper; and from that time the royalist influence was supreme. Accordingly, the junta sent out its first army against this dangerous opponent. By a brilliant victory at Suipacha, General Balcarce forced the royalists back across the Desaguadero, the outlet of Lake Titicaca, which then formed a portion of the Peruvian frontier.

Spaniards' Victory at Huaqui

But this advantage was not maintained. After receiving reinforcements, the Spaniards gained a decisive victory at Huaqui, drove the patriots out of the Bolivian highlands, and followed them into the Argentine Republic. But here Belgrano, who had been appointed general of the northern army, stopped the retreat, defeated the Spanish leader at Tucuman, and some weeks later, at Salta, compelled him and his whole force to lay down their arms.

All these battles were fought with comparatively small armies ; and this explains the transitory nature of the successes attained. Neither party could really dominate the sparsely settled land ; and the inhabitants had no leaning towards either side, but always favoured the victors. Royalists and republicans, even after a number of defeats, were soon able to collect an army of some thousands, and thus to renew the struggle ; hence the manifold fluctuations of fortune in all the campaigns undertaken by the South American patriots against the Spanish royalists.

Belgrano, too, was not permanently favoured by fortune. On his advance into Bolivia he found the enemy reorganised at Huilcapuyo ; and both here and at Ayuma he was so severely defeated that he had again to retreat to Jujuy. He was then for a long time unable to act on the offensive, and although the royalists did not advance into the Argentine Republic itself, all Bolivia was again in their hands at the end of 1813. By reason of a contemporary royalist victory in Venezuela, the cause of Ferdinand VII. never appeared more hopeful than when Napoleon opened the doors of his golden prison to the captive of Valençay and allowed him to return to the throne of his fathers.

Bolivia in the Hands of the Royalists

During the war Spain had passed through many curious experiences ; and the revolutionary trifling of the Cortes at Cadiz, which had introduced a Parliamentary system of government, was not without influence on the movements in the American provinces. But in Spain the people were as little ripe for freedom as in the colonies ; and as the conflict of interests in the mother country was of far less advantage to the new government of Spain than it was to the colonial strivings for independence, the artificial constitution collapsed even before Ferdinand VII. had set foot on Castilian soil, and he lost no time in endeavouring to bring about a similar result in the colonies.

A great expedition, composed of twenty-five warships and sixty transports with 10,000 men, put to sea under General Morillo in March, 1815, to suppress the last efforts of the colonial rising. The original intention was to disembark the troops on the La Plata. But since the fall of Montevideo there was no safe landing-place. Moreover, Buenos Ayres recognised Ferdinand, at least nominally, as its rightful ruler, while in the most recent phase of the war in Venezuela and New Granada an independent republic had been declared. Accordingly, Morillo received instructions to proceed to the subjugation of the northern provinces.

If this was assured, the way to the La Plata region always lay open to him through Bolivia. His first steps gave every promise of success. The island of Margarita, ever the refuge and hiding-place of the patriots of Venezuela in misfortune, was quickly subdued. In the whole of Venezuela there was hardly a troop of patriots that deserved the name of an army; Morillo's march through the province was a military promenade. In order to conquer New Granada, Morillo chose Cartagena as his first point of attack,

Morillo's Long Siege of Cartagena but here he received a foretaste of the difficulties that awaited him. He had already discovered, on endeavouring to embark the Venezuelan army in the fleet, replacing it by Spanish troops for the protection of the province, that the hitherto loyal Llaneros deserted in crowds. Still he had an overwhelmingly superior force when he invested Cartagena by land and water. But the town offered a heroic resistance.

Morillo, who wished to avoid bloodshed as much as possible, tried to reduce it by hunger; but it held aloft the banner of independence for 108 days, although the Spanish general, losing patience, spared neither bombardment nor assault. Even when further resistance was impossible, the town did not capitulate; its defenders broke through the blockade during a storm, and the greater number of them escaped to San Domingo, to renew the struggle from there after a short rest. New Granada, indeed, did not defend itself with the courage of Cartagena. From Quito a second Spanish army was working its way up to meet Morillo, and when it approached Santa Fé there was in this province, too, no patriot

army to oppose it. But even Morillo, though victorious, felt that the ground he stood on was insecure. He therefore abandoned his original system of lenience, and meted out severe treatment to the rebels. But notwithstanding hundreds of sacrifices, he could not firmly establish Spanish rule.

Royalists Defeated on the Apure Wherever the Spanish arms did not penetrate, rebellion broke out anew. The island of Margarita was the first to throw off the unaccustomed yoke; and on the llanos of Casanare an army of horsemen from the plains under the half-breed, Paez, responded for the first time to the cry of freedom and gained its first victory over the royalists on the Apure.

But the fierce warriors of the prairies spared the lives of their prisoners, and thus induced most of these to join them. After a renewed disturbance in Cumana, Morillo began to fear for the safety of Venezuela, and removed his headquarters, then at the foot of the Cordilleras on the east side, to Varinas. But as yet there was no apparent connection between the different risings. Finally, there landed in Margarita the old leaders and the defenders of Cartagena who had prepared in Haiti for a fresh struggle with the aid of the British and of the president of the negro republic. But Bolivar still showed himself to be no strategist.

While troops of horsemen scoured the llanos and kept the plains in a ferment, while his compatriots conquered in the east a district on both banks of the Orinoco, where they enjoyed absolute security, Bolivar remained in the charmed circle of the capital, Caracas, and in the autumn of 1816 attempted to advance on it from Ocumare with an insufficient force. But, most disgraceful of all, on the false report of a

Bolivar's Flight and Return defeat, he took flight on board ship, abandoning his followers to destruction. His reputation had sunk so low that, banished a second time, he was compelled to seek refuge in Haiti. However, he was recalled a few weeks later, for of the leaders of the numerous bands none was held in so high esteem as he; and, above all, no one else was possessed of a definite and fixed political and military plan of campaign.

SCENES IN THE SOUTH AMERICAN REPUBLIC OF PERU

The illustration at the top of this page represents the cathedral at Cuzco, while the bottom picture shows the modern capital of Lima, with the stately cathedral in the background. Bolivar's statue at Lima is also reproduced.

Photos: W. H. Rau, and others

AMERICA

INDEPEND-
ENCE OF
SOUTH AND
CENTRAL
AMERICA II

THE LIBERATION OF THE SOUTH
BOLIVAR'S TRIUMPHS ^{AND}_{THE} NEW REPUBLICS

BOLIVAR'S TRIUMPHS AND THE NEW REPUBLICS

IN the year 1817 the revolution began to gain a firm footing in the north. The idea of creating a safe base for the champions of independence on the right bank of the Orinoco had not originated with Bolivar; but he immediately recognised the importance of the plan. While the investment by land of Angostura and Guayana Vieja, which commanded the river, was attended by only a moderate amount of success, he succeeded, with the help of English sailors, in overthrowing the Spanish supremacy by sea, and in forcing the royalists to evacuate both places.

The Orinoco, and farther west the Apure, now separated the independent territory from the Spanish. Morillo had meanwhile been wasting his time in a fruitless attempt to reconquer the island of Margarita. He brought the coast as far as the peninsula of Paria under his power, but this had no great importance. At this time Bolivar had with **Bolivar's Unlimited Power** difficulty succeeded in getting his authority recognised by the leaders of the different revolutionary parties; he now felt the need of establishing his position on a more legal basis. Accordingly, in the autumn of 1817, he created a council of state and a supreme court of justice, and held out hopes of further political organisation. At the same time he declared his dictatorship a necessity, and, as before, exercised practically unlimited power.

The war still led to no definite result. Bolivar now advanced from the middle Apure against Caracas. He himself defeated Morillo at Calabozo, and Paez at the same time conquered San Fernando, the last bulwark of the royalists on the Apure; but these successes were counterbalanced by a series of unsuccessful undertakings which encouraged the opposition still secretly kept alive against the dictator. However, he was once more able to blunt the edge of the opposition. He won over the discontented generals by the way in which he succeeded in providing them with troops, war material and money to renew the struggle; the politicians he disarmed by summoning a congress to form a constitution at Angostura. This congress was, in reality, a mere spectacular farce; but it **English Troops in the Fight for Independence** gave his dictatorship an appearance of legality by unanimously electing him president of the Venezuelan Republic. Of at least as great importance to Bolivar as this confirmation of his position was the arrival of a considerable number of trained English and German soldiers who had enlisted to fight for the cause of independence.

They formed a nucleus about which the brave, but less valuable, troops of the South American provinces collected, and from which they could receive their military training. The English legion played a prominent part in all later campaigns, and enjoyed Bolivar's confidence to such a degree as repeatedly to call forth expressions of jealousy from the South American patriots. For the campaign of 1818, Bolivar settled on a plan calculated to decide the course of events. Once before he had carried the war from New Granada into the plains of Venezuela to fight for the freedom of the former in the territories of the latter; now he resolved to strive for the emancipation of his fatherland from beyond the Andes.

This idea was suggested to him by the victories of José de San Martin, but, be that as it may, his success proved the correctness of his calculations. Even before the floods **Bolivar Surprises His Enemies** that during the rainy season render the llanos impassable had entirely subsided, Bolivar moved southward from the Apure, which protected his flank from the royalists, and crossed the Andes by the route taken by the traders of the Chibchas and the first conquerors of Bogota. He did, indeed, suffer considerable losses before he reached a settled district at Sogamoso; but his plan of surprising the enemy in the very centre of their sphere of power was completely successful. Everything now depended on his being able to gain a decisive victory before his opponents could summon their full strength. By rapid marches and countermarches he succeeded in so completely outwitting the hostile **The Royalist** advance guard that he was **Army** able to seize the town of Tunja, **Annihilated** and thus to cut off a large portion of his foes from the capital. But the Spaniards, trusting to their superiority in numbers, tried to force their way back to Santa Fé. A decisive battle was fought at the bridge of Boyaca ; it ended in the annihilation of the royalist army. The viceroy evacuated the capital and retired to Cartagena with the remainder of his troops, while the patriots took possession of Santa Fé de Bogota, and re-established the independence of New Granada. Bolivar created here, as in Venezuela, a new civil government at the side of his military dictatorship, and paved the way for the union of the two sister provinces into one republic under the name of Colombia.

The news of this victory reached Angostura, the temporary capital of Venezuela, just when Bolivar for the third time had been deposed as a deserter and banished as a traitor solely because there were others who were covetous of his power. But in the lustre of his recent victory he could treat such proceedings with contempt. The congress, doubly compliant from the consciousness of its offence, adopted without debate the proposal of the liberator that Venezuela, New Granada and Quito should be combined into one republic named Colombia, whose president would naturally be Bolivar, while in each of the three provinces there was to be a vice-president at the head of the civil administration. The constitution of the new state was to be framed in detail by a congress to **The New** meet at Cucuta for this pur- **Republic of** pose as soon as a truce **Colombia** could be declared. This soon occurred. The news that reached South America in the summer of 1820 gave the situation a completely different aspect. The army which had been collected in the neighbourhood of Cadiz to give General Morillo the means of completely subduing the rebels had revolted ; and as it felt compelled to find some pretext in justification of its action,

it adopted as its watchword the restoration of the Constitution of 1812. With this all who had fought for the restoration of the Spanish dominion since 1814 lost once more their legal basis.

The immediate consequence was a cessation of hostilities, leading the way to a peaceful understanding between the mother country and the colonies. But the latter had already gone too far : too large a number of the colonists had with all their interests been compromised by the revolution for an agreement to be possible under a constitution whose liberality, so far as the colonies were concerned, was known to be influenced by the desire of the whole Spanish nation for their continued dependence. The negotiations served rather to bring out the conviction that a return to the old state of affairs was impossible. Both parties took advantage of the truce to prepare for the inevitable renewal of hostilities, and the war broke out anew in the spring of 1821.

The supremacy of the patriots was so far assured in the highlands that Bolivar had now better prospects of success in **Another** attacking the economic centres **Triumph for** of Venezuela, Caracas and **Bolivar** Valencia, so often fought for with varying fortune. As matters then stood, these districts were the last stronghold of the royalists ; even the west of Venezuela, hitherto loyal, had been lost to them ; and apart from the coast towns, all of which, from Cartagena to Cumana, were in their hands, the Spaniards were masters only of the territory occupied by their forces.

At Carabobo, where Bolivar had once before gained a victory, the Spaniards awaited him in a position deemed impregnable ; but the natives were now on the side of the patriots, and led a part of their army by secret paths to the right flank of the enemy, whose position was easily carried from this side. The victory was complete. The Spanish were forced to evacuate the central part of the province and to take refuge under the walls of Puerto Cabello, while Bolivar once again made a triumphal entry into Caracas, whose freedom from this time suffered no further attack.

The opening of the congress at Cucuta was almost contemporaneous with the victory of Carabobo. Now met for the first time in the history of the northern provinces a legislative assembly really possessed of power ; and it showed itself worthy of its calling by not submitting unconditionally to the dictator, as its predecessor had done. But it did not on this account undervalue the indisputable services Bolivar had rendered to the cause of freedom in the Republic of Colombia, and was far from accepting the resignation of all his offices and titles which he handed in to it, as he had done to its predecessors. Neither did it place itself unconditionally in his hands, but, with the best intentions, drew up a constitution which gave free scope to the ambition of the Liberator without placing him above the constitution.

His position as president of Colombia was confirmed by the congress. But it was laid down by law that he could not exercise civil authority in this capacity while at the head of the army in the field. To provide for this eventuality, a vice-president for the whole republic was appointed; and it was only in such provinces as he should afterward free from the Spanish yoke that Bolivar was to exercise dictatorial power. In other respects the new constitution differed widely from Bolivar's ideal. It rejected the scheme of an **Colombia's** upper house, composed of life-**President and** members, which Bolivar had **Constitution** projected for Venezuela at Angostura; nor did it make the presidency hereditary or tenable for life, but followed the example of the United States in limiting the tenure of office of the head of the state to four years. Hitherto no constitution had had a fair test, since every successful partisan had considered himself competent to overthrow it; so, to secure a practical trial for its own work, the congress passed a law forbidding any change in the constitution for the next ten years.

Bolivar submitted to the decisions of the congress of Cucuta. The fortune of war also seemed to favour the new republic. After a siege of fourteen months one of Bolivar's generals had captured Cartagena, and the loss of this stronghold rendered the royalists in the district about the isthmus powerless. Chagres and Portobello drove out their Spanish garrisons; and the isthmus provinces not only made themselves independent of Spain, but even asked to be admitted to the Colombian Republic. The last remnants of the army, with which Morillo once seemed to have brought all New Granada and Venezuela to absolute obedience, now held only Puerto Cabello and Cumana. All danger had disappeared in the north.

In 1814 the cause of freedom in the southern theatre of war had stood on very slender supports. West of the Cordilleras the Spanish viceroy of Peru held sway **The Coming** over all the Pacific provinces **of José de** from Cape Horn to the Gulf **San Martin** of Guayaquil and the tableland of Quito. The province of Buenos Ayres alone still held aloft the flag of freedom; and even it had suffered considerable losses of territory. While Bolivia had been brought back under the rule of the Spanish authorities, Paraguay in the north, and Uruguay in the east, had separated themselves from Buenos Ayres.

The aimless policy of its leading men was quite calculated to keep alive the strife in the province itself; and the Spaniards had reason to hope that the colonies, exhausted by suicidal wars among themselves, would fall an easy prey to them. The prospects of such an issue would have been even more favourable had not there come to the aid of the patriots at this time of internal dissension a man who, by the influence of his personality, became the rescuer of the threatened independence to a greater degree than even Bolivar.

José de San Martin did not return to his South American home in Buenos Ayres until the close of the Peninsula War, during which he had fought bravely on the side of the Spaniards. In Spain he had largely imbibed the liberal ideas then prevalent in the Peninsula, which found their embodiment in the Cortes at Cadiz. He, too, was inspired by a lively ambition, which expressed itself, not as in Bolivar's case by a morbid longing for the outward signs of power, but by an idealistic desire to distinguish himself in the service of his country, and to secure for it a brighter future. San Martin, like most of the far-**San Martin's** sighted politicians of the **Zeal for** South, was not a republican **His Country** in the sense that Bolivar was. He and others like him were convinced that Spanish South America was not sufficiently advanced either in politics or civilisation for a republican form of government like that of the United States.

What he had learned of republican institutions in the colonies of the North, and in part in the provinces of his own country, had roused in him an aversion from any outward show of liberty instituted for the selfish ends of particular individuals, that at times stirred up civil war and at best only replaced Spanish tyranny by another as bad.

Even in Buenos Ayres San Martin found powerful influences which, in his opinion, worked against the true interests of the state. After he had had for a short time an opportunity of rendering his country valuable though modest services, partly on the banks of the La Plata, and partly in the provinces of the Bolivian highlands, the idea arose in his mind of placing himself in the service of freedom and of fighting not merely for the liberty of his country, but for that of all Spanish America. The plan he formed for the attainment of this object proves his capacity as a general. He recognised immediately that the fate of all the southern provinces depended on the expulsion of the Spaniards from their stronghold, the Peruvian highlands on both sides of the Cordilleras; for, secure in their command of the Pacific, the Spaniards could at any time use the ocean as a base for attacks on the patriots by land in three directions. The shortest way from Buenos Ayres to Lima lay through Upper Peru (Bolivia). But this route was the most difficult on account of the extraordinary breadth of the line of advance, and because the Spaniards could always obtain supplies by sea. For this reason, San Martin chose another point of attack. In Chili, during the early years of the colonial rising, the cause of freedom had found numerous and enthusiastic adherents. The Spaniards had been compelled to employ a considerable force in order to bring back the province to its allegiance; and they would not have succeeded at all had not the despotic spirit of the pronunciamentos split the friends of independence into two parties. San Martin accordingly demanded from the government of Buenos Ayres means for collecting and arming the nucleus of a force to be employed first in liberating Chili and afterwards to be used against the Spaniards throughout the southern part of the continent.

Internal dissensions had not yet so blinded the rulers of Buenos Ayres that they were unable to recognise the splendid prospects opened up by San Martin's plan for the cause of freedom; so, in accordance with his own desire, he was entrusted with the government of the district of Mendoza, on the boundary of Northern Chili, so that, without unnecessarily attracting attention, he might collect the means of carrying out his plan, and proceed to its execution at what seemed to him the proper time. San Martin possessed what was wanting in almost all the other champions of independence—a strictly methodical military training complete in all respects; a definite scheme harmonious from both a political and a military point of view, and conscientiously worked out in every detail; and an enthusiasm for the cause he served, which was exhibited by his personal readiness to make every sacrifice for it. He spent fully two years in collecting and training the troops for his campaign and in preparing the district in which he intended to begin operations; and when he gave the signal to march every detail had been foreseen and provided for so definitely that he was able to proceed step by step with mathematical precision, and saw his efforts crowned by complete success.

ADMIRAL LORD COCHRANE
Admiral of the Brazilian fleet in 1823-5, he figured conspicuously in the struggle for independence of the South American states, achieving a series of successes against the Spaniards in their war against Chili, Peru and Brazil.

In the autumn of 1816 San Martin received authority from the government of Buenos Ayres to lead his army across the Cordilleras into Chili, and from there to attempt to reconquer Bolivia. During the last months of the year extraordinary activity prevailed in the district of Mendoza, and the government did all that it could to furnish the expedition with the best possible equipment. On January 14th, 1817, San Martin divided his force of 4,000 picked troops of all arms, with a train of 10,000 mules, into two sections, and set out from Mendoza to cross the Cordilleras by the passes of Aconcagua and Putaendo. The two divisions were to meet at Santa Rosa de los Andes, 210 miles from Mendoza; the greatest height to which they had to ascend was about 12,000 feet. On February 8th the divisions arrived at the rendezvous within such a short time of one another that the royalist outposts at the mouths of the passes did not know from which direction the real attack was to be expected. A short fight forced them to retreat. The first bold step of the plan of campaign had been successful. But the army was still in the heart of the mountains, and it could neither adopt a proper formation nor gain support from a rising in the land until great distances had been traversed. San Martin knew that a rapid advance meant a victory half won, and that the shortest way to Santiago, the capital, was imposed on him by necessity. He allowed his exhausted troops to rest but a short time, and then advanced against the enemy, whose main force barred his way at Chacabuco. By a skilfully executed flank attack San Martin routed the hostile army in a few hours. Panic spread everywhere. The governor evacuated the capital, taking with him the remainder of the army, the treasury, the government officials, and many of the inhabitants of royalist leanings; and on February 14th the troops of the liberator entered Santiago in triumph. In the weeks following

JOSÉ DE SAN MARTIN

Fighting in the war of independence, he displayed great capacity as a general, and, defeating the Spaniards in many engagements, became the liberator of Chili and Peru.

the victory San Martin's character was put to a severe test. He had come to give the people freedom, and indeed all Northern Chili rose for the cause of independence as soon as the Spaniards had retreated. What had been done was now to be justified by a legislative body, and a congress was therefore called together at Santiago. But the new republicans could not conceive that a foreign general would fight for their cause for any other reason than to place himself at their head, and San Martin was almost unanimously elected president with dictatorial power. But he considered that he had taken only the first step on the road to fame, and refused the position unconditionally. He recommended the congress to appoint in his stead General O'Higgins, a Chilian who had fought under him at Chacabuco; he would accept for himself only the position of commander-in-chief of the army. But the civil affairs of the republic had prevented the leader from following up the enemy with the rapidity necessary for complete victory. The royalist party had recovered from its first panic; the viceroy of Peru had sent reinforcements; and as the Spaniards had complete command of the sea they were able to land the latter without molestation in the fortress of Talcahuano, which commanded the Bay of Concepcion. The cause of freedom was directly menaced when an attack on Talcahuano with an insufficient force failed, and on their retreat

HEROES OF THE WAR OF INDEPENDENCE

Belgrano   Sucre

Manuel Belgrano was a commander of singular ability, his talents towering high above many of those who took part in the historic struggle for independence, while, after going through the entire civil war, José de Sucre won the last great battle in 1824 at Ayacucho, and in his honour the town of Chuquisaca was called Sucre.

5971

the patriots were completely defeated at Talca, not far from the Maule. Fear and dismay spread even to the capital. The imminent danger finally roused San Martin from his inactivity. His force, continually kept in strict training, was undoubtedly superior to that of the enemy in military capacity, if not in numbers.

San Martin's Great Victory at Maipu This fact, combined with his ability as a leader, led, after a long and fierce struggle at Maipu, to a victory so complete that even the more southerly provinces took heart and threw off the Spanish yoke. It was not San Martin's fault that he allowed a long time to pass after the victory of Maipu before again taking the offensive.

Immediately after the battle he hastened back across the Andes to secure the approval of the government of Buenos Ayres for his plan of campaign against Peru. It was now time for the patriots to create a fleet in order to dispute the supremacy of the Spaniards on the Pacific, and thus to secure the possibility of attacking Peru by sea. The rulers of Buenos Ayres, like the new government of Chili, were quite ready to approve of San Martin's plans in theory; but neither government was in a position to give effective aid to their prosecution.

In Buenos Ayres the federalistic loosening of old ties set in just at this time. The government had so much to do in providing for its own safety, which it saw, or imagined it saw, threatened from within and without, that for the time at least it could lend no aid to projects which were quite outside its sphere of action. All San Martin could obtain was a number of English ships that were being fitted out by the Chilian patriots to be used almost as much against the newly established government as against the Spaniards.

But this laid the foundation of a sea power which, led with unprecedented boldness by a Scotsman, Cochrane, did not a little to **Spain's Sea Power Challenged** break the power of Spain at sea. For the army San Martin could do nothing in Buenos Ayres. He felt this the more keenly inasmuch as Chili at the same time placed considerable obstacles in his way. It goes without saying that the troops which San Martin had led across the Cordilleras and from victory to victory in Chili were attached to their leader with unshaken loyalty; the Chilian regiments, too, that he had formed and trained before

the battle of Maipu, followed him with blind obedience. President O'Higgins was also among the general's closest friends. But when once the danger from the royalists had been obviated, the majority of the Chilian patriots saw in the presence of the liberating army only an oppressive burden on the badly filled treasury of the young republic and a constant menace to republican freedom. These circumstances served only to spur San Martin to greater exertions for the realisation of his plan of campaign against Lima.

But, as it was at that moment impossible to obtain the means for this, he had no alternative but to arrange for the return of the liberating army across the Andes. This measure, which apparently was only the result of the difficulty in provisioning and paying the army, had also great political significance. It was calculated to deceive the Spaniards in Peru as to the direction from which attack was to be expected; at the same time it deprived the Chilians of all grounds for complaint against their Argentine deliverers, and also let them know how, in the absence of **Fleet of the Spanish Patriots** any effective protection, their existence as a state was threatened by the presence on their borders of the still numerous royalists. Finally the return of the troops to the Argentine Republic was calculated to convince the government of Buenos Ayres that the maintenance of the army, even when condemned to inactivity, would prove almost as great a burden to the state as the moderate demands made by San Martin in order that he might be enabled to fight for the cause of independence in the enemy's territory.

These calculations were justified, at least in part, in all directions. The newly formed fleet of the patriots under Admiral Cochrane made a venturesome attack on the Spanish ships at Callao, and, though not in a position to do much damage to the enemy, it proved that the latter were so disturbed and weakened that a campaign undertaken from the coast in accordance with San Martin's plan would have every prospect of success. O'Higgins and other friends of the liberator obtained a freer hand, despite the Chilian patriots, and proceeded to further his plans; they succeeded in procuring for him an invitation to lead his troops once more across the Andes into Chili, in order to prepare for an attack on Peru with the help of the fleet. Nor did San Martin's military policy remain without effect on the people of the Argentine Republic; he succeeded in winning approval for his schemes, and he was even assisted to some extent with money and war material. Nevertheless, it was from Buenos Ayres, and at the last moment, that the greatest danger threatened him; and the premonition that this must inevitably destroy every prospect of his plan being realised finally drove San Martin to take the risk of breaking the bridges behind him and plunging boldly into the unknown, though his equipment was defective and he had no security for the future.

The party of patriots, which claimed that the authority of the government of Buenos Ayres extended over the whole of the region formerly included in the Spanish colonies province, had found itself compelled to resort to force almost from the beginning. In Paraguay, however, it had not attained its object; on the east bank of the La Plata, in Uruguay, it saw itself driven to hazardous concessions; and even in the north-west the victorious **San Martin Opposed to Civil War** army had had to fight republican opponents as well as Spanish royalists. The opposition in this last quarter finally increased to such an extent that the government believed its rights could be maintained only by force. Thus it was that San Martin, after making preparations for his advance into Peru, received orders to return and protect the government from danger within the republic itself.

San Martin was among the very few patriots who saw clearly that a quarrel as to a greater or less degree of liberty meant the death-warrant of the new republics, if it should degenerate into civil war before the Spaniards had been finally and completely driven from South American soil. He and others of like mind were undoubtedly republicans at heart; and if, notwithstanding, they repeatedly attempted, at different phases of the struggle for independence, to give the newly formed states a monarchical form of government, it was only because they had come to the conclusion that even among the leaders the great majority were as yet quite unfit for a true republican constitution. They saw that when once independence was secured, the land would benefit more by a strong central power on a liberal basis—an enlightened despotism —than by unbridled freedom. San Martin accordingly declared plainly to the government that even his own army, which under stricter discipline would yet be a still more powerful factor in the struggle against the enemy, would, if involved in the civil war, inevitably fall a prey to demoralisation, and in the long **The Noble Appeal of the Great Leader** run would be no more a protection to the government than the troops and the population on which the republic had hitherto relied. He also entered into direct communication with rebel leaders that he might induce them to use their forces in the service of their country, and to postpone the struggle over political opinions until their common enemy had been overcome.

As this noble warning fell on deaf ears, and the government, shaken to its very foundations, kept repeating more insistently than ever the order to return to Buenos Ayres to its support, San Martin finally decided to renounce his allegiance to it. In an address to the army he called on his soldiers to turn their backs on the civil war, and to seek glory and honour in the struggle against an enemy from whom they had already conquered a flourishing province. The appeal was enthusiastically received. A few days later the army assembled on the other side of the Cordilleras; the Chilian government took it under its protection; and in Valparaiso the Chilian-Argentine expedition, which was given the name "Exercito Libertador del Peru," embarked in Cochrane's fleet.

San Martin hoped that the population of Peru would revolt for the cause of independence, as the Chilians had done, as soon as the patriot army afforded it a point of support against the Spaniards. He had accordingly taken advantage of the last raid made by Cochrane's fleet to distribute thousands of copies of a proclamation along the coast. But on landing at Pisco he discovered that the **Liberating Army in Peru** Peruvians maintained an attitude which, if not actually hostile, was as indifferent as that of the Venezuelans had been towards Miranda's proclamation. Besides this, immediately after his arrival news was received from Spain that the rule of the Cortes had been restored, and that this body had strongly recommended the Spanish governors to enter into negotiations with the champions of liberty. These negotiations, which, on account of San Martin's well-known opinions, were begun with far better prospects of success than those between Morillo and Bolivar in the north, made very slow progress; but this did not displease either party. San Martin hoped that time would thus be gained for a movement to arise among the people in favour of the liberating army.

The signs of any such movement had at first been surprisingly small, and it was against San Martin's principles to force upon the country the necessary change in its system of government. The royalists, on the other hand, considered that every day's delay was a distinct advantage to them, and would weaken the little San Martin's operations. Thus the Spaniards saw themselves shut in at Lima before they had once come into contact with San Martin's army. Since the threatened attacks from the coast and from the mountains rendered his position untenable, the viceroy finally resolved to abandon the capital. This was no very severe loss, as without the possession of the port of Callao, which the royalists still held, Lima possessed a moral rather than a strategic value.

San Martin did not display the activity in Peru that had been expected from him; but there were numerous and weighty reasons for this. He could not overcome his conviction that the mass of

THE MAIN STREET IN ASUNCION, THE CAPITAL OF PARAGUAY

expedition, which was disproportionately small for the important task it had undertaken. The landing at Pisco had the double object of finding out the disposition of the people and of sending an expedition into the Peruvian highlands. When these objects had been attained the troops were again embarked and landed at Huachi nearer the capital. The movement now began to make progress. The patriots came into touch with the enemy, even in the coast districts; and a Spanish regiment, in which the liberal tendencies then dominant in Spain had strongly developed, came over to them. Good news was also received from the highlands; the districts of Huaylas, Truxillo, Piura and others, formed patriotic detachments to support the people had no sympathy for the cause for which he was fighting. As long as he had to rely solely on his small command he could not risk a vigorous attack on the enemy, who outnumbered him many times. For him defeat meant annihilation, and even a victory on the field of battle implied no real progress. Besides this, his little force was weakened by the unhealthy climate of the coast; and finally the negotiations, conducted with great diplomatic ability on the Spanish side, gave hopes that the object in view could be attained without bloodshed. None the less, San Martin's waiting policy came in for much blame. Thus the evacuation of Lima occurred at the right time for impressing on his opponents the

GENERAL VIEW OF THE CITY, SHOWING THE HARBOUR IN BACKGROUND

THE PALACE OF THE URUGUAYAN GOVERNMENT

CHURCH OF THE MATRIZ, ONE OF THE CITY'S FINEST BUILDINGS

MONTEVIDEO, THE COSMOPOLITAN CAPITAL OF URUGUAY

5975

necessity for patience, though it was not, as soon became evident, accompanied by the important political and strategic consequences expected from it by the patriots.

The latter had hoped that the fall of the capital would be followed by a rising throughout the country, but in this they were once more deceived. They themselves could not actively follow up the Spaniards, whom the Peruvians allowed to retreat to Cuzco unmolested. Here the connection with Bolivia permitted the royalist army to be reconstructed in a very short time ; and it was even put in a condition for taking the offensive. San Martin had not dared to entrust the future of the country to a congress at Lima ; for it was by no means certain that such an assembly, if it did not degenerate into a mere farce, would not reject the aid of the liberators. Thus he had to content himself with declaring the independence of Peru without the sanction of the people, and with exercising an almost dictatorial power under the title of " protector." But the new government received little support from the people, and found itself in a position of constant danger, threatened both by Callao, the bulwark of the royalists, and by the army advancing to the attack from Cuzco, which far outnumbered its own.

San Martin Protector of Peru

The situation became worse when the royalists gained a victory at Ica and for a short time menaced the safety of Lima. Politically this event was a deliverance. What success had failed to do, necessity accomplished : the population of Lima rose for the cause of freedom and willingly attached themselves to San Martin's forces. The fruits of this movement were immediate victories. Callao had long been invested both by land and water, and the advance of the royalists was for the special object of reprovisioning it. San Martin allowed the Spanish Army to approach the immediate neighbourhood of the fortress ; but there he surrounded it from all sides ; and only a retreat, much resembling flight, saved it from the fate of being involved in the capitulation of Callao, which was now inevitable.

The Spanish Army Forced to Retreat

Nevertheless, San Martin saw the impossibility, with the limited force at his disposal, of securing the province against renewed attacks of the Spaniards from the highlands. As the struggle for independence had always seemed to him a common cause of all the colonies, he lost no time in seeking to come to an understanding with Bolivar as to a mutual plan of campaign, since united action was more likely to lead to swift and sure success than the separate operations, which had almost come to a standstill in both theatres of war. The two heroes of the War of Independence had for some time been in communication with each other, but had not got beyond the exchange of expressions of reciprocal good will.

The immediate occasion of this closer understanding was the circumstance that the harbour of Guayaquil, on the boundary between Peru and Quito, had risen for the cause of freedom, and had been placed by its junta under the joint protection of the two liberators. The object of the patriots of Guayaquil in taking this step was to avoid all dispute as to what province their town belonged to ; for though it was politically a part of the province of Quito it was geographically situated in the viceroyalty of Peru, with which its administration had been closely connected.

Strongholds of the Spanish Royalists

Cochrane's Pacific fleet had rendered the inhabitants of Guayaquil no little help in attaining their independence ; and Bolivar, too, had sent a small force to their aid. No one could then foresee that, in spite of the joint protectorate, consequences by no means favourable to the cause of freedom were to follow.

The victory of Boyaca had not led to the result Bolivar had expected from it. The Spanish flag still waved over Quito, and the fanatically royalist population of the provinces Popayan and Pasto placed insuperable obstacles in the way of the patriots' advance. It was this that caused Bolivar to agree to send a division of his army under Antonio José de Sucre to Guayaquil, in the hope that an attack on Quito from the east would divert the attention of the royalists and facilitate his advance from the north. But Sucre's first campaign was a failure.

After winning two battles, which caused him to under-estimate the strength of the enemy, he suffered a severe defeat at Huachi, the consequences of which he avoided only by skilfully arranging an armistice. Bolivar's attack also failed in its object. He had hoped to slip by the royalist positions at Pasto without attracting attention, and to seize Quito from the

A STRANGE PERUVIAN FESTIVAL: THE ANNUAL PROCESSION OF THE CHRIST OF THE EARTHQUAKE AT CUZCO

A famous annual procession of Cuzco is that of the Christ of the Earthquake, which is held every Easter Monday. The dawn of the day is heralded with joyous peals of bells from cathedral and churches, and before long a crowd of 10,000 Indians has taken possession of the square. In the gaudily draped balconies are the rich and wealthy, who, as the crucified Christ is borne by on a litter, throw baskets of flowers at the image. The first figure in the procession is that of San Blas, over whom an angel with folded wings holds a rose silk parasol. The second image is San Benito, the third is San Cristoval, leaning on a palm-tree, and the fourth San José. Next comes the Virgin Mary, strangely arrayed in Elizabethan costume.

north-east; but the enemy barred his way at Bombona and forced him to battle. He emerged victorious from the contest, but his plan became known to the enemy and was thus rendered impracticable. He was once more compelled to postpone the conquest of Quito, and retreated to the north-west. The liberators of the north

Quito in the Hands of the Patriots were freed from this embarrassing situation by San Martin's help. The latter had repeatedly suggested that he and Bolivar should take common action against either Quito or Cuzco, since in this way only would it be possible for their armies, each too weak for its own task, to overthrow the Spaniards in one of their strongholds.

But Bolivar, as usual, could not make up his mind to share the laurels he expected to win with an ally of equal rank, and constantly put off decisive action. Sucre, however, had little or nothing to risk in this respect, so he willingly accepted San Martin's unselfish offer to assist him in undertaking an offensive movement against Quito by handing over to him a part of his troops. With 1,500 Peruvian soldiers, and about the same number of his own, Sucre, in February, 1822, made an incursion into the districts of Loja and Cucenca, which had hitherto been held by the royalists.

When the latter gave him an opportunity of stopping their retreat at Riobamba he gained a decisive advantage, chiefly with the aid of his cavalry. Then, by a bold outflanking movement, he forced them to a decisive battle on the slopes of the volcano Pichincha. Here, again, the fortune of war favoured the combined patriots of the north and south, and Quito fell into their hands as the prize of victory. With this the back of the Spanish resistance in Ecuador was broken; and Bolivar could now hasten up to deck himself out with the laurels gained under the leadership of his subordinate. In the

Bolivar's Unbounded Ambition hope that the victory in Quito would be followed by a second united campaign against Cuzco and Bolivia, San Martin arranged for a meeting with Bolivar at Guayaquil. But this was not the way in which Bolivar's unbounded ambition could be satisfied.

There was some excuse for his incorporating Quito in the Colombian republic —though it had been conquered only by reason of the energetic support of the Peruvian-Chilian army—for Quito had always formed a part of New Granada. But the case of Guayaquil was not so simple; under the Spaniards there had been doubts as to which province it belonged to, and now it had set up an independent government. San Martin included this among the questions to be discussed at his meeting with Bolivar. But in Bolivar's mind the matter was already legally settled in favour of Colombia, and he actually put his idea in force. He did not wait for the appearance of his rival, but, to the surprise of all, suddenly appeared in Guayaquil and settled the matter with one word of command. While still on the way, San Martin received the news that Bolivar would be glad to receive him, as his guest, on Colombian soil.

Such circumstances as these did not augur well for the meeting between the two liberators in Guayaquil, and the fears entertained proved only too well grounded. The mystery surrounding their negotiations has never been fully cleared up; but so much is certain, that the two generals were unable to come to an understanding. To the astonish-

The Two Liberators in Conference ment of all concerned, San Martin suddenly departed from Guayaquil; nothing more was heard of a common plan of campaign; and San Martin now resolved on a step which he had not indeed contemplated for the first time at Guayaquil, but which was certainly hastened by the result of his interview with Bolivar.

After the victories of Callao and Quito, San Martin had arranged for the election of a congress to draw up a constitution for Peru. He had also the intention of resigning all his extraordinary powers in favour of this body. The latter step, however, was taken in accordance with certain concealed objects. San Martin did not believe in the possibility of establishing vigorous republics in the Spanish-American provinces. He saw the whole of the north in the hands of a dictator who, if enthusiastic for the cause of liberty, was nevertheless consumed by vanity and a thirst for fame. In the south he saw the attempt at a republican form of government in Chili and in Buenos Ayres on the verge of ruin, and the old provinces more or less involved in the general dissolution. On the other hand, the resistance of Peru had shown him how firmly monarchical sentiments were rooted in the hearts of the people ; and the introduction of a constitutional monarchy into the neighbouring empire of Brazil, which was accomplished without any serious political disturbance, furnished an additional argument in favour of this form of government. San Martin was in complete agreement with those of his countrymen in the Argentine Republic who had aimed at setting up a Spanish-American empire with a younger prince of the royal house at its head, at first through the agency of the Infanta Carlota, but afterwards through independent effort. He now worked, both

monarchic proposals. His character as little fitted him to play the part of Providence, after the manner of Bolivar, in the state he was at the time directing, as to take part in the inevitable civil war.

Thus he came to the conclusion that the only course open to him was to retire from public life. He seized on this way of escape the more readily because he was firmly convinced that, after his retirement, Bolivar's ambition would leave no stone unturned to complete the work of liberation and to add Peru and Bolivia to his Colombian republic. Thus San Martin

CELEBRATING THE BIRTHDAY OF AN ARGENTINE PRESIDENT
This illustration shows a review of troops in the Government Square at Buenos Ayres on the occasion of the seventy-first birthday of Señor Manuel Quintana, who assumed office on October 12th, 1904, and was, perhaps, the most popular president which the Argentine Republic has ever had. An admirer of Great Britain, Señor Quintana strove with considerable success to encourage commercial relations between the United Kingdom and the South American republic

in America and in Europe, by means of an ambassador sent across the ocean for this special purpose, at a scheme for establishing a great South American constitutional monarchy, in opposition to the South American Republic planned by Bolivar ; and he even hoped to see the Republic of Colombia incorporated in it. The meeting with Bolivar dashed all his hopes to the ground. Though the European outlook seemed to point to the rapid fulfilment of his plan, he found the general opinion in Peru, as well as in the allied states, decidedly unfavourable to his

resigned all his offices and titles into the hands of the congress that met on September 20th, 1822. Some of the delegates considered this a mere theatrical trick, such as Bolivar was wont to indulge in ; others expected that he would at least continue to act as commander-in-chief ; but he departed suddenly and secretly from Peru, and, disgusted with his experiences in Chili and the Argentine Republic, retired to Europe. Here he spent the remainder of his life in seclusion. San Martin's prophecies were largely justified by the course of events. If Bolivar did not immediately take his place in Peru, it was because of the strong current of public opinion which regarded his devouring ambition with strongly marked distrust. But circumstances proved to be more powerful than the weak government which had undertaken the guidance of Peru. Their contemptuous rejection of Bolivar's proffered aid deprived **Peru Lost to the Patriots** the Peruvians of a great part of their trained troops, and the military expeditions they attempted on their own account led to two severe defeats at Torata and Moquegua. Finally, they had no other resource than to beg humbly for the aid they had once refused to accept, and to appoint the president of the united Republic of Colombia dictator of Peru. But this step led to the outbreak of civil war in the latter country. Even a part of the army revolted against being handed over to Bolivar ; Callao again raised the Spanish banner above its impregnable walls ; and Lima was once more compelled to open its gates to the royalists. The immediate consequence of calling in Bolivar was that Peru was lost to the patriots.

Reorganising his army among the mountains of the north, Bolivar renewed his campaign in August, 1824. His first operations were favoured by fortune. He moved toward the south, through the valleys between the two chains of the Cordilleras, screened by swarms of guerrilla warriors, who appeared from all sides on the approach of the patriots. South of Pasco, on the Lago de Reyes, he came in touch with the enemy, who had advanced to meet him. The Battle of Junin was, in fact, a great cavalry engagement, in which the royalists were at first completely successful. But in their eagerness to pursue the retreating enemy they rushed by a body of Bolivar's cavalry without dispersing it. This body attacked them in the rear, riding down their scattered ranks ; and the Spanish suc- **Bolivar's Great Victory Over the Royalists** cess was thus converted into a disastrous defeat. The royalist leader, who thought that victory was in his grasp, was forced to fall back into the neighbourhood of Cuzco, a distance of 466 miles.

Bolivar was unable to move so rapidly, and when he again met with the enemy, on the Apurimac, the rainy season set in and put an end to operations. At this time Bolivar's dictatorial powers were considerably curtailed by the Congress of Colombia. He therefore resigned his position as commander-in-chief in favour of Sucre and returned to the northern provinces. From there he still directed military operations as long as communications could be maintained. At the end of November the Spaniards seized a position between Sucre and his base, so that he had no alternative but to fight. The royalists considered themselves sure of victory : Sucre was compelled to retreat by forced marches in order to avoid being cut off completely, and suffered considerable losses in the days preceding the battle. But neither he nor his army lost courage, however threatening the situation ; they knew that the safety of more than one expedition depended on their fate. On December 9th, 1824, the Spaniards—unfortunately for themselves —accepted the opportunity of joining battle repeatedly offered to them.

Sucre had chosen his position on the plain of Ayacucho with the greatest skill, and he directed the contest, which was almost entirely a hand-to-hand struggle, with extraordinary military talent. The victory was complete. The last **South America Achieves Independence** royalist army was entirely dispersed, and fourteen Spanish generals, with the few troops remaining on the field, laid down their arms. The independence of South America, fought for at Chacabuco and Maipu, Carabobo and Boyaca, was rendered certain at Ayacucho.

The surrender at Ayacucho was accepted by almost all the military posts still in possession of the royalists. Sucre did not disgrace his victory by unnecessary bloodshed, and an honourable capitulation secured for the defenders of Spanish claims an unmolested withdrawal from the country. Owing to his clemency he secured more than he could ever have expected.

Only in Callao did the Spanish commander continue his opposition for almost a year longer, although hostilities had now become practically without object ; for not only had the Spanish troops evacuated the land, but even the fleet had given up the hopeless contest in American waters. As a matter of fact, independence had been won at the beginning of the year 1825 ; the negative part of the war for freedom was over. Nothing further was necessary except to secure positive recognition for the new states and to constitute them into actual political structures,

AMERICA

INDEPEND-
ENCE OF
SOUTH AND
CENTRAL
AMERICA III

THE INDEPENDENT SOUTH SINCE THE REVOLUTION
THE NEW REPUBLICS IN PEACE AND WAR

AS might have been expected, the Spanish colonies, even during an early stage of their revolt, had applied for the support of the United States of North America, whose example they considered themselves to be imitating in their struggle for liberty and independence. There, however, they met with a distinct refusal. The United States, whose own political status was as yet by no means firmly assured, declared themselves determined to hold aloof from any interference which might entangle them with other Powers.

Various deputations, which in the course of the year made applications to England, met with a similar reply. There can be no question that both the United States and England were benevolently disposed towards the Spanish colonies, and they gave evidence of this feeling by not taking strict measures for preventing the despatch **Pan-American Congress at Panama** of private support from their harbours to the insurgent states. England, however, declared that the struggle of the colonies against the mother country was an internal matter in which, owing to her own close relations with Ferdinand VII., she was the less in a position to interfere. Thus the only open support given to the combatants came from the negro republic of Haiti, and was accorded the more readily owing to the fact that the revolted colonists had everywhere proclaimed the freedom of negro slaves in order to fill with them the thinned ranks of their own regiments, and had made slavery illegal. They did not suspect that by this action they were forfeiting the friendship of their nearest neighbours.

After his great victories in New Granada and Quito, Bolivar summoned a Pan-American congress at Panama, to which, besides the Spanish colonies, the North Americans also were invited. And, indeed, there was at the time a great party in the United States who were enthusiastic in their support of the idea of a Pan-American federation. One of the principal reasons put forth by the United States for not participating in this congress—which afterwards proved a deplorable failure—was that, by being **Ferdinand VII. Restored to the Throne of Spain** represented, they would be virtually sanctioning the abolition of negro slavery, and that their own representatives at the congress would in all probability be placed on an equal footing with the delegates of the Haitian Republic.

The revolution in Spain first brought about a change in public opinion, more especially when Ferdinand VII. was for a second time restored by the Holy Alliance to the throne of his fathers as absolute monarch. The revolutionary government was inclined, from principle, to make large allowances to the colonies, and when it saw that its power was becoming increasingly endangered it was willing to grant even the independence of a portion of the colonies in return for their support against France. The Argentine Republic might at that time have obtained recognition by severing itself from the rest of the colonies; but it refused offhand every offer of separate treatment.

The interference of the Holy Alliance next had the effect of separating Great Britain from the other Powers. That country declared that it would have to regard any attempt at a restoration of the status quo in the colonies as an unfriendly **The Famous Monroe Doctrine** act. Encouraged by this declaration, the president of the United States, James Monroe, enunciated in his message to congress the so-called Monroe Doctrine—frequently reiterated since then in utterly different circumstances—to the effect that the United States would view any attempt on the part of European Powers to conquer territories on American soil as an

INDEPENDENCE SQUARE: A SCENE IN QUITO, THE CAPITAL OF ECUADOR

unfriendly act towards itself. This declaration had at first little significance, for as yet Spain had not officially recognised the independence of South America, nor had the South American republics met with such recognition on the part of the United States. It was, however, a long step in that direction; for, Spain being forbidden to make any attempts at the restoration of its power over the seceded colonies, the full recognition of the independence of the latter could be a question only of time and expediency, subject to the one consideration as to what use the newly emancipated states would make of their liberty.

At that time, when the victory of Ayacucho had destroyed the last vestige of the Spanish power in America, not a single one of the old colonial provinces was organised on a firm basis. Buenos Ayres at first, without any real disturbances, gave signs of developing into a republic with the promise of vitality, though here, too, a rapid change took place in the form and personnel of the supreme executive. After the independence of the republic had been recognised in 1816, however, a congress was elected by a free popular vote, and at times, too, the Budget of this young state, which was still struggling for

GOVERNMENT BUILDINGS AND SQUARE AT TEGUCIGALPA IN THE HONDURAS REPUBLIC

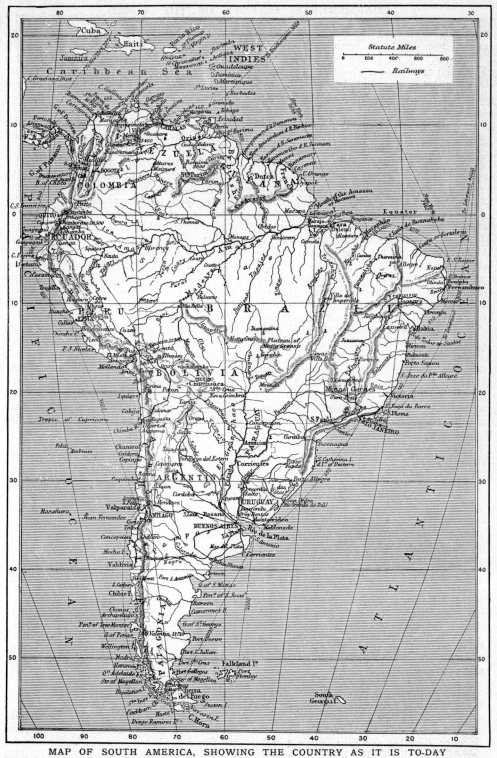

MAP OF SOUTH AMERICA, SHOWING THE COUNTRY AS IT IS TO-DAY

South America, since those days when the Spanish conquistadors found the country uncultivated and inhabited by a sparse population of Indians, has made gigantic strides along the paths of progress. The map on this page shows the country as it is to-day, with its many populous cities, its immense railroad systems, and every other sign of prosperity.

recognition, showed a balance. All these gains, however, were again entirely lost on the advent to power, in 1820, of the Federal party, which abolished the unity of the constitution, and not only acknowledged the independence of the seceded provinces of Bolivia, Paraguay and Uruguay, but also dissolved all connection

Collapse of Constitutional Authority
between the different provinces of the Argentine state *inter se* and with Buenos Ayres. The latter owed its endurance as the predominant power only to its geographical position, which brought it more in contact with foreign Powers than the inland provinces. Though historical tradition repeatedly led those in power for the time being at Buenos Ayres to assert the predominance of that province, yet for a considerable time its alliance with the neighbouring states rested on the basis of the complete sovereign independence of the contracting parties.

At that time the moral status of the government underwent a rapid decline. The revolution had been effected by men destined for leadership by their surpassing capacity. Belgrano, San Martin, Rivadavia, undeniably towered above the majority of their fellow-citizens in abilities and talents. The collapse of all constitutional power was a powerful factor in the production of a class of less honourable politicians. The victory of the federal idea was, in reality, the fruit of the ambition of local party leaders, whose principal aim, amid the general insecurity, was to obtain places for themselves and their supporters. To these aspirations the central party had no higher interests to oppose which might have sufficiently influenced the inexperienced masses.

Hence resulted the collapse of this party and the degeneration of governments. It is in this way only that we can understand the dictatorship of a man like Don Juan Manuel de Rosas, who by cunning and an

Rosas the President of Buenos Ayres
utter absence of principle rose from the office of steward in a hacienda to the presidency of Buenos Ayres ; next succeeded, by more or less doubtful means, in restoring the predominance of the latter state over the other provinces ; and under difficult circumstances maintained his place as dictator for more than twenty years. That during this régime every stir of an independent opinion was stifled in blood, that the security of life and property

was reduced to a mere fancy, and that in spite of this the man was not overthrown, must be simply ascribed to the fact that even the better-minded among the people were as yet absolutely incapable of forming a real idea of the loudly praised blessings of republican liberty.

Nor was Rosas' final overthrow due to a reaction for the restoration of law and order ; on the other hand, he fell in a struggle with people who were no better than himself. The sore point with the Argentine Republic was its relations with the seceded provinces, especially Montevideo, to which, apart from the Independent party in that province, Brazil was repeatedly making claims. After a previous struggle for the possession of Uruguay, Brazil and Buenos Ayres agreed to consider that state as independent, and jointly to guarantee its independence. There, too, however, existed different parties, each fighting for the helm of the ship of state ; and the support of a fallen president gave Rosas the welcome pretext of once more making his influence felt over Uruguay also. The war which

Rosas Falls from Power
resulted led, temporarily, even to the interference of France and England. It principally, however, served to bring into the field against Rosas a succession of ambitious party leaders, to whose attack his rule finally succumbed in 1852, on the battlefield of Monte Caceros.

Under the guise of a convinced federalist, Rosas had managed, though by the most violent means, to maintain a government based on a fairly firm policy of union ; his expulsion once more rendered the alliance of the Argentine Republic doubtful, and Buenos Ayres, for a considerable time, severed its connection with the latter. These contests, however, which were far less concerned with the federation of states or the formation of a republican union than with the acquisition of power by political parties, had hardly ceased at any time : revolutions in the republic itself, or civil wars between its various provinces, have endured up to the present day.

The most important of these struggles was with Paraguay. In this country, which was a republic merely in name, the dictatorship of Dr. Francia was followed by those of Carlos Antonio Lopez and his son Francisco Solano Lopez. While Francia had sought salvation for his state by strictly excluding it from all intercourse

Augusto B. Leguia, Peru   E. G. Navero, Paraguay   Colonel I. Montes, Bolivia

Dr. José F. Alcorta, Argentina   General J. V. Gomez, Venezuela   Dr. Claudio Williman, Uruguay

General Eloy Alfaro, Ecuador   Don Pedro Montt, Chili   Dr. Affonso Penna, Brazil

PRESIDENTS OF THE SOUTH AMERICAN REPUBLICS

with its neighbours, the two Lopez, by freely admitting foreigners of all sorts, considerably advanced its economic development. The younger Lopez, however, by interfering in the presidential conflicts of Uruguay, forfeited the friendship of the latter state, and in October, 1864, also that of Brazil; and while endeavouring to injure these opponents he also frivolously challenged the hostility of the Argentine Republic. In this manner arose the alliance of these three powers against Paraguay, which in the course of a five years' war lost almost its entire wealth, a considerable portion of its territory, and its political importance. Since that time, too, dictators appointed for life

Sucre's victory at Ayacucho. A congress summoned to Chuquisaca in August, 1825, declared the independence of the republic of Bolivia without a protest being lodged by either Peru or the Argentine Republic.

The young republic placed itself under the protection of Bolivar, and entrusted its future condition and development to his care. Nor did Bolivar allow the opportunity to escape of putting into substance his ideas of a constitutional government, but presented Bolivia with a constitution in which, as in the case of Angostura, provision was made for a president elected for life, a hereditary senate, and a lower house with limited powers. For himself Bolivar reserved the power of assuming,

THE METHOD OF SHIPPING NITRATE AT PISAGUA IN CHILI TWENTY YEARS AGO

have been replaced in that country by republican presidents. Nevertheless, internal disturbances have been by no means infrequent, even in Paraguay; though revolutions have not in that country become a chronic condition to the same extent as in Uruguay, where the party wars between Colorados and Blanquillos, dating from Rosas' interference down to our own times, have brought matters to such a pitch that hardly a president has ever completed his legal term of office.

Nor did the last of the provinces once belonging to the viceregal province of Buenos Ayres experience a better fate than its sister states. Upper Peru, now known as Bolivia, did not acquire its liberty until

subject to a decree of congress, dictatorial powers whenever he should enter Bolivian territory; but Sucre, the commander-in-chief at Ayacucho, was chosen as the constitutional president. The latter recognised much better than his master the dangers to which the Codice Boliviano exposed the young republic. He accepted the presidential office for only two years, but resigned before the expiration of that period when he perceived the extreme opposition with which the republican patriotic party viewed the aristocratic tendencies of the Colombian dictator.

Thus Bolivia, too, entered upon a period of successive military revolutions, which were interrupted only by the ten years' dictatorship of General Santa Cruz. The

CHILIAN SLOOP O'HIGGINS FIRING ON THE GARRISON IN VALPARAISO HARBOUR

EXCHANGE OF SHOTS BETWEEN SHORE BATTERIES AND CHILIAN IRONCLAD

THE CIVIL WAR IN CHILI IN 1851: HOSTILITIES AT VALPARAISO

latter was of Indian descent, had fought in the wars of liberation, and so greatly distinguished himself at the Pichincha as to merit his election to the highest office in the state. This, however, did not satisfy his ambition ; for, like Bolivar, he had dreams of a federation of all the American republics under his leadership.

Peru Declares its Independence The condition of Peru gave him an opportunity of seeing his plans realised. Though the dictatorship of Bolivar had ousted the National party, it had by no means extinguished it ; and as soon as the Spanish power had received its final blow it at once revived. The province endured with but little relish the guardianship of the Colombian republic, and when the internal complications of the latter called the dictator to the north, it shook off its yoke, and in 1827 declared itself independent.

This, however, was but the signal for the eruption of civil disturbances. Santa Cruz, delighted at having found his long-cherished wish for interference, contrived to bring about a closer connection of Peru with Bolivia, and, as chief of the alliance, wielded the highest power in both republics. In this capacity he rendered important services to the economic development of the states under his authority ; but his foreign policy was not equal to the difficulties of the situation and brought about the fall of his government and the end of the Peru-Bolivian Federation.

Chili was the rock upon which Santa Cruz was shipwrecked. In that state its first president, O'Higgins, had fallen a victim to democratic aims at the moment when San Martin in Peru gave up the struggle for the establishment of a constitutional monarchy in South America. For Chili also, furthermore, the rule of the so-called Liberals brought bad times ; between 1823 and 1831 that state had no less than thirteen governments and seven times changed its constitution. It was not

Chili's Rapid Succession of Governments until the presidency of Joaquin Prieto and the Conservative Constitution of 1833 that the development of Chili attained that stability which until recently has so favourably distinguished it from all the other Spanish-American republics. In the hope of attaching Chili to its confederacy of states, Santa Cruz had supported the attempt of the Chilian ex-president, Freire, who by force of arms aspired to lead the Liberal party to victory against Prieto and the Conservatives. But not only did Freire himself fall before the constitutional government of Prieto, but he also involved Santa Cruz in his defeat, inasmuch as Chili declared war against the Peruvian-Bolivian alliance on account of the interference of the latter in Chilian affairs. The war, which was but feebly conducted on the part of Santa Cruz, culminated in the complete victory of the Chilians at Yungay in 1839, and was followed by the complete independence of all three republics and the resignation of the Bolivian dictator.

Since that time a large number of presidents have followed one another in Bolivia in rapid succession, almost all having been raised to power and hurled from office by military pronunciamentos. Outstripped by all its neighbours, that country has on only one other occasion since played a part in history, and that an essentially passive one—namely, in the war between Chili and Peru in 1879.

The fall of Santa Cruz benefited Peru as little as it did Bolivia. Though more was done in this state for the economic

Presidents Who Failed in Office development of the country than in the other republics, more especially through the efforts of President Ramon Castilla (1844-1854), the internal policy of most of the presidents was nevertheless neither sufficiently prudent nor sufficiently unselfish to place the welfare of the state on a solid foundation. Its great natural resources were either squandered or were made the object of rash speculations which an old-established state could scarcely have survived. To the young republic they meant absolute ruin. When the natural resources of the central states, which had been the first to be exploited, were exhausted, the southern districts began, towards the end of the seventies, to be regarded as specially valuable.

The discovery of inexhaustible deposits of saltpetre and soda led to these barren deserts being looked to as a substitute for the guano deposits of the Chincha Islands, which had become unlicensed mining-grounds. Hitherto the borders of these somewhat dismal regions had received but little attention. Bolivia was, indeed, in possession of a narrow strip of territory extending to the Pacific Ocean and separating Peru from Chili, but had paid so little attention to it that it had almost resigned both its territorial claims and sovereign rights to Chili before the value of this possession was recognised. Thus it came about that not only in Atacama, the Bolivian coast province, but also in Tarapaca, the southernmost part of Peru, almost all industrial interests were in the hands of Chilian and other foreign subjects, who were here amassing riches, to the great envy of the real owners of the land. Having for a long time been in secret agreement, the opponents of Chili began hostilities, Bolivia in 1879 subjecting Chilian industries in Atacama to heavy tolls, and, on refusal of their payment, confiscating all Chilian property. Chili, however, was prepared for the struggle; its troops occupied, without serious resistance, the disputed strip of coast, and Bolivia during the whole war hardly made another attempt to recover its lost territory. The quarrel was really fought out between Peru and Chili, the former having stepped in on behalf of Bolivia in virtue of treaty obligations, and thereby given Chili the desired opportunity of declaring war. As long as the Peruvian fleet was successful in disputing with Chili its supremacy on the sea, the operations of the Chilians on land did not extend beyond investing the coast towns of the extreme south. But after the capture, October 8th, 1879, of the Huascar, the largest and swiftest of the Peruvian battleships, in an unequal fight against the Chilian fleet, both the fighting forces of the southern republic were able to act in concert and enter upon that succession of victories which culminated at Lima in

THE CHILI-ARGENTINA PLEDGE OF PEACE
Standing high in the very heart of the Andes, this colossal statue of Christ was erected in celebration of peace between Argentina and Chili, and on its pedestal bears this inscription: "Sooner shall these mountains crumble to dust than Argentines and Chilians break the peace which at the feet of Christ the Redeemer they have sworn to maintain." Photo: Rider Noble

January, 1881. Both in Peru and Bolivia the defeat was followed by the downfall of the existing government, and it was years before the relations of the conqueror to the conquered were accorded constitutional sanction. In the end, however, Chili was confirmed in the permanent possession of Atacama and Tarapaca, and in the temporary occupation of the provinces of Tacna and Arica; but the pledges given by Chili on that occasion have not been redeemed up to the present day. This victory was a brilliant justification for the Chilian Constitution, which had been decried as an enemy to liberty. To it undoubtedly must be attributed the fact that the government of Chili has since the constitution of 1833 been firmer and more concentrated than that of any other of the Spanish - American republics. The reproach hurled at this government, of being an enemy to freedom, is, however, utterly unfounded. Even under Manuel Montt (1851–1861), the true founder of Chilian prosperity, the development of the constitution on a liberal basis had been seriously begun, and his successors have not stood idle. Whether, however, the advances thus won by Chili have outweighed the disadvantages of subsequent party struggles, more violent and embittered than those experienced under the Conservative constitution of 1833, may well be left open to doubt. Upon them, at any rate, was based the conflict which, after a peace extending over decades, led in 1891 to a revolution and the violent downfall of the government. The experience that a war may be scarcely less dangerous to the conquering party in its

CYPRIANO CASTRO, EX-PRESIDENT OF THE VENEZUELAN REPUBLIC, AND HIS CABINET

industrial life than to the defeated one, once more proved itself true in the case of Chili. The extraordinary increase in the national wealth which had been the outcome of the war with Peru led to an extravagant activity in the industrial sphere. President José Manuel Balmacéda (1886–1891) especially had in this respect strained the resources of the country beyond their capacity. The financial crisis developed, however, into a political one when it was shown that these industrial speculations had been exploited from the public treasury for the personal advantage of the president and his creatures.

This imparted to the revolution, which was founded as much on political as on personal party considerations, an unexpected moral force, and in 1891, in a short time, procured for it an easy victory and one which was not exploited to excess. The fact remains, notwithstanding, that in Chili, too, the regular succession of constitutional governments was in this wise interrupted by a victorious military rising. The few years which have elapsed since then have sufficed to show that the civil power has not emerged from the struggle without having sustained a permanent shock. At the present time Chili has only a qualified claim to its former reputation of being the most trustworthy of the South American republics.

The republic of Colombia, too, the creation of which had been Bolivar's special pride, did not enjoy a long lease of life. While the liberator, reaping the fruits of Sucre's victory at Ayacucho,

THE IMPOSING BUILDINGS OF THE NATIONAL COUNCIL OF EDUCATION AT BUENOS AYRES

LOOKING WEST ALONG THE AVENUE DE MAYO

THE PASEO D' JULIO, WITH THE DOCKS IN THE DISTANCE

SCENE IN THE FASHIONABLE PALERMO PARK

BUENOS AYRES, THE CAPITAL OF THE ARGENTINE REPUBLIC

was holding his triumphal progress through Bolivia, his mind was already occupied with bold plans which again had for their object the expansion of his Colombian republic. At one time he was offering his aid to the Chilians in driving out the last remnants of the Spanish army of occupation from the archipelago of Chiloë ;

Bolivar Under Suspicion
at another he was planning with the Argentines an advance against Brazil, the last remaining division of the South American continent which was still under a monarchical constitution and which had not yet entirely severed its connection with the Old World.

His dictatorial power, however, and the aristocratic constitution which he had introduced in Peru and Bolivia, caused him to be looked upon with suspicion by republicans not only in foreign countries, but even in New Granada ; and, besides, neither in Chili nor in La Plata was there a dearth of ambitious generals who were ready to follow his own example for their own benefit. In the end the growing distrust of the Colombian Congress recalled him from the south, and his unconditional obedience to their behest was, perhaps, the best defence he could offer.

In Venezuela a strong party, with Paez at its head, had, ever since 1826, urged the separation of that country from the Colombian Republic. Indeed, the secession had almost become an accomplished fact when Bolivar yielded, and by all kinds of concessions succeeded in inducing his old comrades in arms once more to recognise his authority and that of the Colombian Congress. In the meantime an exactly similar movement took place in Peru, where, as in Bolivia, the Colombians had, from the beginning, been extremely unpopular.

As soon as the National party in that state saw itself freed from the menacing presence of the dictator, it rose in revolt, abolished

Peru's Revolt Against the Liberator
the government which Bolivar had established at Lima, and invited Bolivia to join it. The latter state responded to the invitation in a qualified manner by rising against Sucre and forcing him to resign. The Peruvians, however, proceeded even further ; they caused pronunciamentos to be issued at Guayaquil and other places in Ecuador. Under the pretext of protecting the latter against oppression, the Peruvian dictator Lamar

declared war against Colombia. Here, however, Sucre again saved the honour of the Colombian arms, and by his victory at Tarqui brought about a revolution against Lamar in Peru. The new government, though insisting, like so many of its predecessors, on the independence of Peru, nevertheless concluded peace on easy terms with its neighbour states.

Even at this time Bolivar had constantly to battle against a strong current of opposition which aimed at his deposition and the abolition of his dictatorship. After he had four times abdicated his government, in order only at the next moment to resume it with the most unlimited powers, his enemies determined to get rid of him by unconstitutional methods. After several unsuccessful attempts at revolution, a military rising took place on September 25th, 1828, at Bogota, having for its object the assassination of Bolivar. His almost miraculous escape, however, so utterly threw into confusion the plans of the conspirators that they were easily conquered, and once again Bolivar's cleverness induced him to seek for reconciliation with the vanquished

Death of the Great Bolivar
rather than for vengeance upon his enemies. He was, however, unable completely to disarm the party which, in the constant renewal of the extraordinary powers of his regime, saw a serious danger to liberty. At last, having once more in the congress of 1830 had recourse to the often-tried trick of a resignation, he had the painful experience of seeing it accepted, accompanied by all imaginable marks of esteem for his great exertions on behalf of liberty, while a successor was appointed in the person of Joaquin Mosquera. After somewhat prolonged hesitation Bolivar decided to submit to the decision of the congress. Having for some time been in ill health, he at length left the country in which he considered himself to have been treated with ingratitude, and died at Santa Marta on December 17th in the same year.

The Colombian Republic had come to an end even before his death. Venezuela shortly afterwards repeated the attempt to sever its connection with Colombia, and in 1830 these efforts assumed a new direction directly in opposition to the policy of Bolivar. Nor was the abdication of the latter able to stop the movement, for Paez and his following exercised

A TYPICAL GAUCHO, SHOWING HORSE PECULIAR TO THE REPUBLIC

THE GAUCHOS AT HOME: VIEW OUTSIDE A RANCH

GAUCHO MUSICIAN WITH THE NATIONAL GUITAR

GAUCHO TYPES OF THE ARGENTINE REPUBLIC

unlimited control over the legislative assembly. All attempts to resist the new order of things were suppressed without much bloodshed, and before the close of the year Venezuela, within the range of the old general captaincy of Caracas, declared itself an independent republic. The same thing happened in Bolivia, with

Republic of New Granada this difference, that that state upheld with gratitude the memory of its liberator and offered him an asylum when he laid down his offices in Colombia; an offer which he refused, as also the invitation to assume once more the government, sent to him after a successful revolution against the régime of Mosquera. In the following year, 1831, the very name of Colombia disappeared; the provinces which still adhered to the government of Bogota constituted themselves into the Republic of New Granada, and, under a Conservative constitution, handled vigorously by a series of energetic presidents, enjoyed until 1857 a fairly undisturbed—indeed almost peaceful—development.

Here also, however, the unfortunate civil war between the Central and Federal parties afterwards broke out afresh, and the cause of the latter party, which was more than usually justified by the extraordinary differences in the geographical features of the separate provinces, was in the end successful. Under the name of the United States of Colombia they adopted, in 1861, a constitution planned on exactly the same lines as that of the United States of North America. Since then the country has, under more peaceful conditions, been able to devote itself largely to the development and the opening up of its many industrial resources.

Venezuela underwent a similar development. During the first twenty years José Antonio Paez, either in the capacity of president (1830-1838, 1839-1842), as dictator (1846), or merely as adviser of the parties in power, virtually directed the destinies of the state for whose liberation he, next to Bolivar, had done the most. His vigorous government assured peaceful times to the republic. Here too, however, a federal constitution on the North American pattern gained an increasing number of supporters, although such a constitution could hardly be said to have arisen out of natural conditions, but had become the watchword of the Liberal party more from a love of imitating North American political institutions. Venezuela belongs to those states of Spanish America which have been least able to establish themselves on a solid basis. After a civil war extending over several years, in which Paez also once more — 1861-1863 — took up arms in defence of the unity of the republic, the provinces, in 1864, formed themselves into the Federal Republic of "the United States of Venezuela." In spite of this, civil commotions broke out over and over again; and it was not until the almost dictatorial régime of Antonio Guzman Blanco (1870-1877, 1879-1884, and 1886-1887) that the republic enjoyed a temporary peace.

During recent years the Argentine Republic has succeeded in restoring the confidence in its financial stability which at one time sank to a very low ebb. Venezuela has succeeded, on the other hand, in attracting the public attention of Europe by her lighthearted disregard of obligations, financial and other; especially under her recently ejected president, Castro. In 1896 her claims in a boundary dispute with Great Britain led to an arbitration under which the British views

President's Vagaries Lead to Ejection were practically confirmed. At a later date President Castro's attitude brought about a visit of German and British warships acting in concert, with some loss of dignity to both those Powers and some histrionics in connection with the Monroe Doctrine on the part of the United States. Subsequently, however, the president's vagaries resulted in his ejection from the country, and Venezuela has once more relapsed into comparative quiescence.

PLAZA MAYO, BUENOS AYRES, WITH GOVERNMENT HOUSE AND STATUE OF LIBERTY

ESSENTIAL INFORMATION ABOUT SOUTH AMERICA

There are in South America ten independent states, of which the areas, populations, and other details are as follow:

State.	Square miles.	Population.	Capital.	Population of Capital.	National Debt (external).	Revenue (1907).	Imports.	Exports.
					£	£	£	£
Argentine Republic	1,113,849	4,794,149	Buenos Ayres	1,057,000	72,366,000	21,112,000	57,172,000	59,240,000
Bolivia	567,430	2,300,000	La Paz	67,235	None	1,132,000	1,691,563	2,461,078
Brazil	3,218,130	18,386,815	Rio de Janeiro	811,265	69,821,057	31,048,960	40,527,603	54,176,898
Chili	290,829	2,712,145	Santiago	378,000	20,200,000	16,500,000	14,175,000	19,875,000
Colombia	504,773	4,600,000	Bogota	100,000	2,700,000	3,198,575	12,088,563	13,791,442
Ecuador	125,000	1,271,000	Quito	80,000	3,320,750	1,319,500	1,573,389	1,856,566
Paraguay	157,000	660,000	Asuncion	60,259	None	614,400	935,703	1,046,554
Peru	695,733	4,609,999	Lima	130,000	None	2,679,266	5,514,787	5,747,732
Uruguay	72,210	900,600	Montevideo	309,390	27,079,985	4,485,081	7,330,833	7,114,444
Venezuela	593,943	2,444,816	Caracas	80,000	5,744,605	2,115,385	1,987,657	3,116,149

In all the South American republics the metric system of weights and measures is the legal standard, although the old Spanish and Portuguese standards still linger in commercial practice. But in all the customs houses the metric system is the standard enforced.

The agricultural and mineral industries of the countries, the chief exports, and the currency are as follow:

ARGENTINE REPUBLIC.

AGRICULTURE. Wheat, maize, linseed, sugar, wool, cattle, sheep, horses.

MINERALS. Manganese, wolfram.

CHIEF EXPORTS. Frozen meat, wheat.

The Argentine Republic is on the point of introducing a gold standard, and the paper dollar will be redeemed at 44 cents gold—that is, 1s. 9·12d. The new monetary unit will be of the same value as the franc.

BOLIVIA.

AGRICULTURE. Rice, barley, oats, maize, cotton, indigo, rubber, coca, potatoes, fruits, and barks.

MINERALS. Tin, gold, silver, copper.

CHIEF EXPORTS. All the above.

The standard of currency is gold, 5 pesos = £1 sterling.

BRAZIL.

AGRICULTURE. Timbers, sugar, coffee, cotton, cocoa, rubber, tobacco, cereals, cassava, and nuts.

MINERALS. Gold, silver, iron, diamonds, topazes.

CHIEF EXPORTS. Coffee, rubber, cotton, cotton seed, hides and skins, cocoa, yerba maté, tobacco, sugar, gold.

The currency is based on that of Portugal. The milreis (1,000 reis) has a par value of 2s. 2½d. A conto is 1,000 milreis, and a conto of contos is 1,000 contos.

CHILI.

AGRICULTURE. Most cereals, wine, tobacco, flax, hemp, Chili pepper, potatoes.

MINERALS. Copper, gold, silver, coal, nitrate of soda.

CHIEF EXPORTS. Nitrate of soda, iodine, copper, silver, corn, flour, hides, guano.

In January, 1910, a gold currency is to be introduced, and the paper money is to be redeemed at 1s. 6d. per peso. At present the English sovereign has a legal value of 13⅓ pesos.

COLOMBIA.

AGRICULTURE. Coffee, cotton, plantains, bananas, tobacco, wheat.

MINERALS. Gold, silver, platinum, copper, lead, coal, emeralds.

CHIEF EXPORTS. Coffee, precious metals, hides, rubber.

The monetary unit is the gold dollar, five of which make £1 sterling.

ECUADOR.

AGRICULTURE. Cinchona, cocoa, vegetable ivory, cotton, coffee, rubber, yarns, tobacco, sarsaparilla, wheat.

MINERALS. Gold, quicksilver, lead, iron, and copper.

CHIEF EXPORTS. Cocoa, rubber, cinchona, panama hats, coffee, cattle.

The gold standard coin is the condor, which is of the exact value of a British sovereign. The sucré is a silver coin, value 2s., and ten make a condor.

PARAGUAY.

AGRICULTURE. Maize, rice, coffee, manioc, tobacco, sugar cane, oranges, rubber, quebracho, Paraguay tea (or maté), cattle.

MINERALS. These are not of commercial importance.

CHIEF EXPORTS. Oranges, hides, tobacco, maté, timber.

The currency is based on the silver dollar, which is normally worth 4s., and contains 100 centavos.

PERU.

AGRICULTURE. Sugar, rubber, medicinal plants, cocoa, coffee.

MINERALS. Gold, silver, quicksilver, copper, coal, petroleum.

CHIEF EXPORTS. Sugar, metallic ores, guano, gold, silver, cotton, wool, rubber.

The standard gold coin is the libra, which is the exact equivalent of a sovereign. A sol (= 2s.) is the tenth part of a libra.

URUGUAY.

AGRICULTURE. Wheat, barley, maize, cattle, wool.

MINERAL. Gold.

CHIEF EXPORTS. Wool, hides, horn, hair, tallow, beef.

The currency is on a gold standard, although the only gold coins in circulation are foreign. The dollar has 100 centavos, and is nominally worth about 4s. of English money.

VENEZUELA.

AGRICULTURE. Sugar cane, coffee, cocoa, cereals, rubber, cattle.

MINERALS. Gold, silver, copper, iron, tin, salt, asphalt, lead, sulphur, coal.

CHIEF EXPORTS. Coffee, cacao, balata, cattle, hides.

The Venezuelan currency is based on the bolivar, which equals 1 franc approximately. Silver dollar = 5 bolivars = 48¼d. The peso is not a coin, but is used in accounts, and equals 4 bolivars.

The South American possessions of European powers are as follow:

—	Square miles.	Population.	Capital.	Population of Capital.	Exports.
UNITED KINGDOM—					£
British Guiana	120,000	283,278	Georgetown	53,176	1,843,107
Falkland Islands	6,500	1,789	Stanley	916	185,227
FRANCE—					
French Guiana	30,450	30,300	Cayenne	12,612	492,094
HOLLAND—					
Dutch Guiana	40,060	66,490	Paramaribo	34,870	395,797
Curacao	403	53,466	Willemstad	10,000	76,854

In British Guiana, the chief industries are sugar, timber and gold. The chief exports are sugar, rum, molasses, balata, timber, gold and diamonds. The colonial currency is the gold dollar, worth 4s. 2d., but British coins also circulate. British weights and measures are used.

In the Falkland Islands industry is entirely stock-raising, and the exports are wool, hides, leather and tallow. The currency and the weights and measures are as in the United Kingdom.

In Dutch Guiana, or Surinam, the industries and exports are chiefly sugar, cocoa, fruits, coffee, rice and gold. Curacao consists of the islands of Curacao, Aruba, St. Martin, St. Eustache and Saba. The chief products are maize, beans, pulse, cattle salt and phosphate of lime. Gold is worked to a small extent. Curacao oranges are used in the manufacture of Curacao liqueur, which is made in Holland. The currency and the weights and measures are as in Holland [see page 5363].

In French Guiana gold is the only export, and the currency and weights and measures are those of France [see page 5398].

POSTAGE. United Kingdom to South America: For letters, printed papers and samples to British Guiana and Falkland Islands, rates are as for New Zealand [see page 1002]; to all other places in South America, as for France [see page 5398]. Parcels to the Argentine Republic, Chili, Colombia (except departments of Cauca and Narino), Peru, Uruguay and Dutch Guiana, are 2s., 3s., and 4s. for 3lb., 7lb., and 11lb. respectively. To British Guiana and Falkland Island, rates are 1s., 2s., and 3s. respectively, and to French Guiana, 3s., 3s. 6d., 4s. The rates to the departments of Cauca and Narino (in Colombia) are 3s., 4s. 6d., and 6s.; to Ecuador, 4s. 6d., 5s., 5s. 6d.; to Venezuela, 3s. 8d., 4s. 1d., and 4s. 6d. Rate to Bolivia is 3s. 6d. for 7lb. or less; to Brazil 3s. 6d. up to 3lb., and 4s. up to 6lb.; to Paraguay, 2s. 8d. up to 3lb., and 4s. up to 7lb. Limit of length, breadth or depth to Bolivia, Brazil, Ecuador, Paraguay and Venezuela, is 2ft., and of length and girth combined, 4ft.. To other countries, former limit is 3½ft.. and latter is 6ft.

TELEGRAMS. Rates per word vary according to routes and according to the place in the countries and colonies. Argentine, Paraguay and Uruguay, 3s. 10d. to 4s. 2d.; Bolivia and Ecuador, 5s. 9d.; Brazil, 3s. to 6s. 5d.; Chili, 3s. 10d. to 5s. 9d.; Colombia, 5s. 6d. to 5s. 9d.; Peru, 5s. 9d. to 7s. 9d.; Venezuela, 7s. 2d. to 7s. 7d.; to British Guiana, 7s.; to Dutch and French Guiana, 6s. 9d.; to Falkland Island, no service.

THE FRENCH ARMY UNDER MARSHAL BAZAINE ENTERING THE CITY OF MEXICO IN 1863

Napoleon III., for the ostensible purpose of obtaining satisfaction for wrongs and injustices done to the foreign population of Mexico, despatched troops under Bazaine to the republic in 1863. He had originally enlisted the co-operation of England and Spain in his enterprise, but the two latter Powers, finding that his real object was not to obtain indemnification for suffered losses, but to overthrow the existing government with a view to replacing it by a monarchy under the protection of France, promptly withdrew their support from the scheme.

From the painting by Beaugé at Versailles

MEXICO AND ITS REVOLUTIONS
THE TRAGIC HISTORY OF MAXIMILIAN

DURING the whole period of the South American wars of liberation Mexico stood aside and pursued its own road. After the overthrow of Hidalgo and his adherents Spanish rule seemed once more established, and even the introduction and re-abolition of the democratic constitution of 1812 passed off without incident. Naturally, the events which were passing all around in states allied by race could not entirely fail to react upon the mind of the population; but the desire for freedom and independence was not strong enough to aim at the subversion of the existing order of things. The revolutionary impulse in this country took its start from an entirely different quarter.

The viceroy had bestowed his confidence in a special degree upon the principal lieutenant, Iturbide, who, though a Mexican by birth, had not only distinguished himself by his energy and zeal, but also by his **Mexico in the Throes of Revolution** cruelty in the struggle against the forces of Hidalgo. Iturbide, however, abused the trust reposed in him. He engaged in secret schemes with the Creole leaders and the scattered partisans of Hidalgo, and, though ostensibly he took the field against one of the latter, he caused the promulgation in the little town of Iguala of a military pronunciamento the point of which was directed against Spanish rule. In the programme of a constitution which he drew up Mexico was declared independent, and a constitutional assembly was held in prospect. The country, however, was declared a monarchy in anticipation, the throne of which was to be offered to Ferdinand VII. and the other princes of his house.

Iturbide's following increased with astonishing rapidity, so that the viceroy and the Spanish party soon saw themselves confined to the capital. At that moment the arrival of a viceroy appointed by a Liberal Spanish Government terminated the revolution without bloodshed. The new regent accepted Iturbide's plan almost in its entirety, and returned to Spain in person in order to exert himself in its behalf at the court of Ferdinand VII. Had one of the king's brothers decided at that time to go over to Mexico, that state would in all probability have been preserved to the Bourbon dynasty. **Republic Proclaimed in Mexico** The rejection of the Iguala plan, on the other hand, pushed its originators farther along on the road to revolution. Since the provisional arrangement threatened in the end to become dangerous to all parties, Iturbide allowed himself to be proclaimed emperor of Mexico by his adherents in May, 1822, in order in this manner to save his constitutional edifice. His following, however, was neither large enough nor his past career sufficiently stainless to force the country to accept his rule. Hostile pronunciamentos were promulgated in the most widely different provinces, and as early as March, 1823, the emperor was obliged to seek refuge on board an English ship.

Thereupon Mexico, too, was proclaimed a republic. It was, however, a republic merely in name, while a succession of more or less fortunate military pretenders were fighting for Iturbide's inheritance. The most prominent figure in this struggle was General Antonio Lopez de Santa Ana—Santana—who had already taken a conspicuous part in the overthrow of the emperor, and afterwards appointed and deposed presidents at his own free will and pleasure until finally he himself accepted the chief office in the state, which he was destined more than once to lose and to recover. He is, however, **Santa Ana the Great Figure of the Struggle** undeniably entitled to the credit of having adhered in his internal administration to a strong policy of centralisation, as opposed to the federal doctrine which had sprung up out of a blind zeal for imitating the North American constitution, a zeal which was entirely unjustified from both geographical and historical considerations; while in his

THE CAPTURE OF THE HARBOUR OF SAN JUAN DE ULUA BY THE FRENCH IN 1838

Mexico, finding herself both on the verge of bankruptcy and in a state of revolution, sought to recover her financial position by laying hands on the property of foreigners, thus violating treaty rights. This led to the interference of France. The above picture shows an incident in the initial stages of the war that followed, when, on November 27th, 1838, a French man-of-war took possession of the harbour of San Juan de Ulua. The war ended with the parties in power agreeing to make no further encroachment upon the property of foreigners.

THE FRENCH TROOPS IN MEXICO: CAPTURE OF THE TOWN OF PUEBLA

A long and bitter struggle followed the entry of the French into Mexico. With a force of 30,000 men Puebla was captured, but only at the expense of many hundreds of lives. Then Mexico opened its gates to the conquerors, thus paving the way for the proclamation of the Archduke Maximilian of Austria as emperor. A series of internal wars marks the history of the republic for the next two years, a condition of affairs which culminated in the evacuation by the French of the country, the downfall of Napoleon, and the execution of Maximilian.

From the painting by A. Beaugé at Versailles

foreign policy he deserves recognition for having manfully and repeatedly, at the risk of his own personal safety, defended the honour and integrity of the country.

Mexico, however, was drawn into international complications to a greater extent than the other Spanish-American republics. As late as 1829 the Spaniards had made an **Mexico Declares** attempt to reconquer the **War on the** country, but had been de-**United States** feated by Santa Ana and forced to capitulate. The rising which occurred in Texas in 1836 was primarily an internal matter, since at that time the borders of Mexico still embraced the Far West of North America.

Santa Ana in his attempt to bring the province back to its obedience was defeated on April 20th, 1836, and taken prisoner, as a result of which the Separatists gained the upper hand. Under the presidency of Houston, an American, Texas formed an independent republic which from its origin linked its fortunes closely with the United States, and in 1845 was, on its own application, actually received into the Union. Mexico was not prepared to accept this rebuff calmly ; it declared war against the United States and entrusted Santa Ana with the chief command. The Mexican Republic, torn by internal factions and on the verge of financial ruin, was, however, no match for the States. The invasion of the northern provinces by the United States troops met with no serious opposition, nor were the Mexicans able to prevent the landing of the enemy's forces at Vera Cruz.

It is true that Santa Ana repeatedly opposed their advance, but he suffered one defeat after another, and finally fled to Jamaica at the very time when the troops of the Union were dictating the terms of peace to their opponents in their own capital. By this treaty Mexico surrendered its claims to Texas and all its northern Pacific provinces against an indemnity of three million pounds.

The Fall In 1853 Santa Ana was once **of** more summoned to undertake, **Santa Ana** as dictator, the management and restoration to order of the exhausted state—a task which he took in hand with his wonted energy ; but he was hardly likely to restore internal order, seeing that since December 17th, 1853, he had openly been aiming at securing himself in a position of permanent authority. Accordingly, in 1855, his fall was brought about by fresh pronuncia-

mentos. Thereupon Mexico was again plunged into a state of revolution which once more drew down upon the unfortunate country the interference of foreign Powers. The prolonged condition of lawlessness had brought the state to the verge of bankruptcy; and, as may be easily conceived, during the period of financial stress the parties in power had not infrequently laid hands on the property of foreigners, in violation of treaty rights. As early as 1838 similar proceedings had led to a war with France, which had temporarily taken possession of the harbour of San Juan de Ulua. In 1861 President Carlo Benito Juarez, after long party struggles, had managed to secure for himself the supreme authority, though by no means without opposition.

When he once more began to make illegal encroachments upon the property of foreigners, Napoleon III., who by the glory of foreign exploits was endeavouring to make people forget the unconstitutional origin of his imperial rule, seized this opportunity and proposed to England and Spain to vindicate the rights of their subjects in Mexico by a common expedi-**French** tion against that country. The **Victories in** proposal was accepted in the **Mexico** first instance by both parties ; and an army composed of contingents from all three states occupied Vera Cruz and advanced to Orizaba. But first England and afterwards Spain withdrew from the enterprise as soon as the allies saw that France was by no means actuated merely by a desire to obtain indemnification for suffered losses, but was in reality aiming at the overthrow of the existing government with the view of replacing it by a monarchy under its own protection.

Deceived by the whispered insinuations of Mexican fugitives, the French believed that the people would flock to them *en masse* and accompany them in triumph to their capital. Instead of this, they received at Puebla so hot a reception that they were only too glad again to reach and hold their former quarters at Orizaba. Nor was the expeditionary force able to resume its advance until it had been reinforced to 30,000 men. After a bitter struggle for the possession of Puebla, which ended with the capitulation of the Mexican garrison, Mexico also opened its gates to the conqueror. With this the object of the expedition seemed achieved. A junta, rapidly summoned, appointed a

THE ALAMEDA, MEXICO'S BEAUTIFUL PUBLIC GARDEN

PLAZA MAYOR, SHOWING THE FAMOUS ZOCALO GARDEN

IN THE CITY OF MEXICO, THE HANDSOMEST CAPITAL OF AMERICA

provisional government which a few days afterwards laid before the congress the plan of a constitution creating a monarchy under the name of an empire. The proposal was accepted by an overwhelming majority—indeed, almost unanimously. The candidate selected by Napoleon, of whose acceptance he had assured himself previous to taking any action, was the Archduke Maximilian of Austria. Hence, when a deputation of the provisional government proceeded to Miramare to offer the archduke the imperial crown of Mexico, the latter readily accepted the new dignity. In April, 1864, in the harbour of Trieste, he went on board the Novara, which was to convey him to Vera Cruz. The voyage was quickly

control. Bazaine was almost a sort of supplementary or accessory king in Mexico, and his powers in this capacity increased in proportion as the mutual confidence between the emperor and the marshal disappeared. The contracts, moreover, showed that the interference of the French in favour of Maximilian was by no means as unselfish as it had appeared to be. The financial demands made upon the country were extremely oppressive and unjustifiable in so far as, under the pressure of French policy, an unworthy speculation for the exploitation of Mexico was carried on with demands of a highly questionable nature. These in themselves were factors foreboding little good to Maximilian's authority. He

GENERAL VIEW OF RIO DE JANEIRO IN THE YEAR 1835

accomplished, and the people greeted their new sovereign with frank and open-hearted joy. On his entry into Mexico the party of opposition, at whose head was ex-President Benito Juarez, seemed practically vanquished.

Its importance, however, revived and increased with astonishing rapidity in consequence of the internal difficulties which the new imperial government was destined to encounter. From the very beginning Maximilian was not his own master. By his contracts with Napoleon III. he was indeed assured of the assistance of the French troops; but in the person of their commander-in-chief, Marshal Bazaine, he was associated with a power over which he exercised only the most limited

himself fully recognised that the protection of a foreign Power would alienate from him the sympathies of an important party in the country. He therefore not only endeavoured to withdraw himself as much as possible from French influence, but also made efforts to keep himself above the parties which divided the country into two hostile camps. The people, however, were not at this time ripe for such a high-minded policy.

While the Conservative party, which had raised Maximilian to the throne, found itself deceived in its expectations, the Liberals looked upon his conciliatory attitude as a confession of weakness, and soon began to take fresh courage, the more so as they had found a support which

IN THE HEART OF THE CITY: THE FIFTEENTH OF NOVEMBER SQUARE

PANORAMIC VIEW SHOWING THE MOST WONDERFUL BAY IN THE WORLD

SCENES IN RIO DE JANEIRO, THE CAPITAL OF THE REPUBLIC OF BRAZIL

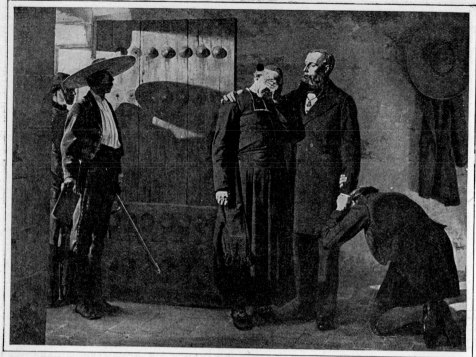

THE LAST MOMENTS OF THE EMPEROR MAXIMILIAN, JUNE 19TH, 1867

The last great tragedy in the history of Mexico occurred on June 19th, 1867. Maximilian, who two years before had been proclaimed emperor by Napoleon III., found himself called upon to defend his empire against the standard of revolt raised by the deposed President Juarez. While defending Queretaro with troops of 8,000 men, he was, on the night of May 19th, betrayed by General Lopez. The above picture shows the ill-starred emperor's last moments; he has breakfasted and taken the sacrament, and is preparing to accompany the two officers to the place of execution.

From the painting by Jean Paul Laurens

promised a much surer protection than France was capable of offering to their opponents. French interference was confessedly directed against the United States, the enormous expansion and rapid rise of which filled the monarchs of Europe with anxious apprehension. Napoleon thought he had seized upon a specially favourable moment for interfering at a time when the war of secession kept the United States busily occupied with their own internal affairs. The rapid and complete victory of the northern states, however, left their hands free, and tended only to make them assume a more vigorous attitude in regard to the Mexican question. They indeed still looked upon Juarez as the sole legal authority in Mexico at a time when the latter, on his own absolute decision, had prolonged the term of his expired presidency, and was actually wandering as an exile on the extreme confines of the country. To Napoleon the prospect that the French support of Maximilian might give to the United States a pretext for invading Northern Mexico seemed extremely annoying. Instead, however, of openly avowing the situation and endeavouring to the best of his power to bring about a solution in some other way, Napoleon made the non-fulfilment of its financial obligations by the Mexican Government the miserable pretext for simply sacrificing Maximilian after leaving him for a long time faltering between hope and fear.

COINAGE OF THE EMPEROR MAXIMILIAN

6004

Maximilian, it is true, had not shown himself equal to the task of controlling the extraordinarily difficult condition of Mexican affairs. His wavering attitude between the Mexican parties and his irresolute policy in regard to France had done much to impair the stability of his throne. To add to these troubles his health gave way, and he was also afflicted by the unfortunate condition of his wife, Charlotte, who had become insane while making vain efforts in Paris and Rome to further her husband's cause. At the time when the French troops began to be withdrawn from Mexico he seemed to have resolved on abdicating. All of a sudden, however, he returned and placed himself at the head of the feeble army which was making painful efforts to maintain his rule. But it was too late. Betrayed by his own generals at Queretaro about the middle of May, after a short informal trial he, in company with the last of his faithful adherents, was shot by the Republicans on June 19th, 1867.

CHARLOTTE, EX-EMPRESS OF MEXICO
The sister of Leopold, King of the Belgians, and the wife of the Emperor Maximilian, she shared with the latter his troubled reign in Mexico. Her husband's tragic fate so affected her that her reason gave way under the grief and excitement, but she is still alive.

Juarez had now an easy task. Once more in possession of power, he showed himself, as a politician, much better adapted for the work than his predecessors. Under the form of a republic, Mexico, since 1866, has been virtually subjected to the dictatorship of two men—Benito Juarez (1867–1872) and Porfirio Diaz (1877–1881, and since 1884 without interruption). Pronunciamentos and revolutions have undoubtedly been as frequent among the orders of the day in that country as in the rest of Spanish America. Nevertheless, through the enlightened despotism of these two men, the country has recovered much that had been lost during the period of continuous revolutions. In alliance with its Spanish sister republics, it has made slow but certain and unmistakable progress on the road to true republican liberty. When Iturbide, in 1821, brought the Spanish dominion in Mexico to a sudden end, the movement in favour of independence also spread to the general captaincy

RUINS OF THE HOUSE WHERE MAXIMILIAN STAYED DURING THE SIEGE OF MEXICO CITY

THE HISTORIC RESIDENCE OF THE RULERS OF MEXICO: THE PALACE OF CHAPULTEPEC

Towering on a rocky hill and surrounded by a magnificent grove of cypresses, the palace of Chapultepec dates from 1783-85, and occupies the site where once stood the palace of the mighty Montezuma. For long it was the residence of the Mexican rulers, but of recent years it has been devoted to the housing of some of the executive departments of the government, including the official offices of the president. The inset picture shows the throne from which the ill-fated Emperor Maximilian directed his brief but momentous rule over Mexico.

of Guatemala, which embraced the states north of the Isthmus of Panama as far as the boundaries of the kingdom of New Spain. Here, though the revolution, so far as separation from Spain was concerned, was accomplished without bloodshed, civil war at once broke out between the two parties of the Serviles and the Liberals.

The former began, in opposition to the constitutional assembly, to carry through the union of Central America with the empire of Iturbide. This, however, involved them in the fall of the latter, which followed soon after, and destroyed their influence in the country, the separate divisions of which now took up the management of their own affairs under the guidance of the Liberals and became the small republics of Central America. Even this, however, did not entirely destroy the feeling of their kinship. Only Chiapa severed its connection with its old allies and attached itself to the Mexican republic. Guatemala, Honduras, San Salvador, Nicaragua and Costa Rica, on the other hand, formed themselves, April 1st, 1823, into a federal union which in 1825 chose its first president in the person of General Acre. This, however, was the **The States of Central America** signal for the beginning of an incessant civil war which, while professedly defending the cause of federal or central principles, was in reality merely a struggle of self-seeking party-leaders for the possession of power.

Continuous attempts have been made, either by diplomatic methods or by resort to arms, to revive a confederation of all or some of the old states of Central America. While, however, these complications have in many cases seriously interrupted the steady progress of the republics concerned, the advantages which their union was to have produced have not been attained. It has never yet been possible to discover a form of government providing safeguards against the subjection of the weaker members of the union by the stronger states. For this reason, hitherto, every attempt at combination has shortly afterwards been followed by a revolution tending towards decentralisation.

The last attempt in this direction, the "Republica Mayor de Centro-America," created in 1896–97, although it left complete internal autonomy to the separate states, came to an end after a brief existence in 1898. The collapse of the throne of Maximilian marked the triumph of republican principles over the whole of the American continent except Brazil. The threat of a French invasion under Junot in 1808 had, indeed, induced the Portuguese royal family to transfer the seat of government to Rio de Janeiro ; but this was considered merely a temporary precautionary measure which was to make no change in the **Triumph of Republican Principles** political relations between the mother country and the colonies. Circumstances, however, rendered the continuance of this state of affairs impossible. The revolutionary wave which passed over the Pyrenean state after the expulsion of Napoleon, the struggle for independence which was proceeding in the surrounding sister states, could not fail to exercise a strong influence on Brazilian affairs. As early as 1815, Brazil was raised to the dignity of a kingdom, an event which could not otherwise than considerably advance the efforts which were directed towards a separation from Portugal. Again, however, the issue was brought about by the condition of affairs in Portugal, and not by the situation in Brazil.

The movement in favour of a parliamentary form of government, which was set on foot in 1820 by Riego in Spain, spread also to the kingdom of Portugal, and thence across to Brazil. King John VI. was completely taken by surprise ; and as his successor to the throne, Dom Pedro, placed himself at the head of the Liberal party, the latter easily attained its object— namely, the promise of a separate parliamentary constitution for Brazil. However, though the Liberals in the colony felt themselves conjointly responsible with those of Portugal, they were soon to learn that the Cortes of the mother country had ends in view quite different from those corresponding with their desires ; for the latter asked for no less than the return of the court to Lisbon and the restoration of the Portuguese dominion in Brazil. **Brazil's Struggles for Independence** The first of these objects was actually attained ; John VI. returned to Lisbon, and Dom Pedro, who had renounced his succession in favour of his brothers and sisters, stayed behind in the first instance at Rio de Janeiro as viceroy.

The more manifest it became that the Cortes was aiming at again reducing Brazil to the condition of a province, the looser became the tie which united the colony to the mother country. At last nothing was left to Dom Pedro himself but to tear the bond, and, on September 7th, 1822, to proclaim the complete independence of Brazil, which, a month later, was declared an empire.

Up to this point Dom Pedro, carried along by the national movement, had remained in accord with the large majority of his people. In the disputes, however, which in the following years arose in regard to questions of internal and foreign policy, this agreement began to be more and more disturbed. Finally, when the populace endeavoured to intimidate him by raising commotions, as it had done successfully and with his co-operation under John VI.,

inextinguishable hotbed hearth of constantly renewed republican agitations. The victorious campaign against Paraguay, though it raised the prestige of the country abroad, on the other hand involved it in serious financial difficulties, which were still further increased by the expenses arising out of the abolition of slavery, which had been resolved upon in 1871. The discussions connected with the passing of this measure filled up the political life of Brazil for years, and have also exercised a determining influence on the last remodelling of the constitution of the country. After Dom Pedro had long endeavoured, with the aid of Conservative

DOM PEDRO, EMPEROR OF BRAZIL AND KING OF PORTUGAL, AND HIS CONSORT
The invasion of Portugal by the French drove the royal family to Brazil. When Brazil gained its independence in 1822 Dom Pedro became emperor as Pedro I. But internal discontent causing his abdication in 1831 in favour of his son, he returned to Portugal, to find that the crown had been usurped by his brother, Dom Miguel, whereupon Dom Pedro issued a decree in favour of his daughter, with complete success. He died in 1834.

he resigned in 1831 in favour of his son, and soon afterwards ended his days at Lisbon. Nor was Pedro II. destined to die in his empire. Even during the time of his minority the adherents of a federal-republican party had attracted considerable notice amid the passionate struggles of party warfare. Their influence naturally fell again into the background during the time that Pedro II., who had been declared of full age before the proper time, was administering with great tact a remarkably liberal government. But even at that time the country did not enjoy a perfect or permanent peace. The province of Sao Paulo especially seemed to be an

Ministries, to solve the slavery question in such a way as to preserve all interests as far as possible, he found himself obliged, in 1888, to call in a Liberal Ministry which, immediately after its accession to office, declared for the unconditional abolition of slavery. By this measure it drove so large a portion of the population into the ranks of the Opposition that the latter was able, on November 15th, 1889, to organise a revolution to which the capital surrendered without an attempt at resistance. The combined Conservative and Federalist parties thereupon forced Dom Pedro to abdicate, and set up the republic of the United States of Brazil. KONRAD HAEBLER

Manuel A. Guerrero, Panama

General Miguel R. Davila, Honduras

General Antoine Simon, Haiti

Don Cleto G. Viguez, Costa Rica

Manuel Estrada-Cabrera, Guatemala

General Porfirio Diaz, Mexico

General José Miguel Gomez, Cuba

General Fernando Figueroa, Salvador

Rafael Reyes, Colombia

José Santos Zelaya, Nicaragua

General Ramón Cáceres, Dominica

PRESIDENTS OF CENTRAL AMERICA AND THE ISLANDS

INFORMATION ABOUT CENTRAL AMERICA & MEXICO

There are six republican states in Central America, and their areas, populations, resources, and other details, are as follow :

State.	Area, Square miles.	Population.	Capital.	Population of Capital.	National Debt (external).	Revenue.	Exports.
					£	£	£
Costa Rica	22,996	351,176	San José	25,000	2,000,000	757,557	1,870,820
Guatemala	46,774	1,647,300	Guatemala la Nueva	96,560	1,493,950	578,653	2,034,897
Honduras	43,000	500,136	Tegucigalpa	34,690	5,398,570	237,125	425,456
Nicaragua	49,200	600,000	Managua	34,872	463,000	1,335,000	730,458
Panama	31,580	360,542	Panama	33,584	None	486,773	392,132
Salvador	7,225	1,006,848	San Salvador	60,000	None	764,362	1,469,239

The interest on the national debts of Costa Rica, Guatemala and Honduras is hopelessly in arrear. In the case of Honduras, the worst of the lot, the overdue interest is about £20,000,000, which is four times the amount of the principal of the debt. Nicaragua has made default in past years, but her finances seem to be in a more satisfactory position at present, and she is negotiating a new loan for £1,200,000 at the moment. Panama is not yet a state old enough to have contracted financial obligations like her neighbours, and perhaps American dollars received on behalf of the Panama concession will keep the new state in the path of solvency. Salvador had a foreign debt of £726,420, but in 1899-1900 this was converted into securities of the Salvador Railway Company, to which the government pays £24,000 a year for eighteen years from 1899.

The resources and currency of these states are as follow :

COSTA RICA.

AGRICULTURE. Timber, coffee, fruits, cocoa, stock-raising.

MINERAL. Gold.

CHIEF EXPORTS. Coffee, bananas, cocoa, cedarwood, fustic, hides.

The monetary unit is the gold colon, which is worth 1s. 10½d. Foreign gold is legal tender. The metric system of weights and measures is the legal standard, although the old Spanish weights and measures are still in commercial use.

GUATEMALA.

AGRICULTURE. Timber, coffee, tobacco, sugar, fruit, rubber, cereals, potatoes, stock-raising.

MINERALS. Gold, silver, salt.

CHIEF EXPORTS. Coffee, timber, sugar, rubber, hides, bananas.

The dollar, or peso, has a nominal value of 4s., but has been as low as 3½d. in the exchange value. The metric system of weights and measures is the legal standard.

HONDURAS.

AGRICULTURE. Fruit, rubber, coffee, tobacco, sugar, cereals, stock-raising, timber.

MINERALS. Silver, gold, copper, lead.

CHIEF EXPORTS. Bananas, cattle, hides, coconuts, timber, silver, gold and metallic ores, rubber, and coffee.

The unit of money value is the silver peso, which is worth about 1s. 6d. ; the gold dollar is worth 4s. The metric system of weights and measures is legal, but the old Spanish weights and measures are still in use commercially.

NICARAGUA.

AGRICULTURE. Coffee, fruit, cocoa, tobacco, rubber, timber, horses, cattle, pigs.

MINERALS. Gold, silver.

CHIEF EXPORTS. Coffee, timber, gold, rubber, bananas, cattle.

The silver dollar, or peso, is worth about 1s. 8d. ; the exportation of silver pesos is forbidden. The metric system of weights and measures is legal.

PANAMA.

AGRICULTURE. Timber, fruit (chiefly bananas), rubber, coffee, cocoa, coconuts, livestock.

MINERAL. Gold (small).

CHIEF EXPORTS. Bananas, timber, rubber, coffee, hides, pearls, turtle-shell.

The monetary unit is the gold balboa, which is equivalent to the gold dollar of the United States. Two silver pesos are equal to a gold dollar. The metric system of weights and measures is the legal standard.

SALVADOR.

AGRICULTURE. Coffee, cocoa, indigo, balsam, sugar, cotton, rubber.

MINERALS. Gold, copper, silver, iron, mercury.

CHIEF EXPORTS. Coffee, indigo, sugar, rubber.

The dollar of 100 centavos has a nominal value of 4s., but an actual value of only 1s. 7d. The weights and measures are metric.

BRITISH HONDURAS

The only European Power possessing territory in the Central American mainland is Great Britain, to whom pertains British Honduras. The area of this Crown colony is 7,560 square miles, and the population is 41,010. The capital is Belize, with a population of 10,397. The other chief towns, with populations, are Corozal (1,722), Stann Cruk (2,575), and Orange Walk (1,286). The revenue in 1906-7 was £80,629, the imports £452,786, and the exports £415,433. The most productive section of the colony is in the west, away from the coast. The chief exports are mahogany, logwood, bananas, cedarwood, coconuts and coffee. Cattle-raising is a not unimportant industry. There is also a good transit trade. The monetary standard is the United States gold dollar, and English gold is legal tender at the rate of $4·86 for the sovereign, and $2·43 for the half-sovereign. The British imperial weights and measures are used.

MEXICO

The area of Mexico is 767,005 square miles, and the population is 18,000,000. The republic is divided into 27 states, 3 territories, and the Federal district. The Senate has 56 members, and the House of Representatives is elected for two years on a universal suffrage, the basis of representation being one member for every 40,000 inhabitants. Each state has its own legislature and governor, and controls its own affairs. The capital is the city of Mexico, which has a population of about 400,000. Other chief cities, with their populations, are : Guadalajara, 101,208 ; Puebla, 93,521 ; Leon, 63,263 ; Monterey, 62,266 ; San Luis Potosi, 61,019 ; Merida, 43,630 ; Guanajuato, 41,486 ; and Pachuca, 37,487. The external gold debt is £31,051,558. The estimated revenue for 1908-9 was £10,338,500. For the year 1906-7 the value of imports was £23,222,958, and the value of exports was £24,801,801. Under the autocratic but enlightened rule of President Diaz, Mexico has made rapid progress during the last half century. The chief agricultural produce consists of wheat, sugar, oranges, maize, henequen, cotton, dyewood, coffee, tobacco, and coca. Stock-rearing is a most important industry, and the variety of stock includes cattle, horses, mules, asses, sheep, goats and pigs. Mexico has great mineral wealth, and the minerals worked are gold, silver, copper, lead, iron, coal, antimony, zinc, graphite, marble (onyx), salt and asphalt. Precious stones are also found. The principal manufactures include textiles, chiefly cotton (which claims some 130 factories, employing over 30,000 hands), and tobacco. The chief exports are silver, gold, henequen, copper, coffee and hides. Mexico purchased over £3,000,000 worth of British produce and manufactures last year.

The Mexican currency is based on the silver dollar, or peso, of 100 centavos, the legal value of which is ·75 gramme of pure gold, and is therefore worth 48½d. The weights and measures are metric, although the use of the old Spanish weights and measures has not been entirely discontinued.

POSTAGE AND TELEGRAM RATES

POSTAGE. Great Britain to Central America and Mexico : For letters, printed matter, and samples, postage rates to British Honduras are as to other British colonies [see page 1002], and to all other places as to other foreign countries [see page 5398]. The parcel-post rates to Costa Rica, Guatemala, Honduras, and Panama (except United States territory in Panama, which is subject to the same conditions as the United States official service) are 2s., 3s., and 4s. for 3lb., 7lb., and 11lb. respectively. To British Honduras the rates are 1s., 2s., and 3s. respectively ; to Nicaragua and Salvador, 3s., 4s. 6d., and 6s. ; and to Mexico, 1s., 2s. 6d., and 3s. 6d. The limit of length, breadth, or depth is 3½ft., and the limit of length and girth combined 6ft. to all places except Mexico, where the limits are 2ft. and 6ft. respectively, with a maximum girth limit of 4ft.

TELEGRAMS from United Kingdom to Costa Rica and Nicaragua, 4s. 2d. per word ; to Guatemala, 3s. 1d. to 3s. 4d. ; to Honduras, 3s. 9d. ; to British Honduras, no service, telegrams being sent by post from New Orleans ; to Panama, 3s. 1d. or 3s. 2d. ; to Salvador, 3s. 6d. or 3s. 9d. ; and to Mexico, 1s. 6d. to 2s. 1d.

COLONISATION OF NORTH AMERICA
THE CENTURY AFTER COLUMBUS
AN AGE OF EXPLORATIONS AND DISCOVERIES

THE North American continent during the sixteenth century, especially in those districts situated on the eastern seaboard, was a free field for discoverers of all nations ; but during several generations no one of the rival Powers succeeded in rendering its possession effective by a permanent settlement. The reason for this was the unpromising appearance of the coasts, on which were to be found a pleasant climate, green meadows, and vast forests, but, in addition, powerful and warlike natives, who vigorously opposed the landing of strangers, and who, by their poverty and the simplicity of their customs, showed clearly the absence of treasure to be won without exertion.

The first Europeans to set foot on North American soil had been the Vikings under Leif Erikson and Thorfinn Karlsefne, who were driven thither while on a voyage from Iceland to Greenland about the year 1100. But their temporary settlements in Vinland, Markland and Huitramannaland had been long forgotten when the discovery of Columbus unveiled a new world. It was the efforts to raise interest in his project, made by the discoverer at the various courts **John Cabot's Great Discovery** of Western Europe years before the realisation of his hopes, that drew attention to his discovery and led to the opening up of the New World some years later. The honour of having been the first among the discoverers of that day to reach the mainland of North America belongs to Giovanni Gabotto, or, as he was called in England, John Cabot. He was specially sent out in 1497 on a voyage to the West, to seek, after the manner of Columbus, the treasures of the Indies and to take possession, for England, of any unknown lands he might come across. It was in fulfilment of this commission that John Cabot in the years 1497–1498 made two voyages between England and America. The first time he **Importance of Cabot's Voyages** landed in Labrador and followed the coast northward. On his second journey he reached the American coast at a point somewhat farther south, and, sailing southward, made a rough exploration of the Atlantic seaboard till he reached the latitude of Florida. Then, for nearly a century, the English paid no further attention to this land, in which their race was to have so great a future, except by sending occasional ships to the inexhaustible fishing-grounds of the Newfoundland Banks ; but even there they did less than most other nations.

The news of Cabot's landing showed the Portuguese that there were undiscovered lands in the north, similar to Brazil in the south, which, according to the delimitation of the spheres of discovery, belonged to them. This was, at any rate, the incentive for the voyages of the brothers Gaspar and Miguel Cortereal. To them King Manuel granted a charter giving them exclusive possession and trading rights in whatever lands they might find to the north of the Spanish colonial sphere and beyond the line of demarcation agreed upon. These claims were recognised and remained in their possession, or in that of their heirs, till 1579, though no effective settlement of the newly discovered region was made by the Portuguese. On his first voyage,

THE FIRST DISCOVERY OF GREENLAND: THE FAMOUS VOYAGE OF KING ERIC THE RED IN 983

Although sighted by Gunnbjörn as far back as 870, Greenland was not visited by Europeans until a century later, when the Icelandic king, Eric the Red, and a small company of followers landed on its shores and established a colony, naming it Grönland. Davis rediscovered the country in 1585-87; but all traces of its early Norse settlers had disappeared, only a few ruins of their towns remaining. The Danes obtained a footing on its west coast in 1721, and a new colony was again founded, which continued to increase and thrive. The above picture shows the sailor-king, Eric the Red, sighting land after many months' weary voyaging. Much of the country still remains unknown.

From the painting by Carl Rasmussen

in 1500, Gaspar Cortereal discovered the island of Newfoundland, with its imposing forests and its bays teeming with fish. In his second journey, in the following year, he was led away by the phantom of a north-west passage to the treasures of India, and following the coast of Labrador north-ward, he and his companions became the first victims of the Arctic ice.

Early Victims of the Arctic Ice They perished, in all proba-bility, in Hudson Strait. During a long period the Portuguese made expeditions to the New-foundland Banks. The first of these, under-taken by Miguel Cortereal to ascertain the fate of his brother, supplied a second party of victims for the ice-deserts of the north. Then these voyages were restricted more and more to the exploitation of the fisheries ; and it was only occasionally that Portuguese sailors assisted the progress of discovery in North America. Among those who did so was João Alvarez Faguendez, who in 1521 sailed round the peninsula of Nova Scotia and into the Gulf of St. Lawrence.

The French followed the example of the Portuguese with especial zeal. From the year 1508, at least, the shipowners of Dieppe and Honfleur took a prominent part in the fishing on the Newfoundland Banks. These fishing expeditions led to occasional visits to the neighbouring coasts, where supplies were taken in, repairs made, and the spoil of the sea dried and smoked for transport. From such settlements Cape Breton received the name it bears to-day, and " Tierra," " Bahia," and " Rio de Bretones " are names that frequently occur in old maps of Canada. Early in the third decade of the sixteenth century these trans-Atlantic lands attracted the attention of the French Government.

Commissioned by it, Giovanni de Veraz-zano, in 1524, made an extended voyage of discovery, following the east coast from Florida nearly up to what is now the northern boundary of the United States.

Opening up of North America Perhaps this undertaking would not have been the only one had not the Portuguese made diplomatic protest. But the Spaniards did incomparably more for the opening up of North America, though their activity was confined principally to the southern part of it. Through slave-hunts among the Bahama Islands the Spaniards made acquaintance with the southern extremity of Florida ; but so uninviting did it seem that for years no one took the trouble to investigate whether this cape belonged to an island or to the mainland. It was not till 1512 that Juan Ponce de Leon, governor of Porto Rico, set out with three ships to investigate what truth there was in the fabulous reports that were current about the land in the north. On Whitsunday, " Pascua Florida," he reached an unknown coast and named it Florida. From there Ponce sailed along the east coast as far as what was later the site of St. Augustine. But, as the flat shore stretched ever before him in unending monotony, he turned, sailed round the southern extremity of the sup-posed island, and followed the west coast for a considerable distance ; but at last, finding neither a strait nor fertile land, but everywhere hostile Indians, he re-turned to Porto ·Rico, and let years pass before renewing the attempt to open up the lands he had discovered.

That he did so at all was due to the fact that districts which he included among those discovered by himself were touched at by other sailors whose competition he wished to exclude. In particular, Francisco Fer-nandez de Cordova, after com-

Historic Voyages of Discovery pleting his voyage of discovery along the coasts of Yucatan and Mexico as far north as Panuco, took, on his return journey, a course too nearly due east, and reached a point that we cannot fix, on the west coast of Florida. This discovery seemed so interesting that Francisco de Garay ordered his pilot, Pineda, who was then about to convey a number of colonists into the district of Panuco, newly claimed by him, to pay more attention to the north coast of the Gulf of Mexico. On this occasion Pineda not only came to the firm conclusion that the coast from Panuco to the peninsula of Florida was continuous, but he also discovered the mouth of the Mississippi, without inferring, however, the extra-ordinary extent of the " hinterland " from the volume of the stream, as Columbus had done in the case of the Orinoco.

Ponce de Leon considered his own claims as a discoverer endangered by these enterprises. He accordingly made applica-tion to the Spanish Government, and was granted, in the usual manner, rights over the territory he had discovered, conditional upon his rendering his possession effective and actually colonising the land. In the year 1521 he made fresh preparations, and shipped 600 persons, besides cattle and supplies, to start a colony; but his attempts to effect a landing on the west coast of Florida were all failures; and at last, mortally wounded by the arrows of the enemy, he decided to return. The greater part of his company perished on the return journey, and he himself reached Cuba only to die. The hostility

Florida's Warlike Indians of the Indians was just what kept Florida from being forgotten. Of the Indians of the islands, some had been pacified, and others had fled before the Spaniards, who had continually to go farther afield to obtain slaves. Two slaveships belonging to the licentiates Matienzo and Ayllon met accidentally off one of the Northern Bahamas, and made an agreement to venture on an expedition against the warlike Indians of Florida. They did, in fact, bring some booty back to San Domingo, and at the same time gave such favourable reports of the land that the licentiate Lucas Vasquez de Ayllon resolved to continue the exploration and eventually to proceed to colonisation.

From the court he obtained without trouble exclusive rights over the territory left without a master by Ponce's death. After preparations lasting several years, during which his pilots explored the Atlantic coast as far as the Santee River, he set out from Hispaniola (San Domingo) in 1526 for his new province, with three ships and 600 men. But he was not favoured by fortune. Sea and shore were hostile to him: the largest of his ships was wrecked, and the Indians opposed his attempts at landing at Rio Jordan or San Mateo so vigorously that he was master only within the range of his muskets.

The colonists, furthermore, had much to suffer in the swampy coast districts, and when Ayllon himself succumbed to fever the rest of his crew betook themselves to their ships and returned to Hispaniola. After this the colonisation of the Atlantic

Expeditions in North America coast was given up for years; but, on the other hand, the Gulf Coast of Florida, a name then applied to the whole of the North American continent so far as it was known to the Spaniards, was the scene of further expeditions which were of great importance in opening up North America. As early as 1528 Panfilo de Narvaez, governor of the Gulf Coast of Florida, the well-known rival of Cortes, cruised from Cuba to Appalachee Bay, to explore, by land and water simultaneously, the territory promised to him in the west. But the land force and the fleet soon got out of touch. The latter returned to Cuba after waiting for months in the neighbourhood of the Mississippi for Narvaez and his company.

When the expedition returned to the coast completely exhausted, nothing remained for them but to build the best vessels they could, and by means of these to make their way out of this inhospitable wilderness to more civilised parts. Imagining himself nearer to Panuco than to the Spanish Islands, Narvaez steered his craft westward; but almost the whole expedition perished in the delta of the Mississippi. Only a few escaped; they continued their journey by land, and, being favoured by fortune, succeeded in reaching the Spanish settlements in New Mexico.

It has been already mentioned how their highly exaggerated stories gave quite a new impulse to expeditions to the fabulous cities of Tusayan and Quivira. The adventurous expedition of Fernando de Soto took in still more of the interior

De Soto's Adventures in the Interior of the continent. It is almost incredible how, despite repeated disasters, companies of considerable size assembled again and again to make the journey into the unknown with hearts as light as if it were a mere pleasure-trip. So strong was the attraction of the personality of De Soto, one of the richest conquistadors of Peru, that, despite the fact that he took only picked men for the expedition, his company on leaving Seville numbered a thousand men. After completing his preparations in Cuba, De Soto crossed over to Tampa Bay on the west coast of Florida, where he had the rare good fortune to meet with a friendly reception from the natives and was able to prepare in peace for his journey into the interior. But it was not long that the Spaniards enjoyed the friendship of the natives. As soon as they began to press forward in a northerly direction they met with Indians who had sworn hostility to the Europeans from the time of Narvaez.

During the course of their three years' wandering the Spaniards were able to gain the friendship of the natives only when they allied themselves with a tribe and helped it in war against its neighbours. The sum total of adventures and privations that reduced De Soto's splendid company to a band of little more than three hundred half-naked and wholly exhausted adventurers was indeed extraordinary.

But incidents of this kind are not what give the expedition its historic importance. What is most interesting for posterity about De Soto's expedition is the geographical and ethnographical aspect of the country traversed, which can be fixed, at least approximately, by the accounts that have come down to us. The Spaniards first made their way northward, at a fixed distance from the marshy coast, till they reached the head of Appalachee Bay. Then they turned their backs to the sea and pressed on towards the north and north-east, through Georgia and South Carolina, till they reached the country where the rivers Altamaha and Savannah rise. Neither here nor farther south did they dare to cross the thickly wooded range of the Alleghanies, so terrible did its forest solitudes seem to them.

Nor did the north attract them; they turned towards the west and south-west. Making their way through the present state of Alabama, they reached the river **Disappointed** of that name, and, striking **Hopes** the sea at Pensacola, estab- **of De Soto** lished temporary communication with the fleet that brought them supplies. In spite of the long, fruitless wandering De Soto could not be persuaded to give up the expedition. After a protracted rest at Mobile, then situated considerably more north than the modern town of the same name, he struck out again into the wilderness and reached the Mississippi not far from where Memphis stands to-day. The passage across the " Father of Waters " occasioned a long delay, but with the help of the Indians and by means of some improvised boats it was finally accomplished. Then the expedition continued its wearisome journey through the present Arkansas and southern Missouri as far as the upper reaches of the White River.

Finding that as he advanced towards the north-west the land was less fertile and more sparsely settled, De Soto changed his course and continued his journey southward and westward over the Washita to the Red River, only to learn that neither treasure nor civilised settlement was to be found in the forests. His decision to return to the Mississippi was a tacit abandonment of all his hopes. He reached that mighty watercourse just above its junction with the Red River, and here, almost exactly three years after his departure from Cuba, he succumbed to fever and to depression at the failure of his plans. His companions imagined themselves so near to New Mexico that they at first attempted to make their way thither by land; but the lack of food **The Fate of** supplies in the west compelled **De Soto's** them once more to make for the **Companions** Mississippi. Finally, they were so fortunate as to be carried out to sea by the stream in their frail improvised craft before they had become too weak to resist the attacks of the ever-hostile Indians. The tedious journey along the Gulf Coast had still to be accomplished before they could reach Panuco, the nearest Christian settlement, and there recuperate from their fatigue and privations. Of De Soto's 1,000 companions only 311 reached the journey's end. So little had been gained by the sacrifice of life that the Spanish Government issued a decree forbidding further exploring expeditions into this unfriendly land.

Though Florida had fallen into discredit with the Spaniards, it had not the same bad name among other nations. Religious discord in France had once before driven men to seek a land of peace and toleration beyond the ocean, when Villegaignon founded his colony in Brazil. But while the object of this first attempt was to establish a colony where toleration should be extended to men of both creeds, the second, undertaken by Ribault and Laudonnière, in the years 1562–1565, aimed at establishing on the coast of Florida a settlement which, though not exclusively Protestant, was to be a place of refuge for those who in their own land were subjected to bitter persecution and oppression.

There was, to begin with, not the slightest difficulty in finding a place on the then deserted coast of Florida where the fleet could land its crews with their stores. **A French** For this purpose the leaders **Settlement in** chose Charleston Bay, called by **Florida** them May River, and by the Spaniards Rio de San Mateo, and named their settlement, overlooked by a fortified hill, " Arx Carolina " in honour of the French sovereign, Charles IX. If the settlers had had no other end in view than to live in peace and tolerance on the distant shore, tilling the land and seeking a peaceful livelihood, it is probable that they could have established themselves and founded a colony undisturbed, as did the English at this and at other points on the coast at a later date. But among the colonists workers were in a minority, and their favourite mode of earning a livelihood was to scour the seas around the Antilles in swift and lightly built craft, and, like pirates, to attack wherever there was a prospect of success. By such proceedings they drew upon themselves the wrath of the Spaniards.

Spain's Hereditary Enemy

Philip of Spain considered it a serious matter that a foreign nation, and especially Spain's hereditary enemy, should dare to establish itself so near to the Spanish colonial possessions and within the Spanish colonial sphere.

More serious in his eyes was the circumstance that they were heretics who thus threatened the Christianising work which Spain regarded as her historic mission. Accordingly, Menendez de Aviles, one of the best seamen then at Spain's disposal, received a commission to root out at all costs this foreign settlement on Spanish soil. He was specially instructed, as a matter of principle, to show no mercy to heretics. The accusation of treacherous cruelty raised by the French against the Spanish leader is scarcely justified. During their own religious struggles they showed themselves scarcely less fanatical than was Menendez towards them. But the latter's action was truly the cause of the transplantation of fanaticism in religious strife to the New World. Even before Menendez had reassembled his forces, which were scattered by a storm in crossing the ocean, he gained an important success. He succeeded in creeping in by night between the French fleet, anchored at San Mateo, and the land, and in driving it from the coast.

Instead of attacking Fort Carolina from the sea, Menendez surprised it from the land side after a difficult march through the forest, and, meeting with scarcely any resistance, overmastered the garrison,

Frenchmen Slain as Heretics

suffering very slight loss himself. Meanwhile the French fleet had been wrecked during the storm, and the crews were thrown on the coast in so defenceless a condition that they had no alternative but to surrender unconditionally. Menendez showed no pity to them in their helplessness, and spared only those who professed the Catholic faith; the rest he slew, "not as Frenchmen, but as heretics." This was barbarous

severity; but he was only obeying his sovereign's orders, and he had never concealed the fact that every heretic he could lay hands on was doomed.

But Menendez's work was not one of destruction only; he was commissioned to colonise Florida for Spain. Accordingly, on the spot where he first landed, he founded the little town of St. Augustine, the oldest town in the United States, which, though several times shifted, has had an uninterrupted existence up to the present day. A second settlement that he founded on the site of Arx Carolina had a less happy fate. It was taken by assault some years later by French Protestants under De Gourgues, who, to avenge his fallen countrymen and co-religionists, mercilessly put to death all Spaniards who fell into his hands, "not as Spaniards, but as murderers"—a grim retort to Menendez.

But Charles IX. disclaimed this deed as an act of unjustifiable piracy, and made complete and express renunciation of his claims to the coast of Florida, where the Spanish settlement of St. Augustine slowly developed and long resisted all foreign encroachments. Here in the

France's Great Ambitions in North America

south, France lightly gave up all her colonial aspirations; but on the other hand she had already begun to establish herself, beginning in the extreme north-east. These latter claims she persisted in much more tenaciously, and had indeed the idea of using the ground gained as a starting-point to bring the whole of the North American continent under her sway. As early as 1535 Jacques Cartier undertook a voyage of discovery along the coasts of Newfoundland and Labrador, and though those regions showed little wealth, he returned the following year to continue his exploration. On this second journey he went farther up the Gulf of St. Lawrence than before, and discovered the great river of the same name that flows into it. Cartier followed the river upstream and, with his ships, reached the site of Quebec; then he pushed on with smaller vessels as far as the Indian capital, Hochelaga, the modern Montreal.

The swiftness of the impetuous stream prevented him from continuing his exploration farther, so he returned to the fleet and spent a severe winter at its anchorage, suffering heavy losses. Next year he returned to France with the first cargo of Canadian furs, carrying with him some Indian chiefs, who pined under the change of scene and climate and died in Europe. In 1541, Cartier returned to the St. Lawrence, built a fort at Cape Rouge seven miles above Quebec, and thence proceeding to Hochelaga, spent in all nearly a year in the country. As he sailed out of the St. Lawrence Gulf, De Roberval sailed in. The latter had been despatched by Francis I. as governor of the newly found territory; and after building a fort at Charlesbourg, close to Quebec, and spending an extremely uncomfortable year with an unruly company, he evacuated the country and returned to France. The quest of precious metals would

carrying their explorations far to the north; and Cartier's first attempts at starting a North-American colony had come to an end before the sixteenth century was half over. The English had rested content with the expeditions of the Cabots. But the spirit was stirring which, early in the 'fifties, sent Willoughby and Chancellor to search for a north-east, instead of a north-west, passage to the Indies, and to "discover" Muscovy.

Yet for another twenty years the English exploits were limited to those expeditions to the Spanish Main and the Spanish seas for the purpose of compelling the Spaniards

ARX CAROLINA: THE HUGUENOT SETTLEMENT AT CHARLESTON, IN SOUTH CAROLINA

Religious persecution in France during the latter half of the seventeenth century compelled a company of French Huguenots to emigrate to North America, where, in South Carolina, they first settled, choosing as their home the site on which Charleston is now situated, and naming their settlement "Arx Carolina." Here they lived for a number of years in peace, free to worship in their own way, and on a footing of equality with the rest of the population.

seem to have been the main inspiration of these early expeditions, which now ceased altogether for the rest of the century, in any serious sense, owing to the internal distractions which agitated France. Fishermen from several European nations, however, resorted even thus early to the waters about Newfoundland, and many from various motives penetrated to the shores of the mainland and into the Gulf of the St. Lawrence. A number of French traders had even settled at Tadoussac, at the mouth of the Saguenay. The Spaniards had made themselves masters of the southern continent without

to trade with them, which reached their climax in the affair of John Hawkins—with Drake—at San Juan d'Ulloa and Drake's raid on Nombre de Dios. With 1575 the horizon enlarged; for in that year John Oxenham built ships on the Isthmus of Panama, and launched them in the Pacific Ocean. In 1578, Drake passed the Straits of Magellan, and discovered that Tierra del Fuego was not a portion of a fabled continent in southern seas; and after harrying the South-American ports, he had sailed, in 1579, to a more northerly point on the Californian coast than any Europeans had hitherto reached, where the natives offered him divine honours; after which he completed his circumnavigation of the globe. In these same years, Martin Frobisher had taken up the search for the north-west passage, visiting Greenland and discovering Frobisher Sound. It is curious to note

Newfoundland the Oldest English Colony

that on the first of his three voyages, the larger of his two ships was of no more than twenty-five tons burden. And before England and Spain fought out the great Armada duel, John Davis had matched Frobisher's exploits in three Arctic voyages, and had given his name to Davis Strait. But raids in Spanish waters, and discoveries in the frozen regions, did not by any means conduce to the establishment of settlements. The Englishman whose imagination first conceived the idea of real colonial expansion was Humphrey Gilbert, the elder half-brother of Sir Walter Raleigh.

The codbanks of Newfoundland—which, together with an indefinitely wide expanse of the continent, had received the somewhat unintelligible name of Norumbega—had become a resort for fishing-fleets of all nations; but since Cartier's day no one had tried to effect a permanent settlement. The English, however, had a kind of first claim, in virtue of Cabot's discoveries made in the English service. Humphrey Gilbert got from Elizabeth a patent for the colonisation of Norumbega; to which he attempted to give effect in 1578, and again in 1583. To this attempt Newfoundland owes her claim to be " the oldest English colony." But the attempt itself failed hopelessly; and Gilbert himself perished on the voyage home.

But Gilbert's inspiration had possessed the soul of his half-brother. Walter Raleigh never set foot in North America himself, in spite of his two Guiana voyages, of which the first was so valuable and the second so disastrous. Nevertheless, it was on persistent attempts to realise Gilbert's ideal that Raleigh sank most of his fortune. Adventurers enough were ready to seek for El Dorados, Tom Tiddler's grounds, where gold and silver could be picked up—with the chance, in default thereof, of sacking a Spanish galleon or two.

The golden city of Manoa had attractions for Raleigh himself. But he was emphatically the prophet—forthteller and fore-teller, too—of the only true doctrine of expansion; of settlement on the soil; of conquering Nature in the new land and making her yield store of other wealth than precious metals; of finding new homes for the English people beyond the limits of their little island. In the year after Gilbert's disaster, Raleigh sent an expedition which established a settlement at Roanoake, in what is now Carolina, giving it the name of Virginia, in honour of Elizabeth. A reinforcement was sent the next year; but when a third company went out, in 1586, they found that their predecessors had thrown up the cards, and had come away on the ships with which Drake had just raided Cartagena.

A party remained; but each time that a relief was sent it found desolation. Raleigh's efforts had failed; colonisation had not proved a short cut to unlimited wealth. When the seventeenth century opened, neither English nor French, nor Dutch, had succeeded in securing a footing on

The Seed of the Coming Harvest

American soil. But the seed had been sown in the minds of all there, to bear harvest in the coming centuries. We shall follow first the French expansion, and then the English—the latter including the Dutch interlude—until the two forces come into direct collision, and the two narratives coalesce in the story of the struggle *à outrance* between the rivals.

KONRAD HAEBLER

THE FRENCH DOMINION IN AMERICA
THE RISE AND DEVELOPMENT OF CANADA

A LONG time passed after Cartier's day before attempts at settlement were renewed by the French Government; but there were always French vessels on the Newfoundland Banks, that traded also in furs on the St. Lawrence, and this trade turned out to be so profitable that early in the seventeenth century a number of Breton traders combined and succeeded in obtaining a monopoly for their company from the French king, Henry IV. The form of this Canadian colony was peculiar from the beginning. It was intermediate between a trading company and a Crown colony.

The intention of the founders, Pontgravé, Chauvin and De Monts, was only to carry on the fur trade more vigorously and to organise it on a better footing. Their settlement, Tadoussac, at the junction of the Saguenay and the St. Lawrence, was intended to be nothing more than a trading station. But when **Beginning of French Colonisation** Samuel de Champlain entered the service of the company in 1603, not only were the aims of the undertaking widened, but its political status was gradually altered, the state gaining more influence, and at the same time assuming more responsibility. In 1612 Count de Soissons was set at the head of the Canadian enterprise as viceroy; and the fact that a second prince of the royal family followed him in this position tended in no small degree to impress upon the colonial enterprise a more and more official character.

But, however, the economic conditions of the colony stood in strange contradiction to this. Till well into the eighteenth century the French Canadian settlements kept their character as trading factories and mission stations. Women, with the exception of nuns, were as rare as true settlers. The population was principally composed of soldiers, traders and priests; and for many years the colonies remained dependent on their imports from Europe and on barter with the natives. The colonies were not in a position to feed themselves till they passed into the hands of the English, when their constitution underwent a radical change. In spite of this a thoroughly characteristic feature of French colonial administration was the **The French Colossus with Feet of Clay** need for expansion, and that to an almost unlimited extent, out of all proportion to the strength of the colony. This was partly the consequence of the economic state of the colony. The receipts from the fur-trade had to cover the expenditure, which, in spite of the moderate number of the colonists, continually increased.

This was possible only so long as a trade monopoly in an extensive region was assured; and, to accomplish this, effective possession became more and more necessary as the advance guard of Dutch and English colonies made its way over the Alleghanies and entered into competition with the French hunters and fur-traders. But in considering the disproportionate need for expansion we must not under-estimate the influence of a number of individual discoverers, possessed of marked characteristics, who acidentally came together in this Canadian movement, and who, in spite of temporary failure, were continually giving a new impulse for advance. Thus the provinces of Canada and Louisiana developed in time into the colossus with feet of clay that the French colonial empire proved to be when put to the actual test. The first of the discoverers who played so great a part in the expansion of New France, **Champlain the Real Founder of Canada** the real founder of Canada, was Samuel de Champlain. From 1603 to 1616 he was connected with the French colonial government, being either in its service or at its head. But the interests of the government or of the trading company never tied his hands, even where his own interests were most intimately connected with them. The unfailing spell that drew him across the ocean into the solitudes of the West was an ardent desire to unravel the secrets of those remote tracts, and to claim as French all that might come to light in their primeval forests.

Champlain was born at Brouage in 1567, and came of a family of fishermen. In the year 1603 De Chastes, governor of Dieppe, **French Pioneers in Canada** having persuaded Henry IV. to sanction the opening up of Canada for trade, despatched two vessels to the St. Lawrence, under the command of a Breton merchant, Pontgravé, with whom, as navigator, he sent Champlain, the latter having already had considerable experience of the North American coast. On this occasion they only visited Hochelaga, and did some surveying in the neighbourhood, among other things making an unsuccessful attempt to pass the Lachine rapids, which have become so familiar to the modern tourist. On returning to France they found that De Chastes had died in their absence; but a new company was immediately formed for trade and colonisation under the presidency of the Sieur de Monts, a personal friend of the king.

It was now decided to confine their attention to La Cadie (Acadia) and abandon for the present the St. Lawrence country, which was already known as Canada, its Indian name, or sometimes as New France, both terms being used irrespectively till it was lost to the French Crown. Associated with De Monts were the Baron de Pontrincourt, a nobleman of Picardy, and Champlain. The venture was supported by Protestant merchants of Rochelle.

The suspicions of the Catholics were allayed by a grant to them of a monopoly in the matter of Indian conversion, while De Monts and his friends were given a monopoly of the fur-trade, a scarcely equitable division of interests according to modern ideas; but the ardour among the Latin Catholic nations of that period for converting the heathen, if **The French Zeal in Trade and Missions** only in outward symbolic form, was almost as strong as the love of gain which among the Spaniards disfigured their missionary zeal and was disgraced by deeds of appalling cruelty. The adventurers made their first settlement on the west shore of the Bay of Fundy, at the mouth of a river which they named St. Croix, and which now separates the state of Maine from the province of New Brunswick.

De Monts, who held the king's commission as lieutenant of Canada, now made a grant to his friend Pontrincourt of territory on the eastern shore of the bay, adjacent to the site of what afterwards became Annapolis in Acadia, the modern Nova Scotia. He named it Port Royal, and sailed to France for the purpose of collecting settlers. Here he found small interest shown in the new colony; but, in the meantime, De Monts arrived with the news that the St. Croix site had proved unsatisfactory, and that the settlers had moved across to the Annapolis River.

The two now set to work to enlist colonists, and in May, 1606, Pontrincourt sailed for Acadia with a heterogeneous and turbulent company. Arriving at Port Royal, he found the fort there occupied only by a faithful Indian and a couple of Frenchmen, and learned that Champlain, Pontgravé, and the rest had just sailed for France. The little company spent a pleasant if unprofitable time fraternising with the Indians, improving land, fishing, exploring, and keeping up the social amenities with jest and song, and good living. But as **Struggle for Territory in North America** Protestants, and even more, perhaps, as monopolists, home jealousies proved too strong; and, to their sorrow, they soon learned from dispatches sent by a ship that their charter was withdrawn. This was in 1607, and there was nothing for it now but to abandon the settlement.

Though De Monts and Pontrincourt succeeded after three years in reconciling the government to their claims in a more restricted form, and renewing the thin thread of French occupation in Acadia, little more can be said of it here. The English, on the strength of the Cabot voyages, never gave up their claims to this region. Armed with government authority, and sometimes with territorial charters of land, they frequently attacked the French, and sometimes turned them out, to occupy their seats till the wheel of fortune or some treaty between the nations restored the status quo. The labours of devout ladies and Jesuit priests among the Micmac Indians give some colour to this earlier period, as do the dreams of gentlemen adventurers who vainly fancied that titles to a vast wilderness were a road to territorial importance in the New World. The English, too, associated their efforts at Acadian settlement with an aristocratic flavour, which produced the well-known order of Nova Scotia baronets. But Acadia, wrapped as it was in its forest mantle, remained profoundly irresponsive to the claims of English baronets or the dreams of grand seigneurs.

Its story, till it was handed over definitely to Great Britain in 1713 at the Treaty of Utrecht, with a thousand or two isolated unlettered French settlers on the western shore, is largely one of trifling events, and lies almost wholly outside the course of French Canadian history proper, with which its isolated community had scarcely any concern whatever.

New France was in reality founded at Quebec by Champlain, after his prospects in Acadia had been interfered with in the manner just described. While De Monts was in France endeavouring to get a renewal of his monopoly of the fur-trade, Champlain and Pontgravé went out as his representatives in 1608, and, making for their old haunts up the St. Lawrence, fixed their headquarters on the site now covered by the lower town of Quebec, and there erected buildings and storehouses. In this year, 1608, too, it may be of interest to note that the only attempts at European colonisation north of Mexico were represented by the struggling handful of English at Jamestown in Virginia, and a small colony of Spaniards at St. Augustine, Florida. By 1610, De Monts had secured his trading monopoly, though not till Champlain had crossed the ocean to assist him. For most of the next twenty-four years Champlain remained in Canada, exploring, working up the fur-trade, and dealing both in peace and war with the Indians, on whose friendship the trade, not to say the existence of the handful of French, depended. At the beginning of his enterprise Champlain was convinced that the friendship of the Indians was absolutely necessary to him if he was to carry out his plans. The natives who came down the St. Lawrence to Quebec and Tadoussac to barter furs belonged chiefly to the Huron race and to some Algonquin tribes who lived near the Hurons, and were allied with them against their common enemy,

Champlain's Relations with the Natives

SAMUEL DE CHAMPLAIN
When Quebec was taken by the British, in 1629, he was carried to England, but on the restoration of Canada to the French, in 1632, he was re-appointed governor.

the Iroquois, who lived to the east and south-east. As the way to the unknown west belonged to them, Champlain did not hesitate to ally himself with them, and he even went so far as to buy their services by helping them against the Iroquois, a decisive step which was to influence Canada for generations. Like all adventurers of his day, he lived in hopes of discovering the great western sea, which was the route to China, and, like the rest, believed the continent at this point to be comparatively narrow. The first campaign, undertaken in the region where Lake Champlain still keeps alive the memory of the discoverer, was so successful that it greatly increased the consideration in which the Europeans were held by their savage allies. In this respect Champlain had completely carried out his intentions. That he had drawn upon his fellow countrymen the undying hostility of the Iroquois did not appear a matter worthy of consideration to him or to anybody else; nor, considering the superiority of European weapons, would it have become so serious a matter as it did but for the fact that European enemies of France now naturally allied themselves with the Iroquois and provided them with weapons that placed them on equal terms with the whites in battle, and rendered them very dangerous opponents to the scattered and sparsely populated French settlements. Champlain could now, under the protection of the Hurons and their allies, explore the country about the St. Lawrence in all directions. The limits to which he extended French influence were Lake Champlain in the south-east, the middle Saguenay in the north, and in the west Lake Huron, which he reached by way of the Ottawa and Nipissing, without, however, gaining any clear conception of the great system of North American lakes.

The Iroquois Hostile to the French

Champlain did even more to strengthen French influence; he summoned missionaries to Canada. Those interested in the trading company looked unfavourably upon the extra expense entailed by this, the more so because the endeavours of the missionaries to get the Indians to settle were prejudicial to the fur-trade ; but the influence of the French Government and Champlain's lofty views gained a complete victory over the narrower opinions of the traders. Some priests of the order of Rècollets arrived in 1615, and they built at Quebec the first permanent church in North

The First Church in Canada America. But although Protestant interests were strongly represented in the company, and hostility to the Jesuits was most pronounced, yet this order, which deserves all praise for its missionary work, could not be permanently kept out of the Canadian settlements. From 1625 they worked side by side with the Franciscans.

How zealously they engaged in the conversion of the Indians of the north is shown by the extent of the literature which the brothers of the order have published on their work in Canada. A change took place with the interference of Richelieu in Canadian affairs. The Company of New France, commonly known as the " Hundred Associates," was formed, and received a monopoly of the fur-trade from Florida to the Arctic Seas. Above all, after the fall of Rochelle, that fatal interdict on Huguenot immigration was decreed, which perhaps lost North America to France, and changed the history of the world.

Even in these early times Canada had once been in danger of falling into the hands of the English. In 1621, Sir William Alexander received from James I. a charter to found a colony under the name of Nova Scotia. Its boundaries included the greater part of the French colony. When war broke out between England and France, Alexander attempted to enforce his claims. His ships repeatedly forced a passage up the St. Lawrence, and, by capturing French ships, almost completely cut off communication between Quebec and the Mother Country. In 1628 Alexander's ships appeared before Quebec

Canada in the Hands of the English and demanded its surrender; and it was only Champlain's ability that caused them to retreat with their object unattained. But they returned next year, and the colonists, exhausted by a severe winter, which was doubly hard on account of the absence of help from Europe, offered no resistance. The colonists, and Champlain himself, were carried off to Plymouth. Canada was at this moment in the hands of the English. But a treaty of peace had

already been concluded in Europe, and by it the possessions of both parties were to remain unchanged. Both Acadia and Canada were thus given up by the British, and French Canada by this means was enabled to prolong an honourable existence for more than a hundred years.

Champlain again returned to Quebec, and did much for the Canadian colony before he ended his life there in 1635. The English claims were practically nullified ; the peace with the Hurons was again confirmed ; and far up the St. Lawrence, at Three Rivers, a new settlement was founded. Still greater deeds were projected by him, but he received no news of their fulfilment before his death. Jean Nicolet, one of his most distinguished followers, had meanwhile revisited Lake Huron by the old route, and had then gone on through the Strait of Mackinac into Lake Michigan and far along its western shore.

He failed, indeed, to discover the geological structure of the basin of these lakes and their peculiar connection ; but in making alliances with the Indians as far as the Fox River he paved a way that

Canada's Slow Growth Under the French became of great importance in the future. The failure so far to make anything more than a trading centre of the St. Lawrence is shown by the fact that there were at this date only some 200 Frenchmen in the whole country. The population, in fact, were merely servants of a trading-company, quartered for the most part in wholesale barrack fashion. Between the years 1632 and 1640 nearly 100 genuine farmers, mainly from Perche, Normandy, Picardy and Champagne, arrived, and were the original progenitors of the modern Canadian habitant. Nearly all of them either brought wives or found them in the colony. In the next twenty years, until the end of the company's rule, about 200 more came. They were prolific, and prospered, and by this time understood how to face the harder conditions of life in the colony. Nineteen-twentieths of them, says M. Sulte, who has exhaustively studied the question, have descendants in the colony to-day.

The Indians were now more formidable, from the fact that they were acquiring firearms from the traders of New England, particularly the Iroquois and the five nations, whose territory lay to the south of the great lakes Erie and Ontario. North of the lakes were Algonquins and

Hurons, while Acadia and what is now New Brunswick, speaking broadly, were occupied by Micmacs and Abernakis, who took no part in the struggle for Canada as here understood. These nations were highly organised, their various tribes living in stockaded villages, each being represented in the general council by two chiefs, one for peace and one for war. All of them, except the Micmacs and Abernakis, were tillers of the soil, and cultivated maize, pumpkins and tobacco.

The sub-tribe dwelt in its separate village, divided again into clans, each of which had its own long house. Chastity not being held in repute, relationship counted only on the mother's side, and each clan thus derived and held together had its badge or token, which was tattooed on the bodies of the males, and displayed over the entrance of the Long Hall. These nations—the Algonquins, Hurons and Iroquois—spoke different languages ; while their several tribes spoke dialects of the same tongue, differing more or less, but at all events sufficiently alike to admit of common discussion. Such, broadly speaking, were the savage nations, among whom the lot of the French Canadians were cast, **The Fearless French Missionaries** and who played such a vital and important part in their history. For it was not in trade only that the relations of the two races became so intimate, but in almost every Indian village, from the great western lakes to the Saguenay, the fearless and indefatigable Catholic missioner in his black robe became a familiar spectacle.

Even among the friendly Hurons and Algonquins, however, his offices were regarded for a long time with suspicion. But men who were ready to face torture and death among the hostile Iroquois, and did so, were not likely to be discouraged by the mere obstinacy of their allies. Those outward forms, at any rate, of conversion, which at that period had a significance for the Jesuit that to us appears almost incredible, were accepted by an ever-increasing number of savages. Pictures seem to have been the most efficacious means of influence, while in the far-scattered mission chapels the fathers did not disdain to add material hospitality to the attractions of their religious ritual.

Nor did they, like their New England contemporaries, show indifference to the Indian dialects and insist, as it were, that the learning of the European tongue must be concurrent with the learning of Christianity. The French priests were, beyond doubt, intellectually superior to the others. They toiled at the various Indian dialects, and addressed each tribe in its own tongue, thus winning the confidence of the natives not merely for themselves, but for their nation, and by **Indians Under French Influence** their far superior enterprise carried its reputation into the remote and distant regions. The English colonists, on the other hand, though not devoid of missionary zeal, and more exacting in some show of practical morality from their converts, were content with slower and more thorough work in the neighbourhood of their own settlements.

The French, as might be expected, acquired by these means, and with some further advantage in national temperament, an influence over the Indians far greater than that of their English neighbours, who owed such as they had rather to their traders than to their preachers. The one exception to this, as we have said, was the most powerful of all the Indian combinations, that of the five nations, commonly known as the Iroquois. With these the French, as allies of their inveterate enemies, the Hurons and Algonquins, could make no headway. They made overtures to the New Englanders for some kind of union against the dreaded people who lay at the back of both colonies ; but the English, fortunately for themselves, declined.

For many a time in after years the Iroquois could have turned the scale in Anglo-French disputes. As it was, their consistent attachment to the English, chiefly as the better customers in trade, remained one of the great facts of North American politics till the Indian had ceased to count. It was in 1648 that the Iroquois crossed into Canada and set to work to exterminate the Huron nation, who were scattered over what is now the great province of Ontario, **Iroquois' Slaughter of the Hurons** and were more numerous than their foes. The latter, however, practically succeeded in their bloody task, one remnant of the Hurons seeking permanent refuge on the Isle of Orleans under the very guns of Quebec. Even then they were not safe, for in 1656 the Iroquois fell upon them and carried off their women in sight of the French, who were not strong enough to interfere, and already had fifty prisoners in the hands of the savages. The destruction of the Hurons came to very nearly destroying for a time the French fur-trade. Montmagny had succeeded to the governorship on Champlain's death. The enterprise of the Jesuits had become known in France, and stimulated a great interest in Canada, particularly of a religious kind. Devout women of good family had arrived in Quebec, bringing money and enthusiasm to the building of churches and hospitals, Madame de la Petrie and Marie Gugard being among the most prominent. It was in 1641, too, that Montreal was founded by a band of enthusiasts, though actually a sub-company of the Hundred Associates, with a title to the land, headed by Maisonneuve and Mlle. Mance, another devotee.

Religious Enthusiasts Found Montreal

They were detained by the winter in Quebec, where many objections were raised to their enterprise. With forty men and four women, however, they persevered, and a granite monument to their success may to-day be seen amid the busy stir of Montreal where its first rude buildings, then known as the Ville Marie, clustered round their protecting battery. In 1659, under the influence of Mlle. Mance and the Sulpitians, Montreal was reinforced by some 200 souls, including thirty marriageable maidens and some nuns. The Jesuit interest pounced upon them, but they were nevertheless soon absorbed into a population which then contained 150 men, fifty of whom were married. The new town, it may be remarked, was not yet even palisaded. A stone windmill formed its chief refuge of defence, and the lurking Iroquois made it unsafe to venture beyond the small area of cleared ground.

The Jesuits were now almost dominant in the colony, and religious fervour is the leading note of all contemporary chronicles. The Hotel Dieu was already founded at Quebec; so also was the now noted convent of the Ursulines with the Jesuit church and college. Fort St. Louis, the permanent seat of government, bristling with cannon, towered above all other buildings, and the whole aspect of the place must have been that of the crusading missionary rather than the trader. Agriculture, from the attractions of the fur-trade on the one hand, and the vigilance of the hostile Iroquois on the other, made slow way, and nearly all supplies were imported from France.

St. Louis the Seat of Government

Montreal was already becoming the chief point of trade, fronting as it did the western wilderness whence issued the Indians, laden with their annual toll of which the beaver-skin was the principal staple—the unit, too, of value and currency in the colony, as tobacco was in Virginia.

Religious exaltation, generated by fearless Jesuit priests and lay devotees, often of noble blood, both men and women, was the electric current which nerved these isolated communities to face incredible hardships and continual dangers. Material fortune, the natural aim of colonists in all times, seems here to have been almost in abeyance. The bulk of the population employed in the fur-trade were, in fact, only servants of the companies.

If the ascetic and missionary side of the life did not appeal to them in spirit, they had outwardly to conform to it, and there is no doubt that the discipline of the settlements lent a contrasting charm to the liberty of the wild woods and made hopeless nomads of innumerable Frenchmen who might, under other conditions, have become useful farmers. A blend of natural gallantry and religious fanaticism gave rise to many heroic deeds other than that notorious and frequent courting of death and torture by the missionaries themselves. Here is one of them : In 1660 there was a rumour that 1,000 Iroquois were together at the mouth of the Ottawa for the destruction of Montreal ; whereupon a band of sixteen enthusiasts, with arms and ammunition, left the town, and at the rapids of the Long Sault ensconced themselves within a log redoubt and, pledged to neither give nor take quarter, calmly awaited certain death. They maintained a heroic and bloody resistance against hundreds of savages till they met their inevitable fate. The motive of this exalted heroism was to sober the Iroquois by some striking exhibition of French valour ; nor, it should be said, did they die in vain.

Brave Deeds of Gallant Frenchmen

In 1663 the able Colbert was put in charge of the French colonial department by the young king, Louis XIV., and at once set to work sweeping changes in Canada, which contained up till now no more than 2,000 French inhabitants, 800 of whom were in Quebec. He annulled the charter of the Hundred Associates, which had till then enjoyed a monopoly of trade with Canada, transferring the

LAVAL, AFTER LANDING, VISITING A CHAPEL IN THE FOREST

THE BAPTISM BY LAVAL OF THE IROQUOIS INDIAN CAPTAIN, GARAKONTIE

THE VICAR OF THE POPE AT THE COURT OF LOUIS XIV.

SCENES IN BAS-RELIEF FROM THE LIFE AND WORK OF LAVAL

Photos Neurdein

privilege to the great French West India Company, which, by its activity did much to infuse new life into Canadian enterprise.

The lake region was soon thoroughly explored in all directions, and the ascendancy of French influence was assured by the establishment of mission-stations and trading depots. Of these the most important were at Sault Sainte-Marie, between Lake Superior and Lake Huron ; near Mackinac, between Lake Huron and Lake Michigan ; and at Niagara Falls. De Courcelles was sent out as governor with a much abler man, the famous Talon, as intendant, to keep an eye on him in the king's interest—a mistrustful form of government that was continued to the end of the French regime. The Carringnan regiment, which had distinguished itself against the Turks, was also sent with a view to ultimate settlement in the country, and many batches of emigrants, male and female, amounting in all, with the soldiers, to some 2,000 souls, arrived there within a few years. The fortifications at Quebec, Montreal and Three Rivers—the last midway between the two towns, and now acquiring importance—were strengthened, and forts were built along the line of the Richelieu to watch the Iroquois.

The king himself took an active interest in the colony, while another great name in Canadian history made its appearance at this time—namely, that of Laval, first as Pope's vicar, then as bishop. The Sulpitians, who were strong in Montreal, had attempted to dispute the Jesuit supremacy. But the arrival of Laval, wholly in sympathy with the latter, high born, wealthy, able and arrogant, settled the matter. Pledged to uphold the supremacy of the Church in Canada, he proved on many occasions too much for the secular government. Hostility to the liquor trade, which was demoralising the Indians, but was considered as one of the mainsprings of the fur-trade, and the endowing of those seminaries in Quebec, now represented by the famous university that bears his name, are the chief actions that occur to one in connection with this powerful and ascetic ecclesiastic. It was his influence, too, that caused the dissolution of the company of the Hundred Associates.

He endeavoured to enforce, and sometimes succeeded in so doing, the outrageous doctrine that the Church should control the secular as well as the religious affairs of the colony, and he had one governor recalled at his own dictation. His name is remembered as the most powerful exponent of those Ultramontane doctrines for which French Canada in a greater or less degree has been distinguished up to the present day.

It was at this epoch, indeed, that the scheme of government and social organisation was planned under which French Canada for good or ill was to work out its destiny. This, in short, was an absolutism, and may be described as a triumvirate, consisting of the governor, the bishop and the intendant, who managed the finances, besides reporting confidentially to the king on the governor's actions and conduct. The three often pulled different ways in settling a decree, but when issued, it had to be unquestioningly obeyed. The land was divided into districts, parishes and seigneuries—the first for purposes of defence, in which an enrolled militia played an important part ; the second for ecclesiastical convenience ; while the third, the seigneuries, were large tracts of several square leagues apiece, mostly fronting on one or other bank of the St. Lawrence, granted to individuals, who constituted an order of noblesse. These people were sometimes officers, members themselves of the *petite noblesse* of France, but quite as often men of no birth, who could afford the moderate sums to qualify for enrolment in this somewhat curious aristocracy.

The land was held from the Crown in quasi-feudal fashion, though not by military service, as the militia was separately organised under distinct captains, who were only incidentally, though almost inevitably, seigneurs. But the seigneur was looked upon as holding his estate in trust, as it were, for the Crown. So much, at least, of dignity was conceded to him, if his rents were microscopic. He could not dispose of it in part, while even the transfer of the whole carried a very heavy fine. The whole country being heavily timbered, the tenants, or *censitaires*, of these seigneuries had to hew their little farms painfully out of the woods, and, of course, erect their own buildings. Theirs was not the energy and ambition of Anglo-Saxon freeholders in the forests to the south of them. Many causes—temperament, the fascinations of the fur-trade, a reactionary government, a stagnant industrial atmosphere—kept the clearings small and the seigneuries

Progress of Trade and Missions

Laval's Great Work for Canada

New Scheme of Social Government

mainly wrapped in unproductive forest. Rents, such as they were, were paid in kind. Corn had to be ground at the seigneural mill, and certain fines were due to the lord on sale or transfer of his tenants' holdings. But for a generation or two the seigneur, if he held no commission or small office, was almost as poor as his tenantry. He had absolutely no part in the government of his country, nor was his opinion asked upon any single question, while his judicial powers were confined to the pettiest matters. Nevertheless, he played a necessary and not ignoble part.

In those dangerous and arduous exploits against either white or Indian foes, whether as militia captain or otherwise, he made the very best of partisan leaders ; while as an explorer he was equally in his element. With the spirits of such rude health as a simple life in a bracing climate generates, and the pride of caste, whether inbred or acquired, he made an ideal instrument for such work as the peculiar French system for developing Canada required, and is a highly picturesque, historical figure when viewed against his wild and romantic background.

The Early Builders of Canada The seigneurs as a unit of organisation served to keep the tillers of the soil in touch and in hand. The latter could not straggle out in solitary clearings all over the country beyond the reach of the military or ecclesiastical authority, to be a constant mark to the Indian tomahawk. They were practically tied to the soil, though all had more of it for a long time than they could clear and cultivate, and it was reasonably fertile, the restraint was mainly theoretical. Certainly it was not felt. The social instinct of the French, too, was by this system preserved and encouraged then as now, for the French Canadian holding was long and narrow, so that the dwellings, which stood at the end of it upon the road— or more often river—as the chief artery of travel, were in neighbourly propinquity, and the banks of the St. Lawrence began in time to assume the form they do to-day, of a continuous, if somewhat disconnected, street.

The Iroquois all this time had been more than aggressive—they were contemptuous. They had wiped out the Hurons—the allies of the French—and confined the industrial and domestic life of the latter to the range of their own guns. Even more ; for the Onondagas, who were the nearest and the least inimical of the five nations, had

virtually compelled the presence of a mission settlement in their country, the members of which lived in daily peril of their lives. De Courcelles, the first Crown governor, in 1665, with the rashness of inexperience, had marched in the dead of winter with 600 men against the Mohawk village. But he never got there. After floundering for weeks in the **Frenchmen Assassinated by the Mohawks** wintry wilderness, harassed by Indians, he returned ignominiously, with considerable loss. The murder of several French officers by Mohawks stirred the French to a greater effort, and an experienced soldier, the Marquess de Tracy, now headed a force of 1,300 men, regulars and militia, against this tribe—the fiercest of the Iroquois confederacy. The Indians flinched from the unequal contest, and Tracy destroyed their villages, though these had been fortified under the guidance of the Dutch, who had that very year been handed over to the British Crown. This led to a peace for twenty years. Canada had rest, and was enabled to extend those settlements in the manner we have already treated of and to organise the nucleus of her seigneuries and parishes.

Four thousand fresh emigrants were despatched to the country between 1667 and 1672 by the efforts of the king and his minister, including several batches of respectable girls, who were placed in charge of the nuns during the extremely brief period it required to find husbands for them. The last-mentioned year, too, saw the end of assisted emigration to Canada. Throughout the remaining century of the French regime the current flowed feebly. It is safe to say that the vast majority of modern French Canadians are descended from the 8,000 men and women who at this time were crystalised into a small nation, utterly distinct from those other varieties of another civilisation that were forming to the south **Ancestors of Modern French Canadians** of them. They represented the habits and ideas of the rural France of the seventeenth century, and no fresh influences except those engendered by mere physical surroundings ever contaminated them. Without education to speak of, or political life of any kind, or intercourse with other communities but savage ones, docile to an Ultramontane Church, ruled absolutely by a succession of officials from France, they remained in effect

6027

provincial Frenchmen, and, save for that special alertness which comes of familiarity with the wilderness, stereotyped seventeenth century France on the far-off shores of the River St. Lawrence.

An overwhelming majority of these settlers had come from Normandy and the northern provinces; the rest mainly **Canada** from the south-west, sailing from **Before the** Rochelle. The south and south-**Conquest** east of France had nothing to do with peopling Canada, and, strange to say, the sea-going Breton took but a trifling part. The Norman was the best settler. He was hardy and used to growing at home the ordinary grain and grass crops that were suited to the soil of Canada. By the middle of the century there were already 3,000 cattle in the country besides a proportionate number of pigs and sheep, but as yet no horses, nor were these at all numerous till after the English conquest. Not all the settlers, however, came from the rural districts; indeed, quite a number unused to agricultural pursuits were imported, and these, by the not unwise paternalism of the government, were placed with farmers to learn the trade. Nor were the country people permitted to move into towns. Bounties were given for large families, and obdurate bachelors were heavily fined. So, in spite of a considerable infant mortality and a more than normal adult death rate from war and hardship, the 8,000 persons that Count Frontenac found in Canada in 1672 multiplied themselves eight times in the eighty years that ensued before the war of the English conquest, in 1756.

About this time, too, France, in the person of the Sieur de Lusson, accompanied by the noted explorers Perrot and Joliet, took ceremonious possession, at the Sault St. Marie, of the great western lakes and territories; nor could a spot for making formal proclamation of such import, though responded to only in the moan of illimitable forest and the roar of mighty waters, have been selected more singularly appropriate than the shores of that broad, rocky channel where the frigid waters of Lake Superior in a mile of seething foam rush down into Lake Huron.

JOHN LAW

This financier, popular and powerful at the court of the regent, was at the head of the India Company, and under his régime speculation was indulged in which resulted in a great financial collapse.

Hitherto the French explorers had been spurred on by the hope of finding by way of the Great Lakes a western passage to the seas of Cathay. But as travellers to the west found land ever before them, and rivers flowing east, more credit was given to the stories told by Indians about the "Father of Waters," whose name, Mississippi, was first learned by Europeans in 1670. Its exploration was then the problem before the adventurous French discoverers. With its solution the colonial power of France reached its highest point.

The first Europeans to reach the Mississippi from the north were Joliet and Marquette. The former was, at Colbert's instigation, sent out by the new Canadian governor, Frontenac, in 1673, with express orders to fathom the mystery of the "Western Water." Marquette, a missionary in Mackinac, volunteered to join him. The two followed the beaten track through Green Bay and up Fox River. There their Indian guides brought them to a place where they had only to carry their canoes two miles overland to reach a branch of the Wisconsin, and now they had but to trust themselves to the stream in order to reach the Mississippi itself in a few weeks. At the mouth of the Ohio they recognised the great waterway mentioned in the hazy reports of the Iroquois. When they reached the great confluence of the Missouri the problem they were attempting was solved. A tributary of this magnitude implied extensive tracts of land and a large watershed in the north and north-west; and the Mississippi itself, flowing ever southward, could lead nowhere else than to the Gulf of Mexico. They followed the river as far as the mouth of the Arkansas, **European** which was a further con-**Discovery of the** firmation of their supposi-**Mississippi** tions. Then, not wishing to run the risk of incurring Spanish hostility, which might render their discovery fruitless, they began the return journey and made their way slowly along the Illinois and the Des Plaines to the site of Chicago.

In France the prospects which Joliet's discovery opened up for French colonial expansion were only gradually comprehended ; but in Canada there were plenty of far-seeing men who were resolved to follow up these discoveries at once. Among these was the governor, Frontenac.

It was through his interposition that René Robert Cavelier, Sieur de la Salle, the possessor of one of the small feudal domains of which a number were established round about Montreal, received letters patent from the Crown, granting him the monopoly of trade on the Illinois and the right to establish trading factories there. It was thus that La Salle became the pioneer of western exploration and the discoverer of Louisiana, to the possession of which he attached great importance, believing that the future of French trade and of French colonisation depended on it.

La Salle then proceeded to erect forts at the mouth of the Mississippi, to render Louisiana safe against attacks by the Spaniards from the Gulf of Mexico, just as Fort Louis was to render it safe against English attacks from the Iroquois territory. His successes now aroused interest in France. No fewer than four ships set out to take him and his colonists to the mouth of the **La Salle's Fate** Mississippi, which, unfortu- **at the Hands of** nately, he failed to recognise **his Followers** from the sea. After sailing much too far west he landed in Texas, at the mouth of the Colorado, which he took to be a branch of the Mississippi. When he recognised his error the ships were already beyond recall.

He endeavoured to reach the Mississippi by land, but was killed by his own followers during the journey. The colonists on the Colorado succumbed to the climate and to the attacks of the natives. When Raphael de Tonty, La Salle's most faithful adherent, made his way from the Illinois to the lower Mississippi to bring help to his leader, all he could learn was that the expedition had been a complete failure. Still La Salle's achievement had decided the future of Louisiana. Where Joliet and La Salle had shown the way, missionaries, fur-traders, hunters and adventurers followed in their footsteps into that rich and extensive region to the west.

Small settlements sprang up on the Illinois, on the Kaskaskia, and on the Arkansas. Here, just as at first in Canada, the French did not, indeed, take root as true settlers and tillers of the soil, but, by adapting themselves to the customs of the natives, they gained great influence over them and were able to keep them on the French side in the struggle which was becoming inevitable between the French colonies in Canada and the English on the Atlantic coast. The knowledge possessed by the Indians played no small part in disseminating information as to the extraordinary richness of the land. It is only by thinking of its subsequent development **First French** that one can fully realise the **Town on the** glamour which was connected **Mississippi** for a short time with the name of Louisiana. In 1699 Lemoine d'Iberville sailed from France to the Gulf of Mexico, to attempt once more to carry out the scheme for which La Salle had given his life. He met with better fortune, and, after experimenting and feeling his way for several years, founded the settlement of Rosalie, the first French town in the district about the mouth of the Mississippi. For years it remained nothing more than a starting-point for the expeditions of fur-traders, fortune-hunters and others ; but even their occasional successes were sufficient to attract renewed attention in France. The monopoly of trade in Louisiana was leased by the Crown to a merchant named Crozat for a term of two years. After this it passed into the hands of the India Company under the management of John Law ; and under the regime of this financier, who for a time was all powerful at the court of the regent, the wildest speculation was indulged in.

The result, of course, was a financial collapse—one of the greatest the world has ever seen. But during this period not a little was done for Louisiana. There were a large number of colonists sent out, though the majority of them were not of the most desirable class, and it was by these that New Orleans was founded. But the incapacity of the French for colonial enterprise, combined with Law's unscrupulous procedure, put an abrupt end to the great expectations entertained for Louisiana. As is always the case, **The Great** the depression following the **Failure of** collapse was proportioned to the **Louisiana** inflation before it, and the colony, out of which, under sound management, much more might have been made than out of inhospitable Canada, was left to itself for half a century. Before its development had been taken up again, the blow was struck that put an end for ever to La Salle's dream of a French colonial empire extending from the Atlantic Ocean to the Gulf of Mexico.

THE MAKERS OF FRENCH CANADA
STRUGGLE AND PROGRESS UNDER FRONTENAC

IN the meantime, Count Frontenac, a strong, soldierly, middle-aged man, was seated in the Chateau St. Louis on the Rock of Quebec. He is the best remembered and most distinguished of the French governors of Canada, as are his contemporaries, Laval and Talon respectively, of its long list of bishops and intendants. His administration, too, bears one singular resemblance to that of Lord Dorchester, the most distinguished of the English occupants of the Chateau St. Louis. Both were divided by a considerable interval into two distinct periods. Each pro-consul had left Canada for good, but was sent back as the only man capable of facing a difficult situation. Furthermore, the many years covered by Frontenac's rule, as well as the length of interval, very nearly corresponded in the one century to those of Dorchester in the next. It fell to each of them, too, to defend Quebec against the only serious attacks ever made upon it by a civilised enemy outside those famous years of 1759-1760. Save in military capacity, however, there was little resemblance. Frontenac had not to handle the susceptibilities of an alien race smarting from defeat. He had no tact. He was arrogant and unyielding. He did not like Jesuits, and resented ecclesiastical dictation as much as he did the prying activity of the intendant. He was a bold and brave soldier, fertile in resource and prompt in action, and the period of his government in Canada was one in which such qualities were needed. He gave La Salle and other explorers his full sympathy and support. In money matters he was not over-scrupulous, for he came out to Canada impoverished and intended to mend his fortunes.

Frontenac Governor of Canada

Memorials of a Strong Governor

Nevertheless, if not actually a great man, he was in every sense a strong one, and his name is cherished to-day in statues and buildings. His first term, from 1672 to 1682, was not eventful, and was chiefly marked by friction in civil affairs. Though a grand seigneur and autocrat in his way, the count disapproved of the highly centralised autocracy which kept all popular expression absolutely mute. He went so far as to revive an assembly after the fashion of the old three estates of France, and in Quebec itself created a sort of quasi-popular municipal government. The intendant Talon, would have nothing to do with these innovations, and when the king learned from him what was going forward, Frontenac was severely censured and curtly ordered to refrain from all future experiments of such a nature. He understood the Indians, however, was popular with the friendly nations, and was feared by the Iroquois ; while the fur-trade, after a ten years' trial in the hands of the new company, was now resumed by the Crown, who granted licences to traders, reserving to itself a fourth of the produce.

The Recall of Frontenac

Frontenac, however, had sufficient enemies among his colleagues and subordinates to bring about his recall in 1682 after ten years of useful service. And, no doubt, the colony soon wished him back again, for two incapable governors, La Barre and Denonville, proceeded to demonstrate by contrast for the next seven years how valuable the shrewd if fiery soldier had been to it.

The English colonists, increasing at a far greater rate than their French neighbours, were beginning to cause that friction on the borders inevitable to the clashing of traders' interests and the presence of warlike Indians always watching their opportunity. La Barre made an ineffectual expedition against the Iroquois, whose tactics at this moment were to destroy the Illinois, and thereby deal a serious blow at the French fur-trade. The governor was recalled, and the Marquess de Denonville, who succeeded to the lowered prestige of his governancy, did no better, and in an active sense much worse. His administration, however, was illuminated by one of those brilliant feats of courage, enterprise and endurance that give a romance peculiarly its own to the French regime, though effected in this case at the expense of the British. For in 1685 the Chevalier de Troyes, an elderly army captain, and the three famous sons of a notable father, Charles le Moyne, a Canadian seigneur, with some eighty soldiers and coureurs de bois, marched through the trackless northern wilderness and captured several of the English trading posts on the Hudson's Bay.

This was the beginning of a dramatic struggle on those remote and lonely shores and the cold seas adjoining them. It was not finally settled, nor were the sufferings of the Hudson's Bay Company, whose loss was considerable, terminated till the Treaty of Utrecht, in 1713, restored the British traders again to full possession and peace. The chief hero of these enterprises was Pierre, the eldest of the Le Moyne brothers, commonly known as the Sieur d'Iberville, who became afterwards the most famous Canadian of his day. But Denonville, who at least had personal courage, had no credit for this audacious enterprise, which was inspired by a newly formed company, eager to capture the trade of Hudson's Bay. His own chief exploit was an expedition against the Seneca tribe of the Iroquois, which, thanks to money and men despatched from France for the purpose, was on far the largest scale of anything undertaken yet in Canada. Here were already 800 regulars in the colony, and as many more were now landed; and it may be here noted incidentally that the ranks of the Canadian noblesse were now greatly augmented by the officers of these corps, who, being **Denonville's** mainly poor gentilhommes with **Betrayal of** nothing but their birth and **the Iroquois** their swords, were tempted by the grants of seigneuries to remain in the colony. With 800 of these regulars, swelled to 2,000 by militia and the Christian Indians of the settlements, Denonville marched against the Senecas. On the way he seized, maltreated, and shipped to France for service in the galleys a number of friendly Iroquois settled under

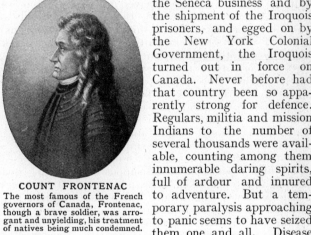

COUNT FRONTENAC

The most famous of the French governors of Canada, Frontenac, though a brave soldier, was arrogant and unyielding, his treatment of natives being much condemned.

the French guns at Fort Frontenac, Kingston, for which treacherous act, everywhere denounced, a terrible reckoning was taken. Yet, with this powerful force, the governor did little more than destroy the villages of the Senecas, a matter of mere temporary inconvenience to the Indians, while he failed to reach their **Iroquois'** fighting-men, who had retired **Terrible** with their families and mov- **Revenge** ables to give a sanguinary account of themselves on a later occasion. The Iroquois had now come formally under the ægis of the British Crown, and the situation grew yet more complicated. The governor of New York, too, began to threaten retaliation on account of certain English traders who had been plundered and seized. In the following year, maddened by the Seneca business and by the shipment of the Iroquois prisoners, and egged on by the New York Colonial Government, the Iroquois turned out in force on Canada. Never before had that country been so apparently strong for defence. Regulars, militia and mission Indians to the number of several thousands were available, counting among them innumerable daring spirits, full of ardour and innured to adventure. But a temporary paralysis approaching to panic seems to have seized them one and all. Disease from bad provisions was raging among the soldiers, and one of those quasi-famines to which the country, from its uneconomic constitution, was peculiarly liable hampered its energies. To shorten a long tale, on the night of August 4th, 1689, further screened by a tempest of hail, 1,500 Iroquois warriors crossed Lake St. Louis just above Montreal, and hid themselves among the settlements at La Chine.

Then ensued the worst massacre recorded in Canadian history, for some 200 persons were killed on the spot, and nearly as many more carried off to a far worse death. In spite of troops and forts, the savages held for two months the region that they had decimated. The terror spread all through Canada; no man knew where some scattered bands of the dreaded Iroquois might next strike, and the tidings flew far away through the western wilderness, to the detriment everywhere of the French prestige and the power of " Onontio," as the French king was called.

These two years were sad ones. Denonville was recalled, and Frontenac, though in his seventieth year, went again in his place. But the glory of Louis XIV. was waning;

Scheme to Capture New York
his vassals, the Stuarts, had been driven from the English throne, and his able and relentless foe, William of Orange, was now seated upon it. The schemes that were to check the power of France, and, finally, through the genius of Marlborough, to shatter its armies, were in progress. There would be no more troops or money for Canada, and Frontenac understood that he had to face the situation with such material as was already in the colony. But the plan of action conceived by the king and himself was an altogether novel and audacious one, and well suited to the grim old soldier's temperament.

This was nothing less than the capture of New York itself, the heart and brain of the English power against Canada and the source of all warlike supplies to the Iroquois. A thousand regulars and 600 militia were to march from Canada by Lake Champlain to Albany and descend the Hudson, with whom two ships of war were to lie off New York and co-operate.

The little town, weak as was supposed in fighting men, once taken, every inhabitant of the province, English and Dutch, save any few Catholics there might be, was to be forcibly deported—a proposition which may be commended to those taking the more emotional view of the removal of Acadians in the next century, a people who were aggressively troublesome and who steadily refused to take the oath of allegiance to a government that for forty years had treated them with singular consideration. By this pretty scheme, New England would be cut off from her sister colonies, and, above all, the

Canada Quaking with Terror
Iroquois isolated. But it all came to nothing, though Frontenac sailed with two ships of war and the best of intentions. So many delays occurred that when he landed in Quebec, to the disgust of the Jesuits and other leaders, but to the joy doubtless of the people generally, he had abandoned his plans, for that season at least. When he discovered the state of the colony, still helpless and quaking with the Indian

terror, and its border desolate, the capture of New York passed into the domain of dreams. His first move, nevertheless, after restoring some confidence to the colony, was to harass the frontiers of New England and New York with various war parties of French and mission Indians and all the horrors of the torch and the scalping knife, his object being to restore the French prestige in the eyes of the Iroquois. The French of this period never understood their English neighbours, but interpreted their industry and comparatively unadventurous temperament to mean a lack of fighting instinct, and Frontenac thought he had given them a salutary and sufficient lesson by his war parties. But he soon found his mistake.

Additional impetus was now given to Anglo-French hostilities, for the two nations were at open war. The English colonists were, moreover, represented to the Canadians and Indians as rebels against their own king, who had been, as everybody knows, a good enough friend to France. The mission Indians, too, who were now a valuable support to the Canadian arms,

Massacres in the Name of the Cross
had sufficiently mastered the externals of the Roman faith to regard themselves as religious crusaders, and tomahawked and tortured their English prisoners in the name of the Cross, while their squaws told their beads on the Island of Orleans and the outskirts of Quebec. The picture of a Pilgrim Father being roasted by an Abernaki Indian for his lack of Christian faith will doubtless commend itself to the modern readers as the quintessence of grim humour. It must be said at once, however, that the priests and seigniors who accompanied their half-tamed flock to battle did their best to curb these amenities, which the Indian regarded as the chief object of war, and cheerfully submitted to himself when the luck went against him.

Frontenac's position was interesting. He had relieved the colony from its terror and tension, and the grim old man could now afford to amuse himself with the ecclesiastics and laymen that formed his council, all of whom he had flouted or imprisoned in former days, and who hated him cordially, though compelled to abase themselves. Trade, however, had returned ; clouds of canoes—a welcome sight—laden with furs once more floated down to Montreal. Frontenac went up there to welcome them, and, brandishing a hatchet, sang the war song and ate dog, seasoned with prunes, round the same fire with their chiefs. This was the kind of complex personality who made himself felt in the North America of that day ; it was not only trade, though, but war, that the count had in his mind, for an English armament from Albany, unknown to most of them, was at that very moment in movement against Montreal.

The expedition in question, which was to be reinforced by Iroquois, was baulked of its fruition, partly by inter-colonial jealousies, and partly by smallpox, which thinned its numbers and frightened off the Indians. But a part of it ravaged the neighbourhood of Montreal, and before Frontenac could avenge the insult much graver news reached him by a hurried messenger in the almost incredible report, as it seemed to him, of a Massachusetts fleet and army in the St. Lawrence beating up towards Quebec. Before he reached that city, a matter of four days' stiff paddling against driving rain in a canoe, the news met him that the New England **Hostile** fleet had passed Tadoussac. In **Fleet before** his absence his deputy had **Quebec** completed the palisade defences he had begun on the two weak sides of the city. The count was greeted with enthusiasm ; men had flocked into Quebec, and Frontenac found himself with 3,000 regulars and militia behind fortifications that Nature and his own foresight had made proof, he might well think, against all the farmers of New England.

Two days later, on October 16th, thirty-four vessels of divers sorts sailed past the Island of Orleans and anchored in the basin of Quebec. They represented the military and naval power of Massachusetts, her patience worn out by frontier wars and burning with religious fervour as strong as the Jesuits to capture Quebec and stamp out the Popish idolaters and instigators of the Indian horrors. The expedition was commanded by Sir William Phips, a rough but able New England sea-dog recently knighted. He had first captured Port Royal in Acadia, and, being badly informed, thought Quebec would fall a ready prey.

Frontenac's feelings were those of amazement and indignation, sobered by the significance of the spectacle. Here was a surprise visit from a single one of those unmartial colonies he and Louis XIV. had proposed to depopulate in part, and altogether to overawe with 1,600 men and two ships. Frontenac's choler was to be further tried. A boat, carrying a white flag, put off from the admiral's ship and landed an officer, who was led blindfolded through demonstrative and jeering crowds to the chateau, where, in the great hall, he opened **Phips's Famous** his eyes on the scowling faces **Message** of the grim old governor and **to Frontenac** his suite, gorgeous in the lace and gold and finery that the French maintained in the New World with punctilious ceremony. This is, perhaps, one of the most picturesque and suggestive scenes in North American history. The young New Englander in his simple uniform might well flinch at the message he had to deliver. He soon recovered his composure and delivered Admiral Phips's letter, which was read aloud by an interpreter to the indignant company.

It was, indeed, well calculated to rouse the Frenchman's ire, for, after reading them a lecture on their barbarities towards English settlers, Phips went on to demand in detail an immediate surrender of all Canada and everything in it, promising in such case a general exercise of King William's clemency towards its inhabitants, Frontenac included. Otherwise, he was prepared to avenge all injuries and reduce the colony to subjection to the British Crown. A definite answer in writing was demanded within an hour, and as if to support his commander's brave words, the envoy, now restored to his native British sangfroid, intensified by the New England atmosphere, took out his watch and handed it to Frontenac.

The gorgeous company were, not unnaturally, furious, crying out that Phips was nothing but a pirate, and demanding that his messenger should be hanged on the spot. Frontenac, however, stifled his feelings, and answered quietly that he should not require an hour to prepare his answer. **Frontenac's** As to William of Orange, a **Reply to** usurper and violator of **Admiral Phips** family ties and destroyer of the true religion, he did not recognise him as king of England at all. In Phips himself he merely saw a traitor to his rightful king, and most assuredly would write to him no letter, but answer him by the mouths of his guns. After this the envoy was again blindfolded and conducted back to his boat. Space forbids any account of the siege which was conducted with more vigour and courage than skill for several days by these 2,000 farmers and fishermen against a place of notorious strength held by 3,000 regulars and militia under skilled leadership.

Phips himself did not shine. He fired away all his ammunition in a furious and ill-directed bombardment from his ships, which **Failure of the Siege of Quebec** was replied to with equal vigour and more success. The men were landed on the Beaufort shore, and though undisciplined amateurs led by amateurs with much more zeal than discretion, half fed and sickening with smallpox, managed to maintain themselves for two or three days and fight a number of fairly successful skirmishes. But the ford over the St. Charles below the city they had neither the dash nor leading to cross, nor, if they had, would success against such odds have been likely. A French chronicler within the city, however, relates that they fought with as much courage as ignorance, and thinks that, with better discipline and leading, they might even have been successful. At any rate, they gave Quebec a very bad fright, and the city gave itself up to transports of Te Deums and bell-ringing when the crestfallen Phips, with his fleet and army, sailed away.

Partisan warfare, however, went on merrily along the frontier, between the French and their Indians, the Iroquois and the English. Bounties were paid in scalps and prisoners, while burning homesteads and ravaged villages marked each little battle. The Ottawa was the great artery of the Canadian fur-trade, and the efforts of the Iroquois were constantly directed to cutting their connections. The unproductive element in Canada was numerically out of proportion to the industrial peasantry. Scarcity was chronic, and the supply ships from France were frequently captured by the English. Frontenac raged at the Anglo-Americans, and urged the king to **Frontenac the Right Man for Canada** attack Boston and New York and extirpate "those old Puritans." At home he supported the Recollets, and thwarted the Jesuits, who vigorously denounced the plays and dances which, being a sociable old man, he loved to encourage.

But he was the right man for Canada in those troublous times. Yet even Frontenac could not tame the Iroquois, who successfully maintained, as it were, the balance of power between French and English, and kept all the neighbouring Indian nations in terror. Cruel and blood-thirsty as they were, it is difficult to withhold one's admiration for the influence wielded by this handful of naked warriors and politicians over so many rival races, red and white. Their loyalty to the English stood many severe tests; their traditional enmity to the French was interrupted occasionally by treaties which, to the Iroquois, were regarded as mere pauses in which to gather breath for a more effectual spring upon their old enemies' still bleeding flanks.

Nor was it merely the individual power of these numerically inconsiderable tribes. Their renown and their fixed policy was an example and a support of disaffection from the far north to the farthest west. Far away on the Mississippi, when the dearness or scarcity of French brandy was weighed against the cheapness and abundance of English rum, the dissatisfied Kickapoo, Fox or Masoucin Indian bethought him of the Iroquois, and took heart to exact his terms. In his seventy-sixth year, carried in a chair, Frontenac, at the head of over **Death of Canada's Great Governor** 2,000 men, made his last attack on the confederacy, and destroyed the village of the Onandagas and Oneidas. But the warriors had vanished, to return again at the appointed hour. Soon after came the peace, cemented by the Treaty of Ryswick.

Te Deums were sung in the cathedral of Quebec, and the envoys from New York were dined in great state by Frontenac at the chateau, where, by an irony of fate, the last public act of the fiery old veteran was to drink the health of Dutch William. He might as well have sung his own death-song that night, for death's mark was already upon him; and a few weeks later, reconciled to some of his bitterest enemies on his death-bed, beloved by the common people—the soldiers and the mission Indians, admired and even mourned as a brave foe, it is said, by the very Iroquois themselves, he was buried in the church of the Recollets.

With his last breath he flouted the Jesuits by refusing burial in the official quarter of the cathedral. His last letter to the governor of New York on the subject of the Iroquois, written with apparent difficulty, breathed his feeling about them, which may be briefly summarised as *Delenda est Carthago.*

Callières, a friend of Frontenac, succeeded him with ability and success. He could not destroy the Iroquois, but he succeeded nevertheless in making an enduring peace with them, helping the latter's growing consciousness that the New Yorkers, though desirable fair-weather friends, were an uncertain support in war. The increasing population of Canada, its quasi-martial organisation, its military support from France and consistent policy, enabled the country to outgrow the fear of the Iroquois which had been its curse throughout the seventeenth century.

The Peace of Ryswick had only lasted five years when the wars of Marlborough began, and lit the torch of strife once more in the remote and sombre forests of North America. Both before and after the peace, Acadia, with its still scant French population of about a thousand, had been the scene of constant fighting; the small posts on the coast had been often taken and retaken. Its Micmac Indians of Acadia proper and the Abernakis of the mainland greatly harried the outermost New England settlers in what is now the state of Maine.

The French take Newfoundland Fishing disputes even then were frequent. Phips, on his way to Quebec, had taken Port Royal (Annapolis), and practically annexed the province. The famous D'Iberville, already mentioned, and now in command of a French ship, harried the New England coast, and with a considerable armament conquered Newfoundland, which had gradually grown from an extensive fishing station, in which the British element was strongest, to an actual British possession. From thence he sailed to Hudson's Bay, the scene of his earlier triumphs, won a naval victory in the bay, and took all the forts.

In 1711 the British Government, at the instigation of the colonies, organised a serious attempt on Canada. It was the greatest failure in American history. A fleet of eighty-eight sail, under Sir Hovenden Walker, carrying several thousand troops, was to be joined in Canada by 4,000 provincials marching by way of Lake George. The latter were duly mustered on that historic lake. But Walker's fleet was scattered by a storm in the Gulf of St. Lawrence, where eight transports and 900 men were lost. On collecting his ships again at Cape Breton, though still strong and with another land army awaiting him, the admiral's heart or judgment failed

him and he sailed for home, where he was ill-received for bringing not only disgrace, but ridicule, on an armament that had contained the veteran soldiers of Marlborough ; and Quebec rang its joy bells to some purpose. But with the Treaty of Utrecht in 1713 there was a fresh shuffling of the cards. Hudson's Bay was restored ;

Newfoundland Restored to England so was Newfoundland, while the whole of Acadia, except the island of Cape Breton, was ceded to England. The latter could do little with it. A weak garrison at Mount Royal, now called Annapolis, was the only footing in a province where the Micmacs and French settlers did practically as they pleased. The retention of Cape Breton by the French was indeed a fatal concession on the part of England.

They at once began building by far the strongest fortified town in North America, at a cost of £2,000,000 sterling, on one horn of a splendid harbour; and Louisbourg, the " Dunkirk of the North," became the key to all Canadian waters and the scourge of New England shipping. During the thirty years' peace which followed, the Acadians, increasing rapidly in numbers and nominally under the benign rule of the Georges, were kept French at heart by the tireless efforts of Canadian priests, who assured them that the country would ultimately be retaken. The great fortress town of Louisbourg, with its fleets, garrison and considerable civic population, to the north of the province, was in truth a better evidence of their compatriots' power and intentions than was the company or two of New England militiamen squatting forlorn upon the southern bay of their conquerors' might.

But what of Canada proper during Walpole's long peace between 1713 and 1743 ? The march of events in Acadia only affected the future of the territory concerned. Canada, with its two growing towns of Quebec and Montreal, and now steadily increasing hardy rural populace,

Canada During the Long Peace was throwing out offshoots characteristic of its peculiar genius that were full of mighty portent. The English had now resigned all hope of the great north-west, and the French sat secure in their fortified posts and in their understanding with the Indians for hundreds of miles along the frontiers of civilisation at Niagara, Detroit, Michillimackinac. But there was much more than this. Posts sprang up in the Illinois, the Wabash, and on the

Ohio. The mouth of the Mississippi had been constituted into a French province, and under the name of Louisiana had the brave D'Iberville for its first governor.

The Canada of the French Régime From thence to the northern lakes was forged a gradually strengthening chain of French influence, marked at longer or shorter intervals by palisaded forts, mounted with French guns and flying the Fleur-de-Lys. They were somewhat more, too, than mere forts, for they were usually surrounded by numerous small villages of traders with Indian wives or their equivalent, and frequented by small groups of Indian warriors, that by conversion—for the priests were everywhere—or still more, perhaps, by the brandy and ammunition always in stock, were attached to these remote oases. As to Canada itself, little need be said of the period leading up to the great war. Of progress, not much except in the number of inhabitants, the increase of seigniors, the gradual development of a narrow fringe of continuously settled country along both banks of the river, from below the island of Orleans to the island of Montreal. This 200 miles of river front, with a strip of seigniories up the Richelieu and an important town at either extremity, together with the secondary one of Three Rivers, about midway, constituted the Canada of the French régime. The habitant — for the name of peasant was resented—multiplied rapidly, lived in quite reasonable comfort, obeyed his priest and his seignior, and was content to be treated as a pawn by an absolute government, only grumbling a little, perhaps, at the frequent corvées.

His religious ardour and well-developed hatred of the heretic Bastonnais reconciled him to marching to battle whenever and wheresoever he was ordered, altogether making an excellent irregular soldier. He often failed to raise crops sufficient to feed a colony weighted with regular garrisons and yet more by clouds of coureurs de bois, who followed the fur-trade only with or without licences, for his agriculture was both primitive and frequently interfered with by the beat of drum. In Quebec and Montreal there was a gay and even brilliant, if limited, social circle of officers, civil servants and the more affluent seigniors. Corruption flourished immediately at the expense of the French king, and indirectly at the expense of the common people, whose channels of supply were often tapped or diverted at headquarters. Religious houses prospered and acquired property, though against them no corruption, to be sure, was ever charged ; while churches rose at shorter intervals along the banks of the St. Lawrence with a dignity of fabric somewhat disproportionate to the humble one-storied, thatched and white-washed buildings extended beside them. But in 1743 England and France were at war again in Europe and the long period of comparative peace for Canada was over.

A. G. BRADLEY

SIEUR D'IBERVILLE
Formed one of the party which, in 1685, marched through the wilderness of Northern America, capturing several of the English trading-posts on the Hudson's Bay.

A VIEW OF NEW AMSTERDAM IN THE SEVENTEENTH CENTURY

ENGLISH COLONIES IN THE SOUTH
HISTORY OF THEIR RISE AND PROGRESS

AS the permanent French occupation of North American territory began with Champlain in 1603, though Champlain had been preceded by pioneers, so the permanent English occupation began in 1606; and rivalry between the colonising schemes of French and English did not become acute till the expulsion of James II. from England converted that country into the most dangerous of the opponents of Louis XIV. at the end of the century.

In 1606 Raleigh was shut up in the Tower of London, and his Virginian settlement had been wiped out. But his ideas had taken root in the minds of others besides the adventurers who would be satisfied with nothing but gold-mines. In that year a company was formed which obtained from James I. charters for founding two colonies on the North American coast between Nova Scotia and Florida. One of the two schemes was **Town Named After the Stuart King** dropped; the second was carried out by the establishment on the Chesapeake Bay of a settlement which was named Jamestown, after the first Stuart king of England. Raleigh's name of Virginia was adopted for the colony. The promoters meant business; it was not a Crown affair, a scheme for providing the king with estates after the Spanish model.

The Dutch were already setting an example of commercial colonisation in the East Indies, and English merchants had started their own East India Company. Now an experiment was to be tried which might develop into a materialisation of the dreams of Gilbert and Raleigh. But it was an experiment with no precedents to serve as guide. The Elizabethan experiments had failed, partly from want of detailed elaboration. It is not surprising that the next was over-elaborate to begin with. There was to be a governing body at home, and another in the colony, the former nominated by the Crown, and selecting the latter from among the settlers,

leaving it to choose its own president. The settlers arrived in 1607; among them was Richard Hakluyt, the famous author and editor of the narratives of the Elizabethan explorers. Most of them were of the adventurer type, younger sons, or **John Smith and the Indian Princess** men of broken fortunes; and the start of the colony was not very promising. Fortunately, one of them, Captain John Smith, was endowed with the qualities of a born leader, and it was mainly due to his energy that the attempt did not collapse.

He is the hero of the romantic story of the Indian " princess " Pocahontas, who saved him from death at the hands of her tribe, and subsequently herself married an Englishman. John Smith kept the community from going to pieces, and the company in London were resolute. A revised charter, granted in 1609, placed the administration on a more practical basis, and newcomers arrived who were better fitted for the work that had to be done—not mere adventurers, but real farmers and mechanics.

The advantages possessed by the members of the company were that they had absolute possession of the land they had settled, that they remained English citizens, and that they had the right of unrestricted trade in colonial produce. This last privilege, which stood in strange contradiction to the usage of other nations, seemed to free the Virginia Company from the necessity of disposing of its products to the Mother Country or by its agency. The full effect of this privilege was certainly not foreseen **A Source of Colonial Friction** by James I., and he made some efforts to render it ineffective. Later on, the navigation acts of the commonwealth and Restoration limited its application considerably; and the attempt to enforce more strictly in the English colonies the generally admitted principle of exclusive trade with the Mother Country was one of the many causes that led to the eventual breaking away of the United States from Great Britain. At first the colony was carried on on a communistic basis. Captain Smith introduced—for a time at least—compulsory labour of six hours daily. But the settlement did not begin to prosper till the land was divided among the colonists as private property. The discovery, in tobacco culture, of an industry that could be pursued on a large scale caused the settlements in Virginia to progress rapidly. Many of the colonists had been brought over at the cost of the company, and had to repay their debts before they could acquire property of their own ; but, thanks to the high price of tobacco, especially in Holland, they were soon able to render themselves independent and to add, by purchase, new lands to what had already been granted them. The profitableness of the tobacco industry was the best advertisement for the colony, and enticed over many more emigrants, among them not only the shipwrecked and indigent, but also wealthy and enterprising men, who began tobacco culture on a larger scale and so brought it into better repute. The scarcity of women was soon remedied by the rapid industrial progress. In 1619 the company tried the experiment of sending to Virginia, at its own expense, a number of young women. Anyone marrying one of these had to repay the passage-money to the company, tobacco being sometimes taken in payment. Very soon the young women were all married, and the company was enabled to repeat the experiment and even increase the charge for passage-money.

The system of transporting to the colonies criminals condemned to hard labour, which flourished to such an extent in the Antilles, was also tried in Virginia, which was at first occasionally used as a convict settlement. This might have gone on to a very much greater extent had not the spirit of the colonists risen to such a degree that they most emphatically refused to allow such an undesirable element to be brought among them.

CAPTAIN JOHN SMITH
A native of Lincolnshire, Smith in 1609 became the leader of the band of colonists who settled on James River, in Virginia. Keeping the colony alive for two years, an accident necessitated his return to England for surgical aid.

On the other hand, they eagerly welcomed another undesirable addition to their population. In 1620 a Dutch vessel landed the first negro slaves at Jamestown. The demand for these was so great that not only were Dutch ships with richer freight attracted thither, but English and even Virginian traders undertook the sale of the blacks. Thus, as early as the seventeenth century that plantation life grew up which was afterwards characteristic of the southern states of the Union. Soon the whites in Virginia formed only the aristocracy ; they lived as plantation owners on their extensive estates, or as mechanics in the not very numerous towns. But the bulk of the work, and especially of the work on the tobacco plantations, and on the cotton plantations that more than a century later surpassed them in importance, was, except where prison labour was employed, performed by negro slaves, whose number continued to increase as the colony developed.

Political circumstances also played their part in the rapid development of the colony. Under the second charter James I. renounced, in favour of the company, many of the rights stipulated for by the Crown. The choice of the directors was left to the members of the company. These nominated, in place of the colonial manager, a governor of the province, who had almost unlimited power on account **The Rapid Development of the Colony** of his great distance from his superiors at home. For this reason much depended on the choice of suitable persons for this position, and the company's selection was not always a happy one ; but its directors were sensible enough to pay heed to the remonstrances of the colonists, whose influence on the management not only continually increased, but was soon afterwards regulated by law.

In 1612 the management of the company was transferred from the board of directors to the shareholders themselves, with the provision that four general meetings were to be held yearly, to settle matters connected with the management of the colony ; and seven years later this general assembly granted to the colonists a share in the management of their internal affairs.

Each of the eleven settlements then existing in Virginia was to send two deputies to Jamestown. These deputies, the "assembly of burgesses," were, in conference with the governor and his nominated council, to discuss the affairs of the colony, and to take action accordingly. The assembly of burgesses rapidly **Virginian** developed in importance; but **Assembly of** the company's control in **Burgesses** London was unsatisfactory. In 1623 the charter was revoked, and a third constitution was framed and proclaimed in 1625. The ultimate control still lay with a council in London; but it was virtually a committee of the privy council. This council appointed a governor and a council of twelve, who were to be the responsible executive in the colony, some of these being chosen from among the colonists; and in effect the assembly of burgesses was permitted to exercise the functions of the English House of Commons. The council in London, though the actual ultimate authority, in practice abstained from interfering in the affairs of the colony. Very much as in England, the assembly proceeded gradually to insist on acquiring a practical and definite control over the executive. Materially the development of the colony was very rapid; but in other matters complete indifference prevailed. The economic conditions gave an aristocratic tone to the colony. Thus, during the struggle of Charles I. against the rising democracy in the Mother Country, the sympathies of the colonists were entirely on the side of the monarch; and when the Roundheads' victory was complete, many a Royalist made his way to Virginia. But this did not prevent the colonial assembly from maintaining its own parliamentary privileges, nor from employing on the plantations the labour of the prisoners of war sent over by Cromwell. The Restora-

PRINCESS POCAHONTAS
The daughter of an Indian chief, she befriended the early Virginia settlers, and eventually married an Englishman. Embracing Christianity, she sailed with her husband for England, but died off Gravesend in March, 1617.

tion, on the other hand, was followed by most disadvantageous consequences for Virginia. Charles II. enforced the provisions of the Navigation Act more strictly, and thus almost destroyed the freedom of trade enjoyed by Virginia, and placed it in this respect in a position very similar to that of the Spanish colonies. This did not seriously affect the Virginians, who did not carry on a large trade; but other measures, that affected their interest more, roused their indignation.

The extravagance characteristic of Charles II. led him to attempt to hand over all Virginia to two of his favourites for a period of thirty-one years, and though the colony maintained its constitutional rights, it had to submit to be saddled with additional expenditure. The king's Virginia representatives were of as dull conscience as himself. An Indian rising that broke out after the two races had lived peaceably side by side for half a century was by some attributed to the shameless manner in which the governor, for his own personal profit, used his creatures to plunder and oppress the Indians. Matters went so far that a section of the colonists rose against the governor. During this civil war, which was put down with much bloodshed, the capital was burned. Still the greater part of the population remained apathetic as before. The typical Virginian sat, like a pasha, in the midst of his extensive estates, and kept himself apart from everything that did not bear upon his own well-being. His wealth enabled him to widen his intellectual horizon. Of all the colonists the Virginians had perhaps the most intellectual intercourse with the Old World. Among them it was the fashion to travel, and to show to guests from Europe a really princely hospitality worthy of the name. But the Virginians of that time took no further part in politics than the maintenance of their ancient constitutional liberties rendered necessary. The second of the Southern or "planter" colonies to be founded was Maryland.

We shall see presently how the northern group was in effect the creation of that spirit of ecclesiastical intolerance which drove Puritans, even those who had no wish to secede from the established Church, to seek in other regions freedom to worship as their consciences required. Maryland was the product, in like manner, of the hos-

The Roman Catholic Colony of Maryland tility of law and of popular sentiment to Roman Catholicism. The Romanist Lord Baltimore proposed to establish in the New World a colony where his co-religionists should have free play. Charles I., absolutely loyal as he was to Anglicanism, was far from hostile to the religion of his wife, Henrietta Maria.

Lord Baltimore was granted a charter, and Maryland came into being in 1632, when the first Puritan colony in the north had already been in existence for more than a decade. Its founder, learning from the persecution to which he himself had been subjected on account of his faith, made absolute freedom in matters of religious belief a basic principle in the colony, whose foundation was readily authorised by his royal friend. Maryland is the only one of the English colonies whose possessors were not Protestants, and even there the majority of the inhabitants belonged to one or other of the reformed sects. But while, in New England, fanatical Puritan intolerance prevailed, while even in the tolerant southern states Catholics were rigidly excluded, Maryland, on principle, opened her doors to men of all creeds, and that without ever endangering her own liberties.

Here, as in most of the other colonies, the proprietary rights of the founders were gradually relaxed before the self-reliance and self-government of the colonists, who organised themselves on the democratic model of their neighbours. The struggle to obtain recognition from the proprietors lasted perhaps a little longer in Maryland; but here, as elsewhere, the goal was reached. In consequence

Maryland an Example of Good Government of its geographical position, Maryland developed into a plantation state; but large accessions of the humbler classes to its population saved it from the evils of the plantation system as known in Virginia, while the kindly spirit that hovered over its foundation saved it from the degeneracy that accompanies cultivation by slave labour. Moreover, friendly relations with the natives were established, so that in all respects Maryland afforded an example of wise moderation and good government. The third of the great southern colonies, Carolina, was not actually occupied till Charles II., in 1663, gave the district between Florida and Virginia to eight proprietors in perpetuity.

What is most interesting about this colony is the history of its constitution. It was specially provided in the royal deed of gift that the colonists should have a share in the management of local affairs; further, the philosopher John Locke had drawn up for this province a constitution which was to unite a patriarchal aristocracy with parliamentary privileges. But Locke's scheme was so complicated and so unpractical in detail that it was never fully carried out. Only two of the principles of Locke's constitution survived—tolerance in religion, and slavery.

As for the rest, the influence of her neighbour Virginia was of far more importance to North Carolina than the sovereign rights of its aristocratic possessors, which were revoked in 1729. Some settlers had migrated from Virginia to the northern

Virginia's Internal Struggles districts of Carolina even before the royal letters patent had been granted; the Virginia plantation system also spread there. The governors of Virginia repeatedly interfered in the management of North Carolina, and the northern part of the colony was often involved in the internal struggles of Virginia. The principal difference between the two colonies was that in Carolina, during the first decades of its existence, no effective provincial government was established, and that a most undesirable class of immigrants were introduced, who made use of their rights of self-government only to perpetuate the unsettled state then existing.

This was changed only when the province was constituted a Crown colony. As such Carolina advanced rapidly, developing on the same economic lines as her older sister Virginia, and becoming a dangerous rival to her in the tobacco markets. The eight proprietors of Carolina turned their attention chiefly to the south. Here, in 1670, the town of Charleston was founded, with settlers of whom the greater number came from Barbados Island. In accordance with the aristocratic and centralising tendency of Locke's proposals the rulers attached great importance to developing the strength of

LANDING A CARGO OF NEGRO SLAVES AT JAMESTOWN IN 1619

To such an extent did the tobacco industry flourish in Virginia that within a few months of the division of land among the natives it became necessary to employ additional labour. With this object in view, the, system of transporting criminals condemned to hard labour was tried, but with indifferent results, the settlers protesting against this undesirable element. Then a Dutch man-of-war landed at Jamestown and sold twenty negroes as slaves. Later on, that number was increased, the presence of the slaves eventually playing an important part in the life of the settlements.

Specially drawn for the HISTORY OF THE WORLD by J. Walter Wilson, R.I.

the colony in a town community, and to the avoidance of the scattering of the population characteristic of Virginia and North Carolina. For this reason Charleston sprang up more rapidly than Jamestown. Its better regulated government and its religious toleration attracted to Carolina elements that were wanting in its northern **The Rapid** neighbours — Puritans from **Advance of** New York, Huguenots from **Charleston** France, Presbyterians from Scotland—every element that desired to work its way upward by its own strength and was opposed to the development of the plantation system. Further, the proximity of the Spanish colony of St. Augustine (Florida) caused the development of South Carolina to differ in many respects from that of the northern provinces.

The contests occasionally engaged in by the neighbouring Spanish and English colonists were indeed, as a rule, of little or of no importance, and both parties finally agreed to remain at peace even if war should break out between the home countries. Still, the proximity of the Spanish colonies was a strong incentive to buccaneering—an established institution among those of the colonists who came from the islands. Finally, Carolina followed the example of its Spanish neighbours in employing large numbers of Indians as slaves, generally such as had been captured on Spanish territory or dragged from Spanish ships.

About the same time another new province, under management of a quite different kind, was mapped out to the south of the English colonial possessions. The philanthropic movement made its appearance very early in England, and its influence, thanks to the example of the New England colonists, and of William Penn, had been already felt several times in America. Pity for those languishing in the debtors' prisons of England induced Oglethorpe to start a movement in their **How Georgia** favour. When public and **Came to** private support had enabled **be Founded** him to collect the necessary funds, he secured from George I. a charter giving the grantees exclusive rights of colonisation for twenty-one years in the territory that lay between the rivers Savannah and Altamaha, stretching from ocean to ocean.

The colony received, as had her northern neighbours, the name of the reigning sovereign, and was called Georgia Augusta.

To South Carolina the establishment of this colony, which lay between her and the Spaniards, was of great importance ; for the new province undertook the defence of the southern boundary (Oglethorpe himself twice took the field against the Spaniards) and rendered possible to its northern neighbours a prosperous and undisturbed development. Alliances were made with the Indians, and few white settlers have been held in such esteem by their red-skinned neighbours as was the mild and worthy Oglethorpe.

At first the province developed according to his ideas. It was a place of refuge for the oppressed and persecuted, and toleration, religious and political, was extended to all. But, as time went on, natural influences proved stronger than human will. It was impossible that the land, whose physical character specially fitted it for an agricultural development on the same lines as Virginia's, should remain for ever in the possession of the poor and disinherited. In Georgia, as elsewhere, the planters got more and more of the land into their possession, brought their slaves thither, and **Slaves in** thus crushed out the attempts **the English** of small holders to carry on a **Colonies** different system. By the middle of the eighteenth century Georgia had become a plantation state like Virginia and the Carolinas, and as such it continued its political development side by side with them.

The origin and development of the southern states of the North American Union differ widely from the picture usually regarded as typical of English colonisation in North America. Geographical conditions decisively influenced the course of development. Even in cases where it was the intention of the colonists to found settlements similar to those in New England there was a gradual transition to the system which developed first and in its most perfect form in Virginia. Most of the colonies were, for a time at least, under the influence of Old World feudal institutions.

They soon freed themselves from these ; but the aristocratic spirit, characteristic of feudalism, with its classification of mankind according to their possessions and rank, came to life again in changed form. The place of the English feudal aristocracy was taken by the large landed proprietors, who kept not only their troops of slaves, but also the greater part of the free white

THE NATIVE TOWN OF POMEIOCK SURROUNDED BY A WALL OF POLES

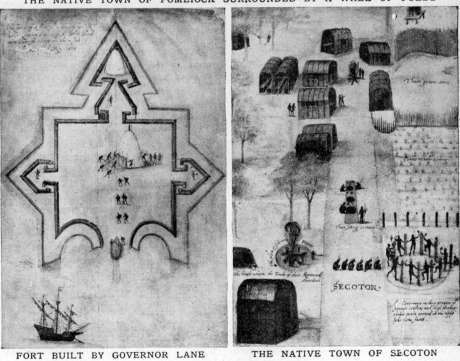

FORT BUILT BY GOVERNOR LANE   THE NATIVE TOWN OF SECOTON

THE FIRST ENGLISH COLONY IN VIRGINIA
From the original drawings made in 1585

6043

population in a state of dependence. The doctrine of the equality of all did not prevail either in ethics or in law.

The planters had practically unlimited power on their own estates, and, in combination, they made use of the parliamentary privileges granted to the landed interests to dominate almost without opposition the government of the province. Thus the southern colonies, with their special views and special needs, were more closely related to the Spanish colonies than to the New England provinces in the north. Settlement often took place as in the Portuguese colonies ; with this difference, that the latter had not the right, common to both English and French feudal colonies, of granting titles and dignities—a right that did much to strengthen the aristocratic tendency of the southern states. The right of possession, as in the Spanish, Portuguese and French colonies, was conferred by conquest. In the treatment of the natives in South Carolina the worst Spanish examples were followed : if hostile, they were made slaves ; but even if they submitted peacefully to the rule of the strangers, they were not, as in the Spanish colonies, granted the rights of subjects.

Oppression of the Natives in South Carolina

The North Americans make the claim for their forefathers that they treated the Indians better than others did. The Spaniards took possession, not only of the land, but also of the persons of the natives, compelling them to pay taxes and to labour in the fields. The French did not interfere with the personal liberty of the natives, but they took the land from them solely by right of conquest. The English, on the contrary—and with them must be classed the Dutch—neither interfered with the liberty of the natives nor contested their rights to the land, but often gained possession of it by purchase ; yet a common view then, and the prevailing legal theory later, was that the Indians' rights were merely those of occupation. The kings of Spain and Portugal, it is true, raised the claim that all this land with its people had become their property by virtue of the papal Bull dividing the unknown half of the world between them ; and when the natives contested these claims they were often very badly treated, especially at the time of the conquest and before the native question had been

The Ambitious Claims of Spain and Portugal

settled by law. In principle, however, Spain had, in accordance with the provisions of Queen Isabella's will, placed the natives in her colonial possessions on the same legal footing as her own subjects ; and in return for the services they were bound to render the state they could claim from it justice and protection.

The French did not go so far. The privilège of becoming French subjects was not granted to the Hurons, Illinois, etc.; but, from the days of Champlain, France had regarded the Indians as allies and friends, and recognised that, as such, they had claims to the friendship and protection of their white allies. Times without number the French allowed these claims by taking the field, with or without Indian aid, against the Iroquois, the sworn enemies of all natives who were allied with the French. Besides this, the Spaniards and the French, by their missions, did more than words can express for the material and intellectual well-being of their protégés.

The activity of the Indian missions carried on by the English was, in comparison, extraordinarily small, and belonged in general to a period we need not consider ; and as for the purchases of land, the great majority of these have been creditable neither to the people of the United States nor to their fathers before them. In former times a large tract of land could be purchased from the Indians, who scarcely understood the nature of the transaction, for a little spirits, gunpowder, or some European finery. But then there was room enough in the broad continent of North America, and it was not so very difficult for a tribe that had thus disinherited itself to find a new home farther west.

The Indians Robbed of Their Land

As civilisation followed them westward, the space left to the Indians, whose mode of life required free expansion, was more and more limited. The unavoidable and by no means unrecognised consequence of the policy of dispossessing the Indians of their lands was that the tribes, now crowded together, carried on endless bloody feuds to preserve their very existence, except when opportunity offered of attacking their neighbours across the boundary of the district claimed by the state. The fundamental distinction, however, in the native question is that in law the Indian was to the Spaniard a brother, to the Frenchman a friend, and to the Englishman a stranger.

THE NEW ENGLAND COLONIES
HOW THE PURITANS AND QUAKERS LAID
THE FOUNDATIONS OF MODERN AMERICA

CONTEMPORANEOUSLY with the Virginia Company, James I., in 1606, had recognised, as we have noticed, a second trading company which was to colonise the territory lying between latitudes 41° and 45° N. This company was called the Plymouth Company, since its most influential members belonged to Plymouth, England. Nothing was done, however, beyond making preliminary inquiries, even when James I., in 1620, organised a new company, the Council for New England, giving it all the land between latitudes 40° and 48° N., and granting it feudal privileges.

This company itself did practically nothing; but it was in this district, and at this same time, that the New England colonies were founded, and from it, not from the Virginia Company, the colonists obtained their concession. These were, in fact, religious refugees. Single groups and communities to whom the Reformation, as officially carried out in England, did not appear to go far enough, separated themselves very early from the English High Church. As their number increased these Puritans formed new sects, Presbyterians, Independents, etc.; but in doing this they drew upon themselves the active persecution of the dominant Church. Before its power they fled, for the most part, to Holland. But when general attention was drawn to trans-Atlantic colonial enterprises, there ripened among the Puritans a plan of seeking a place of refuge across the ocean where they could exercise their faith in perfect freedom and security.

The Famous Voyage of the Mayflower

With the support of like-minded friends in England, their representative obtained first from the Virginia Company the right to found settlements across the ocean. It was in the autumn of 1620 that the Mayflower carried to America the first colonists of the North, the founders of the town of New Plymouth. The concession was then obtained from the Council of New England, the spot selected being in the region allotted to them. Despite Puritanic strictness and simplicity, this colony, too, had to pass through a time of severe struggle before it began to grow strong and make progress. Its agreement with the English company assured to the immigrants almost complete independence. From the beginning the Pilgrim Fathers were almost exclusively their own rulers. Though they had fled before Anglican intolerance, this did not prevent them from establishing in their midst a régime at least as intolerant. Any deviation from their Puritan orthodoxy was unrelentingly punished by expulsion from the settlement. At a time when every strong arm should have been welcome to help to build up the struggling colony, they more than once rejected settlers because they would not submit to the religious conditions.

Intolerance of the Pilgrim Fathers

Political consolidation was attained only by combination with a later undertaking of the same kind which was more favoured by fortune in this respect. In 1629, Charles I. granted to the Massachusetts Bay Company a charter which gave it the right to found colonial settlements. The form of a chartered company was chosen in accordance with current practice. What was really aimed at here was, as in Puritan New Plymouth, a place of refuge for the hard-persecuted Puritans. The Crown had no sort of desire to trouble itself with the Puritan exiles; it was only too well pleased to be rid of them out of England. The new colonists were not, in the main, sectarians, and comprised a large proportion of country gentlemen, well-to-do farmers and professional men, of the same type as the Puritan Churchmen in the House of Commons. But no long time

Puritans' Place of Refuge

passed before they, like many of their compeers at home, were transferred to the ranks of the Independents. In 1630 the whole administration was placed in the hands of those colonists who were members of the corporation. From that time the colonists chose their own governor and his councillors. There was, besides, an

Where Religious Intolerance Flourished assembly, in which every town was represented by two delegates elected by the freemen. The colony successfully defended its rights against the Plymouth Company. At a later date Charles I., aiming at centralisation, took steps to alter the constitution of the colony; but he fell before it had become necessary for the colonists to defend, by open opposition to the royal will, the privileges they had won for themselves. Under Cromwell a benevolent guardianship was extended to all the Puritan communities of the New World: Charles II. failed to overcome the passive resistance of the colony, which, under James II., was forced to submit to the judicial revocation of its charter rights. William of Orange restored all its privileges; and when next they had to be defended against attacks by the government it was in alliance with all the other American colonies.

Religious intolerance, which had once driven the Puritans to New Plymouth and Boston, continued to thrive in their midst. In 1635 the Massachusetts Assembly banished a much-respected preacher, Roger Williams, only because he attacked the frequent amalgamation of Puritan orthodoxy with political rights in the colony and stood up for perfect toleration. With the help of the Narragansett Indians he fled to Rhode Island. Many of like mind came to him from the neighbouring colonies and from England, and he founded new settlements which politically followed, in all respects, the model of Massachusetts, the popular

Roger Williams and his New Colony vote being all powerful; but the principle was maintained that a man's religious beliefs are his own private concern, so that in law all faiths were actually equal. The struggle for an independent existence of the little colony of Rhode Island, situated among the intolerant Puritan colonies, was the more severe since the latter allowed it no place in the confederation established in 1643; but finally it succeeded in obtaining a charter from

Charles II., in 1663, thus securing its continued independent existence. Meanwhile, quite a number of little settlements had sprung up on the New England coast, founded, some from older colonies, some direct from England.

New Hampshire, granted to English merchants under several patents, had drawn so close to the intolerant Massachusetts that it was united to it in 1642 temporarily. Connecticut, too, was largely a Puritan settlement constituted on more purely democratic principles than was Massachusetts. With the exception of New Plymouth, these settlements progressed with surprising rapidity. They protected themselves against the Indians by their generally peaceful policy and by their confederation established in 1643. Against the home government they had at times scarcely any need of protection.

The confusion of the civil war, and the changing fortunes of the two parties, gave the rulers in England so much to do that they were glad to leave the colonies to themselves. These same causes gave a great impetus to emigration, for not only did the

Factors in the Popularity of Emigration conquered seek refuge under the freer rule of the colonies, but many others crossed the ocean only because the political disturbances which convulsed the Mother Country scarcely affected the progress of prosperous development in the colonies. The colonial policy of Cromwell, which found its complete expression in the Navigation Act, curtailed to a great extent the freedom of trade enjoyed by the colonies; but this measure was in agreement with the spirit of the age, and it was chiefly the trade with Holland that was affected. From France and Spain the colonies felt themselves separated by the same national and religious differences as the Mother Country, and the sense of their connection with England was still so strong that the idea seldom occurred of offering the Navigation Act that resistance which had so successfully prevented all interference whatever with the internal affairs of the colonies.

The internal constitution of all these colonies was similar. In general but secondary importance was attached to trade, the true basis of the community being found in labour. There was no search for the precious metals, no barter with the natives, no attempt at their subjugation. When it was impossible to come to a peaceful agreement with them, they were, it is

THE MAYFLOWER, IN WHICH THE PILGRIM FATHERS VOYAGED TO AMERICA

On September 6th, 1620, the Mayflower, a vessel of 160 tons, spread her sails from Plymouth harbour, carrying forty-one men and their families, 102 persons in all. It had been decided to make the passage in the company of the Speedwell, but the captain of the latter lost courage, with the result that the Mayflower made the voyage alone.

From the painting by W. F. Halsall

PILGRIM FATHERS SIGNING THE COMPACT IN THE CABIN OF THE MAYFLOWER

Two days after casting anchor at Cape Cod, Massachusetts, the famous compact was drawn up and duly signed by the leaders of the small band of Puritans in the cabin of the Mayflower. The covenant agreed, among many other things, to "constitute just and equal laws, that shall be thought most meet for the general good of the colony."

From the painting by Edwin White

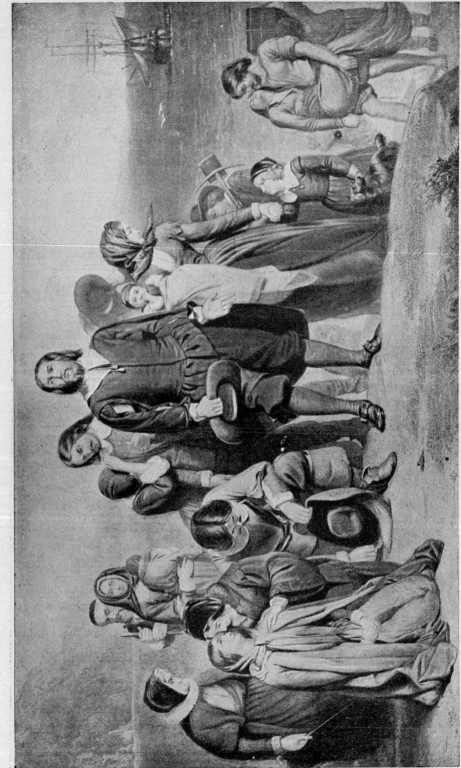

THE END OF THE MAYFLOWER'S HISTORIC VOYAGE : THE PURITANS' SAFE ARRIVAL IN THE NEW WORLD
From the painting by Charles Lucy

THE FIRST THANKSGIVING OF THE PILGRIM FATHERS ON ARRIVAL IN AMERICA

Having survived a particularly stormy passage lasting sixty-three days, the Pilgrim Fathers landed in Massachusetts on November 11th, 1620. Hardly had they set foot on the soil of the New World when a few of them gathered together, gave earnest thanks for safe deliverance from the perils of the sea, and asked a blessing upon their new colony.

From the painting by G. H. Boughton, R.A.

true, driven back by force; but the colonists did not take more land than was necessary to secure their own livelihood by agriculture and the cultivation of a few staple products. Slavery and prison labour were no more excluded than in the southern English settlements; but the natural and economic conditions necessary for their extensive employment were absent.

Agriculture here demanded harder work than was to be obtained by compulsory labour; further, the climate was unhealthy for blacks and unsuited for those products whose cultivation could be carried on on the large scale common in the south. Since every man lived, as a rule, on the returns of his own labour, the little communities required comparatively little space. They forced their way into the

spirit of the Americans turned were the Dutch, whose attention had been first drawn to the North American coast by English sailors. It was under the Dutch flag that Henry Hudson, in 1609, discovered the river that bears his name

Though no actual settlement was yet made, Dutch vessels, during the next few years, paid frequent visits to the river and to the island of Manhattan lying at its mouth, considering that Hudson's voyage gave them claims over it. These were made good when the district about the Hudson was included in the sphere of action of the Dutch West India Company, founded in 1621. Then arose on Manhattan Island permanent buildings in place of the temporary huts in which the Dutch traders had stored their wares for barter with the

IN THE OLD COLONIAL DAYS: ON THE WAY TO CHURCH
It was a long time before the Indians developed anything like friendly relationship towards the white men and women who had landed on their shores from the Mayflower. The above picture shows a party of worthy Puritans trudging across the snow to church, each of the men, except the pastor, armed in case of attack from man or beast.
From the painting by S. H. Boughton, R.A,

interior but slowly, and for a long time did not come into conflict with the inhabitants. On the other hand, they rooted themselves to the soil more firmly than the colonists in any other part of America. The population was denser, and, owing to the smaller admixture of foreign elements, more compact than in the other colonies. Almost all of the settlers came with wife and child to the New World, with the settled purpose of remaining there and establishing a home for their descendants.

Thus there developed there the earliest and strongest manifestation of an American national spirit, which was greatly furthered by the forms of local government which grew up in the colonies. The first against whom the awakening national

Indians; and when, in 1626, the whole island was bought from the Indians for sixty gulden, or florins, there stood among the houses of New Amsterdam the first stone church. Still, Dutch rule did not take firm root on the Hudson.

There were several reasons for this. First, the West India Company strove to promote trade rather than settlement; secondly, wishing to gain more profit from their possessions, the company allowed feudal baronies to be created, thus preventing the rise of a sturdy race of colonial citizens; finally, the company was not fortunate in the choice of its governors. It dismissed Peter Minuit, who had contributed so much to the prosperity of New Amsterdam, and

AN EARLY RELIGIOUS SERVICE OF THE PURITANS AFTER SETTLING IN THEIR NEW HOME

To these English colonists in America, the fathers of the present American race, religious worship was the essence of life. Having escaped from the intolerant ecclesiastical rule of James I. and the persecution to which they were subject from his Ministers, it was with a peculiar sense of gratification that they found themselves able to exercise their faith in freedom and security, and to worship God in the manner approved of by conscience. The above picture shows the first religious service of the Pilgrim Fathers in their new home.

From the painting by George Schwartze

INTERVIEW BETWEEN THE ENGLISH AND THE NATIVES: WILLIAM PENN IN TREATY WITH THE INDIANS

This picture shows William Penn, the leader of the Quakers, in the act of holding his historic interview with the Delaware Indians, on the site of which later sprang the city of Philadelphia. The treaty, the fairness of which appealed to the heart of his strange audience, provided among other things that the colony should be governed by laws of its own making.

From the painting by Benjamin West

drove him into the arms of the Swedes, whose colony on the Delaware lasted only so long as it was supported by Minuit's zeal and care. But even the inclusion of the Swedish colonial territory did not supply to the Dutch settlement that vigorous life which was wanting. Its New England neighbours on the north contested with it the possession of the land, and even within the Dutch boundaries the English element became predominant. On the appearance of four English ships before New Amsterdam in 1664, war having just broken out between Holland and England, the governor, left in the lurch by the West India Company, did not dare to make any resistance, and, before a drop of blood had been shed, he surrendered the town and all the Dutch territory to his opponents. In honour of the Duke of York, afterwards James II., the capital was named New York. Though the influence of the less favourable conditions due to the rule of the West India Company was felt for a long time, yet from the time of its conquest New York was intimately connected with the New England states. In 1673 and 1674 the Dutch succeeded in regaining temporary possession of it; but at the Peace of Westminster they had finally to abandon their claims, and their possessions were absorbed in the English colonial empire. The Dutch wedge thrust in between the northern and southern groups of colonies was assimilated, and from Nova Scotia to Florida the whole coast-line was now politically English.

Another of the neighbouring states—Pennsylvania—owes its origin to the religious intolerance that was manifested against the Quakers not only in England, but, with even greater vehemence, in the New England provinces. As a religious sect, the Quakers, with their rejection of all ceremonies and their unbounded philanthropy, are rather a curiosity; their dogma is almost entirely negative; but from a social point of view the foundation of their state was an interesting if not a particularly successful experiment. What specially excited the hostility of those who differed from them in belief was the interference of their doctrines in the region of politics, as manifested by their refusal to take oaths or to perform military service.

In England the Quakers first came into notice in 1655. It goes without saying that the High Church party persecuted them with the same relentlessness with which it tried to drive out or subdue all who differed from it. It was from such persecution that the Quakers fled to New England; but there they made the disheartening discovery that, despite all their fine phrases about brotherhood and equality, the Puritans were even more intolerant towards them than the High Church. In England it was considered sufficient to imprison Quakers who refused to take the oath; in Boston they were beaten as disturbers of the public peace, and four of them were even executed. It was therefore a deliverance for them when William Penn's action rendered it possible for them to found a colony of their own. The son of an English admiral, Penn had wealth as well as high connections. His father and many others considered it inexplicable eccentricity on his part that he should associate rather with the poor and persecuted Quakers than with the voluptuous court of Charles II.; but it was as a Quaker that he attracted attention in the highest circles, without which it would have been very difficult for his sect to obtain the royal sanction for their projected settlement. With money partly supplied by himself and partly collected by his friends, he acquired a part of the territory which the English had taken from the Dutch, and which the Duke of York, with the extravagant liberality common under Charles II., had presented to two of his friends. For this colony, named New Jersey, Penn drew up a constitution on Quaker principles, and set about obtaining a charter from Charles II. Curiosity mixed with interest

WILLIAM PENN

Son of an English admiral, religious intolerance towards his co-religionists induced him to acquire the territory of Pennsylvania, and found the city of Philadelphia, both of which became headquarters of the Quakers.

caused this to be granted him. Penn himself wished to call the colony Sylvania; the king added the name of the founder, making it Pennsylvania, for, according to the charter, Penn, like the former possessors, was to have the rights of a feudal lord over the new colony. Quaker emigration to America had much increased

Philadelphia the City of Brotherly Love before Penn himself could go there; and when he appeared in person, in 1683, to found Philadelphia, "the City of Brotherly Love," some thousands of his co-religionists had already settled in New Jersey and in Pennsylvania proper. Penn made most honourable use of his power.

The colony was organised on the same democratic basis as its New England neighbours; still Penn, despite the contradiction to the democratic principles of Quakerdom, did not abandon his rights, and did his best to recover them when James II. temporarily withdrew them. He died as possessor of Pennsylvania; but it must be added that the possession did not compensate him for the expenditure he had made for its benefit.

Pennsylvania long preserved its Quaker characteristics, though the Quaker element formed a smaller and smaller proportion of the rapidly increasing population. This exerted a favourable influence on the development of the colony in two respects. True to the principles of his religion, Penn laid great stress on the establishment of friendly relations with the natives. The land was bought from them and cultivated in European fashion; but the colonists did not on that account drive out its old possessors with selfish harshness, but kept up friendly patriarchal relations with them.

Thus it was that for a long time the colonists of Pennsylvania had nothing to fear from their red-skinned neighbours, even when the latter and the inhabitants of the neighbouring colonies were separated by fierce and bloody feuds. It was only when the prosperous development of

The Open Door in Quaker Pennsylvania Pennsylvania had attracted elements that did not admit the peaceful and brotherly doctrines of the Quakers that the good understanding between white and red men suffered. The immigration of those of different faiths early made itself felt. The love and toleration to all enjoined by the Quaker doctrines made it impossible for them to prevent the entrance to the colony of those of other beliefs. Elsewhere, even in the New World, religious tolera-

tion was a conception little understood, still less practised. Thus it was that sects of all kinds, persecuted in other colonies, sought refuge in Pennsylvania's Quaker toleration. Thus came, at Penn's own instigation, the first German immigrants— Calvinists from the Palatinate, pietists and mystics; later came numerous Huguenots—all capable, hard-working people, who sought nothing but the opportunity of working at their callings in freedom from religious and political oppression.

What they sought they found here in full measure; and in return they helped on, in no small degree, the development of Pennsylvania, which was more vigorous and more rapid than that of the other colonies. But by degrees they took away from the colony its exclusively Quaker character. All that remained of it, as common property of the whole province, was the friendly tolerance exercised there, and a certain political difference, caused, in some cases, by the colourlessness of the Quakers' beliefs and their renunciation of all worldly entanglements; in others by the tendency to put everything aside that could interfere with the pursuit

Boundary Disputes in the Colonies of an exclusively material prosperity. Differences in origin, differences in their political conditions, and finally the great distances separating the settlements, made it for a long time impossible in North America, as it was in the Spanish South, that the colonies should possess a common history. In the early days of settlement the different provinces were in almost every case confined to a narrow strip on the coast, and, though not very far from one another, separated by dreary forest-clad tracts.

Increase of population increased the opposition among the colonies instead of abolishing it. Contact with neighbours led to boundary disputes, and the several colonies repeatedly carried on tedious lawsuits over the possession of certain boundary lands. Even in North America the different settlements had no common history except when they came into contact with the subjects of other nations, who were much more numerous here than in Spanish South America. This circumstance may not have been without effect in causing the spirit of union to develop much more strongly in the English colonies than in the Spanish. From the beginning the supporters of the idea of union were the New England states, and they have continued to play this estimable part until the most recent times. It has been already mentioned that as early as 1643 they combined to meet on the one hand enemies at home, and on the other the threatened dangers arising from the political complications in the Mother Country.

The following year they endeavoured to get the southern colonies to join their confederation; but differences in the political and economic conditions of North and South prevented this, and for a long time what may be called the common history of the English colonies is really only the history of the New England states, the southern colonies having no part in it. The conquest of New Amsterdam and the expulsion of the Dutch were, it is true, accomplished from England. It led, not to the extension of the New England colonies, but to the establishment of a number of new communities, which, however, as they developed, were drawn closer and closer to New England. The whole Atlantic coast, from Maine to Georgia, was now in English hands; not a single foreign station remained on it. This circum-
England's Vast Possessions in America stance did not remain without influence on the feeling of union between the English colonies. This time it was the English Government that tried to bring about its realisation. Both Charles II. and James II. made attempts to remedy the complexity of the English colonial relations, and to unite the colonies under a central government; but before the resistance of the colonists their efforts came to naught, and when the English Revolution of 1688 swept away the Stuarts with their centralising tendencies, William and Mary recognised the old colonial constitutions as established by charter.

At this time the rivalry between the French and English colonies made itself more and more noticeable. It was chiefly owing to the differences in their economic conditions that this had not happened before. The English settlements existed almost exclusively by agriculture; and their population was not so large but that the fertile district between the coast and the Alleghanies was amply sufficient for them. They had thus little inducement to penetrate farther into the interior, and did comparatively little to open it up. The French settlements, on the other hand, depending almost entirely on the fur trade, required complete control of an extensive "hinterland"; and every step in the progress of the colonies, every increase in their commercial activity, increased the need for territorial expansion.

This necessity had led them across the continent from the mouth of the St. Lawrence to the delta of the Mississippi. The first to enter into competition with them had been the Dutch of
The Iroquois Armed by the Dutch New Amsterdam. They, too, were traders rather than tillers of the soil, and the opposition between their interests and those of the French was the more accentuated in that their settlements were not far distant from one another and were separated by no natural barriers. As the fur trade was to a large extent carried on by barter with Indian hunting tribes (" voyageurs " and trappers, though we often hear of them, were rare), competition in trade was naturally accompanied by rivalry for the good will of the Indians.

As chance had made the French, under Champlain, the allies of the Hurons, the Dutch naturally allied themselves to the Hurons' enemies, the Iroquois. Unrestrained by political reasons, as the French had been, the Dutch, without thought as to the consequences, supplied their allies with arms more freely than ever the French had, and thus rendered them not only formidable opponents to the Indians between the lakes, the Alleghanies and the Mississippi, but a permanent danger to all European settlements that did not enjoy the friendship of the Iroquois tribes. At the conquest of New Amsterdam the English inherited these friendships and enmities; the Dutch trading spirit remained a characteristic of the colony of New York.

Thus, we find it soon afterwards as hostile to the French as ever the Dutch had been; and on the French side the feeling of hostility was now more strongly manifested than it had ever been against the unimportant Dutch colony. At first
The Founding of the Hudson's Bay Company the contest was confined to commerce. But in 1670, at the instigation of two Frenchmen, who, discontented with the Canadian Government, had entered the service of the English, the Hudson's Bay Company was founded. This company, which extended its operations as far as the Saguenay, was for a time a dangerous competitor with the French in the fur trade. But the boundary war, carried on for a long

time on a small scale, became of greater and greater importance when England and France, at war in Europe, tried to injure each other by attacks on the colonies.

These colonial wars, of which there were no fewer than five between 1688 and 1763, had all much the same character. At the beginning the French with their **Bloodthirsty** Indian allies made their way **Cruelty of** through the marshy forests **the Indians** south of the St. Lawrence to the English villages near the boundary, and there, fighting against the defenceless and scattered farmers, gained easy victories, disgraced, however, by the bloodthirsty cruelty of the Indians. The New England colonists sought to take revenge on the French mission and trading stations in the same manner ; but they could not inflict the same amount of damage on the enemy because the posts attacked were not so valuable as the New England plantations, and not so helpless against attack.

Besides, it was very difficult to win over to a common and energetic plan of action the many minds directing the affairs of the provinces, now united into the Confederation of New England States. The colony of Massachusetts became a kind of leader, chiefly owing to the fact that its capital, Boston, was the seat of the federal assembly. That, however, meant little more than that Massachusetts claimed the leadership, and occasionally assumed it in cases where it was not sure of the agreement of the federated colonies, and did not obtain their support; but it gained real authority neither for itself nor **The Leading** for the federal assembly. **State of** Still, Boston became more **New England** and more the point where the forces sent across the ocean from England to carry on the colonial struggle collected and prepared to take the offensive.

Naturally, it was not to the interest of the English to split up their forces by small expeditions in the backwoods, for which their troops were not prepared, and which, even if successful, could have little effect on the result of the war. They had a decided preference for a point of attack where the fleet that had served to transport the troops could co-operate. Such a point presented itself in the peninsula which lay between the St. Lawrence and the northern boundary of the New England states, called by the French Acadia, and by the English Nova Scotia. It had been settled by the French at the beginning of the seventeenth century; but some decades later it was included in the grant of land made to Sir William Alexander, and was even taken possession of by the English.

But the treaty of peace that restored to the French Quebec, which was taken at the same time, placed them once more in possession of Acadia, where, after a long period of unrest, a number of settlements began to flourish. The most important of these, Port Royal, was the capital of the province. But the New **The Historic** England colonists kept a watch- **Peace** ful eye on this district, and did **of Utrecht** not let slip an opportunity of attempting its reconquest. An English fleet had come over to conquer New Amsterdam, but had been condemned to inaction by the astonishing rapidity with which peace had been concluded. This fleet, at the instigation of the New England colonies, made an expedition against Acadia, and conquered it without much difficulty; neither was it restored to France until 1667, some time after Charles II.'s accession.

In 1713, however, the Peace of Utrecht, following the War of the Spanish Succession, finally transferred Acadia to the British, though without any adequate definition of boundaries. The French withdrew to Cape Breton Island, and erected there the fort of Louisbourg, a fortress of such importance that it was known to the New England colonists as " the Northern Dunkirk." Like Dunkirk, it was the starting-point of piracies and raids, and its commanding position rendered it a perpetual menace to the unprotected New England coast.

KONRAD HAEBLER

✳BRITISH NORTH AMERICA✳
THE STRUGGLE FOR CANADA
WOLFE'S HISTORIC VICTORY AT QUEBEC AND DOWNFALL OF THE FRENCH POWER
By A. G. Bradley

ENGLAND was already at war with Spain and had been victorious at Portobello when Louis XV. joined issue with her in the dispute over the Austrian succession. The victory of Dettingen followed at once, but in 1745 she suffered the defeat of Fontenoy, and in the same year was paralysed for the moment by the rising on behalf of the Young Pretender. But what mainly affected the Canadian situation was her naval weakness in North American waters and the disastrous havoc that French privateers, issuing from the impregnable harbour at Louisbourg, wrought upon the now numerous merchant shipping of New England. At length the colonists could stand it no longer. At a moment of infinite gloom, when England was smarting from defeat by land and sea, and quivering with a Jacobite rebellion at home, the welcome but astounding news crossed the Atlantic that a colonial force had captured Louisbourg.

It was in truth a great feat of arms for raw militia led by lawyers, traders and skippers. Four thousand men had sailed from Boston under John Pepperrell, a leader of some genius, but of no experience, and the movement had been inspired **Louisbourg Captured from the French** by Governor Shirley of Massachusetts, another man of mark. A small English fleet under Commodore Warren, with supplies, joined them at the scene of action. The tale of the siege cannot be told here. Exceptional courage and no little skill with their heavy artillery, were shown by these hardy Puritans, stimulated by that crusading fervour which still burned in a New Englander when he beheld before him a Papist and a Frenchman. The siege lasted forty days, when a breach sufficient to admit of an assault was effected, and 400 men got a lodgment within the works. About the same time, a ship from **Short-lived Triumph of New England** France, carrying reinforcements in men and much needed supplies, was captured by Admiral Warren, which proved a finishing blow to the hopes of the garrison, who, to the number of 1,500, then surrendered to the English, and, together with 2,000 citizens, were shipped to France. New England sounded pæans of triumph, and her militia had the novel satisfaction of garrisoning works fashioned with the skill and on the scale of a great European fortress.

Though the glory remained, its fruits were short-lived. For though the French had in the meantime sent a powerful expedition to retrieve their loss, which was defeated by winds, waves and disease, Louisbourg was restored to them at the hollow Treaty of Aix la Chapelle in 1748, to the despair of the English colonists and the indignation of all conversant with North American politics.

An uneasy lull of seven years succeeded the treaty. The mutterings of the coming storm, trifling in volume though they were, and almost inarticulate amid the thick mantle of boundless forests which still muffled this vast land of the future, nevertheless reached the ears of some few prescient leaders. The outposts of both countries were, in fact, confronting one another even then in menacing attitude at the edge of the promised land in a fashion that only the sword could settle. The crisis had arrived. It was not this valley or that territory that was to be contested, but in effect the greater and most fertile part of what is now the United States of America. Europe was seething with territorial and dynastic complications

The French Hold on Canada which have filled countless volumes of history but left small mark on the world's future. In these wild woods, however, the momentous issue whether North America was to be in effect Gallic and Papist, or Anglo-Saxon and Protestant, was to be fought out. In Canada, the nature of the crisis was well understood.

She had her finger on the pulse of the west; her leaders were urgent, bold and sanguine; her plans defined. The British were to be confined to the narrow seaboard strip that the thirteen colonies then occupied. The deep mountain chain of the Alleghanies, which shut them off from the interior, and over which they had only just begun, in the persons of the land speculator and the trader, to cast longing eyes, was to be their perpetual and everlasting limit. Everything else was to be French, and, so far as the foundation of such things then went, they already were French. Tin plates nailed on trees in remote forests proclaimed the frontier, while forts and trading villages marked it more effectually.

With the English it was otherwise, though simply as traders they were welcome enough. But they did not stop at that; they came with axes, cleared the country, and drove away the game, and with it the Indians' means of existence. Upon the natural hostility of the latter, on the division of the British into so many separate and often jarring commonwealths; upon the industrial and generally unwarlike character of the settlers, France counted, and not without reason. If she had granted religious toleration to Canada,

What France Lost by Her Blunders and admitted the thrifty Huguenots, who would have swarmed into those fertile regions across the Atlantic where their own standard flew, the map of North America would most likely have been painted in different colours. But Canada was nothing if not fanatical.

By the virtues of her creed she had in great measure laid the foundations of her Western empire. By its very vices to an equal degree she threw that empire away.

By the English on the east of the Alleghanies, with a few exceptions, all this was but dimly realised. Governor Shirley, who had organised the capture of Louisbourg, sounded the first note of warning, and with some difficulty stirred up the apathetic legislatures of the inharmonious, disintegrated, struggling groups of colonies into feeble action.

The government of Quebec, then under Gallisoniere, had, on the other hand, a clear enough policy—namely, to resist all encroachments of the English upon the west of the Alleghanies; and acted upon it. This first point of aggression was the Ohio Valley, where the Virginians had already surveyed lands and were preparing to settle them; and it may be remarked incidentally that both nations—France and England—claimed the whole west.

The struggle broke out formally, locally, and on a small scale in 1744 at the forks of the Monongahela and the Alleghany, where Pittsburg, the Birmingham of America, now spreads her miles of resounding industry under a canopy of smoke. The French erected in the following year a single lonely fort, which, under the name of Duquesne,

Beginnings of the Great Struggle became the key of the west. The following year, though England and France had not actually declared war, the ill-fated General Braddock arrived with two regiments, and, marching against the new fort with these and a handful of rangers, met with that sanguinary defeat on the Monongahela at the hands of the Indians, led by and leavened with French Canadians, that usually bears his name. Shirley himself led 1,500 men against the French fort at Niagara, but got no farther than Oswego, where he was checkmated by a French force from across the lake at Fort Frontenac.

Johnson, an Anglo-Irish gentleman, who controlled large estates in the Mohawk Valley, and acquired a singular influence over the Iroquois, though he could not prevent some of them joining the French, led 3,000 militiamen to Lake George with a view to seizing the strong points on the main route to Canada. A French force under a European, General Diskiau, was repulsed by Johnson on Lake George and the general captured; for 3,000 regular troops had now been sent to Canada, and the last French governor of the colony as it proved, the Marquess de Vaudreuil, was seated at Quebec. Technically, he was a Canadian, as he was born in the country

THE DESPERATE STAND OF GENERAL BRADDOCK AT FORT DUQUESNE: A STIRRING EPISODE IN ANGLO-AMERICAN HISTORY

The defeat of General Braddock while attacking Fort Duquesne, on the present site of Pittsburg, is one of the most stirring episodes in Anglo-American history. Starting out with a force of 2,000 men on July 8th, 1755, Braddock, after crossing the Monongahela, found himself attacked by a party of 900 French and Indians. Two hours severe fighting followed, the English, owing to the enemy having ambuscaded the surrounding forest, proving living targets for the destructive fire of the French and their allies. Vainly trying to rally his men, Braddock had four successive horses shot under him before being mortally wounded himself, dying a few days later. Out of the 2,000 men who set out that fateful morning, only 977 returned to camp.

From the painting by Howard Pyle

while his father was governor; and he made the most of it. He was a vain man, without force or any military capacity, but not without patriotism. The population of Canada was then about 60,000.

The Acadians, in the meantime, leading peaceful, isolated lives upon a fertile soil, had increased to 10,000, and had been now **Halifax Founded by the British** for some forty years British subjects. When Louisbourg was restored to France, in 1748, the English Government atoned somewhat for their folly by founding the town of Halifax as a counterpoise. It is the only instance of an organised and successful effort at colonisation on a generous scale ever achieved by the British Government, and at the breaking out of the great war Halifax contained a population of 4,000. The agricultural settlements it naturally threw out into the woods behind created the difficulty which brought about that wholesale deportation of Acadians which Longfellow has made famous with a full measure of poetic sympathy and licence.

Hitherto no question had disturbed the calm of the Acadians' existence, settled as they all were on the opposite shore of the province on the Bay of Fundy. Peaceful and industrious, if backward people, they lived outside the stream of North American life and racial friction. They were British subjects on the fringe of an otherwise unpeopled British province. They led their own primitive lives, while the English flag only flew over a trifling garrison or two of bored colonial militiamen. In 1713 they had been offered the oath of allegiance or a year's notice to quit as an alternative. They did not object to the oath, but demanded a qualified one, which excused them from serving against the French flag. Canadian priests had continually stiffened their backs about this, assuring them that Acadia would be reconquered while the propinquity of Louisbourg gave **The Simple Peasants of Acadia** colour to the notion. It is pretty certain that these simple peasants cared little what flag they were under so long as they were let alone, and the English Government had let them absolutely alone. They had been easy even in the matter of the oath. There were no seigniors, no taxes, no corvées, no military expeditions, as with their brothers on the St. Lawrence, with whom, however, they had no more intercourse than they had with France, which

was nil. The origin, too, of the others is known with precision, but no one knows for certain the districts of France from which the original Acadians came. To this day they speak a slightly different vernacular, and have different characteristics from the Canadian French proper, due in part no doubt to their respective environments. When Halifax was founded and Acadia was renamed Nova Scotia, the province threatened to become English in blood as well as government. This changed the aspect of affairs for those who cherished the hope of its reversion to France; Canadian officials and priests, that is to say, and incidentally, too, the Micmac Indians, bloodthirsty, numerous, and with strong French sympathies.

Word went out that the British settler from the eastern shore, carving out a farm in the backwoods of this, his own province, was to be intimidated. This was done in Micmac fashion, not to be tolerated, of course, for a moment. The officials of Louisbourg and two or three fanatic bloodthirsty priests were the instigators. How far the Acadians were involved is **Acadia's Historic Exodus** doubtful. Some few were, beyond doubt, reckless characters; others were merely hounded on by their superiors. The French, too, had erected forts at the gut of Cansean, that narrow neck which joins Nova Scotia to the mainland, but then a disputed boundary. In 1755, 2,000 armed men, French Canadians and local Micmacs, congregated here on war intent. New England answered in sufficient force and there was some little fighting. The wretched Acadians were now between the hammer and the anvil. They had consistently refused the unqualified oath now really vital to the British Government.

They refused it still, under threats for the most part of eternal damnation from their priests endorsed by the Bishop of Quebec, the fierce Le Loutre being a foremost agent in the business. Colonel Laurence was governor of the province; Colonel Winslow, a New Englander and distinctly humane man, of the troops. To these two belongs the responsibility for the historic exodus. The greater blame at least lies in the heartless fashion in which Canadian priests and officials had used these simple people as their tools. To the British authorities there seemed no alternative if life was to be made possible for their own settlers. All who had refused

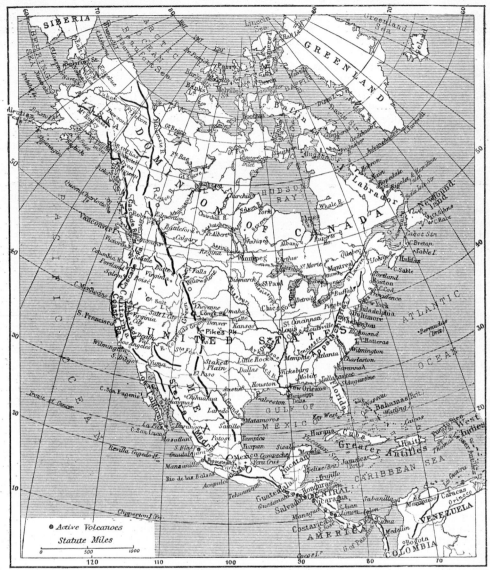

MAP OF NORTH AMERICA, SHOWING THE UNITED STATES AND THE DOMINION OF CANADA

Although Columbus is generally given the distinction of discovering North America, it is practically certain that the Norsemen had landed on its shores nearly five centuries earlier. When John Cabot navigated the coast in the neighbourhood of Cape Breton, in 1497, the population of this vast continent, with an area, inclusive of outlying lands and islands, of 8,300,000 square miles, was counted by thousands, whereas to-day it is 105,000,000 souls.

the oath, numbering, with their families, some 6,000 souls, were forcibly deported with their money and movables. They were taken by sea and distributed in the various colonies, keeping families together as much as possible. It was a lamentable business, but the verdict of those who have not studied the question from the Treaty of Utrecht onward is worthless. The lot of the exiles was almost everywhere unhappy, and most of all in the case of those who went to the prime authors of their

misery at Quebec. Some went to Louisiana, and it is sad to think these peaceful souls became in their poverty and despair themselves a terror to the peaceful. The most fortunate, strange to say, were those who fell among the Puritans of New England.

In 1756, though already for this long time quite active in North America, war was formally declared between France and England. New France, with about 4,000 regulars—for she never succeeded in getting many more—and some 15,000 militia, but virile and compact, and half-conscious, was staking her very existence for an empire ; England, with her brood of a dozen somewhat un-

Montcalm the Leading Figure in Canada
gracious, ill-assorted offspring, blundering into the American part of the business without any very clear ideas,
but chiefly because she was fighting France in Europe. Old France, unfortunately for herself, had lost her enthusiasm for Canada at the wrong moment, and only Canadians measured the stake. It would take a chapter to define the various local considerations which tugged this way and that at the thirteen British colonies and prevented their common action ; only a few persons among them all grasped the great issue. France, at least, sent one of her best soldiers to Canada, and Montcalm becomes henceforth its leading figure. He had little talent pitted against him. Loudon, the English commander-in-chief, and a poor one, too, did not turn up till August, while Abercromby and Webb, who

GENERAL MONTCALM
Montcalm was appointed commander of the French troops in Canada, where, in defending Quebec against the English, with General Wolfe at their head, he was mortally wounded, dying within a few hours of the fall of the city.

in the meantime represented him, were below mediocrity. Some good partisans, like Sir William Johnson, were active, but the details of a big war were for the moment too much for provincial officers.

New England, however, girded her loins, and had several thousand brave but ill-disciplined militia in the field. The more southern colonies were selfish and backward, even in their own defence, for Braddock's defeat had let loose swarms of Indians, egged on by France, upon their frontiers, which were swept bare by the torch and tomahawk amid unspeakable horrors, and here the young George Washington, commanding a few Virginia militia, was engaged in futile but plucky efforts to stem the ravage.

The season for campaigning in these northern forests was short. The summer of 1756 saw Montcalm entrenched with 6,000 men at Ticonderoga, at the head of Lake Champlain, and Loudon with nearly twice as many, a third of whom were

regulars, at the head of Lake George, both posts being on the direct route from Montreal to Albany on the Hudson. The ostensible object of either general was to drive his adversary back and capture the town, which was his base. But neither felt equal to the task, and the summer passed in irregular skirmishing.

Montcalm, however, slipped round with another force, and captured Oswego, on Lake Ontario, the chief north-western frontier post of the English, together with 1,600 men and 160 guns, and razed it to the ground. So far the French had all the best of it. The following year, 1757, Loudon, at his own suggestion, was ordered, with the pick of his British regiments, to sail for Nova Scotia, and attack Louisbourg as a step towards a later expedition by sea against Quebec. It will be enough to say that Loudon and his army, reinforced by 6,000 men from England, spent the summer at Halifax, and did not attack either Louisbourg or Quebec. It must at the same time be said that the short seasons, the immense extent and roughness of the country, the enormous difficulties of transport and victualling, and even of getting news, account for much of what, on paper, often looks like culpable inertia. Montcalm saw with joy this foolish policy, and in the absence of Loudon and his army, moved down the Lakes with a large force and artillery, and captured Fort William Henry, after a brave defence by Colonel Monroe.

Two thousand prisoners were taken, but Montcalm's Indians got out of hand, and the victory was marred by a massacre of about 100 captives. Though Albany, the chief entrepot of the British western fur-trade, lay practically open, the unforeseen exigencies of eighteenth century backwoods warfare on a big scale dashed Montcalm's hopes. A famine was impending in Canada, and a ripening grain crop lacked hands to cut it. Thus ended a year disastrous to British prestige in America, but with no other great result.

Montcalm's fame, in the meantime, had travelled westward on the wings of the wind, and Indians from remote nations with bows and arrows had flocked to Montreal to serve under him, eat of his scanty store, and drink his brandy. His mission Indians, skilled riflemen, were invaluable, but these capricious, uncontrollable hordes were more than a doubtful blessing. Yet for policy's sake they could not be summarily rejected. Official Canada showed at this moment a strange mixture of vice and virtue, of vigour and apathy. The notorious Bigot was intendant, with a gang of harpies who shared his peculations; Vaudreuil, if not himself implicated, was indifferent, but was furiously jealous of Montcalm and frequently thwarted him.

The last was above reproach, and looked with disgust on the commercial baseness of those about him in this supreme hour of stress and trial; but, unlike Frontenac, he kept his temper and pursued at the same time his difficult task unflinchingly. For the government of France had now passed into hands that could not realise North America, or see the dazzling prospects or the ruin which at the moment presented themselves as alternatives. Yet with all the peculation and heartless corruption rife among Canadian officials, and many of the military long stationed there, an ardent patriotism and *esprit de corps* nevertheless animated all alike, the just and the unjust. This was well, for France either could not or would not send further help. Great Britain, on the contrary, had awakened from her slough of lethargy and jobbery to life, and Pitt was at the helm. In the next year, 1758, a fleet and army, in which James Wolfe figured prominently, recaptured Louisbourg. But as an offset, in this same July, at Ticonderoga, on the neck of the land between Lakes George and Champlain, Montcalm won his last and greatest victory. General Abercromby, one of the few

Montcalm Wins his last Victory

incompetents that Pitt had been unable to remove, was approaching Canada by the Lake route, with 6,000 regulars and 9,000 provincials, the largest and best-equipped force yet seen in North America. Montcalm, with his able lieutenant, Levis, with but 3,400 men, mostly regulars, awaited this formidable host.

Rejecting the stone fortress of Ticonderoga, he threw up a circular palisade near by, and surrounded it with a *chevaux de frise* of fallen trees, with their branches pointing outwards. From within this, on platforms, his men could shoot in comparative security. Artillery would have blown this otherwise formidable entrenchment away in an hour; but Abercromby, who was well supplied, left his guns in the rear, and for three hours of a blazing July day hurled his regulars on ramparts impregnable to rifle and bayonet, the 42nd Highlanders, whose American record became one of the proudest, losing just half their numbers; 2,000 men fell valiantly in the hopeless task. At sunset the general abandoned not only his fatuous attack, but the campaign, scuttling back to the head of Lake George with a still large army in semi-panic, as if the enemy were at his heels. Such was Ticonderoga. Astonished and justly elated as were Montcalm and Canada, it was their last flash of glory. An expedition this same summer under Forbes, with George Washington upon his staff, and following more or less on the steps of Braddock, captured Fort Duquesne. Pitt had now set his mind not merely on driving the French power from the west, but from North America altogether, and in 1759 his final effort was made for the capture of Canada. He had now found young and ardent leaders, who caught his fire and communicated it to the private soldier, while the nation was behind him to a man. Sir Jeffery Amherst took the command in America, and with a strong force was himself to move up the Lakes, over the scene of Abercromby's disgrace, on

GENERAL WOLFE

Born in a Kentish vicarage on January 2nd, 1727, General Wolfe was a soldier of distinction even before his victory at Quebec, having fought at the Battle of Dettingen in 1743, at Culloden in 1746, and at Lawfeldt in 1747.

THE BATTLE THAT WON CANADA: GENERAL WOLFE'S CAPTURE OF QUEBEC, ON SEPTEMBER 13TH, 1759
The struggles between England and France for the possession of Quebec came to a conclusion at day-dawn on September 13th, 1759. Twice before the British had attempted to re-capture the city, but without success. In February, 1759, General Wolfe sailed from England, landing opposite Quebec in June. The attack proved one of tremendous difficulty. On the eve of the 13th, Wolfe and his troops, at a point insufficiently guarded, mounted the Heights of Abraham, where a short, decisive battle followed, the French being completely routed. The above picture shows the scene on that historic morning, which decided the fate of Quebec, the British forces obtaining their great victory over the French regulars.

THE DEATH OF GENERAL WOLFE IN THE HOUR OF VICTORY, ON THE PLAINS OF ABRAHAM, SEPTEMBER 13TH, 1759

General Wolfe's supreme moment of victory came with that of his death. The bitter struggle for Quebec was at last over, the French forces were vanquished, the British flag would shortly wave over the city after an interval of 130 years, and Montcalm's dream of a French-Canada lay shattered, himself at the point of death. Foremost in the fighting on the Plains of Abraham, General Wolfe, who had emerged scatheless from the battles of Dettingen, of Culloden, and of Lawfeldt, was mortally wounded, and the above picture shows the great English soldier, the son of a Kentish vicarage, breathing his last in the presence of a few of his faithful followers. His body was brought home, and buried in Greenwich Church.

Montreal. Another expedition was to march on Niagara, the French key to the north-west. Lastly, and most notable of all, was that force of 8,000 men, mainly veteran troops, under General Wolfe, which was borne by a British fleet under **Canada** Admiral Saunders against **Fighting for** Quebec. Canada, by this time **Her Life** almost wholly cut off from the Mother Country by British fleets, had now to fight for her life, and braced every sinew for the struggle. If but one-twentieth of the 100,000 men France was devoting to useless war in Europe had been sent earlier to her aid she might have given another account of herself. Levis was in command at Montreal, but his hour was not yet.

Quebec was the vital spot, the heart and key of Canada. Here sat Montcalm himself, with nearly 4,000 regulars and 12,000 militia, greatly doubting indeed if a fleet of battleships could be safely navigated up the treacherous currents of the St. Lawrence by seamen having no acquaintance of it. But on June 27th that question was settled, and the British fleet lay beneath the city, discharging redcoats on the Isle of Orleans, which there parts the wide stream. The fortifications of the town had been made good. Crowning the point of a lofty promontory parting the St. Lawrence from its small tributary, the St. Charles, its landward or western side was defended by walls, and was held, moreover, as impracticable by the almost perpendicular cliffs which, for some miles up the St. Lawrence, alone gave access to it.

The foot of the town fronting the waters bristled with fixed and floating batteries. Across the St. Charles the low ridge of Beauport, lying back from the St. Lawrence and rising from its flats—these last half covered at high tide—stretched for five miles to where the great cataract of the Montmorency leaped down it with a sheer drop of nearly 300 feet and made a natural flank defence. Crowning this **The British** long ridge of Beauport, and **Attack** heavily intrenched, lay 12,000 **on Quebec** to 14,000 men, the majority, to be sure, no match for regulars in the open, but quite as effective with rifles in their hands behind a strong position. Here, too, was Montcalm, with Vaudreuil, the governor ; for the city, deemed unapproachable save by way of their intrenched Beauport lines, rose just across

the St. Charles on their right, and was garrisoned by 2,000 men. Not six persons, probably, in all that British host had ever before set eyes upon Quebec, and it was a sufficiently formidable prospect as now presented to them with a well-found garrison of nearly twice their number, animated by patriotism and religious fervour, and led by a general of renown.

What Wolfe—now just thirty-one—thought, with the eyes of Pitt and England on him, and barely four months in which to crown or ruin his reputation, he has told us. But space imperatively forbids any full description of this famous siege. How the British artillery from across the river at Point Levis pounded the city to ruins ; and how Wolfe, seeking in vain for a weak spot, flung 2,000 over-eager men upon the steep, embattled ridge of Beauport to their heavy punishment.

Montcalm had tried fireships ; otherwise he wisely sat tight awaiting his wintry ally, whose very approach would drive the English out of the St. Lawrence. Fighting in the open, even at odds, he knew to be in Wolfe's favour, while behind his works **Wolfe's** he had him at an enormous **Brilliant** advantage. Eight weeks thus **Ruse** passed ; the early winter was in sight, but success no nearer. The fleet under Saunders, contrary to the usual custom of those times, acted in perfect harmony with the general, but could advance the great object no further. At length the young leader, sick in body almost unto death from chronic disease, rose with great difficulty from a fevered bed with a new and daring resolve, though its import he kept to himself, not even confiding it to his brigadiers—Monckton, Townshend and Murray.

The batteries by land and sea still held the attention of the besieged ; while on September 7th 4,000 men were marched up the south shore of the river, accompanied by some ships to Cap Rouge, seven miles above the city, where De Bougainville, a capable officer, lay with 2,000, mostly good, troops to guard the upper country. The ruse was admirably maintained. Montcalm was even unaware that a serious body of troops had gone upstream, while Bougainville thought they meditated an attack on himself. Wolfe still kept his own secret till he issued his general orders on the night of the 12th. Some time before he had noticed a foot track leading up the cliff a mile and a half

A RIVER SCENE IN THE PROVINCE OF QUEBEC: LOGS IN TOW

LUMBER CAMPS IN THE FORESTS OF BRITISH COLUMBIA

CUT LOGS IN THE ASSINIBOINE RIVER THAT HAVE FLOATED HUNDREDS OF MILES

SCENES IN CANADA'S GREAT LUMBER INDUSTRY

above the city on to the plateau behind it, known as the Plains of Abraham. In the dark of the early morning of the 13th his force was dropped into boats and crept silently down-stream under the cliffs, narrowly escaping discovery by the sentries stationed there, to the appointed spot known as Wolfe's Cove. Here they were

The Fight That Won Canada landed in relays, the ships following at a distance. Dragging themselves up the steep ascent, and overcoming one or two weak French posts at the summit, the whole 4,000 men were ultimately drawn up on the plateau before either Quebec and Montcalm to the east, or Bougainville to the west, knew anything about it. Montcalm only heard the news at six, and was thunderstruck. Hurrying all the troops he dare withdraw from the Beauport lines through the city, he marched out to meet the British, with about 5,000 men.

They met on the plateau a mile back of the city, now familiar to the world as the Plains of Abraham. Discipline soon settled the matter. Two withering volleys, followed by a charge of bayonet and Highland claymore, sent the French flying, with the loss of about 1,500 men, in panic to the city after about twenty minutes' confused fighting. All was practically over when Bougainville and his force arrived at the English rear, where a regiment had been held in reserve to stop him. The brave Wolfe, however, fell in the great hour of victory, and his eyes closed on the success of his scheme. Montcalm, too, was mortally wounded and died that night.

All was now panic within the French lines. Vaudreuil and the surviving troops hurriedly abandoned Quebec and made their way by inland roads up the river

What Wolfe's Victory did for North America towards Montreal, the militia mostly scattered to their homes, and the city a day or two later surrendered to Townshend, who had succeeded to the command. The British loss in the battle was about 600 killed and wounded. Canada was now virtually won. That brief struggle on the Plains of Abraham was one of the world's most decisive, as it was one of its most dramatic, conflicts.

It finally settled the question whether North America was to be French or English. Incidentally, too, by the removal of the French power it made possible the birth of the United States.

But Canada was not yet literally conquered. Prideaux had captured Niagara ; but the middle and third expedition against Montreal, under Amherst, delayed by obstacles both of Nature's and Levis's making, failed to get through that year. Levis, with the remnant of the French and colony regulars, continued to make a brave, if futile, struggle, including a gallant attempt to recapture Quebec from its English garrison under Murray in the following spring. But in the same summer he laid down his arms at Montreal, and Vaudreuil formally surrendered Canada to Amherst, then at the head of three British columns, which from three different quarters had, by skilful planning, arrived there upon the same day.

The initial terms here granted to the French Canadians were generous, nor did

Britain's Awards at the Treaty of Paris their formal ratification by treaty and subsequent Acts of Parliament entail any substantial alteration. They were guaranteed in the free exercise of their religion, while the property of their religious houses, with the exception of the Jesuits and two or three others to be reserved for the king's pleasure, was secured to them.

The war in Europe closing two years later, the Treaty of Paris was ratified in February, 1763. By this, Canada, Cape Breton, and the whole country east of the Mississippi was ceded to England, leaving only New Orleans and Louisiana to France, or, rather, to Spain, as they were transferred to her by way of compensation for her cession of Florida to England.

Unfortunately, in the teeth of Pitt's opposition, the small barren islands of St. Pierre and Miquelon, and certain fishing rights in Newfoundland, were also yielded at a moment when Great Britain, then at the height of her power and glory, could have resisted far greater demands than this with impunity.

A. G. BRADLEY

A MOUNTAIN STREAM IN THE ROCKIES

FRASER CAÑON, NEAR YALE, B.C.

TAKAKHSA FALLS AND TOHO VALLEY

THE HOMATHCOH RIVER

BY MOUNTAIN AND STREAM IN CANADA

Photos by courtesy of London "Canada" newspaper

BRITAIN'S TAXATION OF HER COLONIES: PATRICK HENRY'S FAMOUS SPEECH OF PROTEST

The passing of the Stamp Act by the British Parliament gave rise to much opposition in the American colonies, contravening, as it did, the recognised principle that taxation should only be by assent of representatives, and showing that the Mother Country claimed to legislate for the colonies to her own advantage and to their disadvantage without consulting the people of the colonies. The above illustration shows the ardent orator, Patrick Henry, making his famous speech, in which he denied the right of Britain's taxation, before the House of Burgesses, in May, 1675.

AMERICA ON THE VERGE OF REVOLT
THE RIFT BETWEEN THE OLD
COLONIES & THE MOTHERLAND

THE Peace of Paris left only two European Powers with a footing on the North American Continent—Great Britain and Spain, which had ceded Florida in exchange for Havana, captured by the British during the war, and had received Louisiana from France. Spanish rivalry was a negligible quantity. The French in Canada acquiesced in the transfer of the sovereignty from Versailles to Westminster. If their goodwill were retained, North America might be regarded as practically British. That the whole of it did not remain a part of the British Empire was only due to a schism in the British race itself, which led to the establishment of a new Britannic nation quite independent of the British Empire.

British North America, then, consisted of two main divisions—the thirteen British colonies which had attained the organisa-

Britain's American Empire tion of self-governing states, subject to certain rights of control retained by the Mother Country; and the new dominion, with its French population, religion, language, customs and institutions; to which must be added the communities of Nova Scotia and Newfoundland, as well as Florida, which had not yet emerged into a form of organisation sufficiently advanced to entitle them to be described as states. The great question of the future, unrecognised at Westminster, was that of establishing between the Mother Country and these two main divisions of her American empire relations which should give that empire permanence—for if the great war had finally secured it from serious attack by a foreign foe or rival, it had by that very fact introduced an element of disintegration.

The presence of the French had in itself served to enforce the dependence of the colonies on the Mother Country. Their individualism or particularism was far too strong to permit of their subjecting themselves voluntarily to a common control for the purpose of resisting French aggression, so long, at least, as the Mother Country recognised an obligation to hold French aggression in check with her own fleets and armies. It was worth while to pay a substantial price to be free from the strain of

The Price Paid for Protection maintaining an efficient military organisation. A degree of submission to a central authority was involved, but it was the authority under whose ægis the several states had come into being. Submission to authority was the price paid for protection. On the other side, it had been worth while for the Mother Country to extend that protection, not from altruistic motives, but on account of benefits received. She had no inclination to interfere with the normal autonomy of the colonies; but if her own interests and those of the colonies clashed, it was natural that she should insist on giving her own the precedence.

The colonists might protest, grumble, evade, but they could not afford to repudiate. The difference which the great war had made was precisely that it was no longer worth while for the colonies to pay the old price for protection. In effect, this price was the regulation of trade, imposing restrictions on the colonies in the interest of the Mother Country. The navigation acts of the commonwealth—Cromwell, to whom they are commonly attributed, was not yet lord protector, and, after a year in

Restrictions on Colonial Commerce Scotland, had been fighting the Battle of Worcester only a month before they were enacted—inflicted little injury on the colonies; the more stringent form given to the Act after the Restoration was more serious in its effects.

Direct trading between the colonies and foreign countries was prohibited, while imports and exports were virtually restricted to English, or, after the union with Scotland, to British shipping. Moreover, the government at Westminster forbade in the colonies the manufacture of goods which entered into competition with English products. The grievance was so marked that the laxity of colonial officials in enforcing the regulations was habitually and deliberately winked at,

Walpole's Method with Grievances
and a huge illicit traffic was permitted to grow up under the regime of Walpole. For it was a cardinal tenet of that Minister to remedy grievances not by legislation, which might rouse angry opposition, but by administrative disregard of breaches of the law—by going as far as possible in the direction of treating the law as a dead letter.

But that laxity would have been superfluous unless it was intended to palliate a serious grievance. A grievance which required to be palliated in Walpole's time, when the need of English protection was growing daily more palpable, was quite certain to require something more than palliation when the need of protection had disappeared altogether. Next it is to be observed that the administration of the colonies was liable to be directed from the Mother Country, which appointed the governors, who were the executive chiefs. In practice, there was ordinarily nothing to invite antagonism between the administrative and the representative assemblies.

But in England the representative assembly had been in possession of practical control of the executive for half a century. If it should be brought home to the colonial assemblies that they did not possess this control, that the executive might set them at naught, it was morally certain that they would follow the precedent of the English House of Commons and would not be contented to leave the effective control in the hands either of the Crown or of a parliament in which they were unrepresented. The English Parliament in its struggle with the

Why the Colonials Grumbled
Crown during the previous century had based its claims on fundamental rights of citizenship which it could not logically deny to the colonists. The average colonial might grumble, and had, in fact, grumbled to some purpose, on occasion ; but agitation was not likely to reach a dangerous stage at such times, as agitators had nothing more serious to denounce than a theoretical subjection. It would be another matter if the theoretical subjection

developed into a practical antagonism, as would happen if the administration became actively engaged in enforcing the will of the sovereign of England against the will of the colonists. In like manner, parliament had accepted the administrative autocracy of the Tudors, which was in accord with the popular will, but challenged and overthrew that of the Stuarts, because it set itself in antagonism to the popular will.

Here, then, were two great grievances—one actual and of long standing, the other potential. And the effect of the war had been to place the colonies in the very position to resent grievances ; or at least it had removed one very strong deterrent to active resentment.

On the other hand, it is a good deal easier for us to-day to realise the extent to which the conditions were changed than it was for politicians in England in 1763. It was less obvious that the colonists had been set free from the need of protection ; it was still supposed that forces would have to be maintained on American soil—not only in Canada—for that purpose. The axiomatic truth that France could not

The North American Indians
be dangerous to our American dominions so long as we held command of the sea was not appreciated. Moreover, a very few months after the Peace of Paris an Indian rising occurred which pointed to a possibility, at least, that the American continent itself contained enemies powerful enough to force the settlers to appeal to the Mother Country for aid.

In the altered political condition of North America, brought about by the Peace of Paris, none was worse off than the Indians. Under French rule the Indians were doubly favoured, because the French settlements, in which agriculture played quite a secondary part, had need of them in two ways—first, to obtain by barter articles of food and trade ; secondly, to aid in resisting the overpowering competition of the English settlements.

Thus the Indians were not only not driven out by the French, but were often encouraged to settle under the protection and in the immediate neighbourhood of the French boundary forts. The English backwoodsmen who now forced their way into this region brought with them an utter want of consideration for the Indians ; and the conflict which soon broke out was occasioned rather by the colonists than by the natives. The latter were, it is true, not wholly free from blame. For generations the Indians had been accustomed to the idea of the unlimited power of their fatherly patron, the distant French king. There may have been, among the Canadian settlers and among the French fur-traders and rangers who lived in the closest intimacy with the Indians, some who really believed that the present state of things was only transitory. At any rate, the Indians were in many cases led to believe that the great king was only asleep, and that when he awoke he would certainly remember his children 'in the distant wilderness and free them once more from the heavy yoke of the stranger.

The general ferment caused by these circumstances threatened to become dangerous to the English. A determined Indian chief of clear judgment tried to take advantage of the situation to stir up a rising of his countrymen which should place him in a position of power and honour. A chief of the Ottawas named Pontiac had during the period of French rule played a considerable part as representative of a powerful tribe. After the **Failure of the Indian Rising** defeat of the French, he, too, had made peace with the English; but when he was disappointed in his hopes of gaining honour and influence among them, he resolved to be revenged on them. He was able, by means of his messengers, to persuade the Indian tribes of the west, from the Lakes to the Mississippi, to join in a great conspiracy against the English. In May, 1763, he himself was to give the signal for a general rising by surprising Fort Detroit, between Lake Huron and Lake Erie.

A number of English forts were actually stormed, and laid waste with the usual barbarities. But the failure of Pontiac's attack on Fort Detroit, which he besieged for months, paralysed the movement. It was completely checked when reinforcements, sent out from Pennsylvania to relieve Fort Erie, which was also besieged, gained a decisive victory over the Indians at Bushy Run. Next year Pontiac went farther towards the southwest and tried to get the Indians on the Illinois and Mississippi to join in the struggle. How dangerous an opponent he was is shown by his endeavours to get the French garrisons, which in many cases had not yet been broken up, to take his part against the English. But in this he failed, and as the English troops were at his heels,

he wisely enough gave up his warlike plans and submitted, as most of the chiefs allied to him had already done.

The interpretation placed upon this object-lesson encouraged the idea that considerable military expenditure would still be demanded from the Mother Country by the colonies. And, in addition to this, **The Colonies' Debt to Great Britain** it was easy to feel a strong conviction that in any debit and credit account between colonies and Mother Country the balance of debt was heavily against the colonies. Not the colonial militia, but ships and regiments from Great Britain, and money out of the national exchequer, had overthrown the French power and secured freedom to the colonists for westward expansion. Though there were colonies such as Massachusetts which had made substantial sacrifices, the burden of the expenditure had been borne not by the colonies but by England; and the bulk of the profit was to be reaped not by England but by the colonies. That is to say in effect that the colonies had not yet discharged their debt for protection in the past. But when moral obligations come to be measured after this fashion, the parties are apt to apply different standards of value, and English politicians left out of the scale what the colonies had paid to England by the commercial regulations.

Now, in dealing with the newly acquired Canadian dominion, the policy adopted aimed at reconciling the French population to the new government. They were not offered self-government on the English analogy—they had never had it, or dreamed of it, nor would they have understood it if it had been granted them. What they got, however, was a paternal government, which sought to disturb them as little as possible, with the result that the end was successfully achieved. But with their own kith and kin the English Ministers dealt altogether otherwise. George Grenville, who became the ruling **Grenville's Strong Hand on the Colonies** spirit after Bute's withdrawal, was appalled by the expenditure which the war had entailed, and was eager to fill the depleted treasury. He looked to the colonies, for whose sake the war had been waged, and found that they were not paying their share. On the contrary, he found that by the illicit traffic they were evading the payment even of that share for which the law had already provided. He resolved in the first place to enforce the law; goods must pay their dues at the ports, and smuggling must cease. To that end the ships of his Majesty's navy were deputed to perform the functions of revenue cutters; and the lucrative trade, in which the most respectable citizens had shared extensively and hardly surreptitiously, became on a sudden extremely precarious. However annoyed the colonists might and did feel, men of British race always have a strong prejudice against putting themselves technically in the wrong, always endeavouring to believe in a technical justification for resistance to constituted authority, to find precedents for showing that the authority is acting *ultra vires*.

Passing of the Contentious Stamp Act

Here Grenville was palpably within his rights. No one had ever disputed the right to impose customs duties for the regulation of trade; the duties being imposed, no one could dispute the right to enforce them. The colonists would have found it extremely difficult to find any technical plea on which his action could be challenged. But his next step, however, gratuitously provided that much sought for technical plea. The Stamp Act was passed, ordering government stamps to be affixed to all legal documents for the purpose of providing revenue.

There was nothing in the colonial charters to bar the British Government from imposing such a tax; but there was no precedent for it. Customs for the regulation of trade had always been held to be distinct from taxes for purposes of revenue. In England, the Crown's prerogative of imposing customs without leave of parliament had been upheld by the courts, and had ultimately been surrendered to parliament for valuable consideration. But taxes for revenue had lain with parliament for centuries, and the Bill of Rights in 1689 had expressly laid down the principle of taxation only by assent of representatives. Yet here was parliament claiming to tax the citizens of the colonies in total disregard of that principle, a fundamental principle to maintain which the English had cut off the head of one king and sent another packing to France.

Taxation Without Representation

It was no doubt true that the circumstances differed in the very material point that there existed no practicable method of providing the colonists with representation, a possibility which the Bill of Rights had not included in its purview; but that did not invalidate the proposition that to ignore the principle was to stultify that charter of English liberties. "Taxation without representation" was not the real colonial grievance; but it was the technical plea behind which the colonial grievance was gratuitously enabled to take cover.

It must be remembered that before the passing of the Stamp Act itself, Grenville had not been content with enforcing the existing import duties; additional duties had been scheduled, and it had been expressly stated that the object of these additional duties was to raise revenue. This was in itself sufficient at least to provide a handle for raising the question of constitutional principles. The fight between Crown and parliament in England had begun on a precisely similar point.

At the accession of the Stuarts, the exaction of the established customs for the regulation of trade by royal prerogative was recognised without qualification. James I., being in want of funds, extended the duties by what were known as the "impositions."

The Essential Grievance of the Colonies

Parliament had at once claimed that such extension was in the nature of taxation, and required the consent of the people's representatives. The law courts had supported the Crown; but parliament by resolution had traversed the decision of the judges, and had never admitted the validity of the claims of the Crown. Protest now on the part of the colonies was on all fours with the old protest of the English Parliament against the impositions. But the effect of the Stamp Act was to give their protest the same basis, in principle, as the Petition of Right, the Declaration of Right, and the Bill of Rights. But the essential grievance of the colonies went much deeper than the technical point. It amounted to this: that the Mother Country—the people of England—claimed to legislate for the colonies to her own advantage and to their disadvantage, without consulting the people of the colonies; whereas the people of England had fought a great civil war rather than submit to legislation which they had not sanctioned.

For their own submission to such legislation in the past the colonists had received value; but they did not see how they were going to receive value for it in the future. They were perfectly certain, sooner or later, under these circumstances, to claim the rights of free men which their fellow citizens in England had asserted very decisively for themselves in the previous century. In England, however, as in every European country, colonists were regarded as having abrogated the full rights of citizenship ; they were, so to speak, people who had been authorised to exploit the territories on which they were permitted to settle, on such terms, and only on such terms, as the Mother Country deemed sufficiently profitable to itself ; they had no right to claim a revision of the terms of contract in their own favour, on the ground of abstract political doctrines, none to assert that restrictions which their charters permitted constituted legitimate grievances.

The letter of the law warranted the maximum claim of the Ministers in England ; but what was novel in these claims was in direct defiance of constitutional principles affirmed in English statutes ; and even what was not novel was liable to be challenged on general principles. But there was still a serious **Great Britain** difficulty in the way of accept-**in a** ing the colonial argument in **Difficulty** practice. If the British Parliament surrendered its technical right of taxation out of consideration for constitutional principles, how was Great Britain to be indemnified for expenditure incurred on behalf of the colonies ?

The only method available was that of voluntary contribution based on the recognition of a moral obligation, each colony contributing what it thought fit. For the colonies possessed no common central authority which could apportion their shares in a common fund ; and, under such conditions, each individual colony was likely to discover very good reasons for paying less than its neighbours. The alternative—the representation of the colonies in the British Parliament—offers, even at the present day, obstacles which seem insuperable. In the days before steamships it was manifestly quite outside the region of practical politics.

In modern days we have accepted the principle—not without some warrant for the old expectation that the colonial translation of moral obligation into pounds, shillings and pence would leave the Mother Country's share disproportionately large. The politicians of the eighteenth century did not accept it, in spite of the

declamation of Burke and the elder Pitt, both of whom declared vehemently in favour of the colonial appeal to fundamental constitutional principles. Ministers took their stand on the letter of the law. They did not believe that the colonists would set them at defiance, and had no doubt whatever that if they did Great **Grenville's** Britain would have no difficulty **Flagrant** in bringing them to reason. **Innovation** There is ground for believing that if Ministers had relied in the first instance on the moral appeal, the answer from the colonies would not have been inadequate, for an unwonted warmth of sentiment had been aroused by the triumphs of the British arms, and the name of William Pitt inspired the utmost enthusiasm.

Grenville chose the other course, and with the most exasperating methods. Before introducing the Stamp Act, he invited an expression of opinion from the colonies, although there had never been any intention of allowing their views to carry any weight. The Stamp Act itself was futile, because the amount of revenue which it would raise could not at the best be more than insignificant : a minimum of value was to be obtained at the cost of a maximum of irritation. To make matters worse, this flagrant innovation was accompanied by a " Quartering Act," requiring the colonies to provide barracks and free quarters for the officers of the troops to be maintained, although the colonists did not admit the necessity for their retention.

There was a violent outburst of indignation, which had been provided with the constitutional formula so invaluable to the agitator. There were already signs that American markets would be closed to British goods, and British merchants were uneasy. The great mass of the colonials would have passionately repudiated any suggestion that they were disloyal to the British connection. When the ardent **The Colonies** orator, Patrick Henry, ex-**Opposed** claimed " Cæsar had his **to "Tyranny"** Brutus, Charles I. had his Cromwell, George III. "—the cries of " Treason ! Treason ! " prevented him from continuing for some moments, and were really allayed only by the ingenuity of his evasion—"George III. may profit by their example." But perfectly honest professions of loyalty were compatible with a very stubborn defiance of "tyranny." In the interval between the passing of the Stamp Act and the day when it was to come into force popular feeling had expressed itself so vigorously, not to say riotously, that no one was found ready to discharge the official functions without which the new act could not be given effect; no one, evidently, could have done so except at the risk of his life. But even

Protest to King and Parliament

more significant of the character of the approaching crisis was the action of Massachusetts, with its Puritan political traditions. Massachusetts invited the colonies to send delegates to a representative congress, in effect for the purpose of protesting, and thus set a precedent which might in the future provide means to concerted action. Delegates assembled from nine states, and those from six of them signed a petition to the king, together with a memorial to parliament, in which the right of parliament to tax the colonies was repudiated.

In the meanwhile, events in England were taking a more favourable turn. The Grenville Ministry had been obliged to resign almost immediately after the passing of the Stamp Act, owing to a serious disagreement with the king over the Regency Bill. Pitt himself could not be induced to form a Ministry; but the government was undertaken by the more Liberal group of Whigs, who were headed by the Marquess of Rockingham, whose secretary, Edmund Burke, was now to appear for the first time in parliament.

In full accord with Pitt, and, indeed, at this time with popular sentiment—for the quarrel with the colonies was having an extremely disturbing effect on the mercantile interests—the Rockingham Ministry repealed the Stamp Act; and although at the same time a Declaratory Act was passed affirming the abstract right of taxation, the immediate effect was most pacificatory. For, simultaneously, a number of existing duties were materially

The Brief Rockingham Ministry

reduced—a measure which, while it pleased the Americans, benefited the revenue more than the Stamp Act could have done, owing, first, to the increased demand for the cheapened goods, and secondly to the disappearance of the main inducement to smuggling.

But the Rockingham Ministry lacked prestige and influence with the country, and was in political disagreement with the king. It was forced in turn to resign, and

Pitt at last accepted office, only to construct an amazingly miscellaneous cabinet and then leave it to anarchy. For the great Commoner accepted a peerage, which withdrew him from the arena of the House of Commons, and was then so sorely gripped with disease that he became wholly incapable of taking part in public affairs. In Chatham's name, the Grafton Ministry proceeded to leave undone every project of the great statesman, and to do everything which he would have most emphatically condemned. The Stamp Act had been passed in 1765 and repealed in 1766; in 1767 Charles Townshend, as Chancellor of the Exchequer, set the mischief at work again, and having done so, died, leaving to others the reaping of the whirlwind which he had sown.

Townshend's Revenue Act could not have been more ingeniously contrived if it had been his deliberate intention to irritate for the sake of irritating. He imposed six new duties, apparently with the object of emphasising the abstract right to tax, seeing that the return expected from them collectively was not more than

America Indignant at the Tea Tax

£40,000. Of the six, one only, that upon tea, was of any commercial importance. The grotesqueness of the thing becomes the more apparent when we realise that the effect of the impost was not to increase but to diminish the price which the Americans had to pay for their tea.

For hitherto, under the navigation laws, tea was not carried direct to a colonial port from India; it had to pass, on its way, through an English port, where it had to pay duty. Its price at the colonial port was consequently enhanced by the amount of that duty. Townshend's Act granted a drawback of this amount—that is, the duty paid on entering the English port was returned, while the new duty imposed at the colonial port was only one-fourth; so that, in effect, three-fourths of the old duty was remitted to the colonial purchaser. But it was exacted at the American port, merely to exemplify the right of exacting it. And thus it once more set ablaze the flame which the Rockingham Ministry had all but quenched. The monstrosity of the tax lay in its sheer wantonness, not in the hardship it involved.

The effect was immediate. The colonies were pervaded with a fixed determination to boycott the taxed goods, and all goods imported from England, until the obnoxious taxes should be withdrawn. Non-importation agreements became the order of the day, with disastrous effects on British trade, accompanied by increased activity in home manufactures. The Massachusetts assembly passed resolutions, sent petitions and protests, and took the lead in inviting plans and schemes for concerted action. The governor, Bernard, required them to withdraw the circular letter in which the invitation had been conveyed, but the assembly flatly refused, by a majority of more than five to one. The governor dissolved the assembly, and refused to issue writs for a new one, whereupon a convention was called together, attended by delegates from every settlement. The convention had no legal standing, but the people of Massachusetts recognised its authority, while it conducted its proceedings skilfully enough to avoid any technical breach of the law.

Other provincial assemblies followed the Boston example in passing strongly expressed resolutions. Troops began to arrive in Boston from England, in response to Governor Bernard's demands, but it was **Murmurings of the Coming War** only with the utmost difficulty that provision could be made for them; the colonists entirely refused to comply with the terms of the Quartering Act. Viewing their conduct as little short of veiled rebellion, the English Parliament passed resolutions in favour of reviving an obsolete statute of Henry VIII., and applying it in the colonies, so that trials in which the action of government officials was involved might be removed for hearing from the province concerned. George Washington in Virginia was already feeling that armed resistance might prove necessary, in 1769, though he was as yet as far as possible from advocating the idea of independence. But it can hardly be doubted that, beneath the surface, that idea was beginning to strike root.

This was the moment chosen for the most fatuous of all the government measures. Of Townshend's six taxes, five were withdrawn; but the sixth—that on tea—was retained. Chatham had already recovered sufficiently from his illness to protest and retire from the Ministry; Grafton, its nominal head, now followed suit; and at the beginning of 1770 Lord North began his disastrous Ministry. It was almost at this moment that a riot occurred in Boston, in which

some of the soldiery were forced to fire on the mob; half a dozen persons were injured, and three were killed. Demagogues exaggerated the incident into a "massacre," though a jury of Bostonians acquitted the soldiers. For the moment, however, agitation was driven beneath the surface. Hutchinson, a Boston man, **Boston's Reply to the Tea Tax** was made governor in place of the somewhat exasperating Bernard, and the English Ministers seem to have come to the conclusion that there was no more serious trouble in store. An awakening came in 1772, when the royal schooner Gaspee, on revenue duty, was boarded by night as she lay aground at Providence, in Rhode Island, and was burnt, while no evidence could be procured as to the perpetrators of the outrage. And now plans which had been slowly maturing took shape in overt action.

The towns in all the New England states, in Virginia and in South Carolina, established correspondence committees; the boycott of British-borne tea was made practically complete. At Charleston tea was landed, but found no purchasers. At New York it was not allowed to be landed at all; ships and cargoes were dismissed from the harbour. At Boston, the people would not allow the tea ships to land their cargoes, and the governor refused to let them leave the port till they had paid duty. After a great public meeting, a party of Bostonians, dressed for the occasion as Red Indians, boarded the tea ships in the presence of an applauding multitude, and emptied their contents into the sea.

This was in December, 1773. It was the signal for a series of repressive measures enacted in 1774. British sentiment, once not unfavourable to the colonies, had swung completely round, in consequence largely of the illegality of the methods which the Americans were now adopting; moreover, the losses to English trade were **Franklin's Breach of Honour** now arousing not merely perturbation, but active resentment. And this was intensified by the action of Benjamin Franklin, who was acting in London as agent for several colonies. By some means never explained, Franklin had obtained possession of a private correspondence between Whately, George Grenville's secretary, and the governor and the chief justice of Massachusetts. Those letters he sent to America, and in America they were published. The Americans were furious on account of the opinions expressed; the British were not less disgusted at the breach of honour involved in their publication.

Three " penal " Acts, then, were passed against Boston. The Boston Port Act closed the port entirely. A second Act removed from Massachusetts the trial of any official who should be indicted for acts performed in the course of his official duties. A third in effect cancelled the charter of the colony. In addition to these, another general Quartering Act was passed. And at the same time the suspicions of the Americans were intensified by an Act which was not directed against them in any way, being concerned entirely with the administration of Canada.

Protestant Feeling in New England

There, as we remarked at the beginning of the chapter, representative government on the English model would not even have been appreciated; and the population was Roman Catholic. The Quebec Act was in effect a measure for the administration of Canada as a Crown Colony, and for the official establishment of Roman Catholicism. New England abhorred Romanism, and imagined the measure to be a political experiment intended to be applied at an early date to the older colonies who were claiming the right of free citizens. The Quebec Act aggravated the effects of the penal legislation.

Massachusetts had stood in the van, and was paying the penalty; but the rest were determined to stand by her. The Virginian assembly passed a resolution of protest and appointed a public fast for the day on which the Boston Port Act was to come into force. The governor dissolved the assembly, but it continued its meetings on its own account. Virginia and Massachusetts agreed in calling for a general congress, to meet in Philadelphia. The congress met in September; every state except Georgia was represented. Among its members were Patrick Henry, Samuel Adams and George Washington. It drew up a Declaration of Rights embodying the principles which need not again be rehearsed, and citing the series of Acts by which it was held that those principles had been violated. It adopted non-importation resolutions. But it still definitely declared its loyalty, and George Washington still believed that independence was " not

American Declaration of Rights

desired by any thinking man in all North America." Even so the Long Parliament had entered upon the great civil war with a firm belief that it was not disloyal to the monarchy. The Massachusetts Charter Act had deprived the assembly of the right of nominating the council. The assembly was summoned by the new governor, General Gage, in October.

The members now nominated by the Crown to the council either refused appointment or resigned immediately. The governor thereupon countermanded the writs for the assembly; but his proclamation was ignored, the elections were held, and the members assembled. Its authority, though without legal sanction, was universally recognised. Prompt steps were taken for the organisation of a militia, called " minute men." In connection with it a " committee of public safety " and a second committee of supplies were organised. Massachusetts was working its own administration, as though a governor were a mere superfluity—even a governor who was also commander-in-chief of his Majesty's forces in America. And in the meantime every provincial assembly, except that of New York was ratifying the resolutions of the " Continental Congress " at Philadelphia, which had adjourned after a sitting of seven weeks. Parliament met at Westminster, and the King's Speech expressed a resolute refusal to yield to the American spirit of disobedience and resistance. Once more Chatham appeared to plead for conciliation, " not for indulgence but for justice," to demand the repeal of the obnoxious measures. This appeal fell on deaf ears.

Colonies Preparing For War

In the commons, North brought forward a childish proposal that the taxes should be withdrawn in the case of colonies which voluntarily made adequate offers of contribution to the treasury. At the same time, since the closing of Boston Port had failed of its object, a string of other ports were treated more or less after the same fashion. The resolutions of the Opposition, presented with splendid eloquence by Edmund Burke, were as useless as the eloquence of Chatham in the other chamber. And the colonists, following the example of Massachusetts, continued on all hands to organise their militia, and to collect provisions and munitions of war.

A. D. INNES

THE FIGHT FOR INDEPENDENCE
THE TRIUMPH OF THE COLONIES AND THE FOUNDING OF THE UNITED STATES REPUBLIC

THE breach between the American colonies and the Mother Country was, in no reasonable sense of the term, "inevitable"; it was the outcome of a purblind policy based on an untenable theory. That theory, common to all the nations which had attempted colonisation, was, in effect, that colonists had no rights as against the parent state.

The idea that the colony will break away from the parent state as soon as it can stand alone has no inherent justification. The family bond is not necessarily severed when the son grows up, but if the son is treated as still *in statu pupillari* he is tolerably certain to rebel. While the colony feels the need of protection by the mother country it will submit to having its own interests subordinated; when it feels capable of standing alone, it will not. The bond has become one of mutual

Restrictions that Troubled the Colonies sentiment and mutual advantage, demanding mutual consideration, and the extent of central control to be exercised must be adjusted on that basis; but there is no essential impossibility about effecting such an adjustment. Moral obligations continue to subsist, but only under a moral sanction, and if another sanction is applied the moral sanction dwindles to the vanishing point.

The American colonies had reached a stage of development at which they were capable of working out their own salvation; they were quite certain sooner or later to insist on the removal of restrictions which interfered with that operation. Commonsense demanded the removal of such restrictions when their existence had no moral warrant. Moderation, tact, appreciation of the other point of view, were required for the readjustment. But King George and his Ministers demanded a readjustment in the direction of British claims for which there was no precedent.

They were not without justification in claiming an indemnity from America; but, if they elected not to trust to the colonial conscience, it was their business to aim at getting the maximum return for the minimum of irritation. Instead, they contented themselves with asking for a return so small as to be not worth having,

Fanning the Flame of Ill-feeling and doing so in the most exasperating manner possible. They gave themselves away to the disloyalists, who fanned the flame of ill-feeling and waited their own time to turn it to account. Both sides had at last gone so far that neither could draw back without some degree of ignominy. In the spring of 1775, it is doubtful if one man in twenty among the serious public in America was desirous of severing the ties with England. But in the then state of tension, a collision between colonial and British troops might occur at any moment

The Provincial Congress of Massachusetts—the acting governing body—had collected its war material at Concord. Thither, on April 18th, 1775, General Gage, governor of Massachusetts and commander-in-chief in America, despatched a party of redcoats to take possession of the stores. The militia had warning of his intention; and when the English troops reached Lexington Common they found themselves face to face with a

The First Engagement in the War hostile force. Here the first shots were exchanged; here the war began. At first the militia retired, and the English entered Concord without resistance. But in a short time their position there became critical; a retreat was inevitable, and it was not unaccompanied by danger. Once a shot had been fired, the colonists rose on all sides. The English troops were hard pressed, suffered severe losses, and continued their retreat

WASHINGTON, HENRY AND PENDLETON ON THEIR WAY TO THE FIRST CONGRESS

THE FIRST PRAYER IN CONGRESS, HELD AT PHILADELPHIA IN 1774

The first mention of a congress for North America was made in 1690 by Jacob Leisler, a suggestion that was renewed eighty-three years later by Benjamin Franklin, who at that time was in London. The following year the colony of Virginia proposed that all the other colonies should send representatives to a congress held at Philadelphia. The proposal was accepted, and the first real American Congress met on September 5th, 1774, sitting until October 26th.

From the painting by Matterson

THE FIRST ENGAGEMENT IN THE AMERICAN WAR OF INDEPENDENCE

THE HISTORIC STRUGGLE ON CONCORD BRIDGE, APRIL 19TH, 1775

The differences between the American colonies and the Mother Country culminated on April 18th, 1775, in an engagement between the colonial and British troops at Lexington. The Provincial Congress of Massachusetts had dispatched troops to take possession of its war material at Concord, and on the way thither the English redcoats found themselves face to face with a hostile force at Lexington Common. After entering Concord, the position of the English troops became critical, and a retreat was inevitable, hence the historic struggle on Concord Bridge.

to the trenches before Boston. In the next few days the investment of the town began, and continued almost a year, during which nothing more important occurred than an occasional skirmish between the opposing forces. Such was the state of affairs when congress renewed its sittings at Philadelphia.

Britain's Sharp Measures with Her Colonies Its petition to the king had been contemptuously rejected; the English Parliament had given its consent to the employment of force to bring the colonies back to obedience, and had voted considerable sums for the strengthening of the fleet and the engagement of mercenaries, drawn chiefly from the smaller German principalities.

Detachments of troops were arriving in America, and the fleet committed occasional acts of hostility on the American coast. The congress, in which all the thirteen states were now represented, could no longer persist in the humble attitude of the preceding year. It took up the position, not as yet of fighting for independence, but of defending itself until England should give compensation for the damage done, re-establish the infringed rights of the colonies, and recognise their constitutional demands.

One more vain effort was made to avoid the final and fatal appeal to arms. An address known as the " Olive-branch Petition " went to London; it expressed readiness to accept all the regulations which had been in force down to 1763. It went as far as it was possible to go in the way of concession. But the king and his Ministers did not want concessions. They would have nothing short of uncompromising submission; and plain submission was out of the question. Lexington had been followed by open hostilities, and the Battle of Bunker's Hill had been fought before the Olive-branch Petition arrived. It was not rejected; for it was not allowed to be presented at all. The practical answer to it was a proclamation against sedition, **Congress in a Difficult Position** and the raising of German mercenaries. The outbreak of war placed the congress in an exceedingly difficult position.

Though recognised by all the North American colonies, it possessed no technical authority. It was a deliberative assembly devoid of all inherent power, and its resolutions could only be put into execution when the provincial assemblies indirectly responsible for them had given their consent. In most respects each of the provincial assemblies was supreme in its own district; and the petty jealousies between the provinces soon led them to keep watch most jealously over this local supremacy. It was only in taking action against England that the authority of congress was fully recognised.

Congress appointed George Washington commander-in-chief of the forces of the thirteen colonies, and Montgomery and Schuyler leaders of the army which was to induce Canada to join the revolutionary movement. As money as well as men was necessary for an army, it established a war fund to which each state was to contribute proportionately. Congress went a step farther in rejecting the English proposals for mediation and sending agents to several courts of Europe in order to dispose them favourably towards the cause of the colonies. A declaration of independence was as yet intentionally avoided; but in reality the congress already claimed for itself the rights of an independent power. **Leaders in the War of Independence** Meanwhile, the struggle was continued in the north. In 1774, the Quebec Act had finally settled the form of government for Canada. The province was given a decidedly centralising organisation, and was placed under a military governor.

It was further decided to extend the southern boundary of the province as far as the Ohio. In resolving to make its first move in this direction, the congress had two objects in view: first, to reconquer the territory which the change in the boundary threatened to take from the New England states; and second, to induce Canada, if possible, to join the other thirteen provinces. Immediately after Lexington a bold stroke had placed the Americans in possession of Ticonderoga, Crown Point and Lake Champlain, and opened up to them the way into Central Canada. In August Montgomery and Schuyler took the offensive; but the movement was crippled by disagreements among the leaders of all ranks.

Schuyler resigned his command. Montgomery besieged and took St. John's, and then pressed on towards Montreal. Before this town he made a long halt, and thus prevented a third corps, which had marched against Quebec under Arnold,

THE FAMOUS BATTLE OF BUNKER'S HILL ON JUNE 17TH, 1775, IN THE AMERICAN STRUGGLE FOR INDEPENDENCE.

The Battle of Bunker's Hill was in reality the first of the many hard-fought battles which marked America's struggle for independence. The Americans, having successfully repulsed two severe attacks from General Gage, who occupied the city of Boston, were only dislodged from the heights of Bunker's Hill and the adjoining Breed's Hill after much severe fighting. Although victory rested with the British, their death-roll amounted to 1,054, while that of the Americans was 449. The above picture shows the death of Joseph Warren, the American patriot.

THE DECLARATION OF INDEPENDENCE OF THE UNITED STATES ON JULY 4TH, 1776

The Declaration of Independence marks a dramatic stage in the war which was ended only by Britain abandoning her colonies, with the exceptions of Canada and the island of Newfoundland. "We," ran the declaration, "solemnly publish and declare that these United Colonies are, and of a right ought to be, Free and Independent States."

PROCLAIMING THE DECLARATION OF INDEPENDENCE FROM THE STATE HOUSE

Immediately after the Declaration of Independence had been agreed to by Congress, the announcement of this epoch-making step in American history was publicly made from the outside of the State House in Philadelphia.

from accomplishing anything. When, in December, the two detachments at last united to make an attack on Quebec, it was repulsed with great loss, Montgomery himself falling. In so far as the campaign had in view the stirring up of revolution in Canada, it was a complete failure. It was only with difficulty that the position gained could be maintained.

Boston, however, was the main theatre of conflict. Fifteen thousand men of the New England militia had gradually collected there, and so shut in the English garrison that its maintenance began to be a matter of difficulty. This induced Gage to push forward bodies of troops in various positions. The besiegers replied by an advance towards Charleston. The opposing forces met at Bunker's Hill on June 17th, 1775. The progress of the combat was typical of the War of Independence. The militia fought bravely, but their leaders had so little capacity for their task that the battle ended with the abandonment of all the positions taken up. From a military point of view the English had gained a victory, but they reaped no advantage from it. The American losses were replaced, and both leaders and men burned with the desire to renew the struggle. At the beginning of July, Washington arrived in the camp before Boston, and took over the command of the army of the united provinces. This made no change in the progress of the siege. The evil results of the militia system were already making themselves felt among the Americans. The colonists were quite prepared to go through a short struggle, but the long inactivity involved in the reduction of a hostile position undermined their discipline and made them unwilling to remain under arms longer than the time

GEORGE WASHINGTON
The greatest figure in the American War of Independence, he displayed remarkable powers of leadership as commander-in-chief of the colonial army, and in spite of defeats, led his forces to ultimate triumph. In 1789 he was elected the first president of the United States of America.

of service agreed upon. It is true that some of the provinces were ready to send fresh men to take the places of those discharged; but, with these, training and exercise had to be begun all over again, and when they were proficient their term of service was nearly ended. Thus it was that the capabilities of the American Army were by no means what was to be expected considering its numbers. The leaders must have possessed the highest ability, both as regards diplomacy and strategy, to attain with such poor material the excellent results they did. The English Government gradually came to the conclusion that it was a mistake to keep its main force shut up in Boston. General Howe, who succeeded Gage in command, was ordered to evacuate the town, and withdrew his forces to Halifax, in Nova Scotia. The British, it should be remarked, had complete control of the sea, and their fleet was under the command of Lord Howe, the general's brother. It was a triumph, however, for the Americans to be able, after nine months' siege, to enter the town which had been first selected for punishment by the home government. In May, 1776, congress met at Philadelphia, for the fourth time, under most favourable auspices. The prevailing elation found expression in a proposal brought before congress some weeks later, that the colonies should separate from the Mother Country and form an independent state. Congress was not elected by popular vote; each state legislature sent as many delegates as it thought fit.

This peculiar composition of the deliberative body rendered it impossible to ascertain how far the proposal embodied the general desire of the inhabitants of the thirteen states. Public opinion, as known in England, did not exist at this time in the colonies. What appears to be the expression of the popular will was generally but the action of a small number of determined politicians who knew what they were aiming at, and who played a prominent part in the correspondence committees and in congress. Under these circumstances it is specially significant that inquiries made led to the conclusion that the proposal to put forth a declaration of independence would not command a majority, even in congress. But the party for independence was in this case excellently led. Hitherto the leaders had not refused assent to the most conciliatory measures, convinced that every failure would bring those who hesitated nearer to their position; and now once more they found a diplomatic way of escape. To withdraw the proposal would be nearly as severe a check as to have it rejected; it was quite safe, however, to postpone discussion and voting for several weeks, as was done on June 10th. How little the leaders doubted that victory would ultimately be theirs was shown by their appointing a commission to discuss the steps which the declaration of independence would render necessary. They were justified by success; and when the proposal was again brought up a number of the opponents of separation from England withdrew from the congress, so that on July 4th the Declaration of Independence, which the committee had meanwhile carefully prepared, was solemnly proclaimed as the unanimous decision of the congress. Among the colonists the

THE BELL THAT DECLARED INDEPENDENCE

Hung in the dome of the old State House, Philadelphia, this bell announced the signing of the Declaration of Independence. Brought from England in 1752, it was, owing to an accident in transit, recast in Philadelphia, when the words "Proclaim liberty throughout all the land unto all the inhabitants thereof" were inscribed on it.

result of the struggle that had meanwhile broken out in different places was awaited with the greatest anxiety. Even those who from the outbreak of the war had looked on separation as its necessary consequence felt clearly that it was too early to give themselves up to rejoicing.

After the evacuation of Boston, Washington went, as early as April, 1776, to New York, in the expectation that this important port, whose population included a numerous royalist party, would be the next object of the British attack. At first it seemed that this expectation would not be justified. A part of the English fleet directed its course southward, and tried to take possession of Charleston, in South Carolina. But on its being repulsed, the British forces again united, and, under Sir William Howe, effected a landing on Long Island towards the end of August. This Washington with his militia was unable to prevent; nor could he offer serious opposition to their advance. He was fortunate in being able to lead his over-matched force across the East River back to New York without serious loss, it being useless for him to hope to hold New York, and thence continued his celebrated retreat, which, considering the difficulties he had to contend with, was a great achievement even for one so talented. Nevertheless, the retreat seemed a severe blow to the cause of American independence.

More dangerous to Washington than his English foe, who followed him from one position to another with deliberate slowness, was the condition of his own army. In each of the numerous letters in which

INDEPENDENCE HALL, SHOWING THE CHAIRS AND PORTRAITS OF THE SIGNATORIES

The plain low building which sheltered the first American Congress was the scene of the signing of the Declaration of Independence. The portraits on the wall are those of the signatories, and the chairs those which were used on that occasion. In this room also Washington was appointed commander-in-chief of the colonial forces. Independence Hall is now kept as a museum of historical relics. It was outside this building that the Declaration was announced to the public.

he informs congress of the course of events at the seat of war Washington returns to the point that with the militia, badly disciplined and unwilling to serve a day more than their short term, he can gain no success against Howe's army, which was composed of well-trained professional soldiers. He repeatedly demands, at least for the period of the war, a standing army and a trained corps of officers.

The thirteen states had declared themselves independent; but congress had still to draw up a scheme for their internal organisation. A considerable time must elapse before this could be approved of by the legislatures of the several states. At first each state turned to congress with its own claims and appeals for help; but all left it to congress to find help for their necessities and misfortunes. The separate states did not always recognise the paper money that congress was forced to issue to cover the expenses of the war, and yet it was precisely money and soldiers that all demanded from that body. Though the

army and its commander had often just ground to complain of the congress, it must not be forgotten that the latter, though having the best of intentions, was often unable to give help.

Washington understood perfectly how to take advantage of Howe's slowness to protract his retreat as much as possible. The British took possession of New York on September 15th; but immediately thereafter were decisively checked by the Americans at Harlem Heights. A month later, after the British had moved by water to Westchester County and had thus swung towards the rear of the American position, the two armies met at White Plains. The result of battle there was to give the British the control of a portion of the country between Long Island Sound and the Hudson, thus enabling their land forces to keep in touch with their naval forces on both bodies of water, and, on the other hand, to restrict further the lines of the Americans and to separate them from their allies on the upper Hudson and in New Jersey. Finally, in November, the Americans at Fort Washington, being attacked from three directions, were forced to abandon the east side of the Hudson in its lower course, and to withdraw into New Jersey.

Washington had now to make a rapid retreat to the Delaware, and with forces disorganised by continued retreat he could no longer hold the enemy in check. At the beginning of December congress believed the capital, Philadelphia, no longer secure, and fled to Baltimore before the approach of the hostile army. But this time it was able to return without the enemy having set foot in the American capital. The most serious thing was that with such ideas prevalent the cause of freedom was losing many adherents. Only after Washington, at the end of 1776, had surprised and defeated the enemy at Trenton did the spirits of his men begin to rise a little. The persistent inactivity of the British general is only explicable on the theory that he was confident that the "Continental" Army would break up of itself; and in fact it was only the indomitable patience and the iron resolution of its great chief that prevented it from doing so. Disappointed in his expectation of the collapse of the enemy's forces, Howe apparently resolved to adopt a less opportunist plan of campaign for 1777, in conjunction or co-operation with the forces now in Canada. We have seen that the attempt to coerce Canada into joining the thirteen colonies ended in a disastrous fiasco; the French habitants were quite satisfied with the British Government, whereas their feeling towards the New Englanders in particular was anything but friendly. In 1776, the British were in possession of Crown Point, and a British flotilla controlled Lake Champlain. The plan of operations then was that General Burgoyne should descend from the lakes, while General Clinton

ADMIRAL LORD HOWE

Fighting in the American War of Independence, Admiral Lord Howe nobly maintained the British prestige on the sea, out-manœuvring the French force in American waters, and proving the greater skill and confidence of the British sailors even when opposed to an enemy much stronger in numbers.

advanced with a column from New York to meet him, thus completely cutting off the New England states. Properly carried out, the effect of the scheme would probably have been decisive.

But Howe attached still more importance to the capture of Philadelphia, counting on the moral effect, for it had no strategical value. Washington with his army lay between New York and Philadelphia, and a direct advance would be almost certain to meet with a repulse. But the control of the sea gave Howe an alternative course. Leaving Clinton in command at New York—although that general should have been on the point of starting to carry out the concerted movement with Burgoyne—Howe embarked the bulk of his forces and sailed for the Chesapeake. Thus Washington's position was turned, and he was no longer master of the road to Philadelphia. Enthusiasm for the war had now reached its lowest ebb in the colonies. The news that arrived from England had not a little to do with this. The amnesty which Howe had promised the New England states if they would submit was now assured by parliament to all who returned to their allegiance. The prospect was also held out of measures which would remedy the most oppressive evils complained of by the colonies. Not only in great part of America, but also in the European states, which followed the progress of the War of Independence with strained attention, a reconciliation between the Mother Country and the rebellious colonies was confidently believed to be impending.

Such expectations naturally drove all the lukewarm to the English side. Even the presence of congress, which had returned to Philadelphia, failed to keep public opinion unwavering in the Quaker city. Washington, by the resistance he offered during his skilfully conducted retreat, delayed the English advance; but in the middle of September

SURRENDER OF THE BRITISH UNDER GENERAL BURGOYNE AT THE BATTLE OF SARATOGA

Burgoyne's surrender of Saratoga on October 17th, 1777, was not the least of the defeats which Britain suffered at the hands of the Americans. It was after this humiliation, which fell like a thunderbolt on British ears, that Chatham made his famous declaration: "You cannot conquer America. If I were an American as I am an Englishman, while a foreign troop landed in my country, I would never lay down my arms; never, never, never!"

BURIAL OF GENERAL SIMON FRASER, WHO WAS KILLED AT SARATOGA

Fighting under General Burgoyne at the Battle of Saratoga, General Simon Fraser was wounded in the thigh, and, dying on the following morning, was buried in one of the British redoubts. As the last rites were being performed, and while the chaplain was reading the service for the dead, the Americans, ignorant of the motive of the small group of people, opened a heavy fire, which they continued until not a solitary person remained.

From the painting by J. Graham

he had to announce to congress that he was no longer in a position to protect the way to Philadelphia. On September 26th, 1777, the English Army occupied the revolutionary capital.

But this apparently brilliant success soon appeared in another light. A few days later, Washington returned to the attack, and succeeded in cutting off all Howe's communications with the interior. The latter was now forced to attack the forts on the Delaware that were still in the hands of the Continental Army and threatened his line of communication with the sea. These forts were neither sufficiently fortified nor strongly enough garrisoned to be able to hold out long, but they withstood the English Army and fleet for almost five weeks. Even this was a decided advantage, for the season was now so far advanced that both armies had to go into winter quarters. The condition of the Continental Army, which had to undergo privations of every kind, and in consequence suffered severely both in numbers and in morale, would have been serious had not fortune in the meantime favoured the arms of the Americans in the north and thus brought about a decisive change in the entire situation. For the movement against Philadelphia had ruined the northern plan of campaign. It had kept Clinton locked up in New York long after he should have been on the march, and the American general, Gates, had in consequence been left to conduct his operations unhampered. Burgoyne himself had advanced from the north with an effective army of regular troops, part British and part German, numbering 8,000 men, and the beginning of his campaign was a series of uninterrupted successes.

Burgoyne's Series of Successes

He met with no serious resistance at the outset, and if Clinton had been moving from the south, serious resistance might have been altogether prevented. Ticonderoga, which the Americans considered the impregnable key of the north, fell into his hands almost without bloodshed. The garrison, which began its retreat partly by land and partly by water, was dispersed. Until they reached the upper Hudson, the English met with no serious opposition from the Continental troops; General Schuyler had only time to destroy roads and bridges, and to withdraw all supplies out of the reach of the English. But in accomplishing so much he changed the whole course of events. When Burgoyne reached the Hudson his force was considerably reduced, as he had to leave garrisons behind him to keep open his lines of communication. Moreover, the troops were too exhausted by the excessive exertions they had to make in the heat of the summer to render passable the roads through the marshes between Lake George and the Hudson. To make matters still worse, they were quite destitute of supplies. Misfortune suddenly broke on Burgoyne from all sides.

Checks to British Forces

Here in the north the war was a great deal more popular than in the Quaker state, Pennsylvania; and with the approach of danger the leaders of the Continental Army received daily fresh accessions of strength. It was the British right wing that received the first check. It was ordered to take Fort Stanwix on the Mohawk; but after a fruitless siege of some weeks' duration it had to begin a retreat to Canada that much resembled flight. A detachment that Burgoyne sent into Vermont to forage was almost annihilated in open combat; all its war material fell into the hands of the Continentals. Finally, Burgoyne himself had to advance, if only to obtain provisions; he crossed the Hudson and met the main army, commanded by General Gates, at Freeman's Farm. The first indecisive encounter was equivalent to a severe defeat for Burgoyne; and when, a few days later, he made a second attempt to gain breathing space for his starving soldiers, he was so thoroughly beaten that his only course was to retreat.

But even this was no longer open to him. Encouraged by their victory, the Continental troops surrounded him on all sides, and when Gates, with the main army, offered battle a third time before Saratoga, Burgoyne and his army, seeing the uselessness of further bloodshed, laid down their arms, on October 17th, 1777. The armies that faced each other in this campaign were not very large according to modern ideas. But apart from the fact that England could not often replace an army of 8,000 men, the Americans gained great strategic advantages. Burgoyne's capitulation meant much more than the failure of the plan to divide the American forces by occupying the line of the Hudson;

Surrender of Burgoyne and His Army

AN AMERICAN TRAITOR: THE ESCAPE OF BENEDICT ARNOLD

The above picture depicts a stirring incident in the life of the famous adventurer and traitor, Benedict Arnold. Originally a surgeon, Arnold, at the outbreak of war between Great Britain and her colonies, joined the latter, and considerably distinguished himself. Towards the close of the war he made a secret offer to General Clinton for surrendering West Point to the British, employing Major Andre, a British officer, to negotiate. The plot was discovered. Andre was shot as a spy, Arnold himself barely managing to escape with his life into the British lines.

From the painting by Howard Pyle

the Canada frontier was now secure for a time at least against British attack, and the British garrison in New York was isolated, having no means of communication with the other British armies, except by sea.

Viewed simply as an incident in the war between the British Government and the recalcitrant colonies, Burgoyne's disaster was serious, but very far from being decisive. It was, in fact, the turning-point of the war, because it introduced a new factor on the American side. Hitherto, the presumption that Great Britain must, in the course of time, overwhelm the colonists had held back foreign Powers from intervention. Saratoga gave the impression that the Americans might win on their own merits. There was one European Power which was athirst for revenge on England : France found the temptation to throw her sword into the scale too strong, and the French intervention secured the colonial victory.

Since the earliest signs of serious dissension between England and the colonies, France had watched events in America with the closest attention. Her leading statesmen waited longingly for the opportunity to take revenge for the losses and humiliation inflicted on her by the peace of 1763. As early as 1767 a French agent had been sent to North America to obtain information, not only on the state of

public opinion there, but also upon the means the colonists had at their disposal in the event of war with England, and as to what kind of help they would most urgently require. But French policy was then considerably in advance of the claims put forward by the colonists. The reports which the agent, De Kalb, sent from America did much to cool French eagerness to support the colonies. The plan of taking revenge on their enemy by promoting an American revolt had to be abandoned for a time. But as soon as the first congresses

French Support for America were convinced that their rights could be maintained against the Mother Country only by force, they remembered the disposition displayed by France ; Paris was the first and most important point to which the congress had sent its agents ; nor did it send them in vain.

Naturally, the French Government could not, in 1775, enter into open communication with the agents of the still quite unorganised rebel provinces ; but it nevertheless gave the Americans much secret support. As soon as war had openly begun, the Americans started hostilities at sea. It was quite in accord with the strongly developed business spirit of the northern provinces that they should be much more eager to do injury to British trade at sea by privateering than to carry

GENERAL WASHINGTON AMONG HIS SOLDIERS AT VALLEY FARM

WASHINGTON AND THE FRENCH MARQUESS DE LAFAYETTE AT MOUNT VERNON

In their struggle for independence the American colonies had the sympathy and support of the French nation, not a few of whose bold sons crossed the ocean to fight against their hated enemy, the British. Chief amongst them was the youthful Marquess de Lafayette, shown with Washington in the above picture, who commanded an American division with conspicuous ability and success, and was publicly thanked by Washington for his military skill and valour.
From the painting by T. P. Rossiter

on an honourable, though less profitable, war by land against the British Army. Soon after the Declaration of Independence, the first American privateers ventured across the ocean into British waters. The ship which in the autumn of 1776 brought Benjamin Franklin to France as accredited representative of the new republic, brought

Privateers Under French Protection into Havre, as prizes, two English vessels which it had captured on the way. This constituted on the part of France a breach of the peace then existing between her and a "friendly nation"; but American privateers continued to take refuge secretly in French harbours. Though the American delegates were not officially recognised, it was an open secret, especially after Franklin's arrival, that they had the direct support of the French Government in buying war material, fitting out ships, and enlisting officers and crews which were taken to America secretly, or under a false flag.

Franklin, from the beginning, felt sure of the favourable issue of the negotiations for a treaty of trade and friendship with which the newly organised Foreign Office had entrusted him; but these sanguine expectations were not altogether realised. There can be no doubt that not

only the French Government, but the whole French people, sympathised with the cause of the United States. This was not for any love they bore the Americans, but principally because they saw in a successful American rising a means of injuring the hated English, and they only too eagerly seized the chance of taking revenge on them. Thus Franklin was permitted to visit Paris, and in his private capacity could speak his mind freely to the leading French Minister, Vergennes.

But a public reception was avoided; the more so because the campaign following the Declaration of Independence was unfortunate to such an extent that the final victory of the Americans was seriously doubted. France's attitude during the year 1777 was purely expectant. Even the amount of secret assistance given to the rebels was insignificant. The only event attracting attention was the departure for America of the youthful Marquess de Lafayette, who, with De Kalb and other Frenchmen, crossed over in a ship he had fitted out to join the enemy of his national foe.

France had at that time almost permitted Great Britain to gain the advantage of her. The American agents negotiated not only with France; they also sought to get into touch with other Powers, and even maintained relations with England. These threatened to take a peculiar turn immediately before and after the capitulation of Saratoga. After the capture of Philadelphia, England had offered the colonies an amnesty and the removal of their principal grievances; after the capitulation of Saratoga she went a step further and held out the prospect of the recognition of a certain degree of independence in return for a permanent and intimate union between the colonies and the Mother Country. The American agents were hardly empowered to make such an agreement with England. But the danger threatened by this combination, together

have been ready to make peace even on those terms. But the spirit of the nation rose; at whatever cost, it would not bear to submit to Bourbon threats and Bourbon dictation. Chatham, almost dying, had himself come down to the house to protest against that last ignomy, the rending of the empire in submission to France.

In the midst of his speech—he was permitted to speak sitting—he fell back in a fit; a month later, he, who had raised his country to the highest pinnacle of triumph—he, to whose voice a purblind king and an infatuate Ministry had refused to hearken—was laid in Westminster Abbey: and England was still fighting for very life.

PAUL JONES IN A NAVAL FIGHT OFF THE COAST OF SCOTLAND IN 1779

A native of Scotland, the bold John Paul Jones adopted the role of naval adventurer, and in 1775, obtaining a commission in the American Navy, he cruised round the British shores while the War of Independence was in progress, attacking the shipping. In 1779, as shown in the above picture, he captured the king's ship Serapis in a naval fight off the Scottish coast

with the improved prospects of the campaign, led France to take a decisive step. The treaty of friendship and commerce over which the Americans had been kept in suspense for more than a year was concluded in a few weeks—February 6th, 1778. This amounted to an official recognition of the United States.

The knowledge of the impending alliance alarmed even North's Ministry into making proposals which the Americans would have welcomed at an earlier stage; but now there were very few who would be content with anything short of independence. The Rockingham Whigs would

For folly and incapacity had played havoc with every department. The navy, which swept the seas with might irresistible in 1760, had not been maintained; while France, guided by Choiseul, had been acting on the lesson she had learnt at such bitter cost, and had been creating her own navy anew. Now, on paper at least, the odds hardly lay with the British, and the British prospect of victory in America depended on the retention of naval supremacy

On American soil, the immediate result was the evacuation of Philadelphia and withdrawal to New York, Howe retiring, and Clinton taking the chief command.

WASHINGTON ON THE BATTLEFIELD AT TRENTON, DECEMBER 8TH, 1776
The varied fortunes of the American colonists in the early stages of the war with the Mother Country did not augur well for the ultimate triumph of their rising, and gradually the cause of freedom and independence lost many adherents; but when, at the end of 1776, Washington, by a series of brilliant manœuvres, surprised and defeated the enemy at Trenton the spirits of his men began to revive, and they followed him with renewed hope and confidence.
From the painting by John Faed

That the withdrawal from the Chesapeake to New York was successfully effected was due to the skill of the admiral, Lord Howe, who outmanœuvred the now superior French force in American waters and accomplished the transference of the troops before D'Estaing had realised the situation. From the British point of view, the one redeeming feature of the war lay in the still superior skill and confidence of the English sailors, which nearly neutralised the greater numbers of the French. Thus, later in the same year, it was the inability of the French fleet to intervene which allowed Clinton to despatch an army to the south, with a view to creating a diversion by a campaign in those provinces which had not hitherto felt the stress of war. But the British fleet could no longer sail when and where it would. Its chief business came to be that of keeping the French out of action. It was not only by sea — that is, on the British line of communication — that the French intervention took effect. Already a considerable number of foreign officers had taken service in the United States. Lafayette and his friends had been fighting with the Americans since the preceding year, though originally received with such ill-concealed distrust that some of them returned to France bitterly disappointed.

Lafayette's enthusiastic advocacy, however, was not without effect in bringing the French Government to consent to the despatch of an auxiliary corps under Rochambeau. Their presence did not prove an unmixed blessing to Washington ; for the colonial officers regarded the Frenchmen with considerable jealousy, while the chief was painfully alive to the diplomatic necessity for treating them in a manner which made the jealousy more acute. Still, the Americans found themselves compelled to recognise that the

THE MARQUESS OF CORNWALLIS
Son of the first Earl of Cornwallis, he served in the American War even while disapproving of it ; but though he gained several notable successes he was finally compelled to surrender at Yorktown, Virginia, on October 19, 1781.

foreign contingent and the foreign officers were a valuable addition to their forces. Both Rochambeau and Lafayette, young as the latter was, were endowed with military capacity, which Washington could not have afforded to despise, even had he attached less importance to the French alliance than he actually did.

From that alliance great wonders were at first expected, not only by Washington and the army, but to an even greater extent by the congress, which had returned in triumph to Philadelphia. It was already so convinced that a decisive victory was impending that it considered it superfluous to do anything more towards it. The disillusionment was the greater when a peculiar combination of unfavourable circumstances rendered the joint campaign of the Americans and the French almost fruitless. From the beginning there had been a party in congress that did not look with favour on the French alliance. It found support in the New England states, which transferred their old antipathy to the Canadians to the French, who were now about to fight as their allies for colonial independence. Moreover, the offers on the part of England to enter into negotiations with the rebels as to the removal of their grievances had caused the idea to take root that a reconciliation was imminent on the basis of the recognition of their independence.

The prospects of peace were seriously affected by the French alliance, for though the Americans interpreted the agreement in the sense that France would only secure their independence, and, this done, make no opposition to a direct understanding between the colonies and the Mother Country, yet the French Government, in continuing negotiations at Paris with the delegates of congress, especially with Franklin, and also, by means of its accredited representatives, with the

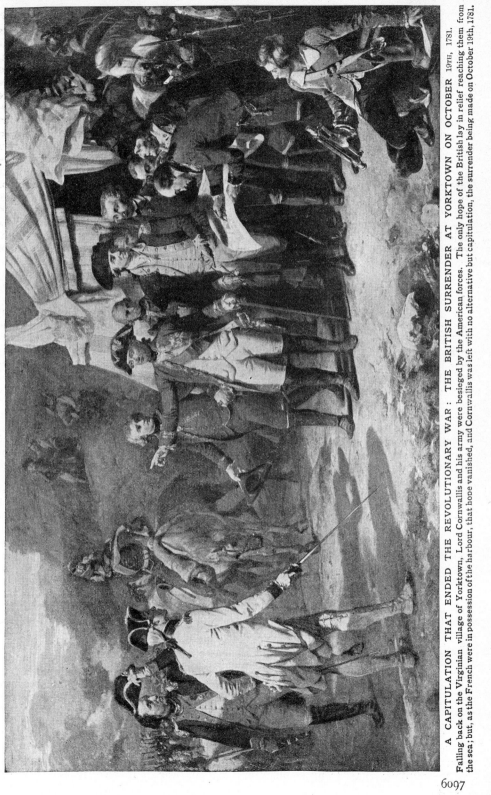

A CAPITULATION THAT ENDED THE REVOLUTIONARY WAR : THE BRITISH SURRENDER AT YORKTOWN ON OCTOBER 19TH, 1781.

Falling back on the Virginian village of Yorktown, Lord Cornwallis and his army were besieged by the American forces. The only hope of the British lay in relief reaching them from the sea; but, as the French were in possession of the harbour, that hope vanished, and Cornwallis was left with no alternative but capitulation, the surrender being made on October 19th, 1781.

congress at Philadelphia, took care that the principle should be recognised that none of the contracting Powers should make peace without the concurrence of the others. This made the termination of the war no longer solely dependent on the recognition of the independence of the United States. These business politicians now forgot how remote this had been before the French alliance, and tried to persuade the states that the continuance of the war was solely due to the French. Though they undoubtedly overshot the mark in this, the congress and an overwhelming majority of the American people were of the opinion that since France, as was natural, was seeking by this war to gain advantages for herself and her allies, especially for Spain, which joined the alliance in 1779, it was only right that she should bring the war to a conclusion with her own money and troops. The demands made on the French Government by the leading statesmen of congress were almost incredible. Their only possible excuse is the political and diplomatic inexperience of men suddenly transformed from lawyers and merchants into the responsible leaders of a mighty state.

There was, it is true, a small circle of really statesmanlike characters among the men who helped to found the United States. Foremost among these stood George Washington. The course of events suddenly placed this conscientious and peaceful country gentleman at the head of the union army; but in his case circumstances served only to develop great **Washington** capacities and to bring to light splendid **at the Head** talents. At the outbreak of war, Washington was in his forty-third year. He was not a professional soldier, and his only experience of war had been as an officer of the Virginia militia; but so successful was he in this capacity that he was appointed its commander-in-chief in 1755. He entered public life more from a sense of duty than from inclination,

BENJAMIN FRANKLIN
To Franklin, perhaps more than to any other man, belongs the distinction of bringing the War of Revolution to a successful issue, for it was owing to his efforts that France interfered and gave to the colonists the support necessary to turn the scales in their favour.

and he retired to his rich estates as soon as possible. He typified all that was noblest in the Virginia planters. His appearance was striking—almost too aristocratic for a republican; but none was more enthusiastic than he for the cause of American liberty.

His sound education and his knowledge of the world fitted him for a diplomat; his wide knowledge of national economies for a statesman. Nor was the limited experience gained in little wars his only qualification for the military position he held; for he possessed two distinguishing qualities that render him, in all respects, one of the most remarkable men America has ever seen. These qualities were the power of taking a clear and unprejudiced view of the situation, which enabled him, even in the most trying circumstances, to calculate and consider with imperturbable composure, and to await the right moment with an iron patience; and an extraordinary energy that enabled him not only to accomplish much himself, but to move all around him to put forth their utmost strength.

At the beginning his position was difficult; even his rank as commander-in-chief, which the first impulse of national enthusiasm had given him, was not quite safe from the envy of jealous rivals or the eagerness of selfish place-hunters. He himself was perhaps the least concerned about his position; for he learned daily how many duties it imposed on him and **Washington** how little real power he **at the Head** possessed. But he was even **of the Army** greater as a diplomat than as a strategist, and was thus enabled to solve the difficult problem before him, and to stand continually between the inexperienced politicians of congress and the European diplomats schooled in the political etiquette of the Old World. From the time of the alliance with France he maintained, not only at the seat of war, but also in the field of politics, a kind of government independent of congress ; but in both spheres his characteristic reserve enabled him to avoid all dangers.

There was no other man of his nation who could be compared with him. Even Benjamin Franklin, with his homely honesty, stood far behind him in political

Franklin's Share in the Revolution
far-sightedness. Despite this, no one, perhaps, played a greater part than Franklin in bringing the revolution to a successful issue. Born in humble circumstances, he had worked his way slowly and laboriously upwards by his own efforts ; and throughout his life he preserved something of the manners said to be characteristic of the inhabitants of Philadelphia, where he had spent his youth and middle age. He was not a man of great actions, but the long experience he had gained at the English court as agent for the colonies enabled him, more than all others, to win the sympathy of other nations for his struggling country ; and the credit of having induced France to side openly with the United States belongs chiefly to him. But his attitude during the peace negotiations showed how much he was affected by the shrewdness that usually characterised the politicians of the youthful state. Many efforts have been made to clear him of the charge of having taken part in the negotiations with England which, though contrary to the agreement with France, were carried on in secret by the American diplomatists. But no amount of explanation can get rid of the fact that Franklin's characteristic appearance of confidential frankness and good-natured honesty served to screen the double-dealing of his fellow diplomatists, though he had perhaps no direct part in deceiving the allies he himself had gained. During the war he exerted little direct influence on affairs at home ; but his sober and practical commonsense and his business

JOHN ADAMS
Representing Massachusetts in the first congress, this statesman proposed the appointment of Washington as commander-in-chief on the outbreak of the war ; after holding the office of vice-president, he succeeded Washington as President of the United States in 1797.

experience helped in no small degree to remove the formidable difficulties that lay in the way of diplomatic success.

Beside these two leaders stood a number of less important personages of similar political views ; but among the influential politicians there were scarcely any others so clear-sighted or so unprejudiced. The significance of this soon appeared when, on the conclusion of the French alliance, weightier events took place in the field of diplomacy than on the field of battle.

In accordance with their plan of campaign, the British transferred their operations to the south. In January, 1779, they conquered Savannah and defended it successfully against the French fleet. In February, 1780, the English commander-in-chief, Clinton, landed in South Carolina and forced the American troops in Charleston to capitulate after a siege of five weeks. It appeared as if British supremacy would be re-established in the south ; and for a time not a single detachment of organised American troops opposed the English. But the object aimed at soon showed itself unattainable. Except on the coast, the land was sparsely populated and but little cultivated. This rendered permanent military occupation impossible, and placed great difficulties in the way of all military operations. This was very well known at Washington's headquarters. Thus, instead of following the British to the south, the leader of the American Army kept in view operations on the Hudson against New York as most likely to decide the issue of the campaign. Clinton was thus compelled to come north again, while in the south a partisan war went on with varying results.

This was stirred up from both headquarters by the despatch of regular troops under approved leaders, so that the British were never in undisturbed possession and still could never be driven out. During these cross-expeditions a number of important battles

6099

were fought in North and South Carolina. At Camden the English gained a victory in which the brave De Kalb lost his life; at King's Mountain and at Cowpens the Americans were successful; other battles, such as that at Guilford, were claimed as victories by both sides. But the situation remained essentially unchanged. The English maintained their hold on the thickly populated coast districts; but in the interior bands of Americans carried on a guerrilla warfare, making unexpected attacks on outposts and cutting off small detachments of British troops.

Cornwallis Surrenders at Yorktown

In 1781, however, Cornwallis, who held the southern command, was ordered to fall back on Yorktown, the British no longer having the control of the sea necessary to enable them to send him reinforcements. Clinton himself was held fast in New York by Washington, who was threatening the place with an assault in force. But such was not his real design; Clinton learned suddenly that the siege was practically abandoned and the army on its way to the south. It was at this point that the aid of the French proved decisive. Lafayette had been largely responsible for paralysing the operations of Cornwallis, whose position now depended on the maintenance of communications by sea. The appearance of a French fleet, newly arrived, under De Grasse, turned the scale.

The British Admiral Hood also arrived, with the intention of relieving Yorktown; but the French were already in possession of the harbour and were not to be enticed into an engagement. On October 19th, 1781, Cornwallis found himself with no possible alternative but capitulation. With the fall of Yorktown, the last hope of mastering the colonists was gone. From this point, interest centres entirely in the naval war between Great Britain and France; its striking feature was the British recovery of naval ascendancy. Since Spain had joined the allies, nearly all her energies had been employed on desperate efforts to reduce Gibraltar, which had held out with grim determination, while at rare intervals British fleets had succeeded in throwing in supplies.

Britain's Ascendancy on the Sea

But in 1782 she despatched a fleet to the West Indies to join De Grasse, who was already in force considerably greater than the British. Their one hope was to force an engagement under conditions which would give the chance of crippling a portion of his fleet. Reinforced by the Spaniards his numbers would be overwhelming. He was determined not to risk an engagement till those reinforcements had joined him. He started on a race with the English Admiral Rodney to reach the point of rendezvous; but by a fortunate co-operation of breezes and calms Rodney overtook him, and, although in less force, attacked him. The battle of "The Saints" is famous, among other things, for the adoption of the plan of attack, thenceforth a favourite manœuvre with the British, known as "breaking the line"—that is, piercing the enemy's line, enveloping his rear, and destroying it before the van can come to its aid.

Rodney annihilated the fleet of De Grasse in what was, in some respects, the most critical engagement in English history. For defeat would have meant the irrevocable loss of a naval supremacy which was tottering; its ultimate recovery gave Great Britain the victory over Napoleon. Five months later, the allies made their last tremendous assault on Gibraltar; but the Rock remained in the possession of its garrison. Much as these events served to excite those on the spot, and important as they were to Great Britain, they had comparatively little influence in determining the final result of the war as it concerned the Americans. The leading French statesmen soon came to the conviction that, instead of having gained an active ally in the struggle against England by their alliance with the United States, they had in reality only gained permission to carry on the war for the Americans with French money, French soldiers, and French ships.

The New Union in Danger

From the fall of Yorktown till the conclusion of peace the negotiations in this connection occupied the attention of congress much more than the concerns of the war had ever done. The debates were carried on with such vehemence that on more than one occasion the newly-made union of thirteen states threatened to fall asunder into groups with divided interests. What American politicians would naturally have preferred was that Great Britain should give up all her North American possessions and renounce all her claims in the northern continent in favour of the

United States. In negotiations with the agents by whom the British throughout the war strove to bring about an understanding, they based their claim on the statement that the proximity of the United States and a British Canada would be a perpetual cause of discord between the two nations of the same blood. Benjamin Franklin deserves the credit of having skilfully put forward this view during the negotiations he conducted with the British agent, Oswald; but in the final settlement the point was not again brought up, so that it was scarcely necessary for Great Britain to reject the demand.

In regard to their southern boundary the Americans were less greedy for territory. They had become quite accustomed to the idea of giving back Florida to Spain as payment for her participation in the war, and especially for the subsidies which had been continually solicited, though without success, from the court of Charles III. But this point was not the true source of discord in the congress. There were two other conditions, to one of which the representatives of the **Discussing the Terms of Peace** southern states clung with as much tenacity as those of the North did to the other. How far-sighted the politicians of the southern states were on points affecting their future interests is shown by the fact that they wished to have the cession of the interior as far as the Mississippi, and the right of free navigation of this stream down to the Gulf of Mexico, regarded as indispensable preliminaries to the conclusion of peace. The British Colonial Office had organised the land west of the Alleghanies independently of the old provinces, and the settlement of this territory on any considerable scale had been but recently begun from the southern provinces. Nevertheless, the leaders in the southern states perceived perfectly the immense importance for this district of the waterway to the Gulf of Mexico, and were resolved not to give up this security for the future.

For a long time discussions upon the conditions of peace possessed a purely theoretical interest. The efforts of the leader of the army, on the one hand, and of the representatives of France, on the other, succeeded in restraining the embittered war of words and in obscuring those subjects on which utterly irreconcilable views were held. When, in March, 1782, by means of Franklin's personal relations with some of the members of the newly formed English Cabinet, the general desire for peace was finally confirmed, strife broke out afresh in the congress. The party of the northern states, which would have preferred that Franklin, the friend of the French, should be deprived of all share in the **Recognising the Independence of the States** negotiations, were so far successful that they placed beside him two representatives of their own views—John Adams and John Jay. The history of the peace negotiations shows once more the total absence of a real executive in the young state. The congress had indeed established a department for foreign affairs; but its representatives, during the peace negotiations, never received definite instructions, and, once on French soil and removed from the interference of congress, they were really independent. That the negotiations were so quickly concluded, and that in a manner exceeding the expectations of the most sanguine American politicians, was due to the weakness of the English negotiators.

The peace ratified at Versailles, September 3rd, 1783, recognised the thirteen United States of North America as an independent state. Almost all the demands of the American party politicians were conceded by the British. Florida, which was restored to Spain, formed the southern boundary of the states; the Mississippi the western; and navigation on this river was to be free to Americans and to the British. The northern boundary ran from the St. Croix River across the watershed between the Hudson and the St. Lawrence, and then through the Great Lakes to the source of the Mississippi. The right of participating in the fisheries on the Newfoundland Banks was expressly conceded. As for the rest, a treaty of peace and commerce between Great Britain and the United States was to restore as **The Republic of the United States** far as possible the relations interrupted by the war. The recognition of the United States by the remaining European Powers was delayed; but this was of little importance to the young state, as it enjoyed not only the recognition but also the goodwill of the Powers which were of most importance to it. Thus, as far as the outside world was concerned, the Republic of the United States was firmly established. KONRAD HAEBLER

THE AMERICAN ATTACK ON QUEBEC IN 1775: THE DEATH OF GENERAL MONTGOMERY IN LEADING THE ASSAULT

The American attack on Quebec occurred on the last morning of the year 1775, when in a bitter wind General Montgomery and his men made for the lower corner of the town. At the Près de Ville barrier they were stopped by the discharge of a battery, Montgomery and a dozen others falling dead in the snow, and the remainder flying for their lives into the darkness.

From the painting by J. Trumbull

CANADA DURING THE GREAT WAR
BRITISH TRIUMPHS AGAINST THE AMERICANS

WHEN Canada was ceded to Great Britain by France all the military and most of the civil officials of Canada returned to France ; the latter, with Bigot at their head, to be heavily and justly punished for their egregious frauds. A good many of the Canadian noblesse went, too, being offered commissions in the French Army. War-sick and impoverished by the presence of contending armies, Canada now resigned herself without difficulty to the just and lenient rule of the English officers who governed her for many years after the peace.

The habitants, forming probably five-sixths of the 70,000 souls by this time in the country, settled down in their parishes to increase and multiply under the mildest regime they had ever experienced. There were no more corvées and no more wars ; otherwise everything went on much as before. They paid their dues to the parish priest, and their trifling rents to the seigniors. The English criminal law, milder than their own code, was administered by the military authorities. Civil law remained as before in spite of edicts intended to encourage the English customs. Thirty to forty seigniorial families, much more than half the total number, remained in the colony, while in Quebec, Montreal and Three Rivers were a goodly sprinkling of traders and professional men.

Canada in the Hands of the British

Murray remained for six years as governor, assisted by a nominated advisory council, and, as regards the French, proved a just and popular administrator. Sentiment apart, there was complete harmony between the English garrison and the small French upper class and clergy. The losers in a stand-up fight did not expect in those days to be put into the seat of the victors, while the habitants, almost wholly illiterate, did not know what votes meant. The disturbing, or at least dissatisfied, element was composed of the few hundred British traders, mostly from the American provinces, who settled in Quebec and Montreal. For it should be said that the Americans, particularly in New England, with its Puritan traditions, had greatly resented the religious toleration that had been granted to the Canadians. The newcomers to Canada shared that view, and being naturally of republican tendencies, as, in fact, were most of the Anglo-American colonists long before their rebellion, objected to living under a government that had no elections and gave no scope for political activity. Their views of popular government, however, did not extend to the 70,000 French, but only to the few hundred not generally very good specimens of Anglo-American settlers.

Puritans Opposed to Toleration

From their body they considered an elective assembly should be chosen to legislate for the rest and control the supplies, while the French laws, religion, and even language should so far as possible be suppressed. This point of view did not commend itself to the British Government, but its exponents, whose numbers slowly increased, caused most of the friction to be found in Canada at that period; and when the great revolutionary agitation began south of the border, its promoters worked hard to stir up the French Canadians to like endeavours.

Here, too, it will be necessary to remind the reader that the destiny of Canada, such as we have seen it fulfilled, could not have been foreseen in 1763. Settlers upon its soil from England seemed then quite unlikely. The fertile colonies to the south, with their enterprising English population, religious affinities, and milder climate, offered overwhelmingly greater attractions to the British immigrant. Canada seemed destined to remain a small French nation under English rule, and to reconcile the

Canada a French Nation

Canadians to that rule seemed so obviously politic, it was almost inevitable that the hearts of the earlier British officials should be in accord with that policy. Montcalm, when he foresaw the conquest of Canada, wrote in private letters to friends, which are still extant, to the effect that the English would be fools if they tried to **Montcalm's** Anglicise their new sub- **Faith in Canada's** jects. He—Montcalm— **Loyalty** foretold the revolt of the "republicans" of the other colonies, and that an Anglicised Canada would surely go with them; whereas, if the Canadians were encouraged to retain their homogeneity under the British Crown, and were well treated, the latter would have a loyal, brave and docile race that would stand staunchly by it against those ancient enemies and neighbours with whom they had so little in common.

Nor was Montcalm by any means alone in reading the handwriting on the wall. Many Frenchmen familiar with North America found consolation for defeat in the prospect of their rival's future difficulties. There were Englishmen, too, who were against the retention of Canada for that very reason, and nothing probably but the intoxication of those glorious years of universal victory prevented there being many more. With a limited Canada in the hands of a French king, the English colonies would not have dreamed of an independence immediately exposed to his always restless sword, his fleets, and his armies. For against French Canada alone, and a mere handful of regulars, their powerlessness, without British aid, had been too glaringly exposed. The French Revolution was then in the womb of the future; what effect that might have had on a French Canada is of necessity a matter of mere speculation, but, like the other, does not here concern us. English troops, too, at the peace, had taken the place of the French garrisons **Pontiac the** throughout the far western **Leader** posts, some of which they were **of Revolt** several months in reaching, and they had hardly settled down in them when there broke out the great rising of the western Indians, known as Pontiac's War. The English, with some truth, were regarded as potential land-grabbers, and the numerous bodies of French fur-traders throughout the west, being human and naturally sore, had painted their rivals' designs in the most lurid colours to their credulous Indian friends, and persuaded them that the French king, their father Onontio, was not vanquished, but sleeping to gather strength for a mighty revenge.

Pontiac was the man produced by the hour—diplomat, orator, warrior and leader of men. First and last he set all the Indians on the war-path from Michillimackinac in the remote North to the tribes on the Mississippi in touch with New Orleans. A glance at the map and the scale of distances will give a notion of the range of his power. All the English outposts had now to fight for their lives. There were heroic defences like Gladwyn's at Detroit, and many massacres. The western French were treated throughout as neutrals, the frontiers of the middle colonies were ravaged from end to end, and hundreds of families, flying from burning homes, cowered in doubtful shelters of weak, ill-victualled forts, often leaving as many behind them tomahawked or tortured to death in the woods.

This did not directly concern the government at Quebec, the campaigns which finally quelled the rising being directed from the **The Good** North American military **Work of Lord** centre of New York. But the **Dorchester** peace which followed established the English garrisons, and opened again the fur trade of the west, which for long remained the mainstay of Canada. In 1766, Sir Guy Carleton, a distinguished soldier of American experience and friend of Wolfe's, afterwards Lord Dorchester, came out as governor to the Château St. Louis, and proved the greatest of its English occupants. Other men as distinguished have held the post, but none had the opportunity to show their mettle under such continually difficult circumstances and for so long a period. Nothing occurred in Canada calling for notice here till the passing of the Quebec Act by the British Parliament. A peck of minor troubles, however, was in progress. Incapable persons, the product of English political jobbery, were planted on the colony, knowing neither its language nor even their own business. The small English community in the towns continued their agitation for popular government administered by themselves. The clashing of the legal codes, too, was a chronic source of minor trouble. The Quebec Act was passed in 1774. This substituted an oath of allegiance in place of a test oath for Roman Catholics. The French civil law, with certain modifications, and the English criminal code, were definitely established, while the tithe, literally a twenty-fifth, always an unwritten law, was now secured to the clergy by statute from all professing the old faith. The administration was to be continued in a governor and council nominated by the Crown. The idea of an elective assembly of British Protestants only, which was urged by representatives of the latter before parliament, found little support in debate. Carleton threw his influence strongly on the side of those concessions to the French, which have been regarded as their charter, and are the base of the political and religious liberties they have ever since enjoyed, though not, however, without some friction.

By the light of after knowledge, much indeed may be urged against this course. But the united empire loyalist refugees, who became such a strong element later, were then undreamed of. Ontario was still a wilderness only trodden by the Indian and the trapper, its fertility buried under dense forests, and its capacities not yet within the prophets' visions. The Quebec Act tied the **The Canadians** Church and the small upper **Faithful to** class of French Canadians **Great Britain** firmly to the government, but gave great discontent to a majority of the British. The condition of the habitant remained much as before, and, being what he was, he had every reason to be content, and indeed actually was so.

Now, however, the feverish agitation which preceded the American War was seething in the colonies. The Canadian British in the main sympathised with it, some violently so. The French gentry and clergy, on the contrary, were from every motive hostile to it; while, as regards the peasantry, they were profoundly ignorant even of its meaning. The American leaders, who had so raged at the religious liberty granted to the French-Canadian Papists at the conquest, now addressed them in flamboyant proclamations as the down-trodden slaves of a tyrannical government, and urged them with unctuous flattery to unite their fortunes to their true friends and brethren.

To the educated French-Canadians this was, of course, only so much nonsense, while the others could not read it. So the American agitators, through their agents and Anglo-Canadian friends, now set to work by means of travellers on commercial pretexts to corrupt their simple and illiterate neighbours. The credulity of the habitant was unfathomable, and his hereditary hatred of the heretic " Bastonnais " now broke down before the unblushing mendacity of these peripatetic politicians. They played on the Quebec Act, and twisted the retention of the tithe and seigniorial rents into a badge of slavery.

Canada in It was given out that the cor-
a Precarious vées were to be resumed, and
Position that the territorial militia, which was retained by the English in its original form for defence of the country, was to be utilised for fighting England's battles in Europe.

Nothing, in short, within the scope of an American demagogue's imagination running riot among a hopelessly uncritical and credulous audience was omitted, in order to alienate the habitant; should the advice of their new friends be rejected, it was darkly hinted that an American army of 50,000 men would sweep the province and make its inhabitants deplore their obstinacy. The success of the agitators was tolerably complete, as was quickly shown when the crisis came, and the militia were called out. Carleton, who had incurred much criticism for his activity in securing what he thought fair treatment for the French, felt this apparent ingratitude of their peasantry most bitterly. Town meetings, too, were held in Quebec and Montreal, in which the disaffected British declaimed against the Quebec Act. Nothing, indeed, could have been more precarious than the situation of Canada at this time, for, in spite of Carleton's warnings, there were not 1,000 regulars in the whole colony.

The first shot of the war was fired at Lexington, in April, 1775. In May, the Champlain forts on the route to Canada had been seized, and it was soon known that an invasion of the colony was impending. Martial law was proclaimed, and a portion of the militia called out.

The First It will be enough to say here
Stages of the that the response to this call
Great War to arms was almost nil. It was in vain that the seigniors and the militia captains waved their swords, and the priests, whose influence, for the only time in Canadian history, had been undermined, called on their flocks. The few that mustered, and still fewer that marched, defied their officers and dispersed. The American General Montgomery, an ex-British officer, having

captured in the meantime most of the British regulars sent to obstruct his way in frontier forts, arrived with an army at Montreal. Carleton, who had vainly endeavoured to raise a sufficient force there was compelled to abandon it, and with some risk and difficulty made his way back alone to Quebec. Here was the last resource and defence of **American Attack on Quebec** Canada, which everywhere else was soon overrun and occupied by the Americans. It was now mid-November, 1775, for we have had to hurry over two or three months thick with events and small fights of no vital consequence. The young American, Arnold, of sinister fame in later days, had executed a daring march to Quebec through the rude wilderness trail from Kennebec, arriving before the city after a struggle of three weeks with half the 1,400 picked men he started with.

He got there just before Carleton, and awaited the arrival of Montgomery. Turning every man out of the city who would not arm, Carleton found himself with about 700 French and 500 English volunteers of a most miscellaneous description, 200 regulars, half of them recruits, and some sailors, about 1,500 in all, and a total population of 5,000. The defences had been previously looked to; the artillery was adequate, and the city was victualled. When Montgomery joined Arnold early in December, their united force was somewhat under 2,000 men, with sufficient guns. The Americans expected the fall of Quebec to follow almost at once upon Montgomery's challenge, like the walls of Jericho before Joshua's trumpets.

That general, though a brave and able soldier, treated Carleton to some rare flights of threatening and offensive bombast, which were received by the latter, who regarded the ex-British officer as a traitor, with silent contempt. After three weeks of futile cannonading and rifle fire, **British Victory at Quebec** Montgomery delivered his famous attack about four o'clock in the last morning of the year, 1775. He himself led a small division from Wolfe's Cove along the margin of the frozen river under the cliff against the barricade that defended the town at the lower corner beneath Cape Diamond. Arnold, in the meantime, made an almost simultaneous attack at the far side, and on a barrier protecting another narrow entry to the town by the St.

Charles River. A bitter wind, laden with fine snow, was blowing, and it was pitch dark. The garrison, who, under Carleton's stimulating leadership had shown surprising vigour, were all alert.

Montgomery was met at the Près de Ville barrier by the unexpected discharge of a battery, which stretched him and a dozen of the foremost with him dead upon the snow, while the remainder fled into the darkness. Arnold's corps had more success, at first forcing the outer barrier quite easily, and getting into the lower town. There, however, they found themselves enclosed in narrow streets between cross fires, and after an hour or two of brisk fighting were repulsed, leaving about 600 dead, wounded, and prisoners behind them. The British loss was trifling, and their triumph complete.

American reinforcements, however, came up from Montreal, and the siege dragged wearily on till the following May. But this amateur garrison—French and English—showed amazing spirit, while the besieging force suffered greatly from cold and disease, and the city was never again **Americans Chased Out of Canada** in danger. Early in May a British fleet arrived bringing that fine army which, in the following year, was to surrender under Burgoyne at Saratoga, and the Americans were chased not merely from Quebec, but completely out of Canada.

For, if the city had fallen on December 31st, the Canadian peasantry, who directly and indirectly had greatly helped the Americans, would have openly sided with them, and it is practically certain that the colony would have been made the fourteenth state of the Union and been lost to the British Crown. As it was, the habitant before the close of winter had tired of his new friends. Four thousand alien and ill-disciplined soldiers—even if well-intentioned—of a traditionally hated race and creed, especially when they were paying for food in almost worthless currency, could easily outstay their welcome.

So the Canadian returned to the fold of his priestly shepherd and his former state of content and political indifference a wiser and sometimes a sadder man. No further attack was made on Canada throughout the war; while Carleton, who had saved her to the British Crown, resigned in disgust at his treatment by that incapable and unprincipled Minister, Germaine.

ATTEMPTED CONQUEST OF CANADA
THE GREAT WAR OF 1812 AND WHAT
IT DID FOR THE BRITISH COLONY

WHEN the English troops evacuated the territory of the new republic in 1783, there were thousands of inhabitants of the various colonies who had openly sympathised and generally fought on the side of the Crown in one or other of the numerous irregular corps raised during the war. The feeling between them and their successful opponents was now so bitter that there was nothing left to the loyalist but exile. The vindictive attitude towards their defeated brethren whose motives of action, though often mixed like their rivals', were quite as worthy of respect, is admitted now by American historians to have been, if not a crime, at least a most egregious political blunder.

No terms worth the paper they were written on were secured to them by Great Britain at the peace. Their property was confiscated and their persons insulted.
The Sad Cry of the Colonist Some remained and endeavoured to live it down, but without success. England is not seldom an ungrateful mother to her colonial children who risk their lives and fortunes for her flag. The cry of the colonist that it does not pay to be loyal is as old as the eighteenth century, and, unfortunately, only too true—the result largely, one need hardly remark, of our system of party government. In this case the Crown voted a sum of money, which after long years some of the survivors in part received. Of private sympathy and generosity to the numbers who had no refuge but England little was shown.

Their correspondence is significant and melancholy reading, for they found themselves too often treated with supercilious neglect even by those who should have befriended them. Their elemental principles, too, were further shocked by discovering a country one-half of whose people rejoiced openly or secretly at the defeat of its own armies. It is a sad and little-known tale, but the brighter side of it, full of hardship and suffering though it was, need only be told here. Fortunately for all concerned, the provinces of Nova Scotia, New Brunswick then
New Homes for the Loyalists carved out of it, and the fertile Prince Edward Island, were still British, still practically undeveloped and eminently suited for settlement. Free grants of land were now offered in these provinces to any loyalist refugees who should apply for them, and ships were provided to convey them there, as well as sufficient supplies and farm implements to tide over the first necessarily unproductive year.

This would have been a comparatively advantageous start for companies of English peasants. But these people had lost in hundreds of cases valuable estates, in most instances comfortable farms or homes. They came from every colony, where many had been social and political leaders, and several thousands were already, in 1782, within the British lines at New York, where Carleton, now commander-in-chief and charged with the military evacuation of the country, refused to move till he had safely embarked the last one of them.

By way of this and other ports, over 30,000 men, women and children were landed in their new homes in these maritime provinces alone. Scarcely any had much more than their wearing apparel in the way of
Nova Scotia the New Name for Acadia property. The reputation of Nova Scotia and the adjoining mainland, all till then called Acadia, stood low as a place of agricultural settlement. In this particular, however, the newcomers were pleasantly surprised; but they had long years of toil, want and suffering to endure before they had carved themselves out new homes in the woods and entered into

comfortable possession of the great provinces, the bulk of whose people to-day are proud to call themselves descendants of the " united empire loyalists."

Of this same exodus another ten or fifteen thousand went to Canada proper, mainly to what is now the province of Ontario. The principal settlements here were at old Fort Frontenac, now Kingston, and away to the west on the Niagara peninsula.

Opening up the Province of Ontario

In this case to the rigours of backwoods settlement were usually added the hardships of many weeks of weary march thither by batteau and canoe and Indian trails through the forest. Acadia had, of course, been well known, though still sparsely settled. Halifax was already a small British town and port. But the northern shores of Lakes Ontario and Erie had been regarded by the American colonists as a forbidding wilderness of indifferent soil, held in the grip of winter for most of the year. French Canadian settlement had reached no further than Montreal. All beyond was part of that vast, shaggy, boundless hinterland which suggested nothing present or future to contemporary man but beaver skins.

There had, in fact, been no incentive to test this country. The French land system held the people to their own seigniories, of which not a tenth part were cleared. Now, however, reports came to the American refugees of another character altogether regarding this wild western country. Experts went to report on it, and reported favourably, and the immigration thither began. As in the maritime provinces, so here the remnant of loyalist regiments settled in many instances together.

Nor were these all English. Germans who had served the king removed here wholesale in their military companies, from choice in their case and a sentiment of gratitude for the treatment they had uniformly received from the Crown, while there were, of course, numbers of New York Dutch loyalists who had lost their all, as well as Scottish highlanders, recent settlers in the Carolinas, whose natural instincts had kept them on the loyalists' side. In short, English Canada, in its origin, may be almost regarded as a military colony. To these original bands large additions were quickly made. Numbers of people, flinching from exile, clung, in spite of all, to the land of their

How Canada Became Populated

birth till the unrelenting persecution of their republican neighbours made their lives unendurable. And it is only fair to add that the contest between the two factions during the many years of war had been conducted on both sides with singular ferocity. The conditions of the war, too, and of the country, had been such that it was almost everywhere safer at the moment, whatever the remote disadvantage might be, to take the popular side when not actually under the British guns.

The majority of the colonial manhood did not personally carry a musket, and it was generally safer for those who " sat on the fence " to shout, at any rate, for the patriot side. It followed, therefore, that the bulk of the exiles were men of force, character and independence ; men, too, who in most cases had themselves disapproved of the British policy, while at the same time deprecating an appeal to arms. When the rupture came, however, they had shown the courage of their convictions, and their sad case proved that they had resisted the frequent opportunities to retract and change sides which offered themselves during the struggle. Thus it happened that the intolerance of the Americans, sometimes stimulated by private commercial indebtedness, an intolerance endorsed by their government in cold blood, proved to them the curse that it well deserved to be.

Canadian Hatred of America

That they hoped to possess the vast country now known as Canada was undoubted and reasonable. But they had inadvertently placed upon it a picked garrison who hated them with a hatred inconceivable to the ordinary Englishman or Frenchman of modern times, and proved the means of permanently alienating Canada ; a hatred, too, which in a modified degree endured to their children's children. Nay, its echoes are there yet, and are a constant source of surprise to the travelling Briton who is unfamiliar with the history of Canada, and hears these sentiments from persons in themselves more like Americans than Englishmen.

To be a united empire loyalist, as immigration from Europe swelled the population, came to be a badge of honour. It was seriously proposed that the significant letters " U.E.L." should be granted by patent, and retained as an hereditary affix to the names of individuals and their descendants who are now legion. Both in the maritime provinces and Ontario it is at this day accounted a matter of pride to be of "U.E.L. stock." In the seaboard British provinces this large influx presented no race problems. Nova Scotia had already a British majority when its population was trebled in a couple of years by the British loyalist influx.

The pleasant fertile island of Prince Edward was practically virgin ground. But in Canada proper the whole conditions were altered. The British element, from a handful of merchants, had been suddenly increased by 20,000 energetic and able people. For, in addition to large settlements in the upper country, numbers were demanding land in Quebec, notably in the eastern townships. What is more, the climate had been proved as bearable, and the soil much better than that of populous New England. Many Americans of the humbler sort, misdoubting the unsettled state of their own country, disliking the new taxation, or merely attracted by good and cheap land, crossed the border. Nor was it merely the phase of the moment, for it was quite evident

Canada Divided into Provinces that Canada was going to be a British as well as a French colony, and the whole machinery would require reconstruction. Carleton, now created Lord Dorchester, had been sent again as governor in 1786 to face these difficulties. He was assisted by many competent lawyers, though they did not all agree.

It was obvious that the large and increasing English community from self-governing colonies would not long tolerate the autocratic government which had really suited the French. To create an assembly with a small minority of skilled parliamentarians sitting among a majority of another race and creed, and quite unused to public affairs, would be to invite friction and deadlock. The result of much agitation and many conflicting opinions was the "Canada Act," dividing the country into the provinces of Lower Canada (Quebec), and Upper Canada (now Ontario), thus separating to a great extent the French and English.

Each province was allotted a governor with a nominated council, from which the executive was selected, and an elective assembly. The principal opposition naturally arose from the English in the old province of Quebec, who, though greatly increased, were still but a trifling minority. The Act was passed, however, in 1791,

after considerable discussion in the British Parliament, and Simcoe, an English officer who had commanded a colonial corps in the American War, was the first lieutenant-governor of Upper Canada. As the legislative assemblies had very limited power of the purse, and as the executive was independent of them, while the council, or upper

Niagara the Temporary Seat of Government house, could veto all their Bills at will, this was a faint reflection of the British model of popular government. With really responsible government, and only a nominal power of veto at this early date, there would have been more friction between the races, numerically unequal as they were, and much more danger.

The only hope of impartiality lay in the governor. Dorchester, for instance, was inclined to favour the French as a pure matter of personal judgment. Imagine an executive responsible to an English or French majority inclined to favour its rivals! The very thought is an absurdity. In Lower Canada there were, of course, both grievances and difficulties. The latter were caused mainly by the dual code of laws and disagreements between the English influence and the always ultramontane Church in efforts for a wider education. The former were experienced by the French later on in their exclusion from the principal offices of state. In Upper Canada the seat of government was temporarily at Niagara, but in due course, and after not inconsiderable discussion, was removed to York, the nucleus of the present city of Toronto.

The years between 1791 and the war of 1812 would represent a distinct epoch in Canada if only for the fact that its establishment for all time as an English as well as a French colony was then in progress. The destitution of some of the earlier immigrants had been relieved by the half-pay granted to those who had held commissions through the American War, while

Ontario Governed by Settlers the offices necessary to carry on the provincial government were mainly and capably filled by the refugees. Indeed, the earlier united empire settlers in Ontario, combining among them most of the talents, developed a virtual oligarchy, and acquired such a grip of the provincial government that for half a century it made a pliant tool of most lieutenant-governors, and held the growing democracy at arm's length till, in 1837, as we shall see, its arrogance provoked a rebellion. The bitter anti-American feelings of the refugees who founded Upper Canada stimulated a proportionate enthusiasm for the British connection.

It was a curious situation. Men whose families for generations had lived in Massachusetts or Virginia, who had themselves grown up and taken part in one or other of the democratic self-governing colonies, and on whom the Western Continent, in appearance and speech, had set its unmistakable mark, displayed a fervour of loyalty that extended itself to every external sign and symbol of British rule, and encouraged the quasi-aristocratic atmosphere that for so long influenced the province. The earlier loyalists again professed distrust of these later waves of immigration from the United States, and regarding themselves alone as founders of the country, succeeded to a large extent in retaining much of the power.

Evolution of the Warlike Iroquois

These tendencies, however, served a useful purpose in their day, being favourable to the martial virtues, and indeed they saved Canada in 1812, though subsequently they proved wholly obstructive to its healthy growth. Hither, too, had retired the remnant of the Iroquois, who, true to their ancient traditions and the leadership of the Johnsons, had fought for the Crown under their great chief Brant. And here to-day, near the town of Brantford, to which he gave its name, may be seen the descendants of his race, who so long were the terror of North America, now seated on the banks of the Grand River, and cultivating the arts of peace in the guise of farmers.

While in Upper Canada, steadily recruited by all sorts and conditions of settlers—mostly English and Germans—from the United States, men of various creeds and impelled by various motives, were busy hewing out their own homesteads, the external affairs of Canada, more particularly as affecting the French province, were again extremely critical. The French Revolution had shaken the world, and England was once more at war with France. One party in the new American republic, led by Jefferson, was enthusiastically pro-French, clamouring for war with England, and was held with difficulty in check by the more cool-headed northern states, supported by Washington and Hamilton. A combination of France and America must

Pro-French Party in America

inevitably have overwhelmed Canada. Hateful as the principles of the Revolution were to the clerics and seigniors, the French-Canadian people would almost certainly not have fought against their old compatriots. The martial habit, too, was lost; a new generation had arisen unaccustomed to war, and unwilling to fight at all. It was fortunate that the cool, experienced veteran Dorchester was at the helm, for between 1790 and 1793 the two countries were more than once on the verge of war.

There were several causes of irritation, one of them being that some of the far western forts in American territory were still held by England on the plea of certain unfulfilled treaty conditions. An American and Indian war was raging around these remote outposts of British regulars, and the situation in the west was a highly inflammable one. One-half of the American people had abandoned themselves to an orgie of enthusiasm for the emancipated French, while the latter had agents in every state, as well as in Canada, who worked upon the credulous habitant with all the more success that the emissaries this time were Frenchmen. The militia in great part refused point-blank to attend their musters, despite priests and seigniors, and after all, as Lord Dorchester pithily informed his government, it was not wholly surprising that peaceful, ignorant peasants no longer used to handling a gun should object to being called from their farms to help Englishmen and heretics shoot one another.

American Settlers in the New Colony

A further cause of anxiety was the great number of Americans that of late years had settled in the colony, particularly in that fertile and beautiful district of Quebec, on the Vermont frontier, which was set apart for them and, popularly known as the Eastern Townships, is still mainly British. These people were no longer united empire loyalists, and their action in case of war was doubtful, though such very natural uncertainty has never for a moment attached to their descendants. The scantiness of the regular garrison kept in Canada through these precarious years was the despair of its governors. In 1794, however, "Jay's Treaty" between Great Britain and the United States relieved the strain for a few brief years.

Though there were many undoubted causes of friction it has always seemed to the student of that period as if another fight between the Mother Country and her offspring was imperative before the air could be thoroughly cleared and their relations properly adjusted. The war of 1812 was the work of the same old Jefferson party, represented mainly by the more Southern and agricultural states and now in power under the presidency of Madison, another Virginian statesman. The more enlightened, vulnerable and commercial states of New England now, as before, were strongly opposed to it.

Great Britain was then engaged with Napoleon in a death grapple which was to decide whether the nations of Europe were to be French or free, and she could not always afford to be over-nice in her treatment of neutrals on the high seas. It is impossible to treat fully here of the points at issue. The chief of these were the famous "orders in council" of the British Government, which ultimately proclaimed a blockade of all countries under France, the right to seize neutral ships carrying supplies to enemies and to search them for deserters, and the answering decrees of Napoleon, futile as they were for lack of ships. Various international episodes, mainly by sea, and the increasing irritation of the Americans on shore at the decline of their commerce, at length, in June, 1812, produced the long-looked-for rupture. In anticipation of it soldiers had been sent out to Canada as rulers; Sir George Prevost was governor-general at Quebec, and Sir Isaac Brock temporary lieutenant-governor of Ontario. The former was popular in his province, which had increased in population to 220,000. The latter was an able **Britain and America Again at War** soldier, had been for ten years in the country and was idolised in Upper Canada, where there were now nearly 80,000 souls. The brunt of the strife fell on the Upper Province. The population of the Canadas was now about 300,000, of which some two-thirds were French. The maritime provinces, whose story throughout this quarter of a century had been an uneventful one of steady development, remained outside the sphere

STEPHEN VAN RANSSELAER
In the war of 1812, Van Ransselaer, commanding the northern frontier, captured Queenstown heights, but because of his militia refusing to cross the Niagara the place was retaken by the British, and Ransselaer resigned in disgust.

of war save in their sea-borne commerce. The Americans were unquestionably weakened by the persistent protests against war made by the New England states and their virtual abstention from any share in it. Still the most martial **American Attacks on Canada** and best organised of the old colonial groups, they had been the backbone of Washington's armies, but were utterly averse to the Napoleonic conception of the welfare of the world, and as a sea-going people could make more allowance for the seemingly high-handed measures into which England in her desperate struggle against such great odds was forced. It was a good thing for Canada that New England took up this attitude. As it was, the Americans came surging against her in three separate divisions composed of troops mainly from the Middle and Southern states, all obsessed with the notion that the Upper Province was seething with discontent, that a majority of its people would welcome them, and, in short, that the enterprise would be a promenade terminating in rewards of land and loot. They came on under Napoleonic designations and with Napoleonic thunder. The "army of the West" made for Niagara, that of the "North" by the Albany and Oswego route for Kingston. There is almost a comic opera flavour about the opening scenes of this really critical struggle. But for the Canadians at the moment there was certainly nothing of comedy in the matter, particularly the Canadians of the Upper Province, who were the sole objects of attack.

There were 1,400 regular troops in the colony and about 2,000 enrolled militia to defend a frontier hundreds of miles in length against a nation with already nearly half the population of Great Britain. It may be doubted if any country has ever been confronted with such apparently hopeless odds as was Upper Canada. "On to Canada!" was the war-cry of the American armies, who, most fortunately, were both ill-disciplined and ill-led. General Hull with 2,500 men occupied Detroit on the American side of the river, which then formed the international boundary, and issued a proclamation that for exuberance of bombast is among the curiosities of military literature. The Americans had either assumed or been misled into the extraordinary notion **Ignominious American Surrender** that a majority of Canadians were eagerly awaiting them as deliverers from a tyrant's yoke. They were soon undeceived. The first blow was struck by the British far away in the north-west, where they captured the important post of Michillimackinac, with its garrison and stores. Brock, in the meantime, who had been detained by a meeting of the legislature at York, now hastened against Hull with 330 regulars and 400 militia.

Tecumseh, the famous chief, with 600 Indians, captured Hull's convoys and cut his connections. Brock crossed the river to Detroit and with not misplaced audacity summoned his opponent to surrender ; which he did with his entire force, guns and stores and very little demur. So vanished this Napoleonic meteor and his corps d'armée from the scene of war in the middle of August. An armistice proposed by the two governments for the interchange of negotiations which proved futile had somewhat checked Brock's movements, but in October he confronted the American force under General Van Ransselaer at Niagara and fought the ever memorable Battle of Queenstown heights, where he lost his life in the supreme hour of victory.

Queenstown heights is a lofty ridge over the Niagara River, between the Falls and Lake Ontario. General Van Ransselaer was on the American side with 6,000 men and headquarters at Lewiston. Brock was on the opposite shore, with about 1,200 regulars and militia somewhat scattered from an uncertainty **Brock's Death in the Hour of Victory** as to the point at which a crossing might be attempted. Before daybreak on October 13th, 1,300 Americans effected a landing at Queenstown after some skirmishing with a few hundred British posted there and a good deal of artillery fire from both sides of the river. Before Brock could reach the scene some of the enemy had gained the crest of Queenstown heights, and the brave general at once led 200 men up the slope against them, but fell dead in the attempt with a ball in his breast. Brock was not only a splendid soldier of considerable European experience, but one of those rare Englishmen who succeeded in winning the devotion of the colonists both in peace and war. His loss in the struggle just begun was simply irreparable.

A lofty obelisk on Queenstown heights keeps his memory green, and two biographers have told the tale of a noble life. Colonel Sheaffe had now arrived on the spot with reinforcements, and, gathering others of the British already in action, scaled the heights to the west of the Americans with about 1,000 men, half regulars and half militia, and a few Indians. Van Ransselaer hurried across the river for reinforcements, but the New York militia exhibited the most unblushing poltroonery, and protested that they had only been enlisted to serve in their own country. The American regulars and militia already on the heights were now charged in front by a judicious combination of volleys and bayonets, while behind them was a precipice with only one place of escape. Numbers threw themselves over **Fate of a Bombastic General** it, more were shot and bayonetted, others drowned in the river, and the loss altogether was about 400. The remaining 900 surrendered as prisoners of war, while the British loss was about 70 killed and wounded. General Smythe now took command of the Americans, and after issuing a proclamation to the men of New York, which began with indecorous diatribes against his two predecessors, and continued in bombastic flights of rhetoric that even poor Hull had not reached, started to put his scheme of occupying and regenerating Canada into operation.

All his attacks, however, were repulsed, and when his army retired into winter quarters the eloquent general was consigned by his government to private life and oblivion. It must be remembered, however, that the Americans were engaged in a war of invasion, always difficult for raw troops, for even their regulars had no serious experience. The militia were badly officered, and all were miserably led. Their inspiring motives, again, were not elevated, while numbers, doubtless, were half-hearted. The Canadians, on the other hand, were fighting for their homes and against an enemy whom they had reason to regard with especial resentment, while the few regulars who aided them were of fine quality, belonging mainly to the 41st Regiment. With the next year, the Americans, smarting under ignominious defeat, braced themselves for greater efforts, got rid of their political generals, and discovered more efficient officers. Michigan was now in the hands of the British.

Proctor, at Detroit with 1,000 men, and the valuable but somewhat intermittent help of Tecumseh and his Indians, was opposed to General Harrison with an army of 7,000, having defeated his colleague, General Winchester, with a loss of nearly 1,000 men, including prisoners. A campaign of varying fortune was conducted on the Michigan side, till a defeat of the British by the American fleet on Lake Erie left Detroit isolated and forced Proctor into Canada and a retreat up the River Thames. He had with him 800 regulars and militia, and 500 Indians. Harrison followed with 3,500 men, including 1,500 mounted riflemen from Kentucky. When Proctor was compelled to make a stand his force was reduced to about 440 regulars and about fifty local dragoons and Tecumseh's Indians. It is

General Harrison's Boast enough to say that he was overwhelmed. The gallant soldiers of the 41st, who had borne the brunt of two arduous campaigns and accounted for at least four times their number in Americans killed, wounded and prisoners, were wearied, ill fed, and overstrained.

They were at last ridden down by a charge of 1,200 horse, supported by over 2,000 infantry, as shown by the official figures of General Harrison, who, in the same breath and in the amazing phraseology of his generation, ascribed the victory over this poor remnant to "superior valour." Tecumseh, whose Indians offered a longer resistance, was slain. Proctor escaped, and was sent into retirement after a court-martial which, though not forgetful of his former merits, censured him for blunders, chiefly of delay. Harrison after his victory evacuated Canada.

Sir George Prevost, who had the general supervision of operations, proved extremely inefficient, and added greatly to the difficulties of his subordinates in their struggle against great odds; while when he himself led in action it was only to failure. Operations on the Niagara frontier were carried on briskly throughout the second summer, the enemy making much better use of their superior numbers. They burned York, the little capital of Upper Canada, in contravention of the terms of its surrender, which cost them their more valuable capital at Washington, destroyed by the British in retaliation. Generals Sheaffe and Vincent commanded on the British shore with about a third of the number of troops

Rout of the American Army opposed to them, for the Canadian militia were mostly farmers, and had to save their crops as well as fight, while the regulars could be but feebly reinforced, as the strain on Great Britain in 1813 left few to spare. The Battle of Stoney Creek was the most notable engagement this year, and was fought in the Niagara district when Colonel Harvey, with a small force, made a night attack, and routed the American army of 2,500 men near the site of the modern city of Hamilton.

Lake Ontario, too, had been the scene of many engagements between the small fleets which struggled for mastery on a sea which meant so much to either. By land and lake, however, the year closed without definite results, nor had anything been accomplished by the American general, Wilkinson, with the 8,000 men that constituted his "Army of the North." Its object in 1814 had been the capture of Kingston, at the east end of Lake Ontario, with a view to descending the river upon Montreal. Another division of 4,000 strong under the South Carolinian generals, Wade, Hampton and Izard, suffered the remarkable defeat of Chateauguay, fought on the river of that name just south of the St. Lawrence.

The heroes of this engagement were 380 French-Canadians under Colonel de Salabery, an officer of that nationality holding a commission in the 60th Regiment, who checked the advance of the enemy on Montreal. It is famous in Canadian annals, and was won partly by skilful shooting from cover and partly by a ruse

A Famous Canadian Victory of bugle-blowing which suggested the advance of a large force and created a panic. It was a saying long afterwards in the American Army that no officer who valued his reputation would admit to having been there at all.

Simultaneously with Chateauguay, Wilkinson descended the St. Lawrence with his 8,000 men and designs upon Montreal. Colonel Morrison, however, followed him from Kingston with as many hundred, and fought the victorious rearguard action of Chrystler's Farm. This, with the news of Hampton's check at Chateauguay, averted all further thoughts of an attack on Montreal, and sent both these incompetent generals into winter quarters. After two years of fighting the Americans did not hold a foot of Canadian ground. In 1814, however, there were about 8,000 British regulars and 4,000 militia, French and English, in arms in Canada. Wilkinson, with 5,000 men, now made another unsuccessful attempt on the Lower Province. The British now held the naval supremacy of Lake Ontario and captured Oswego. There was some heavy fighting, too, on the Niagara frontier, and the American troops by experience had now become much more formidable. The Battle of Lundy's Lane was the most severe of the war, 3,000 British being engaged against 5,000 Americans without any result but a loss of 800 men to either side.

Fighting on the Niagara Border

Michillimackinac had been successfully held against a formidable attack and the war, of which both sides were thoroughly weary, for only the principal engagements have been enumerated here, was terminated in December. The Americans by their success in naval duels on the ocean somewhat redeemed their lack of it on the Canadian frontier. But with these, the British attacks on the American seaboard, their capture of Washington, and their repulse by General Jackson at New Orleans, which was the closing scene, we have nothing to do here. The Canadas, at any rate, emerged triumphant. Even the maritime provinces, though not themselves invaded, had contributed

The End of a Bitter Struggle

their modest quota of troops to the common cause; while the faint boom of contending arms off their stern and foggy coasts was for two years a quite familiar note in their seaport towns, and the pursuit of its quarry by the privateer a frequent and exciting episode.

As regard the issues upon which the war was fought, they remained precisely as they were when it began. But Napoleon was in Elba, peace at length reigned, and the original causes of offence were automatically in abeyance. American commerce had suffered frightfully, but it is often said that the war, in spite of the malcontent states who had at one time threatened secession and a separate peace, had given a certain confidence and patriotism to the new republic. That the Canadas had gained enormously in these qualities is beyond dispute. Indeed, the war of 1812 may in a sense be called the making of Canada. Both races and all classes had fought side by side. No fight for existence that ever was made by a weak against a powerful foe left more cause for pride and satisfaction.

Canada's Gains in the War

There were many domestic troubles in store, but that is another thing and the lot of all communities. If there had been any doubt before as to the destiny of Canada, she had now spoken with a voice that no one could misunderstand, and sealed her decision with her blood. In more senses than one the war of 1812—which was declared by the United States just after the ordinances, which were her principal grievances, had been repealed, and was stimulated by the expectation of an easy conquest of Canada—proved in very truth the making of that country.

QUEENSTOWN HEIGHTS, SHOWING MEMORIAL TO GENERAL BROCK

CANADA OF THE PIONEERS
ASCENDANCY OF THE "FAMILY COMPACT"
THE PAPINEAU REBELLION SUPPRESSED

AFTER an existence of half a century, always at the edge of peril when not in its throes, Canada was now for twenty years or more to be absorbed in the peaceful labours of assimilating succeeding waves of immigration and gathering strength. The times in Great Britain were extraordinarily propitious for furthering these aims. The peace had thrown an enormous number of persons, civil and military, out of employment, and bad times had accentuated that congestion of population which has been more or less chronic ever since.

The British Government took the lead, and brought their schemes to a successful issue. Military settlements were formed of disbanded soldiers in the eastern part of Upper Canada towards Montreal. Highlanders, always an important element in the colony, came in fractions of clans; one such, accompanied **Canadian Life in the Early Pioneer Days** by its chief "the Macnab," who kept for a time on the banks of the Ottawa his authority, his piper, his feathered bonnet and tartan clothes. But Canadian life in those days was deplorably practical and laborious, and though the Highland settlements kept their Gaelic—not yet quite extinct—they quickly shed their feudal reverence and the kilt.

The "eastern townships" of Southern Quebec, the Anglo-American oasis in the French province, were reinforced chiefly from Southern Scotland. The greatest influx, however, was naturally into Upper Canada, with its less rigorous climate and British affinities. The improvement in machinery at this time, too, added to the number of the unemployed in Great Britain, while Ireland, though the great Catholic exodus of modern times did not really begin till after the famine of 1847–48, always had a surplus she could more than spare. In return for a small payment, government, in most instances, conveyed the emigrants out, and gave them a free grant of land, together with implements and provisions for a year. This was generous measure. The hardships incidental to settlement in the primeval forests of Canada in those days are quite beyond **Hardships of Bush Life** the power of English readers to realise. Even by such as know the still rough and unsettled portions of those older provinces to-day it can only be in part appreciated, unless they make some mental effort and recall the prodigious inventions of modern science which have robbed even the wilderness of half its terrors.

Every acre of Canada was originally covered with dense forests, and had to be laboriously cleared by the settler's axe. The Canadian bush, the trunks growing close together above and matted below with the riotous tangle and decay of unnumbered years, was an intimidating foe to the simple British immigrant, whether used or not to manual toil, a child, at any rate for the moment, in that important science of the axe which can alone, and even then not at once, be acquired in the backwoods.

From a world into which he could look out for a greater or less number of miles every day of his life, the emigrant found himself suddenly dropped, as it were, into the bottom of a well, the green walls of which, though picturesque for the moment, or to the passing stranger, stood ever challenging him, so to speak, **The Settlers' Struggle with Nature** to a life struggle. The early French had settled gregariously, their houses set in rows along a river, their farms stretching back in thin strips for a mile or so. The Briton squatted in convenient but cheerless solitude upon his hundred or five hundred acres on the chessboard principle. More often than not, for many years he saw nothing from his log or frame house but the four walls of forest receding slowly over a gradually increasing area, bristling with stumps two or three feet high, which for long years defied decay, obstructed his ox-drawn plough, or harrow, and defaced his limited domain even to his untutored eyes. The forest had some romance for the *coureur de bois*. The more open wood-

Clearing the Pitiless Forests
lands of the Alleghanies again held the mute affection of the pioneer settler, hunter and Indian fighter. But the piti-less Canadian forest had no romance at all for the men who so laboriously cleared it from the flat or undulating surface of Ontario. It was their life-long foe.

Through the long isolated winter, and for every spare day in summer, they carried on in some form or other, with axe, fire and handspike, their everlasting on-slaught, sometimes alone, happier by far in a family of sons. There were consolations, to be sure, in the slowly opening clearing, with the wheat, oats, or maize crop hiding the stumps ; for the land was mostly rich, and carried a certain assurance for the future, however hard might be the present. But for long there were no roads but trails through the forests, and in the richer parts of the province none of the innumerable lakes and few of the navigable rivers that in the vast wilderness to the north of it carried the canoe of the light-hearted voyageur for almost unlimited distances in all directions.

The united empire loyalists of a genera-tion earlier had suffered much, but they were at least North American bred, and settled in more gregarious fashion along the Great Lakes. Their troubles were now over, but these later waves of immigration from over-seas went for the most part deep into the country, and to the average pioneer the " freedom of the woods " meant something like imprisonment in the woods for a long term of years. The days of the well-horsed waggon, the

The Hard Lot of the Pioneers
church, the store, the post-office, the newspaper, the schoolhouse, the market and the doctor were not yet. In the new settlements the fierce Canadian winter smote heavily the tender, the weak and the old, often ill-equipped to face it. Wolves prowled round their rude shanties, and in the hot summers the mosquito and the still worse black fly, battened on their rich English blood. This is no over-drawn picture. To those of us who have

known these same woods in later days and under happier auspices, and have some acquaintance with the drift of these earlier nineteenth century waves of settlement, and the conditions of that period, it is easy enough to picture.

Better evidence than this abounds within easy memory from the lips of those who could recall a youth spent among it, and, better still, in the many printed records of those who endured and ultimately con-quered, or, as many did, went under. To the masses of humble extraction who cleared the first timber from regions that for long have presented the appearance, save for mere technical differences, of Hampshire or Kent, the early struggles, though arduous, were not so severe, while the reward was relatively greater than in the case of hundreds of gently nurtured people of education, who went out dreaming of broad acres which they got but could not handle, and of the romance of the forest which vanished before its stern realities.

Many of these people, of whom the half-pay officer was a frequent type, drifted ultimately into one or other of the little

Aristocrats in Democratic Colonies
towns that arose where a small but congenial society of necessarily simple but some-what exclusive habit of life took a lead in local affairs. Their sons, with a clear start of the millions who were cutting their slow way to comfort and competence in the woods, not only in time, but in education and interest, became the bankers, officials, lawyers, doctors and merchants of the colony. Every colony of Great Britain, including the old states of the Union, however democratic, developed an aristocracy, displaced within easy memory by a plutocracy. Upper Canada developed one which, in the anti-republican fervour natural to its origin and experience, became almost a caste. For half a century it was all powerful, and its rise came about somewhat in this way.

Among the U. E. loyalists who founded the colony, those who had belonged to the governing classes of their old provinces by training and education took a natural lead in their new life. The Canadian wilder-ness had shown itself unsuited to the life of a gentleman farmer or country gentle-man, which was not the case in most of the old American states. The French Cana-dian seignior was an exotic creation in a colony run on mediæval lines, and econo-mically a complete failure. The Upper

AN EARLY SETTLEMENT AMID THE HARDSHIPS OF THE BACKWOODS

THE LABORIOUS METHOD OF WORKING A CANOE UP A RAPID

SCENES IN CANADIAN PIONEER LIFE SEVENTY YEARS AGO

Canadian aristocracy—using the term in a qualified sense for convenience—gathered wholly in towns, were in touch with one another, the government and with England, and therefore monopolised the professions and the offices. The mass of the people, now some 200,000 in number, were leading the laborious isolated lives

Rise of the Family Compact already described, and were in no condition to unite against a powerful oligarchy, securely intrenched in such centres of civilisation as they were. The government at York, rechristened Toronto, consisted of a royal lieutenant-governor, an advisory council, including an executive and an elective house of assembly. But the executive practically held the power of the purse, which was now well replenished. The Canadian Company alone paid the government a quarter of a million sterling for the block of country settled by their immigrants, and now represented by the flourishing districts around Guelph, Galt and Goderich. Nor was the executive responsible to its parliament. It could veto bills with impunity, and, moreover, elections in Canada, as at that time in England, were easily influenced by powerful people.

So it came about that there arose what is known in Canadian history, not only on account of its power and existence, but for the era it marked, roughly the first half of the nineteenth century, as the Family Compact, a group of U. E. loyalist families—that is to say, practically captured the government of Upper Canada in its infancy, and held it. They were mainly, of course, of North American birth and descent, but assumed in miniature something of the airs of an English aristocracy to whom power, offices and pensions of right belonged. Their claim, however, was by no means based wholly on social position, but on the more reasonable one of having done most to found the

Rulers of Upper Canada colony, and so borne the burden and heat of the day. Within limits, this was equitable ; but the Compact came in course of time to exceed all bounds. The not very capable governors who came to Toronto fell naturally under the influence at once of the most agreeable and most accessible society of the province, and adopted their views of men and things. The able and resolute leaders of the oligarchy ruled Upper Canada in their own

interests, while its governors became their puppets. The Compact was not literally confined to a group of families, but extended its friendship and patronage to newcomers and others whose social and political affinities met their approval, and to others who worked or voted in their interests.

It was altogether a curious situation in a colony nominally democratic and just struggling out of poverty by hard toil. But having regard to the cheapness of necessaries, and the absence of all ostentation, the salaries of a somewhat superfluous number of offices were liberal, and patronage remained rigidly in the hands of the Family Compact. For a time their exclusiveness protested against the appointment to a salaried position of any of the later emigration, whatever their ranks or qualifications, and held to the view that all power and privilege were the just inheritance of the U. E. loyalist of their particular class.

The grievances which most rankled in the mind of the powerless and scattered populace were those connected with religion and land. The ruling caste were

Church of England Dominant strongly Church of England, the mass of the people were Presbyterians, Catholics, Nonconformists, or German Lutherans. One-seventh of the wild land of the province had been set apart for the support of a Protestant clergy. The party in power interpreted that to mean an Episcopal clergy ; the people, represented by a minority, and later on by an almost equally powerless majority in the house of assembly, contended that the act implied all Protestant ministers. As a matter of fact, for technical reasons, irrelevant here, it could be read either way. What it did do, however, was to leave blocks of uncleared, unoccupied land in the middle of settlements, causing great inconvenience and hardship.

The inarticulate masses, represented by the reform, or radical, members in the house of assembly, demanded that these lands should be sold and the proceeds applied to education. This became a chronic and burning political question, and was not finally settled till 1857. But much worse than this was the scandalous jobbery that went on in government lands. These were in the power of the ruling party, and were granted wholesale and in great blocks to their friends and relations, carrying no conditions of residence or improvement, which were, of course, never contemplated by the grantee. These forest tracts were simply held for sale when the work of others should have made them of value, and greatly retarded the development of the country, cutting off settlers from market and one another, necessitating miles of useless road and the harbouring of destructive animals.

A few men of good education or social position championed the cause of the people; newspapers opposed to the Compact were started for that minority of the population which was reached by a mail delivery. When their editors got too abusive, the Crown prosecutors and judges made short work of them by fine or banishment. When in time the assembly held a majority of reformers numbering among them many able men, and remained still powerless before an irresponsible and contemptuous executive, the exasperation of the popular party broke out in the insurrection of 1837, which coincided with the rising of Papineau in Lower Canada for somewhat similar reasons. The strongest influence in the Compact was a clever Scotch divine and schoolmaster who became the first Bishop of **The First Bishop of Toronto** Toronto. At his private school many of the sons of the ruling clique attended, and afterwards became its leaders. Robinsons, Boultons, Cartrights, Jessups, Bethunes and others, were his devoted pupils, and found in the astute politician and capable man of affairs the counsel and support which they had found in the schoolmaster.

Bishop Strachan was the incarnation of the Family Compact principles, which may be summed up in a detestation of the methods obtaining to the south of the Lakes, coupled with the pre-eminence of the Church of England. These stout Tories who ruled Canada with such self-satisfied absolutism must not be judged too hardly. They had behaved like heroes in the war of 1812. They dreaded a popular licence which, to be candid, did not present in the United States of that period a very favourable picture.

The senseless abuse of England in some states, the threatened secession of New England, the slavish adulation of the French Revolution and its excesses by southern slave-owners, had not contributed to inspire respect. Canada, too, was filling up with a mixed population other than English and Scotch—Irish Catholics, doubtful Americans, besides Mennonites and Quakers. In four years the enormous total of 160,000 souls landed at Quebec, bound for the two provinces, but chiefly for the upper one. Governors had come and gone and proved as wax in the hands of the Compact. One of them, Sir Francis Head, was a quite humorous appointment, and so utterly lacked every antecedent **The Compact as the Country's Safeguards** qualification that it is supposed he was nominated in mistake for another person of the same name. Plenty of petitions, and even petitions against Compact absolutism, reached England and provoked commissions of inquiry, but the oligarchy was always too much for them. Once or twice appointments to important offices in Upper Canada were made by the English Government and ignored by the Compact. It should be remembered, too, that these people, in spite of certain phases of corruption which were no worse than those obtaining in English political life, had a conviction that they were the safeguards of the country as genuine as their patriotism, which was beyond suspicion.

Though the Upper Canadians had been too much occupied in making life tolerable to bring their full strength against their absolute government, the Quebec house of assembly, being largely French, was under no such disadvantage, and their energies were mainly directed to a futile struggle with the executive, which was chiefly English and composed of the governor's nominees. The constitution of 1791 was, in fact, worse than the straightforward bureaucratic system of the Quebec Act of 1774, for it was illusory in that it created a parliament with power to vote laws and none to create them.

In 1818 the Quebec assembly were given power of supply in the civil list, but when they attempted to coerce the governor by this means he helped himself out of the military fund and went on as before. The bureaucracy, though differing in detail from **How the French were Regarded** the Compact of the other province, was of somewhat the same type and followed the same exclusive methods, in this case directed more particularly against the French. The latter had secured their laws, religion and liberty, but were made to feel an inferiority, both political and even social, which rankled deeply and was lashed into rage by that eloquent radical and ultimate rebel Papineau. Outside the small group of old noblesse, and merging with it, a quite considerable educated class had now sprung from the peasantry. Joseph Papineau was the son of one of them, a notary who had succeeded in purchasing a seigniory on the Ottawa.

The son Joseph was a leading figure in the assembly and the political life of the province from the war of 1812 to the

Papineau the Leader of Revolt rebellion of 1837, which he rashly provoked and took a rather inglorious part in. A brilliant scholar, he became a brilliant orator and the successful leader of the " patriot " party in the province to which a few of the English minority, now numbering about a sixth of the population, belonged. Under various governors, Craig, Lord Aylmer and Lord Dalhousie, the struggle for power waged unceasingly in Press and parliament.

The deadlocks which ensued goaded the British Government into a scheme for uniting the two provinces, which was met by such frantic protests from the French, who saw in it the certain loss of their numerical majority, that it was for the time abandoned. The leader of the small band of English reformers was a physician of character and fortune, Dr. Nelson, who had a good service record in the war of 1812. So, indeed, had Papineau, who had commanded a French company; but with all his oratorical brilliancy and many lovable qualities he was somewhat vain, arrogant and ill-balanced. He became the idol of the French Canadians, and his powers are best shown by the way in which he stirred up the apathetic habitants, who led happy, untaxed lives and neither cared for nor understood the niceties of popular government.

The townspeople and better class felt the grievances keenly enough and required no particular stimulus to agitation. They entered into covenants not to wear English goods, and appeared on the streets and

Outbreak of the Rebellion in parliament arrayed in wondrous homespuns of flamboyant patterns. But for Papineau, however, they would never have gone the length of open rebellion. Incendiary harangues, civic broils, and much drilling of men, in spite of the thunders of the Catholic Church, brought Sir John Colborne and all the troops down from Upper Canada to the assistance of Lord Gosport, their governor-general. In November the rebellion broke

out at St. Denis, to the south of Montreal. The insurgents under Dr. Nelson repulsed an attack of the troops. At St. Charles, however, in the same district and at the same time, 1,300 insurgents with some guns were utterly routed with a loss of 150 killed and 300 wounded, which practically ended the business, though there was a little more skirmishing. Papineau injudiciously yielded to Nelson's advice to leave St. Denis on the eve of the skirmish, and thereby somewhat tarnished his reputation. He got away to the States himself, but Nelson was captured; while, as a last word on this ill-judged insurrection in Lower Canada, it must, at any rate, be said that a majority of the people, whatever their grievances, strongly disapproved of so rash a resort to arms.

Among several incentives to rebellion in Upper Canada was the removal of most of the troops to assist Sir John Colborne in the French province; another was the incapacity of Governor Head. The chief of all, however, was William Lyon Mackenzie, the ill-balanced firebrand who expounded the just grievances of the

Mackenzie the Firebrand Agitator people in outrageous and incendiary language, and finally induced a poor handful of rustics to follow an extremely incapable and quite unprincipled leader. Mackenzie enjoys a spurious and ill-deserved fame. He had much more than the vanity, impudence and arrogance of Joseph Papineau, and few of his compensating qualities; while of political pluck he had an abounding store.

Of humble Scottish origin, diminutive and ungracious physique, without means or connection, but with an insatiable thirst for learning, he arrived in Upper Canada in 1820 at the age of twenty-five, and almost immediately began to constitute himself the mouthpiece of Canadian grievances. Settling at York under the nose of the government, he became, through the agency of the newspaper he published, a very thorn in the sides of the Compact. For twelve years, with tireless energy as a writer and agitator, and with an unbridled and virulent pen, he championed the cause of reform. He was regarded by the Tories almost as a wild beast, and his office and plant were wrecked on one occasion by a gang of well-born youths.

Elected again and again to the assembly by a radical constituency, he was refused admission on various pleas, though he went to London and got a verdict in his favour from the British Government. But even when backed by this and a great mob, he was still rejected. He was elected the first mayor of Toronto when York was incorporated as a city under that name, and was the most popular man in Canada, though such a distinction was perhaps more creditable to his enterprise than to the perception of the democracy who shouted for him. The arrogance of the Family Compact might perhaps justify their opponents in looking more to the end than to the means of withstanding it. Some reactionary measures introduced by the British Government, and a sweeping election victory of the Tories, turned

were killed and wounded; the rest fled, together with Mackenzie, who escaped to the States. With culpable folly he had left behind him a full list of all those implicated, which enabled the authorities to lay by the heels as many as they pleased.

Numbers were imprisoned, and several condemned, of whom two were hanged. Mackenzie then raised a force of ruffians and wastrels on the American side, who for some time continued to make plundering raids into the Niagara country with a good deal of bloodshed, to the greater detriment, fortunately in these skirmishes, of the raiders than of their opponents. Mackenzie was at length arrested by the United States authorities, tried at Albany,

KINGSTON, ON LAKE ONTARIO, AS IT WAS SEVENTY YEARS AGO

Mackenzie from a violent reformer to an annexationist and to American intrigues. This detached the more substantial and sober of his party, and left him the leader, together with Dr. Nelson, a reputable physician, of only an extreme left wing.

With seven or eight hundred of these, mostly country people, Mackenzie raised the flag of rebellion at Montgomery's tavern, ten miles north of Toronto. The latter had then 12,000 souls, but it was denuded of troops, and the citizens were apathetic. Mackenzie was a wretched leader, and lost his only and faint chance by dallying till a body of militia was collected, who very soon scattered his ill-armed rustics. Half a dozen of them

imprisoned for a time, and then released. He remained in miserable circumstances for some years in the United States, and was ultimately pardoned in 1843 and permitted to return to Canada. His rashness and mismanagement had caused much misery. There was nothing that was noble, heroic or self-sacrificing in his career. As a politician on the side that had most justice, and that any poor man with talent would have taken, he was an indomitable fighter, not particular about his methods, or very loyal to his friends, and of an uncontrollable temper. However that may be, Papineau and Mackenzie at least proved, if at a bloody cost to their supporters, that there were grievances in

Canada of a nature that could not longer be ignored, and in 1840 Lord Durham was sent out as governor-general with unprecedentedly wide powers and instructions to report fully on the state of the country. We must pause here for a moment to make some allusion to the maritime provinces of New Brunswick, Nova Scotia and Prince Edward Island. Not much indeed can be said of them in so brief a survey of so large a subject as the history of Canada, for the good reason that these provinces were not burdened with the racial and religious rivalry, or the near neighbourhood of an alien Power, and other complications which vexed the two Canadas.

Social Life in the Maritime Provinces

They were comparatively isolated and self - contained, and practically homogeneous. They had nothing to do but increase and multiply and endure their domestic troubles, which were a milder repetition of the disputes in Upper Canada between the people represented by an assembly and an oligarchy supported by royal governors. They also had a Family Compact, but it was less marked and not seriously fought till after the famous Durham report. Though emigration flowed steadily into these provinces, there was nothing like the stream that swept into the more fertile lands of Upper Canada, while there was no serious problem of the great American settlers to disturb these remote countries.

They were partly a maritime people, too, had ready access to the world's markets, and if they moved more slowly than their sister colonies, progressed more comfortably and with somewhat less hardship to the pioneer. Their French population, though increased considerably from the remnant of the Acadians left in 1754, had no aggressive separate qualities or *esprit de corps* like those of Quebec, and gave no trouble. There were simple-minded loyal Highlanders in Cape Breton, whose descendants to this day speak Gaelic, and Germans, who, like those of Upper Canada, made admirable settlers, though sometimes retaining their nation-

Cape Breton's Loyal Highlanders

ality with mild but harmless persistency. But the united empire loyalists remained a greater proportion of the population, and still do so for the reasons already stated, than even in Ontario. The face of the country resembled that of the Canadas, clad originally with the all-pervading forests, and was slowly cleared and farmed by the same methods and in the same fashion; and to-day it so greatly resembles the landscape of Ontario in its normal and prosperous districts and country towns that only a person familiar with British North America would pick out the technical differences. The inhabitants had their own land troubles, however, as huge grants had been given in early days to favoured persons in England, whose rights made difficulties in a country where freehold settlement were vital to success.

Halifax became a prosperous city and a great naval and military station, and on that account retained, and still retains, a certain flavour of the Old Country in manners and speech less obvious in the Canadas. It was not till 1847 that Nova Scotia shook off an irresponsible executive, and the leader of the Reform party in this case was Joseph Howe, a man far superior in every particular to Papineau or Mackenzie. Howe was the son of a united empire loyalist, and a man of erudition and culture, and, what is more, of surprising eloquence and sound sense.

Howe the Most Eminent Nova Scotian

Nova Scotia, though relatively small, was the most prolific of the British North American colonies in men of intelligence and political ability, and even during the forty years that the dominion of Canada has enjoyed federal government, has contributed more than her share to its political leadership. Howe is the most eminent of Nova Scotians, and in some ways the most distinguished of Canadian—using the term broadly—statesmen. The struggle for reform led by him in Nova Scotia was the chief feature of its provincial life, and, though a long one, it was effected by purely constitutional means, without either disloyalty or annexationist clamour, and calls for no further notice here.

THE MAKERS OF MODERN CANADA

Sir Richard Cartwright, 1835

Sir Thomas Shaughnessy, 1853

Sir Charles Tupper, 1821

Sir Wilfrid Laurier, 1841

Lord Strathcona, 1820

Sir John A. Macdonald, 1815-1891

Hon. Joseph Howe, 1804-1873

Hon. George Brown, 1818-1880

Lord Mountstephen, 1829

Sir George Cartier, 1814-1873

THE MAKING OF MODERN CANADA
AND EXPANSION OF THE NEW DOMINION

IN May, 1838, Lord Durham arrived in Quebec with great pomp and a large retinue. But behind the glitter of externals was a quality rare enough then among Englishmen, and not too common now. The new governor had an intuitive grasp of colonial feeling. He could see all sides, and some way into the future. He was free from that unreasoning bias against foreigners which was the heritage of most Englishmen then—a human enough failing, at least, if a mischievous one. Nor was he cursed with that unworthy and unnatural animus against his own countrymen of Greater Britain which seems inherent and is the stock-in-trade of some modern British politicians who do not know them. He was only in the country five months.

But to the outside world no name stands out so prominently and so favourably in Canadian history as that of Durham, and even among those of more intimate know-**Two Nations Warring in a Single State** ledge it is safe to say that it stands second only to Dorchester. Durham does not live, however, as an administrator or a soldier, but by the single masterly report of the state of the country that he drew up with the assistance of Charles Buller. On his arrival he found eight leaders of the recent rebellion in prison and excluded from the amnesty. These he released and sent into exile in Bermuda, exceeding thereby his powers, and exciting the wrath of the British Government, and a quarrel which provoked his speedy resignation.

But he had time, nevertheless, to draw up that famous report which directed British policy in Canada, and by which his name lives. It fills a considerable volume, and is the most lucid account of Canada, so far as it goes, ever written. He found, he declared in a sentence that has become memorable, not, as he expected, a contest between a government and a people, but two nations warring in the bosom of a single state. There were 600,000 people now in Lower Canada, of whom 150,000 were British. The latter, from whom must be deducted many thousand Irish Catholics, controlled the executive, held most of the offices, had an overwhelming preponderance of capital and energy in the cities of Quebec and Montreal, and as farmers occu-**The French Supreme in the Assembly** pied the exclusively English districts of the eastern townships and a few other regions outside the seigniorial tenures. The bitterness between the races in all classes had become so intense that the very dread of what a collision might mean actually kept the peace between them by tacit consent. The French dreaded the English strength in the cities, and the latter feared the overwhelming habitant majority in the country. Trial by jury had become a farce ; the verdict went by race, not evidence, and the system of challenging weeded out every juryman of the hostile faction.

The French dominated the assembly and refused money for all public works, canals, and such like, that the energetic English regarded, and justly, as vital to the progress of civilisation. The immense increase of the French peasant farmers had not overflowed into new districts, but had merely subdivided on the old seigniories, and the spectacle of congestion and worn-out lands could be seen almost on the edge of an illimitable and fertile wilderness.

The priests, to whom Lord Durham pays an eloquent tribute, were, from those natural motives of self-interest concerned with fees such as obtain in Ireland to-day, opposed to the shifting of their flocks. The English, in fact, looked upon Canada **Canada From Two Points of View** with the enterprising colonial genius of the race—a land to be settled, civilised and developed, and worthy to rank with the numerous states of the rival nation to the southward. The French had altogether another point of view. Immigration, so far as their nation was concerned, was a word without meaning. They regarded Canada as an old

THE CAMP OF A SPORTING PARTY IN NEW BRUNSWICK

LADY EVELYN LAKE IN THE PROVINCE OF QUEBEC

TYPICAL VIEWS OF CANADA'S BEAUTIFUL WOODS AND LAKES

Photos: Canadian Pacific Railway

ON KIPAWA LAKE: HUNTERS RETURNING TO CAMP WITH MOOSE HEAD

MOOSE CAMP AT KIPAWA LAKE IN THE PROVINCE OF QUEBEC

MOOSE-HUNTING IN CANADA: SCENES ON KIPAWA LAKE
Photos: Canadian Pacific Railway

settled country, and objected to innovation and disturbance. Their farmers were mostly without skill or ambition, and at the same time saw the skilled agriculture of such British settlers as were under their observation with irritation and jealousy. The French of the cities had engaged to a certain extent in trade, but were altogether surpassed by the English with their more abundant capital and greater aptitude for business. The late rebellion had made the English more determined to keep the upper hand. Rather than submit to what they considered the blighting and cramping influence of French domination, they would even carry the province over to the hated republic, which would

LORD DURHAM
First earl of Durham, he was appointed governor-general of Canada in 1838, where his brief rule was denounced as high-handed, but his famous Report became the basis for the constitution of the new Canadian Dominion.

at least assure to them the sympathetic laws and certain prosperity. Curiously enough, there was no trace of sectarian animosity between French and English. The creeds did not clash. Each took the other for granted. Half the seigniories, too, were now owned by prosperous Englishmen, and their views of improving their properties irritated the French peasantry, who inherited the purely feudal traditions of their tenure. Social intercourse, which, in the upper classes at least, had once been considerable, was dead, likewise intermarriage. Lord Durham found leading Englishmen who had never once in their lives been under a private roof with Frenchmen, though the latter of this class had a little advantage of their rivals

SIR CHARLES TUPPER
Canadian statesman, born in Nova Scotia in 1821, Sir Charles Tupper earned for himself considerable distinction as surgeon before adopting politics, becoming in 1864 Premier of Nova Scotia and in 1896 of the Dominion.
Elliot & Fry

in the matter of breeding and culture. But being snubbed politically and socially they took refuge in a proud and sore aloofness. The two races frequented different hotels, they even ran passenger steamers against one another. At agricultural shows they competed for different prizes, and conducted their very ploughing matches in different fields. Mostly they could not speak each other's language or read each other's newspapers. It is needless to say that a French-Canadian nation was dreamed of, but in such a situation, hemmed in by a vast North America, all seething with Anglo-Saxon enterprise and traditions, it was an idle dream. Annexation, again, for the British would only have been a rupture of sentiment. To the French, however, it would have meant the destruction of everything they held dear, as it would be to-day. Any longing the French might then have felt for renewed connection with their mother country was equally vain. France of the post-Revolution period was not the France they had known and come from, and had ruled them with an iron, but never resented, rule. The Church of Canada, powerful and absolute, was staunchly loyal to the Crown, for palpable reasons, however she might sympathise with political grievances, and she had done her utmost to stay the rising of '37. When Durham went home to a somewhat ungrateful government and a premature death, he gave his advice, and it was accepted. His prescient mind had foreseen the federation of all the provinces, but the time for this was not quite ripe; and, in the meanwhile, he urged a legislative union of Upper and Lower Canada. In 1839 a bill to that effect was introduced into parliament by Lord John Russell, and at the same time submitted to the two provinces. The constitution of Quebec had been suspended after the rebellion, or the assembly would have most strenuously opposed a union which annihilated their numerical supremacy, and left them on about even terms with their rivals, though with a certainty of being ultimately outstripped through immigration.

The council, however, naturally enough, accepted it, and the assembly of Upper Canada did the same after much demur. For though they would be at no racial disadvantage, Upper Canada had a considerable element whose loyalty was doubtful, and who might conceivably hold the balance of power. The Bill became law in 1840. It was a makeshift and a compromise. The moderate opponents of the Family Compact were the only section thoroughly pleased with it. The united provinces now, at any rate, secured popular government with only a rather less reluctance than how to use the veto on the part of the governor-general. Mr. Paulet Thompson, who had cleverly conducted all the negotiations to a successful issue, became the first governor, as Lord Sydenham. The new legislature from the combined provinces met at Kingston, Montreal, Toronto and Quebec, successively. There we must leave them, to twenty-seven years of a somewhat ill-assorted union. The affairs of the British province were in a certain sense sacrificed to make political existence possible for the Franco-British province. It was the best that could be done, and the races were at any rate of about equal voting strength, which gave an opportunity for some questions to be settled on other than racial cleavages. The points at issue, though discussed at fever heat, and productive of a great deal of passion between classes as well as between races, are not of vital moment to the reader.

The great fact of the epoch now inaugurated, as of most in Canada, was the continuous stream of immigration and the rapid development of the country. The clergy reserves, which had a flavour of state endowments, were transferred to the government for educational purposes, and the rights of the seigniors, who, both French and English, had in many cases provoked their tenantry by assuming the rôle and exactions of mere landlords, were bought out for half a million sterling. Canada was not, however, without external alarms and interests during this epoch. The Ashburton Treaty, in 1842, created that preposterous wedge of the state of Maine into Lower Canada and New Brunswick, the very look of which upon the map is a standing reminder of a careless surrender of Canadian territory by the British Government to the United States. In 1857-1858 the discovery of gold in British Columbia, and the emigration consequent upon it, laid the foundations of that province; and in 1861, the American Civil War, though far removed from the Canadian frontier, gave for four years a great stimulus both to immigration and trade in the British provinces, and on the famous occasion of the Trent affair so nearly embroiled Great Britain and Canada that the Guards were sent out in the dead of winter to Halifax, and marched for hundreds of miles through the snowy wilderness to Quebec. Lastly, in 1866, at the close of the war, two bands of Fenians, mostly old soldiers, made a futile attack on Canada, and were repulsed with slight loss on either side. In spite of

THE GREAT SEAL OF THE DOMINION OF CANADA
The centre of the shield, five inches in diameter, represents Queen Victoria seated under a Gothic canopy, holding the sceptre and orb, and wearing the robe and collar of the Garter. Underneath are the arms of Great Britain, and on the sides are shields bearing the coats-of-arms of Ontario, Quebec, Nova Scotia and New Brunswick.

the great numbers of Catholic Irish settled in Canada, there has been little of that spirit among them, and they have been most loyal citizens, engaging in nothing worse than those local faction fights with their Orange neighbours which distinguished some districts even within the memory of middle-aged people, and might almost be classed under the head of diversions. The upper province grew in time to twice the population of the other, and aroused cries for a re-adjusted representation, which threatened the French with a hopeless minority in Parliament, and the country with another impasse. The federation of all the provinces under something like the American system was the only solution; and with, for the most part, the cordial co-operation of the maritime provinces, the great scheme was carried through, and the new dominion launched in 1867. Each province retained its local autonomy and separate legislature under a lieutenant-governor, always a Canadian, nominated by the federal executive. To the latter was reserved all great affairs, such as defence, customs, Crown lands, Indians, and the organisation of the vast western territories now just beginning to open up.

The famous Sir John Macdonald, the most illustrious of Canadian statesmen, was prominent in the federal movement, as also was Sir Charles Tupper. A final meeting was held in London, and

SIR JOHN A. MACDONALD

For many years a conspicuous figure in Canadian politics, Sir John Macdonald, then a practising barrister, was elected to the Canadian Parliament in 1844, becoming in 1847 a Cabinet Minister, and in 1857, Premier. Upon the establishment of the Dominion of Canada in 1867, he was appointed the first Prime Minister of the Dominion. Above is the statue erected to him outside the Parliament Buildings, Ottawa.

early in 1867 the British North America Act was passed through the Imperial Parliament. The new capital was fixed at Bytown, a small town up the Ottawa well removed from the frontier, fairly central to all the provinces, and felicitously rechristened Ottawa. Here were erected the stately houses of parliament for senate, commons, and the entire government staff, familiar to all travellers, and there, too, the governor-general of all British North America took up his residence, Lord Monck being the first to hold this high office, and Sir John Macdonald the first premier. It only remains to say that Prince Edward Island, British Columbia and Manitoba—not then organised—came into the federation shortly afterwards. And in the meantime, the great north-west was awakening. The term "west," to the agriculturist of that day, suggested nothing in Canada beyond the fertile peninsula washed by the waters of Lake Huron, which, by 1870, was practically settled up. All beyond, as far as the Rocky Mountains some 1,500 miles distant, was sacred to the trapper or the Indian, and the monopoly of its trade was enjoyed with some jealousy by the Hudson's Bay Company, whose lonely posts at intervals broke the waste. Part of this territory was operated by the North-west Company. After the war of 1812, Lord Selkirk, an influential director of the Hudson's Bay Company, with a taste for

MORAINE LAKE, IN THE VALLEY OF THE TEN PEAKS. NEAR LAGGAN

WIND MOUNTAIN, IN THE CANADIAN ROCKIES, NEAR BANFF, ALBERTA

PICTURESQUE LAKE AND MOUNTAIN SCENERY IN CANADA

Photos: Canadian Pacific Railway

colonisation, settled a small group of Highland and Irish farmers near Fort Garry, now Winnipeg, and these were the first people to test the famous wheat lands of the north-west. The fur-traders of the North-west Company were hostile, on one occasion even to bloodshed; there was no market, of course, for grain in those days, but there was no difficulty in self-support, and the little colony became a permanent element among the employes of the two fur companies— Scots, French, half-breeds and Indians. It was sixty years, however, before Manitoba became a province and the north-west was seriously open for agricultural settlement. It was to the obvious interest of the Hudson's Bay Company to discourage the settler, and encourage the superstition that the country was unfit for farming, the climate too severe for serious settlement, and the land never free from frost;

LOUIS RIEL
Riel in 1884 led a party of half-breeds against the Dominion Government, was captured, tried and convicted for treason, and was executed on November 16th, 1885.

and judicially murdered one of the leaders of the small British settlement there. This caused immense excitement in Canada, and brought about the well-known Red River expedition under Lord Wolseley, then but a rising colonel. The long march of regulars and volunteers through the wilderness, and the prompt collapse of the rebellion, was long remembered in Canada, and virtually marked the founding of Winnipeg and the great north-west. The old Rupert's Land became Manitoba, a federal province with the adjoining and more western territories of Assiniboia, Saskatchewan and Alberta, reaching to the Rocky Mountains, and since admitted to provincial rank. This vast fertile grain and stock country was even then but faintly appreciated. The writer can well remember the heated arguments for and against it that were heard all over Canada. For a whole

when at length, by efforts of certain individuals, the eyes of the Federal Government were opened, though only in part, to what we see now as one of the world's great facts and factors. The Hudson Bay monopoly was broken by purchase and arrangement. In surveying the country for settlement in 1869, the government officials were injudicious and unconciliatory, and alarmed the French, mostly half-breeds, who

HALF-BREED SCOUTS BRINGING RIEL AS PRISONER

decade it was still so remote that immigration was limited, and markets yet in the future. That stupendous work, the Canadian Pacific Railway, now came on the political arena. The dominion of Canada, though numbering in 1870 nearly four million souls, and containing a high average of individual well-being, was still and for long afterwards remained in effect a poor country. It was, moreover, an attenuated strip reaching from the Atlantic

formed a majority of its 7,000 people. An ignorant, isolated, lawless community, they rose under the celebrated half-breed leader Louis Riel, seized Fort Garry, to the Pacific, and the United States threatened it commercially all along the line. Parallel railways of prodigious length, running through whole territories of

LOOKING UP THE BOW RIVER AT BANFF, ALBERTA

NATIONAL PARK, WITH AN AREA OF 5,400 SQUARE MILES, AT BANFF

THE ALPINE BEAUTIES OF CANADIAN SCENERY

Photos: Canadian Pacific Railway

unproductive wastes to the sea-board, seemed vital to its industrial independence unless it were to become commercially tributary to the more flourishing nation to the south of it, and railways now became the leading political question that agitated the country and divided parties. The Grand Trunk from Quebec to Toronto, with various off-shoots, had already done good internal service, though with small profit to its shareholders. The government, with imperial guarantee, now ran the inter-colonial road for nearly 900 miles from Quebec to Halifax.

A Factor in Canada's Prosperity

Its profits were dubious when the Conservative party conceived the audacious scheme of running a road through some 700 miles of wooded, rocky barrens to Winnipeg, across the 1,000 miles of prairie beyond, of climbing the Rockies, and thence dropping down to the Pacific. Everyone now knows what a work this is, and that it made the north-west, and lifted Canada into its present stage of prosperity. Its promoters were called madmen ; they are now called patriots. Their stockholders were regarded as dupes ; they have long been in the receipt of dividends. Governments went in and out on the great question ; passing strangers declared jestingly that Canadian politics consisted of railroads, as indeed they mostly did. But railroads in a new country mean more than the inhabitants of old ones can well realise. This one was not only to open a greater and more fertile Canada, but to bind the Atlantic to the Pacific by an " all-British " railroad that would be valuable both in peace and war as an Imperial highway between Europe and Asia. Both in an engineering and financial sense it was the greatest undertaking yet achieved by man, and the first through train reached the Pacific Ocean in 1886. But some years prior to this, when the railroad first reached Winnipeg and the prairie country, the rush to the north-west began. Though a due proportion of Europeans were among the newcomers, the backbone of the movement were farmers and farmers' sons from Ontario and the maritime provinces, hardy men, accustomed to laborious days, sons and grandsons of those who had turned the dense and formidable wilderness of Upper Canada into a smiling country equal to the best provinces of older America. They

The Rush to the North-west

had come out of the struggle with its mark strong upon them in the shape of a grim devotion to hard practical work, of a certain dourness, partly due to much Scottish blood, and an austerity of life that regarded work as the Puritan regards religion, incompatible with most of those accessories that brighten existence.

These and their type were the men who founded the prairie provinces, though recruited by all sorts and conditions of men. There was a " boom " of a more than usually inflated kind, and a great influx of British emigrants, not generally of a very suitable kind, and not usually successful. Indeed, there were hard times yet to be faced, a fiercer climate than even Canadians were accustomed to, plagues of grasshoppers, of hail, of early frosts, and untried conditions, above all of continuous low prices.

There was for long a half-conscious and sometimes openly expressed feeling that the north-west was still an experiment. Winnipeg grew to 30,000, and then nearly stood still. Small towns of 3,000 to 5,000 population were scattered along the solitary railroad to the Rocky Mountains. Grain growers spread for considerable areas round them, and grew good crops, though often damaged ; but there was a good deal against these pioneers of the 'seventies and 'eighties which hardly concerns an historical survey. The stockmen, too, of the ranching countries lost heavily from a lack of understanding of the climate. Men of good judgment protested their stout faith in the great future of the country ; others, whose opinion seemed equally entitled to respect, held grave doubts. We know now which were right. But for nearly twenty years the north-west, considering its extreme fertility and easily worked soils, progressed comparatively slowly, and, indeed, had not a very good name in European emigration circles or even in Old Canada, whose sons had done better there than any other.

A Period of Slow Progress

It had caused, however, no little drain on the rural districts of Ontario and the maritime provinces, all of whose better-class lands at the opening of the north-west had been long occupied, fenced, and built upon. The Eastern Canadian had nothing left near home to pioneer in but third-rate lands, covered with heavy and then almost valueless timber, for the timber merchants, then perhaps the wealthiest and most successful class in Canada, had eliminated the marketable trees far back into the

LAST GREAT COUNCIL OF THE WEST: THE MARQUESS OF LORNE PRESIDING AT A CONFERENCE WITH HOSTILE INDIANS

In 1881 a great council was held between the governor-general of Canada, then the Marquess of Lorne, and the hostile Indians, who for several years had been in a state of open rebellion, which had partly culminated in the terrible Custer massacre of 1876. With a view to pacification, and for the purpose of hearing their grievances, the governor-general invited the Indian chiefs to a conference, which proved to be the last great council of the west. The ceremony began with weird dances, then young Indians would boast of their prowess in war, and finally the orators of the tribes told, in flowery and flamboyant language, of the injustices their people had suffered at the hands of the white man.

From the painting by Sidney P. Hall, by permission of C. E. Clifford & Co.

interior. In the prairies was the richest soil in the world, into which he could immediately thrust his plough. The backwoods of Old Canada altogether ceased to attract. The improved farms, partly for the same reasons that depressed English agriculture, and partly from the drain to the west, went down in value. There was

Vain Hope of French Canadians no more emigration from Europe worth mentioning to Ontario, New Brunswick or Nova Scotia, while all those provinces sent out emigrants themselves. Nor was the drain from Old Canada confined to that of her farming class to the north-west ; but there was a much more serious exodus of the flower of her youth to the United States, where every form of industry then offered better openings. For a long time Canada scarcely maintained the normal birth-rate increase of an old country. She lost more by emigration than she gained by immigration.

In 1886, Louis Riel, the half-breed leader of the Red River affair, went on the warpath again at the head of an Indian and half-breed force on the Saskatchewan. The volunteers, both local and from Old Canada, were called out. Some brief but sharp fighting took place, to the complete discomfiture of the rebels and the capture of Riel, who this time met death, the fate that he deserved. A curious feature of its earlier development was the vain but ardent hope of the French-Canadians, particularly of their Church, to acquire supremacy there, and form a kind of second French-Canadian nation. Outnumbered in the east, they dreamed of finding compensation in the virgin west.

It was a short-lived and pathetic dream, and one may well wonder now how shrewd and able men could have brought themselves to indulge in it, but they did. Its echoes remained in the furious strife over sectarian education in the north-west that agitated the whole of Canada, known

Wonderful Prosperity of North-west as the Manitoba school question. It was not till the closing years of the last century that the Canadian north-west really "found itself," and began that prodigious advance in development and prosperity which has transformed it from the Cinderella of British colonies to the most envied and most talked about of all.

Immigration at the rate of from one to over two hundred thousand a year has passed in there, something like a third of

which has consisted of American farmers, bringing not only experience but capital. Whatever political effect such a movement may have in the future, its practical effect on stimulating development has been greater in proportion than the corresponding influx of less trained and unacclimatised Europeans. These things belong, perhaps, rather to the concerns of to-day than to history. It will be enough to say that Winnipeg, with its nearly 150,000 inhabitants, bids fair to fulfil her early ambition, not always treated respectfully in the long lean years of the 'eighties and 'nineties, of becoming another Chicago. The 800 miles of tributary prairie to the Rockies is filling rapidly and expanding to a broader belt.

The small towns along it that for nearly two decades held out bravely and hopefully, but from a western standpoint unprogressively, have leaped forward. The aggregate output of the finest wheat lands in the world has quadrupled. The grain itself is not only in the greatest demand by millers, but commands the highest price. Experience, too, has immensely modified the climatic drawbacks once felt so

Linking Old Canada to the Pacific Coast keenly both by crops and men. The fierce winters that pierced the ill-built wooden houses and makeshift stabling of the earlier settlers, and caused many of them to think and tell the world that life there was not worth living, now beat harmlessly upon good brick houses warmed under the latest principles and barns as imposing and snug as those of Ontario.

The winters are no longer seasons of dread and weariness to the majority. Farming is more scientific and more mixed. The cattle on the ranches under the Rocky Mountains no longer die by the thousands in a hard winter, but are so handled and fed that the life of a north-western steer is almost as assured as if it were in an Ontario barnyard. New conditions have assured the land a new life. New territories to the northward, quite recently regarded as Arctic and uninhabitable, on a nearer acquaintance are showing themselves in an altogether different light. One great railroad with its branches that only a generation ago a whole Canadian political party and thousands more clear-headed men thought could never pay its way is now utterly insufficient ; and in a few more years two more will link Old Canada to the Pacific coast.

A. G. BRADLEY

SCENES of AGRICULTURAL LIFE IN CANADA

A TYPICAL PLOUGHING SCENE IN THE WEST OF CANADA

WHEAT-REAPING IN THE PROVINCE OF MANITOBA

The photos on these pages are reproduced by the courtesy of the Canadian Pacific Railway

THRESHING GRAIN IN WESTERN CANADA: FIRST STAGE

THRESHING GRAIN: SECOND STAGE—FILLING THE BAGS

THRESHING GRAIN: THIRD STAGE—LOADING UP

AN ABUNDANT CROP OF THE GOLDEN GRAIN IN MANITOBA

STACKING WHEAT IN WESTERN CANADA

TYPICAL HOME OF THE PROSPEROUS CANADIAN FARMER

FARM BUILDINGS IN THE FAR WEST

GRAIN ELEVATOR AT FORT WILLIAM, ONTARIO

ARRIVAL OF GRAIN AT AN ELEVATOR IN WESTERN CANADA

HERD OF CATTLE BY GULL LAKE, SASKATCHEWAN

"ROUND-UP" OF BROOD MARES, AT CALGARY, ALBERTA

SHEEP GRAZING ON A CANADIAN PRAIRIE FARM

READY FOR THE SHEARER: THE WEALTH OF A CANADIAN FARMER

A WELL-ESTABLISHED APPLE ORCHARD IN ONTARIO, FORTY YEARS OLD

HOEING GOOSEBERRY PLANTS, FONTHILL, ONTARIO

CANADA IN OUR OWN TIME
A VAST LAND OF PROGRESS AND PROSPERITY
By A. G. Bradley

ACROSS the huge range of the Rockies the province of British Columbia lies on the Pacific Coast, save for a few interludes of high-lying park-like prairie, a rugged, mountainous, densely-wooded country. It includes the large adjacent island of Vancouver, also wooded, mountainous and wild, save for a corner of settled country, on which Victoria, the capital of the province, is somewhat inconveniently placed, while facing it on the mainland is the more progressive city of Vancouver, the terminus of the Canadian Pacific Railway.

The minerals, as already indicated, gave her an earlier start than the prairie provinces ; but it was a start on a small scale, a mere mining population about the mouth of the Fraser River and on the opposite island of Vancouver, just large enough to require a government. These early fathers of the province, half a century **British Columbia's Mission** ago, had not, for the most part, come through from Canada, for there was no way, and they had nothing in common with her. They came from Great Britain and elsewhere, at haphazard, by way of the Pacific. Strong traces of this remain, particularly in speech and accent, but are only of academic interest. British Columbia is now a typical province of the federation, filling up these many years from the eastward, though, unlike her neighbour, subject to a large influx of Orientals, which the scarcity of white labour has encouraged, and raised a somewhat difficult race problem.

British Columbia has a distinct mission. Her rivers abound in salmon. She is almost stifled under heavy pine, cedar and hemlock timber, of which the great prairie provinces that require it in every phase of their lives have practically none. The less severe climate of her upland valleys and the Devonian climate of her sea-coast are eminently suited to the culture of fruit, which is one product of the temperate zone that the prairie provinces with their coming millions cannot cultivate successfully. Lumber, fruit, minerals and fish are the basis of British Columbian prosperity, as are grain and stock of the prairie **Attractions of British Columbia** provinces. Each will be necessary to the other, apart from their respective sea-borne trade. One more service, too, the Pacific province can render to the interior to its own advantage. There will always be a certain proportion of people, constitutionally averse to a cold climate. Some of these will at once cross the Rockies and settle for this reason in British Columbia. Many more, when they have made a competence in Manitoba, Assiniboia or Alberta, will seek the mild climate of the transmontane province to enjoy it and spend the evening of their days. Thus it will be seen that this vast British territory, stretching from Winnipeg and the Red River to the Pacific Ocean, contains every element of human happiness and virtually every product necessary to man.

Politics in these lusty young provinces are of but small account. In the old story of Canada, soldiers and statesmen have played the leading part laying seeds of future greatness. Some day statesmen will be required in the North-west. In the meantime, the latent talent and brains of the country find what is now the nobler outlet. The politician, with rare exceptions, remains comparatively obscure ; his **The Career of Politics in Canada** work can be done by men of second-rate ability, who do not lead but may be called rather the professional delegates of contending interests, and whose rewards, when honestly adhered to, are small compared to those of other careers, and do not include the prestige which attaches to political life in older countries. And, in the meantime, Ontario and Quebec handle all its eastern-going trade and supply the west with those articles which it is yet a long way from being able to produce. Both these provinces abound in water-power produced by innumerable lakes and streams which from their wild northern back-country flow down to the Great Lakes and the St. Lawrence. Ontario is incomparably the foremost in such industries. Such advance as Quebec has made is mainly due to alien enterprise, the genius of the French-Canadian having no strong bent in that direction.

But though Montreal, the greatest and wealthiest Canadian city, is a short way within the French province, the heart and life of the dominion beats in the province

or rather prejudice, entertained by many Englishmen towards the United States, but is at once greater and less. The superficial differences that mainly excite some Englishmen to unfriendly criticism touch the Canadian only slightly, as he shares most of them himself ; but he has a latent hereditary antagonism of another kind and much more personal—a relic of the bitter moments of 1782 and 1812.

Ontario, though settled by mixed races, has rather a Scottish than an English tone and flavour. She began to manufacture before the federation, but between the high American tariff and British competition had not made great way. Nor have reciprocity treaties with the United States

LOADING TRUCKS WITH TIMBER IN THE MOUNTAINS OF BRITISH COLUMBIA

of Ontario, now containing 2,000,000 souls that show an individual average of well-being, intelligence, industry, sanity of conduct and opinion not surpassed by any country of that size in the world, and rarely equalled. Like the maritime provinces, it is much more American—of the Eastern type—than English in appearance and habit of life, naturally enough not merely from its situation, but from the fact that it was originally settled by Americans. The bitterness of these old U. E. loyalists still lingers in a certain antagonism to the great republic that sometimes puzzles the British visitor. It is not quite the same as the vague dislike,

proved greatly to her advantage. In 1877 Sir John Macdonald introduced the " national policy," which was one of comparatively high protection. This stimulated manufactures greatly, and when the recent development of the west burst upon her she made gigantic strides and practically abandoned all talk of free trade, which had formerly been the creed of the Canadian Liberal party. Not only the cities, but most of the country towns, are now the seats of mills and busy industries which supply the west, export to Europe, and of course serve their own rural districts. The latter, which till the 'seventies, like so much of England, made

WHEEL FOR CATCHING SALMON ON THE COLUMBIAN RIVER OREGON

SALMON JUMPING: THE FISHERS HAULING IN THEIR NETS

A FINE CATCH OF ROYAL CHINOOK SALMON

SALMON FISHING IN CANADIAN WATERS

grain its principal crop, like Great Britain, suffered sorely, till at last it had to confess itself beaten in this phase of agriculture by western competition.

Now, however, the Ontario farmer, who is the freeholder of from one to two hundred acres, with buildings equal to those of an English farm twice the size, has readjusted his system. Dairying, co-operation, fruit, mixed products and careful stockbreeding have made him once more a prosperous man, and his farm, speaking generally, worth as much as it was in 1873. He may send his surplus sons out to the west, but he now no longer wants to go himself. All the religious creeds flourish

The province of Quebec, with 1,648,898 population, is to-day more French than ever, and differs wholly in character from Ontario. The exodus to the north-west has affected those few portions of it that were in part or whole English, notably the eastern townships, far more than the others, for the sufficient reason that the man of British origin is much readier than the other definitely to sever home ties and advance his fortune in distant countries Where the British farmer steps out, the French Canadian steps in, and a considerable displacement of this kind has been proceeding for a generation. The city of Montreal is not typical of the province of

THE WINTER SEASON IN CANADA: A CHARACTERISTIC SNOW SCENE

in the province, so does education. Besides the common free schools, intermediate schools, and a few of the English public school type, there is a flourishing university at Toronto, to which various colleges are affiliated, and the MacGill University at Montreal, which is quite as important. The chartered banks, originated largely by the Family Compact, and increasing with the growth of the country, are the one branch of commerce in which the Canadians are indisputably in advance of the United States ; and the Bank of Montreal, the chief of many sound and old-established banks, has no equal in North America.

Quebec save for the fact that about five-sixths of its population are French. It is the commercial capital and the wealthiest and finest city of Canada, the summer port for ocean navigation, and the distributing point for all winter freights that come from the open ports of Halifax and St. John.

The commercial wealth of the city is mainly in Anglo-Canadian hands, though there is a large element of well-to-do and educated French Canadians. With the exception of Ottawa in political circles, and Quebec on a smaller scale, Montreal is the only part of Canada where French and English in great numbers live as

MEDICINE HAT: A VILLAGE ON THE CANADIAN PACIFIC RAILWAY

immediate neighbours, and in the upper classes the majority of the former are bilingual. Yet in no class, strange to say, to any extent worthy of mention, do they mix together socially or intermarry. The bitter feeling of the past is practically dead, but the continuous cleavage and utter inability to coalesce, particularly among the more enlightened and wealthier elements living side by side and so interested materially in the welfare of their common city and country, are noteworthy and curious facts. It should be said, however, that religion accounts for this in a great measure, which again will seem somewhat paradoxical when the fact is stated that there is practically no sectarian bitterness such as distinguishes Protestant and Roman Catholic in Ireland, or even Nonconformist and Anglican in Wales.

The two races take each other's faiths simply as a matter of course, and as individuals at least give no further thought to the matter. But the Roman Church in Canada, for doctrinal reasons, throws every impediment in the way of intermarriage, and the French Canadian, unlike the European Frenchman, with a few exceptions is a staunch and obedient son of his Church, which in Montreal possesses the most splendid cathedral in North America. This alone must discourage social fusion. That the French Canadians, in the cities at least, could remain uninfluenced by Anglo-Canadian and American influences is of course out of the question. But the cleavage is very marked, and is due also to yet other reasons. The French Canadian is educated in different schools and universities, and is fed on the literature of Old France, much as he abominates the political and religious methods of modern France.

The great and finely equipped University of Laval, in Quebec, with a branch in Montreal, is the Alma Mater of all the college-bred, and is the leading Roman Catholic institution of North America. Something also must be attributed to the ancient habit of separation, which in the higher circles was mainly the fault of the English. The French have the credit of being, on the whole, the more cultured, as they are the less materially vigorous, of

CANADIAN OATFIELD, SHOWING BY CONTRAST THE GREAT HEIGHT OF THE GRAIN

RED SUCKER TRESTLE BRIDGE ON LAKE SUPERIOR

MOUNTAIN CREEK BRIDGE, CONTAINING ONE AND A HALF MILLION FEET OF TIMBER

SCENES ON THE CANADIAN PACIFIC RAILWAY

THE GRAND TRUNK RAILWAY STATION AT HAMILTON, ONTARIO

THE TERMINAL YARDS OF THE SYSTEM AT FORT WILLIAM

Photos on this page and pages 6069, 6152, 6158 and 6174 by courtesy of the London "Canada" newspaper

SCENES ON THE GRAND TRUNK RAILWAY

THE RACECOURSE ON THE FROZEN RIVER ST. LAWRENCE AT MONTREAL

the two. But that has nothing to do with the cleavage, nor must the reader who has followed this story contract the notion that there is any remnant of the old noblesse cherishing exclusive sentiments. The latter were not strong enough or splendid enough to send down a surviving caste through four or five generations of a democracy. Descendants of the old seigniorial families enjoy just such distinction as attaches to the descendants of the quasi-military U. E. loyalist, and other English families of the Family Compact type. But it is purely sentimental, as both, like all Canadians, have had to earn their living in professions or in trade, and have intermarried freely with others who have not their particular claims.

To sum up the question of modern French Canadians' feeling, so far as the subject can be dealt with in a few words, the attitude of the enlightened classes in Montreal, Quebec, Ottawa and various small towns —for the peasantry think nothing about the matter—implies neither cordiality nor yet ill-will between the races. They live apart as people of different ideas and tastes, not as enemies who have quarrelled, though there is sometimes friction. On the other hand, there are, of course, innumerable exceptions to prove a rule which is a matter of Nature, instinct and tradition rather than of design or culpable bigotry. In all things that really matter, the French Canadian nowadays is a quite sound element in the British Empire. His destiny is virtually fixed for him. Any thought of political affiliation to modern France is utterly distasteful. And if it were not so his Ultramontane Church, to which he is entirely devoted, would regard such a possibility with abhorrence. Annexation to the United States has not a single attraction to recommend it.

Such dislike as he may feel for the Anglo-Saxon would be there intensified, while his peculiar privileges, such as an endowed religion, his laws and his language would be in the utmost peril. Canadian independence is not an impossibility at some future day. The French Canadian, however, would probably hail it with less enthusiasm than the other. For this kind of independence would chiefly centre on the Anglo-Saxon, whose preponderance increases yearly. It is unreasonable, again, to expect the French Canadian to have the same zeal for the empire outside Canada that most of us have ourselves. To expect him to volunteer to cross the seas and fight our battles like the Anglo-Canadian is to expect too much of human nature.

LITTLE CHAMPLAIN STREET: QUEBEC'S QUAINT AND PICTURESQUE THOROUGHFARE

The French habitant is in almost full possession of the soil of Quebec, both of the old seigniories and of the regions outside them, which was settled by British immigrants who since then have shifted westward. The province has a less fertile soil and a more rigorous climate than Ontario. In some districts agriculture is fairly progressive. But for the most part the habitant on his long farms of fifty acres or so, though still reckoned by him in the ancient French measure of *arpents*, is unimproving and unambitious. Content with his surroundings, attached to his native country, submissive to his priest, loyal to all observances of his Church, including its holidays, cheerful and prolific, and possessed of a sufficiency of simple comfort, he is a complete contrast to the typical, strenuous English-speaking farmer of Canada or the United States. He usually knows no English, and his speech, with certain modifications, is that of the seventeenth century peasant of Northern France. He is fond of music and dancing, which help to beguile the long winters, and still sings the songs his ancestors brought over from Normandy and Picardy. Though the tendency of the habitant, who occupies the picturesque country along both shores of the St. Lawrence for a hundred miles below Quebec and for more than that between Quebec and Montreal is conservative and home-staying, he sends out two classes of wanderers in great numbers, who keep him and his in frequent touch with the wider world. Nearly a million French Canadians are scattered about New England, working in the factories, and remaining as a rule homogeneous in large groups with their own priests. All through the lumber-camps and saw-mills of Canada, too, " Jean Baptiste " is in great demand. These wanderers, however, keep in touch with their old homes to an infinitely greater extent than British Canadians in the same situation, frequently returning there to settle down, bringing money with them ; and not only money, but ideas somewhat modifying the old elementary conditions and causing anxiety to the excellent priests, whose influence, speaking generally, has always been, and most effectively, exerted in the excellent cause of law and order. Education in French Canada, though administered as elsewhere by a department of the provincial government, is by common consent controlled by the Church ; which owns, moreover, an immense amount of property in the province. If the practical results are for obvious reasons inferior to those obtained in the common schools of Ontario, there are compensations from the French

SNOW-SHED ON THE CANADIAN PACIFIC RAILWAY
The protection of the line during the winter months is a matter of serious importance to the engineers of the Canadian Pacific Railway in the Rockies. The scene of the above picture is particularly exposed to snowslides and avalanches ; hence to meet this emergency snow-sheds are built, which carry the accumulation of snow and ice over the track.

Catholic point of view which are no concern of their British Protestant neighbours. The English districts of Quebec have their own government schools as in Ontario, and there is no friction whatever between the creeds.

Higher education in the province is admirable, with Laval University at its head. The latter is conservative, and still makes the classical and literary standard too prominent in the opinion of many for the North American atmosphere, while the convents educate the women of the same class. The provincial government

THE DOMINION HOUSE OF PARLIAMENT AT OTTAWA

BRITISH COLUMBIA'S HOUSE OF LEGISLATURE AT VICTORIA

ONTARIO'S SEAT OF GOVERNMENT AT TORONTO

THE DOMINION PARLIAMENT AND PROVINCIAL LEGISLATIVE BUILDINGS

QUEBEC, CANADA'S QUAINT AND PICTURESQUE CITY

HALIFAX, NOVA SCOTIA'S IMPORTANT SEAPORT

WINNIPEG, THE FLOURISHING SEAT OF THE MANITOBAN GOVERNMENT

Photos: Valentine

CANADIAN PROVINCIAL LEGISLATIVE BUILDINGS

buildings are at Quebec, the only province except Nova Scotia that has an upper house nominated for life by the governor in council. The legislators and executive are mainly, though not all, Frenchmen, that language being chiefly used in debate; and here, as in the other provinces, lawyers are the strongest element both in the provincial and federal councils. It must be admitted, too, that there is undoubtedly more political corruption all over Canada than would now be tolerated in Great Britain.

It is a happy dispensation, on the whole, that the French Canadians are virtually confined to their ancient province, and, outside Montreal, have control of it, the English being too few to arouse any racial friction. As a member of the

they have agreed to differ, while in the essentials of federal life and Canadian unity and prosperity they are heartily in accord, and have nothing now of serious moment to quarrel about.

As regards the maritime provinces the recent strides made by the dominion have not been felt to the same extent as in Ontario and the west. For the last half century or more they have shared very little in the vast stream of immigration into Canada. They have lived upon their own increase, and upon that there has been a continuous drain to the more fertile and progressive regions. Little Prince Edward Island, with 100,000 souls, has long filled up as a purely agricultural country. New Brunswick, with 350,000, has received

A CHARACTERISTIC FRUIT FARM IN NOVA SCOTIA

federation at Ottawa, Quebec plays a worthy and patriotic part. The new prosperity of the dominion has been sensibly felt even by this, its least active member, and a great deal of American capital has been expended in mills and mines. The French vote, though apt to go nearly solid under a leader like Sir Wilfrid Laurier, simply from racial pride in his achievements, in normal times has before, and doubtless will again, divide on other than racial lines. There seems no reason to anticipate any more of the old bitterness and civic strife between the races. Their difference in temperament and habit has now free scope without clashing. In all their domestic concerns

in its open port for ocean business of St. John an immense access of trade and prosperity; but the province generally pursues an uneventful agricultural existence in method and manners like Ontario, with less of its push, and unrelieved by the pressure of large and small industrial centres. Its forests, like those of the latter, still yield a revenue to the lumberman, whether for sawn timber or the pulp and paper manufacture that has recently converted into a valuable asset thousands of square miles of timber, hitherto only fitted for firewood, and practically valueless.

There is a vast area of land in New Brunswick that if cleared of forests would carry a farming population. But the

A PRETTY VIEW NEAR SYDNEY, ON THE ISLAND OF CAPE BRETON

GENERAL VIEW FROM CAPE BLOMIDON, LOOKING ACROSS MINES BASIN

SCENES IN THE CANADIAN PROVINCE OF NOVA SCOTIA

Photos on this page and pages 6067, 6144, 6154 and 6156 by courtesy of the Canadian Emigration Office

THE TOWN OF RAT PORTAGE, ON THE LAKE OF THE WOODS, ONTARIO

best has long been cleared and occupied, and, as in old Ontario, men with all North America to select from will no longer laboriously clear timber from second or third rate land when unencumbered first-class land can be had in the west. The population includes many races, the old Acadians among them, but by far the prevailing stock is British, mostly sprung from the original U. E. loyalists.

The same general description will apply to Nova Scotia, with rather less than 600,000 inhabitants; but to both, more particularly to the latter, must be added a fishing population and a fishing industry. Nova Scotia is the more attractive country, while both have a climate of much the same quality, but more foggy and milder than Quebec. Halifax, a naval station and commercial port, but no longer of its old military importance, is less progressive than St. John; but Sydney, on Cape Breton, near the scene of the old fortress town of Louisbourg, now vanished, is assuming important dimensions as a busy centre of the coal and iron industry. To the ordinary agricultural industry of Nova Scotia, which has long ago cleared all

the land at present worth clearing, must be added the famous apple orchards of the Annapolis Valley, and other districts so well known in the English market.

As a last word on Canada one may say that it is a country which from the time of the loyalists' influx, the true beginning of modern Canada, grew slowly and surely by hard work. Till a dozen years ago it was accounted, and actually was, a relatively poor country, a land of simple but widely diffused comfort, where individual wealth was rare, and individual expenditure through all classes on a proportionately modest scale, quite different from that of the United States, or, again, of Australia, where great fortunes were accumulated early in her history. The average individual, whether farmer, trader or professional man, of course only does as well or a little better than he did before, but his opportunities are greater and more varied. He feels he is part of a country that has made a solid leap forward, which has astonished the world, and, I may add, himself. But beyond the average man there are now great numbers of wealthy capitalists and millionaires

AUTUMN PLOUGHING IN CARLTON COUNTY, NEW BRUNSWICK

PINE-FOREST SCENERY ON THE RAILWAY SYSTEM OF WESTERN CANADA

PASSENGER STEAMBOAT IN THE LACHINE RAPIDS ON THE ST. LAWRENCE RIVER

TRAVELLING BY RAIL AND RIVER IN CANADA

CAPE BRETON'S CAPITAL TOWN: GENERAL VIEW OF SYDNEY

and corporations, almost a new element in the country created not by gold discoveries or booms, but by the development of solid assets that have lain hitherto partly dormant; why they have done so is something of a mystery, even to the most experienced Canadians, though a dozen reasons, irrelevant here, may be suggested. The Canadian Pacific road was unquestionably the foundation of the new era. But for many years after its completion the country scarcely moved beyond its old slow and measured rate.

It was still half despised, not only by its great neighbour but a little sneered at as well by the more feverish new countries and by European capitalists who operated in such arenas. Nor was it even rated highly by the intending emigrant of enterprise and means, and much abused by many who went there. But in a fashion, and with a suddenness unexpected and unexampled in the history of colonisation, a country intimately known for a century seemed all at once in the closing years of the last to discover its true resources, not merely to the outside world but to its own people. A certain congestion of prosperity and population, if one may use the word advisedly, in the United States, which found a profitable outlet in Canada, was a powerful factor in the movement.

A great and successful effort to turn emigration to Canada from Great Britain and Europe seconded the other, while this concentration of forces was encouraged by a succession of fat crop years. All these things stimulated the Canadians, and stirred to exceptional energy a people who had in themselves an enormous latent power of work that had hitherto only met with moderate encouragement. But, whatever the causes, the sudden rise of Canada to an altogether higher scale of material importance is a permanent fact. Whatever commercial reaction, inevitable to all countries, may be in store for it can make no difference to this. Only Canadians, perhaps, or those who have known their country well, can fully realise the gulf that lies between the Canada of the twentieth and that of the nineteenth century.

A. G. BRADLEY

NORTH BATTLEFORD BRIDGE, ONE OF THE LONGEST IN CANADA

CANADA PAST AND PRESENT

Valentine

GENERAL VIEW OF THE CITY, LOOKING FROM VICTORIA TOWER

PANORAMA OF THE CITY AND RIVER FROM PARLIAMENT BUILDINGS

OTTAWA, THE CAPITAL OF THE DOMINION OF CANADA

6159

MASSES OF FLOATING LUMBER IN THE OTTAWA RIVER

OTTAWA'S FLOURISHING AGRICULTURAL MARKET

SCENES OF TO-DAY IN CANADA'S CAPITAL CITY

THE RIVER SOURIS NEAR ITS ENTRANCE INTO THE GULF OF ST. LAWRENCE

A PRETTY VIEW OF POWNAL, WITH THE BAY IN THE DISTANCE

Valentine

ON THE ROAD: A CHARACTERISTIC SIGHT IN PRINCE EDWARD ISLAND

PRINCE EDWARD ISLAND, CANADA'S ISLAND PROVINCE

THE CITY AS IT LOOKED SEVENTY YEARS AGO

A VIEW TAKEN FROM MOUNT ROYAL IN 1840

THE MARVELLOUS GROWTH OF THE CITY OF MONTREAL

GENERAL VIEW OF MONTREAL, WITH THE ST. LAWRENCE IN THE BACKGROUND

MONTREAL'S PRINCIPAL THOROUGHFARE, SHOWING G.P.O. AND BANK

GENERAL VIEW OF MONTREAL'S EXTENSIVE HARBOUR   Valentine

MONTREAL TO-DAY: THE COMMERCIAL METROPOLIS OF THE DOMINION

BRITISH MEN-OF-WAR AT QUEBEC IN 1840

THE WORLD-FAMOUS VIEW FROM THE CITADEL IN 1840

QUEBEC AT THE BEGINNING OF QUEEN VICTORIA'S REIGN

THE MODERN CITY, AS SEEN FROM PARLIAMENT BUILDINGS   Valentine

THE CHATEAU FRONTENAC AND PART OF THE LOWER TOWN   C. P. R.

QUEBEC'S WAREHOUSES AND WHARVES, WITH CITADEL TO EXTREME LEFT

QUEBEC TO-DAY: THE THIRD LARGEST CITY IN CANADA

QUEEN'S AVENUE, FROM PARLIAMENT BRIDGE

A PICTURESQUE VIEW OF THE CITY IN 1840

YONGE STREET, ONE OF THE CITY'S CHIEF THOROUGHFARES

TORONTO, THE BEAUTIFUL CAPITAL OF ONTARIO

VANCOUVER'S SPACIOUS HARBOUR AND WHARVES

THE COMMODIOUS DOCK OF THE CANADIAN PACIFIC RAILWAY

THE CITY AS SEEN FROM THE CANADIAN PACIFIC RAILWAY HOTEL

VANCOUVER, THE PROSPEROUS CAPITAL OF BRITISH COLUMBIA

TOWN AND RIVER AS THEY WERE IN 1840

THE HARBOUR FRONT AS IT IS TO-DAY

ST. JOHN, NEW BRUNSWICK: PAST AND PRESENT

REVERSIBLE FALLS, SHOWING TIDE RUNNING DOWN THE ST. JOHN RIVER

Valentine

THE WEST END, THE FAVOURITE RESIDENTIAL QUARTER

SCENES OF TO-DAY IN THE PICTURESQUE CITY OF ST. JOHN

THE VILLAGE OF WINNIPEG FORTY YEARS AGO

MAIN STREET, WINNIPEG'S CHIEF THOROUGHFARE

WINNIPEG AS IT WAS IN 1870, AND AS IT IS TO-DAY

THE UNION BANK OF CANADA AND THE CITY HALL, WINNIPEG

GENERAL VIEW, WITH THE MUNICIPAL BUILDINGS IN THE MIDDLE DISTANCE

WINNIPEG, THE CAPITAL OF THE PROVINCE OF MANITOBA

6171

BIRD'S-EYE VIEW OF HALIFAX, SHOWING ITS FINE HARBOUR

Valentine

HALIFAX IN 1849, WHEN IT WAS JUST A HUNDRED YEARS OLD

GENERAL ASPECT OF THE HARBOUR FROM THE CITADEL

CITY AND SEAPORT OF HALIFAX, THE CAPITAL OF NOVA SCOTIA

A BEAUTIFUL VALLEY SCENE IN BRITISH COLUMBIA

AN EXPERIMENTAL FARM AT AGASSIZ

A TOWNSHIP OF BRITISH COLUMBIA, ON THE FRASER RIVER

TYPICAL SCENES IN BRITISH COLUMBIA

EDMONTON, THE IMPORTANT FUR-TRADE CENTRE OF ALBERTA

CALGARY, A THRIVING AGRICULTURAL TOWN

TWO PROSPEROUS CANADIAN COMMUNITIES

INFORMATION ABOUT CANADA AND NEWFOUNDLAND

CANADA

AREA AND POPULATION. The Dominion of Canada comprises the whole of British North America except Newfoundland and Labrador, which belongs to Newfoundland. The total area of the dominion is estimated at 3,745,574 square miles, which includes 125,756 miles of water surface. The area is about as large as that of Europe. The population of Canada, in 1901, was 5,371,315, and the estimation of the present population is about 7,000,000. The provinces and territories of Canada, with their land areas and populations, are as follow :

—	Area. Square miles.	Population.	Capital.	Population of Capital. (1901).
Nova Scotia	21,068	459,574	Halifax	40,832
New Brunswick	27,911	331,120	Fredericton ..	7,117
Prince Edward Island..	2,184	107,259	Charlottet wn	12,080
Quebec	341,756	1,648,898	Quebec	72,840
Ontario	220,508	2,182,947	Toronto	208,040
Manitoba	64,327	360,590	Winnipeg ..	43,340
British Columbia	383,300	178,657	Victoria	20,816
Saskatchewan	242,332	91,460	Regina	2,645
Alberta	251,180	72,841	Edmonton ..	2,626
Keewatin (district) ..	500,191	9,800	—	—
Yukon (territory) ..	196,327	27,219	Dawson	27,219
North-west Territories :				
Mackenzie	562,182	5,216	—	—
Ungava	354,961	5,113	—	—
Franklin	500,000	—	—	—

Keewatin is the district to the west and south-west of Hudson Bay, and is administered by the Lieutenant-Governor of Manitoba. The only permanent settlements in it are trading stations of the Hudson Bay Company. There are some Esquimaux in the north. The same conditions of settlement and population prevail in Mackenzie and Ungava, although these territories are at least as habitable as Yukon.

The figures of population given above are now much under the actual facts, especially in Manitoba, Saskatchewan and Alberta, whither during recent years the great streams of Canadian immigration have gone. Winnipeg has now over 150,000 inhabitants, and the other towns have received great increases.

Ottawa, in the province of Ontario, is the capital of the dominion (population 59,928). The other chief towns, with their populations at last census, are as follow :

NOVA SCOTIA. Sydney, 10,000 ; Yarmouth, 6,500 ; Truro, 6,000 ; Springfield, 5,200 ; Amherst, 5,000 ; Dartmouth, 4,800 ; New Glasgow, 4,500.

NEW BRUNSWICK. St. John (including Portland), 40,711 ; Monckton, 9,026.

PRINCE EDWARD ISLAND. Summerside, 3,000.

QUEBEC. Montreal, 270,000 ; St. Henri, 21,192 ; Hull, 13,993 ; Sherbrooke, 11,765 ; Valleyfield, 11,055 ; St. Louis de Mile End, 10,933 ; St. Cunegonde, 10,912 ; Three Rivers, 9,981.

ONTARIO. Hamilton, 52,000 ; London, 37,000 ; Kingston, 18,000 ; Brantford, 17,000 ; Windsor, 12,000 ; St. Thomas, 11,500 ; Guelph, 11,500.

MANITOBA. Portage la Prairie, 3,900 ; Brandon, 5,380 ; Selkirk, 2,190.

BRITISH COLUMBIA. Vancouver, 26,196 ; New Westminster, 8,000 ; Nanaimo, 5,000.

ALBERTA. Calgary, 4,152.

In the other territories there are no settlements worthy of the designation of towns.

GOVERNMENT. Canada is a constitutional self-governing colony of the United Kingdom. The executive authority is vested in the Sovereign of Great Britain and Ireland, and is exercised by a Governor-General and a Privy Council. The Canadian Parliament is composed of a Senate (the Upper Chamber) and a House of Commons. The members represent the provinces in the following proportion :

	Senate.	Commons.		Senate.	Commons.
Nova Scotia	10	18	Manitoba	4	10
New Brunswick ..	10	13	British Columbia	3	7
Prince Edward Isl'd	4	4	Alberta	4	7
Quebec	24	65	Saskatchewan ..	4	10
Ontario	24	86	Yukon	—	1

The life of a parliament is not longer than five years. The qualification for the vote varies in different provinces, but the franchise is low in all. Members are paid £500 a year, with a reduction of £3 for each day's absence during the session. The king's Privy Council consists of 14 heads of departments, each of whom receives a salary of £1,400 a year, with £2,400 for the Prime Minister, these salaries being in addition to the sessional fees. The Leader of the Opposition in the House of Commons (but not in the Senate) is also paid a salary of £1,400 a year. The provinces have each a separate parliament and a Lieutenant-Governor, who is appointed by the Governor-General.

REVENUE. The revenue for 1908 was £19,210,901, and the expenditure was £15,328,290. More than half of the revenue is derived from customs, and the other chief sources are excise, public works, post-office and lands. The total public debt in 1907 was £75,993,365. The annual charge, including sinking fund, is over £2,500,000 annually.

TRADE. The total imports for 1906 (the last year of which complete figures for twelve months are available) were of the value of £59,000,000, and the total exports were £51,320,000. The chief articles of export are wood and its manufactures, wheat, cheese, cattle, bacon, gold quartz, silver ore, copper ore, flour, butter, fruit, coal, codfish, wood, pulp, furs, hides and skins, salmon, oats, lobsters, sheep, and leather goods. The Canadian preferential tariff admits goods from Great Britain and British colonies at a rate of duty lower than that upon similar goods from other countries. The rebate was formerly one-third of the duty, but in 1906 this general rebate was cancelled, and a specific rebate applied to the different items in the schedule. The effect of the preferential tariff has been to stay the decline in the importation of British goods proportionate to the total imports. Canada has made immense progress in developing her manufactures, which in aggregate value excel the total value of the produce of her mines, forests and fisheries.

WEIGHTS, MEASURES AND CURRENCY. The weights and measures are as in Great Britain, but the hundredweight contains only 100 lb., and the ton 2,000 lb. The currency is based on a dollar of 100 cents, one sovereign equalling 4·86 dollars. British and United States gold coins are legal, and United States notes and coins circulate freely.

NEWFOUNDLAND

Newfoundland, Britain's oldest colony, has an area of 43,734 square miles, and a population of 217,037. Labrador, which is under the government of Newfoundland, has an area of about 120,000 square miles, and a population of 3,634. The capital of the colony is St. John's, with a population of 29,594 ; and the other towns, with their populations, are : Harbour Grace, 5,184 ; Carbonear, 3,703 ; Twillingate, 3,542 ; and Bonavista, 3,696.

GOVERNMENT. Government is vested in the Sovereign of Great Britain, and is exercised through a Governor appointed by the King, and assisted by a two-chambered Parliament. The Legislative Council, or Upper House, consists of 18 life members appointed by the Crown ; and the House of Assembly has 36 members, who are elected for four years by the 18 districts into which the colony is divided. There is manhood suffrage. There is also an Executive Council of not more than nine members, who constitute the Cabinet. Members of the Executive Council and of the Legislative Council are paid.

FINANCE. The revenue of Newfoundland for 1906-7 was £567,428, and the expenditure was £542,358. The public debt is £4,474,374.

RESOURCES AND TRADE. The principal industry of Newfoundland is fishing—cod-fishing in summer, and seal-fishing in spring and winter. Herring and lobster fishing are also of some importance. The value of fish and fish products, including sealskins, exported in 1906, was almost £2,000,000. Agriculture is pursued by small farmers, but, on account of climatic conditions, can never be a predominant industry. The timber wealth of the island is great, and a large wood-pulp industry is being established. Minerals abound. Coal exists, but is not largely worked. Copper and iron are worked, and the value of these exported in 1906 was about £300,000. The riches of the interior of the island have long been neglected, but are now attracting capital and enterprise. There are many attractions for the sportsman—caribou, trout, and salmon abounding. Manufactures are almost negligible, and the only ones worth mentioning are the manufacture of seal and cod-liver oil, and lobster canning. The exports in 1906-7, consisting almost entirely of fish, fish products, and metallic ores, were of the value of £2,420,230, of which Great Britain took about 12 per cent. The total value of imports for the same year was £2,085,208, of which Great Britain supplied about 24 per cent.

CURRENCY, WEIGHTS AND MEASURES. These are similar to the Canadian. [See above.]

POST AND TELEGRAPH RATES

POSTAGE. Great Britain to Canada and Newfoundland : For letters, papers, etc., as to other British colonies [see page 1002], but to Canada there is a special magazine post rate of 1d. per lb. or fraction thereof above 1 lb. Parcel post to Canada, 8d. for 1lb., and 6d. for each excess lb. or fraction thereof up to 11lb. To Newfoundland, 1s., 2s., and 3s. for 3, 7, and 11lb. respectively.

TELEGRAMS. To Canada from 1s. to 3s. 2d. per word, according to destination ; to Newfoundland, 1s. per word.

INFORMATION ABOUT BERMUDAS AND WEST INDIES

BERMUDAS

The Bermudas, or Somers' Islands, consist of some 360 small islands and rocks in the North Atlantic, 600 miles east from Cape Hatteras. About twenty of them are inhabited. The total area is about 20 square miles, of which the largest island contains 16 square miles. The population, excluding army and navy, is 17,535, of which 6,718 are white. The chief town and capital is Hamilton, with a population of 2,246. The islands are a British colony, and an important naval station. There is a Governor, assisted by an Executive Council of six members appointed by the Crown, a Legislative Council of nine members appointed by the Crown, and a House of Assembly consisting of 36 members elected on a property qualification (£60). The average strength of the military and naval force stationed in the islands is about 3,000. There are 4,000 acres under cultivation, and the chief products are onions, potatoes, early vegetables, lily bulbs and arrowroot, almost all of which go to the United States. In 1906 revenue was £53,213 ; expenditure, £69,064 ; exports, excluding specie, £121,295; and imports, £398,176. The islands are a favourite winter resort for Americans.

WEST INDIES

The West India Islands, in the wider definition of the term, include the island and state of Cuba, the island of Hayti, which contains the two republics of Hayti and San Domingo, and the islands claimed as possessions by several of the Powers of Europe and the United States of America, which now own Porto Rico. Geographically, the islands are divided into the Bahamas, the Greater Antilles and the Lesser Antilles, and the last named are divided into the Leeward Islands and the Windward Islands. The total area of the whole is about 95,000 square miles, 83,000 of which belong to the Greater Antilles. The total population is about 4,000,000.

CUBA.

Cuba is the largest of the West India Islands, with an area of about 44,000 square miles and a population of a little under 2,000,000. The island is divided into six provinces. The capital is Havana, with a population of 262,395 ; and other chief towns, with populations, are : Cienfuegos, 59,128 ; Santiago, 45,478 ; Matanzas, 45,282 ; Cardenas, 26,448 ; Puerto Principe, 25,102. The island is an independent republic under the suzerainty of the United States of America. On account of internal disturbances the United States intervened in 1906 and appointed a provisional governor ; but Cuban autonomy will be restored whenever the moment seems propitious. The revenue for 1908–9 was £6,128,159. A loan of £7,000,000 at 5 per cent. was authorised in 1902. The exports for 1907 were of the value of £24,290,124. There is a reciprocal fiscal arrangement with the United States. The chief crops are sugar, tobacco and fruit, and timber is a valuable resource. Iron, copper, and manganese are mined. American capital and enterprise are fast developing the resources of the island state.

HAYTI.

The Republic of Hayti, which forms the western and smaller portion of the island of Hayti, has an area of about 10,200 square miles, and a population, chiefly black and mulatto, the estimates of which vary from 1,500,000 to 2,500,000. The capital is Port-au-Prince, with a population of 101,133. The president is elected by the Senate (39 members elected indirectly for six years), and the Chamber of Representatives (95 members elected for three years on a manhood suffrage). The chief products are coffee, cocoa, cotton, logwood, gaic-wood and hides. Political and revolutionary turmoil hinders progress. There are both import and export duties. Revenue, 1906–7, £957,045 ; public debt, £5,712,268; exports are estimated at about £3,000,000, but the exact figures are not available.

SAN DOMINGO.

The Republic of San Domingo, the eastern and larger portion of the island of Hayti, has an area of 18,045 square miles, and an estimated population of 300,000. The capital is San Domingo, with a population of 20,000 ; other towns, with their populations, are : Santiago, 12,000 ; Puerto Plata, 6,000 ; Macoris, 5,000. There is a President, chosen for four years, and a Cabinet Council of six members who form the Executive, also a National Congress of 24 deputies elected for four years by the provinces and districts. Revenue, 1906, £933,140 ; external debt, £3,885,350 ; exports (1907) £1,525,670. The chief products and exports are sugar, cocoa, tobacco, bananas, coffee, hides, wax, honey, timber, fibres.

BRITISH WEST INDIES.

The British West India Islands have an area of about 13,750 square miles, and a population of about 1,350,000.

Politically, the West Indian Islands are divided as follows :

—	Area. Sq. Miles.	Population.	Capital.	Population of Capital.
Jamaica, with Turk and Caicos Islands, Cayman Islands	4,424	639,491	Kingston	46,542
Bahamas	5,794	57,714	Nassau	10,000
Leeward Islands ..	701	127,536	St. John	9,262
Barbados ..	166	196,287	Bridgetown	22,000
The Windward Islands ..	358	35,464	St. George	5,188
Trinidad and Tobago ..	1,868	334,543	Port of Spain	54,100

The area, population and products of the individual islands are as follow :

—	Area. Sq. Miles.	Population.	Principal Products.
Jamaica	4,207	830,261	Bananas, oranges, sugar, rum, coffee, cocoa, dyewoods.
Turk and Caicos Islands	170	5,287	Salt, sponges, sisal-hemp.
Cayman Islands ..	55	5,919	Coconuts, turtles and turtle-shells, cattle, fibre.
Bahamas	5,794	54,714	Cattle, sponges, turtles, pine-apples, oranges, sisal-hemp.
Leeward Islands—			
Antigua	108	34,953	Sugar, pineapples.
Barbuda	62½	775	Cattle, salt, phosphates.
Redonda		120	
St Kitts ..	65	30,876	Sugar, rum, cotton.
Nevis ..	50	13,087	
Anguilla ..	35	3,699	Garden produce, salt phosphates, cattle.
Dominica	291	30,790	Cocoa, lime-juice, spices, fruit, coffee.
Montserrat	32	13,127	Sugar, limes, cocoa, coffee.
Virgin Islands ..	58	4,639	Sugar, cotton.
Barbados	166	196,287	Sugar, molasses, aloes.
Windward Islands—			
St. Lucia	234	54,599	Sugar, cocoa, spices, tobacco.
St. Vincent ..	132	51,779	Sugar, cocoa, arrowroot, vegetables, fruit, poultry.
Grenadines ..	25	6,400	Cocoa, spices, cotton, sugar.
Grenada ..	133	69,784	
Trinidad ..	1,754	315,343	Cocoa, sugar, asphalt, fibre, coconuts.
Tobago.. ..	114	19,200	

For the forms of government of these, see page 5439.

FRENCH WEST INDIES.

The possessions of France in the West Indies, with their areas and populations, are as follow :

—	Area. Sq. Miles.	Population.	Capital.	Population of Capital.
Martinique	390	182,024	Fort Royal, or Fort de France	27,069
Guadeloupe, consisting of the islands of Basseterre and Grandterre, and several small islands	688	190,273	Basseterre ..	8,626

Each of the two colonies is represented in Paris by a senator and two deputies, and each is administered by a Governor and a Council. The chief products are sugar, rum, coffee, cotton, cocoa, bananas and logwood. Exports in 1907; from Martinique, £759,889 ; from Guadeloupe, £650,757.

DUTCH WEST INDIES.

The islands owned by Holland are Curaçao, Buen Ayre or Bonaire, Aruba, St. Eustatius and Saba, with part of the island of St. Martin. See page 5363.

DANISH WEST INDIES.

The Danish West Indies are Santa Cruz, St. Thomas and St. John. See page 5415.

UNITED STATES' POSSESSION in WEST INDIES.

Porto Rico, which has an area of 3,435 square miles and a population of about 1,000,000, has belonged to the United States since 1898. The chief towns are San Juan, with a population of 32,048; and Ponce, with a population of 27,952. It is administered by a Governor, with an Executive Council of 11 members (six official and five non-official), and a Legislative Assembly of 35 members elected for two years on a low property and educational qualification. The chief products are coffee, fruit, tobacco and sugar. Exports in 1906–7, £5,550,756.

POSTAGE RATES AND TELEGRAMS

POSTAGE. Great Britain to West Indies : To British possessions as to other British colonies [see page 1002], and to other points as to foreign countries [see page 5398]. Parcels post to Cuba, and French and Danish West Indies, 2s., 3s., and 4s. for 3lb., 7lb., and 11lb. respectively ; to all British possessions in West Indies, half of these rates ; to Dutch West Indies, 3s. 6d., 4s., 4s. 6d. ; to San Domingo, 3s., 4s., and 5s.

TELEGRAMS from 1s. 8d. to 7s. 5d. per word, according to destination.

NEWFOUNDLAND, THE WEST INDIES AND BRITISH CENTRAL AMERICA

By W. H. Woodward

ENGLISH rights over Newfoundland date from the discovery of the "New Found Isle" by Cabot in 1497. But the first attempt at effective occupation was made under patent of Elizabeth, by Sir Humphrey Gilbert, in 1583. His venture, however romantic as an incident in the history of plantation, was a failure. A Bristol merchant, named Guy, received an independent grant from James I., but permanent settlement dates from the expedition of Lord Baltimore in 1623.

Meantime, the island seas, and especially the "great banks" off the eastern coast, had become the seat of the finest deep-sea fishery of the world. From 1500 onwards, French, Basque and English vessels had made yearly voyages for the cod fishery. Of the 400 vessels which in 1580 were engaged in it, the majority sailed from Norman and Breton ports. With the turn of the century Englishmen rapidly outnumbered their rivals.

The English fishery was conducted by merchants and shipowners of the West Country ports, who found the capital and organised the annual voyages, which were of the nature of great oversea "adventures." To afford shelter and **A Colony in the Making** the needful premises for curing and storing the catch, rough stagings and sheds were from year to year erected at suitable points along the coast. But it early became the object of the adventurers at home to prevent permanent settlement, the growth of proprietary rights and organised administration, as being likely to restrict the free use of the shore-line. Hence the develop-ment of the colony has been largely determined by the interests, British or other, which have gathered round the fisheries.

Early in the seventeenth century the French cast about for a site for plantation, which would at once serve as a port of refuge and refit, and establish a territorial claim. From Placentia Bay, on **English and French Adventurers** the south side of the island, which was, about 1620, chosen for the purpose, the shore-men so harassed the struggling English settlements that Lord Baltimore, the proprietor, abandoned Newfoundland for Maryland. Placentia was recognised in 1662 as a French possession, with undefined boundaries. Hence, in the absence of active settlement from England, arose vague and conflicting claims to the whole island. The Peace of Utrecht—1713—put an end to French territorial rights; in return, France was accorded the right to share the fishery of the north and west coasts, permanent settlement being forbidden within these limits. Two-fifths of the coast-line were thus shut off from exploitation by the colony; and, further, it soon became evident that the French were ready to claim an exclusive and not concurrent right to the fishery itself.

The colony had, however, by this time attained recognised status. The first governor was appointed in 1728. The settlers, though few, were of a sturdy type, tenacious of their rights as against the Bristol adventurers, on the one hand, and the encroaching French fishermen on the other. By the Treaty of Paris—1763—the fishery rights conceded at Utrecht were confirmed, and in addition the two small islands, St. Pierre and Miquelon, off the south coast, were granted as the sole compensation for the loss of the vast North American domain of France. New England protested, as did the colony, and also, with considerable vigour, the great Chatham. But the English in America had won so much that they could scarcely press their complaint, which passed unheeded. At this period the settlers, chiefly in and near St. John's, numbered 8,000 in all ; but, in addition, 5,000 fishermen visited the island each summer. The apparently undue preference given to the fishing industry is explained by the fact that from English fishermen were drawn the strongest elements in our naval force. In 1765 the coast-line of Labrador facing

SEBASTIAN CABOT

Born probably at Venice in 1474, Cabot accompanied his father, John Cabot, on the famous voyage in the Matthew in 1497, when, in June of the same year Newfoundland was discovered.

turn swept from the seas. From this period dates the firm establis'ment of the prosperity of the colony. At the peace of 1815 the population reached 80,000. It was not until 1832 that a representative assembly was set up, with the usual rights over supply, but without control of the executive. Quarrels with the nominated upper house were constant, until, in 1843, the two were merged, to be again separated in 1848. Full responsible government on the Canadian model was attained in 1855. Internal progress made considerable strides. Roads were formed, a geological survey — 1838 — organised, and oversea communication developed. The great fire of 1846 destroyed St. John's, which was rebuilt on a more dignified plan. New sources of wealth

the island was added to the colony. The influence of the troubles with Massachusetts is seen in the passing of Palliser's Act of 1776, under which a bounty was offered to British seamen visiting the fishery, colonial fishermen being excluded from its benefits. The expressed object was that thereby trustworthy sailors might be trained for the defence of the realm. English prowess during the wars of the French Revolution enabled Newfoundland to command the world's market for fish, as all competitors were in

JOHN CABOT AT THE COURT OF KING HENRY VII.

Failing to enlist the support of Spain and Portugal, Cabot at last succeeded in obtaining audience with Henry VII., who, on March 5th, 1497, authorised him by letters patent to take possession on behalf of England of any countries he might discover. With his three sons, Cabot set sail in the Matthew and, on June 24th, sighted Newfoundland.

were growing up in the seal and lobster fisheries. At least a fourth of the population is still engaged directly or indirectly in the harvest of the seas. With the growth of railways the interior of the island, of which much remains unexplored, is about to be opened up. Valuable mineral areas are already defined. But the persistent assertion by French and American citizens of special rights remained acute till the year 1904, when the former finally surrendered their preferential claims, and thus enabled the western shore to be

THE CABOT MEMORIAL ON SIGNAL HILL, ST. JOHN'S, NEWFOUNDLAND

Towering on Signal Hill, 520 feet above the water and overlooking both sea and city, stands the majestic **Cabot** Tower, erected to the memory of John Cabot, the discoverer of Newfoundland. It now serves for the more practical, if more prosaic, purpose of signalling to the people of St. John's the approach of vessels into the harbour.

opened up for settlement. The privileges exercised by fishermen of Maine and New England are a subject of negotiation in 1909. Up to the present time Newfoundland has shown no desire to apply for admission to the dominion of Canada, nor does she forget that she is the oldest British possession outside the home seas. English occupation of a continuous character in the region of the Caribbean Sea dates from 1623. During the century that elapsed between the first West Indian voyage of Sebastian Cabot (1516) and the last expedition of Raleigh to Guiana (1617), men of English race appeared at intervals in Central American waters, but as marauders, illicit traders, or open enemies of Spain, not as settlers. For it was thoroughly

SIR HUMPHREY GILBERT

In 1583, Gilbert set out from Plymouth harbour to take possession of Newfoundland. On his return journey three out of his five vessels foundered off Cape Breton, himself going down in the fourth, on September 9th, 1583.

understood in London, as in Madrid, during this period, that "the Spaniards account all other nations for pirates, rovers and thieves that visit any heathen coast that they have once sailed by or looked on." But after the death of Philip II. and the English peace, Spain rapidly declined in vigour, and became tacitly content with exclusive possession of her last provinces on the American mainland, with the addition of the larger Antilles, Cuba, Hispaniola, Porto Rico and Jamaica. England and the other Western Powers were no longer disposed to recognise title which did not rest upon occupation, and the Spanish administrators had never attempted plantation upon the Lesser Antilles or the Bahamas, which were,

GROSSWATER BAY AS VIEWED FROM LESTER'S POINT

A PLEASANT BACKWATER ON THE HUMBER

ON THE BEAUTIFUL HUMBER RIVER: SCENE NEAR THE LITTLE RAPIDS

BY SEASHORE AND STREAM IN NEWFOUNDLAND

BURIN HARBOUR, REPUTED TO BE THE BEST IN NEWFOUNDLAND

A VIEW OF PLACENTIA, THE OLD FRENCH CAPITAL

QUIDI-VIDI, A PICTURESQUE FISHING SETTLEMENT NEAR ST. JOHN'S

TOWNS AND HARBOURS OF NEWFOUNDLAND

in fact, ignored by them as insignificant and economically worthless. Not until it was too late did they awaken to the agricultural possibilities and strategic importance of the outer fringe of islands which bounded their peculiar seas.

It is to be noted that the English, the Dutch, and the French took their first steps towards effective occupation of the Caribbean islands within the same decade. The Dutch West Indian Company was incorporated in 1621, the French in 1626, whilst the first English patents which led to plantation in this region fell between 1623 and 1627. The difference which characterises the activities of the four chief European Powers concerned in the colonisation of the West Indies deserves attention.

cutting off the sources of her national wealth. But they became rather the merchant traders of the islands, and having no surplus population for purposes of plantation, were content to gather in the riches won from carrying the produce of their neighbours. In fact, the development of their rich domain in the Eastern seas was, from 1620, a more urgent attraction than American colonisation.

English sovereignty in Western seas was from the first based on settlement, conducted in our national fashion by somewhat haphazard methods of private or corporate ventures. In matters of defence, the planters were largely left to themselves. War in Europe did not necessarily imply hostility between the belligerents in

BAY OF ISLANDS ON THE WEST COAST OF NEWFOUNDLAND

The prime object of Spain was to exploit the mineral wealth of her American possessions; settlement was wholly subordinate to this end. Strong military occupation, rigid government control of production, naval security of ocean routes, and a slave system were essential to her purpose.

Hence the determination of Philip II. to hold the Caribbean Sea and the Mexican Gulf as a *mare clausum*, a policy which survived as a doctrine long after Spain had lost the power of enforcing it. The French went to the West Indies as settlers and traders, working through a royal chartered company, under strict regulation, and with effective protection from the home government. The original purpose of the Dutch was to harry and cripple their ancient enemy, Spain, by

colonial waters. Planters set up their own institutions, borrowed the slave system of Spain, sent out ventures to hoist the British flag on unclaimed islands, joined in buccaneering raids against the ports and treasure fleets of the Spanish West. Two things, however, knit the English settlers into closer connection with the Mother Country—namely, the necessary dependence of the islands upon the home navy, and the ties of commerce, defined and strengthened by the Acts of Navigation.

Viewed in a strict historical sense, the West Indian possessions of England fall into the following groups : (a) the Leeward Islands; (b) Barbados ; (c) Jamaica ; (d) the Bahamas ; (e) the Windward Islands ; (f) Trinidad and Tobago ; (g) British Guiana and Honduras.

"THE NARROWS," FROM CHURCH HILL, SHOWING BRITISH WARSHIPS

ICE IN THE ENTRANCE TO ST. JOHN'S HARBOUR

THE LAND-LOCKED HARBOUR AND TOWN OF ST. JOHN'S

SCENES IN AND NEAR THE CAPITAL OF NEWFOUNDLAND

GOVERNMENT HOUSE: THE ADMINISTRATOR'S RESIDENCE, ST. CHRISTOPHER

St. Kitts, or St. Christopher, received its first English settlers in 1623, and from it other islands of the Leeward group were "planted." At some time within two years a French privateer's crew landed on the opposite end of St. Kitts, which by arrangement was, in 1627, divided between the two nationalities. From St. Kitts, Nevis was settled in 1623, Montserrat in 1632, Antigua in the same year. Dominica had already been occupied by French settlers, whose principal plantations were those of Guadeloupe (1635), and Martinique in the same year. The growth of the Leewards in prosperity and population was remarkable. Tobacco was the main crop, and a profitable one. After fifteen years of occupation, St. Kitts was said to have 12,000 inhabitants — probably

an extreme estimate. But a Spanish raid in 1629, which nearly destroyed the settlements, French and English alike, brought home to the colonists their dependence upon the strong arm of the mother countries. With the exception of Barbados, the Leeward Islands were the most progressive plantations in the West Indies throughout the seventeenth century.

Barbados was formally occupied in 1625 by a company of adventurers fitted out by William Courten, under the Marlborough patent of James I. Other overlapping patents were granted in the usual careless fashion of the time to the Earl of Carlisle and the Earl of Pembroke, and these conflicting rights left their mark upon the economic history of Barbados until 1832. The reputed fertility of the island drew

A STREET SCENE IN ST. JOHN, THE CAPITAL OF ANTIGUA

THE METHOD OF DRYING FISH AT LITTLE BAY ISLAND

LANDING A HUGE "HUMP-BACKED" WHALE FOR USE IN THE OIL INDUSTRY

A BUSY TIMBER MILL AT BONNE BAY

THE FISHING AND LUMBER INDUSTRIES OF NEWFOUNDLAND

settlers from the Bermudas, and from Virginia, as well as from home. By 1636 they numbered 6,000 of British stock. In or soon after 1639, Captain Philip Bell, the governor, summoned an elective assembly, which, with the nominated executive council, became the standing type of administration in the islands.

Sugar cultivation was introduced by Dutch traders from Brazil about 1640. It should be noticed that the relations of the English colonists with the merchant seamen of Holland were always friendly, to the great profit of both. Sugar-growing developed

of substance brought their families and took up land, as Puritans did in New England. The island received also prisoners of war, certain sorts of civil offenders, and other lawless or workless folk ; all these were indentured, and such as survived forced service became free citizens. But the negro race, harder and cheaper, outstripped the rest, and by 1700 formed two-thirds of the population.

The royalist sentiment of Barbados led to hostilities with the English Parliament. In 1650, Charles II. was proclaimed in Barbados. Puritan settlers took their

A FAIR IN THE WEST INDIES: THE MARKET-PLACE AT ROSEAU, DOMINICA

rapidly, and in a few years had ousted the production of cotton and tobacco in Barbados. This was facilitated by negro slavery. Negro slavery in the West Indies dates from 1503, and was firmly established in Spanish America a century before the English settlement. The Dutch landed a cargo of negroes from Lisbon at Barbados in 1627, or soon after ; and from that time slave labour became the dominant factor in West Indian industry as in its population. Barbados, however, drew no little strength from the course of politics at home. Dissatisfied royalists

grievances to London. Led by Governor Lord Willoughby of Parham, the colonists boldly claimed the right of self-government, refused to debar the Dutch from the island ports, and met the fleet of the commonwealth with open resistance. But on January 11th, 1652, a compromise was reached. The settlers, accepting the commonwealth, were left in control of their internal affairs. Peace once established, industrial interests again absorbed the attention of the colony, which advanced in population and in esteem at home. The planters took an active part

GENERAL VIEW OF FORT-DE-FRANCE, THE CAPITAL OF THE COLONY

ST. PIERRE, FORMERLY THE PRINCIPAL TOWN, AND THE HARBOUR

RUINS AT TROIS-ILETS: THE HOUSE IN WHICH EMPRESS JOSEPHINE WAS BORN

VIEWS IN MARTINIQUE, THE SCENE OF A GREAT EARTHQUAKE

in the capture of Jamaica by Cromwell's fleet. The Restoration was welcomed, and the high-water mark of prosperity (1670-1675) attained. The little island, which is slightly larger than the Isle of Wight, was to the fore in every venture that made for British expansion in the Caribbean Sea. It was the social and political centre of the English power in the West Indies. Like Virginia, it boasted of established families of the best English blood. Barbados has never passed under foreign rule, and its development has been of a purely British type. Jamaica, though held by the Spanish administrators as a place of call, was in most other respects neglected by its rulers. It was captured by the English fleet in pursuance of Cromwell's policy in increasing the national wealth at the expense of her European enemies. Charles II. sent out its first governor, who set up the usual executive council and representative assembly. An attempt to subordinate the legislature to the English Parliament was sturdily resisted. The population of the island was of mixed origin; the best element was the New Englander and the planter from Barbados and the Leewards. But there was haste to get labour, and emigrants of worthless sort from the prisons of English towns were hurried out. Sugargrowing was from the outset the main industry of Jamaica; and as it commanded a preferential price negroes were imported on a large scale. The standing dread of a negro rising, characteristic of West Indian life, was peculiarly felt in Jamaica. The Maroons, a mixed slave race, who fled to the mountains on the English conquest, threatened the security

TYPES OF BRITISH WEST INDIAN SOLDIERS

of the planters for 200 years. The buccaneers, an organised piratical community of varied elements, had their headquarters in Jamaica and the Bahamas, whence they carried on unceasing warfare against the Spanish-American coast towns.

Their lawless violence was for a time condoned by colonial governors, both French and English. Henry Morgan, the Welshman, who led a plundering attack on Panama, and was knighted by Charles II., acted as deputy-governor of Jamaica, but was ultimately made a scapegoat to satisfy Spanish importunity. There was obviously risk as well as discredit in connivance at piracy, which was in the end sternly suppressed after the Peace of Utrecht in 1713. Meantime, Jamaica throve apace. Settlers from Guiana, and from the ill-fated enterprise of Darien, and political victims of risings against or for the Stuarts, helped in their various ways in the development of the island. By the end of the seventeenth century Jamaica had outstripped Barbados. The early associations of the Bahamas were discreditable. English occupation appears to date from 1655; but the work of plantation was first taken in hand by the Carolina Company in 1670. The islands already had a bad name for piracy, and New Providence, which alone had the semblance of a permanent settlement, was the gathering ground of outlaws and ruffians. The American Revolution brought fresh blood to the struggling islands, which suffer from poorness of soil and lack of good water. Their trade is mainly with the United States.

Before treating of the Windward Islands, whose history falls rather within the eighteenth century, it will be useful to

SHIPPING AND SEA-FRONT WAREHOUSES, BRIDGETOWN

PANORAMIC VIEW OF THE CAPITAL FROM THE CATHEDRAL

BRIDGETOWN'S PROMENADE, SHOWING GOVERNMENT BUILDINGS

SCENES AT BRIDGETOWN, THE CAPITAL OF BARBADOS

6189

allude to the purpose and the consequences of the Acts of Navigation to which reference has been made. To understand their importance in colonial history two considerations must be borne in mind. The first is that British statesmen, watching the growth of the power of Holland, had once for all accepted the doctrine that " a flourishing marine is the sole defence of the realm." The second, that no European nation was wealthy enough to allow her rivals to appropriate the economic benefit accruing from her

mercantile marine was unequal to the demands thus thrown upon it. Hence a sudden check to colonial export trade, and temporary disorganisation of industry and production in the islands. But this method of protection of British shipping brought about the result aimed at.

The growth of our merchant shipping and of our home seaports dates from the Act of 1651, and with them grew also the naval resources of the kingdom. The Act of 1660 is the historic instrument upon which was built up the mercantile system as it

A COUNTRY LANE IN JAMAICA, SHOWING THE LUXURIANCE OF THE FOLIAGE

colonial trade. The Act of Navigation of 1651 was based upon the first doctrine, that of 1660 upon the second. The former required that all produce imported into England from Asia, Africa and America should be carried to the port of entry in vessels owned, captained, and, in the main, manned by British subjects, including in these the colonists. Now, the Dutch were at this time the carriers of Europe and America. The British West Indian trade was wholly dependent upon them. England by this Act took it into her own hands. For a long time her

concerned the colonies. Its enactments cover two complementary purposes. First, certain enumerated articles, which included practically all West Indian products, must on export from any colony be consigned either to England or to some colony of England. Next, all commodities imported by any colony must be shipped from England only. The object of the first was to render England the central market for the disposal of colonial produce ; of the second, to make England the source or the channel of European shipments for colonial consumption. The

GENERAL VIEW OF KINGSTON, THE CAPITAL OF JAMAICA

STREET TRAVELLING IN KINGSTON: A TYPICAL TRAMCAR

THE CITY AS VIEWED FROM THE SEA

KINGSTON, THE PRINCIPAL COMMERCIAL TOWN OF JAMAICA

Acts were in reality no new departure. But the policy they embodied had not been clearly defined, and certainly not enforced, since the rise of British communities beyond the seas. It was, however, in accord with the practice of the age in colonial relations, and though naturally disliked, was acquiesced in by the islanders. The naval defeats of the Dutch in 1554 and 1664, the capture of Jamaica and New Amsterdam, and the presence of a powerful British squadron in the Caribbean Sea were visible compensations for the loss of the " free trade."

The history of the West Indies during the century that separates the English from the French Revolution is characterised by—first, the steady growth of

1760. Kingston, as the naval station of the English fleet, and a favourite port of call, surpassed Bridgetown as a social centre.

From Jamaica adventurers went forth to Dominica, St. Vincent and St. Lucia. But the Windward Islands were, up to 1756, either tacitly allowed to be French, like Grenada and Dominica, or were practically unappropriated, save on paper, like St. Vincent. During the Seven Years War and subsequent conflicts, they passed from France to England and back again as diplomatists determined. Their settlement was slow, and belongs to the latter period of West Indian history. They are less healthy, more densely wooded, and were the home of a fiercer race of Caribs than the Leewards to the north.

THE GOVERNMENT BUILDINGS AT NASSAU, BAHAMAS

settlement and of cultivation ; second, a marked increase in negro slavery ; third, recurring dangers arising from European wars ; fourth, the decline of the Spanish power and the growth of French interests in the islands. Reviewing these in order, attention is first demanded by the position of Jamaica, which outstripped Barbados in population and in production. The earthquake of 1693 destroyed Port Royal, whereupon a new capital was built at Kingston, itself to fall victim to a like disaster in 1906. Jamaica was the best customer for African slaves, which indicates the reliance of the planters upon the staple crop, and explains their peril in presence of the great rising of the blacks in

The business of providing America with negro slaves was mainly in English hands at this period, partly as a result of the Asiento with Spain. The number annually exported from West Africa to America grew from 25,000 in 1700 to 100,000 a century later. Repellent as is the slave system to our moral sense, two facts must be recognised—that without it the agricultural development of tropical and sub-tropical America would have been impossible ; and that it was obviously consistent with a fine type of citizenship in the planter class. On the other hand, the cheapness and efficiency of the negro slave tended to the supersession of white labour. The slave gang was fitted only for

GENERAL VIEW OF ST. GEORGE, THE CAPITAL OF GRENADA

tasks that were uniform and mechanical. Experiment and enterprise were thereby discouraged. The colonies became dependent on a staple crop, and made little progress in industries which lay outside routine. The limited number of capitalist white men needful to develop the productive areas tended steadily to decrease. Hence the vigour and elasticity of Massachusetts were never reproduced in the West Indies. The economic dilemmas of the islands during the past fifty years are a direct legacy of the slave-holding era. The fortunes of war during the eighteenth century, in spite of constant interruption of peaceful industry, worked steadily in English favour. St. Kitts became wholly English at Utrecht. In the Seven Years War Guadeloupe, Martinique and St. Lucia were won for a time and restored at the peace of 1763; but Tobago, Grenada, Dominica and St. Vincent were retained to Great Britain. Havana was taken but not held.

In the war of 1778–1783, the French harried the Antilles till their defeat by Rodney off Martinique in 1782. The wars of the French Revolution gave Trinidad and Guiana to Britain. The effects of the French Revolution in the islands were for a time disastrous, for the " rights of man " proved to have a sinister meaning for planters living at the mercy of negro slaves who outnumbered them by ten or

GROUP OF WORKERS ON A SUGAR PLANTATION, GUADELOUPE

KAIETEUR FALL, THE MOST WONDERFUL IN THE WORLD

With a height of 741 feet and a breadth varying from 350 feet in the dry season to 400 feet in the rainy season, the Kaieteur Fall, shown in the above picture, is the most wonderful in the world, being five times as high as Niagara. Set in majestic scenery on the Potaro River, in British Guiana, the river at the distance of a quarter of a mile above the fall has a depth of 35 feet, while the volume of water is computed to supply 2⅛th million horse-power.

STABROEK MARKET AND THE STELLINGS AT GEORGETOWN, BRITISH GUIANA

fifteen to one. San Domingo, the wealthy centre of French sovereignty, was the scene of unspeakable horrors. Every island in which a French element existed, notably the Windwards, suffered from armed risings, with much destruction of property. Down to 1789 French interests in the West Indies increased. At that date the trade of their American colonies exceeded by a third that of the British West Indies. The prolonged struggle with France, which closed in 1815, left the ownership of the archipelago as it stood on the eve of the Spanish-American War of 1898.

The problems of the nineteenth century, therefore, have been chiefly economic and administrative. The event of first importance was the abolition of slavery. The import of new slaves from Africa was suppressed by the Act of 1807. Thereafter the extinction of slavery was only a question of time, and in 1833 the Act for the Abolition of Slavery was passed. The operation of the measure was facili-

tated by the proviso that slaves might be retained as " apprentices " until 1838 or 1840, and by the parliamentary grant of £20,000,000 sterling payable as compensation to the slave-owners.

An immediate result of the Act was the search for fresh sources of imported labour. The emancipated slaves worked " in an uncertain and desultory manner." Hence during the period from 1835–1890 nearly 300,000 East Indian coolies were landed in the islands and in British Guiana. The latter colony and Trinidad absorbed an unusual proportion. The export trade of the West Indies has suffered both in British and in foreign markets from two causes. First, the free trade policy of the United Kingdom involved the abolition of the preferential position of the colonies in respect to duties on produce, and the repeal of the whole series of Navigation Acts (1846–1849). Secondly, the growth of competing substitutes for cane sugar, latterly protected by state bounties upon

GENERAL VIEW OF SAN DOMINGO, THE BURIAL PLACE OF COLUMBUS

THE BUSY MARKET-PLACE AT CAYENNE, THE CAPITAL OF THE COLONY

DEVIL'S ISLAND, WITH CONVICTS' BATHING-PLACE AT ILE ROYAL IN FOREGROUND

A CONVICT COLONY AT UPPER SINNAMARY

SCENES IN FRENCH GUIANA

SCENES IN HAVANA, THE CAPITAL OF CUBA

Havana harbour, seen in the first picture, with its imposing buildings overlooking the sea, is protected on the west by Punta Castle, and on the east by Moro Castle and La Cabaña, the latter being shown in the bottom illustration. Inset is the famous cathedral, built in 1764, where the ashes of Columbus rested until their removal to Spain in 1898.

production or export, rendered the sugar industry of the West Indies steadily less profitable. The difficulty of producing and marketing other products has proved to be very great, so that the transition stage of West Indian agriculture has involved disaster to the planter, and grave embarrassment to the finance of the dependencies themselves. A turning-point has probably been reached in the agreement known as the Brussels Convention on sugar bounties, by which the shrinkage in selling prices has been stayed.

At the same time the cultivation of additional products, fruit, coffee, cotton, and especially cocoa, is perceptibly improving the economic outlook. The United States demand has become an important factor. Their imports from Jamaica, for example, are 60 per cent. of the total exports from the island. Disasters such as the great hurricane of 1800, the eruption of La Souffrière in St. Vincent in 1902, and the earthquake which destroyed Kingston in 1906, are typical of the natural calamities which beset the fortunes of our West Indian colonists. The entire elimination of Spanish rule

from the Caribbean Sea and the probable completion of the Panama Canal by the United States are the factors of most serious weight in the future—economic, political and strategic—of the Central American region. In respect of government and administration the constitution of the West Indian groups bear, as we should expect, obvious marks of their origin and their history.

Jamaica's Natural Calamities

The Bahamas have enjoyed representative government since 1806; Jamaica, for fifty years (1678–1728) was involved in an unequal struggle with the Crown before the same privileges were securely won.

The negro outbreak of 1865, sternly suppressed by Governor Eyre, led the planters to desire the stronger government of a Crown colony, which in 1884 was replaced by a constitution in which a representative element was, in modified form, re-introduced. An attempt at a federal type of administration for the Leewards was made in 1671, when Nevis and Antigua became in turn the seat of the executive; but it was ineffective, and the various islands retained separate

A TYPICAL TOBACCO PLANTATION IN THE PROVINCE OF HAVANA, CUBA

A STREET IN TRINIDAD, SHOWING THE ANGLICAN CHURCH

institutions until 1871, when Antigua, St. Kitts, Nevis, Dominica (once reckoned with the Windwards), Montserrat and the Virgin Islands united to set up a common legislature with specific powers, though remaining four presidencies for local purposes. In the same way the Windwards are under one governor-in-chief, with separate administrators; but since 1876 the elective principle has been superseded in Grenada and St. Vincent, which, with St. Lucia, are now ruled as Crown colonies. The Barbados house of assembly ranks with the old Virginian house of burgesses and the assembly of

Government in the West Indies Bermuda, as typical representatives of the English parliamentary principle. Its powers are still much like those enjoyed by the parliament of the Mother Country at the date of the settlement of the colony. Trinidad and Tobago have a legislative council in common, nominated by the Crown; they have never had representative institutions.

British Guiana and British Honduras, though mainland possessions, are integral portions of the West Indian sovereignty of England. Both were brought definitely under the Crown during the wars of the French Revolution. "Guiana" was the name given to the vast but undefined area to the east of the Orinoco, which infringed upon the uncertain borderland

of the Portuguese Brazils. Dutch, English and French adventurers had settled along the estuaries of its great rivers during the seventeenth century.

The early attempts of English settlers, of whom Lord Willoughby of Parham deserves remembrance, came to an end with the Treaty of Breda in 1667. But planters from the English islands by degrees found their way to the Essequibo, the Demerara and the Berbice settlements of the Dutch, who made them welcome. When Holland was dragged into the sphere of French revolutionary politics, in 1796, it was obvious that her people were giving ample hostages to the naval power of Britain. Hence she lost the Cape of Good Hope, Ceylon and her Guiana settlements. The Barbados men promptly attacked the Essequibo and took the fort; the Dutch made but formal resistance. The conquerors made little change in institutions and forms of government; proprietary rights were respected. The Dutch settlers gained the security of the English sea-power.

The cession was ratified in 1814. The colony to-day is of the same area as the British Isles. Its constitution is still essentially that of the Dutch era; only in a very indirect sense can it claim to rest upon a representative basis. The staple crops are sugar and cotton; and the negro and coolie elements are unusually preponderant in the population. British Honduras arose out of settlements effected by wood-cutters, mainly of British origin, who migrated in the eighteenth century to the coast of Yucatan. These maintained a precarious independence of the Spanish rulers of Mexico, but were on friendly terms with the vigorous native stock which inhabited the mountainous hinterland. From 1756, or thereabouts, Britain began to extend her protection to the Belize Baymen, but without disputing Spanish rights of territorial sovereignty. Belize was the port of shipment for the dye-woods and other timber exported. There a form of self-government grew up. In 1798 Spain made a determined effort to put an end to an anomalous situation, and led an attack on the intruders. But the Baymen, aided by English sailors, repelled the assault and, established an independence henceforward formally recognised by both Powers. In 1862 British Honduras attained the status of a colony under the governor of Jamaica, a connection which lasted until 1884. It is now a Crown colony with its own governor, and owes its chief prosperity to its inexhaustible supplies of mahogany. Most of the accessible forests, however, have been so well worked that of recent years the quality of the wood has steadily declined; but it is to be hoped that the cultivation of fruit, cocoa, sugar and indiarubber, which, as yet, is in its infancy, will be extended. In spite of the hot, moist climate, there are comparatively few epidemics, though hurricanes and earthquakes are not unknown.

W. H. WOODWARD

THE MUNICIPAL BUILDINGS AT PORTO RICO

A VIEW LOOKING EAST FROM HAMILTON, THE CHIEF TOWN OF THE BERMUDAS

THE UNITED STATES

BIRTH OF THE GREAT REPUBLIC
THE PRESIDENCY OF GEORGE WASHINGTON
By Professor Konrad Haebler

THE condition of the United States as regards internal affairs left much to be desired when their independence was recognised. The people in general were untrained for the political independence they had gained. Even some men who had for years been striving for these lofty ends and had played the rôle of party leaders in the provincial assemblies showed themselves little fitted for the task of government. They had hitherto had experience only of the negative side of political life as members of an opposition that upheld the real and supposed rights of the provinces against the governors appointed by the Crown. A vehement and radical spirit often characterised the discussions in congress, and it became the more pronounced in that it was not counteracted by the presence of a settled government maintaining an established course of procedure.

In the face of petty jealousies between the states, and the conflict of interests between the two groups of Northern and Southern states, it was no easy task to draw up a constitution for the thirteen united states. When the congress first met, in 1774, its authority was quite undefined. It was constituted, normally, by the revolutionary assemblies of the provinces, and thus lacked a strictly legal basis; and its object, its duration, and the scope of its authority were undetermined. If its course during the early years of the war, though calling into existence most stringent measures, met with no

The First Meeting of Congress

serious opposition, this was due less to its claims of authority than to the force of circumstances. The weakness of its organisation was felt by congress itself, and even before the declaration of independence it appointed a committee to place the management of the common concerns of the colonies on a definite basis. The work of the committee, the articles of confederation, was approved by congress in the autumn of 1777, and was submitted to the legislatures of the separate states for ratification. At the end of fifteen months twelve states had accepted the articles.

America's Spirit of Independence

Maryland withheld its assent for two years longer. But congress had gained nothing by this definition of its authority; rather the contrary. In the closing years of the war congress sank lower and lower in the public estimation. It was to be feared that congress, and with it the idea of unity, would fall into complete discredit as soon as the war was over, and the pressure from without, causing the states to hold together, was withdrawn. This was the feeling of all clear-sighted politicians, both those who wished well to the states and those who speculated on their breaking up. It was in the full consciousness of this that Washington, before giving up his position as leader of the army—the embodiment of the union—and retiring into private life, wrote to the legislatures of the different states that celebrated letter in which he urged on them to hold together, as this was the only basis for a great future; but for the time

WASHINGTON'S FIRST ENTRY AS PRESIDENT INTO NEW YORK CITY IN 1789

The great war over and peace having been restored in the American Republic, George Washington, who had led the forces with such conspicuous success, found himself acclaimed as a national hero. His rare public appearances were marked by tremendous demonstrations; wherever he went, men and women crowded his path, bent on paying homage to the great soldier and statesman. The above picture shows his first entry into New York City after taking up the duties of presidentship the latter event occurring on April 30th, 1789.

6202

his warning was without appreciable effect. The spirit of independence had been greatly strengthened in the various states during the war. Before the revolutionary steps of 1774 only two provinces, Rhode Island and Connecticut, had been completely republican. In all the others the representatives of the people had been controlled by a governor appointed by the proprietor or by the Crown.

The states under governors had, during the war, remodelled their constitutions on a republican basis; and they were too proud of their newly-won rights of self-government to be ready to give them up so soon for the common good. When peace and independence had been established, the important work of congress, representing the states as a whole, was considered as ended. Each of the thirteen states began to adapt itself to the new situation in the way it considered most advantageous to its own particular interests. Common concerns were meanwhile most shamefully neglected. The congress was not in a position to pay off the army, nor was it able to take over the **Congress in Discredit** military posts on the northern and western frontiers. The impotence of the central government created an unfavourable impression abroad. American diplomacy often failed completely in its objects on account of the discredit into which the national government had fallen.

Even at home congress fell into discredit. Pennsylvania looked quietly on while the body representing the union of the states was driven from the capital by eighty mutinous reservists and forced to continue its sittings at Princeton. Each of the states was against all the others. New York set the example by erecting about itself a bulwark of protective duties, not only against foreign states, but, upon its own strict interpretation of the articles of confederation, against its immediate neighbours. These duties were strictly enforced with a total lack of consideration for the interests of neighbouring states. This gave rise to the question whether it would not be desirable to transfer to congress the power of regulating commerce.

It was solely because congress did not possess this power that the desired treaty of commerce with Spain was not concluded; and Great Britain, which now enforced the Navigation Act against the United States, could not be combated because,

while the New England states replied by bringing in a navigation act of their own, Connecticut willingly placed its harbours at the disposal of the British; and the Southern states also declared against a navigation act, because they feared that when the New England shipowners had crushed all competition they would raise **Discontent Among the States** freights on the staple products of the south so high as to ruin southern industry. Old boundary disputes also cropped up again. From the beginning of the war the United States had laid claim to the territory beyond the Alleghanies; but they had not settled among themselves which state it should belong to. Massachusetts and Connecticut claimed a share on the ground that their colonial charters granted them the land from ocean to ocean.

New York claimed all the land which had owed its tribute to their allies, the Iroquois; and Virginia claimed all the land to the "west and north-west," as indefinitely granted in her charter. North Carolina had established government in Tennessee, as had Virginia and Kentucky. Now, Virginia was at that time, apart from new acquisitions, the most populous and richest of the states, so that the small states whose geographical position precluded further expansion were little inclined to let the power of this one state increase indefinitely, as they had seen in the case of New York what dangers to its smaller and poorer neighbours would follow.

The legislature sought to find a way out of this difficulty in 1777 by making a proposal to congress that the latter should not decide upon the claims of the states to the territory between the Alleghanies and the Mississippi, but should treat the whole tract as national territory, out of which new states might later be formed. The proposal was quite unsupported, and was rejected; but Maryland now made its ratification of the articles **Maryland Faithful to the Union** of confederation dependent on the acceptance of this proposal respecting the territory in the west. This was the real reason why this state, otherwise so faithful to the principle of union, delayed its assent to the articles of confederation till 1781.

In the same year Virginia, following the example of New York and Connecticut, declared itself ready to abandon its claims, and was then followed by Massachusetts, North Carolina and Georgia.

The settlement of the territorial dispute led to important constitutional consequences. Hitherto congress, without power and without means, had had a precarious existence ; but the abandonment by the single states of their claims to the hinterland handed over to it a region not only of great extent, but, as the flourishing settlements showed, **Jefferson's Proposal Rejected** of considerable wealth. In what form now was congress to exercise its power over this region ? The proposal put forward by the Virginian governor, Thomas Jefferson, to divide the territory into ten new states, was rejected ; but already in Tennessee and Kentucky communities of such strength had sprung up that soon after the definite constitution of the United States they succeeded in getting themselves admitted as constituted states.

But, on the other hand, the land north of the Ohio was placed under the direct control of congress, partly that it might have the means of paying the interest and capital of the war debt by the sale of land, and partly that it might be able to give the soldiers discharged at the close of the war an opportunity of establishing homes for themselves under favourable conditions. All that was laid down for the constitution of this region was that the rights of individuals, and the religious liberty common to the constitutions of the thirteen states, should be maintained. In other respects also congress was free to arrange the provisional government as it saw fit, thus excluding slavery from the territory and making possible the gradual organisation of these new territories as commonwealths of the union.

This procedure did little to increase the consideration in which congress was held ; but it was of much more importance in that it afforded an example of an extensive territory actually ruled by a central authority. The most enlightened politicians—and before all others **Washington's Plan of Development** Washington—were convinced that the only remedy for the unmistakable stagnation existing in the United States was complete unification. Government by congress was a shadow. The future of America, as was even then recognised, lay in the development of its boundless resources. This was impossible so long as the petty jealousies of the states continually acted in opposition to the common interest—to-day

encouraging the British to cripple the American carrying trade, to-morrow giving the Spaniards an opportunity of closing the mouth of the Mississippi against the Southern states. A first attempt to entrust to congress the supervision of the trade interests of all the states led to such a wonderful confusion of claims and admissions that nothing useful could be accomplished, and the attempt failed. But it was from this direction that the impulse came to which the constitution of the United States owes its origin.

Washington took a lively interest in the economic development of the country, as in all other political questions. Before giving up his post as commander of the army he made a tour in the north to see for himself what communication there was by water between the Hudson and the Great Lakes. After his retirement into private life he took great interest in the project of making a waterway from Chesapeake Bay, through the Potomac, to the Ohio ; for, as he well saw, community of interest was the best means of holding the states of the union together. The **Convention of Annapolis** canal project rendered an understanding among the different states of the union necessary, and, after a meeting of delegates from the four states directly concerned, had been agreed to in principle. It was proposed to invite delegates from all the states to this convention, and to consider, not merely the projected canal, but the economic and especially the commercial needs of the United States.

Thus originated the Convention of Annapolis, which met in September, 1786. It produced no tangible results ; but it passed a resolution, attended by the weightiest consequences, that congress be requested to summon a new convention to deal, not merely with commerce, but with everything bearing on the national welfare and particularly on the form of government of the United States.

Congress was not indisposed to comply with the request of the Convention of Annapolis ; but before it had done so the news was spread abroad that Virginia had already chosen its delegates for the new convention, and that Washington had consented to act in this capacity. The popularity of this name worked wonders ; in a short time four other states nominated their delegates, and congress, at the instigation of Massachusetts, hastened to send out invitations to a convention which was to meet at Philadelphia in May, 1787. The convention, whose work was the constitution of the United States, comprised fifty-five delegates, representing twelve states (Rhode Island not being among them). At the first sitting Washington was elected president. The proceedings were secret, and were not binding on the states represented. But it was exactly this knowledge, that their work could become law only after having been approved by congress and by the states, that gave the delegates the courage to put aside all timid compromise and bring forward a thoroughly new constitution on an essentially altered basis.

The majority of the delegates, though they did not openly express their conviction, knew well that the object of their assembling was to strengthen the union of the thirteen states, and place it on a firmer basis ; but as the sittings proceeded, new groupings were formed among the members, and the final resolutions of the convention were the result of a long series of compromises. No dogmatic policy was **Virginia's Scheme for Reform** pursued ; but by mutual concessions the interest of all groups in the work of the constitution was maintained, a circumstance that bears witness to the great political wisdom displayed. Virginia, which had largely given the impulse that led to the assembling of the convention, was now the first to bring forward a definite scheme.

Governor Edmund Randolph laid before the convention a plan, worked out in the main by James Madison, to establish a more effective central government. Congress was to be elected by a direct vote throughout the United States, in order that expression might be given to the sovereignty of the people. Following the example of most of the states, it was to consist of two houses. The lower house was to be directly elected ; the members of the upper house were to be chosen by the lower house from persons proposed by the state legislatures ; in both cases the number of delegates was to be proportioned to population and to the amount contributed to the revenue. Further, in both houses a motion was to be carried by a majority of members, not by a majority of states, as hitherto ; and a bare majority was now sufficient, whereas a two-thirds majority had often been required before.

Finally, congress, in addition to its power of deciding all matters of common concern, was to have the right of vetoing any resolution of a state legislature dangerous to the interests of the union.

This scheme was, as a whole, too centralising to be acceptable to the anti-Federalists. But its essential feature, the **The Negro and Indian Problem** formation of a bicameral legislature with a different basis of representation for each chamber, was saved for the future constitution by one of those statesmanlike compromises. The anti-Federalists had urged a scheme called the New Jersey Plan, according to which all the states, large and small, rich and poor, were to be represented by the same number of delegates in each house. By a third plan, suggested by a member from Connecticut, it was finally concluded, by way of compromise, to apply in the upper house the anti-Federalist theory of equal representation of the states, and to form the lower house according to the federalist scheme of apportioning representatives among the states according to population. Equally significant was the agreement that in both houses a vote should be allowed to each member, and not, as formerly, to each state delegation. The choice of delegates on a population basis led to further differences of opinion. What was to be taken as the population of a state ? In deciding the number of delegates to be elected by each state, were Indians and negroes to be included in the population ?

This question at once renewed the dissension between north and south, and would perhaps have seriously hampered the convention had not the parties agreed to a compromise based on the precedents of 1783 ; and now, when the southern representatives wished the negro population to be counted in full in settling the number of delegates for each state, the northern opposition finally forced the south to be **Five Negroes Equivalent to Three Whites** content with the system of counting five negroes as equivalent to three white men in the apportionment both of direct taxes and of representatives. The principle that congress should have complete control of all matters connected with foreign trade had been generally recognised as the chief reason for the meeting of the convention. It was therefore considered right that the convention should come to a final decision on the

WASHINGTON'S FAREWELL TO HIS GENERALS

It was Washington's intention at the end of the American War to retire to the seclusion of his country estates at Mount Vernon, and the above picture shows the famous soldier and statesman taking final leave of his generals with this intention, a resolution which the new American nation, having need of his services, would not allow him to fulfil.

From the painting by Matterson

point. But the subject of slavery was involved in the matter, and the question was raised whether congress should have the power of prohibiting the slave trade.

Many states were opposed to the continuation of the traffic; but in the face of the great division of interests in the congress a compromise was once more agreed upon. The Southern states consented that congress should, after a period of twenty years, have power to abolish the slave trade. and the Northern commercial states consented that congress, acting by the vote of a majority instead of by the vote of two-thirds, should have exclusive control of commerce between the states and between other nations.

After a series of far-reaching regulations had defined the authority of congress and of the several states, the form of the executive had still to be decided on. Despite the prevailing anti-monarchical spirit the idea rapidly gained ground among the members of the convention that a single person should be placed at the head of the government. But the question as to how this person should be elected gave rise to endless discussions, during which the half-finished work was more than once endangered. It was finally settled that the president of the

United States should hold office for four years, but be eligible for re-election ; and that he should be chosen by colleges of electors specially constituted for the purpose. The composition of the colleges of electors was left to the separate states. It was not until 1868 that the practice of choosing the electors by the direct vote of the people became general.

The Convention of Philadelphia had done all its work with a feeling that it was binding on no one. This helped it, especially at first, over many difficulties. **Triumph of the Federalists** But though two delegates from New York ostentatiously retired in the course of the proceedings, and at the close three more—two from Virginia and one from Massachusetts—refused their signatures to what had been the result of months of discussion, the majority were quite well aware that the current of public opinion in the young nation went with them. The subsequent treatment of their proposals showed that they were not mistaken.

On September 20th, 1787, Washington laid before congress the work of the convention. The anti-Federalist party would have liked to neutralise by it the proposal to reconsider the constitution in congress, and, if need be, to alter it.

But the Federalists, by an overwhelming majority, carried their proposal that the work of the convention should at once be submitted to the different states without change. The first state to decide in favour of the new constitution was Delaware, whose convention accepted it unanimously on December 6th. Delaware was followed in the same month by Pennsylvania and New Jersey, by Georgia and Connecticut in January, and by Massachusetts, after heated debates, in February, 1788. According to the old articles the consent of every state was necessary before a new form could be established. This constitutional requirement was ignored, and by procedure quite analogous to that of revolution it was provided that the new constitution should be in force upon ratification by only nine states.

Washington Elected President

Efforts were a'so made to qualify the several ratifications by conditions directed to securing more explicitly the civil rights of the individual. But Washington rightly pointed out that to impair what had just been accomplished was equivalent to rejecting it; that the constitution itself afforded the means by which it could be supplemented and improved; and that the proper course for those states whose wishes the constitution did not meet was to use these means to amend it. These arguments told in Massachusetts, and were not without effect on other conventions; and by June, before Virginia had come to a decision, nine states had agreed to the new constitution. Arrangements were then made for the presidential election in which, on January 7th, 1798, all the states, with the exception of New York, North Carolina and Rhode Island, took part. The sixty-nine electors chose Washington as first president of the union. Without doubt the United States possessed no citizen, other than George Washington, in whose hands they could place their fortunes with equal confidence. He combined the tact of a man of the world with an unselfishness that had stood every test, and a firm faith in the future of his country, to whose service he devoted his intellectual talents and his wide practical

ALEXANDER HAMILTON
Founding the National Bank and forming the protective tariff of the United States, he died in 1804 from a wound received in a duel with a political opponent.

experience. His unsought elevation to the position of president was but the just reward of his long public services.

Throughout the Revolutionary War he had kept himself independent of party; and he wished to remain so now that he was the chosen ruler of the nation, and to unite all its forces around him in common activity. But experience soon taught him how impracticable this high ideal was. The struggles about the constitution had led to the establishment of sharply defined party differences. These naturally manifested themselves among the men Washington had chosen as his fellow-workers. The most pressing task that lay before the new government was the re-establishment of the credit of the United States, and with it their repute both at home and abroad. In finance Washington had at his disposal a great force in Alexander Hamilton, a leading member of the convention, and so keen an advocate of a strong central executive that he was the recognised head of the Federal party.

His first measures, the funding of the debt of the United States, and the assumption of the debts of the separate states by the union, were in accord with his expressed centralising tendencies. The objection his opponents made to these measures was that they gave an opportunity to the rich merchants of the north of carrying on a profitable if not particularly honourable business. The merchants bought up great quantities of the practically worthless bonds issued to cover the debts of the different states, and made great profits when these were taken over and redeemed by the central government. In order to provide the means of carrying out these financial operations Hamilton now proposed a tax which he admitted would remind every citizen of his connection with the union by touching him in his most sensitive spot, his pocket; but in this he appeared so clearly as a party politician that the anti-Federalists at once declared themselves against him, and so bitter was the opposition that a revolt against the authority of the union broke out in the west. This turn of affairs made it necessary for Washington to put an imposing force in the field to crush the rising ; and also afforded an opportunity through which the power of the central government was early demonstrated.

According to his political convictions, Washington was a Federalist, but not in the party sense in which Hamilton was. Thus he was able to choose as one of his Ministers

Washington as Politician
the man who afterwards became the leader of the anti-Federalists—Thomas Jefferson. When the latter returned from his position as Minister to France, Washington offered him the post of Secretary of State, which Jefferson accepted. He helped Hamilton with his plans for the assumption of the state debts by the national government. But just as Hamilton was a " Northerner," Jefferson had unconsciously become a " Southerner "; and Hamilton had to buy his support by inducing his own party to agree that the future capital of the union should be situated in the south, on the Potomac.

The unfortunate thing about the party system was that the parties were not based on ideal principles and firm convictions, but were divided chiefly by conflict of interests. Thus it was that the union was always geographically divided into two hostile camps, the interests of the commercial Northern states being always different from those of the agricultural south. The opposition between Federalists and anti-Federalists had justification and significance only during the struggles about the constitution.

After the constitution had been completed and put into operation, these party names had less significance, for in reality the predominant party was always more or less Federalist, while the Opposition made use of the decentralising tendencies of those who held out for the rights of single states as a cloak to cover its own selfish aims. Washington was very desirous of retiring to private life at the close of his four

America's Friendship to France
years' term of office; but at the request of all parties he consented to hold the presidency for another four years, and was once more unanimously elected. This was a piece of good fortune for the young nation ; for this period brought difficulties that were overcome only by Washington's tact and foresight. The friendship of France was still an important factor in United States politics ; the

more because the Revolution tended to establish political conditions in many respects analogous to those of the United States. But these conditions became critical when the abolition of the monarchy and the establishment of a republic involved France in war. The Southern states, which had been so eager for the French alliance in 1782, were now intoxicated by the high-sounding and revolutionary phrases of the French Republicans, and were eager and ready to stand shoulder to shoulder with them in their struggle against the despots.

But this would have been bad policy for the United States ; for their economic connection with France was slight, while the prosperity of the Northern states was largely dependent on trade with England. For this reason Washington declared the strictest neutrality. The French Republicans, it is true, took no notice of this, and their diplomatists showed the same bold assurance that those of the United States had formerly shown. The French plenipotentiary held himself justified in enlisting soldiers and fitting out privateers in American towns, as he was received with tumultuous applause by the people,

England's Drastic Measures
not only in the south, but even in New York. But Washington did not deviate from the path he had chosen, and when he was forced, by the tactless behaviour of the French Minister, to maintain the dignity of the American nation against him, the mass of the people was united in supporting the president.

The position of the government of the union would have been much simpler had it not, at the same time, had to maintain certain claims against Great Britain. The British still held a number of posts in the west under circumstances which laid them open to criticism ; and the regulations by which they endeavoured to check the trade of neutrals with France, and to monopolise all trade with their own land for themselves, injured the business of the United States in many very different respects. But it was difficult to remedy this completely so long as the war between France and England lasted. Washington succeeded in gaining partial relief by an agreement arranged by John Jay ; but many sources of annoyance remained untouched, and succeeding presidents had for years to contend with these difficulties.

CONSOLIDATION OF THE REPUBLIC
UNDER THE VIRGINIAN PRESIDENTS

AT the close of his second term of office, Washington emphatically declined re-election, so that a new head of the state had to be chosen. In this matter the Federalist party began to dig its own grave. Hamilton indulged in electioneering tactics in order to keep John Adams, who was personally unacceptable to him, out of the presidency. He failed in this; but the factional controversy within the Federalist party made possible the election of an anti-Federalist president in 1800.

The United States now seemed to be drifting, much against its inclinations, into war with France. The Directory, by its insolent proceedings, had forced the United States to discontinue diplomatic relations; and under the favourite pretext of searching for contraband, it carried on a more vigorous war against American commerce than Britain had ever done. Then the Federalist party collected its strength, and **Federalists'** demanded a resolution declar-**High-handed** ing war on France; but before **Policy** war had been formally declared, Adams took advantage of the first slight signs of concession on the part of France to effect a reconciliation. This was a severe defeat for the Federalists, and it was made worse by the fact that at the same time they took a disastrous step in home affairs. To guard against foreign agitation in the country, they introduced a severe law against this, and against insults to the government, which they carried in spite of vigorous opposition. The anti-Federalist party considered this the height of illegality, and the legislatures of Kentucky and Virginia held sittings to protest against it.

During these sittings the famous resolutions were passed in which the champions of the rights of single states claimed the right of actively resisting illegal resolutions of congress. The resolutions had no immediate significance, but later they served as a basis for the arguments of secessionists. The new presidential election placed Jefferson at the head of the government. As the result of mismanaged electioneering tactics on the part of the anti-Federalists, Jefferson and Burr, who had been selected for the vice-presidency, received the same number of votes. The unscrupulous Burr **Jefferson** would gladly have displaced **in the** Jefferson; but the Federalists **White House** who helped him in his attempt only succeeded in gaining contempt for themselves by their efforts. Jefferson emerged from the contest doubly victorious. His government gave proof that acting in opposition is a very different thing from leading a government.

The policy of the government was still determined by its relations to the belligerent Powers in Europe. Ever since the Declaration of Independence there had been differences between Spain and the United States about the free navigation of the Mississippi. This had been conceded by England to the United States at the Peace of Versailles; but England had at the same time given up Florida to Spain. Thus the mouth of the Mississippi became exclusively Spanish, and the government at Madrid unconditionally refused to allow foreign ships to pass through its territory. It was only in 1795, after protracted negotiations, that New Orleans was declared a free port for American ships.

Almost immediately after this negotiations were begun which led to a further change at the mouth of the Mississippi—the cession of Louisiana to France by Spain. The union government had several times considered the best means of meeting **Annexation** the danger that the territories **of** on its boundary, Louisiana **Louisiana** and Florida, might pass from the weak hands of Spain into those of England or France; and Jefferson did not delay coming to an understanding with the new owner of Louisiana upon their neighbouring relations. In so doing he made the surprising discovery that the First Consul, Napoleon, was by no means disinclined to rid himself of this territory, which possessed but doubtful value for him. Now, Jefferson had not the least doubt that the constitution did not permit him to acquire new territory for the union; but he had no thought of letting slip such an exceptional opportunity of extending and securing the boundaries of the union. He therefore gave his unqualified approval to the act of his envoy, who purchased the territory in question from France for something like £3,000,000. Of course, there was very considerable opposition, especially on the part of the Northern states, which feared their trade would suffer by the opening of the mouth of the Mississippi; but Jefferson's enemies were not so blind as to think seriously of annulling this profitable transaction.

Jefferson's Profitable Transaction

In the autumn of 1804, Jefferson was elected to the presidency for a further term of four years. During his second term of office the political situation was graver. As Napoleon more and more revealed himself, so the Old World became more and more plunged in war. The United States were affected by it, as each of the sea Powers, Great Britain and France, persistently harassed the commerce of the citizens of the union with that of its enemies. In this the attitude of the British may have been more unfriendly than that of France, though both nations captured American ships almost in their own harbours. But the old leaning of the Southern states towards France, and Jefferson's enthusiasm for that country, were responsible for the union government's directing its anger chiefly against Britain.

From the time of the War of Independence the idea had survived that the interruption of commercial relations was a specially effective and dangerous weapon against that Power. As those on the American side who would suffer most from this were the commercial Northern states, the party of the Southern states, then predominant, immediately carried the proposal of an embargo of several months' duration. But in reality it was only American trade that suffered seriously from it; for even in American waters Great Britain was supreme, and so was able to protect an illicit trade which almost compensated for the loss of the regular commerce. The complaints of the north, continually becoming louder, were not

Great Britain Protects Illicit Trade

without effect on congress. Jefferson himself was considering the removal of the embargo; but towards the end of his term of office he had lost control over congress to such an extent that his opponents carried its immediate repeal greatly against his will.

The change in the presidency made no change in the situation either at home or abroad. Madison, like Jefferson, was one of the leaders of the southern party, that championed the rights of the separate states; but, like his predecessor, he was forced more and more towards the Federalists by the duties of the office he had taken up. One thing was unmistakable—that his personal influence over the southern party was appreciably less than that of his predecessor. On becoming president he had found relations with Great Britain and France unchanged.

Great Britain did not respond to the removal of the embargo by any serious attempt to remedy the grievances complained of by the Americans; on the contrary, the negotiations entered upon ended in her rejecting all the American claims and refusing all concessions until the United States should take up a more decided attitude towards France. Now the latter deserved no consideration from America. Her attitude was quite as unfriendly as England's. But on account of the traditional friendship between France and the union, ever kept alive by skilfully turned phrases, the government could not make up its mind to buy British friendship by a change of front towards France. Thus negotiations were continued with both Powers on the subject of the abolition of the regulations which crippled the trade of neutrals; but the Americans still had to put up with their ships being treated as hostile by both sides, without daring to make reprisals. In this dilemma help came to the government from a quarter whence it was least expected.

French or British Friendship?

In the south there had formed within the anti-Federalist party a new group that held more firmly to the one-sided policy of the party. The leaders of this group, Clay and Calhoun, were intoxicated with pan-American ideas, the first aim of which was the conquest of Canada. Accordingly, they threatened to withdraw their support from Madison in the forthcoming presidential election if he did not adopt a more energetic policy against Great Britain. Now, Madison's ambition was to serve

A VIEW OF THE NIAGARA RIVER ABOVE THE FALL

THE FAMOUS HORSESHOE FALL. WITH A DESCENT OF 158 FT.

THE RAPIDS BELOW THE FALL

Photochrome

SCENES OF THE WONDERFUL NIAGARA FALLS

two terms as president, like his predecessors; and to this desire he sacrificed his love of peace. On April 1st, 1812, he renewed the trade war by an embargo; but as the north was not inclined to a war policy, or willing to bear its expenses for the south, the embargo was weakly enforced, and once again remained ineffective. The war party, **War Declared Against Great Britain** however, was insistent, and Madison yielded. As if in mockery of the American plans, the abolition of the decrees pressing hardly upon the trade of neutrals was consented to exactly at this time by both Great Britain and France; but before definite news of this could reach America the pliant majority of the congress had decided on war against England, and declared it on June 18th, 1812.

If the War of Independence, in spite of the community of interests then existing, had exhibited the military resources of the union in a very unfavourable light, still more so did this war, which the Northern states stigmatised as a party war of their opponents. It is possible that the British Government for a time cherished the hope of breaking up the union and forming the Northern states in a separate union friendly to England. This charge against the Northern states has been founded chiefly on the proceedings of the Hartford Convention. But this assembly, in which, moreover, only Rhode Island, Connecticut and Massachusetts were officially represented, did, in reality, no more than the Southern states had done against Adams by the Kentucky and Virginia resolutions. It claimed for the several states the right of refusing to recognise as binding unjust and pernicious resolutions of congress, and maintained the principle of opposing such resolutions, if need be, by force.

But it did not consider that such a necessity had already arisen, and, though refusing to take active part in the war, had no thought of entering into separate **Madison's Plan of Campaign** negotiations with the British. The course of the war showed how little preparation had been made for it, and how small was its popularity on the whole. Madison had announced that his plan of campaign was to maintain the defensive on the coast, but, by energetically taking the offensive in the north, to try to add Canada to the possessions of the United States. But he was unable to obtain the means of doing this. The recruiting and

enlistment resolved on by congress proved totally inadequate; even the militia avoided service as much as possible.

Matters were made worse by the apparent incapacity of the generals, and the first campaign ended in most disgraceful losses, which were only partially retrieved by the two which followed. The war of defence on the coast also brought to light a melancholy state of affairs. In privateering the ships and seamen of the Northern states proved themselves no despicable opponents, as they had already done in the War of Independence, and it was owing to their bravery in many encounters between single ships that the union government turned its attention more seriously to the creation of a navy.

But where the British appeared with fleets and not with single ships, they scarcely ever met with serious resistance. This many coast towns found to their cost in the first two campaigns; and in 1814 the British landed on the shores of the Potomac and captured and partly burned Washington, the capital of the union, without once having to fight a serious engagement. **Washington Captured and Burned** The union government was broken up and had almost ceased to exist. In this state of affairs the union received unexpected help from the south. Already in the War of Independence both British and Americans had called in the Indians to their aid, but with very different results. Even when the Americans offered the greatest inducements, the redskins did not forget the bad treatment they had received in the past, and still received from the British colonists; thus they were reluctant and untrustworthy allies.

The British, on the other hand, stepped into the shoes of the French in Canada, and to some extent maintained their wise Indian policy. Besides this, even long after the War of Independence, the British held posts in the west, and thus kept in touch with the Indians, against whom Washington had already had to wage a war of several years' duration, in which, after repeated severe losses, success was attained only by the employment of overwhelming force. In the war of 1812 the Indians took the British side in large numbers. The warlike eloquence of Tecumseh, which spread from the northern lakes to Florida, gave rise to the scheme of a general Indian rising. In the north the project led to no very important results; but in the Southern and South-western states a rising of the Creeks threatened to become a serious danger to the Americans. It was here, in the south, that Andrew Jackson fought his first battle. He had decidedly military talents, and he was able, with the comparatively small means at his disposal, to combat the danger, in spite of the secret support the Indians received from Florida.

These struggles attracted the attention of the British to the southern and western boundaries. Knowing well the importance of the mouth of the Mississippi to the Americans, who were rapidly spreading westward, they resolved to try to gain a footing there. The boundary of the Spanish possessions in Florida had long been a subject of dispute between Spain and the union. The Spaniards could not deny that New Orleans was a part of Louisiana; but otherwise they laid claim to the east bank of the Mississippi, while the United States strove to get possession of both banks, and were not disinclined to purchase, if necessary, all West Florida. The British took advantage of this uncertainty of the boundary.

Serious British Defeats They landed at Pensacola and used this Spanish town as a base for their attacks. But they found their match in Jackson, who held command on this boundary. He was as little restrained by international rights as the British. He took for his headquarters Mobile, which was also Spanish, and from this base attacked Pensacola so successfully that the British were forced to abandon it and withdraw to their fleet. New Orleans was the next object of the British attack; but Jackson fortified and defended it successfully, repulsing the British with heavy losses on January 8th, 1815. After this they had no desire to try conclusions with him a third time.

Before these successes became known, peace had been concluded at Ghent, on December 24th, 1814. The frivolous origin of the struggle, and its still more disgraceful course, gave the Americans little claim to favourable conditions of peace. But the political situation in Europe came to their aid once again, and they reaped where they had not sown. Negotiations were entered upon during the second year of the war, and anxiety on account of a menacing grouping of the European Powers caused Great Britain to drop the imperious tone with which she had at first repulsed every approach. As there were scarcely any real points of difference, peace was quickly concluded, and, considering the situation, the Americans could demand nothing better than the re-establishment of the *status quo*.

An immediate consequence of the conclusion of peace was the acquisition of Florida by the United States. Madison was not **Florida Ceded to the Union** destined to accomplish this rounding off of United States territory. This was left to his successor, Monroe, who was especially fitted for the work, as, on account of his diplomatic missions to the courts of Europe, he knew all sides of the question better than any other. The war had shown that Spain was not able to defend the few localities from which her officials were supposed to rule Florida; it was the continual complaint of the Americans that Spain was quite powerless over the country, and that her province was the haunt of all criminals from the neighbouring states. Troops of filibusters had established themselves on some of the islands off the coast, and, under the pretext of fighting for the freedom of the Spanish colonies, they made piratical attacks on both Spanish and American vessels.

The union government was forced to take action here, and, having once begun to establish order in Florida, found it difficult to determine how far it ought to go. On land the Seminoles were as great an annoyance to the neighbouring states as the pirates by sea. They had been furnished by England with money, powder and officers during the war; and here the Peace of Ghent put no end to the strife. Finally, Monroe entrusted the subjugation of the Seminoles to Jackson, and when the latter interpreted his task as the conquest of all Florida the government placed no hindrance in his way.

On the contrary, it tried to justify his action by diplomacy. This pressure sufficed to bring to the desired conclusion the **Monroe's Brilliant Régime** negotiations with Spain which had been pending for years. In October, 1820, Spain ceded to the United States, for the sum of £1,000,000, this territory, which had really slipped from its grasp long before and had for long been of no real use to it. This removed from the path of the United States the last obstacle to the completion of their territorial development in that direction. After the acquisition of Florida nothing remained that was likely to involve the

United States in diplomatic complications with foreign Powers. A long period followed, during which their rulers had leisure to devote their whole attention to the development of the country, which made such progress as exceeded the wildest hopes of the founders. As early as 1806, Jefferson had been able to announce that the revenue of the government exceeded its expenditure, and the complications of the following years caused but a transitory interruption of this favourable state of affairs. By reason of the rapidly increasing immigration the population increased enormously and spread itself over a larger and larger area. By 1818 nine new states had been added to the thirteen original ones, and further admissions to the union were impending.

Besides this, in Monroe the nation had the rare good fortune to have at its head a president who was not merely a party politician. Monroe was the last of the great Virginians, and was elected as the candidate of the anti-Federalists upon a platform essentially Federalist; but the division between the old parties had completely disappeared, the all-powerful organisation of the Republican party had gained complete control of the political situation, and now within that party were gradually being formed those sectional and personal factions which were to become the nucleus of future parties.

Monroe followed Washington's example in not limiting the choice of his advisers to one faction, but rather in seeking to enlist in the service of the state the most capable men of all groups. It is true that he could not crush out the dangerous germs of discord which had their origin in the great economic differences in the development of north and south; but it was a distinct advantage to the land that a serious attempt was once more made to further its general interests.

THE NIAGARA FALLS ICE-BOUND　　　Underwood

THE DEVELOPMENT OF PARTIES
AND THE PRESIDENCY OF ANDREW JACKSON

IT has become customary to regard the recent history of the United States of America exclusively in the light of the struggle over slavery; but this process is not in this case so accurate as when applied to the last three decades of the history of Brazil. The abstract question whether slavery was admissible or justifiable had, indeed, been debated, and in some communities negatived, even at the time of the cessation of British rule in the American continental colonies, and was thereafter discussed quite continuously by individuals and corporate bodies.

Nevertheless, the government of the United States, as such, had, far into the nineteenth century, regarded the enslavement of negroes as a legal institution wherever established by commonwealth enactment; and thus the struggle between north and south could never turn upon the legality of slavery, but only upon the ethical status of the institution.

The Legal Status of Slavery It was not only a defensive struggle for the protection of certain purely economic interests, but it also by degrees assumed such a character that the preservation of slavery seemed to become a *sine qua non* to the south as clearly as did the destruction of the preponderance of the slave-holding Southern states appear essential to the beneficial progress of the north.

A government in which a man's vote upon national affairs was relatively influential in proportion to the number of slaves within his commonwealth; which allowed to a slave-holder the unrestricted pursuit of his slaves even into states where the institution did not exist; a government, finally, which permitted slavery in the small federal district over which it exercised direct control, and in certain of the territories governed by congress—such a government naturally entertained no doubts as to the legal status of slavery. In the Northern states, for reasons of climate, topography and industrial develop-

ment, slavery naturally was not very widely spread; in Massachusetts, in fact, soon after the adoption of its constitution in 1780, slavery was made impossible by judicial decision. In New York, on the other hand, it was to be found for a half-century more, and similar conditions pre-

Slave Traffic Universally Condemned vailed in other Northern states. The slave trade, which was more universally and less reservedly condemned than slavery itself, was vigorously carried on not only legally during the twenty years fixed by the constitution after the adoption of that instrument, but also illegally, far beyond that period, and that, too, by the very merchants who were otherwise fully conscious of the industrial antagonism between north and south.

By the terms of the constitution a measure became law if passed in the house of representatives by a majority of the members, who were apportioned among the states on the basis of population, and in the senate by a majority of the members, who were apportioned equally among the states. As long as the conflict was undecided, a serious danger to both parties lay hidden in this complex system of representation. In the house of representatives the Northern states, owing to their larger population, possessed from the beginning a small majority.

Nor could this be affected by the constitutional concession to the southerners by which, in computing population for purposes of representative apportionment, five

Slaves as Factors in Politics slaves were made to count as three inhabitants. In spite of this, the majority grew; for, notwithstanding the importation and the rearing of slaves, the Southern states were unable to keep pace with the increase of population of the north. Thus the only protection of the south lay in the senate, whose membership consisted of two senators from each state, and not of state delegations, varying in size according to the population of each state. The south, if industrially and politically it was not to be handed over to the north, was compelled to find means of maintaining a balance in the senate. The New England states had, indeed, before this, in the most undisguised fashion, paraded their own sectional arguments and interests as a justification for

Northern and Southern Conflicts possible separation. And even after the establishment of the constitution and the later accession of Jefferson, a perverted federalism was for some years vainly used to further certain of their interests. But after the Hartford Convention the entire policy of the north-eastern group, drawn together by similarity of interests, left no room to doubt what the south would have to expect when once it should no longer be able, of its own weight, to counterbalance the self-centred industrial policy of the Northern states.

Thus the " planter " states had to guard their common life interests against the " industrial " states. These interests, indeed, were not exclusively bound up with the maintenance of slavery. Nevertheless, this institution, so essential to their industry, furnished an outward, visible sign which became more and more a distinguishing mark of the section. Later, the Northerners complacently made the alleged evils of an institution which they themselves had once by no means despised a pretext for attacking the south, while in reality they were seeking to protect their own political and industrial interests.

At the time when the thirteen North American provinces had joined together in a federal union, the industrial opposition of the planter states to the commercial and manufacturing states was by no means so marked as to enable one to speak of a majority of either of these groups. Later, however, the division assumed from year to year a more definite character. It was probably not a mere accident that in the

Slave Labour on the Plantations nine new territories received as states into the union up to 1818 —as in the case of the thirteen original states—the states with an essentially free, industrial and agricultural population exactly balanced those in which plantation industry and slave labour were predominant. This balance seems to have been threatened for the first time when Missouri applied for admission into the union, on which occasion it was proposed by certain Northerners to make the

prohibition of slavery a preliminary condition of such admission. The question was, indeed, still an open one ; for although, according to the North-west ordinance, slavery was to be prohibited in the territories north of the Ohio, no definite limit in this respect had been as yet fixed on the other side of the Mississippi.

From its natural conditions and the manner in which it had been colonised, Missouri was evidently marked out for another planter state. Accordingly the representatives of these states in both houses protested energetically against the resolution, and, in conformity to the doctrine of public law, which from the beginning had recognised slavery as an institution exclusively within the jurisdiction of the states, demanded that the question of slavery should be left to the decision of the new state in its constitution, and that under no pretence should congress be allowed to reserve to itself the right of attaching to the admission of a new state such conditions as it might determine. On the other hand, the north in reality was not concerned merely with the question

Rising Power of the South whether there were to be slaves in Missouri or not—a matter, indeed, of complete indifference to the great merchants ; their real apprehension was whether, by surrendering this territory to the southern interests, the latter might not thereby acquire in the senate such a decided preponderance as might possibly be used in a manner hostile and damaging to the north.

Hence as long as there was danger of such a majority the north offered an obstinate and energetic resistance ; but this at once disappeared when the territory of Maine likewise applied for admission to the union, whereby a check might be afforded to the north against the rising power of the south. In this connection, what is known as the Missouri Compromise was effected in 1820 and 1821, which, on the one hand, admitted the two territories into the union without conditions and recognised the inability of congress to impose such conditions and, on the other hand, fixed the boundary between the slaveholding and non-slaveholding territories west of the Mississippi at 36° 30′ of latitude.

The acuteness with which this Missouri question was fought out by the two parties was in some measure due to another matter—the development in the same years of another approaching conflict of interests between the north and the south. We have already stated that New York, before its acceptance of the federal constitution, had, for the purpose of supporting its young industry, surrounded itself with a system of protective tariffs. As this policy was gradually approved, and as industrial centres began to appear in all the states of the north-east, the desire for protection by the laws of the union became more general. This desire also found adherents in the states of the north-west, in which the farmers were principally engaged in wheat culture.

To the south, on the other hand, free trade seemed a distinctly beneficial policy; for whereas the productions of the Southern states were limited to a small number of commodities which were exported as raw products, they drew the whole of the manufactured articles they required from abroad, and could therefore view only with displeasure a protective tariff which rendered the competition of foreign countries in their markets more difficult, and which increased the cost of all articles which to them were indispensable. It was, **Southern** moreover, doubly annoying to **Struggle for** them, not only that they had **Free Trade** to support, as they argued, by means of a protective tariff, the industry of the Northern states, which formed the principal factor in their rapid increase of population, but also that, by the exclusion of foreign competition, they should render themselves directly dependent for all manufactured articles upon the states of the north.

Nevertheless, in 1824, a bill was passed in both houses of congress, by a majority of a few votes, according to which a moderate protective tariff became a law of the union. This, so far from terminating the struggle between free-traders and protectionists, did not even produce a temporary pause in the agitation; for while the north fought for a further increase of tariffs, the south contended for their abolition or modification. Monroe, on retiring into private life in 1825, after the completion of his second term of office (1821-1825), was justified in reviewing his work with satisfaction. The reputation of the government had been strengthened at home and abroad, the industrial development of the country had been led into appropriate channels, and its financial condition had been placed on a satisfactory basis. These conditions

remained unchanged also under his successor, John Quincy Adams (1825-1829), during whose administration both the favourable external development and the unfortunate internal conflict continued.

John Quincy Adams, the candidate of the Northerners, was far from seeking to conduct his office in a sectional spirit; **Protectionist** but the Protectionists returned **Majority** to each successive congress with **in Congress** increased majorities, and the political situation seemed to them to be a justification of their efforts. Great Britain was still the principal purveyor to the United States, with an annual importation of five million sterling. Instead, however, of treating the commerce of so important a customer with consideration, Great Britain once more resorted to a strict application of the navigation acts, refused the conclusion of a commercial treaty, and endeavoured to exclude the Americans completely from the trade of her West Indian possessions. Hence a protective tariff against British manufactures became a measure as much of political as of industrial necessity. Signs of vigorous opposition, however, became more and more evident among the southern minority and in various fields of political action. Indeed, on one occasion during Adams's presidency the authority of the national executive was directly assailed.

Georgia, in order to rid itself of the remnants of its Indian population, had concluded a treaty with Creek chiefs which turned out to be an undoubted violation of the law, the contracting parties having acted without any authority on behalf of their whole tribe, and, moreover, having unmistakably been bribed. In spite of this, the governor and the state legislature not only upheld the treaty against the president, but also against the judgment of the United States Supreme Court; and they furthermore expressed themselves in **Georgia's** so defiant a manner against the **Illegal** national authorities that the **Treaty** constitution was held up almost to contempt. Finally, they not only succeeded in their expulsion of the Indians, but also were countenanced and aided by President Jackson in his delinquent omission to enforce the decision of the federal Supreme Court.

In these proceedings the doctrine of the sovereignty of the separate states had been much used; immediately afterwards it was applied in a still more forcible manner by another of the Southern states. Already, in John Quincy Adams's time, South Carolina had declared its absolute unwillingness to submit to the policy of increased tariffs ; it had, however, for the moment contented itself with a protest, since a presidential election was imminent

Opposition of South Carolina
and the choice was expected to fall on a man who, it was hoped, would consent to the abolition of the protective tariffs. Andrew Jackson, the hero of the war against the Seminoles and the victor of New Orleans, having at the previous election obtained a plurality of votes, asserted that he had been defeated solely through an unworthy manœuvre concerted between Adams and Clay when the election of president was thrown into the house of representatives. There was no doubt that he would be the favourite candidate at the coming election ; for by his doctrinaire impartiality Adams had managed to estrange even his friends.

Jackson being a pronounced Southerner, the party of the south expected that the administration of a general so high in popular favour would not only abolish the protective tariffs, but would shape its general policy decisively in the interests of the Southern states. Jackson's election, which followed with a crushing majority in 1828, did undoubtedly produce a radical change in the history of the United States ; but, in spite of this, the champions of southern rights did not realise their fulfilment of their ultimate expectations.

Jackson was a man of thoroughly honest and well-meaning character, and one who, as the south found to its cost, valued the welfare of the union much higher than might have been expected after the eccentricities of his earlier career. It seemed true that his intellectual acquirements were not equal to the important task which the administration of the government imposed on him. The

Overthrow of the National Bank
very fact that he entered the White House as the chosen of the masses was, in this sense, an omen of failure ; for he was neither able to gauge the true motives of the bold demands made upon him by demagogic leaders, nor capable of holding himself aloof from them in a dignified manner. While showing himself too readily accessible to influences operating through irregular channels, he must also be blamed

621⁸

for having during his presidency given recognition to that fatal system under which a newly elected president might feel free to reward his faithful adherents with promotion to lucrative offices of state.

But, on the whole, Jackson, in his administrative policy, allowed himself to be guided by that healthy commonsense which was so characteristically his own. The hatred with which he pursued the United States Bank, which he hampered in an autocratic fashion, and finally overthrew, was undeniably short-sighted from the point of view of public finance, and led to a financial crisis in which business men sustained heavy losses. But the ideal which controlled him in this course of action was perfectly reasonable and justifiable in the views of Jackson and his associates ; for, as then organised, the bank was charged with being little else than a support for some of the wild speculations and questionable enterprises which characterised the times.

In regard to the tariff question, Jackson had cautiously refrained from interfering in any particularly incisive manner. Con-

Jackson's Healthy Administration
gress, in fact, continued the system of protective tariffs, in its main features, in the year 1832, although somewhat reducing certain especially unpopular duties in order to deprive the Opposition of its weapons of attack. Most of the Southern states quietly accepted these facts, although they had, without exception, voted with the Opposition, or were satisfied with merely formal protests.

In South Carolina, however, the antiprotectionist movement had begun to assume a more and more radical character. The constituent convention of the state finally declared explicitly that the tariff enactments of 1828 and 1832 were not binding within their territory, and fixed February 1st, 1833, as the date after which it would treat the tariff as abrogated unless congress should before then remove the difficulty.

Although Jackson, in the earlier stages of his career, had not taken too strict views as to the obedience due to the central authority, yet now, when placed at the head of the union, he entertained no doubts as to the criminality of all resistance to its laws ; and he, rough-and-ready soldier that he was, would have much preferred to overcome with the sword any such resistance. Nevertheless, in spite of the strength of his personal impulses, his course of action

THE OLDEST HOUSE IN THE UNITED STATES, BUILT BY THE SPANIARDS IN 1564

Begun by the Huguenots and finished by the Spaniards, this old house in St. Augustine, Florida, has stood the wear and tear of nearly 350 years. It once housed the picturesque monks of St. Francis, who only vacated it when Sir Francis Drake and his band of adventurers burnt and sacked the little town. Of all the houses, it alone remained, and, with the exception of the wood finish, which is quite modern, it is the same to-day as it was in those troublous times.

with reference to South Carolina proceeded in legal channels ; for after that state had defiantly rejected his advice and persisted in its illegal resolutions, his supporters introduced a bill into congress by which the federal executive was charged with the power and duty of providing, under certain circumstances, for carrying into effect the laws of the union by force of arms.

It might, undoubtedly, have been fortunate for the future development of the United States if the conflict had at that time been thus decided. In spite of secret support in certain circles of Southerners, South Carolina at that time stood almost alone ; and its cause was undoubtedly a bad one. No one could have been found more fitted for defending the national idea by force of arms than Jackson, who himself belonged to the party of the south, and personally enjoyed uncommon popularity. If South Carolina had at that time been

forced into obedience, the conflict between national and state sovereignty might possibly have been decided as early as 1838, and the War of Secession would have been rendered less probable.

The national element and the Northerners had neither the courage nor the indiscretion to take up the gauntlet thrown down by South Carolina. The dispute was settled by an arrangement which left the real question at issue an open one, and therefore, though it secured an immediate victory, was considered by many as really a compromise of the authority of the union. The basis on which an agreement was effected was a law in favour of a gradual, moderate reduction of the duties ; this was first passed through congress, so that South Carolina was enabled to withdraw its Nullification Ordinance, while the "Force Bill" which was passed was thus rendered aimless before even it became law.

Jackson, more conspicuously than the majority of his predecessors, during two terms of office (1829-1837), asserted his position at the head of affairs, though he was the last president for a considerable time who maintained himself as the really controlling force in national politics. Thus there appeared a marked tendency **Evils of** towards a presidential, as dis-**Party** tinguished from a parliamentary, **Systems** form of government. The regularly recurring change of the presidency, however, has operated to weaken the president and to harm the state, especially because almost all the presidents, from Jackson's time, adopted his method of removing officials in order to appoint their own adherents to the vacant posts. This system could not fail to exercise a most damaging effect upon the conscientiousness and honesty of civil servants ; capacity for an office being measured, not by personal experience or fitness, but by the services which the individual might have rendered to his party or to the person of the president.

Hence it tended to lead to the disappearance in official circles of the stable or conservative element. The commercial spirit, which from the beginning had attained considerable development in American life, seemed now about to invade also the governing classes ; and thus by degrees large elements in the nation became habituated to have some regard for those principles according to which tangible success is the sole measure of all things.

In the eyes of professional politicians, however, these defects were amply balanced by the advantages which party organisation derived from general recognition of this political standard. The system had first been put into operation on an especially extensive scale in the state of New York, and under its influence not only had a distinct line of separation been drawn between different parties, **The Downfall** but it had produced, always **of the** with a view to the immediate **Federalists** spoils accruing from a victory, a strict party discipline, in which every difference in the views of separate members or groups within the parties was made to give way unconditionally to the " platform " put up in the name of the whole party. Similar processes were next repeated on a far greater scale when this system of plunder and exploitation began to invade the administra-

tion of the federal government and produced that party system by which the United States is still distinguished.

The great party in the country whose fame became historical was that of the Democrats. It embodied in the fullest sense the views of the founders of North American independence. The latter, indeed, had created the constitution of 1787 merely as a preventive measure against the threatening tide of evils which had been the outcome of excessive decentralisation ; by its means they had endeavoured to solve the difficult problem of combining an effective central authority with the highest possible amount of unrestricted liberty.

The Federalist party took its rise during the transactions connected with the drafting of the constitution, and its importance was largely temporary. Finding no support among the masses of the population, and being incapable of creating such support, it soon became disintegrated, its distinctive theory was adopted by its opponent, and after its apparently unpatriotic opposition to the war of 1812, it **Evolution** sank into insignificance. On the **of the** other hand, the Republican **Democrats** party, later known as the Democratic-Republican, and then as the Democratic party, arose by a quite natural process of evolution from the party of the anti-Federalists, whose principal demand—the unlimited sovereignty and the freest self-government of the separate states—it still recognised as a chief principle. The Democratic party was originally by no means the party representing the interests of the Southern states, though men from the Southern and Central states certainly did, from the first, play a leading part in it.

It was the abnormal preponderance of sectional influences, earlier discountenanced, which, in the second phase of the development of the Federalists, weakened permanently the power of that party, while the Democrats, representing a progressive, nationalist and conservative policy, grew steadily in strength. It is true that, certainly as early as the insubordination of South Carolina, that party, having completely overthrown its opponent, had become divided into two wings with quite widely divergent views. But the Radical-Democratic faction of extreme state sovereignty principles, which gave the first proof of its strength during that conflict, formed at that time a minority of little importance. The vast majority of the southern politicians repudiated its claims, not only from tactical reasons, but because they believed that these claims endangered the continued adherence of the northern section of their party, and also because they viewed them in the same light as did their northern confederates—namely, as a departure from the genuine traditional dogma of their party.

In their capacity of champions of the interests of the separate states the Democrats were opposed to the high tariffs which, though largely in the interests of the commercial and industrial north, were cast upon the whole union. They demonstrated, however, by the policy of their members who were elected to the presidency that they were by no means unconditional free-traders, although free trade was as increasingly essential to the interests of the Southern states as was protection to those of the north. They insisted only that the system of tariffs should remain subordinate to the administrative and fiscal needs of the union. They demanded that whenever the surpluses derived from the duties began to accumulate—and this happened a number of times in the first half of the century—those duties which were essentially beneficial only to certain sections should be lowered to such a rate as would make their net return correspond to the actual needs of the United States. The hostility of the Democrats to the United States Bank had its origin in a similar source. This bank, in the hands of their political opponents, was considered a dangerously demoralising force which was supposed by them to be operated solely in the interest of northern speculators. It had actually only a short existence.

Democrats Opposed to Tariffs

The withdrawal of the government moneys from the national bank, and their distribution among a large number of local banking concerns organised under state laws, produced temporarily an unhealthy speculative fever which of necessity was followed by an extensive crash. Accordingly, under Jackson's successor, the bank was replaced by an independent treasury established as a branch of the federal government. By this significant measure the bank question was made a dead issue in party politics.

The opponents of the Democrats were at first thoroughly disorganised. All opposition disappeared in the collapse of the Federalist party, and thereafter any possible opponents were long unable to form a platform which might have effected a reunion of the scattered elements. The interest in a strong central authority could no longer be used as a distinctive party programme, even in the north, and the question became so far immaterial that the new combination of politicians, who appeared under the name of " Whigs," were willing, as had been the Democratic-Republicans earlier, to assign the furtherance of works of general public utility, such as canals and public roads, to the government of the union and not to the separate states. In addition to this the protective tariff and contemporary financial questions formed points on which the new party was able to announce its attitude. It regarded as its principal task, however, merely the maintenance of an unconditional opposition to the Democrats, and it thus became substantially a party of negative opposition, with no positive programme.

The Rise of the Whigs

From this arose the introduction into electoral contests of vigorous discussions with reference to the personalities of candidates, and from it also arose a tendency to minimise the discussion and explanation of political principles. Such features of the political situation serve to make easily explicable the strong control secured and maintained by Jackson and his followers. Even at the end of his second term of office Jackson was still so high in the popular favour that his designation of a successor amounted almost to a nomination. By an overwhelming majority Martin Van Buren was elected to the presidency (1837–1841). A northern Democrat from New York, where the organisation of the party and the comprehensive accomplishment of the policy of plunder were regarded as particularly his work, Buren made good his assurance to continue in all respects the policy of his predecessor.

Van Buren Succeeds Jackson

SELLING SLAVES BY AUCTION IN VIRGINIA

NEGRO MEN AND WOMEN DISPLAYED FOR SALE IN NEW ORLEANS

During the days of slavery in America scenes like these, which are from sketches of the time, were common. In such colonies as Virginia, where, on account of the tobacco plantations, an enormous amount of slave labour was required, a flourishing trade in the traffic was conducted. It was the usual custom to exhibit the unfortunate negroes, well dressed and groomed, outside the sale-rooms early in the morning, so as to attract the attention of possible buyers. Prices fluctuated with the credentials of the slave; a good specimen would fetch £300, an inferior one £10, or less.

IN THE DARK DAYS OF AMERICAN SLAVERY

THE BEGINNING OF ABOLITIONISM
AND THE EXPANSION TO THE PACIFIC

THE inheritance which Van Buren now entered upon was by no means a wholly pleasant one. Jackson's financial policy had let loose a flood of wild speculation which directed its aims principally upon the still undeveloped treasures of the Far West. In the course of a few years many millions had been spent on the purchase of lands in the still unopened western territories, and the value of these lands in a short time increased tenfold.

In spite, however, of the marvellous expansion of the means of communication and the rapid growth of settlements, years had to be spent upon the land before these imagined values could be realised by actual development, and these years had not entered into the calculations of those who were the last to find themselves loaded with mortgages. Accordingly, when the money scarcity from which Europe had been suffering affected sympathetically **Ruinous Financial Policy** the United States also, these fictitious land values began to drop, and this, coupled with such administrative steps as the "Specie Circular," led to the general crash which dragged all enterprises, real and fictitious, down with it into the vortex of general financial confusion.

Now, although the government was almost, and Van Buren himself entirely, free from blame in these transactions, the popularity of the latter and the reputation of his party could not escape a decided shock. As early as 1837 there were signs that Van Buren would have little chance of securing a second period in the presidential office. Nor, indeed, did he secure this in spite of all the artifices of the administrative machine and the party organisation, both of which he, like no other, knew how to manipulate in his own interest. He did not, at all events, succumb because the platform of the Democratic party was rejected or because it was possible to bring out another giving promise of greater vitality. It became,

however, at this time once more apparent how thoroughly the principles of the Democratic party coincided with those of almost the entire people ; so that the election of 1840 was significant because of the conflict of personalities rather than because **Superiority of the White Man** of any popular decision upon questions of public policy or political theory. Even in the time of Jackson a small but active band of idealists had called into being a movement the final aim of which was the abolition of slavery.

Its first steps on this road, to be sure, had been in no way precipitate. But the very appearance of a party which desired, even if from mere principle, to recognise the negro slaves as men and citizens with equal rights aroused wide-spread regret and indignation, both in the south— where such chimæras were usually passed over with laughter—and in the north. The north, almost without exception at that time, shared in the aristocratic consciousness of the superiority of the white skin—a consciousness which in the slave states caused even the most miserable to look down with contempt upon a black man. Among the rich merchants and shippers this feeling was stimulated by their personal and business relations with the large landed proprietors of the south, from whose industrial requirements the north to a large extent derived advantage.

The Central states were less bound by considerations of self-interest. There, too, slavery was legal according to the state laws, but the natural conditions were not **Slavery Legal in the Central States** especially favourable to slave labour. The population consisted mainly of small independent landowners; and their neighbours, the adjoining " free " states, took care that this element should grow larger from year to year and exert a greater influence on the legislatures. But wherever slave labour was compelled to enter into direct competition with free labour it was perceptible, even to the dullest comprehension, that it could not prevail against the latter for any length of time.

Thus we find that only a small part of the population carried on the slave trade in the true sense of the word. What the planters really engaged in more especially was the business of rearing negro slaves. Owing to hard labour and inconsiderate treatment, the naturally high rate of increase of the actual labouring population among the negro slaves had fallen very low. The general course of industrial development, however, was tending in such a direction as to make slave labour relatively less and less profitable, so that the slave-holders could acquire wealth and maintain their position only by constantly extending and enlarging their industries. For this purpose, however, they needed a constant supply of fresh slaves. The slave trade with Africa having been almost suppressed by severe prohibitory laws, the idea arose of producing this urgently needed material in the country itself. Naturally, the Central states, in which slave labour did not yield sufficient profit, and which, moreover, were affected by the proximity of the industrial north, became the chief field of operations. Here an abolitionist movement at most could have effected only a change in the object of their commercial activity, but could not have destroyed the commerce itself. Hence although the movement was watched with anxiety, no very serious fears about it were entertained.

Dearth of Slaves

But even in the north, amidst a population almost exclusively free, the movement met with nothing but bitter opposition. Here the advantages and disadvantages of the slave trade were known only in name, but all the ire of true-born Americans was poured out upon those who proposed to make the despised negro, who was hardly considered a human being, a living member of a state whose constitution all parties never tired of proclaiming as a sacred and inviolable possession. The mob, easily roused, made short work of those who dared to avow themselves Abolitionists. Excesses occurred in different places, in which the lives and property of the opponents of slavery were threatened; but after a time the agitation of the extremists gradually subsided, and its character became radically different.

Murmurings of Emancipation

In congress affairs took a different turn, for there was in that body an overwhelming majority that would have nothing to do with the movement. It was by no means composed exclusively of parties having direct interests at stake, although the radical wing of this majority assumed, perhaps, the most uncompromising attitude towards the Abolitionists.

The majority, moreover, was so large, and kept its ranks united for so long, partly because certain features of the abolitionist movement were unquestionably opposed to the constitution. In the latter, indeed, the word " slave " was not actually expressed, but by it all citizens of the union were in clearly expressed terms guaranteed the enjoyment of the whole of their property, and that not only in the state in which such property might be situated, and where by the constitution of such state it might be recognised, but unconditionally in all states of the union. In so far, then, every state law which aimed at preventing a slave-owner from migrating with his slaves from one state to another was considered by the extremists as being in a strict sense a violation of the constitution. This view found partial expression in the laws for the rendition of fugitive slaves which were established by the federal government and enforced upon the states. From this point of view as well, the abolitionist movement, however justified from a moral standpoint, was, in its opposition to the enforcement of the Fugitive Slave Law, directed against both the law and the constitution.

Drastic Laws Against Slave-holders

Whatever help the abolitionist movement received in congress must be ascribed to John Quincy Adams, who was untiring in bringing before it petition after petition directed against slavery. On the other hand, congress endeavoured to resist this flood of petitions by measures which were branded with the name of " Gag Laws," and which brought their originators into moral discredit. Aside from the vital matter of the freedom of petition, the secondary cause for which Adams professed to be fighting was not ripe for solution, since it could be dealt with conclusively only by adding an amendment to the fundamental law of the land

The way in which Adams conducted his campaign served only to accentuate already existing differences instead of conciliating them, and to rob congress of precious time which it required for other more urgent affairs. Even before the middle of the century the entire development of the union left no doubt that throughout the United States the days of slavery were numbered. In a large number of the states, without being proscribed by their constitutions, the institution had nevertheless become quite extinct. In others, in spite of the extensive protection it enjoyed under the laws, it was undergoing a slow but steady decline ; and even in those states whose whole industrial existence was dependent on it, it continued to occasion discussions which rendered even its most zealous defenders personally sensible of the short-comings of the whole institution.

Hence slavery seemed doomed in time to die out gradually and disappear. In the natural course of things the process of decay would, however, have been so slow that America would have groaned under the evils of slavery long after the rest of the world had shaken off its fetters. But the movement which in our century led to the abolition of slavery over the greater part of the earth's surface could **Loosening the Fetters of Slavery** not have failed, from the mere consideration of their own advantage, to influence the United States, even if the latter had not found the moral courage to rouse them-selves for a decisive effort. From the manner in which it was fought out, the struggle against slavery not only exempli-fies the victory of a lofty ideal, but also affords a proof of how this ideal, through the admixture of political and material in-terests, had lost much of its original purity.

Throughout the whole struggle against slavery the Southern states were acting on the defensive. They were in the posi-tion of defenders of a besieged fortress, who, however well provided for the moment with all the necessary material of war, were yet able to calculate with almost mathematical exactness the date on which they would have to surrender. Their natural shrewdness impelled them to make attacks and sorties in order to procure means for prolonging their re-sistance ; but the ultimate defeat of their opponents lay entirely beyond their power.

The Northern states were able to carry on the struggle under the firm conviction that time, at all events, would finally bestow on them the victory. Meanwhile, they not only steadily grew in strength internally, but they were constantly being joined by new allies—the territories, not yet admitted to the union, which after-wards grew into states. It was an open secret that even in the states and terri-tories in which slavery was still unre-stricted it had found a dangerous com-petitor in free labour : the frontier farm **Free Labour versus Slave Labour** life offered such ample oppor-tunities for the development of the individual that slavery could hardly have achieved a complete victory in the newly constructed states. Sending settlers from the states which strictly protected slavery to the western territories did not help matters, for there, under the favourable influence of the local conditions, a portion of them were led to adopt free labour, while it was beyond the powers of governments or magistracies to keep out free settlers.

The matter, moreover, gained further im-portance from the fact that efforts con-tinued to be generally made to maintain in the senate an exact balance of the geographical divisions of the country as a check upon the house of representa-tives, in which the north retained a decided preponderance, by making the admission of a state belonging to one party always depend on the simultaneous inclu-sion of one belonging to the other side.

The slavery struggle acquired its pecu-liar complexion from the fact that during almost the whole time the agitation was carried on under the leadership of men who in some aspects were standing on the defensive. These were not, however, always Southerners whom the Democratic party sent to Washington as presidents. Nevertheless, northern Democrats could only hope to attain the highest office in the state by so adapting their democratic creed as to give no offence to the party of the south, which was possessed of a much stricter and more united organisation. First of all, indeed, Van Buren had **Defeat of the Democrats** managed affairs in a thoroughly sound manner. But towards the end of his term suggestions of irregularities were made so definite that the responsibility for such, coupled also with the administration's alleged responsibility for the financial collapse, made it impossible for the Democratic party to entertain any prospects of making one of its own men Van Buren's successor. The Whigs, how-ever, were still far from being in a position to send to Washington anyone whom they could rightly reckon to belong to their party. Accordingly, they put up for the presidency William Henry Harrison, an old general, politically almost unknown, and associated with him as vice-president John Tyler, who, though no longer actually a member of the Democratic party, counted far more personal adherents and friends in that than among the Whigs. It was largely by this manœuvre that the Whig party succeeded in getting its candidate elected by an overwhelming majority. But this apparent success was soon reduced to its true proportions. Harrison entered the White House only to succumb there to his last illness — April, 1841 — whereupon Tyler became reunited to those members of the Democratic party with whom he had all along remained in touch. Under the pressure of financial conditions a majority both in the senate and in the house of representatives had, in 1841, once more succeeded in passing a resolution in favour of the re-establishment of a United States bank, which still formed an important item in the political programme of the Whig party.

John Tyler, who was now president— 1841-45—vetoed both this proposal and a subsequent similar resolution of congress, and by these acts effected what was looked upon as an open secession from the party which had raised him to office. On the whole, Tyler's presidency ran its course unattended by any special events. Diplomatic difficulties with England, financial measures intended to remove the evil consequences of the crash, and a gradual reconstruction of the personnel of the administration in favour of the Democrats, by whose aid Tyler had been elected to the presidency, filled up the time, while events of far greater importance were quietly but steadily approaching, though the time was not yet ripe for their appearance in energetic action.

When President Monroe sent his famous message to congress, which until recently had been regarded as the guiding thread of the foreign policy of the United States, though later a quite different interpretation was put upon it, the leading

GENERAL Z. TAYLOR

Mainly on account of the success of his Mexican campaign, he became the Whig president of America in 1848, and during his term of office he headed the pro-slavery faction.

statesmen were of opinion that the territory of the United States had probably reached the extreme limits of its extension consistent with the republican form of government contemplated by the framers of the federal constitution. Two decades, however, sufficed completely to correct this view. It may have seemed justified as long as the vast basin of the Mississippi was still thinly peopled, and while the great roads and means of communication were still in their early development. Such doubts, however, as arose out of considerations of vast separation in space were soon set aside by the rapid utilisation—much furthered by the invention of the steamboat—of suitable waterways, such as the North American lake system furnishes in connection with the Hudson, on the one side, and the Ohio and the Missouri, on the other ; and towards the middle of the century by the construction of railways, which in America were taken up much sooner and more energetically than in the Old World. Even in the middle of the 'thirties the possession of a strip of coast on the Pacific was seen to be as indispensable to the prosperous development of the union as the possession of the mouth of the Mississippi had once been considered. The wild speculation in the public lands of the west, which had conjured up such serious commercial dangers for the union, had not only been far less fatal to the west, but at a time when it was a question of drawing some sort of profit from the less valuable titles to landed property, this speculation had actually had a stimulating and encouraging effect on the settlement of those sections. The far remote districts recovered rapidly from the effects of the crash, and their natural riches constantly attracted fresh emigrants to the borders of civilisation.

Material and Physical Progress

These events naturally reacted on the old states of the union in such a manner as to make a further advancement of the western frontier desirable, and an extension of area came to be regarded as synonymous with national enrichment. The western frontier of the union had never been definitely settled. In the Florida

Treaty Spain had renounced her rights from ocean to ocean; this, however, was a paper claim to an indeterminate territory. The north-western frontier was also under dispute with Great Britain, and at a time when no serious value was attached to the Far West the United States had by treaty agreed to a joint administration of Oregon by British and American officials. Thus the claims of the United States to the possession of an outlet towards the Pacific Ocean were up to that time still very questionable. For a long time, however, doubts had ceased to exist as to the manner in which they were to be improved.

The Separation of Texas

The separation of the republic of Texas from Mexico was to a large extent promoted by men from the United States, whose aim from the beginning had been the inclusion of these territories in the union. The states of the north-east were probably but little concerned about the matter, since they could not hope to derive any commercial advantages from this region. The south may have been influenced to some extent by the profit and political strength, unduly brought into the foreground, which might accrue from the acquisition of territories likely to become future slave states. But among the real influences towards this end were the populations of the young states of the west. Here, on soil reclaimed within the life of the union, which even in that brief space had undergone an astonishing development, a party had come into existence under the watchwords of "a great America," which, though in the first instance confining its ambition to the mere acquisition of Texas, in the next place aimed at the possession of the whole country as far as the Pacific, and finally at the possible absorption of the whole of the decayed republic of Mexico even as far as Tehuantepec.

From among the ranks of this party defenders had arisen to protect the Texan Government, completely powerless from constant want of money, against the attacks of the Mexicans; and their demands that the repeated applications of Texas for admission to the union should at last be entertained, even at the risk of a war with Mexico, became the more urgent in proportion as the untenable conditions of this pseudo-state threatened to make possible the interference of other Powers. Texas, in its then unproductive condition, was not rich enough to furnish the means required by the government. At first the credit of the young state had been abused, and debts had been incurred recklessly in the hope that they would be covered by the reception of the country into the union. This reception, however, was delayed, because Mexico refused either to acknowledge the independence of Texas or to sell the country. The Texans became tired of confining their petitions to the United States; they also applied to France and—so it is asserted, at least—to England. Thus there arose upon the political horizon of the union the threatening spectre of a foreign Power establishing itself in the south-west and perhaps shutting them out from access to the Pacific. Even Tyler had made

GENERAL WINFIELD SCOTT

General Scott early obtained a commission as artillery captain, and defeated Santa Anna in Mexico. At the death of General Taylor, he was nominated for the presidency, without, however, being successful. He was commander-in-chief of the army up to the eve of the Civil War.

efforts to meet this danger by renewed negotiations with Mexico, which were conducted in a tone of so much provocation

6227

that the Young America party was daily hoping for an outbreak of hostilities. Tyler, however, could not summon either sufficient courage or the necessary rashness to attempt to force a declaration of war.

In the electoral contest of 1844 the Texas question was made one of the two great points at issue. To it, and to the

Texas Received into the Union plank in the platform on the Oregon question, James Knox Polk (1845–1849), a Democrat of little influence, owed his victory over Henry Clay, the Whig candidate, as well as over President Tyler. Clay had originally pronounced himself against the admission of Texas, but in the end offended the anti-annexationists by veering around, from electioneering motives, to a policy in favour of admission. Tyler, by his feeble policy on the Texas question, had completely forfeited his already slender chances of re-election. Nevertheless, it was permitted him, during the last days of his term, virtually to carry into effect the admission of the neighbouring republic.

Although the bill bearing on this matter shortly before had been rejected by the senate, he now caused its reintroduction into congress on the ground that the result of the presidential election of 1844 had shown that the majority of the people were in favour of annexation, a plea which so impressed the representatives that the bill was this time passed in both houses. Tyler approved the joint resolution providing alternative methods of annexation during the last days of his official career, and in the following year Texas was received into the union as the twenty-ninth state.

This, however, settled only the relations between Texas and the United States. Mexico still considered the country as its own by right, and refused to enter into negotiations with the United States concerning it. But the federal government sent a division of troops to what was

Mexicans' First Shot in the War claimed as the western border of the new state, and thus attempted to solve the question whether the Rio Grande del Norte or the Nueces River formed the boundary by advancing its forces to the former. The first blood was shed in a surprise by the Mexicans of a troop of dragoons that had been cut off from the main body; and this was looked upon as tantamount to a declaration of war. Throughout the country few voices ventured to protest

against the general cry for vengeance against this provocation by the Mexicans. At the seat of war in the north, General Zachary Taylor achieved a series of brilliant victories against the Mexicans in quick succession; and by the beginning of the year 1847 their resistance in the districts bordering on Texas was completely overcome. This was as yet, however, far from bringing matters to a decisive issue, for the American Army was still some hundreds of miles away, and separated by immeasurable deserts from Mexico proper; and the losses suffered hitherto had made little impression. Polk was therefore obliged to determine on a more effectual move. It took the shape of an advance by General Winfield Scott from Vera Cruz upon the capital. Here, too, the Mexicans were unable to offer any serious resistance to the Americans.

Vera Cruz capitulated in March, 1847, after a brief bombardment; and on each occasion that Santa Anna ventured to oppose the progress of the enemy's advance upon the city of Mexico he suffered heavy defeat. Nevertheless, these very victories

Collapse of Santa Anna's Dictatorship almost robbed the president of the possibility of gathering the harvest of his discredited policy. The vigorous onslaught of the American arms led to the collapse of Santa Anna's feebly supported dictatorship, and when the United States troops entered the capital they found no longer a government with which peace might be concluded. The victors, in fact, had to assist in establishing a government before they could attain their real object, the restoration of international relations between the United States and Mexico.

In the meanwhile, owing to circumstances, the prize to be won had been increased to an extraordinary degree. In addition to the army of Texas and the Vera Cruz division, a third army corps had been equipped for the purpose of invading California. This division had the most marvellous good fortune, for on entering the country it found its work half done. Captain John Charles Frémont had, in 1844, during an exploring expedition, arrived on the borders of California; but he had so participated in politics that he had been expelled from Santa Fé. As soon, however, as war was declared, he returned, took possession of the town of Sonoma, and there hoisted the flag of the union. At the same time, an American man-of-war touched at Monterey on the Bay of California, and there, too, met with so little serious resistance that its commander, with the assistance of the American residents, was able to take possession of this important place. The military occupation of California and New Mexico by the union was thereupon announced, and in the face of this *fait accompli* the Mexican Government had to strike its colours.

In the treaty of peace the United States allowed the acquisition of the new provinces to take the form of a purchase, Mexico relinquishing these vast territories for an indemnity of £3,000,000, recognising Texas as belonging to the union, and agreeing to acknowledge the Rio Grande as the western frontier of the United States. In the meantime, the Oregon question had been settled by negotiation with Great Britain in an arrangement by which the 49° of latitude was recognised as the boundary line between the possessions of the two countries. Thus the United States acquired in the Far West the frontiers which have remained substantially unchanged to the present day. The importance of this acquisition was made at once apparent when, only a year afterwards, the first discoveries of gold were made in California. In congress the Mexican victories had a significant sequel. By what is known as the Wilmot Proviso, it was proposed that the grant of £3,000,000 was to be made subject to the condition that slavery should be forbidden in all the newly acquired territories. This proposal led to prolonged and embittered discussions.

Nor did its first defeat indicate the end of the struggle. It was, in fact, the beginning of the struggle over congressional control of the territories, which was to become a conspicuous issue for the next decade. The nature of the soil of New Mexico and California almost excluded any industry in which slave labour would have yielded profitable results. Besides this, California rapidly acquired a peculiar stamp of its own from the immigration *en masse* of the gold-diggers, who were almost without exception free labourers. Even in Texas,

CAPTAIN FRÉMONT
A supporter of the anti-slavery party, he was the first Republican candidate for the presidency, and was again nominated in 1864, but withdrew in favour of Lincoln.

where slavery was considered as holding a legal status since the admission, it scarcely managed to prolong its existence.

The only significance attached to the proceedings in congress lay in their affording evidence of the growing opposition to slavery, which was as much the outcome of the moral condemnation of the institution, aroused by the opponents of slavery, as of the recognition of its disadvantages from an industrial standpoint. That in the end the majority, in this instance also, agreed to a decision apparently in favour of slavery must again be attributed to the feeling that repeated attacks on the institution itself might develop into broader and more serious controversy relative to the constitution of the union. From the course of the debates, however, the slave-holding south could not fail to detect the remarkable growth of the dangers which threatened its industrial particularism. Hence it is hardly to be wondered at that at this time there was revived in some quarters a discussion of the idea of a secession from the union in which the Southern states considered themselves justified according to extreme democratic principles, and of a closer union between that group of states whose welfare was most intimately connected with the continued existence of slavery. For the time being, these ideas did not lead to actual results. This state of affairs, moreover, was not without its effect on the presidential election. Polk had paid too little respect to the Democrats to be able to entertain hopes of re-election. The whole party was at the time in so disjointed a condition that it had little hope of coming victorious out of the electoral campaign; and its candidate, Cass, a Northerner, was not a sufficiently striking personality to cover up the present weakness of the party.

It was just in this respect, furthermore, that their opponents had been especially fortunate. Their candidate, General Taylor, was of southern origin, was himself a slave-owner, and had never taken a decided part as a politician, though he counted himself as belonging to the right wing of the Whig party.

His campaign in Mexico, moreover, had rendered him popular; like Jackson and Harrison, he was a "people's" candidate. By their own exertions alone the Whigs would never have been able to procure his election, for as a party they were weaker than ever. Their whole programme consisted in ranging on their side all those

Taylor the People's Candidate opponents of the Democrats who were unwilling either to throw in their lot with the enemies of slavery, who formed an insignificant minority, or to attach themselves to the so-called "Know-nothings," or American party. Both these groups were, in a sense, fragments of the dismembered Whig organisation; and the chief aim of the leaders was to devise a means of erecting a platform on which the discontented of all other parties might be able to fight by their side. It was necessary to put up a "ticket" which would also be conformable to such a collectivist policy after the election, and for this purpose the choice of Taylor and Fillmore was a decidedly skilful one.

The victory of these candidates signified the defeat of the Democrats, without, however, implying a victory for the Whig principles. For the time being, politics were still exclusively centred upon the organisation of the newly acquired territories; and the struggle carried on by slaveholders on behalf of their theory, even more than their real interests, was long and violent. Before it was brought to a close, President Taylor died (July 9th, 1850).

For the second time the place of a president chosen by the Whigs was occupied, before the completion of his official

Slavery in Columbia Abolished term, by a vice-president who lacked even the small attachment which Harrison and Taylor had shown for the politicians who had prepared for them the road to the presidency. Millard Fillmore (1850–1853) did not, indeed, renounce the principles of the Whig party to the same extent as Tyler had done, but in his advances towards the representatives of the south he went as far as he possibly could, in the hope of thereby rendering himself an acceptable candidate at the next election. Particularly did he co-operate, more or less directly, with Southerners, with Middle-state men like Clay, and with Northerners like Webster, in sanctioning the important compromise of 1850, by which the principle of "squatter sovereignty" was applied to the territories recently acquired, the slave trade in the district of Columbia was abolished, and the federal Fugitive Slave Law was re-enacted.

By this arrangement it was supposed that slavery was made a dead issue, and this fiction was persistently maintained in the "finality" planks of the campaign of 1852. The effect of the compromise, its relation to the compromise of 1820, and the extent of the doctrine of "squatter sovereignty" were, however, to become the most engrossing problems of the decade, as soon as the introduction of the Kansas-Nebraska bill projected the whole subject of slavery once more into the sphere of congressional politics.

Doctrine of Squatter Sovereignty Fillmore's term of office was almost entirely occupied by preparations for the approaching election; but his hopes were not realised. Some Whigs, indeed, entertained the notion of his re-election; but the nominating convention of the party gave preference to General Scott, without succeeding, however, in making the latter a people's candidate.

The Democrats, in imitating the electioneering tactics of the Whigs, were more fortunate, having nominated Franklin Pierce, and having tied him down to a platform which proposed nothing more than the dropping of all contested matters, to which so much time had been devoted during the last presidency, and which adhered to the compromise of 1850 as an arrangement of the slavery question which was to be treated as a "finality." Such a programme was likely to find numerous adherents even outside the Democratic party. To the general wish of seeing these disputes finally brought to an end, Pierce unquestionably owed a considerable part of the majority with which he achieved success in the electoral campaign of 1852.

RISE OF THE REPUBLICAN PARTY
AND THE APPROACH OF THE STRUGGLE

IT was by the very irony of fate that the first official acts of the president, who had been especially chosen to settle internal strife, happened to turn upon the very question which finally kindled the Civil War. By the admission of California as a non-slavery state the north had obtained a temporary preponderance. In order to balance this as speedily as possible, application was made for the creation of the two territories, Kansas and Nebraska, in the hope of seeing at least one of them develop early into a slave state.

The territories in question, indeed, stretched northward far beyond the line of the Missouri Compromise (36° 30′); but it was argued that the terms of the latter could no longer be legally maintained, inasmuch as, by the Compromise of 1850, it had been agreed to leave the question of slavery in certain territories to be settled entirely by their own legislatures. Nevertheless, the Kansas-Nebraska question at one blow put an end to all peaceful sentiments.

Movement to Abolish Slavery

It aroused a cry of general indignation that in this wise slavery should be allowed to advance farther to the north. It was significant, too, that the movement in support of the Missouri Compromise was confined not only to Whigs and Abolitionists; a split became distinctly apparent in the very camp of the Democrats. A faction of northern origin, opposed to slavery, began to develop, and a second larger one in which the Democrats of the slave states stood up as before for the "peculiar institution" of their section.

The logical consequence implied in the national policy proved itself still stronger than the movement against slavery; the bill which provided for the organisation of Kansas and Nebraska became law, according to the spirit in which the Compromise of 1850 had been interpreted, without restrictions being made as to slavery. But the triumph of the slave-holders was only apparent. The bill inflicted a formidable blow to the cohesion of the Democratic party; and in the Northern states it set on foot the movement which eliminated the feeble party of the Whigs from the ranks of political factors. Amid its ruins arose the Republican party. The latter now came forward with youthful vigour as the supporter of an idea, which, owing to contemporary events, forcibly aroused the attention of all classes of the people. In the Northern states several attempts had been made at infusing fresh vigour into the life of political parties; but neither the Abolitionists nor the American party had succeeded in calling forth any deep or lasting emotion in party life.

Birth of a New Party

The impossibility of reconciling their aims with the fundamental principles of the constitution made impossible for the Abolitionists a general political ascendancy. The conviction as to the harmful nature of slavery and the desire to strive for its abolition were steadily gaining ground in wider and wider circles of the American population; but they were not prepared to accept the platform of the Abolitionist party, which, owing to some illegal proceedings, lost much in the general esteem.

The American party for a short time gained largely in numbers, owing especially to the attraction which the secret element in its organisation exercised upon the masses. Its platform, however, the most essential item of which lay in a demand for rendering the acquisition of the rights of citizenship more difficult for new immigrants, met with a cold reception from the general public. It was especially directed against those immigrants who were coming to America as the forerunners of that large swarm of political malcontents who were seeking an asylum from administrative harshness, civil inequalities and even famine. These, it is true, were by no means a wholly desirable addition

Opposition to Immigrants

to the population. They were, almost without exception, in a lower stage of educational training, and their moral and ethical development was deficient. The fact that these immigrants almost invariably attached themselves to the side of the Democrats did not cause them to be regarded with much favour by anti-Democratic politicians; and, naturally, for the same reason the Democratic majority was opposed to the enactment of such an immigration law as was desired by the American party. In this latter particular the Democrats were also supported by the Whigs, especially as the character of alien immigration had undergone considerable change in consequence of the revolutions which about the middle of the nineteenth century convulsed the Old World.

Aliens in American Politics

The entrance of the foreigners into political life marks a point at which the development of party politics assumed fresh vigour. These men, especially those who came over after 1848, could under no conditions become adherents of the Democratic party. Those who in their old home had fought and suffered for the universal rights of men, as handed down in the formula of the French Revolution, could not possibly attach themselves to a party which through force of circumstances was compelled to give increasing prominence in its political programme to the maintenance of slavery. Though in theory they were thus largely Abolitionists, they were too little acquainted with the actual political conditions of the union to join the Abolitionist party in large numbers. Still less was there a place for them in the party of the " Know-nothings," which desired to close to their countrymen an asylum so much longed for and so much appreciated.

Amid such influences new life was infused into the ranks of those who once composed the Whig party. However much the foreigners may have imparted that leaven which by its fermentation produced the Republican party, they had nothing whatever to do with the formation of that party. The men who beheld with grief and anxiety the disintegration of the anti-Democratic organisation had already made several attempts to bring together all the vital tendencies of the day in such a manner as to engage the concerted efforts of a great and vigorous

Decline of the Whigs

party. In its incipient stages the formation of the republican organisation was nothing more than the renewed attempt of the more intelligent politicians of Whig leanings to found their platform upon an idea which might awaken their party, endow it with greater strength, and help it towards final victory.

In different places attempts of this kind were made simultaneously under different names; but even in the early days the name " republicans " came into prominence. The basis of their platform was formed by the slavery question; but they did not propose to seek for its solution in the radical manner of the Abolitionists. The new party adopted a thoroughly conservative view; but while declaring that the rights of man, as ideally expressed in the Declaration of Independence, should be placed above the letter and spirit of the federal constitution, they demanded that the union should no longer lend a hand in enacting laws, which were designed for the benefit of all, in the interests of a portion of the citizens. The greater part of the platform was devoted to the elaboration of this idea. The party, however, at the same time proclaimed itself the inheritor of the Whig traditions by impressing upon the federal government the assumption of all internal improvements, more especially the construction of a transcontinental railway—tasks similar to those which had been assigned to the federal government by the Whigs, and before that by the Federalists.

Attempts at Party Making

At the presidential election which had resulted in the elevation of Pierce, the Republican party, as such, had scarcely come into life, and it figured in no way as a national factor. It gained considerable strength, however, owing to the events which happened during the succeeding four years (1853–1857), and more especially owing to the affairs of Kansas. The proposal to make the introduction or rejection of slavery in that territory dependent on the decision of its inhabitants led to a contention between the friends and opponents of slavery, which, though at first conducted on constitutional lines, soon degenerated into an open struggle which set all law at defiance.

Societies were formed in different states of the north for the purpose of organising methods for effecting the settlement of Kansas by free farmers; and their efforts

THE BEGINNING OF AMERICA'S VAST RAILROAD SYSTEMS: THE FIRST TRAIN IN THE UNITED STATES

Although railways for the purpose of carrying stone, gravel and other heavy materials were used in America as early as the beginning of the nineteenth century, it was not until August 9th, 1829, that Horatio Allen, a civil engineer, took the first locomotive from Hopendale, Pa., to Carbondale, a distance of twenty-seven miles. On this trip Mr. Allen ran the engine himself, allowing no one else on it, as he considered the risk of life too great. The line was begun two years previously, and both locomotive and rails were procured from England.

From the painting by G. L. Henry, by permission of C. Klackner, 20 Old Bond Street, London

had a decided success. Partly owing to the great immigration from Europe there was no lack of men who were quite prepared to undertake in the Far West their share of the struggle against wild Nature and the southern foe. Now it seemed beyond all doubt that in communities where free settlers had once opened up **Emigration** the soil slave-holders would in **to the** vain attempt to gain a foot-**Far West** hold. A settlement of this kind could not, however, be effected by leaps and bounds, nor could it occupy the whole territory in one single rush. The journey to Kansas from the states of the east was long and expensive, and the means of the colonisation societies were as yet very limited.

For the slave-holders the position of affairs was much more favourable. The inhabited portion of the lands by which Kansas was bordered was almost entirely occupied by slave-holding states, and the people of Missouri, who entered the territory in especially large numbers, were thus enabled to keep in continuous touch with their friends on the other side of the border, and could, if necessary, call in their help. Accordingly, when the governor of the territory issued the writ for the election of a legislative assembly, the people from the adjacent southern districts poured in, and by participation in the voting, falsification of votes, and the use of violence against their opponents, brought about an election which everyone knew did not in the least represent the real condition of affairs.

The federal government not only confirmed the election of the chosen candidates, but actually allowed the latter to draw up a constitution for the territory, which was formed entirely in the interests of the slave-holders and with the object of suppressing their opponents. Indeed, the federal government actually went so far as to place federal troops at the service of the **American** pro-slavery administration, al-**Civil War** though in the meantime the free **Inevitable** settlers, too, had demonstrated, by means of a free popular vote, the presence of an anti-slavery population at least as strong as their opponents, and had organised by electing a legislative body and proclaiming a constitution. Under such conditions a permanent peace became impossible. The first blood was shed probably by the slave party; but their opponents also soon resorted to reckless violence. Thus for years before Lincoln's election, a civil war turning on the question of the permission or prohibition of slavery was raging in the very heart of the union.

The federal government seemed openly to sympathise with the slave-holders. The Democratic party, as such, was forced to do so according to its principles and its past history. Even the northern wing of the party, which, under the leadership of Douglas, did not indeed contend for the maintenance of slavery, but for the extreme consequences of the right of self-government of the separate states and territories, was, nevertheless, by recognising the validity of the first elections in Kansas, logically bound to support the policy of the president.

Even in the Democratic camp no one any longer failed to see that the discipline of the party in congress could in future be maintained only with difficulty; that the reputation of the party among the people had been severely shaken; and that by its policy in the Kansas questions it had placed a formidable weapon in the hands **Feeble** of its opponents. This was **Democratic** made plain to all who could see **Victory** by the next presidential election. This, it is true, once more resulted in the victory of the Democratic candidate, James Buchanan (1857–1861), an old man of seventy-one years, who had spent a long time as ambassador in England, completely removed from political struggles. But of the 4,000,000 votes returned, only 1,800,000 had been recorded for him; and he was elected only because it was still found impossible to gather all the anti-Democrats into one fold.

The old Whigs and the "Know-nothings" had again nominated Fillmore; and though his name clearly enough proclaimed the feeble condition and want of principle of the party, his candidature nevertheless served to withdraw some hundreds of thousands of votes from the third party, and thus to put it in a minority. In spite of this, the election contest was of far-reaching importance to the Republicans, and through it they took a considerable step forward on the road to victory. Even during the negotiations for the nomination of a candidate, an agreement had been effected between the old group of the Free-Soilers, the Abolitionist "Know-nothings," and the true Republicans. The selection of Frémont, the discoverer of the Far West and the conqueror of California, as a candidate for the presidency, seemed a very fortunate move. He embodied the ideas of the Young America party, which would have nothing to do with the old struggle between the defenders of state rights and the nationalists, but which had inscribed on its banners the greatness of their common country in a free republican development.

The Republicans this time remained faithful to the old conservative spirit, not, however, in the sense of a retrogressive stagnation, but in that of a steadily progressive development advancing in definite legal channels towards the highest ends. With his 1,300,000 votes, Frémont had so nearly approached the goal of victory that not only his adherents, but also his opponents, looked upon the success of the Republicans at the next election as certain.

This prospect loomed like a spectre upon the southern Democrats. Hitherto the only way in which their opponents had attained or had hoped to attain a victory had been by putting up a candidate to whom even a Democrat might still be able to give his vote. Now, however,

Success of the Republicans for the first time, the Republicans had put up against them a man in whose programme not a spark of Democratic principle was to be discovered, and one who uncompromisingly placed the union above the states, and the spirit of the Declaration of Independence on an equality with that of the constitution. It was only by a mere chance that this programme had failed to secure the victory, and even before the result of the election was known the slave states recognised that this was the beginning of the end. As had happened earlier, a conference of the Southern states was once more summoned, but it was poorly attended and insignificant in results. Nevertheless, the slave states fully realised the seriousness of the situation.

In the south, the industrial contrast between free and slave states, which rendered any community of interests impossible, had been recognised much earlier and more distinctly than in the north. In times more remote it may not have been so easily perceived how the south, in such a struggle, was far less favourably placed than the north, but the events of the last few years and their thorough and business-like discussion had opened the eyes of the slave-holders on this point. They could not

fail to notice what a difference was observable in the relative increase of population in the two sections of the union, and how the wealth of the north was increasing in a proportion totally different from that of the south. Finally, they must have come to appreciate the reason why the value of land was so essentially different on the

Bankruptcy Facing Slave-holders opposite sides of the border of the slave states. In Kansas and many other border districts they had learned from personal experience how much superior free labour was to the "peculiar institution" of the south; for of the settlers whom they sent to these districts at their common expense for the purpose of opposing free labour not a few went over into the enemy's camp. If only at one and the same stroke they could have abolished slavery and possessed themselves of the industrial conditions of the north! As things were, the abolition of slavery meant nothing less than the ruin of the slave-holders and the bankruptcy of all the propertied classes of the south.

It was not their haughtiness as slave-holders which so often, inside and outside of congress, provoked the Southerners to words and acts unworthy of a highly civilised nation; it was rather the feeling of their own impotence, the certainty of being ruined men as soon as the federal government should be used to put the ban upon the system of slavery. It was such feelings which impelled the firebrands of the south to more and more exorbitant demands, and spurred them on to increasingly bitter struggles.

In reality, the policy adopted by the government, which has often been criticised as displaying a desire to please the slave-holders, arose from a desire to modify to some extent, by favourable enactments, the industrial disadvantages from which the southern half of the union was suffering. It was the same desire which prompted so

Concessions to Southerners large a section of the Northern politicians to feel kindly disposed toward the Southerners. On the other hand, if the majority of the people should renounce these sentiments, and the voting at the presidential election had shown that this was the case, and if they should succeed in filling the administration with men of similar opinions, the only natural result would be the commercial and political bankruptcy of the south. Its only choice then would be to break with its past, to secede from the union, and to form a confederation of states whose interests rested on the common foundation of slave labour.

Such a confederacy would have become rapidly impoverished, and must have succumbed in the competition with its neighbour states, unless, indeed, an internal revolution had forced it to change its system. For the moment, however, the slave-holders indulged the hope that by these means they might save their property and delay its inevitable overthrow. To the men of the south their method of proceeding did not appear revolutionary. The doctrine of state rights had led many politicians, particularly in the south, to regard the union merely as a compact between the states which the contracting parties were entitled to rescind. South Carolina had already openly expressed a similar view in its conflict with Jackson ; but its procedure at that time had been considered by many as incorrect and illegal, even though the government on that occasion had preferred to attain its end by means of what some chose to call a compromise.

End of Slavery in Sight

Of course, in the meantime the feeling of an indissoluble connection had gained considerable strength among widespread classes of the population, and the secessionist longings of individual Southern states only aroused in some sections a feeling in favour of union. Nevertheless, there were those in the north-east, where the contrast of interests with the south was sharpest, who began to regard the separation of industrially dissimilar groups as being as much of an advantage as did the Southerners themselves, and to draw conclusions from the doctrine of state rights, according to which a peaceful dissolution of the union appeared the most desirable way out of the difficulty. President Buchanan first of all made efforts to postpone this question, in the hope that such a course might bring counsel and deliverance. From his predecessor he had received other problems, the solution of which might be supposed to claim general interest, and he was in hopes that by taking such matters in hand he might turn the current of politics into another channel. For a long time past the island of Cuba had been one of those territories whose acquisition by the United

Doctrine of State Rights

States had been particularly desired by many. Its geographical position of necessity brought it in many ways into contact with the United States, and the weakness of Spanish rule in the island made its eventual sale appear by no means impossible.

In such an event, however, it was of vital importance to the United States that the island should not fall into the hands of a Power which understood better how to utilise the industrial resources of the island in competition with their own products. Whether Buchanan really did entertain higher expectations from the future must be left undecided ; at any rate, he now made use of this question for the purpose of diverting attention from internal affairs, and he attained his object—in so far, at least, as his proposition to place eight million pounds for this purpose at the disposal of the government for some time occupied the attention of the senate and imparted a different character to the debates.

The Mormon difficulty was employed for a similar purpose. Pierce had already called out the federal troops against the Mormons, in order to force the submission of Brigham Young's theocratic régime to the federal laws; and Buchanan had to carry through congress the acceptance of the agreement by which matters were settled, at least apparently, in a satisfactory manner. Nevertheless, Buchanan did not succeed by these diversions in appeasing the internal feud. The slavery question kept knocking louder and louder at the doors of congress, which was neither able nor willing to refuse it admittance.

Shameless Electoral Frauds

In Kansas, parties were still facing each other for the fight. The party of the slave-holders had once more, by means of the most shameless electoral frauds, pretended to be alone empowered to speak for the territory, and at Lecompton had drawn up a constitution on the basis of which Kansas applied for admission as a state. But although the Free State party discovered the fraud, and on their side, with the so-called Topeka constitution, which prohibited slavery, made a similar application to congress, Buchanan favoured the Lecompton constitution, and also got the senate to accept it.

But the house of representatives could not be won over by straightforward means ; a majority was finally obtained by parliamentary manœuvres, but only after

THE UNITED STATES SENATE DISCUSSING HENRY CLAY'S FAMOUS "COMPROMISE OF 1850"

In 1847 David Wilmot brought a bill before congress prohibiting the introduction of slavery into newly acquired territories, against which the Southern leaders vehemently protested. The campaign, conducted by them on behalf of their theory was long and violent, culminating in 1850 with Henry Clay's famous compromise, which has since become known as the "Compromise of 1850." This picture depicts congress of that period discussing the final stages of the compromise, the principles of which in the meantime had become important factors in party politics.

it had been agreed to submit once more the question of the constitution to the vote of the people. On this occasion, however, the slave-holders' party was completely defeated. The consequence was that Kansas had to wait several years longer before it was admitted as a state; but it had already rendered an important service to the cause of liberty.

Slave-holders' Party Defeated It had already been for some time a matter of considerable difficulty to hold to the policy of the majority those northern Democrats who at that time were led by Stephen Arnold Douglas. The question of the constitution of Kansas served to effect their complete separation.

The Democratic party defended in principle the right of self-government of the states. Douglas followed out the consequences of this policy in so far as he voted for submitting the Lecompton constitution to the popular vote. It was, however, well known in congress that Douglas's demand would seriously call in question the recognition of slavery in Kansas, and the Democrats of the south accordingly looked upon his action as a secession from the party and used every effort to make the split irremediable. They thus probably hoped merely to expel the unreliable elements from the party, and thereby consolidate it. But, unfortunately, with the disruption of the Democratic party the connection between north and south was once more torn asunder, and the unavoidable conflict of interests was again recognised in a new sphere. Thus was typified the greater fact that the country, in entering upon the campaign of the next presidential election, was divided into two opposite and completely separated groups of states.

On this occasion the Democratic party, as already stated, was no longer united. Its first convention at Charleston adjourned without arriving at a nomination. Later, the northern wing of the party nominated Douglas as its candidate, while the southern delegates put up John C. Breckenridge. The Constitutional Union party nominated Bell. The Republicans held their convention in the western city of Chicago, and here a western candidate, Abraham Lincoln, was nominated for the presidency. Lincoln was a self-made man who had become known only in recent years through a contest which in 1858 he fought with Douglas for

Fruitless Democratic Convention

a seat in the United States Senate. He was, above all, a typical man of the world, who, as backwoodsman, small store-keeper, village postman, and deputy surveyor, had well learnt the lesson which only diverse experience can teach. At the outset of his career his growing reputation as a lawyer nearly compelled him to abandon politics altogether; nor was it until Douglas repealed the Missouri Compromise, and reopened the question of slavery in the territories that his party began to realise his undoubted ability and his strength. His calm circumspection, his humour, and his readiness as a debater had already made him one of the foremost politicians of the young party. Moreover, his many qualities characteristic of a "man of the people" made him a candidate more desirable than the average parliamentarian.

The voting was even less decisive than at Buchanan's election. Though Lincoln, on November 6th, 1860, received a majority of electoral votes, by which he was legally elected to the presidency, he fell short of a majority of popular votes by more than twice as many votes as did his predecessor. The significant feature of the election, however, was that its result was due entirely to the enormous numerical preponderance of the north. In the south Lincoln had not been presented as a candidate at all, and even in the border states he had obtained only a few thousand votes.

Lincoln Elected President

South Carolina, then as much as ever the leader of the extremists, responded to the election with an ordinance of secession from the union. At first it stood alone in taking this step. Soon afterwards, however, a convention of several Southern states was held at Montgomery, for the purpose of deciding upon some common course of action whereby the interests of the south might be safeguarded against a northern president. It was in vain that Virginia summoned a convention for the purpose of bringing about a reconciliation; the most she could effect in that direction was to suggest a moderate course of action for the Central states and to take measures for preventing a further spread of the secession movement. That it would be impossible to win back the Southern states by negotiation was not only expressed by the latter, but was also clearly perceived by some in the north.

THE CIVIL WAR IN AMERICA
AND THE ABOLITION OF SLAVERY

BUCHANAN considered it his duty, during the last months of his period of office, to preserve a passive attitude. He, who as a Democrat had early defended the principle of state rights out of conviction, found no difficulty in acknowledging the claim of the south to the right of secession. But he was destined, before leaving the scene, to execute another complete political *volte-face*. The February convention of the Southern states at Montgomery had for its immediate consequence the formation of a separate confederacy, which elected Jefferson Davis as its president and claimed the rights of an independent state. Buchanan felt disposed to acknowledge this claim.

The idea of allowing the apostate states to withdraw peacefully from the union was so widespread among the Democrats of the North-eastern states that the south was already led to entertain hopes of such an issue. The secession, how-**Integrity of the Union at Stake** ever, had caused the retirement of some of the Ministers from Buchanan's Cabinet; and the men who stepped into their places were not only themselves resolved to maintain the integrity of the union, but they also managed to convince the president of the necessity of such a policy. The latter, therefore, suddenly refused any further negotiations with the confederacy, and though he could not be induced to adopt an active policy against the latter, his temporary advisers managed at least to prevent his yielding another step.

It was under such conditions that Lincoln entered upon office on March 4th, 1861. His inaugural address was entirely animated by that conservative spirit on which the Republican party had built up its platform ; but he declared as his first principle the preservation of the union and the enforcement of all its laws. He expressly guarded against giving utterance to abolitionist longings, which, indeed, then seemed contrary to his personal inclinations ; but he held the Southern states so much the more responsible if by their proceedings they should stir up a civil war. It soon became evident that these were not mere empty words. A deputation which desired to treat with the federal government in the name of the confederate states was refused **The Demands of the Secessionists** formal audience by the Secretary of State on the ground that the government did not recognise the existence of an independent republic of the confederate states. In other respects, however, he preserved a temporising attitude until events forced him to adopt another policy.

The Secessionists had already demanded from Buchanan the delivery into their hands of all federal property in the confederate states, but more especially the forts of Charleston ; and though they had met with a formal refusal they had nevertheless practically succeeded in attaining their object. The Charleston forts were so feebly garrisoned that their commandant, Major Anderson, declared it impossible to defend them against even the slightest attack. But as the government did not promptly send him reinforcements he retired to Fort Sumter, built on an island, and thus capable of being most easily defended, while the enemy occupied the other forts.

Already, in the beginning of January, 1861, shots had been exchanged here. On one occasion, when a federal steamer endeavoured to convey supplies to Anderson, she had been obliged by **The South's First Victory** the shore batteries to return without having effected her object, leaving Anderson to his fate. Nevertheless, it was not until April 12th that the South Carolina troops found sufficient courage to direct their fire on Fort Sumter, which after a two days' bombardment was obliged to capitulate. The south considered it a great victory when the federal flag was hauled down from the last fort on its Atlantic coast-line. But it was considerably mistaken in its calculations. As long as the Secessionists had sought severance from the union by peaceful methods the federal government had to reckon with the fact that a powerful party in its northern dominion was disposed to agree with this demand, and was certainly not prepared to take up arms for the sake of upholding the union.

When, however, the south had shed the first blood a storm of indignation arose in the whole north, and the people demanded that the sword should not be sheathed until the south had been brought back to obedience to the laws. This fighting ardour, turned to good account by the call for volunteers, placed in the hands of the government the means of extricating itself from the awkward position in which Lincoln's hesitation, as opposed to the resolute measures of the Southerners, had placed it. Until now only eleven states had joined the confederacy. Among the border states, however, several were undecided; the side they would finally take would depend, in all probability, on the issue of the initial engagements. Virginia was at first among the waverers; but her importance to the Southern states was so considerable that the congress of the south used every effort to win her over to its cause. It was essentially on this account that Richmond, on the James River, was chosen as the capital of the confederacy, although it was situated not far from the border and was exposed to the attack of the enemy.

The situation of the national government at the beginning of the Civil War was somewhat critical. The federal troops, in themselves inconsiderable, were in a state approaching disorganisation. The Secretary for War, before he resigned, had intentionally placed a portion of the war material in the hands of the Southerners, and the rest seemed to have been dissipated. A large number of the officers had left the federal army and had taken

JEFFERSON DAVIS

Distinguishing himself in the Mexican War, Davis became a powerful advocate of slavery, and president of the confederate states. During the Civil War he was made prisoner, but after two years was released.

service with the south. Even the numerical superiority of the north was at the beginning of no weight. So completely had people in the free states mistaken the character of the impending struggle that some at first believed it would be settled by means of regular soldiers and the militia, while many citizens persisted in their national repugnance to everything military and went about their ordinary business.

The danger threatened most immediately the federal capital. The neighbouring states of Maryland and Delaware were slave states and largely in sympathy with the south. Though the loss of Washington would have been of little military importance, its moral effect would have been more serious inasmuch as in the Northern states the war party had, as a matter of fact, only an uncertain control. Fortunately, it was possible to prevent such a catastrophe, for the militia regiments which had been rapidly summoned arrived at the capital in time. When Maryland prepared to offer armed resistance to the transportation of further reinforcements, its capital, Baltimore, was occupied by the federal troops, and the pro-Secessionist government was replaced by one favourably disposed to the union. This was the first blow received by the Secession, preventing once for all the attachment of the states of Maryland and Delaware to their cause. In the west things were assuming a similar shape. Here, also, the confederacy had reckoned on winning over to its side such slave-holding central states as Kentucky, Missouri and Kansas.

It was the more justified in this hope since almost throughout the region the government was in the hands of Democratic majorities; but in spite of this they were nowhere successful. The western counties of Virginia adhered to the union; in Kentucky the firmness of the federal officials prevented any false step on the part of the local government; and though Missouri could not, in its entirety, be

JEFFERSON DAVIS SIGNING GOVERNMENT ACTS BY THE ROADSIDE

The above picture shows a quaint incident towards the end of the Civil War. The fugitive Cabinet has halted by the roadside, and the president is signing documents which his Secretary of State is handing to him. This was the last official business which was conducted by the Confederate Government, the end of the war being in sight.

THE PRESIDENT OF THE SOUTH BIDDING FAREWELL TO HIS ESCORT AND STAFF

The virtual end of the Civil War came with the disbandment of the Confederate forces in the early part of 1865. Jefferson Davis and his men met for the last time at Washington, Georgia, and in the above picture he is seen bidding farewell to his escort and staff. Assembled around him are men who have sacrificed their all to the cause, and he is urging them to seek their own safety and to leave him to his fate. Forty-eight hours later he was taken prisoner.

preserved to the union, it was nevertheless prevented from formally going over to the Secessionists. Beyond the Mississippi, in fact, even the Democrats were good Unionists, and with the exception of the Gulf states of Louisiana, Arkansas and Texas, the whole of this division of the country remained faithful to the union. Here, indeed, the conservative unionist idea had become firmly rooted. The inhabitants of these regions had lived under the union laws from the time of their first settling, and had always supported a Great-American policy, and were by no means inclined to allow the will of discontented citizens to determine whether the state was to continue a united whole, rich in future possibilities, or was to be divided into separate halves, each restraining the other's development. In the west the union idea flourished; and from the western territory began that succession of victories which, coupled with the parallel campaigns in the east, led to the final overthrow of the confederacy. The first attack by the north had a lamentable result. An army of 60,000 men under McDowell advanced into Virginia, and, falling in with the enemy at Bull Run, was disastrously defeated, and retreated in a state of panic to Washington (July 21st, 1861). In the east the struggle thereafter for years consisted in backward and forward movements of mighty armies between the two capitals of Richmond and Washington, which were only about a hundred miles distant from each other. Numerous battles were fought, lasting sometimes for days, in which the losses on both sides reached uncommonly high figures. And

GENERAL JOHNSTON
After quelling the Mormon rebellion in Utah, Johnston joined the southern forces, and during an attack on Grant at Shiloh on April 6th, 1862, was mortally wounded.

GENERAL LEE
General Lee, at the outbreak of the Civil War, fought in Virginia, and was soon placed at the head of the confederate army. His surrender to General Grant at Richmond in 1865 was the last decisive engagement of the war.

yet neither side was able to win any permanent success. The operations, as a rule, ended fatally to the attacking party, without, however, providing the defenders with an opportunity of pushing matters to a decisive issue. In generalship, the south was undoubtedly superior. The leadership of Joseph Eccleston Johnston and of Robert Edward Lee, the wonderful expeditions of Thomas Jonathan (otherwise known as "Stonewall") Jackson and of his so-called "foot-cavalry," far exceeded the performances of the north. But even these leaders were unable to organise a plan of campaign laid out on an extensive scale and conducted with energy. No doubt they had to struggle with special difficulties. Inasmuch as the south, even during the first phase of the war, had been shut out from the sea, it was compelled to confine its operations exclusively to the land. As long as the scene of these operations lay between Richmond and Washington, the confederate troops enjoyed the advantage of having the population on their side. Nevertheless, for their commissariat, and in many cases, too, owing to the almost entire absence of roads in the European sense of the word, for their transport, the large army divisions were obliged to keep close to such few railway lines as were then in existence. This dependence naturally increased the difficulty of advancing for considerable distances; though, indeed, no advantage could have been derived from such movements in the conditions under which the war was being conducted. The events of the first year of the war had shown that Washington was secure from occupation by the south as long as the power of the union remained permanently unshaken. But apart from the federal capital the army of Richmond seemed to have no serious object of attack. The capture of the commercial and industrial towns of the north-east would indeed have been a highly desirable prize; but to advance on them by land, with the centre of the enemy's force in the rear, was a task to which the armies of the south were not equal. True, they might succeed in temporarily subjecting to southern sway some more or less extensive portions of the Central states; or they might, by successful raids, ravage and alarm the neighbouring Northern states of Pennsylvania or West Virginia; but neither of these moves could appreciably affect the result of the war. Indeed, General Lee twice made the attempt, but without any success whatever. Such operations could only have had a decisive effect if corresponding successes had been obtained simultaneously in the other theatres of war. The principal obstacle to the success of the north was the deplorable absence of good leaders. True, in the first two years of the war the troops themselves were so poor in quality that even better generals could not have achieved victories with them. This, however, no longer applied in the later years of the war, when bodies of tried and picked men and officers had become available among the volunteer regiments. But the hesitating tactics of such men as George Brinton McClellan and the dogged resolution and indomitable courage of Ulysses Grant fell far short of the skill and ability of their southern antagonists. The north, however, enjoyed the advantage of free access

"STONEWALL" JACKSON

Jackson, on May 1st, 1863, made a brilliant attack on the national troops, succeeding in repulsing Hooker at Chancellorsville. In returning from that engagement he was accidentally shot by one of his own party.

to the sea, and McClellan endeavoured to make this the base of his campaign; but the attempt proved unsuccessful and was not repeated at the seat of war in Virginia. In addition to this, the power of the north, especially during the first years of the war, was weakened by political considerations. Lincoln refused to regard the rebels as other than fellow-countrymen who had strayed from the right path. He was unwilling to fight with the confederate states, whose existence he did not recognise, but was only endeavouring to bring those to submission who were in arms against the union. In spite of this consideration, however, he was by no means successful in maintaining among his followers of the north that solid cohesion which on the side of the south was the natural outcome of events. In the east, in particular, and in a less degree also at the other theatres of war, the first two years of hostilities, while involving nothing but sacrifices, had produced no visible results. Instigated by southern agents, the party of those who were in favour of allowing the south to secede peacefully from the union now began to lift up its head in a manner which threatened danger. A time arrived when the Democrats in the east obtained ominous majorities and in some cases got possession of the state governments; and in New York the mob rose up against the "infamous" draft, and a resolution was actually brought forward in congress calling on the president to commence negotiations with the government of the confederate states for the purpose of putting an end to the quarrel. Lincoln's position was indeed one of the utmost difficulty. It would have been almost untenable had not the middle west remained firm to the Unionist

GENERAL McCLELLAN

Driving the confederate troops out of West Virginia, he was sent to reorganise the army of the Potomac, and in November, 1861, was appointed commander-in-chief.

AN IRONCLAD FRIGATE AND TWO ERICSSON BATTERIES GOING INTO ACTION

GUN AND MORTAR BOATS ON THE MISSISSIPPI ENGAGING THE FORTS AND BATTERIES

NAVAL ENGAGEMENTS IN THE AMERICAN CIVIL WAR

The siege of Vicksburg was one of the most memorable in the history of the Civil War. Realising the importance of closing up the Mississippi River, the Confederates in 1862 strongly fortified the place, and from this time on succeeded in repulsing attack upon attack, only surrendering on July 4th after a hard siege by land and water, which began on May 18th, 1863. The lower picture shows a number of gun and mortar boats on the Mississippi River attacking the forts and batteries on the island and mainland, while the first depicts two of the Ericsson batteries going into action.

THE CONFEDERATE MERRIMAC RUNNING INTO THE FEDERAL CUMBERLAND

THE MERRIMAC AND MONITOR IN AN ENGAGEMENT IN HAMPTON ROADS

SCENES IN THE STRUGGLE BETWEEN NORTH AND SOUTH

The second year of the war was marked by a number of defeats for the Union navy, not the least of them being the sinking of the Cumberland on March 8th, 1862, by the confederate Merrimac. For some time the Merrimac, originally attached to the United States Navy, which vessel the confederates had rendered almost invulnerable to artillery, was supreme on the water, sinking more than one Federal ship before meeting a worthy opponent in the Monitor. The latter was built by a Swede named Ericsson, and with its low armoured deck carried two guns of the heaviest calibre.

programme of the Republican party, and had not the governments of the Western states, which at the outbreak of the war were still partially in the hands of the Democrats, been succeeded by others of unionist principles.

In the east the danger would have been immeasurably greater had it not been that there, too, the war gained adherents. The south had obtained a temporary superiority, owing to the fact that before Lincoln's accession to office it had acquired possession of very much of the war material of the union. However, owing to the limited amount of human material it had at its disposal, it was incapable, at least during the years of the war,

benefited by these conditions. The few frigates and revenue cutters which constituted the United States Navy had before the war been ordered partly to southern and partly to far-distant foreign ports, so that in this respect also the union was rendered virtually powerless. The Unionists, however, fully realised that the only way of preventing constant accessions of fresh power to the south was by shutting it out from the sea.

In Washington it was well known what importance the Secessionists attached to this matter. They felt assured that, being unable to do without the cotton supplies of the south, the European Powers, and especially Great Britain, would, in the

FORT LAFAYETTE, THE FEDERAL BASTILLE FOR POLITICAL PRISONERS
During the early part of the Civil War the grim fortress of Lafayette, situated on Hendrick's Reef in the Narrows at the entrance to New York Harbour, served as federal Bastille for political prisoners.

of establishing an industrial independence, and its position in consequence could not fail to become more and more unfavourable. This fact in itself served to stimulate the north towards exerting itself to the utmost of its powers, and provided the North-eastern states with an opportunity of immensely improving their industries and of employing their activities in an exceedingly profitable manner.

The factories engaged in the manufacture of ammunition, military outfits, articles of clothing, etc., were suddenly overwhelmed with orders, and, naturally, obtained most favourable contracts. The shipping industry, which had at all times given employment to thousands of hands on the North Atlantic coast, was especially

event of the north gaining the upper hand, at once hasten to their assistance. In the south, cotton, as a matter of fact, was king. It formed the wealth of the large landowners; for its sake it was necessary to uphold slavery even at the risk of a serious war; with it the costs of that war were to be defrayed; and for its sake, too, the south hoped to obtain the recognition, if not the support, of Europe. Nor were they altogether wrong in the last of these calculations. Napoleon III. felt drawn to the side of the confederates more from a feeling of selfish jealousy of the United States than from any other interests; but in the case of England a similar leaning, due largely to industrial conditions, was counteracted mainly by the strength of

THE GREAT FEDERAL DEFEAT AT THE BATTLE OF FREDERICKSBURG

The defeat of the Union forces at the Battle of Fredericksburg was one of the most desperate episodes in the whole of the Civil War. At sunset, on December 13th, 1862, General Burnside opened fire with every available battery on the Confederate position. A sharp and decisive battle followed, lasting until the night of the 15th, when the national troops, defeated and humiliated, retreated across the river, after suffering a loss of some 10,000 men.

SURRENDER OF GENERAL LEE AT RICHMOND, APRIL 9TH, 1865

Lee's surrender at Richmond was the last and greatest triumph of the northern forces. The decreasing resources of the south had begun to have a despairing influence upon his troops. Reaching Richmond on April 9th, 1865, after a series of engagements which had reduced his infantry to 8,000 muskets, he found himself surrounded by the enemy. Escape was impossible, and to avoid further bloodshed in a hopeless cause, General Lee yielded to the inevitable.

the anti-slavery sentiment. An enormous number of operatives were thrown out of employment by the cotton famine consequent on the blockade of the southern ports.

The strict neutrality preserved by the British Government was the cause of indignant complaints in the south; but the lack of vigilance which permitted the Alabama and other cruisers to escape to sea was regarded by the Federals as warranting on their part an attitude which very nearly brought about a breach of diplomatic relations, and created an intensity of irritation between the two nations which was not allayed for many years. With an energy which compels our admiration, the north set to work to

The decisive stroke came from the west. The formation of the confederacy had once more placed the western states in a position similar to that which they held before the cession of Louisiana. Even at that time the free navigation of the Mississippi down to the Gulf of Mexico had been recognised as indispensable to the prosperity of the inland states of the continent.

Still more was this now the case, when, in place of isolated forts and trading-stations, between which the Indian roamed, flourishing towns and villages had arisen, while sturdy farmers had converted thousands of square miles of virgin soil into rich arable land. As yet only a few railways connected the Father of Waters with

THE CIVIL WAR: DESTRUCTION OF THE CONFEDERATE FLOTILLA OFF MEMPHIS

organise a navy which should be equal to the great task before it, and by the end of 1862 the blockade of the southern ports began to have a telling effect.

A few vessels commanded by daring seamen managed, even down to the end of the war, to run the blockade either undetected, or without sustaining any serious damage. The lucky parties thereby earned large sums of money; but with a few shiploads they were able neither to exercise any appreciable influence on the European demand for cotton, nor, by their occasional and insufficient importations, to keep up the war supplies of the south. Thus, although the naval war exercised a direct influence on the struggle, it was not able to determine the issue.

the provinces of the east; and the project of a railway to the Pacific Ocean had not advanced beyond the preliminary stage. Thus the Mississippi formed the principal artery of traffic for the vast region which is watered by it and its tributaries; and even at that time a large fleet of steamers was employed in the exchange of the products of the inland states and of the east. The Secessionists threatened to close this road, both shores of the Mississippi from the mouth of the Ohio to the Gulf of Mexico being in their hands; and by a complete series of fortifications it was proposed to bar the stream against every foreign vessel. Owing to the fact that at the outset of the war Kentucky was preserved to the union, the Ohio, at least

THE SUMTER CAPTURING TWO FEDERAL MERCHANTMEN OFF GIBRALTAR

THE FIGHT BETWEEN THE ALABAMA AND THE KEARSAGE

CONFEDERATE VESSELS IN VICTORY AND DEFEAT

The final combat between the Alabama and the Kearsage occurred off Cherbourg, on the morning of Sunday, June 19th, 1864, the Alabama being sunk. One of the finest acquisitions of the Confederate navy, the Alabama, during her destructive career, burned or captured no fewer than a hundred American vessels. Of a then more modern type, the Kearsage was one of the nine gun-boats which were completed for the United States within a period of three months.

nearly as far as its mouth, did not come into the possession of the Southerners. On the other hand, the Confederates completely blocked the Cumberland and the Tennessee, at the place where these two rivers approach within a few miles of each other, by means of the two forts Henry and Donelson, and in this manner created for

Modern Methods in the War themselves a fortified camp of immense importance. This point formed the first object of attack for the Unionists.

It was here, even more than in the east, that the war acquired that character which so strikingly distinguishes it from all the wars of the Old World. With the high value that the Americans attach to all practical matters, and with their highly developed commercial instincts, the technical arts and sciences had in the United States attained a development such as one would have looked for in vain in the Old World.

Even at that time railways and steamers played a part in the traffic of the United States which they did not acquire in Europe till many years later. In the War of Secession industry came to embrace a wide field, and northern mechanics and artisans took up the new problems which presented themselves with an energy which attracted the attention of all foreign Powers. Technical inventions found greater application in this war than in any other, both by being employed for the first time on a much larger scale, and by actually owing their origin to the necessity of the moment. In a country without roads, railways acquired a high strategic importance. Not only their destruction, but, above all, their restoration, were among the important tasks of the contesting armies ; and railways were applied even more directly to military purposes, as with armoured trains.

The requirements of war had a still greater effect upon the shipbuilding industry, as was illustrated when the fleet

The War's Effect on Shipbuilding conveying the northern army under McClellan to the James River was met by a vessel of a hitherto unknown type. The Southerners had, it appeared, cut down nearly to the water's edge a steam frigate belonging to the United States Navy, and had then rendered her almost invulnerable to artillery—such as it was then—by means of armour plates, while the principal weapon of this ocean monster consisted of a tremendous ram. More than

one ship of the federal fleet succumbed to the Merrimac before she was met by a worthy opponent. The latter appeared under the name of Monitor, and was built by a Swede named Ericsson. This vessel, likewise, had a low armoured deck, from the midst of which, however, rose a rotary armoured tower, which carried two guns of the heaviest calibre. This period marks the beginning of that competition between heavy armour and guns in naval warfare which has assumed larger and larger proportions, and which appears only within recent years, owing to the tremendous effects of modern explosives, to have been decided in favour of guns.

In the western campaign also technical science was immediately called into requisition. The Unionists built a fleet of heavily armed and armour-plated gunboats which provided both a movable support for the land forces and a floating siege train for attacking the forts. To the performances of this river flotilla are in a large part ascribable the successes won by the western forces on the Mississippi. While a force from the north, after the opening up of the Tennessee and the Cumberland,

Victories of the Federals entered the Mississippi itself, another sent by sea from the east entered the mouth of the river, and captured New Orleans as

early as the beginning of 1862. The second half of this year and the beginning of 1863 were for the union the most depressing period of the war. In the east the Confederates assumed the offensive ; in the centre of the theatre of war they advanced far northwards beyond the line of the Tennessee, which had been wrested from them in the previous year, and threatened the union frontier ; while on the Mississippi the federal forces were for months vainly besieging the bastions of Vicksburg on the left bank of the river.

By a happy chance Vicksburg fell on the same day (July 4th, 1863) that Lee's army in front of Gettysburg was obliged to fall back into Virginia. The more decisive result was that achieved in the west ; it opened the Mississippi completely, and thus separated the south-west from the other secession states. The importance of this success was fully recognised in the north-east, and Grant, the conqueror of Vicksburg, was placed in charge of those armies which, in the autumn of the same year, engaged their opponents so decisively in the battles around Chattanooga. Early

THE CONSUMMATION OF THE AMERICAN CIVIL WAR: PROCLAMATION OF FREEDOM FOR THE NEGRO SLAVES

The proclamation emancipating the slaves of North America was signed by Abraham Lincoln and his Cabinet on September 2nd, 1862, and came into force on the first day of the following year. At this juncture feeling against the Abolitionists became very strong, and rewards were offered for the capture of the leaders of anti-slavery societies. In view of the threatened insurrection of the negroes, the proclamation enjoined them to abstain from violence, and to work faithfully for fair wages. It also announced that a number of them would be taken into the United States military and naval services for which act its framers invoked the "considerate judgment of mankind and the gracious favour of Almighty God."

JOHN BROWN, THE HERO OF THE ANTI-SLAVERY MOVEMENT, GOING TO EXECUTION

The execution of John Brown, the famous American Abolitionist, was one of the direct forces which hastened on the great Civil War. An intensely religious personality, Brown early in life conceived a hatred for slavery, and in 1859, with a band of twenty-two men—mostly negroes—and some arms, organised a plot to free the slaves of Virginia. Hiring a farmhouse near Harper's Ferry, on the night of October 16th they seized the arsenal and took possession of the village. In the ensuing fight several of the party were killed, Brown himself surrendering only after receiving severe injuries. He was taken prisoner, tried, convicted, and, along with his four sons, hanged on December 2nd.

in the following year Grant was given the chief command of all the federal armies, and then began, on a large scale, those two movements by which Lee and Johnston were to be overpowered and the confederacy crushed.

Fortunately for the union, Grant found in William Tecumseh Sherman, also a Westerner, a worthy coadjutor. A succession of victories led him in September,

1864, to the city of Atlanta; and thence he marched straight across the enemy's country to the Atlantic coast. By this movement the war was carried through Georgia into the heart of the enemy's country, the arrogant state of South Carolina, which now was to feel the sufferings of the war. With the progress of Sherman north from Savannah and the establishment of connection with the sea

PRESIDENT FOR THE SECOND TIME: LINCOLN'S GREAT SPEECH IN FRONT OF THE CAPITOL

Lincoln's second inauguration as President of the United States, which took place within a few weeks of the end of the Civil War, marked at once the crowning moment in the history of the Republican party and also in the life of the famous western lawyer. His overwhelming majority of 416,000 on election day proved conclusively that the people were with him. The picture on this page shows the front of the Capitol at Washington as it appeared on that occasion, when Lincoln gave utterance to what has come to be regarded as his greatest and noblest speech.

forces in December, 1864, and thus with the army in Virginia, the war at last entered upon its final stage.

With simultaneous advances on the seat of the enemy's government by Grant from the north and by Sherman from the south, the armies of Lee and Johnson became more and more endangered. On April 9th, 1865, Grant compelled Lee to surrender at Appomattox Court House; and a few days later, on April 26th, the last army of the south, under Johnson, which was opposed to Sherman, relinquished its useless resistance. Thus the North had saved the existence of the union.

African colony of Liberia on an extensive scale; but none of his proposals met with immediate acceptance. Meanwhile, the time for a new presidential election had arrived; and, although Lincoln's re-election was contested both by opponents of slavery and by Democrats from opposite standpoints, he emerged victorious from the contest, with an overwhelming majority. In the meantime, slavery had been abolished in the district of Columbia by law, and in Maryland virtually. At last the administration proposed the Thirteenth Amendment to the federal constitution, which in terms abolished slavery through-

THE BODY OF PRESIDENT LINCOLN ARRIVING AT THE CITY HALL, NEW YORK

The rejoicing of the American nation with the approaching end of the Civil War was suddenly turned to sorrow when, on the evening of April 14th, 1865, Abraham Lincoln was shot at Ford's Theatre, Washington, by John Wilkes Booth. In this picture we see the arrival of the body of the great statesman at the City Hall, New York, whence, after an imposing and impressive service, it was conveyed to Springfield, Illinois, for burial, which took place on May 4th.

On September 22nd, 1862, Lincoln, in his capacity as commander-in-chief of the United States forces, issued a declaration announcing that on January 1st, 1863, all slaves within the portions of the revolted states occupied by federal troops should be free. Under the prevailing circumstances a demand for the abolition of slavery could not fail to be raised in congress also. Lincoln, however, still tried to make terms, as by the offer of money indemnities to the states affected by abolition, and by plans for aiding the emigration of liberated slaves to the

out the whole of the United States. Its acceptance by congress on January 31st, 1865, was followed by its ratification by the requisite number of states, and thus the victory of the Republicans, both military and political, seemed complete.

It was dimmed, however, by the fact that almost at the same moment Lincoln, the man who had served them as a prudent, unimpassioned, but absolutely reliable leader, was, by the cowardly pistol of an assassin on April 14th, 1865, deprived of the fruits of his well-earned victory.

KONRAD HAEBLER

UNITED STATES SINCE THE CIVIL WAR

THEIR SOCIAL AND INDUSTRIAL PROGRESS
THE NATION'S PLACE AMONG THE POWERS

LINCOLN'S death was a great misfortune for the whole union, and to the Republican party it brought an unmistakable crisis. The platform on which Lincoln had been elected in 1860 had not only been fulfilled in all essentials during the few years of the war, but through the course of events had been carried far beyond its original limits. At the decisive moment when, after an unexampled victory, all those meaner spirits were crowding to the victorious side when the time comes for dividing the spoils, the party had neither a definite programme which set forth its higher aims, nor a leader with sufficient influence to keep it in the right path.

Johnson the Successor of Lincoln From Lincoln's just and fair-minded character it might be expected that he would have completed the restoration of the union and the reconstruction of the Southern states in the same spirit which had marked his policy during the whole course of the war. The man, however, who by Lincoln's death was called to the presidency—Vice-President Andrew Johnson—neither stood as high above the views of the party as his predecessor had done, nor possessed enough power over it to keep in check its more radical elements. The Republican party now included such extremists as would strive, casting aside all ideal views, to take exemplary vengeance on the south for the five years' civil war and to render it incapable of ever again playing a part in the inner life of politics. Johnson himself by no means represented these aims, but he entirely failed to recognise the danger with which they threatened the union, and therefore missed the right moment for averting it.

He afterwards proceeded against it and battled with it strenuously to the end of his term of office, but unfortunately he did not succeed in conquering it. Like the Radical Republicans, Johnson had not con-

The President and the Rebel States sidered it advisable forthwith to reinstate the rebel states in their former place in the union ; and the amnesty law proclaimed by him marked out such an extraordinarily large number of those who were to be excluded, by act of the executive, from political privileges, that it acted as a direct encouragement to the Radicals. Johnson, however, made such a vigorous use of the measure and endeavoured so earnestly to control the affairs of the south that in connection with his amnesty policy the quarrel between him and the Radical majority broke out immediately on the meeting of congress. The president had decided to readmit the Southern states to their former relations, subject to the condition that they recognised the abolition of slavery and their obligations with reference to the federal debt, while declaring the debt of the confederate states void.

A number of the Southern states had actually been reconstructed on this basis and had sent their representatives to congress. They were unconditionally sent back by congress ; and the moderate attitude of the president now began to be assailed by an embittered Opposition, the end of which, apparently, was to make the readmission of the Southern states conditional on their agreeing to admit negroes to all the rights of white citizens. Johnson made vain efforts to frustrate the accomplishment of such a policy by means of **Johnson Impeached and Acquitted** his veto. His indiscretion, leading him so far as to malign congress, gave some justification to the Radicals in impeaching him before the senate, where he was finally acquitted by a single vote. One after another of the Southern states was forced to accept the conditions imposed by the Radical party, and its complete victory was thus assured.

THE LAST RESTING-PLACE OF PRESIDENT GRANT, ON THE BANKS OF THE HUDSON
President Grant's tomb, on the banks of the beautiful Hudson River, is one of the most magnificent edifices ever erected to the memory of man. Begun on April 27th, 1892, it was not completed until five years later, when, on April 27th, 1897, the president's remains were removed from their temporary resting-place and interred here. Altogether, 60,000 people contributed to the building fund, which realised a sum approaching £600,000.

In this course of action congress was actuated not exclusively by an ideal enthusiasm for the equality of all men.

The elections, which had been conducted on the basis of Johnson's plan of reconstruction, had shown that, in spite of their reverses in the war and the damage inflicted on their industry, the political influence of the south and of the Democratic party was by no means crushed, but would, under favourable conditions, rapidly reassume its normal position in the political life of the union. It was this result, however, which the Republicans feared as likely to be specially followed by their own defeat, and it was to prevent this that the democratic south was to be rendered politically impotent. Hungry professional politicians now began to swarm to the south. With all kinds of demagogic tricks the party managed to appropriate all the different branches of government and administration, and, by the unscrupulous manner in which they dealt with state property, they actually succeeded in hastening the bankruptcy of some of the Southern states.

Johnson did not see the victory of " carpet-bag " politics during his term of office ; but the manœuvres of the Radicals succeeded in putting in his place a man entirely after their own heart. Hitherto parties had been fortunate in their choice of victorious generals for the presidency ;

THE UNITED STATES MINT AT PHILADELPHIA

and the services which Grant had rendered in the Civil War were undoubtedly more potent than those of all the previous military candidates. As a statesman, and more especially as an administrator, however, Grant was certainly not less incapable than Jackson or any other of his predecessors. In 1869, he entered upon office as the chosen representative of the party which was determined upon gathering in for itself the fruits of victory, and during his career he seemed unable to prevent widespread corruption, not only in the Southern states, but also in other parts of the union. Almost the sole guiding principle of the Republican party now seemed to be that the government was to be used for the purpose of enriching the party in power. A system of high protective tariffs was introduced, ostensibly for the purpose of meeting the financial needs of the country, which had been greatly increased by the war; but it was abused for the purpose of providing certain industrial and commercial rings and companies with an opportunity for exploitation and speculation, by which even officials were supposed to have enriched themselves in the most open manner. Even during Grant's first term of office these proceedings had increased to such an extent as to call forth in many places a vigorous opposition ; but the coherence of the party, aided by those unprincipled followers who held the mastery in the south, was still so powerful that Grant's re-election in 1872 was accomplished without special exertions. During his second term of office, 1873–1877, the Republican party was split asunder.

A faction, the so-called Liberal Republicans, formulated as their primary demand the establishment of an honest administra-

THE GARFIELD MONUMENT AT CLEVELAND
At the outbreak of the Civil War, Garfield received the command of a regiment of volunteers, and was promoted brigadier-general after winning the Battle of Middle Creek. Resigning his commission in 1860, he became, in March, 1881, the twentieth President of the United States.

tion. This section was composed to a considerable extent of that German-American element which had already played an important part in the early development of the Republican party.

The influence of the Liberal Republicans was indeed not sufficiently important to hold out hopes of victory to a candidate of their own ; but neither the old Republicans nor the Democrats, who now were once more energetically coming to the front, could do without these independent votes, and they both were accordingly obliged to propose candidates capable of effecting a moral and healthy cleansing of the administration. It was not until the advent to office of President Rutherford Burchard Hayes (1877–1881) that the insurrectionary epoch of the United States came to an end. From a material point of view the union undoubtedly began to flourish very rapidly after the war, as was shown in a conspicuous way by the financial measures of the administration. In consequence of high protective tariffs and an increase of internal taxation during the war, the treasury found itself face to face with a steadily increasing surplus. The federal debt, which after the war had reached the amount of £500,000,000, was reduced by half in the course of twenty years, the interest thereon, moreover, being reduced from 6 to 3 per cent. Thus a reduction in internal taxation and a lowering of the import duties were rendered possible, though political prejudices rather than financial needs as yet prevented a repeal of the protective tariffs.

Hayes was succeeded in 1881 by James Abram Garfield, a president who gave every promise of leading the country farther on the road to moral regeneration, when, on

YOSEMITE FALLS IN CALIFORNIA

GLACIER POINT, YOSEMITE VALLEY

GRAND CAÑON OF THE COLORADO

TWIN PALMS IN A CALIFORNIAN ORCHARD

CONTRASTS OF AMERICAN SCENERY

MOUNT RAINER, A DORMANT VOLCANO IN PIERCE COUNTY, WASHINGTON

GATE OF THE MOUNTAINS: A SCENE IN THE WONDERFUL YELLOWSTONE PARK

A SCENE FROM COLUMBIA POINT AT YOSEMITE IN CALIFORNIA

MOUNTAIN SCENERY IN THE UNITED STATES

July 2nd, 1881, the bullet of the assassin proved the means of retarding this forward movement. Garfield's successor, Chester Alan Arthur, once again permitted a return to the policy of exploitation ; and, though under his administration things did not become as bad as under Grant, the policy of regeneration suffered a serious check. It was on this account largely that the Republican party completely lost its hold over men's minds. In 1884, for the first time since the Civil War, the Democrats succeeded in obtaining a majority for their candidate for the presidency, Grover Cleveland, with a platform which demanded a tariff for revenue only, an honest and trustworthy financial administration, and the restriction of the spoils system in the appointment of officials. Since 1884 Republican and Democratic presidents have succeeded one another almost in regular alternation. The maintenance of this balance between the great parties has contributed considerably towards rendering impossible such conditions as had existed earlier. The union then entered upon a new stage of its development. The strengthening of the central authority which resulted from the defeat of the supporters of state rights in the War of Secession did not remain without its effect upon the spirit of American politics. The attention of the government still continued, it is true, to be occupied primarily with the internal conditions of the union, which, indeed, are so varied and peculiar as to justify such a policy. Under a republican system of protection carried to an extreme development the industry of the United States has reached dimensions which place it almost at the head of the productive nations of

THE STATUE OF LIBERTY
This colossal bronze statue on Bedloe's Island, New York Harbour, was designed and cast in France and presented to the American people in commemoration of the Franco-American Union of 1874. It weighs 225 tons and reaches a height of 151 ft.

the world. In no country are the technical advances of modern times put to such immediate and comprehensive use as in America. Steam and electricity are the dominating factors, not only in all branches of industry, but also in agriculture.

The inexhaustible wealth of the country is exploited with iron energy ; and nowhere is the struggle for advancement keener than in the United States. Undoubtedly the more ideal elements in human life have had to suffer somewhat thereby, for the fine arts have not long enjoyed a home there ; nor has the advancement of the sciences tended to the improvement of any of the branches of science, other than those devoted to practical purposes, on the same scale as in the Old World. Woman in America has enjoyed a more really independent position than in any other country, and, in the nature of things, feeling herself equal, if not superior, to man, has striven also to share in the activities and the rights of the male sex. Thus in America, more than elsewhere, she early created for herself the possibility of a freer movement in both social and municipal life. Not resting content with this, the more she actually employed herself as a fellow-labourer with man on equal terms, the more she aimed at being placed on an equality with him in other spheres. Social conditions in which material factors gained increasing prominence led in many cases to a restriction of marriages, or to marriages of such a kind as made the wife less a guardian of the home than a co-operating partner of the husband. Many professions were opened to her ; in consequence of her higher culture she finally developed the ability of filling at first a few and then an increasing

THE UNITED STATES HOUSE OF REPRESENTATIVES IN SESSION £dwards

The legislature of the United States consists of a Senate and House of Representatives, the former having 42 members, one-half of whom are elected every two years to hold office for four years, while the House of Representatives is composed of 94 members, elected biennially for terms of two years. This lower House possesses the sole power to originate measures affecting taxation and finance, although the Senate has the right to amend such measures.

number of minor public offices of the clerical and administrative classes. Thus there arose a class of wage-earning women, some of whom, not without reason, claimed to have an equal voice with men in public affairs. The peculiarity of the American Constitution, which leaves the conditions attached to the franchise entirely to the control of the separate states, considerably facilitated the movement towards political rights for women. They early obtained in several states the right of voting merely upon school matters ; and upon this foundation there has been a marked development.

At the present day women in only four states of the union enjoy, in regard to the exercise of the suffrage, the same political rights as do men ; and it is hardly open to doubt that in America as in Australia the emancipation movement will gradually decline. American conditions will be hardly likely to alter the fact that in the end the female sex will have nothing to gain, but everything to lose, by stepping upon the same footing with man into all the different branches of industrial life. Whether or not the United States will always maintain their industrial affairs

in a sound and healthy condition is difficult to foretell. The Socialist danger, which has caused so much anxiety to the governments of the Old World, has not been present in America on the same scale. It has there been counteracted by the overthrow of all social barriers, the Republican equality of all citizens, and the fact that up to the most recent times it has **Restricting** been possible for individuals in **the Flood of** the humblest ranks, by skill and **Immigrants** energy, to work their way up into the circles of the all-powerful aristocracy of wealth. With the increasing density of the population, this possibility is growing less. Though by no means overpopulated in proportion to area, the United States has even at the present day a considerable proletariat of unemployed.

For some time these conditions have exercised a considerable effect upon the question of immigration. The period from 1830 to 1850, during which America encouraged by all the means in its power the influx of immigrants, has been succeeded by another in which the country is beginning to close its doors to improperly qualified foreigners. This movement at first was directed against the Chinese. In

THE WORLD-RENOWNED LICK OBSERVATORY ON MOUNT HAMILTON, CALIFORNIA

Standing on the summit of Mount Hamilton at an altitude of 4,280 ft., this famous astronomical establishment was founded under the provisions of a deed made in 1876 by James Lick, a San Francisco philanthropist. A sum was also provided for the erection of the most powerful telescope in the world, an instrument which for many years had no rival.

LOOKING FROM THE OLD SPANISH FORT OVER THE PACIFIC AT PANAMA

the negroes and Indians the union already had in its midst two foreign elements of population whose improvement and absorption presented difficult and expensive problems. It was therefore justified in refusing to burden itself with another foreign element, and one, moreover, which from its peculiarity seemed unlikely to become assimilated to the rest of the population. The union, however, is beginning to close its doors to European immigration also. It is not, of course, trying to effect this indirectly in the manner once aimed at by the " Knownothings "—by rendering more difficult the acquisition of the rights of citizenship.

Where Wealth is Power But, on the other hand, now that its social conditions are no longer such that physical powers alone are sufficient for obtaining a livelihood, it more particularly refuses to receive those whose bodily and mental constitution would lead one to expect that, so far from benefiting the country, they would become a burden to it.

The republican equality of all citizens is, in the United States even more than in other republics, modified by the power of wealth. In no country is the influence of capital so great as in the United States. Its " trusts " and " rings " have succeeded more than once not only in wresting to themselves monopolies for the New World, but also in threatening the Old World with them. Nor is either the tariff or the financial policy of the United States free from the reproach of having been abused for the business purposes of large commercial associations.

We cannot, however, deny the enormous capacity for development in the vast natural resources of the country. It is the growing recognition of this fact which helped to induce the United States to adopt an entirely new foreign policy at the end of the nineteenth century. It is, of course, professed that the policy first laid down and followed out by Monroe is still, as in 1823, the guiding thread of American statesmanship, but a wholly new interpretation is nowadays placed upon Monroe's original declarations. Monroe, in those days, laid stress on the fact that the guiding principle of the foreign policy of the United States should be non-interference in American affairs by other

DISASTROUS RESULT OF FRENCH MANAGEMENT ON THE PANAMA CANAL

SOLDIERS GUARDING THE PANAMA RAILWAY, NEAR OBISPO

A GREAT ENTERPRISE: SCENES ON THE PANAMA CANAL

The first picture depicts a by no means rare scene on the banks of the Panama Canal. Bribery and corruption had so characterised the efforts of the French company that many hundreds of thousands of pounds' worth of machinery were ordered in excess of any reasonable need, to be dumped down by the wayside and allowed to rot and rust. The second picture shows United States soldiers guarding the railway near Obispo, one of the many military stations along the line.

MONSTER AMERICAN STEAM SHOVEL IN POSITION TO TAKE A "BITE"

WEST INDIAN NEGROES AT WORK ON THE CULEBRA CUT

SCENES IN THE CONSTRUCTION OF THE PANAMA CANAL

The construction of the Panama Canal is the greatest physical undertaking the world has ever seen. When finished, it will have a length of about forty-five miles, thirteen of which will run through Lake Bohio, and it will have a minimum depth of 35 feet. The most important engineering feat in this huge enterprise is the Culebra cut, which necessitates levelling down to 250 feet a rocky ground seven miles long. The bulk of the work is being done by West Indian negroes.

nations. The declaration that they would consider the interference of foreign Powers for the restoration of the Spanish dominion in Central and South America as an unfriendly act against the United States was directed, as was the policy of Great Britain, more especially against the Holy Alliance, which was ready to support

Purpose of the Monroe Doctrine
Ferdinand VII. by the aid of an international force. The union beheld with indifference more than one attempt of the Spaniards to reconquer their colonial empire, without regarding it as other than an internal affair of the provinces affected.

The Monroe doctrine was first introduced into diplomacy at the time of the Panama Canal enterprise. The North Americans had for a long time made efforts to subject the industrial conditions of the isthmus to their control, and became uneasy when there seemed a probability of the enterprise being carried out without their participation. They also have made continuous efforts for the construction of a Nicaragua Canal, and at present it seems as if one of these projects would be realised under the protection of the American Government.

Still in another way did the United States attempt to obtain a firm footing in the neighbouring provinces of the south. In 1848, Yucatan, having once more severed its connection with the Mexican Republic, and being unable to settle a revolt of its disaffected Indian subjects, applied to the United States for help, offering in return to acknowledge their sovereignty. The offer, however, met with a refusal. Next, in the middle of the 'fifties, a plan for the incorporation of Nicaragua was under consideration. The interests of North American commercial companies had repeatedly provoked lively diplomatic discussions, and finally an adventurer from Tennessee, named William Walker, had raised himself to the presidency of Nicaragua. Regarded with suspicion by almost

The Problem of the Union Expansion
the whole of the native population, Walker was obliged to look for support to his own country; and his compatriots in the west repeatedly supported him, in the hope that his adventure would end in the admission of Nicaragua into the union.

In this case, however, the object desired failed to be carried into effect. Another time, under Grant, in 1870, the expansion of the union was brought under discussion. In the Republic of San

6266

Domingo, which forms the eastern part of the island of the same name, a large party in whose hands was the presidential authority asked for admission into the United States. Ever since 1868 deputations in regard to this matter had been going backwards and forwards between the two countries ; but it was not until Grant began to evince a lively interest in the matter that a treaty of annexation was arranged. While, however, in San Domingo the treaty was passed by a vote of a majority of the people, congress assumed a hostile attitude. Three times Grant introduced the scheme into the senate, and as many times was he obliged to withdraw it before the opposition of that body.

These failures were due to the same cause. The view prevailed quite generally in the United States that the territorial area of the union had reached an extent large enough for its development, and that the acquisition of territories situated outside the present well-drawn boundaries could only prove a source of danger to the state. It was not until the last decade of the nineteenth century that

America for the Americans
their industrial development tended to force the United States to modify this conception of the original Monroe doctrine. The extension of its industry is such that the union at present not only amply supplies its own requirements, but produces far in excess of these, and hence is obliged to seek other markets.

It is natural that its attention should be primarily directed towards those other states of the American continent which, owing to their inferior economic development, are still dependent upon Europe for their industrial needs. In this connection a new and amplified expression of the Monroe doctrine has been called into existence. It was now proposed to restrict the activity of the European Powers upon the American Continent even in the industrial sphere, as it had formerly been checked in the political, and to conquer " America for the Americans."

To this end the United States endeavoured to bring about a closer union of the independent American states. The centennial anniversary of the Declaration of Independence (July 4th, 1876) first caused a revival of the idea of a Pan-American Federation ; and in connection with the celebration of the four-hundredth anniversary of the discovery of America

(October 12th, 1892), a limited Pan-American arrangement was called into existence in the Bureau of American Republics.

The fruits of such a connection could not, however, be reaped immediately in such a manner as to satisfy the existing conditions of the labour market. Hence the United States, like the countries of the Old World, were forced to adhere to the policy of protection for their national industry. A protective tariff had, of course, been in force for a long time before this in the United States. But hitherto it had been used partly as a means of maintaining good order in the financial

in United States politics was not limited to the industrial sphere. The repeated risings against Spanish dominion in Cuba have more than once rendered certain Americans desirous of acquiring an island so valuable to them from its geographical situation. In their relations to the disaffected population, American citizens have sometimes approached as nearly as possible to the limits of international law. Spain, moreover, had tolerated a shameless misgovernment in the remnants of its once opulent colonial empire. The most justifiable demands of its colonies were either disregarded or were appeased by empty

MR. THEODORE ROOSEVELT AND HIS SUCCESSOR, MR. WILLIAM H. TAFT
Mr. Theodore Roosevelt, being then Vice-President, succeeded to the Presidency of the United States at the death of President McKinley on September 14th, 1901, and was re-elected by an overwhelming majority in 1905, this time defeating the democratic candidate, Mr. W. J. Bryan. His term of office was marked by a number of excellent reforms, notable among which was his vigorous opposition to American trust methods. His successor, Mr. W. H. Taft, is by profession a lawyer, and has for many years played a conspicuous part in the administration of the great republic.

economy of the state as a whole, and partly for the purpose of supporting growing industries. The tariff of 1890, on the other hand, which is specially connected with the name of President McKinley, betokened a complete change in the tariff policy of the union. Its object was to remove foreign competition from home markets, and to render home industries capable of competing in foreign markets. This policy was approved by the majority of the citizens of the United States, and in 1896 McKinley was chosen president (1897-1901). The first year of McKinley's presidency, however, sufficed to show that the change

promises, while the Spanish Government, allowing its governors to enrich themselves by extortions, in the meanwhile derived only insignificant profits from its colonies.

The Cubans had already, in 1868, risen against this state of things, and it was only after a ten years' struggle, accompanied by the expenditure of much blood and treasure, that Spain succeeded in bringing the island to obedience. When this promise was left unfulfilled, Cuba revolted anew in 1896. It was thereafter that occasion was given for the United States to intervene. Thus pressed, Spain renewed its promises of autonomous government, and, as earlier,

AMERICA'S NAVAL STRENGTH: THE UNITED STATES SQUADRON FOR SERVICE IN THE PACIFIC

AN INCIDENT IN THE SPANISH-AMERICAN WAR: THE DESTRUCTION OF ADMIRAL CERVERA'S FLEET OUTSIDE SANTIAGO HARBOUR

The Destruction of Admiral Cervera's Fleet Outside Santiago Harbour. Admiral Cervera was dispatched to Cuba to defend Spanish interests, taking refuge on May 19th, 1898, in the inner harbour of Santiago. In the early stages of the Spanish-American War, Admiral Cervera, under the command of Admiral Sampson, effected either the destruction of Santiago. When, on July 3rd, he attempted to escape, acting under orders from his superiors, the Americans, under the command of Admiral Sampson, effected either the destruction or the capture of every one of the Spanish ships. A third of the men met their death, the remainder, with Cervera, being taken prisoners of war, but were soon afterwards released.

with no result of accomplishment. The American Government demanded, in the interests of humanity, that the state of war in Cuba should cease. The American Government also took the position that the independence of Cuba ought to be recognised ; diplomatic relations were severed ; and war against Spain was declared to exist in April, 1898.

On the one hand, the United States possessed both a fleet and an army superior to those of the Spaniards ; they excelled the latter in their facilities for procuring material resources, and the natural

Cuba, while Puerto Rico was ceded directly to the United States, as were also, for an indemnity, the Philippines.

For years past the United States had had their eyes set on the Farthest West ; and, owing to the position of the latter region opposite to their own Pacific coast, the Americans had become better acquainted with the methods of its development than had some of the countries of the Old World. At Samoa they had, it is true, earlier yielded to the combination of European and colonial Powers, although the check, even there, was only temporary.

THE UNITED STATES PURCHASE OF THE PANAMA CANAL

The mismanagement which had characterised the affairs of the two French Panama companies, and culminated in the prosecution of the De Lesseps Company for fraud, brought the scheme to the verge of ruin, with the result that the American Government agreed to pay the sum of £8,000,000 for certain concessions and for the work already accomplished. This picture shows the signing of the £8,000,000 warrant in payment of the Panama Canal, in November, 1903.

theatre of the war lay at their very doors. On the other hand, the misgovernment of Spain weakened the administration both in the mother country and in the colonies, and rendered quite impossible a vigorous or even adequate conduct of such a campaign. When, finally, its fleets were forced to engage in the contest, they suffered complete and speedy defeat. After the destruction of the Spanish fleet before Santiago, the islands of both Cuba and Puerto Rico were occupied and controlled by the military force of the Americans. Spain, as a result, was compelled to recognise the independence of

The manner, furthermore, in which in 1897 they succeeded in accomplishing the annexation of Hawaii showed how the United States were determined to obtain a position in the Pacific Ocean. Here, again, the unforeseen results of the Spanish War seemed to coincide with the development of American policy ; for by the treaty of peace of December 10th, 1898, America took the title to the Philippine Islands.

It is at present impossible to foretell how these astonishing changes will affect the future of the United States. Their new acquisitions serve in a marked degree to satisfy the need for industrial expansion,

BRITAIN'S DISPUTE WITH VENEZUELA: PRESIDENT ROOSEVELT AND HIS CABINET

On account of British and German subjects failing to obtain compensation from the Venezuelan Government for property destroyed and concessions violated, Great Britain and Germany instituted a blockade of Venezuelan ports. Matters were assuming an ugly aspect when the United States intervened, and the picture on this page shows President Roosevelt discussing the question with his Cabinet, through which an understanding was arrived at in 1903.

and in the changes which the Japano-Chinese war of 1894 initiated in Eastern Asia, America for the first time shows herself prepared to enter into competition with European exporting countries. In view of the results of the Spanish War she is enabled to do so under exceptionally favourable conditions. But the colonies will, on the other hand, in all probability be a source of many future difficulties, both administrative and diplomatic, to the union; and whether or not all these difficulties can be solved without shaking the foundations or altering the structure of the constitution we must leave for the future to determine.

On his way to Guam he also raised the flag on Wake Island, and thus two additional naval stations were secured in the Pacific. The year 1899 was one of unusual calm, excepting for the determined resistance of several of the wilder Filippino tribes to the new régime. These, however, had never been reconciled to Spanish rule, and now demanded absolute independence, under Aguinaldo, a brave and very able guerrilla leader. Throughout 1899 sanguinary conflicts occurred in the Philippines, during which many American officers fell, including General Lawton. The struggle was protracted till the capture of Aguinaldo on March 23rd, 1901. But

A STRIKING SCENE IN ALASKA: LOOKING DOWN ON MUIR GLACIER
This magnificently developed and picturesque ice-sheet of Alaska rises from 150 ft. to 220 ft. above the surface of the water, and occupies an area of from twenty to thirty miles. As the result of the earthquake of 1899, a considerable portion of it was destroyed, its front wall previously terminating into a majestic ice-cliff of 1½ miles in width.

The acquisition of the new insular appanages was quickly to compel the nation to assert herself as a great Pacific Power. Indeed, the closing period of the last century and the opening of the new marked a most memorable transition, which set an indelible stamp on the history of the great republic and irresistibly changed the whole attitude of international policy, involving momentous departures from the old rule of non-intervention in the affairs of the Old World.

On February 1st, 1899, Commander Taussig took possession of the picturesque little island of Guam, the largest member of the Marianne, or Ladrones, Archipelago.

the American Government had, throughout the campaign, used conciliatory means, proclaiming in the summer of 1900 an amnesty for the Filippino insurgents.

The dramatic and startling episodes of the years 1900 and 1901 rendered the inaugural period of the twentieth century one of the most striking of American historical landmarks. Indeed, the whole world was stirred by phenomenal records. "The war which staggered humanity," to use Krüger's phrase, led the Boers to appeal to the United States; but the government saw no justification for interference, even diplomatically. But in China the appalling Boxer insurrection rendered the

TOTEM POLES OUTSIDE THE HOUSES OF CHIEFS AT FORT WRANGELL

THE MAIN STREET IN SITKA, ALASKA'S BEAUTIFULLY SITUATED CAPITAL

A VOLCANIC ISLAND OF RECENT ORIGIN NEAR FORT WRANGELL

SCENES IN ALASKA, THE NORTH-WESTERN PART OF NORTH AMERICA

John Pierpont Morgan

Mark Twain

Thomas A. Edison

Booker T. Washington

John D. Rockefeller

William J. Bryan

Andrew Carnegie

Admiral George Dewey

NOTABLE FIGURES IN THE UNITED STATES: LEADERS IN VARIOUS DEPARTMENTS OF LIFE AND BUSINESS

situation terribly lurid and the outlook ominous. The news of the siege of the legations in Pekin roused intense excitement throughout the states, as in other lands, and brought not only the European Powers but also the United States Government to feel the instant necessity of armed intervention. When

America's Interference in China

Pekin was captured by the allied forces, under General von Waldersee, the American contingent was the first to enter the city. The emperor and empress-dowager had fled, and Li Hung Chang asked for an armistice, which was refused, as also was a special appeal by the Tsung-li-yamen to Washington. China was given to understand that the full demands of the American Government must be complied with and General Chaffee was allowed full power to act. On February 19th, 1901, the United States protested against further military expeditions to China, and on February 21st the Powers agreed to acquire no Chinese territory without international consent.

In the midst of the world's general unrest occurred a momentous presidential election in America. William McKinley was, on November 6th, 1900, chosen president for a second term, with Theodore Roosevelt, of New York, as vice-president, on the republican ticket. The eloquent William Jennings Bryan, of Nebraska, thus for the second time sustained a crushing defeat, which perhaps settled for ever the fate of his silver standard movement. Thus also was reduced to comparative impotence the great Democratic party, which had been intrenched in power under the two administrations of Grover Cleveland, 1885–1889, and 1893–1897, yielding in 1897 to the republican onslaught that placed McKinley in power.

In this election of 1900 the money issue was the paramount factor of the campaign. A dark cloud soon rolled over the fair

Tragic Fate of President McKinley

prospect. The nation was shocked almost to frenzy in a few months by the dastardly assassination of the beloved president. While McKinley was holding a reception in the Temple of Music at the Pan-American Exposition, Buffalo, he was shot by Leon Czolgosz, an anarchist. Though not killed on the spot, he died, on September 19th, 1901, from his wounds. According to settled law, Theodore Roosevelt became president, and this extra-

ordinary man soon displayed, in increasing measure, those capacities as a statesman which had been already successfully tested in other offices. He rapidly proved himself to be the "strong man" of America, the implacable enemy of the trusts and gigantic, corrupt corporations ; and also a foremost representative of constructive policy.

Early in his occupancy of the supreme office President Roosevelt recommended to congress the purchase of the rights of the French Panama Canal Company for £8,000,000, and this led to the inauguration of the greatest engineering enterprise ever undertaken by the great republic. The stupendous cutting was planned to be completed by 1905. Important incidents rapidly followed each other. In 1903 the Pacific cable was completed, and the dispute with Britain over the Alaskan boundary was settled in favour of America by an arbitration

Roosevelt at the White House

award. But 1904 was a "Roosevelt year," for, by a sweeping majority, the president was re-elected, defeating Judge Allen B. Parker. William H. Taft, who had been Governor of the Philippines, became Secretary of War.

One of President Roosevelt's last measures was to summon a great conference for the consideration of the incalculable waste of national resources, especially through the wanton destruction of the magnificent forests and the reckless consumption of coal. Finally, he firmly refused the multitudinous solicitation to accept nomination for a third term, but openly and strenuously commended the candidature of William H. Taft, of Cincinnati, O., his celebrated Secretary of War. Once more W. J. Bryan tried his fortune, but Taft won a magnificent victory over America's most gifted orator, and entered the White House as President on March 4th, 1909.

Other notable incidents of the first decade of the twentieth century were the addition of a forty-sixth star to the "Old Glory" flag by the creation of a new state, Oklahoma—out of the united Oklahoma and Indian territories—in June, 1906 ; the sailing on his ninth trip to the Arctic of Commander R. E. Peary, July 6th, 1908 ; the adoption of a penny postal rate by Great Britain and the United States on October 1st, 1908.

KONRAD HAEBLER
WILLIAM DURBAN

AMERICA'S UNCROWNED KING: MR. TAFT DELIVERING HIS FIRST PRESIDENTIAL ADDRESS

Inauguration Day in the United States falls every four years on March 4th, a date originally selected by Benjamin Franklin on account of the fact that for the next two hundred years it would less frequently fall on a Sunday than any other. It is usual for the new president to take the oath outside the Capitol at Washington, but Mr. William H. Taft, who is seen delivering his inaugural address in the picture on this page, was sworn inside, because of a sudden storm.

THE PRESIDENT'S HOUSE SIXTY YEARS AGO

THE HOUSE OF THE PRESIDENT AS IT IS TO-DAY

6277

THE STATELY CAPITOL. HEADQUARTERS OF THE UNITED STATES GOVERNMENT

A SCENE OF SIXTY YEARS AGO : LOOKING TOWARDS THE CAPITOL

CONGRESSIONAL LIBRARY THE LARGEST LIBRARY BUILDING IN THE WORLD

WASHINGTON, THE CAPITAL CITY OF THE UNITED STATES OF AMERICA

BIRD'S-EYE VIEW OF UNION STOCK YARDS

AN EVERYDAY SCENE IN STATE STREET

CHICAGO, THE SECOND LARGEST CITY IN AMERICA

NEW YORK BAY FROM TELEGRAPH STATION

HOW BROOKLYN FERRY LOOKED FORTY YEARS AGO

THE OLD CITY HALL, WITH THE PARK IN THE FOREGROUND

NEW YORK AT THE TIME OF THE CIVIL WAR

"FLAT-IRON" BUILDING, FIFTH AVENUE

BROADWAY, THE CHIEF THOROUGHFARE

WATER FRONT OF NEW YORK CITY, AS SEEN FROM JERSEY CITY

"TIMES" BUILDING ON AN ELECTION NIGHT

THE FAMOUS "GREAT WHITE WAY"

SCENES IN NEW YORK, THE COMMERCIAL METROPOLIS OF THE UNITED STATES

STATE STREET, BOSTON'S MAIN THOROUGHFARE, FORTY YEARS AGO

BOSTON HARBOUR, WITH BUNKER HILL ON THE RIGHT

A QUAINT CORNER IN THE OLD CITY

BOSTON AS IT WAS IN THE EARLY 'SIXTIES

THE OLD STATE HOUSE

OLD SOUTH CHURCH

TREMONT STREET, ONE OF THE LEADING THOROUGHFARES

BOSTON, THE CENTRE OF AMERICAN CULTURE AND EDUCATION

6283

RUINS OF THE HALL OF JUSTICE

THE DEVASTATION OF TELEGRAPH HILL

A STRIKING SCENE OF DESTRUCTION

OVERLOOKING KEARNY STREET

SAN FRANCISCO: SCENES IN THE RUINED CITY

UNION SQUARE, WITH ST. FRANCIS HOTEL

NEWSPAPER SQUARE

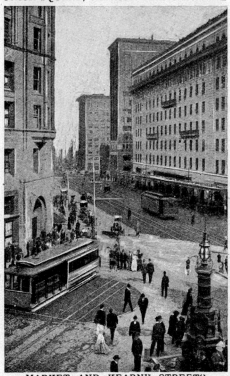

MARKET AND KEARNY STREETS

TYPICAL BUILDINGS OF THE NEW CITY

SAN FRANCISCO: THE REMAKING OF THE CITY

THE IMPOSING NEW MORMON TABERNACLE

MAIN STREET, THE PRINCIPAL STREET IN THE CITY

SALT LAKE CITY, THE CENTRAL SEAT OF MORMON POWER

SOCIAL CONDITIONS & THE SOCIAL FUTURE IN THE UNITED STATES

BY H. G. WELLS

THE POPULATION OF THE UNITED STATES

THE social conditions and social future of America constitute a system of problems quite distinct and separate from the social problems of any other part of the world. The nearest approach to parallel conditions, and that on a far smaller and narrower scale, is found in the British colonies and in the newly settled parts of Siberia. For while in nearly every other part of the world the population of to-day is more or less completely descended from the prehistoric population of the same region, and has developed its social order in a slow growth extending over many centuries, the American population is essentially a transplanted population, a still fluid and imperfect fusion of great fragments torn at this point or that from the gradually evolved societies of Europe. The European social systems grow and flower upon their roots, on soil which has made them and to which they are adapted.

The Mixed Races of America

The American social accumulation is a various collection of cuttings thrust into a new soil and respiring a new air, so different that the question is still open to doubt, and, indeed, there are those who do doubt, how far these cuttings are actually striking root and living and growing; whether, indeed, they are destined to more than a temporary life in the new hemisphere. We propose to discuss and weigh certain arguments for and against the belief that these 80,000,000 people who constitute the United States of America are destined to develop into a great distinctive nation with a character and culture of its own. Humanly speaking, the United States of America—and the same is true of Canada and all the more prosperous, populous and progressive regions of South America—is a vast sea of newly-arrived and unstably-rooted people.

Of the 76,000,000 inhabitants recorded by the 1900 census, 10,500,000 were born and brought up in one or other of the European social systems, and the parents of another 26,000,000 were foreigners. Another 9,000,000 are of African negro descent; 14,000,000 of the 65,000,000 native born are living not in the state of their birth, but in other states to which they have migrated. Of the 30,500,000 whites whose parents on both sides were native Americans, a high proportion probably had one, if not more, grandparents foreign born. Nearly 5,500,000 out of 33,500,000 whites in 1870 were foreign born, and another 5,250,000 the children of foreign-born parents. The children of the latter 5,250,000 count, of course, in the 1900 census as native born of native parents. Immigration, naturally enough, varies enormously with the activity of business, but in 1906 it rose for the first time on record above a million.

These figures may be difficult to grasp. The facts may be seen in a more concrete form by the visitor to Ellis Island, the receiving station for the immigrants into New York harbour. One goes to this place by tugs from the United States barge office in Battery Park, and in order to see the thing properly one needs a letter of introduction to the commissioner in charge. Then one is taken through vast barracks littered with people of every European race to a central hall in which the gist of the examining goes on. The floor

At the Receiving Station

6287

of this hall is divided up into a sort of maze of winding passages between lattice work, and along these passages, day after day incessantly, the immigrants go—wild-eyed gypsies, Armenians, Greeks, Italians, Ruthenians, Cossacks, German peasants, Scandinavians, a few Irish still, impoverished English, occasional Dutch.

The Steady Stream of Immigration They halt for a moment at little desks to exhibit papers, at other little desks to show their money and prove they are not paupers, to have their eyes scanned by this doctor and their general bearing by that. Their thumb-marks are taken, names and heights and weights and so forth are recorded for the card index, and so slowly they pass along towards America, and at last reach a little wicket—the gate of the New World.

Through this metal wicket drips the immigration stream; all day long, every two or three seconds, an immigrant with a valise or a bundle passes the little desk and goes on past the well-managed money-changing place, past the carefully organised separating ways that go to this railway or that, past the guiding, protecting officials into a new world. The great majority are young men and young women between seventeen and thirty—good, youthful, hopeful peasant stock. They stand in a long string, waiting to go through that wicket, with bundles, with little tin boxes, with cheap portmanteaux, with odd packages, in pairs, in families, alone, women with children, men with strings of dependents, young couples. All day that string of human beads waits there, jerks forward, waits again; all day and every day, constantly replenished, constantly dropping the end beads through the wicket, till the units mount to hundreds and the hundreds to thousands.

In such a prosperous year as 1906 more immigrants passed through that wicket into America than children were born in the whole of France. This figure

Europe the Feeding-place of America of a perpetual stream of new stranger citizens will serve to mark the primary distinction between the American social problem and that of any European or Asiatic community. The vast bulk of the population of the United States has, in fact, only got there from Europe in the course of the last hundred years, and mainly since the accession of Queen Victoria to the throne of Great Britain. This is the first fact that

6288

the student of the American social future must realise. Only an extremely small proportion of its blood goes back now to those who fought for freedom in the days of George Washington. The American community is not an expanded colonial society that has become autonomous. It is a great and deepening pool of population accumulating upon the area their predecessors freed, and since fed copiously by affluents from every European community. Fresh ingredients are still being added in enormous quantity, in quantity so great as to materially change the racial quality in a score of years. It is particularly noteworthy that each accession of new blood seems to sterilise its predecessors.

Had there been no immigration at all into the United States, but had the rate of increase that prevailed in 1810–1820 prevailed to 1900, the population, which would then have been a purely native American one, would have amounted to 100,000,000; that is to say, to more than 23,000,000 in excess of the present total population. The new waves are for a time amazingly fecund, and then comes a rapid fall in the birth-rate.

Old World's Surplus Population The proportion of colonial and early republican blood in the population is therefore probably considerably smaller even than the figures I have quoted would suggest. These accesses of new population have come in a series of waves, very much as if successive reservoirs of surplus population in the Old World had been tapped, drained and exhausted. First came the Irish and Germans, then Central Europeans of various types; then Poland and Western Russia began to pour out their teeming peoples, and more particularly their Jews; Bohemia, the Slavonic states, Italy, and Hungary followed, and the latest arrivals include great numbers of Levantines, Armenians, and other peoples from Asia Minor and the Balkan Peninsula. The Hungarian immigrants have still a birth-rate of forty-six per 1,000, the highest birth-rate in the world.

A considerable proportion of the Mediterranean arrivals, it has to be noted, and more especially the Italians, do not come to settle. They work for a season or a few years, and then return to Italy. The rest come to stay.

A vast proportion of these accessions to the American population since 1840 has, with the exception of the East European

IMMIGRANTS SHOWING THEIR CREDENTIALS

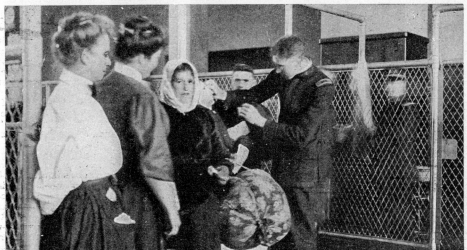

EXAMINING THE EYES OF WOULD-BE AMERICAN CITIZENS

WAITING THEIR TURN: A TYPICAL BATCH OF ALIEN IMMIGRANTS

AT THE GATE OF THE NEW WORLD: AMERICAN IMMIGRATION

Immediately upon arrival in New York harbour aliens are taken direct to the United States Immigration Offices in Ellis Island, where they undergo a rigid examination before being permitted to pass through the gates into the New World. Thumb-marks are taken and, with names, heights and weights, are recorded for the immigration index.

Jews, consisted of peasantry, mainly or totally illiterate, accustomed to a low standard of life and heavy bodily toil. For most of them the transfer to a new country meant severance from the religious communion in which they had been bred and from the servilities or subordinations to which they were accustomed.

A Pool of Mixed Humanity They brought little or no positive social tradition to the synthesis to which they brought their blood and muscle. The earlier German, English and Scandinavian incomers were drawn from a somewhat higher social level, and were much more closely akin in habits and faith to the earlier founders of the republic. Our inquiry is this: What social structure is this pool of mixed humanity developing or likely to develop?

If we compare any European nation with the American we perceive at once certain broad differences. The former, in comparison with the latter, is evolved and organised; the latter, in comparison with the former, is aggregated and chaotic. In nearly every European country there is a social system, often quite elaborately classed and defined; each class with a sense of function, with an idea of what is due to it and what is expected of it.

Nearly everywhere you find a governing class, aristocratic in spirit, sometimes no doubt highly modified by recent economic and industrial changes, with more or less of the tradition of a feudal nobility; then a definite great mercantile class; then a large, self-respecting middle class of professional men—minor merchants and so forth; then a new industrial class of employees in the manufacturing and urban districts, and a peasant population rooted to the land. There are, of course, many local modifications of this form. In France the nobility is mostly expropriated; in England, since the days of John Ball, the peasant has lost his common

Degrees of Social Orders rights and his holding, and become an "agricultural labourer" to a newer class of more extensive farmer. But these are differences in detail; the fact of the organisation, and the still more important fact of the traditional feeling of organisation, remain true of all these older communities.

And in nearly every European country, though it may be somewhat despoiled here and shorn of exclusive predominance there, or represented by a dislocated "reformed" member, is the Church; custodian of a great moral tradition, closely associated with the national universities and the organisation of national thought. The typical European town has its castle or great house, its cathedral or church, its middle class and lower class quarters. Five miles off one can see that the American town is on an entirely different plan. In his remarkable "American Scene" Mr. Henry James calls attention to the fact that the Church as one sees it and feels it universally in Europe is altogether absent, and he adds a comment as suggestive as it is vague. Speaking of the appearance of the churches, so far as they do appear amidst American urban scenery, he says:

Looking for the most part no more established or seated than a stopped omnibus, they are reduced to the inveterate bourgeois level—that of private, accommodated pretensions merely—and fatally despoiled of the fine old ecclesiastical arrogance. . . .

The field of American life is as bare of the Church as a billiard-table of a centre-piece; a truth that the myriad little structures "attended" on Sundays and on the "off" evenings **No Church in America** of their "sociables" proclaim as with the audible sound of the roaring of a million mice. . . . And, however one indicates one's impression of the clearance, the clearance itself, in its completeness, with the innumerable odd connected circumstances that bring it home, represents, in the history of manners and morals, a deviation in the mere measurement of which hereafter may well reside a certain critical thrill. I say hereafter because it is a question of one of those many measurements that would as yet, in the United States, be premature. Of all the solemn conclusions one feels as "barred," the list is quite headed in the states, I think, by this particular abeyance of judgment. When an ancient treasure of precious vessels, over-scored with glowing gems and wrought artistically into wondrous shapes, has, by a prodigious process, been converted, through a vast community, into the small change, the simple circulating medium of dollars and "nickels," we can only say that the consequent permeation will be of values of a new order. Of *what* order we must wait to see.

America has no Church. Neither has it a peasantry nor an aristocracy; and until well on in the Victorian epoch it had no disproportionately rich people.

In America, except in the regions where the negro abounds, there is no lower stratum. There is no "soil people" to this community at all; your bottomest man is a mobile freeman who can read, and who has ideas above digging and pigs and poultry-keeping, except incidentally for his own ends. No one owns to subordination. As a consequence, any position

REFUGEES FROM LIBAU SEEKING FREEDOM IN AMERICA

IMMIGRANTS WITH THEIR COMPLETE BELONGINGS AFTER PASSING THE AUTHORITIES

EUROPE'S DREGS ENTERING THE NEW WORLD

It is estimated that over a million foreigners seek admission into the United States every year. They represent all the races under the sun, coming mostly from China, Japan and Russia. Only those who are fit to battle with life, who have a clean record, and who are not paupers, are allowed to land; the rest—thieves, anarchists, imbeciles, and persons suffering from disease, so far as can be ascertained, are sent back to their own countries in the steamships that brought them over. Of this group of undesirables between 6,000 and 12,000 are excluded within the course of a twelvemonth.

which involves the acknowledgment of an innate inferiority is difficult to fill ; there is, from the European point of view, an extraordinary dearth of servants, and this endures in spite of a great peasant immigration. The servile tradition will not root here now; it dies forthwith. An enormous importation of European serfs and peasants goes on ; but as they touch this soil their backs immediately begin to stiffen with a new assertion. And at the other end of the scale, also, one misses an element. There is no territorial aristocracy, no aristocracy at all, no throne, no legitimate and acknowledged representative of that upper social structure of leisure, power and state responsibility which in the old European theory of society was supposed to give significance to the whole. The American community, one cannot too clearly insist, does not correspond to an entire European community at all, but only to the middle masses of it, to the trading and manufacturing class between the dimensions of the magnate and the clerk and skilled artisan. It is the central part of the European organism without either the dreaming head or the subjugated feet.

A Country Without an Aristocracy

Even the highly feudal slave-holding "county family" traditions of Virginia and the south pass now out of memory. So that in a very real sense the past of the American nation is in Europe, and the settled order of the past is left behind there. This community was, as it were, taken off its roots, clipped of its branches, and brought hither. It began neither serf nor lord, but burgher and farmer ; it followed the normal development of the middle class under progress everywhere, and became capitalistic. The later immigration has converged upon the great industrial centres, and added merely a vast non-servile element of employees to the scheme. America has been, and still very largely is, a one-class country. It is a great sea of human beings detached from their traditions of origin. The social difference from Europe appears everywhere, and nowhere more strikingly than in the railway carriages. In England the compartments in these are either " first class," originally designed for the aristocracy ; or " second class," for the middle class ; or " third class," for the populace. In America there is only one class, one universal

The Seat of Triumphant Democracy

simple democratic car. In the Southern states, however, a proportion of these simple democratic cars are inscribed with the word " White," whereby 9,000,000 people are excluded. But to this original even-handed treatment there was speedily added a more sumptuous type of car, the parlour car, accessible to extra dollars ; and then came special types of train, all made up of parlour cars and observation cars, and the like. In England nearly every train remains still first, second and third, or first and third. And now, quite outdistancing the differentiation of England, America produces private cars and private trains, such as Europe reserves only for crowned heads.

The evidence of the American railways, then, suggests very strongly what a hundred other signs confirm, that the huge classless sea of American population is not destined to remain classless, is already developing separations and distinctions, and structures of its own. Monstrous architectural portents in Boston and Salt Lake City encourage one to suppose that even the churchless aspect, which so stirred the speculative element in Mr. Henry James, is only the opening, formless phase of a community destined to produce not only classes, but intellectual and moral forms of the most wonderful and remarkable kind.

America's Vast Area of Land

It is well to note how these 80,000,000 of people whose social future we are discussing are distributed. This huge development of human appliances and resources is here going on in a community that is still, for all the dense crowds of New York, the teeming congestion of East Side, extraordinarily scattered. America, one recalls, is still an unoccupied country, across which the latest developments of civilisation are rushing. We are dealing here with a continuous area of land, which is, leaving Alaska out of account altogether, equal to Great Britain, France, the German Empire, the Austro-Hungarian Empire, Italy, Belgium, Japan, Holland, Spain and Portugal, Sweden and Norway, Turkey in Europe, Egypt, and the whole Empire of India ; and the population spread out over this vast space is still less than the joint population of the first two countries named, and not a quarter that of India. Moreover, it is not spread at all evenly. Much of it is in undistributed clots. Neither is it upon the soil; barely half of it is in holdings and homes and authentic communities. It is a population of an extremely modern type. Urban concentration has already gone far with it; 15,000,000 of it are crowded into and about twenty great cities; other 18,000,000 make up 500 towns. Between these centres of population run railways indeed, telegraph wires, telephone connections, tracks of various sorts; but to the European eye these are mere scratchings on a virgin surface. An empty wilderness manifests itself through this thin network of human conveniences, appears in the meshes even at the railroad side.

Essentially, America is still an unsettled land, with only a few incidental good roads in favoured places, with no universal police, with no wayside inns where a civilised man may rest, with still only the crudest of rural postal deliveries, with long stretches of swamp and forest and desert by the track side, still unassailed by industry. This much one sees clearly enough eastward of Chicago. Westward it becomes more and more the fact. In Idaho, at last, comes the untouched and perhaps invincible desert, plain and continuous through the long hours of travel. Huge areas do not contain one human being to the square mile, still vaster portions fall short of two.

It is upon Pennsylvania and New York state and the belt of great towns that stretch out past Chicago to Milwaukee and Madison that the nation centres and seems destined to centre. One needs but examine a tinted population map to realise that. The other concentrations are provincial and subordinate; they have the same relation to the main axis that Glasgow or Cardiff has to London in the British scheme.

NEW YORK'S GHETTO: AN EVERY-DAY SCENE IN THE JEWISH COLONY

One of the most notable features in the social life of the United States is the yearly increase of the Jewish population, which, since 1840, when it numbered only 50,000 souls, has reached 1,200,000. Of these it is estimated that no fewer than 500,000 have made their homes in New York State, a large proportion living in the city itself. Mostly refugees from Poland and desperately poverty-stricken, they follow almost every industrial pursuit, frequently at sweating wages and under most unfavourable conditions. The above picture shows a typical every-day scene in the Jewish colony, New York City, where the frugal housewife does her marketing.

MILL SURROUNDED BY GROWING COTTON

IN A GREAT COTTON-SPINNING ROOM

"DOG BOYS" EMPLOYED IN THE FACTORIES

GIRLS WHO RUN SPINNING-FRAMES

Photos: H. C. White

CHILD LABOUR IN THE UNITED STATES: SCENES OF FACTORY LIFE

THE AMERICAN TRADITION
A STUDY OF NATIONAL CHARACTERISTICS

WHEN I speak of this vast multitude, these 80,000,000 souls of the United States of America, as being for the most part peasants de-peasantised and common people cut off from their own social traditions I do not intend to convey that the American community is, as a whole, traditionless. There is in America a very distinctive tradition indeed, which not only animates the entire nation, but gives a unique idiom to its Press and all its public utterances, and is manifestly the starting point from which the adjustments of the future must be made.

The mere sight of the stars and stripes serves to recall it; "Yankee" in the mouth of a European gives something of its quality. One thinks at once of a careless abandonment of any pretension, of tireless energy and daring enterprise, of immense self-reliance, of a disrespect for the past so complete that a mummy **Democracy** is in itself a comical object, **Freedom and** and the blowing out of an **Confidence** ill-guarded sacred flame a delightful jest. One thinks of the enterprise of the skyscraper and the humour of "A Yankee at the Court of King Arthur," and of "Innocents Abroad." Its dominant notes are democracy, freedom and confidence. It is religious-spirited without superstition, consciously Christian in the vein of a nearly Unitarian Christianity, fervent but broadened— broadened as a halfpenny is broadened by being run over by an express train—substantially the same, that is to say, but with a marked loss of outline and detail.

It is a tradition of romantic concession to good and inoffensive women and a high development of that personal morality which puts sexual continence and alcoholic temperance before any public virtue. It is equally a tradition of sporadic emotional public-spiritedness, entirely of the quality of gallantry, of handsome and surprising gifts to the people, disinterested occupation of office and the like. It is emotionally patriotic, hypothetising fighting and dying for one's country as a supreme good, while inculcating also that working and living for oneself is quite within the sphere of virtuous action. It adores the flag, but suspects the state. One sees more **The Only** national flags and fewer national **National** servants in America than in **Costume** any country in the world. Its conception of manners is one of free plain-spoken men revering women and shielding them from most of the realities of life, scornful of aristocracies and monarchies, while asserting simply, directly, boldly and frequently, an equal claim to consideration with all other men. If there is any traditional national costume at all it is shirt-sleeves. And it cherishes the glorious rights of property above any other right whatsoever.

Such are the details that come clustering into one's mind in response to the phrase, the American tradition.

From the War of Independence onward until our own times, that tradition, that very definite ideal, has kept pretty steadily the same. It is the image of a man and not the image of a state. Its living spirit has been the spirit of freedom at any cost, unconditional and irresponsible. It is the spirit of men who have thrown off a yoke, who are jealously resolved to be unhampered masters of their "own," to whom nothing else is of anything but secondary importance. That was the spirit of the English small gentry and **The Living** mercantile class, the comfort-**Spirit** able property owners, the par-**of Liberty** liamentarians, in Stuart times. Indeed, even earlier, it is very largely the spirit of More's Utopia. It was the spirit that sent Oliver Cromwell himself packing for America, though a heedless and ill-advised and unforeseeing king would not let him go. It was the spirit that made taxation for public purposes the supreme wrong and provoked each country, first the Mother Country and then in its turn the daughter country, to armed rebellion. It has been the spirit of the British Whig and the British Nonconformist almost up to the present day. In the Reform Club of London, framed and glazed over against Magna Charta, is the American Declaration of Independence; **The Thirst for Freedom at any Cost** kindred trophies they are of the same essentially English spirit of stubborn insubordination. But the American side of it has gone on unchecked by the complementary aspect of the English character which British Toryism expresses.

The War of Independence raised that Whig suspicion of and hostility to government, and the freedom of private property and the repudiation of any but voluntary emotional and supererogatory co-operation in the national purpose, to the level of a religion; and the American Constitution, with but one element of elasticity in the Supreme Court decisions, established these principles impregnably in the political structure. It organised disorganisation. Personal freedom, defiance of authority, and the stars and stripes have always gone together in men's minds; and subsequent waves of immigration—the Irish fleeing famine, for which they held the English responsible, and the Eastern European Jews escaping relentless persecutions—brought a persuasion of immense public wrongs as a necessary concomitant of systematic government, to refresh without changing this defiant thirst for freedom at any cost whatsoever.

In my book, " The Future in America," I have tried to make an estimate of the working quality of this American tradition of unconditional freedom for the adult male citizen. I have shown that from the point of view of anyone who regards civilisation as an organisation of human interdependence and believes that the stability of society can be secured only **Weaknesses of the National Tradition** by a conscious and disciplined co-ordination of effort, it is a tradition extraordinarily and dangerously deficient in what I have called a "sense of the state." And by a sense of the state I mean not merely a vague and sentimental show of public-spiritedness—of that the states have enough and to spare—but a real sustaining conception of the collective interest embodied in the state as an object of simple duty and as a determining factor in the life of each individual. It involves a sense of function and a sense of " place," a sense of a general responsibility and of a general well-being overriding the individual's well-being, which are exactly the senses the American tradition attacks and destroys.

For the better part of a century the American tradition, quite as much by reason of what it disregards as of what it suggests, has meant a great release of human energy, a vigorous, if rough and untidy, exploitation of the vast resources that the European invention of railways and telegraphic communication put within reach of the American people. It has stimulated men to a greater individual activity, perhaps, than the world has ever seen before. Men have been wasted by misdirection, no doubt, but there has been less waste by inaction and lassitude than was the case in any previous society.

Great bulks of things and great quantities of things have been produced, huge areas brought under cultivation, vast cities reared in the wilderness. But this tradition has failed to produce the beginnings or promise of any new **The Selfish Policy of Individualism** phase of civilised organisation; the growths have remained largely invertebrate and chaotic, and concurrently with its gift of splendid and monstrous growth it has also developed portentous political and economic evils. No doubt the increment of human energy has been considerable, but it has been much less than appears at first sight. Much of the human energy that America has displayed in the last century is not a development of new energy, but a diversion. It has been accompanied by a fall in the birth-rate that even the immigration torrent has not altogether replaced. Its insistence upon the individual, its disregard of the collective organisation, its treatment of women and children as each man's private concern, has had its natural outcome.

Men's imaginations have been turned entirely upon individual and immediate successes, and upon concrete triumphs; they have had no regard, or only an ineffectual sentimental regard, for the race. Every man was looking after himself, and there was no one to look after the future. Had the promise of 1815 been fulfilled, there would now be in the United States of America 100,000,000 descendants of the homogeneous and free-spirited native population of that time. There are not, as a matter of fact, more than 35,000,000. There are probably, as I have pointed out, much less. Against the assets of cities, railways, mines, and industrial wealth won, the American tradition has to set the price of 75,000,000 native citizens who have never found time to be born, and whose place is now more or less filled by alien substitutes. Biologically speaking, this is not a triumph for the American tradition. It is, however, very clearly an outcome of the intense individualism of that tradition. Under the sway of that it has burnt its future in the furnace to keep up steam.

The next and necessary evil consequent upon this exaltation of the individual and private property over the state—over the race, that is, and over public property— has been a contempt for public service. It has identified public spirit with spasmodic acts of public beneficence. The American political ideal became a Cincinnatus whom nobody sent for, and who therefore never left his plough. There has ensued a corrupt and undignified political life, speaking **Corruption in American Politics** clap-trap, dark with violence, illiterate and void of statesmanship or science, forbidding any healthy social development through public organisation at home, and, every year that the increasing facilities of communication draw the alien nations closer, deepening the risks of needless and disastrous wars abroad.

And, in the third place, it is to be remarked that the American tradition has defeated its dearest aims of a universal freedom and practical equality. The economic process of the last half century, so far as America is concerned, has completely justified the generalisations of Marx. There has been a steady concentration of wealth and of the reality, as distinguished from the forms, of power, in the hands of a small energetic minority, and a steady approximation of the condition of the mass of the citizens to that of the so-called proletariat of the European communities. The tradition of individual freedom and equality is, in fact, in process of destroying the realities of freedom and equality out of which it rose.

Instead of the 600,000 families of 1790, all at about the same level of property and, excepting the peculiar condition of 700,000 blacks, with scarcely anyone in the position of a hireling, we have now as the most striking though by no means the most important fact in American social life, a frothy confusion of millionaires' families, just as wasteful, foolish and vicious as irresponsible human beings with unlimited resources have always shown themselves to be. And concurrently with the appearance of these concentrations of **Poverty and Slums on the Increase** great wealth we have appearing also poverty—poverty of a degree that was quite unknown in the United States for the first century of their career as an independent nation. In the last few decades slums as frightful as any in Europe have appeared with terrible rapidity, and there has been a development of the viler side of industrialism, of sweating, and base employment of the most ominous kind.

In Mr. Robert Hunter's " Poverty " one reads of " not less than 80,000 children, most of whom are little girls, at present employed in the textile mills of this country. In the south there are now six times as many children at work as there were twenty years ago. Child labour is increasing yearly in that section of the country. Each year more little ones are brought in from the fields and hills to live in the degrading and demoralising atmosphere of the mill towns . . ."

Children are deliberately imported by the Italians. I gathered from Commissioner Watchorn at Ellis Island that the proportion of little nephews and nieces, friends' sons and so forth, brought in by them is peculiarly high, and I heard him try and condemn a doubtful case. It was a particularly unattractive Italian in charge of a dull-eyed, emaciated little boy of no ascertainable relationship.

In the worst days of cotton-milling in England the conditions were hardly worse than those now existing in the south. Children, the tiniest and frailest, of five and six years of age, rise in the morning and, like old men and women, go to the **Child Slaves in the South** mills to do their day's labour ; and, when they return home, " wearily fling themselves on their beds, too tired to take off their clothes." Many children work all night, " in the maddening racket of the machinery, in an atmosphere insanitary and clouded with humidity and lint.

" It will be long," adds Mr. Hunter, in his description, " before I forget the face of a little boy of six years, with his hands stretched forward to rearrange a bit of

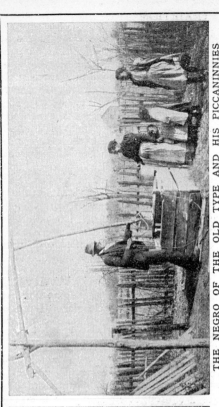

THE OLD-TIME NEGRO AND HIS ILL-BUILT PLANK HUT

THE NEGRO OF THE OLD TYPE AND HIS PICCANINNIES

HOUSE OF A WELL-TO-DO NEGRO IN A SOUTHERN CITY

THE CHILDREN OF A PROSPEROUS NEGRO OF TO-DAY

THE OLD AND THE NEW: THE EVOLUTION OF THE AMERICAN NEGRO

In 1790 the coloured population numbered less than 700,000. At the present time there are more than 10,000,000 negroes in the States. Since the dark days of slavery the black man's status has also improved. The old nigger and his plank hut are things of the past; to-day he takes active interest in the administration of the republic, and has his own colleges and churches.

machinery, his pallid face and spare form already showing the physical effects of labour. This child, six years of age, was working twelve hours a day."

From Mr. Spargo's "Bitter Cry of the Children" I learn this much of the joys of certain among the youth of Pennsylvania: "For ten or eleven hours a day children of ten or eleven stoop over the chute and pick out the slate and other impurities from the coal as it moves past them. The air is black with coal-dust, and the roar of the crushers, screens and rushing mill-race of coal is deafening. Sometimes one of the children falls into the machinery and is terribly mangled, or slips into the chute and is smothered to death. Many children are killed in this way. Many others, after a time, contract coal-miners' asthma and consumption, which gradually undermine their health. Breathing continually day after day the clouds of coal-dust, their lungs gradually become black and choked with small particles of anthracite . . ."

The Hard Lot of the Children

In Massachusetts, at Fall River, the Hon. J. F. Carey tells how little naked boys, free Americans, work for a well-known New York millionaire, packing cloth into bleaching vats, in a bath of chemicals that bleaches their little bodies like the bodies of lepers.

Altogether it would seem that at least 1,500,000 children are growing up in the United States of America stunted and practically uneducated because of un-regulated industrialism. These children, ill-fed, ill-trained, mentally benighted, since they are alive and active, since they are an active and positive and not a negative evil, are even more ominous in the American outlook than those five and sixty million of good race and sound up-bringing who will now never be born. It must be repeated that the American tradition is really the tradition of one particular ingredient in this great admixture and stirring up of peoples. This ingredient is the colonial British, whose seventeenth century Puritanism and eighteenth century mercantile radicalism and rationalism manifestly furnished all the stuff out of which the American tradition is made.

Source of the American Tradition

It is this stuff planted in virgin soil, and inflated to an immense and buoyant optimism by colossal and unanticipated material prosperity and success. From that British middle-class tradition comes the individualist Protestant spirit, the keen self-reliance and personal responsibility, the irresponsible expenditure, the indiscipline and mystical faith in things being managed properly if they are only let alone. "State-blindness" is the natural and almost inevitable quality of a middle-class tradition, a class that has been forced neither to rule nor obey, which has been concentrated and successfully concentrated on private gain.

The middle-class British section of the American population was, and is to this day, the only really articulate ingredient in its mental composition. And so it has had a monopoly in providing the American forms of thought. The other sections of people that have been annexed by, or have come into, this national synthesis are silent so far as any contribution to the national stock of ideas and ideals is concerned. There are, for example, those great elements, the Spanish Catholics, the French Catholic population of Louisiana, the Irish Catholics, the French Canadians —who are now ousting the sterile New Englander from New England —the Germans, the Italians, the Hungarians. Comparatively, they say nothing. From all the ten million of coloured people come just two or three platform voices, Booker Washington, Dubois, Mrs. Church Terrell, mere protests at specific wrongs.

American German and His Beer

The clever restless Eastern European Jews, too, have still to find a voice. Professor Münsterberg has written with a certain bitterness of the inaudibility of the German element in the American population. They allow themselves, he remonstrates, to count for nothing. They did not seem to exist, he points out, even in politics until prohibitionist fury threatened their beer. Then, indeed, the American German emerged from silence and obscurity, but only to rescue his mug and retire again with it into enigmatical silences.

If there is any exception to this pre-dominance of the tradition of the English-speaking, originally middle-class, English-thinking Northerner in the American mind, it is to be found in the spread of social democracy outward from the festering tenement houses of Chicago into the mining and agrarian regions of the middle west. It is a fierce form of Socialist teaching that spreads throughout these regions, far more closely akin to the revolutionary Socialism of the continent of Europe than to the constructive and evolutionary Socialism of Great Britain. Its typical organ is " The Appeal to Reason," which circulates more than a quarter of a million copies weekly from Kansas City. It is a Socialism reeking with class feeling and class hatred, and altogether anarchistic in spirit ; a new and highly indigestible contribution to the American moral and intellectual synthesis. It is remarkable chiefly as the one shrill exception in a world of plastic acceptance.

Now, it is possible to believe that this vast silence of these imported and ingested factors that the American nation has taken to itself is as acquiescent as it seems. No doubt they are largely taking over the traditional forms of American thought and expression quietly and without protest, and wearing them ; but they will wear them as a man wears a misfit, shaping and adapting it every day more and more to his natural form, here straining a seam and there taking in a looseness.

A force of modification must be at work. It must be at work in spite of the fact that, with the exception of social democracy,

A Great Living Force for Righteousness it does not anywhere show as a protest or a fresh beginning or a challenge to the prevailing forms. How far it has actually been at work is perhaps to be judged best by an observant stroller, surveying the crowds of a Sunday evening in New York, or read in the sheets of such a mirror of popular taste as the Sunday edition of the " New York American " or the " New York Herald." In the former just what I mean by the silent modification of the old tradition is quite typically shown. Its leading articles are written by Mr. Arthur Brisbane, the son of one of the Brook Farm Utopians, that gathering in which Hawthorne and Henry James senior and Margaret Fuller participated, and in which the whole brilliant world of Boston past, the world of Emerson, Longfellow, Thoreau, was interested. Mr. Brisbane is a very distinguished man, quite over and above the fact that he is paid the greatest salary of any journalist in the world.

He writes with a wit and directness that no other living man can rival, and he holds up constantly what is substantially the American ideal of the past century to readers who evidently need strengthening in it. It is, of course, the figure of a man and not of a state ; it is a man, clean, clean-shaven, and almost obtrusively strong-jawed, honest, muscular, alert, pushful, chivalrous, self-reliant, non-political, except when he breaks into shrewd and penetrating voting—" you can fool all the people some of the time," etc., and independent—independent—in a world which is therefore certain to give way to him. His doubts, his questionings, his aspira-

Leaders that are Read by Millions tions are dealt with by Mr. Brisbane with a simple direct fatherliness, with all the beneficent persuasiveness of a revivalist preacher. Millions read these leaders and feel a momentary benefit, en route for the more actual portions of the paper. He asks : " Why are all men gamblers ? " He discusses our longing for Immortal Imperfection, and " Did we once live on the moon ? "

He recommends the substitution of whisky and soda for neat whisky, drawing an illustration from the comparative effect of the diluted and of the undiluted liquid as an eye-wash (Try whisky on your friend's eyeball, is the heading), sleep ; (The man who loses sleep will make a failure of his life, or at least diminish greatly his chances of success), and the education of the feminine intelligence (The cow that kicks her weaned calf is all heart). He makes identically the same confident appeal to the moral motive which was for so long the salvation of the Puritan Individualism from which the American tradition derives. " That hand," he writes, " which supports the head of the new-born baby, the mother's hand, supports the civilisation of the world."

But that sort of thing is not saving the old native strain in the population. It moves people, no doubt, but inadequately. And here is a passage that is quite the quintessence of Americanism, of all its deep moral feeling and sentimental untruthfulness. I wonder if any man but an American or a British Nonconformist in a state of rhetorical abandonment ever

What is the Purpose of Life ? believed that Shakespeare wrote his plays or Michael Angelo painted in a mood of humanitarian exaltation, " for the good of other men " ?

What *shall* we strive for ? *Money ?*
Get a thousand millions. Your day will come, and in due course the graveyard rat will gnaw as calmly at your bump of acquisitiveness as at the mean coat of the pauper.
Then shall we strive for *power ?*
The names of the first great kings of the world are forgotten, and the names of all those whose

NEGRO HOME-LIFE IN THE OLD PLANTATION DAYS

THE TYPICAL HOME OF A MODERN WELL-TO-DO NEGRO

THE SOCIAL EVOLUTION OF THE AMERICAN NEGRO

Few people imagined, probably least of all the small band of Virginian colonists who bargained for the first batch of negroes from a Dutch man-of-war in 1619, that the coloured man was to become such a factor in the social life of America. The picture on the top of this page shows him in the old days, shortly after his emancipation, when he toiled and struggled on the land; the second as he is to-day, not the laughing negro of plantation lore, but the American citizen who takes the business of life in grim earnest, and who enters into open competition with his white brothers.

power we envy will drift to forgetfulness soon. What does the most powerful man in the world amount to standing at the brink of Niagara, with his solar plexus trembling ? What is his power compared with the force of the wind or the energy of one small wave sweeping along the shore ?

The power which man can build up within himself, for himself, is nothing. Only the dull reasoning of gratified egotism can make it seem worth while. Then what is worth

Working for the Good of Others while ? Let us look at some of the men who have come and gone, and whose lives inspire us. Take a few at random : Columbus, Michael Angelo, Wilberforce, Shakespeare, Galileo, Fulton, Watt, Hargreaves—these will do.

Let us ask ourselves this question : " Was there any *one thing* that distinguished *all* their lives, that united all these men, active in fields so different ? "

Yes. Every man among them, and every man whose life-history is worth the telling, did something for *the good of other men.* . . . .

Get money if you can. Get power if you can. Then, if you want to be more than the ten thousand million unknown mingled in the dust beneath you, see what good you can do with your money and your power.

If you are one of the many millions who have not, and can't get, money or power, see what good you can do without either.

You can help carry a load for an old man. You can encourage and help a poor devil trying to reform. You can set a good example to children. You can stick to the men with whom you work, fighting honestly for their welfare.

Time was when the ablest man would rather kill ten men than feed a thousand children. That time has gone. We do not care much about feeding the children, but we care less about killing the men. To that extent we have improved already.

The day will come when we shall prefer helping our neighbour to robbing him—legally— of a million dollars.

Do what good you can *now*, while it is unusual, and have the satisfaction of being a pioneer and an eccentric.

It is the voice of the American tradition strained to the utmost to make itself audible to the New World, and cracking into italics and breaking into capitals with the strain. The rest of that enormous bale of paper is eloquent of a public void of moral ambitions, lost to any sense of comprehensive things, deaf

A Public Void of Moral Ambitions to ideas, impervious to generalisations, a public which has carried the conception of freedom to its logical extreme of entire individual detachment. These tell-tale columns deal all with personality and the drama of personal life. They witness to no interest but the interest in intense individual experiences. The engagements, the love affairs, the scandals of conspicuous people are given in pitiless

detail in articles adorned with vigorous portraits and sensational pictorial comments. Even the eavesdroppers who write this stuff strike the personal note, and their heavily muscular portraits frown beside the initial letter.

Murders and crimes are worked up to the keenest pitch of realisation, and any new indelicacy in fashionable costume, any new medical device, any new dance or athleticism, any new breach in the moral code, any novelty in sea bathing, or the woman's seat on horseback, or the like, is given copious and moving illustration, stirring headlines and eloquent reprobation. There is a coloured supplement of knockabout fun written chiefly in the quaint dialect of the New York slums. It is a language from which " th " has vanished, and it presents a world in which the kicking by a mule of an endless succession of victims is an inexhaustible joy to young and old. " Dat ole Maud ! "

There is a smaller bale dealing with sport, and another with the political prospects of the purely personal independence party of Mr. Hearst. In the advertisement

Excitement the Object of Life columns one finds nothing of books, nothing of art ; but great choice of bust-developers, hair restorers, nervous tonics, clothing sales, self-contained flats, and business opportunities. Individuality has, in fact, got home to itself, and, as people say, taken off its frills. All but one ; Mr. Arthur Brisbane's eloquence one may consider as the last stitch of the old costume. Excitement remains the residual object in life. The " New York American " represents a clientèle, a clientèle to be counted by the hundred thousand, manifestly with no other solicitudes, just burning to live and living to burn.

The modifications of the American tradition that will occur through its adoption by these silent foreign ingredients in the racial synthesis are not likely to add to it or elaborate it in any particular way. They tend merely to simplify it to bare irresponsible non-moral individualism. It is with the detail and qualification of a tradition as with the inflexions of a language ; when another people takes it over, the refinements entirely disappear. But there are, however, other forces of modification at work upon the American tradition of an altogether more hopeful kind. It has entered upon a constructive phase. Were it not so, then the American social outlook would indeed be hopeless. The effectual modifying force at work is not the strangeness or the temperamental maladjustment of the new elements of population, but the conscious realisation of the inadequacy of this tradition on the part of the more intelligent sections of the American population. That blind national conceit that would hear no criticism and admit no deficiency has disappeared. In the last decade such a change has come over the American mind as sometimes comes over a vigorous and wilful child. Suddenly it seems to have grown up, to have begun to weigh its powers and consider its possible deficiencies.

There was a time when American confidence and self-satisfaction seemed impregnable ; at the slightest qualm of doubt America took to violent rhetoric as a drunkard resorts to drink. Now, the indictment I have drawn up harshly, bluntly and unflatteringly would receive the endorsement of American after American. The falling birth-rate of all the best elements in the state, the cankering effect

A Great Epoch-Making Book
of political corruption, the crumbling of independence and quality before the progressive aggregation of wealth —he has to face them, he cannot deny them. There has arisen a new literature, the literature of national self-examination, that seems destined finally to modify the American tradition profoundly. To me it seems to involve the hope and possibility of a conscious collective organisation of social life.

If ever there was an epoch-marking book it was surely Henry Demarest Lloyd's "Wealth against Commonwealth." It marks an epoch not so much by what it says as by what it silently abandons. It was published in 1894, and it stated in the very clearest terms the incompatibility of the almost limitless freedom of property set up by the constitution with the practical freedom and general happiness of the mass of men. It must be admitted that Lloyd never followed up the implications of this repudiation. He made his statements in the language of the tradition he assailed, and foreshadowed the replacement of chaos by order in quite chaotic and mystical appeals. Here, for instance, is a typical passage from " Man the Social Creator " :

Property is now a' stumbling-block to the people, just as government has been. Property

will not be abolished, **but,** like government, **it** will be democratised.

The philosophy of self-interest as the social solution was a good living and working synthesis in the days when civilisation was advancing its frontiers twenty miles a day across the American continent, and every man for himself was the best social mobilisation possible.

But to-day it is a belated ghost that has overstayed the cock-crow. These were frontier morals. But this same everyone for himself becomes most immoral when the frontier is abolished and the pioneer becomes the fellow-citizen, and these frontier morals are most uneconomic when labour can be divided and the product multiplied. Most uneconomic, for they make closure the rule of industry, leading not to wealth but to that awful waste of wealth which is made visible to every eye in our unemployed— not hands alone, but land, machinery, and, most of all, hearts. Those who still practise these frontier morals are like criminals who, according to the new science of penalogy, are simply reappearances of old types. Their acquisitiveness, once divine like Mercury's, is now out of place, except in gaol. Because out of place, they are a danger. A sorry day it is likely to be for those who are found in the way when the new people rise to rush into each other's arms, to get together, to stay together, and to live together. The labour movement halts because so many of its rank and file—and all its leaders— do not see clearly the golden thread of love on which have been strung together all the past glories of human association, and which is to serve for the link of the new Association of Friends who Labour, whose motto is " All for All."

The establishment of the intricate cooperative commonwealth by a rush of 80,000,000 flushed and shiny-eyed enthusiasts, in fact, is Lloyd's proposal. He will not face, and few Americans to this day will face, the cold need of a great science of social adjustment and a disciplined and rightly ordered machinery to turn such enthusiasms to effect. However, he did express clearly enough the opening phase of American disillusionment towards the wild go-as-you-please that had been the conception of life in America for a vehement wasteful expanding century. And he was the precursor of what is now a bulky and extremely influential literature of national criticism.

America's Reserve Forces
A number of writers, literary investigators one may call them, or sociological men of letters or magazine publicists—they are a little difficult to place—have taken up the inquiry into the condition of civic administration, into economic organisation, into national politics and racial interaction, with a frank fearlessness and an absence of windy eloquence that has been to many Europeans a surprising revelation of the

reserve forces of the American mind. President Roosevelt, that magnificent reverberator of ideas, that gleam of wilful humanity, that fortunate interruption to the succession of machine-made politicians at the White House, has echoed clearly and fearlessly to this movement and made it an integral part of the general intellectual movement of America. It is to these first intimations of the need of a " sense of the state " in America that I would particularly direct the reader's attention in this discussion. They are the beginnings of what is quite conceivably a great and complex reconstructive effort. I admit they are but beginnings. They may quite possibly wither and perish presently ; they may much more probably be seized upon by adventurers and converted into a new public cant almost as empty and fruitless as the old.

The fact, however, remains that through this busy and immensely noisy confusion of 80,000,000 of people these little voices go on intimating more and more clearly the intention to undertake public affairs in a new spirit and upon new and sounder principles, to strengthen the state and the law against individual enterprise, to have done with those national superstitions under which hypocrisy and disloyalty and private plunder have sheltered and prospered for so many long years.

Just so far as these reform efforts succeed and develop is the organisation of the United States of America into a great, self-conscious, civilised nation, unparalleled in the world's history, possible ; just so far as they fail is failure written over the American future. The real interest of America for the next century to the student of civilisation will be the development of these attempts, now in their infancy, to create and realise out of this racial hotchpotch, this human chaos, an idea of the collective commonwealth as the datum of reference for every individual life.

TRAINING THE NEGRO: THE LARGEST BLACK MAN'S COLLEGE IN THE WORLD

Brought to America first of all to work as plantation slaves, the African negroes have gone on steadily increasing in numbers, and what to do with their gigantic black population has for many years been a serious problem with the United States. In some ways, the negro is himself striving to settle the difficulty, endeavouring by education to fit himself to take his stand by the side of his white brother. The Normal and Agricultural Institute at Hampton, in Virginia—the carpentry shop of which is shown in the above picture—has done much to improve the status of the coloured man, while at Tuskegee, in Alabama, the institution founded by Mr. Booker T. Washington on the plan of Hampton has developed in quite a remarkable way, and is turning out yearly a large number of highly efficient men.

THE PROBLEMS OF SOCIALISM

FACTORS IN THE MAKING OF THE CIVILISED AMERICAN STATE

A THIRD influence that may also contribute very materially to the reconstruction of the American tradition is the Socialist movement. It is true that so far American Socialism has very largely taken an anarchistic form, has been, in fact, little more than a revolutionary movement of the wages-earning class against the property owner. It has already been pointed out that it derives not from contemporary English Socialism, but from the Marxist social democracy of the continent of Europe, and has none of the constructive spirit that has been developed by the English Socialists of the Fabian and Labour party group or by the newer German evolutionary Socialists.

Nevertheless, whenever Socialism is intelligently met by discussion, or whenever it draws near to practicable realisation, it becomes, by virtue of its inherent implications, a constructive force, **Anarchism the** and there is no reason to sup- **Alternative** pose that it will not be in- **to Socialism** telligently met, on the whole and in the long run, in America. The alternative to a developing Socialism among the labouring masses in America is that revolutionary anarchism from which it is slowly but definitely marking itself off. In America we have to remember that we are dealing with a huge population of people who are for the most part, and more and more evidently, destined under the present system of free industrial competition to be either very small traders, small farmers on the verge of debt, or wages-earners for all their lives. They are going to lead limited lives and worried lives; and they know it.

And it has to be borne in mind also that these people are so far under the sway of the American tradition that each thinks himself as good as any man, and as much entitled to the fulness of life. Whatever social tradition their fathers had, whatever ideas of a place to be filled humbly and seriously, and duties to be done, have been left behind in Europe. No church dominates the scenery of this new land and offers in authoritative and convincing tones **Labour's** consolations hereafter for lives **Gloomy** obscurely but faithfully lived. **Outlook** Whatever else happens in his national future, upon one point the patriotic American may feel assured, and that is of an immense general discontent in the working class, and of a powerful movement in search of a general betterment.

The practical forms and effects of that movement will depend almost entirely upon the average standard of life among the workers and their general education. Sweated and ill-organised foreigners, such as one finds in New Jersey, living under conditions of great misery, will be fierce, impatient and altogether darkened. They will be acutely exasperated by every picture of plutocratic luxury in their newspaper; they will readily resort to destructive violence. The western miner, the western agriculturist, worried beyond endurance between the money-lender and railway combinations, will be almost equally prone to savage methods of expression. "The Appeal to Reason," for example, which voices the feelings of a quarter of a million of subscribers, chiefly in the middle west, is furious to wreck the present capitalist system; but it is far too angry and impatient for that satis- **Angry and** faction to produce any clear **Impatient** suggestion of what shall re- **Discontent** place it. To call this discontent of the seething underside of the American system Socialism is a misnomer. Were there no Socialism there would be just as much of this discontent, just the same insurgent force and desire for violence, taking some other title, and far more destructive methods.

This discontent is a part of the same planless confusion that gives on the other side the wanton irresponsible extravagances of the smart people of New York. But Socialism alone, of all the forms of expression adopted by the losers in the economic struggle, contains constructive possibilities and leads its adherents towards that ideal of an organised state, planned and developed, from which these terrible social stresses may be eliminated ; which is also the ideal to which sociology and the thoughts of every constructive-minded and foreseeing man in any position of life tend to-day. In the Socialist hypothesis of collective ownership and administration as the social basis, there is the germ of a sense of the state that may ultimately develop into comprehensive conceptions of social order, conceptions upon which enlightened millionaires and enlightened workers may meet at last in generous co-operation.

The chances of the American future, then, seem to range between two possibilities, just as a more or less constructive Socialism does or does not get hold of and inspire the working mass of the population. In the worst event—given an emotional and empty hostility to property, as such, masquerading as Socialism— one has the prospect of a bitter and aimless class war between the expropriated many and the property-holding few, a war not of general insurrection, but of localised outbreaks, strikes and brutal suppressions, rising to bloody conflicts and sinking to coarsely corrupt political contests in which one side may prevail in one locality and one in another, and which may even develop into a chronic civil war in the less settled parts of the country or an irresistible movement for secession between west and east.

That is, assuming the greatest imaginable vehemence and short-sighted selfishness and the least imaginable intelligence on the part of both workers and the plutocrat-swayed government. But if the more powerful and educated sections of the American community realise in time the immense moral possibilities of the Socialist movement, if they will trouble to understand its good side instead of emphasising its bad, if they will keep in touch with it and help in the development of a constructive content to its propositions, then it seems to me that popular Socialism may

Shadows of a Class War

The Hope of the Socialist Movement

count as a third great factor in the making of the civilised American state. In any case it does not seem to me probable that there can be any national revolutionary movement or any complete arrest in the development of an aristocratic phase in American history. The area of the country is too great, and the means of communication between the workers in different parts inadequate for a concerted rising, or even for effective political action in mass.

In the worst event—and it is only in the worst event that a great insurrectionary movement becomes probable—the newspapers, telephones and telegraphs, all the apparatus of discussion and popular appeal, the railways, arsenals, guns, flying machines, and all the material of warfare, will be in the hands of the property owners ; and the average of betrayal among the leaders of a class, not racially homogeneous, embittered, suspicious, united only by their discomforts and not by any constructive intentions, will necessarily be high. So that though the intensifying trouble between labour and capital may mean immense social disorganisation and lawlessness, though it may even supply the popular support in new attempts at secession, I do not see in it the possibility and force for that new start which the revolutionary Socialists anticipate ; I see it merely as one of several forces, making, on the whole, and particularly in view of the possible mediatory action of the universities, for construction and reconciliation.

Forces that Make for Construction

What changes are likely to occur in the more intimate social life of the people of the United States ? Two influences are at work that may modify this profoundly. One is that spread of knowledge and that accompanying change in moral attitude which is more and more sterilising the once prolific American home ; and the second is the rising standard of feminine education. There has arisen in this age a new consciousness in women. They are entering into the collective thought to a degree unprecedented in the world's history, and with portents at once disquieting and confused.

I enumerated above what I called the silent factors in the American synthesis, the immigrant European aliens, the Catholics, the coloured blood, and so forth. I would now observe that in the making of the American tradition the women also have been to a large extent and quite remarkably a silent factor. That tradition is not only fundamentally middle class and English, but it is also fundamentally masculine. The citizen is the man. The woman belongs to him. He votes for her, works for her, does all the severer thinking for her. She is in the home behind the shop, or in the dairy of the farmhouse with her daughters. She gets the meal while the men talk.

The American imagination and American feeling centre largely upon the family and upon "mother." American ideals are homely. The social unit is the home, and it is another and a different set of influences and considerations that are never thought of at all when the home sentiment is under discussion, that indeed it would be indelicate to mention at such a time, which are making that social unit the home of one child or of no children at all.

That ideal of a man-owned, mother-revering home has been the prevalent American ideal from the landing of the Mayflower right down to the leader writing of Mr. Arthur Brisbane. And it is clear that a very considerable section among one's educated women contemporaries do not mean to stand this ideal any longer. They do not want to be owned and cherished, and they do not want to be revered. How far they represent their sex in this matter it is very hard to say. In England, in the professional and most intellectually active classes, it is scarcely an exaggeration to say that all the most able women below five and thirty are workers for the suffrage and the ideal of equal and independent citizenship, and active critics of the conventions under which women live to-day.

Passing of a Cherished Ideal

It is plausible to suppose that a day is approaching when the alternatives between celibacy or a life of economic dependence and physical subordination to a man who has chosen her, and upon whose kindness her happiness depends, or prostitution, will no longer be a satisfactory outlook for the great majority of women, and when with a newly aroused political consciousness they will be prepared to exert themselves as a class to modify this situation. It may be that this is incorrect, and that in devotion to an accepted male and his children most women do still and will continue to find their greatest satisfaction in life. But it is the writer's impression that so simple and single-hearted a devotion is rare, and that, released from tradition—and education, reading and discussion do mean release from tradition—women are as eager for initiative, freedom and experience as men. In that case they will persist in the present agitation for political rights, and these secured, go on to demand a very considerable reconstruction of our present social order.

Woman's Political Agitation

It is interesting to point the direction in which this desire for independence will probably take them. They will discover that the dependence of women at the present time is not so much a law-made as an economic dependence due to the economic disadvantages their sex imposes upon them.

Maternity and the concomitants of maternity are the circumstances, exhausting energy and earning nothing, that place them at a discount. From the stage when property ceased to be chiefly the creation of feminine agricultural toil—the so-called primitive matriarchate—to our present stage women have had to depend upon a man's willingness to keep them in order to realise the organic purpose of their being. Whether conventionally equal or not, whether voters or not, that necessity for dependence will still remain under our system of private property and free independent competition. There is only one way by which women, as a class, can escape from that dependence each upon an individual man, and from all the practical inferiority this dependence entails, and that is by so altering their status as to make maternity and the upbringing of children a charge not upon the husband of the mother, but upon the community.

The public endowment of maternity is the only route by which the mass of women can reach that personal freedom and independent citizenship so many of them desire. Now, this idea of the endowment of maternity—or, as it is frequently phrased, the endowment of the home—is at present put forward by the modern Socialists as an integral part of their proposals, and it is interesting to note that there is this convergent possibility which may bring the feminist movement at last altogether into line with constructive Socialism. Obviously, before anything in the direction

Proposed Endowment of the Home

of family endowment becomes practicable, public bodies and the state organisation will need to display far more integrity and efficiency than they do in America at the present time. That is the trend of things in all contemporary civilised communities, and it is a trend that will find a powerful reinforcement in men's solicitudes as the increasing failure **The Cry Against Race Suicide** of the unsupported private family to produce offspring adequate to the needs of social development becomes more and more conspicuous. The impassioned appeals of Mr. Roosevelt have already brought home the race suicide of the native-born to every American intelligence, but mere rhetoric will not in itself suffice to make people, insecurely employed and struggling to maintain a comfortable standard of life against great economic pressure, prolific.

Presented as a call to a particularly onerous and quite unpaid social duty, the appeal for unrestricted parentage fails. Husband and wife alike dread an excessive burden. Travel, leisure, freedom, comfort, property and increased ability for business competition are the rewards of abstinence from parentage, and even the disapproval of Mr. Roosevelt and the pride of offspring are insufficient counterweights to these inducements. Large families disappear from the states and more and more couples are childless. Those who have children restrict their number in order to afford those they have some reasonable advantage in life. This, in the presence of the necessary knowledge, is as practically inevitable a consequence of individualist competition and the old American tradition as the appearance of slums and a class of millionaires.

These facts go to the very root of the American problem. I have already pointed out that, in spite of a colossal immigration, the population of the United States was, at the end of the nineteenth century, over **How Long will Europe Feed America?** twenty millions short of what it should have been through its own native increase had the birth-rate of the opening century been maintained. For a hundred years America had been "fed" by Europe. That feeding process will not go on indefinitely. The immigration came in waves, as if reservoir after reservoir was tapped and exhausted. Nowadays, England, Scotland, Ireland, France and Scandinavia send hardly any more people—they have no more

to send. Germany and Switzerland send only a few. The South European and Austrian supply is not so abundant as it was. There may come a time when Europe and Western Asia will have no more surplus population to send, when even Eastern Asia will have passed into a less fecund phase, and when America will have to look to its own natural increase for the continued development of its resources. If the present isolated family of private competition is still the social unit, it seems improbable that there will be any greater natural increase than there is in France.

Will the growing idea of a closer social organisation have developed by that time to the possibility of some collective effort in this matter ? Or will that only come about after the population of the world has passed through a phase of absolute recession ? The peculiar constitution of the United States gives a remarkable freedom of experiment in these matters to each individual state, and local developments do not need to wait upon a national change of opinion ; but, on the other hand, the superficial impression of an English visitor is **A Democracy of Untutored Individualists** that any such profound interference with domestic autonomy runs counter to all that Americans seem to hold dear at the present time. These are, however, new ideas and new considerations that have still to be brought adequately before the national consciousness, and it is quite impossible to calculate how a population living under changing conditions and with a rising standard of education, and a developing feminine consciousness, may not think and feel and behave in a generation's time. At present, for all political and collective action, America is a democracy of untutored individualist men who will neither tolerate such interference between themselves and the women they choose to marry as the endowment of motherhood implies, nor view the "kids" who will at times occur even in the best regulated families as anything but rather embarrassing, rather amusing by-products of the individual affections.

I find in a London weekly paper for August 15th, 1908, a description by Mr. Jerome K. Jerome of "John Smith," the average British voter. John Smith might serve, I think, in some respects, for the common man of all the modern civilisations. Among other things that John Smith thinks and wants, he wants :

A little house and garden in the country all to himself. His idea is somewhere near half an acre of ground. He would like a piano in the best room; it has always been his dream to have a piano. The youngest girl, he is convinced, is musical. As a man who has knocked about the world and has thought, he quite appreciates the argument that by co-operation the material side of life can be greatly improved. He quite sees that by combining a dozen families together in one large house better practical results can be obtained. It is as easy to direct the cooking for a hundred as for half a dozen. There would be less waste of food, of coals, of lighting. To put aside one piano for one girl is absurd. He sees all this, but it does not alter one little bit of his passionate craving for that small house and garden all to himself. He is built that way. He is typical of a good many other men and women built on the same pattern. What are you going to do with them? Change them—their instincts, their very nature, rooted in the centuries? Or, as an alternative, vary Socialism to fit John Smith? Which is likely to prove the shorter operation?

That, however, is by the way. Here is the point at issue:

He has heard that Socialism proposes to acknowledge women's service to the state by paying her a weekly wage according to the number of children that she bears and rears. I don't propose to repeat his objections to the idea; they could hardly be called objections. There is an ugly look coming into his eyes;

Mr. Jerome on John Smith something quite undefinable, prehistoric, almost dangerous, looks out of them. . . . In talking to him on this subject you do not seem to be talking to a man. It is as if you had come face to face with something behind civilisation, behind humanity, something deeper down still among the dim beginnings of creation . . .

Now, no doubt Mr. Jerome is writing with emphasis here. But there is sufficient truth in the passage for it to stand here as a rough symbol of another factor in this question. John Smithism, that manly and individualist element in the citizen, stands over against and resists all the forces of organisation that would subjugate it to a collective purpose. It is careless of coming national cessation and depopulation, careless of the insurgent spirit beneath the acquiescences of Mrs. Smith, careless of its own inevitable defeat in the economic struggle, careless because it can understand none of these things; it is obstinately muddle-headed, asserting what it conceives to be itself against the universe and all other John Smiths whatsoever. It is a factor with all other factors.

The creative, acquisitive, aggressive spirit of those bigger John Smiths who succeed as against the myriads of John Smiths who fail, the wider horizons and more efficient methods of the educated man, the awakening class-consciousness of women, the inevitable futility of John Smithism, the sturdy independence that makes John Smith resent even disciplined co-operation with Tom Brown to achieve a common end, his essential incapacity indeed for collective action; all these things are against the ultimate triumph and make for the ultimate civilisation even of John Smith. It may be doubted if the increasing collective organisation of society to which the United States of America, in common with all the rest of the world, seem to be tending, will be to any very large extent a national organisation. The constitution is an immense and complicated barrier to effectual centralisation. There are many reasons for supposing the national government will always remain a little ineffectual and detached from the full flow of American life, and this notwithstanding the very great powers with which the president is endowed.

The Seat of National Government

One of these reasons is certainly the peculiar accident that has placed the seat of government upon the Potomac. To the thoughtful visitor to the United States, this hiding away of the central government in a minute district remote from all the great centres of thought, population and business activity, becomes more and more remarkable, more and more perplexing, more and more suggestive of an incurable weakness in the national government as he grasps more and more firmly the peculiarities of the American situation.

I do not see how the central government of that great American nation of which I dream can possibly be at Washington, and I do not see how the present central government can possibly be transferred to any other centre. But to go to Washington, to see and talk to Washington, is to receive an extraordinary impression of the utter isolation and hopelessness of Washington. The national government has an air of being marooned there. One goes from the abounding movement and vitality of the Northern cities to this sunny and enervating place through the negligently cultivated country of Virginia, and one discovers the slovenly, unfinished promise of a city, broad avenues lined by negro shanties and patches of cultivation, great public buildings and an immense post-office, a lifeless museum, an inert university, a splendid desert library, a

Disappointing Capital of the States

street of souvenir shops, a certain industry of " seeing Washington," an idiotic colossal obelisk. It seems an ideal nest for the tariff manipulator, a festering corner of delegates and agents and secondary people. In the White House the present writer found a transitory glow of intellectual activity ; the spittoons and glass screens that once made it like a London gin-palace had been removed, and the former orgies of handshaking reduced to a minimum. It was, one felt, an accidental phase.

The assassination of McKinley was an interruption of the normal Washington process. To this place, out of the way of everywhere, come the senators and congressmen, mostly leaving their families behind them in their states of origin ; and hither, too, are drawn a multitude of journalists and political agents and clerks —a crowd of underbred, mediocre men. For most of them there is neither social nor intellectual life. The thought of America is far away, centred now in New York ; the business and economic development centres upon New York ; apart from the president it is in New York that one meets the people who matter, and the New York atmosphere that grows and develops ideas and purposes. New York is the natural capital of the United States, and would need to be the capital of any highly organised national system. Government

from the district of Columbia is in itself the repudiation of any highly organised national system. But government from this ineffectual, inert place is only the most striking outcome of that inflexible constitution the wrangling delegates of 1787–1788 did at last produce out of a conflict of state jealousies. They did their best to render centralisation or any coalescence of states impossible and private property impregnable, and so far their work has proved extraordinarily effective. Only a great access of intellectual and moral vigour in the nation can ever set it aside. And while the more and more sterile millions of the United States grapple with the legal and traditional difficulties that promise at last to arrest their development altogether, the rest of the world will be moving on to new phases. An awakened Asia will be reorganising its social and **America's** political conceptions in the **Internal** light of modern knowledge **Development** and modern ideas ; and South America will be working out its destinies, perhaps in the form of a powerful confederation of states. All Europe will be schooling its John Smiths to finer disciplines and broader ideas. But our present concern is the internal development of the United States of America, and it opens too wide a field to speculate how that may be affected or interrupted by foreign forces.

CHICAGO UNIVERSITY THE LEADING INSTITUTE OF LEARNING IN THE WESTERN STATES

SOCIAL
CONDITIONS
AND THE
SOCIAL
FUTURE

IN THE
UNITED
STATES IV
BY
H. G. WELLS

THE UNITED STATES OF TO-MORROW
REBUILDING THE SOCIAL SCHEME

I HAVE hinted in the last section that there is a possibility that the new wave of constructive ideas in American thought may speedily develop a cant of its own. But even then a constructive cant is better than a destructive one. Even the conscious hypocrite has to do something to justify his pretences; and the mere disappearance from current thought of the persuasion that organisation is a mistake and discipline needless clears the ground of one huge obstacle even if it guarantees nothing about the consequent building.

But, apart from this, are there more solid and effectual forces behind this new movement of ideas that makes for organisation in the American medley at the present time?

The speculative writer casting about for such elements lights upon four sets of possibilities which call for discussion. First, one has to ask: How far is the American plutocracy likely to be merely *Future of the American Woman* a wasteful and chaotic class and how far is it likely to become consciously aristocratic and constructive? Secondly, and in relation to this, what possibilities of pride and leading are there in the great university foundations of America? Will they presently begin to tell as a restraining and directing force upon public thought? Thirdly: Will the growing American Socialist movement, which at present is just as anarchistic and undisciplined in spirit as everything else in America, presently perceive the constructive implications of its general propositions and become statesmanlike and constructive after the fashion of the Socialist movement in England? And fourthly: What are the latent possibilities of the American women? Will women, as they become more and more aware of themselves as a class and the problem of their sex, become a force upon the anarchistic side—a force favouring race suicide—or upon the constructive side, which plans and builds and bears the future? The only possible answer

to each one of these questions at present is guessing and an estimate. But the only way in which a conception of the American social future may be reached lies through their discussion. Let us begin by considering what constructive *Forces in the New Plutocracy* forces may exist in this new plutocracy, which already so largely sways American economic and political development. The first impression is one of extravagant expenditure, of a class irresponsible and wasteful beyond all precedent.

One gets a Zolaesque picture of that aspect in Mr. Upton Sinclair's "Metropolis," or the fashionable intelligence of the popular New York Sunday editions; and one finds a good deal of confirmatory evidence in many incidental aspects of the smart American life of Paris and the Riviera. The evidence in the notorious Thaw trial, after one has discounted its theatrical elements, was still a very convincing demonstration of a rotten and extravagant, because aimless and functionless, class of rich people. But one has to be careful in this matter if one is to do justice to the facts. If a thing is made up of two elements, and one is noisy and glaringly coloured, and the other is quiet and colourless, the first impression created will be that the thing is identical with the element that is noisy and glaringly coloured.

One is less likely to hear of the broad plans and the quality of the wise, strong and constructive individuals in a class than of their foolish wives, their spendthrift sons, their mistresses if *Rich Men in the Making* they lapse from virtue, or their own moments of folly. In the making of very rich men there is always a factor of good fortune and a factor of design and will. One meets rich men at times who seem to be merely lucky gamblers, who strike one as just the thousandth man in a myriad of wild plungers, who are, in fact, chance nobodies washed up by an eddy. Others, again, strike one as exceptionally lucky half-knaves. But there are others of a growth more deliberate and of an altogether higher personal quality. One takes such men as Mr. J. D. Rockefeller or Mr. Pierpont Morgan—the scale of their fortunes makes them public property—and it is clear that

Types of America's Rich Men we are dealing with persons on a quite different level of intellectual power from the British Colonel Norths, for example, or the South African Joels. In my "Future in America" I have taken the former largely at Miss Tarbell's estimate, and treated him as a case of acquisitiveness raised in Baptist surroundings.

But I doubt very much if that exhausts the man as he is to-day. Given a man brought up to saving and "getting on" as if to a religion, a man very acquisitive and very patient and restrained, and indubitably with great organising power, and he grows rich beyond the dreams of avarice. And having done so, there he is. What is he going to do? Every step he takes up the ascent to riches gives him new perspectives and new points of view.

It may have appealed to the young Rockefeller, clerk in a Chicago house, that to be rich was in itself a supreme end. In the first flush of the discovery that he was immensely rich he may have thanked heaven as if for a supreme good, and spoken to a Sunday-school gathering as if he knew himself for the most favoured of men. But all that happened twenty years ago or more. One does not keep on in that sort of satisfaction; one settles down to the new facts. And such men as Mr. Rockefeller and Mr. Pierpont Morgan do not live in a made and protected world with their minds trained, tamed and fed, and shielded from outside impressions as royalties do. The thought of the world has washed about them; they have read and listened to the discussion of themselves

Questions that Trouble the Millionaire for some decades; they have had sleepless nights of self-examination. To succeed in acquiring enormous wealth does not solve the problem of life—indeed, it reopens it in a new form. "What shall I do with myself?" simply recurs again. You may have decided to devote yourself to getting on, getting wealthy. Well, you have got it. Now again comes the question: "What shall I do?" Mr. Pierpont Morgan, I am told, collects

works of art. I can understand that satisfying a rich gentleman of leisure, but not a man who has felt the sensation of holding great big things in his great big hands. Saul, going out to seek his father's asses, found a kingdom, and became very spiritedly a king; and it seems to me that these big industrial and financial organisers, whatever in their youth they proposed to do or be, must many of them come to realise that their organising power is up against no less a thing than a nation's future. Napoleon, it is curious to remember, once wanted to run a lodging-house, and a man may start to corner oil and end the father of a civilisation.

Now, I am disposed to suspect at times that an inkling of such a realisation may have come to some of these very rich men. I am inclined to put it among the possibilities of our time that it may presently become clearly and definitely the inspiring idea of many of those who find themselves predominantly rich. I do not see why these active rich should not develop statesmanship, and I can quite imagine them developing very considerable

New Career for the Active Rich statesmanship. Because these men were able to realise their organising power in the absence of economic organisation, it does not follow that they will be fanatical for a continuing looseness and freedom of property. The phase of economic liberty ends itself, as Marx long ago pointed out. The American business world becomes more and more a managed world with fewer and fewer wild possibilities of succeeding. Of all people, the big millionaires should realise this most acutely, and, in fact, there are many signs that they do.

It seems to me that the educational zeal of Mr. Andrew Carnegie and the university and scientific endowments of Mr. Rockefeller are not merely showy benefactions; they express a definite feeling of the present need of constructive organisation in the social scheme. The time has come to build. There is, I think, good reason for expecting that statesmanship of the millionaires to become more organised and scientific and comprehensive in the coming years. It is plausible at least to maintain that the personal quality of the American plutocracy has risen in the last three decades, has risen from the quality of a mere irresponsible wealthy person towards that of a real aristocrat with a sense of the state.

THE COLUMBIA UNIVERSITY, NEW YORK: VIEW OF THE LIBRARY

PRINCETON UNIVERSITY, NEW JERSEY: THE BLAIR HALL

THE CORNELL UNIVERSITY AT ITHACA IN NEW YORK STATE

AMERICA'S SEATS OF LEARNING: VIEWS OF WELL-KNOWN UNIVERSITIES

That one may reckon the first hopeful possibility in the American outlook. And intimately connected with this development of an attitude of public responsibility in the very rich is the decay, on the one hand, of the preposterous idea once prevalent in America that politics is an unsuitable interest for a " gentleman,"

New York's Idea of Gentlemen and, on the other, of the democratic jealousy of any but poor politicians. In New York they talk very much of "gentlemen," and by gentlemen they seem to mean a rich man " in society " with a college education. Nowadays, gentlemen seem more and more disposed towards politics, and less and less towards a life of business or detached refinement. Theodore Roosevelt, for example, was one of the pioneers in this new development, this restoration of virility to the gentlemanly ideal. His career marks the appearance of a new and better type of man in American politics, the close of the rule of the idealised nobody.

The prophecy has been made at times that the United States might develop a Cæsarism, and certainly the position of president might easily become that of an imperator. No doubt, in the event of an acute failure of the national system such a catastrophe might occur, but the more hopeful and probable line of development is one in which a conscious and powerful, if informal, aristocracy will play a large part. It may indeed never have any of the outward forms of an aristocracy or any definite public recognition.

The Americans are as chary of the coronet and the known aristocratic titles as the Romans were of the word king. Octavius, for that reason, never called himself king, nor Italy a kingdom. He was just the Cæsar of the republic, and the empire had been established for many years before the Romans fully realised that they had returned to monarchy. The American

Education Assisted by the State universities are closely connected in their development with the appearance and growing class-consciousness of this aristocracy of wealth. The fathers of the country certainly did postulate a need of universities, and in every state congress set aside public lands to furnish a university with material resources.

Every state does possess a university, though in many instances these institutions are in the last degree of feebleness.

From the very beginning, side by side with the state universities, were the universities founded by benefactors ; and with the evolution of new centres of population, new and extremely generous plutocratic endowments appeared. The dominant universities of America to-day, the treasure-houses of intellectual prestige, are almost all of them of plutocratic origin ; and even in the state universities, if new resources are wanted to found new chairs, to supply funds for research or publication or what not, it is to the more state-conscious wealthy, and not to the state legislature, that the appeal is made almost as a matter of course. The common voter, the small individualist, has less constructive imagination, is more individualistic, than the big individualist.

This great network of universities that is now spread over the states, interchanging teachers, literature and ideas, and educating not only the professions, but a growing proportion of business leaders and wealthy people, must necessarily take an important part in the reconstruction of the American tradition that is now in

The Good Work of the Universities progress. It is giving a large and increasing amount of attention to the subjects that bear most directly upon the peculiar practical problems of statecraft in America, to psychology, sociology and political science. It is influencing the Press more and more directly by supplying a rising proportion of journalists, and creating an atmosphere of criticism and suggestion. It is keeping itself, on the one hand, in touch with the popular literature of public criticism in those new and curious organs of public thought, the ten cent magazines, and, on the other, it is making a constantly more solid basis of common understanding upon which the newer generation of plutocrats may meet. That older sentimental patriotism must be giving place under its influence to a more definite and effectual conception of a collective purpose.

It is to the intellectual influence of sustained scientific study in the universities, and a growing increase of the college-trained element in the population, that we must look if we are to look anywhere for the new progressive methods, for the substitution of persistent, planned and calculated social development for the former conditions of the systematic neglect and corruption in public affairs varied by epileptic seizures of " reform."　　H. G. WELLS

AMERICA'S PREMIER UNIVERSITY FOR WOMEN: BARNARD COLLEGE, NEW YORK

THE AMERICAN GIRTON: THE FAMOUS WOMEN'S COLLEGE AT BALTIMORE

THE UNIVERSITY OF PENNSYLVANIA AT PHILADELPHIA, SHOWING COLLEGE HALL

NOTABLE UNIVERSITIES IN THE UNITED STATES

6315

LEADING DATES IN THE HISTORY OF THE AMERICAN CONTINENT

A.D.	
1000	Discovery of Vinland by Leif Eriksen
1200	Rise of the Incas in Peru
1300	Reign of Maita Capak
1330	Reign of Capak Yupanki
1360	Inca Roca : traditional organiser of the Inca system
1390	Yahuar Capak : the reign of tears
1400	Tecpanec supremacy in Mexico. Tezozomoc emperor of Anahuac. Chibcha pentarchy on the Magdalena
1403	Huitzilihuitl in Mexico
1410	Huiracocha restores the Inca supremacy
1419	Fall of Ixtlilxochitl. Rise of Aztecs
1427	Maxtla succeeds Tezozomoc
1431	Alliance of Aztecs and Chichimecs to overthrow Tecpanecs. Intellectual ascendancy of Chichimecs. Progress of kingdom of Quito
1440	Yupanki Pachacutek expands the Inca empire. Montezuma I. organises the Aztec kingdom
1450	Supremacy of Tunja and Bogota on the Magdalena. Development of Aztec military ascendancy in Mexico
1460	Tupak Yupanki extends Inca empire
1468	Axayacotl succeeds Montezuma I.
1470	Tenochtitlan (Aztec : Mexico) absorbs Tlatelulco. Incorporation of Chimu with Inca empire
1480	Quito incorporated by the Incas
1492	Columbus reaches the West Indies
1493	Second voyage of Columbus
1497	John Cabot discovers Labrador
1499	The Cabots explore North American coast-line. Voyage of Amerigo Vespucci
1500	Cabral discovers Brazil. Huana Capak Inca emperor. Extension of Bogota supremacy on the Magdalena under Nemequene
1502	Bishoprics founded in Spanish dominion
1503	Casa de Contratacion founded. Bull of Pope Alexander VI.
1511	Audiencia of San Domingo established.
1512	Discovery of Florida. Montezuma II. supreme in Anahuac (Mexico)
1513	Balboa sights the Pacific from Panama
1514	Rio de la Plata discovered
1515	Bermudas discovered
1517	First importation of negro slaves. Yucatan discovered by Francesco de Cordoba
1519	Cortes invades Mexico
1520	Magelhaes passes Straits of Magellan, on the first voyage of circumnavigation
1526	Edict of Granada. Plate fleet organised
1527	Fishing fleets congregate off Newfoundland
1530	Struggle between Tunja and Bogota
1531	Brazil : capitanries established
1532	Atahualpa usurps the Inca sovereignty. Pizarro invades Peru
1534	Cartier on the St. Lawrence
1535	Mendoza founds Buenos Ayres
1536	Queseda's expedition. Submission of Bogota to Spain
1539	De Soto's Mississippi expedition
1545	Silver mines of Potosi discovered
1549	Jesuits in Brazil
1562	French Huguenot settlement in Florida
1568	Hawkins and Drake at San Juan d'Ulloa
1572	Drake's raid on Nombre de Dios
1576	John Oxenham on the Pacific. Frobisher's first Arctic voyage
1577	Drake sails on voyage of circumnavigation
1583	Humphrey Gilbert in Newfoundland
1584	Raleigh's first colony at Roanoke
1587	Discovery of Davis Strait by John Davis
1595	Raleigh's Guiana voyage
1600	French settlement at Tadoussac
1602	Gosnold's attempt to colonise Virginia
1603	Champlain's first voyage to the St. Lawrence
1604	Champlain's second voyage
1605	Port Royal (Annapolis) founded
1606	Charter of Virginia and Plymouth Companies
1607	Colony of Virginia at Jamestown
1608	Quebec founded. Jesuits in Paraguay
1609	Bermudas annexed. Second Virginia charter : Lord Delaware governor
1612	Hudson's Bay claimed for England
1615	Recollet Fathers in Canada
1620	New Plymouth founded by Pilgrim Fathers
1621	Grant of Nova Scotia to Sir W. Alexander. Dutch West India Company ; origin of Dutch Guiana

A.D.	
1622	Dutch found New Amsterdam (New York)
1625	Settlement of Barbados
1625	New constitution proclaimed for Virginia. Settlement of Lord Baltimore in Newfoundland
1627	Company of the Hundred Associates
1629	Charter of Massachusetts Company. Capture of Quebec by English
1630	Winthrop governor of Boston
1632	Maryland granted to Lord Baltimore. Canada and Acadia restored to France
1633	Champlain governor of Canada
1634	First committee of the Privy Council for control of plantations
1635	Colony of Connecticut. Death of Champlain
1636	Roger Williams at Providence
1637	David Kirke's settlement in Newfoundland
1639	Colony of Maine
1641	Montreal founded
1643	Confederation of New England colonies
1651	Commonwealth Navigation Act. De Lanson governor of " New France "
1654	English take possession of Acadia, which is ceded to them by treaty next year
1655	Capture of Jamaica by Penn and Venables
1661	Restoration Navigation Act. Colonies more stringently restricted
1663	Rhode Island Charter. Beginning of Carolina. Abolition of the Hundred Associates
1664	First Assembly in Jamaica. English capture New Amsterdam, renamed New York
1665	De Courcelles governor of New France
1666	Iroquois checked by De Tracy
1667	Carolina established as a colony. Treaty of Breda
1670	Acadia restored to France. Hudson's Bay Charter. Prince Rupert president
1672	Frontenac governor of New France
1673	French Mississippi expedition
1675	Indian wars of New England states
1676	Rising against the government in Virginia
1682	Pennsylvania Charter. Frontenac replaced in Canada by De la Barre
1683	Massachusetts Charter annulled
1685	De la Barre replaced by Denonville
1686	French attacks on Hudson's Bay Company
1687	French Iroquois war
1688	Andros appointed governor of all northern colonies
1689	Frontenac returns as governor of Canada. English colonies claim restoration of their old constitutions
1690	Expedition of Phipps against Acadia and Quebec
1691	New Massachusetts Charter
1695	French recover Acadia
1697	Anglo-French hostilities suspended by European Treaty of Ryswick
1698	Death of Frontenac
1699	D'Iberville's Mississippi expedition. Beginning of Louisiana
1702	Contests between South Carolina and Florida
1713	Treaty of Utrecht : Newfoundland acknowledged British ; Acadia ceded (except Cape Breton) and becomes Nova Scotia. Asiento, giving monopoly of slave trade with Spanish colonies, with other trading rights, transferred to Great Britain
1719	Bahama pirates suppressed
1725	French establish Fort Niagara
1728	A government established in Newfoundland : Osborne first governor
1731	French fort at Crown Point
1733	Georgia Charter
1745	British capture Louisbourg
1748	Louisbourg restored by Peace of Aix-la-Chapelle
1754	French establish Fort Duquesne
1755	Braddock's disaster
1756	Montcalm in Canada ; he captures Fort Oswego
1757	Montcalm captures Fort William Henry
1758	Montcalm defeats Abercrombie at Ticonderoga. British capture forts Frontenac and Duquesne, and Louisbourg
1759	Capture of Quebec by Wolfe
1760	Capture of Montreal
1763	Treaty of Paris : France cedes Louisiana to Spain, and the rest of her North American colonies to Britain. Spain cedes Florida to Britain. In the West Indies, Grenada, St. Vincent, Dominica and Tobago ceded to Britain

LEADING DATES IN THE HISTORY OF THE AMERICAN CONTINENT

A.D.		A.D.	
1764	Grenville enforces existing commercial regulations. Pontiac's insurrection	1822	Retirement of San Martin. Iturbide becomes Emperor of Mexico
1765	George Grenville's Stamp Act	1823	Monroe doctrine enunciated. Fall of Iturbide ; Mexican Republic
1766	Rockingham Ministry repeals the Stamp Act and reduces Customs duties, but passes Declaratory Act affirming the abstract right of taxation. Carleton (afterwards Lord Dorchester) governor at Quebec	1824	Bolivar dictator in Peru. Bolivia constituted
		1825	John Quincy Adams president U.S.A. Independence of Uruguay. Federal Union of Central America
1767	Townshend's taxes	1827	Independence of Bolivia
1768	General Gage governor of Massachusetts. Massachusetts recognises a Convention in place of the suppressed Assembly. Expulsion of Jesuits from Paraguay.	1829	Andrew Jackson president U.S.A.
		1830	Venezuela separates from Colombia. Bolivar resigns
1769	Prince Edward Island separated from Quebec. Bedford's Resolution for changing the venue of trials. Repeal of Townshend's taxes except that on tea	1831	Colombia becomes Republic of New Granada
		1833	S. Carolina repudiates tariff imposed by congress. Chilian constitution established
		1835	Rosas dictator at Buenos Ayres
		1837	Van Buren president U.S.A. Papineau's revolt in Canada
1770	Lord North's Ministry. The Boston massacre	1838	Lord Durham in Canada
1772	Burning of the Gaspee	1839	Lord Durham's report. Central American Union dissolved. Chili, Peru and Bolivia separate states
1773	DEC. : The " Boston Tea-party "		
1774	Penal Acts against Boston. Quebec Act makes Canada a Crown colony, and establishes Roman Catholicism. Continental Congress meets at Philadelphia	1840	Canadian Act of Reunion
		1841	Harrison president (dies April 4th). Vice-president Tyler becomes president U.S.A.
1775	American War of Independence begun by Battle of Lexington. Battle of Bunker's Hill. Washington commander-in-chief. Invasion of Canada by Montgomery and Benedict Arnold	1842	Ashburton Treaty
		1845	Polk president U.S.A. Annexation of Texas
		1846	War between U.S. and Mexico
1776	Collapse of Invasion of Canada. Boston evacuated. JULY : Declaration of Independence. British occupy New York. Battles of Brooklyn and Trenton	1848	Mexican War ended. U.S. victorious
		1849	Repeal of British navigation acts. Zachary Taylor president U.S.A.
		1850	Millard Fillmore president U.S.A.
1777	Battles of Princeton and Brandywine Creek. British take Philadelphia. Burgoyne's surrender at Saratoga. Benjamin Franklin in Paris	1852	" Uncle Tom's Cabin " published
		1853	Franklin Pierce president
		1855	Slavery question in Kansas
1778	French alliance with Americans. North's conciliation proposals rejected. Death of Chatham. Beginning of Naval War	1857	Buchanan president U.S.A. Dred Scott case
		1858	Colony of British Columbia
		1860	Secession of South Carolina
1779	Spain joins the War ; siege of Gibraltar	1861	Lincoln president U.S.A. War of North and South. Capture of Fort Sumter. Battle of Bull Run. The Trent affair. New Granada becomes United States of Colombia
1780	Campaign in the Southern colonies		
1781	Surrender of Yorktown assures American independence [Saints		
1782	Rodney recovers naval ascendancy at Battle of the	1863	Lincoln's Slave Emancipation Proclamation
1783	Peace of Versailles ; independence of the United States acknowledged. Emigration of U. E. Loyalists to Canada. Florida restored to Spain	1864	Ulysses Grant Federal commander. Archduke Maximilian made emperor of Mexico
		1865	Surrender of Lee and Johnston ends Civil War. Assassination of Lincoln. Andrew Johnson president. Jamaica disturbances suppressed by Governor Eyre
1778	American Constitution ratified		
1789	George Washington first president of U.S.A.		
1791	Canada Act ; separation of Upper and Lower Canada	1867	U.S. Reconstruction Act. Purchase of Alaska. British North America Act. Execution of Emperor Maximilian ; Juarez president of Mexican Republic
1792	Washington re-elected president		
1794	Jay's Treaty		
1795	San Domingo partly ceded to France by Spain		
1796	Toronto becomes capital of Upper Canada. British Guiana annexed	1869	Grant president U.S.A. Red River Rebellion
		1870	Blanco dictator of Venezuela
1797	John Adams president U.S.A., Washington having refused re-election. Capture of Trinidad by	1871	British Columbia in B.N.A. Confederation
		1877	Hayes president U.S.A. Diaz president Mexico
1798	British Honduras secured [British	1879	Canada adopts protection, under Sir J. Macdonald. War between Chili and Peru
1799	Death of Washington		
1800	Franco-American Treaty	1880	B.N.A., except Newfoundland, included in the dominion of Canada
1801	Thomas Jefferson president of U.S.A.		
1803	Louisiana Purchase	1881	Garfield, president U.S.A., assassinated. Vice-President Arthur becomes president. Canadian Pacific Railway begun. End of Chili-Peruvian War
1807	Whitelock defeated at Buenos Ayres		
1808	Portuguese monarchy at Rio de Janeiro		
1809	Madison president U.S.A. Risings in Spanish colonies	1885	Grover Cleveland president U.S.A. Riel's second rebellion
1810	Hidalgo's unsuccessful revolt in Mexico. Independent government proclaimed at Buenos	1886	Balmacéda president of Chili
		1889	Harrison president U.S.A. Republic of Brazil established
1811	Venezuela declares independence [Ayres		
1812	War between U.S.A. and Great Britain. Invasion of Canada repulsed	1891	Fall of Balmacéda
		1893	Cleveland (2) president U.S.
1813	Bolivar at head of revolt in Northern Spanish colonies	1896	Venezuela Boundary Arbitration
		1897	McKinley president U.S.
1814	Capture of Washington. Peace of Ghent. Francia dictator of Paraguay	1898	War between Spain and U.S.
		1899	Castro president of Venezuela. Annexation of Philippines by U.S.A.
1815	Repulse of New Orleans. Brazil constituted a kingdom		
1816	Argentine Republic established	1900	Canadian contingent in South African War
1817	Monroe president U.S.A. Family Compact in Upper Canada. San Martin's invasion of Chili. O'Higgins president of Chili. Brazil declared independent	1901	McKinley assassinated. Vice-President Theodore Roosevelt becomes president U.S.A.
		1903	Application of Monroe Doctrine in Venezuela
1819	Florida acquired by U.S.	1905	Roosevelt re-elected president U.S.A.
1821	Missouri Compromise. Independence of Spanish colonies assured by battle of Carabobo. Bolivar president of Colombia	1908	Expulsion of president Castro from Venezuela
		1909	W. H. Taft inaugurated president U.S.A.

AREA AND POPULATION. The area of the United States is 3,025,600 square miles, and the population at the census of 1900 was 75,994,575, including 66,893,405 whites and 8,840,388 negroes or coloured. The outside territories belonging to the United States are as follow :

	Population.	Population.	
Alaska	590,884 ..	63,592 ..	[see page 6319]
Porto Rico	3,435 ..	953,243 ..	[see page 6176]
Hawaii	6,449 ..	154,001 ..	[see pages 968-974]
Philippine Islands	127,853 ..	7,635,426 ..	[see page 936]
Guam (Ladrones)	200 ..	10,879 ..	
Part of the Samoan Islands	102 ..	5,800 ..	[see page 979]
Total	728,923	8,822,941	

Thus the grand total area is 3,754,523 square miles and the grand total of population is 84,817,516. It is probable that the present grand total (1909) of population is not far short of 100,000,000, and perhaps exceeds it.

The territory of the United States proper is divided into states and territories, as follow :

	Postal Contraction.	Area. sq. Miles.	Population, 1900.	Capital.	Population of Capital, 1900.
Alabama	Ala.	51,540	1,828,697	Montgomery	40,308
Arizona	Ariz.	112,920	122,931	Phœnix	5,544
Arkansas	Ark.	53,045	1,311,564	Little Rock	39,959
California	Cal.	156,172	1,485,053	Sacramento	30,732
Colorado	Colo.	103,645	539,700	Denver	151,920
Connecticut	Conn.	4,845	908,420	Hartford	95,822
Delaware	Del.	1,960	184,735	Dover	3,329
District of Columbia	D.C.	60	278,718	Washington	278,718
Florida	Fla.	54,240	528,542	Tallahassee	2,981
Georgia	Ga.	58,980	2,216,331	Atlanta	104,984
Idaho	Ida.	84,290	161,772	Boisé	20,000
Illinois	Ill.	56,000	4,821,550	Springfield	38,933
Indiana	Ind.	35,910	2,516,462	Indianapolis	233,277
Iowa	I. or Ia.	55,475	2,231,853	Des Moines	78,323
Kansas	Kan.	81,700	1,470,495	Topeka	41,886
Kentucky	Ky.	40,000	2,147,174	Frankfort	9,487
Louisiana	La.	45,420	1,381,625	Baton Rouge	11,743
Maine	Me.	29,895	694,466	Augusta	12,379
Maryland	Md.	9,860	1,188,044	Annapolis	9,077
Massachusetts	Mass.	8,040	2,805,346	Boston	595,380
Michigan	Mich.	57,430	2,420,982	Lansing	20,276
Minnesota	Minn.	79,205	1,751,394	St. Paul	203,815
Mississippi	Miss.	46,340	1,551,270	Jackson	7,816
Missouri	Mo.	68,735	3,106,665	Jefferson City	9,667
Montana	Mont.	145,310	243,329	Helena	16,770
Nebraska	Neb.	76,840	1,066,300	Lincoln	48,232
Nevada	Nev.	109,740	42,335	Carson City	2,100
New Hampshire	N.H.	9,005	411,588	Concord	21,210
New Jersey	N.J.	7,525	1,883,669	Trenton	86,355
New Mexico	N. Mex.	122,460	195,310	Santa Fé	5,603
New York	N.Y.	47,620	7,268,894	Albany	98,374
North Carolina	N.C.	48,580	1,893,810	Raleigh	13,543
North Dakota	N. Dak.	70,195	319,146	Bismark	3,319
Ohio	O.	40,760	4,157,545	Columbus	145,414
Oklahoma	Okla.	38,830	398,331	Guthrie	11,652
Indian Territory	Ind. T.	31,000	392,060		
Oregon	Ore.	94,560	413,536	Salem	4,258
Pennsylvania	Pa.	44,985	6,302,115	Harrisburg	55,725
Rhode Island	R.I.	1,053	428,556	Providence	203,243
South Carolina	S.C.	30,170	1,340,316	Columbia	24,564
South Dakota	S. Dak.	76,850	401,570	Pierre	2,306
Tennessee	Tenn.	41,750	2,020,616	Nashville	84,703
Texas	Tex.	262,290	3,048,710	Austin	25,290
Utah	U.	82,190	276,749	Salt Lake City	61,202
Vermont	Vt.	9,135	343,641	Montpelier	6,266
Virginia	Va.	40,125	1,854,184	Richmond	87,246
Washington	Wash.	66,880	518,103	Olympia	4,082
West Virginia	W.Va.	24,645	958,800	Charleston	13,715
Wisconsin	Wis.	54,450	2,069,042	Madison	19,164
Wyoming	Wyo.	97,575	92,531	Cheyenne	13,570

In 1906 the Indian reservations had an area of 87,237 square miles, and a population of 291,581. The chief Indian reservations are in Oklahoma, Arizona, South Dakota and Montana. Of the foreign-born population of the United States, totalling over 10,000,000, more than 50 per cent. went from the United Kingdom and Germany —the number from the former being slightly greater than that from the latter—and the next most important countries providing the United States with immigrants are Canada and Newfoundland, Sweden, Italy, Russia, Poland, Norway, Austria, Denmark, Bohemia, Hungary, Switzerland, Holland and France.

The chief cities and towns in the United States, with populations over 50,000, and not including the capitals of the states mentioned above, are as follow :

California.—San Francisco, 364,677 ; Los Angeles, 160,000 ; Oakland, 72,670.

Connecticut.—New Haven, 121,227 ; Bridgeport, 84,274 ; Waterbury, 61,903.

Delaware.—Wilmington, 85,140.

Georgia.—Savannah, 68,596.

Illinois.—Chicago, 2,367,000 ; Peoria, 66,365.

Indiana.—Evansville, 63,957 ; Terre Haute, 52,805 ; Fort Wayne, 50,947.

Kansas.—Kansas City, 77,912 (adjoining Kansas City, Missouri, but a different municipality).

Kentucky.—Louisville, 226,129.

Louisiana.—New Orleans, 314,146.

Maine.—Portland, 55,167.

Maryland.—Baltimore, 553,669.

Massachusetts.—Worcester, 128,135 ; Fall River, 105,762 ; Cambridge, 97,434 ; Lowell, 94,889 ; New Bedford, 79,078 ; Lynn, 77,042 ; Lawrence, 76,616 ; Springfield, 75,968 ; Somerville, 69,272.

Michigan.—Detroit, 317,591 ; Grand Rapids, 95,718.

Minnesota.—Minneapolis, 273,825 ; Duluth, 67,337.

Missouri.—St. Louis, 649,320 ; Kansas City, 182,376 (adjoining Kansas City, Kansas, but a different municipality) ; St. Joseph, 118,004.

Nebraska.—Omaha, 124,167.

New Hampshire.—Manchester, 64,703.

New Jersey.—Newark, 289,634 ; Jersey City, 237,952 ; Paterson, 112,801 ; Camden, 84,819 ; Hoboken, 66,689 ; Elizabeth, 62,185.

New York.—New York City, 4,013,781 (comprising Manhattan, 2,112,380 ; Bronx, 271,630 ; Brooklyn, 1,358,686 ; Queens, 198,240 ; Richmond, 72,845) ; Buffalo, 376,587 ; Rochester, 181,666 ; Syracuse, 117,503 ; Troy, 76,910 ; Utica, 62,934 ; Yonkers, 61,716 ; Schenectady, 58,387.

Ohio.—Cleveland, 460,327 ; Cincinnati, 345,230 ; Toledo, 159,980 ; Dayton, 100,799 ; Youngstown, 52,710 ; Akron, 50,738.

Oregon.—Portland, 109,884.

Pennsylvania.—Philadelphia, 1,441,735 ; Pittsburg, 375,082 ; Allegany, 145,240 ; Scranton, 118,692 ; Reading, 91,141 ; Wilkesbarre, 60,121 ; Erie, 59,993.

Tennessee.—Memphis, 125,018.

Texas.—San Antonio, 62,711 ; Houston, 58,132 ; Dallas, 52,793.

Virginia.—Norfolk, 66,931.

Washington.—Seattle, 200,000 ; Tacoma, 80,000 ; Spokane, 80,000.

Wisconsin.—Milwaukee, 317,903.

GOVERNMENT. Politically the United States of America is a federation of forty-six sovereign states, united for purposes of defence and imperial objects, but separate in respect to local administration. The constitution of the United States provides for three distinct authorities in the functions of government—the Executive, the Legislative, and the Judicial. The chief officer is the president (salary £10,000), who holds office for four years, the elections taking place on every fourth year—on the Tuesday after the first Monday in November—and the electors being chosen by the individual states. Each state can appoint as many electors as it has members in both Houses of Congress, but no senator or member of the House of Representatives may be an elector. The president is commander in chief of the army and navy ; he can veto measures passed by congress, although his power of veto vanishes when a measure, once vetoed, is afterwards passed by a two-thirds majority of each house. The vice-president (salary, £2,400) is elected at the same time as the president, and by the same electorate. He is, ex-officio, president of the senate, and in the event of the death or resignation of the president, the vice-president assumes his office. The executive is in the hands of the president and the Cabinet. The Cabinet, which is composed of nine heads of departments, is nominated by the president and confirmed by the senate. The heads of departments constituting the Cabinet are the Secretaries of State, of the Treasury, of War, of the Navy, of the Interior, of Agriculture, and of Commerce and Labour, the Postmaster-General and the Attorney-General. Each of these Ministers receives a salary of £2,400.

CONGRESS. Legislative power is vested in a congress, which is composed of a senate—the Upper House—and a House of Representatives. Senators, who must be at least 30 years of age, citizens for nine years previous to election, and residents of the states which they represent, are appointed by the state legislatures for six years—two from each state. Members of the House of Representatives are elected every two years by the electors in the different states. Every representative must be at least 25 years old, must have been a citizen for at least seven years prior to election, and must reside in the state that he represents. Each organised " territory "—i.e., a district not admitted to the privileges of a state, sends a delegate

THE UNITED STATES OF AMERICA

to the house, who may talk, but may not vote. Practically, votes are held by all male citizens, irrespective of race or colour, but in some states a residence qualification, in others the payment of taxes, in yet others a low educational qualification, are necessary to possession of the vote. There are 92 senators and 391 members of the House of Representatives, the numerical representation of each state in the latter assembly being proportionate to population and determined by the decennial census. Thus, New York State has 37 representatives, and several states have only one each. The senate considers all treaties made by the president with foreign Powers, and to become law a treaty provisionally made must be ratified by the votes of two-thirds of the senators present when it is considered. Each senator, representative and delegate in congress receives a salary of $7,000 (=£1,400) per annum, with a travelling and expense allowance additional.

JUDICIARY. The supreme judicial power is in the hands of a SUPREME COURT, the members of which are appointed by the president for life. The court decides all disputed points between the states and the federal government. There are also about 60 federal courts, each possessing jurisdiction in its own district, and nine circuit courts. Many legal matters, such as offences against the person and property, divorce, bankruptcy and probate, come under the jurisdiction of the state courts, and thus many of the criminal and civil laws differ widely in the different states of the union.

FINANCE. The revenue for the fiscal year 1907 was $846,725,340 (=£169,345,068), and the expenditure was $762,488,753 (=£152,497,750). The customs duties are high and provide half of the total revenue. The national debt in 1907 stood at $2,457,188,062 (=£491,437,612), but deducting the cash in the treasury the net debt was $878,596,755 (=£175,719,351).

FORESTRY. About one-third of the area of the United States is woodland, and about half of the woodland area is covered with marketable timber. The lumber districts are California, Washington, Oregon, the Rockies, the lake states of Minnesota, Wisconsin and Michigan, and the Eastern and Southern states. The lumber industry takes fourth place among American industries, coming behind iron and steel manufacture, textiles, and the meat industry.

AGRICULTURE. In 1900, 21·6 per cent. of the area of the United States was farm land, and 65 per cent. of the farms were owned by their proprietors. The chief cereal grown in the United States is maize, or Indian corn, the area under which (99,931,000 acres in 1907) is more than twice the acreage under wheat (45,211,000 acres in 1907). Oats comes third in importance, with 31,837,000 acres, and the next most important cereal and vegetable crops are barley (6,448,000 acres), potatoes (3,124,000 acres), flax (2,864,000 acres), and rye (1,926,000 acres). Hay claimed 44,028,000 acres, and rice 627,300 acres. The United States provide three-quarters of the world's supply of cotton, in spite of efforts to grow cotton within the British Empire. In 1907, 820,000 acres were under tobacco. The output of sugar is about 700,000 tons, two-thirds of which is beet sugar. Nearly every state grows maize, but the most is grown in the valley of the Mississippi. The principal wheat and oats states are the western and northern. Cotton is grown principally in the Southern states upon the Atlantic and upon the Gulf of Mexico. The chief tobacco growing states are the Virginias and Carolinas, Kentucky and Tennessee.

Many varieties of fruit and vegetables are grown and marketed, both in the fresh state and preserved. Recent annual figures relating to the chief products were as follow : Apples, 23,990,000 barrels ; raisins, 100,000,000 lb. ; oranges and lemons, 15,304,000 boxes ; prunes, 185,000,000 lb. ; hops, 63,576,000 lb. ; wine, 35,658,000 gallons. The principal states where fruit and vegetable canning is prosecuted are California, New York and Maryland.

STOCK RAISING. The number of farm animals, according to statistics of 1907, were as follows :
Cattle, 72,533,996 ; swine, 54,794,439 ; sheep, 53,240,282 ; horses, 19,746,583 ; mules, 3,816,692.

The output of the meat-packing factories, of which Chicago is the chief centre, was of the value of £156,756,000 in 1900, and in 1905 it had risen to £182,783,000. The chief states for the manufacture of dairy produce—butter, cheese, and condensed milk—are New York, Wisconsin and Iowa. The wool clip in 1907 was 298,294,750 lb.

MINING. The United States produce all the commercial minerals, except nickel and diamonds. The importance of the various metallic minerals, judged by the value of the annual output, is as follows : iron, copper, gold, lead, silver, zinc, aluminium, quicksilver and antimony. The quantities of tin and platinum are negligible. Nickel is refined in the United States, but the ore is Canadian imported into the United States in the form of matte. The total value of metallic minerals for 1906 was £173,220,000. The non-metallic minerals in the order of their importance, judged

by value of output, are soft coal, hard coal, petroleum, stone, cement, natural gas, phosphate rock, salt and borax. The chief iron ore fields are in the Lake Superior region, Alabama, New York, Pennsylvania, Virginia, Tennessee, Ohio, Colorado and Wyoming. Gold and silver are found in the Rocky Mountains and Pacific states, copper in Arizona, Montana, and Michigan ; lead and zinc in Missouri and Kansas ; quicksilver in California. Coal is widely distributed, but anthracite coal is found only in the north-east of Pennsylvania. Petroleum and natural gas are found in Pennsylvania, New York, Ohio Indiana, Texas and California.

FISHERIES. The fisheries of the United States employ about 220,000 people, and the annual value of fish products is about £12,000,000, including the seals of Alaska. About one-fifth of the value comes from the Pacific coast and Alaska ; about one-twelfth from the Great Lakes, the inland waters, and the Mississippi and its tributaries ; about 7 per cent. from the Gulf states, and the remainder (about 60 per cent.) from the Atlantic states. Fish curing and preserving provide occupation for about 7,000 persons—sardines in Maine ; cod, mackerel and herring in Massachusetts ; and salmon in Washington, Oregon and Alaska.

TRADE.—For the fiscal year 1907, the imports were of the value of $1,434,421,425 (= £286,884,285), and the exports were of the value of $1,880,851,078 (=£376,170,216). The imports from the United Kingdom were of the value of $246,112,047 (= £49,222,409), and the exports to the United Kingdom were of the value of $607,783,255 (= £121,556,651). The chief article of export is raw cotton, and the next, in order of importance, are meat and dairy produce, breadstuffs, iron and steel manufactures, copper and copper goods, mineral oils, wood and wooden ware, leather and leather goods, tobacco, coal, manufactured cotton and agricultural implements.

ALASKA. The population, which was 63,592 in 1900, was 85,670 in 1907. The capital is Sitka, with a population of 1,396. The largest town is Nome (population 3,500), and the other towns are Fairbanks (3,500), Juneau (1,864), and Skagway (1,100). The chief industry is gold-mining, with copper, lead and silver much less important. The timber wealth is great, and the salmon and seal fisheries are valuable. Government is administered by a governor, appointed by the President of the United States for four years.

CURRENCY. The monetary unit is the dollar, containing 25·8 grains of gold ·900 fine. The value of the American dollar in British currency varies from $4·84 to $4·87, to the British sovereign, but $4·86 may be taken as the average. The dollar is worth approximately 4s. 1½d. The coins in general use are :

Bronze.	Nickel.	Silver.		Gold	
1 cent. = ½d.	5 cents. = 2½d.	10 cents. = 5d.	5 dollars = 20/7½		
		25 ,, = 1/0½.	10 ,, = 41/3		
		50 ,, = 2/1.	20 ,, = 82/6		
		1 dollar = 4/1½			

Gold does not circulate much. Its place is taken by paper notes, sometimes filthy and torn.

WEIGHTS AND MEASURES. The British weights and measures are used, but the cwt., or cental, contains 100 lb., and the short ton contains 2,000 lb., while the ton of 2,240 lb. (the British ton) is called a long ton. The only other difference is that the wine gallon is ·83333 imperial gallon, the ale gallon is 1·01695 imperial gallon, and the bushel is ·9692 imperial bushel.

POST AND TELEGRAPH RATES.

POSTAGE. The United Kingdom to the United States (including Alaska) : letters, 1d. per oz. ; printed papers, commercial papers, and samples ½d. per 2 ozs., with a minimum of 2½d. for commercial papers, and of 1d. for samples. Letters from the United Kingdom to Porto Rico, Hawaii, Samoa, Guam, and the Philippine Islands, 2½d. for first oz. or part thereof, and 1½d. for each additional oz. or part thereof. Papers and samples to United States non-continental possessions as to the United States, given above. Parcel post is by two services—the official and the semi-official. By the official service, 3lb., 1s. 6d. ; 7lb., 2s. 6d. ; 9lb., 3s. 6d. ; 11lb., 4s. 6d., to all places in the United States, Porto Rico, United States territory in Panama, Hawaii, Philippines and Samoa. By the semi-official service (American Express Company), to New York City, Brooklyn, Jersey City, and Hoboken, 3lb., 2s. 6d. ; 7lb., 3s. 6d. ; 11lb., 4s. 6d. ; to all other places in the United States (but not in the islands or colonies), 3lb., 3s. 6d. ; 7lb., 4s. 6d. ; 11lb. 5s. 6d.

TELEGRAMS. Great Britain to United States : 1s. to 1s. 6d. per word, according to destination, the cities on the east being 1s., and the far west 1s. 6d., with the intervening places roughly proportionate to their distance west. To Porto Rico, 4s. 2d. per word ; to Honolulu, 3s. ; to Philippines, 4s. 2d. to 4s. 10d. according to destination.

6319

MAP OF THE ARCTIC REGIONS, SHOWING THE ROUTES OF NORTH POLE EXPLORERS

Although Arctic exploration began with Alfred the Great and the discovery of Greenland in the tenth century, it was not until after John Cabot sighted the coast of Labrador in 1497 that the possibilities of a North-east Passage and a North-west Passage suggested themselves to sea-going adventurers. Since that period our geographical knowledge of the northern regions has vastly increased with each successive century, the nineteenth being notable on account of the excellent work accomplished in this direction. In this map the farthest points attained in each of the forty-five expeditions of the last 400 years are indicated by a +, the record being that of R. E. Peary in 1903-6.

⌐THE WORLD AROUND THE POLES⌐
A RECORD OF POLAR EXPLORATION
By George Sandeman, M.A.
THE GLAMOUR AND ROMANCE OF THE SEARCH FOR THE NORTH POLE

THE story of Polar exploration is one of rich and varied interest, just as it has always been a rich and complex interest that has led the adventurer into high latitudes. We have often seen elaborate arguments in defence of Arctic and Antarctic enterprise, but these apologies have appeared to us equally unnecessary and inadequate. Unnecessary, because the impulse to go and see is as deep and unquestionable as human nature itself. Inadequate, because the apologists appeal to one or two partial interests, such as the interest of trade at one period, the interest of naval efficiency at another, or, as in our own time, to the interest of international rivalry or of scientific investigation. The real interest is more concrete and complex than any of these things or all of them together.

No one, for instance, can spend an hour with an Arctic explorer without realising the enormous imaginative spell which these mysterious desolations have cast over his mind. They call him incessantly, and he inevitably returns to them. Their vast simplicity accords with some profound mode of the human spirit, such as is mirrored in the "Ancient Mariner" or in the majestic phantasms of northern mythology. The mind once touched with the North seems to turn to it as certainly as the compass-card; and doubtless the same fascination enters deeply into the interest with which we follow the voyages of a Barentz or a Nansen. Or, again, no one

The Call of the North

can follow these voyages, even in their barest records, without realising that those who have accomplished such arduous and even heroic labours have been men indeed, and that because they have been such men they have sought such labours. "There increaseth in my heart," says Sebastian Cabot, "a great flame of desire to attempt some notable thing." "It was the only thing of the world," says Martin Frobisher, "that was left yet undone, whereby a notable mind might be made famous and fortunate."

Explorers of the Polar Seas

Is it too much to say that this magnanimous ardour and fortitude, which have been a hundred times proved through unimaginable sufferings and endurance to the threshold of death, and still characterise, as nobly as ever, the explorers of to-day, are worth incomparably more than any results whatever that may be achieved by them? Is it too much to say that our interest in Polar exploration is inevitably first of all the human interest, centring round intrepid men and the great maritime nations that have bred them, and only afterwards round the geographical features that have been mapped and the scientific observations that have been recorded?

We no longer seek commercial openings through Polar seas, and it is possible that Arctic enterprise has done all that it will ever do for trade. But it has done a great deal. It gave us trade with Russia, and established the Hudson's Bay Company

ARCTIC SEA AT MIDNIGHT: SCENE AT THE MOUTH OF THE COPPER MINE RIVER

A WINTER VIEW OF FORT ENTERPRISE

A CAMP IN THE FOREST: THE EXPLORERS PREPARING A RESTING PLACE

FRANKLIN AND HIS PARTY IN THE ARCTIC REGIONS, 1819-22

THE EXPEDITION CROSSING LAKE PROSPEROUS

THE EXPLORERS DOUBLING CAPE BARROW ON JULY 25TH. 1821

SCENES IN FRANKLIN'S FIRST GREAT POLAR EXPEDITION

in the heart of Canada. It led directly to the cod fishery of the Newfoundland coast, and to the enormous whale industry of the Spitzbergen seas.

The chief results to be expected from Arctic and Antarctic exploration are now of a scientific nature, and the observations that have been obtained, and will yet be obtained, are of peculiar import-

What Science Gains by Exploration ance to a considerable group of sciences. Geography, geology, oceanography, magnetism, meteorology and biology are outstanding examples. Sir John Murray has well said that " every department of natural knowledge would be enriched by systematic observations as to the order in which phenomena co-exist and follow each other in regions of the earth's surface about which we know very little or are wholly ignorant. It is one of the great objects of science to collect observations of the kind here indicated, and it may be safely said that without them we can never arrive at a right understanding of the phenomena by which we are surrounded, even in the habitable parts of the globe." It is this indissoluble unity of natural conditions over the face of our planet that gives such very high significance to the scientific study of Polar regions. To take an example. We learn during the year 1909 that the centre of the Antarctic region, far from being, as was generally supposed, an area of peculiar calm, is, in fact, swept by terrific gales; and this involves a new interpretation of those weather conditions elsewhere, from which that region of calms had been erroneously inferred.

In the same year we learn that coal measures had been discovered in the Antarctic continent, showing that this region has at one period been characterised by a warm climate—a fact which inevitably modifies our estimate of the history of the globe. It is because of this interdependence of Polar conditions with those in all other parts of the earth

King Alfred's Interest in the Arctic that a modern expedition to high latitudes is in itself a microcosm of the sciences. The impulse to penetrate the northern seas is as old as English history, and the first chronicler of an Arctic expedition was King Alfred the Great. But we may take it as certain that in the early days there was a great deal more discovery than we shall ever know of. From the eighth to the tenth centuries the adventurous Scandinavians were ranging over the northern ocean and descending on every coast. In 861 they discovered Iceland ; but when, a few years later, many Norwegian colonists made their home there, they found the remains of an even earlier Christian settlement. A regular traffic sprang up between Norway and Iceland, and Iceland, in its turn, became a centre of geographical discovery. Thus Eric the Red, sailing thence in 983, fell in with the east coast of Greenland, and here, also, little colonies were quickly established. Another Icelandic ship, driven far southwestward out of her course in 1000, reached at length a finely wooded country and ascended a river, certainly in Newfoundland or Canada, and brought back reports of a land which, because of its wild grapes or berries, was called Vinland.

A more deliberate kind of exploration followed these fortuitous expeditions. Richard III. of England sent ships to Iceland for purposes of discovery, and within a century later the question of navigation to the North Pole was seriously discussed. In the notable enterprises which followed, England took a

The Cabot Family of Explorers leading part. Henry VII., who had failed to secure the services of Columbus, granted in 1497 a patent of discovery to the Venetian John Cabot, who had settled in Bristol with his three sons, of whom Sebastian was the most famous. " Understanding," says the latter, " by reason of the sphere that if I should sail by way of north-west I should by a shorter tract come into India, I thereupon caused the king to be advertised of my desire, who immediately commanded two caravels to be furnished with all things appertaining to the voyage." Together, the father and son sailed to the west, and discovered Newfoundland, which they named Prima Vista ; but they did not pursue the American coast north of 56°.

Newfoundland had already been visited, and named Terra de Baccalhaos, or " Land of Cod-fish," by the Portuguese Cortereal in 1464, under the patronage of Alfonso V. ; and his son, Gaspar Cortereal, set out from Lisbon with two ships in 1500 for the northwest passage, and visited and described Greenland, Labrador and the River St. Lawrence. In subsequent voyages Gaspar, and later his brother Miguel, were lost ; but these expeditions, and another sent in search of them, secured for Portugal

F. W. Beechey   Sir Edward Belcher   Robert McCormick   Sir Horatio T. Austin

Sir Henry Kellett   Sir Robert M'Clure   Sir Richard Collinson   Sir John Richardson

William Kennedy   William Penny   Dr. John Rae   Sir F. Leopold McClintock

Sir Erasmus Ommanney   Sir George H. Richards   Sir Edward A. Inglefield   Sherard Osborn

Sir Allen Young   Alexander Stewart   William R. Hobson   David Walker

BRAVE EXPLORERS OF THE ARCTIC SEAS

The above group contains the portraits of hardy sailors who commanded expeditions of exploration to the Arctic regions as well as of some of the many daring seamen who went in search of the missing Sir John Franklin.

the valuable Newfoundland fisheries. King Henry VIII., persuaded by Mr. Robert Thorne, of Bristol, "with very weighty and substantial reasons to set forth a discovery even to the North Pole," sent out the Dominus Vobiscum and another ship in 1527, "having in them divers cunning men," of whom one was a canon of St. Paul's, London,

Unfortunate Enterprise of Henry VIII. and a great mathematician. This genuinely scientific enterprise met with ill-fortune; one of the ships was cast away north of Newfoundland, and the other returned after less than five months. The attempt was repeated in 1536, when the Trinity and Minion sailed from Gravesend with a company of six score, of whom thirty were gentlemen "desirous to see the strange things of the world." Having reached Newfoundland, they fell into the extremity of distress for want of food, and were only saved by the welcome arrival of a French vessel, which they immediately seized upon, and so returned to England.

It should be made clear that the central idea in all Polar exploration until the end of the eighteenth century was the discovery of a practicable trade route by sea from the Atlantic to the Pacific, either round the north of America, or round the north of Russia, or straight across the Pole. It should also be made clear that this project, which appears so fantastic now, was not at that time in the least fantastic, because the theory was universally held, unquestioned, that ice could not be formed in the open sea. It was accepted as a matter of course that ice was formed only in rivers and along coast-lines.

It is obvious that if this theory had been in accordance with fact there was every reason to expect an open route somewhere between the Atlantic and the Pacific through Polar seas. Not until the early years of the nineteenth century was it thoroughly realised that the Arctic

Navigation Blocked by Ice-packs ice-pack is, so far as navigation is concerned, practically a solid body. Of course, both the north-east and the north-west passages exist, and have been traversed by ships. But they do not exist in that sense in which they were sought for by early mariners. For all practical purposes, however, they are non-existent. They are not ice-free routes. A well-organised expedition set out from England in 1553 for the discovery, not of

the north-western passage—which had been sought hitherto—but of the north-east passage to Cathay. The plan was due to Sebastian Cabot, whom Edward VI. had created " grand pilot of England " and " Governor of the Mystery and Company of the Merchants Adventurers for the discovery of regions, dominions, islands, and places unknown."

Sir Hugh Willoughby commanded the Bona Esperanza (120 tons), Richard Chancellor and Stephen Burrough were in the Edward Bonadventure (160 tons), and Cornelius Durfoorth was in the Bona Confidentia (90 tons). Willoughby and the whole of the company of the Bona Esperanza and of the Bona Confidentia perished on the eastern coast of Lapland during the following winter ; but Chancellor, who had missed his consorts, reached Archangel in safety, and having visited the tsar at Moscow, brought his ship back to England in the following spring, carrying a letter from the tsar to Edward VI.

The prospect thus opened of trade with Muscovy led Queen Mary to send a commission in return. Chancellor sailed again

Tragic Fate of Queen Mary's Commission on this errand in 1555, with instructions to "use all ways and means possible to learn how men may pass from Russia, either by land or by sea, to Cathay." He was followed, in 1556, by Stephen Burrough in the Searchthrift, whose mission it was to explore the sea to the eastward. Burrough reached and discovered Novaya Zemlya, Vaigach Island and the Kara Strait, and returned in safety.

The other ships, after accomplishing the voyage to Archangel, came to a disastrous end. Returning with a Russian envoy on board, the Edward Bonadventure was cast away on the Scottish coast, where the ambassador was with difficulty saved, but Chancellor and most of his crew perished ; and the two other ships were lost with all hands in the North Sea. But a very considerable step had been made in Arctic discovery, and the beginning of the Russian trade by the Muscovy Company had been established.

The next attempt was in the direction of the north-west passage. Martin Frobisher, one of the most adventurous seamen of a most adventurous period, had urged the project for many years before he was placed in command of the Gabriel (35 tons), the Michael (30 tons), and a pinnace of 10 tons. He sailed in June,

"BEYOND MAN'S FOOTSTEPS": IN THE ICY WILDERNESS AROUND THE NORTH POLE

From the painting by Briton Rivière in the Tate Gallery

TO FACE PAGE 632

1576, from Greenwich, Queen Elizabeth waving her hand to them from the shore. Reaching the coast of Labrador, he sailed northward among the ice, and discovered the bay which is known by his name.

This voyage, in which Frobisher thought, erroneously, that he had found promise of gold, was followed by two others, in the two following years, to the same region and to the west coast of Greenland; but their results, however, were regarded as discouraging in respect both of the north-west passage and of the gold-mines. In 1580, the Muscovy Company sent Arthur Pet in the George (40 tons), and Charles Jackman in the William

the Cumberland peninsula, where he named Mount Raleigh and Exeter Sound, as well as the two forelands of that sound—viz., Cape Dyer and Cape Walsingham. He returned in the two following years, sailing up Cumberland Sound, and exploring the coasts of Labrador and of Greenland; and in his third voyage he discovered the strait which is known by the name of Hudson.

Davis's observations rightly confirmed his belief in a north-west passage, but he failed to persuade the merchant adventurers to support further attempts. A great advance towards the discovery of the north-eastern passage was next

IN SEARCH OF A NORTH-WEST PASSAGE: PARRY'S EXPEDITION AT WINTER ISLAND
By calling a sailor, Sir Edward William Parry made altogether five expeditions to the Arctic regions, the second, in 1819, being in search of a north-west passage, earning for him the sum of £5,000 offered by parliament. His last, and perhaps most famous, voyage was that of 1827, when he and his party made a gallant though unsuccessful attempt to reach the Pole on sledges from Spitzbergen. This picture shows an exciting incident during his second voyage, which lasted three years, to the Arctic regions, and during which the Fury and Hecla Strait was discovered.

(20 tons) to the north-eastern sea. Reaching Vaigach Island, the two explorers discovered and passed through Yugor Strait between it and the mainland, but they were stopped by the ice in the Kara Sea, and had to return through the strait a month later. The George returned to England, but the William was lost on her way to Iceland.

The sanguine and intrepid John Davis, in his three voyages towards the north-west passage, now made important geographical discoveries in the strait which bears his name. In 1585 he proceeded with the Sunshine (50 tons) and the Moonshine (35 tons) to the west coast of Greenland, and thence northward to

made by William Barentz, the Dutch pilot, in the last of his three famous voyages of 1594, 1595, and 1596. For twenty years before that time, the merchants of Amsterdam had been trading round the north of Scandinavia to Archangel; and wishing to extend their operations farther eastward they had been advised by Peter Plancius, a celebrated geographer, to seek a passage round the northern end of Novaya Zemlya, because the course through the Kara Strait, at the southern end of that island, and through the Kara Sea beyond, was so often impracticable because of ice. This suggestion was in accordance with the theory which we have already noticed,

A WINTER VIEW OF FORT FRANKLIN

LAUNCHING BOATS ACROSS A REEF OPPOSITE MOUNT CONYBEARE

SCENES IN FRANKLIN'S SECOND EXPEDITION TO THE ARCTIC SEAS, IN 1825–27

as generally accepted at that time. In the expeditions which the merchants now sent out for that purpose, Barentz, who was a well-educated man, besides being a first-rate seaman, contributed to geographical science the first real knowledge of the conditions of the ice between Novaya Zemlya and Spitzbergen. His first voyage, sailing June 4th, 1594, was in the Mercurius (100 tons), accompanied by a fishing smack. They sighted Novaya Zemlya a month later, and sailed up to its north-eastern extremity, vainly seeking an eastward passage through the ice-pack.

The second expedition, of the following year, in which seven vessels took part, started too late in the season, and only reached the entrance to the Sea of Kara, at the southern end of the great island, when it had to return. The third voyage, which set out on May 13th, 1596, was that on which Barentz secured his great celebrity, and on which he died. A large reward had been offered by the Dutch Government to anyone who should complete a voyage to China by the north-eastern route, a feat only accomplished by Nordenskiöld in 1878. The **Notable Discoveries of Barentz** Amsterdam merchants commissioned two ships, in one of which Barentz sailed as chief pilot. Because of the erroneous impression above mentioned, Barentz determined to keep far out to westward, in order to secure open water. In doing so he discovered Bear Island, south of Spitzbergen, and a few days later found himself on the west coast of Spitzbergen, a land of which he was the first discoverer.

Returning to Bear Island, the two ships parted company, one proceeding northward, and the other, with Barentz, steering eastward. From July 2nd they beat against head winds, and among packs of drifting ice, until, on the 17th, they came upon the west coast of Novaya Zemlya at 74° 40′ N., and thence sailed northward along it. Rounding its northern extremity they were, on August 26th, imprisoned by the ice in Barentz Bay, or "Ice Haven," on the eastern coast. "Here," writes De Veer, the chronicler of the expedition, "we were forced, in great cold, poverty, misery and grief to stay all that winter."

Realising that their ship had sustained such damage by the pressure of the ice that she could not take the sea again, the seventeen stout-hearted Dutchmen abandoned her, and built a strong and capacious timber house out of driftwood, which they found in abundance, and out of planks torn from the ship. Great drifts of snow surrounded the house, and protected it from cold. Bears and white foxes visited them in great abundance; the fat of the bears was used for lamps, the flesh of the foxes for food, and their skins for clothing.

Explorers Imprisoned by the Ice Nearly three centuries later this house was discovered intact. On September 9th, 1871, Elling Carlsen, a Norwegian shipmaster, having entered Ice Haven, found the place exactly as they had left it, with the old Dutch clock on the wall, the cooking pots on the fireplace, and the weapons and instruments and books lying about as if in an inhabited cabin. Among the books was a "History of China," which Barentz had been studying because China was to be the ultimate end of his voyage. These relics are now in the Foreign Office at the Hague.

On January 16th the little company perceived "a certain redness in the sky," and on the 27th "we saw the sun in his full roundness above the horizon, which made us all glad, and we gave God hearty thanks for His grace showed unto us, that that glorious light appeared to us again." But the weather grew colder yet, and it was not until June 13th that their two open boats were repaired and provisioned for a boat voyage. Setting forth on the same day to return by the way that he had come, Barentz, who was so ill that he had to be carried to the boats, died on the seventh day. Those who remained, after enduring extraordinary hardships, brought their open boats into harbour at Kola.

No success having attended the attempts to discover either a north-east or a north-west passage, the Muscovy Company commissioned Henry Hudson, in 1607, to sail to Japan straight across the North Pole. He set out from Greenwich, on May 1st, in the Hopewell (80 tons), on this astonishing enterprise. **Hudson's Fruitful Voyage** The voyage led to considerable commercial results. Hudson's reports of the abundance of whales and sea-horses in the Polar seas were the beginning of a great and valuable industry. Its scientific results were also notable. Hudson was the first of the northern explorers to observe the dip of the magnetic needle, and he added not a little to geographical knowledge. Falling in with the east coast of Greenland, which

PLANTING THE BRITISH FLAG ON THE POSITION OF THE MAGNETIC POLE

THE VICTORY UNDER PROTECTING WALLS OF SNOW IN FELIX HARBOUR

THE UNION JACK IN GRAHAM'S VALLEY

THE EXPEDITION THAT LED TO THE DISCOVERY OF THE MAGNETIC POLE

This Arctic expedition, fitted out in 1829 by Sir Felix Booth, was under the command of Sir John Ross and his nephew, Sir James Clark Ross. It was during this expedition that the latter explorer discovered the North Magnetic Pole.

H.M.S. TERROR ICEBOUND IN FOX'S CHANNEL

BUILDING SNOW WALLS AROUND THE SHIP: THE CREW CAUGHT IN A GALE

THE BREAKING UP OF THE ICE AROUND THE SHIP

SCENES IN SIR GEORGE BACK'S ARCTIC EXPEDITION, 1836–37

Before his Arctic voyage of 1836–37, illustrated in the above pictures, Sir George Back had shared in three Polar expeditions under Sir John Franklin, and had gone in search of Sir John Ross when that explorer was supposed to be lost.

THE ARCTIC COUNCIL DISCUSSING PLANS FOR THE RELIEF OF SIR JOHN FRANKLIN
On May 18th, 1845, Sir John Franklin, then almost sixty years of age, set out on what proved to be his last voyage, the expedition having for its object the discovery of a north-west passage through Lancaster Sound and Bering Strait. When the famous explorer failed to return, numerous expeditions vainly set out in search of him, the above picture showing a council of Arctic experts discussing ways and means for reaching the missing party.

he named "Hold with Hope," he explored it northward until stopped by ice in 73° N. Thence he proceeded north-east and followed the western coast of Spitzbergen to its northern point. Steering again north-west, with the intention of rounding the north of Greenland, he passed **The Fate** the 80th parallel, but failed to **of the Brave** find a passage through the **Hudson** ice, and returned to England after discovering an island, which he called "Hudson's Tutches," but which was afterwards named Jan Mayen.

His second voyage, in 1608, in which he attempted to find a passage through the ice between Spitzbergen and Novaya Zemlya, ended in disappointment; in the following year he explored the east coast of North America southward from Newfoundland and discovered the Hudson River. His fourth and most notable voyage was undertaken in the Discovery (55 tons) in 1610, with a view to finding the north-west passage. Passing the northern point of Labrador, Hudson entered the great enclosed sea which is known as Hudson Bay, where he hauled the ship aground and was frozen in. In the following June, as he was working the Discovery out of the bay, the ship's

company suddenly mutinied and abandoned Hudson, his son, and seven others in a small boat amid the ice.

It was now that the English and Dutch whalers began to frequent every year the seas about Spitzbergen, and soon increased to great numbers, so that knowledge with regard to that group of islands, and especially with regard to the seasonal conditions and yearly variations of the Polar ice-pack, gradually accumulated during the next two centuries from their reports. The names of many skippers, such as Poole, Baffin, Fotherby, Edge, and especially Scoresby, are associated with various discoveries and generalised observations made by these whaling expeditions It became gradually established, for instance, that ice is formed in deep and open sea, far from land, and **The Truth** even in rough weather; that **About the** the Polar ice-pack is absolutely **Ice-pack** impenetrable; that its southern limits vary considerably from one season to another, and that the 81st degree of latitude, or at most the 82nd, is the highest to which ships can go in any year. But these conclusions were not fully realised for two centuries after the time when Hudson's discoveries brought the whaling fleets into being. A great advance was made to the north-west by William Baffin, in the Discovery, in the year 1616. Passing through Davis Strait into Baffin Bay, he entered, and named, Wolstenholme Sound and Smith Sound, on the north-west coast of Greenland, reaching the latitude of 78° N.; and then, turning westward and southward, he discovered and named Jones Sound and Lancaster Sound. In the latter, though he did not know it, he had found the actual gate to the north-west passage. Baffin **Gate to the** was followed in 1631 by Luke **North-west** Fox, who had obtained from **Passage** Charles I. a pinnace, the Charles (80 tons), and a letter to the Emperor of Japan. Fox, whose garrulous and vainglorious narrative is exceedingly entertaining, passed through Hudson Strait, and coasted round a considerable portion of Hudson Bay, and, returning, discovered the channel and the promontory that bear his name. In the bay he fell in with Captain James, a somewhat incompetent navigator, who was on the same quest and carried a similar letter. An unsuccessful voyage by Captain Wood

to Novaya Zemlya in 1676 completes the story of Arctic exploration to the end of the seventeenth century.

The Hudson Bay Company, which had been formed in 1670 for trade with the North American Indians in furs and skins, and had received the absolute concession of all lands which might be discovered through Hudson Strait, was expressly bound by its charter to continue the work of exploration and in particular to search for a passage to the South Seas. For this purpose, as well as to follow up a native report of copper mines, an expedition in the Albert and the Discovery was sent out under Knight in 1719, but was never heard of again. Later voyages under Scroggs in 1722, and Middleton in 1741, failed in their main object, and in 1742 a reward of £20,000 was offered by the British Government for the discovery of a route to the Pacific through Hudson Strait. William Moor and Francis Smith in 1846, and Samuel Hearne in 1769, undertook unsuccessful voyages with this purpose.

In the meantime, active researches were being promoted on the North Siberian coast by Peter the Great, who commissioned Vitus Behring, a Dane, in 1725,

GRAVES IN THE ARCTIC ICE: THE BURIAL PLACE OF FRANKLIN'S COMRADES

Though many search expeditions, public and private, British and American, beginning in 1848, set out in quest of Sir John Franklin and his party, it was not till 1859 that traces of the unfortunate voyagers were discovered. It was then ascertained that Sir John Franklin had died on June 11th, 1847, and that every member of the party had perished.

A MOUNTAIN OF ICE OFF THE COAST OF GREENLAND

AN ICE WALL, SHOWING ARCH, NEAR ST. JOHN'S, NEWFOUNDLAND

ON THE LABRADOR COAST: A BERG WITH ITS CONNECTION UNDER WATER

THE FROZEN TERRORS OF THE POLAR SEAS

Photos: Shepstone

ON THE DANGEROUS COAST OF ST. JOHN'S, NEWFOUNDLAND

A HUGE ICE-CLIFF OFF THE SHORES OF LABRADOR

FLOATING MASS ON THE EXTREME NORTH OF NEWFOUNDLAND

FLOATING ICE MOUNTAINS IN THE NORTH ATLANTIC

Photos : Shepstone

6335

to sail northward from Kamchatka. Shipwrights were sent with Behring to the Pacific coast, and there two vessels, the Gabriel and the Fortuna, were built. Sailing in 1728, Behring discovered the strait between America and Asia. In a later voyage, 1740, he set out from Okhotsk with the St. Peter and St. Paul, explored the American coast and the Aleutian Islands, and discovered and named Mount St. Elias. His ship was wrecked on Bering Island, where the great seaman died in December, 1741. The New Siberian Islands, rich in fossil ivory, were discovered in 1770 by a Russian merchant in a sledge journey over the frozen sea, and were surveyed by officers of the Russian Government in 1809.

Behring's Discoveries and Death

During the eighteenth century the whole of the northern coast-line of Russia and Siberia was systematically explored by government expeditions. Thus, the sea passages from Archangel to the River Obi and from the latter to the Yenesei River were successfully made in 1738; though the great northern promontory of Taimyr, terminating in Cape Chelyuskin, was not rounded by a ship for more than a century afterwards. It was, however, nearly doubled by Pronchishchef in 1736, who died in winter quarters near the cape; and his lieutenant, Chelyuskin, reached the cape in sledges in 1742.

The rise of Polar exploration as a definite, determined and continuous aim may be traced to the year 1773, when a Mr. Daines Barrington, having collected all available knowledge on the subject, read a series of papers to the Royal Society. Arctic research now began to enter on its scientific era. The society petitioned the king; the government's reply was favourable, and the bombs Racehorse (Captain Phipps) and Carcass (Captain Lutwidge) sailed from the Nore in June, 1773. Horatio Nelson, then a midshipman, accompanied the expedition. The two ships reached 80° 48′ N., north of Spitzbergen, and worked closely along the edge of the ice-pack throughout twenty degrees of longitude, without finding any passage through the ice. This conclusion was confirmed by other expeditions which followed. Captain Buchan, with the whalers Dorothea and Trent, the last-named being commanded by the

Scientific Era of Arctic Research

celebrated Franklin, sailed in 1818, and attacked the ice-pack to the north of Spitzbergen in vain; Captain Clavering, in the brig Griper, made the same attempt in 1823, with the same failure; and Admiral Lutke, of the Russian Navy, in the following year, found the ice barrier equally impenetrable in the seas between Novaya Zemlya and Spitzbergen. These surveys of the ice established once for all the important principle that no ship could sail to the Pole, and that all further exploration northward must be made by sledges. This principle, which has been only partially modified by Nansen, determined the epoch-making enterprise of Parry, with whom the modern era of Arctic exploration begins.

Edward Parry had taken part in four Arctic expeditions before he sailed, in 1827, in the Hecla, with a view to travelling in sledge-boats from Spitzbergen to the Pole. Leaving his ship in Hecla Cove, on the north shore of Spitzbergen, he set out on Midsummer Day with two flat-bottomed boats on runners, each boat having fourteen men on board. They travelled 200 miles by water, and then dragged their boats for 92 miles over broken ice-floes; but they never reached the solid pack at all, and the drift of the ice southward soon made further progress impossible. Parry realised that he had left his base several months too late in the season. On July 23rd he reached his highest point, at 82° 43′ N., a latitude which remained the "farthest north" for many years to come.

The Great Sir John Franklin

Early in the nineteenth century the tide of discovery set strongly towards the labyrinth of promontories, islands and channels to the north of Canada, and gradually, by one experiment after another, a track was found through the maze, and the north-west passage was accomplished. The central figure in this chapter of Arctic exploration will always be that of the gallant Sir John Franklin, whose disaster was the occasion of a swarm of expeditions to these waters, so that his death did more for geographical knowledge than his life had done. Actually, however, Franklin, when he died on the coast of King William Land, had solved the great problem, and had found a passage by sea from Davis Strait to the straits south of Wollaston and Victoria Land, which were known to lead to Bering Strait. That is to say, he had united a known track on the east with

Sir John Ross   Sir John Franklin   Sir William E. Parry

Sir Edward Sabine   Sir James Clark Ross   Rochfort Maguire

Thomas E. L. Moore   Sir George S. Nares   B. Leigh Smith

FAMOUS BRITISH EXPLORERS OF THE POLAR SEAS

a known track on the west. The expeditions which took part in the exploration of the north-west during last century are far too numerous even for mention ; for instance, more than forty went out to seek for Franklin within the ten years which followed his death. We can only name the most important enterprises in a great series which lasted throughout the century. John Ross, a naval commander, sailed in 1818 with the Isabella (385 tons) and the Alexander (252 tons) to Baffin Bay, to inquire into the probability of a north-west passage. Parry was in command of the smaller vessel. Ross confirmed Baffin's observations of Wolstenholme Sound and of Smith Sound, and named the two capes at the entrance to the latter, Cape Isabella and Cape Alexander. Parry, in the following year, in the first of his memorable voyages, did better service with the Hecla (375 tons) and the Griper (180 tons). With orders particularly to explore Lancaster Sound, he entered it August 1st, 1819, and ran up it before an easterly gale. Passing through a strait which he named Barrow Strait, he found his ship's compasses at first sluggish, and then dominated merely by the attraction of the ship. He discovered and named Wellington Channel, and on September 26th, as the ice was closing around them, the Hecla and Griper went into winter quarters on the south coast of Melville Island. During this winter, Captain Sabine, who had sailed with Parry as astronomer, made observations on magnetism, on the pendulum and on the flora and fauna of the coast ; indeed, all Parry's voyages were notable for the most assiduous attention to scientific

ROALD AMUNDSEN

Mate of the ship Belgica, which conveyed the Belgian expedition of 1897, under the command of M. de Gerlache, to the Polar regions, Roald Amundsen made a number of important scientific and geographical discoveries.

work. In the following summer, the commander, with a land party, explored the island. It was not until August 1st that the ships were free, and after coasting westward for three weeks, in great danger from the ice, they turned eastward to Lancaster Sound, and so to England. In this important expedition, North Devon, Cornwallis, Bathurst, Byam Martin and Melville Islands had been named and charted on the north of Parry's course, and North Somerset and Banks Land on its southern shores. Parry's second voyage, in 1821 to 1823, with the Hecla and the Fury (377 tons), was due to his conjecture, which was in accordance with fact, that a passage might exist between Barrow Strait and Hudson Bay. Having reached North Southampton Land in Hudson Bay, he passed through Frozen Strait into Repulse Bay, and proved, by a searching examination, that the latter had no outlet northward, in other words that Melville Peninsula was continuous with the mainland. He was forced to winter near Lyon's Inlet, on the south-east coast of the peninsula, where he obtained geographical information of great value from the Esquimaux. In the following summer he entered and named Fury and Hecla Strait, but was unable to force his way through it, and returned to England after wintering once more in Fox Channel. Again, in 1824, the same explorer sailed with the Fury and the Hecla, under orders to try for a passage through Lancaster Sound, Barrow Strait and Prince Regent's Inlet. It was an unusually bad season, and Parry only reached the inlet in time to take up winter quarters. Released in July following, he

A TYPICAL VIEW OF THE COAST

DANISH HARBOUR

THE GOVERNOR'S HOUSE

PEARY'S HOUSE AND TENT

CAPE CLEVELAND, N.-W. COAST

STONE HUTS OF THE NATIVES

GREENLAND'S ICY REGIONS: VIEWS TAKEN AT MIDNIGHT

sailed southward through waters hitherto unexplored; but the ships were much beset with ice, and the Fury was so damaged that she had to be abandoned, and Parry turned homeward.

Dolphin and Union Strait, and Wollaston Land to the north of it, were charted by Richardson in 1826, and twelve years later Dease and Simpson continued the discovery of this channel eastward, through Dease Strait, south of Victoria Land, to Simpson Strait, south of King William Land. In his researches with the Victory, from 1829 to 1833, Sir John Ross entered the Gulf of Boothia by Prince Regent's Inlet; and James Ross, his nephew, explored the James Ross Strait and the Boothia Peninsula, and discovered the North Magnetic Pole. John Rae, a doctor in the service of the Hudson Bay Company, made a close examination of the shores of the Gulf of Boothia in 1845. In the same year Franklin set out on the voyage from which neither he nor any one of his 134 companions was to return.

Sir John Franklin had seen much varied service; he had fought in the battles of Copenhagen and of Trafalgar, and in the attack on New Orleans; he had served under Buchan in the Arctic expedition of 1818; and in 1819 and again in 1825 he had led exploring expeditions in the interior and on the north coast of Canada. He had been employed, as a young naval officer, in a survey of the Australian coasts, and returned to the same region in later life as Lieutenant-Governor of Tasmania from 1834 to 1843. No more competent commander could have been entrusted with the Erebus (Captain Fitzjames) and the Terror (Captain Crozier) in the attempt to seek the north-west passage. Sailing on May 19th, 1845, his ships were seen in Baffin Bay, for the last time, two months later. From the records discovered years afterwards in a cairn at Point Victory it was learned that the two ships had passed through Lanaster Sound, Wellington Channel,

DR. NANSEN

He was only twenty-one years of age when he visited Greenland in 1882, and had crossed the vast elevated ice-field from east to west of Greenland, in 1888, before devising his daring and original scheme for approaching the Pole.

Penny Strait and Crozier Channel, and had then wintered at Beechey Island, off the south-west corner of North Devon, in Barrow Strait. Thence they had sailed through Peel Sound and Franklin Strait to King William Land, where they had been prevented from further progress by pressure of ice. Franklin having died here in June, 1847, the survivors abandoned the ships in the following summer and attempted to make their way southward by the Adelaide Peninsula to outposts of the Hudson Bay Company, but all perished. Their skeletons were afterwards found scattered along the route. Of the many expeditions which sought for the lost company and their relics, we may mention those of the Prince Albert, 1850, and of the Fox, 1857, both fitted out by Lady Franklin; the Grinnell expedition in the Advance, which discovered Grinnell Land; and that of the Assistance, with four other ships under Sir E. Belcher, in 1852. By these and others the north shores of America, the Parry Islands, and the intricate channels of these Arctic waters were assiduously explored. Subsequently the Polaris, under Captain Hall, passing in 1871 through Smith Sound towards the Pole, reached 82° 16' N.; and commander A. H. Markham, of the Nares expedition in the Alert and Discovery, 1875, which pursued the same course, succeeded in attaining by sledge a latitude of 83° 20' N. The north-east passage was now accomplished, in 1878 by Nordenskiöld. This explorer, who was a highly trained scientific man, had led several important expeditions to Greenland, Spitzbergen, Novaya Zemlya and the North Siberian coast before he equipped the Vega (300 tons), in 1877, for his successful voyage from Sweden to Japan. He proved that the north-east passage is perfectly practicable with adequate knowledge and equipment. Leaving Karlskrona on June 22nd, 1878, accompanied by three other ships bound for the North Siberian rivers, the Vega anchored off Cape Chelyuskin

NANSEN'S EXPEDITION TO THE NORTH POLE: THE FRAM AFTER ITS RETURN

Nansen set out on his voyage in August, 1893, reaching the New Siberia Islands in September. Here the Fram was made fast to an ice-floe, and allowed gradually to drift north, until on March 5th, 1895, a latitude of 84° 4' was reached. Here he left the Fram, and pushing across the ice succeeded in advancing as far north as 86° 13·6' on April 7th, 1895.

on August 20th, and was frozen in at Kuliutchin Bay at the end of September, only 120 miles from Bering Strait. During the ten months of winter imprisonment scientific observations were carried on and overland excursions were undertaken. The ship was free on July 18th, 1879, rounded the East Cape two days later, and on September 2nd entered Yokohama harbour. We may here mention the important discovery made in Russian Polar seas by the Austrians, Payer and Weyprecht, in 1873. This was the archipelago known as Franz Josef Land, about 200 miles north of Novaya Zemlya, and 250 miles east of Spitzbergen. Franz Josef Land was further explored by Leigh Smith in 1880. Here, also, the Jackson-Harmsworth expedition was engaged, from 1894 to 1897, in scientific investigations, and welcomed Nansen and Johansen, in June, 1896, on their return from their adventurous journey over the ice. The name of Fridtjof Nansen will always stand among those of the greatest Arctic explorers. A

CAPTAIN SVERDRUP

Accompanying Nansen on his Polar journey of 1893, Sverdrup commanded an Arctic expedition in 1898, succeeding in carrying his country's flag as far as 85° 42'

naturalist by training, and curator successively of the Bergen Museum and of the Museum of Comparative Anatomy at Christiania, he had visited Greenland at the age of twenty-one, in 1882, and had crossed the vast elevated icefield from east to west of Greenland, in 1888, before he devised his daring and original scheme for approaching the Pole. This project was based largely on conclusions drawn from the disastrous experience of De Long's expedition in the Jeannette. It was in 1879 that De Long, commissioned by Mr. Gordon Bennett, sailed northward through the Bering Strait to seek the Pole. He believed in the existence of a Japanese current flowing northward through the strait, and along the east coast of Wrangel Land, which was then supposed to extend far northward; and he thought that the warm water of this current would keep an open passage that might be followed to a very high latitude. Whaling ships had always found that when caught by the ice in the neighbourhood of Bering Strait they drifted north-ward. Pushing, therefore, as far north as possible, the Jeannette was ice-bound in September, 1879, in 71° 35′ N. and 175° 6′ E., south-east of Wrangel Land, and drifted for two years with the ice, until the ship was broken by the pressure, and foun-dered, to the north-east of the New Siberia Is-lands. A few men reached Yakutsk by way of these islands, though De Long and most of his com-panions lost their lives. But certain relics of the Jeannette continued to drift slowly, at the esti-mated rate of about two miles a day, with the vast movement of the ice-pack, until the ice-floe on which they were carried reached the Greenland coast, where they were discovered. Professor Mohn was the first ·to point out the great significance of these far-travelled fragments, and his conclusions were confirmed by a study of the driftwood which is thrown in great quantities on the Greenland shores and is much used by the Esquimaux. This timber was found to belong to Siberian species; and, further, an examination of the Greenland flora revealed numerous plants of undoubted Siberian origin. The theory of the constant current from Bering Strait and the Siberian coast, across the Pole, to the shores of Greenland and the Atlantic Ocean was strengthened by the fact that the Polar Sea is not large, and is for the most part very shallow; yet an enormous mass of water moves continually from it into the Atlantic, and this water must come, at least in part, from the Bering Strait. Nansen and his crew sailed in the Fram (402 tons) in August, 1893, rounded Cape Chelyuskin, and entering the ice at the New Siberia

THE DUKE OF THE ABRUZZI
The Duke of the Abruzzi headed an expedi-tion that left Christiania in June, 1899, and planted the Italian flag on a spot within 230 miles of the North Pole, thus getting nearer the goal than any of his predecessors.

ROBERT E. PEARY
Under the auspices of the Peary Arctic Club, R. E. Peary set out on an Arctic expedi-tion in the Roosevelt in 1906, reaching a point within 203 miles of the North Pole.

Islands, was carried northward for two years. In 1895 he left the Fram in the charge of Sverdrup, and, accompanied by Johansen, made a forced march north-ward, attaining the latitude of 86° 13·6′. After spending the winter in the north of Franz Josef Land, he joined the Jackson-Harmsworth ex-pedition, in May, 1897, and was by them brought back to Norway, whither the Fram also returned in safety. Nansen's "farthest north" was surpassed by Captain Cagni, of the Duke of the Abruzzi's expedition, in the Polar Star. This whaling vessel left Chris-tiania for Archangel in June, 1899, and thence proceeded to Franz Josef Land, where she wintered in Teplitz Bay, on Prince Rudolph Island. Thence an admirably organised sledge journey was under-taken to the north under great difficulties; and the latitude of 86° 33′ 49″ was attained on April 24th, 1900. This latitude, in its turn, has been exceeded by Commander Robert E. Peary, of the United States Navy, whose admirable researches in Greenland, Ellesmere Land and Grant Land were begun in 1886. Peary is a master in sledge travel, and owes much of his success to the excellent relations which he has established with the Es-quimaux. He has made a study of the Greenland ice-cap, was the first to prove that Greenland is an island, and has charted the islands to the north of it. With the support of the Peary Arctic Club he set out in 1905 with the Roosevelt, and, sailing northward to the west of Greenland, wintered at Cape Sheridan. Leaving the ship in February, he pushed northward with a party consisting of six Americans and twenty-one Esquimaux, and succeeded in reaching 87° 6′ on April 21st, 1906.

ANDREE'S ILL-FATED EXPEDITION: DEPARTURE OF THE BALLOON FROM SPITZBERGEN

The most conspicuous attempt to reach the North Pole by means of a balloon was that made by Salomon August Andree, a Swedish engineer, in 1897. With two companions he set out from Dane's Island on July 11th, but beyond a message received two days later by carrier pigeon nothing definite has been heard of the ill-fated enterprise. The balloon was capable of travelling from 15 to 16 miles an hour, and had a capacity of 170,000 cubic feet.

THE AIRSHIP AMERICA LEAVING ITS SHED

A VIEW SHOWING THE AIRSHIP'S GAS APPARATUS

THE HEADQUARTERS AT VIRGO BAY, SPITZBERGEN

TO THE POLE BY AIRSHIP: WELLMAN'S FUTILE ATTEMPT IN 1907

A notable aerial attempt to reach the North Pole was made on September 2nd, 1907, by Walter Wellman, an American journalist, in his airship, the America, an attempt, however, which utterly failed in its object, the airship being beaten back by storms and forced on to an Arctic glacier, the party returning a few weeks later.

THE LURE OF THE SOUTH POLE
HEROIC STRUGGLES WITH THE ANTARCTIC ICE

THE history of Antarctic exploration is comparatively modern, and may be said to begin with the voyages of the illustrious James Cook in 1768 and 1772. Before his time the myth of a great Austral continent had been handed on from one generation of map-makers to another, on the ground, apparently, that a vast continental mass was necessary in the southern hemisphere as an equipoise to the continents north of the Equator.

The Terra Australis was therefore charted right round the world, its northern limits coming up to the Strait of Magellan, in South America, and approaching near the Cape of Good Hope and the Malay Archipelago ; and though expeditions, such as that of Bouvet in 1739, pushed its coast-line farther south, they tended rather to confirm than to dissipate this fallacious conjecture. Cook's voyage in the Endeavour, in 1768, did much to shake the inveterate error.

The Famous Voyages of Captain Cook His ship had been sent with an astronomical party to Tahiti to observe the transit of Venus ; and on his way back Cook circumnavigated New Zealand, surveyed the east coast of Australia and claimed it for Britain, and passing through Torres Strait established the insularity of New Guinea.

He had thus done much to disprove the existence of the supposed great continent, and his next voyage was to dispose of the matter finally. Sailing in 1772 with the Resolution and the Adventure, he took a southerly course from the Cape of Good Hope, was the first to cross the Antarctic Circle, and pushed on until he was stopped by ice. Proceeding eastward, he now circumnavigated the world in high latitudes, breaking his Antarctic voyage by retreats to the north, during which he made important surveys.

"The importance of this voyage," says Captain R. F. Scott, of the Discovery, " can scarcely be exaggerated ; once and for all the idea of a populous fertile southern continent was proved to be a myth, and it was clearly shown that whatever land might exist to the south it must be a region of desolation, hidden beneath a mantle of ice and snow. The vast extent of the tempestuous southern seas was revealed, and the limits of the habitable globe were made known." Cook himself described the regions of the south as "countries condemned to everlasting rigidity by Nature, never to yield to the warmth of the sun, for whose wild and desolate aspect I find no words." Cook's feat was repeated in 1819 by the Russian Bellingshausen, who crossed the Antarctic Circle six times during his circumnavigation, and discovered and named Peter I. Island and Alexander I. Land.

Desolate Regions of the South

About this time, also, the large but short-lived whaling and sealing industries in these waters were responsible for important discoveries, which are associated chiefly with the names of Weddell, Biscoe, and Balleny. Weddell's " farthest south " (74° 15') was achieved in 1823 in an open sea which has been called by his name ; Biscoe, in 1831, discovered Enderby Land and Graham Land ; and Balleny, in 1839, reported the Balleny Islands and Sabrina Land.

A French expedition, sailing in 1837, under Dumont d'Urville, added Joinville Land and Louis Philippe Land to the map in 1838, and two years later Adélie Land and the Côte Clarie also ; Commodore Wilkes, of the American Navy, sailing in 1837 with five ships, discovered Wilkes Land; and these expeditions were immediately followed by an important British enterprise in the interests of magnetic science. Captain James Ross, who was appointed to this government expedition, sailed from Hobart in November, 1840, with the Erebus (370 tons), and the Terror (340 tons). Crossing the Antarctic Circle at 171° E., he came upon a great expanse

National Scientific Enterprises

ANTARCTIC NAVIGATORS ICEBOUND: HUNTING FOR SEALS

THE ASTROLABE AND THE ZÉLÉE SURROUNDED BY ICEBERGS

THE EXPLORERS AMID THE TERRORS OF THE ANTARCTIC

ADMIRAL D'URVILLE'S FRENCH EXPEDITION TO THE ANTARCTIC IN 1837

6346

THE GAUSS IN ITS WINTER QUARTERS OFF WILHELM II. LAND

CAMPING-OUT IN THE ANTARCTIC REGIONS

MEMBERS OF THE PARTY ON A SLEDGE JOURNEY

VON DRYGALSKI'S GERMAN EXPEDITION TO THE ANTARCTIC IN 1903

of broken ice, and ploughing southward through it for five days, he broke into an open sea that was to be thereafter known by his name. Steering westward, he discovered and followed the long coast of Victoria Land, from Cape North to Cape Crozier, and then followed the great ice barrier into which it passed. In this voyage, which did more for Antarctic discovery than any which preceded or has followed it, Ross reached a latitude of 78° 11′, discovered and named the volcanoes Erebus and Terror, and determined the position of the South Magnetic Pole. Little was now done in these regions until the close of the century, when a general revival of interest led to several well-equipped expeditions which have achieved very considerable results. Thus, the Norwegian Antarctica entered Ross Sea in 1894, and effected the first landing in Victoria Land. Mr. C. F. Borchgrevink, commissioned by Sir George Newnes, sailed in the Southern Cross for the same region in 1898, and wintered at Cape Adare. The Belgica, under Captain de Gerlache, coasted in 1898 along Graham Land and Alexander Land, and becoming ice-bound in Bellingshausen Sea, drifted in the ice throughout the winter. A German expedition in the Gauss, under Professor Von Drygalski, discovered in 1902 Kaiser Wilhelm II. Land, off which the Gauss wintered, returning home in the following year.

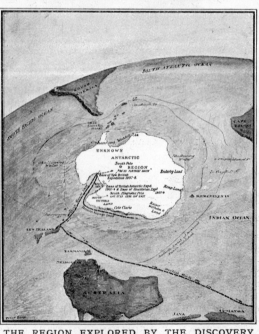

DR. OTTO NORDENSKIOLD

Nephew of Baron Nordenskiöld, the famous Arctic explorer, he led a Swedish expedition to the Antarctic in 1901; two years later his ship was crushed in the ice, and with his party he was rescued by an Argentine gunboat.

The Swedish vessel Antarctica made a close survey of the west coast of Danco Land and Graham Land in 1902 and 1903, and at the same time the Scotia, under W. S. Bruce, made an oceanographical study of the Weddell Sea, and discovered and named Coats' Land. A vast accretion to scientific knowledge of Polar conditions has resulted from these expeditions. Simultaneously with these, a British expedition was sent out to the Ross Sea in the Discovery (485 tons), under Captain Robert F. Scott, R.N. The undertaking was promoted jointly by the Royal Society and the Royal Geographical Society, and was partially subsidised by the British Government. The vessel, a wooden auxiliary steamship, was specially built for this work, and was manned by a naval crew. Leaving England in August, and New Zealand in December, 1901, the Discovery worked up the coast of Victoria Land from Cape Adare to McMurdo Sound, making close observations of the mountains along the coast. Thence they sailed eastward along the great ice barrier, which was found to vary from 30 feet to 280 feet in height. It was observed that the edge of the barrier was considerably to the south of Ross's determination of it, and that this enormous field of ice rises and falls with the tide, and is therefore floating for an undetermined distance southward. By following

THE REGION EXPLORED BY THE DISCOVERY

THE DISCOVERY AS IT APPEARED WHEN FOUND BY THE RELIEF SHIPS

OFFICERS OF THE TERRA NOVA RETURNING FROM A SEAL HUNT

THE RELIEF SHIP, MORNING: SOLID ICE TO LEFT AND BROKEN PACK ICE TO RIGHT

AMID THE SOUTHERN SNOWS: SCENES IN THE DISCOVERY RELIEF EXPEDITION

6349

LETTERS FROM HOME: "POSTMEN" ON THE ANTARCTIC ICE

Captain Scott's expedition to the Antarctic left England in August, 1901, and New Zealand the following December, and the party had suffered extreme hardships before welcome relief was brought them in January, 1904, by the Morning and Terra Nova, two government ships. The above picture shows four stalwart members of the Morning on ski, conveying the Discovery's well=filled letter-bag from the Terra Nova to be loaded on dog sledges

the edge of the barrier, the Discovery arrived at King Edward VII.'s Land, a region of peaks and glaciers hitherto unknown, and then, returning westward, Captain Scott established the fact that Mounts Erebus and Terror constitute an island, which was named Ross Island. The ship was put into winter quarters at Cape Armitage there. On November 2nd, 1902, Captain Scott, accompanied by Messrs. Wilson and Shackleton, started on his southward sledge party over the ice. Amid great difficulties, due chiefly to the deterioration of the food which they carried for the dogs, and also to the insufficiency of their own food supply, they travelled to a latitude of 82° 16' 33", which was reached on December 30th.

STUDYING THE HIDDEN LIFE OF THE ANTARCTIC DEEP

How the explorers with Captain Scott's expedition employed the scientific drag-net, which was frequently lowered through a hole cut in the ice, in their examination of the life of the Antarctic Ocean, is illustrated in the above picture. While engaged in this operation the men sheltered themselves behind a semi-circular wall of snow.

JAMES WEDDEL

LT. A. DE GERLACHE

C. BORCHGREVINK

W. S. BRUCE

CAPTAIN SCOTT

LIEUTENANT SHACKLETON

ADML. D'URVILLE

LT. WILKES, U.S.N.

BENJAMIN MORRELL

ADML. BELLINGSHAUSEN

THE QUEST OF THE SOUTH POLE: INTREPID EXPLORERS OF THE ANTARCTIC

Photos by Thomson, S. J. Beckett and Alston Rivers

6351

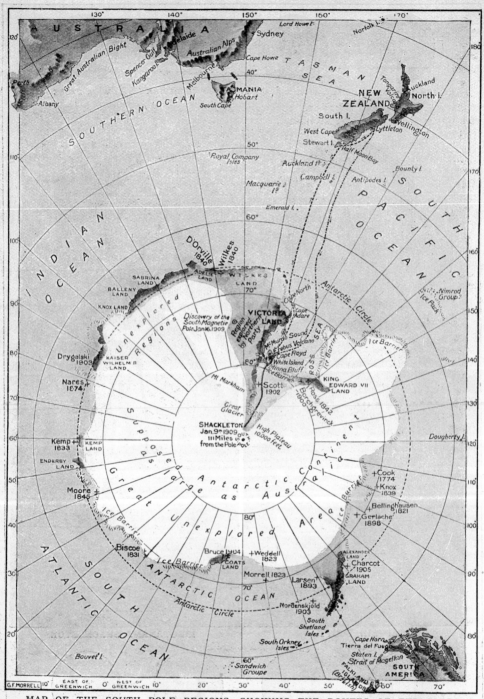

MAP OF THE SOUTH POLE REGIONS, SHOWING THE ROUTES OF EXPLORERS

The history of Antarctic exploration is comparatively modern, beginning with Captain Cook's memorable voyage in the Endeavour in 1768, and subsequently with the Resolution and the Adventure in 1772, on which latter occasion the famous explorer succeeded in crossing the Antarctic Circle. With the exception of Captain Ross's voyage in 1840, little of importance was done in these regions until the close of the nineteenth century, when several well-equipped expeditions were sent out by various governments and geographical societies, the greatest success being achieved on January 9th, 1909, when Lieutenant Shackleton reached a point within 111 miles of the South Pole. Lieutenant Shackleton's route in the above map has been carefully traced from details supplied by himself.

The route lay along the ice to the east of the coast of Victoria Land, on which the mountains Longstaff, Markham and many others were named. The little party returned to the ship, extremely worn, on February 3rd, 1903. In the following summer Captain Scott travelled westward with two companions over a high, desolate plateau, the summit of Victoria Land, to 146° 33′ E., covering in eighty-one days 1,098 miles.

These daring ice journeys were emulated in a later South Polar expedition, by Lieut. Ernest H. Shackleton, who has succeeded in reaching 88° 23′ S., 162° E., a point within 111 statute miles of the Pole. This explorer, who had accompanied Captain Scott in his southward

Nimrod on March 4th. A second party, the Northern, succeeded, amid great difficulties and dangers in locating the Magnetic Pole in 72° 25′ S., 154° E.; and the Westward, or third, party explored and mapped the coast.

Among the most important results of this expedition have been the complete reversal of the old theory of a region of Polar calm; the discovery that the South Polar region is an elevated plateau; the discovery of coal measures in the Antarctic continent; the surveying of a considerable range of coastline to the west of Victoria Land; and the ascent of Mount Erebus, the height of which has been determined at 13,120 feet. In all probability the North and the

THE HARDSHIPS OF ANTARCTIC EXPLORATION: AN EPISODE IN SHACKLETON'S EXPEDITION
Lieutenant Shackleton's Antarctic expedition of 1907–9 was marked by many hardships, not the least of them being a shortage of food, which made it necessary for the explorers to kill the small, hardy ponies which accompanied them one after the other, until at last the original number had been reduced to three, as shown in the above picture.

journey to a point within 450 miles of the Pole in December, 1902, fitted out the Nimrod, a whaling vessel of 227 tons, in 1907, and proceeded to the Ross Sea. The leader with three companions, who constituted the "Southern party," leaving the coast on October 29th, 1908, pressed southward as rapidly as possible over a mountainous plateau at an elevation of 10,000 feet. Glaciers intersected by frequent crevasses, treacherous snow-drifts, fearful blizzards, and temperatures of from 40 to 90 degrees of frost, made the journey incomparably arduous. After ten weeks of continuous travelling, they reached their farthest south on January 9th, 1909, and, returning, joined the

South Poles will have been reached before many years have passed. The impression left on one's mind by a review of the history of Polar exploration is that the scientific study of these regions is still only in its beginnings, and that the remarkable interest in Arctic and Antarctic research which has characterised the early years of the twentieth century can only increase with every fresh accession of knowledge. It is greatly to be desired, and can hardly be doubted, that British explorers will continue in the future, as they have done in the past, to play a pre-eminent part in this high enterprise.

GEORGE SANDEMAN

FIGHTING ITS WAY TOWARDS THE POLE: THE NIMROD IN A HEAVY STORM

Weekly Press, N.Z.

ARRIVAL OF THE EXPEDITION AT NEW ZEALAND: THE NIMROD NEARING LYTTELTON

NEAREST APPROACH TO THE SOUTH POLE: THE SHACKLETON EXPEDITION

The copyright of the top picture is reserved by Lieutenant Shackleton

THE WORLD TO·DAY

BEING A FOOTNOTE TO THE HARMSWORTH HISTORY OF THE WORLD

By W. Kinnaird Rose

SINCE the publication of this History began, history has been in the making. Has not one of the greatest historians of the last century said that there are many longitudinal feet of small printed history in every veracious daily newspaper ? The currents of human affairs never cease to flow ; and although we were able to trace with illumination the course of these with all their tributaries, even to their issue into the ocean of present experience, that present was the date of publication of the respective volumes of our work. Therefore, to change the metaphor, the narrative of our explorations must, as it were, be rounded off so as to bring the epitome of the world's events down to the veritable present, and thus make this History of the World the most exhaustive in modern literature.

Perhaps it is well to remind our readers that the plotting of the History was designed on what was not inaptly termed the lines of sequence of Orientation—an entirely original plan, it will be admitted, in the world's record. The dawn in the historic, as in the physical. sphere arises in the East, and the full day follows the circle of the sun to the West. So we began with Japan, and ended with the races and countries of the Occident.

We continue the scheme in what may be called this footnote to our general narrative history, so as to make the whole complete, not only unto the day, but almost the hour, of going to the press.

JAPAN

Japan, from the swaddling clothes of its new birth—the analogue is drawn from the dominant religion of the country—at the close of the great and victorious war with Russia on the plains and rivers, the coasts and mountains of Manchuria, has shot up into lusty manhood in the family of nations, and the demand was made and is being accorded that due recognition should be made of it as a first-class Power.

After the visit of the American fleet to Japanese waters and its magnificent reception by all classes of the Japanese, there was a diplomatic exchange of notes defining the relations between the United States and Japan with reference to (1) the encouragement of the free and peaceful development of their commerce in the Pacific ; (2) the maintenance of the *status quo* on these matters, and an equal opportunity for the commerce and industry of all nations in China ; (3) respect for each other's territorial position ; (4) the support of the independence and integrity of China by all peaceful nations.

On the material side of things, Japan is making steady if silent progress. Like the nations of the West, it has been feeling the pressure of vast expenditure on armaments, and on its army and navy. There was strong opposition in the House of Representatives at the proposed imposition of new and additions to existing taxes, and this led to the fall of the Saionji Ministry. A new administration was formed in the latter end of 1908 by the Marquis Katsura, a former Premier, whose genius for organisation during the war with Russia will be remembered. Economies were effected, and the credit of the country was restored.

Korea. But it is in Korea that Japan has seized the opportunity of developing its ideas of extra territorial expansion, and finding an outlet for its surplus population. It might almost be said that Korea has become an appanage of Japan under the dexterous manipulation of the Marquis Ito. His persistent efforts during the past two years to promote the political supremacy of Japan and the welfare of the Koreans were rewarded by the rank of prince being conferred upon him by the Emperor of Japan. In October, 1907, the crown prince of Japan visited Korea, and was received by the emperor and crown prince of that country almost as a suzerain, and later in the same year the crown prince of Korea, a boy of eleven years of age, was sent to Japan for his education.

The Korean Emperor's father is in semi-banishment, and the emperor himself is in semi-tutelage to Prince Ito, who—or Viscount Sone, the prince's assistant—always accompanies him when his Majesty travels throughout his own dominions. What was officially described as an armed rising was suppressed by Japanese troops, and, according to a statement in the "Times," between July, 1907, and August, 1908, 12,916 Korean "insurgents" were killed, with a loss of only 196 men by the Japanese forces. The Press is under censorship, and the publication of articles "detrimental to public security or morals" is prohibited. Material prosperity, however, is increasing by the reform of taxation, the arrest of corruption in the court, and the transfer to the state of property formerly in charge of the imperial household. Railway extension is proceeding apace between Wiju in the north and Fusan in the south, and by branch lines east and west.

Siberia. Siberia has no recent history, except the increase of population by the import of some 70,000 political exiles and convicted criminals from European Russia, and the shadowy development of much-

belauded, but altogether disappointing from the speculator's point of view, goldfields on the edge of the Frozen Sea and near the borders of Northern Manchuria.

Malaysia. In Malaysia there is little beyond peaceful commercial progress to be recorded. In the Federated Malay States there has been the only real accession to the extent of the British Empire for several years past. On March 10th, 1909, an Anglo-Siamese Treaty was signed at Bangkok, by which Siam ceded to Great Britain Siamese rights of suzerainty over certain provinces to the north of the Federated Malay States, the whole comprising an area of about 15,000 square miles, and a population of nearly half a million. As a *quid pro quo*, Great Britain agreed that all registered British subjects should be amenable to the Siamese International Courts, subject to certain safeguards ; and, further, to support financially the extension of railway construction, so as to connect Siamese lines with those of the Federated Malay States. The progress of the British Protectorate in North Borneo is notable. Java and Sumatra, which constitute the richest portions of the Dutch East Indies, are showing the fruits of the new colonial policy introduced by the Netherlands Government. In Java an era of agricultural prosperity has followed the cultivation of tea rather than coffee, for which the island was long famous.

The discontent in Sumatra, the root of which was the method of raising revenue by the purchase from the natives of produce at fixed prices, has been in great measure allayed by the introduction of a just and adequate system of taxation. In Achin, where there has been incessant war for many years, the pacification of the natives is all but complete. The power of the tyrannical petty chiefs has been broken. Dutch officials have been appointed in every district on the island ; improved roads have been opened ; the natives enjoy a fair administration of justice, and gladly devote their activities to the cultivation of their holdings rather than to fighting.

CHINA

The awakening of China has been accompanied by many portents and incidents. Our detailed outline of the history of China was brought down to the end of October, 1907. The health of the emperor was then known to be indifferent, and the announcement of his death, which was said to have taken place on November 14th, caused no great surprise; but the demise of the empress - dowager, which happened on the following day, came as a shock to both natives and foreigners. The birthday of the empress - dowager had been celebrated with unusual magnificence ten days before, and it was rumoured that she had taken part in the choice of a successor to the throne, and that the emperor's valedictory edict had been drawn up on her instructions.

The new emperor, an infant of only five years of age, is a son of Prince Chun, a younger brother of the late emperor, who has been appointed regent. The succession was generally accepted by the people, a mutinous outbreak at Nanking in favour of appointing a Chinese rather than a Manchu prince being immediately suppressed. The representatives of the foreign governments at Peking attended the ceremonial of the lying-in-state of the late emperor and dowager empress within their palaces, and took part in the long procession which conveyed their remains to their final resting-place in the mausoleums, built long ago in anticipation, in the City of the Tombs of the dynasty.

The infant emperor has been recognised by the Great Powers. The *de facto* emperor, Prince Chun, who is only twenty-six years of age, is credited with very considerable ability, and is said to be actuated by the reform spirit. At any rate, he has some knowledge of the West, acquired during the mission on which he was dispatched in 1901 to Germany, to convey the regret of the Chinese Government for the murder of the German ambassador at Peking in 1900—the first time in history that a Chinese prince of the blood had visited Europe. The belief in his reforming tendencies was rather checked by his dismissal of Yuan Shih-Kai, the viceroy of the metropolitan province of Chi-Li, and by far the ablest of Chinese administrators. The dismissal was said to be on account of the ill-health of Yuan Shih-Kai, but it is generally believed that it was because of his opposition to Manchu prerogatives, and to the power of the eunuchs.

So much was this step of the regent regarded as retrograde that friendly representations were made against the dismissal by the Great Powers. One reform, however, the regent carried out early in 1909 was the impeachment and cashiering of Chen Pi, Minister of Commerce, for corruption. A reform perfected by Yuan Shih-Kai, the dismissed viceroy, has been left untouched. Its object is no less than the merging of the Manchu population, which constitutes only one per cent. of the whole, in the Chinese population of the empire; and the appointment of Chinese officers in Manchuria with the same form of administration in Manchuria as in the other provinces.

Constitution building has seized the Mongolian imagination. The new government has announced to the outside world the intention of granting a constitution in 1917. This constitution, drafted by a special commission, was presented to the throne in the autumn of 1908, and sanctioned by the new government by rescript at the beginning of 1909. It provides for a constitutional assembly, to include princes, dukes, hereditary nobles, imperial clansmen, officials, certain persons possessed of property worth at least £150,000, and representatives of the provincial councils. These latter are to be formed of representatives chosen on an educational diploma, of men of official rank or possessed of property of the value of £1,250. The commission also recommended to the throne to command the introduction of judicial and administrative reforms in the provinces. The foreign Powers have given the Chinese Government the assurance that when the constitutional régime is set up, the foreign troops will be withdrawn from Peking.

The announcement of the determination of the United States Government to forgo the payment of the £2,500,000 of the indemnity of 1900 induced the Chinese Government to send Tang Shao-Yi as special ambassador to the United States with a letter of thanks to President Roosevelt, and to give a special official welcome to the United States fleet at Amoy by Prince Yu Lang, and his Excellency Liang-Tung Yen.

Chinese sovereign rights in Manchuria have been asserted with the help of the United States as against Russian claims to the absolute right of administration over Chinese and foreign residents at Harbin; and also with regard to the evacuation of the Japanese army of occupation. The popular feeling in China, which came to a head in the beginning of 1908, of "China for the Chinese," so far as railway policy is concerned, had to be faced by the government. After much negotiation and the payment of certain indemnities, China recovered rights previously granted to concessionaries for the construction of certain railways and also for the working of specific coal-mines.

Nothing is more striking than the re-awakened passion for education displayed by the progressive element in the government of China. Money is freely forthcoming for this purpose, however stinted the grants may be in other directions.

In February, 1909, an international conference was held at Shanghai on the opium question. The conference sat for three weeks, and Sir Alexander Hosie, speaking on behalf of the British delegation, said that "fair progress had been made in several provinces in combating the opium evil, but much remained to be done. The sincerity of the Chinese Government was beyond question, and had the sympathy of the conference in its efforts to eradicate the opium evil from the empire." Resolutions were adopted by the conference, that each government should investigate scientifically anti-opium remedies, take measures to prevent smuggling of opium, and all preparations from it ; to prevent opium smoking in its own territory, and to enter into negotiations with the Chinese Government to take and promote effective measures for the suppression of the opium traffic, and smoking in their own foreign settlements in China.

The relation of Tibet to China came prominently into notice by the arrival at Peking on September 28th, 1908, of the Dalai Lama, with a large retinue, and valuable presents for the Chinese Court. He was received with great ceremony during his stay of two months, and is understood to have endeavoured to negotiate with the Chinese Government for his recognition by China as sovereign of Tibet. However, it has been alleged on authority that the aspirations of the Dalai Lama were not only sharply rebuked, but hints were thrown out that even his spiritual authority would henceforth be dependent upon his recognition by China. The latest accounts of the Dalai state that 10,000 Lamas, instigated by him, had risen in rebellion against Chinese authority, but that they had been defeated by the imperial troops. The only other points of interest in the recent history of China are the proposal for the adoption of a big programme of naval construction and the re-modelling of the army on European lines ; the departure of Sir Robert Hart, the famous financial adviser to the Chinese Government on customs, and the appointment in his room of Sir Walter C. Hillier.

AUSTRALIA

In the commonwealth of Australia, and in the constituent states of which it is composed, constitutional principles have recently been crystallised into practical statecraft, which must have far-reaching consequences in the future. They established precedents which are bound to modify in a marked degree the evolution of colonial constitutions, and the relation of the dominions beyond the seas to the Imperial Government. It will be remembered that Mr. Deakin became Prime Minister of the commonwealth after the general election in 1906, with Sir William Lyne as Treasurer. But he was head of only one of three parties—the full-blooded Protectionists, the Liberal and Labour party under Mr. Fisher, and the Conservatives, mostly free traders, under Mr. J. H. Reid. In order to secure himself in office, Mr. Deakin had to come to terms with the Labour party, who agreed to his high protective tariff if a share of its advantages were conceded to the consumer and the worker. The result was the elaboration, under the manipulation of Sir William Lyne, of what was known as the "New Protection," and its embodiment in the Excise Tariff Act of 1906. Under that act local manufacturers, protected by heavy duties upon British and foreign imports, were compelled to sell their goods at a "fair price," and to pay their workmen "a fair rate of wages" ; or, alternatively, the local manufacturers were to pay to the Commonwealth Government a high excise duty on their manufactured goods.

After the act had been put into operation, the employees in the agricultural machinery industry, which was then in a flourishing condition, complained that they were not receiving "a fair rate of wages," and appealed to the Commonwealth Arbitration Court for the enforcement of the Excise Tariff Act. The case was tried before Mr. Justice Higgins, who gave a judgment which will become historical in the annals of labour and fiscal arrangements of the commonwealth.

The judge decided in favour of the workmen, fixed a fair rate of wages for each class, and further decreed that the men should be paid " back wages " equal to the excise duty for the whole period covered by the act. The employers appealed to the Commonwealth High Court, on the ground that the Excise Tariff Act was a violation of the constitution of the commonwealth, a contention maintained by three out of the five judges of the High Court. Mr. Deakin then introduced a bill to amend the constitution, but the details of that measure were obnoxious to the Labour party, whose leader, Mr. Fisher, with the support of the Conservatives, moved and carried by a majority of 49 to 13 a vote of want of confidence in the Deakin Government.

On the fall of the Deakin-Lyne Ministry, the governor-general, Lord Northcote, sent for Mr. Fisher, who formed an administration—the sixth in the eight years of the life of the commonwealth. Mr. Fisher's Government devoted itself to promoting measures mainly for the benefit of the proletariat. During this fair political weather, the term of office of Lord Northcote as governor-general expired, and he was succeeded by the Earl of Dudley.

In what may be called internal politics, the most outstanding feature was the conflict between the commonwealth and the constituent states with regard to the financial relations between them. According to what is known as the Braddon Clause in the commonwealth constitution, the customs revenues in all the states were collected by the national government, but three-fourths of the amount derived from each state was returned to it, the remaining fourth being retained to meet national expenditure.

An endeavour was made to compose differences at a conference of the state Premiers, which took place in Melbourne in 1908. Sir William Lyne's proposals, representing the view of the National party, were that all the state debts should be placed under the control and administration of a council of finance and consolidated as they fell due into a 3 per cent. consols with a sinking fund, while £6,000,000 should be credited out of the customs fund to the different states in equitable proportions. The counter proposals of the States Rights' party were : (1) Payment to the states of a fixed annual sum, plus a proportionate part of the increase of revenue from customs and excise ; (2) the states to retain the right to raise loans without interference from the Council of Finance ; (3) in the event of the states' debts being taken over by the Council of Finance, the indebtedness of the states to be reduced to the extent of the value of the property transferred from the states to the commonwealth.

The last view found most favour, but legislation will be required by the parliaments of the different states to carry it out before the close of 1910, when the Braddon Compact in the commonwealth constitution expires.

It is a striking fact that the visit of the American fleet to Australian waters, and the rhetorical wave of alarm which struck Australian shores from the Old Country as to the threatened mastery of the ocean by a German armada, which was increasing by squadrons of Dreadnoughts, had in no inconsiderable degree an effect on the fate of the Commonwealth Government. Mr. Deakin's record at the last Imperial Conference, and since, has been characterised by the imperial instinct. Perhaps it was this which prompted a not ungenerous envy of the kudos which had come to New Zealand from far and near throughout the British Empire by its electric offer of a Dreadnought, and a second, if necessary, to the imperial government, at the psychological moment of the fleet crisis in the Old Country. Mr. Deakin played on this feeling, in Victoria especially, in the most skilful manner. Mr. Fisher, the commonwealth Premier, belongs to the school whose motto is " an Australian fleet for Australia," and cares less for imperial Dreadnoughts. Parliament was not then in session, but on Independence Day in 1909 he expounded his programme in a great speech to the people of all Australia at Gympie, Queensland.

The points of the programme were : (1) Efficient local defence by a universally trained citizen army, and a local squadron of large destroyers ; (2) a contribution to the cost of imperial defence in the form of relieving the Admiralty within four years of the responsibility of defending the Australian coast and policing the Western Pacific ; (3) a progressive land tax to pay the cost of defence ; (4) no federal borrowing until consolidation of state debts ; (5) " new protection " to be enforced by an amendment of the constitution ; (6) nationalisation of the iron industry ;

(7) a commonwealth note issue ; a silver coinage by a commonwealth mint ; a commonwealth high commissioner for London ; the taking over of the northern territory ; the rearrangement of the sugar bounties ; and the building of a capital.

When the federal parliament met in Melbourne on May 26th, 1909 — the session being opened by the governor-general, Lord Dudley—Mr. Pearce, Minister for Defence, announced that the government had telegraphed to the imperial government that the flotilla of destroyers proposed to be built for Australian defence would be placed under the command of the admiral on the Australian station as soon as war was declared. This did not meet the imperialistic ideas of Mr. Deakin, while the Conservative members were opposed to the progressive land tax, the " new protection," and the Socialistic nationalisation of the iron industry. A motion for the adjournment of the debate, which was carried by 39 to 30, was taken by Mr. Fisher to be a vote of want of confidence in his ministry, and he thereupon demanded a dissolution. The governor-general, however, refused a general election, and the Fisher Ministry resigned. Mr. Deakin was sent for, and he succeeded in forming a new coalition Cabinet, which at once cabled on behalf of the Commonwealth Government to the imperial government an offer of a Dreadnought or its equivalent in a scheme of imperial defence.

So much for the commonwealth. A great deal that is of striking historical and economic interest took place in the different constituent states. In New South Wales a Wages Dispute Bill was passed in the session of 1908, but that did not prevent strikes among the government tramway employees in Sydney, the miners and unskilled labourers in Newcastle, and the men employed in the Broken Hill silver mines ; and in the last-named locality there were scenes of violence. A Local Government Act came into operation at the beginning of 1908, which compelled municipalities to strike a rate of a penny in the pound upon the unimproved value of land alone, the state remitting land tax to that amount. It is said that the effect has been to give an impetus to building operations in and around Sydney.

Victoria. In Victoria there have been no labour troubles, but the land question has been forced to the front by the rapid depopulation of the vast agricultural districts of the state. Sir Thomas Bent, the Premier, was harassed by the growing Labour party in the Legislative Assembly in view of his proposals to meet the difficulty, and on a crucial division he was not supported by the representatives of the old squatting interests, and suffered defeat. He thereupon obtained the consent of the governor to an appeal to the country, and, with great dexterity, ran the election on the lines of " anti-Socialism versus Labourism," with the result that his party won thirty-nine seats, the Labourites twenty-one and Independents, five. This was the first occasion on which women had a right to vote under the Adult Suffrage Act of 1908, which previously had been annually rejected for years by the Legislative Council. When the new state parliament was opened in its first session on June 30th, by Sir Thomas Gibson Carmichael, who had succeeded Sir Reginald Talbot as governor, it was announced that the governments of Victoria and New South Wales had informed the imperial government that, failing action on the part of the commonwealth, they were prepared to share jointly the cost of a Dreadnought on a *per capita* basis ; and now that the new commonwealth administration had also offered a Dreadnought, he was confident that the citizens of Victoria would bear a proportion of the cost.

Queensland. Queensland has been almost as fruitful in constitutional crises as Melbourne, and out of these events have arisen which will govern the future course of Australian history. In the parliamentary session of 1907 a bill was passed by a large majority in the Legislative Assembly extending the provisions of the Wages Board Act to agricultural labourers, and fixing a minimum wage and the maximum hours of labour for all farm and station hands. When the bill went to the nominated Legislative Council, which is largely conservative and representative of the squatting interest, it was twice thrown out. The Premier of the Labour Government, Mr. Kidston, had the support of a solid majority in the elective chamber, which was fresh from the constituencies, and he requested Lord Chelmsford, the governor, to appoint a sufficient number of nominee members to the Legislative Council which would carry the bill into law. This the governor declined to do, and the refusal created not only great excitement throughout Queensland, but was generally condemned in the other states.

Mr. Kidston resigned, and Lord Chelmsford sent for Mr. Philp, the leader of the Opposition ; but he was unable to form a Ministry with any chance of carrying on the business of parliament. Mr. Philp demanded and obtained a dissolution, and the result of the elections to the new parliament was : Kidstonites, 25 ; Labourites, who, on the constitutional and wages question, are really supporters of Mr. Kidston's policy, 22 ; with only 25 Philpites. Mr. Kidston, having already the power, was called to office, and the address in reply to the governor's opening speech to the new parliament contained a clause which was a vote of censure on Lord Chelmsford, as it expressed regret that the governor should have dissolved a newly elected parliament capable of carrying on the business of the country. It may be as well to state here that Lord Chelmsford was afterwards transferred as governor to New South Wales on the retirement of Admiral Sir Harry H. Rawson.

This frank criticism smoothed the passage of another far-reaching amendment to the Queensland Constitution. This was a bill, which has received the royal assent, providing for a referendum to the whole state electors in case of disputes between the two chambers.

The discussion of this measure gave rise to a strong agitation throughout the whole of the states of Australia for the appointment of the state governors, as in Canada, by the respective states, and not by the imperial government, i.e., the Colonial Office in London. It may be mentioned at this point that in the parliament of South Australia, where there was a Liberal and Labour Ministry in power, under the Hon. Tom Price, who visited England in 1908, and who died in 1909, a motion recommending the local appointment of the state governor was carried by a large majority of the Legislative Assembly, though it was rejected in the Legislative Council with more than a hint that it was disloyal. In Western Australia, the Legislative Assembly found means to express their views on the appointment of local instead of imperial governors by carrying an amendment during the discussion on the governor's salary to reduce it by £1. There has scarcely been a ruffle in the local history of the South Australian state, which since our last record has been in a condition of enviable general prosperity.

It was in West Australia that a serious demand was made for secession from the commonwealth a few years ago on the question of state rights. In the elective chamber the democratic sentiment was so strong as to demand the local appointment of its own state governor, and to pass progressive land measures for the encouragement of close settlement, the improvement of small holdings, and the development of the pastoral industry. Yet the old Conservative leaven still works, and makes its influence work, even in the Legislative Assembly, to which alone in the Australian states the constituents have failed to return a powerful Labour party. Withal public works and railways are being extended with a free hand, and the increasing yield of the goldfields, under judicious and sober management, contrast favourably with that during the " wild cat " mania of a few years ago.

New Zealand. On the death of Mr. Seddon, Sir Joseph Ward, as Premier, carried on the administration of the dominion on the lines which led for years to unchecked prosperity. In 1908, by the effluxion of time, the government had to appeal to the constituencies, and Sir Joseph Ward came back with a majority of 45 supporters, as against 25 members of the Opposition and five Independents. By a clause in the constitution the local option poll was taken at the same time as the election for members of parliament, with the result that " no licence " was carried by increasing majorities in those districts where the policy had been previously adopted ; total prohibition was carried in seven new districts ; and in ten districts there was a reduction of licences amounting in all to 150.

The anomalous thing is that the consumption of liquor in the dominion as a whole is increasing, and so also is the number of convictions for drunkenness. The only possible explanation offered is that liquor can be bought wholesale if not by retail, and that so-called temperance legislation has therefore become not a panacea, but a delusion and a snare. It was, however, on the imperial plane that New Zealand and its Premier, Sir John Ward, swam into the ken of an admiring empire. The visit of the American fleet had duly impressed the

New Zealanders, who were exuberant in their reception alike of the tars and of the officers of the quarter-deck. Interest in a squadron unparalleled in its numbers and strength, which, thus far, had safely accomplished more than half a memorable voyage, was increased by the fact that it represented the naval power of their cousins on the other side of the Pacific. Then came the cabled cry that the age-long rule of Britannia as mistress of the seas was being challenged by an alien Power. This cut straight to the heart of the sons and daughters not only of the island gem of the Pacific, but of the continental shores swept by " the long wash of the Australasian seas."

The unbidden response was immediate ; Sir Joseph Ward only gave magic inter-pretation to it. It was the pride no less than the duty of the daughter states to come, if need be, to the help of the Mother-land, which had given them of her best in territory, in language, in literature, in laws and in undying love of freedom. And so the message, " New Zealand offers one battleship, and two if necessary, as an addition to the guardian fleet of the Homeland," was flashed to an astonished and satisfied people along the floor of the ocean, the rule of which had been contested, at least tacitly. New Zealand's offer fired the imagination of all classes in Great Britain, and even struck the tumultuous thoughts of other nations. It was acknow-ledged with warmth of gratitude by king, lords and commons, by the imperial government officially, and by the leading corporations of the country ; and the offer of not only New Zealand but of the Australian Commonwealth and the Aus-tralian states of their notable gifts has been duly recorded in the archives and the heart of the empire.

Oceania. In Papua (formerly known as British New Guinea and now a depen-dency of the Australian Commonwealth) there have been further discoveries of gold, and new valuable discoveries of copper ; and an ordinance has been passed by the Papuan Council " to en-courage the natives in habits of industry." The long-standing dispute between the German Government and British traders in the Marshall Islands has been amicably settled, and the latter have received compensation. The convention between Great Britain and France, which settled the division of interest between the two

countries in the New Hebrides, came into force on December 1st, 1907, by a pro-clamation made by Sir Everard Im Thurn, high commissioner for the Western Pacific ; and a joint court for the ad-ministration of justice has been appointed. The islands, moreover, have derived con-siderable benefit from the existence of a settled administration.

INDIA

Not since the Mutiny has India bulked so largely in the contemporary history of the British Empire as during the past eighteen months or two years. Since the close of our historical survey in 1907 there has been a sinister increase in the number of riots and manifestations of sedition in widely scattered districts of the Indian Peninsula. In some places in the Bombay Presidency the military had to be employed in restoring order, but it was in Bengal that the most serious indications of a deep-seated political unrest appeared. There has not been anything like a concocted mutiny, even on a small scale, like that of 1857, either amongst the native troops or segregated numbers of the civil population, but only solitary acts of revolt against the ruling authorities. These, however, have been regarded in some quarters as the har-bingers or the preparations for more audacious and wider plans of rebellion.

The most sinister augury was the attempt to assassinate Sir Andrew Fraser, Lieu-tenant-Governor of Bengal, by a bomb. Shells were also thrown at railway trains, fortunately with little loss of life ; but greater horror was, in May, 1908, created by the cruel murder of Mrs. and Miss Kennedy by an explosive thrown at the private carriage in which they were driving in open daylight along the roadway at Muzafferpur. Numerous arrests were made, and a large quantity of bombs and seditious literature seized in Calcutta and other large cities, which showed how widespread and formidable the anarchical conspiracy was. The Legislative Council took speedy means to deal with the grave situation. Two bills were rapidly passed.

One was directed against the manufacture or possession of explosives, and the other dealt with Press offences, such as instiga-tion to murder or outrage. The latter contained provisions for confiscating the plant of newspapers against which a con-viction was obtained. The murder of witnesses who had given evidence against prisoners tried for these crimes, and especially of an approver named Gossain, in the gaol at Alipur, a second attempt at the assassination of Sir Andrew Fraser in a public meeting in Calcutta, and the murder of a Bengal inspector of police who had been active in tracing the members of the conspiracy, induced further repressive measures to be taken by the viceroy and his advisers.

The Legislative Council, on December 11th, 1908, at a single sitting passed the Indian Criminal Law Amendment Act, which became immediately operative in the provinces of Bengal and Eastern Bengal and Assam, and which might be extended by the governor-general-in-council to any part of India. There are special stringent provisions for dealing with sedition, murder, outrages and disturbances of the public peace ; while a special procedure for trying prisoners in the High Court by a bench of three judges without a jury is also provided. The act likewise gives extensive powers for dealing with unlawful associations. Many persons, believed to be leaders in the seditious agitation, were promptly arrested and deported, or placed in confinement without trial under Regulation 3 of 1818.

A durbar of vast historical importance and interest was held at Jodhpur on November 2nd, 1908, which date was the fiftieth anniversary of the assumption by the Crown of the direct government of India. At this assembly the viceroy, Earl Minto, read a message from the king-emperor "To the princes and peoples of India." This momentous state document repeated and confirmed the declaration and assurance contained in Queen Victoria's message of 1858 when assuming the sovereignty, and, after pointing out in some detail the evidences of the material prosperity of India during the last half century, his Imperial Majesty went on to pay, in language of dignified sincerity and lofty sentiment surpassed by no state document in the annals of any nation, tribute to the loyalty of the feudatory chiefs and the native army, and to the work of the world-famous and unique Indian Civil Service. Of course, reference was made to the seditious agitation and disorders that had recently occurred in certain parts of India, and the necessity for their firm suppression ; but the imperial message went on in the same

noble strain to add that such unhappy events would not deter his Majesty from giving effect to the plans of reform to be formulated by the Secretary of State in co-operation with the viceroy and government of India.

In redemption of the promises contained in the latter part of the message, Lord Morley, Secretary for India, on December 17th, 1908, expounded in a memorable speech his Indian Reform measure. In briefest outline it was that no attempt would be made to set up parliamentary institutions in India, or anything which would lead to them. Nor was there to be any material change in the general system of government. But the people of India were to be admitted to a wider share in the government of the country by the enlargement of the powers of legislative councils, provincial and central. Native members were to be nominated both to the provincial and executive councils, and to the Executive Council of the Viceroy. The scheme met with almost unanimous favour both among the native princes and peoples and in the British community.

When the imperial parliament met, the measure embodying Lord Morley's scheme was introduced into the House of Lords and passed, with the exception of the third clause, which gave power to set up new provincial councils. The clause was restored in the House of Commons, but was finally amended in the Lords, so that no new council should be set up without the scheme being first laid before both Houses of Parliament. The next step was the appointment of Mr. Sinha, an eminent member of the Indian Bar, and a man of distinguished learning, eloquence and lofty character, as the first native member of the Viceroy's Council.

So far it was hoped that these measures, generous beyond record in the history of a governing race to the congeries of conquered peoples which make up the hundreds of millions of dwellers in British India, would have arrested the spirit of sedition and the cultivation of political murder as a brutal art. But these hopes were dashed, though not, it is firmly trusted, utterly blasted, by a fiendish transfer of the stage of premeditated assassination from India to the heart of the empire

The foul murder of Lieutenant-Colonel Sir William Hutt Curzon Wyllie, K.C.I.E., C.V.O., political A.D.C. to Lord Morley, Secretary of State for India, on the evening of July 1st, 1909, in the hall of the Imperial Institute, London, came as a shock of surprise and indignation, while compassion and sorrow stirred the feeling of the people in these islands in a greater degree than any public event since the assassination of Lord Frederic Cavendish and Mr. Burke in the Phœnix Park, Dublin, on May 6th, 1882, or the shooting of Mr. Spencer Perceval in the Lobby in the House of Commons on May 11th, 1812.

That feeling had instant and sympathetic response in India, in every centre of civilisation in the West, in the distant southern hemisphere, and in the Farthest East. For Sir Curzon Wyllie stood high in the regard of his sovereign, in the confidence of his political superiors, in the esteem and honour of an ever-widening circle of friends in every quarter of the globe, and in the tenderest affection of his domestic hearth. And the pity of the dark deed was increased by the fact that his murder was accompanied by that of a distinguished Parsee physician, who had nothing whatever to do with the political government of India, and was only in this country on holiday from his home in China.

For nearly half a century ambitious natives of India of various nationalities have made it their business to come to British universities with the object of acquiring the learning of the West, of studying for the Bar, or for the practice of medicine, engineering and other professions. London, Oxford, Cambridge, Edinburgh, have their circle of students in sufficient numbers to form clubs. It is not believed that more than a very few of these students were permeated with thoughts of revolt against British rule in India. On the contrary, the vast majority were known to be as staunch as their profession in their loyalty. Some time ago, with the view of surrounding native Indian students in this country with good influences, a society was formed under the name of the Native Indian Association, by ex-Indian officials and friends of India, and of this association Sir Curzon Wyllie was treasurer. It held meetings and social functions, and promoted intercourse between earnest and loyal native students and their English friends. It had the friendly sanction of the authorities of the India Office, as was shown by the official position of Sir Curzon Wyllie. It was at an " At Home " of the association that the tragedy occurred.

The function was a brilliant one and the company were dispersing after a happy evening spent in the gorgeous Jehangir Hall of the Imperial Institute, South Kensington, which had been built and decorated, there is a pathetic irony in reflecting, by an eminent Parsee, a native of India. Sir Curzon Wyllie, as he was leaving, was accosted in the vestibule by a young engineering student named Madar Lal Dhingra, with whom he had been in communication, and before anyone could effectively intervene, the wretched youth drew a revolver, and at close quarters fired at Sir Curzon Wyllie's face four or five shots. Death was instantaneous. A fifth shot took effect on Dr. Cawas Lalcaca, who had made a gallant attempt to arrest the hand of the assassin, and who died on being removed to the hospital.

Madar Lal Dhingra attempted to shoot himself, but the pistol missed fire, and, on being seized and searched, a second fully loaded revolver and dagger knife were found upon him. When charged at the police-court on the following morning, the prisoner made no response, except to say that he did not intend to murder Dr. Lalcaca. Dhingra was sentenced to death at the Central Criminal Court on July 22nd. Expressions of condolence with Lady Wyllie were sent by the king and queen, Lord Morley and the Premier, while repudiations of all sympathy or association with the crime were at once forthcoming from the father of the prisoner, Dr. Dhingra, Allahabad, meetings of Indian students and others, Mohammedans as well as Hindus, and from leaders of the so-called reform movements in England and India.

North=West Frontier. At the end of 1907 and beginning of 1908 there were repeated raids across the frontier from Afghanistan, of Zakka Khels, Afridis and Mohmands. These tribes were punished by two brilliant expeditions of native and British troops, led by General Sir James Willcocks, in February and May of the latter year. Operations took place mainly in the Bazar Valley.

Afghanistan. A plot originated in Kabul in March of 1909 among some members of the old Shere Ali faction, to cause an outbreak against the authorities of the amir, Habid Ullah Khan, to murder him on a journey he was about to make from Kabul to Jellalabad, and also to murder the heir-apparent, Inaya Ullah Khan, and the brother of the amir. The plot was discovered, two of the conspirators were blown from guns, while the others met their death by execution.

Tibet. A convention between Great Britain and China relating to the affairs of Tibet was signed at Calcutta on April 20th, 1909. Its main provisions are that the trade regulations of 1893 are to remain in force, except where specially modified. Provision is made for the trial of disputes between British subjects and Tibetans and Chinese. China undertakes to protect the telegraph line from India to Gyantse, Great Britain undertaking to consider the question of making over the line to China when her telegraph system reaches that point. British officers and subjects are prohibited from travelling in Tibet, without permission, otherwise than to and from trade marts ; and the protection of travellers on these routes is made incumbent on the local authorities. The regulations are to remain in force for ten years, and are then to be terminable at six months' notice.

PERSIA

In our sketch of Persia, which was brought down to the beginning of 1908, it was stated that the Shah Mohammed Ali had brought his country to the edge of a revolution. At the present moment it is in a state of complete anarchy. The reconciliation between the shah and the mejliss (the national assembly) was only a blind for plots and counter-plots. In February, 1908, an attempt was made to assassinate the shah by a bomb thrown beneath his motor-car. Disorder followed. The old Cabinet, under Nazin-es-Sultanah, was supplanted by another under Mushir-es-Sultanah, who, however, proved a minister of reaction. The shah fled from his capital ; the House of Assembly in Teheran was bombarded by the shah's troops in June, who then looted the city, and hanged two of the leaders of the popular party. The mejliss was dissolved by a manifesto, and martial law was established in the capital.

On his return to Teheran, the shah repeatedly declared his intention of maintaining the constitution, but a new mejliss was not elected. Later in the year the shah solemnly abolished the constitution, whereupon an identical note was presented by the representatives of Great Britain and Russia, disclaiming any intention of interfering in the internal affairs of Persia, but advising the shah to re-establish constitutional rule as the only effectual means of restoring order. The provinces broke into complete anarchy. The important city of Tabriz was taken possession of by the revolutionaries, and royalist troops surrounded and bombarded it. Again joint representations were made to the shah by England and Russia to restore constitutional rule, and grant a general amnesty, and a force of Russian troops was sent to Tabriz to protect the foreigners and the 100,000 starving population.

Meanwhile, the numerous and well-armed Bakhtiari tribes, under a chief named Sirdar-as-Sad, joined the revolutionaries, or Nationalists, as they called themselves, under Sipahdar, and advanced towards Teheran, where a stiff battle was fought between the royal forces and the Nationalists—the latter obtaining the victory with comparatively little loss and practically no fatal results to the European population, and taking possession of the capital on July 16th, 1909. In the meantime, the Russian Government had dispatched a strong force of troops from Baku to Kasvin, eighty-six miles from Teheran, with assurance to the Great Powers that they would retire immediately on the safety of the foreign diplomatic representatives, and their nationals and institutions being assured. On July 17th, the shah sought refuge in the Russian Legation—a step which his Majesty distinctly stated, through the British and Russian Ministers, was an act of abdication.

A national assembly, composed of the chief mujtehids and notables and of the Nationalist chiefs, proclaimed the crown prince as shah, and appointed Azad-ul-Mulk, who is the head of the Kajar tribe, as regent. The new shah, only eleven years of age, but a very bright lad, is Ahmed Mirza, known as Valiahd, the second son of Mohammed Ali Shah, the eldest son not being eligible as heir-apparent because his mother is not a Kajar princess. The Sipahdar was appointed Minister and Governor of Teheran. Strong protests have been made in the British Parliament against the dispatch of the Russian forces to Persia, and in view of the report that a Council of the Empire of Russia, convened on July 5th by the Premier, M. Stolypin, had decided " to maintain by all possible means Russian prestige in Persia."

Arabia. There have been the usual tribal revolts in the Yemen, but these, for the most part, have been promptly checked by the Turkish garrison. By far the most interesting event in the period covered by our footnote was the opening, in September, 1908, of the railway constructed by Turkish soldiers as a religious duty and from subscriptions given by Mohammedans in all parts of the world, from Damascus to Medina. The main line is 750 miles in length. The opening ceremony was performed by the governor-general of Arabia, Kiazim Pasha, with wonderful demonstrations of religious enthusiasm; and among the banners were many bearing the strange device for despotic and fanatical Arabia—"Liberty, Equality and Fraternity."

Since then the railway has been attacked at several points by various tribes, and the garrisons for the defence of the line have had to be strengthened. A branch is in course of construction to connect Aleppo with the proposed Anatolian and Bagdad railway, and another to run to Mecca with a loop to the port of Jeddah on the Red Sea. These railways will no doubt result in consolidating the power of the Central Turkish Government in Arabia.

Asiatic Turkey and Asia Minor. In the north-west of Asiatic Turkey Kurdish tribes under Ibrahim Pasha seized the opportunity of the revolt of the Young Turk Party in Constantinople against Abdul Hamid to raid Nestorian and Armenian villages. There was also an outbreak in favour of the old régime at Mosul in the Euphrates Valley. Simultaneously with Abdul Hamid's final *coup d'état* there was a terrible outbreak of Moslem fanaticism in Asia Minor against the Christian population, in which Turkish troops enlisted under the old régime unquestionably took part. The greatest massacres occurred at and around Adana, Mersina, Larnaca and Aleppo, and official reports of the foreign consuls state that throughout the province 30,000 Christians, mostly Armenians and Nestorians, were killed, while 35,000 inhabitants were rendered homeless.

The Christian quarters in Hadjin and Tarsus were also looted and fired. In all the places mentioned the destruction of property was almost complete, and the looting soldiers paid no respect to the property of foreigners. American schools and mission stations and French schools and convents were destroyed. The Constantinople Government, on the accession of Mohammed V., dispatched troops from Salonica to restore order, and the sultan made a large subscription from his Civil List towards the relief funds which had been raised in America and England for feeding, clothing and sheltering the victims.

EGYPT

Since our detailed history of the land of the Pharaohs appeared, a general census was taken which showed that the total population of Egypt in 1908 was 11,287,359, as against 9,717,228 in 1897, or an average of 939 inhabitants per square mile. Of the population, 91·8 are Mussulmans, and 41 per cent. of the male population are engaged in agriculture. Sir Eldon Gorst, in his report to the British Foreign Office, states that the revenue for the year was £E15,522,000 and the expenditure £E14,408,000. The outstanding capital debt amounted to £95,834,000. The economic crisis continues, and the value of the imports fell a million, while the exports were nearly £6,000,000 short in value. Cotton, which forms the largest export, amounted in value to £E17,092,000.

Sir Eldon Gorst, in his general review, states that "the general movement against autocratic government in the neighbouring Mohammedan countries has not been without its effect upon the state of public opinion in Egypt. There is a limited but gradually increasing class which interests itself in matters pertaining to the government and administration of the country, and aspires, quite rightly, to help in bringing about the day when Egypt will be able to govern itself without outside assistance." This, Sir Eldon Gorst declares, is also the end to which British policy is directed; but, in his opinion, Egypt is by no means yet ripe for a parliamentary régime.

Parenthetically, it may be stated that a great "national demonstration" in Cairo, held in April, attended by 3,000 people, and at which incendiary speeches were made against Ministers and the British army of occupation, was dispersed by using the hose of the fire-engines on the demonstrators. While the non-official and educated classes had been somewhat restless in British leading strings, the masses of the people were contented and happy with a progressive agriculture and a greater supply of water, which is the very life of the fellaheen, rendered possible by the erection of more barrages and the regulation of the supply of the Nile floods for irrigation purposes.

The Esneh barrage, erected in Upper Egypt, a hundred miles north of Assouan, at a cost of a million pounds, was opened by the khedive on February 9th, 1909. This barrage will save the province of Keneh from all danger of drought, and bring a large area of land under cultivation. Sterling progress has been made under the régime of the sirdar, Sir Francis Wingate, in consolidating the Anglo-Egyptian power in the Sudan. In April the khedive opened the new port and harbour on the Red Sea which are to form the commercial entrepôt for the Sudan, and are united with Berber and Khartoum by railway.

His Highness, in his speech at the ceremony, which was made the occasion of a large assemblage of Arab chiefs, said that the "port was a striking evidence of the great advance made in the Sudan, and would tend, by improving communication, to unite the more remote districts, enlarge the sphere of trade, and promote the development of the resources of the country, and thereby bring the blessings of peace and prosperity to the inhabitants." The Blue Nile has been bridged at Khartoum, and the railway is to be carried southward in order to tap the great gum forests of Kordofan. The Moslems have built a mosque in Khartoum at a cost of £30,000, and the Copts have completed a grand cathedral. Sir Francis Wingate has made an appeal in England for subscriptions for the erection of an Anglican cathedral, and his Majesty the King sent in the early days of July a donation thereto of two hundred guineas.

NORTH AFRICA

Nothing has to be added to our history of Tunis and Algiers. The centre of interest lies in Morocco. The late Sultan Abd-el-Aziz met with his Waterloo at Marrakesh at the hands of his half-brother, Mulai Hafid, who thereupon entered Fez, where he seized, without further opposition, the reins of government. Abd-el-Aziz escaped to Stettat, where the French forces under General d'Amade were concentrated.

This happened in August, 1908. Immediately after, Mulai Hafid was proclaimed sultan at Tangier, and he made it known that he would accept the Algeciras Act and be responsible for the debts of the maghzen. The European Powers recognised him as sultan, both *de facto* and *de jure,* and Abd-el-Aziz was banished. The French troops, who had been aligned along the Algerian frontier in the neighbourhood of Casa Blanca, at one time numbered 15,000, but were reduced in December, 1908, to 3,000. The difficulty which had arisen between France and Germany with regard to the desertion of Germans from the French Foreign Legion and their capture by the French troops from the German Consulate in Casa Blanca was settled by a reference to the Hague Convention and by the expression of mutual regrets. It seemed as if Morocco at last had settled down, but new complications suddenly arose in the middle of June, 1909.

A new competitor for the throne appeared in El Roghi, said to be Mulai Mohammed, the One-Eyed Khalifa, eldest son of Mulai Hassan, and brother of Abd-el-Aziz, the late sultan. With a large following of tribesmen he met the forces of Mulai Hafid only a few miles distant from Fez, and completely defeated them in several engagements. His troops are accused of inflicting horrible injuries on dying and wounded enemies.

A report, dated July 13th, 1909, stated that El Roghi had stormed and looted Fez, but the fate of Mulai Hafid is unknown. El Roghi is not the only Richmond in the field. The sultan's brother, Mulai Hebir, has succeeded in raising an army, and also threatens to march on Fez. A third candidate for the throne, Bu Hamara, the Pretender, as he has been called, is encamped with a large force south of Fez, and Abd-el-Aziz has once more reappeared from banishment and makes a second bid for the throne from which he had been displaced. In fact, Morocco is in a state of anarchy, and may produce an embroglio among some of the European Powers.

Abyssinia. The Emperor Menelik has had his difficulties with frontier and outlying tribes, involving negotiations with the British and Italian Governments. These have been settled. A convention between Abyssinia and Italy has defined the limits of Italian Somaliland and Daucalia. The Emperor Menelik has nominated a successor in the person of Lidj Eyassa, a son of Ras Mikhael. He has also appointed a Cabinet Council.

The Congo. After long debate in the Belgian Parliament, the bill to transfer the sovereignty of the Congo from the Free State, *i.e.*, from the personal sway of King Leopold, to Belgium was carried in September, 1908. But, according to the Berlin Act the assumption of sovereignty by Belgium has to be notified to the signatory Powers in case they have any objection. It is alleged that the old atrocities under the Leopold régime are continued as badly as ever. Germany has recognised the annexation; but before the British Government consents to this, Sir Edward Grey, the Foreign Secretary, insists upon guarantees being given by the Belgian Government for the better treatment of the natives. His latest dispatch, issued on June 11th, 1909, takes a firm stand on the question of forced labour and taxation in kind, which is, in fact, as he puts it, " indistinguishable from slavery." The latest proposal, however, of the Belgian Government is the establishment in one of the provinces of the Congo territory of a model colony based on economic development, where the colonial system which Great Britain desires to see established throughout the country might be given a trial.

Nigeria. The development of both Northern and Southern Nigeria is progressing by leaps and bounds. The extension of the railway to Kano and Iloru is being pushed forward. In the beginning of 1909, when the German and British Commissions were delimiting the frontier between the British Protectorate and the German possessions near Lake Chad and the Kameruns, they were attacked by the natives, and they fought side by side during military operations, which lasted several days.

SOUTH AFRICA

The remarkable feature in connection with public life in South Africa during the past two years has been the gradual softening of the racial feeling between Briton and Boer. General Botha, Premier of the Transvaal, has done much to smooth over matters by the cordial recognition of the supreme generosity of the imperial government in conceding self-government to the Transvaal and Orange River Colony.

The seemingly impassable gulf between the two sections of the people in all the four colonies has been bridged by the judicious action of the leaders of both parties; and the gratifying result is that the Boers as

well as the Britons are inspired by an almost passionate loyalty to the British connection. Dr. Jameson, the erstwhile protagonist of British supremacy, has publicly admitted this. " Of course," he said, in June, 1909, " the racial feeling still lingers to a certain extent among the ignorant and badly informed people; but even among these there are marked signs of its disappearance as they see that the leaders of both parties are of one accord. Among these latter it has absolutely disappeared." There were economic as well as sentimental reasons for this remarkable and desirable change.

In the Cape Colony finances there was a deficit of £3,000,000; and at the general election in 1908, when Mr. Merriman was returned to power by a large majority of the Bond party, defeating Dr. Jameson, he took that as a mandate to form a united South Africa, judging that the only way out of the difficulties of the colony was reform of finance, economy in administration, and closer union of all the colonies. The Transvaal was recovering from the long continued depression, aided by a large increase in the gold output and the abundance of native labour following the repatriation of the Chinese; while agriculture was prosperous in both Natal and the Orange River Colony.

The course of events which led up to the union was as follows. A conference of representatives of the four colonies met at Pretoria, and afterwards at Cape Town, and recommended the election of a national convention to consider the issues underlying the federation or unification of the South African colonies. This convention met on October 12th, 1908, at Durban, when a message was read from the king, expressing his Majesty's deep interest in the subject of the convention, and conveying his cordial good wishes for the success of the deliberations of the delegates in their efforts to advance the common good of South Africa.

The imperial government also sent a message on behalf of the people of the United Kingdom. The convention was held with closed doors; but a unanimous vote was taken on the fundamental principle of union, and then the convention adjourned to meet in Cape Town. There, after prolonged deliberation, extending into the beginning of 1909, a draft bill was prepared " for the union of those colonies which might assent thereto, and for the eventual admission into the union as provinces or territories of such parts of South Africa as are not originally included therein."

The draft bill embodying the constitution was afterwards submitted to the parliaments of the different colonies. It was adopted by the Cape House of Assembly with only two dissentients ; unanimously by the Transvaal and Orange Parliaments. The Natal Parliament passed an act referring the decision to the whole body of the electorate, with the result that 11,121 votes were cast for union and 3,701 against—a majority of 7,420. The convention again met at Bloemfontein, and the constitution was signed by all the delegates ; and all that remains now is its final adoption by the imperial parliament and the sign-manual of the king.

The constitution provides for a governor-general, an executive council to advise him, and officers, members of the executive council, to administer the departments of state. The parliament will consist of (1) the king, whose assent to legislative measures will be required ; (2) a senate, partly nominated and partly elected—a property qualification being proposed for the elected senators ; (3) a house of assembly, consisting of members chosen directly by the voters of the four provinces. The number of members for each province will be proportioned to the number of voters. Each member will receive a salary of £400 a year. Each province shall have an administrator, appointed for five years by the governor-general, and a council, whose members shall be elected by the voters. Each council shall elect from three to five persons to form with the administrator an administrative committee. The duties of the provincial councils will relate to finance, education, local institutions, roads and other local matters. Free trade will be maintained throughout the union. Detailed provision is made for the administration of justice by a supreme court of South Africa, and various courts in the provinces. The financial arrangements include the formation of a railway and harbour fund and a consolidated reserve fund.

As soon as possible after the union a commission will be appointed to inquire into what financial arrangements should exist between the union and the provinces, temporary arrangements being provided in the draft constitution. All harbours, ports and railways belonging to the colonies are to vest in the governor-general, and the sanction of parliament will be required for new ports, harbours or railways. A practical commission will control and manage the railways and ports. Both Dutch and English will be official languages. Native affairs are to be administered by the governor-general in council. Finally, provision is made for the repeal or alteration, under specified conditions, of any of the provisions of the act of parliament completing the union.

In regard to other matters of historic interest in South Africa, the leading facts are : An agreement was concluded in April between the Transvaal Government and the Portuguese Government of Mozambique, appointing a joint board of control for the management of the port of Delagoa Bay and the railway thence to Pretoria and Johannesburg, and fixing the share of the railway traffic between these points. It provides also for free trade in local products between the two countries. The Portuguese Government undertakes to facilitate recruiting operations in Mozambique of native labour for the Transvaal mines, and the Transvaal Government undertakes to repatriate the labourers. The agreement is for ten years.

In Natal an Indemnity Act was passed for the proclamation by the executive government of martial law during the native troubles. The trial of Dinizulu for high treason and abetting treason, by a specially appointed court, consisting of Mr. Justice Smith and two commissioners, excited great interest in Natal and in England. The trial lasted seventy days, beginning on November 19th, 1908, and ending on March 4th, 1909. Two hundred witnesses were examined, and the indictment consisted of twenty-three counts. The court found Dinizulu guilty of harbouring Bambaata's family during the native rising, and a number of rebels after the rebellion. Dinizulu was sentenced on the former charge to a fine of £100, or to undergo twelve months imprisonment, and on the latter charge to four years imprisonment— the sentence to take effect from the date of Dinizulu's arrest fifteen months before.

German South African Colonies. The British and German Governments have asked King Alfonso of Spain to act as arbitrator in the long-standing dispute regarding the boundaries between Walfish Bay in German South-west Africa and the Cape Colony territory.

RUSSIA

Our detailed review of historic events in Russia was brought down to May 1st, 1909. An important bill, dealing with the navy and curtailing the prerogatives of the tsar, was passed by both chambers of the Duma. To this bill the tsar definitely refused his assent on May 11th, and at the same time refused to accept the resignation of the Premier, M. Stolypin. His Imperial Majesty, however, issued a rescript which charged Ministers to draw up rules which would determine what legislative affairs of the war and marine departments were subject to his Majesty's immediate decision, and what were to be submitted for his sanction. The meaning of this is that the rules are to decide what the tsar can do in virtue of his prerogatives, and what may be subject to discussion and agreement by the Duma.

A government bill was introduced early in June into the Duma to transform a part of Eastern Poland into a Russian government. The measure was hotly opposed by the Polish deputies and the Socialists ; and, although they could not secure its rejection, the bill was shelved by being remitted to a committee. No other business of outside interest was done by the Duma, and on its prorogation the leading members paid a visit to Great Britain, which is referred to in another section. A Russo-Finnish commission has been appointed to delimit imperial from Finnish local legislation. It held a meeting in the last week of June, 1909, when an extraordinary scene occurred. M. Kharitonoff, on behalf of the Council of the Empire, in opening the sitting, said that a reorganisation of the legislative relations between Russia and Finland was absolutely necessary. Thereupon Archbishop Johannson, a Finnish member, declared that the Finnish nation prized most highly, next to the Gospel, their constitution ; and he insisted that in any change in Finnish law the fundamental laws of Finland and its constitution should not be impaired. M. Dietrich, on behalf of the Russian members, insisted that, according to the fundamental laws of Russia, Finland was an inseparable part of Russia, and the latter had only legislative power in regard to internal affairs. There was an impasse, and the Finnish members being unable or unwilling to speak Russian, the views of the members were agreed to be taken in writing at some future date.

The eyes of Europe were directed to the meeting early in June, 1909, of the tsar and German Emperor on board the Russian royal yacht, which was anchored in one of the bays of the Finnish Skerries in the upper reaches of the Gulf of Finland, whither the emperor had voyaged in his own yacht, the Hohenzollern. Curiously enough, the Emperor William gave the only authentic account of what took place at the meeting of the two powerful sovereigns. Addressing a meeting at Cuxhaven on June 22nd, immediately on his return from the interview, the Emperor William, after referring to the "warm and hospitable reception given him by the Emperor of All the Russias," said : "The Tsar Nicholas and I agreed that our meeting is to be regarded as a vigorous re-enforcement of the cause of peace. We feel ourselves, as monarchs, responsible to our God for the joys and sorrows of our people, whom we desire to lead forward as far as possible on the path of peace, and to raise to their full development. All peoples need peace, in order, under its protection, to fulfil undisturbed the duties of civilisation for their economic and commercial development. We will both, therefore, continually endeavour, as far as lies in our power, to work, with God's help, for the furtherance and maintenance of peace."

TURKEY

The old régime in Turkey has vanished even more completely than the most sanguine reformer of less than a decade ago could have hoped or dreamt of. The Young Turk, with his striving for the light of the Western world, has come into his own, and the spirit of the East which has brooded over the empire of the kalif, with its seat on the Golden Horn, since the fall of Byzantium, has taken flight. There was infinite disquietude in Constantinople towards the end of March. The air was full of terror, murder was rife, suspicion reigned in parliament, where no born leader seemed capable of taking occasion by the forelock and at the same time ruling with a sense of responsibility the elected chamber and defying the intriguing despot of Yildiz. On April 13th, 1909, a military revolt suddenly broke out. Two battalions of troops surrounded the parliament house. The Minister of Justice was killed; the Minister of Marine wounded; Kiamil, the unready Premier, resigned; Tewfik, a man of action at least, was appointed Grand Vizir. Abdul Hamid had accomplished his coup with apparent success. The sultan issued a decree granting a general amnesty to the revolting and murdering troops, adding, with characteristic hypocrisy, his intention of a strict observance of the Sheri law and the preservation of the constitution. The troops kept the astonished and terrified inhabitants of Constantinople awake the whole night by firing a *feu de joie* every few minutes.

The committee of the Young Turk party, at a meeting at Salonika, decided on resistance to Abdul's counter revolt; and the Third Army Corps stationed there proceeded at once on its march to Constantinople under Shevket Pasha, commander-in-chief at Salonika. San Stefano was reached on the 20th, on which day the national assembly, which had changed its venue from Constantinople to that pretty town on the shores of the Sea of Marmora, historically interesting as the scene of the signing of the Treaty of Peace at the close of the Russo-Turkish War in 1878, decreed the deposition of Abdul Hamid.

On the following day Abdul paid a visit to the mosque near Yildiz, and, contrary to all precedent, made an appearance at the windows of the Kiosk to receive the paid plaudits of the troops, whom he had bribed with £T100,000, and numerous softas, among whom he had distributed £T10,000. That night Shevket's troops secretly seized the outposts of Constantinople, vacated by the sultan's troops during the Selamlik. Just at dawn Constantinople was attacked by Shevket's army in three columns.

The most serious opposition was met with at Tashkislla and Taxim barracks, near the sultan's palace of Yildiz, which were defended with fanatical bravery for some time, and only captured with the assistance of artillery and maxims; and many hundreds were killed and wounded. The whole operation was planned and carried out with consummate skill and wonderful bravery. The city was in possession of Shevket and his highly disciplined troops, a strong detachment of which surrounded Yildiz for the purpose of preventing the escape of the sultan. The national assembly returned to Stamboul on the 26th, and appointed Essad Pasha and Carasso Effendi, deputies, with Ahran Effendi and Arif Pasha, senators, a deputation to announce to Abdul Hamid his deposition and effect his arrest. The scene at Yildiz when the deputation arrived to discharge their commission presented the action and the emotion of historical drama. Abdul, who had taken refuge in an inner chamber of the harem, was pale, and trembling with terror, asked: "What do you want? Do you want my life?" Essad Pasha said: "We have come to inform you that in virtue of the Fetva of the Sheri, countersigned by the Sheik-ul-Islam, the nation dethrones you." The sultan said: "May God confound those who have been the cause of this misfortune." Whereupon Carasso Effendi rejoined: "Yes, God is just; and we may be certain that he will confound the guilty."

The sultan, trembling: "I have reigned for thirty-three years; but I have done ill to nobody. Why do you want my life? I made war with Greece successfully; why then do you want my life? For thirty years I have treated my brother Mamoud well; any other sultan would have had him killed. So why do you want my life?" Whining pitifully: "Only let me live, and I will do all you wish."

Then he sank down in a state of collapse on the divan. Think of this man who was responsible for the massacres of hundreds of thousands of Bulgarians, Armenians, and even of his own race in almost every part of his empire, pleading pitifully for his life on the ground that he had done ill to nobody; he had not even killed his brother! There was nothing heroic about this man. When stripped of his tinsel talents, his petty soul was laid bare. The only touch of pathos about the whole scene was his cry: "Take me to the palace of Cheragan with my family. I was born there; let me die there."

The deposed sultan was afterwards conveyed to Salonika, where he is now confined as a prisoner in a spacious villa.

Rechad Effendi, the late sultan's younger brother, was proclaimed sultan, under the title of Mohammed V., and on May 2nd, 1909, his Highness issued an imperial hatt, in which he said:

"By the will of the Eternal, who is above all monarchs, I have been raised to the throne of my ancestors, in accordance with the stipulations of the constitution and the unanimous wish of the whole Ottoman people." Having set forth that the grand vizirate had been conferred upon Tewfik Pasha, the hatt went on to say : " The aim of my government will always be to guarantee liberty, equality and justice to all my subjects, and to apply the Sheriat Law and the codes of the state in their entirety in order that the foundations of the empire may be strengthened." His first duty would be to suppress disorder, to take measures to enable " the different nationalities of the empire to live in concord as befits the children of the fatherland, so that they may enjoy the benefits of liberty, equality and justice."

Determination is expressed to improve the condition of the land and sea forces, improve the administration of justice and finance, and to provide the provinces with schools. Commerce, industry and agriculture are to be encouraged. Treaties with foreign Powers are confirmed, and are to be conscientiously observed, and good, friendly relations with them are to be strengthened. So ends the story of the wonderful counter revolution of Abdul Hamid and his downfall. Mohammed V. was, with imposing ceremony, invested with the Sword of Osman on May 10th, and ten days later he visited the Turkish Parliament, witnessed the deputies taking the oath of loyalty to himself and the constitution, and handed to the grand vizir his speech from the throne. In that speech his Majesty expressed the conviction that the progress and prosperity of the country depended upon the maintenance of the constitution. He deeply regretted the recent disorders at Adana, the authors of which would be punished severely. The remainder of the speech dealt with the necessity of reform in every department of the state.

It need only be said that the subject of Crete was vigorously debated in the national assembly on June 21st, 1909, when insistence was made that when the international troops were withdrawn from the island, on July 27th, the sovereign rights of Turkey must be maintained.

Greece and the Balkan States. Greece pursues its peaceful development, except for occasional aspirations by irresponsible Hellenists after territorial extension in Lower Macedonia and the annexation of Crete ; neither of which, in the present mood of rejuvenated Turkey and the Great Powers, whose professed sole desire is peace, is likely to be realised. In the second week of July, 1909, a series of earthquakes shook the mainland on the western side of the Peloponnesus, and also in the islands of Crete and Canea. Several hundred people were killed and many villages completely destroyed.

All questions in dispute between Bulgaria and Turkey in regard to the independence of Bulgaria and the declaration of Ferdinand as king are now at an end. The protocol which settles the compensation to be paid to Turkey in lieu of tribute, and for the railways and the educational and Church property in Roumelia, was signed on April 19th, 1909, in the presence of the British, French and Russian ambassadors at Constantinople. King Ferdinand gave a banquet at Sofia to the diplomatic corps on May 1st to celebrate the auspicious event, and he asked his guests to transmit to their respective governments the sincere thanks of himself and his queen for their good wishes for his dynasty and the prosperity of his kingdom.

Servia. Servia passed through a period of turmoil during the spring of 1909. When Austria-Hungary assumed sovereign rights over Bosnia and Herzegovina, the government of Servia demanded territorial compensation and threatened war. The army was mobilised and aligned along the Bosnian frontier ; sympathy was felt by the Slavophiles in Russia, and many volunteers from that country joined the Servian Army. Pressure was brought to bear on Servia by the Great Powers to renounce its claim for territorial compensation, and by none more than the government of Great Britain through the Foreign Secretary, Sir Edward Grey.

Some time in March, Servia, in response to a note from Russia, agreed to abandon its territorial claim, but requested the Powers to grant it political and economic independence. This did not satisfy Baron von Aehrenthal, the Austro-Hungarian Minister of Foreign Affairs, and pressure was brought to bear by Germany upon Russia, which thereupon ceased to support Servian demands, a result which was regarded as a great diplomatic triumph for Germany. Eventually the terms of a formula were agreed upon by Sir Edward Grey and Baron von Aehrenthal, and accepted by all parties. Servia then demobilised its troops, as did Austria, and peace was secured. During the excitement over these events Prince George, the crown prince of Servia, intimated his renunciation of succession to the throne in favour of his younger brother, Alexander. The end of the Servian troubles is not yet. King Peter had an apoplectic fit in June, and fell from his horse; and an anti-dynastic proclamation had been circulated throughout the country declaring that King Peter and his family have forfeited the Servian throne.

GERMANY

Practically the recent history of Germany has been the debates on the navy, and the deficit in the imperial budget, which latter amounted to £25,000,000, caused by the extraordinary naval and military expenditure of late years. Prince Bülow, the German Chancellor, proposed in the Reichstag additional indirect taxes to the amount of £20,000,000, which were generally accepted, and to raise the additional £5,000,000 from land taxes on the unearned increment, and by succession duties. These latter were bitterly opposed by the Conservatives and Agrarian party, and in the parliamentary struggle Prince Bülow was defeated, and placed his resignation in the hands of the emperor. It is reported that a compromise has been arrived at in regard to land taxes which will enable the government to balance the Budget.

On July 13th, 1909, the resignation of Prince Bülow was finally accepted by the emperor, and Dr. von Bethmann-Hollweg appointed Imperial Chancellor. It was as Minister for the Interior for Prussia, that Dr. von Bethmann-Hollweg, who is descended from an old Dutch family of financiers, began his official career, and as successor to Posadowsky as Minister of the interior for Germany that he passed from Prussian to imperial politics. Prince Bülow stated on July 6th to a deputation from the Federal Council that "he handed over affairs to Dr. von Bethmann-Hollweg with a full confidence which was founded, not only on his recognition of the high gifts of his successor, but also with regard to his personal qualities."

During the spring and early summer the chief cities of Germany have given a wonderful manifestation of friendly good feeling towards the citizens of Great Britain. There have been visits and interchange of courtesies between the Burgomaster of Berlin and the Lord Mayor of London with members of their respective councils. Representatives of various associations in England, interested in workmen's dwellings and town planning, paid a visit to Cologne, Düsseldorf, Frankfort, Berlin and other cities with the object of seeing for themselves and studying the methods of municipal control of suburban extension. Everywhere they went they were received with cordiality, furnished with every information and plans, and entertained with gracious hospitality.

Then came the visit during the Whit Sunday recess of the English Labour parliamentary representatives. They, too, were received in the chief cities of Germany with hearty goodwill, not only by representatives of their own class, but by influential parliamentarians and government officials. Every facility was offered them, and they took full advantage of it to study the German system of labour exchanges and of the pension schemes which prevail in the different Germanic states.

But, in some respects, the most important party which visited Germany was that representing all the Christian Churches of Great Britain. It consisted of three bishops of the Church of England, several Catholic clergymen, the president of the Free Church Union, and many Nonconformist ministers. The party were conveyed to Hamburg from Dover in a special steamer, and their reception was kind and brotherly beyond measure by court chaplains, high-placed clergy of the Protestant Churches, representatives of the Roman Catholic hierarchy, and laymen of every religious persuasion.

Public meetings were held, at which the duty of the cultivation of peaceful relations between Germany and England was earnestly insisted upon, sermons in the same direction were preached, and services were held in churches and cathedrals in Berlin and in other cities.

But the crowning event in the Church Pilgrims' Progress was their reception at Potsdam on June 14th by the German Emperor and Empress, who had specially travelled from Kiel to meet them. His Imperial Majesty delighted the pilgrims by making a charming speech, in which he expressed the hope that this visit, like that of the previous year, would tend to promote good feeling between the two great kindred nations.

Holland. On April 30th, 1909, the Queen of Holland gave birth to a daughter in the Palace of the Woods, at the Hague. This proved an occasion of great rejoicing to the people of the Netherlands, not only on account of the youth and beauty of the young queen, but of the hopes which had been entertained by them during the eight years of her marriage with Duke Henry of Mecklenburg-Schwerin of a direct heir to the throne of William of Orange, who had a passionate dislike, amounting, one would almost say, to a horror, of the succession passing to a foreign prince. The sober, grave, matter-of-fact people of Holland for once cast off all their usual national characteristics, and the nation gave itself over to the most frantic joy.

Italy. There is nothing to add to the historic record of this country, except that earthquake shocks were renewed, with some loss of life, at Messina, where a beginning had been made in rebuilding the city. In the political sphere, the meeting of the king and the German Emperor at Brindisi had no further signification except as a proof that the Triple Alliance remains unshaken. Plans for the addition of several first-class battleships to the Italian Navy have been approved of.

FRANCE

The relations of France to other countries continue to be happy ; even the chaos in Morocco has ceased to cause excitement. There was a tendency in some quarters, after the massacres at Adana in Asia Minor, from which many French subjects and their property suffered, to reassert the old claim—a claim which ranked prominently among the causes which led to the Crimean War—that the protection of Christians in the Near East was the special right and duty of France.

Little, however, has been heard of it since a semi-official announcement in the German Press emphatically insisted that " each of the Powers has an exclusive right to protect its own subjects and proteges." In the Paris Press a French interviewer reported the German Emperor, whom he had seen at Kiel, as having expressed " satisfaction at the present condition of the relations between France and Germany, and declared that he was determined from the outset that the Casa Blanca incident should be amicably settled. France and Germany should only meet one another in the sphere of economics, industry and commerce." In home affairs, the Chamber of Deputies was engaged in tariff revision. The Minister of Marine, M. Picard, has presented a report on the state of the French Navy, and demanding votes for the year for the complete reorganisation of the ships, including new artillery, for shipbuilding, port extensions and general equipment amounting to £7,725,000.

Strict inquiry is to be made into recent accidents, to losses of various ships, and also into allegations of prevalent corruption in the navy. A shipbuilding programme has also been put forward, which provides for the construction of 45 vessels of large type, at a cost of £120,000,000.

Much excitement was caused, and some inconvenience to the whole country, by the strikes in March and May of the post and telegraph employees. An attempt was made by revolutionaries and anarchists to make use of the strikes for the purpose of overthrowing the existing régime ; but the government, under the Premier, M. Clemenceau, taking a firm stand, checked the strikes completely, while at the same time the grievances of the operatives were fairly met.

Spain. The record of Spain has been uneventful. The Cortes have passed a bill for the building of a new navy, and the contract for the same has, after long, sometimes acrimonious, discussion, been given to an Anglo-Spanish company. On June 22nd, 1909, her Majesty the Queen gave birth to a daughter at the Palace of La Granja. The queen-mother and the Princess Henry of Battenberg were with her Majesty. King Alfonso, dressed in the uniform of captain-general, presented the infant to ministers and other dignitaries in the ante-chamber, and received their hearty congratulations.

Portugal. The country is settling down under the new king. Certain differences have arisen in the Cortes, but these have been smoothed over. The only incident of external interest is the reform of the labour regulations in the colonial island of St. Thomé for the cocoa plantations. This reform has been rendered necessary by the action of British, German and American cocoa manufacturers refusing to purchase St. Thomé cocoa, which they alleged was grown under disgraceful slavery conditions.

Sweden and Norway. The only question that has arisen between these two countries since they peacefully dissolved partnership has been a slight dispute over the rights of nomad Lapps in their annual migration to pastures to and from Sweden and Norway. The matter is to be referred to arbitration.

THE UNITED KINGDOM

Since the close of our historical survey, two great questions have bulked in the public mind of the people of Great Britain—the fleet and the budget. The question of the fleet was first brought into prominence when the Navy Estimates were introduced into the House of Commons, showing a large increase over those of the previous year. In justification of this increase, both the First Lord of the Admiralty, Mr. McKenna, and, at a later stage, the Premier, Mr. Asquith, delivered weighty speeches, in which direct reference was made not only to the number of first-class battleships of the Dreadnought type which were being built in Germany under their shipbuilding programme, but to the acceleration at an unprecedented rate of construction in the German yards. Of course, this gave rise to demands by the Opposition for additional naval expenditure. The Government proposed to lay down at once four new Dreadnoughts, and under certain contingencies to lay other four later on in 1909, or at any rate to make preparations therefor.

The Opposition, led by Mr. Balfour, insisted that the activity in the German dockyards, and the rapid increase in the number and power of their new line-of-battle ships could only be directed against Great Britain, and was meant to challenge the supremacy of the ocean, held for centuries by Great Britain. They demanded that provision should be made for the beginning of the building in 1909 by this country of at least eight Dreadnoughts; otherwise, they alleged, this country would be in a position of naval inferiority to Germany in 1912, and possibly in 1914. On this question the Opposition moved a vote of censure on the Government, and statistics were produced by Mr. Balfour and others to prove this contention.

The Government had not only to meet the case of the Opposition, but to satisfy economists on their own side that their increased naval expenditure was absolutely necessary.

Sir Edward Grey, the Foreign Secretary, in the course of the debate, delivered a speech which caused something of a sensation, not only in this country, but in the colonies; and no doubt roused the latter to make the magnificent offer of assistance to which reference has already been made. "It is essential to us," he said, "that we should not fall into a position of inferiority. It is essential that we should keep, as regards our navy, a position of superiority. . . . If I were asked to name one thing which might reassure the world, or certainly Europe, with regard to the prospect of peace, it would be that the naval expenditure in Germany was being diminished; and that ours was following suit, and being diminished also."

He admitted "that when the German programme is completed, Germany, a great country close to our own shores, will have a fleet of 33 Dreadnoughts. That fleet will be the most powerful the world has ever seen. . . . There is no dispute as to the issue. In order to meet the German fleet when it is completed, we shall have to build a new fleet of our own more powerful than we have ever yet built." The vote of censure against the Government was defeated by 353 to 135. During the debates Mr. Asquith stated that his Government had approached that of Germany with a view to coming to some understanding as to mutual arrest of naval armaments, but that the German Government, clearly within their rights, did not see their way to accept the suggestion.

About this time, when the German naval programme was under discussion in the Reichstag Budget Commission, the Foreign Secretary, on behalf of Prince Bülow, made a statement that "the British Government let their readiness to enter into an Anglo-German understanding as to the scope and cost of the naval programme be known in a general way, but it made no formal proposition to that effect. No British proposal has ever been made which, in our opinion, could serve as a basis for official negotiations. Our legally established naval construction has been fixed solely in accordance with the requirements of our own defence; and, as has been repeatedly asseverated, involves no threat to any nation." Prince Bülow, a few days afterwards, reiterated the assurance that the German Navy was no special menace to Great Britain.

In spite of these statements, the battle of the Dreadnoughts went on in England. A great meeting was held in the City of London, and others in the country, to enforce the demand upon the Government to build this year eight and not four battleships; and the expression was common that every Englishman ought to be proud to spend his last shilling to maintain England in her traditional position of mistress of the seas. Admiral Lord Charles Beresford, after hauling down his flag as Commander-in-Chief of the Home Fleet, made an important speech in the City, in which he insisted that this country was unprepared for war; that in March, 1914, the Germans would have 21 Dreadnoughts and cruisers, as against 16 which Great Britain would have.

He maintained the immediate necessity of 10 battleships, 18 second-class cruisers, 18 commerce protection cruisers, 24 sea-going torpedo-boat destroyers, 52 torpedo-boat destroyers and 4 floating docks, with an addition of 16,000 men to the personnel of the fleet—the whole to cost £60,000,000.

As the Budget is under discussion at the time of writing, and likely to be for many months, it need not here be touched upon. In the last week of June there was a remarkable visitation to this country. It consisted of a delegation of members of the Russian Council of the Empire and the Russian Duma, headed by M. Nicholas A. Homyakoff, the President of the Duma. They had been invited by letter signed by the Archbishops of Canterbury and York; members of the House of Lords, headed by the Duke of Northumberland; members of the House of Commons, headed by Mr. Speaker; the Lord Mayor of London and Lord Provost of Edinburgh, and the mayors and provosts of the leading cities of England and Scotland; professors of universities; leading scientists and others.

The letter of invitation said that it was intended as a welcome from the British public to that of Russia, and that it seemed that a visit from members of the various shades of political thought in the Council of the Empire and in the Duma would be a fitting beginning to closer relations between the two countries. The members of the party were conducted to all the principal sights of London, after a reception by Lord Weardale on behalf of the invitation committee on June 21st, and on the following day they were entertained to luncheon in the House of Commons, Lord Weardale in the chair. Mr. Asquith, in a graceful speech, welcomed the guests as colleagues and representatives of the Russian people. He referred to the happy change that had recently taken place in the relations between the two countries; but they appreciated it could not be lasting unless it were accompanied by an understanding between the two peoples. For that reason, they felt special gratification at the presence of the visitors. Mr. Balfour said that Great Britain had looked with admiration upon the work which the Russian Parliament had done during its brief years, and he anticipated, as a result of these new developments in Russia, a perpetuation of the friendly feeling which now happily existed between the two countries.

M. Homyakoff, on behalf of the delegation, briefly replied in appropriate terms, and raised his glass to " Great and friendly England." The visitors afterwards attended a party given by Mrs. Lowther and the Speaker on the terrace of the Houses of Parliament. On subsequent days there were receptions in their honour by the king at Buckingham Palace, at the Foreign Office, the Russian Embassy, by the London Chamber of Commerce, etc.; and during a provincial tour they were entertained at Oxford, Cambridge, Edinburgh, etc. On their departure, a letter, signed by the President of the Duma and all the members of the Council of the Empire and of the Duma comprised in the deputation, was addressed to the British people and the Press, thanking them for their delightful visit, which had given them " one of the most real ways of drawing our two countries together, and therefore helps to realise the ardent wish which we believe is entertained both in England and Russia."

THE BRITISH EMPIRE

The movement initiated some years ago by the Earl of Meath to bring before the imagination of the citizens of the British Empire some conception of its extent and importance, physically, politically, socially and ethically, on a special day, to be called " Empire Day," has caught on; and this year, 1909, on May 24th—the date fixed because it was the birthday of the late Queen Victoria—no fewer, it is estimated, than 16,000,000 British subjects, who adopted the watchword of the movement " Duty, responsibility, sympathy and self-sacrifice," took an active part in the celebration. Nearly 7,000 sermons and addresses were delivered in the British Isles, and about 4,000,000 scholars from nearly 19,000 schools paraded with music and banners.

But the most striking illustration of the unity of the empire was the meeting in London of the Imperial Press Conference. This was attended by over 150 representative newspaper editors from every section of the empire, be it dominion, commonwealth, dependency, colony or protectorate. The conference met in June, and was inaugurated on Saturday, the 5th, by a great banquet attended by a thousand representatives, not only of British journalism, but of literature, art and politics. Lord Rosebery, who presided, bade the editors from beyond the seas "Welcome Home."

He dwelt on the importance of the gathering, transcending that of any conference of Prime Ministers, who were essentially transient bodies, whereas the newspapers were eternal. He emphasised the value of the Press as an instrument of closer union, and urged that the most vital topic to be discussed was Imperial defence. There was never a time in the history of the world so threatening and of so overpowering a preparation as if for some great Armageddon. We live in the midst of a silent warfare in which not a drop of blood is shed in anger, but in which the last drop is extracted from the living body by the lancets of European statesmen. Where was all this to stop ? Was it going to bring back Europe into a state of barbarism, or would it cause a catastrophe in which the working men of the world would say : "We will have no more of this madness, this foolery which is grinding us to powder." The message which the guests were to take back to their homes across the sea was : "The Old Country is right at heart ; there is no failing or weakness of heart. She rejoices in renewing her youth in her giant dominions beyond the seas. For her salvation she must look to herself, and, that failing, she must look to you."

In session, the conference discussed for more than a week "Cable news and inter-Press Communication," "The Press and the Empire," "Imperial Defence," "Literature and Journalism," "Wireless Telegraphy and Cable Rates," and other subjects. Probably the most striking speeches were those made by Lord Morley, Lord Milner, Lord Roberts, Mr. Winston Churchill and Sir Edward Grey. One practical effect was that the Pacific Cable Board agreed to reduce cable rates to Australia, and that Mr. Marconi consented to a reduction of wireless telegraph messages to 2d. a word. Unbounded hospitality was extended to the members of the conference by public bodies and private individuals, and official recognition was given by the Government in the shape of a banquet in the Grafton Galleries, at which the Prime Minister delivered a sympathetic speech, by a grand naval review at Portsmouth, and a mimic battle, in which all branches of the army took part, at Aldershot.

The members of the conference also spent a week motoring to the leading centres of industry and historic interest in the provinces. Before breaking up, the executive committee of the conference addressed a letter of thanks on the part of the conference to the reception committee, in which they said : "There is a general feeling that an immense amount of vigour is shown in your great manufacturing and commercial concerns. We were much struck with all we saw, and we have come to the conclusion that anybody who takes the view that the industrial life of England is on the decline is extremely pessimistic. We are not taking that view back with us ; quite the reverse. An impression had got abroad that the industries of Great Britain were on the decline. The visits we have paid to the great manufacturing centres have undoubtedly produced in the minds of the delegates a feeling that that decline, if it existed at all, has been very much exaggerated. We certainly saw no sign of it."

South America. The only facts worth noting in regard to the South American Continent are the death, at Rio de Janeiro, on June 14th, of Dr. Penna, President of the Republic of Brazil ; and the signing of a Treaty of Arbitration between Great Britain and Brazil, by Signor Nilo Pecanha, who had succeeded to the presidency, on June 18th. In Venezuela, President Gomez agreed to refer the settlement of all outstanding American claims against the republic to the arbitration of the Hague Tribunal. For some years there has been a dispute between the Republics of Peru and Bolivia as to the boundaries between the two states. The matter was finally referred to the arbitration of Dr. José Alcorta, President of the Argentine Republic, who recently issued his award dividing the contested territory and giving to each disputant about an equal area. The award also required Bolivia to restore to Peru a portion of the territory which the former sold to Brazil about 1907 for a sum of £2,000,000. The award created great sensation in Bolivia as too favourable to Peru, and the Argentine Legation at La Paz was surrounded by irate Bolivians on July 10th, 1909, who attacked the buildings with stones. The Bolivian Government called out troops for the defence of the Argentine and Peruvian Legations; but the Bolivian president has since refused to accept the award.

Newfoundland. After a prolonged negotiation by Mr. Bryce, British Ambassador at Washington, Mr. Root, U.S. Secretary of State, Sir Robert Bond, Premier, and Mr. Kent, Minister of Justice of Newfoundland, a treaty was negotiated and signed for the settlement at the Hague of the fisheries disputes with the United States. A general election took place in the colony in May, 1909, during which there was hot disputation, and charges made against Sir Robert Bond of having entered into secret negotiations for joining Newfoundland to the Dominion of Canada. The Newfoundlanders prefer to remain as an independent self-governing colony, as was shown by the result of the election, which gave twenty-six supporters to Sir Edward Morris in the Legislative Assembly, and only ten to Sir Robert Bond.

THE POLES

It is not too much to say that the civilised world was astounded on the morning of March 24th, 1909, to read of the safe arrival of Lieutenant Ernest H. Shackleton and his Antarctic exploring expedition on board the whaler Nimrod at Stewart Island, off the south coast of South Island, New Zealand. The news came in a dispatch forwarded to the "Daily Mail"—the longest and probably the most interesting, scientifically and imaginatively, ever cabled to any newspaper. The results of the Shackleton Expedition may be summarised as follows : (1) That the Magnetic Pole has been reached ; (2) eight mountain chains discovered ; (3) 100 mountains surveyed ; (4) volcano of Mount Erebus, 13,120 ft. high, ascended ; (5) new coast and high mountains located running west from Victoria Land ; (6) coal measures discovered on the Antarctic Continent ; (7) the most southerly point reached was 88° 23' ; South longitude, 162° East— that is to say, 1° 37', or 111 statute miles from the South Pole, at which spot the Union Jack, presented by her Majesty the Queen to Lieutenant Shackleton, was hoisted. Lieutenant Shackleton and his indomitable comrades arrived in England in June, and met with the most enthusiastic reception from his Majesty the King, who has since conferred upon him the decoration of the Victorian Order, the Royal Geographical Society, which presented them with gold and silver medals, and from numerous other scientific societies and social clubs.

Our task is done. Our historic survey of the circle of the sun is complete.

History, as Carlyle said, is "a looking both before and after, as, indeed, the coming Time already waits, unseen, yet definitely shaped, predetermined and inevitable, in the Time to come ; and only by the combination of both is the meaning of either completed. . . . Man lives between eternities, and warring against oblivion, he would fain unite himself in clear conscious relation, as in dim unconscious relation he is already united with the whole future and the whole past."

In this history the reader has at his command a beautiful instrument by which he can plumb every mystery and passion, every motive and action of man. It is a book which presents in vivid outline the whole past of man, from the origins of savagery to the attainment of the highest civilisation ; and the student by its careful perusal is enabled, with gathered wisdom, to forecast in some measure the whole future, and to realise to himself some ideal of the best that is to be, not for this race or that nation, but for humanity. In it, if he seeks with a seeing eye, he can find the nearest approach which mortals can make to Omniscience. In no very exaggerated sense it may be cited as a book of revelations of the spirit of all the ages and all the countries, and possessed of it he may declare in the language of Goethe :

My inheritance, how lordly wide and fair,
Time is my fair seed field, to Time I'm heir.

W. KINNAIRD ROSE

HARMSWORTH HISTORY
OF THE WORLD
EIGHTH GRAND DIVISION

THE TRIUMPH
OF THE MIND OF MAN

EIGHTH GRAND DIVISION
THE TRIUMPH OF THE MIND OF MAN

Our record of the World's history down to the present year is closed. For a brief ten thousand years we have traced the doings of Man, the social animal, the organiser of communities; a small span in that space of time wherein the earliest forms of life on this planet developed and differentiated into the species of which man is himself the highest product; an infinitesimal fraction of the æons since our globe began to take form; a mere moment in the history of the universe. Even of this it has been attempted to give an idea in our opening sections.

What remains for our closing section—the epilogue at this particular moment of a story still in its beginnings? Our theme is Man: the infinite universe is but the setting to Finite Man— if Man be Finite! And man is so, in the sense that material life on this material globe will one day have faded into "the infinite azure of the past."

But the study of the Past is valuable precisely because Finite Man has before him a future of incalculable vastness. If in ten, twenty, nay, fifty thousand years a Shakespeare and a Newton have been evolved out of pithecanthropus, what may not be evolved in another fifty thousand years?

It is not our part in this epilogue to prophesy. But glancing on the future from contemplation of the past, realising the story which is that of the Triumph of the Mind of Man, there are three points of view which present themselves.

The historian reviews the records of our social animal, marks that wherein would seem to lie the progress of communal life, the solution of problems in the relation of Man to his fellow man; and thus he can formulate the problem of the immediate future, even hint at the method of its solution; point the next step forward, but nothing more.

The man of science, biologist or physicist, concerns himself mainly with the evolution not of the State but of the Race, with development and degeneration, amelioration and deterioration, with the victory of intelligence over material obstacles, with the relations of man to the material universe.

And last it remains to feel and know the Infinite in the Finite, the Spiritual revealed in the Material, the Eternal which is when Time was not and shall have ceased to be, the soul of man which knows not death.

PLAN

THE SOCIAL FABRIC OF THE MODERN WORLD
By W. Romaine Paterson, M.A.

THE TRIUMPH OF THE MIND OF MAN
By Dr. C. W. Saleeby

THE END OF THE WORLD
By Harold Begbie

THE SOCIAL FABRIC OF THE MODERN WORLD

A SURVEY OF INDUSTRIAL PROGRESS
By W. Romaine Paterson, M.A.

THE END OF FEUDALISM

HISTORIANS have discussed the question as to the date at which the modern era may be said properly to begin, but their answers have not been unanimous. And the truth is that no genuine answer can be given to that question, for the stages of any process of development are never sharply divided. They lie embedded in each other, and as they unfold themselves in history the student of their growth discovers their independence.

Some of the ideas, which are characteristic of the modern world, even its scientific inventions and its theories of government, are unrelated to the past. Rather, they are the consummation of centuries of obscure, obstructed, but unwearied effort. Sometimes it is in antiquity that we discover the most perfect expression of ideas which we suppose to be wholly modern. What more admirable definition of the function of the state, for example, could be found than Aristotle's remark that the state is created for the sake of mere life, but continues to exist " for the sake of the good life " ?

Here we are presented with a social ideal which has not even yet been realised. The roads of progress were suggested long ago; some of them were even

The Process of Social Evolution laid out and partly built ; but frequently they were left broken off or overgrown. When, as in the case of human history, the process of social evolution has taken place over an immense area and among alien races living in territories widely separated, the divergence between the different national systems at a given moment may be profound. Institutions which have perhaps been abolished by one people may linger among another. The modern era in Japan, for instance, began only about fifty years ago, and to-day in many Asiatic and African communities archaic

The Slow March of Civilisation and barbarous customs are still in existence. Even in Europe, where the social systems of the various states have, during a long period, been tending towards uniformity, some states have lagged centuries behind others. In Russia, representative government is a creation of yesterday—if, indeed, it may be said to exist in that country as yet in any effective form at all.

The march of civilisation has, on the whole, been painful and slow, and its victories have frequently had merely local value. The abolition of abuses came piecemeal, and often the passage of a frontier meant either greater happiness or greater misery for the individual. Feudal influence has extended itself far into our own day. It was, for instance, only a few years ago that towns like Bolton, Oldham and Rochdale, in Lancashire, were able to purchase their freedom from the lord of the manor.

Or take the history of the abolition of serfdom. Louis X. of France enfranchised the serfs of the royal domain in the year 1315; but in the domains of the French seigneurs the serfs remained unenfranchised during many hundreds of years afterwards. In England the serfs received personal liberty after the Black Death (1349), and their manumission was due to economic rather than to moral causes. In Germany it was not till 1702 that Frederic I. of Prussia liberated his own serfs, whereas in the other German states the oppressed peasantry were compelled to wait for their charter of freedom until the day when all Europe was vibrating with the French Revolution (1789). And in Russia the serfs were not emancipated until 1861. This is an instance of

When did the Modern Era Begin? the irregular and intermittent action of the forces of progress. Such facts enable us to see that the light of the modern era did not shine simultaneously or with equal strength throughout Europe, and that it is therefore impossible to fix upon any event which had an immediate and universal effect in breaking down the mediæval and building up the modern world.

Those writers who, like Bluntschli, believe that the modern era began in the year 1740, because in that year Frederic the Great ascended the throne of Prussia, lay themselves open to the charge of being too exclusively occupied with the affairs and fortunes of a single European state. In like manner, the more plausible view that it was the Reformation which marked the cleavage between the mediæval and the modern world must be in turn dismissed as an inadequate explanation. For the Reformation did not affect Europe as a whole. Doubtless, it was a powerful manifestation of the modern spirit, and its influence reached beyond the limits of the religious world ; but, after all, it was only a single manifestation.

The modern spirit had already been working obscurely in other ways. A jurist might point out that it had betrayed itself in the reascendancy of public law over the private law of the Middle Ages, or a statesman might claim that its most significant triumph was the disentanglement of the State from the Church. Or, again, a student of military science might urge that it was the invention of gunpowder and the use of artillery which, in having rendered obso-

Scientific Discoveries of Antiquity lete the methods of the warfare of chivalry, brought the feudal period to a close. All such theories, however, could present nothing but an incomplete picture of the historical situation. The truth is that the numerous factors of modern civilisation already lay scattered and isolated throughout the ages, and that what distinguishes the modern era is their combined utilisation. Scientific discoveries were made even in antiquity. The

invention of the compass is attributed to the Chinese about the year 2634 B.C. ; a primitive microscope in the form of a convex lens made of rock crystal was discovered in the ruins of Nineveh ; the telescope, at least in the shape of rude optic glasses, was probably known before the thirteenth century ; clocks were in use before the beginning of the Middle Ages ; the invention of printing took place in the fifteenth century, and in the same age watches with mainsprings were being worn ; while during thousands of years metal implements were being gradually improved, until at length they made way for modern machinery, which is really a combination of separate tools—not that we believe that modern machinery is an unmixed blessing. It is the modern spirit which has gathered together and perfected these and innumerable other instruments of material progress, and has thus organised the results of the accumulation of knowledge for the service of mankind.

Every human society is, in its primary aspect, a collective effort to exploit material resources for the purpose of gain-

The State's Immediate and Final Goal ing the means of subsistence, which in turn become the means of leisure. In that exploitation the modern has far surpassed the ancient and the mediæval world. But the factors of civilisation are spiritual and æsthetic as well as material. If mere being is the state's immediate, well being is its ultimate goal. Hence, if the distinguishing mark of modern activity were merely its greater success in accumulating gigantic material resources, we should be compelled to conclude that mankind had misspent centuries in mistaking the means for the end. In attempting to sketch the historical development of some of the main social facts of to-day, we shall chiefly concern ourselves, therefore, with the question how far, in comparison with the past, modern conditions tend to make life not only a more comfortable, but a more dignified thing for the mass of human beings engaged in daily toil. For history is a record either of the happiness or the unhappiness of communities.

In antiquity, as in the case of the slave states, almost the entire burden of industrial creation rested upon an enslaved mass shut out from citizen's rights ; in the mediæval period the majority of Europeans were sunk in a servitude which impoverished in the end not only themselves, but their lords; in the modern world labour is paid in wages, and the working class is at least politically, if not economically, free. Those three opposed systems correspond to three different schemes for the distribution of social well-being. A fundamental change has thus gradually been introduced into the understructure of civilised society, and even the most pessimistic Socialist does not deny the gain in rights. Hence, from our present point of view, it is in the region of political and social principles that the real significance of the modern world lies.

And since it was the French Revolution which gave those principles their most sudden and their widest diffusion, we may fix upon 1789 as the date at which the break with the political past became visible. That date brings us face to face with a new social demand. For although elsewhere, and especially in England, important victories had already been won for human freedom, yet the peculiar character of the French Revolution was that it gave to the doctrine of human rights the most insistent, most articulate, most universal form which it had as yet received. We shall see later, indeed, that the Revolution appears to have promised more than it performed, and that from the point of view of modern socialistic agitation its economic results are judged to be inadequate. But there can be no doubt that it was by means of the French Revolution that the formidable voice of modern democracy first made itself distinctly heard.

Consequences of the French Revolution

If we wish to acquaint ourselves with the most vivid and uncompromising statement of the early aims of the Revolution, we cannot do better than study the pamphlet of Siéyès, " Qu'est-ce que le Tiers État ? " In a few sentences Siéyès brings the entire situation before us. The Tiers État, or Third Estate, was the third of the three great orders or classes which constituted the French nation. It comprised the commons, that is to say, the bulk of the people as distinguished from the clergy and the nobility. These latter were the privileged orders, and enjoyed an immunity from taxation. It was upon the Third Estate that the economic and industrial burden rested, and the weight of that burden had become intolerable. Almost two hundred years had passed since the States-General had been convoked, and the social problem of France had, during the interval, become exceedingly grave. But the States-General in their ancient constitution could do nothing to solve that problem. Summoned by the king, they did not form a parliament in any strict sense, for they possessed neither legislative nor executive powers. The king, whenever he chose, might call them to his aid when the affairs of state seemed to require their presence, but especially when the Treasury was in need of supplies. The chief object of the assembly had been to assist the Crown in discovering new sources of taxation.

France in the Days of its Kings

The three orders sat in separate chambers, and the votes were taken, not per capita, but by estates. Hence the two superior orders might combine in order to outvote the third. This is what had always happened when the interests of the nobles and the clergy were identical. Thus, even although the representatives of the Third Estate had outnumbered the bishops and the abbots and the feudal aristocracy by ten to one, their voting power would not thereby have increased.

The mediæval character of these assemblies is made strikingly evident if we remember that the deputies of the Third Estate were required, when presenting petitions, to be on their knees. Since 1614, when they were last convoked, social abuses had grown apace, but the Third Estate had also grown in power. What was more ominous was that it already possessed a consciousness of its power, and was groping its way towards the manifestation of it. The weapons of political agitation were already being forged.

At the moment when the financial situation was felt to be most acute and when bankruptcy threatened the court and the nation, Necker, the Finance Minister of Louis XVI., invited all French writers to publish their views on the best means of convoking the States-General. For the real constitution of that body was unknown, and there seemed to be no fixed tradition regarding its procedure. The Abbé Siéyès was one of those who availed themselves of Necker's invitation, and his response was the most remarkable political pamphlet of that time. We seem to hear in it the first bugles of the Revolution. Siéyès asks three definite questions, to

The First Bugles of the Revolution

which he gives three very definite answers. (1) What is the Third Estate ? Everything. (2) What position has it hitherto held in the political world ? None at all. (3) What does it demand ? To assume its rightful position. He then goes on to identify the Third Estate with " the nation," for its interests, he says, are ident-

Privileged Classes versus the People

ical with national as opposed to merely particular interests. A privileged order is, he maintains, " a chimæra " if judged from the point of view of the public weal. If all privileged orders were abolished the work of the state could still be carried on by the people themselves. The highest offices should be filled only by men of superior talent. Therefore, Siéyès declares war on the hereditary principle. " Who," he asks, " will deny that the people form the nation ? But they resemble a strong man one of whose arms has been pinioned." Remove the privileged class from the state, and the state would continue to exist. On the other hand, remove the people and the state would perish. For such reasons he demands that only men chosen from the people should be sent as their representatives to the States-General.

" The people desire," he continues, " to make themselves of some account, and in truth they ask the least that is possible." Their influence in the national councils should be at least equivalent to that of the other two orders combined.

The number of their representatives should balance the number of those who stand for the Church and the noblesse. Besides, the voting should take place per head and not per estate. For Siéyès knew that the minor clergy and even some of the members of the aristocracy would be found on certain occasions to vote with the people. When he pours ridicule on the hereditary principle, which he calls " a Gothic invention," when he

France Under Agents of Feudalism

attacks, without restraint, those " agents of feudalism " who were governing, or rather misgoverning, France, when, in a curious phrase, he declares that the people have lived only in a kind of ante-chamber of the state in which they were compelled to await in patience and submission the commands of their masters, we are listening to a voice which had been hitherto unheard in the political world. Or, rather, Siéyès was only turning into practice the

theories of Rousseau. And when he says that the national will (la volonte commune) can be recognised only in the vote of the majority, and that that maxim is " indisputable," we feel that the mediæval theory of government has suddenly become obsolete.

" It follows," adds Siéyès, " that the representatives of the people are the real depositories of the national will, and that they are entitled to speak in the name of the entire nation." This is the revolution and this is modern politics in a sentence. Already, indeed, in 1762 Rousseau, like a good Republican, had in his Contrat Social announced the doctrine that the real sovereignty belongs to the people. But it was by other and later hands that that doctrine was made to assume a formidable because a practical shape. In the writings of men like Siéyès we feel the perilous imminence of a vast social change.

" I believe," said Burke, " that were Rousseau alive and in one of his lucid intervals, he would be shocked at the practical frenzy of his scholars." It is no part of our task to re-tell the old tale

Rising of the French Democracy

of the excesses of the Revolution. The democracy of to-day would not justify all that the democracy of 1789 was driven to do. But Burke was probably too near the Revolution to be able to understand its real meaning. Although he admits the existence of enormous abuses, he does far less than justice at least to the first leaders of the revolt. And yet it is clear that in the earlier stages the representatives of the Third Estate were even eager for compromise. They waited patiently for an answer to their invitation to the clergy and the noblesse to join them in a real National Assembly.

But how little the temper of the time was understood may be measured by the fact that the ruling class still gravely insisted that the representatives of the people should, in accordance with the ancient usage, kneel while presenting their addresses. It was only when the commons were at last wearied out by a delay caused by the discussion of mediæval and puerile formalities that, on June 10th, 1789, and on the initiative of Siéyès, they took the bold step of summoning the clergy and the noblesse to a common deliberation on the nation's affairs. There seemed to be no hope, however, of a union between interests so fundamentally antagonistic, and on

June 15th, the commons proclaimed themselves as the National Assembly. Later, on June 20th, came the famous oath which bound each member not to separate from the others until a constitution had been devised and set upon a firm basis. At length the Third Estate triumphed when, by order of the king, the clergy and the noblesse united themselves on June 27th for common deliberation with the representatives of the people. It was easy for Burke to pour ridicule on those upstarts in the business of framing a constitution. He describes their decrees as "the polluted nonsense of licentious and giddy coffee-houses."

He laughed at their metaphysics and at their schedule of the Rights of Man. "They have a power given to them," he says, "like that of the evil principle to subvert and destroy; but none to construct, except such machines as may be fitted for further subversion and further destruction." Yet it was precisely because their rulers had during centuries of misgovernment and oppression failed to do the work of political construction **The French** that the people in haste, and **Declaration** therefore in violence, attempted **of Rights** to undertake that task for themselves. It is true that many of the deputies of the Third Estate were only petty provincial lawyers. Burke regrets the absence of "leading advocates and renowned professors."

But it was sufficient that the people should find a voice, and it is absurd to affirm that the voice of the National Assembly was incapable of expressing the national suffering. When we turn to the famous declaration of the Rights of Man we are struck, not by the excess, but by the moderation and even caution of the language used. Carlyle objects to a statement of rights unaccompanied by a statement of duties. But Michelet points out that hitherto the people had heard everything about duties, and nothing whatever about rights. It is false to say that it was the declaration of rights which was responsible for the ensuing violence. The Bastille had already fallen. The declaration did nothing but make articulate vast social forces which were already in motion, and which no assembly could control. Lord Morley says that "no set of propositions framed by human ingenuity and zeal has ever let loose more swollen floods of sophism, fallacy, cant

and rant." Yet he maintains that the social conditions of the moment demanded that declaration, and that it contains vital truths. With all its faults it stands, together with the American Declaration, as the most important pronouncement of modern democracy. Perhaps its real significance is best seen, **Burke's Work** not in its own clauses, but in **on the French** some of the preliminary documents in which the deputies **Revolution** received their instructions. For instance, in the "Cahier" of Paris the representatives of that city are to demand the abolition of various abuses, such as personal servitude, and to refuse to accede to any proposal for indemnifying the owners of serfs. They are to secure the freedom of the Press, the liberty of conscience, and the abolition of privilege.

The declaration, which came as the result of a long debate, is really an earnest attempt to express certain elementary human rights which had been destroyed during the Middle Ages. Behind its seventeen articles lay centuries of fruitless struggle. Thomas Paine said that Burke's work on the French Revolution was "a tribute of fear"; and the phrase seems to be justified. He convicts the great rhetorician of ignorance of the springs and principles of the entire movement. And he points out that the Revolution involved an attack not merely upon a single despotism, but upon a thousand despotisms which had grown up under the Crown, and had become in large measure independent of it. Between the monarchy, the noblesse and the Church there was a competition of despotism.

The Revolution was not aimed solely, or, indeed, at first at all against the king. There was something impersonal in its beginnings, and it was only later that violence ran loose, and seized as its victims those who by rank and privilege were identified with a system which had reduced **What the** the nation to economic ruin. **Revolution** In the very remarkable words **Aimed at** of Paine, every office in the state had its despotism, every place its Bastille and every Bastille its despot. Burke had said that the age of chivalry was gone. But in truth the feudal spirit had survived till the end of the eighteenth century, and it still expressed itself in serfdom, in the corvée, and in the financial exploitation of the people. The majority of the seventeen articles which form the Declaration of the Rights of Man have now the appearance of political platitudes, and there are few men who would not assent to them.

Thus, when public law is defined as the expression of the national will, or when it is affirmed that every society has the right to hold its officers responsible for their administration, or even when liberty is vaguely declared to consist in doing whatever does not injure others, we feel that these are reasonable propositions. Nevertheless, at the time when they were promulgated they formed something of the nature of a discovery. It is impossible to pardon all the errors of the constituent assembly, but we should not forget that its members were attempting to bring order out of a vast social and political disorder.

Errors of the Constituent Assembly

Judged by some of the socialistic standards of our own age, those men are even convicted of timidity. For they did not attack property. In the second and in the seventeenth article the rights of property are specially safeguarded. Property is, together with liberty and personal security, declared to be one of the natural rights of man. In the seventeenth article property is even defined as "an inviolable and sacred right, of which no one should be deprived." And there is a clause which declares that if in the public interest expropriation is demanded it ought to be accompanied by a just indemnification of the expropriated individual. But these are precisely the opinions, and this is the language of the propertied classes and of all moderate men. "There is no reason," said Siéyès "why each man, making use of his natural and his acquired powers, and running the ordinary hazards of life, should not increase his property by all available means, and so raise himself in the social scale." Now it is important to remember these words because they embody a political and social principle which triumphed over both the Revolution and the reaction in which the Revolution ended. In his imperial policy Napoleon transformed for his own purposes all the agents of the Revolution, and most of the doctrines of 1789 were forgotten. The Napoleonic system broke down, and during a long period, which came to an end less than forty years ago, the government of France suffered numerous oscillations

Yet throughout all the dynastic and political changes we observe the steady growth of the bourgeois conception of the state such as we find expressed by writers like Siéyès. Moreover, that conception of the state is not confined to France. It is, in its completed form, essentially modern, and it has spread into every country in which the methods of modern industry have been developed. Briefly, we may say that the great political principle for which the men of 1789 fought was the equality of all citizens before the law. This principle is now recognised in every civilised state.

The Fight for Equality

FALL OF THE LAST STRONGHOLD OF FEUDALISM: THE FRANCHISE IN TURKEY

AGE OF ECONOMIC RECONSTRUCTION
COMMERCE EMERGING FROM ITS SHACKLES

BUT while privilege may be abolished by a stroke of the pen, the great economic forces which accumulate within every society are not so easily controlled. Silently and secretly they create new privileges. Although fruitful in the region of politics, the doctrines of the Revolution were not fruitful in the region of economics. Equality was affirmed but was not achieved. In France, as in every other European country, political reform was not necessarily accompanied by sudden social improvement.

All men have become equal in the eyes of the law, but that fact does not abolish poverty. All men are allowed to compete freely with each other for the goods of life, but that competition never results in an equal share. And, as we shall see, the vast development of modern industry has brought back the old problem in a new form. We are apt to suppose that the Third Estate, who formed the driving power of the Revolution, comprised a single uniform mass. **The Driving Power of the Revolution** But this is by no means true. The great unprivileged order included not only the labouring population, but the bourgeoisie and the small capitalists, in whose hands were the trade and commerce of the country. And it was this latter class who gained most by the Revolution. The rights of man turned out in the sequel to be only the rights of the bourgeoisie.

The political freedom which was won became an instrument for advancing the interests mainly of the upper ranks of the Third Estate. We have already seen that the leaders of the Revolution—if we except men like Babeuf—did not propose the abolition of private property so long as that property was not held by the old aristocracy. They confiscated and they partitioned the estates of the clergy and the noblesse, but they did not nationalise the land. They sold it to the highest bidder, so that it merely changed hands.

In the preamble to the constitution, which was completed on September 3rd, 1791, the feudal régime is declared to be no longer in existence, the aristocracy has disappeared, their titles and prerogatives are gone for ever. But "the inviolability" **A New Order in France** of the property of the ordinary French citizen is guaranteed. And it is expressly stated that no attack is made on "natural rights," and the power to acquire property is recognised as one of those rights. The conception of the state as an arena for free competition for the prizes of life lies behind the constructive efforts of the Revolution. And it is this idea which has governed the political and the economic development of the modern world.

In 1791 the National Assembly divided the citizens into those who paid direct and those who paid only indirect taxation. The franchise was reserved for citizens who paid direct taxes to the amount of three shillings. The wage-earners were excluded. In other words, a new privileged order was created out of those members of the Third Estate who possessed a certain amount of property. It is true that this property qualification amounted to a trifling sum ; nevertheless, it carried with it an important distinction which separated those who had political power from those who had none.

Thus in the attempt at social reconstruction which followed the Revolution, the old principle that a man's place in the state depends upon the amount of his property **How the Franchise was Bestowed** was not really abandoned, although it assumed a more democratic guise. That principle was simply set to work at a lower level. Moreover, the right to the franchise was afterwards made more difficult to acquire. In 1814, when the theories of the Revolution had spent themselves and the Napoleonic discipline had borne fruit, the franchise was bestowed only upon those who paid direct taxation to the amount of 300 francs, or £12. After the Revolution of 1830 the amount was lowered to 200 francs, or £8. During the reign of Louis Philippe (1830–1848) out of a population of 30,000,000 only some 200,000 persons exercised the right to vote. This was a paltry result of the tremendous upheaval of 1789. Even, however, although there had been no Napoleonic dynasty and no Restoration, the political development of France would not probably have been different. The work of enfranchisement would have proceeded as slowly.

Founders of the New Republic

In the latter half of the nineteenth century the founders of the new republic granted universal suffrage, and by that measure they showed themselves to be more revolutionary than the men who drew up the constitution of 1791. From the point of view of the proletariat, the Revolution was somewhat barren. No doubt the corvée was abolished. Labour was emancipated, but it was given no voice in the government of the country. Power had simply been transferred from the old aristocracy of birth to the new aristocracy of money. And, again, we must add that what took place in France was fairly typical of what had happened, was happening, or was about to happen, in every other modern state.

Capital in its modern form did not exist in the Middle Ages. To-day capital is mobile, and may be transferred from one industry to another. But throughout the mediæval period it remained immobile, for it was expressed in the ownership of land. The economic situation was therefore not the result of the fluctuations of the markets. There were no great markets. Such trade as existed was local, and had no wide ramifications. Manufactures were carried on not in large factories, but in the houses of master workmen, who were surrounded by their apprentices. There was no machinery, and therefore production was slow. Moreover, whereas to-day the supply usually outruns the demand, the reverse was the case in mediæval Europe. Trade waited upon demand, and since, owing to the existence of serfdom, the purchasing power of the vast majority was infinitesimal, there was little stimulus towards production. Mediæval life was controlled by the landed interest. Agriculture was the chief concern, and it was

Commerce in Mediæval Europe

carried on by servile labourers. The result was economic stagnation. To-day trade is fluid, but in the Middle Ages movable property hardly existed. Commodities which are now manufactured in endless quantity either did not then exist, or were exchanged only on the smallest scale.

According to mediæval private law, real estate was not transferable. On the other hand, goods and chattels might be alienated or bequeathed. But they formed only an insignificant part of the wealth of that time. The feudal organisation tended towards rigidity. The land remained changeless, and something of its immobile character affected the entire social system. The serfs who tilled the land were forbidden to emigrate; they remained on the soil from generation to generation, and were only the animated implements of its exploitation. Likewise in the towns which grew up within the shadow of the great domains the local industries were subjected to the same kind of restriction. And the trade guilds which formed the units of the commercial system hindered the expansion of trade. While at every point commercial enterprise was taxed by the seigneur, the action of the trade corporations, which were not suppressed in France until the Revolution, was no less injurious. In every locality the number of apprentices which a master workman might employ was fixed by law. This meant that the volume of his production remained steadily at the same point. His business could not grow.

The Law's Restrictions on Trade

There was, besides, a minute subdivision of industry, so that no overlapping of trades was permitted. Thus, for example, a man who made locks was forbidden to make the nails which fastened the locks. The tailor who made clothes was not allowed to mend them. Whereas, again, to-day multifarious activities are carried on in one and the same business, no such system prevailed in the early days of the handicrafts. We may see, therefore, why there was no opportunity for a large accumulation of capital. Speculation and investment did not exist, and there were no stocks and shares. A manufacturer's capital consisted in his tools and in a small quantity of raw material.

Likewise, rent was unknown. The income of a landowner was made up of tolls and fines, and many of these were extracted from industrial workers as well as from villeins and serfs. There is a long list of exactions, by means of which commercial activity was penalised and paralysed. A merchant could not undertake a journey without protection, and often he had to pay a high price in order to reach his destination in safety. There is a typical case from Burgundy which happened in the year 1374, when a certain feudal noble undertook to conduct an Italian merchant from Dijon to Maurice-en-Chablais, and to guarantee him against all damage and robbery by the way in return for thirty francs in gold, which were equivalent to sixty English sovereigns.

In those days it required more than average courage in order to become a commercial traveller. Vexatious fines met the merchant at every stage of his journey. There was even a tax, called *pulveraticum*, which was levied on any carrier whose waggon raised dust on the road which belonged to a seigneur. During centuries throughout Europe commerce was shackled; every attempt at innovation was crushed. Even as late as the reign of James I. of England a proclamation was issued forbidding the use of a machine for making needles. And

Europe's Shackled Commerce a naive enactment of Charles I., which prohibited the use of brass buckles because " those who cast the brass buckles can make more in one day than ten of those that make the iron buckles can do " lets us see even in this trivial case how great have been the odds against which the inventive and progressive spirit of man has struggled. Even on agriculture feudalism exerted an influence as paralysing as its influence on trade.

There can be no doubt that it is in the gradual removal of one restriction after another that we should find the main explanation of the immense industrial activity and wealth of the modern world. In mediæval France, as in mediæval England, " there could be," as Dr. Cunningham says, " little desire of accumulation when the ever-recurring tallages, aids and fines were sure to empty the hoards that had been filled during several preceding years. There could be no enterprise in seeking out a new line of life, for each villein was bound to the land, and no lord would willingly part with his services; there could be no high farming while the custom of the manor and the collective ownership of the teams forced all to adopt the same system. Even in trade there was little opportunity of

raising oneself, for the prices of articles of native production, for which there would be much competition, were regulated by authority; and merchants, too, were subject to special risks or to special fines for protection as well as to heavy trading dues." All this has been changed. It would be impossible in the present sketch to trace

Charlemagne as a Trading Farmer the causes of the victory of commerce over the mediæval restrictions which had attempted to strangle it. That victory was not complete until the bourgeoisie obtained a share in government. Hence the history of modern economic development is related to the history of the franchise.

But even during the reign of feudalism signs of the coming power of a new class in the state were by no means absent. Gradually it began to appear that the economic basis of feudalism—the exploitation of the land by servile labour—was unsound. Unlike Charlemagne, who was not too proud to sell the eggs and other produce of his farms, the nobles had a contempt for trade, and the feudal usage forbade them to engage in it. Nevertheless, in times of financial difficulty many a great baron called to his aid the despised Jew or the petty bourgeois. It was in the hands of these latter that such capital as existed in the Middle Ages began to accumulate, and it formed the nucleus of the capital which exists to-day. But both the wealthy commune and the wealthy individual trader were in perpetual danger of being plundered.

Expensive and unproductive wars, together with an expensive and unproductive tillage, brought about the bankruptcy of feudalism. Yet the bourgeois became aware of his power when a great lord, in defiance of feudal custom, offered to share with him the risks and profits of commercial speculation. In the protocols of Burgundy there are numerous instances which prove that men

Merchants Protected by Lords of rank and title entered into negotiations with men of the merchant class. While the bourgeois was thriftily amassing his small savings, the seigneur was misspending in luxury and barren war the income which he extorted from serf and bourgeois alike. Owing to the anarchy of the period, the travelling merchant was often, as we have seen, compelled to put himself under the protection of some powerful lord, who in return received a percentage on the results of the expedition. Sometimes, for greater safety, merchants travelled in companies both by land and sea. What this new corporate activity which laid the foundations of the vast modern system of production and exchange was able to achieve may be discovered in the history of the communes of France, and especially **Great Days** of the Hansa towns of Ger- **of the Hanseatic** many. Originally, Hansa **League** meant a military company. But the object of those companies was not military but commercial. They placed outposts and depots in the great towns, and at last they attained to such power that they were able to dictate treaties to kings.

A silent reconstruction of the economic basis of European life was taking place. Frequently the work was impeded by reactionary forces and especially by war, but it was never wholly arrested. It is a striking truth, however, that the tendency of this new factor of progress was to create social privileges not fundamentally different from those of the system which it was secretly overthrowing. That tendency was aristocratic. For instance, in the yearly assemblies of the Hanseatic League, which generally took place at Lübeck, no one below the rank of councillor might take his seat. Moreover, if any town displayed democratic leanings it was punished by expulsion from the league.

Wealth, in fact, which had been created not out of the land but out of commerce, became the instrument for creating and maintaining a new hierarchy. We may measure the change which had occurred when we recall the fact that Louis XIV., at Versailles, raised his hat to a wealthy merchant of that day from whom he required financial aid. The interests of the capitalist class and of the aristocracy had become less and less antagonistic. According to some writers, indeed, the economic revolution which the development **Results of** of trade brought with it suc- **Trade** ceeded only in creating a new **Development** "commercial feudalism," which benefits the producers at the expense of the consumers. "In vain," says Blanqui, "the French Revolution abolished the trade guilds and emancipated labour if wages tend to fall and the price of commodities tends to rise." And in the opinion of Lassalle there is an exact parallel between the historical significance of the bourgeoisie and the mediæval

noblesse. He maintained that the bourgeoisie, as soon as it had secured power, transformed itself into a privileged class, whose feudal character was expressed in terms of capital.

In the Middle Ages the ruling orders were untaxed. Every privileged order in every age has attempted to place the burden of taxation, whether in the form of labour or of money, on the shoulders of the classes who possess no property. It is true that the capitalists take their share in taxation, but that share, say the Socialists, is out of all proportion to the amount of their incomes. By the device of indirect taxation they lighten the burden for themselves in those countries in which trade monopolies are fostered. A man who is twenty, or fifty, or a hundred times as rich as another, does not for that reason, says Lassalle, require twenty, or fifty, or a hundred times as much food and shelter. We shall deal later with the question of modern poverty.

Meantime, it is sufficient to point out that the great leading factors in the creation of modern conditions—the use of machinery, **The Three** the discovery of America **Broad Divisions** and other great markets for **in Society** trade, the facility of locomotion by land and sea, the numerous inventions of applied science in all industries, together with new political theory and practice—have transformed beyond recognition the great divisions of ancient and mediæval society. The social organisation has become more flexible. Instead of slaves and serfs there are men and women who sell their labour for wages.

The omnipotence of the owner of land has been checked and the powers which he once exercised have passed to the state. In the words of the distinguished historian of English industry, "Economically we have three broad divisions in society, for men arrange themselves according to the things which they own and exchange; they may exchange their labour for wages, or they may exchange the use of their capital for interest, or they may exchange the use of their land for rent. In modern societies, labourers, capitalists and landlords are the three classes which group themselves round the possession of the power to labour, the possession of wealth and the possession of land. This is the social structure we habitually assume, but it is strangely unlike the manorial life it has superseded."

THE ERA OF INDUSTRIAL SLAVERY
HARDSHIPS OF FACTORY LIFE IN ENGLAND

EVERY progressive modern state has thus been the scene of a political and economic transformation, by means of which many of the principles which governed collective action in the past have been abandoned. Representative government, the great political principle of modern democracies, was unknown in antiquity. Ancient democracies were direct ; that is to say, their component members legislated not by proxy, but in their own persons in the national assemblies.

In the ancient Germanic tribes, for instance, all the freemen met together in council. In the Athenian ecclesia the entire body of free citizens above twenty years of age transacted political business. But this system was adapted only to small communities in which public opinion could be easily and quickly ascertained. As nations grew larger it became impracticable to summon all the citizens for common deliberation, and

How Grotius Defined the State many hundreds of years elapsed before men discovered and perfected the methods of representative government. The definition of the state which Grotius formulated expresses the modern social ideal, which is still in process of realisation. " The state," said Grotius, " is the perfect union of free men for the purpose of enjoying common rights and a common welfare."

The history of the franchise is the history of the extension of this sphere of rights and also of the attempt to discover within the vast masses which constitute modern nations that unanimity of public opinion which was so simply expressed in the national councils of the ancient tribes. In some countries universal suffrage actually reproduces, although in an indirect form, the ancient referendum, while in others political development has been marked by a steady widening of the electoral basis. Even in a country such as England, which is not nominally a democracy, a democratic representative system has been grafted upon a constitutional monarchy, and the public business is initiated by a committee of the nation in the form of a Cabinet responsible to the people. But this mechanism of government was

The Voice of the Industrial Population known neither to the ancient nor to the mediæval world, although, indeed, the procedure of the Athenian ecclesia appears in some instances to have approximated to the methods of a parliament. Whereas, in antiquity and during the Middle Ages numerous interests were left inarticulate and unrepresented in the state, in modern times the industrial population makes its voice heard in public affairs.

The nations have long outgrown their earlier organisations. In the western world the system of castes has broken down, and the idea of common citizenship is fully developed. The functions of the state are regarded as purely secular, and the old conceptions of theocratic government have disappeared. Sovereigns, whether as hereditary monarchs or as elected presidents, are no longer supposed to rule by divine authority, but only as embodiments of the concentrated national will.

Whereas in mediæval society each group of privileged persons was governed by a code of law peculiar to itself—the clergy by the canon law ; the barons, the knights, the vassals, the burghers, the villeins and the serfs by customs belonging to their respective ranks—to-day the national consciousness expresses

The Main Duty of the State itself in statutes before which all men are equal. And thus we return to that conception of the state which has controlled both the political theory and practice of some of the most advanced modern nations—the principle, namely, that the main duty of the state is the maintenance of the rights and the property of all its members. This principle found remarkable expression, especially in England in the nineteenth century, in the doctrine of *laissez faire*, according to which the state should interfere as little as possible with the activity of the individual.

That activity found vent in every form of industrial enterprise, and it is to the system of unrestricted competition that the accumulation of modern wealth is **Doctrine** due. The conception, however, **of Modern** that the chief function of the **Democracy** state is to protect property, or, in other words, to prevent burglary—a conception to which Immanuel Kant, among others, gave expression—has been attacked by the opponents of the bourgeois ideal, who have pointed out that it converts the modern state into a mere policeman. And, as we shall see, this indictment against the materialistic view of national life is not unjustified. In the attempt to accumulate property and to defend it, the modern world has forgotten that the state in its highest and noblest aspects should represent not only the physical, but also the intellectual and the moral energy of man.

The great doctrine of modern democracy embodied in the triple formula, liberty, equality, fraternity, contains inherent contradictions which will always prevent its full realisation. In any case political liberty has had little effect upon the economic foundations of modern society. And if we examine the origin of modern wealth, we shall find that the emancipation of industry did not involve the emancipation of the industrial workers. The immense development of modern manufactures and commerce has been the result of the enterprise of individuals who have been more or less unshackled by the interference of the state. But in the pursuit of his own interests the individual is tempted to sacrifice the interests of others. During a long period the modern methods of acquiring wealth were not fundament- **Slavery** ally different from those of **in the** antiquity and of the Middle **Colonies** Ages. The history of colonial slavery and of modern factories amply demonstrates how long political theory may remain unrelated to actual social conditions.

Many years after the French Revolution the colonial possessions of Britain and of France were, like America, the scene of servile labour as degrading as the servile labour of ancient times. No doubt, slavery was abolished in Western Europe towards the close of the twelfth century. But as soon as Europeans began to colonise the New World they did not scruple to make use of a tyranny which in Europe had been already condemned. Fortunes destined to be spent in Europe were extorted from the labour of slaves in the rice-fields and the cotton-fields, and in the indigo and the tobacco plantations of another continent. Men who attended Christian churches in Europe did not consider it to be incompatible with their religious beliefs to enrich their families by help of a tyranny which was the negation of Christian doctrine.

In the official journal of Martinique for June 22nd, 1840, we read as follows : " In the name of the king, of law and of justice.—Be it known to all whom it may concern that on Sunday, June 26th, 1840, in the market-place of the Holy Spirit, there shall be sold at auction immediately after Mass the slave-woman Suzanne, a negress, together with her six children, aged respectively thirteen, eleven, eight, seven, six and three years." A proclamation like this was a strange commentary on eighteen hundred years of Christianity. **When the** And it would be interesting to **Slave Trade** attempt to discover what **Flourished** proportion of modern wealth can be traced directly to slave labour. There are at least sufficient data to prove that even in our own day, as recent events on the Congo bear witness, the ancient dogma of man's property in man is by no means extinct. The men who drew up the Black Code and who ordained for the fugitive slave the punishment of lopping his ears and of branding his shoulder with the fleur-de-lis, and the punishment of death if the attempt to escape were repeated, were, *mutatis mutandis*, using the language of the slave laws of antiquity.

In a French journal of July, 1843, we even find the statement that the proposal for the abolition of slavery was " atheistical " because it attacked the most sacred of all rights, the right of property. And this belief that an inferior race may be exploited as implements for the production of wealth to be consumed by their masters was held universally in every country which had acquired colonial possessions. In the London newspapers towards the end of the eighteenth century there are to be seen advertisements for fugitive slaves, and high rewards are promised to the captors. Throughout that century there was continued a great discussion as to whether a slave who had landed on the shores of Great Britain should be considered to be free. In 1729 the following was announced as the official decision of the attorney-general and the solicitor-general of the day : " We are of opinion that a slave, by coming from the West Indies into Great Britain or Ireland, either with or without his master, does not become free, and that his master's right and property in him is not thereby determined (i.e., ended) or varied, and that baptism doth not bestow freedom on him nor make any alteration in his temporal condition in these kingdoms. We are also of opinion that the master may legally compel him to return to the plantations."

It was not until January, 1772, and after prolonged investigation that Mansfield and his coadjutors declared that " as soon as ever any slave set his foot upon English territory be became free." In this case, however, English territory meant only the shores of Great Britain, and the abolition of slavery throughout the British dominions did not take place till 1834. Such facts bring **The Coming of Machinery** before us in a striking way the overlapping of the ancient on the modern world. In the frantic effort to create capital, Europeans, who enjoyed a charter of political liberties which it had taken centuries to win, revived outside Europe an industrial system in which liberty had no place.

If we now turn to consider for a moment the development of modern manufactures in Europe itself, we shall find that during a long period the factory system was responsible for the sacrifice of the industrial population merely for purposes of economic gain. The condition of the workers who spun cotton in the English factories was hardly better than that of the negro slaves who had first raised the cotton in the American plantations. Owing to the invention of steam and the steam engine and Arkwright's spinning-frame a revolution took place in many important industries. Machinery not only destroyed the old handicrafts, but it produced great changes in the habits of the people.

Manufactures which used to be carried on in cottages, where the head of a family had his family or his apprentices as co-workers, were now transferred to large buildings in which men, women and children were congregated under the supervision of overseers who were responsible only to the owners. The history of the cotton and woollen factories is, unfortunately, full of data which prove that the new inventions and the new industrial organisation which they involved resulted in a ruthless exploitation of adult and child labour. In a speech delivered in the **Child Slaves in the Cotton Factories** House of Commons in 1796, William Pitt pointed out the advantages which might be derived from the employment of children in the great staple industries. He spoke of " the addition which by the fruits of their toil might be made to the country's internal opulence." And the manufacturers were quick to utilise a form of labour so abundant and so cheap.

Yet it would be wrong to suppose that it was in the great factories that for the first time children were set to do the work of adults, and to perish by thousands in the process. As early as the reign of Elizabeth it was enacted by the Poor Law of 1601 that pauper children and orphans should be apprenticed to various trades. So that when at the end of the eighteenth century the new discoveries in machinery had given a great stimulus to the spinning and weaving industries, the manufacturers simply pressed into their service the apprentice system which they found ready to their hands. We cannot attempt, however, to describe the abuses which the new methods of manufacture introduced, or the slow and halting attempts at interference and control on the part of the state. It was pointed out by Spencer Walpole that it required twenty-five years of legislation to restrict a child of nine to a sixty-nine hours' week, and that that restriction applied only to the cotton-mills.

And it is part of the irony of those abuses that attention was drawn to them only when, owing to the insanitary conditions in which the children worked, a serious outbreak of fever threatened **Industry's Frightful Cruelties** the public health. The memoir of Robert Blincoe, a cotton apprentice, who served his time while the system was doing its maximum mischief, allows us a glimpse of the frightful cruelties which attended the earliest stage of modern industry. Blincoe declares that he was often compelled to work almost naked throughout a winter's day, and to work, moreover, loaded with two half-hundredweights of iron slung to each shoulder. Those apprentices who, like the slaves of antiquity, were suspected of a desire to escape were kept in chains, and their ankles were shackled. The duration of the hours of labour would be incredible unless the facts were fully authenticated, as, in the present case, they happen to be by a number of official documents.

Unchecked Abuses in the Cotton Mills The first Sir Robert Peel stated that, from his personal knowledge, children seven years old were compelled to work thirteen and fourteen hours a day. Sir Samuel Romilly declared that he knew of cotton mills where the apprentices were murdered in order that fresh premiums might be secured with new apprentices. The Poor Law overseers and the justices of the peace appear to have been able only on the rarest occasions to check the abuses that existed within the walls of factories which, since they were private concerns, were not yet liable to inspection by the state.

It was in the year 1802 that the first great attempt was made by the state to establish a control over the factory system. An act called the Health and Morals of Apprentices Act was passed without much opposition, and it reduced the working hours to twelve per diem. Night work was to cease in June, 1804. This measure marked an important stage in social progress. Provision was made for an improvement in the sanitary condition of the factories, inspectors were appointed, and all mills were to be registered. The justices of the peace were empowered to impose penalties for violation of the act. But the act applied only to cotton and woollen factories, and even in these it was soon found to be inefficient.

The reduction of the working time was inadequate, and in many cases evasion of the statute was easy. It required the legislation of exactly a hundred years to establish in the interests of the **Beginning of State Interference** workers an effective control over the great industries of the country. And it was not until 1901 that, in the Factory and Workshop Act of that year, a large number of statutes regulating the hours and the conditions of labour were consolidated. The history of state interference was at first marked by great caution and timidity. The acts of 1802, 1819 and 1825 were soon found to be wholly insufficient. For instance, the act of 1819

forbade any person under sixteen to be employed more than twelve hours a day, exclusive of meal times. But it had no application beyond cotton mills. Although it prohibited the labour of children less than nine years old, nevertheless, in other industries, children of five and six years were still being employed. And the hours for adult labour were intolerable. In Manchester in 1825 the average working day extended beyond fourteen hours. During the meal hours the children were not allowed to go free, but were compelled to clean the machinery and, thus engaged, to eat their miserable food in a suffocating temperature. A meagre advance was made in 1831, when a twelve hours' working day was prescribed for all persons under eighteen, and night work was prohibited except for those who were above twenty-one years of age. But again only the cotton mills were included in the act.

The goal of reform was still far off. The letters of Richard Oastler to the " Leeds Mercury " in 1830, although somewhat wildly written, were justified by the facts which they disclosed. " The pious and able **Victims of Industrial Slavery** champions of negro liberty," said Oastler, " should, before they had travelled so far as the West Indies, have sojourned in our own immediate neighbourhood—i.e., Yorkshire—and have directed attention to scenes of misery, acts of oppression, and victims of slavery on the threshold of our homes. Thousands of little children, both male and female, but principally female, from seven to fourteen years of age, are daily compelled to labour from six o'clock in the morning to seven in the evening, with only thirty minutes allowed for eating and recreation."

These and similar passages referring to the condition of labour in the Bradford worsted mills, and in many other factories during the first half of the nineteenth century, prove the truth of the view that the ancient and the mediæval methods of exploiting human labour have been extended far into the modern era. They expressed themselves in a new form in the new industrial organisation, but they reproduced the old results. And if we look closely enough at the foundation of the social fabric of the modern world we shall be compelled to admit that the accumulation of modern as of ancient wealth has not been made without a great and unnecessary sacrifice of human life.

THE EMANCIPATION OF LABOUR
AND THE STATE'S DUTY TO THE WORKER

IN our own day, however, we are happily able to observe new social forces at work. The doctrine of *laissez faire* is, as we have already said, now discredited, and the state no longer remains indifferent to the welfare of its labouring class. No doubt much remains to be done. Mr. Sidney Webb has pointed out that " the sweated trades remain at the opening of the twentieth century as free from any effective common rules as was the factory system at the beginning of the nineteenth."

In the report of the Select Committee of the House of Lords on the sweating system in 1890 it is stated that the hours of labour in the sweated industries " are such as to make the lives of the workers periods of ceaseless toil," and the sanitary conditions under which the work is done are described as wretched. Even as we write, however, attempts are being made to establish control over private workshops, **Industries Under the Eye of the State** and the inevitable goal of recent social legislation will be the extension of protection to the sweated worker. Perhaps the most hopeful characteristic of modern legislative effort consists in the fact that reform is now undertaken not merely for economic but for direct moral reasons.

Sometimes slaves and serfs were emancipated because their emancipation became a source of profit to their masters. To-day, however, as soon as social abuses become known the public conscience is stirred. If we examine the Factory Act of 1901, which was the consummation of a century of philanthropic effort, we shall be able to measure the social progress which has been made. The provisions of that act apply no longer merely to factories and workshops, but to laundries and warehouses, docks, wharves and quays and railways. All the great national industries have come under the eye of the state. The hours of labour both in textile and in non-textile facotries are definitely regu-

lated. For instance, it is enacted that for women and young persons the working hours shall be from 6 a.m. till 6 p.m., or from 7 a.m. till 7 p.m., with two hours, of which one hour is before 3 p.m., for meals. And on Saturdays work stops at **A Better Day for the Workers** 11.30 in the forenoon. The clauses which relate to " Health and Safety," " Overtime and Night work," " The Fencing of Machinery," " The Education of Children," " Dangerous and Unhealthy Industries," and numerous other matters indicate to what great purpose the state has interfered in the organisation of industry.

Moreover, the spirit of the English factory acts has spread into all other civilised countries. The most minute provisions are made for the maintenance of the health of the workers. For instance, by the Act of 1901 every factory—except, indeed, the domestic factory—is required to " be kept in a cleanly state," and " it must not be so overcrowded while work is carried on therein as to be dangerous or injurious to the health of the persons employed therein." In section 13 of part I. it is enacted that " a child must not be allowed to clean in any factory (a) any part of any machinery, or (b) any place under any machinery other than overhead mill gearing, while the machinery is in motion by the aid of steam, water or other mechanical power."

Again, " a woman or young person shall not be employed continuously for more than four hours and a half without an interval of at least half an hour for **The State's Care for the Children** a meal." By the Act of 1903, regulating the employment of children, night work is forbidden, and a child under the age of eleven " shall not be employed in street trading." To the men of the middle half of the nineteenth, all such enactments would have appeared to be an infringement of the rights of property. To us they mark only a tardy act of justice, and they involve a new conception of the function of the state. For the state can no longer be supposed to be merely a machine for the production of material goods which are to be enjoyed by a minority of its members. Rather, its true life is attained only when there exists between all its members a collaboration for moral as well

The Wage-earner Versus the Capitalist as for material purposes. We have mentioned some of the obstacles which throughout many centuries have prevented the realisation of this ideal. Let us now ask if our own age appears to be any nearer the solution of the social problem.

When Saint Just said that " wealth is an infamy " he was denouncing it as the possession of the few, and his cry is being re-echoed in the twentieth century. It is the tendency of capital as well as of land to accumulate within the hands of a minority. And the complaint of the industrial wage-earner to-day is far more bitter against the capitalist than against the owner of land. Socialism desires, above and before all things, the destruction of the middle class. To-day the great economic struggle lies between the wage-giver and wage-earner. Below the wage-earners are the wageless, who make up the great pauper population. Although it has been estimated that the sum paid in wages in the United Kingdom amounts annually to £500,000,000, yet seven out of every ten persons live in a state of semi-starvation.

One thing is clear—the working class is no longer satisfied merely with the political franchise. Political equality has not brought with it, they say, that wider extension of social well-being which is the ultimate aim of democracy. And when democracy expresses itself in the terms of Socialism, the reason is that it is no longer content with a political, but insists as well upon an economic revolution. Throughout the nineteenth century it was the great

Power of the Industrial Population middle class which played the leading political rôle. But the transfer of power from the old aristocracy to the middle class has been followed by the transfer of power from the middle class to the industrial population. And just as at the opening of the French Revolution the Third Estate determined to be represented by members chosen from itself, so to-day the working class finds its political representatives within its own ranks. As Lassalle pointed

out, there lay concealed within the middle class of all European nations a fourth class, which has only recently become articulate. Whether it calls itself the Labour or Social Democratic Party, it will develop independently, and will use politics only as an instrument for the advance of its own aims. Democracy does not necessarily mean Socialism ; but, like the latter, it dreams of the overthrow of that powerful individualism which lies at the basis of the modern capitalistic system.

Socialism professes to supply democracy with an economic theory, according to which collective production and collective distribution should form respectively the means and the goal of human activity. The social problem to-day centres, therefore, round the conflicts of capital and labour. The long and victorious struggle of the trade unions for recognition, and the improved conditions of labour which the factory acts have secured, do not by any means mark the limit of the democracy's ambitions. The modern world has abolished personal property in human beings. But the question is now asked

What are the Rights of Labour? whether, if one man has no right to exploit another as his slave or serf, he has any better right to exploit that other's labour ? If it is labour which bestows the right to own property, it is maintained that the workman's claim is not satisfied by the payment of a wage which affords him only a bare subsistence. His interest in the product of his labour should, it is declared, be cumulative under the industrial régime. His labour forms his only property, but it perishes in the process of work. He describes a weary circle. Although he is paid in wages, the wages are sufficient only to provide him with food, whereby his labouring power is daily renewed. And so on till his death, he, the producer, is shut out from the enjoyment of the results of his production. His political freedom seems to be nothing more or less than an idle and useless gift.

According to Karl Marx, the effects of the modern industrial system have been the physical and moral deterioration of the workman, the intensification of labour, and the creation of a surplus value which is appropriated by the capitalist. The Marxian theory of value, based upon some statements of Adam Smith and Ricardo, has now been discredited. His view was that value is created only by labour, and he neglected other important factors, such as scarcity and abundance, the varying demand for different commodities, and the different quality of the raw material upon which labour is spent.

Laveleye points out that the wine known as Château-Lafite may be worth twelve shillings a bottle, whereas the produce of the neighbouring vineyard may be worth only tenpence a bottle, although in the latter case double the amount of labour may have been expended in the cultivation. Labour, therefore, is not the sole factor in the creation of value. Besides, Marx has not touched upon the effect of competition in raising or reducing values, irrespective of the labour employed in the production of commodities of the same kind. Marx objects to the surplus profit which falls to the employer. He says that capital, like a great sponge (Kapital Schwamm), sucks up the surplus value drop by drop.

The work which the labourer performs in the course of a single day creates a value only a portion of which returns to him as a wage. He may be compelled to work twelve hours, while only three hours would be sufficient to earn that wage. **Problem of Surplus Labour** But if an employer were not to retain part of the realised value of the product he could neither preserve nor enlarge his business, which, as a source both of income and of wages, would thus soon cease to exist. It cannot be true to say that the capitalist simply " steals " the profits which accrue from what Marx calls " surplus labour."

No doubt, the labourer may create by his day's work a product the value of which, when realised in the market, will more than liquidate the day's wage. But other expenses of production are to be met. And is the man whose energy and foresight creates and maintains an organised industry not to be paid a wage in proportion to the value of his services? It is certainly no longer possible to hold the old and exploded theory of a wages fund. Wages are ultimately paid out of sources which labour has itself created. But apart from a controlling and organising force, labour would be impotent, and it would be unfair to equalise wages between agents who contribute disproportionate services.

All these, however, are questions which we cannot discuss here. We are more concerned with the general fact that the development of modern industrialism has been accompanied by an ever growing antagonism between the forces to which it owes its birth. What has been called " the iron law of wages " is supposed by Socialistic economists to be the inevitable result of the reigning system of capitalism. This law, the operation of which was implied in the writings of French economists **The Iron Law of Economics** like Turgot, and also in those of Malthus, Ricardo and Adam Smith, was re-expressed by Lassalle in the following passage : " The iron law of economics (das eherne ökonomische Gesetz), which, under the modern conditions of supply and demand, regulates the rate of wages, is this, that the average wage must always remain at the amount which, in accordance with the customary standard of living, is necessary to make mere subsistence and propagation of the species possible. It is about this point that, like a pendulum, the real wage— that is, the purchasing power of wages— oscillates without being able either to rise above it or to fall below it for any lengthened period. It cannot permanently raise itself above this average because, if it did, there would take place, owing to the improved condition of the workers, an increase of population which would have the effect of reducing wages again, since the supply of labour would have become abundant. Likewise, wages cannot permanently fall below the amount necessary for subsistence, because in that case there would follow emigration, the reduction of the marriage and of the birth-rate, and, lastly, as a necessary consequence, a diminution of labour supply resulting in a rise of wages to the former level."

Now, if this " law " operated eternally and invariably, the outlook for the working class would certainly be hopeless. Social and moral stagnation would be their destiny. Happily, recent criticism and a closer observation of the conditions of labour have resulted in a considerable modification of **Factors in the Rate of Wages** this theory, according to which wages are fixed by " a natural law." As a matter of fact, the rate of wages is determined by varying causes, such as the workman's efficiency, the needs of the market, supply and demand, etc. Professor Marshall has pointed out that local variations of weekly wages and of efficiency generally correspond. He maintains that the tendency of economic freedom and enterprise—that is, the competitive system—is generally to equalise efficiency earnings in the same district. It is not, therefore, merely the standard of comfort common to the labouring class in a given locality which regulates the amount of their wages. It often happens that common labourers and mechanics receive wages as high as, if not higher than, the salaries of clerks and **High Wages Mean Efficient Production** curates, whose standard of living is, nevertheless, superior. Besides, the fluctuation in the rate of wages and the price of commodities are not simultaneous. The researches of Brentano and Schoenof have proved that there is a close connection between the high wages and efficient production, and, indeed, that fact was already expressed by Adam Smith, who said that "the liberal reward of labour increases the industry of the common people." There is a saying in America that he is the best man of business who continues to pay the highest wages. For the highest wages attract the highest skill, and the result is seen in an improvement in the quality of the products. Professor Marshall says that "highly paid labour is generally efficient, and therefore not dear labour, a fact which is more full of hope for the future of the human race than any other that is known to us."

Various statistics prove the correctness of this view. In the year 1872 the great increase in the wages of Prussian miners was followed by a remarkable increase in the productivity of the miners. Whereas, too, in Austria, a miner's daily wage in 1870 was two shillings and sevenpence and his yearly output 1,952 cwt., in 1872, when the wage had risen to three shillings and sixpence, the individual output had correspondingly risen to 2,323 cwt. Schoenof has written a book to prove the economy of high wages, and to disprove the dogma that cheap labour means a gain to the employer of it. But let it not be supposed that high wages mean necessarily an immoderate price for the products of labour. For more efficient labour accomplishes more in a given time, and hence, although more

highly paid, actually reduces the cost of production. The following table of average annual earnings and average prices in some American coal-mines is of special interest :

	Yearly Earnings (Dollars)		Wages Per Ton (Cents)		Value Per Ton (Dollars)	
	1880	1890	1880	1890	1880	1890
Tennessee	332	392	68	82	1·27	1·21
Kentucky	261	334	73	70	1·20	0·99
Ohio	320	352	86	69	1·29	0·94

Those figures, which are quoted by Schoenof from the census of 1880, prove that the labour cost per ton was lowest where the average of day wages was highest, and that the price of coal fell, although the rate of wages rose. And he shows that, in many other industries, along with an increase in earnings there has gone a decrease in the hours of labour. These facts are of the deepest importance, and they have been corroborated by numerous independent observers. Lord Brassey points out that where wages are low the work done is, as a rule, correspondingly small.

It is precisely in the countries in which wages are highest and the working hours shortest that the greatest productivity prevails. It is more than probable that the adoption of an eight hours' day, advocated as early as the beginning of the nineteenth century by Robert Owen, would result, not only in improved social, but in improved economic conditions. When it was proposed to restrict **The Road of Social Progress** the hours of factory hands there was an outcry that the industries of the country would be ruined. What is the truth? It is that the steady reduction of hours has been accompanied by an increase both in the quantity and the quality of the products. These few facts at which we have glanced appear to prove that even political economy, which has been called "the dismal science," is able to indicate for us the road of social progress.

THE SOCIAL PROBLEMS OF TO-DAY
AND THE REMEDIES OFFERED BY SOCIALISM

IT is not necessary to be a Socialist in order to believe in the urgent need of a wider distribution of the means of human well-being. Socialism does not appear to have yet discovered economic principles which are sound, but neither can it be said that the present industrial system, which has created on the one hand vast wealth, and on the other vast poverty, is capable of satisfying the conscience of the civilised world.

A recent writer, Sir H. Wrison, who betrays alarm concerning the dominance of democracy, asks the question: "What are the poor going to do with the rich?" But we should also ask what have the rich been doing with the poor? Rodbertus pointed out long ago that pauperism and a glutted market are the chief causes of the economic distress of modern times. And there is profound suggestion in the theory that there exists **The Sequel to Rapid Production** likewise a close interaction between poverty and the state of the markets for commodities. In spite of the increased productivity of human labour, aided as it is by machinery and scientific processes, the industrial class receive only what is sufficient to support their existence.

But the industrial class is the most numerous in the state. In other words, they ought to form the largest body of consumers. What, however, is the real situation? The purchasing power of the poorer classes is greatly restricted. Hence the rapid production of modern industry is not met by a corresponding consumption. Rather, it is followed by an economic deadlock. The creation of commodities suddenly stops because the market becomes full of superfluous goods. Expansion is succeeded by contraction of production, by a scarcity of employment, and a further decline in the purchasing power of the working class. Thus, we have a commercial crisis bringing with it pauperism as a necessary result. In the meantime the purchasing power of the capitalists and landholders continues relatively to increase; but as they have already had enough to buy all the comforts of life, they spend more in the purchase of luxuries, the production of which increases. Such phenomena are the result of what some Socialistic writers call "the competitive anarchy" of the capitalistic system. They propose to replace that system by collective ownership of capital, collective production and collective distribution of the products of industry. The state is to become a vast factory or assemblage of factories, and every citizen is to take his place as a working unit.

The State According to the Socialists

Private speculation is to cease. There would be neither profits nor wages, but each individual worker would be paid by the community in labour cheques. Money would be abolished. Land and machinery, together with the entire means of production, would be collectively owned. All workers would be on the same level, for, according to the crude doctrine of Proudhon, a piece of work done in one place balances a piece of work done in another, no matter how different the two kinds of work may be, provided that the same amount of time is consumed.

Those individuals who would be incapable of producing material things, but could serve the community as officials, teachers, physicians or artists would be remunerated by a share in commodities proportioned to the time spent by them in work socially useful. Credit and loan, lease, stocks and shares would no longer exist. But it is difficult to see how the result of such a system could be anything else than economic stagnation. Private enterprise would be crushed, for private enterprise is the result of private interest, which Socialism disallows. Equality would mean the death of liberty. If an individual possesses superior powers

Socialism the Death of Liberty

of invention and energy, to forbid him the enjoyment of the fruits of those powers would be tyrannical and unjust.

To compel the more highly endowed to remain for ever on the same dead level as the more lowly endowed would be to abolish justice in the name of an equality whereby only mediocrity would gain.

A Lesson From Argentina In his book on foreign work and English wages Lord Brassey narrates the history of a highly instructive experiment in Socialism which took place in Argentina, and which came under his own observation. "Large numbers of colonists," he says, "were sent out from all parts of Europe. To each was allotted an equal area of land ; for each a house was built, a well dug and seeds and implements provided. Nature gave to each an equal portion of sunshine and of rain, and at the end of a short term of years you find some in penury, many struggling to maintain a bare subsistence ; a few, but only a few, had prospered. The unsuccessful regarded themselves as the victims of undeserved misfortune and viewed with envy the growing prosperity of their neighbours."

If Socialism means the abolition of distinction for all who succeed, it will kill not only the desire to succeed, but even the desire to work. Exaggerated individualism has produced economic tyranny, but the worst of all despotism is collective despotism, for it is impersonal. It is not really true that one man is as valuable to the state as another, or that one man is equal to another. To equalise fortunes which have been created by unequal talent would convert the state into a poor-house. We cannot believe that when the state is rechristened "Socialistic" the mainsprings of human activity will be fundamentally changed.

He who supposes that, as long as characters and talent remain diverse, it is possible to create and to maintain a uniformity **Eternal Struggle For Life** in human fortune, knows little of human nature. A mass of human beings idly leaning upon each other is not a state. Let us admit that at the present moment it is difficult to see any solution for the social problem. It appears to be inevitable that there should go on within the limits of the state that war for life, which is the main fact of human and of all other existence. Even Lassalle declared that "History is a struggle against Nature"

(Die Geschichte ist ein Kampf mit der Natur). But that fact does not prevent the interference of mankind for the purpose of mitigation and appeasement. What characterises the social action of the modern world is the perception that there is no necessary antagonism between moral and economic reform. The abolition of abuses has proved that the reverse is true. More and more we have come to see that in voluntary collaboration lies the true life of the state, and that if the state is an organism, every member who contributes to its combined life requires to be rewarded according to his contribution.

We may not be able to discover in Socialism a practicable theory of government. But we cannot blind ourselves to the fact that that doctrine contains a noble truth. Schäffle has said that "Socialism is a question of the stomach" (eine Magenfrage). But so is individualism. If the two great efforts of the state are still, as in the words of Aristotle, the attainment of mere life, and then of the good and harmonious life, a certain share of material comfort is necessary for all its members. **Where the Poor Live** Recent investigations into modern poverty prove that national health and security are not compatible with the existence of a vast proletariat half fed, half clothed, and, we may add, half housed. The slave and the serf received food and clothing and shelter from their masters, but to-day the pauper and the unemployed workman are required to provide these things for themselves.

In the slums of all great modern cities extraordinary efforts are daily made by millions of men and women to procure even the most wretched and the most repulsive conditions of bare existence. Beneath the glittering fabric of civilisation lies this immense, foul and rickety foundation of poverty. Whatever our theories of economics may be, and howsoever we may apportion the moral responsibility for the long antagonism between labour and capital, the fact remains that, owing to a combination of moral and economic causes, every modern state suffers from the same social disease. Says Emerson :

'Tis the day of the chattel,
　Web to weave and corn to grind,
Things are in the saddle,
　And ride mankind.

But "things," or economic causes, have been in the saddle since the beginning of human history, and they have ridden many generations to death. Not only emotional philanthropists, but economists with cool heads have examined the lower strata of modern society, and have pointed out that the amount of wretchedness to be discovered in the great pauper areas is a national danger.

Professor Marshall, in his "Principles of Economics," says that children of the working classes are imperfectly fed and clothed. They are housed in a way that promotes neither physical nor moral health; they receive an education which, though in modern England it may not be very bad so far as it goes, yet goes only a little way; they have few opportunities of getting a broader view of life, or an insight into the nature of the higher work of business, or of science, or of art; they meet hard and exhausting toil early on the way, and for the greater part keep to it all their lives. At last they go to the grave, carrying with them undeveloped abilities and faculties, which, if they could have borne full fruit, would have added to the national wealth of the country—to say **Signs of Physical Decadence** nothing of higher considerations —many times as much as would have covered the expense of providing adequate opportunities for their development." But the point on which we have here specially to insist is that the evil is cumulative.

An anæmic generation can have only an anæmic progeny. If we examine the returns for recruiting for the British Army we shall discover grave reasons for believing that the national energy is being sapped. In 1900, out of 88,402 recruits medically inspected, no fewer than 23,105 were rejected as physically unfit. And the standard required is, unfortunately, by no means high. When we remember, too, that many of the recruits are only provisionally accepted, and that a considerable number break down during training, and are sent back as useless, the symptoms of a low vitality in the proletariat are still more evident. The causes of rejection are defective eyesight and hearing, weight and chest and height under-developed, deformed limbs, heart disease, skin disease, decayed teeth, and unsound lungs. What do such facts mean?

They mean that generations of the progenitors of those recruits have been imperfectly fed, imperfectly housed, and imperfectly clothed. The victories of a handful of picked British athletes at the Olympic games cannot be accepted as a proof that the great mass of the people enjoy physical health. On the contrary, the researches of Mr. Charles Booth, of Mr. Seebohm Rowntree, and of many other trained observers, make the truth painfully manifest that, in spite of free **High Rate of Infant Mortality** trade, the nutrition of a great portion of the labouring class is wholly inadequate. In London the percentage of pauper population is 30·7, in York it is 27·84, and in other industrial cities the same average is reached. How is it possible to provide the nation with a virile working class when families earning wages below twenty shillings weekly live upon a diet far less nutritious than what is supplied to the inmates of the workhouse?

In the poorest districts of our great cities, out of every 1,000 children 250 die before they are twelve months old. And that this high rate of infant mortality is due to poverty and its attendant dangers and discomforts seems to be proved by the fact that among the better paid section of the working class only about 94 out of every 1,000 children die below the age of twelve months. It has been calculated that the death rate among children in the poorer parts of London is almost three times higher than the corresponding rate in the richer districts. Conditions of life under which one child out of every four dies before it is twelve months old are a menace to national well-being. We are told that only 12 per cent. of the working class population in York are living in sanitary houses.

Comparatively high rents are paid for hovels. A family of six, with an income of less than eighteen shillings a week, find it necessary to deny themselves food and clothing in order to pay three shillings in rent. And even that amount of rent is too high if we consider the kind of accommodation provided in the slums. **Profits of Slum Property** There are cases in which there is only one water-tap to fourteen tenements, and a single closet is shared by fifteen families. Anyone who wishes to study the budgets of the poor will find abundant material in the pages of Mr. Booth and Mr. Rowntree. And he will learn that one of the most ironical facts of the social life of to-day is that slum property is highly profitable to the owner. We are told that wherever a room is, owing to its bad state of repair or its dampness and general unhealthiness, to be had at a low rental, there is an eager demand for it among the poorest classes. It is impossible to deny that such a fact is nothing less than a disgrace to modern civilisation, especially in a country in which the national income reaches approximately the sum of

The Hard Lot of the Poor £1,350,000,000. No doubt, a great part of that sum is represented by wages. But it is only in the ranks of the higher artisans that the rate of wages is sufficient to allow a margin for saving. And, as Mr. Hobson points out, a low wage is not accompanied by a low price for commodities.

To begin with, the rent absorbs a large fraction of the wage. It is calculated that in certain pauper areas in London 86 per cent. of the inhabitants pay more than one-fifth of their weekly wages in rent. If, during the last fifty years, wages have risen, rents have also risen. Moreover, since the poor buy in small quantities, they are compelled to pay higher prices for their food. The price of fresh vegetables, such as carrots, parsnips, etc., in East London is not infrequently ten times the price at which the same articles can be purchased wholesale from the grocers. The results of a loss of employment or of sudden illness may be imagined in the case of men and women who exist in such conditions as these. Extra expenditure is met by savings on necessaries, and in order to purchase a pair of boots the family frequently goes without a dinner.

It has been estimated that out of a population of 40,000,000 only three out of every ten persons in the United Kingdom are able to live above the poverty line. On the first day of January an old-age pension scheme, for providing for the aged poor, came into force. This measure is essentially socialistic. It may even be the beginning of a disastrous era for British finance and national security. But all

Millions Spent in Charity parties in the state are in agreement that the time was ripe for some such provision. Yet we wonder whether it would not be wiser, both in the interests of the nation and of the individual, to aid the poorest of the working class not at the end, but at the beginning of their lives.

The millions annually spent in charity are often spent too indiscriminately, and too late. And the state would receive a more adequate return, in the form of the higher physical and moral development of her weakest members, if her activities in social amelioration were better organised. Meantime, those writers are scarcely to be convicted of unreasonable pessimism who, after they have examined modern pauperism, doubt whether, in spite of all contrary appearances, modern civilisation marks any real social advance on ancient and mediæval slavery and serfdom.

Let us not forget that the social problem is universal, and that no nation is unaffected by it. Modern industrialism has produced in Germany, in America and in France, and, indeed, wherever it has spread its roots, exactly the same economic results which are found in Great Britain. But it is precisely in its international character that we may perhaps find the best promise of a mitigation if not of an ultimate cure of the great social disease of the modern world. At first sight, indeed, the reverse would appear to be the case.

For the armed condition of modern nations is the result not only of immemorial antagonisms, but also of rivalries engendered by the struggle for industrial and

If War Should Cease? commercial supremacy. *Prima facie*, therefore, the working class of one country is the natural enemy of the working class of another. Nevertheless, internationalism, which is a wholly modern idea, was first proclaimed by the representatives of the industrial population of all the great European countries. It was by them that war was denounced as a crime against the essential solidarity of mankind. What would be the economic result of the abolition of war is difficult to forecast. But since that abolition would at least involve an immense reduction in taxation, and would divert industrial activity from wasteful production to a production socially useful, the moral and economic gain might be incalculable.

At any rate, there exists the closest connection between the internal conditions and the external relations of a state. If, then, an international harmony could be discovered, each state would be left free to apply its energies and to devote its wealth to the solution of its own social problems. This, we should like to believe, is the consummation which lies before all the modern peoples. The ideal goal of history is the collaboration of states in the great tasks of a common humanity. The cost of the retardation of inter-racial and international justice is too vast for measurement. Let us not forget that, although climatic influences, age-long habits, and many other complex causes have created a sense of actual physical repulsion between various breeds of men, the war which goes on between races erroneously supposed to be absolutely divergent is really the same kind of war which goes on within the limits of a single race, and, for that matter, within the frontiers of a single nation. It is the war for food. And yet the earth is capable of providing food for all. Every national group has reproduced within itself a minor and more or less modified form of the struggle for existence. The conflict between individuals for the means of subsistence and for liberty is the same kind of conflict which rages between states for territorial possessions. Empire is only a colossal form of landowning, and the history of war forms part of the history of property.

It was a perception of these permanent factors of disturbance in human society which caused Immanuel Kant to say that

Ideal Goal of Human History " at the sight of the actions of men displayed on the great stage of the world, it is impossible to escape a certain feeling of disgust." Yet in his remarkable essay on " Universal History," Kant foreshadowed a set of inter-racial and international conditions which have been the dream and hope of less practical and more visionary minds. The last and the greatest task, he tells us, which will be offered to men will be the creation of a civil society founded upon justice, and embracing the entire earth. In spite of the fact that during the period which has elapsed since Kant's death the world has frequently vibrated with the shock of revolution and war, it cannot be said that this ideal goal of human history has wholly vanished out of human thought.

On the contrary, there are signs that civilised peoples are becoming more impatient with the doctrine that the work of the world must be inevitably accompanied by an eternal homicide. The gradual elimination of the idea that man, like any other living thing, is only a form of prey, meant a new route for human destiny. That idea, as expressed in the slave system, was the dominant principle of ancient society in its industrial aspect ; and it lingered far into the Christian era. But in modern times the labourer is a free man, and he sells his labour for wages. The basis of human society has by this single fact been so revolutionised that only ignorance of history could make us deny that the relations existing within states and between them are infinitely more humane in the

The Secret of Social Harmony modern than they were in the ancient world. The doctrine that *réciprocité c'est justice* is, at least in practice, a purely modern idea, and it contains the secret of social harmony. The modern state is the result of a voluntary co-operation between its members. Sooner or later, amid all social conflagrations and confusions, the end has been the same, and that end has been the triumph of liberty.

And it seems time to ask whether it is not just here in this common goal of states that we may be able to detect some promise of union in the broken history of man ? For if they are all striving to be free, it is in the interests of every one of them that none shall be enslaved by another. The Bill of Rights which each of them has won or is winning must, unless human society is to remain fundamentally irrational, cover inter-racial and international relations. It is not unreasonable to suppose that just as the feuds of families and of clans gave way before the conception of national unity, so the feuds of nations and of races may be at last lost in a general collaboration of mankind. This would be the true *Foedus Amphictyonum*.

One of the remarkable facts of history is that, on the whole, all social systems at any given period tend towards uniformity. In Greece and in Italy the age of the despots was followed by the age of the democracies. Thus, too, during the mediæval period various forms of feudalism were simultaneously spread throughout a wide European area. In

What History Teaches other words, political and social ideas have always been contagious, and to-day a common conception of human rights is being diffused through the world. History teaches us that out of the most disordered forces order has actually been created, and that in the world of man, as in the world of Nature, chaos is the first stage of cosmos. Although the stairs of human progress are broken, nevertheless they are stairs. WILLIAM ROMAINE PATERSON

6403

PROGRESS

From the painting by G. F. Watts, by permission of Fredk. Hollyer

THE TRIUMPH OF THE MIND OF MAN

By Dr. C. W. Saleeby

THE MASTER KEY OF PROGRESS OR
HISTORY IN THE LIGHT OF BIOLOGY

THE spectacle offered to the historian is not merely a succession of persons and scenes; it is not a panorama, nor a pageant, nor a phantasmagoria, but a sequence, or medley of sequences, which have direction and tendency. The happenings with which he deals are not merely events to be placed and dated, but processes. It is the difference between a succession of music-hall " turns " and an organic drama.

Being human, the historian inevitably applies to the spectacle before him criteria derived from the human sense of worth or value. He speaks of the decline and fall of an empire; he distinguishes between savagery and civilisation, barbarism and culture, ignorance and knowledge.

Here or there he witnesses processes which he calls progress or retrogression, advance or decadence. Whatever the meaning that he attaches to these terms, history unquestionably presents phenomena to which they may be applied, and for man as a spiritual being the questions that centre around the word " progress " are the vital questions of history, and those by which it is exalted to a rightful place above the purely physical sciences. However defined or conceived, progress has at least been observed at certain **Biology's** times and in certain places, and **Relation** it is the supreme interest of **to History** the historian. In the present essay it is our business to consider the new conceptions of history which, as it seems to the writer, must necessarily follow from our new perception of the facts of biological science. It is biology after all, and not archæology, nor anthropology, that has given new dignity

to history. It is the study of life as a whole, the study of all life—vegetable, animal, human—as a single fact, and the only important fact of the earth's surface, that has made for ever ridiculous the conception of the history of the world as **Man as** neither more nor less than the **Part of a** history of man during the last **Process** few thousand years. The doctrine of organic evolution has revealed to us the continuity of man with his inferiors in the scale of life. The whole of human history may thus, for some purposes, be rightly conceived as only a chapter in the history of life—the greatest chapter, and that which gives meaning to all the rest, and perhaps the longest chapter when it is completely written, if it is to be ended at all, but at the time of writing, probably the shortest chapter in the history of important species.

The thesis of the writer is that in the light of the revelations of the nineteenth century it is impermissibly short-sighted any longer to conceive of human history as if it were not the latest term in a long series. We have to conceive a man as part and product of a process which is older than he. We derogate nothing from his dignity and from his unique position in thus conceiving him.

If, for instance, throughout the whole living world, apart from man, we find certain principles under which life has advanced here and degenerated there, multiplied or diminished, left the sea for the land or the land for the air, we are bound to ask ourselves whether man as a living being must not also be subject to these principles, though with profound modifications due to his unique character.

6405

It is not merely that modern biology desires to trace the very earliest stages in the history of man. Certainly it is desirable that the historian, in attempting to write, for instance, the earliest pages of the history of the New World, should recognise the conclusion of the biologists that the human species arose in the Old

A Creature Older than Man World. It would be inconsistent with the largeness of our scheme if we failed to realise the weight of the fact that man claims a common ancestry with the anthropoid apes, and that these are exclusively confined to what we find it still convenient to call the Eastern Hemisphere.

Plainly, also, biology has a right to be heard in these days when it claims that not even the anthropologist is entitled to write the first chapter of human history. Older even than primitive man, older than the earliest or palæolithic civilisation, there was a creature, neither ape nor man—to be called the missing link, however, only by those who ignorantly think that man is descended from one of the present species of anthropoid apes—which had his history; and since every present time has all the future in its womb, the history of even the ape-man is part of the planetary epic. That history, however, it seems safe to say, will never be written. At present, indeed, we have only the scantiest evidence regarding the characters of the most primitive erected mammal. Nevertheless, a history of the world which contained no allusion to that evidence nor even to that period would be ludicrously imperfect. Yet there is no general historical work extant other than this one which alludes to this missing chapter, or, rather, this prologue to human history.

The positive evidence, then, which we actually possess regarding the first period in human history consists of the imperfect remains of a fossil skeleton discovered by

The Old World's Erect Ape-man Dr. Dubois in Pliocene deposits in Java in the year 1892. The creature thus suggested to us has been called *Pithecanthropus erectus*—the erect ape-man. It is not the immediate concern of the historian to study the characters of this skeleton; it is, at all events, his concern to note the fact that we are possessed of evidence showing an erected creature, neither ape nor man, to have lived in the Old World at the period indicated by these

deposits. This fact, coupled with the contrast between the monkeys of the New World and the apes of the Old World, is the first great fact of human history.

It is not my purpose here, however, to dwell upon this matter. Suffice it that, at any rate in the twentieth century, we formally repair the omission of the first chapter of human history, which our predecessors during the last half century sanctioned, and of which their predecessors were, of course, wholly unaware. But I repeat that modern biology is of immeasurably greater importance to the historian than that involved in its contributions to the very earliest stages in the history of man. The point is that modern biology sees its principles illustrated in human history, sees them determining the lives not merely of individuals, but also of races and empires and civilisations.

Above all, it is the science of life, and that alone, from which we may obtain any real and fruitful understanding of the supreme fact of history, which is progress—not uninterrupted, continuous, inevitable, irresistibly cumulative progress, but progress sometimes, somewhere,

History's New Definition and, on the whole, nevertheless. It is high time, indeed, that worthy conceptions of history, conceptions worthy of the spirit of age, should find due recognition amongst us. Never again must it be possible for any historian, distinguished or undistinguished, to pen those famous and monstrous words so often quoted from Gibbon's "Decline and Fall of the Roman Empire": "History, which is, indeed, little more than the register of the crimes, follies, and misfortunes of mankind."

On the contrary, the present writer would define history as the record of the ascent of man. Such a definition would have been impossible for Gibbon, who had no evidence of such ascent, and no conception of the emergence of man from the sub-human world. If the reader would estimate the services of biology to human thought, let him contrast the definition of history which was possible for a great genius like Gibbon and the definition which only requires a moment's reflection to be regarded as commonplace to-day, or if not to-day, at any rate to-morrow.

But in any discussion of progress we shall achieve less than nothing unless we successfully define this great term in which our interest centres. It is possible to use the word " progress " concerning facts on many planes. Any change in the direction of differentiation, any passage from the homogeneous to the heterogeneous, might conceivably be referred to as progress But this is not a sense of the word that can have any real value for us.

There was a time, we know, when not only was the earth's surface destitute of life, but even its crust was destitute of structure. Such structure was achieved in the course of ages, yet there is something incongruous in the term " geological progress." Again, in the course of time life appeared upon the earth, its first forms, as we must infer from the facts of nutrition, being vegetable, that is to say, forms capable of feeding wholly upon inorganic material. From these earliest beginnings there may be traced upwards the evolution of the vegetable kingdom, which has at last flowered, in what we call the flowering plants, including, of course, the mightiest trees.

In the course of this history there has been much advance from the homogeneous to the heterogeneous, much differentiation, **What is Meant by Progress** much achievement of complexity; there has been everything that answers to Herbert Spencer's definition of his word " evolution." There has been what we might call anatomical or morphological progress, there has as certainly been physiological progress, increase in complexity and efficiency of function as well as of structure, yet is there not a something lacking, which causes us to regard the term " vegetable progress " as somehow incongruous ? It is less so, perhaps, than geological progress, because at least it deals with life. Yet, in spite of all, we feel that the word is not worthily used.

Plainly, then, our definition of progress must not be in terms of the physical. Physical evolution, whether mechanical or anatomical, is not progress. The evolution of the motor-car mechanism with six cylinders from that with one is not progress, nor yet the evolution of the many-celled anatomico-chemical mechanism called the oak from the one-celled plant. Our definition must be in terms of the intangible. It must have " thoughts of things which thoughts but tenderly touch." It must be in terms of mind. By progress we mean no series of physical changes, however admirable or perfect their physical result.

Yet if without any physical changes that seem noteworthy there appears but the barest rudiment of the psychical, the merest glimmering of sentiency, the scarcely recognisable emergence of anything that feels, there is the very fact of progress before us. As a preliminary definition, then, let us take it that by progress we mean the emergence and **Vegetable and Animal Kingdoms** increasing predominance of the psychical over the physical. Only in terms of mind—using that word in its widest sense—can we frame any definition of progress that appeals to us who are minds. Plainly, then, geological evolution is out of court. More noteworthy, however, is the fact that one-half of all biological evolution is out of court.

It is not easy to frame any final definition of the difference between an animal and a plant. Yet if we compare the animal and the vegetable kingdoms, it is possible to declare one overwhelming fact of contrast between them. The vegetable kingdom, with all its power and achievements, shows no growth of mind. On every other score but this the oak is vastly superior to the alga ; yet if we are to apply the criterion of the psychical to them the difference is naught. Everything has been achieved, but the one thing—the oak displays no unified consciousness, let alone self-consciousness, no volition, not even the scantiest, or any but the scantiest, differentiation of the primary sentiency which we are compelled to attribute to the first vegetables. So far as any psychical evolution is concerned, the history of the vegetable kingdom is substantially blank. This it is which, to my mind, constitutes the one difference that matters between the vegetable and the animal kingdoms.

We dismiss, then, as beneath our present notice the whole course of vegetable evolution, and turn to recognise the overwhelming contrast displayed in animal evolution. This displays a series of increasing complexities for the **Complexities of Animal Evolution** physicist, yet another for the chemist, yet another for the comparative anatomist, and another for the student of the cell. To all of these, however, a parallel might be found in the vegetable kingdom, but there is no vegetable parallel to that evolution which the psychologist discerns in the history of the animal world, and that psychical evolution is the only worthy thing that we can possibly mean by the

6407

word progress. I say psychical rather than mental, because it is not merely intelligence of which we must think, but all the attributes of the psyche.

It is the historic fact that upon the earth long ago there was nothing of the psychical, or, at any rate, no more than the hylozoist may attribute, like Empedocles,

Man and Insect Compared
to the atoms with their " loves and hates." Later, there was no more of the psychical than is displayed by the bacterium or the oak to-day, and now there are intelligence and will and motherhood. Consider that if we study any kind of sentiency that may be found in the oak, we regard it as existing to serve the oak itself, and by the oak itself we mean the bodily, physical, material oak ; similarly, also, in the case of the sensitive plant or the sea anemone or the worm. Any powers of sensation or discrimination or response that such creatures possess we describe as appanages or faculties useful for the plant or animal itself, and the self is still the physical being.

But now pass upwards. I do not say that there is presented to us a picture of animal species placed on the successive rungs of a ladder of intelligence, and I even remember that Father Wasmann declares, erroneously, I believe, that if there were such a ladder, we should have to put ants on the highest rungs above any monkey. But I will pass right up to man, and then we shall surely agree that the relation of things has been reversed. Such a mind as the insect has exists for its body. But the body of a man exists only to serve the man himself, and by the man himself we do not mean the bodily, physical, material man. We do not even require to pass up to man in order to realise this fashion in which the psychical has turned the tables upon the physical. Let the reader compare, for instance, his dog with a tree and a caterpillar, and con-

Progress the Supreme Fact of History
sider the case of physical mutilation. If the branches of the tree be lopped off, part of the tree is gone ; so with the caterpillar. But who that has a pet dog would consider that the creature he loves has partly vanished because a leg is amputated ? It is its psyche that is the dog, it is its body that is the caterpillar ; the psychical has turned the tables upon the physical— and that is progress. Its highest form is found in man, to whom were addressed

the words : " If thy hand or foot offend thee, cut them off, and cast them from thee." The man is not composed of hand and feet and viscera—these are his body-servants.

Progress is therefore not an illusion of youth, but the supreme fact of the earth's history, and the final demonstration of that truth is the first service of biology and of the nineteenth century to mankind. Progress is possible because it has occurred. It is not an illusion, but a scientific truth. The common cant about the " illusion of progress " may make attractive literature or rhetoric, but to deny the reality of progress is as definitely to flout scientific truth as to deny the motion of the earth, and is an error immeasurably more grave. Even if we care to play with the terrible idea of Aristotle, that every art and every philosophy has probably been found out many times, up to the limits of the possible, and again destroyed, even then we have to reckon with the finding out, which is an aspect of progress.

The converse error is no less noteworthy. It consists in the teaching that science demonstrates progress to be constant and

Survival of the Fittest
inevitable. This error, however, was long ago exposed. We may remember that during those years when Spencer was working towards his conception of universal evolution he wrote, in 1857, an essay called " Progress : Its Law and Cause." When he saw, however, that all change is not progressive, he introduced the word " evolution " as a term which does not commit us to any moral concept. We must remember, also, that his familiar phrase is not " survival of the best," but " survival of the fittest," and that fitness may at times be constituted by characters which are irrelevant to progress, such as vegetable characters ; or by others which, so far from being the best, are the worst.

If we are inclined to believe that progress is constant and inevitable, let us recall the evolution of the intestinal parasites as proof of the possibility of degradation even under the action of natural selection. The survival of the fittest now becomes equivalent to the survival of the worst. Yet, again, biologists are familiar with what may be called survivals from the past in the plant world. Change in no direction can occur if there be nothing to cause it, and thus you may find species extant to-day which seem to have undergone no change for untold ages. On the one hand, organic evolution asserts that progress is possible and has occurred, and on the other hand that it is neither constant nor inevitable under all conditions. Evolution demonstrates and has achieved, but is not synonymous with, progress.

This, of course, the historian knows full well, and one of the reasons why, during the last half century, he has failed to realise what organic evolution means for him is that he has been misled as to what the doctrine asserts. He knows that progress is not inevitable ; he knows that the mightiest empires, having reached unexampled heights, have fallen. Where, he asks, are " the glory that was Greece and the grandeur that was Rome " ? He has pushed back his inquiries to Babylon, and yet more clearly he sees that progress is not inevitable. As Spain fell, and Rome and Greece, so did Egypt and Babylon. When, therefore, the doctrine of organic evolution is presented to him as asserting that progress is a constant law of Nature, can he be blamed for declining to waste his time upon what **Is there a Goal to Progress?** he knows to be false ? It is our business in these pages to state the facts and the theory based upon them in a more correct fashion, and in the course of doing so to show that there is absolutely no conflict whatever between the teachings of biology and the facts of history. If there were such a conflict, which would have to go to the wall, does the reader fancy—the theories or the facts ?

But before we turn more closely to examine the historical facts let us endeavour to complete our concept of progress. We have agreed that, considered from afar, it is at any rate clearly discernible to be the increasing predominance of the psychical over the physical, and that, if it exists at all, it is involved in psychical evolution. We remind ourselves also that evolution under all its aspects is a change from the homogeneous to the heterogeneous. Is it possible, then, to conceive of any finality, any goal to progress ? Is there any ideal that seems to be indicated ?

Plainly, I think, psychical evolution can result in nothing higher than what we call personality or individuality. If evolution is to result in the production of the heterogeneous, its ideal is most completely achieved in personality—" the most distinctive quality we know," as Professor Höffding says. Progress, then, must be such a series of changes as increase the conscious life of the individual. We can by no means plumb the depths which the conscious life may reach here or hereafter, but along this path and no other is our goal to be sought. If the machinery **The Real Proofs of Progress** of a motor-car is not proof of progress, no more is the machinery of a society. The products of progress are not mechanisms, but men. Physical complexity, physical differentiation—all this as such is nothing to us. The life of the beehive, for instance, has to be judged by the ideals which we have formulated and not by any mechanical standards. If the machinery of the beehive does not make for individuality, it has nothing to do with the subject we are discussing, though as an achievement in vital mechanics it may be considerably more interesting than a motor-car. So much, then, by way of definition.

The older theory of organic evolution, which is commonly named after Lamarck, and which was expounded by him at length in 1809, the year of Charles Darwin's birth, asserted that characters acquired by the parent, such as the effects of use and disuse, are transmitted to the offspring. One of his examples was the case of the giraffe, which owes its long neck, he presumed, to the gradual stretching of the necks of many ancestors in their efforts to reach the leaves of trees. Now, it needs but the smallest consideration to recognise that this question of the transmission of acquired characters, commonly regarded as a quarrel of the biologists, is of the utmost moment to the philosophic historian.

In general, it is fair to say that historians have hitherto accepted, as popular opinion commonly accepts, the Lamarckian doctrine of the inheritance of acquirements. For many generations **Doctrine of Inherited Acquirements** a race is disciplined, and so at last there is produced a people to whom discipline is native ; or for many generations a nation finds it necessary to make adventure upon the water, and so at last there is produced a generation with blue water in its blood.

The theory applies equally to retrogression—a fact of history scarcely less salient than the fact of progress. Every historian has asserted that the vices of a people will, in course of time, produce moral and physical degeneration in their posterity. Historians like to compare the history of a nation to the history of an individual, and this leads them to the very familiar assertion, repeated and believed almost everywhere, that the life of a species or race or nation, like the life of an individual, must inevitably **Biology an Aid to History** show a period of growth followed by maintenance, and, as in the individual, ultimately by decadence and death. Now, modern biology has to be reckoned with in these interpretations of history, with its periods of progress and retrogression. And in the first place, for the case may be more briefly dealt with, let us observe that the argument from the necessity of death for the individual to the necessity of death for a species or race is, biologically considered, not merely false but ridiculous. On the contrary, between the individual and the race there exists only one overwhelming difference, which is precisely that, whilst the individual is necessarily mortal, the race is not, and the analogy between the life of the individual and the life of a nation belongs entirely to the domain not of science, but of rhetoric or poetry.

Every living man at this moment bears within him living elements which may trace back a continuous ancestry to the beginnings of life upon our planet. Life as a whole phenomenon does not die; it is only the individual that dies. To assert that because an individual dies a species or a nation must die is to prove oneself blind to the most salient fact that distinguishes the species from the individual.

Turn we now to the still more serious questions involved in the truth or falsity of the Lamarckian doctrine concerning the inheritance of acquired characters. Let us state in a concrete and striking form the magnitude of the contrast between the interpretations of history that respectively assert and deny this proposition. **The Case of a "Dying Nation"** Let us imagine a nation which for many generations has lived in ever-increasing luxurious sloth and ease. Let us take this nation at a period when it would seem that decadence could no further go. But still, of course, there are many babies being born. Now, the question is as to the state of those babies at birth. According to the Lamarckian view, the new generation is predestined to failure; it is imbued with character acquired and accumulated by its ancestors. This is a " dying nation." Like an individual it has entered on its period of decadence, and, as in the case of the individual, no social medicine will restore either its adult manhood or its youth.

But suppose that we are empowered summarily to deny the transmission of acquired characters. Words can scarcely picture the contrast in our interpretation. The new generation, then, is, on the whole, not much better, not much worse, except through the slow operation of any form of selection for parenthood than was the new generation of centuries before. The baby makes a fresh start, the sins of the parent are not visited upon it in the direct fashion asserted by the other theory. If, then, something outside the new generation could be changed ; if each baby could be born into the social environment into which its ancestors of centuries before were born, then, in an instant, so to speak, that nation would become again as great and worthy as in the days of old. It contains the constant possibility of recovery, which the individual who is " dying " in the course of Nature does not. Now, the answer to the question whether or not **History and Biology in Agreement** acquired characters are transmitted cannot be left to the historian. It is to be answered by the students of heredity; it is to be answered after experimental inquiry by the microscope, and by statistics. If the facts so obtained are incompatible with the facts of history, then further inquiry must show why it is that what is true of the dog or the chestnut is not true of man ; but we shall find that there is no incompatibility with the facts of history. Let us see how we can defend that assertion.

It is the conclusion of modern biology, and one which we are now compelled to accept, that acquired characters are not transmissible. We now recognise a principle that makes for organic evolution without requiring us to assume that acquired characters are transmissible. This principle we are about to study. But it is not merely that we do not need the transmission of acquirements ; it is that on inquiry we find that it does not occur. To this statement there are some very dubious exceptions, derived, for instance, from the realm of immunity to disease ; but these are quite irrelevant to the interpretation of history. So far as the historian is concerned, acquired characters are not transmissible and are never transmitted. He has to reckon with this.

The result of this conclusion of the biologists is in a sense to enhance the importance of that department of history which is outside the sphere of biology. This is to say that in denying the transmission of acquirements by heredity we greatly restrict the importance of biological heredity in the study of history, whilst to do so is proportionately to increase the moment that must be attached to the facts of history that lie outside all biological heredity. In other words, whilst in explaining the degeneration of a people the historian might formerly transfer his burden to the shoulders of the biologist, as, for instance, by saying that a species must die as an individual dies, he is now compelled to explain the phenomenon in social terms and historical terms, in terms of events and customs and

History's Tremendous Phenomena morality, and especially of environment, as the selector of parenthood. The transmission of acquired characters being denied, Lamarckian heredity will no longer bear the burden of explaining these tremendous phenomena of history. In effect, the biologist says to the historian: " No, you must not come to me for explanations ; I will give you the great assistance, if you recognise it as such, of denying absolutely that I can give you any assistance at this point, and of asserting that you must find explanations for these facts in your own proper sphere."

Now, certainly, if the historian found it impossible to make history reasonable without resort to the doctrine of the transmission of acquired characters or the doctrine that nations, like individuals, must die, then, as we have hinted above, the biologist would have to reconsider his position. He would have to ask himself whether, in the total absence of any other conceivable explanation, the decadence of Rome must not be explained in terms of such transmission. But there is no such necessity. On the contrary, the historian

must be purblind who fails to see, staring him in the face, causes totally independent of the transmission of acquired characters or the supposed necessity for the death of a nation, which abundantly account for all the phenomena that he has

The Historian's Debt to the Biologist to explain. What are these causes, I shall be asked, which to my mind so easily account for the tremendous phenomena hitherto found unaccountable by historians, except by recourse to biological doctrines now discredited ? To this I answer that whilst the historian has recorded battles and intrigues and enactments, and so forth, he may possibly have neglected matters of greater moment. And here, also, he has to learn from the biologist ; he has to be taught, and is, indeed, now learning, which are the potent and which the trivial factors of history.

In an early chapter of the HISTORY OF THE WORLD it has been shown how history may be conceived as a history of knowledge, as a history of culture, as a history of liberty, as a history of political institutions. But if the present writer is assured of anything at all, it is that history may be conceived not only under these headings, but also, for instance, as a history of motherhood or as a history of morality.

Human history, after all, is the history of man the individual, in co-existence and in sequence with other individuals. It is a history of individual specimens of human nature, and the factors that have made it must necessarily be the factors that most nearly affect the individual. How, then, can history be rightly interpreted if, for instance, we have as yet no historian of childhood, as we have yet no historian

How to Interpret History of motherhood ? Many have devoted themselves to the influence of the geographical environment upon history, the influence of the sea or the mountains ; many to the influence of the mental environment ; some have even deliciously conceived the history of mankind to be but a series of marginal notes upon the history of machinery.

THE SURVIVAL OF THE FITTEST
BEING LESSONS OF THE PAST
FOR THE WORLD OF TO-DAY

IT is obvious that the inquiries raised have their value, but how relatively limited that value is we realise when we come to ask how far, in terms of mountains or machinery, there can be explained the great facts of history, which are, of course, the rise

The Rise and Fall of Peoples

and fall of peoples. The evident answer is, to take the case of a mountain alone, that this constant and unchanging factor is plainly irrelevant. And the case of machinery is very little better. If history is to be interpreted in terms of human nature, we must interpret its greatest phenomena by the study of those factors which most closely influence human nature.

It is for the reader to decide whether, in the case of this man or that, in the case of this society or that, it is a mountain or a mother, the weather or the home, that is most worthy of his study. This question of the social interpretation of history, one of the most luminous and momentous ideas of this age, must be duly recognised elsewhere. Here we introduce it in order to note that the historian who seeks to explain progress and retrogression, and who is no longer allowed to find simple but false explanations in terms of Lamarckian heredity, need by no means be gravelled for lack of matter.

He has yet to study adequately marriage and motherhood, parentage, social and domestic morality, all the factors that most nearly influence the growing generation; he has to study the progressive

Darwin's Theory of Evolution

modifications in those influences when, for instance, a nation finds it necessary to struggle for its life, or when, having gained success, it ceases to struggle. These subjects are inexhaustible and of inexhaustible moment. Turn we now to the modern theory of organic evolution as conceived and demonstrated by Charles Darwin. We now realise that

the absolute ruler of all organic evolution is that all-important reality which Darwin calls "natural selection" and Spencer "the survival of the fittest." We must closely study these phrases if we are to understand the conditions which, as we saw in the preceding chapter, have resulted in the predominance of the psychical. As we saw, biology can tell us positively that this new predominance of the psychical, which is progress, has occurred. But that would be a small service if it could not proceed to tell us how it has occurred. We are interested in the past, of course; but it is onwards that our eyes are most commonly turned if we are really to justify ourselves as historians for this age, and the question is whether biology can pilot us.

Now, what is the theory of natural selection? It depends upon the existence

The Laws of Heredity and Variation

of two facts, heredity and variation. Like begets like, but commonly not exactly like. The inborn degree of unlikeness is called variation. There are more born than can survive, survival including the idea of parenthood on their part—survival and reproduction in offspring; and therefore those variations which constitute superior fitness for whatever the environment may be are automatically or naturally selected, and those same variations will tend to be transmitted to posterity by the law of heredity. Observe that a variation is an inborn character—inborn, innate, inherent, fundamental, which you will, and as such tends to be perpetuated or transmitted.

This, of course, is an old and very long controversy, but for our present purpose it will suffice if we recognise that the distinction between variations and acquirements is a real one, and that it is variations the selection of which is of value, because it is variations, as distinguished from acquirements, which, being selected, can perpetuate themselves. Now, natural selection in no sense creates—it selects. If there were no variation there would be nothing for it to select from ; it would have no choice. Without variation there would have been no organic evolution.

What is it, then, that in any individual natural selection selects ? The answer is that, with absolute indifference as to all other considerations, natural selection selects whatever has survival value, and in proportion as it has survival value.

Let us begin with the variations upon which it acts. We do not understand their production, but at least we find no more evidence to-day than Darwin found of the existence of any determinate character in them. When we call them fortuitous we must not imagine a "chance" outside the realm of law. On the contrary, the Mendelians find variations to be capable of analysis and prediction. No one who is acquainted with the work of this young school of biologists can speak of fortuitous variations without at any rate an unspoken reminder of the mathematical analysis of what we call **Conditions of Natural Selection** chance. Further, only certain variations are possible for any species. The "fortuity" of natural selection is anything but the "law of higgledy-piggledy," as an academic opponent of Charles Darwin once called it.

Secondly, when we come to study the conditions under which natural selection acts—its dependence upon certain conditions, not merely as regards the production of variations but also as regards the degree to which the environment exercises stringent preference—we see how monstrous is the notion of chance having been set up as an idol and superstitiously worshipped by Darwin, as some would have us believe, and we see also that the law is not a blind law, but, from this point of view at any rate, a very reasonable and discerning one.

Thirdly, as we shall see when we come to study survival value more closely, the demands made by the law of natural selection are absolutely constant, notwithstanding the contrasts between the various fashions in which they are met. I have said that natural selection selects whatever has survival value, and in proportion as it has survival value. The word "value," as Ruskin himself reminds us, is derived from *valere*, to be strong, which is itself an idea derived from life. Now, life, despite its varying manifestations, is at bottom a constant thing, and it is this constant thing, life, and characters that have survival value, that natural selection invariably requires. Natural selection knows what it wants, and invariably gets it. Higgledy-piggledy is, plainly, not the word. **Ruskin's Condemnation of Competition** I will grant that the manifestations of life answer so varyingly to our ethical judgments that we are liable to forget the absolute fundamental consistency which I have tried to indicate. Since life manifests itself in the microbe as well as in man, natural selection may be found selecting the microbe, if that be found to have more value, or, to translate the word into English, more strength.

Hence the superficial aspect of higgledy-piggledy which the law may assume in our eyes if we confine our study to any given moment instead of surveying the whole epic of life. For it is true that the character which possesses survival value may vary indefinitely and offer terrible contrasts to any ethical judgment such as that involved in the idea of progress. Hence the vehemence with which Ruskin condemns the law of competition as anarchy, the law not of life but of death.

In the microbe the characters having survival value are its poisons, or toxins ; in the oak, green leaves, amongst other things, of course ; in the tiger, teeth, claws and muscles ; in the ox, a complicated stomach ; and so on. In so far as the character makes for life it must perpetuate itself ; its might constitutes its right. Nature makes no explicit avowal of any bias towards what we have defined as progress ; she does not declare outright that she is after quality rather than quantity, after the psychical rather than the physical. Thus, though, as we are about to see, the psychical commonly triumphs, simply because it has superior survival **Why the Psychical Triumphs** value, it is not spared if the physical characters of some lower form of life can conquer it. The crab, a crawling invertebrate, may eat the bird. It is said that "on sandbanks among the Laccadive Islands land crabs often kill the nestling terns by the hundred." Yet more striking, man himself, and often the finest souls amongst mankind—a Spinoza or a Schubert—may be killed by a despicable fungus, the tubercle bacillus. The bacillus has some character which is of superior survival value, and accordingly it survives. Thus, so far as natural selection is concerned, there is no right but might. Yet, somehow, the right, as, for instance, the conception of right, has emerged. We can only conclude, then, that if our principle be correct, the right, **Process of Animal Evolution** everything that we admire, or more comprehensively, the psychical, must possess might. Even in a world of claws and toxins it must have possessed sufficient survival value to survive. This is the great thesis of Carlyle in other words. If it be true that natural selection has no prejudices, we can only explain in terms of survival value the present dominance of the psychical.

It is evident enough, if we come to think in terms of this concept of survival value, that lowly psychical characters, such as sensory acuity, sensory discrimination, sensory memory, would constitute factors having survival value for the creature that displayed them. Such creatures would tend to succeed in the struggle for life and to transmit their powers to their offspring. More and more we might expect to find creatures living by their wits rather than by force of bone or muscle. The survival value of such aptitudes is self-evident, and the increasing part they play in the course of animal evolution is one of the most easily explicable of facts.

In short, the evolution of instinctive and intelligent powers is a necessary consequence of their high survival value. Given the action of natural selection upon all vital characters, and given the indisputable, if mysterious, fact that such vital characters may include intelligence, then the emergence and dominance of intelligence is inevitable. The "fluke" theory of its history is untenable. The very reverse is the truth. The only possible theory of the emergence of intelligence is a **Successful Struggle of Intelligence** necessitarian theory. It was given no unfair start; on the contrary, it has not been favoured by the judge; it has not been allowed to emerge without a struggle; it has emerged only where there has been struggle, and it has emerged because it could— because of its superior survival value. It has the right which belongs to might. When, then, man is described as the

"poor fluke or sport of the anthropoid ape," this conclusion, which is advanced as the inevitable inference from biology, seems to me to assert everything that biology denies. So far as the intellectual powers of man are concerned, their emergence and dominance in the light of the concept of survival value seem to me to have been inevitable, not under any conditions, but under the conditions that have obtained. If we believe with Tyndall that their promise and potency must be discerned by the scientific imagination in the primeval nebula, then they must out. When out, as we have seen, they may have to compete even with the tubercle bacillus. Nature never gives a final verdict, but out they must.

This is as much as to say that though progress is not constant, and though evidence of retrogression is only too easy to find, yet, given certain conditions which have obtained, progress was fore-ordained. Contrast with the assertion that man is a "fluke" Sir E. Ray Lankester's "specific assertion that he is the predestined outcome of an orderly, and to a large **Love's Survival Value** extent perceptible, mechanism." But hitherto we have considered the survival value of the psychical only in so far as discrimination, memory, instinct and intelligence are concerned. We turn now to what is infinitely more important for us here, progress being really an ethical term—the psychical characters which may be summed up under the word love.

Now, if it is possible to assert the survival value of intelligence, it is immeasurably easier to assert the survival value of love, and this in direct contravention of the Nietzschean misinterpretation of the Darwinian theory, and also in direct contravention of the famous opinion of Huxley that "cosmic evolution is incompetent to furnish any better reason why what we call good is preferable to what we call evil than we had before." According to Huxley, as to Ruskin, moral or ethical evolution is opposed, radically opposed, to cosmic evolution. But let us look at love in terms of survival value, and let us, if you please, begin with the lowest vertebrates, and we shall end with man.

Sutherland found that so soon as the slightest trace of parental care emerges amongst the fishes, the chance of survival is increased and, as we should expect, the birth rate lowered. This advance may be traced right through the vertebrate kingdom, increase of parental care, that is, of love, being associated with a lower birth rate and a lower infant mortality, this meaning a greater proportion of life to death and a greater possibility of individuation for the parent individual, in consequence of the economy effected in reproduction; whilst the offspring, though fewer, increase in individual power, especially since parental care, in the highest stages of evolution, is concentrated upon a few instead of scattered upon many, and, therefore, weakened for each.

This sequence may be traced through the fishes, amphibia, reptiles, birds and mammals progressively, the birth rate of the anthropoid apes and man being the lowest known. In man the period of gestation, the period of what we may call organic morality, is, in proportion to weight, the longest known, and the natural lactation period of three or four years is also the longest known. Sociologists tell us that the same sequence is to be observed in the human race itself. "Diminutions in the number of deaths and child-births per family accompany advances in parental care from society to society or from class to class in the same society." In short, the psychical fact called love is demonstrated to constitute a factor of supreme survival value. Natural selection actually selects morality, and we come to realise that man is the highest product of morality. Without love no baby can live for a week. Every one of the 1,600 millions of human beings on the earth at this moment is a product of mother-love, and I am entitled to say "no morals, no man." So far is Darwinism from reducing morality to the level of a superstition that natural selection, which is the Darwinian principle, actually selects morality, because of its superior survival value. The creature in whom, as the comparative facts of gestation and lactation show, organic morality is at its height has become the lord of the earth.

Man the Highest Product of Morality

I have no space to discuss the argument that the prolongation of infancy, depending upon parental care—that is to say, upon love—has made possible the transmutation of instinct into intelligence and educability, the instruments of man's dominance. There still remains the fact, seeming to confirm Huxley, that the indiscriminate extension of sympathy, involving the abrogation of the law of the survival of the fittest, would lead to the multiplication of the unfit. This is a very small difficulty, however, since it is quite possible to extend every kind of sympathy and care to the unfit whilst meanwhile forbidding them just one thing, and that is parenthood. This is to effect mercifully what natural selection would, in a former age, have effected unmercifully. Our argument requires completion now only by one further proposition, which is that not only has the psychical a survival value, but this demonstrates itself increasingly to outweigh that of the physical. Obviously, by no other means could the psychical have emerged and become dominant.

Creations of the Mind of Man

This proposition is absolutely vital to our argument, but, fortunately, it requires no labouring. Man daily achieves by means of his mind what the lower animals have to achieve by physical means. If he cannot run so fast, his mind creates a train; if his teeth do not last so well, he makes false ones, and so on. It was so from the first. The Drift-men of Taubach, living in the Interglacial Period, could kill the full-grown elephant and rhinoceros. Says Ranke: "It is the mind of man that shows itself superior to the most powerful brute force, even where we meet him for the first time." Furthermore, whilst the physical methods are all self-limited, whether as to the achievement of speed by means of muscles, or cutting power by means of teeth, the method of mind is not limited; it is even more than cumulative, and multiplies its capacities by geometrical progression. That dominance of the psychical which we call progress is due to its dominant survival value.

If this sometimes fails us, still, when measured with the physical, as when it is pitted against the toxins of the tubercle bacillus, that is only for a season. Carlyle despised the evolutionists, and there is, therefore, all the more interest and piquancy in the fact that during the years when he produced "Past and Present," and "Heroes and Hero Worship," with their magnificent assertion of the survival value of the psychical, Darwin was filling his note-books with facts supporting the idea of natural selection. In the whole of Carlyle's

Carlyle and the Evolutionists

philosophy there are few ideas more important, more characteristic and more frequently expressed than the idea of natural selection. Indeed, Carlyle believed in natural selection unqualified; he does not care that Mohammed propagated his religion by the sword:

I care little about the sword; I will allow a thing to struggle for itself in this world, with **Nature** any sword or tongue or implement **Can Do No** it has, or can lay hold of. We will **Wrong** let it preach, and pamphleteer, and fight, and to the uttermost bestir itself, and do, beak and claws, whatsoever is in it; very sure that it will, in the long run, conquer nothing which does not deserve to be conquered. What is better than itself it cannot put away, but only what is worse. In this great duel, Nature herself is umpire, and can do no wrong; the thing which is deepest-rooted in Nature, what we call *truest*, that thing, and not the other, will be found growing at last.

Parallel passages are to be found—need we remind ourselves?—in the wonderful second chapter of " Past and Present." There are few more interesting passages of literature for the biologist, who knows how profoundly true they are. Yet one more point as to competition. Ruskin tells us that in all things anarchy and competition are the laws of death. Modern biology declares, on the other hand, that it finds no anarchy in the world of life, but that it finds competition to be the law of life, even if it be the competition of mother and child together against foes which do not so co-operate. The antithesis between competition and co-operation is obviously superficial. In Carlyle, on the other hand, we find it constantly asserted that by competition, and only by competition, can any kind of progress, physical or psychical, be effected. Up to this present, competition has been in all things the law of life, for it has been the necessary factor of all progress.

That is what the doctrine of natural selection and survival value asserts. It is a matter of infinite moment to the **Success** historian, who so frequently **Fatal to** observes that no nation can **Nations** survive complete success. It advances until, perhaps, it is mistress of the world, and from that moment the historian may trace its decline. We have seen already that, misled by deceptive analogies from biology, historians have interpreted this phenomenon as really identical with the yielding of adult strength to senility in the individual. Though that analogy is

false, the historian may, nevertheless, find assistance in biology for the phenomenon which he deplores, and it is in terms of selection for parenthood that he will find the true biological explanation of the facts.

Here is, indeed, a whole conception of history which has yet to be used by historians. The historians must not ask the biologists to undertake the task, for they have not the historical knowledge. The historian, however, can hear and accept the biological principle in a single breath, and the application is plainly his duty. We have to realise that natural selection did not cease to operate with the production of man. In every generation, including those which initiated new epochs in history, natural selection has been at work. Always some have been taken and others left; those taken were the least fit for the environment in question, and those left were the fittest.

It is the duty of the historian to apply the idea of survival value to history. What were the factors that possessed survival value in the age of Pericles, in **Factors in** the periods of religious perse- **Rome's** cution in Sparta? He must **Greatness** answer the question for every place and every time. Observe the value of this process, apart from its explanation of history. Take, for instance, the case of religious persecution. The characters that, so far from having any survival value, make directly for death are the courage and the something immeasurably nobler than courage which will make a man willing to die for what he believes to be true. Religious persecution is, therefore, condemned by biology because it takes the worthlessness of the hypocrite and gives it survival value, whilst it confers a value for death alone upon all that is really valuable. A form of selection continues to operate, but the circumstances are such that its whole tendency is reversed, and it is made to work for the evil and against the good.

But observe, furthermore, the services of the idea of natural selection in the understanding of history. Take, for example, the case of Rome. There was a time when the factors which possessed survival value in Rome were such as courage, devotion, hardihood and the patriotism that did not fear death. The babies born in that generation were very much like the babies a hundred years before and a hundred years after. But those which displayed these characters were selected— and so much the better for Rome.

Take a somewhat later generation. The material upon which selection is to operate is much the same; there has been no time for marked consequences to follow the previous selection. In a given number of babies of that age you will find just about as many potential patriots and potential traitors as before. But there has been what Nietzsche would call a "transvaluation of values." Patriotism and hardihood and honour are at a discount. Smooth speaking and elegance and worse things are selected, and so much the worse for Rome. I follow the convention in speaking of the men first, but I might speak of the women also. What if in one age motherliness gives a woman survival value, but in another is regarded as a nuisance, and is rejected for smartness? There is no substantial difference between the girl babies in the two cases, for this transvaluation may take place in a single generation. But observe the immediate consequences.

The Meaning of Racial Deterioration Nay, more, observe remoter consequences, for motherliness tends to be transmitted, and so does its nameless opposite. If the valuations agreed upon persist for generations you will indeed have real consequences in the blood of the people. If patriots alone have been selected for fathers, and motherly women for mothers, you will indeed have produced a race with patriotism and motherliness in its blood. I need not state the converse case.

Here, at last, we have before us, in a form that biology not merely accepts but demands, a true conception of racial degeneration as distinguished from racial deterioration. The issue between the meanings of these two terms is one which is not merely of vital importance to every civilised community of to-day, but also to the historian who holds fast to the idea that the characters of the individual human being are the key to history.

We shall use the term racial deterioration to mean the worsening of the individuals of the race after their birth and in consequence of their environment. Such deterioration is to be witnessed in every city in the world, and might have been so witnessed throughout the whole course of history. We shall use the term racial degeneration to involve a process which

acts in the blood of the people, or, to use technical language, which acts upon the germ-cells themselves, a process producing change which will show itself entirely apart from environment. This restriction in the use of the term will help us to avoid many misapprehensions. A bad environment may cause deterioration in one who is also a degenerate, but also in one who is not. Now, observe the overwhelmingly important judgment of biology upon these distinctions. In any time or place the individuals of a race may be deteriorated by a bad environment in consequence of its direct action upon the individual. The case is simplicity itself so far, and no theory of heredity needs to be invoked to explain it. We are faced with our problem, however, directly we ask what the consequences will be for the next generation. Will the children of these deteriorates be degenerates?

What of the Next Generation?

The popular answer is and always has been affirmative, the same being true of the ascent as well as the descent of a people, because the deteriorate and the degenerate have not been distinguished till very recently. But the answer of modern biology is definitely negative, and the historian in his future interpretations must accept that negative. In general, each generation, now or in the past, makes a fresh start so far as its inborn characters are concerned. It may, in its turn, be deteriorated by the environment; but in a healthy environment it would have utterly surpassed in every way its deteriorated parents.

This proposition is generally true, not merely of physical, but also of psychical characters. Ideals of patriotism, to take an instance, may be taught to any generation at school though its ancestors have lost them for centuries, or have never had them. The critics, including some historians, may reply that these assertions are monstrous, it being the historical fact that races do alter in type, thus making history, whether for better or for worse. This, however, is not for a moment denied by biology. Only it is asserted that the factors of this change differ radically from those asserted in the Lamarckian conception which has held sway for so long. The biologist is now compelled to believe, and the historian must follow suit,

Alteration in the Type of Races

that the inherent, inborn characters of any species or race or nation—vegetable, animal, or human—are altered for better or for worse only under the influence of selection, selecting those inborn characters, new or old, which are the fittest for the environment in question. Observe that this does not deny the im-

The Place of Selection in Progress portance of the environment any more than the Lamarckian view does, for it is the environment that determines fitness, which may vary from the abominable to the admirable, ethically considered. What, then, are the conditions under which modern biology permits us to recognise that a nation will ascend or degenerate in so far as the inborn characters of its people are concerned ? Let us note the importance of this last phrase.

It involves the proposition that natural selection is the only essential factor of progress, because the characters which it selects are inborn and transmissible. The happy adjustment of the environment so as to make the most of every individual, but such as to abrogate selection, will also make for progress, but it is only superficial progress. Change the environment for the worse, and you instantly discover that you have not radically improved your stock. That can only be achieved by what we soon learn to call eugenic selection, and for the simple reason that acquired characters are not transmissible. History offers terrible instances of these truths.

A nation will ascend under the influence of natural selection such that the fittest are also the best ; a nation will degenerate under the influence of natural selection such that the fittest are also the worst. More than this, a nation will degenerate if natural selection be abrogated altogether, and universal survival or indiscriminate survival be substituted for any process of selection at all. Let us consider these propositions. If a nation

Babylon's Fall after 4,000 Years can ascend in any sure way— its surety being dependent upon the fact that the ascent is in the very blood of the people —only when natural selection actively operates in the choice of the best, then we begin to realise why it is that in the whole course of history hitherto this sure ascent has not been realised. Babylon may have lasted for 4,000 years, as the historians tell us ; yet at last it fell. If natural selection had been operating in

6418

Babylon throughout that time, choosing only the best, the noblest and the wisest, conferring upon them, and upon them alone, the supreme privilege and duty of parenthood, Babylon could not have fallen. It would have had a population fit to excite the admiration of all ages, and one from which would have been recruited the dominant peoples of all time thereafter.

The overwhelming truth for the historian is this : that natural selection, the sole factor of efficient and permanent progress, the factor which has definitely evolved man from the brute, and has definitely awarded him the sceptre of this, his planet, is constantly thwarted, if not entirely abrogated, or even inverted, by man himself—" Nature's insurgent son."

In human society, the natural state has necessarily been altered by a thousand factors. The fittest will survive ; but fitness may mean anything. More than this, the fitness which is chosen may be, and very often is, only an acquired fitness, not dependent upon any inborn characters, and therefore not transmissible. Nature takes the fitness and rewards it.

No Enduring Empire in History But she is deceived ; she expects it to be transmissible, and so she expects to achieve her great purpose—I speak in figure. But, suppose the fitness has been acquired merely in consequence of a legacy of monetary wealth ; is it not plain that the whole value of the process of selection is utterly destroyed ? Or, suppose that the fitness has been due not to anything inherent in the individual, nor yet to anything acquired, but to the well-meaning kindness of others or the state, who have given room and food and mercy to an imbecile—and that he has thereby been enabled to exercise the privilege of parenthood, which, in a state of nature, would have been necessarily and with real mercy to the future, denied him. Processes which are typified in these examples are not merely characteristic of human society, but are absolutely peculiar to it. There is no parallel to them in the case of any other living creature than man.

We are faced, then, with the fact that the conditions necessary for the secure ascent of any race, an ascent secured in its very blood, made stable in its very bone, have not yet been achieved in history. I advance this as the true reason why history records no enduring empire. This is the biological conclusion, and it is made all the stronger when we discover how stringent selection requires to be in order to produce substantial results. In the case of the lower animals, and in the whole vegetable kingdom, natural selection is stringent, and stringent within the species. Let us quote from the most authoritative of recent pronouncements, Sir E. Ray Lankester's Romanes Lecture of 1905. He says :

The world, the earth's surface, is practically full—that is to say, fully occupied. Only one pair can grow up to take the place of the pair, male and female, which have launched a dozen, or it may be as many as a hundred thousand, young individuals on the world. . . . One pair in a new generation, only one pair, survive for every parental pair. Animal population does not increase. The struggle for existence takes place not . . . between different species, but between individuals of the same species, brothers and sisters and cousins. . . . In Nature's struggle for existence death, immediate obliteration, is the fate of the vanquished, whilst the only reward to the victors—few, very few, but rare and beautiful in the fitness which has carried them to victory—is the permission to reproduce their kind ; to carry on by heredity to another generation the specific qualities by which they triumphed. It is not

Nature's Severe Competition generally realised how severe is the pressure and competition in Nature, not between different species, but between the immature population of one and the same species, precisely because they are of the same species and have exactly the same needs.

Contrasted with these facts, the struggle for existence and the process of selection within human society can scarcely be recognised at all. It is still survival value that determines survival and parenthood. But Nature can scarcely distinguish survival value as it has been transvalued by her insurgent son.

As regards the other aspect of the account. It follows from these principles that a nation will degenerate with surety, in a stable fashion which is beyond repair, only if natural selection selects the worst and breeds from them ; not, as all but the instructed few believe, under the accumulated and transmitted influence of a bad environment. We must recognise the bright as well as the dark aspect of our principles. If they explain to us why progress has been so unstable and ascent so unsure in human history, they also assert that deterioration in a people is also unsure and unstable. The historian cannot name a people in which the selection of the worst has been consistently carried out, any more than he can name a people in which the selection of the best

has been consistently carried out. Therefore, he can no more assert that any people have irredeemably fallen, assuming that they are still in existence at all, than he can assert that any past or present people have risen to heights from which they cannot fall. Whilst the abrogation of anything like natural selection in human

Prevalent Conception of Spain society denies the permanence of historical ascent, it also denies the permanence of historical descent. A contemporary instance of very great magnitude is the case of Spain. We have been brought up to believe that there is no possible future for Spain ; it is a dying nation, a senile individual, a people of degenerates ; it has had its day, which can never return. This has been explained by the false analogy between a race and an individual, and by the false Lamarckian theory of heredity.

To these the biologist can now retort with comments upon their falsity, and with the conviction that since Spain has not been subjected to the only process which can ensure real degeneration, viz., the consistent and stringent selection of the worst, she is yet capable of regeneration. Regeneration is not really the word, because there has been no real degeneration, but only the successive deterioration of successive and undegenerate generations. The corresponding term to deterioration should be amelioration.

If we took an animal species that has degenerated, such as the intestinal parasites, and endeavoured to regenerate them, we should begin to realise the magnitude of our task. That is not the task for Spain, the biologist asserts. Merely the environment must be altered, not the mountain ranges and the rivers, but the really potent factors in the environment, the spiritual and psychical and social factors, and the deterioration, for it is only a deterioration, will give place to amelioration. I

Where the Biologist is Right am using these opposed terms with great care and of set purpose. And the biologist is right. The facts concerning which so many historians have shaken their heads, and upon which they have based so many moralisings and theories of history, the facts which they have cited in support of their false analogies and misconceptions of heredity—due, of course, to the errors of former biology—turn out to be not facts at all, or, at any rate, only facts of the moment. The "dying nation," as Lord Salisbury called it, has occasion to alter its psychical environment. It introduces the practice of education ; it begins to shake off that ecclesiasticism which has uniformly cursed

Spain's Brighter Future mankind since the days when the first Palæolithic savage persuaded his fellows that he was a witch doctor. And what are the consequences ? The new generation — which the casual and scarcely directed action of natural selection, acting on ten or twelve generations, has not affected in any substantial way— is found to be potentially little worse and little better than its predecessors of the sixteenth century. There has been no national or racial degeneration. The environment is modified for the better, and Spain, as they say in misleading phrase, "takes on a new lease of life."

The historian of the present day, basing his theories upon sound biology, knowing as a historian what qualities of blood have been in the Spanish people, may confidently assert that that blood, incapable, as he knows, of degeneration by any Lamarckian process, may still retain its ancient quality and will yet make history. The signs that he is right are to be followed almost week by week in the world's chronicles, and not least by those who realise how inevitable is the importance of South America in the making of future history.

I have deliberately taken Spain as a contemporary test case because of its magnitude and because of the manner in which it is now falsifying the assertions which the contrast between its recent past and its already passing present have drawn from so many historians.

But the historian might well write a volume upon the same thesis as applied to China and Japan. We know historically what were the immediate effects in one generation of a total change of environment in Japan. That change

The Change in China and Japan has not yet occurred in China, but must inevitably occur. Consider for a moment how the historian, made far-sighted and clear-sighted by biology, must contemplate the history of this astounding people. The popular belief used to be that China illustrated the so-called law of nations. It was the decadent, though monstrous,

relic of an ancient civilisation ; it had had its day. Inevitable degeneration, which must sooner or later befall all peoples, had come upon it. Behold it in the paralysis which precedes death !

But in the light of the facts of Japan, the man in the street and the historian alike have in this case found modern biology superfluous in enabling them to arrive at sound conclusions. They now believe what the Darwinian has been compelled to believe for close upon half a century, and more strongly than ever during the latter part of that period, when the doctrine of the transmission of acquired characters was finally discarded. A clever writer invents the phrase " the yellow peril," and people discard their old theories. The metaphor must be changed. This is not paralysis, but merely slumber. Doubtless, it is an unnatural slumber ; doubtless, it is not the slumber which brings renewed strength. It is suspense, not recuperation ; but assuredly it is not paralysis. Is there a man who now would dare to say that China has had its day, even if he still

Biology Supported by History clings to the old fictions about Spain ? I repeat that the contemporary facts of history are all on the side of modern biological theory, and that the historian is not incompetent, if he will look at all the facts and discard all preconceptions, to reach true principles for himself. I will go further, and say that if biologists, as it happens, had not already discarded their old ideas and arrived at sounder ones, they would now have been in the position of learners, as to the fundamental facts of heredity, at the feet of the historians. It is scarcely more than an accident—the birth of a certain baby in the year 1809— that the historians are not now turning round upon the biologists and saying, " Your doctrine of the transmission of acquired characters must be false, for look at Spain and Japan and China."

In the demonstrable absence of stringent selection of the worst, true racial or national degeneration has not occurred in human history. That peoples do not degenerate is false ; deteriorate they may, and often do. The difference between the two words is exactly the difference between the former assertions regarding, for instance, Spain and China, and the facts which we are witnessing to-day.

INDIVIDUALITY AND PROGRESS
FACTORS IN MANKIND'S UPWARD MARCH

SO much, then, at present, for matters which cannot be studied at too great length. At least we have seen nothing that causes us to question our original proposition, that the emergence and even the dominance of the psychical can be recorded in accordance with the principle of selection and the concept of survival value. Let us now go back to the very beginning and see whether we can discern throughout the whole history of life another principle which has worked itself out, and is still working itself out, under the influence of natural selection, and which has most conspicuously played into the hands of the psychical.

Let us attempt, then, to set before our eyes the drama of the earth, and, if possible, to interpret as we observe. Looking without keen interest upon the changes wrought in the earth before the appearance **Before Life Appeared on the Earth** of life, we find much to rouse us in what followed. We may ignore the vegetable world, which has devoted itself to synthetic chemistry, apparently at the cost of the psychical, and which now is of no intrinsic worth, but simply serves the animal kingdom. If we look upon this last, or, indeed, upon the whole kingdom of life, we see what suggests, as someone has observed, some impulse in Nature towards obtaining at any cost just so much life as may be. We seem to see what Shelley imagined in "Adonais":

> . . . The one Spirit's plastic stress
> Sweeps through the dull, dense world, compelling there
> All new successions to the forms they wear;
> Torturing th' unwilling dross that checks its flight
> To its own likeness, as each mass may bear;
> And bursting in its beauty and its might
> From trees and beasts and men into the Heaven's light.

The chief concern of life seems to be to multiply and magnify itself, and whatever device will make for more life Nature will welcome. It is, one can safely assert, the fact that in so far as we may speak quantitatively of life at all there is more life upon the earth at this moment than ever before in any period of her history. But whilst all living things attempt to obey the command to be fruitful and **Spencer's Great Law of Multiplication** multiply, we find ourselves compelled to recognise, what Malthus did not see, viz., that as individuality, which is obviously correlated with the psychical, increases, so fertility diminishes. This is the great law of multiplication which we owe to Herbert Spencer. It is as much as to say that the older method of achieving the utmost life, the method which trusts in numbers, becomes gradually superseded by the method which trusts in quality, a word which has psychical connotations. Amongst the bacteria or the fishes we see the older method, that to which we are besought to return by those, bachelors and others, who are alarmed at our falling birth-rate.

We find this "antagonism between individuation and genesis" illustrated even up to man himself, where the process of genesis is actually so slow that commonly only one new being is produced at a birth, whilst the period of gestation in proportion to the body weight is, as we have seen, the longest known. Yet this creature is lord of the earth, and his lordship constitutes the triumph of the psychical as well as the satisfaction of Nature's demand for fulness of life. For increasing individuation culminates at **Quality Before Quantity** last in human personality. This great fact, the ousting of quantity by quality, and quality is practically a psychical conception, is worthy of a little closer study. It implies a steadily falling birth-rate from the unicellular organisms up to man who, as we have seen, has the lowest birth-rate known— on the average about one child to each female every two years. The higher orders of mammals taken together yield a corresponding figure of rather more than one per annum. Go lower amongst the mammals, and the figure is three per annum, amongst the birds five, amongst the reptiles seventeen, amongst the amphibia 441, and amongst the fishes 646,000. As for the multi-

The World's Declining Birth-rate plication of bacteria it is really quite unthinkable. Surveying the animal world as a whole, then, we recognise the observed fact, not a theory, of a falling birth-rate. We have already observed how this makes for individual development, since the fewer the offspring the greater the proportion of parental care and parental education that is available for them. Observe, also, that it makes for individuation because of the vital economy effected for the parent. Amongst not a few lowly forms of animal life the act of reproduction terminates the life of the parent. What an unthinkable contrast to our case! Amongst bacteria the act of reproduction involves the absolute and complete disappearance of the parent. To use Herbert Spencer's own terminology, here is the maximum of genesis and the minimum of individuation. Survey the whole animal world, then, and we see that a falling birth-rate is a factor associated with, involved in, and making for, progress.

Yet again, consider the death-rate, and especially the infant mortality, which is the dominant factor in all death-rates. We hear much nowadays of infant mortality, though not nearly enough; but infant mortality, if the term may be used, is a phenomenon which is common to the whole living world. The high rate of infant mortality among fishes is astounding. If it were not 99 in 100 the ocean would be solid with fish from shore to shore. But as life ascends and the birth-rate falls the infant mortality falls also, and

Appalling Infant Mortality with it, obviously, the general death-rate. I have not the slightest doubt that our own infant mortality, appalling though it be, is considerably lower than any to be found amongst any animal species apart from human care. This low death-rate goes with the low birth-rate which accompanies increasing individuation.

Already we have expressed in terms of parental care the fashion in which this falling birth-rate plays into the hands of

the psychical by giving it increased importance as a factor of survival value, plays into the hands of quality as against quantity. If we are prepared to look further into these relations observed in the sub-human world, we will be interested to discover that they hold in our own society to-day.

The dominant classes are not those which excel in production of quantity, but those the birth-rate of which is lowest, but the products thereof the most highly developed individually. We shall find also that a high death-rate, and especially a high infant mortality, is constantly found associated with a high birth-rate, just as amongst the bacteria or the fishes. Indeed, the more one tries to work out this wonderful law of multiplication, which is so simple and which yet had to wait so long for its recognition, the more its value becomes apparent. If progress means anything, it means the deepening and the broadening of the conscious and self-conscious life of the individual, and this most certainly involves, as the whole history of life proves, a decline in his

Conditions that Make for Progress fertility. But observe that this decline and this increasing individuation are absolutely reconcilable with Nature's demand for the maximum of life, for they involve the attainment of a state of things in which the amount of life shall be the greatest possible, and the births and deaths the fewest possible. This is surely clear enough, nor need I ask the reader to delay for more than a moment in looking at the matter in another way.

Would not progress be served if the enormous amount of human energy now expended in giving birth to, and subsequently burying, the children who die before they have completed one year of life were devoted to the development of life in the adult population—if the energy and labour spent by the mother in producing the thirteenth and fourteenth child, let us say, which will very likely die, were expended upon the older children? Is it not better to bring up four children with a mother's loving care than to leave ten motherless? Which, then, makes most for progress? After all, I am only saying what everyone with any practical acquaintance with the subject believes—that, except, perhaps, from the merely military point of view, the birth-rate amongst the lowest classes of our population is higher than is compatible with the maximum rate of progress. Nor am I by any means sure that the military point of view is incompatible with that proposition.

When we come to discuss the great eugenic idea of Sir Francis Galton we shall see how utterly remote these assertions are from meaning that all is well with the birth-rate in what we call the upper classes—or in such of them as have any birth-rate.

It would seem that by following these principles a race might apparently improve itself off the earth altogether. If we consider, however, that sterility is palpably the very last thing that natural selection can select, the very first thing that it rejects, we will see that nothing so stultifying as that can ever be the final result of the process of individuation. If we push the matter further and argue that, reproduction being necessary if a race is to continue at all, there therefore appears to be a limit to the degree to which the individuals of the race may develop their individualities, then the reply is : Are we sure that, except in a few abnormal, **Malthusian** I do not say morbid, cases, the **Principle of** individual can develop his or **Multiplication** her personality to the utmost and the best without parenthood ? Now, it is most important to observe that this law of multiplication constitutes a very potent modification of the principle of Malthus. This, enunciated in 1798, asserts that human population multiplies faster than the supply of food and that, apart from deliberate control, it will continue to do so. Man must go on multiplying in geometrical progression, his food only in arithmetical progression, nor is there anything to correct the appalling struggles between men for food which must inevitably follow. •

This idea has enormous interest for the historian of thought, since it was the reading of Malthus that independently gave both to Darwin and to Wallace the idea of natural selection. Spencer's law of multiplication, however, supplies the missing half of the Malthusian principle, which is only a half truth. For we find that the unlimited multiplication which Malthus observed leads to its own correction. It provides an abundance of material for natural selection to work upon, and then the survival value of individuation, wherever it appears, asserts itself, with the consequence that

the rate of multiplication declines. This process has been in evidence throughout the whole course of animal evolution. Malthus desired to lower the birth-rate; but under the influence of natural selection and the dominant survival value of individuation, which is inimical to a high birth-rate, the birth-rate has **Civilisation's** fallen, and continues to fall. **Effect** Malthus desired that we should **on Marriage** postpone marriage to later ages so as to lower the birth-rate. Yet, though not one in a thousand of the population has ever heard of Malthus, and though it is incredible that there should ever have been any individual so impersonal in his outlook as to postpone his own marriage on Malthusian principles, we find that the increasing necessity and demand for individuation are actually leading to that postponement in marriage which Malthus desired. This is a progressive tendency in both sexes in our own country during the last thirty years; and not only so, but as civilisation advances the age of marriage becomes later and later, a fact some aspects of which Professor Metchnikoff has discussed in his wonderful book "The Nature of Man." Thus, we must observe that there is no excuse whatever at the present day for accepting the Malthusian principle as if it were the whole truth.

For the sake of completeness we must add a second qualification to the Malthusian principle in the case of man—which is that he is a creator, and can achieve amongst other things what is practically equivalent to the creation of food. Just in so far as man makes his environment, moulding Nature to provide him with the means of sustenance, just in so far the Malthusian principle requires correction. We may say, then, that one of the results of progress has been, is, and will be, persistently to lower the importance of the Malthusian principle **Man's** until it becomes of purely his-**Physical** torical interest. Turn we now **Variation** to the specific case of man. It is possible in our thought to distinguish between physical variation and psychical variation, and it is man himself who most clearly illustrates the distinction. Some biologists tell us that man is the least variable of animals, but in so saying they are thinking exclusively of physical variation. His physical variation seems to have very nearly lapsed with the practical completion of his physical evolution. That is an easily told story. From the chaos of the invertebrates there emerged the first vertebrates. To this new kind of being there were added four limbs, two in front and two behind. Lastly, the anterior pair of limbs, originally locomotor, was entirely freed from that function which, in the case of man, is performed by the posterior limbs alone. To this end, the centre of gravity of the body had to be somewhat modified in position so that, whereas the vertical line from it to the ground falls in front of the hip joints in the case of the lower vertebrates, it falls behind the hip joints in the case of man. Hence man is erect and erected, as Stevenson said.

At the Goal of Physical Evolution

Thus, we may admit without alarm as to the possibility of future progress that variations are the indispensable raw material of organic evolution, and yet that man is the least variable of animals—with the all-important qualification that we are speaking of physical variation only. There is no need for physical variability, so to say, for there is no further goal in particular that we want the body of man to reach. So far as physical evolution is concerned, the goal has been attained with the erect attitude. There doubtless will be a certain lightening of the ship, casting overboard the superfluities, but that is all.

It is worth noting, perhaps, as not entirely irrelevant to the question of progress under its æsthetic aspect, that the superfluities to which I have referred do not necessarily include everything that is without immediate utility. No biologist could assent for a moment to the monstrous pictures that have been drawn of the man of the future, without hair or teeth or nails, only with difficulty supporting his enormous head upon his puny trunk and limbs. Let him who would entertain such a notion, and declare that here as elsewhere progress is only another name for the supersession of the beautiful, turn to Darwin's "Descent of Man," and there learn how the particular form of natural selection, which he called sexual selection, has endowed even beauty as such with survival value. It is sexual selection that has encouraged and developed physical beauty, both for its own sake and indirectly because of the correlation between grace and ease, between beauty

Darwin's "Descent of Man"

of movement and efficiency of movement. Now, to suppose that the future evolution of man will involve the total destruction of everything that we call beauty is, in the first place, to ignore the possibility of changes in the canon of beauty, and, in the second place, to suppose, against Darwin and the facts, that beauty is without survival value. On the contrary, few will doubt that the skin-deep variety of beauty in women has, in the past, like claws and tearing teeth, been possessed of too great survival value.

This will shrink, it is now shrinking, to more reasonable proportions. "The saying that beauty is but skin-deep is but a skin-deep saying," remarked Spencer somewhere. We know well that facial beauty, at any rate, may be the direct outcome of beauty of mind or character. We have only to read Darwin's "Expression of the Emotions" to see that this is and must be so. That consideration is my answer to the critic who may reply to my argument regarding sexual selection, that on my own assumptions sexual selection must surely be transferred to the psychical from the physical plane, and that, since men and women will no longer choose each other for characters of body, but for characters of character, physical beauty and all structures which are now without any other value will become decadent. The argument may be admitted in part, but with the comment that all the beauty which is not skin-deep will persist and increase under the new conditions in consequence of the increasing survival value of those psychical characters of which it is the expression.

Will Physical Beauty Become Decadent?

I may not depart so far from my proper subject as to inquire whether, for instance, front teeth will persist, on account of their æsthetic value, in smiling, whilst back teeth, having no æsthetic value, and having lost, as nails have already lost, their original function, will disappear. But at least this digression will serve to modify the first conception which we form of physical superfluity, and also to complete the assertion that in the future history of man physical selection would seem to be of little moment, except, perhaps, as Dr. Archdall Reid would insist, in respect of evolution against disease by the natural selection of the least susceptible. Physical selection will be of little moment, I say ;

but more, even now it is scarcely occurring as compared with the past. In our present epoch man seems to have lost most of the variability upon which the possibility of selection depends. Having attained his goal, he can practically dispense with physical selection, and, in point of fact, physical selection has been superseded in the main by something else.

We may grant as much as we please that man is the least variable of animals physically. For all we know or care, as students of society, that is true enough ; but beyond a doubt he is the most variable psychically. We may question this when we see the sheep-like behaviour of a crowd. But I am not now talking of man as moulded by social life and imitation ; I am writing, not of psychical acquirements but of psychical variations, and for them we must go to the nursery. That is where we will find character ; that is where we will find individuality that is inborn, and being inborn is transmissible. There, certainly, we will be content to believe—what, indeed, I think no one will question—that man is psychically the most variable of animals.

Individuality the Goal of Progress We may put it this way, then, that what in man we call individuality is the psychical analogue of physical variation in the lower animals. At bottom individuality is inborn, as the nursery demonstrates against the market-place, and, being inborn, it is transmissible. Just, then, as the natural selection of physical variations has been the factor of organic evolution, so the natural selection of psychical variations, expressed in man as personality, may be submitted to be the factor of psychical evolution. Individuality is thus at once the goal of progress and its instrument.

Now, before we devote ourselves to this proposition, with all that it involves, let us clear the way by contemplating a new fact which emerges with man, or, to be more accurate, with *homo sapiens*, with man the speaker, and immeasurably more so with man the writer. I have already asserted that organic evolution has proceeded without any aid from that transmission of acquired characters in which Lamarck and Spencer, and even Darwin himself to some extent, believed. We seem nowadays to be compelled to credit the Darwinian principle of natural selection, or survival of the fittest, as bearing the whole burden of organic change upon its shoulders, the fundamental fact of inborn variation being taken for granted. Now, this natural selection is a terribly slow process so far as substantial results are concerned, and this even in the most favourable circumstances for its operation. Even to-day,

Nature Never in a Hurry when we read of the work of Mendel and De Vries and Bateson, who rather qualify Darwin's adherence to the principle that Nature does nothing by leaps —even to-day we have to recognise organic evolution as an exceedingly slow process. But suppose we had been able to watch its course from a great distance, we should have contemplated slow, æonian change, involving, together with degeneration and stagnation, slow æonian advance, until at last there appeared an erected mammal who learnt to communicate with his fellows by speech.

The process, so far, has occupied, we seem compelled to believe, scores at least— hundreds possibly—of millions of years ; further ages elapse between the men who made the eoliths and the beginnings of recorded history, and then, in what is relatively scarcely more than the twinkling of an eye, such a long-lived observer would recognise the achievement of the amazing thing which we call civilisation. It is man, the historian or recorder, who has made human history possible. It is man, the historian, who has made possible what history now records. No historian—i.e., no recording—no history. Thus, in a new sense, the historians have made history. By his trick of recording his speech, man has succeeded, in a sense, in achieving that transmission of psychical acquirements which is otherwise impossible.

Nevertheless, however fully we recognise this, the importance of individuality remains. The acquirements which have been thus transmitted to us by a sort of heredity acting out-

If Natural Selection were to Cease side the germ-plasm were the deeds of individuals. As Mill says : " Nothing was ever yet done which someone was not the first to do." Yet, further, if the process of natural selection were to cease, we can readily understand how there would eventually be produced a race which cared for none of these things, and so the idea of Aristotle would be realised, and all that had been accomplished would be lost.

6425

NATURE AND MAN

THE SOCIAL RESULTS OF NATURAL SELECTION

WE must not allow ourselves to lose hold of the valid distinction that still remains between an acquirement and a variation. Natural selection, as we have observed, has no means of distinguishing between the inborn and the acquired, the transmissible and the non-transmissible. If the acquirement makes for life, it will prosper just as much as if it had been an inborn character. Except in the case of the products of genius or talent, such prosperity, however, is of little value to the future, because the acquirement on which it was based is not transmissible. From the point of view of natural selection, then, it is the variations, the inborn characters, the transmissible characters, that we desire to see made the most of.

The Theory of Organic Evolution

So far as the theory of organic evolution will carry us, it seems to me absolutely plain that we must condemn anything that tends towards the suppression of individuality or psychical variation, and therefore towards the obliteration of its natural function, which is to provide material for natural selection. Anything that interferes with the natural selection of variations seems to me to interfere with the essential factor of all progress ; anything that resulted in the practical suppression of individuality would put a stop to progress for ever. This remains true even if you choose to ignore the theory of natural selection, or, with Huxley, to deny that it is applicable to human society. Let us now observe how this bears on certain of our questions. In the first place, it bears profoundly upon the theory of education, which I like to define as the provision of an environment. Since we are aiming at individuality, whether as an end in itself—which it is—or as affording material for natural selection, or as the means by which the race makes its acquirements; and since psychical variation is, in fact, so great that no two

Education the Provision of an Environment

children are quite identical, and since for each child you can provide only one environment that will most completely educe all its most worthy potentialities, it follows that the ideal of uniformity in education is quite the worst that can be conceived. This applies not only within the sexes but as between the sexes, and is, moreover, relevant to the current question of co-education.

If biology teaches us anything at all, it is that sexual differentiation has been an instrument of progress, and it is incredible that progress can be served by any attempts to minimise or abolish this. I do not believe that co-education constitutes such an attempt, but I do say that we ought to recognise what we want to obtain.

Then, again, this view, that the realisation of the potentialities in all psychical variation, except in so far as they may be anti-social, is the object of education, suggests that the home environment rather than the school environment will serve our purpose best. Since the boy tends to be a chip of the old block, the environment which his parents have created, and of which, indeed, they are the most important part, will be, on the average, the most suitable for him. This is one more argument for the home, which has all the arguments for it, and against it none. Unfortunately, there is no present space for going further into this matter of the principles of education as they are taught us by biology. At least, however, we find new warrant, if it were needed, for rejecting the principle of uniformity, which, I suppose, we all reject in principle, yet very nearly all of us accept in practice, if not for our own children, at any rate for other people's children.

Helpful Environment of the Home

Secondly, all these foregoing considerations must lead us to regard, even with more detestation than formerly, our infant mortality. In the present stage of progress, with so little done and so much to do, we have every reason for making the most of the selective opportunities afforded by the birth-rate. The enormous slaughter of children, amounting in practice to a virtual reduction of our birth-rate by more than one-half, would at least serve the selective purpose if the children slain were, as has been asserted, the least fit. But every doctor knows that this is pure myth. It is not a question whether the child is less or more inherently fit, but whether the mother gives it her own breast or a feeding-bottle with a long tube. The weakliest child, nursed by its mother, will probably survive, and the strongest, if poisoned long enough, will certainly die. If we are to have a birth-rate as high as ours is, at least let us make the most of it. At present we slay quite blindly.

Thirdly, we find amongst those practices of ours which interfere with natural selection all such as prejudice the fairness of the start ; and with the best desire in the world one finds it impossible to meet the argument of Mr. Alfred Russel Wallace that the inheritance of property is incom-patible with the principle of **Problem of Inherited Wealth** selection in that it makes the start unfair. To accept this conclusion of Mr. Wallace's is not merely to part company with Spencer, the great exponent of the principles which I am trying to lay before the reader, but it is to run counter to almost universal practice. Therefore, if I saw any possible means whereby the inheritance of property could be reconciled with principles which, so far as I can see, are indefeasible, I would gladly welcome it.

Another reason for welcoming such an escape is that, if you are going to abolish the inheritance of wealth, you are faced with the problem of dealing with that wealth, and at this point the collectivist comes up to you with open arms. And so, with many apologies, I must leave this point, which it would, perhaps, have been more politic to ignore. That, how-ever, was really impossible. If it be true that throughout the ages organic advance has been effected by the choice of inhe-rent fitness as against inherent unfitness, then it seems absolutely impossible to deny that that advance is interfered with by anything which makes it possible that inherent unfitness shall be given a practical advantage over inherent fitness. And now we must approach a larger

question still. I suppose the word indi-vidualism is still associated in many minds with the extreme political doctrines of Herbert Spencer or Mr. Auberon Her-bert—opinions which there is really no one to uphold to-day. But, after all, there may still be a use for the word, even though it should designate nothing so extreme. We **Progress in Terms of Machinery** must have some word to express the doctrine which is opposed to the modern forms of Socialism or collectivism. Let us sup-pose for a moment, then, that we accept a definition of progress in terms of machinery, and achieve our end. We obtain com-plete social efficiency and internal order.

If we are fortunate we shall have a society or social machine as perfect as the beehive. We shall doubtless require to follow the bees' example, and distinguish between the workers and the breeders. I am informed that the Japanese are trying experiments in that direction now. We shall completely realise the idea of the social organism—its parts nicely balanced, the whole practically self-regulating, no disorder, perfect discipline, life, regarded as a series of physico-chemical reactions, perfectly achieved. Now you have to reckon with two facts.

The first is that you have barred the onward road. How much room do you think there is for variation in the bee-hive ? There, any variation is, as such, a monstrosity. But if no kind of individ-uality, nothing new or original, is to be permitted, since, of course, it would inter-fere with the balance of your machine, our first principles make it quite evident that you never go any farther. "Genius," which is an extreme variation, "can only breathe freely in an atmosphere of free-dom," said John Stuart Mill; and John Milton has the same idea when he speaks of "Liberty, which is ever the nurse of great wits." But, well and good, the collectivist may reply ; there is no farther **After Perfection— What ?** to go. Do you not see that when we have perfected this machine, with a place for everyone, and everyone in his place, progress will have reached its goal ? If this machine is so constructed that it will run indefinitely, like the societies of the social bees, what more do you want ? Perfection has been realised and arrange-ments for its perpetuation completed with it. The answer is that the reason why we desire to see some possibility of change,

6427

which may mean progress, in such a society is that nothing further from our ideal can possibly be conceived. For what is our ideal ? The goal of progress, we declared, is the realisation of the utmost for the conscious life of the individual : the products of progress are not mechanisms but men. We will welcome any machine that makes **The Ideal of Progress** for that, but we have no interest in any machine that does not ; we are not mechanics. Here, in the admirable words of Professor Höffding, is the ideal of progress, including, of course, social progress :

If the single individual, in developing itself in its own peculiar way, gives the best possible contribution to the whole life of society, and if, on the other hand, society is organised in such a manner that a free and full development is possible for all individuals, then we are approaching to the ethical ideal.

And again in his " Philosophy of Religion," he says :

The ideal is a kingdom of personalities, in which each individual unfolds his personality in such a manner that in this very act he helps others to unfold their own.

We may remember Herbert Spencer's discussion of what he called the social organism, and of how the analogy between a society and an organism may be worked out ; you will remember also that at the last point it breaks down, thus demonstrating, Mr. Kidd tells us, its weakness. But to my mind the point at which the analogy breaks down, and the fact that it does so break down, is just what gives it its value. In a society " the living units do not, and cannot, lose individual consciousness, since the community, as a whole, has no corporate consciousness."

This is the condemnation of the beehive, or the collective state. We have chained the individual in order to make a good machine—and we have got it. Now, in the case of the individual cells of my body, that is worth while, because somehow there realises itself in this machine **The Social Machine and its Value** a mode of consciousness higher than that which any of the individual cells of my body could display. But in our social machine, with our system of standardisation and an endless supply of " spare parts," like the motor-car makers, what have we achieved ? Nothing but the machine—nothing more interesting and valuable than the human body would be if it were simply a walking *automaton.*

That is not progress, but its absolute stultification. The society that follows this path will run into its miserable little *cul de sac* as the bees have done.

The bee, as we have seen, is an insect of far older genealogy than any vertebrate, let alone man. Well, we may run our human society off the main rails in this fashion, and let it play with itself at the top of a siding, and if it waits long enough there will be evolved from the races which keep to the open road a society of the future as superior to our piece of machinery as we are to the bees ; and, just as we use the bees' honey, so that society of the future will use our collective machine to turn out whatever it has a use for. But it will doubtless be a good machine.

If this is not to be our sorry end, we have no choice but to recognise and even improve upon Nature's method of rewarding capacity. " Never, no never, did Nature say one thing and Wisdom say another." " Nature is to be commanded only by obeying her," says one writer. " The law," says Spencer, " that each creature shall take the benefits and the evils of its own nature has been **Improving Upon Nature** the law under which life has evolved thus far. Any arrangements which, in a considerable degree, prevent superiority from profiting by the rewards of superiority, or shield inferiority from the evils it entails, any arrangements which tend to make it as well to be inferior as to be superior are arrangements diametrically opposed to the progress of organisation and the reaching of a higher life." I have suggested that we can improve upon Nature, and so undoubtedly we can. We can reconcile cosmic with ethical evolution by extending to the unfit all our sympathy, but forbidding them parenthood, a solution of Huxley's dilemma so simple and obvious that one reads his famous lecture on " Evolution and Ethics " with ever-increasing astonishment at the difficulties he has made for himself. Should the reader be scandalised let him remember that already wise societies provide for the permanent care of the feeble-minded, at once giving them love, and averting misery and disaster from the future, reconciling Nature and love.

Yet, again, if once we realise that worth of any kind is always worth something to others than its possessor, we may provide for the survival of those whose worth does not directly make for life, and for whom sub-human nature would find no room; for whom, alas, society itself has too often found no room—for a Mozart and a Keats, and for all who can create anything that serves the psychical life of man. But, at all costs, we must do what Nature has done: wherever there is a scrap of anything new it must have a hearing. Only so can we achieve the true and good. If it be not the real thing it will come to naught; "but if it be of God ye cannot overthrow it, lest haply ye be found even to fight against God." You must have freedom of thought for progress—that is to say, you must allow psychical variation to express itself.

If, then, we look to no machinery for our salvation, but to the potentialities of human nature itself, and if we agree that human nature is a thing which is displayed in individuals, let us focus in the individual our hope for the future, or if in such things as laws, only in them because they may make for progress through the individual. "The soul of all improvement is the improvement of the soul." We

The Workings of Man and Nature have agreed already that the future evolution of man the individual, which is the necessary condition of progress, is to be psychical and not physical. It is this that Sir Francis Galton has recognised in his prosecution of the science which he calls eugenics, the science which promises to realise Huxley's suggestion that some day theoretical biology would become useful, just as physics and chemistry are. The aim of eugenics, says Sir Francis, is "to bring as many influences as can be reasonably employed to cause the useful classes in the community to contribute more than their proportion to the next generation." "This science," he says, "co-operates with the workings of Nature by securing that humanity shall be represented by the fittest races. What Nature does blindly, slowly and ruthlessly, man may do providently, quickly and kindly."

This whole conception has been criticised in anticipation by Huxley in the lecture to which I have already referred. He says, we may remember:

There is another fallacy which appears to me to pervade the so-called ethics of evolution, It is the notion that, because, on the whole, animals and plants have advanced in perfection of organisation by means of the struggle for existence and the consequent "survival of the

fittest"; therefore men in society, men as ethical beings, must look to the same process to help them towards perfection. I suspect that this fallacy has arisen out of the unfortunate ambiguity of the phrase "survival of the fittest." "Fittest" has a connotation of the "best"; and about "best" there hangs a moral flavour. In cosmic nature, however, what is "fittest" depends upon the conditions.

The answer to that, I take it, is simply **Man the Product of Eugenics** that eugenics propose to establish such conditions, social, sentimental, legal, whatever are necessary, that the best shall be the fittest, and the fittest the best. Of course, Sir Francis Galton is no pioneer, for Plato set the same object before him more than two thousand years ago; but he is the pioneer of this great idea in the age of science. A word invented by him, *stirpiculture*, is now familiar, especially in America; but later he substituted for it another term, *eugenics*, which literally means good breeding. In brief, he maintains that, as his cousin Charles Darwin proved, man is the product of eugenics; and therefore that in eugenics must now be recognised the essential factor of progress, not in legal enactments, nor in mechanical discovery, but in the extension and facilitation of the process which has already brought us thus far— the process which made man man.

In his own writings, and in his choice of a title for his proposals, Galton has laid stress almost exclusively upon what, for myself, I prefer to call the positive aspect of eugenics, the selection, by means later to be considered, of the best members of the community to do more than "their share" in the infinitely responsible task of continuing the species. But in a short paper which I published in 1904 I ventured to employ the terms "positive eugenics" and "negative eugenics," thus including both the encouragement of the propagation of the best and the discouragement of the propagation of the **Nature's Method in Reproduction** worst. Sir Francis Galton approved highly of that little paper, and the terms which it instructed are now generally accepted. Indeed, the controversy between those who insist upon the exclusive importance of either aspect of eugenics as against the other seems to me to be without a logical basis. Some say that the method of Nature is to choose the best for reproductive purposes; others, that the method is simply to destroy the worst. By some the latter method is declared incapable of achieving progress, and capable merely of preventing retrogression; by others, the former method is characterised as utterly impracticable. But, candidly, I cannot see that there is any real basis for controversy. Surely our terms are relative. Surely the elimination of the worse necessarily implies the selection of the better; surely the encouragement of the better implies the relative discouragement of the worse. Complete encouragement of the better and complete discouragement of the worse would surely be identical in result. I hold, therefore, that this claiming of Nature as being definitely in favour of the one side or the other is a mere confusion of thought.

Factors in Race Extinction

In answer to those who assert that natural selection is entirely in abeyance in human society, let us observe that both the negative and positive factors of eugenics are already in operation, and will doubtless continue to operate amongst us as throughout the past ages. The relative unfitness which is implied by disease obviously tends to its own extinction, since disease shortens life and in other ways lessens fertility. Mental inferiority also tends towards extinction, since it certainly lessens the chances of marriage. Even moral inferiority, though with many and salient exceptions, tends towards extinction, since imprisonment and other forms of punishment interfere with the possibility of fertility.

Since I insist elsewhere upon the principle of the worth of individuality, it is hardly necessary to reply to the critics who expend themselves against propositions of their own imagining, such as "Sir Francis Galton desires to create a dull uniformity of type"; as if this great student of heredity did not know the value of variation. Allusion has already been made to our obvious duty in respect of the hopelessly unfit, such as the insane. It can scarcely be doubted that one feature which distinguishes our present civilisation from all past civilisations is our attitude, not consciously but effectively, in looking with favour upon the reproduction of such persons. It is probably to be questioned whether such reproduction has ever occurred in time past to a degree sufficient to be of any great historical moment. It

Our Duty to the Unfit

is another question whether the historian of the future would make the same statement of to-day.

If now we turn away from the definitely unfit and look more at the positive aspects of eugenics, we shall do well to recall what has already been said at length regarding the antagonism between individuation and genesis. The truth that the higher the individual type the less is its fecundity is illustrated not only throughout the whole organic world, but also in human society, and it is impossible to doubt that it has played an enormous part in history.

"Society," as the writer has said elsewhere, "is an organism that reproduces itself from below. One cannot eat one's cake and have it; cannot write a system of philosophy and successfully bring up a large family. The energy available by any one of us is finite, and if it be expended upon the race it cannot remain for the service of the individual; if expended for the individual it is not available for the race. No eugenic system will alter this fact; but it surely lends added force to the contention that, at any rate, we should do what we can by way of removing any difficulties that may affect the marriage of the worthy. The granting of eugenic certificates for marriage, the development of social opinion in the direction of added respect for the parents of worthy children, the establishment, after the fashion of the Chinese, of a Golden Book wherein will be recounted the names and achievements of worthy families—these and many other measures, some easy, others difficult, some in more or less vigorous action to-day, and others novel, will serve for that encouragement of the best which is as certainly part of Nature's method as the destruction of the hindmost."

The One Qualification for Parentage

This, of course, is not the place for anything more than an allusion to Galton's great ideas. I am tempted, however, to make one comment. I am not quite comfortable in my mind about any kind of exterior device for persuading people to become parents, neither a tax on bachelors, nor a golden book of merit, nor any of Sir Francis's suggestions. Assuming physical and psychical health and adequate means, there seems to me to be just one qualification for parentage that overrides all others, and that is the love of children for their own sweet sake.

THE FUTURE OF THE HUMAN RACE
SCIENTIFIC VIEWS OF THE WORLD'S DESTINY

IF, then, it be in terms of individual worth, in terms of the value of the individual life, the self-conscious life, that progress is to be measured, what limits may we set to its course ? It seems to me that there are no limits discernible. I love to turn over in my mind Spencer's remark that what is possible for human nature here and there is possible for human nature at large. This is the promise of the deathless dead. A Newton shows what is possible for the intellect of man ; a Buddha or Socrates or St. Francis what is possible for his soul ; a Shakespeare and a Beethoven what is possible for his artistic capacity. "The best is yet to be."

Surely it is no longer possible for us to accept the doctrine of organic evolution, yet fail to see its magnificent implication that man is not a finished product, but is in climax. To do so, as has well been said,

Man Yet in the Making would be to commit the folly of the man who sets forth to tell a good story, but leaves out the point. The truth is that we get from science not only a promise, but also the means by which that promise may be made good at no late date. The writer has failed utterly in his endeavour if he has not persuaded the reader to protest with him against the common opinion, very forcibly expressed by a great thinker, only just departed, in one of his greatest works.

In the prelude to "The Egoist," Mr. George Meredith says of our request for aid from the doctrine of evolution : "We were the same, and animals into the bargain. That is all we got from science. Our disease was hanging on to us again with the extension of a tail. . . . We have little to learn from apes, and they may be left." Another noble-minded thinker, John Ruskin, compared Darwin to "some dim comet, wagging its tail of phosphorescent nothing against the steadfast stars." We have seen also that Carlyle, whom Ruskin well describes as "the greatest

historian since Tacitus," despised the teachings of modern biology, even though he had independently reached its salient conclusions himself. Amongst the distinguished figures of the nineteenth century who denied that biology had any lessons

Lessons of Biology Denied for man were Carlyle, Ruskin, Gladstone, Salisbury, Disraeli, Manning and Newman. For names of equal weight on the other side we have only Tennyson and Emerson. But it is high time that even amongst that great majority who are not directly concerned with biology, and the greatest of whom in recent times we have just named, there should be realised the truth foreshadowed by Huxley that the science of life would one day be as useful to living man as, let us say, the science of electricity, and ineffably more so.

Assuredly "the best is yet to be," but there is no student of natural science who would not demur if I were to make another quotation from the great optimist who wrote those words, and declare that "man has for ever."

He said : "What's time? Leave now for dogs
  and apes !
 Man has For ever ! "

It is not that we fear the coming of the year 2000, like our ancestors, who thought that the year 1000 would usher in the end of the world, nor is it that we fear to be brushed off the earth by the tail of some chance comet, not yet need we expect to be drowned in the rising sea of carbonic acid gradually accumulating in the atmosphere and driving our descendants to the

Possible End of the World mountains, higher than which they cannot go. Superstitions and speculations like these are not seriously to be regarded. Much graver, though infinitely remote and dubious, is the suggestion seriously countenanced by no less an authority than Professor Simon Newcomb that in the course of the apparent journey of the solar system towards Vega, or at the end of it, we may encounter some star, perhaps some dark star which the astronomers cannot see, but the disturbing gravitational influence of which upon the planets they may detect—and that the ensuing collision, by no means an unprecedented occurrence in the stellar world, may teach us "what shadows we are and what

The Threat of the Physicists shadows we pursue," and slay us in the teaching. This, however, is possible, but not inevitable. The sun, for instance, may have an orbit and may not reach Vega or any other star. There remains, however, an end apparently inevitable.

For there hangs over us the threat of the physicists. If I ask the physicists whether, in their sinister predictions, they have reckoned with mind, some of them may answer that they have not reckoned with mind because mind needs not to be reckoned with. It is, they say, quoting Maudsley and Huxley, an "epiphenomenon," or by-product of cerebral chemistry, the impotent but interested spectator of a drama in which its own destinies are decided.

This was the view of Huxley; yet in the very essay in which he denies that man can ever arrest the procession of the great year, he tells us that there lies within man "a fund of energy, operating intelligently, and so far akin to that which pervades the universe, that it is competent to influence and modify the cosmic process." The physicists cannot dispose of mind in their predictions on the ground of its impotence, and so much the worse for the epiphenomenal theory of mind. More acceptable to the psychologists of the present day is the doctrine of psycho-physical parallelism, which we commonly associate with the name of Wundt, of Leipsic. According to this, mind and matter—or shall we say the physics of the brain and the psychics of the mind?—proceed in two parallel lines,

Teaching of Great Thinkers the psychical never being able to influence the physical, nor the physical the psychical. This is plausible teaching, and it comes to us with the authority of great thinkers, but it is difficult to reconcile with admitted facts. It must seriously be asked whether the doctrine of Wundt, now current, is compatible with the known facts of the spiritual history of mankind, or with each man's consciousness of purpose and volition within himself, or

even with the manufacture of a thimble. Materialists, idealists, or whatever we be, we know, as an inalienable first-hand fact, that purpose and the effecting of purpose do verily exist, if not in the world around us, at any rate in ourselves. Hence, I will venture to declare that there are no schools of philosophy, however mutually hostile, which can bring the philosophical argument, at any rate, against my view that in forecasting the future of the evolutionary process as we may observe it in the external world, or in what passes for us as the external world, the human intelligence has hitherto failed to reckon with itself.

Man has a good deal to learn, you will say, before he can remould this "scheme of things entire" as he would please, and meanwhile the sun grows cold. But the latest developments of physics tell us that even if the sun is already beginning to grow cold, the process will take far longer than used to be thought. The estimate of Helmholtz, based upon the assumption that the solar energy is due to gravitation alone, is undergoing

The Doubtful Future profound modification, and instead of three, five, or seven million years to go, we hear talk of a minimum of thirty millions. Also we are finding a source of heat in radium in the earth's crust which is not self-cooling, but self-heating. The sun and the earth, we are beginning to suspect, are not old, but young. As for man, it is but a brief period that comprises his whole history, and he is self-conscious already. If this past be compared with the future promised him, even apart from any extension by his intelligence, man is not merely not yet adult, he has scarcely begun to be at all.

Once we cease to accept the law of the dissipation of energy, we are face to face with the possibility that the human mind is not threatened with necessary extinction. If our own race alone can produce a Newton, a Darwin, a Kelvin already, and if much of their work—though not, we now suspect, the theory of the dissipation of energy—remains, who will venture to say what we shall achieve when we begin to grow up? I take it that "What's past is prologue," and that, for the future.

Our Friends are exultations, agonies,
And love, and man's unconquerable mind.

C. W. SALEEBY

HOPE

One star, one string, and all the rest
  Darkness and everlasting space,
Save that she shelters in her breast
  The travail of the race.

Borne thro' the cold and soundless deep
  With ruin riding down the air,
She bows, too heavenly to weep,
  Too human to despair.

And ever on her lonely string
  Expects the music from above,
Some faint confirming whispering
  Of fatherhood and love.

One star, one string, and thro' the drift
  Of æons sad with human cries
She waits the hand of God to lift
  The bandage from her eyes.
            HAROLD BEGBIE

From the painting by George Frederick Watts, R.A., photographed by Hollyer.

THE END OF THE WORLD
THE THOUGHT OF MASTER MINDS ON THE
FINAL DESTINY OF THE HUMAN RACE
By Harold Begbie

THE PROBLEM OF LIFE BEYOND THE GRAVE

Even as, heavy-curled,
Stooping against the wind, a charioteer
Is snatched from out his chariot by the hair
So shall Time be ; and as the void car, hurled
Abroad by reinless steeds, even so the world :
Yea, even as chariot dust upon the air,
It shall be sought, and not found anywhere.
ROSSETTI

Though earth and man were gone,
    And suns and universes ceased to be ;
And Thou were left alone,
    Every existence would exist in Thee.
EMILY BRONTË

" In the year 626 of our era," says Emerson, " when Edwin, the Anglo-Saxon king, was deliberating on receiving the Christian missionaries, one of his nobles said to him, ' The present life of man, O King, compared with that space of time beyond, of which we have no certainty, reminds me of one of your winter feasts, where you sit with your generals and ministers. The hearth blazes in the middle and a grateful heat is spread around, while storms of rain and snow are raging without. Driven by the chilling tempest, a little sparrow enters at one door and flies delighted around us till it departs through the other. Whilst it stays in our mansion it feels not the winter storm ; but when this short moment of happiness has been enjoyed, it is forced again into the same dreary tempest from which it had escaped, and we behold it no more. Such is the life of man, and we are as ignorant of the state which preceded our present existence as of that which will follow it. Things being so, I feel that if this new faith can give us more certainty, it deserves to be received.' "

The Dark and Doubtful Future

But what was before us, we know not,
And we know not what shall succeed.

In spite of centuries of religion, in spite of centuries of science, in spite of immemorial and increasing rhetoric, man knows nothing of the great central mystery of existence—its origin, its purpose, and its end. Theology can produce no document of immortality, and Science can formulate no explanation of life. We are still in the sad case of that sparrow of the year 626 of our era, now, undoubtedly dead ; we are still surrounded by a great darkness that does not lift ; and in spite of Sir Thomas Browne's gallant gospel—" For the World, I count it not an Inn, but an Hospital ; and a place not to live, but to die in "—the vast majority of the human race consider this life as a warm and cheerful hearth at which they warm themselves for a little, with the door of birth open to one darkness and the door of death open to another.

What Follows Death?

What is beyond ?

As we warm our hands at the blaze, as we draw our chairs nearer to the human hearth, from which so many that we once knew have departed and to which so many more of whom we know nothing are approaching, we ask ourselves more and more the question which no man has yet answered with certainty : What is beyond?

Many rebuke us for these anxious glancings towards the dark door where the storm rages and the darkness abides. Solomon and Epicurus and Omar Khayyam have each their good reason why we should keep our faces to the fire, the cup to our lips, and our ear to the song :

Come, fill the cup, and in the fire of spring
Your winter garment of repentance fling :
    The Bird of Time has but a little way
To flutter, and the Bird is on the wing.

Emerson, too, that high and lofty soul, has his own reproach for us : " You shall not say, ' O my bishop, O my pastor, is there any resurrection ? What do you think ? Did Dr. Channing believe that we should know each other ? Did Wesley ? Did Butler ? Did Fenelon ? ' What questions are these ? Go read Milton,

The Soul's Eternal Question Shakespeare, or any truly ideal poet. Read Plato, or any seer of the interior realities. Read St. Augustine, Swedenborg, Immanuel Kant. Let any master simply recite to you the substantial laws of the intellect, and in the presence of the laws themselves you will never ask such primary-school questions."

But in despite of these differing rebukes the soul of man still asks : What is beyond ? And not on all the congregated inspiration of Milton, Shakespeare, Plato, Augustine, Swedenborg, Kant and Emerson can he rest his soul and feel secure with certainty.

"The human mind," says Pasteur, " actuated by an invincible force, will never cease to ask itself : What is beyond ? It is of no use to answer : Beyond is limitless space, limitless time, or limitless grandeur ; no one understands those words." The question is not in rhetoric, but in the simple longings of the human heart. When I close the eyes of my child, when I fold her hands, and when, shut down in darkness, the little body so dear to me is borne out of the house she made like heaven, and lowered into the silence and ruin of the tomb—is *that* the end ? I want to know that. I want to know : Is she as if she had never been ? I do not want limitless space, limitless time, limitless grandeur ; I only want to know if *somewhere* and in *some state* the soul of my child is conscious and still sensitive to my love. Victor Hugo, who leaned upon the cold

Man's Quest After Certainty stone of death and cried to his child : " Feelest thou that I am there ? " uttered his lamentation and his surrender to God in these words :

Je sais que vous avez bien autre chose à faire
  Que de nous plaindre tous,
Et qu'un enfant qui meurt, désespoir de sa mére,
  Ne vous fait rien, à vous.

Je sais que le fruit tombe au vent qui le secoue,
  Que l'oiseau perd sa plume et la fleur son parfum ;
Que la création est une grande roue
  Qui ne peut se mouvoir sans écraser quelqu'un.

" I know that You have many other things to do than pitying us, and that the child who dies and breaks his mother's heart makes no difference to You. I know that the fruit falls in the wind that shakes it, that the bird loses its plumage, and the flower its scent ; that creation is a great wheel which cannot move without crushing someone."

This is the attitude of the contemporary mind. The vastness of God is acknowledged, the insignificance of man is admitted, the terrible silence and cold-bloodedness of natural law is accepted ; but human love still ventures to ask the Infinite whether perhaps He has no use for it. Victor Hugo said that when he threw angry cries at God he was like a child who throws a stone at the sea ; and he bowed and said : " Humble as a child and soft as a woman, I come to adore You."

It was apprehension of the Infinite that bowed the god-like soul of Victor Hugo ; it is the suspicion of the Infinite that keeps the ordinary man reverent and obedient to his conscience. " He who proclaims the existence of the Infinite— and none can avoid it—accumulates in that affirmation more of the supernatural than is to be found in all the

Mystery of the Infinite miracles of all the religions ; for the notion of the Infinite presents that double character that it forces itself upon us and yet is incomprehensible. When this notion seizes upon our understanding, we can but kneel . . . I see everywhere the inevitable expression of the Infinite in the world ; through it the supernatural is at the bottom of every heart. The idea of God is a form of the Idea of the Infinite. As long as the mystery of the Infinite weighs on human thought, temples will be erected for the worship of the Infinite, whether God is called Brâhma, Allah, Jehovah or Jesus ; and on the pavement of those temples men will be seen kneeling, prostrated, annihilated in the thought of the Infinite."

Thus Pasteur, who studied the Infinite, not through a telescope, but through a microscope ; who knew, not the infinitely great, but the infinitely little, and saw marvel, miracle, and annihilating infinity in the invisible kingdom of bacteriæ.

There are men of science who tell us that the unconquerable hope is vain, that the inviolable shade is a mirage. Pasteur is dead ; he believed with Victor Hugo that the tomb which shuts out the earth opens the firmament, and that this which we take to be the end is the beginning ;

but he produced no proof, and he has not come back to tell us of the beyond. Another occupies his chair at the great Institute in Paris ; and this man, Metchnikoff, tells us that " a man is as old as his arteries," that we only desire immortality because our manner of living abridges the natural term of life by some sixty or seventy years ; and that if by right living we reached a hundred and fifty human years —mortality's natural span—we should have no desire at all for immortality, only a tired leaning towards eternal sleep.

There are also men of science who look away from the individual end of the world—the death of a man—and, speculating on the cosmical end of the world, lose all sense of personal identity, and show us the destruction of the planet on which we live and kneel and bury our dead as an event of trivial significance, if significant at all, to the rest of the universe. We have traced in these volumes the history of the world. From the beginning of things to the present day we have followed the march of humanity from barbarism to civilisation. Such an

Secrets of the Dim and Distant Past undertaking, never attempted before, staggers the mind and fills one with an awful sense of vastness and despair. We have seen peoples rise and fall like the waves of the sea, mighty empires and historic dynasties go out like candles, age-long religions expire like last season's popular novel, philosophies, customs, morals, manners and laws that seemed eternal change with climate and with race, and lose all likeness to their origins ; nay, we have seen that before recorded history began uncountable centuries stretched behind—æons in which continents of which we know nothing bore under the stars the palaces and temples of civilisations which were blotted out, and left not a rack behind, and when the present configuration of our planet was a little dust at the bottom of the ocean.

But even as human history is only as a day to the history of a blade of grass, so is the total history of our earth but as the trembling of an eyelid to the history of the universe in which it swims.

The birth of our planet was a trivial and late event in the history of the universe ; its destruction would be to the rest of the universe only like the falling of a child's kite which for a few moments hung in the blue air of a summer day.

And again, the total history of that whole swarm of worlds which we call the universe, to the eternity which saw its birth, and which, according to some, is quite indifferent to its death, is like the splutter of a catherine wheel. " We must admit," says Sir Oliver Lodge, in " Man and the Universe,"

Where Science is Ignorant " that science knows nothing of ultimate origins. Which first — the hen or the egg ? is a trivial form of a very real puzzle. That the world in the sense of this planet, this homely lump of matter we call the earth—that this had an origin, a history, a past, intelligible more or less, growingly intelligible to the eye of science, is true enough. The date when it was molten may be roughly estimated. The manner and the mechanism of the birth of the moon has been guessed : the earth and moon, then, *originated* in one sense ; before that they were part of a nebula, like the rest of the solar system ; and some day the solar system may again be part of a nebula, in consequence of collision with some at present tremendously distant mass. But all that is nothing to the universe ; nothing even to the visible universe. The collisions there take place every now and then before our eyes.

" The universe is full of lumps of matter of every imaginable size : the history of a solar system may be written—its birth and also its death, separated perhaps by millions and millions of years ; but what of that ? It is but an episode, a moment in the eternal cosmogony, and the eye of history looks to what happened before the birth and after the death of any particular aggregate ; just as a child may trace the origin and the destruction of a soap-bubble, the form of which is evanescent, the material of which is permanent. While the soap-bubble lived it was the scene of much beauty, and of a kind of law and order impossible to the mere water and soap out of which it

History of the Solar System was made, and into which again it has collapsed. The history of the soap-bubble can be written, but there is a before and an after. So it is with the solar system ; so with any assigned collocation of matter in the universe. No point in space can be thought of 'at which if a man stand it shall be impossible for him to cast a javelin into the beyond.' Nor can any epoch be conceived in time at which the mind will not instantly and automatically inquire, 'and what before' or 'what after'?" Science is quite emphatic that the end of the world is a definite event of the future. Whatever may be the end of the world in the individual sense, the physical end of the great globe itself is inevitable.

The Earth Moving to Destruction This misshapen ball, with its atmosphere and clouds, swinging in perfect silence round an immense conflagration which we call the sun, this little star, this planet, this earth, with its varying languages, climates, morals, manners and religions, which, like a moth in the universal ether, flies round the candle of the sun, will, at some awful moment in the womb of time, perish, and be as if it had never been.

Our history of which we are so proud, man's struggle for political liberty, his advance from slavery and ignorance, his conflicts with other nations, his beheadings of tyrannical kings, his French Revolutions, which fill libraries with the documents of their achievements—these things, which have meant nothing to the earth on which they were enacted, are but like the buzzings of flies. They have scratched with a pin the earth's crust during her silent circlings of the sun; they are merely the movements of parasites swarming on the monster that is moving, wholly indifferent to us, to his own destruction. The central, absolute, and dwarfing fact is the destiny of the earth itself, and that destiny is destruction.

How will it end?

Although it is Science that makes us certain of the world's end, long before there was exact science men of the ancient world had foreseen, prophesied, and speculated

upon this vast event. We will examine some of these inspirational notions before we proceed to consider the definite predictions of dogmatic Science. The phrase of Sir Oliver Lodge, that the question, Hen or egg—which first? represents a trivial form of a very real problem will suggest to the reader that there is an element of immodesty in attempting to discuss the end of something about whose origin we are ignorant. This is quite true. But man is immodest whenever he opens his mouth to historise yesterday, to prophesy to-morrow, or to dogmatise the present. We do not know which came first, the hen or the egg.

On the Outskirts of the Infinite We can weigh the stars, measure the heavens, elaborate our thesis of evolution; but we cannot for the life of us tell whether in the beginning an egg hatched the first hen, or a hen laid the first egg. We are, in fact, concerning origins, concerning certainty, as much in the dark as our earliest ancestors.

Therefore at the head of all our inquiries we set the words of the writer of the Book of Job:

These are but the outskirts of His ways:
And how small a whisper do we hear of Him!
But the thunder of His power who can understand?

Standing in the outskirts of the Universal Infinite, knowing that we hear but a faint whisper of His Being, acknowledging that it is utterly beyond our finite understanding to comprehend the fulness of His Power, we may with reverence contemplate the destiny of the apparently self-captained vessel whereon humanity, like a party of excursionists, makes sixty or seventy journeys round the sun, and consider how it will end.

"WHEN THE SEA GIVES UP ITS DEAD"
From the painting by Lord Leighton, P.R.A.

HOW WILL THE WORLD END?
THE VOICE OF LITERATURE AND OF SCIENCE ON THE FINAL CATACLYSM

ONE central fact of all ancient speculations on this head is their apprehension of an everlastingness outside of man and his earth. It is well to bear this in mind.

From the days of the Psalmist, with his cry, " From everlasting to everlasting Thou art God . . . a thousand years in Thy sight are but as yesterday when it is past, and as a watch in the night," down to the days when Shakespeare uttered sweetest melancholy in the sonnet beginning—

When I consider everything that grows
  Holds in perfection but a little moment,
That this huge stage presenteth nought but
  shows
Whereon the stars in secret influence comment—

down to our time, when Science has made infinity and existence as absolutely

Man's Brief Span of Life facts of the universe as the transitoriness of the globe on which we speculate—man has *always* been conscious of some Vast surrounding him with majestic incomprehensibility.

Of old hast Thou laid the foundations of the earth,
And the heavens are the work of Thy hands.
They shall perish, but Thou shalt endure ;
Yea, all of them shall wax old like a garment ;
As a vesture shalt thou change them, and they
  shall be changed :
But Thou art the same,
And Thy years shall have no end.
PSALM cii., 25-27.

Behold, God is great, and we know Him not :
The number of His years is unsearchable.
JOB xxvi., 26.

It would be tedious to multiply instances of this conviction of the human heart. Man from the first has felt that he is like the grass of the field, that the earth and the stars shall perish ; but that the Power which called them into existence will continue for ever. We find also in some of those millennial prophecies which distinguish ancient

literature the idea of an end to the world in its present form :

Isaiah, who said—
They shall not hurt nor destroy in all My holy mountain, for the earth shall be full of the knowledge of the Lord, as the waters cover the sea.—xi., 9.

said likewise—
Lift up your eyes to the heavens, and look upon the earth beneath ; for the heavens shall vanish away like smoke, and the earth shall wax old like a garment ; and they that dwell therein shall die in like manner, but my salvation shall be for ever, and my righteousness shall not be abolished.—li., 6.

Christ himself, in His own unique fashion, prophesied the end of the world.

As [Jesus] sat upon the Mount of Olives, the disciples came unto Him privately, saying : Tell us . . . what shall be the sign of Thy coming, and of the end of the world ? [The consummation of the age.]

And Jesus answered, and said unto them : Take heed that no man lead you astray. For many shall come in My name, saying, I am the Christ ; and shall lead many astray. And ye shall hear of wars and rumours of wars: see that ye be not troubled ; for these things must needs come to pass ; but the end is not yet. For nation shall rise against nation, and kingdom against kingdom ; and there shall be famines and earthquakes in divers places. But all these things are the beginning of travail. Then shall they deliver you up unto tribulation, and shall kill you ; and ye shall be hated of all the nations for My name's sake. And then shall many stumble, and shall deliver up one another, and shall hate one another. And many false prophets shall arise, and shall lead many astray. And because iniquity shall be multiplied, the love of the many shall wax cold.

But he that endureth unto the end, the same shall be saved. And this gospel of the kingdom shall be preached in the whole world for a testimony unto all the nations ; and then shall the end come.

As the lightning cometh forth from the East, and is seen even unto the West, so shall be the coming of the Son of Man. Wheresoever the carcase is, there will the eagles [vultures] be gathered together.

But immediately after the tribulation of those

days the sun shall be darkened, and the moon shall not give her light, and the stars shall fall from heaven, and the powers of the heavens shall be shaken ; and then shall appear the sign of the Son of Man in heaven ; and then shall all the tribes of the earth mourn, and they shall see the Son of Man coming on the clouds of heaven with power and great glory .

Heaven and earth shall pass away, but My words shall not pass away. But of that day and hour knoweth no one, not even the angels of heaven, neither the Son, but the Father only. . . . For as in those days which were before the flood they were eating and drinking, marrying and giving in marriage, until the day that Noah entered into the Ark, and they knew not until the flood came, and took them all away ; so shall be the coming of the Son of Man.

ST. MATTHEW, xxiv.

Take heed to yourselves, lest haply your hearts be overcharged with surfeiting and drunkenness, and cares of this life, and that day come on you suddenly as a snare, for so shall it come upon all them that dwell on the face of all the earth.

ST. LUKE, xxi., 34.

And so we go on to the Apostles, and find the same prophecy, strengthened by the conviction that upon them the ends of the world were already come.

In the last days mockers shall come with mockery, walking after their own lusts, and saying : Where is the promise of His coming ? For, from the day that the fathers fell asleep, all things continue as they were from the beginning of the creation. For this they wilfully forget that there were heavens from of old, and an earth compacted out of water and amidst water, by the word of God ; by which means the world that then was, being overflowed with water, perished ; but the heavens that now are, and the earth, by the same word have been stored up for fire [stored with fire], being reserved against the day of judgment and destruction of ungodly men.

But forget not this one thing, beloved, that one day is with the Lord as a thousand years, and a thousand years as one day. The Lord is not slack concerning His promise, as some count slackness ; but is long-suffering to usward, not wishing that any should perish, but that all should come to repentance.

But the day of the Lord will come as a thief ; in the which the heavens shall pass away with a great noise, and the elements [heavenly bodies] shall be dissolved with fervent heat ; and the earth and the works that are therein shall be burned up. Seeing, then, that all these things are thus to be dissolved, what manner of persons ought ye to be in all holy living and godliness, looking for and earnestly desiring the coming of the day of God, by reason of which the heavens being on fire shall be dissolved, and the elements shall melt with fervent heat ? But, according to His promise we look for new heavens and a new earth wherein dwelleth righteousness.

2 ST. PETER, iii., 5.

And I saw a new heaven and a new earth : for the first heaven and the first earth are passed away, and the sea is no more.—REV. xxi., 1.

Ever since the days of the Apostles men have attempted to prophesy the end of the world, every generation containing some who looked for the Second Coming of Christ.

The end of the world, we learn from Hallam's "The Middle Ages," ought to have occurred, according to Cardinal Nicolas de Cusa, in 1704. He demonstrated his thesis in this manner : The Deluge happened in the thirty-fourth jubilee of fifty years from the Creation (A.M. 1700), and, therefore, the end of the world should properly occur on the thirty-fourth jubilee of the Christian era, or A.D. 1704. The four grace years are added to compensate for the blunder of chronologists respecting the first year of grace.

The most popular dates of modern times for the end of the world, or, what is practically the same thing, the Millennium, are the following : 1757, Swedenborg ; 1836, Johann Albrecht Bengel, Erklärte Offenbarung ; 1843, William Miller of America ; 1866, Dr. John Cumming ; 1881, Mother Shipton.

It was very generally believed in France and Germany that the end of the world would happen in the 1,000th year after Christ ; and, therefore, much **Preparing** of the land was left uncultifor the vated and a general famine World's End ensued. Happily, it was not agreed whether the 1,000 years should date from the birth or the death of Christ, or the desolation would have been much greater. Many charters begin with these words : " As the world is now drawing to its close." Kings and nobles gave up their state ; Robert of France, son of Hugh Capet, entered the monastery of St. Denis ; and at Limoges princes, nobles, and knights proclaimed " God's truce," and solemnly bound themselves to abstain from feuds, to keep the peace towards each other, and to help the oppressed.

Another hypothesis is this : As one day with God equals 1,000 years (Psalm xc., 4), and God laboured in creation six days, therefore the world is to labour 6,000 years, and then to rest. According to this theory, the end of the world ought to occur in A.M. 6000, or A.D. 1996 (supposing the world to have been created 4,004 years before the birth of Christ).

Turning from foolish speculations, we come to the prophecies of literature concerning the final cataclysm, and see how man (whose immortality is an open question) can occupy his transitory days with attempts to visualise the final destruction — the strangest diversion, surely, unless, as the Preacher says, God hath set eternity in man's heart.

Few descriptions can vie with the extraordinary rhetoric of Philip James Bailey, in "Festus," a book, unfortunately, so little known that we shall quote his prophecy in full. It is Bailey, by the way, who has the fine lines :

Tremble ! Ye dare not believe.
No, cowards ! Sooner than believe ye would die ;
Die with the black lie flapping on your lips,
Like the soot-flake upon a burning bar.

Here is the picture from "Festus" :

BAILEY'S PICTURE OF THE CATACLYSM

It is earth shall head destruction. She shall end.
The worlds shall wonder why she comes no more
On her accustomed orbit ; and the sun
Miss one of his apostle lights ; the moon,
An orphaned orb, shall seek for earth for aye,
Through time's untrodden depths, and find her not.
No more shall morn, out of the holy east
Stream o'er the amber air her level light ;
Nor evening, with the spectral fingers, draw
Her star-sprent curtain round the head of earth.
Her footsteps never thence again shall grace
Heaven's blue, sublime. Her grave, Death's now at work,
Gaps in space. See tombwards gathering, all
Her kindred stars in long process, night-clad ;
Each lights his funeral brand, and ranks him round.
And one by one shall all yon wandering worlds,
Whether in orbed path they roll, or trail
Gold-tressed, in length inestimable of light,
Their train, returnless from extreme space, lease ;
The sun, bright keystone of Heaven's world-built arch,
Be left in burning solitude ; the stars
As dewdrops countless on the ætherial fields
Of the skies, and all they comprehend shall pass ;
The spirits of all worlds shall all depart
To their great destinies ; and thou and I,
Greater in grief than worlds, shall live, as now.
And let the worst come to the worst, you say,
There always will be time to turn ourselves,
And cry for half an hour or so to God.
Salvation, sure, is not so very hard ;
It need not take one long ; and half an hour
Is quite as much as we can spare for it.
We have no time for pleasures. Business ! business !
No ! ye shall perish suddenly and unsaved.
The world shall stand still with a rending jar,
As though it struck at sea ; or as when once
An arm Titanian, say not whose, but jogged
By earthquakes, wryed the pole, and o'er the dry
Poured competitive mains. The unsleepful sea,
Mooning and bellowing now round caverned coasts,
Now, drawing hard through thirty thousand teeth,
Upon the shingly shore, his pauseful breath,
Like some monogamous monster which hath lost,
Poor fool ! his mate ; and every rock-hole searched

By torch of foam-light, dogs her steps with sad,
Superfluous faithfulness, shall rest at last,
Nor wist which way to turn him ; ebb nor flow
No more to choose. All elements as though smote
With reasonablest disloyalty to man's
Usurpful claim, their constrained suit shall cease,
And natural service ; men their mightiest wont,
Their meanest use and craft. The halls where parle
The heads of nations shall be dumb with death.
The priest shall dipping, die. Can man save man ?
Is water God ? The counsellor, wise fool,
Drop down amid his quirks and sacred lies.
The judge, while dooming unto death some wretch,
Shall meet at once his own death, doom and judge.
The doctor, watch in hand and patient's pulse,
Shall feel his own heart cease its beats, and fall.
Professors shall spin out, and students strain
Their brains no more. Art, science, toil, shall cease,
Commerce. The ship shall her own plummet seek,
And sound the sea herself and depths of death.
At the first turn, death shall cut off the thief,
And dash the gold-bag in his yellow brain.
The gambler, reckoning gains, shall drop a piece ;
Stoop down, and there see death ; look up, there God.
The wanton, temporising with decay,
And qualifying every line which vice
Writes bluntly on the brow, inviting scorn,
Shall pale through plastered red ; and the loose sot
See clear, for once, through his misty, o'er-brimmed eye.
The just, if there be any, die in prayer.
Death shall be everywhere among your marts ;
And giving bills which no man may decline,
Drafts upon hell one moment after date,
Then shall your outcries tremble amid the stars ;
Terrors shall be about ye like a wind ;
And fears fall down upon ye like four walls.

Thomas Campbell with feebler power has attempted to show the condition of the dying world inhabited by a solitary survivor of the human race. The poem is called, "The Last Man."

THE LAST MAN

All worldly shapes shall melt in gloom,
  The sun himself must die
Before this mortal shall assume
  Its immortality.
I saw a vision in my sleep
That gave my spirit strength to sweep
  Adown the gulf of Time ;
I saw the last of human mould
That shall Creation's death behold,
  As Adam saw her prime.

The sun's eye has a sickly glare
  The earth with age was wan,
The skeletons of nations were
  Around that lonely man.
Some had expired in fight—the brands
Still rusted in their bony hands ;
  In plague and famine some !
Earth's cities had no sound nor tread,
And ships were drifting with the dead
  To shores where all was dumb !

Yet, prophet-like, that lone one stood,
  With dauntless words and high,
That shook the sere leaves from the wood
  As if a storm passed by,
Saying, We are twins in death, proud sun !
Thy face is cold, thy race is run,
  'Tis mercy bids thee go ;
For thou ten thousand thousand years
Hast seen the tide of human tears
  That shall no longer flow.

What though beneath thee man put forth,
  His pomp, his pride, his skill,
And arts that made fire, flood, and earth
  The vassals of his will !
Yet mourn I not thy parted sway,
Thou dim discrowned king of day ;
  For all those trophied arts
And triumphs that beneath thee sprang
Healed not a passion or a pang,
  Entailed on human hearts.

Go, let oblivion's curtain fall
  Upon the stage of men,
Nor with thy rising beams recall
  Life's tragedy again.
It's piteous pageants bring not back,
Nor waken flesh upon the rack
  Of pain anew to writhe—
Stretched in disease's shapes abhorred,
Or mown in battle by the sword,
  Like grass beneath the scythe.

Even I am weary in yon skies
  To watch thy fading fire ;
Test of all sumless agonies,
  Behold not me expire !
My lips that speak thy dirge of death,
Their rounded gasp and gurgling breath,
  To see thou shalt not boast ;
The eclipse of Nature spreads my pall,
The majesty of Darkness shall
  Receive my parting ghost !

The spirit shall return to Him
  Who gave its heavenly spark ;
Yet think not, sun, it shall be dim
  When thou thyself art dark !
No, it shall live again, and shine
In bliss unknown to beams of thine,
  By Him recalled to breath
Who captive led captivity,
Who robbed the grave of victory,
  And took the sting from death !

Go, sun, while mercy holds me up
  On Nature's awful waste,
To drink this last and bitter cup
  Of grief that man shall taste.
Go tell the night that hides thy face
Thou saw'st the last of Adam's race
  On earth's sepulchral clod,
The darkening universe defy
To quench his immortality,
  Or shake his trust in God !

Tennyson's end of the world, like all his poetry, is gentle, ideal, and graceful— a millennium and not a cataclysm. Could there be greater contrast than that between "Festus" and the two "Locksley Halls."

TENNYSON'S VISION OF MILLENNIUM

Far I dipt into the future, far as human eye
  could see,
Saw the Vision of the world and all the wonder
  that would be ;
Saw the heavens fill with commerce, argosies of
  magic sails,
Pilots· of the purple twilight, dropping down
  with costly bales ;
Heard the heavens fill with shouting, and there
  rained a ghastly dew
From the nations' airy navies grappling in the
  central blue ;
Far along the world-wide whisper of the south
  wind rushing warm,
With the standards of the peoples plunging thro'
  the thunder-storm ;
Till the war-drum throbbed no longer, and the
  battle-flags were furled
In the Parliament of Man, the Federation of the
  world,
There the common-sense of most shall hold a
  fretful realm in awe,
And the kindly earth shall slumber, lapt in
  universal law.

. . . .

Many an æon moulded earth before her highest
  man was born,
Many an æon, too, may pass when earth is
  manless and forlorn.

. . . .

When the schemes and all the systems, kingdoms
  and republics fall,
Something kindlier, higher, holier—all for each
  and each for all ?
All the full-brained, half-brained races, led by
  justice, love, and truth ;
All the millions one at length with all the visions
  of my youth ?
All diseases quenched by science, no man halt,
  or deaf, or blind ;
Stronger ever born of weaker, lustier· body,
  larger mind ?
Earth at last, a warless world, a single race, a
  single tongue—
I have seen her far away—for is not Earth as yet
  so young ?—
Every tiger madness muzzled, every serpent
  passion killed,
Every grim ravine a garden, every blazing
  desert tilled,
Robed in universal harvest up to either pole she
  smiles,
Universal ocean softly washing all her warless
  isles.

This faith in some culminating perfection, some Paradisal baptism of earth in the waters of millennium, was apparently shared by Browning.

My own hope is, a sun will pierce
The thickest cloud earth every stretched ;
  That, after Last, returns the First,
Though a wide compass round be fetched ;
  That what began best, can't end worst,
Nor what God blessed once, prove accurst.

The attitude of Joseph Addison, if he expressed it in "Cato," differed from anything of a millennial character, and concerned only the immortality of a soul infinitely greater than the perishable earth. His beautiful lines march with the hopes of humanty.

It must be so—Plato, thou reasonest well !
Else whence this pleasing hope, this fond desire,
This longing after immortality ?
Or whence this secret dread and inward horror
Of falling into naught ? Why shrinks the soul
Back on herself, and startles at destruction ?
'Tis the divinity that stirs within us ;
'Tis Heaven itself that points out an hereafter,
And intimates eternity to man.
Eternity ! thou pleasing, dreadful thought !

I'm weary of conjectures,—this must end 'em,
Thus am I doubly armed : my death and life,
My bane and antidote, are both before me :
This in a moment brings me to an end ;
But this informs me I shall never die.
The soul, secured in her existence, smiles
At the drawn dagger, and defies its point.
The stars shall fade away, the sun himself
Grow dim with age, and Nature sink in years ;
But thou shalt flourish in immortal youth,
Unhurt amidst the war of elements,
The wrecks of matter, and the crush of worlds.

No man, of course, with greater dignity and nobler restraint of power, has matched Shakespeare's sublime utterance in the familiar passage :

Our revels now are ended. These our actors,
As I foretold you, were all spirits, and
Are melted into air, into thin air :
And, like the baseless fabric of this vision,
The cloud-capped towers, the gorgeous palaces,
The solemn temples, the great globe itself,
Yea, all which it inherit, shall dissolve,
And, like this insubstantial pageant faded,
Leave not a rack behind. We are such stuff
As dreams are made on ; and our little life
Is rounded with a sleep.

There is a sense of mystery in these glorious lines, as though the great and inscrutable master, taking his leave of the stage in a sweet allegory—

Deeper than did ever plummet sound
I'll drown my book——

let himself hint at some knowledge of eternal verities which he possessed and could not more impart. But always in Shakespeare's greatest moments there is this hinting spirit of a profound knowledge of the mystery of existence, as for instance in the lines

There are more things in heaven and earth, Horatio,
Than are dreamt of in your philosophy.

Shakespeare, we may say, is saturated with mystery, and he seems to us to stand at the head of the human race smiling on all children of imagination, and gently and with a large tolerance rebuking those smaller spirits who shout that the universe is merely an inferior machine on a large scale. It has always struck us that Shakespeare, with his large soul and ample powers, his abiding calm, and his profound mystery better answers both in himself and in his works the arguments of a soulless materialism than all the packed logic of theism and transcendentalism.

The Finite and the Infinite Mystery is the quintessence of Shakespeare as it is of all great imaginative work. Sir Thomas Browne spoke for a considerable number of the human race when he said, " I love to lose myself in a mystery, to pursue my Reason to an *O altitudo !* . . . Who can speak of Eternity without a solecism, or think thereof without an extasie ? Time we may comprehend, 'tis but five days elder than ourselves, and hath the same Horoscope with the World ; but to retire so far back as to apprehend a beginning, to give such an infinite start forwards as to conceive an end in an essence that we affirm hath neither the one nor the other, it puts my Reason to St. Paul's Sanctuary : my philosophy dares not say the Angels can do it ; God hath not made a Creature that can comprehend Him ; 'tis a privilege of His own nature. *I am that I am* was his own definition unto Moses ; and 'twas a short one, to confound mortality, that durst question God, or ask Him what He was . . . . In Eternity there is no distinction of Tenses . . . what to us is to come, to His Eternity is present, His whole duration being but one permanent point, without Succession, Parts, Flux, or Division."

This attitude is characteristic of all our literature on the great subject of God and Man, Time and Eternity. While we confess the utterness of our inability to comprehend Infinity, Omnipotence and Eternity, we love to lose ourselves in the mystery and to pursue our Reason to an *O altitudo!* Perhaps this concern with **In the Atmosphere of Science** such tremendous and infinite issues on the part of a finite and insignificant creature, inhabiting so small a planet in the visible universe is a fact as important to science as the teeth of an anthropoid ape, the nature of radium, or the functions of the liver.

When we turn from literature to science we find ourselves in a quite different atmosphere. The reader who is constitutionally averse from rhetoric and prejudiced in favour of the calm, grave, and passionless vocabulary of science will rejoice to escape from Bailey and Tennyson and Addison to listen with reverence and attention to Professor Clifford and Professor Flammarion. But a caution is necessary. "The whole drift of my education," says Professor James, in "The Varieties of Religious **Experience** Experience," "goes to persuade **Preferred** me that the world of our **to Science** present consciousness is only one out of many worlds of consciousness that exist, and that those other worlds must contain experiences which have a meaning for our life also ; and that although in the main their experiences and those of the world keep discreet, yet the two become continuous at certain points, and higher energies filter in. By being faithful in my own poor measure to this over-belief, I seem to myself to keep more sane and true. I *can*, of course, put myself into the sectarian scientist's attitude, and imagine vividly that the world of sensations and of scientific laws and objects may be all. But whenever I do this, I hear that inward monitor of which W. K. Clifford once wrote whispering the word ' Bosh ! ' Humbug is humbug, even though it bear the scientific name, and the total expression of human experience as I view it objectively, invincibly urges one beyond the narrow ' scientific ' bounds. Assuredly the real world is of a different temperament—more intricately built than physical science allows."

It will certainly be well for the reader, in following the man of science in his dogmatic and convincing forecast of cataclysm, to remember that inward monitor of Professor Clifford, and to remind himself of that healthy word, "Bosh!" When we have done with the man of science we shall consult the psychologists and philosophers, who have **" The First** studied that mind and that **and Last** consciousness employed by the **Catastrophe "** man of physical science to arrive at his conclusions. Let us begin by a quotation from one of the most emphatic and brilliant of scientists, Professor W. K. Clifford, who, in "The First and Last Catastrophe," writes :

"The life which exists upon the earth is made by the sun's action, and it depends upon the sun for its continuance. We know that the sun is wearing out, that it is cooling; and although this heat that it loses day by day is made up in some measure, perhaps completely at present, by the contraction of its mass, yet that process cannot go on for ever. There is only a certain amount of energy in the present constitution of the sun, and when that has been used up the sun cannot go on giving out any more heat. Supposing, therefore, the earth remains in her present orbit about the sun, seeing that the sun must be cooled down ,at some time, we shall all be frozen out. . . . . . .

" In any case, all we know is that the sun is going out. If we fall into the sun, that we shall be fried ; if we go away from the sun, or the sun goes out, then we shall be frozen. So that, as far as the earth is concerned, we have no means of determining what will be the character of the end. But we know that one of these two things must take place in time. But in regard to the whole universe, if we were to travel forward as we have travelled backward, in time, consider things as falling together, we should come to a great **When** central mass, all in one piece, **the Sun** which would send out waves of **Cools** heat through a perfectly empty ether, and gradually cool itself down. As this mass gets cool it would be deprived of all life or motion ; it would be just a mere enormous frozen block in the middle of the ether.

"But that conclusion, which is like the one that we discussed about the beginning of the world, is one which we have no right whatever to rest upon. It depends upon the same assumption that the laws of geometry and mechanics are exactly and absolutely true, and that they will continue exactly and absolutely true for ever and ever. Such an assumption we have no right whatever to make. We may therefore, I think, conclude about the end of things that, so far as the earth is concerned, an end of life upon it is as probable as science can make anything ; but that in regard to the universe we have no right to draw any conclusion at all."

In another form we have the end of the world adumbrated by Professor Camille Flammarion in an article which is as reasonable as any prophecy ever yet ventured upon by seer or scientist. We quote it at some length because it is the most representative expression of materialistic opinion which obtains at the present day.

We might say with confidence that if the world is to end at all, this is certainly how it will happen.

"What is the future of our planet and of all that which adorns it now—mankind, plants, animals, birds—of the continents and of the ocean? Will it fall into ruins, as an ancient monument of the firmament, decayed by millions of centuries of existence?

"Yes; without death, for it is not immortal. It has not always existed, and will not always exist. The earth has had a birth, and will consequently die. But as there are as many possible modes of death for a world as for other human beings the question may possibly arise, what will be its end?—and an attempt made to indicate the nature of the crisis that will destroy it.

"On the one hand, water and air diminish; on the other, the plane of the continents is gradually sinking, and certainly reducing the surface of the globe to one general level. Will the earth perish from drought and cold; or, on the contrary, will it be overwhelmed by the conquering ocean? Water sustains the heat and life of the earth. **The World Without Water** Should it disappear this would mean the total extinction of all that lives, breathes, and renders Nature active. Should the liquid element, on the contrary, invade the dry land, such an action, though diametrically opposed to the preceding, would produce, nevertheless, a similar result. In either case it would mean the destruction of the human race.

"On the planet Mars, which is also smaller than the earth, and certainly in a more advanced period of planetary life, without being so aged as the moon, we observe seas reduced to narrow inland straits: the great oceans have disappeared, rain is scarce, and the sky is nearly always clear.

"Doubtless the future will reserve for us a similar destiny, more like that of the present state of Mars than of that of our satellite, the moon; and we may anticipate an inexorable fatal day wherein languishing terrestrial living Nature will be deprived of the element that is indispensable to its maintenance—water.

"Water constitutes the vital part of all living bodies. The human organism contains 70 per cent., whether in the liquid state or in the form of vapour in the atmosphere. It is the element that governs life, and preserves on the surface of the globe the heat that is necessary to the development of all beings. The suppression thereof signifies, therefore, a death warrant; and it is in the power of Nature to inflict such a sentence upon us. But doubtless it is not alone the want of water in itself that will cause the end of things; it will be rather the **The Fate Awaiting the Earth** effect this cause will have on the climate. It is the invisible water vapour, spread through the atmosphere, that exercises the paramount influence on the temperature, though its quantity be evidently very small, since to every 200 molecules of oxygen and of azote there is not found one of water vapour. This latter possesses, nevertheless, eighty times more energy and efficacy than the other 200.

"These minute transparent drops, suspended in the atmosphere, act like heat condensers, to concentrate the rays of the sun, and to retain them in the lower layers of the atmosphere. What will happen when this protecting veil shall have disappeared? The temperature of the soil will become glacial, and will render the globe uninhabitable.

"From the summit of the mountains the mantle of the snows will be spread over the valleys, driving before it both life and civilisation. New York, London, Paris, Berlin, Vienna, Constantinople, Rome would successively sleep under the eternal snows. Such towns would only then be arid deserts, split with fissures much more terrible than the solitudes of those Polar regions at present known to us.

"There will be no more spring, no more nests, no more birds, no more luxurious plants, flowers, or fruits; no more bubbling springs, richly stocked rivers, lakes bordered by willows and poplars; no more shall the crested waves sing with monotonous voice their rhythmic chant. The last representatives of the human race **How the End Will Come** will come and expire on the shores of the last remaining equatorial sea, beneath the rays of a feeble sun that from henceforth will only light a moving tomb that shall turn again and again around a light-giving but insufficient heat. At this epoch our planet would have reached a temperature approximating to 273° below zero. Such will be the necessary end of the earth should its vital elements be removed. It appears more than probable that the earth will end thus, as not only the water vapour is diminishing, but also the other elements of the air, such as oxygen and azote, are gradually decreasing. From century to century the atmosphere is becoming poorer, and in consequence the conditions of terrestrial life are themselves becoming weaker. In 10,000,000 of years the great body of the earth—worn, aged, sterile, and solitary—will only bear on its dried surface the ruins of its brilliant past."

A Grim Picture of the Future

But is there no Mind behind all this creation, beauty and destruction ? " Life must have had a beginning," says F. W. Hutton, " and must come to an end." Yes ; very true. But what was before the beginning of life ? Professor Clifford, in a letter to Dr. Martineau, wrote : " The idea of an external conscious being is unavoidably suggested, as it seems to me, by the categorical imperative of the moral sense ; and, moreover, in a way quite independent, by the aspect of Nature, which seems to answer to our questionings with an intelligence akin to our own." The laws of the universe are not accidents, apparently. " It is prima facie," says Newman, in the " Grammar of Assent," " unaccountable that an accident should happen twice, not to speak of it happening always." " The sceptic," says Emerson, " affirms that the universe is a nest of boxes with nothing in the last box."

Here is a great point made by Newman : " A law is not a cause, but a fact ; but when we come to the question of cause, then *we have no experience of any cause but Will*."

" The presence of Mind," says Sir John Herschel, " is what solves the whole difficulty."

Every child thinks that its hand is the visible cause of the swing of the toy in its hand ; but it can be made to see that the hand is merely the obedient servant of its will. Everything that the materialist predicates of the world's creation, and prophesies of its final destruction, the philosopher can subscribe to if only the materialist will place Will at the back of phenomena, without which force—so far as all human knowledge goes—there can be no movement, no ordered action, no law.

The Force Behind the Universe

And now what remains ?

Professor Flammarion tells us what the Psalmist told his contemporaries, what St. Peter told his contemporaries, what almost every intelligent man since the creation of the world has believed, that the earth will perish.

Then at the loud but solemn peal the heavens shall burst away ;
The elements shall melt in flame at Nature's final day.

It does not matter how greatly the theories of Professor Flammarion are affected by the discovery of radium, by the mysteries of radio-active bodies still puzzling the scientist as much as the problem of hen or egg ; it does not matter whether our professor is altogether right or altogether wrong ; the fact stands that in some way or other the physical world will end, and that for each individual man it ends at death.

What remains ?

Consciousness !

The hope of humanity is the despair of the materialist ; it is this mystery of all mysteries, *consciousness*. How man (matter) became conscious, became self-conscious, was able to take pen and write, " I am not immortal," in order to controvert his fellow lump of matter who argued that he was immortal, is a puzzle just as baffling as the hen and the egg. Consciousness, a materialist might say, makes cowards of us all.

Man's Spiritual Nature

What is this mystery of our minds which we call consciousness ? What is its place in the universe ?

One cannot call consciousness a by-product of evolution without making oneself ridiculous. Consciousness is not something without which life would have been very much what it is now. Indeed, it is only by considering the spiritual nature of man that history becomes in the least intelligible. Whether materialists realise the significance of this fact or not, certain is it that history concerns the spiritual nature of man struggling towards fulfilment.

" On the hypothesis of this spiritual nature, superadded to the animal nature of man, we are able to understand much that is otherwise mysterious or unintelligible in regard to him, especially the enormous influence of ideas, principles, and beliefs over his whole life and actions," writes Professor A. R. Wallace. " Thus alone we can understand the constancy of the martyr, the unselfishness of the philanthropist, the devotion of the patriot, the enthusiasm of the artist, and the resolute and persevering search of the scientific worker after Nature's secrets. Thus we may perceive that the love of truth, the delight in beauty, the passion for justice, and the thrill of exultation with which we hear of any act of courageous self-sacrifice are the workings within us of a higher nature which has not been developed by means of the struggle for material existence.''

Evolution, it has been said, can account well enough for the land-grabber, the company promoter, and the sweater ; but it fails to account for the great intellects and lofty souls who have led the advance of humanity from barbarism to civilisation. This world — this physical and material world of man—has been moved infinitely more by spiritual forces than by material and selfish forces. History, if it is anything, is a struggle towards idealism. The animal does not content man. He never is, but always to be blest. *Why?* This question is at the beginning of all theses, confronts all dogmatisms.

"The higher gifts of genius : poetry, the plastic arts, music, philosophy, pure

Nature's Process of Evolution

mathematics—all of these are precisely as much in the central stream of evolution—are perceptions of new truth and powers of new action, just as decisively predestined for the race of man as the aboriginal Australian's faculty for throwing a boomerang or for swarming up a tree for grubs," says F. W. H. Myers in "Human Personality." "There is, then, about these loftier instincts nothing exotic, nothing accidental; they are an intrinsic part of that ever-evolving response to our surroundings which forms not only the planetary but the cosmic history of all our race.

"What inconsistencies, what absurdities, underlie that assumption that evolution means nothing more than the survival of animals fittest to conquer enemies and to overrun the earth. On that bare hypothesis the genus homo is impossible to explain. No one really attempts to explain him, except on the tacit supposition that Nature somehow intended to evolve intelligence—somehow needed to evolve joy ; was not satisfied with such an earth-overrunner as the rabbit, or such an invincible conqueror as the influenza microbe. But *how much* intelligence, *what* kind of joy Nature aimed at ? Is this to be left to be settled by the instinct

of l'homme sensuel moyen ? Or ought we not rather to ask of the best specimens of our race what it is that they live for ? Whether they labour for the meat that perisheth, or for Love and Wisdom " ? Let us endeavour to see this mystery

The First Ancestors of Man

of human consciousness in a steady, unsentimental, and historical manner. Let us try to realise the beginning of this mystery about whose end we are now concerned. " Since the germ of life appeared on earth," the same author goes on to say, " its history has been a history not only of gradual self-adaptation to a known environment, but of gradual discovery of an environment, always there but unknown. " It is probable, to begin with, that the only environment which the vast majority of our ancestors knew was simply hot water. For the greater part of the time during which life has existed on earth it would have been thought chimerical to suggest that we could live in anything else. It was a great day for us when an ancestor crawled up out of the slowly cooling sea— or say, rather, when a previously unsuspected capacity for directly breathing air gradually revealed the fact that we had for long been breathing air in the water, and that we were living in the midst of a vastly extended environment—the atmosphere of the earth.

" It was a great day again when another ancestor felt on his pigment-spot the solar ray—or say, rather, when a previously unsuspected capacity for perceiving light revealed the fact that we had for long been acted upon by light as well as by heat, and that we were living in the midst of a vastly extended environment— namely, the illumined universe that stretches to the Milky Way. It was a great day when the first skate (if skate he were) felt an unknown virtue go out from him towards some worm or mudfish —or say, rather, when a previously unsuspected capacity for electrical excitation demonstrated the fact that we had long

Stages in Evolution's March

been acted upon by electricity as well as by heat and by light ; and that we were living in an inconceivable and limitless environment—namely, an ether charged with infinite energy, overpassing and interpenetrating alike the last gulf of darkness and the extremest star. All this—phrased perhaps in some other fashion—all men admit as true. May we not then suppose that there are yet other environments, other interpretations, which a further awakening of faculty still sub-liminal is yet fated by its own nascent response to discover ? Will it be alien to the past history of evolution if I add : It was a great day when the first thought or feeling flashed into some mind of beast or

The Dawn of Thought man from a mind distant from his own ? When a previously unsuspected capacity of tele-pathic percipience revealed the fact that we had long been acted upon by telepathic as well as by sensory stimuli; and that we were living in an inconceivable and limitless environment—a thought-world or spiritual universe charged with infinite life, and interpenetrating and overpassing all human spirits—up to what some have called world-soul, and some God" ?

From that extraordinary moment in history when the first thing *thought to itself*, up to this day, when physicians study nervous diseases and the alienist writes his reports from the lunatic asylums, what has history been but a continual change in the nervous cells, a continual movement in the brain, a perpetual straining forward of faculties nowhere to be found in the animal kingdom ? Our bodies are very like those of the first man ; but the differ-ence which separates the soul of Shake-speare, the soul of Newton, and the soul of Darwin from the souls not only of our earliest ancestors but the souls of the greatest Greeks, the greatest Romans, and *their own souls* (*i.e.*, the difference between the knowledge of Newton and Darwin, both men of science, fellow-countrymen, and born within a few years of each other), is so considerable that no form of words can express it. One has only to think quietly for a moment or two to perceive that history in its totality is the record of change in the spiritual and intellectual outlook of the human race. Before pro-ceeding to consider what modern science has to tell us about conscious-

History a Record of Change ness, it will be useful to our argument if we confront the protagonists of materialism with the consequence of their thesis. If consciousness is a by-product, the accident of an accident, how can we trust the conclusions of our men of science ?

They tell us how the world came into existence, and inform us emphatically that man is not an immortal soul; their elaborate arguments, their bold deductions,

the closeness of their reasoning, fill us with respect. But to believe their conclusion, arrived at by means of a by-product of evolution, . how ridiculous ! We know that man can examine his environment only with human senses so imperfect that instruments are necessary for all work but the coarsest ; but the work of these im-perfect senses is reflected upon, matured, and presented for our belief by *conscious-ness*—a mere accident. Is it reasonable to suppose that such work can be true, can represent the eternal verity of facts ?

It is like a watchmaker making a watch to tell, not the time, but that there is no such thing as time. This at the outset of our consideration. But even if we can believe that accidental con-sciousness reports truly on the facts of existence, even if we perfectly agree that human consciousness is an accident, and functions only till the moment of death, when it ceases as absolutely as the beating of the heart or the move-ments of the blood corpuscles—dare any man in any nation in any degree of civilisation propose that humanity should

Where Materialism Fails act upon this thesis ? This is the test at which materialism absolutely breaks. There is no question about it. Brought to this place, no materialist dares to act. And on this ground the plain man may take his stand and reply to the materialist : " Your arguments are all very fine, but their consequence in practical life is impossible."

Moral restraints are essential to society ; moral aspirations are essential to society's progress. "From the time he can under-stand what is said to him," writes Protagoras, " nurse, and mother, and teacher, and father, too, are bending their efforts to this end—to make the child *good ;* teaching and showing him as to everything he has to do or say, how this is right and that not right, and this is honourable and that vile, and this is holy and that unholy, and this do and that do not." Is this to cease, this illogical education of moral qualities which are unreasonable in a soulless world ? No man dare say so. No father, no teacher, no statesman, no man of science dare announce that right and wrong are distinctions without sanction of some spiritual kind. David's struggle with his nature has been unquestionably one of the greatest levers in evolution; the Psalms have strengthened and encouraged generations of the human race to live up to their conscience. Is it contended that he was a fool, and that the world would have done just as well if he had lived like a satyr? No materialist can deny that India without religion would be ungovernable, or that Christianity—the religion and not the ecclesiasticism—has been of the essence of European progress. Without conscience nothing is logical except anarchy. Philanthropy, which is not merely a relief of the poor but rather the exercise of a divine and formative function of the soul, would cease to play its part in evolution, would cease to be. Instead of self-denial, we should have self-assertion. Instead of wisdom we should have brute force. Instead of love and help, egotism of the most terrible kind.

Professor Goldwin Smith has a remarkable passage which must surely give pause to blank materialism:

"The Christian doctrine of fraternity is, at all events for many of us, more comfortable than that of mutual jostling and the survival of the strongest. We cannot all be foremost in the race of competition, we cannot all thrust **Carlyle on** each other aside, we cannot **the Spread of** all climb over each other's **Christianity** heads. But we can all do our duty in our place; and if duty is the pledge of happiness, we can all in a measure be happy . . . .

"Nobody could be more free from orthodox superstition of any kind than Carlyle, who in one of his essays, after speaking of other agencies of progress, says:

Or, to take an infinitely higher instance, that of the Christian religion, which, under every theory of it, in the believing or unbelieving mind, must ever be regarded as the crowning glory, or rather the life and soul, of our whole modern culture. How did Christianity arise and spread abroad among men? Was it by institutions and establishments and well-arranged systems of mechanism? Not so; on the contrary, in all past and existing institutions for those ends its divine spirit has invariably been found to languish and decay. It arose in the mystic deeps of man's soul, and was spread abroad by the "preaching of the word," by simple, altogether natural, and individual efforts; and flew, like hallowed fire, from heart to heart, till all were purified and illuminated by it; and its heavenly light shone, as it still shines, and (as sun or star) will ever shine, through the whole dark destinies of man.

"It happened that when I laid down Carlyle there met my eyes a gilt cross on the spire of a Catholic church illumined by the sun. The cross was the emblem of all that was materially weak, of slavery and the shameful death of the slave. The eagle was the emblem of the Roman Empire, the greatest embodiment of force which the world has ever seen. The eagle and the cross encountered each **Is Man** other. Which prevailed?" In **Only an** no subject more than in this **Animal?** question of man's nature is it essential for the reader to guard himself against the persuasions of the *technical* or the *expert* mind. When such a man as Metchnikoff shuts himself up in a library, and, safeguarded by the police, and nourished by food and warmed by raiment which others have produced for him, proceeds to prove that man is only an animal, other people reading the result of his labour in a comfortable seclusion may easily come to consider that he is perfectly correct.

But if Metchnikoff stood up in the open streets, exposed to the elements and surrounded by the extraordinary atmosphere of the "full air," which is so much more real than the artificial atmosphere of stove-warmed rooms, and there attempted to enunciate his doctrine, the ordinary citizen would feel something lacking in this dogmatism, would be conscious of large and potent verities of life lying altogether outside physiology and chemistry, and would desire the orator to turn his attention from phagocytes and bacteria to explain the hard struggle of Plato for virtue, the grandeur of Michael Angelo, the sweetness of Fenelon, and the consciousness in animal man of disturbing moral responsibility.

We believe we are stating the firm conviction of the best modern minds when we say that materialism as a thesis **Mind at the** of existence cannot be ap- **Back of** plied to social life without **the Universe** destruction, and that it provides no explanation whatever of human consciousness. We are still in the position of Bacon: "I had rather believe all the fables in the Legend, and the Talmud, and the Alcoran, than that this universal Frame is without a Mind"; materialism only succeeds in making the universal Frame, which includes everything, even materialism itself—*irrational*.

THE IMMORTALITY OF THE SOUL
THE MYSTERY OF HUMAN CONSCIOUSNESS

TO begin with, a caution is necessary as to any use of the term Man in a fixed and generic sense, as if he has always been what he is now, and always will remain precisely the same : as if the average man, and not the genius, is of importance to psychology : " The word normal in common speech is used almost indifferently to imply **The Human Race in Evolution** either of two things, which may be very different from each other—conformity to a standard and position as an average between extremes," says F. W. H. Myers in " Human Personality." " Often, indeed, the average constitutes the standard—as when a gas is of normal density ; or is practically equivalent to the standard— as when a sovereign is of normal weight. But when we come to living organisms, a new factor is introduced. Life is change ; each living organism changes ; each generation differs from its predecessor.

" To assign a fixed norm to a changing species is to shoot point-blank at a flying bird. The actual average at any given moment is no ideal standard ; rather, the furthest evolutionary stage now reached is tending, given stability in the environment, to become the average of the future. Human evolution is not so simple or so conspicuous a thing as the evolution of the pouter pigeon. But it would be rash to affirm that it is not even swifter than any variation among domesticated **Physical Changes in Man** animals. Not a hundred generations separate us from the dawn of history ; about as many generations as some microbes can traverse in a month ; about as many as separate the modern Derby winner from the war-horse of Gustavus Adolphus.

" Man's change has been less than the horse's change in physical contour— probably only because man has not been specially bred with that view ; but,

taking as a test the power of self-adaptation to environment, man has traversed in these thirty centuries a wider arc of evolution than separates the race-horse from the eohippus.

" Of all creatures man has gone furthest both in differentiation and in entegration ; he has called into activity the greatest number of those faculties which lay potential in the primal germ, and he has established over those faculties the strongest central control."

To come a little nearer to this mystery of consciousness, we would remind the reader of a simple passage from " De Profundis," which is science, literature, and common-sense : " I said in ' Dorian Gray ' that the great sins of the world take place in the brain ; but it is in the brain that everything takes place. We **The Soul after Death** know now that we do not see with our eyes or hear with the ears. They are really channels for the transmission, adequate or inadequate, of sense impressions. It is in the brain that the poppy is red, that the apple is odorous, that the skylark sings."

Here is an admirable figure from McTaggart's " Some Dogmas of Religion." " If a man is shut up in a house, the transparency of the windows is an essential condition of his seeing the sky. But it would not be prudent to infer that, if he walked out of the house, he could not see the sky because there was no longer any glass through which he might see it."

" After death," says Kant, " the soul possesses self-consciousness, otherwise it would be the subject of spiritual death, which has already been disproved. With this self-consciousness necessarily remains personality and the consciousness of personal identity."

We can present a modern view of the mystery of consciousness as it strikes a distinguished contemporary, qua philosopher and qua physicist, by a few extracts from Sir Oliver Lodge's "Man and the Universe."

"We display ourselves to our fellows in a certain garb, artificially constructed of animal and vegetable materials, and in the form of a certain material organism, put together by processes of digestion and assimilation, and likewise composed of terrestrial materials. The source of these chemical compounds is evidently not important ; nor is their special character maintained. Whether they formed part of sheep or birds or fish or plants, they are assimilated and become part of us ; being arranged by our subconscious activities and vital processes into appropriate form, just as truly as other materials are consciously woven into garments, no matter what their origin.

"Moreover, just as our clothes wear out and require darning and patching, so our bodies wear out ; the particles are in continual flux, each giving place to others and being constantly discarded and renewed. The identity of the actual or instantaneous body is therefore an affair of no importance : the **The Truth about The Body** body which finally dies is no more fully representative of the individual than any of the other bodies which have gradually been discarded en route : there is no reason why it should persist any more than they : the individuality, if there is one, must lie deeper than any particular body, and must belong to whatever it is which put the particles together in this shape and not another. . . .

"The more frankly and clearly the truth about the body is realised, namely, that the body is a flowing and constantly changing episode in material history, having no more identity than has a river, no identity whatever in its material constitution, but only in its form— identity only in the personal expression or manifestation which is achieved through the agency of a fresh and constantly differing sequence of material particles—the more frankly all this is realised, the better for our understanding of most of the problems of life and being.

"The body is the instrument or organ of the soul, and in its special form and aggregation is certainly temporary—exceedingly temporary ; for in the most durable cases it lasts only about a thousand months—a mere instant in the life-history of a planet. But if the body is thus trivial and temporary, though while it lasts most beautiful and useful and wonderful, what is it that puts it together and keeps it active and retains it fairly constant through all the vicissitudes of climate and condition, and through all the fluctuations of atomic constitution ? . . . .

"When the body is destroyed, **The Meaning of Immortality** therefore, the soul disappears from physical ken ; when the body is impaired, its function is interfered with, and the soul's physical reaction becomes feeble and unsatisfactory. Thus has arisen the popular misconception that the soul of a slain person, or of a cripple or paralytic, has been destroyed or damaged : whereas, only its instrument of manifestation need have been affected. The kind of evils which really assault and hurt the soul belong to a different category. . . .

"Now let us consider what is meant by Immortality. Is there anything that is not subject to death and annihilation ? Can we predicate immortality about anything ? Everything is subject to change, but are all things subject to death ? Without change there could be no activity, and the universe would be stagnant ; but without death it is not so clear that its progress would be obstructed, unless death be only a sort of change.

"But is it not a sort of change ? Consider some examples : When a piece of coal is burnt, and brought to an apparent end, the particles of long-fossilised wood are not destroyed ; they enter into the atmosphere as gaseous constituents, and the long-locked-up solar energy is released from its potential form and appears once more as light and heat. The burning of the coal is a kind of resurrection. And yet it is a kind of death too, and to the casual eye nothing is left but ashes. . . .

"Never in physical science do we surmise for a moment that something suddenly springs into being from **Facts of Physical Science** previous non-existence. All that we perceive can be accounted for by changes of aggregation, by assemblage and dispersion. Of material aggregates we can trace the history, as we can trace the history of continents and islands, of suns and planets and stars ; we can say, or try to say, whence they arose and what they will become ; but never do we state that they will vanish into nothingness, nor do we ever conjecture that they arose from nothing."

Huxley, we may notice in passing, answers the question, "What, then, is certain?" with these words: "Why, the fact that the thought, the present consciousness, exists. Our thoughts may be delusive, but they cannot be fictitious. As thoughts, they are real and existent, and the cleverest deceiver cannot make them otherwise. . . . Thought is existence. More than that, so far as we are concerned, existence is thought, all our conceptions of existence being some kind or other of thought."

"Riddles of the Sphinx"

Here follows a passage from "Riddles of the Sphinx," a book by F. C. S. Schiller, a brilliant American of Cornell University, now at Oxford: "Matter is an admirably calculated machinery for regulating, limiting, and restraining the consciousness which it encases . . . If the material encasement be coarse and simple, as in the lower organisms, it permits only a little intelligence to permeate through it; if it is delicate and complex, it leaves more pores and exists, as it were, for the manifestations of consciousness . . . On this analogy, then, we may say that the lower animals are still entranced in the lower stage brute lethargy, while we have passed into the higher phase of somnambulism, which already permits us strange glimpses of a lucidity that divines the realities of a transcendent world. And this gives the final answer to Materialism: it consists of showing in detail . . . that Materialism is a hysteron proteron, a putting of the cart before the horse, which may be rectified by just inverting the connection between Matter and Consciousness.

"Matter is not that which produces consciousness, but that which limits it, and confines its intensity within certain limits: material organisation does not construct consciousness out of arrangements of atoms, but contracts its manifestation within the sphere which it permits. This explanation . . . admits the connection of Matter and Consciousness, but contends that the course of interpretation must proceed in the contrary direction. Thus it will fit the facts alleged in favour of Materialism equally well, beside enabling us to understand facts which Materialism rejected as 'super-

Connection of Matter and Consciousness

natural.' It explains the lower by the higher, Matter by Spirit, instead of vice versa, and thereby attains to an explanation which is ultimately tenable, instead of one which is ultimately absurd.

"And it is an explanation the possibility of which no evidence in favour of Materialism can possibly affect. For if, e.g., a man loses consciousness as soon as his brain is injured, it is clearly as good an explanation to say the injury to the brain destroyed the mechanism by which the manifestation of the consciousness was rendered possible as to say that it destroyed the seat of consciousness. On the other hand, there are facts which the former theory suits far better. If, e.g., as sometimes happens, the man, after a time, more or less, recovers the faculties of which the injury to his brain had deprived him, and that not in consequence of a renewal of the injured part, but in consequence of the inhibited functions being performed by the vicarious action of other parts, the easiest explanation certainly is that, after a time, consciousness constitutes the remaining parts into a mechanism capable of acting as a substitute for the lost parts. And, again, if the body is a mechanism for inhibiting consciousness, for preventing the full powers of the ego from being prematurely actualised, it will be necessary to invert also our ordinary ideas on the subject of memory, and to account for forgetfulness instead of for memory. It will be during life that we drink the bitter cup of Lethe; it will be with our brain that we are enabled to forget. And this will serve to explain not only the extraordinary memories of the drowning and the dying generally, but also the curious hints which experimental psychology occasionally affords us that nothing is ever forgotten wholly and beyond recall."

Psychology and the Memory

To go deeper into the matter:

"The expression, 'field of consciousness,' has but recently come into vogue in the psychology books," writes Professor William James in "The Varieties of Religious Experience." "Until quite lately the unit of mental life which figured most was the single 'idea,' supposed to be a definitely outlined thing. But at present psychologists are tending, first, to admit that the actual unit is more probably the total mental state, the entire wave of consciousness or fields of objects present to the thought at any time ; and, second, to see that it is impossible to outline this wave, this field, with any definiteness. As our mental fields succeed one another, each has its centre of interest, around which the objects of which we are less and less attentively conscious fade to a margin so faint that its limits are unassignable.

" Some fields are narrow fields and some are wide fields. Usually, when we have a wide field, we rejoice, for we then see masses of truth together, and often get glimpses of relations which we divine, rather than see, for they shoot beyond the field into still remoter regions of objectivity, regions which we seem rather to be about to perceive than to perceive actually. At other times, of drowsiness, illness, or fatigue, our fields may narrow almost to a point, and we find ourselves correspondingly oppressed and contracted. Different individuals present constitutional differences in this matter of width of fields.

" Your great organising geniuses are men with habitually vast fields of mental

The Mental Vision of Genius

vision, in which a whole programme of future operations will appear dotted out at once, the rays shooting far ahead into definite directions of advance. In common people there is never this magnificent inclusive view of a topic. They stumble along, feeling their way, as it were, from point to point, and often stop entirely. In certain diseased conditions consciousness is a mere spark, without memory of the past or thought of the future, and with the present narrowed down to some one simple emotion or sensation of the body.

"The important fact which this ' field ' formula commemorates is the determination of the margin. Inattentively realised as is the matter which the margin contains, it is nevertheless there, and helps both to guide our behaviour and to determine the next movement of our attention. It lies around us like a ' magnetic field,' inside of which our centre of energy turns like a compass neeedle, as the present phase of consciousness alters into its successor. Our whole past store of memories floats beyond this margin, ready at a touch to come in ; and the entire mass of residual powers, impulses, and knowledges that constitute our empirical self stretches continuously beyond it. So vaguely drawn are the outlines between what is actual and what is only potential at any moment of our conscious life, that it is always hard to say of certain mental elements whether we are conscious of them or not.

" The ordinary psychology, admitting fully the difficulty of tracing the marginal outline, has nevertheless taken for granted,

Psychology's Notable Discovery

first, that all the consciousness that the person has now, be the same focal or marginal, inattentive or attentive, is there in the field of the moment, all dim and impossible to assign as the latter's outline may be ; and, second, that what is absolutely extra-marginal is absolutely non-existent, and cannot be a fact of consciousness at all. . . .

" I cannot but think that the most important step forward that has occurred in psychology since I have been a student of that science is the discovery, first made in 1886, that, in certain subjects at least, there is not only the consciousness of the ordinary field, with its usual centre and margin, but an addition thereto in the shape of a set of memories, thoughts, and feelings which are extra-marginal and outside of the primary consciousness altogether, but yet must be classed as conscious facts of some sort, able to reveal their presence by unmistakable signs. I call this the most important step forward because, unlike the other advances which psychology has made, this discovery has revealed to us an entirely unsuspected peculiarity in the constitution of human nature. No other step forward which psychology has made can proffer any such claim as this." The reader will perceive from these extracts that a more bold and exhaustive psychology is now at work on the mystery of existence. Psychologists are not debating questions of the schools, but are exploring consciousness itself. An immense advance in this supreme science has been made during

The March of Science

recent years by means of hypnotism and psychical research. It is possible to think that before the world plunges into ruin or gradually chills until life is impossible on its surface man will have discovered the riddle of terrestrial life, perhaps—as some believe—established telepathic communication with other stars. But certainly we may expect that the history of the world from this time onward will lie largely with the discoveries of the psychologist. Far from being at the end of existence, we are only now at the beginning. Interesting as it has been, studying earthworms, classifying beetles, collecting fossils, and examining bacteriæ under microscopes, the real beginning of knowledge, discovery, and excitement for us men and for our salvation lies ahead of us in the exploration of consciousness.

Goethe said : " It is to a thinking being quite impossible to think himself non-existent, ceasing to think and live ; so far does everyone carry in himself the proof of immortality, and quite sponta-neously. But so soon as the man will be objective and go out of himself, so soon as he dogmatically will grasp a personal duration to bolster up in cockney fashion that inward assurance, he is lost in con-tradiction." Upon which Emerson com-ments : " My idea of heaven is that there is no melodrama in it at all ; that it is wholly real. Here is the emphasis of conscience and experience ; this is no speculation, but the most practical of doctrines. Do you think that the eternal **Emerson's** chain of cause and effect which **Idea** pervades Nature, which threads **of Heaven** the globes as beads on a string, leaves this out of its circuit— leaves out this desire of God and men as a waif and a caprice, altogether cheap and common, and falling without reason or merit ? "

The vast majority of human-kind long for personal identity, and cling to it with a sweetness of faith which seems to have the force of reality :

> Life ! I know not what thou art,
> But know that thou and I must part ;
> And when, or how, or where we met
> I own to me's a secret yet.
>
> Life ! we've been long together
> Through pleasant and through cloudy
> weather ;
> 'Tis hard to part when friends are dear—
> Perhaps 'twill cost a sigh, a tear ;
> Then steal away, give little warning,
> Choose thine own time ;
> Say not good-night, but in some brighter
> clime
> Bid me good-morning.

The new psychology, fortified by sane psychical research and utterly uninfluenced by a crazy spiritualism, begins—so it seems to some, at least—to offer reasons for our faith in personal identity after death. Whether it is Eternity or Immor-tality to which we move—the two great

opposing battle-cries of those who follow the Christ and the Buddha—it would appear that most reasonable men look beyond physical death for explanation, satisfaction, and life.

The crash and ruin of worlds can hardly affect the thought which has so far risen above physical things as to comtemplate either eternity or immortality. If the reader will reflect as he reads the following poem by George Eliot, that he is acquaint-ing himself with the deliberate utterance, so far as words can effect it, of a soul's longing, a longing quite free of hunger for personal reward or personal identity, he will feel it difficult to imagine that this pure and spiritual desire is merely a functioning of the material brain, and that it has no more significance than the ravings of a madman or the gibberish of a monkey :

> O may I join the choir invisible
> Of those immortal dead who live again
> In minds made better by their presence : live
> In pulses stirred to generosity,
> In deeds of daring rectitude, in scorn
> For miserable aims that end with self,
> In thoughts sublime that pierce the night like
> stars,
> And with their mild persistence urge man's
> search
> To vaster issues.
>   So to live is heaven :
> To make undying music in the world,
> Breathing a beauteous order that controls
> With growing sway the growing life of man
> So we inherit that sweet purity
> For which we struggled, failed and agonised
> With widening retrospect that bred despair.
> Rebellious flesh that would not be subdued,
> A vicious parent shaming still its child.
> Poor anxious penitence, is quick dissolved ;
> Its discords, quenched by meeting harmonies,
> Die in the large and charitable air.
> And all our rarer, better, truer self
> That sobbed religiously in yearning song,
> That watched to care the burthen of the world,
> Laboriously tracing what must be,
> And what may yet be better—saw within
> A worthier image for the sanctuary,
> And shaped it forth before the multitude
> Divinely human, raising worship so
> To higher reverence more mixed with love
> That better self shall live till human Time
> Shall fold its eyelids, and the human sky
> Be gathered like a scroll within the tomb
> Unread for ever.
>   This is life to come,
> Which martyred men have made more glorious
> For us who strive to follow. May I reach
> That purest heaven, be to other souls
> The cup of strength in some great agony,
> Enkindle generous ardour, feed pure love,
> Beget the smiles that have no cruelty—
> Be the sweet presence of a good diffused,
> And in diffusion ever more intense.
> So shall I join the choir invisible
> Whose music is the gladness of the world.

MAN'S DESTINY AFTER DEATH
AND THE ETERNAL HOPE OF A FUTURE LIFE

AT the beginning of this essay we indulged ourselves in some of those dimensional comparisons which overwhelm the mind and sadden consciousness with the conviction of human littleness and terrestrial insignificance.

Standing on this earth, surrounded by a vast host of marching worlds, and well assured that his journey round the particular sun of his own solar system is only a matter of some sixty or seventy times, man may excusably feel himself so mean and trivial an atom that any assumption of immortality or significance to the universe on his part would be in the nature of absurdity.

The modern mind has been peculiarly exposed to this paralysing humility. A multitude of half-educated and entirely unphilosophic men of science have taken advantage of the cheap Press and that eager demand for knowledge which is **Reflections on the Master-minds** characteristic of our emerging democracy to publish their reflections on the work of the master-minds in science with such dimensional comparisons from astronomy and physics as will so daze the reader as to make him imagine his author a very considerable fellow.

A philosophic mind, however, will not be disturbed by such "showing-off." It will know, for instance, that time and space (by which alone these comparisons can be made) are ideas purely human. London is a long way from Penzance; it is further still from St. Petersburg; compared with this latter distance, that between London and Penzance is trivial—a man in St. Petersburg would call it nothing. Nevertheless, for a man starting out to walk from Penzance to London, the distance *is* considerable. A dog is small beside an elephant, but to his parasites even his tail is an interesting and extensive peninsula; an elephant compared to the county of Yorkshire is a mere beetle, compared with the globe it is less than a parasite on the dog. All these interwindings in relativity may amuse a schoolboy, but they will not disturb the outlook of a Wordsworth, nor humble the godlike imagination of a Shakespeare.

Professor William James refers to one of these modern and unphilosophic ideas **Professor James on Immortality** which disturb men in their contemplation of immortality —the vast numbers of souls already peopling any possible heaven. As this thought is likely to press upon some minds contemplating the end of the world, and as Professor James has corrected this impression in a passage whose lucidity equals its force and beauty, we will do ourselves the pleasure to quote him at some length:

"An immortality from which inconceivable billions of fellow-strivers should be excluded becomes an irrational idea for us. That our superiority in personal refinement or in religious creed should constitute a difference between ourselves and our messmates at life's banquet, fit to entail such a consequential difference of destiny as eternal life for us, and for them torment hereafter or death with the beasts that perish, is a notion too absurd to be considered serious. Nay, more, the very beasts themselves—the wild ones, at any rate—are leading the heroic life at all times. . . .

"If any creature lives for ever, why not all? Why not the patient brutes? So **Is There a Future Life for Animals?** that a faith in immortality, if we are to indulge it, demands of us nowadays a scale of representation so stupendous that our imagination faints before it, and our personal feelings refuse to rise up and face the task. The supposition we are swept along to is too vast; and, rather than face the conclusion, we abandon the premise from which it starts. We give up our own immortality sooner than believe that all the hosts of Hottentots and Australians that have been, and shall ever be, should share it with us *in secula seculorum*. Life is a good thing on a reasonably copious scale ; but the very heavens themselves, and the cosmic times and spaces, would stand aghast, we think, at the notion of preserving eternally such an ever-swelling plethora and glut of it."

Participants in Immortality After saying that he himself was once oppressed by this fallacy, Professor James goes on : " It is the most obvious fallacy in the world, and the only wonder is that all the world should not see through it. It is the result of nothing but an invincible blindness from which we suffer, and insensibility to the inner significance of alien lives, and a conceit that would project our own incapacity into the vast cosmos, and measure the wants of the Absolute by our own puny needs. . . .

" But is not such an attitude due to the veriest lack and dearth of your imagination ? You take these swarms of alien kinsmen as they are *for you ;* an external picture painted on your retina representing a crowd oppressive by its vastness and confusion. As they are for you, so you think they positively and absolutely are. *I* feel no call for them, you say ; therefore there is no call for them. But all the while, beyond this externality which is your way of realising them, they realise themselves with the acutest internality, with the most violent thrills of life. 'Tis you who are dead, stone dead, and blind, and senseless, in your way of looking on.

" You open your eyes upon a scene of which you miss the whole significance. Each of these grotesque or even repulsive aliens is animated by an inner joy of living as hot or hotter than that which you feel beating in your private breast. The sun rises and beauty beams to light his path. To miss the inner joy of him, as Stevenson says, is to miss the whole of him. Not a being

The Passion for a Future Life of the countless throng is there whose continued life is not called for, and called for intensely, by the consciousness that animates the being's form. That you neither realise, nor understand, nor call for it, that you have no use for it, is an absolutely irrelevant circumstance. That you have a saturation-point of interest tells us nothing of the interests that absolutely are. The universe, with every living entity which her resources create, creates

at the same time a call for that entity, and an appetite for its continuance—creates it, if nowhere else, at least within the heart of the entity itself. It is absurd to suppose, simply because our private power of sympathetic vibration with other lives gives out so soon, that in the heart of infinite being itself there can be such a thing as plethora, or glut, or super-saturation. It is not as if there were a bounded room where the minds in possession had to move up or make place and crowd together to accommodate new occupants. Each new mind brings its own edition of the universe of space along with it, its own room to inhabit ; and these spaces never crowd each other—the space of my imagination, for example, in no way interferes with yours."

Not only does this passage completely do away with the particular human notion of an overcrowded heaven, but the spirit which inspires it reveals to us the whole question of eternity, infinity and immortality in the true, reasonable and philosophic light. If man's consciousness, which, as we have seen, seems to represent something super-

The Kingdom of Heaven Within us physical, endures when the body has collapsed, it will find itself not in a place, but in a state of being, where the yard measure, the compass, and the plummet are wholly unnecessary. Our outlook is upon a physical universe, but our identity is a personal feeling. We inhabit ideas rather than houses ; we travel by imagination rather than by tram-car. It is in our spirit, far more than in our muscles and our blood, that we spend the days of our life on earth ; and it is very certain that a man who reflects upon himself can come to no other conclusion than that his happiness or unhappiness is a condition of his feelings, independent altogether of physical circumstance or physical environment.

Christ's startling announcement, *The Kingdom of Heaven is within you,* is almost the foundational thing in all religion. The history of the world, in addition to wars, rebellions and revolutions, tells us of thousands of men and women, called by the religious saints, who in miserable circumstances or in physical pain have preserved the brightest of dispositions, and manifested a sweetness of character which has inspired the most brutal with reverence, respect and imitation. Whether these people delude themselves, or whether they have discovered the secret of existence, they are an incontestable proof of the religious claim, *The Kingdom of Heaven is within you.* They prove to us, if we do not already know it, that the real life of a man resides in his feelings, and that by the disposition of those feelings he can render himself immune from disaster, and independent of exterior influences.

Therefore, the wise man is not disturbed by dimensional comparisons or by scientific or literary prognostications concerning the final cataclysm. We may even imagine a man who would be more concerned by the burning of his house than by the sudden rush of this planet towards the flames of the sun. The destruction of the world does not weigh heavily on our spirits; we are not greatly occupied by the thought of our own death. We are in the position of the first man beholding for the first time Night and the Stars, as Blanco White in his immortal sonnet has pictured him :

Mysterious Night ! when our first parent knew
  Thee from report divine, and heard thy name,
  Did he not tremble for this lovely frame,
This glorious canopy of light and blue ?
Yet 'neath a curtain of translucent dew,
  Bathed in the rays of the great setting flame,
  Hesperus with the host of heaven came
And lo ! Creation widened in man's view.

Who could have thought such darkness lay con-
   cealed
  Within thy beams, O Sun ! or who could find,
Whilst flower and leaf and insect stood
   revealed,
That to such countless orbs thou mad'st us blind.
  Why do we then shun death with anxious
   strife ?
  If Light can thus deceive, wherefore not Life ?

In a word, we feel ourselves conscious of a hope, we feel ourselves to belong to the universe, we cannot think that we shall altogether die ; and in our **Longing for the Fuller Life** brightest and purest moments we have a longing for more and fuller life, which seems to us a divine and quite beautiful desire. "The soul of man is like the world," says Alexander Smith, "one half in day, the other dipped in night ; the one is music and the flying cloud, the other silence and the wakeful stars."

It is quite certain that all pessimism concerning life has come from a misconception of the facts, physical reaction, or a self-delusion almost amusing. To begin with, if existence is a burden, those who say so convict themselves of the most illogical position in taking the trouble to tell us so when they might their own

quietus make with a bare bodkin. This is no *argumentum ad hominem.* The most intellectual of pessimists does, on the face of it, vitiate his whole position by remaining alive to take it at all. Logic forces us to perceive that the whole chain of his reasoning, and all the gloomy majesty of his rhetoric are dissipated by the solitary **The Mysterious "Something after Death"** fact that he deems it *worth while* to remain alive preaching his pessimism. Death is so easily, so painlessly, and so decently to be obtained that no logical pessimist can be excused for remaining in existence. By remaining in existence—eating his breakfast, reading his books, opening his window to the fresh air, taking a walk in his garden, receiving his friends, and by studying the newspaper—he convicts himself of preferring life to annihilation.

Shakespeare's "something after death" makes, for one set of men, "calamity of so long end" ; for another set of men it is the flood and glory of existence.

The fact is the man who condemns life condemns precisely what the believer in immortality condemns—imperfect life. He is not really in love with death and non-existence ; if he were, he would fly to them as a victim to sanctuary—he is only out of love with imperfect life, and his agony is for the perfect thing.

Whatever crazy sorrow saith
No life that breathes with human breath
Has ever truly longed for death.

'Tis life, whereof our nerves are scant,
Oh life, not death, for which we pant ;
More life, and fuller, that I want.

The desire for immortality, therefore, is one with the root cause of all pessimism and despair—a realisation of incompleteness and imperfection in the fragmentary existence of terrestrial experience. But there is this sublime difference between the two conditions of mind, making, the one for joy and the other for despair, that the believer in immortality longs for the larger vision.

This truth within thy mind rehearse
That in a boundless universe
Is boundless better, boundless worse.

Think you this mould of hopes and fears
Could find no statelier than his peers
In yonder hundred million spheres ?

It is perfectly true, as Huxley said, that "we poor mortals have to be content with hope and belief in all matters past and present—our sole certainty is momentary," but hope and belief are real functions of the mind, and, besides possessing an immense significance for psychology, are the moving force in all progress, all morality, all happiness, and all joy.

Dryden's line, " The world's an inn, and Death the journey's end," proves, when pressed, even an insufficient illustra-

Tennyson on the Life After Death

tion for man's place in the universe, as witness the following anecdote from Tennyson's Life, written by his son : " We then went for a three miles' walk, my father talking of the Passion Play at Ober-Ammergau, of religion, of faith, and of immortality. While touching on the life after death he spoke of Carlyle and his dimness of faith in the closing years of his life. He said that when he was stopping at a coffee-house in London, Carlyle had come to smoke a pipe with him in the evening, and the talk turned upon the immortality of the soul ; upon which, Carlyle said : ' Eh, old Jewish rags ; thou must clear your mind of all that. Why should we expect a hereafter ? Your traveller comes to an inn, and he takes his bed ; it's only for one night, he leaves the next day, and another man takes his place and sleeps in the bed that he has vacated.' My father continued : ' I answered, " Your traveller comes to his inn, and lies down in his bed, and leaves the inn in the morning, and goes on his way rejoicing, with the sure and certain hope and belief that he is going somewhere where he will sleep the next night." And then Edward Fitzgerald, who was present, said, " You have him there." Which proves,' said my father, ' how dangerous an illustration is.' "

Carlyle's " dimness of faith " is easily explained. His physical organism had broken down, and it was not his soul but his liver which shrank from the vastness of the universe. All such lines as, " The world is a comedy to those who think, a

Life From Different Standpoints

tragedy to those who feel," and Sir Thomas More's saying, " This world is all a fleeting show," are not the expression of a healthy mind responding to the joy of existence, but the groaning of physical machinery. Shakespeare says, as no man else could say it :

The weariest and most loathed worldly life
That age, ache, penury, and imprisonment
Can lay on nature is a paradise
To what we fear of death.

And then the familiar lines :

Ay, but to die, and go we know not where ;
To lie in cold obstruction and to rot ;
This sensible warm motion to become
A kneaded clod ; and the delighted spirit
To bathe in fiery floods, or to reside
In thrilling region of thick-ribbed ice ;
To be imprison'd in the viewless winds,
And blown with restless violence round about
The pendent world.

Hazlitt, whose studied optimism we all admire, may, with his jaunty essay " On the fear of Death," console a hale and well-fed man in full maturity of his powers, may assure him that he has no more concern with the eternity beyond his death than with the eternity before his birth ; but any man with the smallest scrap of imagination, who will solitary contemplate the thought of death, the intense reality of eternity, and consider well within himself the mystery and the burden of human existence as it is revealed in the pageant of history, the missal of the saint, the language of the poet, and the colours of the painter, must, we think, feel the utter inadequacy of the materialistic thesis, and incline to the theory that Hazlitt's civil

The Joy of Life

and quite-at-my-ease attitude towards the universe was due to lack of imagination. When somebody told Carlyle that a lady in America, famous for transcendental notions, had said, " I accept the universe," he made the very sensible comment : " Gad ; she'd better ! "

No man who has perfect health and unvitiated appetites does anything but rejoice in life ; for him the freshness of the dawn, the grandeur of the tall rock and the round sea, the scent of flowers, the flight of birds, the colours of the clouds, and the gladness of the air, are a source of profound and pervasive joy. And it is only the healthy man, able to respond to life, who really has any right to tell us whether it is a good thing or a bad thing. What is Christianity, in its original essence, but an endeavour to complete the incompleteness of fragmentary or damaged perceptions of existence ?

I am come that they might have life, and that they might have it more abundantly.
Your sorrow shall be turned into joy.
Your heart shall rejoice, and your joy no man taketh from you.
He that cometh unto Me shall never hunger, and he that believeth in Me shall never thirst.
These words have I spoken unto you, that My joy might remain, and that your joy might be full.

Come unto Me all ye that are weary and heavy laden.

I am the Light of the world ; he that followeth Me shall not walk in darkness.

It is, surely, possible that if life here below is a good thing to the healthy man, so to the full and advancing soul of man it is a good thing elsewhere in the universe. We do not now imagine that with the moment of death a man is either plunged into irremediable torture or flashed full into the presence of God ; we have accustomed ourselves to follow evolution into the universe and to believe that the soul of man, refreshed by death, rises to new and delightsome but laborious states of being, stage by stage, for ever fulfilling himself, for ever answering some purpose of his Creator. And as a last word we may say that psychology in its widest sense seems to promise that one day we may have definite evidence that this thesis of the evolving soul is a fact of the universe. On this note we conclude with some extracts from the remarkable synthesis of psychology, " Human Personality," which F. W. H. Myers bequeathed to posterity as his **The Yearning** life's work : " Through the **for** mouth of Diotima, Plato **Immortality** insists that it is an unfailing sign of true love that its desires are for ever ; nay, that love may be even defined as the desire of the everlasting possession of the good.

" And in all love's acts he finds the impress of man's craving for immortality— for immortality whose only visible image us on earth is the birth of children to us for as we ourselves decay—so that when the slow self-renewal of our own ever-changing bodies has worn out and ceased, we may be renewed in brighter, younger bodies which we desire to be born to us from whomsoever we find most fair. ' And then,' says Plato, rising, as ever, from visible to invisible things, ' if active bodies have so strong a yearning that an endless series of lovely images of themselves may constitute, as it were, an earthly immortality for them when they have worn away, how greatly must creative souls desire that partnership and close communion with other souls as fair as they may bring to birth a brood of lofty thoughts, poems, statutes, institutions, laws—the fitting progeny of the soul ?

" ' And he who in his youth that hath the need of these things in him, and grows to be a godlike man, wanders about in search of a noble and well-nurtured soul ; and finding it, and in presence of that beauty which he forgets not night or day, brings forth the beautiful which he conceived long ago ; and the twain together tend that which he hath brought forth, and all bound by a far closer bond than that of earthly children, since the **Heirs of** children which are born to them **the** are fairer and more immortal **Immortals** far. Who would not choose to have Homer's offspring rather than any sons or daughters of men ? Who would not choose the offspring which Lycurgus left behind him, to be the very salvation of Lacedæmon and of Greece ? or the children of Solon, whom we call Father of our Laws ? or of other men like these, whether Greeks or barbarians, who by great deeds that they have done have become the begetters of every kind of virtue ? Ay, and of these men's children have temples been set up, and never to any other progeny of man. . . .

" ' What would it be, then, were it granted to any man to see Very Beauty clear ;—incorruptible and undefiled, not mingled with colour or flesh of man, or with aught that can consume away, but single and divine ? Could man's life, in that vision and beatitude, be poor or low ? or deemest thou not (said she), that then alone it will be possible for this man, discerning spiritual beauty with those eyes by which it is spiritually discerned, to beget no shadows of virtue, since that is no shadow to which he clings, but virtue in very truth, since he hath the very truth in his embrace ? and begetting and rearing Virtue as his child he must needs become the friend of God ; and if there be any man who is immortal, that man is he.'

.   .   .   .   .   .

" Beyond us still is mystery ; but it is mystery lit and mellowed with an infinite hope. We ride in darkness at the haven's mouth ; but sometimes **The Hope** through rifted clouds we see **of the** the desires and needs of many **Future** generations floating and melting upwards into a distant glow, up through the light of the seas by the moon's long silvering ray.

" The high possibilities that lie before us should be grasped once for all, in order that the dignity of the quest may help to carry the inquirer through many disappointments, deceptions, delays. But he must remember that this inquiry must be extended over many generations; nor must he allow himself to be persuaded that there are byways to mastery. I will not say that there cannot possibly be any such thing as occult wisdom, or dominion over the secrets of nature ascetically or magically acquired. But I will say that every claim of this kind

Nature's Well-Kept Secrets which my colleagues or I have been able to examine has proved deserving of complete distrust; and that we have no confidence here any more than elsewhere in any methods except the open, candid, straightforward methods which the spirit of modern science demands.

* * * *

"Science, then, need be no longer fettered by the limitations of this planetary standpoint; nor ethics by the narrow experience of a single life. Evolution will no longer appear as a truncated process, an ever-arrested movement upon an unknown goal. Rather, we may gain a glimpse of an ultimate incandescence where science and religion fuse in one; a cosmic evolution of energy into life, and of life into love, which is joy. Love, which is joy at once and wisdom; we can do no more than ring the changes on terms like these, whether we imagine the transfiguration and apotheosis of conquering souls, or the lower, but still sacred, destiny which may be some day possible for souls still tarrying here. We picture the perfected soul as the Buddha, the Saviour, the *aurai simplicis ignem*, dwelling on one or other aspect of that trinal conception of wisdom, love and joy.

"For souls not yet perfected, but still held on earth I have foretold a growth in holiness. By this I mean no unreal opposition or forced divorcement of sacred and secular, of flesh and spirit. Rather, I define holiness as the joy too high as yet for our enjoyment; the wisdom just beyond our learning; the rapture of love which we still strive to attain.

Order of the Cosmos Inevitably, as our link with other spirits strengthens, as the life of the organism pours more fully through the individual cell, we shall feel love more ardent, wider wisdom, higher joy; perceiving that this organic unity of soul, which forms the inward aspect of the telepathic law, is in itself the Order of the Cosmos, the summation of things. And such devotion may find its flower in no vain self-martyrdom, no cloistered resignation, but rather in such pervading ecstasy as already the elect have known; the vision which dissolves for a moment the corporeal prison-house; ' the flight of the One to the One.'

"' So let the soul that is not unworthy of that vision contemplate the great soul; freed from deceit and every witchery, and collected into calm. Calmed be the body for her in that hour, and the tumult of the flesh; ay, all that is about her, calm; calm be the earth, the sea, the air, and let Heaven itself be still. Then let her feel how into that silent heaven the great soul floweth in. . . . And so may man's soul be sure of vision, when suddenly she is filled with light; for this light is from Him and is He; and then surely shall one know His presence when, like a god of old time, He entered into the house of one that calleth Him, and maketh it full of light. And how,' concludes Plotinus, ' may this thing be for us? Let all else go.'

"These heights, I confess, are above the stature of my spirit. Yet for each of us is a fit ingress into the unseen; and for some lesser man the memory of one

Our Eternal Hope vanished soul may be beatific as of old for Plotinus the flooding immensity of Heaven. And albeit no historical religion can persist as a logical halting-place upon the endless mounting way — that way which leads unbroken from the first germ of love in the heart to an inconceivable union with Divine — yet many a creed in turn may well be close inwrought and inwoven with our eternal hope."

A soul shall draw from out the vast
And strike his being into bounds,

And moved thro' life of lower phase
  Result in man, be born and think,
  And act and love, a closer link
Betwixt us and the crowning race.

Of those that eye to eye shall look
  On Knowledge; under whose command
Is earth and earth's, and in their hand
Is Nature like an open book;

No longer half-akin to brute,
  For all we thought and loved and did,
  And hoped and suffered, is but seed
Of what in them is flower and fruit;

Whereof the man, that with me trod
  This planet was a noble type
  Appearing ere the times were ripe,
That friend of mine who lives in God,

That God, which ever lives and loves,
  One God, one law, one element,
  And one far-off divine event
To which the whole creation moves.

HAROLD BEGBIE

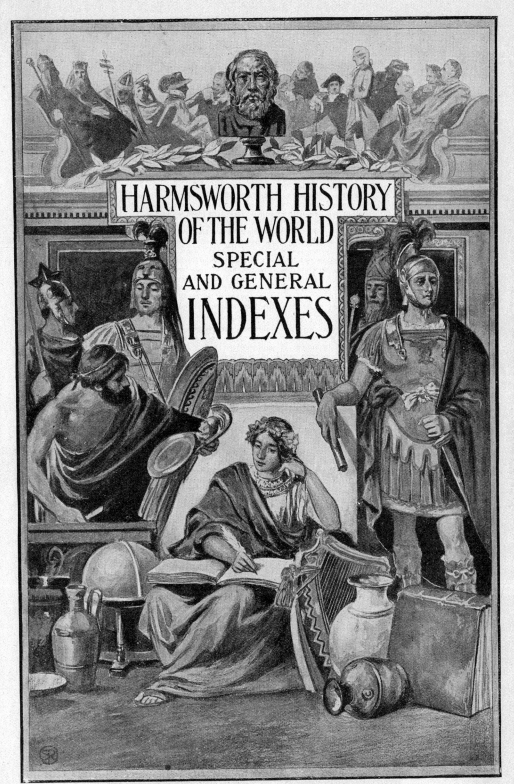

HARMSWORTH HISTORY OF THE WORLD
OF THE WORLD
SPECIAL AND GENERAL
INDEXES

THE SPECIAL INDEX TO EUROPEAN HISTORY

The history of the separate non-European nations has been presented consecutively in Volumes I. to III., and Volume VIII. of this work. Thus, for the history of China, India, or the United States, the story of the particular state from its inception to the present day can be followed without interruption. But this is not the case with Europe. Here, the form which the work has of necessity taken is that of a history (1) of Ancient Europe; (2) of Eastern Europe from the Fall of the Western Roman Empire to the French Revolution; (3) of Western Europe during the same period; (4) of Europe since that period. Hence, to follow out the story of any one particular nation, it is necessary to pick out the chapters which relate to that nation's history and to place them in chronological order. Thus, for instance, in the history of the British Empire, chapters in the history of India or of Canada have to be brought into their chronological sequence with the chapters belonging to the British Isles.

This is what we have done for our readers in this index. Under the name of each country, we have given as nearly as possible in chronological sequence the list of the chapters in which that country's history is narrated. We begin with Greece and the Greek Peninsula as having the earliest start in point of time; and, as subsidiary to this, the Turkish Dominion. For a like reason we follow with Italy and, as subsidiary to this, the Papacy. Next stands the revived Empire of the West—the "Holy Roman Empire," which subsisted for a thousand years. Out of this several modern states have been evolved; thus we have a separate heading for the Austrian Empire and its component parts, and for Prussia and the Modern German Empire.

These are followed by Poland and Russia; the three Scandinavian States; the Low Countries; Switzerland; and then the colonising states whose history is largely colonial Spain and Portugal, France and Great Britain. In the last case we recognise that until the beginning of the 18th century there are three states which demand separate record, England, Scotland and Ireland; from that time, there is a single, undivided history of Great Britain and the British Empire.

Finally, we give the index to our survey of the British Empire, treating the whole story not chronologically, but in a series of specific aspects.

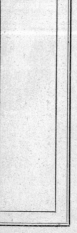

THE GENERAL INDEX

The General Index has been compiled with the greatest care to provide a means of ready reference to the innumerable facts of history chronicled throughout the different divisions of the work. The names of historical characters who figure in the narratives and the places mentioned in the text are all indexed in alphabetical order, the numbers of the pages on which the references occur being given in ordinary numerals; and in cases where an event, a person or a place is the subject of an illustration, that fact is indicated by the page number being printed in italic.

To facilitate reference to any of the special plates, of which a very considerable number appear throughout the work, a special index has been prepared, and a similar index is provided for the numerous maps which occur throughout the text.

LIST OF SPECIAL PLATES IN THE HARMSWORTH HISTORY OF THE WORLD

LIST OF MAPS APPEARING IN THE HARMSWORTH HISTORY OF THE WORLD

GENERAL INDEX

TO THE

HARMSWORTH HISTORY OF THE WORLD